MW00983533

No part of
database a
photocopyi
For licensin

Of

Editing,

Ingram Content Group UK Ltd.
Milton Keynes UK
UKHW020813120323
418334UK00004BA/329

TABLE OF CONTENTS

TABLE OF CONTENTS

ᎧᏏ Foreword: The World of Jewish Prayer ᏓᎧ

The Hebrew Bible is the foundation of the Jewish faith. The closing of the biblical canon in the Second Temple era did not end the vibrant spirituality of the Jewish people. The rabbis responded to the changing conditions of their time by invigorating Jewish life with the ability to survive the catastrophic destruction of the Second Temple in Jerusalem. Consequently, Jewish prayer utilizes the idioms and expressions of the Tanakh, i.e., the Hebrew Bible and the Sages of Israel.

While honoring personal prayer, Judaism is a liturgical religion. Many essential prayers, e.g., the Baruch She'amar, Amidah, Alenu, Kiddush, Havdalah, etc., are ascribed to the Anshei Knesset HaGedolah, the Men of the Great Assembly. According to rabbinic lore, the this Assembly included many biblical prophets of Israel, i.e., Haggai, Zechariah, Ezra, etc. The Assembly stretched over many years into the Maccabean period. The Men of the Great Assembly established many of the Jewish practices that are known to us today. While the rabbis did not invent prayer, they did engineer Jewish rituals with a consciousness of God's presence in a world devoid of the Holy Temple.

Traditional Jewish prayer expresses the fundamental values and beliefs of Judaism. Jewish prayer recollects the historical experiences of the Jewish people affirms the present, and it looks forward to final redemption. While personal prayer is undoubtedly encouraged, Jewish prayer is generally collective. The individual prays "for us" and on behalf of all of the People of Israel. We pray for peace "upon us and all Israel" because each Jew is responsible for one another.

This is not simply an exercise in reminding the individual to notice the needs and sufferings of others. It is intended to make the individual aware that they are part of an extended family. This aspect is a crucial difference between Judaism and other religious traditions. The Jewish people are an ethnoreligious group. Judaism encompasses not only a religious faith in God but includes a unique history, a historic homeland, a language, and a family kinship. When Jews speak of the Patriarchs, Abraham, Isaac, and Jacob, or the Matriarchs, Sarah, Rebekah, Rachel, and Leah, they are not simply invoking their spiritual memory. They also remember their forebears.

Judaism is a well-regulated religious tradition. There are specific laws for observing the commandments of the Torah. This leads to a fundamental question. Is prayer a commandment? If so, how can such a spiritual and personal endeavor be regulated? Why should prayer be structured? Is this not counterintuitive to the spiritual nature of prayer?

To this, the rabbis answer that all fulfillment is derived from a structure. Art is a discipline. Music is a discipline. Notes and instructions are followed to create something beautiful. Yet rules can kill spontaneity. One of the greatest Jewish sages of the medieval period, the Spanish Rabbi Moses ben Maimon (known as the

Rambam or Maimonides), asserted that prayer was a daily obligation prescribed by the written Torah. Deuteronomy 11:13 states:

> *"And it shall come to pass, if ye shall hearken diligently unto My commandments which I command you this day, to love the L-RD your G-d, and to serve Him with all your heart and with all your soul...."*

He interpreted the service of the heart mentioned in the previous passage as referring to prayer. [1] In contrast, another great rabbi of the medieval period from Spain, Rabbi Moses ben Nachman (known as the Ramban or Nachmanides), believed that daily prayer was a rabbinic decree. The Torah only prescribed the obligation to pray in times of emergency. [2]

Rabbi Joseph Dov Soloveitchik reconciled these two positions by noting the sensitivity of the human condition. As humans, we are always in crisis, and hence, we are in desperate need of prayer every day. Both the Rambam and the Ramban experienced severe religious persecution during their lifetimes, and I believe they both would have agreed with Rabbi Soloveitchik's assertion.

This prayerbook provides a unique contribution to the world of Jewish prayer. It provides an accessible tool for individuals from varied Sephardic backgrounds with insights from the Shulchan Arukh and other halakhic sources. It gives the eager student a resource that will allow them to "grow" with the siddur as their Hebrew skills mature. This siddur is particularly noteworthy because it also incorporates elements from historic Spanish-Portuguese communities, historically formed from former Conversos or B'nei Anusim, who returned to Judaism centuries ago and whose spirit and courage continue to draw many Anusim to return to the faith of their fathers.

Rabbi:

רבי יוסי בן מאיר חיים אברהם

Rabbi Dr. Juan Marcos Bejarano Gutierrez
Yeshivat Meor Enaim
B'nei Anusim Center for Education

---

[1] *[The Talmud in Taanit 2a also relates that the service of the heart is accomplished by prayer. See Maimonides' Mishneh Torah, Hilchot Tefilah 1:1.] However, Rabbi Moses ben Maimon asserted that the actual content of prayer and the number of daily prayers was rabbinic. [Hilchot Tefilah 1:1. Hayim Halevy Donin, To Pray as a Jew (New York: Basic Books, 1980), 10. Also see Charles Wengrov, trans., The Chafetz Chayim, The Concise Book of Mitzvoth (New York: Feldheim, 1990), 19-20.]*

[2] *[Commenting on Sefer Ha-mitzvot (mitzvat asei 5), the Ramban states refers to prayer as being mandated only in times of crisis when the Torah (Numbers 10:9) writes, "And when ye go to war in your land against the adversary that oppresseth you, then ye shall sound an alarm with the trumpets; and ye shall be remembered before the LORD your God, and ye shall be saved from your enemies." For the Ramban it is a mitzvah to respond to every crisis by calling out to God in prayer.]*

Introduction: About the Siddur

This siddur is the fruit of about two years of much labor, but truly a labor of love. The intention of creating this came about as a congregational need for helping those with Converso or B'nei Anusim backgrounds (Spanish and Portuguese Jews who accepted Christianity in order to avoid death) to be able to join in with Jewish practice as well as be able to have a great resource to learn and grow with minimal hinderance. While in exile, the Sephardic B'nei Anusim have faced a difficult task of re-entering the world of Judaism and becoming members of often reluctant and even suspicious Jewish communities. Citing Yosef Karo, author of the Shulchan Arukh, in a letter to a community in Kandiyah, Greece:

"...We have heard that Jews who had lived in Spain and were forced to convert have now come to your kehillah in order to live freely as Jews and keep all the mizvot openly. Instead, you remind them of the sins they committed in Spain and, when a disagreement arises between them and the people of your kehillah, you claim these blessed baalei teshuvah are meshumadim (converts to Christianity). This is a terrible sin, because you are slamming the door in the faces of baalei teshuvah. The Mordechai (a Rishon from Ashkenaz) recorded in his sefer that Rabbenu Gershom decreed that any Jew who does not openly accept ba'alei teshuvah should himself be considered menuddeh (not part of the Jewish people). Therefore, from today and henceforth, may every person be exceptionally careful in his dealings with these ba'alei teshuvah, and never again refer to them as meshumadim. And if, has veshalom (may Hashem forbid), the word escapes someone's lips, be he young or old, let him sit completely alone for an entire day and with his own mouth confess his ugly sin. And further, he must undertake never to do so again...Written this 15th of Tammuz, here in Sefat, in the year 5328, (1568), David ben Zimra, Yosef Caro, Moshe miTrani and Yisrael de Kuriel."

- quoted from The Story of Maran Bet Yosef: R Yosef Caro, Author of the Shulhan Aruch (The Sephardic Heritage Series), Artscroll, 1986.

We therefore feel it is our duty and a great mitzvah to bring these souls, as well as anyone closer to the light of Torah and Judaism. This siddur combines a traditional HaMizrach text which generally follows *Tefillat Yesharim*. We've seen with various common scenarios today, that those with B'nei Anusim backgrounds tend to be very zealous and studious when coming to Judaism. Many are not satisfied with the other various nusachim or rites. If attending a Sephardic congregation, more than likely a HaMizrach nusach is utilized. We kept to a format that incorporates customs of different communities, it will generally say "some say:" before a prayer or section that includes the custom of a different community. We kept the kabbalistic prayers, but generally do not translate or transliterate them, except for the "L'shem Yichud" prayer before Sefirat Omer, in the view of Chacham Ovadia Yosef, zt'll. We then provided the transliteration. We utilized a more modern, universal phonetic system, as it seems easier to understand for everyone who is new to hebrew. The translation was compiled predominantly from a combination of *Book of Prayers* by Moses Gaster (Spanish-Portugese), altered, as well as original translation. We put the time into making the translation unique, modern and not just simply using Old-English so that the import can be clear for anyone. We maintained transliterated Hebrew names and words to help in understanding as well as communicating in community. We then provided translation of certain laws from the Shulchan Arukh, as well as a few other sources, for a basic understanding of Sephardic Judaism.

May we continue to feel the importance of כל ישראל ערבים זה לזה / "All Yisrael are responsible for one another", caring for one another within the community, outside of the community, within Eretz Yisrael, and all over the world, a responsibility to all of עם ישראל / the people of Yisrael.

Kelil
President of Eitz Echad

EREV SHABBAT / SHABBAT EVE

Kabbalat Shabbat - Order of Lighting Candles

The Shabbat candles should be lit while the sun is still on the tops of the trees, and on a cloudy day it should be done when the hens roost. (Most traditionally light anywhere from 18-40 minutes before sundown to add from the common to the holy.) One should make sure to have at least one beautiful candle. It is best to light two candles or even one with two wicks to remember the commands to "Remember" and "Keep" the Shabbat. Women are more responsible for it since they are present in the home and engaged in household needs. Both man and the wife bless upon lighting the candle. (SA, OC 263)

When lighting it is ideal to bless before lighting. Light the Shabbat candle(s):

Baruch Attah Adonai Eloheinu	בָּרוּךְ אַתָּה יְהוָה אֱלֹהֵינוּ
Melech Ha'olam Asher	מֶלֶךְ הָעוֹלָם. אֲשֶׁר
Kideshanu Bemitzvotav.	קִדְּשָׁנוּ בְּמִצְוֹתָיו
Vetzivanu Lehadlik Ner Shel	וְצִוָּנוּ לְהַדְלִיק נֵר שֶׁל
Shabbat.	שַׁבָּת:

Blessed are You, Hashem our God, King of the universe, Who has sanctified us with His commandments and commanded us to kindle the lamp of Shabbat.

It is good for a woman to recite the following prayer after lighting the candle. (K"H 263: 34)

Yehi Ratzon Milfaneicha Adonai Elohai	יְהִי רָצוֹן מִלְּפָנֶיךָ. יְהוָה אֱלֹהַי וַאלֹהֵי
Velohei Avotai Shetachus Uterachem	אֲבוֹתַי. שֶׁתָּחוּס וּתְרַחֵם
Alai Vetagdil Chasdecha Immadi Latet Li	עָלַי. וְתַגְדִּיל חַסְדְּךָ עִמָּדִי לָתֵת לִי
Zera Anashim Osei Retzonecha	זֶרַע אֲנָשִׁים עוֹשֵׂי רְצוֹנֶךָ
Ve'osekim Betoratecha Lishmah Veyihyu	וְעוֹסְקִים בְּתוֹרָתְךָ לִשְׁמָהּ. וְיִהְיוּ
Me'irim Batorah Bizchut Nerot	מְאִירִים בַּתּוֹרָה בִּזְכוּת נֵרוֹת
Hashabbat Hallalu Kemo Shekatuv Ki	הַשַׁבָּת הַלָּלוּ. כְּמוֹ שֶׁכָּתוּב. כִּי
Ner Mitzvah Vetorah Or. Vegam Tachus	נֵר מִצְוָה וְתוֹרָה אוֹר. וְגַם תָּחוּס
Uterachem Al Ba'ali (Peloni Ben Peloni)	וּתְרַחֵם עַל בַּעֲלִי. (פלוני בן פלוני).

Vetiten Lo Orech Yamim Ushenot	וְתִתֶּן לוֹ אוֹרֶךְ יָמִים וּשָׁנוֹת
Chayim Im Berachah Vehatzlachah	חַיִּים עִם בְּרָכָה וְהַצְּלָחָה.
Utesaye'ehu La'asot Retzonecha	וּתְסַיְּעֵהוּ לַעֲשׂוֹת רְצוֹנְךָ
Bishleimut Ken Yehi Ratzon Amen: Vihi	בִּשְׁלֵימוּת. כֵּן יְהִי רָצוֹן. אָמֵן: וִיהִי
No'am Adonai Eloheinu Aleinu	נֹעַם אֲדֹנָי אֱלֹהֵינוּ עָלֵינוּ.
Uma'aseh Yadeinu Konenah Aleinu	וּמַעֲשֵׂה יָדֵינוּ כּוֹנְנָה עָלֵינוּ.
Uma'aseh Yadeinu Konenehu. Yihyu	וּמַעֲשֵׂה יָדֵינוּ כּוֹנְנֵהוּ: יִהְיוּ
Leratzon Imrei-Fi Vehegyon Libi	לְרָצוֹן אִמְרֵי־פִי וְהֶגְיוֹן לִבִּי
Lefaneicha Adonai Tzuri Vego'ali.	לְפָנֶיךָ יְהוָה צוּרִי וְגֹאֲלִי:

May it be Your will, Hashem, my God and God of my fathers, that you take pity on and have compassion for me and act with great kindness toward me, by giving me the seed of men who will perform Your will and who will immerse themselves in Your Torah for its own sake; and may they illuminate [the world] with the Torah in the merit of these Shabbat lights, as it is written: "For a mitzvah is a lamp, and Torah is light." (Prov. 6:23) Also take pity on and have compassion for my husband, (husband's name) son of (father's name); give him long days and years of life with blessing and success, and help him to perform Your will in completion. So may it be Your will, Amen. May the pleasantness of Hashem, our God, be upon us; establish the work of our hands for us, the work of our hands establish. And may the graciousness of Hashem our God be on us; Establish also upon us the work of our hands; and the work of our hands, establish it. May the words of my mouth and the meditation of my heart find favor before You, Hashem my Rock and my Redeemer.

Before lighting a Yom Tov candle you will bless:

Baruch Attah Adonai Eloheinu	בָּרוּךְ אַתָּה יְהוָה אֱלֹהֵינוּ
Melech Ha'olam Asher Kideshanu	מֶלֶךְ הָעוֹלָם. אֲשֶׁר קִדְּשָׁנוּ
Bemitzvotav. Vetzivanu Lehadlik	בְּמִצְוֹתָיו וְצִוָּנוּ לְהַדְלִיק
Ner Shel If Yom Tov falls on Shabbat, add:	נֵר שֶׁל אם חל בשבת תוסיף:
(Shabbat Ve) Yom Tov.	(שַׁבָּת וְ)יוֹם טוֹב:

Blessed are You, Hashem our God, King of the Universe, Who has sanctified us with His commandments and commanded us to kindle the lamp of If Yom Tov falls on Shabbat, add: (Shabbat and) Yom Tov.

Some communities, on Yom Tov, except for the last days of Pesach, the women say Shehecheyanu:

Baruch Attah Adonai Eloheinu Melech

Ha'olam Shehecheyanu Vekiyemanu

Vehigi'anu Lazman Hazeh.

בָּרוּךְ אַתָּה יְהֹוָה אֱלֹהֵינוּ מֶלֶךְ

הָעוֹלָם. שֶׁהֶחֱיָנוּ וְקִיְּמָנוּ

וְהִגִּיעָנוּ לַזְּמַן הַזֶּה:

Blessed are You, Hashem our God, King of the universe, Who has kept us in life
and preserved us and enabled us to reach this time.

Shir Hashirim / Song of Songs

Chanted by some shortly before the Kabbalat Shabbat service.

לְשֵׁם יִחוּד קוּדְשָׁא בְּרִיךְ הוּא וּשְׁכִינְתֵּיהּ. בִּדְחִילוּ וּרְחִימוּ. וּרְחִימוּ וּדְחִילוּ.
לְיַחֲדָא שֵׁם יוֹ"ד קֵ"י בְּוָא"ו קֵ"י בְּיִחוּדָא שְׁלִים (יהוה) בְּשֵׁם כָּל יִשְׂרָאֵל.
הנה אנחנו באים לשורר בקול נעים שיר השירים לתקן את שורשה
במקום עליון. וִיהִי נֹעַם אֲדֹנָי אֱלֹהֵינוּ עָלֵינוּ וּמַעֲשֵׂה יָדֵינוּ כּוֹנְנָה עָלֵינוּ
וּמַעֲשֵׂה יָדֵינוּ כּוֹנְנֵהוּ׃

א שִׁיר הַשִּׁירִים אֲשֶׁר לִשְׁלֹמֹה׃ יִשָּׁקֵנִי מִנְּשִׁיקוֹת פִּיהוּ כִּי־טוֹבִים
דֹּדֶיךָ מִיָּיִן׃ לְרֵיחַ שְׁמָנֶיךָ טוֹבִים שֶׁמֶן תּוּרַק שְׁמֶךָ עַל־כֵּן עֲלָמוֹת
אֲהֵבוּךָ׃ מָשְׁכֵנִי אַחֲרֶיךָ נָּרוּצָה הֱבִיאַנִי הַמֶּלֶךְ חֲדָרָיו נָגִילָה
וְנִשְׂמְחָה בָּךְ נַזְכִּירָה דֹדֶיךָ מִיַּיִן מֵישָׁרִים אֲהֵבוּךָ׃ שְׁחוֹרָה אֲנִי
וְנָאוָה בְּנוֹת יְרוּשָׁלָ͏ִם כְּאָהֳלֵי קֵדָר כִּירִיעוֹת שְׁלֹמֹה׃ אַל־תִּרְאוּנִי
שֶׁאֲנִי שְׁחַרְחֹרֶת שֶׁשֱּׁזָפַתְנִי הַשָּׁמֶשׁ בְּנֵי אִמִּי נִחֲרוּ־בִי שָׂמֻנִי נֹטֵרָה
אֶת־הַכְּרָמִים כַּרְמִי שֶׁלִּי לֹא נָטָרְתִּי׃ הַגִּידָה לִּי שֶׁאָהֲבָה נַפְשִׁי
אֵיכָה תִרְעֶה אֵיכָה תַּרְבִּיץ בַּצׇּהֳרָיִם שַׁלָּמָה אֶהְיֶה כְּעֹטְיָה עַל עֶדְרֵי
חֲבֵרֶיךָ׃ אִם־לֹא תֵדְעִי לָךְ הַיָּפָה בַּנָּשִׁים צְאִי־לָךְ בְּעִקְבֵי הַצֹּאן וּרְעִי
אֶת־גְּדִיֹּתַיִךְ עַל מִשְׁכְּנוֹת הָרֹעִים׃ לְסֻסָתִי בְּרִכְבֵי פַרְעֹה דִּמִּיתִיךְ
רַעְיָתִי׃ נָאווּ לְחָיַיִךְ בַּתֹּרִים צַוָּארֵךְ בַּחֲרוּזִים׃ תּוֹרֵי זָהָב נַעֲשֶׂה־לָּךְ
עִם נְקֻדּוֹת הַכָּסֶף׃ עַד־שֶׁהַמֶּלֶךְ בִּמְסִבּוֹ נִרְדִּי נָתַן רֵיחוֹ׃ צְרוֹר הַמֹּר ׀
דּוֹדִי לִי בֵּין שָׁדַי יָלִין׃ אֶשְׁכֹּל הַכֹּפֶר ׀ דּוֹדִי לִי בְּכַרְמֵי עֵין גֶּדִי׃ הִנָּךְ
יָפָה רַעְיָתִי הִנָּךְ יָפָה עֵינַיִךְ יוֹנִים׃ הִנְּךָ יָפֶה דוֹדִי אַף נָעִים
אַף־עַרְשֵׂנוּ רַעֲנָנָה׃ קֹרוֹת בָּתֵּינוּ אֲרָזִים רחיטנו רַהִיטֵנוּ בְּרוֹתִים׃

א Shir Hashirim Asher Lishlomoh. Yishakeni Mineshikot Pihu, Ki-
Tovim Dodeicha Miyayin. Lereiach Shemaneicha Tovim, Shemen
Turak Shemecha; Al-Ken Alamot Ahevucha. Moshcheini Achareicha
Narutzah; Hevi'ani Hamelech Chadarav, Nagilah Venismechah
Bach, Nazkirah Dodeicha Miyayin, Meisharim Ahevucha.
Shechorah Ani Venavah, Benot Yerushalayim Ke'oholei Kedar, Kiri'ot

Shelomoh. Al-Tir'uni She'ani Shecharchoret, Sheshezafatni
Hashamesh; Benei Immi Nicharu-Vi, Samuni Noterah Et-
Hakeramim, Karmi Sheli Lo Natareti. Hagidah Li, She'ahavah
Nafshi, Eichah Tir'eh, Eichah Tarbitz Batzohorayim; Shallamah
Ehyeh Ke'oteyah, Al Edrei Chavereicha. Im-Lo Tede'i Lach, Hayafah
Banashim; Tze'i-Lach Be'ikvei Hatzon, Ure'i Et-Gediyotayich, Al
Mishkenot Haro'im. Lesusati Berichvei Far'oh, Dimmitich Ra'yati.
Navu Lechayayich Battorim, Tzavarech Bacharuzim. Torei Zahav
Na'aseh-Lach, Im Nekudot Hakkasef. Ad-Shehamelech Bimsibo,
Nirdi Natan Reicho. Tzeror Hamor Dodi Li, Bein Shadai Yalin.
Eshkol Hakkofer Dodi Li, Becharmei Ein Gedi. Hinach Yafah Ra'yati,
Hinach Yafah Einayich Yonim. Hinecha Yafeh Dodi Af Na'im,
Af-'Arsenu Ra'ananah. Korot Batteinu Arazim, Rahitenu Berotim.

1. The song of songs, which is Shlomo's. Let him kiss me with the
kisses of his mouth— For your love is better than wine. Your
ointments have a good fragrance; your name is as ointment poured
out; Therefore do the maidens love you. Draw me, we will run after
you; The king has brought me into his chambers; We will be glad
and rejoice in you, We will find your love more fragrant than wine.
Sincerely do they love you. I am black, but suitable, you daughters of
Yerushalayim, As the tents of Kedar, As the curtains of Shlomo. Do
not look on me, that I am dark-skinned, That the sun has tanned
me; My mother's sons were incensed against me, They made me
keeper of the vineyards; But my own vineyard I have not kept. Tell
me, you whom my soul loves, where you feed, where you make your
flock to rest at noon; For why should I be as one that veils herself
beside the flocks of your companions? If you do not know, you,
fairest among women, Go your way out by the footsteps of the flock
and feed your kids, beside the shepherds' tents. I have compared
you, my love, to a steed in Pharaoh's chariots. Your cheeks are
adorned with circlets, your neck with beads. We will make you
circlets of gold with studs of silver. While the king sat at his table,
my spikenard sent out its fragrance. My beloved is to me as a bag of
myrrh, that lies between my breasts. My beloved is to me as a cluster
of henna in the vineyards of Ein-Gedi. Behold, you are fair, my love;
behold, you are fair; Your eyes are like doves. Behold, you are fair,

my beloved, also, pleasant; Also our couch is leafy. The beams of our houses are cedars, And our panels are cypresses.

ב אֲנִי חֲבַצֶּלֶת הַשָּׁרוֹן שׁוֹשַׁנַּת הָעֲמָקִים: כְּשׁוֹשַׁנָּה בֵּין הַחוֹחִים כֵּן רַעְיָתִי בֵּין הַבָּנוֹת: כְּתַפּוּחַ בַּעֲצֵי הַיַּעַר כֵּן דּוֹדִי בֵּין הַבָּנִים בְּצִלּוֹ חִמַּדְתִּי וְיָשַׁבְתִּי וּפִרְיוֹ מָתוֹק לְחִכִּי: הֱבִיאַנִי אֶל־בֵּית הַיַּיִן וְדִגְלוֹ עָלַי אַהֲבָה: סַמְּכוּנִי בָּאֲשִׁישׁוֹת רַפְּדוּנִי בַּתַּפּוּחִים כִּי־חוֹלַת אַהֲבָה אָנִי: שְׂמֹאלוֹ תַּחַת לְרֹאשִׁי וִימִינוֹ תְּחַבְּקֵנִי: הִשְׁבַּעְתִּי אֶתְכֶם בְּנוֹת יְרוּשָׁלַם בִּצְבָאוֹת אוֹ בְּאַיְלוֹת הַשָּׂדֶה אִם־תָּעִירוּ | וְאִם־תְּעוֹרְרוּ אֶת־הָאַהֲבָה עַד שֶׁתֶּחְפָּץ: קוֹל דּוֹדִי הִנֵּה־זֶה בָּא מְדַלֵּג עַל־הֶהָרִים מְקַפֵּץ עַל־הַגְּבָעוֹת: דּוֹמֶה דוֹדִי לִצְבִי אוֹ לְעֹפֶר הָאַיָּלִים הִנֵּה־זֶה עוֹמֵד אַחַר כָּתְלֵנוּ מַשְׁגִּיחַ מִן־הַחֲלֹנוֹת מֵצִיץ מִן־הַחֲרַכִּים: עָנָה דוֹדִי וְאָמַר לִי קוּמִי לָךְ רַעְיָתִי יָפָתִי וּלְכִי־לָךְ: כִּי־הִנֵּה הַסְּתָו עָבָר הַגֶּשֶׁם חָלַף הָלַךְ לוֹ: הַנִּצָּנִים נִרְאוּ בָאָרֶץ עֵת הַזָּמִיר הִגִּיעַ וְקוֹל הַתּוֹר נִשְׁמַע בְּאַרְצֵנוּ: הַתְּאֵנָה חָנְטָה פַגֶּיהָ וְהַגְּפָנִים | סְמָדַר נָתְנוּ רֵיחַ קוּמִי לכי לָךְ רַעְיָתִי יָפָתִי וּלְכִי־לָךְ: יוֹנָתִי בְּחַגְוֵי הַסֶּלַע בְּסֵתֶר הַמַּדְרֵגָה הַרְאִינִי אֶת־מַרְאַיִךְ הַשְׁמִיעִנִי אֶת־קוֹלֵךְ כִּי־קוֹלֵךְ עָרֵב וּמַרְאֵיךְ נָאוֶה: אֶחֱזוּ־לָנוּ שׁוּעָלִים שׁוּעָלִים קְטַנִּים מְחַבְּלִים כְּרָמִים וּכְרָמֵינוּ סְמָדַר: דּוֹדִי לִי וַאֲנִי לוֹ הָרֹעֶה בַּשׁוֹשַׁנִּים: עַד שֶׁיָּפוּחַ הַיּוֹם וְנָסוּ הַצְּלָלִים סֹב דְּמֵה־לְךָ דוֹדִי לִצְבִי אוֹ לְעֹפֶר הָאַיָּלִים עַל־הָרֵי בָתֶר:

ב Ani Chavatzelet Hasharon, Shoshanat Ha'amakim. Keshoshanah Bein Hachochim, Ken Ra'yati Bein Habanot. Ketappuach Ba'atzei Haya'ar, Ken Dodi Bein Habanim; Betzillo Chimmadti Veyashavti, Ufiryo Matok Lechikki. Hevi'ani El-Beit Hayayin, Vediglo Alai Ahavah. Samechuni Ba'ashishot, Rappeduni Battappuchim; Ki-Cholat Ahavah Ani. Semolo Tachat Leroshi, Vimino Techabekeni. Hishba'ti Etchem Benot Yerushalayim Bitzva'ot, O Be'aylot Hassadeh; Im-Ta'iru Ve'im-Te'oreru Et-Ha'ahavah Ad Shetechpatz.

Kol Dodi, Hineh-Zeh Ba; Medalleg Al-Heharim, Mekapetz Al-
Hageva'ot. Domeh Dodi Litzvi, O Le'ofer Ha'ayalim; Hineh-Zeh
Omed Achar Kotlenu, Mashgiach Min-Hachallonot, Metzitz Min-
Hacharakkim. Anah Dodi Ve'amar Li; Kumi Lach Ra'yati Yafati
Ulechi-Lach. Ki-Hineh Hassetav Avar; Hageshem Chalaf Halach Lo.
Hanitzanim Nir'u Va'aretz, Et Hazamir Higia'; Vekol Hator Nishma
Be'artzenu. Hate'enah Chanetah Faggeiha, Vehagefanim Semadar
Natenu Reiach; Kumi Lch Lach Ra'yati Yafati Ulechi-Lach. Yonati
Bechagvei Hassela', Beseter Hamadregah, Har'ini Et-Mar'ayich,
Hashmi'ini Et-Kolech; Ki-Kolech Arev Umar'eich Naveh. Echezu-
Lanu Shu'alim, Shu'alim Ketanim Mechabelim Keramim;
Ucherameinu Semadar. Dodi Li Va'ani Lo, Haro'eh Bashoshanim.
Ad Sheyafuach Hayom, Venasu Hatzelalim; Sov Demeh-Lecha Dodi
Litzvi, O Le'ofer Ha'ayalim Al-Harei Vater.

2. I am a rose of Sharon, A lily of the valleys. As a lily among thorns,
so is my love among the daughters. As an apple-tree among the
trees of the wood, so is my beloved among the sons. Under its
shadow I delighted to sit, And its fruit was sweet to my taste. He has
brought me to the banqueting-house, and his banner over me is
love. Satisfy me with delicacies, refresh me with apples; for I am
love-sick. Let his left hand be under my head, And his right hand
embrace me. I urge you, daughters of Yerushalayim, by the gazelles,
and by the hinds of the field, That you do not awaken, or stir up
love, until it pleases. Behold, My beloved, he comes, leaping upon
the mountains, skipping on the hills. My beloved is like a gazelle or a
young deer; Behold, he stands behind our wall, He looks in through
the windows, He peers through the lattice. My beloved spoke, and
said to me: 'Rise up, my love, my fair one, and come away. For,
behold, the winter is past, The rain is over and gone; The flowers
appear on the earth; The time of singing has come, And the voice of
the turtledove is heard in our land; The fig-tree puts out her green
figs, And the vines in blossom give out their fragrance. Arise, my
love, my fair one, and come away. Oh my dove, that is in the clefts of
the rock, in the covert of the cliff, Let me see your countenance, let
me hear your voice; For sweet is your voice, and your countenance
is pleasant. Catch for us the foxes, the little foxes, that spoil the

vineyards; For our vineyards are in blossom. My beloved is mine, and I am his, That feeds among the lilies. Until the day breathes, and the shadows flee away, Turn, my beloved, and be like a gazelle or a young deer on the mountains of spices.

ג עַל־מִשְׁכָּבִי בַּלֵּילוֹת בִּקַּשְׁתִּי אֵת שֶׁאָהֲבָה נַפְשִׁי בִּקַּשְׁתִּיו וְלֹא מְצָאתִיו: אָקוּמָה נָּא וַאֲסוֹבְבָה בָעִיר בַּשְּׁוָקִים וּבָרְחֹבוֹת אֲבַקְשָׁה אֵת שֶׁאָהֲבָה נַפְשִׁי בִּקַּשְׁתִּיו וְלֹא מְצָאתִיו: מְצָאוּנִי הַשֹּׁמְרִים הַסֹּבְבִים בָּעִיר אֵת שֶׁאָהֲבָה נַפְשִׁי רְאִיתֶם: כִּמְעַט שֶׁעָבַרְתִּי מֵהֶם עַד שֶׁמָּצָאתִי אֵת שֶׁאָהֲבָה נַפְשִׁי אֲחַזְתִּיו וְלֹא אַרְפֶּנּוּ עַד־שֶׁהֲבֵיאתִיו אֶל־בֵּית אִמִּי וְאֶל־חֶדֶר הוֹרָתִי: הִשְׁבַּעְתִּי אֶתְכֶם בְּנוֹת יְרוּשָׁלַ͏ִם בִּצְבָאוֹת אוֹ בְּאַיְלוֹת הַשָּׂדֶה אִם־תָּעִירוּ | וְאִם־תְּעוֹרְרוּ אֶת־הָאַהֲבָה עַד שֶׁתֶּחְפָּץ: מִי זֹאת עֹלָה מִן־הַמִּדְבָּר כְּתִימֲרוֹת עָשָׁן מְקֻטֶּרֶת מֹר וּלְבוֹנָה מִכֹּל אַבְקַת רוֹכֵל: הִנֵּה מִטָּתוֹ שֶׁלִּשְׁלֹמֹה שִׁשִּׁים גִּבֹּרִים סָבִיב לָהּ מִגִּבֹּרֵי יִשְׂרָאֵל: כֻּלָּם אֲחֻזֵי חֶרֶב מְלֻמְּדֵי מִלְחָמָה אִישׁ חַרְבּוֹ עַל־יְרֵכוֹ מִפַּחַד בַּלֵּילוֹת: אַפִּרְיוֹן עָשָׂה לוֹ הַמֶּלֶךְ שְׁלֹמֹה מֵעֲצֵי הַלְּבָנוֹן: עַמּוּדָיו עָשָׂה כֶסֶף רְפִידָתוֹ זָהָב מֶרְכָּבוֹ אַרְגָּמָן תּוֹכוֹ רָצוּף אַהֲבָה מִבְּנוֹת יְרוּשָׁלָ͏ִם: צְאֶנָה | וּרְאֶינָה בְּנוֹת צִיּוֹן בַּמֶּלֶךְ שְׁלֹמֹה בָּעֲטָרָה שֶׁעִטְּרָה־לּוֹ אִמּוֹ בְּיוֹם חֲתֻנָּתוֹ וּבְיוֹם שִׂמְחַת לִבּוֹ:

ג Al-Mishkavi Baleilot, Bikashti Et She'ahavah Nafshi; Bikashtiv Velo Metzativ. Akumah Na Va'asovevah Va'ir, Bashevakim Uvarechovot, Avakshah Et She'ahavah Nafshi; Bikashtiv Velo Metzativ. Metza'uni Hashomerim, Hassovevim Ba'ir; Et She'ahavah Nafshi Re'item. Kim'at She'avarti Mehem, Ad Shematzati, Et She'ahavah Nafshi; Achaztiv Velo Arpenu, Ad-Shehaveitiv El-Beit Immi, Ve'el-Cheder Horati. Hishba'ti Etchem Benot Yerushalayim Bitzva'ot, O Be'aylot Hassadeh; Im-Ta'iru Ve'im-Te'oreru Et-Ha'ahavah Ad Shetechpatz. Mi Zot, Olah Min-Hamidbar, Ketimerot Ashan; Mekutteret Mor Ulevonah, Mikol Avkat Rochel. Hineh, Mitato Shelishlomoh, Shishim Giborim Saviv Lah; Migiborei Yisra'el. Kulam Achuzei Cherev, Melummedei Milchamah; Ish Charbo Al-Yerecho, Mipachad

Baleilot. Appiryon, Asah Lo Hamelech Shelomoh, Me'atzei
Hallevanon. Ammudav Asah Chesef, Refidato Zahav, Merkavo
Argaman; Tocho Ratzuf Ahavah, Mibenot Yerushalayim. Tze'enah
Ure'einah Benot Tziyon Bamelech Shelomoh; Ba'atarah, She'itterah-
Lo Imo Beyom Chatunato, Uveyom Simchat Libo.

3. By night on my bed I searched for him whom my soul loves; I
searched for him, but I did not find him. I will rise now, and go about
the city, In the streets and in the broad ways, I will seek him whom
my soul loves. I searched for him, but I did not find him. The
watchmen that go around the city found me: 'Did you see him
whom my soul loves?' I had just passed them, when I found him
whom my soul loves: I held him, and would not let him go, until I had
brought him into my mother's house, And into the chamber of her
that conceived me. I urge you, daughters of Yerushalayim, By the
gazelles, and by the deer of the field, that you do not awaken, or stir
up love, until it pleases. Who is this that comes up out of the
wilderness like pillars of smoke, perfumed with myrrh and
frankincense, with all powders of the merchant? Behold, it is the
offspring of Shlomo; Sixty mighty men are escorting it, of the
mighty men of Yisrael. They all handle the sword, And are expert in
war; Every man has his sword on his thigh, because of dread in the
night. King Shlomo made himself a palanquin out of the wood of
Levanon. He made the pillars if it out of silver, The top of it from
gold, The seat of it of purple, The inside of it being inlaid with love,
From the daughters of Yerushalayim. Go out, you daughters of
Tziyon, And gaze on King Shlomo, Even on the crown that his
mother has crowned him in the day of his wedding, and in the day
of the gladness of his heart.

ד הִנָּךְ יָפָה רַעְיָתִי הִנָּךְ יָפָה עֵינַיִךְ יוֹנִים מִבַּעַד לְצַמָּתֵךְ שַׂעְרֵךְ
כְּעֵדֶר הָעִזִּים שֶׁגָּלְשׁוּ מֵהַר גִּלְעָד: שִׁנַּיִךְ כְּעֵדֶר הַקְּצוּבוֹת שֶׁעָלוּ
מִן־הָרַחְצָה שֶׁכֻּלָּם מַתְאִימוֹת וְשַׁכֻּלָה אֵין בָּהֶם: כְּחוּט הַשָּׁנִי
שִׂפְתוֹתַיִךְ וּמִדְבָּרֵךְ נָאוֶה כְּפֶלַח הָרִמּוֹן רַקָּתֵךְ מִבַּעַד לְצַמָּתֵךְ:

כְּמִגְדַּל דָּוִיד צַוָּארֵךְ בָּנוּי לְתַלְפִּיּוֹת אֶלֶף הַמָּגֵן תָּלוּי עָלָיו כֹּל שִׁלְטֵי
הַגִּבֹּרִים: שְׁנֵי שָׁדַיִךְ כִּשְׁנֵי עֳפָרִים תְּאוֹמֵי צְבִיָּה הָרוֹעִים בַּשּׁוֹשַׁנִּים:
עַד שֶׁיָּפוּחַ הַיּוֹם וְנָסוּ הַצְּלָלִים אֵלֶךְ לִי אֶל־הַר הַמּוֹר וְאֶל־גִּבְעַת
הַלְּבוֹנָה: כֻּלָּךְ יָפָה רַעְיָתִי וּמוּם אֵין בָּךְ: אִתִּי מִלְּבָנוֹן כַּלָּה אִתִּי
מִלְּבָנוֹן תָּבוֹאִי תָּשׁוּרִי| מֵרֹאשׁ אֲמָנָה מֵרֹאשׁ שְׂנִיר וְחֶרְמוֹן מִמְּעֹנוֹת
אֲרָיוֹת מֵהַרְרֵי נְמֵרִים: לִבַּבְתִּנִי אֲחֹתִי כַלָּה לִבַּבְתִּנִי באחד בְּאַחַת
מֵעֵינַיִךְ בְּאַחַד עֲנָק מִצַּוְּרֹנָיִךְ: מַה־יָּפוּ דֹדַיִךְ אֲחֹתִי כַלָּה מַה־טֹּבוּ
דֹדַיִךְ מִיַּיִן וְרֵיחַ שְׁמָנַיִךְ מִכָּל־בְּשָׂמִים: נֹפֶת תִּטֹּפְנָה שִׂפְתוֹתַיִךְ כַּלָּה
דְּבַשׁ וְחָלָב תַּחַת לְשׁוֹנֵךְ וְרֵיחַ שַׂלְמֹתַיִךְ כְּרֵיחַ לְבָנוֹן: גַּן | נָעוּל
אֲחֹתִי כַלָּה גַּל נָעוּל מַעְיָן חָתוּם: שְׁלָחַיִךְ פַּרְדֵּס רִמּוֹנִים עִם פְּרִי
מְגָדִים כְּפָרִים עִם־נְרָדִים: נֵרְדְּ | וְכַרְכֹּם קָנֶה וְקִנָּמוֹן עִם כָּל־עֲצֵי
לְבוֹנָה מֹר וַאֲהָלוֹת עִם כָּל־רָאשֵׁי בְשָׂמִים: מַעְיַן גַּנִּים בְּאֵר מַיִם
חַיִּים וְנֹזְלִים מִן־לְבָנוֹן: עוּרִי צָפוֹן וּבוֹאִי תֵימָן הָפִיחִי גַנִּי יִזְּלוּ
בְשָׂמָיו יָבֹא דוֹדִי לְגַנּוֹ וְיֹאכַל פְּרִי מְגָדָיו:

ז Hinach Yafah Ra'yati Hinach Yafah, Einayich Yonim, Miba'ad
Letzammatech; Sa'rech Ke'eder Ha'izim, Sheggaleshu Mehar Gil'ad.
Shinayich Ke'eder Hakketzuvot, She'alu Min-Harachtzah; Shekulam
Mat'imot, Veshakkulah Ein Bahem. Kechut Hashani Siftotayich,
Umidbarech Naveh; Kefelach Harimmon Rakkatech, Miba'ad
Letzammatech. Kemigdal David Tzavarech, Banui Letalpiyot; Elef
Hamagen Talui Alav, Kol Shiltei Hagiborim. Shenei Shadayich
Kishnei Ofarim Te'omei Tzeviyah; Haro'im Bashoshanim. Ad
Sheyafuach Hayom, Venasu Hatzelalim; Elech Li El-Har Hamor,
Ve'el-Giv'at Hallevonah. Kullach Yafah Ra'yati, Umum Ein Bach. Iti
Millevanon Kallah, Iti Millevanon Tavo'i; Tashuri Merosh Amanah,
Merosh Senir Vechermon, Mime'onot Arayot, Meharerei Nemerim.
Libavtini Achoti Challah; Libavtini Be'achad Me'einayich, Be'achad
Anak Mitzaveronayich. Mah-Yafu Dodayich Achoti Challah; Mah-
Tovu Dodayich Miyayin, Vereiach Shemanayich Mikol-Besamim.
Nofet Titofenah Siftotayich Kallah; Devash Vechalav Tachat
Leshonech, Vereiach Salmotayich Kereiach Levanon. Gan Na'ul
Achoti Challah; Gal Na'ul Ma'yan Chatum. Shelachayich Pardes
Rimonim, Im Peri Megadim; Kefarim Im-Neradim. Nered

Vecharkom, Kaneh Vekinamon, Im Chol-'Atzei Levonah; Mor
Va'ahalot, Im Chol-Rashei Vesamim. Ma'yan Ganim, Be'er Mayim
Chayim; Venozelim Min-Levanon. Uri Tzafon Uvo'i Teiman, Hafichi
Gani Yizelu Vesamav; Yavo Dodi Legano, Veyochal Peri Megadav.

4. Behold, you are beautiful, my love; behold, you are beautiful;
Your eyes are like doves behind your veil; Your hair is like a flock of
goats, that trail down from Mount Gil'ad. Your teeth are like a flock
of sheep all shaped alike, which have come up from the washing;
And all are paired, and none fails among them. Your lips are like a
thread of scarlet, And your mouth is pleasant; Your temples are like
a pomegranate split open behind your veil. Your neck is like the
tower of David built with turrets, on it there hang a thousand
shields, All the armor of the mighty men. Your two breasts are like
two fawns that are twins of a gazelle, which feed among the lilies.
Until the day breathes, And the shadows flee away, I will go to the
mountain of myrrh, And to the hill of frankincense. You are all fair,
my love; And there is nothing wrong in you. Come with me from
Levanon, my bride, With me from Levanon; Look from the top of
Amana, From the top of Senir and Hermon, From the lions' dens,
From the mountains of the leopards. You have ravished my heart,
my sister, my bride; You have ravished my heart with one of your
eyes, With one bead of your necklace. How fair is your love, my
sister, my bride. How much better is your love than wine. And the
smell of your ointments than all manner of spices. Your lips, my
bride, drop honey—Honey and milk are under your tongue; And the
smell of your garments is like the smell of Levanon. A garden closed
off is my sister, my bride; A spring closed, a fountain sealed. Your
brances are an orchard of pomegranates, With precious fruits;
Henna with spikenard plants, Spikenard and saffron, calamus and
cinnamon, With all trees of frankincense; Myrrh and aloes, with all
the chief spices. You are a fountain of gardens, A well of living
waters, And flowing streams from Levanon. Awake, north wind; And
come, south; Blow on my garden, That the spices of it may flow out.
Let my beloved come into his garden, and eat his precious fruits.

ה בָּאתִי לְגַנִּי אֲחֹתִי כַלָּה אָרִיתִי מוֹרִי עִם־בְּשָׂמִי אָכַלְתִּי יַעְרִי
עִם־דִּבְשִׁי שָׁתִיתִי יֵינִי עִם־חֲלָבֵי אִכְלוּ רֵעִים שְׁתוּ וְשִׁכְרוּ דּוֹדִים:
אֲנִי יְשֵׁנָה וְלִבִּי עֵר קוֹל | דּוֹדִי דוֹפֵק פִּתְחִי־לִי אֲחֹתִי רַעְיָתִי יוֹנָתִי
תַמָּתִי שֶׁרֹאשִׁי נִמְלָא־טָל קְוֻצּוֹתַי רְסִיסֵי לָיְלָה: פָּשַׁטְתִּי אֶת־כֻּתָּנְתִּי
אֵיכָכָה אֶלְבָּשֶׁנָּה רָחַצְתִּי אֶת־רַגְלַי אֵיכָכָה אֲטַנְּפֵם: דּוֹדִי שָׁלַח יָדוֹ
מִן־הַחֹר וּמֵעַי הָמוּ עָלָיו: קַמְתִּי אֲנִי לִפְתֹּחַ לְדוֹדִי וְיָדַי נָטְפוּ־מֹור
וְאֶצְבְּעֹתַי מוֹר עֹבֵר עַל כַּפּוֹת הַמַּנְעוּל: פָּתַחְתִּי אֲנִי לְדוֹדִי וְדוֹדִי
חָמַק עָבָר נַפְשִׁי יָצְאָה בְדַבְּרוֹ בִּקַּשְׁתִּיהוּ וְלֹא מְצָאתִיהוּ קְרָאתִיו
וְלֹא עָנָנִי: מְצָאֻנִי הַשֹּׁמְרִים הַסֹּבְבִים בָּעִיר הִכּוּנִי פְצָעוּנִי נָשְׂאוּ
אֶת־רְדִידִי מֵעָלַי שֹׁמְרֵי הַחֹמוֹת: הִשְׁבַּעְתִּי אֶתְכֶם בְּנוֹת יְרוּשָׁלָם
אִם־תִּמְצְאוּ אֶת־דּוֹדִי מַה־תַּגִּידוּ לוֹ שֶׁחוֹלַת אַהֲבָה אָנִי: מַה־דּוֹדֵךְ
מִדּוֹד הַיָּפָה בַּנָּשִׁים מַה־דּוֹדֵךְ מִדּוֹד שֶׁכָּכָה הִשְׁבַּעְתָּנוּ: דּוֹדִי צַח
וְאָדוֹם דָּגוּל מֵרְבָבָה: רֹאשׁוֹ כֶּתֶם פָּז קְוֻצּוֹתָיו תַּלְתַּלִּים שְׁחֹרוֹת
כָּעוֹרֵב: עֵינָיו כְּיוֹנִים עַל־אֲפִיקֵי מָיִם רֹחֲצוֹת בֶּחָלָב יֹשְׁבוֹת
עַל־מִלֵּאת: לְחָיָו כַּעֲרוּגַת הַבֹּשֶׂם מִגְדְּלוֹת מֶרְקָחִים שִׂפְתוֹתָיו
שׁוֹשַׁנִּים נֹטְפוֹת מוֹר עֹבֵר: יָדָיו גְּלִילֵי זָהָב מְמֻלָּאִים בַּתַּרְשִׁישׁ מֵעָיו
עֶשֶׁת שֵׁן מְעֻלֶּפֶת סַפִּירִים: שׁוֹקָיו עַמּוּדֵי שֵׁשׁ מְיֻסָּדִים עַל־אַדְנֵי־פָז
מַרְאֵהוּ כַּלְּבָנוֹן בָּחוּר כָּאֲרָזִים: חִכּוֹ מַמְתַקִּים וְכֻלּוֹ מַחֲמַדִּים זֶה
דוֹדִי וְזֶה רֵעִי בְּנוֹת יְרוּשָׁלָם:

ה Bati Legani Achoti Challah Ariti Mori Im-Besami, Achalti Ya'ri Im-
Divshi, Shatiti Yeini Im-Chalavi; Ichlu Re'im, Shetu Veshichru
Dodim. Ani Yeshenah Velibi Er; Kol Dodi Dofek, Pitchi-Li Achoti
Ra'yati Yonati Tammati, Sheroshi Nimla-Tal, Kevutzotai Resisei
Lailah. Pashati Et-Kuttonti, Eichachah Elbashenah; Rachatzti Et-
Raglai Eichachah Atanefem. Dodi, Shalach Yado Min-Hachor,
Ume'ai Hamu Alav. Kamti Ani Liftoach Ledodi; Veyadai Natefu-Mor,
Ve'etzbe'otai Mor Over, Al Kapot Haman'ul. Patachti Ani Ledodi,
Vedodi Chamak Avar; Nafshi Yatze'ah Vedabero, Bikashtihu Velo
Metzatihu, Kerativ Velo Anani. Metza'uni Hashomerim Hassovevim
Ba'ir Hikkuni Fetza'uni; Nase'u Et-Redidi Me'alai, Shomerei
Hachomot. Hishba'ti Etchem Benot Yerushalayim Im-Timtze'u Et-

Dodi, Mah-Taggidu Lo, Shecholat Ahavah Ani. Mah-Dodech Middod, Hayafah Banashim; Mah-Dodech Middod, Shekachah Hishba'tanu. Dodi Tzach Ve'adom, Dagul Merevavah. Rosho Ketem Paz; Kevutzotav Taltallim, Shechorot Ka'orev. Einav Keyonim Al-'Afikei Mayim; Rochatzot Bechalav, Yoshevot Al-Millet. Lechayav Ka'arugat Habbosem, Migdelot Merkachim; Siftotav Shoshanim, Notefot Mor Over. Yadav Gelilei Zahav, Memulla'im Battarshish; Me'av Eshet Shen, Me'ullefet Sappirim. Shokav Ammudei Shesh, Meyussadim Al-'Adnei-Faz; Mar'ehu Kallevanon, Bachur Ka'arazim. Chikko Mamtakkim, Vechulo Machamadim; Zeh Dodi Vezeh Re'i, Benot Yerushalayim.

5. I have come into my garden, my sister, my bride; I have gathered my myrrh with my spice; I have eaten my honeycomb with my honey; I have drunk my wine with my milk. Eat, friends; Drink, yes, drink abundantly, beloved. I sleep, but my heart wakes; Behold, my beloved knocks: 'Open to me, my sister, my love, my dove, my undefiled; For my head is filled with dew, My locks with the drops of the night.' I have taken off my coat; How will I put it on? I have washed my feet; How will I defile them? My beloved put in his hand by the hole of the door, And my heart was moved for him. I rose up to open to my beloved; And my hands dropped with myrrh, And my fingers with flowing myrrh, On the handles of the bar. I opened to my beloved; But my beloved had turned away, and was gone. My soul failed me when he spoke. I searched for him, but I could not find him; I called him, but he gave me no answer. The watchmen that go around the city found me, They struck me, they wounded me; The keepers of the walls took my mantle away from me. 'I adjure you, daughters of Yerushalayim, If you find my beloved, what will you tell him? That I am love-sick.' 'What is your beloved more than another beloved, Oh fairest among women? What is your beloved more than another beloved, That you so adjure us?' 'My beloved is white and ruddy, Pre-eminent above ten thousand. His head is as the most fine gold, His locks are curled, And black as a raven. His eyes are like doves Beside the water-brooks; Washed with milk, And fitly set. His cheeks are like a bed of spices, like banks of sweet herbs; His lips are as lilies, Dropping with flowing myrrh. His hands are like rods of gold set with beryl; His body is like polished ivory overlaid with sapphires. His legs are like pillars of marble, Set on sockets of fine gold; His aspect is like Levanon, Excellent as the cedars. His mouth is most sweet; yes, he is altogether lovely. This is my beloved, and this is my friend, daughters of Yerushalayim.'

ו אָנָה הָלַךְ דּוֹדֵךְ הַיָּפָה בַּנָּשִׁים אָנָה פָּנָה דוֹדֵךְ וּנְבַקְשֶׁנּוּ עִמָּךְ: דּוֹדִי יָרַד לְגַנּוֹ לַעֲרֻגוֹת הַבֹּשֶׂם לִרְעוֹת בַּגַּנִּים וְלִלְקֹט שׁוֹשַׁנִּים: אֲנִי לְדוֹדִי וְדוֹדִי לִי הָרֹעֶה בַּשּׁוֹשַׁנִּים: יָפָה אַתְּ רַעְיָתִי כְּתִרְצָה נָאוָה כִּירוּשָׁלִַם אֲיֻמָּה כַּנִּדְגָּלוֹת: הָסֵבִּי עֵינַיִךְ מִנֶּגְדִּי שֶׁהֵם הִרְהִיבֻנִי שַׂעְרֵךְ כְּעֵדֶר הָעִזִּים שֶׁגָּלְשׁוּ מִן־הַגִּלְעָד: שִׁנַּיִךְ כְּעֵדֶר הָרְחֵלִים שֶׁעָלוּ מִן־הָרַחְצָה שֶׁכֻּלָּם מַתְאִימוֹת וְשַׁכֻּלָה אֵין בָּהֶם: כְּפֶלַח הָרִמּוֹן רַקָּתֵךְ מִבַּעַד לְצַמָּתֵךְ: שִׁשִּׁים הֵמָּה מְלָכוֹת וּשְׁמֹנִים פִּילַגְשִׁים וַעֲלָמוֹת אֵין מִסְפָּר: אַחַת הִיא יוֹנָתִי תַמָּתִי אַחַת הִיא לְאִמָּהּ בָּרָה הִיא לְיוֹלַדְתָּהּ רָאוּהָ בָנוֹת וַיְאַשְּׁרוּהָ מְלָכוֹת וּפִילַגְשִׁים וַיְהַלְלוּהָ: מִי־זֹאת הַנִּשְׁקָפָה כְּמוֹ־שָׁחַר יָפָה כַלְּבָנָה בָּרָה כַּחַמָּה אֲיֻמָּה כַּנִּדְגָּלוֹת: אֶל־גִּנַּת אֱגוֹז יָרַדְתִּי לִרְאוֹת בְּאִבֵּי הַנָּחַל לִרְאוֹת הֲפָרְחָה הַגֶּפֶן הֵנֵצוּ הָרִמֹּנִים: לֹא יָדַעְתִּי נַפְשִׁי שָׂמַתְנִי מַרְכְּבוֹת עַמִּי נָדִיב:

ו Anah Halach Dodech, Hayafah Banashim; Anah Panah Dodech, Unevakshenu Imach. Dodi Yarad Legano, La'arugot Habbosem; Lir'ot Baganim, Velilkot Shoshanim. Ani Ledodi Vedodi Li, Haro'eh Bashoshanim. Yafah At Ra'yati Ketirtzah, Navah Kirushalayim Ayumah Kanidgalot. Hasebbi Einayich Minegdi, Shehem Hirhivuni; Sa'rech Ke'eder Ha'izim, Sheggaleshu Min-Hagil'ad. Shinayich Ke'eder Harechelim, She'alu Min-Harachtzah; Shekulam Mat'imot, Veshakkulah Ein Bahem. Kefelach Harimmon Rakkatech, Miba'ad Letzammatech. Shishim Hemah Melachot, Ushemonim Pilagshim; Va'alamot Ein Mispar. Achat Hi Yonati Tammati, Achat Hi Le'imah, Barah Hi Leyoladtah; Ra'uha Vanot Vay'asheruha, Melachot Ufilagshim Vayhaleluha. Mi-Zot Hanishkafah Kemo-Shachar; Yafah

Chalevanah, Barah Kachamah, Ayumah Kanidgalot. El-Ginat Egoz Yaradti, Lir'ot Be'ibei Hanachal; Lir'ot Hafarechah Hagefen, Henetzu Harimonim. Lo Yada'ti, Nafshi Samatni, Markevot Ammi Nadiv.

6. 'Where has your beloved gone, Oh fairest among women? Where has your beloved turned, That we may seek him with you?' 'My beloved is gone down into his garden, To the beds of spices, To feed in the gardens, And to gather lilies. I am my beloved's, and my beloved is mine, that feeds among the lilies.' You are beautiful, my love, as Tirzah, Pleasant like Yerushalayim, Threatening like an army with banners. Turn away your eyes from me, For they have overcome me. Your hair is like a flock of goats, that trail down from Gilead. Your teeth are like a flock of ewes, which have come up from the washing; Which are all paired, And none fails among them. Your temples are like a pomegranate split open behind your veil. There are sixty queens, And eighty concubines, And maidens without number. My dove, my undefiled, is but one; She is the only one of her mother; She is the choice one of her that gave birth to her. The daughters saw her, and called her happy; Even, the queens and the concubines, they praised her. Who is she that appears like the dawn, Beautiful like the moon, Clear like the sun, Threatening like an army with banners? I went down into the garden of nuts, To look at the green plants of the valley, To see whether the vine budded, And the pomegranates were in flower. Before I was aware, my soul set me on the chariots of my princely people.

ז שׁוּבִי שׁוּבִי הַשּׁוּלַמִּית שׁוּבִי שׁוּבִי וְנֶחֱזֶה־בָּךְ מַה־תֶּחֱזוּ בַּשּׁוּלַמִּית כִּמְחֹלַת הַמַּחֲנָיִם: מַה־יָּפוּ פְעָמַיִךְ בַּנְּעָלִים בַּת־נָדִיב חַמּוּקֵי יְרֵכַיִךְ כְּמוֹ חֲלָאִים מַעֲשֵׂה יְדֵי אָמָּן: שָׁרְרֵךְ אַגַּן הַסַּהַר אַל־יֶחְסַר הַמָּזֶג בִּטְנֵךְ עֲרֵמַת חִטִּים סוּגָה בַּשּׁוֹשַׁנִּים: שְׁנֵי שָׁדַיִךְ כִּשְׁנֵי עֳפָרִים תָּאֳמֵי צְבִיָּה: צַוָּארֵךְ כְּמִגְדַּל הַשֵּׁן עֵינַיִךְ בְּרֵכוֹת בְּחֶשְׁבּוֹן עַל־שַׁעַר בַּת־רַבִּים אַפֵּךְ כְּמִגְדַּל הַלְּבָנוֹן צוֹפֶה פְּנֵי דַמָּשֶׂק: רֹאשֵׁךְ עָלַיִךְ

כַּכַּרְמֶ֫ל וְדַלַּת רֹאשֵׁךְ כָּאַרְגָּמָ֑ן מֶ֫לֶךְ אָס֥וּר בָּרְהָטִֽים: מַה־יָּפִית֙
וּמַה־נָּעַ֫מְתְּ אַהֲבָ֖ה בַּתַּעֲנוּגִֽים: זֹ֤את קֽוֹמָתֵךְ֙ דָּֽמְתָ֣ה לְתָמָ֔ר וְשָׁדַ֖יִךְ
לְאַשְׁכֹּלֽוֹת: אָמַ֙רְתִּי֙ אֶעֱלֶ֣ה בְתָמָ֔ר אֹֽחֲזָ֖ה בְּסַנְסִנָּ֑יו וְיִֽהְיוּ־נָ֤א שָׁדַ֙יִךְ֙
כְּאֶשְׁכְּל֣וֹת הַגֶּ֔פֶן וְרֵ֥יחַ אַפֵּ֖ךְ כַּתַּפּוּחִֽים: וְחִכֵּ֕ךְ כְּיֵ֥ין הַטּ֛וֹב הוֹלֵ֥ךְ לְדוֹדִ֖י
לְמֵֽישָׁרִ֑ים דּוֹבֵ֖ב שִׂפְתֵ֥י יְשֵׁנִֽים: אֲנִ֣י לְדוֹדִ֔י וְעָלַ֖י תְּשֽׁוּקָתֽוֹ: לְכָ֤ה דוֹדִי֙
נֵצֵ֣א הַשָּׂדֶ֔ה נָלִ֖ינָה בַּכְּפָרִֽים: נַשְׁכִּ֙ימָה֙ לַכְּרָמִ֔ים נִרְאֶ֞ה אִם פָּֽרְחָ֤ה
הַגֶּ֙פֶן֙ פִּתַּ֣ח הַסְּמָדַ֔ר הֵנֵ֖צוּ הָרִמּוֹנִ֑ים שָׁ֛ם אֶתֵּ֥ן אֶת־דֹּדַ֖י לָֽךְ: הַֽדּוּדָאִ֣ים
נָֽתְנוּ־רֵ֗יחַ וְעַל־פְּתָחֵ֙ינוּ֙ כָּל־מְגָדִ֔ים חֲדָשִׁ֖ים גַּם־יְשָׁנִ֑ים דּוֹדִ֖י צָפַ֥נְתִּי
לָֽךְ:

ז Shuvi Shuvi Hashulammit, Shuvi Shuvi Venechezeh-Bach; Mah-Techezu Bashulammit, Kimcholat Hamachanayim. Mah-Yafu Fe'amayich Bane'alim Bat-Nadiv; Chamukei Yerechayich, Kemo Chala'im, Ma'aseh Yedei Omman. Shorerech Aggan Hassahar, Al-Yechsar Hamazeg; Bitnech Aremat Chitim, Sugah Bashoshanim. Shenei Shadayich Kishnei Ofarim To'omei Tzeviyah. Tzavarech Kemigdal Hashen; Einayich Berechot Becheshbon, Al-Sha'ar Bat-Rabim, Appech Kemigdal Hallevanon, Tzofeh Penei Dammasek. Roshech Alayich Kakarmel, Vedalat Roshech Ka'argaman; Melech Asur Barehatim. Mah-Yafit Umah-Na'amt, Ahavah Batta'anugim. Zot Komatech Dametah Letamar, Veshadayich Le'ashkolot. Amarti E'eleh Vetamar, Ochazah Besansinav; Veyihyu-Na Shadayich Ke'eshkelot Hagefen, Vereiach Appech Kattappuchim. Vechikkech Keyein Hatov Holech Ledodi Lemeisharim; Dovev Siftei Yeshenim. Ani Ledodi, Ve'alai Teshukato. Lechah Dodi Netzei Hassadeh, Nalinah Bakkefarim. Nashkimah Lakeramim, Nir'eh Im Parechah Hagefen Pittach Hassemadar, Henetzu Harimonim; Sham Etten Et-Dodai Lach. Hadduda'im Natenu-Reiach, Ve'al-Petacheinu Chol-Megadim, Chadashim Gam-Yeshanim; Dodi Tzafanti Lach.

7. Return, return, Shulammite; Return, return, that we may look upon you. What will you see in the Shulammite? As it were a dance of two companies. How beautiful are your steps in sandals, Oh prince's daughter, The roundings of your thighs are like the links of a chain, The work of the hands of a skilled workman. Your navel is like a round goblet, where in no mingled wine is absent; Your belly is

like a heap of wheat set around with lilies. Your two breasts are like two fawns that are twins of a gazelle. Your neck is as a tower of ivory; Your eyes as the pools in Cheshbon, By the gate of Bat-rabim; Your nose is like the tower of Levanon which looks toward Dammasek. Your head on you is like Karmel, and the hair of your head like purple; The king is held captive in the locks of it. How beautiful and how pleasant you are, Oh love, for delights, Your stature is like a palm-tree, and your breasts to clusters of grapes. I said: 'I will climb up into the palm-tree, I will take hold of the branches of it; and let your breasts be as clusters of the vine, And the smell of your countenance like apples; And the roof of your mouth like the best wine, That glides down smoothly for my beloved, moving gently the lips of those that are asleep.' I am my beloved's, and his desire is toward me. Come, my beloved, let us go out into the field; let us lodge in the villages. Let us get up early to the vineyards; let us see whether the vine has budded, whether the vine-blossom is opened, and the pomegranates be in flower; there I will give you my love. The mandrakes give out fragrance, and at our doors are all manner of precious fruits, new and old, which I have laid up for you, Oh my beloved.

ח מִי יִתֶּנְךָ֙ כְּאָ֣ח לִ֔י יוֹנֵ֖ק שְׁדֵ֣י אִמִּ֑י אֶֽמְצָאֲךָ֤ בַחוּץ֙ אֶשָׁ֣קְךָ֔ גַּ֖ם לֹא־יָבֻ֥זוּ לִֽי: אֶנְהָֽגֲךָ֗ אֲבִֽיאֲךָ֛ אֶל־בֵּ֥ית אִמִּ֖י תְּלַמְּדֵ֑נִי אַשְׁקְךָ֙ מִיַּ֣יִן הָרֶ֔קַח מֵעֲסִ֖יס רִמֹּנִֽי: שְׂמֹאלוֹ֙ תַּ֣חַת רֹאשִׁ֔י וִימִינ֖וֹ תְּחַבְּקֵֽנִי: הִשְׁבַּ֨עְתִּי אֶתְכֶ֜ם בְּנ֤וֹת יְרֽוּשָׁלִַ֙ם֙ מַה־תָּעִ֣ירוּ ׀ וּֽמַה־תְּעֹֽרְר֛וּ אֶת־הָאַהֲבָ֖ה עַ֥ד שֶׁתֶּחְפָּֽץ: מִ֣י זֹ֗את עֹלָה֙ מִן־הַמִּדְבָּ֔ר מִתְרַפֶּ֖קֶת עַל־דּוֹדָ֑הּ תַּ֤חַת הַתַּפּ֙וּחַ֙ עֽוֹרַרְתִּ֔יךָ שָׁ֚מָּה חִבְּלַ֣תְךָ אִמֶּ֔ךָ שָׁ֖מָּה חִבְּלָ֥ה יְלָדַֽתְךָ: שִׂימֵ֨נִי כַֽחוֹתָ֜ם עַל־לִבֶּ֗ךָ כַּֽחוֹתָם֙ עַל־זְר֣וֹעֶ֔ךָ כִּֽי־עַזָּ֤ה כַמָּ֙וֶת֙ אַהֲבָ֔ה קָשָׁ֥ה כִשְׁא֖וֹל קִנְאָ֑ה רְשָׁפֶ֕יהָ רִשְׁפֵּ֕י אֵ֖שׁ שַׁלְהֶבֶתְיָֽה: מַ֣יִם רַבִּ֗ים לֹ֤א יֽוּכְלוּ֙ לְכַבּ֣וֹת אֶת־הָֽאַהֲבָ֔ה וּנְהָר֖וֹת לֹ֣א יִשְׁטְפ֑וּהָ אִם־יִתֵּ֨ן אִ֜ישׁ אֶת־כָּל־ה֤וֹן

בֵּיתוֹ בָּאַהֲבָה בּוֹז יָבוּזוּ לוֹ: אָחוֹת לָנוּ קְטַנָּה וְשָׁדַיִם אֵין לָהּ
מַה־נַּעֲשֶׂה לַאֲחֹתֵנוּ בַּיּוֹם שֶׁיְּדֻבַּר־בָּהּ: אִם־חוֹמָה הִיא נִבְנֶה עָלֶיהָ
טִירַת כָּסֶף וְאִם־דֶּלֶת הִיא נָצוּר עָלֶיהָ לוּחַ אָרֶז: אֲנִי חוֹמָה וְשָׁדַי
כַּמִּגְדָּלוֹת אָז הָיִיתִי בְעֵינָיו כְּמוֹצְאֵת שָׁלוֹם: כֶּרֶם הָיָה לִשְׁלֹמֹה
בְּבַעַל הָמוֹן נָתַן אֶת־הַכֶּרֶם לַנֹּטְרִים אִישׁ יָבִא בְּפִרְיוֹ אֶלֶף כָּסֶף:
כַּרְמִי שֶׁלִּי לְפָנָי הָאֶלֶף לְךָ שְׁלֹמֹה וּמָאתַיִם לְנֹטְרִים אֶת־פִּרְיוֹ:
הַיּוֹשֶׁבֶת בַּגַּנִּים חֲבֵרִים מַקְשִׁיבִים לְקוֹלֵךְ הַשְׁמִיעִנִי: בְּרַח | דּוֹדִי
וּדְמֵה־לְךָ לִצְבִי אוֹ לְעֹפֶר הָאַיָּלִים עַל הָרֵי בְשָׂמִים:

ח Mi Yitencha Ke'ach Li, Yonek Shedei Immi; Emtza'acha Vachutz
Eshakecha, Gam Lo-Yavuzu Li. Enhagecha, Avi'acha El-Beit Immi
Telamedeni; Ashkecha Miyayin Harekach, Me'asis Rimmoni.
Semolo Tachat Roshi, Vimino Techabekeni. Hishba'ti Etchem Benot
Yerushalayim Mah-Ta'iru Umah-Te'oreru Et-Ha'ahavah Ad
Shetechpatz. Mi Zot, Olah Min-Hamidbar, Mitrappeket Al-Dodah;
Tachat Hatappuach Orarticha, Shamah Chibelatcha Imecha,
Shamah Chibelah Yeladatcha. Simeni Chachotam Al-Libecha,
Kachotam Al-Zero'echa, Ki-'Azah Chamavet Ahavah, Kashah
Chish'ol Kin'ah; Reshafeiha Rishpei Esh Shalhevetyah. Mayim
Rabim, Lo Yuchelu Lechabbot Et-Ha'ahavah, Uneharot Lo
Yishtefuha; Im-Yiten Ish Et-Chol-Hon Beito Ba'ahavah, Boz Yavuzu
Lo. Achot Lanu Ketanah, Veshadayim Ein Lah; Mah-Na'aseh
La'achotenu, Bayom Sheyedubbar-Bah. Im-Chomah Hi, Nivneh
Aleiha Tirat Kasef; Ve'im-Delet Hi, Natzur Aleiha Luach Arez. Ani
Chomah, Veshadai Kammigdalot; Az Hayiti Ve'einav Kemotze'et
Shalom. Kerem Hayah Lishlomoh Beva'al Hamon, Natan Et-
Hakerem Lanoterim; Ish Yavi Befiryo Elef Kasef. Karmi Sheli Lefanai;
Ha'elef Lecha Shelomoh, Umatayim Lenoterim Et-Piryo. Hayoshevet
Baganim, Chaverim Makshivim Lekolech Hashmi'ini. Berach Dodi,
Udemeh-Lecha Litzvi O Le'ofer Ha'ayalim, Al Harei Vesamim.

8. Oh that you were like my brother, that fed on the breasts of my
mother. When I would find you without, I would kiss you; Yes, and
no one would despise me. I would lead you, and bring you into my
mother's house, That you might instruct me; I would cause you to
drink of spiced wine, of the juice of my pomegranate. His left hand
would be under my head, And his right hand would embrace me. 'I

implore you, daughters of Yerushalayim: Why should you awaken, or stir up love, until it pleases?' Who is this that comes up from the wilderness, Leaning on her beloved? Under the apple-tree I awakened you; There your mother was in travail with you; There she was in travail and brought you out. Set me as a seal upon your heart, As a seal upon your arm; For love is strong as death, Jealousy is cruel as the grave; The flashes of it are flashes of fire, A very flame of Hashem. Many waters cannot quench love, Neither can the floods drown it; If a man would give all the substance of his house for love, he would utterly be despised. We have a little sister, And she has no breasts; What will we do for our sister In the day when she will be spoken for? If she is a wall, We will build upon her a turret of silver; And if she is a door, We will enclose her with boards of cedar. I am a wall, And my breasts like the towers of it; Then was I in his eyes as one that found peace. Shlomo had a vineyard at Baal-hamon; He gave over the vineyard to keepers; Every one for the fruit of it brought in a thousand pieces of silver. My vineyard, which is mine, is before me; You, Shlomo, will have the thousand, And those that keep the fruit of it two hundred. You that dwells in the gardens, The companions heed your voice: 'Cause me to hear it.' Make haste, my beloved, And be like a gazelle or a young deer on the mountains of spices.

Some say afterwards:

רִבּוֹן כָּל הָעוֹלָמִים. יְהִי רָצוֹן מִלְּפָנֶיךָ יְהֹוָה אֱלֹהֵינוּ וֵאלֹהֵי אֲבוֹתֵינוּ. שֶׁבִּזְכוּת שִׁיר הַשִּׁירִים אֲשֶׁר קָרָאנוּ וְלָמַדְנוּ. שֶׁהוּא קֹדֶשׁ קָדָשִׁים. בִּזְכוּת פְּסוּקָיו. וּבִזְכוּת תֵּבוֹתָיו. וּבִזְכוּת אוֹתִיּוֹתָיו. וּבִזְכוּת נְקֻדּוֹתָיו. וּבִזְכוּת טְעָמָיו וְצֵרוּפָיו וּרְמָזָיו וְסוֹדוֹתָיו הַקְּדוֹשִׁים וְהַטְּהוֹרִים הַנּוֹרָאִים הַיּוֹצְאִים מִמֶּנּוּ. שֶׁתְּהֵא שָׁעָה זוֹ שְׁעַת רַחֲמִים. שְׁעַת הַקְשָׁבָה. שְׁעַת הַאֲזָנָה. וְנִקְרָאֲךָ וְתַעֲנֵנוּ. נַעֲתִיר לְךָ וְתֵעָתֵר לָנוּ. וְתִהְיֶה עוֹלָה לְפָנֶיךָ קְרִיאַת וְלִמּוּד שִׁיר הַשִּׁירִים כְּאִלּוּ הִשַּׂגְנוּ כָּל־הַסּוֹדוֹת הַנִּפְלָאִים וְהַנּוֹרָאִים אֲשֶׁר הֵם חֲתוּמִים וּסְתוּמִים בּוֹ בְּכָל־תְּנָאָיו.

וְנִזְכֶּה לְמָקוֹם שֶׁהַנְּפָשׁוֹת. הָרוּחוֹת וְהַנְּשָׁמוֹת. נֶחְצָבוֹת מִשָּׁם. וּכְאִלּוּ עָשִׂינוּ
כָּל־מַה־שֶּׁמֻּטָּל עָלֵינוּ לְהַשִּׂיג בֵּין בְּגִלְגּוּל זֶה. בֵּין בְּגִלְגּוּלִים אֲחֵרִים. וְלִהְיוֹת
מִן הָעוֹלִים וְהַזּוֹכִים לְעוֹלָם הַבָּא. עִם שְׁאָר צַדִּיקִים וַחֲסִידִים. וּמַלֵּא
כָּל־מִשְׁאֲלוֹת לִבֵּנוּ לְטוֹבָה. וְתִהְיֶה עִם לְבָבֵנוּ וְאִמְרֵי פִינוּ בְּעֵת מַחְשְׁבוֹתֵינוּ.
וְעִם יָדֵינוּ בְּעֵת מַעֲבָדֵינוּ. וְתִשְׁלַח בְּרָכָה וְהַצְלָחָה וְהַרְוָחָה בְּכָל־מַעֲשֵׂי יָדֵינוּ.
וּמֵעָפָר עָנְיֵנוּ תְּקִימֵנוּ. וּמֵאַשְׁפּוֹת דַּלּוּתֵנוּ תְּרוֹמְמֵנוּ. וְתָשִׁיב שְׁכִינָתְךָ לְעִיר
קָדְשְׁךָ בִּמְהֵרָה בְיָמֵינוּ. אָמֵן:

Ribon Kol Ha'olamim, Yehi Ratzon Milfaneicha Adonai Eloheinu Velohei Avoteinu,
Shebizchut Shir Hashirim Asher Karanu, Shehu Kodesh Kadashim, Bizchut Pesukav,
Uvizchut Tevotav, Uvizchut Otiyotav, Uvizchut Nekudotav, Uvizchut Te'amav
Vetzerufav Uremazav Vesodotav Hakkedoshim Vehatehorim Hanora'im Hayotze'im
Mimenu, Shetehei Sha'ah Zo She'at Rachamim, She'at Hakshavah, She'at
Ha'azanah, Venikra'acha Veta'aneinu, Na'atir Lecha Vete'ater Lanu, Vetihyeh Olah
Lefaneicha Keri'at Shir Hashirim Ke'ilu Hissagnu Kol-Hassodot Hanifla'im
Vehanorah'im Asher Hem Chatumim Usetumim Bo Bechol-Tena'av, Venizkeh
Lemakom Shehanefashot, Haruchot Vehaneshamot, Nechtzavot Misham, Uche'ilu
Asinu Kol-Mah-Shemuttal Aleinu Lehassig Bein Begilgul Zeh, Bein Begilgulim
Acherim, Velihyot Min Ha'olim Vehazochim La'olam Haba, Im She'ar Tzaddikim
Vachasidim. Umalei Kol-Mish'alot Libenu Letovah, Vetihyeh Im Levavenu Ve'imrei
Finu Be'et Machshevoteinu, Ve'im Yadeinu Be'et Ma'abbadeinu, Vetishlach
Berachah Vehatzlachah Veharvachah Bechol-Ma'asei Yadeinu, Ume'afar Aneyenu
Tekimenu, Ume'ashpot Dalutenu Teromemenu, Vetashiv Shechinatecha Le'ir
Kodshecha Bimheirah Veyameinu, Amen.

Kabbalat Shabbat / Receiving Shabbat

Psalms 95

לְכוּ נְרַנְּנָה לַיהוָה נָרִיעָה לְצוּר יִשְׁעֵנוּ: נְקַדְּמָה פָנָיו בְּתוֹדָה
בִּזְמִרוֹת נָרִיעַ לוֹ: כִּי אֵל גָּדוֹל יְהוָה וּמֶלֶךְ גָּדוֹל עַל־כָּל־אֱלֹהִים:
אֲשֶׁר בְּיָדוֹ מֶחְקְרֵי־אָרֶץ וְתוֹעֲפֹת הָרִים לוֹ: אֲשֶׁר־לוֹ הַיָּם וְהוּא
עָשָׂהוּ וְיַבֶּשֶׁת יָדָיו יָצָרוּ: בֹּאוּ נִשְׁתַּחֲוֶה וְנִכְרָעָה נִבְרְכָה לִפְנֵי־יְהוָה
עֹשֵׂנוּ: כִּי הוּא אֱלֹהֵינוּ וַאֲנַחְנוּ עַם מַרְעִיתוֹ וְצֹאן יָדוֹ הַיּוֹם
אִם־בְּקֹלוֹ תִשְׁמָעוּ: אַל־תַּקְשׁוּ לְבַבְכֶם כִּמְרִיבָה כְּיוֹם מַסָּה בַּמִּדְבָּר:
אֲשֶׁר נִסּוּנִי אֲבוֹתֵיכֶם בְּחָנוּנִי גַּם־רָאוּ פָעֳלִי: אַרְבָּעִים שָׁנָה | אָקוּט
בְּדוֹר וָאֹמַר עַם תֹּעֵי לֵבָב הֵם וְהֵם לֹא־יָדְעוּ דְרָכָי: אֲשֶׁר־נִשְׁבַּעְתִּי
בְאַפִּי אִם־יְבֹאוּן אֶל־מְנוּחָתִי:

Lechu Neranenah L'Adonai Nari'ah. Letzur Yish'enu. Nekademah
Fanav Betodah; Bizmirot. Naria Lo. Ki El Gadol Adonai Umelech
Gadol. Al-Chol-'Elohim. Asher Beyado Mechkerei-'Aretz; Veto'afot
Harim Lo. Asher-Lo Hayom Vehu Asahu; Veyabeshet. Yadav Yatzaru.
Bo'u Nishtachaveh Venichra'ah; Nivrechah. Lifnei-Adonai Osenu. Ki
Hu Eloheinu. Va'anachnu Am Mar'ito Vetzon Yado; Hayom. Im-
Bekolo Tishma'u. Al-Takshu Levavchem Kimrivah; Keyom Massah.
Bamidbar. Asher Nissuni Avoteichem; Bechanuni. Gam-Ra'u Fo'oli.
Arba'im Shanah Akut Bedor. Va'omar. Am To'ei Levav Hem; Vehem.
Lo-Yade'u Derachai. Asher-Nishba'ti Ve'appi; Im-Yevo'un. El-
Menuchati.

Come, let us sing to Hashem; Let us shout for joy to the Rock of our
salvation. Let us come before His presence with thanksgiving, Let
us shout for joy to Him with songs of praise. For Hashem is a great
God, And a great King above all gods; In whose hand are the depths
of the earth; The heights of the mountains are His also. The sea is
His, and He made it; And His hands formed the dry land. Come, let
us bow down and bend the knee; Let us kneel before Hashem our
Maker; For He is our God, And we are the people of His pasture,
and the flock of His hand. Today, if you would only heed His voice.

Do not harden your heart, as at Merivah, As in the day of Massah in the wilderness; When your fathers tried Me, Proved Me, even though they saw My work. For forty years I was wearied with that generation, And said: It is a people that do stray in their heart, And they have not known My ways; so I swore in My wrath, That they should not enter into My rest.

Psalms 96

שִׁירוּ לַיהֹוָה שִׁיר חָדָשׁ שִׁירוּ לַיהֹוָה כָּל־הָאָרֶץ: שִׁירוּ לַיהֹוָה בָּרְכוּ
שְׁמוֹ בַּשְּׂרוּ מִיּוֹם־לְיוֹם יְשׁוּעָתוֹ: סַפְּרוּ בַגּוֹיִם כְּבוֹדוֹ בְּכָל־הָעַמִּים
נִפְלְאוֹתָיו: כִּי גָדוֹל יְהֹוָה וּמְהֻלָּל מְאֹד נוֹרָא הוּא עַל־כָּל־אֱלֹהִים:
כִּי כָּל־אֱלֹהֵי הָעַמִּים אֱלִילִים וַיהֹוָה שָׁמַיִם עָשָׂה: הוֹד־וְהָדָר לְפָנָיו
עֹז וְתִפְאֶרֶת בְּמִקְדָּשׁוֹ: הָבוּ לַיהֹוָה מִשְׁפְּחוֹת עַמִּים הָבוּ לַיהֹוָה
כָּבוֹד וָעֹז: הָבוּ לַיהֹוָה כְּבוֹד שְׁמוֹ שְׂאוּ־מִנְחָה וּבֹאוּ לְחַצְרוֹתָיו:
הִשְׁתַּחֲווּ לַיהֹוָה בְּהַדְרַת־קֹדֶשׁ חִילוּ מִפָּנָיו כָּל־הָאָרֶץ: אִמְרוּ בַגּוֹיִם |
יְהֹוָה מָלָךְ אַף־תִּכּוֹן תֵּבֵל בַּל־תִּמּוֹט יָדִין עַמִּים בְּמֵישָׁרִים: יִשְׂמְחוּ
הַשָּׁמַיִם וְתָגֵל הָאָרֶץ יִרְעַם הַיָּם וּמְלֹאוֹ: יַעֲלֹז שָׂדַי וְכָל־אֲשֶׁר־בּוֹ אָז
יְרַנְּנוּ כָּל־עֲצֵי־יָעַר: לִפְנֵי יְהֹוָה כִּי בָא כִּי בָא לִשְׁפֹּט הָאָרֶץ
יִשְׁפֹּט־תֵּבֵל בְּצֶדֶק וְעַמִּים בֶּאֱמוּנָתוֹ:

Shiru L'Adonai Shir Chadash; Shiru L'Adonai Chol-Ha'aretz. Shiru L'Adonai Barechu Shemo; Baseru Miyom-Leyom. Yeshu'ato. Saperu Vagoyim Kevodo; Bechol-Ha'ammim. Nifle'otav. Ki Gadol Adonai Umehulal Me'od; Nora Hu Al-Chol-Elohim. Ki Chol-'Elohei Ha'ammim Elilim; Va'Adonai. Shamayim Asah. Hod-Vehadar Lefanav; Oz Vetif'eret. Bemikdasho. Havu L'Adonai Mishpechot Ammim; Havu L'Adonai Kavod Va'oz. Havu L'Adonai Kevod Shemo; Se'u-Minchah. Uvo'u Lechatzrotav. Hishtachavu L'Adonai Behadrat-Kodesh; Chilu Mipanav. Chol-Ha'aretz. Imru Vagoyim Adonai Malach. Af-Tikon Tevel Bal-Timot; Yadin Ammim. Bemeisharim. Yismechu Hashamayim Vetagel Ha'aretz; Yir'am Hayam. Umelo'o. Ya'aloz Sadai Vechol-'Asher-Bo; Az Yeranenu.

Chol-'Atzei-Ya'ar. Lifnei Adonai Ki Va. Ki Va Lishpot Ha'aretz
Yishpot-Tevel Betzedek; Ve'ammim. Be'emunato.

Sing to Hashem a new song; Sing to Hashem, all the earth. Sing to
Hashem, bless His name; Proclaim His salvation from day to day.
Declare His glory among the nations, His marvelous works among
all the peoples. For great is Hashem, and highly to be praised; He is
to be feared above all gods. For all the gods of the peoples are
nothing; But Hashem made the heavens. Honor and majesty are
before Him; Strength and beauty are in His Sanctuary. Ascribe to
Hashem, families of peoples, Ascribe to Hashem glory and strength.
Ascribe to Hashem the glory due to His name; Bring an offering,
and come into His courts. Worship Hashem in the beauty of
holiness; Tremble before Him, all the earth. Say among the nations:
'Hashem reigns.' The world is also established that it cannot be
moved; He will judge the peoples with equity. Let the heavens be
glad, and let the earth rejoice; Let the sea roar, and the fullness of it;
Let the field exult; and all that is there in; Then will all the trees of
the wood sing for joy; Before Hashem, for He has come; For He has
come to judge the earth; He will judge the world with righteousness,
And the peoples in His faithfulness.

Psalms 97

יְהֹוָה מָלָךְ תָּגֵל הָאָרֶץ יִשְׂמְחוּ אִיִּים רַבִּים: עָנָן וַעֲרָפֶל סְבִיבָיו צֶדֶק

וּמִשְׁפָּט מְכוֹן כִּסְאוֹ: אֵשׁ לְפָנָיו תֵּלֵךְ וּתְלַהֵט סָבִיב צָרָיו: הֵאִירוּ

בְרָקָיו תֵּבֵל רָאֲתָה וַתָּחֵל הָאָרֶץ: הָרִים כַּדּוֹנַג נָמַסּוּ מִלִּפְנֵי יְהֹוָה

מִלִּפְנֵי אֲדוֹן כָּל־הָאָרֶץ: הִגִּידוּ הַשָּׁמַיִם צִדְקוֹ וְרָאוּ כָל־הָעַמִּים

כְּבוֹדוֹ: יֵבֹשׁוּ | כָּל־עֹבְדֵי פֶסֶל הַמִּתְהַלְלִים בָּאֱלִילִים הִשְׁתַּחֲווּ־לֹו

כָּל־אֱלֹהִים: שָׁמְעָה וַתִּשְׂמַח | צִיּוֹן וַתָּגֵלְנָה בְּנוֹת יְהוּדָה לְמַעַן

מִשְׁפָּטֶיךָ יְהֹוָה: כִּי־אַתָּה יְהֹוָה עֶלְיוֹן עַל־כָּל־הָאָרֶץ מְאֹד נַעֲלֵיתָ

עַל־כָּל־אֱלֹהִים: אֹהֲבֵי יְהֹוָה שִׂנְאוּ רָע שֹׁמֵר נַפְשׁוֹת חֲסִידָיו מִיַּד

רְשָׁעִים יַצִּילֵם: אוֹר זָרֻעַ לַצַּדִּיק וּלְיִשְׁרֵי־לֵב שִׂמְחָה: שִׂמְחוּ צַדִּיקִים
בַּיהוָה וְהוֹדוּ לְזֵכֶר קָדְשׁוֹ:

Adonai Maloch Tagel Ha'aretz; Yismechu. Iyim Rabim. Anan
Va'arafel Sevivav; Tzedek Umishpat. Mechon Kis'o. Esh Lefanav
Telech; Utelahet Saviv Tzarav. He'iru Verakav Tevel; Ra'atah Vatachel
Ha'aretz. Harim. Kaddonag. Namassu Millifnei Adonai Millifnei.
Adon Chol-Ha'aretz. Higidu Hashamayim Tzidko; Vera'u Chol-
Ha'ammim Kevodo. Yevoshu Chol-'Ovedei Fesel. Hamit'halelim
Ba'elilim; Hishtachavu-Lo Chol-Elohim. Shame'ah Vatismach
Tziyon. Vatagelenah Benot Yehudah; Lema'an Mishpateicha Adonai
Ki-'Attah Adonai Elyon Al-Chol-Ha'aretz; Me'od Na'aleita. Al-Chol-
Elohim. Ohavei Adonai Sin'u Ra Shomer Nafshot Chasidav; Miyad
Resha'im. Yatzilem. Or Zarua Latzaddik; Uleyishrei-Lev Simchah.
Simchu Tzaddikim Ba'Adonai; Vehodu. Lezecher Kodsho.

Hashem reigns; let the earth rejoice; Let the multitude of islands be glad. Clouds and darkness are around Him; Righteousness and justice are the foundation of His Throne. A fire goes before Him, And burns up His adversaries all around. His lightnings lit up the world; The earth saw, and trembled. The mountains melted like wax at the presence of Hashem, At the presence of Hashem of the whole earth. The heavens declared His righteousness, And all the peoples saw His glory. They are all ashamed that serve graven images, That boast themselves of nothings; Bow down to Him, all you gods. Tziyon heard and was glad, And the daughters of Yehudah rejoiced; Because of Your judgments, Hashem. For You, Hashem, are most high above all the earth; You are exalted far above all gods. Oh you that love Hashem, hate evil; He preserves the souls of His pious-ones; He delivered them out of the hand of the wicked. Light is sown for the righteous, And gladness for the upright in heart. Be glad in Hashem, you righteous; And give thanks to His holy name.

SOME BEGIN KABBALAT SHABBAT WITH PSALMS 99

Psalms 98

מִזְמוֹר שִׁירוּ לַיהֹוָה | שִׁיר חָדָשׁ כִּי־נִפְלָאוֹת עָשָׂה הוֹשִׁיעָה־לּוֹ יְמִינוֹ
וּזְרוֹעַ קָדְשׁוֹ: הוֹדִיעַ יְהֹוָה יְשׁוּעָתוֹ לְעֵינֵי הַגּוֹיִם גִּלָּה צִדְקָתוֹ: זָכַר
חַסְדּוֹ | וֶאֱמוּנָתוֹ לְבֵית יִשְׂרָאֵל רָאוּ כָל־אַפְסֵי־אָרֶץ אֵת יְשׁוּעַת
אֱלֹהֵינוּ: הָרִיעוּ לַיהֹוָה כָּל־הָאָרֶץ פִּצְחוּ וְרַנְּנוּ וְזַמֵּרוּ: זַמְּרוּ לַיהֹוָה
בְּכִנּוֹר בְּכִנּוֹר וְקוֹל זִמְרָה: בַּחֲצֹצְרוֹת וְקוֹל שׁוֹפָר הָרִיעוּ לִפְנֵי |
הַמֶּלֶךְ יְהֹוָה: יִרְעַם הַיָּם וּמְלֹאוֹ תֵּבֵל וְיֹשְׁבֵי בָהּ: נְהָרוֹת יִמְחֲאוּ־כָף
יַחַד הָרִים יְרַנֵּנוּ: לִפְנֵי יְהֹוָה כִּי בָא לִשְׁפֹּט הָאָרֶץ יִשְׁפֹּט־תֵּבֵל
בְּצֶדֶק וְעַמִּים בְּמֵישָׁרִים:

Mizmor Shiru L'Adonai Shir Chadash Ki-Nifla'ot Asah; Hoshi'ah-Lo
Yemino. Uzeroa Kodsho. Hodia Adonai Yeshu'ato; Le'einei
Hagoyim. Gillah Tzidkato. Zachar Chasdo Ve'emunato Leveit
Yisra'el Ra'u Chol-'Afsei-'Aretz; Et Yeshu'at Eloheinu. Hari'u
L'Adonai Chol-Ha'aretz; Pitzchu Veranenu Vezameru. Zameru
L'Adonai Bechinor; Bechinor. Vekol Zimrah. Bachatzotzerot Vekol
Shofar; Hari'u. Lifnei Hamelech Adonai Yir'am Hayom Umelo'o;
Tevel. Veyoshevei Vah. Neharot Yimcha'u-Chaf; Yachad Harim
Yeranenu. Lifnei Adonai Ki Va Lishpot Ha'aretz Yishpot-Tevel
Betzedek; Ve'ammim. Bemeisharim.

A Psalm. Sing to Hashem a new song; For He has done marvelous
things; His right hand, and His holy arm, has worked salvation for
Him. Hashem has made His salvation known; His righteousness He
revealed in the sight of the nations. He has remembered His mercy
and His faithfulness toward the House of Yisrael; All the ends of the
earth have seen the salvation of our God. Shout to Hashem, all the
earth; Break out and sing for joy, yes, sing praises. Sing praises to
Hashem with the harp; With the harp and the voice of melody. With
trumpets and sound of the horn shout before the King, Hashem.
Let the sea roar, and the fullness of it; The world, and they that
dwell there in; Let the floods clap their hands; Let the mountains
sing for joy together; Before Hashem, for He has come to judge the
earth; He will judge the world with righteousness, And the peoples
with equity.

Psalms 99

יְהֹוָה מָלָךְ יִרְגְּזוּ עַמִּים יֹשֵׁב כְּרוּבִים תָּנוּט הָאָרֶץ: יְהֹוָה בְּצִיּוֹן גָּדוֹל
וְרָם הוּא עַל־כָּל־הָעַמִּים: יוֹדוּ שִׁמְךָ גָּדוֹל וְנוֹרָא קָדוֹשׁ הוּא: וְעֹז
מֶלֶךְ מִשְׁפָּט אָהֵב אַתָּה כּוֹנַנְתָּ מֵישָׁרִים מִשְׁפָּט וּצְדָקָה בְּיַעֲקֹב |
אַתָּה עָשִׂיתָ: רוֹמְמוּ יְהֹוָה אֱלֹהֵינוּ וְהִשְׁתַּחֲווּ לַהֲדֹם רַגְלָיו קָדוֹשׁ
הוּא: מֹשֶׁה וְאַהֲרֹן | בְּכֹהֲנָיו וּשְׁמוּאֵל בְּקֹרְאֵי שְׁמוֹ קֹרִאים אֶל־יְהֹוָה
וְהוּא יַעֲנֵם: בְּעַמּוּד עָנָן יְדַבֵּר אֲלֵיהֶם שָׁמְרוּ עֵדֹתָיו וְחֹק נָתַן־לָמוֹ:
יְהֹוָה אֱלֹהֵינוּ אַתָּה עֲנִיתָם אֵל נֹשֵׂא הָיִיתָ לָהֶם וְנֹקֵם עַל־עֲלִילוֹתָם:
רוֹמְמוּ יְהֹוָה אֱלֹהֵינוּ וְהִשְׁתַּחֲווּ לְהַר קָדְשׁוֹ כִּי־קָדוֹשׁ יְהֹוָה אֱלֹהֵינוּ:

Adonai Maloch Yirgezu Ammim; Yoshev Keruvim. Tanut Ha'aretz.
Adonai Betziyon Gadol; Veram Hu Al-Chol-Ha'ammim. Yodu
Shimcha Gadol Venora. Kadosh Hu. Ve'oz Melech Mishpat Ahev
Attah Konanta Meisharim; Mishpat Utzedakah. Beya'akov Attah
Asita. Romemu Adonai Eloheinu. Vehishtachavu Lahadom Raglav.
Kadosh Hu. Mosheh Ve'aharon Bechohanav. Ushemu'el Bekore'ei
Shemo; Korim El-Adonai Vehu Ya'anem. Be'ammud Anon Yedaber
Aleihem; Shameru Edotav. Vechok Natan-Lamo. Adonai Eloheinu
Attah Anitam El Nosei Hayita Lahem; Venokem. Al-'Alilotam.
Romemu Adonai Eloheinu. Vehishtachavu Lehar Kodsho; Ki-Kadosh.
Adonai Eloheinu.

Hashem reigns; let the peoples tremble; He is enthroned on the
cheruvim; let the earth quake. Hashem is great in Tziyon; And He is
high above all the peoples. Let them praise Your name as great and
awful; Holy is He. The strength also of the king who loves justice—
You have established equity, You have executed justice and
righteousness in Yaakov. Exalt Hashem our God, And prostrate
yourselves at His footstool; Holy is He. Moshe and Aharon among
His priests, And Shemuel among them that call on His name, called
on Hashem, and He answered them. He spoke to them in the pillar
of cloud; They kept His testimonies, and the statute that He gave
them. Hashem our God, You answered them; You were a forgiving
God to them, though You took vengeance of their misdeeds. Exalt

Hashem our God, And worship at His holy hill; For Hashem our God is holy.

Mizmor Letodah (Psalms 100)

מִזְמוֹר לְתוֹדָה הָרִיעוּ לַיהֹוָה כָּל־הָאָרֶץ: עִבְדוּ אֶת־יְהֹוָה בְּשִׂמְחָה בֹּאוּ לְפָנָיו בִּרְנָנָה: דְּעוּ כִּי־יְהֹוָה הוּא אֱלֹהִים הוּא־עָשָׂנוּ וְלֹא (וְלוֹ) אֲנַחְנוּ עַמּוֹ וְצֹאן מַרְעִיתוֹ: בֹּאוּ שְׁעָרָיו | בְּתוֹדָה חֲצֵרֹתָיו בִּתְהִלָּה הוֹדוּ־לוֹ בָּרְכוּ שְׁמוֹ: כִּי־טוֹב יְהֹוָה לְעוֹלָם חַסְדּוֹ וְעַד־דֹּר וָדֹר אֱמוּנָתוֹ:

Mizmor Letodah; Hari'u L'Adonai Chol-Ha'aretz. Ivdu Et-Adonai Besimchah; Bo'u Lefanav. Birnanah. De'u. Ki-Adonai Hu Elohim Hu-'Asanu Velo Anachnu; Ammo. Vetzon Mar'ito. Bo'u She'arav Betodah. Chatzerotav Bit'hillah; Hodu-Lo Barechu Shemo. Ki-Tov Adonai Le'olam Chasdo; Ve'ad-Dor Vador. Emunato.

A Psalm of thanksgiving. Shout to Hashem, all the earth. Serve Hashem with gladness; come before His presence with singing. Know that Hashem, He is God; it is He that made us, and we are His, His people, and the flock of His pasture. Enter into His gates with thanksgiving, and into His courts with praise; give thanks to Him, and bless His name. For Hashem is good; His mercy endures forever; and His faithfulness to all generations.

Bameh Madlikin
Mishnah, Shabbat Ch.2

א. בַּמֶּה מַדְלִיקִין וּבַמֶּה אֵין מַדְלִיקִין אֵין מַדְלִיקִין לֹא בְלֶכֶשׁ. וְלֹא בְחֹסֶן. וְלֹא בְכָלָךְ. וְלֹא בִּפְתִילַת הָאִידָן. וְלֹא בִּפְתִילַת הַמִּדְבָּר. וְלֹא בִירוֹקָה שֶׁעַל פְּנֵי הַמָּיִם. לֹא בְזֶפֶת וְלֹא בְשַׁעֲוָה. וְלֹא בְשֶׁמֶן קִיק. וְלֹא בְשֶׁמֶן שְׂרֵפָה. וְלֹא בְאַלְיָה. וְלֹא בְחֵלֶב. נַחוּם הַמָּדִי אוֹמֵר מַדְלִיקִין בְּחֵלֶב מְבֻשָּׁל. וַחֲכָמִים אוֹמְרִים אֶחָד מְבֻשָּׁל וְאֶחָד

שֶׁאֵינוֹ מְבֻשָּׁל אֵין מַדְלִיקִין בּוֹ: ב. אֵין מַדְלִיקִין בְּשֶׁמֶן שְׂרֵפָה בְּיוֹם
טוֹב. רַבִּי יִשְׁמָעֵאל אוֹמֵר אֵין מַדְלִיקִין בְּעִטְרָן מִפְּנֵי כְּבוֹד הַשַּׁבָּת.
וַחֲכָמִים מַתִּירִים בְּכָל הַשְּׁמָנִים בְּשֶׁמֶן שֻׁמְשְׁמִין. בְּשֶׁמֶן אֱגוֹזִים.
בְּשֶׁמֶן צְנוֹנוֹת. בְּשֶׁמֶן דָּגִים. בְּשֶׁמֶן פַּקּוּעוֹת. בְּעִטְרָן וּבְנֵפְט. רַבִּי
טַרְפוֹן אוֹמֵר אֵין מַדְלִיקִין אֶלָּא בְשֶׁמֶן זַיִת בִּלְבָד: ג. כָּל הַיּוֹצֵא מִן
הָעֵץ אֵין מַדְלִיקִין בּוֹ אֶלָּא פִשְׁתָּן. וְכָל הַיּוֹצֵא מִן הָעֵץ אֵינוֹ מְטַמֵּא
טֻמְאַת אֹהָלִים. אֶלָּא פִשְׁתָּן. פְּתִילַת הַבֶּגֶד שֶׁקִּפְּלָהּ וְלֹא הִבְהֲבָהּ.
רַבִּי אֱלִיעֶזֶר אוֹמֵר טְמֵאָה הִיא. וְאֵין מַדְלִיקִין בָּהּ. רַבִּי עֲקִיבָא
אוֹמֵר טְהוֹרָה הִיא. וּמַדְלִיקִין בָּהּ: ד. לֹא יִקֹּב אָדָם שְׁפוֹפֶרֶת שֶׁל
בֵּיצָה. וִימַלְאֶנָּה שֶׁמֶן. וְיִתְּנֶנָּה עַל פִּי הַנֵּר בִּשְׁבִיל שֶׁתְּהֵא מְנַטֶּפֶת.
וַאֲפִלּוּ הִיא שֶׁל חֶרֶס. וְרַבִּי יְהוּדָה מַתִּיר. אֲבָל אִם חִבְּרָהּ הַיּוֹצֵר
מִתְּחִלָּה מֻתָּר. מִפְּנֵי שֶׁהוּא כְּלִי אֶחָד: לֹא יְמַלֵּא אָדָם קְעָרָה שֶׁמֶן.
וְיִתְּנֶנָּה בְּצַד הַנֵּר. וְיִתֵּן רֹאשׁ הַפְּתִילָה בְּתוֹכָהּ. בִּשְׁבִיל שֶׁתְּהֵא
שׁוֹאֶבֶת. וְרַבִּי יְהוּדָה מַתִּיר: ה. הַמְכַבֶּה אֶת הַנֵּר מִפְּנֵי שֶׁהוּא
מִתְיָרֵא מִפְּנֵי גוֹיִם. מִפְּנֵי לִסְטִים. מִפְּנֵי רוּחַ רָעָה. מִפְּנֵי הַחוֹלֶה
שֶׁיִּישָׁן פָּטוּר. כְּחָס עַל הַנֵּר. כְּחָס עַל הַשֶּׁמֶן. כְּחָס עַל הַפְּתִילָה
חַיָּב. וְרַבִּי יוֹסֵי פּוֹטֵר בְּכֻלָּן. חוּץ מִן הַפְּתִילָה. מִפְּנֵי שֶׁהוּא עוֹשָׂהּ
פֶּחָם: ו. עַל שָׁלשׁ עֲבֵירוֹת נָשִׁים מֵתוֹת בִּשְׁעַת לֵדְתָּן עַל שֶׁאֵינָן
זְהִירוֹת בַּנִּדָּה וּבַחַלָּה וּבְהַדְלָקַת הַנֵּר: ז. שְׁלֹשָׁה דְבָרִים צָרִיךְ אָדָם
לוֹמַר בְּתוֹךְ בֵּיתוֹ עֶרֶב שַׁבָּת עִם חֲשֵׁכָה. עִשַּׂרְתֶּן. עֵרַבְתֶּן. הַדְלִיקוּ
אֶת הַנֵּר. סָפֵק חֲשֵׁכָה. סָפֵק אֵינָהּ חֲשֵׁכָה. אֵין מְעַשְּׂרִין אֶת
הַוַּדַּאי. וְאֵין מַטְבִּילִין אֶת הַכֵּלִים. וְאֵין מַדְלִיקִין אֶת הַנֵּרוֹת. אֲבָל
מְעַשְּׂרִין אֶת הַדְּמַאי. וּמְעָרְבִין וְטוֹמְנִין אֶת הַחַמִּין:

1. Bammeh Madlikin Uvammeh Ein Madlikin Ein Madlikin Lo
Velechesh. Velo Vechosen. Velo Vechalach. Velo Biftilat Ha'idan.
Velo Biftilat Hamidbar. Velo Virokah She'al Pnei Hamayim. Lo
Vezefet Velo Vosha'avah. Velo Veshemen Kik. Velo Veshemen
Serefah. Velo Ve'alyah. Velo Vechelev. Nachum Hamadi Omer

Madlikin Bechelev Mevushal. Vachachamim Omerim Echad
Mevushal Ve'echad She'eino Mevushal Ein Madlikin Bo. 2. Ein
Madlikin Beshemen Serefah Beyom Tov. Ribi Yishma'el Omer Ein
Madlikin Be'itran Mipenei Kevod Hashabbat. Vachachamim Matirim
Bechol Hashmanim Beshemen Shumshemin. Beshemen Egozim.
Beshemen Tzenonot. Beshemen Dagim. Beshemen Pakku'ot.
Be'itran Uvenefet. Ribi Tarfon Omer Ein Madlikin Ella Veshemen
Zayit Bilvad. 3. Kol Hayotzei Min Ha'etz Ein Madlikin Bo Ella
Fishtan. Vechol Hayotzei Min Ha'etz Eino Mittammei Tum'at
Ohalim. Ella Fishtan. Petilat Habeged Shekkippelah Velo Hivhavah.
Ribi Eli'ezer Omer Teme'ah Hi. Ve'ein Madlikin Bah. Ribi Akiva
Omer Tehorah Hi. Umadlikin Bah. 4. Lo Yikkov Adam Shefoferet
Shel Beitzah. Vimall'enah Shemen. Veyittnenah Al Pi Haner Bishvil
Shetehei Menattefet. Va'afilu Hi Shel Cheres. Veribi Yehudah Matir.
Aval Im Chiberah Hayotzer Mittechillah Muttar. Mipenei Shehu Keli
Echad. Lo Yemalei Adam Ke'arah Shemen. Veyittnenah Betzad
Haner. Veyiten Rosh Happetilah Betochah. Bishvil Shetehei
Sho'evet. Veribi Yehudah Matir. 5. Hamchabeh Et Haner Mipenei
Shehu Mityarei Mipenei Goyim. Mipenei Listim. Mipenei Ruach
Ra'ah. Mipenei Hacholeh Sheyishan Patur. Kechas Al Haner. Kechas
Al Hashemen. Kechas Al Happetilah Chayav. Veribi Yosei Poter
Bechulan. Chutz Min Happetilah. Mipenei Shehu Osah Pecham. 6.
Al Shalosh Aveirot Nashim Metot Bish'at Lidtan Al She'einan Zehirot
Baniddah Uvachallah Uvehadlakat Haner. 7. Sheloshah Devarim
Tzarich Adam Lomar B'Toch Beito Erev Shabbat Im Chashechah.
Issarten. Eravten. Hadliku Et Haner. Safek Chashechah. Safek Einah
Chashechah. Ein M'aserin Et Havadda. Ve'ein Matbilin Et Hakelim.
Ve'ein Madlikin Et Hanerot. Aval M'aserin Et Hadema. Ume'arvin
Vetomnin Et Hachamin.

1. With what materials may the Shabbat lamp be kindled and with
what may it not be kindled? Not with a wick made of cedar-bast,
uncombed skeined flax or floss-silk, or with a wick made of willow-
bast or wilderness grass, or with water weeds. Not with fuel from
pitch, liquid wax, castor oil, or consecrated oil that has become
defiled and has then been set apart to be burnt, or with the fat from
the tails of sheep, or with tallow. Though Nahum the Mede declares

that it may be lighted with boiled tallow, the other rabbis decide that tallow may not be used, whether boiled or not boiled. **2.** Also on a festival the lights may not be kindled with defiled oil set apart to be burnt. Rabbi Yishmael says that out of respect for the Shabbat the lamp may not be lit with resin. But the other rabbis allow all kinds of oil, such as sesame oil, oil of nuts, oil of radish seed, oil of fish, oil of colocynth seed, as well as resin and naphtha. Rabbi Tarphon is of opinion that it must be lit with only olive oil. **3.** Nothing produced by a plant is proper for a wick except flax, which cannot acquire tent pollution, as other plant products can. As to a slip of cloth which has been folded together but not singed, Rabbi Elazar says it is subject to the law of pollution and must not be used, but Rabbi Akiva declares that it remains clean and may be used for lighting. **4.** One may not perforate an egg shell, fill it with oil and place it so that the oil may drip into the opening of the Shabbat lamp. Or, even, may a vessel of earthenware be used in this way, though Rabbi Yehudah allows it. But if the potter had originally joined the two parts together it is allowable, because they then form one vessel. Similarly, one may not fill a dish with oil and place it by the side of the Shabbat lamp and put the end of the wick into it to draw up the oil (for this also would make two separate vessels), though Rabbi Yehudah permits this also. **5.** He who extinguishes the Shabbat lamp because he fears aggression by non-Jews or robbers, or an evil spirit, or in order that the sick may sleep, is absolved. But if his intention be to save his lamp, oil or wick, he is guilty of Shabbat desecration. Rabbi Yosei allows it, except in the case of saving the wick, because he then forms tinder. **6.** (It was held that) women may die in childbirth for the following three transgressions: for negligence at their time of separation, for not separating the first portion of the dough, and for not lighting the Shabbat lamp. **7.** On the eve of the Shabbat near to dusk, a man must say three things in his home: "Have you separated the tithe?" "Have you prepared the Eruv?" "Light the Shabbat lamp." When it has become doubtful whether or not it be already dark, grain which is certainly untithed may no longer be tithed, or may vessels be immersed for cleansing, or may the Shabbat lamps be kindled; but it is still permitted to tithe that which is doubtfully untithed, to prepare the Eruv, or to cover the Shabbat victuals so that they retain their heat.

אָמַר רַבִּי אֶלְעָזָר אָמַר רַבִּי חֲנִינָא תַּלְמִידֵי חֲכָמִים מַרְבִּים שָׁלוֹם בָּעוֹלָם. שֶׁנֶּאֱמַר וְכָל־בָּנַיִךְ לִמּוּדֵי יְהֹוָה וְרַב שְׁלוֹם בָּנָיִךְ: אַל תִּקְרֵי בָּנַיִךְ אֶלָּא בּוֹנַיִךְ: יְהִי־שָׁלוֹם בְּחֵילֵךְ שַׁלְוָה בְּאַרְמְנוֹתָיִךְ: לְמַעַן אַחַי וְרֵעָי אֲדַבְּרָה־נָּא שָׁלוֹם בָּךְ: לְמַעַן בֵּית־יְהֹוָה אֱלֹהֵינוּ אֲבַקְשָׁה טוֹב לָךְ: וּרְאֵה־בָנִים לְבָנֶיךָ שָׁלוֹם עַל־יִשְׂרָאֵל: שָׁלוֹם רָב לְאֹהֲבֵי תוֹרָתֶךְ וְאֵין־לָמוֹ מִכְשׁוֹל: יְהֹוָה עֹז לְעַמּוֹ יִתֵּן יְהֹוָה | יְבָרֵךְ אֶת־עַמּוֹ בַשָּׁלוֹם:

Amar Ribi El'azar Amar Ribi Chanina Talmidei Chachamim Marbim Shalom Ba'olam. Shene'emar Vechol-Banayich Limmudei Adonai Verav Shelom Banayich. Al Tikrei Banayich Ella Bonayich. Yehi-Shalom Becheilech; Shalvah. Be'armenotayich. Lema'an Achai Vere'ai; Adaberah-Na Shalom Bach. Lema'an Beit-Adonai Eloheinu; Avakshah Tov Lach. Ure'eh-Vanim Levaneicha; Shalom. Al-Yisra'el. Shalom Rav Le'ohavei Toratecha; Ve'ein-Lamo Michshol. Adonai Oz Le'ammo Yiten; Adonai Yevarech Et-'Ammo Vashalom.

Rabbi Elazar in the name of Rabbi Chanina says, that the wise men promote peace in the world: as it is said: "And all your children study the Torah of Hashem: and great will be the peace of your children." Do not read banayich, "your children," but bonayich, "your builders." "May there be peace within your walls, and prosperity within your palaces. For the sake of my brothers and friends, I will now speak of peace within you. For the sake of the House of Hashem our God, I will seek your good. And you will see your children's children, and peace in Yisrael. Abundant peace have they who love Your Torah, and none will obstruct them. Hashem will give strength to His people; Hashem will bless His people with peace."

Some stand and say Kaddish Al Yisrael here, others at the end:

Kaddish is only recited in a minyan (ten men). אמן denotes when the congregation responds "Amen" together out loud. According to the Shulchan Arukh, the congregation says "Yehei Shemeh Rabba" to "Yitbarach" out loud together without interruption, and also that one should respond "Amen" after "Yitbarach." (SA, OC 55,56) This is not the common custom today. Though many are accustomed to answering according to their own custom, it is advised to respond in the custom of the one reciting to avoid not fragmenting into smaller groups. ("Lo Titgodedu" - BT, Yevamot 15b / SA, OC 493, Rema / MT, Avodah Zara 12:15)

יִתְגַּדַּל וְיִתְקַדַּשׁ שְׁמֵהּ רַבָּא. אמן בְּעָלְמָא דִּי בְרָא. כִּרְעוּתֵהּ. וְיַמְלִיךְ
מַלְכוּתֵהּ. וְיַצְמַח פֻּרְקָנֵהּ. וִיקָרֵב מְשִׁיחֵהּ. אמן בְּחַיֵּיכוֹן וּבְיוֹמֵיכוֹן
וּבְחַיֵּי דְכָל בֵּית יִשְׂרָאֵל. בַּעֲגָלָא וּבִזְמַן קָרִיב. וְאִמְרוּ אָמֵן. אמן יְהֵא
שְׁמֵיהּ רַבָּא מְבָרַךְ לְעָלַם וּלְעָלְמֵי עָלְמַיָּא יִתְבָּרַךְ. וְיִשְׁתַּבַּח.
וְיִתְפָּאַר. וְיִתְרוֹמַם. וְיִתְנַשֵּׂא. וְיִתְהַדָּר. וְיִתְעַלֶּה. וְיִתְהַלָּל שְׁמֵהּ
דְקֻדְשָׁא. בְּרִיךְ הוּא. אמן לְעֵלָּא מִן כָּל בִּרְכָתָא שִׁירָתָא. תֻּשְׁבְּחָתָא
וְנֶחֱמָתָא. דַּאֲמִירָן בְּעָלְמָא. וְאִמְרוּ אָמֵן. אמן

Yitgadal Veyitkadash Shemeh Rabba. ^{Amen} Be'alema Di Vera.
Kir'uteh. Veyamlich Malchuteh. Veyatzmach Purkaneh. Vikarev
Meshicheh. ^{Amen} Bechayeichon Uveyomeichon Uvechayei Dechal-
Beit Yisra'el. Ba'agala Uvizman Kariv. Ve'imru Amen. ^{Amen} Yehei
Shemeh Rabba Mevarach Le'alam Ule'alemei Alemaya Yitbarach.
Veyishtabach. Veyitpa'ar. Veyitromam. Veyitnasse. Veyit'hadar.
Veyit'aleh. Veyit'hallal Shemeh Dekudsha. Berich Hu. ^{Amen} Le'ella
Min Kol Birchata Shirata. Tushbechata Venechemata. Da'amiran
Be'alema. Ve'imru Amen. ^{Amen}

Glorified and sanctified be God's great name ^{Amen} throughout the world which He has created according to His will. May He establish His kingdom, hastening His salvation and the coming of His Messiah, ^{Amen}, in your lifetime and during your days, and within the life of the entire House of Yisrael, speedily and soon; and say, Amen. ^{Amen} May His great name be blessed forever and to all eternity. Blessed and praised, glorified and exalted, extolled and honored, adored and lauded is the name of the Holy One, blessed is He, ^{Amen} Beyond all the blessings and hymns, praises and consolations that are ever spoken in the world; and say, Amen. ^{Amen}

עַל יִשְׂרָאֵל וְעַל רַבָּנָן. וְעַל תַּלְמִידֵיהוֹן וְעַל כָּל תַּלְמִידֵי תַלְמִידֵיהוֹן. דְּעָסְקִין בְּאוֹרַיְתָא קַדִּשְׁתָּא. דִּי בְאַתְרָא הָדֵין וְדִי בְכָל אֲתַר וַאֲתַר. יְהֵא לָנָא וּלְהוֹן וּלְכוֹן חִנָּא וְחִסְדָּא וְרַחֲמֵי. מִן קֳדָם מָארֵי שְׁמַיָּא וְאַרְעָא וְאִמְרוּ אָמֵן. אמן

Al Yisra'el Ve'al Rabbanan. Ve'al Talmideihon Ve'al Kol Talmidei Talmideihon. De'asekin Be'orayta Kaddishta. Di Ve'atra Hadein Vedi Vechal Atar Va'atar. Yehei Lana Ulehon Ulechon China Vechisda Verachamei. Min Kodam Marei Shemaya Ve'ar'a Ve'imru Amen. Amen

May we of Yisrael together with our rabbis, their disciples and pupils, and all who engage in the study of holy Torah here and everywhere, find gracious favor and mercy from their Father Who is in heaven; and say, Amen. Amen

יְהֵא שְׁלָמָא רַבָּא מִן שְׁמַיָּא. חַיִּים וְשָׂבָע וִישׁוּעָה וְנֶחָמָה. וְשֵׁיזָבָא וּרְפוּאָה וּגְאוּלָה וּסְלִיחָה וְכַפָּרָה וְרֶוַח וְהַצָּלָה לָנוּ וּלְכָל עַמּוֹ יִשְׂרָאֵל. וְאִמְרוּ אָמֵן. אמן

Yehei Shelama Rabba Min Shemaya. Chayim Vesava Vishu'ah Venechamah. Vesheizava Urefu'ah Uge'ulah Uselichah Vechapparah Verevach Vehatzalah Lanu Ulechol Ammo Yisra'el. Ve'imru Amen. Amen

May abundant peace descend from heaven, with life and plenty, salvation, solace, liberation, healing and redemption, and forgiveness and atonement, enlargement and freedom, for us and all of God's people Yisrael; and say, Amen. Amen

> One bows and takes three steps backwards, while still bowing. After three steps, while still bowing and before erecting, while saying, "Oseh Shalom Bimromav", turn one's face to the left, "Hu [Berachamav] Ya'aseh Shalom Aleinu", turn one's face to the right; then bow forward like a servant leaving his master. (SA, OC 123:1)

עוֹשֶׂה שָׁלוֹם בִּמְרוֹמָיו. הוּא בְּרַחֲמָיו יַעֲשֶׂה שָׁלוֹם עָלֵינוּ. וְעַל כָּל־עַמּוֹ יִשְׂרָאֵל. וְאִמְרוּ אָמֵן:

Oseh Shalom Bimromav. Hu Berachamav Ya'aseh Shalom Aleinu. Ve'al Kol-'Ammo Yisra'el. Ve'imru Amen

Creator of peace in His high places, may He in His mercy create peace for us and for all Yisrael, and say Amen.

Stay standing and say Psalms 29.

Psalms 29

מִזְמוֹר לְדָוִד הָבוּ לַיהֹוָה בְּנֵי אֵלִים הָבוּ לַיהֹוָה כָּבוֹד וָעֹז: הָבוּ לַיהֹוָה כְּבוֹד שְׁמוֹ הִשְׁתַּחֲווּ לַיהֹוָה בְּהַדְרַת־קֹדֶשׁ: קוֹל יְהֹוָה עַל־הַמָּיִם אֵל־הַכָּבוֹד הִרְעִים יְהֹוָה עַל־מַיִם רַבִּים: קוֹל־יְהֹוָה בַּכֹּחַ קוֹל יְהֹוָה בֶּהָדָר: קוֹל יְהֹוָה שֹׁבֵר אֲרָזִים וַיְשַׁבֵּר יְהֹוָה אֶת־אַרְזֵי הַלְּבָנוֹן: וַיַּרְקִידֵם כְּמוֹ־עֵגֶל לְבָנוֹן וְשִׂרְיֹן כְּמוֹ בֶן־רְאֵמִים: קוֹל־יְהֹוָה חֹצֵב לַהֲבוֹת אֵשׁ: קוֹל יְהֹוָה יָחִיל מִדְבָּר יָחִיל יְהֹוָה מִדְבַּר קָדֵשׁ: קוֹל יְהֹוָה | יְחוֹלֵל אַיָּלוֹת וַיֶּחֱשֹׂף יְעָרוֹת וּבְהֵיכָלוֹ כֻּלּוֹ אֹמֵר כָּבוֹד: יְהֹוָה לַמַּבּוּל יָשָׁב וַיֵּשֶׁב יְהֹוָה מֶלֶךְ לְעוֹלָם: יְהֹוָה עֹז לְעַמּוֹ יִתֵּן יְהֹוָה | יְבָרֵךְ אֶת־עַמּוֹ בַשָּׁלוֹם:

Mizmor LeDavid Havu L'Adonai Benei Elim; Havu L'Adonai Kavod Va'oz. Havu L'Adonai Kevod Shemo; Hishtachavu L'Adonai Behadrat-Kodesh. Kol Adonai Al-Hamayim El-Hakavod Hir'im; Adonai Al-Mayim Rabim. Kol-Adonai Bakoach; Kol Adonai Behadar. Kol Adonai Shoveir Arazim; Vayshaber Adonai Et-'Arzei Hallevanon. Vayarkidem Kemo-'Egel; Levanon Vesiryon. Kemo Ven-Re'emim. Kol-Adonai Chotzev. Lahavot Esh. Kol Adonai Yachil Midbar; Yachil Adonai Midbar Kadesh. Kol Adonai Yecholel Ayalot Vayechesof Ye'arot Uveheichalo; Kulo. Omer Kavod. Adonai Lammabbul Yashav; Vayeshev Adonai Melech Le'olam. Adonai Oz Le'ammo Yiten; Adonai Yevarech Et-'Ammo Vashalom.

A Psalm of David. Ascribe to Hashem, sons of might, Ascribe to Hashem glory and strength. Ascribe to Hashem the glory due to His name; Worship Hashem in the beauty of holiness. The voice of Hashem is upon the waters; The God of glory thunders, Even Hashem upon many waters. The voice of Hashem is powerful; The voice of Hashem is full of majesty. The voice of Hashem breaks the cedars; yes, Hashem breaks, in pieces, the cedars of Levanon. He makes them also to skip like a calf; Levanon and Sirion like a young wild-ox. The voice of Hashem hews out flames of fire. The voice of Hashem shakes the wilderness; Hashem shakes the wilderness of Kadesh. The voice of Hashem makes the hinds to calve, And strips the forests bare; And in His Temple all say: 'Glory.' Hashem sat enthroned at the flood; Hashem sits as King forever. Hashem will give strength to His people; Hashem will bless His people with peace.

Lecha Dodi
Shlomo HaLevi Alkabetz

לְכָה דוֹדִי לִקְרַאת כַּלָּה. פְּנֵי שַׁבָּת נְקַבְּלָה:

Lechah Dodi Likrat Kallah. Penei Shabbat Nekabelah.

Come, my beloved, to meet the bride; The presence of Shabbat let us welcome.

שָׁמוֹר וְזָכוֹר בְּדִבּוּר אֶחָד. הִשְׁמִיעָנוּ אֵל הַמְיֻחָד. יְהֹוָה אֶחָד וּשְׁמוֹ
אֶחָד. לְשֵׁם וּלְתִפְאֶרֶת וְלִתְהִלָּה: לכה

Shamor Vezachor Bedibur Echad. Hishmi'anu El Hameyuchad.
Adonai Echad Ushemo Echad. Leshem Uletif'eret Velit'hillah.
(Lecha)

God proclaimed as One, caused us to hear in one utterance, "Observe" and "Remember (the Shabbat)." Hashem is One, and His name One, for fame, glory, and praise.

לִקְרַאת שַׁבָּת לְכוּ וְנֵלְכָה. כִּי הִיא מְקוֹר הַבְּרָכָה. מֵרֹאשׁ מִקֶּדֶם
נְסוּכָה. סוֹף מַעֲשֶׂה בְּמַחֲשָׁבָה תְּחִלָּה: לכה

Likrat Shabbat Lechu Venelechah. Ki Hi Mekor Haberachah. Merosh Mikedem Nesuchah. Sof Ma'aseh Bemachashavah Techillah. (Lecha)

To meet Shabbat, Come, and let us go, For it is the fountain of blessing; From the beginning, of old, it was ordained; though last in creation, yet it was first in the divine design.

מִקְדַּשׁ מֶלֶךְ עִיר מְלוּכָה. קוּמִי צְאִי מִתּוֹךְ הַהֲפֵכָה. רַב לָךְ שֶׁבֶת בְּעֵמֶק הַבָּכָא. וְהוּא יַחֲמוֹל עָלַיִךְ חֶמְלָה: לכה

Mikdash Melech Ir Meluchah. Kumi Tze'i Mitoch Hahafechah. Rav Lach Shevet Be'emek Habacha. Vehu Yachmol Alayich Chemlah.
(Lecha)

Oh Sanctuary of the King, Oh royal city, Arise, go forth from the midst of the overthrow; It is enough for you to dwell in the valley of weeping, And He will have pity on you with compassion.

הִתְנַעֲרִי מֵעָפָר קוּמִי. לִבְשִׁי בִּגְדֵי תִפְאַרְתֵּךְ עַמִּי. עַל יַד בֶּן יִשַׁי בֵּית הַלַּחְמִי. קָרְבָה אֶל נַפְשִׁי גְאָלָהּ: לכה

Hitna'ari Me'afar Kumi. Livshi Bigdei Tif'artech Ammi. Al Yad Ben Yishai Beit Hallachmi. Karevah El Nafshi Ge'alah. (Lecha)

Shake yourself from the dust, arise. Put on the garments of your glory, Oh my people. Through the son of Yishai, the Bethlehemite will redemption draw near to my soul.

הִתְעוֹרְרִי הִתְעוֹרְרִי. כִּי בָא אוֹרֵךְ קוּמִי אוֹרִי. עוּרִי עוּרִי שִׁיר דַּבֵּרִי. כְּבוֹד יְהֹוָה עָלַיִךְ נִגְלָה: לכה

Hit'oreri Hit'oreri. Ki Va Orech Kumi Ori. Uri Uri Shir Daberi. Kevod Adonai Alayich Niglah. (Lecha)

Awake, awake, your light is come, arise and shine out. Awake, awake, chant a song; For the glory of Hashem was revealed upon you.

לֹא תֵבוֹשִׁי וְלֹא תִכָּלְמִי. מַה תִּשְׁתּוֹחֲחִי וּמַה תֶּהֱמִי. בָּךְ יֶחֱסוּ עֲנִיֵּי עַמִּי. וְנִבְנְתָה עִיר עַל תִּלָּהּ: לכה

Lo Tevoshi Velo Tikalemi. Mah Tishtochachi Umah Tehemi. Bach Yechesu Aniyei Ammi. Venivnetah Ir Al Tillah. (Lecha)

Do not be ashamed, or be confounded; Why are you bowed down, and why are you weeping? In you will the poor of my people will find refuge, when the city will be built on her mound.

וְהָיוּ לִמְשִׁסָּה שׁוֹסַיִךְ. וְרָחֲקוּ כָּל מְבַלְּעָיִךְ. יָשִׂישׂ עָלַיִךְ אֱלֹהָיִךְ. כִּמְשׂוֹשׂ חָתָן עַל כַּלָּה: לכה

Vehayu Limshissah Shosayich. Verachaku Kol Mevalle'ayich. Yasis Alayich Elohayich. Kimsos Chatan Al Kallah. (Lecha)

And, as a spoil will be they that spoil you; And far away will they all be that would swallow you; Over you will your God rejoice, As a bridegroom rejoices over his bride.

יָמִין וּשְׂמֹאל תִּפְרוֹצִי. וְאֶת יְהֹוָה תַּעֲרִיצִי. עַל יַד אִישׁ בֶּן פַּרְצִי. וְנִשְׂמְחָה וְנָגִילָה: לכה

Yamin Usemol Tifrotzi. Ve'et Adonai Ta'aritzi. Al Yad Ish Ben Partzi. Venismechah Venagilah. (Lecha)

On the right and on the left you will spread, And Hashem you will revere, Through a man, the son of Peretz*; And we will rejoice and be glad, and rejoice.

בֹּאִי בְשָׁלוֹם עֲטֶרֶת בַּעְלָהּ. גַּם בְּשִׂמְחָה בְּרִנָּה וּבְצָהֳלָה. תּוֹךְ אֱמוּנֵי עַם סְגֻלָּה: לכה

Bo'i Veshalom Ateret Ba'lah. Gam Besimchah Berinah Uvetzoholah. Toch Emunei Am Segullah. (Lecha)

Come in peace, crown of her husband, With joy and with cheerfulness; In the midst of the faithful of the beloved people.

And say aloud:

בֹּאִי כַלָּה:

Bo'i Challah.

Oh come, bride.

Turn right and say:

בֹּאִי כַלָּה:

Bo'i Challah.

Oh come, bride.

Turn left and say:

תּוֹךְ אֱמוּנֵי עַם סְגֻלָּה:

Toch Emunei Am Segullah.

In the midst of the faithful of the beloved people.

When he says Oh, Come Bride a third time he will be prepared to receive the extra soul of Shabbat, and he will say in a whisper:

בֹּאִי כַלָּה. שַׁבָּת מַלְכְּתָא:

Bo'i Challah. Shabbat Malketa.

Oh come, bride. Shabbat Queen.

Mizmor Shir Leyom HaShabbat (Psalms 92)

מִזְמוֹר שִׁיר לְיוֹם הַשַּׁבָּת: טוֹב לְהֹדוֹת לַיהוָה וּלְזַמֵּר לְשִׁמְךָ עֶלְיוֹן:
לְהַגִּיד בַּבֹּקֶר חַסְדֶּךָ וֶאֱמוּנָתְךָ בַּלֵּילוֹת: עֲלֵי־עָשׂוֹר וַעֲלֵי־נָבֶל עֲלֵי
הִגָּיוֹן בְּכִנּוֹר: כִּי שִׂמַּחְתַּנִי יְהוָה בְּפָעֳלֶךָ בְּמַעֲשֵׂי יָדֶיךָ אֲרַנֵּן:
מַה־גָּדְלוּ מַעֲשֶׂיךָ יְהוָה מְאֹד עָמְקוּ מַחְשְׁבֹתֶיךָ: אִישׁ־בַּעַר לֹא יֵדָע
וּכְסִיל לֹא־יָבִין אֶת־זֹאת: בִּפְרֹחַ רְשָׁעִים | כְּמוֹ עֵשֶׂב וַיָּצִיצוּ
כָּל־פֹּעֲלֵי אָוֶן לְהִשָּׁמְדָם עֲדֵי־עַד: וְאַתָּה מָרוֹם לְעֹלָם יְהוָה: כִּי הִנֵּה
אֹיְבֶיךָ | יְהוָה כִּי־הִנֵּה אֹיְבֶיךָ יֹאבֵדוּ יִתְפָּרְדוּ כָּל־פֹּעֲלֵי אָוֶן: וַתָּרֶם
כִּרְאֵים קַרְנִי בַּלֹּתִי בְּשֶׁמֶן רַעֲנָן: וַתַּבֵּט עֵינִי בְּשׁוּרָי בַּקָּמִים עָלַי
מְרֵעִים תִּשְׁמַעְנָה אָזְנָי: צַדִּיק כַּתָּמָר יִפְרָח כְּאֶרֶז בַּלְּבָנוֹן יִשְׂגֶּה:
שְׁתוּלִים בְּבֵית יְהוָה בְּחַצְרוֹת אֱלֹהֵינוּ יַפְרִיחוּ: עוֹד יְנוּבוּן בְּשֵׂיבָה
דְּשֵׁנִים וְרַעֲנַנִּים יִהְיוּ: לְהַגִּיד כִּי־יָשָׁר יְהוָה צוּרִי וְלֹא־(עַוְלָתָה)
עלתה בּוֹ:

Mizmor Shir. Leyom Hashabbat. Tov Lehodot L'Adonai Ulezamer
Leshimcha Elyon. Lehagid Baboker Chasdecha; Ve'emunatecha.
Baleilot. Alei-'Asor Va'alei-Navel; Alei Higayon Bechinor. Ki
Simachtani Adonai Befo'olecha; Bema'asei Yadeicha Aranen. Mah-
Gadelu Ma'aseicha Adonai Me'od. Ameku Machshevoteicha. Ish-
Ba'ar Lo Yeda'; Uchesil. Lo-Yavin Et-Zot. Bifroach Resha'im Kemo
Esev. Vayatzitzu Chol-Po'alei Aven; Lehishamedam Adei-'Ad.
Ve'attah Marom. Le'olam Adonai Ki Hineh Oyeveicha Adonai Ki-
Hineh Oyeveicha Yovedu; Yitparedu. Chol-Po'alei Aven. Vatarem
Kir'eim Karni; Baloti. Beshemen Ra'anan. Vatabet Eini. Beshurai
Bakamim Alai Mere'im. Tishma'nah Oznai. Tzaddik Kattamar
Yifrach; Ke'erez Ballevanon Yisgeh. Shetulim Beveit Adonai
Bechatzrot Eloheinu Yafrichu. Od Yenuvun Beseivah; Deshenim
Vera'ananim Yihyu. Lehagid Ki-Yashar Adonai Tzuri. Velo-Avlatah
Bo.

A Psalm, a Song. For the Shabbat day. It is a good thing to give
thanks to Hashem, And to sing praises to Your name, Most High; To
declare Your lovingkindness in the morning, And Your faithfulness
in the night seasons, With an instrument of ten strings, and with the
psaltery; With a solemn sound on the harp. For You, Hashem, have
made me glad through Your work; I will rejoice in the works of Your
hands. How great are Your works, Hashem. Your thoughts are very
deep. A brutish man doesn't know, Neither does a fool understand
this. When the wicked spring up as the grass, And when all the
workers of iniquity flourish; It is that they may be destroyed forever.
But You, Hashem, are on high forever. For, behold, Your enemies,
Hashem, For, behold, Your enemies will perish: All the workers of
iniquity will be scattered. But my horn You have exalted like the
horn of the wild-ox; I am anointed with rich oil. My eye has also
gazed on them that lie in wait for me, My ears have heard my desire
of the evil-doers that rise up against me. The righteous will flourish
like the palm-tree; He will grow like a cedar in Levanon. Planted in
the House of Hashem, They will flourish in the courts of our God.
They will still bring forth fruit in old age; They will be full of sap and
richness; To declare that Hashem is upright, My Rock, in Whom
there is no unrighteousness.

Psalms 93

יְהֹוָה מָלָךְ גֵּאוּת לָבֵשׁ לָבֵשׁ יְהֹוָה עֹז הִתְאַזָּר אַף־תִּכּוֹן תֵּבֵל
בַּל־תִּמּוֹט: נָכוֹן כִּסְאֲךָ מֵאָז מֵעוֹלָם אָתָּה: נָשְׂאוּ נְהָרוֹת | יְהֹוָה
נָשְׂאוּ נְהָרוֹת קוֹלָם יִשְׂאוּ נְהָרוֹת דָּכְיָם: מִקֹּלוֹת| מַיִם רַבִּים אַדִּירִים
מִשְׁבְּרֵי־יָם אַדִּיר בַּמָּרוֹם יְהֹוָה | עֵדֹתֶיךָ נֶאֶמְנוּ מְאֹד לְבֵיתְךָ
נַאֲוָה־קֹדֶשׁ יְהֹוָה לְאֹרֶךְ יָמִים:

Adonai Maloch Ge'ut Lavesh Lavesh Adonai Oz Hit'azar; Af-Tikon
Tevel. Bal-Timot. Nachon Kis'acha Me'az; Me'olam Attah. Nase'u
Neharot Adonai Nase'u Neharot Kolam; Yis'u Neharot Dochyam.
Mikolot Mayim Rabim. Adirim Mishberei-Yam; Adir Bamarom
Adonai Edoteicha Ne'emnu Me'od. Leveitecha Na'avah-Kodesh;
Adonai Le'orech Yamim.

Hashem reigns; He is clothed in majesty; Hashem is clothed, He has
girded Himself with strength; The world is established, that it
cannot be moved. Your Throne is established from old; You are
from everlasting. The floods have lifted up, Hashem, the floods have
lifted up their voice; the floods lift up their roaring. Above the voices
of many waters, the mighty breakers of the sea, Hashem on high is
mighty. Your testimonies are very sure, holiness suits Your House,
Hashem, forever.

כָּל יִשְׂרָאֵל יֵשׁ לָהֶם חֵלֶק לָעוֹלָם הַבָּא. שֶׁנֶּאֱמַר וְעַמֵּךְ כֻּלָּם
צַדִּיקִים. לְעוֹלָם יִירְשׁוּ אָרֶץ. נֵצֶר מַטָּעַי מַעֲשֵׂה יָדַי לְהִתְפָּאֵר:

Kol Yisra'el Yesh Lahem Chelek La'olam Haba. Shene'emar
Ve'ammecha Kulam Tzaddikim. Le'olam Yiyreshu Aretz. Netzer
Matta'ai Ma'aseh Yadai L'Hitpa'er.

All Yisrael have a portion in the world to come: for it is said: "Your
people also will be all righteous, They will inherit the land forever;
The branch of My planting, the work of My hands, in which I glory.
(Isaiah 60:21)

And some say Kaddish Al Yisrael here, if not recited earlier:

Kaddish is only recited in a minyan (ten men). אמן denotes when the congregation responds "Amen" together out loud. According to the Shulchan Arukh, the congregation says "Yehei Shemeh Rabba" to "Yitbarach" out loud together without interruption, and also that one should respond "Amen" after "Yitbarach." (SA, OC 55,56) This is not the common custom today. Though many are accustomed to answering according to their own custom, it is advised to respond in the custom of the one reciting to avoid not fragmenting into smaller groups. ("Lo Titgodedu" - BT, Yevamot 13b / SA, OC 493, Rema / MT, Avodah Zara 12:15)

יִתְגַּדַּל וְיִתְקַדַּשׁ שְׁמֵהּ רַבָּא. אמן בְּעָלְמָא דִּי בְרָא. כִרְעוּתֵהּ. וְיַמְלִיךְ
מַלְכוּתֵהּ. וְיַצְמַח פֻּרְקָנֵהּ. וִיקָרֵב מְשִׁיחֵהּ. אמן בְּחַיֵּיכוֹן וּבְיוֹמֵיכוֹן
וּבְחַיֵּי דְכָל בֵּית יִשְׂרָאֵל. בַּעֲגָלָא וּבִזְמַן קָרִיב. וְאִמְרוּ אָמֵן. אמן יְהֵא
שְׁמֵהּ רַבָּא מְבָרַךְ לְעָלַם וּלְעָלְמֵי עָלְמַיָּא יִתְבָּרַךְ. וְיִשְׁתַּבַּח.
וְיִתְפָּאַר. וְיִתְרוֹמַם. וְיִתְנַשֵּׂא. וְיִתְהַדָּר. וְיִתְעַלֶּה. וְיִתְהַלָּל שְׁמֵהּ
דְּקֻדְשָׁא. בְּרִיךְ הוּא. אמן לְעֵלָּא מִן כָּל בִּרְכָתָא שִׁירָתָא. תֻּשְׁבְּחָתָא
וְנֶחֱמָתָא. דַּאֲמִירָן בְּעָלְמָא. וְאִמְרוּ אָמֵן. אמן

Yitgadal Veyitkadash Shemeh Rabba. **Amen** Be'alema Di Vera.
Kir'uteh. Veyamlich Malchuteh. Veyatzmach Purkaneh. Vikarev
Meshicheh. **Amen** Bechayeichon Uveyomeichon Uvechayei Dechal-
Beit Yisra'el. Ba'agala Uvizman Kariv. Ve'imru Amen. **Amen** Yehei
Shemeh Rabba Mevarach Le'alam Ule'alemei Alemaya Yitbarach.
Veyishtabach. Veyitpa'ar. Veyitromam. Veyitnasse. Veyit'hadar.
Veyit'aleh. Veyit'hallal Shemeh Dekudsha. Berich Hu. **Amen** Le'ella
Min Kol Birchata Shirata. Tushbechata Venechemata. Da'amiran
Be'alema. Ve'imru Amen. **Amen**

Glorified and sanctified be God's great name **Amen** throughout the world which He has created according to His will. May He establish His kingdom, hastening His salvation and the coming of His Messiah, **Amen**, in your lifetime and during your days, and within the life of the entire House of Yisrael, speedily and soon; and say, Amen. **Amen** May His great name be blessed forever and to all eternity. Blessed and praised, glorified and exalted, extolled and honored, adored and lauded is the name of the Holy One, blessed is He, **Amen** Beyond all the blessings and hymns, praises and consolations that are ever spoken in the world; and say, Amen. **Amen**

עַל יִשְׂרָאֵל וְעַל רַבָּנָן. וְעַל תַּלְמִידֵיהוֹן וְעַל כָּל תַּלְמִידֵי תַלְמִידֵיהוֹן.
דְּעָסְקִין בְּאוֹרַיְתָא קַדִּשְׁתָּא. דִּי בְאַתְרָא הָדֵין וְדִי בְכָל אֲתַר וַאֲתַר.
יְהֵא לָנָא וּלְהוֹן וּלְכוֹן חִנָּא וְחִסְדָּא וְרַחֲמֵי. מִן קֳדָם מָארֵי שְׁמַיָּא
וְאַרְעָא וְאִמְרוּ אָמֵן. אָמֵן

Al Yisra'el Ve'al Rabbanan. Ve'al Talmideihon Ve'al Kol Talmidei
Talmideihon. De'asekin Be'orayta Kaddishta. Di Ve'atra Hadein Vedi
Vechal Atar Va'atar. Yehei Lana Ulehon Ulechon China Vechisda
Verachamei. Min Kodam Marei Shemaya Ve'ar'a Ve'imru Amen. Amen

May we of Yisrael together with our rabbis, their disciples and
pupils, and all who engage in the study of holy Torah here and
everywhere, find gracious favor and mercy from their Father Who is
in heaven; and say, Amen. Amen

יְהֵא שְׁלָמָא רַבָּא מִן שְׁמַיָּא. חַיִּים וְשָׂבָע וִישׁוּעָה וְנֶחָמָה. וְשֵׁיזָבָא
וּרְפוּאָה וּגְאוּלָה וּסְלִיחָה וְכַפָּרָה וְרֶוַח וְהַצָּלָה לָנוּ וּלְכָל עַמּוֹ
יִשְׂרָאֵל. וְאִמְרוּ אָמֵן. אָמֵן

Yehei Shelama Rabba Min Shemaya. Chayim Vesava Vishu'ah
Venechamah. Vesheizava Urefu'ah Uge'ulah Uselichah
Vechapparah Verevach Vehatzalah Lanu Ulechol Ammo Yisra'el.
Ve'imru Amen. Amen

May abundant peace descend from heaven, with life and plenty,
salvation, solace, liberation, healing and redemption, and
forgiveness and atonement, enlargement and freedom, for us and
all of God's people Yisrael; and say, Amen. Amen

> One bows and takes three steps backwards, while still bowing. After three steps, while still bowing
> and before erecting, while saying, "Oseh Shalom Bimromav", turn one's face to the left, "Hu
> [Berachamav] Ya'aseh Shalom Aleinu", turn one's face to the right; then bow forward like a servant
> leaving his master. (SA, OC 123:1)

עוֹשֶׂה שָׁלוֹם בִּמְרוֹמָיו. הוּא בְּרַחֲמָיו יַעֲשֶׂה שָׁלוֹם עָלֵינוּ. וְעַל
כָּל־עַמּוֹ יִשְׂרָאֵל. וְאִמְרוּ אָמֵן:

Oseh Shalom Bimromav. Hu Berachamav Ya'aseh Shalom Aleinu.
Ve'al Kol-'Ammo Yisra'el. Ve'imru Amen

Creator of peace in His high places, may He in His mercy create peace for us and for all Yisrael, and say Amen.

ARVIT L'SHABBAT V'YOM TOV / EVENING PRAYER FOR SHABBAT AND YOM TOV

Barechu

On the Night of Rosh Chodesh some have the custom of saying Psalms 104 before Arvit on Rosh Chodesh and some postpone it to the second night (of Rosh Chodesh) if it lands on Erev-Shabbat. Refer to Rosh Chodesh, Barchi Nafshi for the reading.

Some recite before:

לְשֵׁם יְחוּד קוּדְשָׁא בְּרִיךְ הוּא וּשְׁכִינְתֵּיהּ. בִּדְחִילוּ וּרְחִימוּ. וּרְחִימוּ וּדְחִילוּ.
לְיַחֲדָא שֵׁם יוֹ"ד קֵ"י בְּוָא"ו קֵ"י בְּיִחוּדָא שְׁלִים (יהוה) בְּשֵׁם כָּל יִשְׂרָאֵל.
הנה אנחנו באים להתפלל תפלת ערבית שֶׁל שבת קדש שתקן יעקב אבינו
עליו השלום. עם כל המצות הכלולות בה לתקן את שורשה במקום עליון.
לעשות נחת רוח ליוצרנו ולעשות רצון בוראנו. וִיהִי נֹעַם אֲדֹנָי אֱלֹהֵינוּ עָלֵינוּ
וּמַעֲשֵׂה יָדֵינוּ כּוֹנְנָה עָלֵינוּ וּמַעֲשֵׂה יָדֵינוּ כּוֹנְנֵהוּ:

יִמְלֹךְ יְהֹוָה | לְעוֹלָם אֱלֹהַיִךְ צִיּוֹן לְדֹר וָדֹר הַלְלוּיָהּ: יוֹמָם | יְצַוֶּה
יְהֹוָה | חַסְדּוֹ וּבַלַּיְלָה שִׁירֹה עִמִּי תְּפִלָּה לְאֵל חַיָּי: כֹּל הַנְּשָׁמָה
תְּהַלֵּל יָהּ הַלְלוּיָהּ: וִיבָרְכוּ שֵׁם כְּבֹדֶךָ וּמְרוֹמַם עַל־כָּל־בְּרָכָה
וּתְהִלָּה:

Yimloch Adonai Le'olam. Elohayich Tziyon Ledor Vador.
Halleluyah. Yomam Yetzaveh Adonai Chasdo. Uvallaylah Shiroh
Immi; Tefillah. Le'el Chayai. Kol Haneshamah Tehallel Yah.
Halleluyah. Vivarechu Shem Kevodecha. Umeromam Al-Chol-
Berachah Utehilah.

Hashem will reign forever, Your God, Tziyon, to all generations.
Halleluyah. By day Hashem will command His lovingkindness, and
in the night His song will be with me, even a prayer to the God of my
life. Let everything that has breath praise Hashem. Halleluyah. May
Your glorious name be blessed, exalted though it is above every
blessing and praise. (Psalms 146:10, 42:9, 150:6, Nehemiah 9:5)

And say Hatzi-Kaddish:

Kaddish is only recited in a minyan (ten men). אָמֵן denotes when the congregation responds "Amen" together out loud. According to the Shulchan Arukh, the congregation says "Yehei Shemeh Rabba" to "Yitbarach" out loud together without interruption, and also that one should respond "Amen" after "Yitbarach." (SA, OC 55,56) This is not the common custom today. Though many are accustomed to answering according to their own custom, it is advised to respond in the custom of the one reciting to avoid not fragmenting into smaller groups. ("Lo Titgodedu" - BT, Yevamot 15b / SA, OC 493, Rema / MT, Avodah Zara 12:15)

יִתְגַּדַּל וְיִתְקַדַּשׁ שְׁמֵהּ רַבָּא. אמ״ בְּעָלְמָא דִּי בְרָא. כִרְעוּתֵהּ. וְיַמְלִיךְ מַלְכוּתֵהּ. וְיַצְמַח פֻּרְקָנֵהּ. וִיקָרֵב מְשִׁיחֵהּ. אמ״ בְּחַיֵּיכוֹן וּבְיוֹמֵיכוֹן וּבְחַיֵּי דְכָל בֵּית יִשְׂרָאֵל. בַּעֲגָלָא וּבִזְמַן קָרִיב. וְאִמְרוּ אָמֵן. אמ״ יְהֵא שְׁמֵהּ רַבָּא מְבָרַךְ לְעָלַם וּלְעָלְמֵי עָלְמַיָּא יִתְבָּרַךְ. וְיִשְׁתַּבַּח. וְיִתְפָּאַר. וְיִתְרוֹמַם. וְיִתְנַשֵּׂא. וְיִתְהַדָּר. וְיִתְעַלֶּה. וְיִתְהַלָּל שְׁמֵהּ דְּקֻדְשָׁא. בְּרִיךְ הוּא. אמ״ לְעֵלָּא מִן כָּל בִּרְכָתָא שִׁירָתָא. תֻּשְׁבְּחָתָא וְנֶחֱמָתָא. דַּאֲמִירָן בְּעָלְמָא. וְאִמְרוּ אָמֵן. אמ״

Yitgadal Veyitkadash Shemeh Rabba. ^{Amen} Be'alema Di Vera.
Kir'uteh. Veyamlich Malchuteh. Veyatzmach Purkaneh. Vikarev
Meshicheh. ^{Amen} Bechayeichon Uveyomeichon Uvechayei Dechal-
Beit Yisra'el. Ba'agala Uvizman Kariv. Ve'imru Amen. ^{Amen} Yehei
Shemeh Rabba Mevarach Le'alam Ule'alemei Alemaya Yitbarach.
Veyishtabach. Veyitpa'ar. Veyitromam. Veyitnasse. Veyit'hadar.
Veyit'aleh. Veyit'hallal Shemeh Dekudsha. Berich Hu. ^{Amen} Le'ella
Min Kol Birchata Shirata. Tushbechata Venechemata. Da'amiran
Be'alema. Ve'imru Amen. ^{Amen}

Glorified and sanctified be God's great name ^{Amen} throughout the world which He has created according to His will. May He establish His kingdom, hastening His salvation and the coming of His Messiah, ^{Amen}, in your lifetime and during your days, and within the life of the entire House of Yisrael, speedily and soon; and say, Amen. ^{Amen} May His great name be blessed forever and to all eternity. Blessed and praised, glorified and exalted, extolled and honored, adored and lauded is the name of the Holy One, blessed is He, ^{Amen} Beyond all the blessings and hymns, praises and consolations that are ever spoken in the world; and say, Amen. ^{Amen}

Barechu / Call to Prayer

Barechu / Call to prayer is only recited with 10 men (minyan).

The Chazan says:

בָּרְכוּ אֶת יְהֹוָה הַמְבֹרָךְ:

Barechu Et Adonai Hamevorach.

Bless Hashem, the blessed One.

The kahal / congregation answers:

בָּרוּךְ יְהֹוָה הַמְבֹרָךְ לְעוֹלָם וָעֶד:

Baruch Adonai Hamevorach Le'olam Va'ed.

Blessed is Hashem Who is blessed for all eternity.

The Chazan says:

בָּרוּךְ יְהֹוָה הַמְבֹרָךְ לְעוֹלָם וָעֶד:

Baruch Adonai Hamevorach Le'olam Va'ed.

Blessed is Hashem Who is blessed for all eternity.

Kriyat Shema Uvirchotei'a / The Recital of Shema and Blessings

Ma'ariv Aravim

Baruch Attah Adonai Eloheinu	בָּרוּךְ אַתָּה יְהֹוָה אֱלֹהֵינוּ
Melech Ha'olam. Asher Bidvaro	מֶלֶךְ הָעוֹלָם. אֲשֶׁר בִּדְבָרוֹ
Ma'ariv Aravim Bechochmah.	מַעֲרִיב עֲרָבִים בְּחָכְמָה
Potei'ach She'arim Bitvunah.	פּוֹתֵחַ שְׁעָרִים בִּתְבוּנָה.
Meshaneh Itim. Umachalif Et-	מְשַׁנֶּה עִתִּים. וּמַחֲלִיף אֶת־
Hazmanim. Umesader Et-	הַזְּמַנִּים. וּמְסַדֵּר אֶת־
Hakochavim Bemishmeroteihem	הַכּוֹכָבִים בְּמִשְׁמְרוֹתֵיהֶם
Barakia'. Kirtzono. Borei Yomam	בָּרָקִיעַ. כִּרְצוֹנוֹ. בּוֹרֵא יוֹמָם
Valailah. Golel Or Mipenei	וָלָיְלָה. גּוֹלֵל אוֹר מִפְּנֵי
Choshech Vechoshech Mipenei	חֹשֶׁךְ וְחֹשֶׁךְ מִפְּנֵי
Or. Hama'avir Yom Umevi	אוֹר. הַמַּעֲבִיר יוֹם וּמֵבִיא
Lailah. Umavdil Bein Yom Uvein	לָיְלָה. וּמַבְדִּיל בֵּין יוֹם וּבֵין
Lailah. Adonai Tzeva'ot Shemo.	לָיְלָה. יְהֹוָה צְבָאוֹת שְׁמוֹ:
Baruch Attah Adonai Hama'ariv	בָּרוּךְ אַתָּה יְהֹוָה הַמַּעֲרִיב
Aravim.	עֲרָבִים:

Blessed are You, Hashem our God, King of the universe, At Your word You bring on evening; with Your wisdom You open the gates of the heavens, and with Your understanding You make the cycles of time and progressing seasons. By Your will You set the stars in their watches in the sky. You create both day and night, making darkness recede before light and light before darkness. You make distinction between day and night, causing day to pass away and night to advance, Hashem of hosts is Your name. Blessed are You, Hashem Who brings on evening.

Ahavat Olam

Ahavat Olam Beit Yisra'el	אַהֲבַת עוֹלָם בֵּית יִשְׂרָאֵל
Ammecha Ahaveta. Torah	עַמְּךָ אָהָבְתָּ. תּוֹרָה
Umitzvot Chukkim Umishpatim	וּמִצְוֹת חֻקִּים וּמִשְׁפָּטִים
Otanu Limadta. Al-Ken Adonai	אוֹתָנוּ לִמַּדְתָּ. עַל־כֵּן יְהֹוָה
Eloheinu. Beshachevenu	אֱלֹהֵינוּ. בְּשָׁכְבֵנוּ
Uvekumenu Nasiach	וּבְקוּמֵנוּ נָשִׂיחַ
Bechukkeicha. Venismach	בְּחֻקֶּיךָ. וְנִשְׂמַח
Vena'aloz Bedivrei Talmud	וְנַעֲלוֹז בְּדִבְרֵי תַלְמוּד
Toratecha Umitzvoteicha	תּוֹרָתֶךָ וּמִצְוֹתֶיךָ
Vechukkoteicha Le'olam Va'ed.	וְחֻקּוֹתֶיךָ לְעוֹלָם וָעֶד.
Ki-Hem Chayeinu Ve'orech	כִּי־הֵם חַיֵּינוּ וְאֹרֶךְ
Yameinu. Uvahem Nehgeh	יָמֵינוּ. וּבָהֶם נֶהְגֶּה
Yomam Valailah. Ve'ahavatecha	יוֹמָם וָלַיְלָה. וְאַהֲבָתְךָ
Lo Tasur Mimenu Le'olamim.	לֹא תָסוּר מִמֶּנּוּ לְעוֹלָמִים:
Baruch Attah Adonai Ohev	בָּרוּךְ אַתָּה יְהֹוָה אוֹהֵב
Et-'Ammo Yisra'el.	אֶת־עַמּוֹ יִשְׂרָאֵל:

With love everlasting You have loved the House of Yisrael, Your people. You have taught us Your Torah, its statutes, commandments and judgments; and therefore, Hashem our God, when we lie down and when we rise up, for all time we will speak of what You have ordained, rejoicing and delighting in learning the words of Your Torah, its commandments and statutes. For they are our life and our length of days, and on them we will meditate by day and by night. May Your love never depart from us. Blessed are You, Hashem Who loves Your people Yisrael.

LAWS OF RECITING THE SHEMA

One who recites the Shema, but did not have intention during the first verse, 'Shema Yisrael', one did not fulfill their obligation. As for the rest, if they read during the specified time and did not have intention, they have fulfilled their obligation. One should recite the Shema with intention, awe, fear, shaking and trembling. The custom is to place one's hands over their face during the recitation of the first verse in order that one will not look at something else that will prevent him from directing his heart. (SA, OC 59-61)

The Shema

Deuteronomy 6:4-9

One covers their eyes and says:

שְׁמַ֫ע יִשְׂרָאֵל יְהֹוָה אֱלֹהֵינוּ יְהֹוָה | אֶחָֽד:

Shema Yisrael; Adonai Eloheinu Adonai Echad.

"Hear, O Yisrael, Hashem is our God, Hashem is One."

Whisper silently:

בָּרוּךְ שֵׁם כְּבוֹד מַלְכוּתוֹ לְעוֹלָם וָעֶד:

Baruch Shem Kevod Malchuto Le'olam Va'ed.

Blessed is His name and glorious kingdom forever and ever.

Ve'ahavta

וְאָהַבְתָּ אֵת יְהֹוָה אֱלֹהֶיךָ בְּכָל־לְבָבְךָ וּבְכָל־נַפְשְׁךָ וּבְכָל־מְאֹדֶֽךָ:
וְהָיוּ הַדְּבָרִים הָאֵלֶּה אֲשֶׁר אָנֹכִי מְצַוְּךָ הַיּוֹם עַל־לְבָבֶֽךָ: וְשִׁנַּנְתָּם
לְבָנֶיךָ וְדִבַּרְתָּ בָּם בְּשִׁבְתְּךָ בְּבֵיתֶךָ וּבְלֶכְתְּךָ בַדֶּרֶךְ וּבְשָׁכְבְּךָ
וּבְקוּמֶֽךָ: וּקְשַׁרְתָּם לְאוֹת עַל־יָדֶךָ וְהָיוּ לְטֹטָפֹת בֵּין עֵינֶֽיךָ: וּכְתַבְתָּם
עַל־מְזֻזוֹת בֵּיתֶךָ וּבִשְׁעָרֶֽיךָ:

Ve'ahavta Et Adonai Eloheicha; Bechol-Levavecha Uvechol-
Nafshecha Uvechol-Me'odecha. Vehayu Hadevarim Ha'eleh. Asher
Anochi Metzavecha Hayom Al-Levavecha. Veshinantam Levaneicha.
Vedibarta Bam; Beshivtecha Beveitecha Uvelechtecha Vaderech.
Uveshochbecha Uvekumecha. Ukeshartam Le'ot Al-Yadecha;
Vehayu Letotafot Bein Eineicha. Uchetavtam Al-Mezuzot Beitecha
Uvish'areicha.

And you will love Hashem your God with all your heart, and with all your soul, and with all your might. And these words, which I command you this day, will be upon your heart; and you will teach them diligently to your children, and will talk of them when you sit in your house, and when you walk by the way, and when you lie down, and when you rise up. And you will bind them for a sign on your hand, and they will be for frontlets between your eyes. And you will write them on the doorposts of your house, and on your gates.

Vehayah Im-shamoa

וְהָיָה אִם־שָׁמֹעַ תִּשְׁמְעוּ אֶל־ מִצְוֹתַי אֲשֶׁר אָנֹכִי מְצַוֶּה אֶתְכֶם הַיּוֹם
לְאַהֲבָה אֶת־יְהוָה אֱלֹהֵיכֶם וּלְעָבְדוֹ בְּכָל־לְבַבְכֶם וּבְכָל־נַפְשְׁכֶם:
וְנָתַתִּי מְטַר־אַרְצְכֶם בְּעִתּוֹ יוֹרֶה וּמַלְקוֹשׁ וְאָסַפְתָּ דְגָנֶךָ וְתִירֹשְׁךָ
וְיִצְהָרֶךָ: וְנָתַתִּי עֵשֶׂב בְּשָׂדְךָ לִבְהֶמְתֶּךָ וְאָכַלְתָּ וְשָׂבָעְתָּ: הִשָּׁמְרוּ
לָכֶם פֶּן יִפְתֶּה לְבַבְכֶם וְסַרְתֶּם. וַעֲבַדְתֶּם אֱלֹהִים אֲחֵרִים
וְהִשְׁתַּחֲוִיתֶם לָהֶם: וְחָרָה אַף־יְהוָה בָּכֶם וְעָצַר אֶת־הַשָּׁמַיִם וְלֹא־
יִהְיֶה מָטָר וְהָאֲדָמָה לֹא תִתֵּן אֶת־יְבוּלָהּ וַאֲבַדְתֶּם מְהֵרָה מֵעַל
הָאָרֶץ הַטֹּבָה אֲשֶׁר יְהוָה נֹתֵן לָכֶם: וְשַׂמְתֶּם אֶת־דְּבָרַי אֵלֶּה
עַל־לְבַבְכֶם וְעַל־נַפְשְׁכֶם וּקְשַׁרְתֶּם אֹתָם לְאוֹת עַל־יֶדְכֶם וְהָיוּ
לְטוֹטָפֹת בֵּין עֵינֵיכֶם. וְלִמַּדְתֶּם אֹתָם אֶת־בְּנֵיכֶם לְדַבֵּר בָּם בְּשִׁבְתְּךָ
בְּבֵיתֶךָ וּבְלֶכְתְּךָ בַדֶּרֶךְ וּבְשָׁכְבְּךָ וּבְקוּמֶךָ: וּכְתַבְתָּם עַל־מְזוּזוֹת בֵּיתֶךָ
וּבִשְׁעָרֶיךָ: לְמַעַן יִרְבּוּ יְמֵיכֶם וִימֵי בְנֵיכֶם עַל הָאֲדָמָה אֲשֶׁר נִשְׁבַּע
יְהוָה לַאֲבֹתֵיכֶם לָתֵת לָהֶם כִּימֵי הַשָּׁמַיִם עַל־ הָאָרֶץ:

Vehayah Im-Shamoa Tishme'u El-Mitzvotai. Asher Anochi Metzaveh
Etchem Hayom; Le'ahavah Et-Adonai Eloheichem Ule'avdo. Bechol-
Levavchem Uvechol-Nafshechem. Venatati Metar-'Artzechem Be'ito
Yoreh Umalkosh; Ve'asafta Deganecha. Vetiroshecha Veyitzharecha.
Venatati Esev Besadecha Livhemtecha; Ve'achalta Vesava'eta.
Hishameru Lachem. Pen Yifteh Levavchem; Vesartem. Va'avadtem

Elohim Acherim. Vehishtachavitem Lahem. Vecharah Af-Adonai
Bachem. Ve'atzar Et-Hashamayim Velo-Yihyeh Matar. Veha'adamah.
Lo Titen Et-Yevulah; Va'avadtem Meheirah. Me'al Ha'aretz Hatovah.
Asher Adonai Noten Lachem. Vesamtem Et-Devarai Eleh. Al-
Levavchem Ve'al-Nafshechem; Ukeshartem Otam Le'ot Al-Yedchem.
Vehayu Letotafot Bein Eineichem. Velimadtem Otam Et-Beneichem
Ledaber Bam; Beshivtecha Beveitecha Uvelechtecha Vaderech.
Uveshochbecha Uvekumecha. Uchetavtam Al-Mezuzot Beitecha
Uvish'areicha. Lema'an Yirbu Yemeichem Vimei Veneichem. Al
Ha'adamah. Asher Nishba Adonai La'avoteichem Latet Lahem;
Kimei Hashamayim Al-Ha'aretz.

And it will come to pass, if you will observe My commandments
which I command you this day, to love Hashem your God, and to
serve Him with all your heart and with all your soul, that I will give
the rain of your land in its season, the former rain and the latter
rain, that you may gather in your corn, and your wine, and your oil.
And I will give grass in your fields for your cattle, and you will eat
and be satisfied. Be cautious, in case your heart is deceived, and you
turn aside, and serve other gods, and worship them; and the anger
of Hashem is kindled against you, and He shut up the heaven, so
that there will be no rain, and the ground will not yield her fruit; and
you perish quickly from off the good land which Hashem gives you.
Therefore you will lay up these words in your heart and in your soul;
and you will bind them for a sign upon your hand, and they will be
for frontlets between your eyes. And you will teach them to your
children, talking of them, when you sit in your house, and when you
walk by the way, and when you lie down, and when you rise up. And
you will write them on the doorposts of your house, and on your
gates; that your days may be multiplied, and the days of your
children, upon the land which Hashem swore to your fathers to give
them, as the days of the heavens above the earth. (Deuteronomy 11:13-21)

Numbers 15:37-41

וַיֹּאמֶר יְהוָה אֶל־מֹשֶׁה לֵּאמֹר: דַּבֵּר אֶל־בְּנֵי יִשְׂרָאֵל וְאָמַרְתָּ אֲלֵהֶם
וְעָשׂוּ לָהֶם צִיצִת עַל־כַּנְפֵי בִגְדֵיהֶם לְדֹרֹתָם וְנָתְנוּ עַל־צִיצִת הַכָּנָף
פְּתִיל תְּכֵלֶת: וְהָיָה לָכֶם לְצִיצִת וּרְאִיתֶם אֹתוֹ וּזְכַרְתֶּם
אֶת־כָּל־מִצְוֹת יְהוָה וַעֲשִׂיתֶם אֹתָם וְלֹא־תָתוּרוּ אַחֲרֵי לְבַבְכֶם וְאַחֲרֵי
עֵינֵיכֶם אֲשֶׁר־אַתֶּם זֹנִים אַחֲרֵיהֶם: לְמַעַן תִּזְכְּרוּ וַעֲשִׂיתֶם
אֶת־כָּל־מִצְוֹתָי וִהְיִיתֶם קְדֹשִׁים לֵאלֹהֵיכֶם: אֲנִי יְהוָה אֱלֹהֵיכֶם אֲשֶׁר
הוֹצֵאתִי אֶתְכֶם מֵאֶרֶץ מִצְרַיִם לִהְיוֹת לָכֶם לֵאלֹהִים אֲנִי יְהוָה
אֱלֹהֵיכֶם: אֱמֶת.

Vayomer Adonai El-Mosheh Lemor. Daber El-Benei Yisra'el
Ve'amarta Aleihem. Ve'asu Lahem Tzitzit Al-Kanfei Vigdeihem
Ledorotam; Venatenu Al-Tzitzit Hakanaf Petil Techelet. Vehayah
Lachem Letzitzit Ure'item Oto Uzechartem Et-Chol-Mitzvot Adonai
Va'asitem Otam; Velo-Taturu Acharei Levavchem Ve'acharei
Eineichem. Asher-'Attem Zonim Achareihem. Lema'an Tizkeru.
Va'asitem Et-Chol-Mitzvotai; Vihyitem Kedoshim Leloheichem. Ani
Adonai Eloheichem. Asher Hotzeti Etchem Me'eretz Mitzrayim.
Lihyot Lachem Lelohim; Ani Adonai Eloheichem. Emet.

And Hashem spoke to Moshe, saying: Speak to the children of Yisrael, and command them to make tzitzit on the corners of their garments throughout their generations, and that they put a thread of tekhelet with the tzitzit of each corner. And they will be to you for tzitzit, that you may look upon them, and remember all the commandments of Hashem, and do them; and that you do not go about after your own heart and your own eyes, after which you go whoring; that you may remember and do all My commandments, and be holy to your God. I am Hashem your God, Who brought you out of the land of Mitzrayim, to be your God: I am Hashem your God. It is true.

יְהוָה אֱלֹהֵיכֶם אֱמֶת:

Adonai Eloheichem Emet.
Hashem, your God, is true.

Emet Ve'Emunah

וֶאֱמוּנָה כָּל־זֹאת וְקַיָּם עָלֵינוּ. כִּי הוּא יְהֹוָה אֱלֹהֵינוּ וְאֵין זוּלָתוֹ.
וַאֲנַחְנוּ יִשְׂרָאֵל עַמּוֹ. הַפּוֹדֵנוּ מִיַּד מְלָכִים. הַגֹּאֲלֵנוּ מַלְכֵּנוּ מִכַּף
כָּל־עָרִיצִים. הָאֵל הַנִּפְרָע לָנוּ מִצָּרֵינוּ. הַמְשַׁלֵּם גְּמוּל לְכָל־אֹיְבֵי
נַפְשֵׁנוּ. הַשָּׂם נַפְשֵׁנוּ בַּחַיִּים. וְלֹא נָתַן לַמּוֹט רַגְלֵנוּ. הַמַּדְרִיכֵנוּ עַל
בָּמוֹת אוֹיְבֵינוּ. וַיָּרֶם קַרְנֵנוּ עַל־כָּל־שׂוֹנְאֵינוּ. הָאֵל הָעֹשֶׂה לָנוּ נְקָמָה
בְּפַרְעֹה. בְּאוֹתוֹת וּבְמוֹפְתִים בְּאַדְמַת בְּנֵי חָם. הַמַּכֶּה בְעֶבְרָתוֹ
כָּל־בְּכוֹרֵי מִצְרָיִם. וַיּוֹצִיא אֶת־עַמּוֹ יִשְׂרָאֵל מִתּוֹכָם לְחֵרוּת עוֹלָם.
הַמַּעֲבִיר בָּנָיו בֵּין גִּזְרֵי יַם־סוּף. וְאֶת־רוֹדְפֵיהֶם וְאֶת־שׂוֹנְאֵיהֶם
בִּתְהוֹמוֹת טִבַּע. רָאוּ בָנִים אֶת־גְּבוּרָתוֹ. שִׁבְּחוּ וְהוֹדוּ לִשְׁמוֹ.
וּמַלְכוּתוֹ בְרָצוֹן קִבְּלוּ עֲלֵיהֶם. מֹשֶׁה וּבְנֵי יִשְׂרָאֵל לְךָ עָנוּ שִׁירָה
בְּשִׂמְחָה רַבָּה. וְאָמְרוּ כֻלָּם. מִי־כָמֹכָה בָּאֵלִם יְהֹוָה מִי כָּמֹכָה
נֶאְדָּר בַּקֹּדֶשׁ נוֹרָא תְהִלֹּת עֹשֵׂה פֶלֶא: מַלְכוּתְךָ יְהֹוָה אֱלֹהֵינוּ רָאוּ
בָנֶיךָ עַל הַיָּם. יַחַד כֻּלָּם הוֹדוּ וְהִמְלִיכוּ וְאָמְרוּ. יְהֹוָה | יִמְלֹךְ לְעֹלָם
וָעֶד: וְנֶאֱמַר. כִּי־פָדָה יְהֹוָה אֶת־יַעֲקֹב וּגְאָלוֹ מִיַּד חָזָק מִמֶּנּוּ: בָּרוּךְ
אַתָּה יְהֹוָה גָּאַל יִשְׂרָאֵל:

Ve'emunah Kol-Zot Vekayam Aleinu. Ki Hu Adonai Eloheinu Ve'ein
Zulato. Va'anachnu Yisra'el Ammo. Hapodenu Miyad Melachim.
Hago'alenu Malkeinu Mikaf Kol-'Aritzim. Ha'el Hanifra Lanu
Mitzareinu. Hamshalem Gemul Lechol-'Oyevei Nafshenu. Hassam
Nafshenu Bachayim. Velo Natan Lamot Raglenu. Hamadricheinu Al
Bamot Oyeveinu. Vayarem Karnenu Al-Kol-Sone'einu. Ha'el
Ha'oseh Lanu Nekamah Befar'oh. Be'otot Uvemofetim Be'admat
Benei Cham. Hamakeh Ve'evrato Kol-Bechorei Mitzrayim. Vayotzi
Et-'Ammo Yisra'el Mitocham Lecherut Olam. Hama'avir Banav Bein
Gizrei Yam-Suf. Ve'et-Rodefeihem Ve'et-Sone'eihem Bit'homot Tiba.
Ra'u Vanim Et-Gevurato. Shibechu Vehodu Lishmo. Umalchuto
Veratzon Kibelu Aleihem. Mosheh Uvenei Yisra'el Lecha Anu Shirah
Besimchah Rabah. Ve'ameru Chulam. Mi-Chamochah Ba'elim
Hashem Mi Kamochah Ne'dar Bakodesh; Nora Tehillot Oseh Fele.
Malchutecha Adonai Eloheinu Ra'u Vaneicha Al Hayam. Yachad
Kulam Hodu Vehimlichu Ve'ameru. Adonai Yimloch Le'olam Va'ed.

Vene'emar. Ki-Fadah Adonai Et-Ya'akov; Uge'alo Miyad Chazak Mimenu. Baruch Attah Adonai Ga'al Yisra'el.

Trustworthy is all of this, and binding upon us, that He is Hashem our God with none besides Him, and we Yisrael are His people. He redeems us from the hand of kings, our King Who redeems us from the hand of all oppressors. The God Who ransoms us from adversaries, Who brings retribution on all enemies of our souls. "He set our soul in life, And has not allowed our feet to slip." He has guided us upon high places of our enemies, And has raised our strength above all who hated us. The God Who performed vengeance on Pharaoh or us by signs and wonders in the land of the sons of Cham. In His wrath He struck all the first-born of Mitzrayim, And brought out His people Yisrael to everlasting freedom. He led His children between the divided Sea of Reeds, and sank their pursuers and enemies in the depths. His children praised His power; they sang gave thanks to His name and with willingly accepted His kingship. Then, to You, Moshe and all the children of Yisrael sang, proclaiming with great joy, "Who is like You, Hashem, among the gods, Who is like You, glorified in holiness, You are awesome in praise, working wonders?" By the sea, Hashem our God, Your children beheld Your kingdom; all together they gave thanks to You, proclaiming Your kingship, and it is said, "Hashem will reign forever and ever." And also declared Yirmiyahu, Your prophet, "Hashem will surely redeem Yaakov, And rescue him from the hand of one stronger than him." (Jeremiah 31:10) Blessed are You, Hashem Who redeemed Yisrael.

Hashkiveinu

Hashkiveinu Avinu Leshalom.

Veha'amidenu Malkeinu

Lechayim Tovim Uleshalom.

הַשְׁכִּיבֵנוּ אָבִינוּ לְשָׁלוֹם.

וְהַעֲמִידֵנוּ מַלְכֵּנוּ

לְחַיִּים טוֹבִים וּלְשָׁלוֹם.

Uferos Aleinu Sukkat	וּפְרֹשׂ עָלֵינוּ סֻכַּת
Shelomecha. Vetakenenu	שְׁלוֹמֶךָ. וְתַקְּנֵנוּ
Malkeinu Be'etzah Tovah	מַלְכֵּנוּ בְּעֵצָה טוֹבָה
Milfaneicha. Vehoshi'enu	מִלְפָנֶיךָ. וְהוֹשִׁיעֵנוּ
Meheirah Lema'an Shemecha.	מְהֵרָה לְמַעַן שְׁמֶךָ.
Vehagen Ba'adenu. Uferos	וְהָגֵן בַּעֲדֵנוּ. וּפְרֹשׂ
Aleinu Ve'al Yerushalayim Ircha	עָלֵינוּ וְעַל יְרוּשָׁלַיִם עִירָךְ
Sukkat Rachamim Veshalom.	סֻכַּת רַחֲמִים וְשָׁלוֹם.
Baruch Attah Adonai Hapores	בָּרוּךְ אַתָּה יְהֹוָה הַפּוֹרֵשׂ
Sukkat Shalom Aleinu Ve'al Kol	סֻכַּת שָׁלוֹם עָלֵינוּ וְעַל כָּל
Ammo Yisra'el. Ve'al	עַמּוֹ יִשְׂרָאֵל. וְעַל־
Yerushalayim. Amen:	יְרוּשָׁלַיִם. אָמֵן:

Our Father, lay us down in peace and raise us up, our King, to a good life and peace. And spread over us Your shelter of peace and direct us with good council before You, our King. And save us speedily for Your name's sake. Shield us and spread over us and over Yerushalyim, Your city, a tent of mercy and peace. Blessed are You, Hashem, Who spreads a tent of peace over us, and over Your people Yisrael, and Yerushalayim. Amen.

VeShameru

וְשָׁמְרוּ בְנֵי־יִשְׂרָאֵל אֶת־הַשַּׁבָּת לַעֲשׂוֹת אֶת־הַשַּׁבָּת לְדֹרֹתָם בְּרִית
עוֹלָם: בֵּינִי. וּבֵין בְּנֵי יִשְׂרָאֵל אוֹת הִוא לְעֹלָם כִּי־שֵׁשֶׁת יָמִים עָשָׂה
יְהוָה אֶת־הַשָּׁמַיִם וְאֶת־הָאָרֶץ וּבַיּוֹם הַשְּׁבִיעִי שָׁבַת וַיִּנָּפַשׁ:

Veshameru Venei-Yisra'el Et-Hashabbat; La'asot Et-Ha Shabbat
Ledorotam Berit Olam. Beini. Uvein Benei Yisra'el. Ot Hi Le'olam;
Ki-Sheshet Yamim. Asah Adonai Et-Hashamayim Ve'et-Ha'aretz.
Uvayom Hashevi'i. Shavat Vayinafash.

The children of Yisrael will keep the Shabbat, to observe the Shabbat throughout their generations, for a perpetual covenant. It is a sign between Me and the children of Yisrael forever; for in six days Hashem made heaven and earth, and on the seventh day He ceased from His work and rested. (Ex. 31:16-17)

On a Yom Tov / Festival some recite the following:

אֵלֶּה מוֹעֲדֵי יְהֹוָה מִקְרָאֵי קֹדֶשׁ אֲשֶׁר־תִּקְרְאוּ אֹתָם בְּמוֹעֲדָם: וַיְדַבֵּר מֹשֶׁה אֶת־מֹעֲדֵי יְהֹוָה אֶל־בְּנֵי יִשְׂרָאֵל:

Eleh Mo'adei Adonai Mikra'ei Kodesh Asher Tikre'u Otam Bemo'adam. Vaydaber Mosheh Et Mo'adei Adonai El Benei Yisra'el.

These are the appointed times of Hashem, holy convocations, which you will proclaim in their appointed season. (Lev. 23:4) And Moshe declared to the children of Yisrael the appointed seasons of Hashem. (Lev. 23:44)

And say Hatzi- Kaddish:

Kaddish is only recited in a minyan (ten men). אמן denotes when the congregation responds "Amen" together out loud. According to the Shulchan Arukh, the congregation says "Yehei Shemeh Rabba" to "Yitbarach" out loud together without interruption, and also that one should respond "Amen" after "Yitbarach." (SA, OC 55,56) This is not the common custom today. Though many are accustomed to answering according to their own custom, it is advised to respond in the custom of the one reciting to avoid not fragmenting into smaller groups. ("Lo Titgodedu" - BT, Yevamot 13b / SA, OC 493, Rema / MT, Avodah Zara 12:15)

יִתְגַּדַּל וְיִתְקַדַּשׁ שְׁמֵהּ רַבָּא. אמן בְּעָלְמָא דִּי בְרָא. כִּרְעוּתֵהּ. וְיַמְלִיךְ מַלְכוּתֵהּ. וְיַצְמַח פֻּרְקָנֵהּ. וִיקָרֵב מְשִׁיחֵהּ. אמן בְּחַיֵּיכוֹן וּבְיוֹמֵיכוֹן וּבְחַיֵּי דְכָל בֵּית יִשְׂרָאֵל. בַּעֲגָלָא וּבִזְמַן קָרִיב. וְאִמְרוּ אָמֵן. אמן יְהֵא שְׁמֵהּ רַבָּא מְבָרַךְ לְעָלַם וּלְעָלְמֵי עָלְמַיָּא יִתְבָּרַךְ. וְיִשְׁתַּבַּח. וְיִתְפָּאַר. וְיִתְרוֹמַם. וְיִתְנַשֵּׂא. וְיִתְהַדָּר. וְיִתְעַלֶּה. וְיִתְהַלָּל שְׁמֵהּ דְּקֻדְשָׁא. בְּרִיךְ הוּא. אמן לְעֵלָּא מִן כָּל בִּרְכָתָא שִׁירָתָא. תֻּשְׁבְּחָתָא וְנֶחֱמָתָא. דַּאֲמִירָן בְּעָלְמָא. וְאִמְרוּ אָמֵן. אמן

Yitgadal Veyitkadash Shemeh Rabba. Amen Be'alema Di Vera. Kir'uteh. Veyamlich Malchuteh. Veyatzmach Purkaneh. Vikarev Meshicheh. Amen Bechayeichon Uveyomeichon Uvechayei Dechal-Beit Yisra'el. Ba'agala Uvizman Kariv. Ve'imru Amen. Amen Yehei Shemeh Rabba Mevarach Le'alam Ule'alemei Alemaya Yitbarach. Veyishtabach. Veyitpa'ar. Veyitromam. Veyitnasse. Veyit'hadar. Veyit'aleh. Veyit'hallal Shemeh Dekudsha. Berich Hu. Amen Le'ella Min Kol Birchata Shirata. Tushbechata Venechemata. Da'amiran Be'alema. Ve'imru Amen. Amen

Glorified and sanctified be God's great name ᴬᵐᵉⁿ throughout the world which He has created according to His will. May He establish His kingdom, hastening His salvation and the coming of His Messiah, ᴬᵐᵉⁿ, in your lifetime and during your days, and within the life of the entire House of Yisrael, speedily and soon; and say, Amen. ᴬᵐᵉⁿ May His great name be blessed forever and to all eternity. Blessed and praised, glorified and exalted, extolled and honored, adored and lauded is the name of the Holy One, blessed is He, ᴬᵐᵉⁿ Beyond all the blessings and hymns, praises and consolations that are ever spoken in the world; and say, Amen. ᴬᵐᵉⁿ

LAWS OF AMIDAH

When one gets up to pray if he was standing outside the Land of Yisrael, he should turn his face toward the Land of Yisrael and focus also on Yerushalayim and the Temple and the Holy of Holies. One who is not able to determine the directions, [should] direct one's heart to their Father in Heaven. One should consider oneself as if one is standing in the Beit Hamikdash, and in one's heart, one should be directed upward towards Heaven. One who prays needs to intend in their heart the meaning of the words which are coming out of their mouth. They should think as if the Divine Presence is before them, and remove all distracting thoughts from themselves, until their thoughts and intention are pure in their prayer. (SA, OC 94, 95, 98) These are the blessings at which we bow: in Avot, at the beginning and at the end; in Modim, at the beginning and at the end. And if you come to bow at the end of every blessing or at the beginning, we teach him to not bow but in the middle, one can bow. One needs to bend until all the vertebrae in his spine are bent. His head should stay straight and submissive. One should not bow too much until his mouth is opposite his belt. If he is sick or old and cannot bow, he should humble his head, that is enough. Bow at "Baruch" and stand up at Hashem's name. (SA, OC 113,114) One should position one's feet next to each other as though they are one, in order to imitate angels, as it written regarding them: "their feet were a straight foot" (Ez. 1:7), which is to say their feet appeared as one foot. One should take three steps forward in the way of coming close and approaching a matter that must be done. (SA, OC 95, Rema)

Amidah / Shemoneh Esrei - Arvit

Take three steps forward and say:

Adonai Sefatai Tiftach; Ufi. Yagid
Tehilatecha.

אֲדֹנָי שְׂפָתַי תִּפְתָּח וּפִי יַגִּיד
תְּהִלָּתֶךָ:

Hashem, open my lips, that my mouth may declare Your praise.

Avot / Fathers

Bow at "Baruch Attah" / "Blessed are You". Raise up at Adonai / Hashem.

Baruch Attah Adonai Eloheinu

בָּרוּךְ אַתָּה יְהֹוָה אֱלֹהֵינוּ

Velohei Avoteinu. Elohei

וֵאלֹהֵי אֲבוֹתֵינוּ. אֱלֹהֵי

Avraham. Elohei Yitzchak.

אַבְרָהָם. אֱלֹהֵי יִצְחָק.

Velohei Ya'akov. Ha'el Hagadol

וֵאלֹהֵי יַעֲקֹב. הָאֵל הַגָּדוֹל

Hagibor Vehanorah. El Elyon.

הַגִּבּוֹר וְהַנּוֹרָא. אֵל עֶלְיוֹן.

Gomel Chasadim Tovim. Koneh

גּוֹמֵל חֲסָדִים טוֹבִים. קוֹנֵה

Hakol. Vezocher Chasdei Avot.

הַכֹּל. וְזוֹכֵר חַסְדֵי אָבוֹת.

Umevi Go'el Livnei Veneihem

וּמֵבִיא גוֹאֵל לִבְנֵי בְנֵיהֶם

Lema'an Shemo Be'ahavah.

לְמַעַן שְׁמוֹ בְּאַהֲבָה:

Blessed are You, Hashem our God and God of our fathers, God of Avraham, God of Yitzchak and God of Yaakov; the great, mighty and revered God, most high God, Who bestows lovingkindness. Master of all things; Who remembers the kindnesses of our fathers, and Who will bring a redeemer to their children's children for the sake of His name in love.

During the 10 days of repentance (Rosh Hashanah to Yom Kippur) add:

Zochrenu Lechayim. Melech Chafetz

זָכְרֵנוּ לְחַיִּים. מֶלֶךְ חָפֵץ

Bachayim. Katevenu Besefer Chayim.

בַּחַיִּים. כָּתְבֵנוּ בְּסֵפֶר חַיִּים.

Lema'anach Elohim Chayim.

לְמַעַנְךָ אֱלֹהִים חַיִּים.

Remember us to life, King Who delights in life; inscribe us in the book of life for Your sake, Oh living God.

Bow at "Baruch Attah" / Blessed are You. Raise up at Adonai / Hashem.

Melech Ozeir Umoshia	מֶלֶךְ עוֹזֵר וּמוֹשִׁיעַ
Umagen. Baruch Attah Adonai	וּמָגֵן: בָּרוּךְ אַתָּה יְהוָה
Magen Avraham.	מָגֵן אַבְרָהָם:

King, Supporter, and Savior and Shield. Blessed are You, Hashem, Shield of Avraham.

Gevurot / Powers

> We [in Yisrael] begin to say "Mashiv Haruach" in the second blessing of the Amidah from the Musaf [Additional] Service of the last day of Sukkot, and conclude at the Musaf [Additional] Service of the first day of Pesach. On the first day of Pesach the congregation still says it in the Musaf Service, but the Reader stops saying it then. In lands outside of Yisrael, [in the Birkhat HaShanim / Blessing for the Years,] we begin to pray for rain in the Arvit (Evening) Service of the sixtieth day after the New Moon of Tishrei, and in Yisrael we begin to say it in the evening of the seventh day of Cheshvan, and it is said until the Afternoon Service on the day preceding the first day of Passover. If one prayed for rain in the summer, or if one omitted to pray for it in the winter, he must repeat the Amidah again. If one said "Morid Hageshem" in the summer time, he must repeat again from the beginning of the blessing. If he already concluded the blessing, he must read the entire Amidah again. Likewise in the winter, if he omitted it, he must begin all over again. (SA, OC 117)

Attah Gibor Le'olam Adonai.	אַתָּה גִבּוֹר לְעוֹלָם אֲדֹנָי.
Mechayeh Meitim Attah. Rav	מְחַיֶּה מֵתִים אַתָּה. רַב
Lehoshia.	לְהוֹשִׁיעַ.

You, Hashem, are mighty forever; You revive the dead; You are powerful to save.

B'ketz: Morid Hatal.	בקיץ: מוֹרִיד הַטָּל.
B'choref: Mashiv Haruach Umorid	בחורף: מַשִּׁיב הָרוּחַ וּמוֹרִיד
Hageshem.	הַגָּשֶׁם.

In summer: You cause the dew to fall.

In winter: You cause the wind to blow and the rain to fall.

Mechalkel Chayim Bechesed.	מְכַלְכֵּל חַיִּים בְּחֶסֶד.
Mechayeh Meitim Berachamim	מְחַיֶּה מֵתִים בְּרַחֲמִים

Rabim. Somech Nofelim. Verofei	רַבִּים. סוֹמֵךְ נוֹפְלִים. וְרוֹפֵא
Cholim. Umatir Asurim.	חוֹלִים. וּמַתִּיר אֲסוּרִים.
Umekayem Emunato Lishenei	וּמְקַיֵּם אֱמוּנָתוֹ לִישֵׁנֵי
Afar. Mi Chamocha Ba'al	עָפָר. מִי כָמוֹךָ בַּעַל
Gevurot. Umi Domeh Lach.	גְּבוּרוֹת. וּמִי דוֹמֶה לָּךְ.
Melech Memit Umechayeh	מֶלֶךְ מֵמִית וּמְחַיֶּה
Umatzmiach Yeshu'ah.	וּמַצְמִיחַ יְשׁוּעָה.

You sustain the living with kindness, and revive the dead with great mercy; You support all who fall, and heal the sick; You set the captives free, and keep faith with those who sleep in the dust. Who is like You, Master of power? Who resembles You, Oh King? You bring death and restore life, and cause salvation to flourish.

During the 10 days of repentance (Rosh Hashanah to Yom Kippur) add:

| Mi Chamocha Av Harachaman. Zocher | מִי כָמוֹךָ אָב הָרַחֲמָן. זוֹכֵר |
| Yetzurav Berachamim Lechayim. | יְצוּרָיו בְּרַחֲמִים לְחַיִּים. |

Who is like You, merciful Father? In mercy You remember Your creatures to life.

Vene'eman Attah Lehachayot	וְנֶאֱמָן אַתָּה לְהַחֲיוֹת
Meitim. Baruch Attah Adonai	מֵתִים: בָּרוּךְ אַתָּה יְהֹוָה
Mechayeh Hameitim.	מְחַיֵּה הַמֵּתִים:

And You are faithful to revive the dead. Blessed are You, Hashem, Who revives the dead.

Kedushat HaShem / Holiness of the Name

Attah Kadosh Veshimcha	אַתָּה קָדוֹשׁ וְשִׁמְךָ
Kadosh. Ukedoshim Bechol-	קָדוֹשׁ. וּקְדוֹשִׁים בְּכָל־
Yom Yehalelucha Selah. Baruch	יוֹם יְהַלְלוּךָ סֶּלָה: בָּרוּךְ
Attah Adonai Ha' El Hakadosh.	אַתָּה יְהֹוָה הָאֵל הַקָּדוֹשׁ:

You are holy and Your name is holy, and the holy-ones will praise You every day, selah. Blessed are You, Hashem, The Holy God.

During the 10 days of repentance (Rosh Hashanah to Yom Kippur) say:

Hamelech Hakadosh.   הַמֶּלֶךְ הַקָּדוֹשׁ:

The Holy King.

If one is unsure or forgot if they said, repeat the Amidah. If it was immediately said after, it is fulfilled.

Erev Shabbat / Arvit Blessings

Attah Kidashta Et Yom Hashevi'i	אַתָּה קִדַּשְׁתָּ אֶת־יוֹם הַשְּׁבִיעִי
Lishmecha. Tachlit Ma'aseh	לִשְׁמֶךָ. תַּכְלִית מַעֲשֵׂה
Shamayim Va'aretz. Uverachto	שָׁמַיִם וָאָרֶץ. וּבֵרַכְתּוֹ
Mikol Hayamim. Vekidashto	מִכָּל־הַיָּמִים. וְקִדַּשְׁתּוֹ
Mikol Hazmanim. Vechein	מִכָּל־הַזְּמַנִּים. וְכֵן
Katuv Betoratach:	כָּתוּב בְּתוֹרָתֶךְ:

You have sanctified the seventh day to Your name; the purpose of the work of the creation of heaven and earth. And You blessed it above all days, and sanctified it above all times, and so is it written in Your Torah:

Vaychulu Hashamayim	וַיְכֻלּוּ הַשָּׁמַיִם
Veha'aretz Vechol-Tzeva'am	וְהָאָרֶץ וְכָל־צְבָאָם
Vaychal Elohim Bayom	וַיְכַל אֱלֹהִים בַּיּוֹם
Hashevi'i. Melachto Asher Asah;	הַשְּׁבִיעִי מְלַאכְתּוֹ אֲשֶׁר עָשָׂה
Vayishbot Bayom Hashevi'i.	וַיִּשְׁבֹּת בַּיּוֹם הַשְּׁבִיעִי
Mikol-Melachto Asher Asah.	מִכָּל־מְלַאכְתּוֹ אֲשֶׁר עָשָׂה:

Vayvarech Elohim Et-Yom	וַיְבָרֶךְ אֱלֹהִים אֶת־יוֹם
Hashevi'i. Vaykadesh Oto; Ki Vo	הַשְּׁבִיעִי וַיְקַדֵּשׁ אֹתוֹ כִּי בוֹ
Shavat Mikol-Melachto. Asher-	שָׁבַת מִכָּל־מְלַאכְתּוֹ אֲשֶׁר־
Bara Elohim La'Asot.	בָּרָא אֱלֹהִים לַעֲשׂוֹת:

And the heavens and the earth were finished, and all the host of them. And with the seventh day God finished His work which He had made; and He rested on the seventh day from all His work which He had made. And God blessed the seventh day, and sanctified it; because that in it He rested from all His work which God in creating had made. (Genesis 2:1-5)

Yismechu Vemalchutach	יִשְׂמְחוּ בְמַלְכוּתָךְ
Shomerei Shabbat Vekore'ei	שׁוֹמְרֵי שַׁבָּת וְקוֹרְאֵי
Oneg. Am Mekadeshei Shevi'i.	עֹנֶג. עַם מְקַדְּשֵׁי שְׁבִיעִי.
Kulam Yisbe'u Veyit'anegu	כֻּלָּם יִשְׂבְּעוּ וְיִתְעַנְּגוּ
Mituvech. Vehashevi'i Ratzita	מִטּוּבָךְ. וְהַשְּׁבִיעִי רָצִיתָ
Bo Vekidashto. Chemdat Yamim	בּוֹ וְקִדַּשְׁתּוֹ. חֶמְדַּת יָמִים
Oto Karata. Zecher Lema'asei	אוֹתוֹ קָרָאתָ. זֵכֶר לְמַעֲשֵׂה
Vereishit.	בְרֵאשִׁית.

They will rejoice in Your rule, those who keep Shabbat and call it a delight. A people who sanctify the seventh day, they will all be satisfied and delight in Your goodness. And the seventh, You desired it, and sanctified it, declaring it "the desired of days", a memorial to the work of creation.

Eloheinu Velohei Avoteinu.	אֱלֹהֵינוּ וֵאלֹהֵי אֲבוֹתֵינוּ.
Retzeh Na Bimnuchatenu.	רְצֵה נָא בִמְנוּחָתֵנוּ.

Kadeshenu Bemitzvoteicha. Sim	קַדְּשֵׁנוּ בְּמִצְוֹתֶיךָ. שִׂים
Chelkenu Betoratach. Sabe'einu	חֶלְקֵנוּ בְּתוֹרָתָךְ. שַׂבְּעֵנוּ
Mituvach. Same'ach Nafshenu	מִטּוּבָךְ. שַׂמֵּחַ נַפְשֵׁנוּ
Bishu'atach. Vetaher Libenu	בִּישׁוּעָתָךְ. וְטַהֵר לִבֵּנוּ
Le'avedcha Ve'emet.	לְעָבְדְּךָ בֶּאֱמֶת.
Vehanchilenu Adonai Eloheinu	וְהַנְחִילֵנוּ יְהֹוָה אֱלֹהֵינוּ
Be'ahavah Uveratzon Shabbat	בְּאַהֲבָה וּבְרָצוֹן שַׁבָּת
Kodshecha. Veyanuchu Vah Kol	קָדְשֶׁךָ. וְיָנוּחוּ בָה כָּל
Yisra'el Mekadoshei Shemecha.	יִשְׂרָאֵל מְקַדְּשֵׁי שְׁמֶךָ.
Baruch Attah Adonai Mekadesh	בָּרוּךְ אַתָּה יְהֹוָה מְקַדֵּשׁ
Hashabbat.	הַשַּׁבָּת:

Our God, God of our fathers, be pleased with our rest. Sanctify us through Your commandments and grant our portion in Your Torah. Content us with Your goodness. Rejoice our soul with Your salvation. And make our heart pure to serve You in truth. Cause us to inherit, Hashem our God, Your holy Shabbat with love and favor: and grant rest on it to all Yisrael, who sanctify Your name. Blessed are You, Hashem Who sanctifies the Shabbat.

Avodah / Temple Service

Retzeh Adonai Eloheinu	רְצֵה יְהֹוָה אֱלֹהֵינוּ
Be'ammecha Yisra'el Velitfilatam	בְּעַמְּךָ יִשְׂרָאֵל וְלִתְפִלָּתָם
She'eh. Vehasheiv Ha'avodah	שְׁעֵה. וְהָשֵׁב הָעֲבוֹדָה
Lidvir Beitecha. Ve'ishei Yisra'el	לִדְבִיר בֵּיתֶךָ. וְאִשֵּׁי יִשְׂרָאֵל
Utefilatam. Meheirah Be'ahavah	וּתְפִלָּתָם. מְהֵרָה בְּאַהֲבָה
Tekabel Beratzon. Utehi Leratzon	תְקַבֵּל בְּרָצוֹן. וּתְהִי לְרָצוֹן
Tamid Avodat Yisra'el Ammecha.	תָּמִיד עֲבוֹדַת יִשְׂרָאֵל עַמֶּךָ:

Be favorable, Hashem our God, on Your people Yisrael and regard their prayers. And the service to the Sanctuary of Your House, and the fire offerings of Yisrael, and their prayers accept soon with love. And may the service of Your people, Yisrael, always be favorable.

On Rosh Chodesh and Chol HaMoed Passover and Sukkot say:

Ya'aleh Veyavo

אֱלֹהֵינוּ וֵאלֹהֵי אֲבוֹתֵינוּ. יַעֲלֶה וְיָבֹא. וְיַגִּיעַ וְיֵרָאֶה. וְיֵרָצֶה וְיִשָּׁמַע. וְיִפָּקֵד וְיִזָּכֵר. זִכְרוֹנֵנוּ וְזִכְרוֹן אֲבוֹתֵינוּ. זִכְרוֹן יְרוּשָׁלַיִם עִירָךְ. וְזִכְרוֹן מָשִׁיחַ בֶּן־דָּוִד עַבְדָּךְ. וְזִכְרוֹן כָּל־עַמְּךָ בֵּית יִשְׂרָאֵל לְפָנֶיךָ. לִפְלֵיטָה. לְטוֹבָה. לְחֵן. לְחֶסֶד וּלְרַחֲמִים. לְחַיִּים טוֹבִים וּלְשָׁלוֹם. בְּיוֹם:

Eloheinu Velohei Avoteinu. Ya'aleh Veyavo. Veyagia Veyera'eh. Veyeratzeh Veyishama'. Veyipaked Veyizacher. Zichronenu Vezichron Avoteinu. Zichron Yerushalayim Irach. Vezichron Mashiach Ben-David Avdach. Vezichron Kol-'Ammecha Beit Yisra'el Lefaneicha. Lifleitah. Letovah. Lechein. Lechesed Ulerachamim. Lechayim Tovim Uleshalom. Beyom:

Our God, and God of our fathers, may it rise, and come, arrive, appear, find favor, and be heard, and be considered, and be remembered our remembrance and the remembrance of our fathers, Yerushalayim Your city, the remembrance of Messiah ben David Your servant, and the remembrance of all Your people of the House of Yisrael before You for deliverance, for good favor, for kindness and mercy, for good life and for peace. On this day of:

On Rosh Chodesh:

רֹאשׁ חֹדֶשׁ הַזֶּה.

Rosh Chodesh Hazeh.

Rosh Chodesh (New Moon).

On Pesach:

חַג הַמַּצּוֹת הַזֶּה. בְּיוֹם מִקְרָא קֹדֶשׁ הַזֶּה.

Chag Hamatzot Hazeh. Beyom Mikra Kodesh Hazeh.

The Festival of Matzot. on this day of holy convocation.

On Sukkot:

חַג הַסֻּכּוֹת הַזֶּה. בְּיוֹם מִקְרָא קֹדֶשׁ הַזֶּה.

Chag Hasukkot Hazeh. Beyom Mikra Kodesh Hazeh.

The Festival of Sukkot. on this day of holy convocation.

לְרַחֵם בּוֹ עָלֵינוּ וּלְהוֹשִׁיעֵנוּ. זָכְרֵנוּ יְהֹוָה אֱלֹהֵינוּ בּוֹ לְטוֹבָה. וּפָקְדֵנוּ בּוֹ
לִבְרָכָה. וְהוֹשִׁיעֵנוּ בּוֹ לְחַיִּים טוֹבִים. בִּדְבַר יְשׁוּעָה וְרַחֲמִים. חוּס וְחָנֵּנוּ.
וַחֲמוֹל וְרַחֵם עָלֵינוּ. וְהוֹשִׁיעֵנוּ כִּי אֵלֶיךָ עֵינֵינוּ. כִּי אֵל מֶלֶךְ חַנּוּן וְרַחוּם אָתָּה:

Lerachem Bo Aleinu Ulehoshi'enu. Zochrenu Adonai Eloheinu Bo Letovah.
Ufokdenu Vo Livrachah. Vehoshi'enu Vo Lechayim Tovim. Bidvar Yeshu'ah
Verachamim. Chus Vechanenu. Vachamol Verachem Aleinu. Vehoshi'enu Ki Eleicha
Eineinu. Ki El Melech Chanun Verachum Attah.

to have mercy upon us and save us. Remember us, Hashem our God, on it for good.
Be mindful of us on it for blessing and save us on it for a life of good. With the
promise of salvation and mercy, show us pity, and be gracious to us and have
compassion and mercy on us and save us. For our eyes are lifted towards You, for
You, God, are a gracious and merciful King.

Attah Berachameicha Harabim.	וְאַתָּה בְּרַחֲמֶיךָ הָרַבִּים.
Tachpotz Banu Vetirtzenu.	תַּחְפֹּץ בָּנוּ וְתִרְצֵנוּ.
Vetechezeinah Eineinu	וְתֶחֱזֶינָה עֵינֵינוּ
Beshuvecha Letziyon	בְּשׁוּבְךָ לְצִיּוֹן
Berachamim. Baruch Attah	בְּרַחֲמִים: בָּרוּךְ אַתָּה
Adonai Hamachazir Shechinato	יְהֹוָה הַמַּחֲזִיר שְׁכִינָתוֹ
Letziyon.	לְצִיּוֹן.

And You, in Your abundant mercy, delight in us, and be favorable to
us, so that our eyes may witness Your return to Tziyon with mercy.
Blessed are You, Hashem Who returns His Presence to Tziyon.

Hoda'ah (Modim) / Thanksgiving

On Saying "Modim" / "We are Thankful" One Bows and begins to rise after "Adonai" / "Hashem".

Modim Anachnu Lach. She'attah	מוֹדִים אֲנַחְנוּ לָךְ. שֶׁאַתָּה
Hu Adonai Eloheinu Velohei	הוּא יְהֹוָה אֱלֹהֵינוּ וֵאלֹהֵי
Avoteinu Le'olam Va'ed. Tzurenu	אֲבוֹתֵינוּ לְעוֹלָם וָעֶד. צוּרֵנוּ

Tzur Chayeinu Umagen Yish'enu	צוּר חַיֵּינוּ וּמָגֵן יִשְׁעֵנוּ
Attah Hu. Ledor Vador Nodeh	אַתָּה הוּא. לְדוֹר וָדוֹר נוֹדֶה
Lecha Unsapeir Tehilatecha. Al	לְךְ וּנְסַפֵּר תְּהִלָּתֶךְ. עַל
Chayeinu Hamesurim	חַיֵּינוּ הַמְּסוּרִים
Beyadecha. Ve'al Nishmoteinu	בְּיָדֶךְ. וְעַל נִשְׁמוֹתֵינוּ
Hapekudot Lach. Ve'al Niseicha	הַפְּקוּדוֹת לָךְ. וְעַל נִסֶּיךְ
Shebechol-Yom Imanu. Ve'al	שֶׁבְּכָל־יוֹם עִמָּנוּ. וְעַל
Nifle'oteicha Vetovoteicha	נִפְלְאוֹתֶיךְ וְטוֹבוֹתֶיךְ
Shebechol-'Et. Erev Vavoker	שֶׁבְּכָל־עֵת. עֶרֶב וָבֹקֶר
Vetzaharayim. Hatov. Ki Lo	וְצָהֳרָיִם. הַטּוֹב. כִּי לֹא
Chalu Rachameicha.	כָלוּ רַחֲמֶיךְ.
Hamerachem. Ki Lo Tamu	הַמְּרַחֵם. כִּי לֹא תַמּוּ
Chasadeicha. Ki Me'olam Kivinu	חֲסָדֶיךְ. כִּי מֵעוֹלָם קִוִּינוּ
Lach.	לָךְ:

We are thankful to You, Hashem our God and the God of our fathers, forever. You are our strength and Rock of our life and the Shield of our salvation. In every generation we will thank You and recount Your praise for our lives which are given into Your hand, for our souls which are placed in Your care, and for Your miracles which are daily with us, and for Your wonders and goodness—evening, morning and noon. The Beneficent One, for Your mercies never end, Merciful One, for Your kindness has never ceased, for we have always placed our hope in You.

Al HaNissim

On Purim and Hanukkah an extra prayer is added here:

עַל הַנִּסִּים וְעַל הַפֻּרְקָן וְעַל הַגְּבוּרוֹת וְעַל הַתְּשׁוּעוֹת וְעַל הַנִּפְלָאוֹת וְעַל
הַנֶּחָמוֹת שֶׁעָשִׂיתָ לַאֲבוֹתֵינוּ בַּיָּמִים הָהֵם בַּזְּמַן הַזֶּה:

Al Hanissim Ve'al Hapurkan Ve'al Hagevurot Ve'al Hateshu'ot Ve'al Hanifla'ot Ve'al Hanechamot She'asita La'avoteinu Bayamim Hahem Bazman Hazeh.

For the miracles, and for the triumphant liberation, and the mighty works, and for the deliverances, and for the wonders, and for the consolations which You have done for our fathers in those days at this season:

On Hanukkah:

בִּימֵי מַתִּתְיָה בֶּן־יוֹחָנָן כֹּהֵן גָּדוֹל. חַשְׁמוֹנָאִי וּבָנָיו כְּשֶׁעָמְדָה מַלְכוּת יָוָן הָרְשָׁעָה עַל עַמְּךָ יִשְׂרָאֵל. לְשַׁכְּחָם תּוֹרָתֶךָ וּלְהַעֲבִירָם מֵחֻקֵּי רְצוֹנֶךָ. וְאַתָּה בְּרַחֲמֶיךָ הָרַבִּים עָמַדְתָּ לָהֶם בְּעֵת צָרָתָם. רַבְתָּ אֶת רִיבָם. דַּנְתָּ אֶת דִּינָם. נָקַמְתָּ אֶת נִקְמָתָם. מָסַרְתָּ גִבּוֹרִים בְּיַד חַלָּשִׁים. וְרַבִּים בְּיַד מְעַטִּים. וּרְשָׁעִים בְּיַד צַדִּיקִים. וּטְמֵאִים בְּיַד טְהוֹרִים. וְזֵדִים בְּיַד עוֹסְקֵי תוֹרָתֶךָ. לְךָ עָשִׂיתָ שֵׁם גָּדוֹל וְקָדוֹשׁ בְּעוֹלָמֶךָ. וּלְעַמְּךָ יִשְׂרָאֵל עָשִׂיתָ תְּשׁוּעָה גְדוֹלָה וּפֻרְקָן כְּהַיּוֹם הַזֶּה. וְאַחַר כָּךְ בָּאוּ בָנֶיךָ לִדְבִיר בֵּיתֶךָ. וּפִנּוּ אֶת־הֵיכָלֶךָ. וְטִהֲרוּ אֶת־מִקְדָּשֶׁךָ. וְהִדְלִיקוּ נֵרוֹת בְּחַצְרוֹת קָדְשֶׁךָ. וְקָבְעוּ שְׁמוֹנַת יְמֵי חֲנֻכָּה אֵלּוּ בְּהַלֵּל וּבְהוֹדָאָה. וְעָשִׂיתָ עִמָּהֶם נִסִּים וְנִפְלָאוֹת וְנוֹדֶה לְשִׁמְךָ הַגָּדוֹל סֶלָה:

Bimei Mattityah Ven-Yochanan Kohen Gadol. Chashmona'i Uvanav Keshe'amedah Malchut Yavan Haresha'ah Al Ammecha Yisra'el. Leshakecham Toratach Uleha'aviram Mechukkei Retzonach. Ve'attah Berachameicha Harabim Amadta Lahem Be'et Tzaratam. Ravta Et Rivam. Danta Et Dinam. Nakamta Et Nikmatam. Masarta Giborim Beyad Chalashim. Verabim Beyad Me'atim. Uresha'im Beyad Tzaddikim. Uteme'im Beyad Tehorim. Vezeidim Beyad Osekei Toratecha. Lecha Asita Shem Gadol Vekadosh Be'olamach. Ule'ammecha Yisra'el Asita Teshu'ah Gedolah Ufurkan Kehayom Hazeh. Ve'achar Kach Ba'u Vaneicha Lidvir Beitecha. Ufinu Et-Heichalecha. Vetiharu Et-Mikdashecha. Vehidliku Nerot Bechatzrot Kodshecha. Vekave'u Shemonat Yemei Chanukkah Elu Behallel Uvehoda'ah. Ve'asita Imahem Nissim Venifla'ot Venodeh Leshimcha Hagadol Selah.

Then in the days of Mattityahu ben-Yochanan, High Priest, the Hasmonean and his sons, when the cruel Greek power rose up against Your people, Yisrael, to make them forget Your Torah and transgress the statutes of Your will. And You, in Your great compassion, stood up for them in time of their trial to plead their cause and defend their judgment. Giving out retribution, delivered the strong into the hand of the weak, and the many into the hand of the few, and the wicked into the hand of the upright, and the impure into the hand of the pure, and tyrants into the hand of the devotees of Your Torah. You made for Yourself a great and holy name in Your world. And for Your people, Yisrael, You performed a great salvation and liberation as this very day. Then Your children came to the Sanctuary of Your House, cleared Your Temple, cleansed Your Sanctuary and kindled lights in Your courtyards, and they instituted these eight days of Hanukkah for praise and thanksgiving. And You did miracles and wonders for them, and we give thanks to

Your great name, selah.

On Purim:

בִּימֵי מָרְדְּכַי וְאֶסְתֵּר בְּשׁוּשַׁן הַבִּירָה. כְּשֶׁעָמַד עֲלֵיהֶם הָמָן הָרָשָׁע. בִּקֵּשׁ
לְהַשְׁמִיד לַהֲרֹג וּלְאַבֵּד אֶת־כָּל־הַיְּהוּדִים מִנַּעַר וְעַד זָקֵן טַף וְנָשִׁים בְּיוֹם אֶחָד.
בִּשְׁלֹשָׁה עָשָׂר לְחֹדֶשׁ שְׁנֵים עָשָׂר. הוּא חֹדֶשׁ אֲדָר. וּשְׁלָלָם לָבוֹז. וְאַתָּה
בְּרַחֲמֶיךָ הָרַבִּים הֵפַרְתָּ אֶת־עֲצָתוֹ וְקִלְקַלְתָּ אֶת־מַחֲשַׁבְתּוֹ. וַהֲשֵׁבוֹתָ לּוֹ גְּמוּלוֹ
בְּרֹאשׁוֹ. וְתָלוּ אוֹתוֹ וְאֶת־בָּנָיו עַל הָעֵץ. וְעָשִׂיתָ עִמָּהֶם נֵס וָפֶלֶא וְנוֹדֶה לְשִׁמְךָ
הַגָּדוֹל סֶלָה:

Bimei Mordechai Ve'ester Beshushan Habirah. Keshe'amad Aleihem Haman
Harasha. Bikesh Lehashmid Laharog Ule'abed Et-Kol-Hayehudim Mina'ar Ve'ad
Zaken Taf Venashim Beyom Echad. Bishloshah Asar Lechodesh Sheneim Asar. Hu
Chodesh Adar. Ushelalam Lavoz. Ve'attah Berachameicha Harabim Hefarta
Et-'Atzato Vekilkalta Et-Machashavto. Vahasheivota Lo Gemulo Verosho. Vetalu Oto
Ve'et-Banav Al Ha'etz. Ve'asita Imahem Nes Vafelei Venodeh Leshimcha Hagadol
Selah.

In the days of Mordechai and Ester in Shushan, the capital, the wicked Haman rose
up and sought to destroy, slay and utterly annihilate all of the Yehudim, both young
and old, women and children, on one day, on the thirteenth day of the twelfth
month, which is the month of Adar, and to plunder their possessions. But You in
Your great mercy You broke his plan and spoiled his designs, causing them to recoil
on his own head, and they hanged him and his sons on the gallows. And You did
miracles and wonders for them, and we give thanks to Your great name, selah.

Ve'al Kulam Yitbarach.	וְעַל כֻּלָּם יִתְבָּרַךְ.
Veyitromam. Veyitnasse. Tamid.	וְיִתְרוֹמַם. וְיִתְנַשֵּׂא. תָּמִיד.
Shimcha Malkeinu. Le'olam	שִׁמְךָ מַלְכֵּנוּ. לְעוֹלָם
Va'ed. Vechol-Hachayim	וָעֶד. וְכָל־הַחַיִּים
Yoducha Selah.	יוֹדוּךָ סֶלָה:

For all these acts, may Your name, our King, be blessed, extolled
and exalted forever. And all of the living will thank You, selah.

During the 10 days of repentance (Rosh Hashanah to Yom Kippur) say:

Uchetov Lechayim Tovim Kol Benei
Veritecha.

וּכְתֹב לְחַיִּים טוֹבִים כָּל בְּנֵי
בְרִיתֶךָ.

Inscribe all of Your people of the covenant for a happy life.

Bow at "Baruch Attah" / "Blessed are You". Raise up at Adonai / Hashem.

Vihalelu Vivarechu Et-Shimcha	וִיהַלְלוּ וִיבָרְכוּ אֶת־שִׁמְךָ
Hagadol Be'emet Le'olam Ki	הַגָּדוֹל בֶּאֱמֶת לְעוֹלָם כִּי
Tov. Ha'el Yeshu'ateinu	טוֹב. הָאֵל יְשׁוּעָתֵנוּ
Ve'ezrateinu Selah. Ha'el Hatov.	וְעֶזְרָתֵנוּ סֶלָה. הָאֵל הַטּוֹב:
Baruch Attah Adonai Hatov	בָּרוּךְ אַתָּה יְהֹוָה הַטּוֹב
Shimcha Ulecha Na'eh	שִׁמְךָ וּלְךָ נָאֶה
Lehodot.	לְהוֹדוֹת:

And they will praise and bless Your great and good name sincerely, forever. For You are good, the God of our salvation and our help forever, the Good God. Blessed are You, Hashem, Your name is good and to You it is good to give thanks.

Sim Shalom / Grant Peace

Sim Shalom Tovah Uverachah.	שִׂים שָׁלוֹם טוֹבָה וּבְרָכָה.
Chayim Chein Vachesed	חַיִּים חֵן וָחֶסֶד
Verachamim. Aleinu Ve'al Kol-	וְרַחֲמִים. עָלֵינוּ וְעַל כָּל־
Yisra'el Ammecha. Uvarecheinu	יִשְׂרָאֵל עַמֶּךָ. וּבָרְכֵנוּ
Avinu Kulanu Ke'echad Be'or	אָבִינוּ כֻּלָּנוּ כְּאֶחָד בְּאוֹר
Paneicha. Ki Ve'or Paneicha	פָּנֶיךָ. כִּי בְאוֹר פָּנֶיךָ
Natata Lanu Adonai Eloheinu	נָתַתָּ לָּנוּ יְהֹוָה אֱלֹהֵינוּ
Torah Vechayim. Ahavah	תּוֹרָה וְחַיִּים. אַהֲבָה
Vachesed. Tzedakah	וָחֶסֶד. צְדָקָה
Verachamim. Berachah	וְרַחֲמִים. בְּרָכָה
Veshalom. Vetov Be'eineicha	וְשָׁלוֹם. וְטוֹב בְּעֵינֶיךָ
Levarecheinu Ulevarech Et-	לְבָרְכֵנוּ וּלְבָרֵךְ אֶת־

Kol-'Ammecha Yisra'el. Berov

Oz Veshalom.

כָּל־עַמְּךָ יִשְׂרָאֵל. בְּרֹב
עֹז וְשָׁלוֹם:

Grant peace, goodness and blessing, a life of grace, and kindness and mercy, to us and to all Yisrael, Your people. And bless us, our Father, all as one with the light of Your countenance; for with the light of Your countenance You have given us, Hashem our God, a Torah and life, love and kindness, righteousness and mercy, blessing and peace. May it be good in Your eyes to bless us and bless all of Your people, Yisrael, with abundant strength and peace.

During the 10 days of repentance (Rosh Hashanah to Yom Kippur) say:

Uvesefer Chayim. Berachah Veshalom.

וּבְסֵפֶר חַיִּים. בְּרָכָה וְשָׁלוֹם.

Ufarnasah Tovah Vishu'ah

וּפַרְנָסָה טוֹבָה וִישׁוּעָה

Venechamah. Ugezerot Tovot. Nizacher

וְנֶחָמָה. וּגְזֵרוֹת טוֹבוֹת. נִזָּכֵר

Venikkatev Lefaneicha. Anachnu

וְנִכָּתֵב לְפָנֶיךָ. אֲנַחְנוּ

Vechol Ammecha Beit Yisra'el.

וְכָל עַמְּךָ בֵּית יִשְׂרָאֵל.

Lechayim Tovim Uleshalom.

לְחַיִּים טוֹבִים וּלְשָׁלוֹם.

May we and all Yisrael Your people be remembered and inscribed before You in the book of life and blessing, peace and prosperity, for a happy life and for peace.

Baruch Attah Adonai

בָּרוּךְ אַתָּה יְהֹוָה

Hamevarech Et Ammo Yisra'el

הַמְבָרֵךְ אֶת עַמּוֹ יִשְׂרָאֵל

Bashalom. Amen.

בַּשָּׁלוֹם. אָמֵן:

Blessed are You, Hashem, Who blesses His people Yisrael with peace. Amen.

Yihyu Leratzon Imrei-Fi Vehegyon Libi

Lefaneicha; Adonai Tzuri Vego'ali.

יִהְיוּ לְרָצוֹן | אִמְרֵי־פִי וְהֶגְיוֹן לִבִּי
לְפָנֶיךָ יְהֹוָה צוּרִי וְגֹאֲלִי:

May the words of my mouth and the meditation of my heart find favor before You, Hashem my Rock and my Redeemer.

Elohai. Netzor Leshoni Meira	אֱלֹהַי. נְצֹר לְשׁוֹנִי מֵרָע
Vesiftotai Midaber Mirmah.	וְשִׂפְתוֹתַי מִדַּבֵּר מִרְמָה.
Velimkalelai Nafshi Tidom.	וְלִמְקַלְלַי נַפְשִׁי תִדֹּם.
Venafshi Ke'afar Lakol Tihyeh.	וְנַפְשִׁי כֶּעָפָר לַכֹּל תִּהְיֶה.
Petach Libi Betoratecha.	פְּתַח לִבִּי בְּתוֹרָתֶךָ.
Ve'acharei Mitzvoteicha Tirdof	וְאַחֲרֵי מִצְוֹתֶיךָ תִּרְדֹּף
Nafshi. Vechol-Hakamim Alai	נַפְשִׁי. וְכָל־הַקָּמִים עָלַי
Lera'ah. Meheirah Hafer	לְרָעָה. מְהֵרָה הָפֵר
Atzatam Vekalkel	עֲצָתָם וְקַלְקֵל
Machshevotam. Aseh Lema'an	מַחְשְׁבוֹתָם. עֲשֵׂה לְמַעַן
Shemach. Aseh Lema'an	שְׁמָךְ. עֲשֵׂה לְמַעַן
Yeminach. Aseh Lema'an	יְמִינָךְ. עֲשֵׂה לְמַעַן
Toratach. Aseh Lema'an	תּוֹרָתָךְ. עֲשֵׂה לְמַעַן
Kedushatach. Lema'an	קְדֻשָּׁתָךְ. לְמַעַן
Yechaletzun Yedideicha;	יֵחָלְצוּן יְדִידֶיךָ
Hoshi'ah Yeminecha Va'Aneni.	הוֹשִׁיעָה יְמִינְךָ וַעֲנֵנִי:

My God, guard my tongue from evil, and my lips from speaking deceit. And to those who curse me may my soul be silent; and may my soul be like the dust to all. Open my heart to Your Torah, that my soul may follow after Your commandments. And all that rise to do evil against me, speedily nullify their plan, and spoil their thoughts. Do it for the sake of Your name; do it for the sake of Your right hand; do it for the sake of Your Torah, do it for the sake of Your holiness. That Your beloved may be rescued, save with Your right hand and answer me. (Ps. 60:7)

Yihyu Leratzon Imrei-Fi Vehegyon Libi	יִהְיוּ לְרָצוֹן אִמְרֵי־פִי וְהֶגְיוֹן לִבִּי
Lefaneicha; Adonai Tzuri Vego'ali.	לְפָנֶיךָ יְהֹוָה צוּרִי וְגֹאֲלִי:

May the words of my mouth and the meditation of my heart find favor before You, Hashem my Rock and my Redeemer.

Oseh Shalom

One bows and takes three steps backwards, while still bowing. After three steps, while still bowing and before erecting, while saying, "Oseh Shalom Bimromav", turn one's face to the left, "Hu [Berachamav] Ya'aseh Shalom Aleinu", turn one's face to the right; [face forward and] then bow forward like a servant leaving his master. (SA, OC 123:1)

Oseh Shalom On the 10 Days of

Repentance: (Hashalom) Bimromav,

Hu Berachamav Ya'aseh Shalom

Aleinu, Ve'al Kol-'Ammo

Yisra'el, Ve'imru Amen.

עוֹשֶׂה שָׁלוֹם

בעשי״ת אומ: (הַשָּׁלוֹם) בִּמְרוֹמָיו.

הוּא בְּרַחֲמָיו יַעֲשֶׂה שָׁלוֹם

עָלֵינוּ. וְעַל כָּל־עַמּוֹ

יִשְׂרָאֵל. וְאִמְרוּ אָמֵן:

Creator of On the 10 Days of Repentance: (the) peace in His high places, may He in His mercy create peace for us and for all Yisrael, and say Amen.

Yehi Ratzon Milfaneicha Adonai

Eloheinu Velohei Avoteinu. Shetivneh

Beit Hamikdash Bimheirah Veyameinu.

Veten Chelkenu Vetoratach La'asot

Chukkei. Retzonach Ule'avedach

Belevav Shalem.

יְהִי רָצוֹן מִלְּפָנֶיךָ יְהֹוָה

אֱלֹהֵינוּ וֵאלֹהֵי אֲבוֹתֵינוּ. שֶׁתִּבְנֶה

בֵּית הַמִּקְדָּשׁ בִּמְהֵרָה בְיָמֵינוּ.

וְתֵן חֶלְקֵנוּ בְּתוֹרָתָךְ לַעֲשׂוֹת

חֻקֵּי רְצוֹנָךְ וּלְעָבְדָךְ

בְּלֵבָב שָׁלֵם:

May it be Your will, Hashem our God and God of our fathers, that the Beit HaMikdash be speedily rebuilt in our days, and grant us a share in Your Torah so we may fulfill the statutes of Your will and serve You with a whole heart.

Stay standing and say:

וַיְכֻלּוּ הַשָּׁמַיִם וְהָאָרֶץ וְכָל־צְבָאָם וַיְכַל אֱלֹהִים בַּיּוֹם הַשְּׁבִיעִי
מְלַאכְתּוֹ אֲשֶׁר עָשָׂה וַיִּשְׁבֹּת בַּיּוֹם הַשְּׁבִיעִי מִכָּל־מְלַאכְתּוֹ אֲשֶׁר
עָשָׂה: וַיְבָרֶךְ אֱלֹהִים אֶת־יוֹם הַשְּׁבִיעִי וַיְקַדֵּשׁ אֹתוֹ כִּי בוֹ שָׁבַת
מִכָּל־מְלַאכְתּוֹ אֲשֶׁר־בָּרָא אֱלֹהִים לַעֲשׂוֹת:

Vaychulu Hashamayim Veha'aretz Vechol-Tzeva'am Vaychal Elohim
Bayom Hashevi'i. Melachto Asher Asah; Vayishbot Bayom Hashevi'i.
Mikol-Melachto Asher Asah. Vayvarech Elohim Et-Yom Hashevi'i.
Vaykadesh Oto; Ki Vo Shavat Mikol-Melachto. Asher-Bara Elohim
La'asot.

And the heavens and the earth were finished, and all the host of
them. And with the seventh day God finished His work which He
had made; and He rested on the seventh day from all His work
which He had made. And God blessed the seventh day, and
sanctified it; because that in it He rested from all His work which
God in creating had made. (Genesis 2:1-3)

And the Chazan says Birkhat Me'ein Sheva / The Seven-Faceted Blessing alone:

Baruch Attah Adonai Eloheinu	בָּרוּךְ אַתָּה יְהֹוָה אֱלֹהֵינוּ
Velohei Avoteinu. Elohei	וֵאלֹהֵי אֲבוֹתֵינוּ. אֱלֹהֵי
Avraham. Elohei Yitzchak	אַבְרָהָם. אֱלֹהֵי יִצְחָק
Velohei Ya'akov. Ha'el Hagadol.	וֵאלֹהֵי יַעֲקֹב. הָאֵל הַגָּדוֹל.
Hagibor Vehanorah. El Elyon.	הַגִּבּוֹר וְהַנּוֹרָא. אֵל עֶלְיוֹן.
Koneh Verachamav Shamayim	קוֹנֵה בְרַחֲמָיו שָׁמַיִם
Va'aretz. Magen Avot Bidvaro.	וָאָרֶץ. מָגֵן אָבוֹת בִּדְבָרוֹ.
Mechayeh Meitim Bema'amaro.	מְחַיֶּה מֵתִים בְּמַאֲמָרוֹ.
Ha' El on Shabbat Shuva say: (HaMelech)	הָאֵל בשבת תשובה אומר: (הַמֶּלֶךְ)
Hakadosh She'ein Kamohu.	הַקָּדוֹשׁ שֶׁאֵין כָּמוֹהוּ.
Hameniach Le'ammo Beyom	הַמֵּנִיחַ לְעַמּוֹ בְּיוֹם

Shabbat Kodsho. Ki Vam Ratzah	שַׁבַּת קָדְשׁוֹ. כִּי בָם רָצָה
Lehaniach Lahem. Lefanav	לְהָנִיחַ לָהֶם. לְפָנָיו
Na'avod Beyir'ah Vafachad.	נַעֲבֹד בְּיִרְאָה וָפַחַד.
Venodeh Lishmo Bechol Yom	וְנוֹדֶה לִשְׁמוֹ בְּכָל יוֹם
Tamid Me'ein Haberachot	תָּמִיד מֵעֵין הַבְּרָכוֹת
Vehahoda'ot. La'adon	וְהַהוֹדָאוֹת. לָאֲדוֹן
Hashalom. Mekadesh Hashabbat	הַשָּׁלוֹם. מְקַדֵּשׁ הַשַּׁבָּת
Umevarech Hashevi'i.	וּמְבָרֵךְ הַשְּׁבִיעִי.
Umeniach Bikdushah Le'am	וּמֵנִיחַ בִּקְדֻשָּׁה לְעַם
Medushenei Oneg. Zecher	מְדֻשְּׁנֵי עֹנֶג. זֵכֶר
Lema'aseh Vereshit.	לְמַעֲשֵׂה בְרֵאשִׁית:

Blessed are You Hashem, our God and God of our fathers, God of Avraham, God of Yitzchak, God of Yaakov, the great God, all-powerful and awe-inspiring God supreme, in whose merciful hands heavens and earth rest. The Shield of our fathers by His word will quicken the dead at His command. He is the holy God, on Shabbat Shuva say: (The Holy King), there is none like Him, Who gives rest to His people on His holy Shabbat, the day He desired for giving them rest. Everyday we worship in reverence and awe, and praise Him with the essential form of blessings. But today we add special praise to the Lord of peace Who sanctifies the Shabbat and blesses the seventh day, and in holiness gives rest to a people satiated with delights, as a memorial of the work of creation.

Eloheinu Velohei Avoteinu.	אֱלֹהֵינוּ וֵאלֹהֵי אֲבוֹתֵינוּ.
Retzeh Na Bimnuchatenu.	רְצֵה נָא בִּמְנוּחָתֵנוּ.
Kadeshenu Bemitzvoteicha. Sim	קַדְּשֵׁנוּ בְּמִצְוֹתֶיךָ. שִׂים
Chelkenu Betoratach. Sabe'einu	חֶלְקֵנוּ בְּתוֹרָתָךְ. שַׂבְּעֵנוּ

Mituvach. Same'ach Nafshenu	מִטּוּבָךְ. שַׂמֵּחַ נַפְשֵׁנוּ
Bishu'atach. Vetaher Libenu	בִּישׁוּעָתָךְ. וְטַהֵר לִבֵּנוּ
Le'avedcha Ve'emet.	לְעָבְדְּךָ בֶּאֱמֶת.
Vehanchilenu Adonai Eloheinu	וְהַנְחִילֵנוּ יְהוָה אֱלֹהֵינוּ
Be'ahavah Uveratzon Shabbat	בְּאַהֲבָה וּבְרָצוֹן שַׁבָּת
Kodshecha. Veyanuchu Vah Kol	קָדְשֶׁךָ. וְיָנוּחוּ בָהּ כָּל
Yisra'el Mekadoshei Shemecha.	יִשְׂרָאֵל מְקַדְּשֵׁי שְׁמֶךָ.
Baruch Attah Adonai Mekadesh	בָּרוּךְ אַתָּה יְהוָה מְקַדֵּשׁ
Hashabbat.	הַשַּׁבָּת:

Our God, God of our fathers, be pleased with our rest. Sanctify us through Your commandments and grant our portion in Your Torah. Content us with Your goodness. Rejoice our soul with Your salvation. And make our heart pure to serve You in truth. Cause us to inherit, Hashem our God, Your holy Shabbat with love and favor: and grant rest on it to all Yisrael, who sanctify Your name. Blessed are You, Hashem Who sanctifies the Shabbat.

And now say the Shaliach Tzibur says Kaddish Titkabbal:

Kaddish is only recited in a minyan (ten men). אָמֵן denotes when the congregation responds "Amen" together out loud. According to the Shulchan Arukh, the congregation says "Yehei Shemeh Rabba" to "Yitbarach" out loud together without interruption, and also that one should respond "Amen" after "Yitbarach." (SA, OC 55,56) This is not the common custom today. Though many are accustomed to answering according to their own custom, it is advised to respond in the custom of the one reciting to avoid not fragmenting into smaller groups. ("Lo Titgodedu" - BT, Yevamot 13b / SA, OC 493, Rema / MT, Avodah Zara 12:15)

יִתְגַּדַּל וְיִתְקַדַּשׁ שְׁמֵהּ רַבָּא. אָמֵן בְּעָלְמָא דִּי בְרָא. כִּרְעוּתֵהּ. וְיַמְלִיךְ מַלְכוּתֵהּ.
וְיַצְמַח פֻּרְקָנֵהּ. וִיקָרֵב מְשִׁיחֵהּ. אָמֵן בְּחַיֵּיכוֹן וּבְיוֹמֵיכוֹן וּבְחַיֵּי דְכָל בֵּית
יִשְׂרָאֵל. בַּעֲגָלָא וּבִזְמַן קָרִיב. וְאִמְרוּ אָמֵן. אָמֵן יְהֵא שְׁמֵיהּ רַבָּא מְבָרַךְ לְעָלַם
וּלְעָלְמֵי עָלְמַיָּא יִתְבָּרַךְ. וְיִשְׁתַּבַּח. וְיִתְפָּאַר. וְיִתְרוֹמַם. וְיִתְנַשֵּׂא. וְיִתְהַדָּר.
וְיִתְעַלֶּה. וְיִתְהַלָּל שְׁמֵהּ דְּקֻדְשָׁא. בְּרִיךְ הוּא. אָמֵן לְעֵלָּא מִן כָּל בִּרְכָתָא
שִׁירָתָא. תֻּשְׁבְּחָתָא וְנֶחֱמָתָא. דַּאֲמִירָן בְּעָלְמָא. וְאִמְרוּ אָמֵן. אָמֵן

Yitgadal Veyitkadash Shemeh Rabba. ^{Amen} Be'alema Di Vera. Kir'uteh. Veyamlich Malchuteh. Veyatzmach Purkaneh. Vikarev Meshicheh. ^{Amen} Bechayeichon Uveyomeichon Uvechayei Dechal-Beit Yisra'el. Ba'agala Uvizman Kariv. Ve'imru Amen. ^{Amen} Yehei Shemeh Rabba Mevarach Le'alam Ule'alemei Alemaya Yitbarach. Veyishtabach. Veyitpa'ar. Veyitromam. Veyitnasse. Veyit'hadar. Veyit'aleh. Veyit'hallal Shemeh Dekudsha. Berich Hu. ^{Amen} Le'ella Min Kol Birchata Shirata. Tushbechata Venechemata. Da'amiran Be'alema. Ve'imru Amen. ^{Amen}

Glorified and sanctified be God's great name ^{Amen} throughout the world which He has created according to His will. May He establish His kingdom, hastening His salvation and the coming of His Messiah, ^{Amen}, in your lifetime and during your days, and within the life of the entire House of Yisrael, speedily and soon; and say, Amen. ^{Amen} May His great name be blessed forever and to all eternity. Blessed and praised, glorified and exalted, extolled and honored, adored and lauded is the name of the Holy One, blessed is He, ^{Amen} Beyond all the blessings and hymns, praises and consolations that are ever spoken in the world; and say, Amen. ^{Amen}

תִּתְקַבֵּל צְלוֹתָנָא וּבָעוּתָנָא. עִם צְלוֹתְהוֹן וּבָעוּתְהוֹן דְּכָל בֵּית יִשְׂרָאֵל. קֳדָם אֲבוּנָא דְּבִשְׁמַיָּא וְאַרְעָא. וְאִמְרוּ אָמֵן. אָמֵן

Titkabbal Tzelotana Uva'utana. Im Tzelotehon Uva'utehon Dechol Beit Yisra'el. Kodam Avuna Devishmaya Ve'ar'a. Ve'imru Amen. ^{Amen}

May the prayer and supplication of the whole House of Yisrael be accepted before their Father in heaven, and say, Amen. ^{Amen}

יְהֵא שְׁלָמָא רַבָּא מִן שְׁמַיָּא. חַיִּים וְשָׂבָע וִישׁוּעָה וְנֶחָמָה. וְשֵׁיזָבָא וּרְפוּאָה וּגְאוּלָה וּסְלִיחָה וְכַפָּרָה וְרֶוַח וְהַצָּלָה לָנוּ וּלְכָל עַמּוֹ יִשְׂרָאֵל. וְאִמְרוּ אָמֵן. אָמֵן

Yehei Shelama Rabba Min Shemaya. Chayim Vesava Vishu'ah Venechamah. Vesheizava Urefu'ah Uge'ulah Uselichah Vechapparah Verevach Vehatzalah Lanu Ulechol Ammo Yisra'el. Ve'imru Amen. ^{Amen}

May abundant peace descend from heaven, with life and plenty, salvation, solace, liberation, healing and redemption, and forgiveness and atonement, enlargement and freedom, for us and all of God's people Yisrael; and say, Amen. ^{Amen}

> One bows and takes three steps backwards, while still bowing. After three steps, while still bowing and before erecting, while saying, "Oseh Shalom Bimromav", turn one's face to the left, "Hu [Berachamav] Ya'aseh Shalom Aleinu", turn one's face to the right; then bow forward like a servant leaving his master. (SA, OC 123:1)

עוֹשֶׂה שָׁלוֹם בִּמְרוֹמָיו. הוּא בְּרַחֲמָיו יַעֲשֶׂה שָׁלוֹם עָלֵינוּ. וְעַל כָּל־עַמּוֹ יִשְׂרָאֵל. וְאִמְרוּ אָמֵן:

Oseh Shalom Bimromav. Hu Berachamav Ya'aseh Shalom Aleinu. Ve'al Kol-'Ammo Yisra'el. Ve'imru Amen.

Creator of peace in His high places, may He in His mercy create peace for us and for all Yisrael, and say Amen.

On Pesach recite Psalms 114, on Shavuot, Sukkot, Shemini Atzeret / Simchat Torah recite Psalms 122 next, on Purim recite Psalms 124.

Psalms 23

מִזְמוֹר לְדָוִד יְהֹוָה רֹעִי לֹא אֶחְסָר: בִּנְאוֹת דֶּשֶׁא יַרְבִּיצֵנִי עַל מֵי מְנֻחוֹת יְנַהֲלֵנִי: נַפְשִׁי יְשׁוֹבֵב יַנְחֵנִי בְמַעְגְּלֵי־צֶדֶק לְמַעַן שְׁמוֹ: גַּם כִּי־אֵלֵךְ בְּגֵיא צַלְמָוֶת לֹא־אִירָא רָע כִּי־אַתָּה עִמָּדִי שִׁבְטְךָ וּמִשְׁעַנְתֶּךָ הֵמָּה יְנַחֲמֻנִי: תַּעֲרֹךְ לְפָנַי | שֻׁלְחָן נֶגֶד צֹרְרָי דִּשַּׁנְתָּ בַשֶּׁמֶן רֹאשִׁי כּוֹסִי רְוָיָה אַךְ | טוֹב וָחֶסֶד יִרְדְּפוּנִי כָּל־יְמֵי חַיָּי וְשַׁבְתִּי בְּבֵית־יְהֹוָה לְאֹרֶךְ יָמִים:

Mizmor Ledavid; Adonai Ro'i. Lo Echsar. Bin'ot Deshei Yarbitzeni; Al Mei Menuchot Yenahaleini. Nafshi Yeshovev; Yancheini Vema'gelei-Tzedek. Lema'an Shemo. Gam Ki-'Elech Begei Tzalmavet Lo-'Ira Ra'. Ki-'Attah Immadi; Shivtecha Umish'antecha. Hemah Yenachamuni. Ta'aroch Lefanai Shulchan. Neged Tzorerai; Dishanta Vashemen Roshi. Kosi Revayah Ach Tov Vachesed Yirdefuni Chol-Yemei Chayai; Veshavti Beveit-Adonai Le'orech Yamim.

A Psalm of David. Hashem is my Shepherd; I will not want. He makes me to lie down in green pastures; He leads me beside the still waters. He restores my soul; He guides me in straight paths for His name's sake. Even though I walk through the valley of the shadow of death, I will fear no evil, for You are with me; Your rod and Your staff, they comfort me. You prepare a table before me in the presence of my enemies; You have anointed my head with oil; my cup runs over. Surely goodness and mercy will follow me all the days of my life; And I will dwell in the House of Hashem forever.

And on Chol HaMoed Pesach say:

Psalms 114

בְּצֵאת יִשְׂרָאֵל מִמִּצְרָיִם בֵּית יַעֲקֹב מֵעַם לֹעֵז: הָיְתָה יְהוּדָה לְקָדְשׁוֹ יִשְׂרָאֵל מַמְשְׁלוֹתָיו: הַיָּם רָאָה וַיָּנֹס הַיַּרְדֵּן יִסֹּב לְאָחוֹר: הֶהָרִים רָקְדוּ כְאֵילִים גְּבָעוֹת כִּבְנֵי־צֹאן: מַה־לְּךָ הַיָּם כִּי תָנוּס הַיַּרְדֵּן תִּסֹּב לְאָחוֹר: הֶהָרִים תִּרְקְדוּ כְאֵילִים גְּבָעוֹת כִּבְנֵי־צֹאן: מִלִּפְנֵי אָדוֹן חוּלִי אָרֶץ מִלִּפְנֵי אֱלוֹהַּ יַעֲקֹב: הַהֹפְכִי הַצּוּר אֲגַם־מָיִם חַלָּמִישׁ לְמַעְיְנוֹ־מָיִם:

Betzet Yisra'el Mimitzrayim Beit Ya'akov Me'am Lo'ez. Hayetah Yehudah Lekodsho
Yisra'el Mamshelotav. Hayam Ra'ah Vayanos Hayarden Yissov Le'achor. Heharim
Rakedu Che'eilim Geva'ot Kivnei Tzon. Mah Lecha Hayam Ki Tanus Hayarden
Tissov Le'achor. Heharim Tirkedu Che'eilim Geva'ot Kivnei Tzon. Millifnei Adon
Chuli Aretz Millifnei Eloah Ya'akov. Hahofechi Hatzur Agam Mayim Challamish
Lema'yeno Mayim.

When Yisrael came forth out of Mitzrayim, The house of Yaakov from a people of
strange language; Yehudah became His Sanctuary, Yisrael His dominion. The sea
saw it, and fled; The Yarden turned backward. The mountains skipped like rams,
The hills like young sheep. What ails you, Oh sea, that you flee? You Yarden, that
you turn backward? You mountains, that you skip like rams; You hills, like young
sheep? Tremble, earth, at the presence of Hashem, At the presence of the God of
Yaakov; Who turned the rock into a pool of water, the flint into a fountain of
waters.

And on Chol HaMoed Sukkot; Shavuot, and Shemini Atzeret / Simchat Torah say:

Psalms 122

שִׁיר הַמַּעֲלוֹת לְדָוִד שָׂמַחְתִּי בְּאֹמְרִים לִי בֵּית יְהוָה נֵלֵךְ: עֹמְדוֹת הָיוּ רַגְלֵינוּ
בִּשְׁעָרַיִךְ יְרוּשָׁלָםִ: יְרוּשָׁלַםִ הַבְּנוּיָה כְּעִיר שֶׁחֻבְּרָה־לָּהּ יַחְדָּו: שֶׁשָּׁם עָלוּ
שְׁבָטִים שִׁבְטֵי־יָהּ עֵדוּת לְיִשְׂרָאֵל לְהֹדוֹת לְשֵׁם יְהוָה: כִּי שָׁמָּה | יָשְׁבוּ
כִסְאוֹת לְמִשְׁפָּט כִּסְאוֹת לְבֵית דָּוִד: שַׁאֲלוּ שְׁלוֹם יְרוּשָׁלָםִ יִשְׁלָיוּ אֹהֲבָיִךְ:
יְהִי־שָׁלוֹם בְּחֵילֵךְ שַׁלְוָה בְּאַרְמְנוֹתָיִךְ: לְמַעַן אַחַי וְרֵעָי אֲדַבְּרָה־נָּא שָׁלוֹם בָּךְ:
לְמַעַן בֵּית־יְהוָה אֱלֹהֵינוּ אֲבַקְשָׁה טוֹב לָךְ:

Shir Hama'alot Ledavid Samachti Be'omerim Li Beit Adonai Nelech. Omedot Hayu
Ragleinu Bish'arayich Yerushalayim. Yerushalayim Habenuyah Ke'ir Shechuberah
Lah Yachdav. Shesham Alu Shevatim Shivtei Yah Edut Leyisra'el Lehodot Leshem
Adonai. Ki Shamah Yashevu Chis'ot Lemishpat Kis'ot Leveit David. Sha'alu Shelom
Yerushalayim Yishlayu Ohavayich. Yehi Shalom Becheilech Shalvah
Be'armenotayich. Lema'an Achai Vere'ai Adaberah Na Shalom Bach. Lema'an Beit
Adonai Eloheinu Avakshah Tov Lach.

A Song of Ascents; of David. I rejoiced when they said to me: 'Let us go to the
House of Hashem.' Our feet are standing within your gates, Yerushalayim;
Yerushalayim, that is built as a city that is compact together; Where the tribes went
up, even the tribes of Hashem, as a testimony to Yisrael, to give thanks to the name
of Hashem. For there were set thrones for judgment, the thrones of the House of
David. Pray for the peace of Yerushalayim; May they that love You prosper. Peace
be within your walls, and prosperity within your palaces. For my brothers and
companions' sakes, I will now say: 'Peace be within you.' For the sake of the House
of Hashem our God I will seek your good.

And after say Kaddish Yehei-Shelama:

Kaddish is only recited in a minyan (ten men). אמן denotes when the congregation responds "Amen" together out loud. According to the Shulchan Arukh, the congregation says "Yehei Shemeh Rabba" to "Yitbarach" out loud together without interruption, and also that one should respond "Amen" after "Yitbarach." (SA, OC 55,56) This is not the common custom today. Though many are accustomed to answering according to their own custom, it is advised to respond in the custom of the one reciting to avoid not fragmenting into smaller groups. ("Lo Titgodedu" - BT, Yevamot 13b / SA, OC 493, Rema / MT, Avodah Zara 12:15)

יִתְגַּדַּל וְיִתְקַדַּשׁ שְׁמֵהּ רַבָּא. אמן בְּעָלְמָא דִּי בְרָא. כִּרְעוּתֵהּ. וְיַמְלִיךְ מַלְכוּתֵהּ. וְיַצְמַח פֻּרְקָנֵהּ. וִיקָרֵב מְשִׁיחֵהּ. אמן בְּחַיֵּיכוֹן וּבְיוֹמֵיכוֹן וּבְחַיֵּי דְכָל בֵּית יִשְׂרָאֵל. בַּעֲגָלָא וּבִזְמַן קָרִיב. וְאִמְרוּ אָמֵן. אמן יְהֵא שְׁמֵהּ רַבָּא מְבָרַךְ לְעָלַם וּלְעָלְמֵי עָלְמַיָּא יִתְבָּרַךְ. וְיִשְׁתַּבַּח. וְיִתְפָּאַר. וְיִתְרוֹמַם. וְיִתְנַשֵּׂא. וְיִתְהַדָּר. וְיִתְעַלֶּה. וְיִתְהַלָּל שְׁמֵהּ דְּקֻדְשָׁא. בְּרִיךְ הוּא. אמן לְעֵלָּא מִן כָּל בִּרְכָתָא שִׁירָתָא. תֻּשְׁבְּחָתָא וְנֶחֱמָתָא. דַּאֲמִירָן בְּעָלְמָא. וְאִמְרוּ אָמֵן. אמן

Yitgadal Veyitkadash Shemeh Rabba. **Amen** Be'alema Di Vera. Kir'uteh. Veyamlich Malchuteh. Veyatzmach Purkaneh. Vikarev Meshicheh. **Amen** Bechayeichon Uveyomeichon Uvechayei Dechal-Beit Yisra'el. Ba'agala Uvizman Kariv. Ve'imru Amen. **Amen** Yehei Shemeh Rabba Mevarach Le'alam Ule'alemei Alemaya Yitbarach. Veyishtabach. Veyitpa'ar. Veyitromam. Veyitnasse. Veyit'hadar. Veyit'aleh. Veyit'hallal Shemeh Dekudsha. Berich Hu. **Amen** Le'ella Min Kol Birchata Shirata. Tushbechata Venechemata. Da'amiran Be'alema. Ve'imru Amen. **Amen**

Glorified and sanctified be God's great name **Amen** throughout the world which He has created according to His will. May He establish His kingdom, hastening His salvation and the coming of His Messiah, **Amen**, in your lifetime and during your days, and within the life of the entire House of Yisrael, speedily and soon; and say, Amen. **Amen** May His great name be blessed forever and to all eternity. Blessed and praised, glorified and exalted, extolled and honored, adored and lauded is the name of the Holy One, blessed is He, **Amen** Beyond all the blessings and hymns, praises and consolations that are ever spoken in the world; and say, Amen. **Amen**

יְהֵא שְׁלָמָא רַבָּא מִן שְׁמַיָּא. חַיִּים וְשָׂבָע וִישׁוּעָה וְנֶחָמָה. וְשֵׁיזָבָא
וּרְפוּאָה וּגְאוּלָה וּסְלִיחָה וְכַפָּרָה וְרֶוַח וְהַצָּלָה לָנוּ וּלְכָל עַמּוֹ
יִשְׂרָאֵל. וְאִמְרוּ אָמֵן. אמן

Yehei Shelama Rabba Min Shemaya. Chayim Vesava Vishu'ah
Venechamah. Vesheizava Urefu'ah Uge'ulah Uselichah
Vechapparah Verevach Vehatzalah Lanu Ulechol Ammo Yisra'el.
Ve'imru Amen. Amen

May abundant peace descend from heaven, with life and plenty,
salvation, solace, liberation, healing and redemption, and
forgiveness and atonement, enlargement and freedom, for us and
all of God's people Yisrael; and say, Amen. Amen

One bows and takes three steps backwards, while still bowing. After three steps, while still bowing
and before erecting, while saying, "Oseh Shalom Bimromav", turn one's face to the left, "Hu
[Berachamav] Ya'aseh Shalom Aleinu", turn one's face to the right; then bow forward like a servant
leaving his master. (SA, OC 123:1)

עוֹשֶׂה שָׁלוֹם בעשי״ת אומ: (הַשָּׁלוֹם) בִּמְרוֹמָיו. הוּא בְּרַחֲמָיו יַעֲשֶׂה שָׁלוֹם
עָלֵינוּ. וְעַל כָּל־עַמּוֹ יִשְׂרָאֵל. וְאִמְרוּ אָמֵן:

Oseh Shalom On the 10 Days of Repentance: (Hashalom) Bimromav, Hu
Berachamav Ya'aseh Shalom Aleinu, Ve'al Kol-'Ammo Yisra'el,
Ve'imru Amen.

Creator of On the 10 Days of Repentance: (the) peace in His high places, may
He in His mercy create peace for us and for all Yisrael, and say
Amen.

Barechu

Barechu is only recited with 10 men (minyan).

The Chazan says:

בָּרְכוּ אֶת יְהֹוָה הַמְבֹרָךְ:

Barechu Et Adonai Hamevorach.

Bless Hashem, the blessed One.

The kahal answers:

בָּרוּךְ יְהֹוָה הַמְבֹרָךְ לְעוֹלָם וָעֶד:

Baruch Adonai Hamevorach Le'olam Va'ed.

Blessed is Hashem Who is blessed for all eternity.

The Chazan says:

בָּרוּךְ יְהֹוָה הַמְבֹרָךְ לְעוֹלָם וָעֶד:

Baruch Adonai Hamevorach Le'olam Va'ed.

Blessed is Hashem Who is blessed for all eternity.

Aleinu

> [*] denotes pausing and then bowing when saying "Va'anachnu Mistachavim". **Some take Tefillin off after Aleinu.**

Aleinu Leshabei'ach La'adon	עָלֵינוּ לְשַׁבֵּחַ לַאֲדוֹן
Hakol. Latet Gedullah Leyotzer	הַכֹּל. לָתֵת גְּדֻלָּה לְיוֹצֵר
Bereshit. Shelo Asanu Kegoyei	בְּרֵאשִׁית. שֶׁלֹּא עָשָׂנוּ כְּגוֹיֵי
Ha'aratzot. Velo Samanu	הָאֲרָצוֹת. וְלֹא שָׂמָנוּ
Kemishpechot Ha'adamah. Shelo	כְּמִשְׁפְּחוֹת הָאֲדָמָה. שֶׁלֹּא
Sam Chelkenu Kahem	שָׂם חֶלְקֵנוּ כָּהֶם
Vegoraleinu Kechal-Hamonam.	וְגוֹרָלֵנוּ כְּכָל־הֲמוֹנָם.
Shehem Mishtachavim Lahevel	שֶׁהֵם מִשְׁתַּחֲוִים לְהֶבֶל
Varik. Umitpallelim El-'El Lo	וָרִיק. וּמִתְפַּלְּלִים אֶל־אֵל לֹא
Yoshia. *Va'anachnu	יוֹשִׁיעַ. *וַאֲנַחְנוּ
Mishtachavim Lifnei Melech	מִשְׁתַּחֲוִים לִפְנֵי מֶלֶךְ
Malchei Hamelachim Hakadosh	מַלְכֵי הַמְּלָכִים הַקָּדוֹשׁ
Baruch Hu. Shehu Noteh	בָּרוּךְ הוּא. שֶׁהוּא נוֹטֶה
Shamayim Veyosed Aretz.	שָׁמַיִם וְיוֹסֵד אָרֶץ.
Umoshav Yekaro Bashamayim	וּמוֹשַׁב יְקָרוֹ בַּשָּׁמַיִם

Mima'al. Ushechinat Uzo	מִמַּעַל. וּשְׁכִינַת עֻזּוֹ
Begavehei Meromim. Hu	בְּגָבְהֵי מְרוֹמִים. הוּא
Eloheinu. Ve'ein Od Acher. Emet	אֱלֹהֵינוּ. וְאֵין עוֹד אַחֵר. אֱמֶת
Malkeinu Ve'efes Zulato.	מַלְכֵּנוּ וְאֶפֶס זוּלָתוֹ.
Kakatuv Batorah. Veyada'ta	כַּכָּתוּב בַּתּוֹרָה. וְיָדַעְתָּ
Hayom. Vahasheivota El-	הַיּוֹם וַהֲשֵׁבֹתָ אֶל־
Levavecha Ki Adonai Hu	לְבָבֶךָ כִּי יְהֹוָה הוּא
Ha'elohim. Bashamayim	הָאֱלֹהִים בַּשָּׁמַיִם
Mima'al. Ve'al-Ha'aretz	מִמַּעַל וְעַל־הָאָרֶץ
Mitachat; Ein Od.	מִתָּחַת אֵין עוֹד:

It is our obligation us to praise the Lord of all. To render greatness to the Former of creation. For He has not made us like the nations of the lands, nor set us to be like the families of the earth. Who has not given our portion like theirs and our lot like their masses that bow down to vanity and emptiness, "And pray to a god that does not save." *¹But we bow before the supreme King of kings, the Holy One, blessed is He. Who stretches out the heavens and laid the foundations of the earth and His glorious seat is in the heavens above, and the presence of His might in the most exalted of heights. He is our God, there is no other. In truth our King, there is no one except Him. As it is written in the Torah: "This day know and lay it to your heart, that Hashem, He is God in the heavens above and on the earth beneath. There is no one else."

Al Ken Nekaveh Lach. Adonai	עַל כֵּן נְקַוֶּה לָךְ. יְהֹוָה
Eloheinu. Lir'ot Meheirah	אֱלֹהֵינוּ. לִרְאוֹת מְהֵרָה
Betif'eret Uzach. Leha'avir	בְּתִפְאֶרֶת עֻזָּךְ. לְהַעֲבִיר
Gilulim Min Ha'aretz.	גִּלּוּלִים מִן הָאָרֶץ.
Veha'elilim Karot Yikaretun.	וְהָאֱלִילִים כָּרוֹת יִכָּרֵתוּן.

Letakken Olam Bemalchut	לְתַקֵּן עוֹלָם בְּמַלְכוּת
Shaddai. Vechol-Benei Vasar	שַׁדַּי. וְכָל-בְּנֵי בָשָׂר
Yikre'u Vishmecha. Lehafnot	יִקְרְאוּ בִשְׁמֶךָ. לְהַפְנוֹת
Eleicha Kol-Rish'ei Aretz. Yakiru	אֵלֶיךָ כָּל-רִשְׁעֵי אָרֶץ. יַכִּירוּ
Veyede'u Kol-Yoshevei Tevel. Ki	וְיֵדְעוּ כָּל-יוֹשְׁבֵי תֵבֵל. כִּי
Lecha Tichra Kol-Berech. Tishava	לְךָ תִּכְרַע כָּל-בֶּרֶךְ. תִּשָּׁבַע
Kol-Lashon. Lefaneicha. Adonai	כָּל-לָשׁוֹן. לְפָנֶיךָ. יְהֹוָה
Eloheinu Yichre'u Veyipolu.	אֱלֹהֵינוּ יִכְרְעוּ וְיִפֹּלוּ.
Velichvod Shimcha Yekar Yitenu.	וְלִכְבוֹד שִׁמְךָ יְקָר יִתֵּנוּ.
Vikabelu Chulam Et-'Ol	וִיקַבְּלוּ כֻלָּם אֶת-עֹל
Malchutecha. Vetimloch Aleihem	מַלְכוּתֶךָ. וְתִמְלוֹךְ עֲלֵיהֶם
Meheirah Le'olam Va'ed. Ki	מְהֵרָה לְעוֹלָם וָעֶד. כִּי
Hamalchut Shelecha Hi.	הַמַּלְכוּת שֶׁלְּךָ הִיא.
Ule'olemei Ad Timloch	וּלְעוֹלְמֵי עַד תִּמְלוֹךְ
Bechavod. Kakatuv Betoratach.	בְכָבוֹד. כַּכָּתוּב בְּתוֹרָתֶךָ:
Adonai Yimloch Le'olam Va'ed.	יְהֹוָה	יִמְלֹךְ לְעֹלָם וָעֶד:
Vene'emar. Vehayah Adonai	וְנֶאֱמַר. וְהָיָה יְהֹוָה
Lemelech Al-Kol-Ha'aretz;	לְמֶלֶךְ עַל־כָּל־הָאָרֶץ
Bayom Hahu. Yihyeh Adonai	בַּיוֹם הַהוּא יִהְיֶה יְהֹוָה
Echad Ushemo Echad.	אֶחָד וּשְׁמוֹ אֶחָד:

Therefore we hope in You, Hashem our God, soon to see Your glorious might, to remove idols from the earth and the non-gods will be wholly cut down, to rectify the world with the kingdom of El Shaddai, and all children of flesh will call on Your name and all of the earth's wicked will turn to You. All that dwell on earth will understand and know that to You every knee must bend, and every tongue swear. Before You, Hashem our God, may all kneel and fall and give honor to Your glorious name. And they will all accept the yoke of Your kingdom. And may You speedily rule over them forever. For dominion is Yours, and forever You will reign in glory, as is written in Your Torah, "Hashem will reign forever and ever." For, it is said, "Hashem will be King over all the earth; and on that day Hashem will be One and His name One."

וּבְתוֹרָתְךָ יְהֹוָה אֱלֹהֵינוּ כָּתוּב

Uvetoratecha Adonai Eloheinu

לֵאמֹר. שְׁמַע יִשְׂרָאֵל יְהֹוָה

Katuv Lemor. Shema Yisra'el;

אֱלֹהֵינוּ יְהֹוָה אֶחָד:

Adonai Eloheinu Adonai Echad.

And in Your Torah, Hashem our God, it is written: Hear O Yisrael Hashem our God, Hashem is One.

Yigdal

It is customary after the prayer to recite a summary of the 13 principles of Jewish faith:

יִגְדַּל אֱלֹהִים חַי וְיִשְׁתַּבַּח. נִמְצָא וְאֵין עֵת אֶל מְצִיאוּתוֹ:

Yigdal Elohim Chai Veyishtabach. Nimtza Ve'ein Et El Metzi'uto.

1. Extolled and praised is the living God; He exists, but His existence is not limited by time.

אֶחָד וְאֵין יָחִיד כְּיִחוּדוֹ. נֶעְלָם וְגַם אֵין סוֹף לְאַחְדוּתוֹ:

Echad Ve'ein Yachid Keyichudo. Ne'lam Vegam Ein Sof Le'achduto.

2. He is One, and His unity is unparalleled; His unity is incomprehensible and endless.

אֵין לוֹ דְמוּת הַגּוּף וְאֵינוֹ גוּף. לֹא נַעֲרֹךְ אֵלָיו קְדֻשָּׁתוֹ:

Ein Lo Demut Haguf Ve'eino Guf. Lo Na'aroch Elav Kedushato.

3. He has no bodily form, He is incorporeal, and His holiness cannot be comparable to anything.

קַדְמוֹן לְכָל דָּבָר אֲשֶׁר נִבְרָא. רִאשׁוֹן וְאֵין רֵאשִׁית לְרֵאשִׁיתוֹ:

Kadmon Lechol Davar Asher Nivra. Rishon Ve'ein Reshit Lereshito.

4. He existed prior to everything created, He is the first, but without any commencement.

הִנּוֹ אֲדוֹן עוֹלָם לְכָל נוֹצָר. יוֹרֶה גְדֻלָּתוֹ וּמַלְכוּתוֹ:

Hino Adon Olam Lechol Notzar. Yoreh Gedulato Umalchuto.

5. Behold, He is the Lord of the universe, and to all creation He teaches His greatness and dominion.

שֶׁפַע נְבוּאָתוֹ נְתָנוֹ אֶל. אַנְשֵׁי סְגֻלָּתוֹ וְתִפְאַרְתּוֹ:

Shefa Nevu'ato Netano El. Anshei Segulato Vetif'arto.

6. The inspiration of His prophecy He bestowed on men of His chosen and glorious people.

לֹא קָם בְּיִשְׂרָאֵל כְּמֹשֶׁה עוֹד. נָבִיא וּמַבִּיט אֶת תְּמוּנָתוֹ:

Lo Kam Beyisra'el Kemosheh Od. Navi Umabbit Et Temunato.

7. There never arose in Yisrael a prophet who, like Moshe, beheld the likeness of God.

תּוֹרַת אֱמֶת נָתַן לְעַמּוֹ אֶל. עַל יַד נְבִיאוֹ נֶאֱמַן בֵּיתוֹ:

Torat Emet Natan Le'ammo El. Al Yad Nevi'o Ne'eman Beito.

8. The Torah of truth God gave to His people by the hand of His prophet (Moshe), "the faithful of His house."

לֹא יַחֲלִיף הָאֵל וְלֹא יָמִיר. דָּתוֹ לְעוֹלָמִים לְזוּלָתוֹ:

Lo Yachalif Ha'el Velo Yamir. Dato Le'olamim Lezulato.

9. God will not alter His law, or ever change it for any other.

צוֹפֶה וְיוֹדֵעַ סְתָרֵינוּ. מַבִּיט לְסוֹף דָּבָר בְּקַדְמוּתוֹ:

Tzofeh Veyodea Setareinu. Mabbit Lesof Davar Bekadmuto.

10. He perceives and knows our secrets, and sees the end of all things at their very beginning.

גּוֹמֵל לְאִישׁ חָסִיד כְּמִפְעָלוֹ. נוֹתֵן לְרָשָׁע רַע כְּרִשְׁעָתוֹ:

Gomel Le'ish Chasid Kemif'alo. Noten Lerasha Ra Kerish'ato.

11. He rewards the pious man according to his work, and returns evil to the wicked according to his wickedness.

יִשְׁלַח לְקֵץ יָמִין מְשִׁיחֵנוּ. לִפְדוֹת מְחַכֵּי קֵץ יְשׁוּעָתוֹ:

Yishlach Leketz Yamin Meshicheinu. Lifdot Mechakkei Ketz
Yeshu'ato.

12. At the end of days He will send our Messiah, to redeem those who await with hope his final salvation.

מֵתִים יְחַיֶּה אֵל בְּרֹב חַסְדּוֹ. בָּרוּךְ עֲדֵי עַד שֵׁם תְּהִלָּתוֹ:

Meitim Yechayeh El Berov Chasdo. Baruch Adei Ad Shem Tehilato.

13. The dead, God will in His great mercy quicken: Blessed is His glorious name forever.

אֵלֶּה שְׁלֹשׁ עֶשְׂרֵה לְעִקָּרִים. הֵן הֵם יְסוֹד דַּת אֵל וְתוֹרָתוֹ:

Eleh Shelosh Esreh Le'ikarim. Hen Hem Yesod Dat El Vetorato.

These are the Thirteen Principles of our faith, they are the foundation of the divine faith and of God's Torah.

תּוֹרַת מֹשֶׁה אֱמֶת וּנְבוּאָתוֹ. בָּרוּךְ עֲדֵי עַד שֵׁם תְּהִלָּתוֹ:

Torat Mosheh Emet Unevu'ato. Baruch Adei Ad Shem Tehilato.

The Torah of Moshe is true and his prophecy. Blessed is His glorious name forever.

Continue with Shalom Aleichem.

Shalom Aleichem

Some have the custom (BTH', BT Shabbat 33b:8) of circling, to his right (when he is facing, counter-clockwise) the table with 2 myrtle branches, holding them together, making the appropriate blessing for sweet smelling trees (borei atzei vesamim), smelling them and saying:

זָכוֹר וְשָׁמוֹר בְּדִיבּוּר אֶחָד נֶאֶמְרוּ:

Remember and keep [the Shabbat] were said in one utterance.

And also say:

רֵיחַ נִיחוֹחַ אִשֶּׁה לַיהוה:

A soothing fragrance to Hashem.

שָׁלוֹם עֲלֵיכֶם מַלְאֲכֵי הַשָּׁרֵת מַלְאֲכֵי עֶלְיוֹן מֶלֶךְ מַלְכֵי הַמְּלָכִים
הַקָּדוֹשׁ בָּרוּךְ הוּא: ג׳ פעמים

Shalom Aleichem Mal'achei Hasharet Mal'achei Elyon Melech
Malchei Hamelachim Hakadosh Baruch Hu. 3x

Peace be with you, ministering angels, Angels of the Most High,
Coming from the King Who rules over kings. The Holy One, the
Blessed One. 3x

בּוֹאֲכֶם לְשָׁלוֹם מַלְאֲכֵי הַשָּׁלוֹם מַלְאֲכֵי עֶלְיוֹן מֶלֶךְ מַלְכֵי הַמְּלָכִים
הַקָּדוֹשׁ בָּרוּךְ הוּא: ג׳ פעמים

Bo'achem Leshalom Mal'achei Hashalom Mal'achei Elyon Melech
Malchei Hamelachim Hakadosh Baruch Hu. 3x

Come in peace, ministering angels, Angels of the Most High,
Coming from the King Who rules over kings. The Holy One, the
Blessed One. 3x

בָּרְכוּנִי לְשָׁלוֹם מַלְאֲכֵי הַשָּׁלוֹם מַלְאֲכֵי עֶלְיוֹן מֶלֶךְ מַלְכֵי הַמְּלָכִים
הַקָּדוֹשׁ בָּרוּךְ הוּא: ג׳ פעמים

Barechuni Leshalom Mal'achei Hashalom Mal'achei Elyon Melech
Malchei Hamelachim Hakadosh Baruch Hu. 3x

Bless me in peace, ministering angels, Angels of the Most High,
Coming from the King Who rules over kings. The Holy One, the
Blessed One.

בְּשִׁבְתְּכֶם לְשָׁלוֹם מַלְאֲכֵי הַשָּׁלוֹם מַלְאֲכֵי עֶלְיוֹן מֶלֶךְ מַלְכֵי
הַמְּלָכִים הַקָּדוֹשׁ בָּרוּךְ הוּא: ג׳ פעמים

Beshivtechem Leshalom Mal'achei Hashalom Mal'achei Elyon
Melech Malchei Hamelachim Hakadosh Baruch Hu. 3x

In your rest for peace, ministering angels, Angels of the Most High,
Coming from the King Who rules over kings. The Holy One, the
Blessed One.

בְּצֵאתְכֶם לְשָׁלוֹם מַלְאֲכֵי הַשָּׁלוֹם מַלְאֲכֵי עֶלְיוֹן מֶלֶךְ מַלְכֵי
הַמְּלָכִים הַקָּדוֹשׁ בָּרוּךְ הוּא: ג׳ פעמים

Betzetechem Leshalom Mal'achei Hashalom Mal'achei Elyon
Melech Malchei Hamelachim Hakadosh Baruch Hu. 3x

Peace be your going, ministering angels, Angels of the Most High,
Coming from the King Who rules over kings. The Holy One, the
Blessed One.

כִּי מַלְאָכָיו יְצַוֶּה־לָּךְ לִשְׁמָרְךָ בְּכָל־דְּרָכֶיךָ: יְהֹוָה יִשְׁמָר־צֵאתְךָ
וּבוֹאֶךָ מֵעַתָּה וְעַד־עוֹלָם:

Ki Mal'achav Yetzaveh-Lach; Lishmorcha. Bechol-Deracheicha.
Adonai Yishmor-Tzetecha Uvo'echa; Me'attah. Ve'ad-'Olam.

He will give His angels charge over you, to guard you in all your
ways. Hashem will guard your going out and your coming in, From
this time now and forever. (Psalms 91:11. 121:8)

Continue with Ribon Kol-Ha'Olamim. Some omit lines.

Ribon Kol Ha'Olamim

רִבּוֹן־כָּל הָעוֹלָמִים אֲדוֹן כָּל־הַנְּשָׁמוֹת אֲדוֹן הַשָּׁלוֹם. מֶלֶךְ מַלְכֵי
אַבִּיר. מֶלֶךְ בָּרוּךְ. מֶלֶךְ גָּדוֹל. מֶלֶךְ דּוֹבֵר שָׁלוֹם. מֶלֶךְ הָדוּר. מֶלֶךְ
וָתִיק. מֶלֶךְ זַךְ. מֶלֶךְ חֵי הָעוֹלָמִים. מֶלֶךְ טוֹב וּמֵטִיב. מֶלֶךְ יָחִיד
וּמְיוּחָד. מֶלֶךְ כַּבִּיר. מֶלֶךְ לוֹבֵשׁ רַחֲמִים. מֶלֶךְ מַלְכֵי הַמְּלָכִים.
מֶלֶךְ נִשְׂגָּב. מֶלֶךְ סוֹמֵךְ נוֹפְלִים. מֶלֶךְ עוֹשֶׂה מַעֲשֶׂה בְרֵאשִׁית. מֶלֶךְ
פּוֹדֶה וּמַצִּיל. מֶלֶךְ צַח וְאָדוֹם. מֶלֶךְ קָדוֹשׁ. מֶלֶךְ רָם וְנִשָּׂא. מֶלֶךְ
שׁוֹמֵעַ תְּפִלָּה. מֶלֶךְ תָּמִים דַּרְכּוֹ:

Ribon Kol Ha'olamim Adon Kol Haneshamot Adon Hashalom.
Melech Abbir. Melech Baruch. Melech Gadol. Melech Dover
Shalom. Melech Hadur. Melech Vatik. Melech Zach. Melech Chei
Ha'olamim. Melech Tov Umeitiv. Melech Yachid Umeyuchad.
Melech Kabbir. Melech Lovesh Rachamim. Melech Malchei
Hamelachim. Melech Nishgav. Melech Somech Nofelim. Melech
Oseh Ma'aseh Vereshit. Melech Podeh Umatzil. Melech Tzach
Ve'adom. Melech Kadosh. Melech Ram Venish. Melech Shome'ah'
Tefillah. Melech Tamim Darko:

Lord of all the worlds, Master of all souls, Lord of peace, great,
blessed and glorious King Whose word is peace, King that is pure
and lives forever, You that is good and does good, single and alone,
King of all power yet dressed in mercy, even King of all Kings, King
that is exalted yet sustains those that have fallen, Who renews the
work of the creation, Who redeems and delivers, King of Holiness,
high and exalted, Who hears prayer, King Whose way is perfect.

מוֹדֶה אֲנִי לְפָנֶיךָ יְהֹוָה אֱלֹהַי וֵאלֹהֵי אֲבוֹתַי עַל כָּל־הַחֶסֶד אֲשֶׁר
עָשִׂיתָ עִמָּדִי. וַאֲשֶׁר אַתָּה עָתִיד לַעֲשׂוֹת עִמִּי. וְעִם כָּל בְּנֵי בֵיתִי.
וְעִם כָּל־בְּרִיּוֹתֶיךָ בְּנֵי בְרִיתִי. וּבְרוּכִים הֵם מַלְאָכֶיךָ הַקְּדוֹשִׁים
וְהַטְּהוֹרִים. שֶׁעוֹשִׂים רְצוֹנֶךָ: אֲדוֹן הַשָּׁלוֹם. מֶלֶךְ שֶׁהַשָּׁלוֹם שֶׁלוֹ.
בָּרְכֵנִי בַּשָּׁלוֹם. וְתִפְקֹד אוֹתִי וְאֶת־כָּל־בְּנֵי בֵיתִי וְכָל־עַמְּךָ בֵּית
יִשְׂרָאֵל. לְחַיִּים טוֹבִים וּלְשָׁלוֹם:

Modeh Ani Lefaneicha Adonai Elohai Velohei Avotai Al Kol
Hachesed Asher Asita Imadi. Va'asher Attah Atid La'asot Immi. Ve'im
Kol Benei Veiti. Ve'im Kol Beriyoteicha Benei Veriti. Uveruchim
Hem Mal'acheicha Hakedoshim Vehatehorim. She'osim
Retzonecha: Adon Hashalom. Melech Shehashalom Shelo.
Barecheini Bashalom. Vetifkod Oti Ve'et Kol Benei Veiti Vechol
Ammecha Beit Yisra'el. Lechayim Tovim Uleshalom:

I give thanks before You, Hashem my God and the God of my
fathers, for all the loving-kindness which You have already done for
me and which You will in future do to me and to all my household
and to all of Your creatures who share with me in the covenant.
Blessed are Your Angels, holy and pure, that work Your will, Lord of
peace. King whose possession is peace, bless me with peace and
ordain for me, for my household and for all of Your people, the
House of Yisrael, life, happiness and peace.

מֶלֶךְ עֶלְיוֹן עַל־כָּל־צְבָא מָרוֹם. יוֹצְרֵנוּ יוֹצֵר בְּרֵאשִׁית. אֲחַלֶּה פָנֶיךָ
הַמְּאִירִים. שֶׁתְּזַכֶּה אוֹתִי וְאֶת כָּל־בְּנֵי בֵיתִי. לִמְצֹא חֵן וְשֵׂכֶל טוֹב.
בְּעֵינֶיךָ וּבְעֵינֵי כָל בְּנֵי אָדָם וְחַוָּה. וּבְעֵינֵי כָל־רוֹאֵינוּ לַעֲבוֹדָתֶךָ.
וְזַכֵּנִי לְקַבֵּל שַׁבָּתוֹת מִתּוֹךְ רֹב שִׂמְחָה. וּמִתּוֹךְ עֹשֶׁר וְכָבוֹד. וּמִתּוֹךְ
מְעוּט עֲוֹנוֹת. וְהָסֵר מִמֶּנִּי וּמִכָּל־עַמְּךָ בֵּית יִשְׂרָאֵל. כָּל־מִינֵי חֹלִי.
וְכָל־מִינֵי מַדְוֶה. וְכָל־מִינֵי דַלּוּת וַעֲנִיּוּת וְאֶבְיוֹנוּת. וְתֵן בָּנוּ יֵצֶר טוֹב
לְעָבְדְּךָ בֶּאֱמֶת וּבְיִרְאָה וּבְאַהֲבָה. וְנִהְיֶה מְכֻבָּדִים בְּעֵינֶיךָ וּבְעֵינֵי
כָל־רוֹאֵינוּ. כִּי אַתָּה הוּא מֶלֶךְ הַכָּבוֹד. כִּי לְךָ נָאֶה כִּי לְךָ יָאֶה:

Melech Elyon Al Kol Tzeva Marom. Yotzreinu Yotzer Bereshit.
Achaleh Faneicha Hame'irim. Shetezakeh Oti Ve'et Kol Benei Veiti.
Limtzo Chein Vesechel Tov. Be'eineicha Uve'einei Chol Benei Adam
Vechavah. Uve'einei Chol Ro'einu La'avodatecha. Vezakkeni
Lekabel Shabbatot Mitoch Rov Simchah. Umitoch Osher Vechavod.
Umitoch Mi'ut Avonot. Vehaseir Mimeni Umikol Ammecha Beit
Yisra'el. Kol Minei Choli. Vechol Minei Madveh. Vechol Minei Dalut
Va'aniyut Ve'evyonut. Veten Banu Yetzer Tov Le'avdecha Be'emet
Uveyir'ah Uve'ahavah. Venihyeh Mechubbadim Be'eineicha
Uve'einei Chol Ro'einu. Ki Attah Hu Melech Hakavod. Ki Lecha
Na'eh Ki Lecha Ya'eh:

King that rules on high over all the hosts, Who formed us as You formed all of the world, I implore Your glorious presence that You might account me and my household worthy to find grace and good understanding in Your sight, and in the sight of all the sons of Adam and Chavah, to serve You. Pardon and forgive us and our children for all our sins. Grant us that we may receive each Shabbat in the midst of joy, plenty and honor, but not in the midst of sin. Remove from us and our children and from all Yisrael every manner of sickness, disease, poverty, and dependence on charity. Strengthen our better feelings to serve You in truth, in awe as well as in love, and let us be honored in Your sight and in the sight of those that behold us, for You are the King of Glory, for to You it is suitable, for to You it is fitting.

אָנָּא מֶלֶךְ מַלְכֵי הַמְּלָכִים. צַוֵּה לְמַלְאָכֶיךָ מַלְאֲכֵי הַשָּׁרֵת. מְשָׁרְתֵי עֶלְיוֹן. שֶׁיִּפְקְדוּנִי בְּרַחֲמִים. וִיבָרְכוּנִי בְּבוֹאָם לְבֵיתִי בְּיוֹם קָדְשֵׁנוּ. כִּי הִדְלַקְתִּי נֵרוֹתַי וְהִצַּעְתִּי מִטָּתִי וְהֶחֱלַפְתִּי שִׂמְלוֹתַי לִכְבוֹד יוֹם הַשַּׁבָּת. וּבָאתִי לְבֵיתְךָ לְהַפִּיל תְּחִנָּתִי לְפָנֶיךָ שֶׁתַּעֲבִיר אַנְחָתִי. וָאָעִיד אֲשֶׁר בָּרָאתָ בְּשִׁשָּׁה יָמִים כָּל הַיְצוּר. וָאֶשְׁנֶה וָאֲשַׁלֵּשׁ עוֹד לְהָעִיד עַל כּוֹסִי בְּתוֹךְ שִׂמְחָתִי כַּאֲשֶׁר צִוִּיתַנִי לְזָכְרוֹ וּלְהִתְעַנֵּג בְּיֶתֶר נִשְׁמָתִי אֲשֶׁר נָתַתָּ בִּי. בּוֹ אֶשְׁבֹּות כַּאֲשֶׁר צִוִּיתַנִי לְשָׁרְתֶךָ וְכֵן אַגִּיד גְּדֻלָּתְךָ בְּרִנָּה. וְשִׁוִּיתִיבוּ אֶשְׁבֹּות. כַּאֲשֶׁר צִוִּיתַנִי לְשָׁרְתֶךָ. וְכֵן אַגִּיד גְּדֻלָּתְךָ בְּרִנָּה. וְשִׁוִּיתִי יְהֹוָה לְקִרְאָתִי. שֶׁתְּרַחֲמֵנִי עוֹד בְּגָלוּתִי לְגָאֳלֵנִי. וּלְעוֹרֵר לִבִּי לְאַהֲבָתֶךָ: וְאָז אֶשְׁמֹר לְפִקּוּדֶיךָ וְחֻקֶּיךָ בְּלִי עֶצֶב. וְאֶתְפַּלֵּל כַּדָּת כָּרָאוּי וְכַנָּכוֹן:

Ana Melech Malchei Hamelachim. Tzaveh Lemal'acheicha
Mal'achei Hasharet. Mesharetei Elyon. Sheyifkeduni Berachamim.
Vivarechuni Bevo'am Leveiti Beyom Kadeshenu. Ki Hidlakti Nerotai
Vehitza'ti Mitati Vehechelafti Simlotai Lichvod Yom Hashabbat.
Uvati Leveitcha Lehappil Techinati Lefaneicha Sheta'avir Anchati.
Va'a'id Asher Barata Beshishah Yamim Kol Hayetzur. Va'eshneh
Va'ashallesh Od Leha'id Al Kosi Betoch Simchati Ka'asher Tzivitani

Lezochro Ulehit'aneg Beyeter Nishmati Asher Natatta Bi. Bo Eshbot
Ka'asher Tzivitani Leshortecha Vechein Aggid Gedulatecha Berinah.
Veshivitibo Eshbot. Ka'asher Tzivitani Leshortecha. Vechein Aggid
Gedulatecha Berinah. Veshiviti Adonai Likrati. Sheterachameni Od
Begaluti Lego'oleini. Ule'orer Libi Le'ahavatecha: Ve'az Eshmor
Lefikudeicha Vechukeicha Beli Etzev. Ve'etpallel Kadat Vechara'ui
Vechanachon:

You Who is the Supreme King of Kings, command Your Angels,
Your supreme ministering Angels, to watch over me in mercy and
bless me as they come into my house on this our holy day. For I have
kindled my lights and I have spread my bed and I have changed my
garments for the glory of the Shabbat Day. I have come into Your
House to pour out my supplication to You that You may cause all of
my sorrows to pass away, and I have testified that in six days You
have created all things. Twice again, even thrice, I will bear
testimony over the sacred cup in the midst of my joy, as You have
commanded me, in order to serve You and so I will tell of Your
greatness in song. I have set Hashem before me; may You yet have
mercy on me in my exile, redeem me and arouse my heart to love
You. Then indeed I will keep Your ordinances and statutes without
hindrance, and then I will pray as is truly due and fitting.

מַלְאֲכֵי הַשָּׁלוֹם. בּוֹאֲכֶם לְשָׁלוֹם. בָּרְכוּנִי לְשָׁלוֹם. וְאִמְרוּ בָּרוּךְ
לְשֻׁלְחָנִי הֶעָרוּךְ. וְצֵאתְכֶם לְשָׁלוֹם. מֵעַתָּה וְעַד עוֹלָם אָמֵן סֶלָה:

Mal'achei Hashalom. Bo'achem Leshalom. Barechuni Leshalom.
Ve'imru Baruch Leshulchani He'aruch. Vetzetchem Leshalom.
Me'attah Ve'ad Olam Amen Selah:

Angels of peace, come in peace, bless me with peace, bring your
blessing to my set table, and may your going out be in peace, from
now and forever. Amen, selah.

Continue with the Eshet Chayil.

Eshet Chayil

Proverbs 31:10-31

אֵשֶׁת־חַיִל מִי יִמְצָא וְרָחֹק מִפְּנִינִים מִכְרָהּ: בָּטַח בָּהּ לֵב בַּעְלָהּ
וְשָׁלָל לֹא יֶחְסָר: גְּמָלַתְהוּ טוֹב וְלֹא־רָע כֹּל יְמֵי חַיֶּיהָ: דָּרְשָׁה צֶמֶר
וּפִשְׁתִּים וַתַּעַשׂ בְּחֵפֶץ כַּפֶּיהָ: הָיְתָה כָּאֳנִיּוֹת סוֹחֵר מִמֶּרְחָק תָּבִיא
לַחְמָהּ: וַתָּקָם | בְּעוֹד לַיְלָה וַתִּתֵּן טֶרֶף לְבֵיתָהּ וְחֹק לְנַעֲרֹתֶיהָ:
זָמְמָה שָׂדֶה וַתִּקָּחֵהוּ מִפְּרִי כַפֶּיהָ נטע (נָטְעָה) כָּרֶם: חָגְרָה בְעוֹז
מָתְנֶיהָ וַתְּאַמֵּץ זְרוֹעֹתֶיהָ: טָעֲמָה כִּי־טוֹב סַחְרָהּ לֹא־יִכְבֶּה בליל
(בַלַּיְלָה) נֵרָהּ: יָדֶיהָ שִׁלְּחָה בַכִּישׁוֹר וְכַפֶּיהָ תָּמְכוּ פָלֶךְ: כַּפָּהּ
פָּרְשָׂה לֶעָנִי וְיָדֶיהָ שִׁלְּחָה לָאֶבְיוֹן: לֹא־תִירָא לְבֵיתָהּ מִשָּׁלֶג כִּי
כָל־בֵּיתָהּ לָבֻשׁ שָׁנִים: מַרְבַדִּים עָשְׂתָה־לָּהּ שֵׁשׁ וְאַרְגָּמָן לְבוּשָׁהּ:
נוֹדַע בַּשְּׁעָרִים בַּעְלָהּ בְּשִׁבְתּוֹ עִם־זִקְנֵי־אָרֶץ: סָדִין עָשְׂתָה וַתִּמְכֹּר
וַחֲגוֹר נָתְנָה לַכְּנַעֲנִי: עֹז־וְהָדָר לְבוּשָׁהּ וַתִּשְׂחַק לְיוֹם אַחֲרוֹן: פִּיהָ
פָּתְחָה בְחָכְמָה וְתוֹרַת חֶסֶד עַל־לְשׁוֹנָהּ: צוֹפִיָּה הילכת (הֲלִיכוֹת)
בֵּיתָהּ וְלֶחֶם עַצְלוּת לֹא תֹאכֵל: קָמוּ בָנֶיהָ וַיְאַשְּׁרוּהָ בַּעְלָהּ
וַיְהַלְלָהּ: רַבּוֹת בָּנוֹת עָשׂוּ חָיִל וְאַתְּ עָלִית עַל־כֻּלָּנָה: שֶׁקֶר הַחֵן
וְהֶבֶל הַיֹּפִי אִשָּׁה יִרְאַת־יְהֹוָה הִיא תִתְהַלָּל: תְּנוּ־לָהּ מִפְּרִי יָדֶיהָ
וִיהַלְלוּהָ בַשְּׁעָרִים מַעֲשֶׂיהָ:

Eshet-Chayil Mi Yimtza; Verachok Mippeninim Michrah. Batach Bah
Lev Ba'lah; Veshalal. Lo Yechsar. Gemalat'hu Tov Velo-Ra'; Kol
Yemei Chayeiha. Dareshah Tzemer Ufishtim; Vata'as. Bechefetz
Kappeiha. Hayetah Ko'oniyot Socher; Mimerchak. Tavi Lachmah.
Vatakom Be'od Laylah. Vatiten Teref Leveitah; Vechok.
Lena'aroteiha. Zamemah Sadeh Vatikachehu; Miperi Chappeiha.
Nate'ah Karem. Chagerah Ve'oz Motneiha; Vate'ammetz.
Zero'oteiha. Ta'amah Ki-Tov Sachrah; Lo-Yichbeh Vallaylah Nerah.
Yadeiha Shillechah Vakkishor; Vechappeiha. Tamechu Falech.
Kappah Paresah Le'ani; Veyadeiha. Shillechah La'evyon. Lo-Tira
Leveitah Mishaleg; Ki Chol-Beitah. Lavush Shanim. Marvadim
Asetah-Lah; Shesh Ve'argaman Levushah. Noda Bashe'arim Ba'lah;
Beshivto. Im-Ziknei-'Aretz. Sadin Asetah Vatimkor; Vachagor.

Natenah Lakena'ani. Oz-Vehadar Levushah; Vatischak. Leyom
Acharon. Piha Patechah Vechochmah; Vetorat Chesed. Al-Leshonah.
Tzofiyah Halichot Beitah; Velechem Atzlut. Lo Tochel. Kamu
Vaneiha Vay'asheruha; Ba'lah. Vayhalelah. Rabot Banot Asu Chayil;
Ve'at. Alit Al-Kullanah. Sheker Hachein Vehevel Hayofi; Ishah Yir'at-
Adonai Hi Tit'hallal. Tenu-Lah Miperi Yadeiha; Vihaleluha
Vashe'arim Ma'aseiha.

A woman of valor who can find? For her price is far above rubies.
The heart of her husband safely trusts in her, and he has no lack of
gain. She does him good and not evil all the days of her life. She
seeks wool and flax, and works willingly with her hands. She is like
the merchant-ships; she brings her food from afar. She rises also
while it is still night, and gives food to her household, and a portion
to her maidens. She considers a field, and buys it; with the fruit of
her hands she plants a vineyard. She girds her loins with strength,
And makes her arms strong. She perceives that her merchandise is
good; Her lamp does not go out at night. She lays her hands to the
distaff, And her hands hold the spindle. She stretches out her hand
to the poor; she even reaches out her hands to the needy. She is not
afraid of the snow for her household; For all her household are
clothed with scarlet. She makes for herself bedspreads; Her clothing
is fine linen and purple. Her husband is known in the gates, When
he sits among the elders of the land. She makes linen garments and
sells them; And delivers girdles to the merchant. Strength and
dignity are her clothing; And she laughs at the time to come. She
opens her mouth with wisdom; And the law of kindness is on her
tongue. She looks well to the ways of her household, And does not
eat the bread of idleness. Her children rise up, and call her blessed;
Her husband also, and praises her: 'Many daughters have done
valiantly, But you excel them all.' Grace is deceitful, and beauty is
vain; But a woman that fears Hashem, she will be praised. Give her
of the fruit of her hands; And let her works praise her in the gates.

some say:

מִגְדַּל־עֹז שֵׁם יְהֹוָה בּוֹ־יָרוּץ צַדִּיק וְנִשְׂגָּב: כִּי־בִי יִרְבּוּ יָמֶיךָ וְיוֹסִיפוּ לְּךָ שְׁנוֹת חַיִּים: עֵץ־חַיִּים הִיא לַמַּחֲזִיקִים בָּהּ וְתֹמְכֶיהָ מְאֻשָּׁר: דְּרָכֶיהָ דַרְכֵי־נֹעַם וְכָל־נְתִיבוֹתֶיהָ שָׁלוֹם:

Migdal Oz Shem Adonai Bo Yarutz Tzaddik Venisgav. Ki Vi Yirbu Yameicha Veyosifu Lecha Shenot Chayim. Etz Chayim Hi Lamachazikim Bah Vetomecheiha Me'ushar. Deracheiha Darchei No'am Vechol Netivoteiha Shalom.

The name of Hashem is a strong tower: The righteous run into it, and are set up on high. For by me your days will be multiplied, and the years of your life will be increased. She is a tree of life to those who grasp her, and whoever holds on to her is happy. Her ways are ways of pleasantness, And all her paths are peace. (Prov. 18:10, 9:11, 3:18, 3:17)

Atkinu Seudata - Shabbat Evening

אַתְקִינוּ סְעֻדָּתָא דִּמְהֵימְנוּתָא שְׁלֵימָתָא חֶדְוָתָא דְּמַלְכָּא קַדִּישָׁא: אַתְקִינוּ סְעֻדָּתָא דְּמַלְכָּא. דָּא הִיא סְעֻדָּתָא דַּחֲקַל תַּפּוּחִין קַדִּישִׁין (וּזְעֵיר אַנְפִּין וְעַתִּיקָא קַדִּישָׁא אַתְיָן לְסַעֲדָא בַּהֲדֵיהּ):

Atkinu Se'udata Dimheimnuta Sheleimata Chedvata Demalka Kaddisha: Atkinu Se'udata Demalka. Da Hi Se'udata Dachakal Tappuchin Kaddishin (Uze'eir Anpin V'atika Kaddisha Atyan Lsa'ada Bahadeih):

some say:

אֲהַלְלָה שֵׁם־אֱלֹהִים בְּשִׁיר וַאֲגַדְּלֶנּוּ בְתוֹדָה: יְהֹוָה | עֻזִּי וּמָגִנִּי בּוֹ בָטַח לִבִּי וְנֶעֱזָרְתִּי וַיַּעֲלֹז לִבִּי וּמִשִּׁירִי אֲהוֹדֶנּוּ:

Ahallah Shem Elohim Beshir Va'agadelenu Vetodah. Adonai Uzi Umagini Bo Vatach Libi Vene'ezareti Vaya'aloz Libi Umishiri Ahodenu.

I will praise the name of God with a song, And will magnify Him with thanksgiving. Hashem is my strength and my shield, In Him my heart has trusted, And I am helped; So my heart greatly rejoices, And with my song I will praise Him. (Ps. 69:31, 28:7)

It is a custom for some to say Azamer before kiddush:

אֲזַמֵּר בִּשְׁבָחִין. לְמֵיעַל גּוֹ פִתְחִין. דְּבַחֲקַל תַּפּוּחִין. דְּאִנּוּן קַדִּישִׁין:

Azamer Bishvachin. Lemei'al Go Fitchin. Devachakal Tappuchin. De'inun
Kaddishin:

נְזַמֵּן לָה הַשְׁתָּא. בִּפְתוֹרָא חַדְתָּא. וּבִמְנַרְתָּא טַבְתָּא. דְּנַהֲרָא עַל רֵישִׁין:

Azamer Bishvachin. Lemei'al Go Fitchin. Devachakal Tappuchin. De'inun
Kaddishin:

יְמִינָא וּשְׂמָאלָא. וּבֵינַיְהוּ כַלָּה. בְּקִשּׁוּטִין אַזְלָא. וּמָאנִין וּלְבוּשִׁין:

Yemina Usemala. Uveinayhu Challah. Bekishutin Azla. Umanin Ulevushin:

יְחַבֵּק לָה בַּעְלָה. וּבִיסוֹדָא דִילָה. דְּעָבִיד נַיְחָא לָה. יְהֵא כָתִישׁ כַּתִּישִׁין:

Yechabek Lah Ba'lah. Uvisoda Dilah. De'avid Naycha Lah. Yehe Chatish Katishin:

צְוָחִין אַף עָקְתִין. בְּטֵלִין וּשְׁבִיתִין. בְּרַם אַנְפִּין חַדְתִּין. וְרוּחִין עִם נַפְשִׁין:

Tzevachin Af Aktin. Betelin Ushevitin. Beram Anpin Chadtin. Veruchin Im Nafshin:

חֲדוּ סַגִּי יֵיתֵי. וְעַל חֲדָא תַּרְתֵּי. נְהוֹרָא לָה יִמְטֵי. וּבִרְכָאן דִּנְפִישִׁין:

Chadu Sagi Yeitei. Ve'al Chada Tartei. Nehora Lah Yimtei. Uvirchan Dinfishin:

קְרִיבוּ שׁוֹשְׁבִינִין. עֲבִידוּ תִקּוּנִין. לְאַפָּשָׁא זִינִין. וְנוּנִין עִם רַחְשִׁין:

Kerivu Shushevinin. Avidu Tikunin. Le'appasha Zinin. Venunin Im Rachshin:

לְמֶעְבַּד נִשְׁמָתִין. וְרוּחִין חַדְתִּין. בְּתַרְתֵּין וּבִתְלָתִין. וּבִתְלָתָא שִׁבְשִׁין:

Leme'bad Nishmatin. Veruchin Chadtin. Betartein Uvitlatin. Uvitlata Shivshin:

וְעִטּוּרִין שִׁבְעִין לָה. וּמַלְכָּא דִלְעֵלָּא. דְּתִתְעַטַּר כַּלָּא. בְּקַדִּישׁ קַדִּישִׁין:

Ve'itturin Shiv'in Lah. Umalka Dil'ella. Detit'attar Kalla. Bekaddish Kaddishin:

רְשִׁימִין וּסְתִימִין. בְּגוֹ כָל־עָלְמִין. בְּרַם עַתִּיק יוֹמִין. הֲלָא בָּטִישׁ בַּטִּישִׁין:

Reshimin Usetimin. Bego Chol Alemin. Beram Atik Yomin. Hala Batish Batishin:

יְהֵא רַעֲוָא קַמֵּיהּ. דְּתִשְׁרֵי עַל עַמֵּיהּ. דְּיִתְעַנַּג לִשְׁמֵיהּ. בִּמְתִיקִין וְדוּבְשִׁין:

Yehe Ra'ava Kammeih. Detishrei Al Ammeih. Deyit'anag Lishmeih. Bimtikin
Veduveshin:

אֲסַדֵּר לִדְרוֹמָא. מְנַרְתָּא דִסְתִימָא. וְשֻׁלְחָן עִם נַהֲמָא. וּבִצְפוֹנָא אַרְשִׁין:

Asader Lidroma. Menarta Distima. Veshulchan Im Nahama. Uvitzfona Arshin:

בְּחַמְרָא גּוֹ כַסָּא. וּמְדָאנֵי אַסָּא. לְאָרוּס וַאֲרוּסָה. לְהִתַּקְפָא חַלָּשִׁין:

Bechamra Go Chasa. Umedanei Assa. Le'arus Va'arusah. Lehittakfa Challashin:

נַעֲבֵד לְהוֹן כִּתְרִין. בְּמִלִּין יַקִּירִין. בְּשִׁבְעִין עִטּוּרִין. דְּעַל גַּבֵּי חַמְשִׁין:

Ne'abed Lehon Kitrin. Bemillin Yakkirin. Beshiv'in Itturin. De'al Gabei Chamshin:

(שְׁבִיתִין וּשְׁבִיקִין. מְסָאֲבִין דִּרְחִיקִין. חֲבִילִין דִּמְעִיקִין. וְכָל זִינֵי חַרְשִׁין:)

(Shevitin Ushevikin. Mesa'avin Dirchikin. Chavilin Dim'ikin. Vechol Zinei Charshin:)

שְׁכִינְתָּא תִתְעַטַּר. בְּשִׁית נַהֲמֵי לִסְטָר. בְּוָוִין תִּתְקַטַּר. וְזִינִין דִּכְנִישִׁין:

Shechinta Tit'attar. Beshit Nahamei Listar. Bevavin Titkattar. Vezinin Dichnishin:

לְמִבְצַע עַל רִפְתָּא. כְּזֵיתָא וּכְבֵיעֲתָא. תְּרֵין יוּדִין נַקְטָא. סְתִימִין וּפְרִישִׁין:

Lemivtza Al Rifta. Kezeita Uchevei'ata. Terein Yudin Nakta. Setimin Uferishin:

מְשַׁח זֵיתָא דַכְיָא. דְּטַחֲנִין רֵיחֲיָא. וְנַגְדִּין נַחֲלַיָא. בְּגַוַּהּ בִּלְחִישִׁין:

Meshach Zeita Dachya. Detachanin Reichaya. Venagdin Nachalaya. Begavah Bilchishin:

הֲלָא נֵימָא רָזִין. וּמִלִּין דְּגְנִיזִין. דְּלֵיתְהוֹן מִתְחֲזִין. טְמִירִין וּכְבִישִׁין:

Hala Neima Razin. Umillin Dignizin. Deleithon Mitchazin. Temirin Uchevishin:

אִתְעַטָּרַת כַּלָּה. בְּרָזִין דִּלְעֵלָּא. בְּגוֹ הַאי הִלּוּלָא. דְּעִירִין קַדִּישִׁין:

It'atrat Kallah. Berazin Dil'ella. Bego Ha Hilula. De'irin Kaddishin:

וִיהֵא רַעֲוָא מִן קֳדָם עַתִּיקָא קַדִּישָׁא דְכָל קַדִּישִׁין. טְמִירָא דְּכָל טְמִירִין סְתִימָא דְכֹלָּא דְּיִתְמְשַׁךְ טַלָּא עִלָּאָה מִנֵּיהּ לְמַלְּיָא רֵישֵׁיהּ דִּזְעֵיר אַנְפִּין וּלְהַטִּיל לַחֲקַל תַּפּוּחִין קַדִּישִׁין בִּנְהִירוּ דְּאַנְפִּין בְּרַעֲוָא וּבְחֶדְוָתָא דְכֹלָּא. וְיִתְמְשַׁךְ מִן קֳדָם עַתִּיקָא קַדִּישָׁא דְכָל קַדִּישִׁין טְמִירָא דְּכָל־טְמִירִין סְתִימָא דְכֹלָּא רְעוּתָא וְרַחֲמֵי חִנָּא וְחִסְדָּא בִּנְהִירוּ עִלָּאָה בִּרְעוּתָא וְחֶדְוָא עָלַי וְעַל כָּל בְּנֵי בֵיתִי וְעַל־כָּל־הַנִּלְוִים אֵלַי וְעַל כָּל יִשְׂרָאֵל עַמֵּיהּ. וְיִפְרְקִינַן מִכָּל עָקְתִין בִּישִׁין דְּיֵיתוּן לְעָלְמָא וְיַזְמִין וְיִתְיְהִיב לָנָא וּלְכָל־נַפְשָׁתָנָא חִנָּא וְחִסְדָּא וְחַיֵּי אֲרִיכֵי וּמְזוֹנֵי רְוִיחֵי וְרַחֲמֵי מִן קֳדָמֵיהּ. אָמֵן כֵּן יְהִי רָצוֹן:

Vihe Ra'ava Min Kodam Atika Kaddisha Dechol Kaddishin. Temira Dechol Temirin Setima Decholla Deyitmeshach Talla Illa'ah Mineih Lemalya Reisheih Diz'eir Anpin Ulehatil Lachakal Tappuchin Kaddishin Binhiru De'anpin Bera'ava Uvechedvata Decholla. Veyitmeshaach Min Kodam Atika Kaddisha Dechol Kaddishin Temira Dechol Temirin Setima Dechola Re'uta Verachamei China Vechisda Binhiru Illa'ah Bir'uta Vechedva Alai Ve'al Kol Benei Veiti Ve'al Kol Hanilvim Elai Ve'al Kol Yisra'el Ammeih. Veyifrekinan Mikol Aktin Bishin Deyeitun Le'alema Veyazmin Veyityehiv Lana Ulechol Nafshatana China Vechisda Vechayei Arichei Umezonei Revichei Verachamei Min Kodameih. Amen Ken Yehi Ratzon:

Order of the Friday Night Kiddush

Before Kiddush, some say:

לְשֵׁם יְחוּד קוּדְשָׁא בְּרִיךְ הוּא וּשְׁכִינְתֵּיה. בִּדְחִילוּ וּרְחִימוּ. וּרְחִימוּ וּדְחִילוּ. לְיַחֲדָא שֵׁם יוֹ"ד קֵ"י בְּוָא"ו קֵ"י בְּיִחוּדָא שְׁלִים (יהוה) בְּשֵׁם כָּל יִשְׂרָאֵל. הנה אנחנו באים לקיים מצות עשה דאורייתא לקדש את השבת ולקיים מצות עשה דרבנן לקדש על היין כמו שפירשו רבותינו זכרונם לברכה פסוק זכור את יום השבת לקדשו זכרהו בדברים הנאמרים על היין לתקן שורשה מצות אלו במקום עליון. והרי אנחנו מוכנים להמשיך אורות עליונים לחקל תפוחין קדישין על ידי הכנה בסוד המעשה והכנה בסוד הדבור.

וִיהִי רָצוֹן מִלְּפָנֶיךָ יְהֹוָה אֱלֹהֵינוּ וֵאלֹהֵי אֲבוֹתֵינוּ. שיעלה לפניך כאלו כוננו בכל הכוונות הראויות לכוין בסוד המעשה ובסוד הדבור אשר יסדו לנו עבדיך חכמי ישראל בסדר הקידוש שֶׁל שבת. ויעלה לפניך קידוש זה עם קידושי בניך היודעים ומכונים כהגן וימשך שפע וברכה רבה בכל העולמות הקדושים ומשם ימשך שפע רב לנפשנו רוחנו ונשמתנו לעבדך באמת ולשמר את כל שבתות קדשך כל ימי חיינו במחשבה ודבור ומעשה ביראה ואהבה ושמחה רבה. והרי אנחנו מוכנים לקבל עלינו מצות עשה של התשובה כמו שכתוב ושבת עד יהוה אלהיך ושמעת בקלו: וִיהִי נֹעַם אֲדֹנָי אֱלֹהֵינוּ עָלֵינוּ וּמַעֲשֵׂה יָדֵינוּ כּוֹנְנָה עָלֵינוּ וּמַעֲשֵׂה יָדֵינוּ כּוֹנְנֵהוּ:

וִיהִי רָצוֹן מִלְּפָנֶיךָ יְהֹוָה אֱלֹהֵינוּ וֵאלֹהֵי אֲבוֹתֵינוּ. שיהא עתה עת רצון לפניך וימשך לנו ולנפשותינו ולבנינו ובנותינו ולכל ישראל שפע שלום טובה וברכה חיים חן וחסד ורחמים על ידי כ"ב צנורות עליונים אשר הם פתוחים ומריקים שפע וברכה מבריכה העליונה מראש כל הכתרים. ויהי רצון מלפניך יהוה אלהינו ואלהי אבותינו. שבזכות מצות מזיגת כוס היין של הקידוש במים מלא ידינו מברכותיך מעשר מתנות ידיך ובזכות יעקב תמימך אשר מתק הגבורות בחסדים ככתוב ויבא לו יין וישת דארמי ליה מיא ביינא כן ברחמיך וחסדיך יתמתקו כל הגבורות והדינין וגמלנו חסדים טובים:

וִיהִי רָצוֹן מִלְּפָנֶיךָ יְהֹוָה אֱלֹהֵינוּ וֵאלֹהֵי אֲבוֹתֵינוּ. שֶׁבִּזְכוּת מִצְוַת הַבְּרָכָה שֶׁל קִידּוּשׁ שַׁבָּת עַל כּוֹס יַיִן מָלֵא יִתְמַלְּאוּ אוֹתִיּוֹת כּוֹס שֶׁהֵם כ"ף וא"ו סמ"ך שְׁעוּלִים מִסְפַּר הַבְּרָכָה. וְיִהְיוּ צִנּוֹרוֹת לְקַבֵּל לָנוּ שֶׁפַע הַבְּרָכָה מִן הַבְּרִיכָה הָעֶלְיוֹנָה מִמְּקוֹר הַבְּרָכוֹת. וְיִתְקַיֵּים בָּנוּ מִקְרָא שֶׁכָּתוּב יְצַו יהוה אִתְּךָ אֶת הַבְּרָכָה בַּאֲסָמֶיךָ וּבְכָל מִשְׁלַח יָדֶךָ. וְעַתָּה אֲדֹנָי אֱלֹהִים הוֹאֵל וּבָרֵךְ אֶת בֵּית עַבְדְּךָ וּמִבִּרְכָתְךָ יְבוֹרַךְ בֵּית עַבְדְּךָ לְעוֹלָם. יִהְיוּ לְרָצוֹן אִמְרֵי־פִי וְהֶגְיוֹן לִבִּי לְפָנֶיךָ יְהֹוָה צוּרִי וְגֹאֲלִי:

Some say:

Psalms 23

מִזְמוֹר לְדָוִד יְהֹוָה רֹעִי לֹא אֶחְסָר: בִּנְאוֹת דֶּשֶׁא יַרְבִּיצֵנִי עַל מֵי מְנֻחוֹת יְנַהֲלֵנִי: נַפְשִׁי יְשׁוֹבֵב יַנְחֵנִי בְמַעְגְּלֵי־צֶדֶק לְמַעַן שְׁמוֹ: גַּם כִּי־אֵלֵךְ בְּגֵיא צַלְמָוֶת לֹא־אִירָא רָע כִּי־אַתָּה עִמָּדִי שִׁבְטְךָ וּמִשְׁעַנְתֶּךָ הֵמָּה יְנַחֲמֻנִי: תַּעֲרֹךְ לְפָנַי | שֻׁלְחָן נֶגֶד צֹרְרָי דִּשַּׁנְתָּ בַשֶּׁמֶן רֹאשִׁי כּוֹסִי רְוָיָה אַךְ | טוֹב וָחֶסֶד יִרְדְּפוּנִי כָּל־יְמֵי חַיָּי וְשַׁבְתִּי בְּבֵית־יְהֹוָה לְאֹרֶךְ יָמִים:

Mizmor Ledavid; Adonai Ro'i. Lo Echsar. Bin'ot Deshei Yarbitzeni;
Al Mei Menuchot Yenahaleini. Nafshi Yeshovev; Yancheini
Vema'gelei-Tzedek. Lema'an Shemo. Gam Ki-'Elech Begei
Tzalmavet Lo-'Ira Ra'. Ki-'Attah Immadi; Shivtecha Umish'antecha.
Hemah Yenachamuni. Ta'aroch Lefanai Shulchan. Neged Tzorerai;
Dishanta Vashemen Roshi. Kosi Revayah Ach Tov Vachesed Yirdefuni
Chol-Yemei Chayai; Veshavti Beveit-Adonai Le'orech Yamim.

A Psalm of David. Hashem is my Shepherd; I will not want. He makes me to lie down in green pastures; He leads me beside the still waters. He restores my soul; He guides me in straight paths for His name's sake. Even though I walk through the valley of the shadow of death, I will fear no evil, for You are with me; Your rod and Your staff, they comfort me. You prepare a table before me in the presence of my enemies; You have anointed my head with oil; my cup runs over. Surely goodness and mercy will follow me all the days of my life; And I will dwell in the House of Hashem forever.

יוֹם הַשִּׁשִּׁי: וַיְכֻלּוּ הַשָּׁמַיִם וְהָאָרֶץ וְכָל־צְבָאָם וַיְכַל אֱלֹהִים בַּיּוֹם
הַשְּׁבִיעִי מְלַאכְתּוֹ אֲשֶׁר עָשָׂה וַיִּשְׁבֹּת בַּיּוֹם הַשְּׁבִיעִי מִכָּל־מְלַאכְתּוֹ
אֲשֶׁר עָשָׂה: וַיְבָרֶךְ אֱלֹהִים אֶת־יוֹם הַשְּׁבִיעִי וַיְקַדֵּשׁ אֹתוֹ כִּי בוֹ
שָׁבַת מִכָּל־מְלַאכְתּוֹ אֲשֶׁר־בָּרָא אֱלֹהִים לַעֲשׂוֹת:

Yom Hashishi. Vaychulu Hashamayim Veha'aretz Vechol-Tzeva'am
Vaychal Elohim Bayom Hashevi'i. Melachto Asher Asah; Vayishbot
Bayom Hashevi'i. Mikol-Melachto Asher Asah. Vayvarech Elohim Et-
Yom Hashevi'i. Vaykadesh Oto; Ki Vo Shavat Mikol-Melachto. Asher-
Bara Elohim La'asot.

The sixth day. And the heavens and the earth were finished, and all
the host of them. And with the seventh day God finished His work
which He had made; and He rested on the seventh day from all His
work which He had made. And God blessed the seventh day, and
sanctified it; because that in it He rested from all His work which
God in creating had made. (Genesis 2:1-3)

Lift wine glass and say:

Savri Maranan!   סַבְרִי מָרָנָן:

Gentlemen, with your attention!

And those present answer:

Le'chayim!   לְחַיִּים:

To life!

Baruch Attah Adonai Eloheinu   בָּרוּךְ אַתָּה יְהֹוָה אֱלֹהֵינוּ

Melech Ha'olam Borei Pri   מֶלֶךְ הָעוֹלָם. בּוֹרֵא פְּרִי

Hagefen.   הַגָּפֶן:

Blessed are You, Hashem our God, King of the universe, Who
creates the fruit of the vine.

Wait until after the next prayer before drinking.

Baruch Attah Adonai Eloheinu	בָּרוּךְ אַתָּה יְהֹוָה אֱלֹהֵינוּ
Melech Ha'olam Asher	מֶלֶךְ הָעוֹלָם. אֲשֶׁר
Kideshanu Bemitzvotav.	קִדְּשָׁנוּ בְּמִצְוֹתָיו.
Veratzah Vanu. Veshabbat	וְרָצָה בָנוּ. וְשַׁבַּת
Kodsho Be'ahavah Uveratzon	קָדְשׁוֹ בְּאַהֲבָה וּבְרָצוֹן
Hinchilanu. Zikaron Lema'aseh	הִנְחִילָנוּ. זִכָּרוֹן לְמַעֲשֵׂה
Vereshit. Techillah Lemikra'ei	בְרֵאשִׁית. תְּחִלָּה לְמִקְרָאֵי
Kodesh Zecher Litzi'at	קֹדֶשׁ זֵכֶר לִיצִיאַת
Mitzrayim. Veshabbat	מִצְרָיִם. וְשַׁבַּת
Kodshecha. Be'ahavah	קָדְשְׁךָ. בְּאַהֲבָה
Uveratzon Hinchaltanu. Baruch	וּבְרָצוֹן הִנְחַלְתָּנוּ. בָּרוּךְ
Attah Adonai Mekadesh	אַתָּה יְהֹוָה מְקַדֵּשׁ
Hashabbat.	הַשַּׁבָּת:

Blessed are You, Hashem our God, King of the universe, Who has sanctified us with His commandments and shown us Your favor. With love and favor You have given us Your holy Shabbat, a memorial of Your work of creation. The beginning of the holy convocations, recalling our going out from Mitzrayim. And with loving favor You have given Your holy Shabbat to us. Blessed are You, Hashem, Who sanctifies the Shabbat.

Sit and drink.

Blessing of the Children

The boys should be kissed by their parents. And it is good that the Father puts his hands on their heads and blesses them.

Blessing for son(s):

Yesimcha Elohim. Ke'efrayim	יְשִׂמְךָ אֱלֹהִים כְּאֶפְרַיִם
Vechimnasheh;. Yevarechecha	וְכִמְנַשֶּׁה: יְבָרֶכְךָ
Adonai Veyishmerecha. Ya'er	יְהוָה וְיִשְׁמְרֶךָ: יָאֵר
Adonai Panav Eleicha	יְהוָה ׀ פָּנָיו אֵלֶיךָ
Vichuneka. Yissa Adonai Panav	וִיחֻנֶּךָּ: יִשָּׂא יְהוָה ׀ פָּנָיו
Eleicha. Veyasem Lecha Shalom.	אֵלֶיךָ וְיָשֵׂם לְךָ שָׁלוֹם:

May God make you as Ephraim and Manasseh. Hashem bless You and keep You. Hashem make His countenance shine upon you, and be gracious to You. Hashem lift up His countenance towards You and give You peace.

Blessing for daughter(s):

Yesimech Elohim Kesarah.	יְשִׂמֵךְ אֱלֹהִים כְּשָׂרָה.
Rivkah. Rachel Vele'ah Asher	רִבְקָה. רָחֵל וְלֵאָה אֲשֶׁר
Banu Et-Beit Yisra'el.	בָּנוּ אֶת בֵּית יִשְׂרָאֵל:
Yevarechecha Adonai	יְבָרֶכְךָ יְהוָה
Veyishmerecha. Ya'er Adonai	וְיִשְׁמְרֶךָ: יָאֵר יְהוָה ׀
Panav Eleicha Vichuneka. Yissa	פָּנָיו אֵלֶיךָ וִיחֻנֶּךָ: יִשָּׂא
Adonai Panav Eleicha. Veyasem	יְהוָה ׀ פָּנָיו אֵלֶיךָ וְיָשֵׂם
Lecha Shalom.	לְךָ שָׁלוֹם:

May God make you as Sarah, Rebekah, Rachel, and Leah, who built the House of Yisrael. Hashem bless You and keep You. Hashem make His countenance shine upon you, and be gracious to You. Hashem lift up His countenance towards You and give You peace.

Shabbat Eve Meal

Netilat Yadayim / Washing of Hands

One should first pour water on his right hand and then his left. The water must be poured three times on each hand up to the wrist. Dipping the hands into a vessel filled with water constitutes valid washing for prayers. He who is awake all night should wash his hands without saying the blessing; and the same law applies to a case where one washed his hands before dawn had arisen. If one has no water, he may clean his hands with gravel or earth, and say the blessing: "Al Netilat Yadayim" He who sleeps during the daytime should wash his hands without saying the blessing. The minimum amount of water is a revi'it (approx. 3oz), you should add more water though, as Rav Chisda said "I washed a full hand of water and I was given a full hand of good." It is customary to wash out one's mouth as well. (SA, OC 4,158:10) Some have the practice to wait to make the blessing "Al Netilat Yadayim" until coming to the assembly, and arrange them with the rest of the blessings. The children of Sephardim do not do so. (SA, OC 6:2) Bless before washing, because every mitzvah you should bless before you do the mitzvah. But the custom is to bless after washing, because sometimes your hands aren't clean, so you bless after you clean your hands and before you do the second washing. (SA, OC 158:11) Only wash your hands with a vessel. All vessels are kosher for this, even galalim vessels (stone vessels, earthenware vessels, etc.) The vessel must be able to hold a revi'it of liquid. (SA, OC 158:11, 159:1)

Baruch Attah Adonai Eloheinu	בָּרוּךְ אַתָּה יְהֹוָה אֱלֹהֵינוּ
Melech Ha'olam Asher	מֶלֶךְ הָעוֹלָם. אֲשֶׁר
Kideshanu Bemitzvotav	קִדְּשָׁנוּ בְּמִצְוֹתָיו
Vetzivanu Al Netilat Yadayim.	וְצִוָּנוּ עַל נְטִילַת יָדָיִם:

Blessed are You, Hashem our God, King of the universe, Who has sanctified us with His commandments, and commanded us concerning the washing of hands.

Some authorities hold that one does not need to careful of pausing between Netilat and Hamotzi, and there are those who say that one needs to be careful. It is good to be careful. (Rema': The amount of time equivalent to walking 22 cubits [33 ft.] is considered a pause [Tosefot Perek Elu Ne'emarim]). (SA, OC 166) (REMA: It is a meritorious act to place salt on the table before breaking the bread.)

He will hold two loaves of bread in his two hands, and the giver will bless. And it is customary to say these verses before the blessing:

עֵינֵי־כֹל אֵלֶיךָ יְשַׂבֵּרוּ וְאַתָּה נוֹתֵן־לָהֶם אֶת־אָכְלָם בְּעִתּוֹ: פּוֹתֵחַ אֶת־יָדֶךָ וּמַשְׂבִּיעַ לְכָל־חַי רָצוֹן:

Einei-Chol Eleicha Yesaberu; Ve'attah Noten-Lahem Et-'Ochlam Be'ito. Potei'ach Et-Yadecha; Umasbia Lechol-Chai Ratzon.

The eyes of all wait for You, And You give them their food in due season. You open Your hand, And satisfy every living thing with favor. (Ps. 145:15-16)

Baruch Attah Adonai Eloheinu

Melech Ha'olam Hamotzi

Lechem Min Ha'Aretz.

בָּרוּךְ אַתָּה יְהֹוָה אֱלֹהֵינוּ מֶלֶךְ
הָעוֹלָם. הַמּוֹצִיא לֶחֶם מִן
הָאָרֶץ:

Blessed are You, Hashem our God, King of the universe Who brings forth bread from the earth.

Take a slice of bread and dip it in salt.

Before the meal some say:

לְשֵׁם יְחוּד קוּדְשָׁא בְּרִיךְ הוּא וּשְׁכִינְתֵּיהּ. בִּדְחִילוּ וּרְחִימוּ. וּרְחִימוּ וּדְחִילוּ.
לְיַחֲדָא שֵׁם יוֹ"ד קֵ"י בְּוָא"ו קֵ"י בְּיִחוּדָא שְׁלִים (יהוה) בְּשֵׁם כָּל יִשְׂרָאֵל.
הֲרֵינִי מוּכָן לְקַיֵּים מִצְוַת סְעוּדָה רִאשׁוֹנָה שֶׁל שַׁבָּת לְתַקֵּן אֶת שׁוֹרְשָׁהּ
בְּמָקוֹם עֶלְיוֹן וְהִיא כְּנֶגֶד יִצְחָק אַבָּא קַדִּישָׁא וּבִזְכוּתוֹ נָצוּל מֵחֶבְלוֹ שֶׁל
מָשִׁיחַ וִיקֻיַּים בָּנוּ מִקְרָא שֶׁכָּתוּב וְהִרְכַּבְתִּיךָ עַל־בָּמֳתֵי אָרֶץ. וִיהִי נֹעַם אֲדֹנָי
אֱלֹהֵינוּ עָלֵינוּ וּמַעֲשֵׂה יָדֵינוּ כּוֹנְנָה עָלֵינוּ וּמַעֲשֵׂה יָדֵינוּ כּוֹנְנֵהוּ:

The wine over which the blessing was recited exempts from blessing wine drunk during the meal. Food which are generally partaken of during the meal, such as, meat, fish, eggs, vegetables, cheese, or pickled or salted foods, require no blessing either before partaking of it or after. But if the food is not served in an ordinary course of a meal, such as all kinds of fruit, require a blessing before partaking of it but not afterwards, if they are not eaten together with bread.

Some read Zohar Parashat Yitro (2:88a:3-2:88b:1):

זכור את יום השבת לקדשו. רבי יצחק אמר. כתיב ויברך אלהים את יום
השביעי. וכתיב במן ששת ימים תלקטהו וביום השביעי שבת לא יהיה בו.
כיון דלא משתכח ביה מזוני. מה ברכתא אשתכח ביה. אלא הכי תאנא.
כל ברכאן דלעילא ותתא. ביומא שביעאה תלין. ותאנא. אמאי לא אשתכח

מנא ביומא שביעאה. משום דההוא יומא. מתברכאן מניה כל שתא יומין
עלאין. וכל חד וחד יהיב מזוניה לתתא. כל חד ביומוי. מההיא ברכה
דמתברכאן ביומא שביעאה. ובגיני כך. מאן דאיהו בדרגא דמהימנותא.
בעי לסדרא פתורא. ולאתקנא סעודתא בליליא דשבתא. בגין דיתברך
פתוריה. כל אינון שיתא יומין. דהא בההוא זמנא. אזדמן ברכה. לאתברכא
כל שיתא יומין דשבתא. וברכתא לא אשתכח בפתורא ריקניא. ועל כך.
בעי לסדרא פתוריה בליליא דשבתא. בנהמי ובמזוני. רבי יצחק אמר.
אפילו ביומא דשבתא נמי. רבי יהודה אמר. בעי לאתענגא בהאי יומא.
ולמיכל תלת סעודתי בשבתא. בגין דישתכח שבעא וענוגא בהאי יומא
בעלמא. רבי אבא אמר. לאזדמנא ברכתא באנון יומין דלעלא. דמתברכאן
מהאי יומא. והאי יומא. מליא רישיה דזעיר אנפין. מטלא דנחית מעתיקא
קדישא סתימא דכלא. ואטיל לחקלא דתפוחין קדישין. תלת זמני. מכד
עייל שבתא. בגין דיתברכון כלהו כחדא. ועל דא בעי בר נש. לאתענגא
תלת זמנין אלין. דהא בהא תליא מהימנותא דלעלא. בעתיקא קדישא.
ובזעיר אנפין. ובחקלא דתפוחין. ובעי בר נש לאתענגא בהו. ולמחדי בהו.
ומאן דגרע סעודתא מניהו. אחזי פגימותא לעלא ועונשיה דההוא בר נש
סגי. בגיני כך. בעי לסדרא פתוריה. תלת זמני. מכד עייל שבתא. ולא
ישתכח פתוריה ריקניא. ותשרי ברכתא עליה. כל שאר יומי דשבתא.
ובהאי מלה. אחזי. ותלי מהימנותא לעילא. רבי שמעון אמר. האי מאן
דאשלים תלת סעודתי בשבתא. קלא נפיק ומכרזא עליה. אז תתענג על
יהוה. דא סעודתא חדא. לקבל עתיקא קדישא דכל קדישין. והרכבתיך
על־במתי ארץ. דא סעודתא תנינא. לקבל חקלא דתפוחין קדישין.
והאכלתיך נחלת יעקב אביך. דא הוא שלימו דאשתלים בזעיר אנפין. רבי
שמעון אמר. האי מאן דאשלים תלת סעודתי בשבתא. קלא נפיק ומכרזא
עליה. אז תתענג על יהוה. דא סעודתא חדא. לקבל עתיקא קדישא דכל
קדישין. והרכבתיך על במתי ארץ. דא סעודתא תנינא. לקבל חקלא
דתפוחין קדישין. והאכלתיך נחלת יעקב אביך. דא הוא שלימו דאשתלים
בזעיר אנפין. רבי אבא. (נ״א רב המנונא סבא) כד הוה יתיב בסעודתא
דשבתא. הוה חדי. בכל חד וחד. והוה אמר. דא היא סעודתא קדישא.
דעתיקא קדישא סתימא דכלא. בסעודתא אחרא הוה אמר. דא היא
סעודתא דקודשא בריך הוא. וכן בכלהו סעודתי. והוה חדי בכל חד וחד.

כד הוה אשלים סעודתי. הוה אמר אשלימו סעודתי דמהימנותא. רבי
שמעון. כד הוה אתי לסעודתא. הוה אמר הכי. אתקינו סעודתא
דמהימנותא עלאה. אתקינו סעודתא דמלכא. והוה יתיב וחדי. כד אשלים
סעודתא תליתאה. הוו מכרזי עליה. אז תתענג על יהוה והרכבתיך על
במתי ארץ והאכלתיך נחלת יעקב אביך. אמר רבי אלעזר לאבוי. אלין
סעודתי היך מתתקנן. אמר ליה. ליליא דשבתא. כתיב. והרכבתיך על־במתי
ארץ. ביה בליליא. מתברכא מטרוניתא. וכלהו חקל תפוחין. ומתברכא
פתוריה דבר נש. ונשמתא אתוספת ביה. וההיא ליליא. חדוה דמטרוניתא
הוי. ובעי בר נש למחדי בחדותא. ולמיכל סעודתא דמטרוניתא. ברוך יהוה
לעולם אמן ואמן:

Some study Chapters 1-8 in Tractate Shabbat from the Mishnah.

Pizmonim / Songs for Shabbat

Ki Eshmerah Shabbat
Rabbi Avraham Ibn Ezra

Ki Eshmerah Shabbat El	כִּי אֶשְׁמְרָה שַׁבָּת אֵל
Yishmereni. Ot Hi Le'olemei Ad	יִשְׁמְרֵנִי. אוֹת הִיא לְעוֹלְמֵי עַד
Beino Uveini.	בֵּינוֹ וּבֵינִי:

When Shabbat I duly keep, God will also guard me; For an eternal covenant and "sign it is between Him and me."

Asur Metzo Chefetz. Asot	אָסוּר מְצֹא חֵפֶץ. עֲשׂוֹת
Derachim. Gam Milledaber Bo	דְּרָכִים. גַּם מִלְּדַבֵּר בּוֹ
Divrei Tzerachim. Divrei	דִּבְרֵי צְרָכִים. דִּבְרֵי
Sechorah O Divrei Melachim.	סְחוֹרָה אוֹ דִּבְרֵי מְלָכִים.
Ehgeh Betorat El	אֶהְגֶּה בְּתוֹרַת אֵל
Utechakkemeni.	וּתְחַכְּמֵנִי:

On it, it is prohibited to transact business, to travel, to discuss political, commercial, or private affairs. But I must meditate in the divine Torah, that its instructions may improve my knowledge.
(Repeat Chorus)

Bo Emtze'ah Tamid Noach	בּוֹ אֶמְצְאָה תָּמִיד נוֹחַ
Lenafshi. Hineh Ledor Rishon	לְנַפְשִׁי. הִנֵּה לְדֹר רִאשׁוֹן
Natan Kedoshi. Mofet Betet	נָתַן קְדוֹשִׁי. מוֹפֵת בְּתֵת
Lechem Mishneh Bashishi.	לֶחֶם מִשְׁנֶה בַּשִּׁשִׁי.
Kachah Bechol Shishi Yachpil	כָּכָה בְּכָל־שִׁשִׁי יַכְפִּיל
Mezoni.	מְזוֹנִי:

On that day I find rest for my soul. Behold, to a former generation the Most Holy gave a wondrous sign, by granting them a double portion on every sixth day. May He also on that day forever double my portion. (Repeat Chorus)

Rasham Bedat Ha'el Chok El	רָשַׁם בְּדַת הָאֵל חֹק אֵל
Seganav. Bo La'aroch Lechem	סְגָנָיו. בּוֹ לַעֲרוֹךְ לֶחֶם
Panim Lefanav. Al Ken	פָּנִים לְפָנָיו. עַל כֵּן
Lehit'anot Bo Al Pi Nevonav.	לְהִתְעַנּוֹת בּוֹ עַל פִּי נְבוֹנָיו.
Asur Levad Miyom Kippur	אָסוּר לְבַד מִיּוֹם כִּפּוּר
Avoni.	עֲוֹנִי:

It was commanded to His chiefs and priesthood to arrange on it, according to law, the showbread before Him; but to fast on that day has been prohibited by the sages, except if it is Yom Kippur for our sins. (Repeat Chorus)

Hayom Mechubbad Hu Yom	הַיּוֹם מְכֻבָּד הוּא יוֹם
Ta'anugim. Lechem Veyayin Tov	תַּעֲנוּגִים. לֶחֶם וְיַיִן טוֹב
Basar Vedagim. Hashemechim	בָּשָׂר וְדָגִים. הַשְּׂמֵחִים
Bo Hem Simchah Massigim, Ki	בּוֹ הֵם שִׂמְחָה מַשִּׂיגִים. כִּי
Yom Semachot Hu	יוֹם שְׂמָחוֹת הוּא
Utesamecheini.	וּתְשַׂמְּחֵנִי:

This glorious day is one of delights, which we also honor with bread, wine, good meat and fish. The afflicted must on that day abstain from mourning, for it is a day of joy, on which God caused me to rejoice. (Repeat Chorus)

Mechel Melachah Bo Sofo	מֶחֶל מְלָאכָה בּוֹ סוֹפוֹ
Lehachrit. Al Ken Achabes Bo	לְהַכְרִית. עַל־כֵּן אֲכַבֵּס בּוֹ
Libi Bevorit. Etpallelah El El	לִבִּי בְּבוֹרִית. אֶתְפַּלְלָה אֶל־אֵל
Arvit Veshachrit. Musaf Vegam	עַרְבִית וְשַׁחֲרִית. מוּסָף וְגַם
Minchah Hu Ya'aneni.	מִנְחָה הוּא יַעֲנֵנִי:

He who works on that day will assuredly be cut off. Therefore I will purify my heart of every unseemly thought. I will pray to the Almighty evening and morning, address to Him the additional and afternoon prayers, that He may answer me. (Repeat Chorus)

Yom Zeh Mechubad

Yom Zeh Mechubbad Mikol Yamim. Ki Vo Shavat Tzur Olamim.

יוֹם זֶה מְכֻבָּד מִכָּל יָמִים. כִּי בוֹ שָׁבַת צוּר עוֹלָמִים.

This day is the most precious of all days, Because on it the Eternal ceased from work.

Sheshet Yamim Ta'aseh Melachtecha. Veyom Hashevi'i Leloheicha. Shabbat Lo Ta'aseh Vo Melachah. Ki Chol Asah Sheshet Yamim.

שֵׁשֶׁת יָמִים תַּעֲשֶׂה מְלַאכְתֶּךָ. וְיוֹם הַשְּׁבִיעִי לֵאלֹהֶיךָ. שַׁבָּת לֹא תַעֲשֶׂה בוֹ מְלָאכָה. כִּי כֹל עָשָׂה שֵׁשֶׁת יָמִים.

Six days you are to perform all your work, But the seventh day is your God's Shabbat; On it you must not do any labor, For in six days He accomplished all things. (Repeat Chorus)

Rishon Hu Lemikra'ei Kodesh. Yom Shabbaton Yom Shabbat Kodesh. Al Ken Kol Ish Beyeino Yekadesh. Al Shetei Lechem Yivtze'u Temimim.

רִאשׁוֹן הוּא לְמִקְרָאֵי קֹדֶשׁ. יוֹם שַׁבָּתוֹן יוֹם שַׁבָּת קֹדֶשׁ. עַל כֵּן כָּל אִישׁ בְּיֵינוֹ יְקַדֵּשׁ. עַל שְׁתֵּי לֶחֶם יִבְצְעוּ תְמִימִים.

It is supreme among the holy feasts, The day of rest, the holy Shabbat day; Hence, let each recite Kiddush over wine, Let the faithful say grace over the twin loaves. (Repeat Chorus)

Echol Mashmanim Sheteh	אֱכֹל מַשְׁמַנִּים שְׁתֵה
Mamtakkim. Ki El Yiten Lechol	מַמְתַּקִים. כִּי אֵל יִתֵּן לְכָל
Bo Devekim. Beeged Lilbosh	בּוֹ דְבֵקִים. בֶּגֶד לִלְבּוֹשׁ
Lechem Chukkim. Basar	לֶחֶם חֻקִּים. בָּשָׂר
Vedagim Vechol Mat'ammim.	וְדָגִים וְכָל מַטְעַמִּים.

Come, enjoy the delicacies and drink the sweet, For God provides for all who cling to Him. Clothes to wear and portions of nourishment, meat and fish and all luxurious foods. (Repeat Chorus)

Lo Techsar Kol Bo Ve'achalta	לֹא תֶחְסַר כֹּל בּוֹ וְאָכַלְתָּ
Vesava'eta Uverachta Et Adonai	וְשָׂבַעְתָּ וּבֵרַכְתָּ אֵת יהוה
Eloheicha Asher Ahavta. Ki	אֱלֹהֶיךָ אֲשֶׁר אָהַבְתָּ. כִּי
Verachcha Mikol Ha'ammim.	בֵרַכְךָ מִכָּל הָעַמִּים.

You will not be in want of anything; When you have eaten and are satisfied, You will bless Hashem your God Whom you love, For He has blessed you above all people. (Repeat Chorus)

Hashamayim Mesaperim	הַשָּׁמַיִם מְסַפְּרִים
Kevodo. Vegam Ha'aretz	כְּבוֹדוֹ. וְגַם הָאָרֶץ
Male'ah Chasdo. Re'u Ki Chol	מָלְאָה חַסְדוֹ. רְאוּ כִּי כָל
Eleh Asetah Yado. Ki Hu Hatzur	אֵלֶּה עָשְׂתָה יָדוֹ. כִּי הוּא הַצּוּר
Po'olo Tamim.	פָּעֳלוֹ תָמִים.

The heavens declare His glory, The earth is full of His kindness; Behold, His hand has made all these things. He is God, Whose work is perfect. (Repeat Chorus)

Dror Yikra
Dunash ben Labrat

Deror Yikra Leven Im Bat.	דְּרוֹר יִקְרָא לְבֵן עִם בַּת.
Veyintzarechem Kemo Vavat.	וְיִנְצָרְכֶם כְּמוֹ בָבַת.
Ne'im Shimchem Velo Yushbat.	נְעִים שִׁמְכֶם וְלֹא יֻשְׁבַּת.
Shevu Nuchu Beyom Shabbat:	שְׁבוּ נוּחוּ בְּיוֹם שַׁבָּת:

He grants release to son and daughter: As His eye's apple safe, they play. Their innocence will never pass, Then take your ease this Shabbat day.

Derosh Navi Ve'ulammi. Ve'ot	דְּרוֹשׁ נָוִי וְאוּלָמִי. וְאוֹת
Yesha Aseh Immi. Neta Sorek	יֶשַׁע עֲשֵׂה עִמִּי. נְטַע שׁוֹרֵק
Betoch Karmi. She'eh Shav'at	בְּתוֹךְ כַּרְמִי. שְׁעֵה שַׁוְעַת
Benei Ammi:	בְּנֵי עַמִּי:

Oh seek in love my martyred shrine. And to my eyes, salvation show. In my vineyard plant her vine - And hear my people's cry of woe.

Deroch Purah Betoch Batzerah.	דְּרוֹךְ פּוּרָה בְּתוֹךְ בָּצְרָה. וְגַם
Vegam Edom Asher Gaverah.	אֱדוֹם אֲשֶׁר גָּבְרָה. נְתוֹץ צָרַי
Netotz Tzarai Be'af Ve'evrah.	בְּאַף וְעֶבְרָה. שְׁמַע קוֹלִי בְּיוֹם
Shema Koli Beyom Ekra:	אֶקְרָא:

On Batzrah's sin tread deep Your press, That Your fair world be pure once more. Against Bavel's full-grown wickedness, this day, Your safeguard I implore.

Elohim Ten Bamidbar Har.	אֱלֹהִים תֵּן בַּמִּדְבָּר הַר.
Hadas Shittah Berosh Tidhar.	הֲדַס שִׁטָּה בְּרוֹשׁ תִּדְהָר.
Velammazhir Velanizhar.	וְלַמַּזְהִיר וְלַנִּזְהָר.
Shelomim Ten Kemei Nahar:	שְׁלוֹמִים תֵּן כְּמֵי נָהָר:

On desert hill, Your garden rear. Make bloom the myrtle, fir and pine. Teachers and taught - Your saplings dear - Nurture with streams of peace divine.

Hadoch Kamai Chai El Kana.	הֲדוֹךְ קָמַי חַי אֵל קַנָּא.
Bemog Levav Uvimginah.	בְּמוֹג לֵבָב וּבְמִגְנָּה.
Venarchiv Peh Unemalle'enah.	וְנַרְחִיב פֶּה וּנְמַלְאֶנָּה.
Leshonenu Lecha Rinah:	לְשׁוֹנֵנוּ לְךָ רִנָּה:

Our enemies rage in wrath and pride: Oh turn their hearts, contrite, to You. Then will our mouths, in song, be wide. Our tongues, with them in unity.

De'eh Chochmah Lenafshecha.	דְּעֵה חָכְמָה לְנַפְשֶׁךָ.
Vehi Cheter Leroshecha. Netzor	וְהִיא כֶתֶר לְרֹאשֶׁךָ. נְצוֹר
Mitzvat Eloheicha. Shemor	מִצְוַת אֱלֹהֶיךָ. שְׁמוֹר
Shabbat Kedoshecha:	שַׁבַּת קָדְשֶׁךָ:

By wisdom crowned, in splendrous state. Let quest of wisdom be your goal. As each Shabbat you consecrate. May Shabbat consecrate your soul.

Yom Shabbaton
Rabbi Yehudah HaLevi

Yom Shabbaton Ein Lishkoach.	יוֹם שַׁבָּתוֹן אֵין לִשְׁכּוֹחַ.
Zichro Kereiach Hanichoach.	זִכְרוֹ כְּרֵיחַ הַנִּיחֹחַ.
Yonah Matze'ah Vo Manoach.	יוֹנָה מָצְאָה בוֹ מָנוֹחַ.
Vesham Yanuchu Yegi'ei	וְשָׁם יָנוּחוּ יְגִיעֵי
Choach:	כֹחַ:

Fragrant your memories, Oh sweet Shabbat day. Fragrant as incense, never to fade away; The wandering dove does find her nest. In you, the toilers cease their weary quest.

Hayom Nichbad Livnei	הַיּוֹם נִכְבָּד לִבְנֵי
Emunim. Zehirim Leshomro	אֱמוּנִים. זְהִירִים לְשָׁמְרוֹ
Avot Uvanim. Chakuk Bishnei	אָבוֹת וּבָנִים. חָקוּק בִּשְׁנֵי
Luchot Avanim. Merov Onim	לֻחוֹת אֲבָנִים. מֵרוֹב אוֹנִים
Ve'ammitz Koach:	וְאַמִּיץ כֹּחַ:

Deep in your children's hearts, enshrined lies your fame. Masters and sons faithful, linked, your love proclaim. Linked Your love proclaim. Strong, in never-weakening might, He engraved your name; Engraved on twin tablets, still stands His sure behest.

Yonah Matze'ah Vo Manoach.	יוֹנָה מָצְאָה בוֹ מָנוֹחַ.
Vesham Yanuchu Yegi'ei	וְשָׁם יָנוּחוּ יְגִיעֵי
Choach:	כֹחַ:

The wandering dove does find her nest. In you, the toilers cease their weary quest.

Uva'u Chulam Bivrit Yachad.	וּבָאוּ כֻלָּם בִּבְרִית יַחַד.
Na'aseh Venishma Ameru	נַעֲשֶׂה וְנִשְׁמַע אָמְרוּ
Ke'echad. Ufatechu Ve'anu	כְּאֶחָד. וּפָתְחוּ וְעָנוּ
Adonai Echad. Baruch Hanotein	יְהֹוָה אֶחָד. בָּרוּךְ הַנּוֹתֵן
Laya'ef Koach:	לַיָּעֵף כֹּחַ:

Then to His covenant, abiding in stone, 'We will swear loyalty' answered they all as one. Answered they all as one. 'He is our Lord' they cried, 'eternal is His Throne,' Peace to all care-worn He grants, His name be blessed.

Yonah Matze'ah Vo Manoach.	.יוֹנָה מָצְאָה בוֹ מָנוֹחַ
Vesham Yanuchu Yegi'ei	וְשָׁם יָנוּחוּ יְגִיעֵי
Choach:	כֹּחַ:

The wandering dove does find her nest. In you, the toilers cease their weary quest.

Diber Bekodsho Behar Hamor.	.דִּבֶּר בְּקָדְשׁוֹ בְּהַר הַמּוֹר
Yom Hashevi'i Zachor	יוֹם הַשְּׁבִיעִי זָכוֹר
Veshamor. Vechol Pikudav	וְשָׁמוֹר. וְכָל־פִּקוּדָיו
Yachad Ligmor. Chazek	יַחַד לִגְמוֹר. חַזֵּק
Motnayim Ve'ammetz Koach:	מָתְנַיִם וְאַמֵּץ כֹּחַ:

Once on Hamor's peak He commanded His people to heed; 'Keep my Shabbats, sanctified in word and deed'. Sanctified in word and deed. Sacred her precepts all, for you, for your seed. Strengthen the feeble, comfort my oppressed.'

Yonah Matze'ah Vo Manoach.	.יוֹנָה מָצְאָה בוֹ מָנוֹחַ
Vesham Yanuchu Yegi'ei	וְשָׁם יָנוּחוּ יְגִיעֵי
Choach:	כֹּחַ:

The wandering dove does find her nest. In you, the toilers cease their weary quest.

Ha'am Asher Na Katzon Ta'ah.	.הָעָם אֲשֶׁר נָע כַּצֹּאן תָּעָה
Yizkor Lefokdo Berit Ushevu'ah.	.יִזְכּוֹר לְפָקְדוֹ בְּרִית וּשְׁבוּעָה
Leval Ya'avar Bam Mikreh	לְבַל יַעֲבָר־בָּם מִקְרֶה
Ra'ah. Ka'asher Nishba'ta Al	רָעָה. כַּאֲשֶׁר נִשְׁבַּעְתָּ עַל
Mei Noach:	מֵי נֹחַ:

We are Your chosen flock, remember us still. Long have we wandered, Oh soon Your oath fulfill. Oh soon Your oath fulfill. You who calmed the flood, preserve us from ill, Safe in green pastures, safe by the brooks to rest.

Yonah Matze'ah Vo Manoach,

יוֹנָה מָצְאָה בוֹ מָנוֹחַ.

Vesham Yanuchu Yegi'ei

וְשָׁם יָנוּחוּ יְגִיעֵי

Choach:

כֹּחַ:

The wandering dove does find her nest. In you, the toilers cease their weary quest.

Mizmor Shir (Psalms 92)

Mizmor Shir Leyom Hashabbat.

מִזְמוֹר שִׁיר לְיוֹם הַשַּׁבָּת.

A Psalm, a Song. For the Shabbat day.

Tov Lehodot L'Adonai Ulzameir

טוֹב לְהֹדוֹת לַיהוָה וּלְזַמֵּר

Leshimka Elyon.

לְשִׁמְךָ עֶלְיוֹן.

It is good to praise Hashem, to sing praises to Your name, Most High,

Lehagid Baboker Chasdecha

לְהַגִּיד בַּבֹּקֶר חַסְדֶּךָ

Ve'emunatecha Baleilot.

וֶאֱמוּנָתְךָ בַּלֵּילוֹת.

To declare Your lovingkindness in the morning, And Your faithfulness in the night seasons,

Alei-Asor Va'alei-Navel Alei

עֲלֵי-עָשׂוֹר וַעֲלֵי-נָבֶל עֲלֵי

Higayon Bechinor.

הִגָּיוֹן בְּכִנּוֹר.

With an instrument of ten strings, and with the psaltery; With a solemn sound on the harp.

Ki Simachtani Adonai   כִּי שִׂמַּחְתַּנִי יְהוָה

Befo'olecha Bema'asei Yadeicha   בְּפָעֳלֶךָ בְּמַעֲשֵׂי יָדֶיךָ

Aranen.   אֲרַנֵּן.

For You, Hashem, has made me glad through Your work; I will rejoice in the works of Your hands.

Mah-Gadelu Ma'aseicha Adonai   מַה-גָּדְלוּ מַעֲשֶׂיךָ יְהוָה

Me'od Ameku   מְאֹד עָמְקוּ

Machshevoteicha.   מַחְשְׁבֹתֶיךָ.

How great are Your works, Hashem. Your thoughts are very deep.

Ish-Ba'ar Lo Yeda Uchesil Lo-   אִישׁ-בַּעַר לֹא יֵדָע וּכְסִיל לֹא-

Yavin Et-Zot.   יָבִין אֶת-זֹאת.

A brutish man does not know, neither does a fool understand this.

Bifroach Resha'im Kemo Esev   בִּפְרֹחַ רְשָׁעִים כְּמוֹ עֵשֶׂב

Vayatzitzu Kol-Po'alei Aven.   וַיָּצִיצוּ כָּל-פֹּעֲלֵי אָוֶן.

Lehishomdam Adei-Ad.   לְהִשָּׁמְדָם עֲדֵי-עַד.

When the wicked spring up as the grass, And when all the workers of iniquity do flourish; It is that they may be destroyed forever.

Ve'attah Marom Le'olam   וְאַתָּה מָרוֹם לְעֹלָם

Adonai.   יְהוָה.

But You, Hashem, are on high forever.

Ki Hineh Oyeveicha Adonai Ki-   כִּי הִנֵּה אֹיְבֶיךָ יְהוָה כִּי-

Hineh Oyeveicha Yovedu   הִנֵּה אֹיְבֶיךָ יֹאבֵדוּ

Yitparedu Kol-Po'alei Aven.   יִתְפָּרְדוּ כָּל-פֹּעֲלֵי אָוֶן.

For, behold, Your enemies, Hashem, For, behold, Your enemies will perish: All the workers of iniquity will be scattered.

Vatarem Kir'eim Karni Baloti

Beshemen Ra'anan.

וַתָּרֶם כִּרְאֵים קַרְנִי בַּלֹּתִי
בְּשֶׁמֶן רַעֲנָן.

But my horn You exalted like the horn of the wild-ox; I am anointed with rich oil.

Vatabet Eini Beshurai Bakamim

Alai Mere'im Tishma'nah

Azenai.

וַתַּבֵּט עֵינִי בְּשׁוּרָי בַּקָּמִים
עָלַי מְרֵעִים תִּשְׁמַעְנָה
אָזְנָי.

My eye also has gazed on them that lie in wait for me, My ears have heard my desire of the evil-doers that rise up against me.

Tzaddik Kattamar Yifrach

Ke'erez Ballevanon Yisgeh.

צַדִּיק כַּתָּמָר יִפְרָח
כְּאֶרֶז בַּלְּבָנוֹן יִשְׂגֶּה.

The righteous will flourish like the palm-tree; He will grow like a cedar in Levanon.

Shetulim Beveit Adonai

Bechatzrot Eloheinu Yafrichu.

שְׁתוּלִים בְּבֵית יְהוָה
בְּחַצְרוֹת אֱלֹהֵינוּ יַפְרִיחוּ.

Planted in the House of Hashem, They will flourish in the courts of our God.

Od Yenuvun Beseivah

Deshenim Vera'ananim Yihyu.

עוֹד יְנוּבוּן בְּשֵׂיבָה
דְּשֵׁנִים וְרַעֲנַנִּים יִהְיוּ.

They will still bring out fruit in old age; They will be full of sap and richness;

Lehagid Ki-Yashar Adonai Tzuri

Velo-Avlatah Bo.

לְהַגִּיד כִּי-יָשָׁר יְהוָה צוּרִי
וְלֹא-עַוְלָתָה בּוֹ.

To declare that Hashem is upright, My Rock, in Whom there is no unrighteousness.

Mah Yedidut
Menahem ben Makhir of Ratisbon

Mah Yedidut Menuchatech. At

Shabbat Hamalkah. Bechein

Narutz Likratech. Bo'i Challah

Nesuchah. Levush Bigdei

Chamudot. Lehadlik Ner

Bivrachah. Vatechel Kol

Ha'avodot. Lo Ta'asu Melachah:

מַה יְּדִידוּת מְנוּחָתֵךְ. אַתְּ

שַׁבָּת הַמַּלְכָּה. בְּכֵן

נָרוּץ לִקְרָאתֵךְ. בּוֹאִי כַלָּה

נְסוּכָה. לְבוּשׁ בִּגְדֵי

חֲמוּדוֹת. לְהַדְלִיק נֵר

בִּבְרָכָה. וַתֵּכֶל כָּל־

הָעֲבוֹדוֹת. לֹא תַעֲשׂוּ מְלָאכָה:

How sweet your precious gift of rest Queen Shabbat, cherished far and wide. Let us speed in your quest, Haste, we'll greet our pure bride. Decked in splendid robes to meet her. To our homes, the lamp will be her sure guide. Labor over, we will greet her, Labor over, we will greet her. Cease your toil, at home in peace abide.

Lehit'aneg Beta'anugim.

Barburim Uselav Vedagim:

לְהִתְעַנֵּג בְּתַעֲנוּגִים

בַּרְבּוּרִים וּשְׂלָיו וְדָגִים:

Let's rejoice today with delicacies fairest. Set in choice array, with morsels rarest. Fat chicken, quails and fish. Each upon a royal dish.

Me'erev Mazminim. Kol Minei

Mat'ammim. Mibe'od Yom

Muchanim. Tarnegolim

Mefuttamim. Vela'aroch Bo

Kamah Minim. Shetot Yeinot

Mevussamim. Vetafnukei

Ma'adanim. Bechol Shalosh

Pe'amim:

מֵעֶרֶב מַזְמִינִים. כָּל־מִינֵי

מַטְעַמִּים. מִבְּעוֹד יוֹם

מוּכָנִים. תַּרְנְגוֹלִים

מְפֻטָּמִים. וְלַעֲרוֹךְ בּוֹ

כַּמָּה מִינִים. שְׁתוֹת יֵינוֹת

מְבֻשָּׂמִים. וְתַפְנוּקֵי

מַעֲדַנִּים. בְּכָל־שָׁלֹשׁ

פְּעָמִים:

Each Friday busy housewives all. Bake delicacies for the Shabbat fare. Before the evening shades fall; Plumpest fowls, skillful, they prepare; Crispy pie and sweetest pastry, Spiced cider to drink and wines rare. Morsels rich, candies tasty, Morsels rich, candies tasty. Thrice the poor our Shabbat feasts will share.

Lehit'aneg Beta'anugim.	לְהִתְעַנֵּג בְּתַעֲנוּגִים
Barburim Uselav Vedagim:	בַּרְבּוּרִים וּשְׂלָיו וְדָגִים:

Let's rejoice today with delicacies fairest. Set in choice array, with morsels rarest. Fat chicken, quails and fish. Each upon a royal dish.

Nachalat Ya'akov Yirash. Beli	נַחֲלַת יַעֲקֹב יִירָשׁ. בְּלִי
Metzarim Nachalah.	מְצָרִים נַחֲלָה.
Vichabeduhu Ashir Varash.	וִיכַבְּדוּהוּ עָשִׁיר וָרָשׁ.
Vetizku Lig'ullah. Yom Shabbat	וְתִזְכּוּ לִגְאֻלָּה. יוֹם שַׁבָּת
Im Tishmoru. Vihyitem Li	אִם תִּשְׁמֹרוּ. וִהְיִיתֶם לִי
Segullah. Sheshet Yamim	סְגֻלָּה. שֵׁשֶׁת יָמִים
Ta'avodu. Uvashevi'i Nagilah:	תַּעֲבוֹדוּ. וּבַשְּׁבִיעִי נָגִילָה:

Gain Yaakov's heritage divine, From sorrow set your spirit free. And redemption be yours; Rich or poor though you be. Keep your Shabbat God ordained. Amid His chosen people, He will surely give blessing. Six days' toil not disdained, Six days' toil not disdained. Take your Shabbat in joyous resting,

Lehit'aneg Beta'anugim.	לְהִתְעַנֵּג בְּתַעֲנוּגִים
Barburim Uselav Vedagim:	בַּרְבּוּרִים וּשְׂלָיו וְדָגִים:

Let's rejoice today with delicacies fairest. Set in choice array, with morsels rarest. Fat chicken, quails and fish. Each upon a royal dish.

Chafatzeicha Bo Asurim. Vegam	חֲפָצֶיךָ בּוֹ אֲסוּרִים. וְגַם
Lachashov Cheshbonot.	לַחֲשׁוֹב חֶשְׁבּוֹנוֹת.
Hirhurim Muttarim.	הִרְהוּרִים מֻתָּרִים.
Uleshaddech Habanot. Vetinok	וּלְשַׁדֵּךְ הַבָּנוֹת. וְתִינוֹק
Lelamedo Sefer.	לְלַמְּדוֹ סֵפֶר.
Lammenatzeach Binginot.	לַמְנַצֵּחַ בִּנְגִינוֹת.
Velahagot Be'imrei Shefer.	וְלַהֲגוֹת בְּאִמְרֵי שֶׁפֶר.
Bechol Pinot Umachanot:	בְּכָל־פִּנּוֹת וּמַחֲנוֹת:

From weekday needs you will refrain, Oh Merchant, pondering over your schemes; Soft thoughts are your gain, Daughter's bridal your dreams; Teach your son our ancient glory; (Yisrael's minstrel-king will chant him sweet themes) Yisrael's wanderings your story, Yisrael's wanderings your story. Until your boy with emulation gleams,

| Lehit'aneg Beta'anugim. | לְהִתְעַנֵּג בְּתַעֲנוּגִים |
| Barburim Uselav Vedagim: | בַּרְבּוּרִים וּשְׂלָיו וְדָגִים: |

Let's rejoice today with delicacies fairest. Set in choice array, with morsels rarest. Fat chicken, quails and fish. Each upon a royal dish.

Hiluchach Tehe Venachat. Oneg	הִלּוּכָךְ תְּהֵא בְנַחַת. עֹנֶג
Kera Lashabbat. Vehashenah	קְרָא לַשַּׁבָּת. וְהַשֵּׁנָה
Meshubachat. Kedat Nefesh	מְשֻׁבַּחַת. כְּדָת נֶפֶשׁ
Meshivat. Bechein Nafshi Lecha	מְשִׁיבַת. בְּכֵן נַפְשִׁי לְךָ
Aregah. Velanuach Bechibat.	עָרְגָה. וְלָנוּחַ בְּחִבַּת.
Kashoshanim Sugah. Bo	כַּשּׁוֹשַׁנִּים סוּגָה. בּוֹ
Yanuchu Ben Uvat:	יָנוּחוּ בֵּן וּבַת:

Tread softly, gain Shabbat's calm, Queen Shabbat, happiness her name; Yield to slumber's rare balm—So His Torah heals your frame

—For her rest my soul is pining, Sweet rest I seek, encircled with love's flame. Amid white lilies reclining; Amid white lilies reclining. Sons and daughters, Shabbat Shalom acclaim.

Lehit'aneg Beta'anugim.

לְהִתְעַנֵּג בְּתַעֲנוּגִים

Barburim Uselav Vedagim:

בַּרְבּוּרִים וּשְׂלָיו וְדָגִים:

Let's rejoice today with delicacies fairest. Set in choice array, with morsels rarest. Fat chicken, quails and fish. Each upon a royal dish.

Me'ein Olam Haba. Yom

מֵעֵין עוֹלָם הַבָּא. יוֹם

Shabbat Menuchah. Kol

שַׁבָּת מְנוּחָה. כָּל־

Hamit'anegim Bah. Yizku Lerov

הַמִּתְעַנְּגִים בָּהּ. יִזְכּוּ לְרוֹב

Simchah. Mechevlei Mashiach.

שִׂמְחָה. מֵחֶבְלֵי מָשִׁיחַ.

Yutzalu Lirvachah. Pedutenu

יֻצָּלוּ לִרְוָחָה. פְּדוּתֵנוּ

Tatzmiach. Venas Yagon

תַצְמִיחַ. וְנָס יָגוֹן

Va'anachah: Lehit'aneg

וַאֲנָחָה: לְהִתְעַנֵּג

Beta'anugim. Barburim Uselav

בְּתַעֲנוּגִים. בַּרְבּוּרִים וּשְׂלָיו

Vedagim:

וְדָגִים:

True vision of Paradise to be. Thrice welcome, restful Shabbat day. All whose hearts beat for you, Time unending will play. Earth's hard travail never heeding, Save us before we perish in the dense fray, Our redemption soon speeding, Our redemption soon speeding. Then will tears and sighings fade away.

Lehit'aneg Beta'anugim.

לְהִתְעַנֵּג בְּתַעֲנוּגִים

Barburim Uselav Vedagim:

בַּרְבּוּרִים וּשְׂלָיו וְדָגִים:

Let's rejoice today with delicacies fairest. Set in choice array, with morsels rarest. Fat chicken, quails and fish. Each upon a royal dish.

Baruch El Elyon
Rabbi Baruch bar Shmuel

Baruch El Elyon. Asher Natan	בָּרוּךְ אֵל עֶלְיוֹן. אֲשֶׁר נָתַן
Menuchah. Lenafshenu Fidyon.	מְנוּחָה. לְנַפְשֵׁנוּ פִדְיוֹן.
Mishet Va'anachah. Vehu	מִשֵּׁאת וַאֲנָחָה. וְהוּא
Yidrosh Letziyon. Ir	יִדְרוֹשׁ לְצִיּוֹן. עִיר
Haniddachah. Ad Anah	הַנִּדָּחָה. עַד אָנָה
Tugeyon. Nefesh Ne'enachah.	תּוּגְיוֹן. נֶפֶשׁ נֶאֱנָחָה.

God on high be blessed. Who gives our soul repose. When anguish spoils our rest, He heals all of our woes. To Tziyon sore distressed, His tender mercy shows. How long have you oppressed? He rebukes her raging foes.

Hashomer Shabbat Haben Im	הַשּׁוֹמֵר שַׁבָּת הַבֵּן עִם
Habat. La'el Yeratzu Keminchah	הַבַּת. לָאֵל יֵרָצוּ כְּמִנְחָה
Al Machavat:	עַל מַחֲבַת:

Keep the day divine. Sons and daughters mine, For He will then accept you, As gifts before His shrine.

Rochev Ba'aravot. Melech	רוֹכֵב בָּעֲרָבוֹת. מֶלֶךְ
Olamim. Et Ammo Lishbot. Izen	עוֹלָמִים. אֶת עַמּוֹ לִשְׁבֹּת. אִזֵּן
Bane'imim. Bema'achalei	בַּנְעִימִים. בְּמַאֲכָלֵי
Arevot. Beminei Mat'ammim.	עֲרֵבוֹת. בְּמִינֵי מַטְעַמִּים.
Bemalbushei Chavod. Zevach	בְּמַלְבּוּשֵׁי כָבוֹד. זֶבַח
Mishpachah:	מִשְׁפָּחָה:

Time's eternal Lord, whose chariot spans the spheres. Pleasantness His word, King of all the years. Gave us rest outpoured; then drink the wine that cheers. Bring your delicacies stored, to feast with all of your peers.

Hashomer Shabbat Haben Im
Habat. La'el Yeratzu Keminchah
Al Machavat:

הַשּׁוֹמֵר שַׁבָּת הַבֵּן עִם
הַבַּת. לָאֵל יֵרָצוּ כְּמִנְחָה
עַל מַחֲבַת:

Keep the day divine. Sons and daughters mine, For He will then accept you, As gifts before His shrine.

Ve'ashrei Kol Chocheh.
Letashlumei Chefel. Me'et Kol
Socheh. Shochein Ba'arafel.
Nachalah Lo Yizkeh. Bahar
Uvashafel. Nachalah
Umenuchah. Kashemesh Lo
Zarechah:

וְאַשְׁרֵי כָּל־חוֹכֶה.
לְתַשְׁלוּמֵי כֶפֶל. מֵאֵת כָּל
סוֹכֶה. שׁוֹכֵן בָּעֲרָפֶל.
נַחֲלָה לוֹ יִזְכֶּה. בָּהָר
וּבַשָּׁפֶל. נַחֲלָה
וּמְנוּחָה. כַּשֶּׁמֶשׁ לוֹ
זָרְחָה:

Blessed band, whose double wage, God's promise will assure; A faithful heritage, forever to endure. Above the clouds that rage His Throne abides sure. As the sun satisfies, so His gifts, our rest secure.

Hashomer Shabbat Haben Im
Habat. La'el Yeratzu Keminchah
Al Machavat:

הַשּׁוֹמֵר שַׁבָּת הַבֵּן עִם
הַבַּת. לָאֵל יֵרָצוּ כְּמִנְחָה
עַל מַחֲבַת:

Keep the day divine. Sons and daughters mine, For He will then accept you, As gifts before His shrine.

Kol Shomer Shabbat. Kadat
Mechallelo. Hen Hechsher
Chibat. Kodesh Goralo. Ve'im
Yetze Chovat. Hayom Ashrei Lo.
El El Adon Mecholelo. Minchah
Hi Sheluchah:

כָּל־שׁוֹמֵר שַׁבָּת. כַּדָּת
מֵחַלְּלוֹ. הֵן הֶכְשֵׁר
חִבַּת. קֹדֶשׁ גּוֹרָלוֹ. וְאִם
יֵצֵא חוֹבַת. הַיּוֹם אַשְׁרֵי לוֹ.
אֵל אֵל אָדוֹן מְחוֹלְלוֹ. מִנְחָה
הִיא שְׁלוּחָה:

Stand fast and true, Shabbat's laws obey. Her love will strengthen you. Your love, she will repay. Your loyal duty do, it is your Maker's happy day. His blessings do renew, then this gift before Him lay,

Hashomer Shabbat Haben Im
Habat. La'el Yeratzu Keminchah
Al Machavat:

הַשׁוֹמֵר שַׁבָּת הַבֵּן עִם
הַבַּת. לָאֵל יֵרְצוּ כְּמִנְחָה
עַל מַחֲבַת:

Keep the day divine. Sons and daughters mine, For He will then accept you, As gifts before His shrine.

Chemdat Hayamim. Kera'o Eli
Tzur. Ve'ashrei Litmimim. Im
Yihyeh Natzur. Keter Hilumim.
Al Rosham Yatzur. Tzur
Ha'olamim. Rucho Vam
Nachah:

חֶמְדַּת הַיָּמִים. קְרָאוֹ אֵלִי
צוּר. וְאַשְׁרֵי לִתְמִימִים. אִם
יִהְיֶה נָצוּר. כֶּתֶר הִלּוּמִים.
עַל רֹאשָׁם יָצוּר. צוּר
הָעוֹלָמִים. רוּחוֹ בָם
נָחָה:

Day of pure delights, you did our Lord acclaim, Thrice happy be your knights, your guardians free from blame. Their helmets gleam with lights, with a halo-crown of flame; His Spirit from the heights comes to rest upon their name,

Hashomer Shabbat Haben Im
Habat. La'el Yeratzu Keminchah
Al Machavat:

הַשׁוֹמֵר שַׁבָּת הַבֵּן עִם
הַבַּת. לָאֵל יֵרְצוּ כְּמִנְחָה
עַל מַחֲבַת:

Keep the day divine. Sons and daughters mine, For He will then accept you, As gifts before His shrine.

Zachor Et Yom. Hashabbat
Lekadesho. Karno Ki Gavehah.
Nezer Al Rosho. Al Ken Yiten.

זָכוֹר אֶת יוֹם. הַשַּׁבָּת
לְקַדְּשׁוֹ. קַרְנוֹ כִּי גָבְהָה.
נֵזֶר עַל רֹאשׁוֹ. עַל כֵּן יִתֵּן.

Ha'adam Lenafsho. Oneg Vegam
Simchah. Bahem Lemoshchah:

הָאָדָם לְנַפְשׁוֹ. עֹנֶג וְגַם
שִׂמְחָה. בָּהֶם לְמָשְׁחָה:

Greet the Shabbat morn, mindful of the bride; Exalted is her horn, a diadem of pride. With joy your hearts adorn, and with Shabbat sanctified; A new twin soul reborn comes to bless each Shabbat-tide,

Hashomer Shabbat Haben Im
Habat. La'el Yeratzu Keminchah
Al Machavat:

הַשּׁוֹמֵר שַׁבָּת הַבֵּן עִם
הַבַּת. לָאֵל יֵרָצוּ כְּמִנְחָה
עַל מַחֲבַת:

Keep the day divine. Sons and daughters mine, For He will then accept you, As gifts before His shrine.

Kodesh Hi Lachem. Shabbat
Hamalkah. El Toch Batteichem.
Lehaniach Berachah. Bechol
Moshevoteichem. Lo Ta'asu
Melachah. Beneichem
Uvenoteichem. Eved Vegam
Shifchah:

קֹדֶשׁ הִיא לָכֶם. שַׁבָּת
הַמַּלְכָּה. אֶל תּוֹךְ בָּתֵּיכֶם.
לְהָנִיחַ בְּרָכָה. בְּכָל-
מוֹשְׁבוֹתֵיכֶם. לֹא תַעֲשׂוּ
מְלָאכָה. בְּנֵיכֶם
וּבְנוֹתֵיכֶם. עֶבֶד וְגַם
שִׁפְחָה:

Day of holiness, Shabbat bridal queen, Oh deign our homes to bless and leave a gift unseen. The great your sway confess, you do not disdain the mean. Boys and girls fresh happiness, new rest, from labor glean,

Hashomer Shabbat Haben Im
Habat. La'el Yeratzu Keminchah
Al Machavat:

הַשּׁוֹמֵר שַׁבָּת הַבֵּן עִם
הַבַּת. לָאֵל יֵרָצוּ כְּמִנְחָה
עַל מַחֲבַת:

Keep the day divine. Sons and daughters mine, For He will then accept you, As gifts before His shrine.

Yah Ribon
Israel Najara

Yah Ribon Olam Ve'alemaya.	יָהּ רִבּוֹן עָלַם וְעָלְמַיָּא.
Ant Hu Malka Melech	אַנְתְּ הוּא מַלְכָּא מֶלֶךְ
Malchaya.	מַלְכַיָּא.

Lord of all worlds, all-time comprehending, King of all kings, above all-creation transcending.

Ovadei Gevuretach Vetimhaya.	עוֹבָדֵי גְבוּרְתָּךְ וְתִמְהַיָּא.
Shefar Kodamai Lehachavaya:	שְׁפַר קֳדָמַי לְהַחֲוַיָּא:
Yah Ribon Alam Ve'alemaya.	יָהּ רִבּוֹן עָלַם וְעָלְמַיָּא.
Ant Hu Malka Melech	אַנְתְּ הוּא מַלְכָּא מֶלֶךְ
Malchaya:	מַלְכַיָּא:

Gladly we tell of Your wonders never ending, striving, Your holy name to magnify.

Shevachin Asader Tzafra	שְׁבָחִין אֲסַדֵּר צַפְרָא
Veramsha. Lach Elaha Kaddisha.	וְרַמְשָׁא. לָךְ אֱלָהָא קַדִּישָׁא.
Di Bara Kol Nafsha. Irin	דִּי בְרָא כָּל נַפְשָׁא. עִירִין
Kaddishin Uvenei Enasha.	קַדִּישִׁין וּבְנֵי אֱנָשָׁא.
Cheivat Bera Ve'of Shemaya:	חֵיוַת בְּרָא וְעוֹף שְׁמַיָּא:

In the grey dawn we rise to adore You, In the dark night for help we all implore You; Angel and man, Creator, fall before You, Beast in the field and bird above the sky.

Ravrevin Ovadach Vetakifin.	רַבְרְבִין עוֹבָדָךְ וְתַקִּיפִין.
Makkich Ramaya Zakkif Kefifin.	מַכִּיךְ רָמַיָא זַקִּיף כְּפִיפִין.
Lu Yechi Gevar Shenin Alfin. La	לוּ יְחִי גְבַר שְׁנִין אַלְפִין. לָא
Ye'ul Gevuretach	יֵעוּל גְּבוּרְתָּךְ
Bechushbenaya:	בְּחֻשְׁבְּנַיָּא:

Great are Your works, over time You prevail; Raising the meek, the tyrant You assail. Aeons must fail—but You never fail—Aeons too short, Your strength to glorify.

Elaha Di Leih Yekar Urevuta.	אֱלָהָא דִי לֵיהּ יְקַר וּרְבוּתָא.
Perok Yat Anach Mippum	פְּרוֹק יַת עָנָךְ מִפּוּם
Aryavata. Ve'appik Yat Amach	אַרְיָוָתָא. וְאַפִּיק יַת עַמָּךְ
Migo Galuta. Amach Di Vechart	מִגּוֹ גָלוּתָא. עַמָּךְ דִּי בְחַרְתְּ
Mikol Ammaya:	מִכָּל אֻמַּיָּא:

Glory and strength are Yours, Oh defend us. We are Your flock, see, raging lions rend us. Long is our exile, redeem and befriend us, Chosen from all, Your name to sanctify.

Lemikdashach Tuv Ulekodesh	לְמִקְדָּשָׁךְ תּוּב וּלְקֹדֶשׁ
Kudeshin. Atar Di Veih Yechdun	קוּדְשִׁין. אֲתַר דִּי בֵיהּ יֶחְדּוּן
Ruchin Venafshin. Vizamerun	רוּחִין וְנַפְשִׁין. וִיזַמְּרוּן
Lach Shirin Verachshin.	לָךְ שִׁירִין וְרַחֲשִׁין.
Birushelem Karta Deshuferaya:	בִּירוּשְׁלֵם קַרְתָּא דְשׁוּפְרַיָּא:

Turn again, Lord, to our Temple adored. There our souls rejoice, once more restored; There will our songs again rise to You outpoured. Yerushalayim will echo our voices raised on high.

Menucha VeSimcha
Moshe

Menuchah Vesimchah Or	מְנוּחָה וְשִׂמְחָה אוֹר
Layehudim. Yom Shabbaton Yom	לַיְהוּדִים. יוֹם שַׁבָּתוֹן יוֹם
Machamadim. Shomerav	מַחֲמַדִּים. שׁוֹמְרָיו
Vezocherav Hemah Me'idim. Ki	וְזוֹכְרָיו הֵמָּה מְעִידִים. כִּי
Leshishah Kol Beru'im	לְשִׁשָּׁה כֹל בְּרוּאִים
Ve'omedim:	וְעוֹמְדִים:

Repose and gladness, a light to the Yehudim, The day of Shabbat is a day of bliss; Those who observe it give testimony that in six days all things were created:

Shemei Shamayim Eretz	שְׁמֵי שָׁמַיִם אֶרֶץ
Veyamim. Kol Tzeva Marom	וְיַמִּים. כָּל־צְבָא מָרוֹם
Gevohim Veramim. Tanin	גְּבוֹהִים וְרָמִים. תַּנִּין
Ve'adam Vechayat Re'emim. Ki	וְאָדָם וְחַיַּת רְאֵמִים. כִּי
Beyah Adonai Tzur Olamim:	בְּיָהּ יְהוָה צוּר עוֹלָמִים:

The highest heavens, the land and the seas, All the celestial hosts, lofty and great, Sea-monster as well as man and wild beast; Indeed, God is Creator of all worlds.

Hu Asher Diber Le'am Segulato.	הוּא אֲשֶׁר דִּבֶּר לְעַם סְגֻלָּתוֹ.
Shamor Lekadesho Mibo'o	שָׁמוֹר לְקַדְּשׁוֹ מִבּוֹאוֹ
Ve'ad Tzeto. Shabbat Kodesh	וְעַד צֵאתוֹ. שַׁבָּת קֹדֶשׁ
Yom Chemdato. Ki Vo Shavat El	יוֹם חֶמְדָּתוֹ. כִּי בוֹ שָׁבַת אֵל
Mikol Melachto:	מִכָּל־מְלַאכְתּוֹ:

He it is Who bade His chosen people: Keep it holy from sunset to sunset; The holy Shabbat is His beloved day, For on it He rested from all His work.

Bemitzvat Shabbat El	בְּמִצְוַת שַׁבָּת אֵל
Yachalitzach. Kum Kera Elav	יַחֲלִיצָךְ. קוּם קְרָא אֵלָיו
Yachish Le'ammetzach. Nishmat	יָחִישׁ לְאַמְּצָךְ. נִשְׁמַת
Kol Chai Vegam Na'aritzach.	כָּל־חַי וְגַם נַעֲרִיצָךְ.
Echol Besimchah Ki Chevar	אֱכֹל בְּשִׂמְחָה כִּי כְבָר
Ratzach:	רְצָךְ:

By the Shabbat command, God makes you strong; Arise, call on Him; soon will He strengthen you; Read the prayers, Nishmat Kol-Chai and also the Kedushah, Then eat with joy, for He is pleased with you.

Bemishneh Lechem Vekiddush	בְּמִשְׁנֵה לֶחֶם וְקִדּוּשׁ
Rabah. Berov Mat'ammim	רַבָּה. בְּרוֹב מַטְעַמִּים
Veruach Nedivah. Yizku Lerav	וְרוּחַ נְדִיבָה. יִזְכּוּ לְרַב
Tuv Hamit'anegim Bah. Bevi'at	טוּב הַמִּתְעַנְּגִים בָּהּ. בְּבִיאַת
Go'el Lechayei Ha'olam Haba:	גּוֹאֵל לְחַיֵּי הָעוֹלָם הַבָּא:

Recite the day's Kiddush over twin loaves; Be generous with abundant dainties; All who enjoy Shabbat will merit the future world when the redeemer comes.

Shimru Shabtotai
Rabbi Shlomo Ibn Gavirol

Shimru Shabtotai. Lema'an Tinku	שִׁמְרוּ שַׁבְּתוֹתַי. לְמַעַן
Useva'tem. Miziv Birchotai. El	תִּינְקוּ וּשְׂבַעְתֶּם. מִזִּיו
Hamenuchah Ki Batem: Shabbat	בִּרְכוֹתַי. אֶל הַמְּנוּחָה כִּי בָאתֶם: שַׁבָּת
Hayom L'Adonai. Ulevu Alai	הַיּוֹם
Banai. Ve'idnu Ma'adanai.	לַיהֹוָה. וּלְווּ עָלַי בָּנַי.
Shabbat Hayom L'Adonai:	וְעִדְנוּ מַעֲדַנַי. שַׁבָּת הַיּוֹם לַיהֹוָה:

Keep my Shabbat rest, With rich draughts she feeds you; From her soft sweet flowing breast to repose she leads you.

Ulevu Alai Banai. Ve'idnu	וּלְווּ עָלַי בָּנַי. וְעִדְנוּ
Ma'adanai. Shabbat Hayom	מַעֲדַנַי. שַׁבָּת הַיּוֹם
L'Adonai:	לַיהוָה:

Though you beg, her needs, she will repay; Richest delicacies bring out, be happy, it is my Shabbat, keep your holiday.

Le'amel Kir'u Deror. Venatati Et	לְעָמֵל קִרְאוּ דְרוֹר. וְנָתַתִּי אֶת
Birchati. Ishah El Achotah	בִּרְכָתִי. אִשָּׁה אֶל אֲחוֹתָהּ
Litzror. Legalot Al Yom Simchati.	לִצְרוֹר. לְגַלּוֹת עַל יוֹם שִׂמְחָתִי.
Bigdei Shesh Im Shani.	בִּגְדֵי שֵׁשׁ עִם שָׁנִי.
Vehitbonenu Mizekenai:	וְהִתְבּוֹנְנוּ מִזְּקֵנַי:
Shabbat Hayom L'Adonai.	שַׁבָּת הַיּוֹם לַיהוָה.
Ulevu Alai Banai. Ve'iddenu	וּלְווּ עָלַי בָּנַי. וְעִדְנוּ
Ma'adanai. Shabbat Hayom	מַעֲדַנַי. שַׁבָּת הַיּוֹם
L'Adonai:	לַיהוָה:

Labor's task has ended; See, I send you my blessing. As two brides, soft blended, Singing sweetly simultaneously. So my counsels sage attract your ear. Scarlet silks will be yours to wear, Shabbat's holiday is here.

Ulevu Alai Banai. Ve'idnu	וּלְווּ עָלַי בָּנַי. וְעִדְנוּ
Ma'adanai. Shabbat Hayom	מַעֲדַנַי. שַׁבָּת הַיּוֹם
L'Adonai:	לַיהוָה:

Though you beg, her needs, she will repay; Richest delicacies bring out, be happy, it is my Shabbat, keep your holiday.

Maharu Et Hamaneh. La'asot Et	מַהֲרוּ אֶת הַמָּנֶה. לַעֲשׂוֹת אֶת
Devar Ester. Vechishevu Im	דְּבַר אֶסְתֵּר. וְחִשְּׁבוּ עִם
Hakoneh. Leshalem Achol	הַקּוֹנֶה. לְשַׁלֵּם אָכוֹל
Vehoter. Bittechu Vi Emunai.	וְהוֹתֵר. בִּטְחוּ בִי אֱמוּנַי.
Ushetu Yein Mashmanai:	וּשְׁתוּ יֵין מַשְׁמַנַּי:
Shabbat Hayom L'Adonai.	שַׁבָּת הַיּוֹם לַיהֹוָה.
Ulevu Alai Banai. Ve'iddenu	וּלְווּ עָלַי בָּנַי. וְעִדְּנוּ
Ma'adanai. Shabbat Hayom	מַעֲדַנַּי. שַׁבָּת הַיּוֹם
L'Adonai:	לַיהֹוָה:

Ester's feast you prepare, To the store haste, good cheer provide freely, do not forbear. Anything, to welcome this Shabbat-tide. He who sells will fill your purse anew; Come, buy sweetest wines of ruby hue. Trust His promise, made to you.

Ulevu Alai Banai. Ve'idnu	וּלְווּ עָלַי בָּנַי. וְעִדְּנוּ
Ma'adanai. Shabbat Hayom	מַעֲדַנַּי. שַׁבָּת הַיּוֹם
L'Adonai:	לַיהֹוָה:

Though you beg, her needs, she will repay; Richest delicacies bring out, be happy, it is my Shabbat, keep your holiday.

Hineh Yom Ge'ulah. Yom	הִנֵּה יוֹם גְּאֻלָּה. יוֹם
Shabbat Im Tishmoru. Vihyitem	שַׁבָּת אִם תִּשְׁמֹרוּ. וִהְיִיתֶם
Li Segullah. Linu Ve'achar	לִי סְגֻלָּה. לִינוּ וְאַחַר
Ta'avoru. Ve'az Tichyu Lefanai.	תַּעֲבוֹרוּ. וְאָז תִּחְיוּ לְפָנַי.
Utemalle'u Tzefunai: Shabbat	וּתְמַלְּאוּ צְפוּנַי: שַׁבָּת
Hayom L'Adonai. Ulevu Alai	הַיּוֹם לַיהֹוָה. וּלְווּ עָלַי
Banai. Ve'iddenu Ma'adanai.	בָּנַי. וְעִדְּנוּ מַעֲדַנַּי.
Shabbat Hayom L'Adonai:	שַׁבָּת הַיּוֹם לַיהֹוָה:

Redemption is swiftly speeding, Then My own you once more will be. Hear My Shabbat pleading: "Rest one night, before you pass, with me". In My Presence will your years be blessed. Life's hidden joys all to you confessed. For life's secret is the Shabbat rest.

Ulevu Alai Banai. Ve'idnu	וּלְווּ עָלַי בָּנַי. וְעִדְנוּ
Ma'adanai. Shabbat Hayom	מַעֲדַנַי. שַׁבָּת הַיּוֹם
L'Adonai:	לַיהֹוָה:

Though you beg, her needs, she will repay; Richest delicacies bring out, be happy, it is my Shabbat, keep your holiday.

Chazek Kiryati El Elohim Elyon.	חַזֵּק קִרְיָתִי אֵל אֱלֹהִים עֶלְיוֹן.
Vehasheiv Et Nevati Besimchah	וְהָשֵׁב אֶת נְוָתִי בְּשִׂמְחָה
Uvehigayon. Yeshoreru Sham	וּבְהִגָּיוֹן. יְשׁוֹרְרוּ שָׁם
Renanai. Leviyai Vechohanai.	רְנָנַי. לְוִיַּי וְכֹהֲנַי.
Az Tit'anag Al Adonai: Shabbat	אָז תִּתְעַנַּג עַל יְהֹוָה: שַׁבָּת
Hayom L'Adonai. Ulevu Alai	הַיּוֹם לַיהֹוָה. וּלְווּ עָלַי
Banai. Ve'iddenu Ma'adanai.	בָּנַי. וְעִדְּנוּ מַעֲדַנַי.
Shabbat Hayom L'Adonai:	שַׁבָּת הַיּוֹם לַיהֹוָה:

My walls shattered, Lord of Glory, rebuild again; My exiles scattered, lead in joy to their old domain. Priests and Levites there restored will sing Songs which exiled hearts at last will bring, A joyous welcome to their King.

Ulevu Alai Banai. Ve'idnu	וּלְווּ עָלַי בָּנַי. וְעִדְנוּ
Ma'adanai. Shabbat Hayom	מַעֲדַנַי. שַׁבָּת הַיּוֹם
L'Adonai:	לַיהֹוָה:

Though you beg, her needs, she will repay; Richest delicacies bring out, be happy, it is my Shabbat, keep your holiday.

Yedid Nefesh
Rabbi Elazar Azikri

Yedid Nefesh Av Harachman.	יְדִיד נֶפֶשׁ אָב הָרַחֲמָן.
Meshoch Avdach El Retzonach.	מְשֹׁךְ עַבְדְּךָ אֶל רְצוֹנָךְ.
Yarutz Avdach Kemo Ayal.	יָרוּץ עַבְדְּךָ כְּמוֹ אַיָּל.
Yishtachaveh Mul Hadarach. Ki	יִשְׁתַּחֲוֶה מוּל הֲדָרָךְ. כִּי
Ye'rav Lo Yedidutach. Minofet	יֶעֱרַב לוֹ יְדִידוּתָךְ. מִנוֹפֶת
Tzuf Vechol Ta'am:	צוּף וְכָל־טָעַם:

My soul's beloved, merciful Father, Draw Your surrendered to Your will rendered. Your surrendered will run like a gazelle, He will bow before Your splendor. For to him, Your love is sweeter than the dripping honeycomb, and any taste at all.

Hadur Na'eh Ziv Ha'olam.	הָדוּר נָאֶה זִיו הָעוֹלָם.
Nafshi Cholat Ahavatach. Ana El	נַפְשִׁי חוֹלַת אַהֲבָתָךְ. אָנָּא אֵל
Na Refa Na Lah. Behar'ot Lah	נָא רְפָא נָא לָהּ. בְּהַרְאוֹת לָהּ
No'am Zivach. Az Titchazek	נוֹעַם זִיוָךְ. אָז תִּתְחַזֵּק
Vetitrappe. Vehayetah Lach	וְתִתְרַפֵּא. וְהָיְתָה לָךְ
Shifchat Olam:	שִׁפְחַת עוֹלָם:

Resplendent, beautiful, radiance of the world, My soul is sick for Your love, Please, God, heal her now, By the beauty of Your radiance, by showing her. Then she will be strong, she will be healed, And she will be Your handmaiden forever more.

Vatik Yehemu Rachameicha.	וָתִיק יֶהֱמוּ רַחֲמֶיךָ.
Vechus Na Al Ben Ohavecha. Ki	וְחוּס נָא עַל בֵּן אוֹהֲבֶךָ. כִּי
Zeh Chameh Nichsof Nichsaf.	זֶה כַּמֶּה נִכְסוֹף נִכְסַף.
Lir'ot Betif'eret Uzach. Ana Eli	לִרְאוֹת בְּתִפְאֶרֶת עֻזָּךְ. אָנָּא אֵלִי
Machmad Libi Chushah Na Ve'al	מַחְמַד לִבִּי חוּשָׁה נָא
Tit'alam:	וְאַל תִּתְעַלָּם:

Ancient One, please awaken Your mercy. Please, on Your beloved son, have compassion. For so much has this yearning been, To see Your strength, in its beauty. Please, my God, the delight of my heart. Hurry, please, and do not remain hidden.

Higgaleh Na Uferos Chaviv. Alai	הִגָּלֵה נָא וּפְרוֹשׁ חָבִיב. עָלַי
Et Sukkat Shelomach. Ta'ir Eretz	אֶת סֻכַּת שְׁלוֹמָךְ. תָּאִיר אֶרֶץ
Mikevodach. Nagilah	מִכְּבוֹדָךְ. נָגִילָה
Venismechah Vach. Maher Ahuv	וְנִשְׂמְחָה בָךְ. מַהֵר אָהוּב
Ki Va Mo'ed. Vechaneni Kimei	כִּי בָא מוֹעֵד. וְחָנֵּנִי כִּימֵי
Olam:	עוֹלָם:

Please, be revealed and spread the covering, beloved, upon me, the shelter of Your peace. Illuminate the earth with Your glory. We will be glad and rejoice in You. Hurry, Beloved, for the time has come, And be good to me, like ancient days.

Yom Zeh L'Yisrael
Isaac Luria

Yom Zeh Leyisra'el Orah	יוֹם זֶה לְיִשְׂרָאֵל אוֹרָה
Vesimchah Shabbat Menuchah.	וְשִׂמְחָה שַׁבָּת מְנוּחָה.

This day is for Yisrael light and rejoicing, a Shabbat of rest.

Tzivita Pikudim Bema'amad Har	צִוִּיתָ פִּקּוּדִים בְּמַעֲמַד הַר
Sinai. Shabbat Umo'adim	סִינַי. שַׁבָּת וּמוֹעֲדִים
Lishmor Bechol Shanai.	לִשְׁמוֹר בְּכָל שָׁנַי.
La'aroch Lefanai Mas'et	לַעֲרוֹךְ לְפָנַי מַשְׂאֵת
Va'aruchah. Shabbat	וַאֲרוּחָה. שַׁבָּת
Menuchah.	מְנוּחָה.

You bade us standing assembled at Sinai that all of the years through we should keep Your behest to set out a table fully-laden, to honor the Shabbat of rest. (Repeat Chorus)

Chemdat Halvavot Le'umah	חֶמְדַּת הַלְּבָבוֹת לְאֻמָּה
Shvurah. Linfashot Nich'avot	שְׁבוּרָה. לִנְפָשׁוֹת נִכְאָבוֹת
Neshamah Yeterah. Lenefesh	נְשָׁמָה יְתֵרָה. לְנֶפֶשׁ
Metzerah Yasir Anachah.	מְצֵרָה יָסִיר אֲנָחָה.
Shabbat Menuchah.	שַׁבַּת מְנוּחָה.

Treasure of heart for the broken people, Gift of new soul for the souls distress, Soother of sighs for the prisoned spirit—the Shabbat of rest. (Repeat Chorus)

Kidashta Berachta Oto Mikol	קִדַּשְׁתָּ בֵּרַכְתָּ אוֹתוֹ מִכָּל
Yamim. Besheshet Killita	יָמִים. בְּשֵׁשֶׁת כִּלִּיתָ
Melechet Olamim. Bo Matze'u	מְלֶאכֶת עוֹלָמִים. בּוֹ מָצְאוּ
Agumim Hashket Uvitchah.	עֲגוּמִים הַשְׁקֵט וּבִטְחָה.
Shabbat Menuchah.	שַׁבַּת מְנוּחָה.

You made this day to be holy and blessed, when the work of the worlds in their wonder was finished. And those heavy-laden found safety and stillness, A Shabbat of rest. (Repeat Chorus)

Le'issur Melachah Tzivitanu	לְאִסּוּר מְלָאכָה צִוִּיתָנוּ
Nora. Ezkeh Hod Meluchah Im	נוֹרָא. אֶזְכֶּה הוֹד מְלוּכָה אִם
Shabbat Eshmorah. Akriv Shai	שַׁבַּת אֶשְׁמֹרָה. אַקְרִיב שַׁי
Lammora Minchah Merkachah.	לַמּוֹרָא מִנְחָה מֶרְקָחָה.
Shabbat Menuchah.	שַׁבַּת מְנוּחָה.

If I keep Your command I inherit a kingdom, If I treasure Shabbat I bring You the best—The noblest of offerings, the sweetest of incense—A Shabbat of rest. (Repeat Chorus)

Chadesh Mikdashenu Zacherah	חַדֵּשׁ מִקְדָּשֵׁנוּ זָכְרָה
Necherevet. Tuvecha Moshi'enu	נֶחֱרֶבֶת. טוּבְךָ מוֹשִׁיעֵנוּ
Tenah Lane'etzevet. Beshabbat	תְּנָה לַנֶּעֱצֶבֶת. בְּשַׁבָּת
Yoshevet Bizmir Ushevachah.	יוֹשֶׁבֶת בְּזְמִיר וּשְׁבָחָה.
Shabbat Menuchah.	שַׁבַּת מְנוּחָה.

Restore us our Temple—Oh remember our ruin And save now and
comfort the sorely oppressed, Now sitting at Shabbat, all singing
and praising the Shabbat of rest. (Repeat Chorus)

Shabbat HaYom L'Hashem

Shabbat Hayom L'hashem	שַׁבָּת הַיּוֹם לַיְיָ
Me'od Tzahalu Berinunai.	מְאֹד צָהֲלוּ בְּרְנוּנַי.
Vegam Harbu Ma'adanai. Oto	וְגַם הַרְבּוּ מַעֲדָנַי. אוֹתוֹ
Lishmor Kemitzvot Adonai:	לִשְׁמוֹר כְּמִצְוֹת יהוה:
Shabbat Hayom L'Hashem:	שַׁבָּת הַיּוֹם לַיְיָ:

Keep your holy Shabbat rest before your God today, Come, cry out
with joyful shout, rejoicing in your rest: Pleasures mine, treasures
fine, take with laughter best. Yet be mindful, God's command obey:
Day of rest, Hashem has blessed Yisrael's Shabbat day.

Me'avor Derech Ugevulim.	מֵעֲבוֹר דֶּרֶךְ וּגְבוּלִים.
Me'assot Hayom Pe'alim.	מֵעֲשׂוֹת הַיּוֹם פְּעָלִים.
Le'echol Velishtot Behilulim.	לֶאֱכוֹל וְלִשְׁתּוֹת בְּהִלּוּלִים.
Zeh Hayom Asah Hashem:	זֶה הַיּוֹם עָשָׂה יהוה:
Shabbat Hayom L'Hashem:	שַׁבָּת הַיּוֹם לַיְיָ:

Cease your weary journey, stay and rest beside the road, Toil is
past, your burden cast, for I will bear your load: Sweet-meats I bring

you, eat your fill and say: Day of rest, Hashem has blessed Yisrael's Shabbat day.

Ve'im Tishmerenu.Yah	וְאִם תִּשְׁמְרֶנוּ. יָהּ
Yintzareka Kevavat. Attah	יִנְצָרְךָ כְּבָבַת. אַתָּה
Uvincha Vegam Habat. Vekarata	וּבִנְךָ וְגַם הַבַּת. וְקָרָאתָ
Oneg Leshabbat. Az Tit'aneg Al	עוֹנֶג לְשַׁבָּת. אָז תִּתְעַנַּג עַל
Hashem: Shabbat Hayom	יהוה: שַׁבָּת הַיּוֹם
L'Hashem:	לַיְיָ:

Keep me safe and God will ever guard you in His sight. You, with all your tender ones, will find in me delight. Joyful, in chorus, delight in the festive lay, Day of rest, Hashem has blessed Yisrael's Shabbat day.

Echol Mashemanim	אֱכוֹל מַשְׁמַנִּים
Uma'adanim. Umat'ammim	וּמַעֲדַנִּים. וּמַטְעַמִּים
Harbeh Minim. Egozei Perech	הַרְבֵּה מִינִים. אֱגוֹזֵי פֶּרֶךְ
Verimonim. Ve'achalta	וְרִמּוֹנִים. וְאָכַלְתָּ
Vesava'eta Uverachta Et	וְשָׂבָעְתָּ וּבֵרַכְתָּ אֶת
Hashem: Shabbat Hayom	יהוה: שַׁבָּת הַיּוֹם
L'Hashem:	לַיְיָ:

Bring me finest delicacies, bring me sweets and spices rare: Crispiest nuts and ripest fruit will be our Shabbat fare. Raisins and nuts, see their choice array, Day of rest, Hashem has blessed Yisrael's Shabbat day.

La'aroch Beshulchan Lechem	לַעֲרוֹךְ בְּשֻׁלְחָן לֶחֶם
Chamudot. La'asot Hayom	חֲמֻדֹת. לַעֲשׂוֹת הַיּוֹם
Shalosh Se'udot. Et Hashem	שָׁלֹשׁ סְעוּדוֹת. אֶת הַשֵּׁם
Hanichbad Levarech Ulehodot.	הַנִּכְבָּד לְבָרֵךְ וּלְהוֹדוֹת.

Shakedu Veshimmeru Ve'asu

שָׁקְדוּ וְשִׁמְרוּ וְעָשׂוּ

Vanai: Shabbat Hayom

בָּנַי: שַׁבָּת הַיּוֹם

L'Hashem:

לַיְיָ:

Set twin loaves beside your cup, so He will bless your bread. Feast our guest and with your best thrice let your board be spread. Praise Him Who fed you, turn to Him and pray, Day of rest, Hashem has blessed Yisrael's Shabbat day.

Tzur Mishelo Achalnu

Tzur Mishelo Achalnu Barechu

צוּר מִשֶּׁלּוֹ אָכַלְנוּ בָּרְכוּ

Emunai. Sava'nu Vehotarnu

אֱמוּנַי. שָׂבַעְנוּ וְהוֹתַרְנוּ

Kidvar Adonai.

כִּדְבַר יהוה.

Come, friends, in grateful strains. Give thanks and bless our Lord. Rock, Whose store our life sustains. Whose sure abundance still remains, according to His word.

Hazan Et Olamo Ro'enu Avinu.

הַזָּן אֶת עוֹלָמוֹ רוֹעֵנוּ אָבִינוּ.

Achalnu Et Lachmo Veyeino

אָכַלְנוּ אֶת לַחְמוֹ וְיֵינוֹ

Shatinu. Al Ken Nodeh Lishmo

שָׁתִינוּ. עַל כֵּן נוֹדֶה לִשְׁמוֹ

Unehallelo Befinu. Amarnu

וּנְהַלְלוֹ בְּפִינוּ. אָמַרְנוּ

Ve'aninu Ein Kadosh Kaiya.

וְעָנִינוּ אֵין קָדוֹשׁ כַּיְיָ.

Your abundance mankind feeds, Your flock, Oh Shepherd, guiding; You are the bread that we have eaten, Your rich grace our drink did sweeten, All our wants providing, For all our daily needs, Father, forever abiding, Let us praise Your name: Again, Let us sing with loud refrain, 'None holy like our King.'

Beshir Vekol Todah Nevarech	בְּשִׁיר וְקוֹל תּוֹדָה נְבָרֵךְ
L'Eloheinu. Al Eretz Chemdah	לֵאלֹהֵינוּ. עַל אֶרֶץ חֶמְדָּה
Tovah Shehinchil La'avoteinu.	טוֹבָה שֶׁהִנְחִיל לַאֲבוֹתֵינוּ.
Mazon Vetzedah Hisbia'	מָזוֹן וְצֵדָה הִשְׂבִּיעַ
Lenafshenu. Chasdo Gavar	לְנַפְשֵׁנוּ. חַסְדּוֹ גָּבַר
Aleinu Ve'emet Adonai.	עָלֵינוּ וֶאֱמֶת יהוה.

To God our voice we raise in songs of jubilation. For the land of His bestowing, Land with milk and honey flowing, He gave our ancient nation. His food our hunger stays; His grace our soul's salvation. Strong above us mortals frail Hashem's sure mercies will prevail. His truth will watch our ways.

Rachem Bechasdecha Al	רַחֵם בְּחַסְדֶּךָ עַל
Ammecha Tzurenu. Al Tziyon	עַמְּךָ צוּרֵנוּ. עַל צִיּוֹן
Mishkan Kevodecha Zevul Beit	מִשְׁכַּן כְּבוֹדֶךָ זְבוּל בֵּית
Tif'artenu. Ben David Avdecha	תִּפְאַרְתֵּנוּ. בֶּן דָּוִד עַבְדֶּךָ
Yavo Veyig'alenu. Ruach Apeinu	יָבוֹא וְיִגְאָלֵנוּ. רוּחַ אַפֵּינוּ
Meshiach Adonai.	מְשִׁיחַ יהוה.

Have mercy on Your flock, On Tziyon desolated; Tziyon, once Your glory's Throne, There Your presence dwelt alone, Our splendor, now desecrated. Oh Eternal Rock, For You our hearts have waited; Our life's breath, Messiah, speed, Wandering exiles home to lead, Born of David's stock.

Yibaneh Hamikdash. Ir Tziyon	יִבָּנֶה הַמִּקְדָּשׁ. עִיר צִיּוֹן
Temalle. Vesham Nashir Shir	תְּמַלֵּא. וְשָׁם נָשִׁיר שִׁיר
Chadash Uvirnanah Na'aleh.	חָדָשׁ וּבִרְנָנָה נַעֲלֶה.
Harachaman Hanikdash	הָרַחֲמָן הַנִּקְדָּשׁ
Yitbarach Veyit'aleh. Al Kos Yayin	יִתְבָּרַךְ וְיִתְעַלֶּה. עַל כּוֹס יַיִן

Male Kevirkat Adonai.   מָלֵא כְּבִרְכַּת יהוה.

Our hearts, now mute, will sing new songs, before unspoken, When we see with marveling eyes Yerushalyim's crowds once more arise, To build her walls broken. Loud let your voices ring. In pledge and grateful token. Raise your cups, His grace confessing. Raise your cups, accept His blessing, Yisrael's God and King.

BIRKHAT HAMAZON / GRACE AFTER MEALS

One may wash hands after the meal, known as Mayim Acharonim (The After-Waters). It is a custom, according to the Shulchan Arukh, it is a duty (mandatory). (OC, 181) It is not necessary to wash more than up to the second joints of the fingers. It is permissible to wash hands with any liquid and a blessing is not recited on this. It is required that the fingers be lowered during such washing. Birkhat Hamazon requires no cup of wine. (However it is most proper to recite Birkhat Hamazon over a cup of wine). It may be said only over a cup of wine, beer or upon any liquid that is the beverage of the locality, except water.

Some say before:

Psalms 67 / Lamnatzeach Binginot

לַמְנַצֵּחַ בִּנְגִינֹת מִזְמוֹר שִׁיר: אֱלֹהִים יְחָנֵּנוּ וִיבָרְכֵנוּ יָאֵר פָּנָיו אִתָּנוּ סֶלָה:
לָדַעַת בָּאָרֶץ דַּרְכֶּךָ בְּכָל־גּוֹיִם יְשׁוּעָתֶךָ: יוֹדוּךָ עַמִּים | אֱלֹהִים יוֹדוּךָ עַמִּים
כֻּלָּם: יִשְׂמְחוּ וִירַנְּנוּ לְאֻמִּים כִּי־תִשְׁפֹּט עַמִּים מִישֹׁר וּלְאֻמִּים | בָּאָרֶץ תַּנְחֵם
סֶלָה: יוֹדוּךָ עַמִּים | אֱלֹהִים יוֹדוּךָ עַמִּים כֻּלָּם: אֶרֶץ נָתְנָה יְבוּלָהּ יְבָרְכֵנוּ
אֱלֹהִים אֱלֹהֵינוּ: יְבָרְכֵנוּ אֱלֹהִים וְיִירְאוּ אֹתוֹ כָּל־אַפְסֵי־אָרֶץ:

Lamnatzeach Binginot. Mizmor Shir. Elohim. Yechonenu Vivarecheinu; Ya'er Panav Itanu Selah. Lada'at Ba'aretz Darkecha; Bechol-Goyim. Yeshu'atecha. Yoducha Ammim Elohim; Yoducha. Ammim Kulam. Yismechu Viranenu. Le'ummim Ki-Tishpot Ammim Mishor; Ule'ummim Ba'aretz Tanchem Selah. Yoducha Ammim Elohim; Yoducha. Ammim Kulam. Eretz Natenah Yevulah; Yevarecheinu. Elohim Eloheinu. Yevarecheinu Elohim; Veyire'u Oto. Chol-'Afsei-'Aretz.

For the Leader; with string-music. A Psalm, a Song. May God be gracious to us, and bless us; May He cause His face to shine toward us; Selah. That Your way may be known upon earth, Your salvation among all nations. Let the people give thanks to You, Oh God; Let the peoples give thanks to You, all of them. Let the nations be glad and sing for joy; For You will judge the people with equity, And lead the nations on earth. Selah. Let the people give thanks to You, Oh God; Let the peoples give thanks to You, all of them. The earth has yielded her increase; May God, our own God, bless us. May God bless us; And let all the ends of the earth fear Him.

אֲבָרְכָה אֶת־יְהֹוָה בְּכָל־עֵת תָּמִיד תְּהִלָּתוֹ בְּפִי: סוֹף דָּבָר הַכֹּל נִשְׁמָע
אֶת־הָאֱלֹהִים יְרָא וְאֶת־מִצְוֹתָיו שְׁמוֹר כִּי־זֶה כָּל־הָאָדָם: תְּהִלַּת יְהֹוָה יְדַבֶּר פִּי
וִיבָרֵךְ כָּל־בָּשָׂר שֵׁם קָדְשׁוֹ לְעוֹלָם וָעֶד: וַאֲנַחְנוּ | נְבָרֵךְ יָהּ מֵעַתָּה וְעַד־עוֹלָם
הַלְלוּיָהּ: וַיְדַבֵּר אֵלַי זֶה הַשֻּׁלְחָן אֲשֶׁר לִפְנֵי יְהֹוָה:

Avarechah Et-Adonai Bechol-'Et; Tamid. Tehilato Befi. Sof Davar HaKol Nishma'; Et-Ha'elohim Yera Ve'et-Mitzvtav Shemor. Ki-Zeh Chol-Ha'adam. Tehillat Adonai Yedaber Pi Vivarech Chol-Basor Shem Kodsho. Le'olam Va'ed. Va'anachnu Nevarech Yah. Me'attah Ve'ad-'Olam. Halleluyah. VayDaber Elai. Zeh Hashulchan. Asher Lifnei Adonai.

I will bless Hashem at all times; His praise will continually be in my mouth. The sum of the matter, when all is said and done: Revere God and observe His commandments. For this applies to all mankind: My mouth will speak the praise of Hashem; And let all flesh bless His holy name forever and ever. and he said to me: 'This is the table that is before Hashem.' **(Psalms 31:2, Ecclesiastes 12:13, Psalms 145:21, Ezekiel 41:22)**

Zimmun / Invitation

If there are not 3 or more, go to the first blessing. If there are 3 or more say:

Hav Lan Venivrich Lemalka Illa'ah   הַב לָן וְנִבְרִיךְ לְמַלְכָּא עִלָּאָה

Kaddisha.   קַדִּישָׁא:

Allow us and We will bless the King, Most High and Holy.

The participants answer:

Shamayim!   שְׁמַיִם:

(By) Heaven!

And say the zimmun / invitation:

Birshut Malka Illa'ah Kaddisha   בִּרְשׁוּת מַלְכָּא עִלָּאָה קַדִּישָׁא

On Shabbat: (Uvirshut Shabbat Malketa.)   בשבת: (וּבִרְשׁוּת שַׁבָּת מַלְכְּתָא)

On Yom Tov: (Uvirshut Yoma Tava   ביו"ט: (וּבִרְשׁוּת יוֹמָא טָבָא

Ushepiza Kaddisha.)   אוּשְׁפִּיזָא קַדִּישָׁא.)

On Sukkot: (Uvirshut Shiv'ah Ushepizin   בסוכות: (וּבִרְשׁוּת שִׁבְעָה אוּשְׁפִּיזִין

Illa'in Kaddishin) (Uvirshut Morai   עִלָּאִין קַדִּישִׁין) (וּבִרְשׁוּת מוֹרַי

Verabotai) Uvirshutechem.   וְרַבּוֹתַי) וּבִרְשׁוּתְכֶם.

With the permission of the King, Most High and Holy **On Shabbat:** (And with the permission of the Shabbat Queen.) **On Yom Tov:** (And with the permission of the Holy Festival.) **On Sukkot:** (And with permission of the seven exalted and holy guests) (and with the permissions of, my masters and my teachers) and with your permission.

Nevarech

With Ten Or More: (Eloheinu)

She'achalnu Mishelo.

Let us bless **with ten or more:** (Our God) Him of whose bounty we have eaten.

נְבָרֵךְ

בעשרה או יותר: (אֱלֹהֵינוּ)

שֶׁאָכַלְנוּ מִשֶּׁלוֹ:

Participants respond:

Baruch **with ten or more:** (Eloheinu) **at a marriage supper:** (Shehasimchah Bim'ono)

She'achalnu Mishelo Uvetuvo Chayinu.

בָּרוּךְ בעשרה או יותר: (אֱלֹהֵינוּ) בסעודת

התן: (שֶׁהַשִּׂמְחָה בִמְעוֹנוֹ.)

שֶׁאָכַלְנוּ מִשֶּׁלוֹ וּבְטוּבוֹ

חָיִינוּ:

Let us bless **with ten or more:** (Our God) **at a marraige supper:** (in Whose dwelling place is joy [and]) Him of Whose bounty we have eaten and through whose abundant goodness we live.

Leader responds:

Baruch **with ten or more:** (Eloheinu) **at a marriage supper:** (Shehasimchah Bim'ono)

She'achalnu Mishelo Uvetuvo Chayinu.

בָּרוּךְ בעשרה או יותר: (אֱלֹהֵינוּ) בסעודת

התן: (שֶׁהַשִּׂמְחָה בִמְעוֹנוֹ.)

שֶׁאָכַלְנוּ מִשֶּׁלוֹ וּבְטוּבוֹ

חָיִינוּ:

Let us bless **with ten or more:** (Our God) **at a marraige supper:** (in Whose dwelling place is joy [and]) Him of Whose bounty we have eaten and through whose abundant goodness we live.

First Blessing: Birkhat Hazan / For the Nourishment

[*] denotes opening one's hand and concentrating on the sovereignty of Hashem

Baruch Attah Adonai Eloheinu
Melech Ha'olam Ha'el Hazan

בָּרוּךְ אַתָּה יְהֹוָה אֱלֹהֵינוּ מֶלֶךְ

הָעוֹלָם. הָאֵל הַזָּן

Otanu Ve'et-Ha'olam Kulo	אוֹתָנוּ וְאֶת־הָעוֹלָם כֻּלּוֹ
Betuvo. Bechein Bechesed	בְּטוּבוֹ. בְּחֵן בְּחֶסֶד
Berevach Uverachamim Rabim.	בְּרֶוַח וּבְרַחֲמִים רַבִּים.
Noten Lechem Lechol-Basar; Ki	נֹתֵן לֶחֶם לְכָל־בָּשָׂר כִּי
Le'olam Chasdo. Uvetuvo	לְעוֹלָם חַסְדּוֹ. וּבְטוּבוֹ
Hagadol Tamid Lo Chasar Lanu.	הַגָּדוֹל תָּמִיד לֹא חָסַר לָנוּ.
Ve'al Yechsar Lanu Mazon Tamid	וְאַל יֶחְסַר לָנוּ מָזוֹן תָּמִיד
Le'olam Va'ed. Ki Hu El Zan	לְעוֹלָם וָעֶד. כִּי הוּא אֵל זָן
Umefarnes LaKol Veshulchano	וּמְפַרְנֵס לַכֹּל וְשֻׁלְחָנוֹ
Aruch LaKol. Vehitkin Michyah	עָרוּךְ לַכֹּל. וְהִתְקִין מִחְיָה
Umazon Lechol-Beriyotav Asher	וּמָזוֹן לְכָל־בְּרִיּוֹתָיו אֲשֶׁר
Bara Berachamav Uverov	בָּרָא בְּרַחֲמָיו וּבְרוֹב
Chasadav. Ka'amur. *Potei'ach	חֲסָדָיו. כָּאָמוּר. *פּוֹתֵחַ
Et-Yadecha; Umasbia Lechol-	אֶת־יָדֶךָ וּמַשְׂבִּיעַ לְכָל־
Chai Ratzon. Baruch Attah	חַי רָצוֹן. בָּרוּךְ אַתָּה
Adonai Hazan Et HaKol.	יְהֹוָה הַזָּן אֶת הַכֹּל:

Blessed are You, Hashem our God, King of the universe, Who feeds us, and the whole world with His goodness; with grace, kindness, relief and great mercy, "Who gives food to every creature, for His mercy endures forever." And in His great goodness we have never lacked; and may we never lack food forever and ever, for He feeds and sustains all; and His table is decked for all; He has also prepared nourishment and food for all His creatures, which He has created in His abundant mercy and kindness; as it is written: *"You open Your hand, and satisfy every living-being with favor." Blessed are You, Hashem, Who feeds all. (Psalms 136:25, 145:16)

Second Blessing:
Birkhat Ha'Aretz / For the Land

Nodeh Lecha Adonai Eloheinu	נוֹדֶה לְךָ יהוה אֱלֹהֵינוּ
Al Shehinchalta La'avoteinu.	עַל שֶׁהִנְחַלְתָּ לַאֲבוֹתֵינוּ.
Eretz Chemdah Tovah	אֶרֶץ חֶמְדָּה טוֹבָה
Urechavah Berit Vetorah	וּרְחָבָה בְּרִית וְתוֹרָה
Chayim Umazon. Al	חַיִּים וּמָזוֹן. עַל
Shehotzetanu Me'eretz	שֶׁהוֹצֵאתָנוּ מֵאֶרֶץ
Mitzrayim. Ufeditanu Mibeit	מִצְרָיִם. וּפְדִיתָנוּ מִבֵּית
Avadim. Ve'al Beritecha	עֲבָדִים. וְעַל בְּרִיתְךָ
Shechatamta Bivsarenu. Ve'al	שֶׁחָתַמְתָּ בִּבְשָׂרֵנוּ. וְעַל
Toratecha Shelimadtanu. Ve'al	תוֹרָתְךָ שֶׁלִּמַּדְתָּנוּ. וְעַל
Chukkei Retzonach	חֻקֵּי רְצוֹנָךְ
Shehoda'tanu. Ve'al Chayim	שֶׁהוֹדַעְתָּנוּ. וְעַל חַיִּים
Umazon She'attah Zan	וּמָזוֹן שֶׁאַתָּה זָן
Umefarnes Otanu.	וּמְפַרְנֵס אוֹתָנוּ:

We thank You, Hashem our God, for having caused our fathers to inherit that desirable, good, and spacious land; for a covenant and Torah, life and sustenance; and because You have brought us out from the land of Mitzrayim, and redeemed us from the house of bondage; and for Your covenant which You have sealed in our flesh, and for the statutes of Your gracious will, which You have made known to us, and for the life and food which You feed and sustain us.

On Hanukkah and Purim, Al HaNissim is recited:

Al HaNissim

עַל הַנִּסִּים וְעַל הַפֻּרְקָן וְעַל הַגְּבוּרוֹת וְעַל הַתְּשׁוּעוֹת וְעַל הַנִּפְלָאוֹת וְעַל הַנֶּחָמוֹת שֶׁעָשִׂיתָ לַאֲבוֹתֵינוּ בַּיָּמִים הָהֵם בַּזְּמַן הַזֶּה:

Al Hanissim Ve'al Hapurkan Ve'al Hagevurot Ve'al Hateshu'ot Ve'al Hanifla'ot Ve'al Hanechamot She'asita La'avoteinu Bayamim Hahem Bazman Hazeh.

For the miracles, and for the triumphant liberation, and the mighty works, and for the deliverances, and for the wonders, and for the consolations which You have done for our fathers in those days at this season:

On Hanukkah:

בִּימֵי מַתִּתְיָה בֶן־יוֹחָנָן כֹּהֵן גָּדוֹל. חַשְׁמוֹנָאִי וּבָנָיו כְּשֶׁעָמְדָה מַלְכוּת יָוָן הָרְשָׁעָה עַל עַמְּךָ יִשְׂרָאֵל. לְשַׁכְּחָם תּוֹרָתֶךָ וּלְהַעֲבִירָם מֵחֻקֵּי רְצוֹנֶךָ. וְאַתָּה בְּרַחֲמֶיךָ הָרַבִּים עָמַדְתָּ לָהֶם בְּעֵת צָרָתָם. רַבְתָּ אֶת רִיבָם. דַּנְתָּ אֶת דִּינָם. נָקַמְתָּ אֶת נִקְמָתָם. מָסַרְתָּ גִבּוֹרִים בְּיַד חַלָּשִׁים. וְרַבִּים בְּיַד מְעַטִּים. וּרְשָׁעִים בְּיַד צַדִּיקִים. וּטְמֵאִים בְּיַד טְהוֹרִים. וְזֵדִים בְּיַד עוֹסְקֵי תוֹרָתֶךָ. לְךָ עָשִׂיתָ שֵׁם גָּדוֹל וְקָדוֹשׁ בְּעוֹלָמֶךָ. וּלְעַמְּךָ יִשְׂרָאֵל עָשִׂיתָ תְּשׁוּעָה גְדוֹלָה וּפֻרְקָן כְּהַיּוֹם הַזֶּה. וְאַחַר כָּךְ בָּאוּ בָנֶיךָ לִדְבִיר בֵּיתֶךָ. וּפִנּוּ אֶת־הֵיכָלֶךָ. וְטִהֲרוּ אֶת־מִקְדָּשֶׁךָ. וְהִדְלִיקוּ נֵרוֹת בְּחַצְרוֹת קָדְשֶׁךָ. וְקָבְעוּ שְׁמוֹנַת יְמֵי חֲנֻכָּה אֵלּוּ בְּהַלֵּל וּבְהוֹדָאָה. וְעָשִׂיתָ עִמָּהֶם נִסִּים וְנִפְלָאוֹת וְנוֹדֶה לְשִׁמְךָ הַגָּדוֹל סֶלָה:

Bimei Mattityah Ven-Yochanan Kohen Gadol. Chashmona'i Uvanav Keshe'amedah Malchut Yavan Haresha'ah Al Ammecha Yisra'el. Leshakecham Toratach Uleha'aviram Mechukkei Retzonach. Ve'attah Berachameicha Harabim Amadta Lahem Be'et Tzaratam. Ravta Et Rivam. Danta Et Dinam. Nakamta Et Nikmatam. Masarta Giborim Beyad Chalashim. Verabim Beyad Me'atim. Uresha'im Beyad Tzaddikim. Uteme'im Beyad Tehorim. Vezeidim Beyad Osekei Toratecha. Lecha Asita Shem Gadol Vekadosh Be'olamach. Ule'ammecha Yisra'el Asita Teshu'ah Gedolah Ufurkan Kehayom Hazeh. Ve'achar Kach Ba'u Vaneicha Lidvir Beitecha. Ufinu Et-Heichalecha. Vetiharu Et-Mikdashecha. Vehidliku Nerot Bechatzrot Kodshecha. Vekave'u Shemonat Yemei Chanukkah Elu Behallel Uvehoda'ah. Ve'asita Imahem Nissim Venifla'ot Venodeh Leshimcha Hagadol Selah.

Then in the days of Mattityahu ben-Yochanan, High Priest, the Hasmonean and his sons, when the cruel Greek power rose up against Your people, Yisrael, to make them forget Your Torah and transgress the statutes of Your will. And You, in Your great compassion, stood up for them in time of their trial to plead their cause and defend their judgment. Giving out retribution, delivered the strong into the hand of the weak, and the many into the hand of the few, and the wicked into the hand of the upright, and the impure into the hand of the pure, and tyrants into the hand of the devotees of Your Torah. You made for Yourself a great and holy name in Your world. And for Your people, Yisrael, You performed a great salvation and liberation as this very day. Then Your children came to the Sanctuary of Your House, cleared Your Temple, cleansed Your Sanctuary and kindled lights in Your courtyards, and they instituted these eight days of Hanukkah for praise and thanksgiving. And You did miracles and wonders for them, and we give thanks to

Your great name, selah.

On Purim:

בִּימֵי מָרְדְּכַי וְאֶסְתֵּר בְּשׁוּשַׁן הַבִּירָה. כְּשֶׁעָמַד עֲלֵיהֶם הָמָן הָרָשָׁע. בִּקֵּשׁ
לְהַשְׁמִיד לַהֲרֹג וּלְאַבֵּד אֶת־כָּל־הַיְּהוּדִים מִנַּעַר וְעַד זָקֵן טַף וְנָשִׁים בְּיוֹם אֶחָד.
בִּשְׁלֹשָׁה עָשָׂר לְחֹדֶשׁ שְׁנֵים עָשָׂר. הוּא חֹדֶשׁ אֲדָר. וּשְׁלָלָם לָבוֹז. וְאַתָּה
בְּרַחֲמֶיךָ הָרַבִּים הֵפַרְתָּ אֶת־עֲצָתוֹ וְקִלְקַלְתָּ אֶת־מַחֲשַׁבְתּוֹ. וַהֲשֵׁבוֹתָ לוֹ גְּמוּלוֹ
בְּרֹאשׁוֹ. וְתָלוּ אוֹתוֹ וְאֶת־בָּנָיו עַל הָעֵץ. וְעָשִׂיתָ עִמָּהֶם נֵס וָפֶלֶא וְנוֹדֶה לְשִׁמְךָ
הַגָּדוֹל סֶלָה:

Bimei Mordechai Ve'ester Beshushan Habbirah. Keshe'amad Aleihem Haman
Harasha. Bikesh Lehashmid Laharog Ule'abed Et-Kol-Hayehudim Mina'ar Ve'ad
Zaken Taf Venashim Beyom Echad. Bishloshah Asar Lechodesh Sheneim Asar. Hu
Chodesh Adar. Ushelalam Lavoz. Ve'attah Berachameicha Harabim Hefarta
Et-'Atzato Vekilkalta Et-Machashavto. Vahasheivota Lo Gemulo Verosho. Vetalu Oto
Ve'et-Banav Al Ha'etz. Ve'asita Imahem Nes Vafelei Venodeh Leshimcha Hagadol
Selah.

In the days of Mordechai and Ester in Shushan, the capital, the wicked Haman rose
up and sought to destroy, slay and utterly annihilate all of the Yehudim, both young
and old, women and children, on one day, on the thirteenth day of the twelfth
month, which is the month of Adar, and to plunder their possessions. But You in
Your great mercy You broke his plan and spoiled his designs, causing them to recoil
on his own head, and they hanged him and his sons on the gallows. And You did
miracles and wonders for them, and we give thanks to Your great name, selah.

Al Hakol Adonai Eloheinu	עַל הַכֹּל יְהֹוָה אֱלֹהֵינוּ
Anachnu Modim Lach	אֲנַחְנוּ מוֹדִים לָךְ
Umevarechim Et Shemach.	וּמְבָרְכִים אֶת שְׁמָךְ.
Ka'amur. Ve'achalta Vesava'eta;	כָּאָמוּר. וְאָכַלְתָּ וְשָׂבָעְתָּ
Uverachta Et-Adonai Eloheicha.	וּבֵרַכְתָּ אֶת־יְהֹוָה אֱלֹהֶיךָ
Al-Ha'aretz Hatovah Asher	עַל־הָאָרֶץ הַטֹּבָה אֲשֶׁר
Natan-Lach. Baruch Attah	נָתַן־לָךְ. בָּרוּךְ אַתָּה
Adonai Al Ha'aretz Ve'al	יְהֹוָה עַל הָאָרֶץ וְעַל
Hamazon.	הַמָּזוֹן:

For everything, Hashem our God, we thank You and bless Your
Name. As it says, "And You will eat and be satisfied, and bless
Hashem, Your God, for the good land which He has given to you."
Blessed are You, Hashem, for the land and the sustenance.

Third Blessing:
Binyan Yerushalayim / Building up of Yerushalayim

Rachem Adonai Eloheinu Aleinu	רַחֵם יְהֹוָה אֱלֹהֵינוּ עָלֵינוּ
Ve'al Yisra'el Amach. Ve'al	וְעַל יִשְׂרָאֵל עַמֶּךָ. וְעַל
Yerushalayim Irach. Ve'al Har	יְרוּשָׁלַיִם עִירָךְ. וְעַל הַר
Tziyon Mishkan Kevodach. Ve'al	צִיּוֹן מִשְׁכַּן כְּבוֹדָךְ. וְעַל
Heichalach. Ve'al Me'onach.	הֵיכָלָךְ. וְעַל מְעוֹנָךְ.
Ve'al Devirach. Ve'al Habayit	וְעַל דְּבִירָךְ. וְעַל הַבַּיִת
Hagadol VeHakadosh Shenikra	הַגָּדוֹל וְהַקָּדוֹשׁ שֶׁנִּקְרָא
Shimcha Alav. Avinu. Re'enu.	שִׁמְךָ עָלָיו. אָבִינוּ. רְעֵנוּ.
Zunenu. Parnesenu. Kalkelenu.	זוּנֵנוּ. פַּרְנְסֵנוּ. כַּלְכְּלֵנוּ.
Harvicheinu Harvach-Lanu	הַרְוִיחֵנוּ הַרְוַח לָנוּ
Meheirah Mikol Tzaroteinu.	מְהֵרָה מִכָּל צָרוֹתֵינוּ.
Vena. Al Tazricheinu Adonai	וְנָא. אַל תַּצְרִיכֵנוּ יְהֹוָה
Eloheinu. Lidei Mattenot Basar	אֱלֹהֵינוּ. לִידֵי מַתְּנוֹת בָּשָׂר
Vadam Velo Lidei Halva'atam.	וָדָם וְלֹא לִידֵי הַלְוָאָתָם.
Ella Leyadecha Hamele'ah	אֶלָּא לְיָדְךָ הַמְּלֵאָה
Veharechavah. Ha'ashirah	וְהָרְחָבָה. הָעֲשִׁירָה
Vehappetuchah. Yehi Ratzon	וְהַפְּתוּחָה. יְהִי רָצוֹן
Shelo Nevosh Ba'olam Hazeh.	שֶׁלֹּא נֵבוֹשׁ בָּעוֹלָם הַזֶּה.
Velo Nikalem La'olam Haba.	וְלֹא נִכָּלֵם לְעוֹלָם הַבָּא.

Umalchut Beit David	וּמַלְכוּת בֵּית דָּוִד
Meshichach Tachazirenah	מְשִׁיחָךְ תַּחֲזִירֶנָּה
Limkomah Bimheirah	לִמְקוֹמָהּ בִּמְהֵרָה
Veyameinu.	בְיָמֵינוּ:

Hashem our God, have mercy on us, on Your people Yisrael, and on Your city Yerushalayim, and on Mount Tziyon, the residence of Your glory, and the great and holy house, which is called by Your name. Our Father, tend us, nourish us, sustain us, provide for us, relieve us and us grant relief speedily from all our anxieties, and let us not, Hashem our God, stand in need of the gifts of flesh and blood, or of their loans; But let our dependence be only on Your hand, which is full, plentiful, rich and open; so that we may not be put to shame in this world, or be humiliated in the world to come. And the kingdom of the House of David, Your anointed, restore also speedily in our days.

On Rosh Hodesh, Intermediate days of Passover and Sukkot, and Yom Tov say:

Ya'aleh Veyavo

אֱלֹהֵינוּ וֵאלֹהֵי אֲבוֹתֵינוּ. יַעֲלֶה וְיָבֹא. וְיַגִּיעַ וְיֵרָאֶה. וְיֵרָצֶה וְיִשָּׁמַע. וְיִפָּקֵד וְיִזָּכֵר. זִכְרוֹנֵנוּ וְזִכְרוֹן אֲבוֹתֵינוּ. זִכְרוֹן יְרוּשָׁלַיִם עִירָךְ. וְזִכְרוֹן מָשִׁיחַ בֶּן־דָּוִד עַבְדָּךְ. וְזִכְרוֹן כָּל־עַמְּךָ בֵּית יִשְׂרָאֵל לְפָנֶיךָ. לִפְלֵיטָה. לְטוֹבָה. לְחֵן. לְחֶסֶד וּלְרַחֲמִים. לְחַיִּים טוֹבִים וּלְשָׁלוֹם. בְּיוֹם:

Eloheinu Velohei Avoteinu. Ya'aleh Veyavo. Veyagia Veyera'eh. Veyeratzeh Veyishama'. Veyipaked Veyizacher. Zichronenu Vezichron Avoteinu. Zichron Yerushalayim Irach. Vezichron Mashiach Ben-David Avdach. Vezichron Kol-'Ammecha Beit Yisra'el Lefaneicha. Lifleitah. Letovah. Lechein. Lechesed Ulerachamim. Lechayim Tovim Uleshalom. Beyom:

Our God, and God of our fathers, may it rise, and come, arrive, appear, find favor, and be heard, and be considered, and be remembered our remembrance and the remembrance of our fathers, Yerushalayim Your city, the remembrance of Messiah ben David Your servant, and the remembrance of all Your people of the House of Yisrael before You for deliverance, for good favor, for kindness and mercy, for good life and for peace. On this day of:

On Rosh Chodesh:

רֹאשׁ חֹדֶשׁ הַזֶּה.

Rosh Chodesh Hazeh.

Rosh Chodesh [New Moon].

On Pesach:

חַג הַמַּצוֹת הַזֶּה בְּיוֹם (ביום טוב: טוֹב מִקְרָא קֹדֶשׁ הַזֶּה):

Chag Hamatzot Hazeh Beyom **On Yom Tov:** (Tov Mikra Kodesh Hazeh):

The Festival of Matzot, this day **on Yom Tov:** (appointed for Holy Convocation):

On Shavuot:

חַג הַשָּׁבוּעוֹת הַזֶּה בְּיוֹם טוֹב מִקְרָא קֹדֶשׁ הַזֶּה:

Chag Hashavuot Hazeh Beyom Mikra Kodesh Hazeh.

The Festival of Shavuot, this appointed day of Holy Convocation:

On Sukkot:

חַג הַסֻּכּוֹת הַזֶּה בְּיוֹם (ביום טוב: טוֹב מִקְרָא קֹדֶשׁ הַזֶּה):

Chag Hasukkot Hazeh Beyom **On Yom Tov:** (Tov Mikra Kodesh Hazeh):

The Festival of Sukkot, this day **on Yom Tov:** (appointed for Holy Convocation):

On Shemini Atzeret:

שְׁמִינִי חַג עֲצֶרֶת הַזֶּה בְּיוֹם טוֹב מִקְרָא קֹדֶשׁ הַזֶּה:

Shemini Chag Atzeret Hazeh Beyom Tov Mikra Kodesh Hazeh:

The Festival of Shemini Atzeret, this appointed day of Holy Convocation:

On Rosh Hashanah:

הַזִּכָּרוֹן הַזֶּה בְּיוֹם טוֹב מִקְרָא קֹדֶשׁ הַזֶּה:

Hazikaron Hazeh Beyom Tov Mikra Kodesh Hazeh:

The Memorial, this appointed day of Holy Convocation:

לְרַחֵם בּוֹ עָלֵינוּ וּלְהוֹשִׁיעֵנוּ. זָכְרֵנוּ יְהוָה אֱלֹהֵינוּ בּוֹ לְטוֹבָה. וּפָקְדֵנוּ בּוֹ
לִבְרָכָה. וְהוֹשִׁיעֵנוּ בּוֹ לְחַיִּים טוֹבִים. בִּדְבַר יְשׁוּעָה וְרַחֲמִים. חוּס וְחָנֵּנוּ.
וַחֲמוֹל וְרַחֵם עָלֵינוּ. וְהוֹשִׁיעֵנוּ כִּי אֵלֶיךָ עֵינֵינוּ. כִּי אֵל מֶלֶךְ חַנּוּן וְרַחוּם אָתָּה:

Lerachem Bo Aleinu Ulehoshi'enu. Zochrenu Adonai Eloheinu Bo Letovah.
Ufokdenu Vo Livrachah. Vehoshi'enu Vo Lechayim Tovim. Bidvar Yeshu'ah
Verachamim. Chus Vechanenu. Vachamol Verachem Aleinu. Vehoshi'enu Ki Eleicha
Eineinu. Ki El Melech Chanun Verachum Attah.

to have mercy upon us and save us. Remember us, Hashem our God, on it for good.
Be mindful of us on it for blessing and save us on it for a life of good. With the
promise of salvation and mercy, show us pity, and be gracious to us and have

compassion and mercy on us and save us. For our eyes are lifted towards You, for You, God, are a gracious and merciful King.

Vetivneh Yerushalayim Irach	וְתִבְנֶה יְרוּשָׁלַיִם עִירָךְ
Bimheirah Veyameinu. Baruch	בִּמְהֵרָה בְיָמֵינוּ. בָּרוּךְ
Attah Adonai Boneh	אַתָּה יְהֹוָה בּוֹנֵה
Yerushalayim. Say Quietly: Amen.	יְרוּשָׁלָיִם ואומר בלחש: אָמֵן:

And build Yerushalayim, Your city, speedily in our days. Blessed are You, Hashem, Builder of Yerushalayim. say Quietly: Amen.

If one forgot to say Ya'aleh Veyavo and remembers, he should say the appropriate blessing here. Only pronounce Hashem part on the first days of Pesach and Sukkot and on Shabbat, except 3rd meal. Other wise say "Blessed is He" (SA, OC:188):

בָּרוּךְ (אַתָּה יְהֹוָה אֱלֹהֵינוּ מֶלֶךְ הָעוֹלָם) שֶׁנָּתַן:

Baruch (Attah Adonai Eloheinu Melech Ha'olam) Shenatan:

Blessed (are You, Hashem our God King of the universe,) Who has given us:

For Shabbat:

שַׁבָּתוֹת לִמְנוּחָה לְעַמּוֹ יִשְׂרָאֵל בְּאַהֲבָה לְאוֹת וְלִבְרִית:

Shabbatot Limnuchah Le'ammo Yisra'el Be'ahavah Le'ot Velivrit:

Shabbatot for joy to His people Yisrael with love for a sign and covenant:

For Rosh Chodesh:

(וְ)רָאשֵׁי חֳדָשִׁים לְעַמּוֹ יִשְׂרָאֵל לְזִכָּרוֹן:

(Ve)Roshei Chodashim Le'ammo Yisra'el Lezikaron:

(and) New Moons to His people Yisrael for a memorial:

For Rosh Hashanah:

(וְ)יָמִים טוֹבִים לְיִשְׂרָאֵל אֶת יוֹם הַזִּכָּרוֹן הַזֶּה:

(Ve)Yamim Tovim Leyisra'el Et Yom Hazikaron Hazeh:

(and) festival days to Yisrael, this day of memorial:

For the Shelosh Regalim / Three Pilgrimage Festivals:

(וְ)יָמִים טוֹבִים לְשָׂשׂוֹן וּלְשִׂמְחָה אֶת יוֹם (חַג הַמַּצוֹת הַזֶּה) (חַג הַשָּׁבוּעוֹת הַזֶּה) (חַג הַסֻּכּוֹת הַזֶּה) (שְׁמִינִי חַג עֲצֶרֶת הַזֶּה):

Ve)Yamim Tovim Lesasson Ulesimchah Et Yom (Chag Hamatzot Hazeh) (Chag Hashavuot Hazeh) (Chag Hasukkot Hazeh) (Shemini Chag Atzeret Hazeh):

(and) festival days for happiness and joy, the day of (this feast of Matzot) (this feast of Sukkot) (This feast of Shemini Atzeret).

בָּרוּךְ (אַתָּה יְהוָה) מְקַדֵּשׁ (הַשַּׁבָּת) (וְ) (יִשְׂרָאֵל וְרָאשֵׁי חֳדָשִׁים) (יִשְׂרָאֵל וְיוֹם הַזִּכָּרוֹן) (יִשְׂרָאֵל וְהַזְּמַנִּים):

Baruch (Attah Adonai) Mekadesh (Hashabbat) (Ve) (Yisra'el Roshei Chodashim) (Yisra'el Veyom Hazikaron) (Yisra'el Vehazmanim):

Blessed (are You, Hashem) Who sanctifies (the Shabbat) (and) (Yisrael and the New Moons) (Yisrael and the day of memorial) (Yisrael and the seasons).

Fourth Blessing:
HaTov Vehameitiv / For the Goodness of God

Baruch Attah Adonai Eloheinu	בָּרוּךְ אַתָּה יְהוָה אֱלֹהֵינוּ
Melech Ha'olam Ha'el Avinu.	מֶלֶךְ הָעוֹלָם. הָאֵל אָבִינוּ.
Malkeinu. Adireinu. Bore'enu.	מַלְכֵּנוּ. אַדִּירֵנוּ. בּוֹרְאֵנוּ.
Go'alenu. Kedoshenu Kedosh	גּוֹאֲלֵנוּ. קְדוֹשֵׁנוּ קְדוֹשׁ
Ya'akov. Ro'enu Ro'eh Yisra'el.	יַעֲקֹב. רוֹעֵנוּ רוֹעֵה יִשְׂרָאֵל.
Hamelech Hatov. Vehameitiv	הַמֶּלֶךְ הַטּוֹב. וְהַמֵּטִיב
Lakol. Shebechol-Yom Vayom	לַכֹּל. שֶׁבְּכָל-יוֹם וָיוֹם
Hu Hetiv Lanu. Hu Meitiv Lanu.	הוּא הֵטִיב לָנוּ. הוּא מֵטִיב לָנוּ.
Hu Yeitiv Lanu. Hu Gemalanu.	הוּא יֵיטִיב לָנוּ. הוּא גְמָלָנוּ.
Hu Gomelenu. Hu Yigmelenu	הוּא גוֹמְלֵנוּ. הוּא יִגְמְלֵנוּ
La'ad Chein Vachesed	לָעַד חֵן וָחֶסֶד
Verachamim Verevach	וְרַחֲמִים וְרֶוַח
Vehatzalah Vechol-Tov.	וְהַצָּלָה וְכָל-טוֹב:
And Answer: Amen.	יענו: אָמֵן:

Blessed are You, Hashem our God, King of the universe, the God our Father, our King, our Strength, our Creator, our Redeemer, our Holy One: the Holy One of Yaakov, our Shepherd, the Shepherd of Yisrael; the King Who is good and beneficent to all; Who day by day has been, is, and ever will be beneficent to us. He has dealt bountifully with us, as He does now, and forever will: granting us grace, kindness, mercy, relief, deliverance, and every good. **And answer:** Amen.

הָרַחֲמָן הוּא יִשְׁתַּבַּח עַל כִּסֵּא כְבוֹדוֹ:

Harachaman Hu Yishtabach Al Kissei Chevodo.

May the All-merciful be praised on the Throne of His glory.

הָרַחֲמָן הוּא יִשְׁתַּבַּח בַּשָּׁמַיִם וּבָאָרֶץ:

Harachaman Hu Yishtabach Bashamayim Uva'aretz.

May the All-merciful be praised in heaven and on earth.

הָרַחֲמָן הוּא יִשְׁתַּבַּח בָּנוּ לְדוֹר דּוֹרִים:

Harachaman Hu Yishtabach Banu Ledor Dorim.

May the All-merciful be praised amidst us throughout all generations.

הָרַחֲמָן הוּא קֶרֶן לְעַמּוֹ יָרִים:

Harachaman Hu Keren Le'ammo Yarim.

May the All-merciful exalt the horn of His people.

הָרַחֲמָן הוּא יִתְפָּאַר בָּנוּ לְנֵצַח נְצָחִים:

Harachaman Hu Yitpa'ar Banu Lenetzach Netzachim.

May the All-merciful be glorified amidst us to all eternity.

הָרַחֲמָן הוּא יְפַרְנְסֵנוּ בְּכָבוֹד וְלֹא בְבִזּוּי בְּהֶתֵּר וְלֹא בְאִסּוּר בְּנַחַת וְלֹא בְצַעַר:

Harachaman Hu Yefarnesenu Bechavod Velo Vevizui Behetter Velo Ve'issur Benachat Velo Vetza'ar.

May the All-merciful grant us sustenance with honor, and not with contempt; lawfully, and not by forbidden means; in ease, and not with trouble.

הָרַחֲמָן הוּא יִתֵּן שָׁלוֹם בֵּינֵינוּ:

Harachaman Hu Yiten Shalom Beineinu.

May the All-merciful grant peace amongst us.

הָרַחֲמָן הוּא יִשְׁלַח בְּרָכָה רְוָחָה וְהַצְלָחָה בְּכָל מַעֲשֵׂה יָדֵינוּ:

Harachaman Hu Yishlach Berachah Revachah Vehatzlachah Bechol Ma'aseh Yadeinu.

May the All-merciful send blessing and prosperity to all the work of our hands.

הָרַחֲמָן הוּא יַצְלִיחַ אֶת דְּרָכֵינוּ:

Harachaman Hu Yatzliach Et Deracheinu.

May the All-merciful prosper all our ways.

הָרַחֲמָן הוּא יִשְׁבֹּר עֹל גָּלוּת מְהֵרָה מֵעַל צַוָּארֵנוּ:

Harachaman Hu Yishbor Ol Galut Meheirah Me'al Tzavarenu.

May the All-merciful speedily break the yoke of the nations from off our neck.

הָרַחֲמָן הוּא יוֹלִיכֵנוּ מְהֵרָה קוֹמְמִיּוּת לְאַרְצֵנוּ:

Harachaman Hu Yolicheinu Meheirah Komemiyut Le'artzenu.

May the All-merciful lead us securely to our land.

הָרַחֲמָן הוּא יִרְפָּאֵנוּ רְפוּאָה שְׁלֵמָה. רְפוּאַת הַנֶּפֶשׁ וּרְפוּאַת הַגּוּף:

Harachaman Hu Yirpa'enu Refu'ah Shelemah. Refu'at Hanefesh Urefu'at Haguf.

May the All-merciful grant us perfect healing, healing of soul and healing of body.

הָרַחֲמָן הוּא יִפְתַּח לָנוּ אֶת יָדוֹ הָרְחָבָה:

Harachaman Hu Yiftach Lanu Et Yado Harechavah.

May the All-merciful open for us His bountiful hand.

הָרַחֲמָן הוּא יְבָרֵךְ כָּל־אֶחָד וְאֶחָד מִמֶּנּוּ בִּשְׁמוֹ הַגָּדוֹל כְּמוֹ שֶׁנִּתְבָּרְכוּ אֲבוֹתֵינוּ אַבְרָהָם יִצְחָק וְיַעֲקֹב, בַּכֹּל מִכֹּל כֹּל, כֵּן יְבָרֵךְ אוֹתָנוּ יַחַד בְּרָכָה שְׁלֵמָה, וְכֵן יְהִי רָצוֹן וְנֹאמַר אָמֵן: הָרַחֲמָן הוּא יִפְרוֹשׁ עָלֵינוּ סֻכַּת שְׁלוֹמוֹ:

Harachaman Hu Yevarech Kol Echad Ve'echad Mimenu Bishmo
Hagadol Kemo Shenitbarechu Avoteinu Avraham Yitzchak
Veya'akov. Bakol Mikol Kol. Ken Yevarech Otanu Yachad Berachah
Shelemah. Vechein Yehi Ratzon Venomar Amen. Harachaman Hu
Yifros Aleinu Sukkat Shelomo.

May the All-merciful bless each of us by His great name, even as our
ancestors Avraham, Yitzchak and Yaakov were blessed with every
blessing. So may He bless us all together with perfect blessing. And
so may this be His will, and let us say, Amen. May the All-merciful
spread over us the shelter of His peace.

On Shabbat:

הָרַחֲמָן הוּא יַנְחִילֵנוּ עוֹלָם שֶׁכֻּלוֹ שַׁבָּת וּמְנוּחָה לְחַיֵּי הָעוֹלָמִים:

Harachaman Hu Yanchilenu Olam Shekulo Shabbat Umenuchah Lechayei
Ha'olamim.

May the All-merciful cause us to inherit a world which will be entirely Shabbat, and
rest for eternal life.

On Rosh Chodesh:

הָרַחֲמָן הוּא יְחַדֵּשׁ עָלֵינוּ אֶת הַחְדֶשׁ הַזֶּה לְטוֹבָה וְלִבְרָכָה:

Harachaman Hu Yechadesh Aleinu Et Hachodesh Hazeh Letovah Velivrachah.

May the All-merciful renew upon us this month for good and for blessing.

On Rosh Hashanah:

הָרַחֲמָן הוּא יְחַדֵּשׁ עָלֵינוּ אֶת הַשָּׁנָה הַזֹּאת לְטוֹבָה וְלִבְרָכָה:

Harachaman Hu Yechadesh Aleinu Et Hashanah HaZot Letovah Velivrachah.

May the All-merciful renew upon us this year for good and for blessing.

On Sukkot:

הָרַחֲמָן הוּא יְזַכֵּנוּ לֵישֵׁב בְּסֻכַּת עוֹרוֹ שֶׁל לִוְיָתָן: הָרַחֲמָן הוּא יַשְׁפִּיעַ עָלֵינוּ
שֶׁפַע קְדֻשָּׁה וְטָהֳרָה מִשִּׁבְעָה אוֹשְׁפִּיזִין עִלָּאִין קַדִּישִׁין. זְכוּתָם תְּהֵא מָגֵן
וְצִנָּה בַּעֲדֵינוּ: הָרַחֲמָן הוּא יָקִים לָנוּ אֶת סֻכַּת דָּוִד הַנּוֹפֶלֶת:

Harachaman Hu Yezakenu Leishev Besukkat Oro Shel Livyatan. Harachaman Hu
Yashpia Aleinu Shefa Kedushah VeTaharah Mishiv'ah Ushepizin Illa'in Kaddishin.
Zechutam Tehei Magen Vetzinah Ba'adeinu. Harachaman Hu Yakim Lanu Et Sukkat
David Hanofelet.

May the All-merciful give us the merit to sit in the Sukkah of the skin of Leviathan.
May the All-merciful bestow upon us plenty of holiness and purity from the seven
holy and pure guests, may their merit be a shield and protection for us. May the All-
merciful establish for us the Sukkah of David, that is fallen.

On Sukkot, Pesach and Shavuot:

הָרַחֲמָן הוּא יַגִּיעֵנוּ לְמוֹעֲדִים אֲחֵרִים הַבָּאִים לִקְרָאתֵנוּ לְשָׁלוֹם:

Harachaman Hu Yaggi'enu Lemo'adim Acherim Habai'm Likratenu Leshalom.

May the All-merciful allow us to arrive at other appointed-times that come to greet us for peace.

On Yom Tov:

הָרַחֲמָן הוּא יַנְחִילֵנוּ יוֹם שֶׁכֻּלוֹ טוֹב:

Harachaman Hu Yanchilenu Yom Shekulo Tov.

May the All-merciful grant us a day that is completely good.

הָרַחֲמָן הוּא יִטַּע תּוֹרָתוֹ וְאַהֲבָתוֹ בְּלִבֵּנוּ וְתִהְיֶה יִרְאָתוֹ עַל פָּנֵינוּ לְבִלְתִּי נֶחֱטָא. וְיִהְיוּ כָל מַעֲשֵׂינוּ לְשֵׁם שָׁמָיִם:

Harachaman Hu Yitta Torato Ve'ahavato Belibeinu Vetihyeh Yir'ato Al Paneinu Levilti Necheta. Veyihyu Chol-Ma'aseinu Leshem Shamayim.

May the All-merciful plant His Torah and His love into our hearts. And may His fear be on our faces that we may not sin. And all our works should be for the sake of heaven.

A guest says:

הָרַחֲמָן הוּא יְבָרֵךְ אֶת הַשֻּׁלְחָן הַזֶּה שֶׁאָכַלְנוּ עָלָיו וִיסַדֵּר בּוֹ כָּל מַעֲדַנֵּי עוֹלָם. וְיִהְיֶה כְּשֻׁלְחָנוֹ שֶׁל אַבְרָהָם אָבִינוּ. כָּל רָעֵב מִמֶּנּוּ יֹאכַל וְכָל צָמֵא מִמֶּנּוּ יִשְׁתֶּה. וְאַל יֶחְסַר מִמֶּנּוּ כָּל טוּב לָעַד וּלְעוֹלְמֵי עוֹלָמִים. אָמֵן. הָרַחֲמָן הוּא יְבָרֵךְ בַּעַל הַבַּיִת הַזֶּה וּבַעַל הַסְּעוּדָּה הַזֹּאת. הוּא וּבָנָיו וְאִשְׁתּוֹ וְכָל אֲשֶׁר לוֹ. בְּבָנִים שֶׁיִּחְיוּ וּבִנְכָסִים שֶׁיִּרְבּוּ. בָּרֵךְ יְהֹוָה חֵילוֹ וּפֹעַל יָדָיו תִּרְצֶה. וְיִהְיוּ נְכָסָיו וּנְכָסֵינוּ מֻצְלָחִים וּקְרוֹבִים לָעִיר. וְאַל יִזְדַּקֵּק לְפָנָיו וְלֹא לְפָנֵינוּ שׁוּם דְּבַר חֵטְא וְהִרְהוּר עָוֹן. שָׂשׂ וְשָׂמֵחַ כָּל-הַיָּמִים. בְּעֹשֶׁר וְכָבוֹד. מֵעַתָּה וְעַד עוֹלָם. לֹא יֵבוֹשׁ בָּעוֹלָם הַזֶּה. וְלֹא יִכָּלֵם לָעוֹלָם הַבָּא. אָמֵן כֵּן יְהִי רָצוֹן:

Harachaman Hu Yevarech Et Hashulchan Hazeh She'achalnu Alav Visader Bo Kol Ma'adanei Olam. Veyihyeh Keshulchano Shel

Avraham Avinu. Kol Ra'ev Mimenu Yochal Vechol Tzamei Mimenu
Yishteh. Ve'al Yechsar Mimenu Kol Tuv La'ad Ule'olemei Olamim.
Amen. Harachaman Hu Yevarech Ba'al Habayit Hazeh Uva'al
Hasse'udah HaZot. Hu Uvanav Ve'ishto Vechol Asher Lo. Bevanim
Sheyichyu Uvinchasim Sheyirbu. Barech Adonai Cheilo. Ufo'al
Yadav Tirtzeh;. Veyihyu Nechasav Unechaseinu Mutzlachim
Ukerovim La'ir. Ve'al Yizdakel Lefanav Velo Lefaneinu Shum Devar
Chet Vehirhur Avon. Sas Vesameach Kol-Hayamim. Be'osher
Vechavod. Me'attah Ve'ad Olam. Lo Yevosh Ba'olam Hazeh. Velo
Yikalem La'olam Haba. Amen Ken Yehi Ratzon.

May the All-merciful bless this table at which we have eaten, and
may all the delicacies of the world be served upon it; may it be like
the table of Avraham, our forefather, so that every hungry one may
eat from it and every thirsty one drink from it. And do not deprive
him of all good forever. Amen. May the All-merciful bless the master
of this house, and the host of this meal; him, his children, and his
wife, and all that belongs to him, with children who will live and with
possessions that will multiply. Bless, Hashem, his substance, And
accept the work of his hands; (Deut. 33:11) And may he prosper in all his
possessions; may all his and our possessions be successful and near
to the city; (Berakhot 46a:6) And do not require before him or before us
anything of sin or contemplation of iniquity. May they have joy and
gladness all their days, in wealth and honor now and forever. May
he not be put to shame in this world or be confounded in the world
to come. Amen, yes, may it be His will.

At a circumcision:

הָרַחֲמָן הוּא יְבָרֵךְ אֶת בַּעַל הַבַּיִת הַזֶּה. אֲבִי הַבֵּן. הוּא וְאִשְׁתּוֹ הַיּוֹלֶדֶת.
מֵעַתָּה וְעַד עוֹלָם: הָרַחֲמָן הוּא יְבָרֵךְ אֶת הַיֶּלֶד הַנּוֹלָד. וּכְשֵׁם שֶׁזִּכָּהוּ הַקָּדוֹשׁ
בָּרוּךְ הוּא לַמִּילָה. כֵּן יְזַכֵּהוּ לְהִכָּנֵס לַתּוֹרָה וְלַחֻפָּה וְלַמִּצְוֹת וּלְמַעֲשִׂים
טוֹבִים. וְכֵן יְהִי רָצוֹן וְנֹאמַר אָמֵן: הָרַחֲמָן הוּא יְבָרֵךְ אֶת מַעֲלַת הַסַּנְדָּק
וְהַמּוֹהֵל וּשְׁאָר הַמִּשְׁתַּדְּלִים בַּמִּצְוָה הֵם וְכָל אֲשֶׁר לָהֶם:

Harachaman Hu Yevarech Et Ba'al Habayit Hazeh. Avi Haben. Hu Ve'ishto
Hayoledet. Me'attah Ve'ad Olam. Harachaman Hu Yevarech Et Hayeled Hanolad.
Ucheshem Shezikahu Hakadosh Baruch Hu Lamilah. Ken Yezakehu Lehikanes

LaTorah Velachuppah Velamitzvot Ulema'asim Tovim. Vechein Yehi Ratzon
Venomar Amen. Harachaman Hu Yevarech Et Ma'alat Hasandak VeHamOhel
Ushe'ar Hamishtadelim BaMitzvah Hem Vechol Asher Lahem.

May the All-merciful bless the master of this house, the father of the son - he and
his wife, the mother, from now and forever. May the All-merciful bless the newborn
child, and just as the Holy One, Blessed is He, merited him to circumcision, so may
He let him merit to enter to the Torah, to the Chuppah, to the commandments,
and to good works, and so may it be His will and let us say Amen. May the All-
merciful bless the Sandak and Mohel and the rest of those that strove in the
commandment, them and all that is theirs.

At a wedding meal:

הָרַחֲמָן הוּא יְבָרֵךְ אֶת הֶחָתָן וְהַכַּלָּה. בְּבָנִים זְכָרִים לַעֲבוֹדָתוֹ יִתְבָּרַךְ: הָרַחֲמָן
הוּא יְבָרֵךְ אֶת כָּל הַמְסֻבִּין בַּשֻּׁלְחָן הַזֶּה וְיִתֵּן לָנוּ הַקָּדוֹשׁ בָּרוּךְ הוּא
מִשְׁאֲלוֹת לִבֵּנוּ לְטוֹבָה:

Harachaman Hu Yevarech Et Hechatan Vehakallah. Bevanim Zecharim La'avodato
Yitbarach. Harachaman Hu Yevarech Et Kol Hamesubbin Bashulchan Hazeh
VeYiten Lanu Hakadosh Baruch Hu Mish'alot Libenu Letovah.

May the All-merciful bless the groom and the bride, with male sons for his work,
may he be blessed. May the All-merciful bless all who are seated a this table; May
the Holy One, blessed is He, give us our heart's wishes, for good.

(one may add here a personal prayer)

Harachaman Hu Yechayenu	הָרַחֲמָן הוּא יְחַיֵּנוּ
Vizakenu Vikarevenu Limot	וִיזַכֵּנוּ וִיקָרְבֵנוּ לִימוֹת
HaMashlach Ulevinyan Beit	הַמָּשִׁיחַ וּלְבִנְיַן בֵּית
HaMikdash Ulechayei Ha'olam	הַמִּקְדָּשׁ וּלְחַיֵּי הָעוֹלָם
Haba.	הַבָּא.

May the All-merciful grant us life, and make us worthy and bring us
near to the days of the Messiah, of the building of the Beit
HaMikdash, and of the life in the world to come.

Magdil On a day when Musaf is prayed as well	מַגְדִּיל ביום שמתפללים מוסף וכן במוצ"ש ואמרים:
as on Shabbat and say: **(Migdol)**	(מִגְדּוֹל)
Yeshu'ot Malko; Ve'oseh-Chesed	יְשׁוּעוֹת מַלְכּוֹ וְעֹשֶׂה־חֶסֶד
Limshicho Ledavid Ulezar'o	לִמְשִׁיחוֹ לְדָוִד וּלְזַרְעוֹ
Ad-'Olam. Kefirim Rashu	עַד־עוֹלָם: כְּפִירִים רָשׁוּ
Vera'evu; Vedoreshei Hashem	וְרָעֵבוּ וְדֹרְשֵׁי יְהֹוָה
Lo-Yachseru Chol-Tov. Na'ar	לֹא־יַחְסְרוּ כָל־טוֹב: נַעַר
Hayiti. Gam-Zakanti Velo-Ra'iti	הָיִיתִי גַּם־זָקַנְתִּי וְלֹא־רָאִיתִי
Tzaddik Ne'ezav; Vezar'o.	צַדִּיק נֶעֱזָב וְזַרְעוֹ
Mevakesh-Lachem. Kol-Hayom	מְבַקֶּשׁ־לָחֶם: כָּל־הַיּוֹם
Chonen Umalveh; Vezar'o.	חוֹנֵן וּמַלְוֶה וְזַרְעוֹ
Livrachah. Mah-She'achalnu	לִבְרָכָה: מַה־שֶּׁאָכַלְנוּ
Yihyeh Lesave'ah. Umah-	יִהְיֶה לְשָׂבְעָה. וּמַה־
Sheshatinu Yihyeh Lirfu'ah.	שֶּׁשָּׁתִינוּ יִהְיֶה לִרְפוּאָה.
Umah-Shehotarnu Yihyeh	וּמַה־שֶּׁהוֹתַרְנוּ יִהְיֶה
Livrachah. Kedichtiv. Vayiten	לִבְרָכָה. כְּדִכְתִיב. וַיִּתֵּן
Lifneihem Vayochelu Vayotiru	לִפְנֵיהֶם וַיֹּאכְלוּ וַיּוֹתִרוּ
Kidvar Adonai. Beruchim Attem	כִּדְבַר יְהֹוָה: בְּרוּכִים אַתֶּם
L'Adonai Oseh. Shamayim	לַיהֹוָה עֹשֵׂה שָׁמַיִם
Va'aretz. Baruch Hagever. Asher	וָאָרֶץ: בָּרוּךְ הַגֶּבֶר אֲשֶׁר
Yivtach Ba'Adonai; Vehayah	יִבְטַח בַּיהֹוָה וְהָיָה יְהֹוָה
Adonai Mivtacho. Adonai Oz	מִבְטַחוֹ: יְהֹוָה עֹז
Le'ammo Yiten; Hashem	לְעַמּוֹ יִתֵּן יְהֹוָה
Yevarech Et-'Ammo Vashalom.	יְבָרֵךְ אֶת־עַמּוֹ בַשָּׁלוֹם:
Oseh Shalom Bimromav. Hu	עוֹשֶׂה שָׁלוֹם בִּמְרוֹמָיו, הוּא
Berachamav Ya'aseh Shalom	בְּרַחֲמָיו יַעֲשֶׂה שָׁלוֹם

Aleinu. Ve'al Kol-'Ammo Yisra'el.   עָלֵינוּ. וְעַל כָּל־עַמּוֹ יִשְׂרָאֵל.

Ve'imru Amen.   וְאִמְרוּ אָמֵן:

He gives great salvation to His king: On a day when Musaf is prayed as well as on Shabbat and say: (Great is the salvation of His king) and acts mercifully to His anointed; to David and his seed forever. (Psalms 18:51) Even young lions do lack, and suffer hunger; but they who seek Hashem will not lack any good. (Psalms 34:11) I have been young, and am now old; yet never did I see a righteous man forsaken, or his offspring begging for bread. (Psalms 37:25) All day He is merciful, and lends, and his seed are a blessing. (Psalms 37:26) May what we have eaten, satisfy us; what we have drank, be conducive to our health; and what we have left, be for a blessing; as it is written, "He set it before them, and they did eat and had some left over according to the word of Hashem." (2 Kings 4:44) Blessed are you of Hashem, Who made heaven and earth. Blessed is the man who trusts in Hashem; for Hashem will be his trust. (Jeremiah 17:7) Hashem will give strength to His people: Hashem will bless His people with peace. (Psalms 29:11) He Who creates peace in His celestial heights, may He in His mercy create peace for us and for all Yisrael; and say, Amen.

After concluding Birkhat Hamazon, if it was said over a cup of wine, one should recite the blessing borei pri hagafen, and he who recited the Birkhat Hamazon should taste of the wine, and afterwards all those present should taste it, unless he can provide a cup for each and everyone present.

If Birkhat Hamazon was said over a cup of wine, then say:

Kos Yeshu'ot Essa Uveshem Adonai   כּוֹס־יְשׁוּעוֹת אֶשָּׂא וּבְשֵׁם יְהוָה

Ekra.   אֶקְרָא:

I will lift up the cup of salvation, and call upon the name of Hashem. (Psalms 116:13)

Savri Maranan!

סַבְרִי מָרָנָן:

Gentlemen, with your attention!

And answer:

Le'chayim!

לְחַיִּים:

To life!

Baruch Attah Adonai Eloheinu Melech
Ha'olam Borei Pri Hagefen.

בָּרוּךְ אַתָּה יְהֹוָה אֱלֹהֵינוּ מֶלֶךְ
הָעוֹלָם. בּוֹרֵא פְּרִי הַגָּפֶן:

Blessed are You, Hashem our God, King of the universe, Who creates the fruit of the vine.

After one drinks the cup of Birkhat HaMazon, one blesses the Mein Shalosh [for the wine]. (SA, OC 190:2)

Me'ein Shalosh / The Three-Faceted Blessing

This prayer literally means "a summary of the three" referring to the first three blessings of Birkhat Hamazon. These blessings are made after consuming at least a kezayit (olive size) of : Mezonot (non-bread products made from the 5 grains: wheat, barley, rye, oats and spelt), Wine (or grape juice), the seven species of fruits (wheat, barley, vines, figs, and pomegranates, olive trees and honey - Deut. 8:8), and drinking at least a revi'it (approx. 3oz) of any drink (excluding wine).

Baruch Attah Adonai Eloheinu

Melech Ha'olam:

בָּרוּךְ אַתָּה יְהֹוָה אֱלֹהֵינוּ מֶלֶךְ
הָעוֹלָם:

Blessed are you, Hashem our God, King of the Universe:

After partaking of Mezonot, food prepared from wheat, barley, rye, oats and spelt that were pounded or beaten and cooked food was made out of it, say:

עַל הַמִּחְיָה וְעַל הַכַּלְכָּלָה:

Al Hamichyah Ve'al Hakalkalah;

For the sustenance and the nourishment;

If one drinks wine say:

(וְ)עַל הַגֶּפֶן וְעַל פְּרִי הַגֶּפֶן:

(Ve)'Al Hagefen Ve'al Pri Hagefen;

(And) for the fruit of the vine;

If one ate one of the seven species of fruits, say:

(וְ)עַל הָעֵץ וְעַל פְּרִי הָעֵץ:

(Ve)'Al Ha'etz Ve'al Pri Ha'etz;

(And) for the land and the fruit of the tree;

Ve'al Tenuvat Hassadeh. Ve'al	וְעַל תְּנוּבַת הַשָּׂדֶה. וְעַל
Eretz Chemdah Tovah	אֶרֶץ חֶמְדָּה טוֹבָה
Urechavah. Sheratzita	וּרְחָבָה. שֶׁרָצִיתָ
Vehinchalta La'avoteinu.	וְהִנְחַלְתָּ לַאֲבוֹתֵינוּ.
Le'echol Mipiryah Velisboa	לֶאֱכֹל מִפִּרְיָה וְלִשְׂבֹּעַ
Mituvah. Rachem Adonai	מִטּוּבָהּ. רַחֵם יְהֹוָה
Eloheinu Aleinu Ve'al Yisra'el	אֱלֹהֵינוּ עָלֵינוּ וְעַל יִשְׂרָאֵל

Amach. Ve'al Yerushalayim Irach.

Ve'al Har Tziyon Mishkan

Kevodach. Ve'al Mizbachach

Ve'al Heichalach. Uveneh

Yerushalayim Ir Hakodesh

Bimheirah Veyameinu.

Veha'alenu Letochah.

Vesamecheinu Bevinyanah.

Unevarechach Aleiha Bikdushah

Uvetaharah.

עַמָּךְ. וְעַל יְרוּשָׁלַיִם עִירָךְ.

וְעַל הַר צִיוֹן מִשְׁכַּן

כְּבוֹדָךְ. וְעַל מִזְבָּחָךְ

וְעַל הֵיכָלָךְ. וּבְנֵה

יְרוּשָׁלַיִם עִיר הַקְּדֶשׁ

בִּמְהֵרָה בְיָמֵינוּ.

וְהַעֲלֵנוּ לְתוֹכָהּ.

וְשַׂמְּחֵנוּ בְּבִנְיָנָהּ.

וּנְבָרֶכְךָ עָלֶיהָ בִּקְדֻשָּׁה

וּבְטָהֳרָה:

(And) for the produce of the field, and for the lovely and spacious land which You granted to our fathers as a heritage to eat of it's fruit and enjoy its good gifts. Have mercy, Hashem our God, on Yisrael Your people, and on Yerushalayim Your city, and on Mount Tziyon the abode of Your glory, and on Your Altar and Your Temple. Rebuild the holy city of Yerushalayim speedily in our days. Bring us to it and gladden us in its rebuilding, and may we bless You for it in holiness and purity.

On Shabbat:

וּרְצֵה וְהַחֲלִיצֵנוּ בְּיוֹם הַשַּׁבָּת הַזֶּה.

Urezeh Vehachalitzenu Beyom Hashabbat Hazeh.

And be pleased to strengthen us on this Shabbat day.

On Rosh Chodesh:

וְזָכְרֵנוּ לְטוֹבָה בְּיוֹם רֹאשׁ חֹדֶשׁ הַזֶּה.

Vezacherenu Letovah Beyom Rosh Chodesh Hazeh.

And be mindful of us on this New Moon day.

On Rosh Hashanah:

וְזָכְרֵנוּ לְטוֹבָה בְּיוֹם הַזִּכָּרוֹן הַזֶּה.

Vezochrenu Letovah Beyom Hazikaron Hazeh.
And be mindful of us on this Day of Remembrance.

On Pesach:

וְשַׂמְּחֵנוּ בְּיוֹם חַג הַמַּצּוֹת הַזֶּה. בְּיוֹם טוֹב מִקְרָא קֹדֶשׁ הַזֶּה.

Vesamecheinu Beyom Chag Hamatzot Hazeh. Beyom Tov Mikra Kodesh Hazeh.

And grant us joy on this Festival of Unleavened Bread, this Festival Day of holy convocation.

On Shavuot:

וְשַׂמְּחֵנוּ בְּיוֹם חַג הַשָּׁבוּעוֹת הַזֶּה בְּיוֹם טוֹב מִקְרָא קֹדֶשׁ הַזֶּה.

Vesamecheinu Beyom Chag Hashavu'ot Hazeh Beyom Tov Mikra Kodesh Hazeh.

And grant us joy on this Festival of Weeks, this Festival Day of holy convocation.

On Sukkot:

וְשַׂמְּחֵנוּ בְּיוֹם הַסֻּכּוֹת הַזֶּה. בְּיוֹם טוֹב מִקְרָא קֹדֶשׁ הַזֶּה.

Vesamecheinu Beyom Hasukkot Hazeh. Beyom Tov Mikra Kodesh Hazeh.

And grant us joy on this Festival of Tabernacles, this Festival Day of holy convocation.

On Shemini Atzeret / Simchat Torah:

וְשַׂמְּחֵנוּ בְּיוֹם שְׁמִינִי חַג עֲצֶרֶת הַזֶּה בְּיוֹם טוֹב מִקְרָא קֹדֶשׁ הַזֶּה.

Vesamecheinu Beyom Shemini Chag Atzeret Hazeh Beyom Tov Mikra Kodesh Hazeh.

And grant us joy on this Festival of Eighth Day Feast, this Festival Day of holy convocation.

Ki Attah Tov Umeitiv Lakol.   כִּי אַתָּה טוֹב וּמֵטִיב לַכֹּל.

Venodeh Lecha Al Ha'aretz.   וְנוֹדֶה לְךָ עַל הָאָרֶץ:

For You are good and beneficent to all; and we will give You thanks for the land,

For Mezonot (foods prepared from wheat, barley, rye, oats and spelt, that were pounded or beaten and made cooked food out of it), say:

Ve'al Hamichyah Ve'al Hakalkalah;

וְעַל הַמִּחְיָה וְעַל הַכַּלְכָּלָה:

Of the land of Yisrael: Ve'al Michyatah Ve'al Kalkalatah;

שׁל ארץ ישראל ועל: וְעַל מִחְיָתָה וְעַל כַּלְכָּלָתָ:

And for the sustenance and the nourishment;
Of the land of Yisrael: And for its sustenance and its nourishment.

After wine say:

Ve'al Pri Hagefen.

וְעַל פְּרִי הַגֶּפֶן:

Of the land of Yisrael: Ve'al Pri Gafnah.

שׁל ארץ ישראל: וְעַל פְּרִי גַפְנָה:

And for the fruit of the vine.
Of the land of Yisrael: And for the fruit of its vine.

After the seven species of fruits, say:

Ve'al Haperot.

וְעַל הַפֵּרוֹת:

Of the land of Yisrael: Ve'al Peroteiha.

שׁל ארץ ישראל: וְעַל פֵּרוֹתֶיהָ:

And for the fruit.
Of the land of Yisrael: And for its fruit.

Borei Nefashot

> **After eating if one ate at least a kezayit (approx. the size of an olive), or drank a revi'it (approx. 3oz) of all food not made from grain or the 7 kinds fruits. This includes everything we make the before blessings of "Ha Adamah" or "Shehakol" on, like meat, fish, eggs, drinks (excluding wine), etc. and all fruits not included in the seven species of fruits. (wheat, barley, vines, figs, and pomegranates, olive trees and honey - Deut. 8:8)**

בָּרוּךְ אַתָּה יְהֹוָה אֱלֹהֵינוּ מֶלֶךְ הָעוֹלָם. בּוֹרֵא נְפָשׁוֹת רַבּוֹת וְחֶסְרוֹנָן עַל כָּל־מַה־שֶּׁבָּרֵאתָ לְהַחֲיוֹת בָּהֶם נֶפֶשׁ כָּל־חָי. בָּרוּךְ חַי הָעוֹלָמִים.

Baruch Attah Adonai Eloheinu Melech Ha'olam Borei Nefashot
Rabot Vechesronan Al Kol-Mah-Shebarata Lehachayot Bahem
Nefesh Kol-Chai. Baruch Chai Ha'olamim.

Blessed are You, Hashem our God, King of the universe, Who
creates many living souls with their needs, for all the things You have
created to sustain every living being. Blessed is the Life of all worlds.

Birkhot HaNehenin / Blessings on Enjoyments

Regarding all these blessings, one should not interrupt between the blessing and the eating of the food.

For Mezonot (one of the five species of grain were pounded or beaten and made cooked food out of it), he should say (and the after-blessing: "Al Hamichyah" [in Mein Shalosh]):

Baruch Attah Adonai Eloheinu

Melech Ha'olam Borei Minei

Mezonot.

בָּרוּךְ אַתָּה יְהֹוָה אֱלֹהֵינוּ

מֶלֶךְ הָעוֹלָם. בּוֹרֵא מִינֵי

מְזוֹנוֹת:

Blessed are You, Hashem our God, King of the universe, Who creates various kinds of food.

On the wine, one blesses:

Baruch Attah Adonai Eloheinu

Melech Ha'olam Borei Pri

Hagefen.

בָּרוּךְ אַתָּה יְהֹוָה אֱלֹהֵינוּ

מֶלֶךְ הָעוֹלָם. בּוֹרֵא פְּרִי

הַגָּפֶן:

Blessed are You, Hashem our God, King of the universe, Who creates the fruit of the vine.

On the fruit of the tree, one blesses:

Baruch Attah Adonai Eloheinu

Melech Ha'olam Borei Pri

HaEitz.

בָּרוּךְ אַתָּה יְהֹוָה אֱלֹהֵינוּ

מֶלֶךְ הָעוֹלָם. בּוֹרֵא פְּרִי

הָעֵץ:

Blessed are You, Hashem our God, King of the universe, Who creates the fruit of the tree.

On the fruits of the earth, one blesses:

Baruch Attah Adonai Eloheinu

Melech Ha'olam Borei Pri

Ha'adamah.

בָּרוּךְ אַתָּה יְהֹוָה אֱלֹהֵינוּ

מֶלֶךְ הָעוֹלָם. בּוֹרֵא פְּרִי

הָאֲדָמָה:

Blessed are You, Hashem our God, King of the universe, Who creates the fruit of the earth.

On something that is not from the earth such as meat, fish, milk, cheese, etc. And on drinks (except wine), one blesses:

Baruch Attah Adonai Eloheinu

Melech Ha'olam Shehakol

Nihyah Bidvaro.

בָּרוּךְ אַתָּה יְהֹוָה אֱלֹהֵינוּ

מֶלֶךְ הָעוֹלָם. שֶׁהַכֹּל

נִהְיָה בִּדְבָרוֹ:

Blessed are You, Hashem our God, King of the universe, by Whose word all things came into being.

Blessings over Good Smells

On the good smell of trees, their flowers or shrubs, one blesses:

Baruch Attah Adonai Eloheinu

Melech Ha'olam Borei Atzei

Vesamim.

בָּרוּךְ אַתָּה יְהֹוָה אֱלֹהֵינוּ

מֶלֶךְ הָעוֹלָם. בּוֹרֵא עֲצֵי

בְשָׂמִים:

Blessed are You, Hashem our God, King of the universe, Who creates sweet smelling woods.

On the good smell of herbs, grass, or flowers, one blesses:

Baruch Attah Adonai Eloheinu

Melech Ha'olam Borei Isbei

Vesamim.

בָּרוּךְ אַתָּה יְהֹוָה אֱלֹהֵינוּ
מֶלֶךְ הָעוֹלָם. בּוֹרֵא עִשְׂבֵי
בְשָׂמִים:

Blessed are You, Hashem our God, King of the universe, Who creates sweet smelling herbs.

On a good smell that is not wood or grass, or vegetation, one blesses:

Baruch Attah Adonai Eloheinu

Melech Ha'olam Borei Minei

Vesamim.

בָּרוּךְ אַתָּה יְהֹוָה אֱלֹהֵינוּ
מֶלֶךְ הָעוֹלָם. בּוֹרֵא מִינֵי
בְשָׂמִים:

Blessed are You, Hashem our God, King of the universe, Who creates various kinds of spices.

Kriyat Shema She'Al Hamita / The Bedtime Shema

If one stays awake until after midnight they will read the recital of Shema half an hour before midnight, and if he forgot to read before midnight he can read any Kriyat Shema order after midnight.

Some say before:

לְשֵׁם יְחוּד קוּדְשָׁא בְּרִיךְ הוּא וּשְׁכִינְתֵּיהּ. בִּדְחִילוּ וּרְחִימוּ. וּרְחִימוּ וּדְחִילוּ. לְיַחֲדָא שֵׁם יוֹ"ד קֵ"י בְּוָא"ו קֵ"י בְּיִחוּדָא שְׁלִים (יהוה) בְּשֵׁם כָּל יִשְׂרָאֵל. הריני מקבל עלי אלהותו יתברך ואהבתו ויראתו. והריני ירא ממנו בגין דאיהו רב ושליט על כלא. וכלא קמיה כלא. והריני ממליכו על כל אבר ואבר וגיד וגיד מרמ"ח אברים ושס"ה גידים שֶׁל גופי ונפשי רוחי ונשמתי מלכות גמורה ושלמה. והריני עבד להשם יתברך והוא ברחמיו יזכני לעבדו בלבב שלם ונפש חפצה. אָמֵן כֵּן יְהִי רָצוֹן.

Ribono Shel Olam

Ribono Shel Olam Hareini	רִבּוֹנוֹ שֶׁל עוֹלָם הֲרֵינִי
Mochel Vesoleach Lechol-Mi-	מוֹחֵל וְסוֹלֵחַ לְכָל־מִי־
Shehich'is Vehiknit Oti O	שֶׁהִכְעִיס וְהִקְנִיט אוֹתִי אוֹ
Shechata Kenegdi. Bein Begufi	שֶׁחָטָא כְּנֶגְדִּי. בֵּין בְּגוּפִי
Bein Bemamoni Bein Bichvodi	בֵּין בְּמָמוֹנִי בֵּין בִּכְבוֹדִי
Bein Bechol-'Asher Li. Bein	בֵּין בְּכָל־אֲשֶׁר לִי. בֵּין
Be'ones Bein Beratzon Bein	בְּאוֹנֶס בֵּין בְּרָצוֹן בֵּין
Beshogeg Bein Bemezid Bein	בְּשׁוֹגֵג בֵּין בְּמֵזִיד בֵּין
Bedibur Bein Bema'aseh. Bein	בְּדִבּוּר בֵּין בְּמַעֲשֶׂה. בֵּין
Begilgul Zeh Bein Begilgul	בְּגִלְגּוּל זֶה בֵּין בְּגִלְגּוּל
Acher. Lechol-Bar-Yisra'el. Velo	אַחֵר. לְכָל־בַּר־יִשְׂרָאֵל. וְלֹא
Ye'anesh Shum Adam Besibati.	יֵעָנֵשׁ שׁוּם אָדָם בְּסִבָּתִי.
Yehi Ratzon Milfaneicha Adonai	יְהִי רָצוֹן מִלְפָנֶיךָ יְהוָה

Elohai Velohei Avotai Shelo	אֱלֹהַי וֵאלֹהֵי אֲבוֹתַי שֶׁלֹּא
Echeta Od. Umah-Shechatati	אֶחֱטָא עוֹד. וּמַה־שֶּׁחָטָאתִי
Lefaneicha Mechok	לְפָנֶיךָ מְחוֹק
Berachameicha Harabbim. Aval	בְּרַחֲמֶיךָ הָרַבִּים. אֲבָל
Lo Al-Yedei Yissurin Vechola'im	לֹא עַל־יְדֵי יִסּוּרִין וְחוֹלָאִים
Ra'im. Yihyu Leratzon Imrei-Fi	רָעִים. יִהְיוּ לְרָצוֹן אִמְרֵי־פִי
Vehegyon Libi Lefaneicha;	וְהֶגְיוֹן לִבִּי לְפָנֶיךָ
Adonai Tzuri Vego'ali.	יְהֹוָה צוּרִי וְגֹאֲלִי:

Sovereign of the universe, behold, I freely forgive everyone who has aggrieved or frustrated me, or who has sinned against me, either in my body, property, honor, or in anything else belonging to me; whether by compulsion or choice: whether ignorantly or with intent: whether in word or in deed, during the whole period of my existence; I forgive any Israelite, and I pray that no person may be punished on account of me. May it be acceptable in Your presence, Hashem my God and God of my fathers, that I may sin no more; and whatever I have sinned before You, blot out through Your abundant mercies: but not through means of anguish and severe illness. May the words of my mouth and the thoughts of my heart, be acceptable in Your presence, Hashem, my Rock and Redeemer.

Baruch HaMapil Chevlei

Baruch (Attah Adonai Eloheinu	בָּרוּךְ (אַתָּה יְהֹוָה אֱלֹהֵינוּ
Melech Ha'Olam) Hamapil	מֶלֶךְ הָעוֹלָם.) הַמַּפִּיל
Chevlei Shenah Al-'Einai	חֶבְלֵי שֵׁנָה עַל־עֵינַי
Utenumah Al-'Af'appai. Ume'ir	וּתְנוּמָה עַל־עַפְעַפָּי. וּמֵאִיר
Le'ishon Bat-'Ayin. Yehi Ratzon	לְאִישׁוֹן בַּת־עָיִן. יְהִי רָצוֹן

Milfaneicha Adonai Elohai	מִלְּפָנֶיךָ יְהֹוָה אֱלֹהַי
Velohei Avotai Shetashkiveni	וֵאלֹהֵי אֲבוֹתַי שֶׁתַּשְׁכִּיבֵנִי
Leshalom. Veta'amideini	לְשָׁלוֹם. וְתַעֲמִידֵנִי
Lechayim Tovim Uleshalom.	לְחַיִּים טוֹבִים וּלְשָׁלוֹם.
Veten Chelki Betoratecha.	וְתֵן חֶלְקִי בְּתוֹרָתֶךָ.
Vetargileini Lidvar Mitzvah.	וְתַרְגִּילֵנִי לִדְבַר מִצְוָה.
Ve'al-Targileini Lidvar Averah.	וְאַל־תַּרְגִּילֵנִי לִדְבַר עֲבֵרָה.
Ve'al-Tevi'eni Lidei Chet. Velo	וְאַל־תְּבִיאֵנִי לִידֵי חֵטְא. וְלֹא
Lidei Nissayon Velo Lidei	לִידֵי נִסָּיוֹן וְלֹא לִידֵי
Vizayon. Veyishlot Bi Yetzer	בִזָּיוֹן. וְיִשְׁלוֹט בִּי יֵצֶר
Hatov Ve'al-Yishlot Bi Yetzer	הַטּוֹב וְאַל־יִשְׁלוֹט בִּי יֵצֶר
Hara. Vetatzileini Miyetzer Hara	הָרָע. וְתַצִּילֵנִי מִיֵּצֶר הָרָע
Umechola'im Ra'im. Ve'al-	וּמֵחוֹלָאִים רָעִים. וְאַל־
Yavhiluni Chalomot Ra'im	יַבְהִילוּנִי חֲלוֹמוֹת רָעִים
Vehirhurim Ra'im. Utehei Mitati	וְהִרְהוּרִים רָעִים. וּתְהֵא מִטָּתִי
Shelemah Lefaneicha. Veha'er	שְׁלֵמָה לְפָנֶיךָ. וְהָאֵר
Einai Pen Ishan Hamavet. Baruch	עֵינַי פֶּן אִישַׁן הַמָּוֶת. בָּרוּךְ
(Attah Adonai) Hame'ir La'olam	(אַתָּה יְהֹוָה) הַמֵּאִיר לָעוֹלָם
Kulo Bichvodo.	כֻּלּוֹ בִּכְבוֹדוֹ:

Blessed (are You, Hashem our God, King of the universe,) Who weighs down my eyes with the bonds of sleep, my eyelids with slumber, and illuminates the pupil of my eye. May it be Your will, Hashem my God and God of my fathers, to lay me down in peace, and to raise me up again to good and peaceful life with my portion in Your Torah. Exercise me in the observance of Your commands and do not let me walk in the way of transgression. Do not let me come into the power of temptation, sin or shame. May the good inclination rule me, and may the evil inclination not rule over me.

Deliver me from the evil inclination and from grievous sickness. May bad dreams and evil thoughts not trouble me, but let my bed be perfect before You. Illuminate my eyes again, so I will not sleep the sleep of death. (Blessed are You, Hashem,) Whose glory gives light to the whole universe.

LAWS OF RECITING THE SHEMA

One who recites the Shema, but did not have intention during the first verse, 'Shema Yisrael', one did not fulfill their obligation. As for the rest, if they read during the specified time and did not have intention, they have fulfilled their obligation. One should recite the Shema with intention, awe, fear, shaking and trembling. The custom is to place one's hands over their face during the recitation of the first verse in order that one will not look at something else that will prevent him from directing his heart. (SA, OC 59-61). Some say "El Melech Ne'eman / God Faithful King" before.

One covers their eyes and says:

שְׁמַע יִשְׂרָאֵל יְהוָה אֱלֹהֵינוּ יְהוָה | אֶחָד:

Shema Yisrael; Adonai Eloheinu Adonai Echad.
"Hear, O Yisrael, Hashem is our God, Hashem is One."

Whisper silently:

בָּרוּךְ שֵׁם כְּבוֹד מַלְכוּתוֹ לְעוֹלָם וָעֶד:

Baruch Shem Kevod Malchuto Le'olam Va'ed.
Blessed is His name and glorious kingdom forever and ever.

Ve'ahavta

וְאָהַבְתָּ אֵת יְהוָה אֱלֹהֶיךָ בְּכָל־לְבָבְךָ וּבְכָל־נַפְשְׁךָ וּבְכָל־מְאֹדֶךָ: וְהָיוּ הַדְּבָרִים הָאֵלֶּה אֲשֶׁר אָנֹכִי מְצַוְּךָ הַיּוֹם עַל־לְבָבֶךָ: וְשִׁנַּנְתָּם לְבָנֶיךָ וְדִבַּרְתָּ בָּם בְּשִׁבְתְּךָ בְּבֵיתֶךָ וּבְלֶכְתְּךָ בַדֶּרֶךְ וּבְשָׁכְבְּךָ וּבְקוּמֶךָ: וּקְשַׁרְתָּם לְאוֹת עַל־יָדֶךָ וְהָיוּ לְטֹטָפֹת בֵּין עֵינֶיךָ: וּכְתַבְתָּם עַל־מְזֻזוֹת בֵּיתֶךָ וּבִשְׁעָרֶיךָ:

Ve'ahavta Et Adonai Eloheicha; Bechol-Levavecha Uvechol-
Nafshecha Uvechol-Me'odecha. Vehayu Hadevarim Ha'eleh. Asher
Anochi Metzavecha Hayom Al-Levavecha. Veshinantam Levaneicha.
Vedibarta Bam; Beshivtecha Beveitecha Uvelechtecha Vaderech.
Uveshochbecha Uvekumecha. Ukeshartam Le'ot Al-Yadecha;
Vehayu Letotafot Bein Eineicha. Uchetavtam Al-Mezuzot Beitecha
Uvish'areicha.

And you will love Hashem your God with all your heart, and with all
your soul, and with all your might. And these words, which I
command you this day, will be upon your heart; and you will teach
them diligently to your children, and will talk of them when you sit
in your house, and when you walk by the way, and when you lie
down, and when you rise up. And you will bind them for a sign on
your hand, and they will be for frontlets between your eyes. And you
will write them on the doorposts of your house, and on your gates.

Vehayah Im-shamoa

וְהָיָ֗ה אִם־שָׁמֹ֤עַ תִּשְׁמְעוּ֙ אֶל־מִצְוֺתַ֔י אֲשֶׁ֧ר אָנֹכִ֛י מְצַוֶּ֥ה אֶתְכֶ֖ם הַיּ֑וֹם
לְאַהֲבָ֞ה אֶת־יְהֹוָ֤ה אֱלֹֽהֵיכֶם֙ וּלְעׇבְד֔וֹ בְּכׇל־לְבַבְכֶ֖ם וּבְכׇל־נַפְשְׁכֶֽם:
וְנָתַתִּ֧י מְטַר־אַרְצְכֶ֛ם בְּעִתּ֖וֹ יוֹרֶ֣ה וּמַלְק֑וֹשׁ וְאָסַפְתָּ֣ דְגָנֶ֔ךָ וְתִירֹֽשְׁךָ֖
וְיִצְהָרֶֽךָ: וְנָתַתִּ֛י עֵ֥שֶׂב בְּשָׂדְךָ֖ לִבְהֶמְתֶּ֑ךָ וְאָכַלְתָּ֖ וְשָׂבָֽעְתָּ: הִשָּׁמְר֣וּ
לָכֶ֔ם פֶּ֥ן יִפְתֶּ֖ה לְבַבְכֶ֑ם וְסַרְתֶּ֗ם וַעֲבַדְתֶּם֙ אֱלֹהִ֣ים אֲחֵרִ֔ים
וְהִשְׁתַּחֲוִיתֶ֖ם לָהֶֽם: וְחָרָ֨ה אַף־יְהֹוָ֜ה בָּכֶ֗ם וְעָצַ֤ר אֶת־הַשָּׁמַ֙יִם֙
וְלֹֽא־יִהְיֶ֣ה מָטָ֔ר וְהָ֣אֲדָמָ֔ה לֹ֥א תִתֵּ֖ן אֶת־יְבוּלָ֑הּ וַאֲבַדְתֶּ֣ם מְהֵרָ֗ה מֵעַל֙
הָאָ֣רֶץ הַטֹּבָ֔ה אֲשֶׁ֥ר יְהֹוָ֖ה נֹתֵ֥ן לָכֶֽם: וְשַׂמְתֶּם֙ אֶת־דְּבָרַ֣י אֵ֔לֶּה
עַל־לְבַבְכֶ֖ם וְעַֽל־נַפְשְׁכֶ֑ם וּקְשַׁרְתֶּ֨ם אֹתָ֤ם לְאוֹת֙ עַל־יֶדְכֶ֔ם וְהָי֥וּ
לְטוֹטָפֹ֖ת בֵּ֥ין עֵינֵיכֶֽם. וְלִמַּדְתֶּ֥ם אֹתָ֛ם אֶת־בְּנֵיכֶ֖ם לְדַבֵּ֣ר בָּ֑ם בְּשִׁבְתְּךָ֤
בְּבֵיתֶ֙ךָ֙ וּבְלֶכְתְּךָ֣ בַדֶּ֔רֶךְ וּֽבְשׇׁכְבְּךָ֖ וּבְקוּמֶֽךָ: וּכְתַבְתָּ֛ם עַל־מְזוּז֥וֹת בֵּיתֶ֖ךָ

וּבִשְׁעָרֶיךָ: לְמַעַן יִרְבּוּ יְמֵיכֶם וִימֵי בְנֵיכֶם עַל הָאֲדָמָה אֲשֶׁר נִשְׁבַּע
יְהֹוָה לַאֲבֹתֵיכֶם לָתֵת לָהֶם כִּימֵי הַשָּׁמַיִם עַל־הָאָרֶץ:

Vehayah Im-Shamoa Tishme'u El-Mitzvotai. Asher Anochi Metzaveh
Etchem Hayom; Le'ahavah Et-Adonai Eloheichem Ule'avdo. Bechol-
Levavchem Uvechol-Nafshechem. Venatati Metar-'Artzechem Be'ito
Yoreh Umalkosh; Ve'asafta Deganecha. Vetiroshecha Veyitzharecha.
Venatati Esev Besadecha Livhemtecha; Ve'achalta Vesava'eta.
Hishameru Lachem. Pen Yifteh Levavchem; Vesartem. Va'avadtem
Elohim Acherim. Vehishtachavitem Lahem. Vecharah Af-Adonai
Bachem. Ve'atzar Et-Hashamayim Velo-Yihyeh Matar. Veha'adamah.
Lo Titen Et-Yevulah; Va'avadtem Meheirah. Me'al Ha'aretz Hatovah.
Asher Adonai Noten Lachem. Vesamtem Et-Devarai Eleh. Al-
Levavchem Ve'al-Nafshechem; Ukeshartem Otam Le'ot Al-Yedchem.
Vehayu Letotafot Bein Eineichem. Velimadtem Otam Et-Beneichem
Ledaber Bam; Beshivtecha Beveitecha Uvelechtecha Vaderech.
Uveshochbecha Uvekumecha. Uchetavtam Al-Mezuzot Beitecha
Uvish'areicha. Lema'an Yirbu Yemeichem Vimei Veneichem. Al
Ha'adamah. Asher Nishba Adonai La'avoteichem Latet Lahem;
Kimei Hashamayim Al-Ha'aretz.

And it will come to pass, if you will observe My commandments
which I command you this day, to love Hashem your God, and to
serve Him with all your heart and with all your soul, that I will give
the rain of your land in its season, the former rain and the latter
rain, that you may gather in your corn, and your wine, and your oil.
And I will give grass in your fields for your cattle, and you will eat
and be satisfied. Be cautious, in case your heart is deceived, and you
turn aside, and serve other gods, and worship them; and the anger
of Hashem is kindled against you, and He shut up the heaven, so
that there will be no rain, and the ground will not yield her fruit; and
you perish quickly from off the good land which Hashem gives you.
Therefore you will lay up these words in your heart and in your soul;
and you will bind them for a sign upon your hand, and they will be
for frontlets between your eyes. And you will teach them to your
children, talking of them, when you sit in your house, and when you
walk by the way, and when you lie down, and when you rise up. And
you will write them on the doorposts of your house, and on your

gates; that your days may be multiplied, and the days of your children, upon the land which Hashem swore to your fathers to give them, as the days of the heavens above the earth. (Deuteronomy 11:13-21)

Numbers 15:37-41

וַיֹּאמֶר יְהֹוָה אֶל־מֹשֶׁה לֵּאמֹר: דַּבֵּר אֶל־בְּנֵי יִשְׂרָאֵל וְאָמַרְתָּ אֲלֵהֶם
וְעָשׂוּ לָהֶם צִיצִת עַל־כַּנְפֵי בִגְדֵיהֶם לְדֹרֹתָם וְנָתְנוּ עַל־צִיצִת הַכָּנָף
פְּתִיל תְּכֵלֶת: וְהָיָה לָכֶם לְצִיצִת וּרְאִיתֶם אֹתוֹ וּזְכַרְתֶּם
אֶת־כָּל־מִצְוֹת יְהֹוָה וַעֲשִׂיתֶם אֹתָם וְלֹא־תָתוּרוּ אַחֲרֵי לְבַבְכֶם וְאַחֲרֵי
עֵינֵיכֶם אֲשֶׁר־אַתֶּם זֹנִים אַחֲרֵיהֶם: לְמַעַן תִּזְכְּרוּ וַעֲשִׂיתֶם
אֶת־כָּל־מִצְוֹתָי וִהְיִיתֶם קְדֹשִׁים לֵאלֹהֵיכֶם: אֲנִי יְהֹוָה אֱלֹהֵיכֶם אֲשֶׁר
הוֹצֵאתִי אֶתְכֶם מֵאֶרֶץ מִצְרַיִם לִהְיוֹת לָכֶם לֵאלֹהִים אֲנִי יְהֹוָה
אֱלֹהֵיכֶם: אֱמֶת.

Vayomer Adonai El-Mosheh Lemor. Daber El-Benei Yisra'el
Ve'amarta Aleihem. Ve'asu Lahem Tzitzit Al-Kanfei Vigdeihem
Ledorotam; Venatenu Al-Tzitzit Hakanaf Petil Techelet. Vehayah
Lachem Letzitzit Ure'item Oto Uzechartem Et-Chol-Mitzvot Adonai
Va'asitem Otam; Velo-Taturu Acharei Levavchem Ve'acharei
Eineichem. Asher-'Attem Zonim Achareihem. Lema'an Tizkeru.
Va'asitem Et-Chol-Mitzvotai; Vihyitem Kedoshim Leloheichem. Ani
Adonai Eloheichem. Asher Hotzeti Etchem Me'eretz Mitzrayim.
Lihyot Lachem Lelohim; Ani Adonai Eloheichem. Emet.

And Hashem spoke to Moshe, saying: Speak to the children of Yisrael, and command them to make tzitzit on the corners of their garments throughout their generations, and that they put a thread of tekhelet with the tzitzit of each corner. And they will be to you for tzitzit, that you may look upon them, and remember all the commandments of Hashem, and do them; and that you do not go about after your own heart and your own eyes, after which you go whoring; that you may remember and do all My commandments, and be holy to your God. I am Hashem your God, Who brought you

out of the land of Mitzrayim, to be your God: I am Hashem your
God. It is true.

יְהֹוָה אֱלֹהֵיכֶם אֱמֶת:

Adonai Eloheichem Emet.

Hashem, your God, is true.

The following verses are typically recited:

יַעְלְזוּ חֲסִידִים בְּכָבוֹד יְרַנְּנוּ עַל־מִשְׁכְּבוֹתָם: רוֹמְמוֹת אֵל בִּגְרוֹנָם וְחֶרֶב פִּיפִיּוֹת
בְּיָדָם:

Ya'lezu Chasidim Bechavod; Yeranenu. Al-Mishkevotam. Romemot El Bigronam;
Vecherev Pifiyot Beyadam.

Let the pious rejoice in glory; Let them sing for joy upon their beds. Let the high
praises of God be in their mouth, And a two-edged sword in their hand; (Psalms
149:5-6)

הִנֵּה מִטָּתוֹ שֶׁלִּשְׁלֹמֹה שִׁשִּׁים גִּבֹּרִים סָבִיב לָהּ מִגִּבֹּרֵי יִשְׂרָאֵל: כֻּלָּם אֲחֻזֵי
חֶרֶב מְלֻמְּדֵי מִלְחָמָה אִישׁ חַרְבּוֹ עַל־יְרֵכוֹ מִפַּחַד בַּלֵּילוֹת: ג׳ פעמים

Hineh. Mitato Shelishlomoh. Shishim Giborim Saviv Lah; Migiborei Yisra'el. Kulam
Achuzei Cherev. Melummedei Milchamah; Ish Charbo Al-Yerecho. Mipachad
Baleilot.

There is Shlomo's couch, Encircled by sixty warriors of the warriors of Yisrael, All
of them trained in warfare, Skilled in battle, Each with sword on thigh, because of
terror by night. (3x) (Song of Songs 3:7-8)

יְבָרֶכְךָ יְהֹוָה וְיִשְׁמְרֶךָ: יָאֵר יְהֹוָה | פָּנָיו אֵלֶיךָ וִיחֻנֶּךָּ: יִשָּׂא יְהֹוָה | פָּנָיו אֵלֶיךָ
וְיָשֵׂם לְךָ שָׁלוֹם:

Yevarechecha Adonai Veyishmerecha. Ya'er Adonai Panav Eleicha Vichuneka. Yissa
Adonai Panav Eleicha. Veyasem Lecha Shalom.

Hashem bless you and keep you. Hashem make His countenance shine upon you,
and be gracious to you. Hashem lift up His countenance upon you and give you
peace.

Psalms 91:1-9

יֹשֵׁב בְּסֵתֶר עֶלְיוֹן בְּצֵל שַׁדַּי יִתְלוֹנָן: אֹמַר לַיהֹוָה מַחְסִי וּמְצוּדָתִי |
אֱלֹהַי אֶבְטַח־בּוֹ: כִּי הוּא יַצִּילְךָ מִפַּח יָקוּשׁ מִדֶּבֶר הַוּוֹת: בְּאֶבְרָתוֹ
יָסֶךְ לָךְ וְתַחַת־כְּנָפָיו תֶּחְסֶה צִנָּה וְסֹחֵרָה אֲמִתּוֹ: לֹא־תִירָא מִפַּחַד
לָיְלָה מֵחֵץ יָעוּף יוֹמָם: מִדֶּבֶר בָּאֹפֶל יַהֲלֹךְ מִקֶּטֶב יָשׁוּד צָהֳרָיִם:
יִפֹּל מִצִּדְּךָ אֶלֶף וּרְבָבָה מִימִינֶךָ אֵלֶיךָ לֹא יִגָּשׁ: רַק בְּעֵינֶיךָ תַבִּיט
וְשִׁלֻּמַת רְשָׁעִים תִּרְאֶה: כִּי־אַתָּה יְהֹוָה מַחְסִי:

Yoshev Beseter Elyon; Betzel Shaddai. Yitlonan. Omar. L'Adonai
Machsi Umetzudati; Elohai. Evtach-Bo. Ki Hu Yatzilecha Mippach
Yakush. Midever Havot. Be'evrato Yasech Lach Vetachat-Kenafav
Techseh; Tzinah Vesocherah Amito. Lo-Tira Mipachad Lailah;
Mechetz. Ya'uf Yomam. Midever Ba'ofel Yahaloch; Miketev. Yashud
Tzohorayim. Yippol Mitzidecha Elef. Urevavah Miminecha; Eleicha.
Lo Yigash. Rak Be'eineicha Tabbit; Veshilumat Resha'im Tir'eh.
Ki-'Attah Adonai Machsi.

You that dwells in the shadow of the Most High, And abides in the
shadow of the Almighty; I will say of Hashem, Who is my refuge and
my fortress, My God, in Whom I trust, That He will deliver you from
the snare of the fowler, And from the harmful pestilence. He will
cover you with His wings, And under His wings you will take refuge;
His truth is a shield and a buckler. You will not be afraid of the terror
by night, or of the arrow that flies by day; Of the pestilence that
walks in darkness, or of the destruction that wastes at noon. A
thousand may fall at Your side, And ten thousand at Your right
hand; It will not come near you. Only with your eyes you will behold,
And see the recompense of the wicked. For you have made Hashem
your habitation.

Continue with Hashkivenu.

Some say, without a blessing:

Hashkiveinu

הַשְׁכִּיבֵנוּ אָבִינוּ לְשָׁלוֹם. וְהַעֲמִידֵנוּ מַלְכֵּנוּ לְחַיִּים טוֹבִים וּלְשָׁלוֹם.
וּפְרוֹשׂ עָלֵינוּ סֻכַּת שְׁלוֹמֶךָ. וְתַקְּנֵנוּ מַלְכֵּנוּ בְּעֵצָה טוֹבָה מִלְּפָנֶיךָ.
וְהוֹשִׁיעֵנוּ מְהֵרָה לְמַעַן שְׁמֶךָ. וְהָגֵן בַּעֲדֵנוּ. וְהָסֵר מֵעָלֵינוּ מַכַּת
אוֹיֵב. דֶּבֶר. חֶרֶב. חוֹלִי. צָרָה. רָעָה. רָעָב. וְיָגוֹן. וּמַשְׁחִית. וּמַגֵּפָה.
שְׁבוֹר וְהָסֵר הַשָּׂטָן מִלְּפָנֵינוּ וּמֵאַחֲרֵינוּ. וּבְצֵל כְּנָפֶיךָ תַּסְתִּירֵנוּ.
וּשְׁמוֹר צֵאתֵנוּ וּבוֹאֵנוּ לְחַיִּים טוֹבִים וּלְשָׁלוֹם מֵעַתָּה וְעַד עוֹלָם: כִּי
אֵל שׁוֹמְרֵנוּ וּמַצִּילֵנוּ אַתָּה מִכָּל דָּבָר רָע וּמִפַּחַד לָיְלָה.

Hashkiveinu Avinu Leshalom. Veha'amidenu Malkeinu Lechayim
Tovim Uleshalom. Uferos Aleinu Sukkat Shelomecha. Vetakenenu
Malkeinu Be'etzah Tovah Milfaneicha. Vehoshi'enu Meheirah
Lema'an Shemecha. Vehagen Ba'adenu. Vehaseir Me'aleinu Makat
Oyev. Dever. Cherev. Choli. Tzarah. Ra'ah. Ra'av. Veyagon.
Umashchit. Umagefah. Shevor Vehaseir Hasatan Millefaneinu
Ume'achareinu. Uvetzel Kenafeicha Tastirenu. Ushemor Tzetenu
Uvo'enu Lechayim Tovim Uleshalom Me'attah Ve'ad Olam. Ki El
Shomerenu Umatzilenu Attah Mikol Davar Ra Umipachad Lailah.

Our Father, lay us down in peace and raise us up, our King, to a
good life and peace. And spread over us Your shelter of peace and
direct us with good council before You, our King. And save us
speedily for Your name's sake. And remove from us the strike of an
enemy, pestilence, sword, illness, distress, evil, famine, sorrow and
destruction and plague. Break and remove the Satan from before us
and from behind us. And shelter us in the shadow of Your wings and
guard our going out and our coming in, for a good life and peace
now and forever. For You are God, our Guardian and our Deliverer
from every evil thing and from dread of the night.

Some say:

Psalms 121

שִׁיר לַמַּעֲלוֹת אֶשָּׂא עֵינַי אֶל־הֶהָרִים מֵאַיִן יָבֹא עֶזְרִי: עֶזְרִי מֵעִם
יְהֹוָה עֹשֵׂה שָׁמַיִם וָאָרֶץ: אַל־יִתֵּן לַמּוֹט רַגְלֶךָ אַל־יָנוּם שֹׁמְרֶךָ: הִנֵּה
לֹא־יָנוּם וְלֹא יִישָׁן שׁוֹמֵר יִשְׂרָאֵל: יְהֹוָה שֹׁמְרֶךָ יְהֹוָה צִלְּךָ עַל־יַד
יְמִינֶךָ: יוֹמָם הַשֶּׁמֶשׁ לֹא־יַכֶּכָּה וְיָרֵחַ בַּלָּיְלָה: יְהֹוָה יִשְׁמָרְךָ מִכָּל־רָע
יִשְׁמֹר אֶת־נַפְשֶׁךָ: יְהֹוָה יִשְׁמָר־צֵאתְךָ וּבוֹאֶךָ מֵעַתָּה וְעַד־עוֹלָם:

Shir. Lamma'alot Essa Einai El-Heharim; Me'ayin. Yavo Ezri. Ezri
Me'im Adonai Oseh. Shamayim Va'aretz. Al-Yiten Lamot Raglecha;
Al-Yanum. Shomerecha. Hineh Lo-Yanum Velo Yishan; Shomer.
Yisra'el. Adonai Shomerecha; Hashem Tzillecha. Al-Yad Yeminecha.
Yomam. Hashemesh Lo-Yakekah. Veyareach Balailah. Adonai
Yishmorcha Mikol-Ra'; Yishmor. Et-Nafshecha. Adonai Yishmor-
Tzetecha Uvo'echa; Me'attah. Ve'ad-'Olam.

A Song of Ascents. I will lift up my eyes to the mountains: From
where will my help come? My help comes from Hashem. Who made
heaven and earth. He will not suffer Your foot to be moved; He that
keeps You will not slumber. Behold, He that keeps Yisrael neither
slumbers or sleeps. Hashem is your Guardian; Hashem is Your
shade on Your right hand. The sun will not harm you by day, or the
moon by night. Hashem will keep you from all evil; He will keep your
soul. Hashem will guard your going out and your coming in, From
this time and forever.

Some recite the following verses:

בְּטוֹב אָלִין וְאָקִיץ בְּרַחֲמִים:

Betov Alin Ve'akitz Berachamim:
May I abide in good and arise in compassion.

לִישׁוּעָתְךָ קִוִּיתִי יְהֹוָה: קִוִּיתִי יְהֹוָה לִישׁוּעָתְךָ: יְהֹוָה לִישׁוּעָתְךָ קִוִּיתִי:

Lishu'atecha Kiviti Adonai. Kiviti Adonai Lishu'atecha. Adonai Lishu'atecha Kiviti.
For Your salvation, I wait, Hashem. I wait, Hashem, for Your salvation. Hashem, for
Your salvation, I wait.

Ana Bechoach

אָנָּא בְּכֹחַ. גְּדוּלַת יְמִינֶךָ. תַּתִּיר צְרוּרָה:

Ana Bechoach. Gedulat Yeminecha. Tatir Tzerurah.
By the great power of Your right hand, Oh set the captive free.

קַבֵּל רְנַּת. עַמֶּךָ שַׂגְּבֵנוּ. טַהֲרֵנוּ נוֹרָא:

Kabel Rinat. Ammecha Sagveinu. Tahareinu Nora.
God of awe, accept Your people's prayer; strengthen us, cleanse us.

נָא גִבּוֹר. דּוֹרְשֵׁי יִחוּדֶךָ. כְּבָבַת שָׁמְרֵם:

Na Gibor. Doreshei Yichudecha. Kevavat Shamerem.
Almighty God, guard as the apple of the eye those who seek You.

בָּרְכֵם טַהֲרֵם. רַחֲמֵי צִדְקָתֶךָ. תָּמִיד גָּמְלֵם:

Barechem Taharem. Rachamei Tzidkatecha. Tamid Gamelem.
Bless them, cleanse them, pity them; forever grant them Your truth.

חֲסִין קָדוֹשׁ. בְּרֹב טוּבְךָ. נַהֵל עֲדָתֶךָ:

Chasin Kadosh. Berov Tuvecha. Nahel Adatecha.
Almighty and holy, in Your abundant goodness, guide Your people.

יָחִיד גֵּאֶה. לְעַמְּךָ פְּנֵה. זוֹכְרֵי קְדֻשָּׁתֶךָ:

Yachid Ge'eh. Le'ammecha Feneh. Zocherei Kedushatecha.
Supreme God, turn to Your people who are mindful of Your holiness.

שַׁוְעָתֵנוּ קַבֵּל. וּשְׁמַע צַעֲקָתֵנוּ. יוֹדֵעַ תַּעֲלוּמוֹת:

Shav'ateinu Kabel. Ushema Tza'akateinu. Yodea Ta'alumot.
Accept our prayer, hear our cry, You Who knows secret thoughts.

And say silently:

בָּרוּךְ, שֵׁם כְּבוֹד מַלְכוּתוֹ, לְעוֹלָם וָעֶד:

Baruch, Shem Kevod Malchuto, Le'olam Va'ed.
Blessed is the Name of His glorious kingdom forever and ever.

אַתָּה תָקוּם תְּרַחֵם צִיּוֹן כִּי־עֵת לְחֶנְנָהּ כִּי־בָא מוֹעֵד: בְּיָדְךָ אַפְקִיד
רוּחִי פָּדִיתָ אוֹתִי יְהֹוָה אֵל אֱמֶת:

Attah Takum Terachem Tziyon; Ki-'Et Lechenenah. Ki-Va Mo'ed.
Beyadecha Afkid Ruchi Padita Oti Hashem El Emet.

You will surely arise and take pity on Tziyon, for it is time to be
gracious to her; the appointed time has come. Into Your hand I
entrust my spirit; You redeem me, Hashem, faithful God. (Psalms 102:14,
31:6)

SHABBAT SHACHARIT / SHABBAT MORNING PRAYER

Hashkamat HaBoker / Rising in the Morning

One should be as strong as a lion to rise in the morning for the service of the Creator. At any rate, one should not delay his prayers until after the congregation has prayed. Better are few supplications with kavanah (intention) than many without kavanah. (SA, OC 1:1,4)

Modeh Ani

When awaking from sleep, one should say:

women: (Modah)

האשה: (מוֹדָה)

Modeh Ani Lefaneicha Melech

מוֹדֶה אֲנִי לְפָנֶיךָ מֶלֶךְ

Chai Vekayam Shehechezarta Bi

חַי וְקַיָּם שֶׁהֶחֱזַרְתָּ בִּי

Nishmati Vechemlah. Rabah

נִשְׁמָתִי בְּחֶמְלָה. רַבָּה

Emunatecha.

אֱמוּנָתֶךָ:

I offer thanks to You, everlasting King, Who has mercifully restored my soul within me; Your faithfulness is great.

LAWS OF NETILAT YADAYIM / WASHING OF HANDS

One should first pour water on his right hand and then his left. The water must be poured three times on each hand up to the wrist. Dipping the hands into a vessel filled with water constitutes valid washing for prayers. He who is awake all night should wash his hands without saying the blessing; and the same law applies to a case where one washed his hands before dawn had arisen. If one has no water, he may clean his hands with gravel or earth, and say the blessing: "Al Netilat Yadayim". He who sleeps during the daytime should wash his hands without saying the blessing. The minimum amount of water is a revi'it (approx. 3oz), you should add more water though, as Rav Chisda said "I washed a full hand of water and I was given a full hand of good. It is customary to wash out one's mouth as well. (SA, OC 4,158:10) Some have the practice to wait to make the blessing "Al Netilat Yadayim" until coming to the assembly, and arrange them with the rest of the blessings. The children of Sephardim do not do so. (SA, OC 6:2) Bless before washing, because every mitzvah you should bless before you do the mitzvah. But the custom is to bless after washing, because sometimes your hands aren't clean, so you bless after you clean your hands and before you do the second washing. (SA, OC 158:11) Only wash your hands with a vessel. All vessels are kosher for this, even galalim vessels (stone vessels, earthenware vessels, etc.) The vessel must be able to hold a revi'it of liquid. (SA, OC 158:11, 159:1)

Netilat Yadayim / Washing of Hands

Baruch Attah Adonai Eloheinu

Melech Ha'olam Asher

Kideshanu Bemitzvotav

Vetzivanu Al Netilat Yadayim.

בָּרוּךְ אַתָּה יְהֹוָה אֱלֹהֵינוּ

מֶלֶךְ הָעוֹלָם. אֲשֶׁר

קִדְּשָׁנוּ בְּמִצְוֹתָיו

וְצִוָּנוּ עַל נְטִילַת יָדָיִם:

Blessed are You, Hashem our God, King of the universe, Who has sanctified us with His commandments, and commanded us concerning the washing of hands.

Asher Yatzar

Every day when using the restroom, bless "Asher Yatzar" and not "Al Netilat Yadayim" [every time] even if one wants to learn or pray right away. (SA, OC 7:1)

Baruch Attah Adonai Eloheinu.

Melech Ha'olam Asher Yatzar Et

Ha'Adam Bechochmah. Uvara

Vo Nekavim Nekavim. Chalulim

Chalulim. Galui Veyadua Lifnei

Chisei Chevodecha. She'im

Yisatem Echad Mehem. O Im

Yipate'ach Echad Mehem. Ei

Efshar Lehitkayem Afilu Sha'ah

Echat. Baruch Attah Adonai

Rofei Chol-Basar Umafli

La'asot.

בָּרוּךְ אַתָּה יְהֹוָה אֱלֹהֵינוּ.

מֶלֶךְ הָעוֹלָם. אֲשֶׁר יָצַר אֶת

הָאָדָם בְּחָכְמָה. וּבָרָא

בוֹ נְקָבִים נְקָבִים. חֲלוּלִים

חֲלוּלִים. גָּלוּי וְיָדוּעַ לִפְנֵי

כִּסֵּא כְבוֹדֶךָ. שֶׁאִם

יִסָּתֵם אֶחָד מֵהֶם. אוֹ אִם

יִפָּתֵחַ אֶחָד מֵהֶם. אִי

אֶפְשָׁר לְהִתְקַיֵּם אֲפִלּוּ שָׁעָה

אֶחָת. בָּרוּךְ אַתָּה יְהֹוָה

רוֹפֵא כָל־בָּשָׂר וּמַפְלִיא

לַעֲשׂוֹת:

Blessed are You, Hashem, our God, King of the universe, Who has formed man in wisdom, and created in him many openings and cavities. It is revealed and known before Your glorious Throne, that if one of them were closed or one of them opened, it would be impossible to survive, even for a short while. Blessed are You, Hashem, Who heals all flesh and works wonders.

Elohai Neshamah

Elohai Neshamah Shenatata Bi	אֱלֹהַי נְשָׁמָה שֶׁנָּתַתָּ בִּי
Tehorah. Attah Veratah. Attah	טְהוֹרָה. אַתָּה בְרָאתָהּ. אַתָּה
Yetzartah. Attah Nefachtah Bi.	יְצַרְתָּהּ. אַתָּה נְפַחְתָּהּ בִּי.
Ve'attah Meshamerah Bekirbi.	וְאַתָּה מְשַׁמְּרָהּ בְּקִרְבִּי.
Ve'attah Atid Litelah Mimeni.	וְאַתָּה עָתִיד לִטְּלָהּ מִמֶּנִּי.
Ulehachazirah Bi Le'atid Lavo.	וּלְהַחֲזִירָהּ בִּי לֶעָתִיד לָבוֹא.
Kol-Zeman Shehaneshamah	כָּל־זְמַן שֶׁהַנְּשָׁמָה
Vekirbi. Modeh	בְקִרְבִּי. מוֹדֶה
Women: (Modah) Ani Lefaneicha	האשה: (מוֹדָה) אֲנִי לְפָנֶיךָ
Adonai Elohai Velohei Avotai.	יְהֹוָה אֱלֹהַי וֵאלֹהֵי אֲבוֹתַי.
Ribon Kol-Hama'asim Adon	רִבּוֹן כָּל־הַמַּעֲשִׂים אֲדוֹן
Kol-Haneshamot. Baruch Attah	כָּל־הַנְּשָׁמוֹת. בָּרוּךְ אַתָּה
Adonai Hamachazir Neshamot	יְהֹוָה הַמַּחֲזִיר נְשָׁמוֹת
Lifgarim Meitim.	לִפְגָרִים מֵתִים:

My God, the soul which You have endowed me with is pure. You have created it. You have formed it. You have breathed it into me. You preserve it within me, and You will after reclaim it and restore it to me in the life to come. So long as there is soul within me, I confess before You, Hashem my God and God of my fathers, that You are the Sovereign of all creation, the Ruler of all living, the Lord of all souls. Blessed are You, Hashem, Restorer of the souls to the dead.

Birkhot HaShachar / Blessings of the Morning

When making blessings, one should concentrate on the meaning of the words. When mentioning the name "Hashem", concentrate on the meaning of the proclamation is lordship, that He is the Master of all, and concentrate on the writing of Y-d H-ei that was, is, and will be. And when one mentions "Elohim", concentrate on that He is Powerful, Master over everything and Master of the powers of everything. (SA, OC 5)

Baruch Attah Adonai Eloheinu	בָּרוּךְ אַתָּה יְהֹוָה אֱלֹהֵינוּ
Melech Ha'olam Hanotein	מֶלֶךְ הָעוֹלָם. הַנּוֹתֵן
Lasechvi Vinah. Lehavchin Bein	לַשֶּׂכְוִי בִינָה. לְהַבְחִין בֵּין
Yom Uvein Lailah.	יוֹם וּבֵין לָיְלָה:

Blessed are You, Hashem our God, King of the universe, Who gives even to the rooster understanding to make us recognize day from night.

Baruch Attah Adonai Eloheinu	בָּרוּךְ אַתָּה יְהֹוָה אֱלֹהֵינוּ
Melech Ha'olam Pokei'ach	מֶלֶךְ הָעוֹלָם. פּוֹקֵחַ
Ivrim.	עִוְרִים:

Blessed are You, Hashem our God, King of the universe, Who opens the eyes of the blind.

Baruch Attah Adonai Eloheinu	בָּרוּךְ אַתָּה יְהֹוָה אֱלֹהֵינוּ
Melech Ha'olam Matir Asurim.	מֶלֶךְ הָעוֹלָם. מַתִּיר אֲסוּרִים:

Blessed are You, Hashem our God, King of the universe, Who releases the bound.

Baruch Attah Adonai Eloheinu	בָּרוּךְ אַתָּה יְהֹוָה אֱלֹהֵינוּ
Melech Ha'olam Zokeif	מֶלֶךְ הָעוֹלָם. זוֹקֵף
Kefufim.	כְּפוּפִים:

Blessed are You, Hashem our God, King of the universe, Who raises up those who are bowed.

Baruch Attah Adonai Eloheinu

Melech Ha'olam Malbish

Arumim.

בָּרוּךְ אַתָּה יְהֹוָה אֱלֹהֵינוּ

מֶלֶךְ הָעוֹלָם. מַלְבִּישׁ

עֲרֻמִּים:

Blessed are You, Hashem our God, King of the universe, Who clothes the naked.

Baruch Attah Adonai Eloheinu

Melech Ha'olam Hanotein

Laya'ef Koach.

בָּרוּךְ אַתָּה יְהֹוָה אֱלֹהֵינוּ

מֶלֶךְ הָעוֹלָם. הַנּוֹתֵן

לַיָּעֵף כֹּחַ:

Blessed are You, Hashem our God, King of the universe, Who gives strength to the weary.

Baruch Attah Adonai Eloheinu

Melech Ha'olam Roka Ha'aretz

Al Hamayim.

בָּרוּךְ אַתָּה יְהֹוָה אֱלֹהֵינוּ

מֶלֶךְ הָעוֹלָם. רוֹקַע הָאָרֶץ.

עַל הַמָּיִם:

Blessed are You, Hashem our God, King of the universe, Who stretches out the earth over the waters.

Baruch Attah Adonai Eloheinu

Melech Ha'olam Ha'meichin

Mitz'adei Gaver.

בָּרוּךְ אַתָּה יְהֹוָה אֱלֹהֵינוּ

מֶלֶךְ הָעוֹלָם. הַמֵּכִין

מִצְעֲדֵי גָבֶר:

Blessed are You, Hashem our God, King of the universe, Who guides the steps of man.

Baruch Attah Adonai Eloheinu

Melech Ha'olam She'asah Li

Kol-Tzarki.

בָּרוּךְ אַתָּה יְהֹוָה אֱלֹהֵינוּ

מֶלֶךְ הָעוֹלָם. שֶׁעָשָׂה לִי

כָּל־צָרְכִּי:

Blessed are You, Hashem our God, King of the universe, Who has provided for all my needs.

Baruch Attah Adonai Eloheinu
Melech Ha'olam Ozeir Yisra'el
Bigvurah.

בָּרוּךְ אַתָּה יְהֹוָה אֱלֹהֵינוּ
מֶלֶךְ הָעוֹלָם. אוֹזֵר יִשְׂרָאֵל
בִּגְבוּרָה:

Blessed are You, Hashem our God, King of the universe, Who girds Yisrael with might.

Baruch Attah Adonai Eloheinu
Melech Ha'olam Oteir Yisra'el
Betif'arah.

בָּרוּךְ אַתָּה יְהֹוָה אֱלֹהֵינוּ
מֶלֶךְ הָעוֹלָם. עוֹטֵר יִשְׂרָאֵל
בְּתִפְאָרָה:

Blessed are You, Hashem our God, King of the universe, Who crowns Yisrael with glory.

Baruch Attah Adonai Eloheinu
Melech Ha'olam Shelo Asani
Goy.

בָּרוּךְ אַתָּה יְהֹוָה אֱלֹהֵינוּ.
מֶלֶךְ הָעוֹלָם. שֶׁלֹא עָשַׂנִי
גּוֹי:

women say: (Goyah)   האשה אומרת: (גּוֹיָה)

Blessed are You, Hashem our God, King of the universe, Who has not made me an idolater.

Baruch Attah Adonai Eloheinu
Melech Ha'olam Shelo Asani
Aved.

בָּרוּךְ אַתָּה יְהֹוָה אֱלֹהֵינוּ
מֶלֶךְ הָעוֹלָם. שֶׁלֹא עָשַׂנִי
עָבֶד:

women say: (Shifchah)   האשה אומרת: (שִׁפְחָה)

Blessed are You, Hashem our God, King of the universe, Who has not made me a slave. women say: (a maid-servant)

A man blesses:

Baruch Attah Adonai Eloheinu

Melech Ha'olam Shelo Asani

Ishah.

בָּרוּךְ אַתָּה יְהֹוָה אֱלֹהֵינוּ
מֶלֶךְ הָעוֹלָם. שֶׁלֹּא עָשַׂנִי
אִשָּׁה:

Blessed are You, Hashem our God, King of the universe, Who has set upon me the obligations of a man.

A woman blesses without pronouncing Hashem's name and Kingship:

Baruch She'asani Kirtzono.

בָּרוּךְ שֶׁעָשַׂנִי כִּרְצוֹנוֹ:

Blessed is He Who made me according to His Will.

Baruch Attah Adonai Eloheinu

Melech Ha'olam Hama'avir

Chevlei Sheinah Me'einai

Utenumah Mei'af'appai. Vihi

Ratzon Milfaneicha Adonai.

Elohai Velohei Avotai.

Shetargileini Betoratecha.

Vetadbikeini Bemitzvoteicha.

Ve'al Tevi'eni Lidei Chet. Velo

Lidei Avon. Velo Lidei Nisayon.

Velo Lidei Vizayon. Vetarchikeni

Miyetzer Hara'. Vetadbikeini

Beyetzer Hatov. Vechof Et-Yitzri

Lehishta'bed Lach. Uteneni

Hayom Uvechol-Yom Lechein

בָּרוּךְ אַתָּה יְהֹוָה אֱלֹהֵינוּ
מֶלֶךְ הָעוֹלָם. הַמַּעֲבִיר
חֶבְלֵי שֵׁנָה מֵעֵינָי.
וּתְנוּמָה מֵעַפְעַפָּי. וִיהִי
רָצוֹן מִלְּפָנֶיךָ יְהֹוָה.
אֱלֹהַי וֵאלֹהֵי אֲבוֹתַי.
שֶׁתַּרְגִּילֵנִי בְּתוֹרָתֶךָ.
וְתַדְבִּיקֵנִי בְּמִצְוֹתֶיךָ.
וְאַל תְּבִיאֵנִי לִידֵי חֵטְא. וְלֹא
לִידֵי עָוֹן. וְלֹא לִידֵי נִסָּיוֹן.
וְלֹא לִידֵי בִזָּיוֹן. וְתַרְחִיקֵנִי
מִיֵּצֶר הָרָע. וְתַדְבִּיקֵנִי
בְּיֵצֶר הַטוֹב. וְכוֹף אֶת־יִצְרִי
לְהִשְׁתַּעְבֶּד לָךְ. וּתְנֵנִי
הַיּוֹם וּבְכָל־יוֹם לְחֵן

Ulchesed Ulerachamim	וּלְחֶסֶד וּלְרַחֲמִים
Be'eineicha Uve'einei Chol-	בְּעֵינֶיךָ וּבְעֵינֵי כָל־
Ro'ai. Vegameleini Chasadim	רוֹאָי. וְגָמְלֵנִי חֲסָדִים
Tovim. Baruch Attah Adonai	טוֹבִים. בָּרוּךְ אַתָּה יְהֹוָה
Gomel Chasadim Tovim	גּוֹמֵל חֲסָדִים טוֹבִים
Le'ammo Yisra'el.	לְעַמּוֹ יִשְׂרָאֵל:

Blessed are You, Hashem our God, King of the universe, Who removes sleep from my eyes and slumber from my eyelids. And may it be Your will, Hashem, my God and God of my fathers, to make us familiar with Your Torah and to cause us to adhere to Your commandments. And do not bring us into sin, or to iniquity, or to be tested, or to be dishonored. And distance me from the evil inclination and adhere me to the good inclination. And force my inclination to submit to You. And grant me today, and everyday, grace, loving-kindness, and mercy in Your eyes and in the eyes of all who see me, and bestow loving-kindnesses upon me. Blessed are You, Hashem, Who bestows loving-kindnesses to His nation, Yisrael.

Yehi Ratzon Milfaneicha Adonai.	יְהִי רָצוֹן מִלְּפָנֶיךָ יְהֹוָה.
Elohai Velohei Avotai.	אֱלֹהַי וֵאלֹהֵי אֲבוֹתַי.
Shetatzileini Hayom Uvechol	שֶׁתַּצִּילֵנִי הַיּוֹם וּבְכָל
Yom Vayom. Me'azei Fanim.	יוֹם וָיוֹם. מֵעַזֵּי פָנִים.
Ume'azut Panim. Me'adam Ra'.	וּמֵעַזּוּת פָּנִים. מֵאָדָם רָע.
[Me'ishah Ra'ah.] Miyetzer Ra'.	[מֵאִשָּׁה רָעָה.] מִיֵּצֶר רָע.
Mechaver Ra'. Mishachein Ra'.	מֵחָבֵר רָע. מִשָּׁכֵן רָע.
Mipega Ra'. Me'ayin Hara'.	מִפֶּגַע רָע. מֵעַיִן הָרָע.
Umillashon Hara'. [Mimalshinut.	וּמִלָּשׁוֹן הָרָע. [מִמַּלְשִׁינוּת.

Mei'edut Sheker. Misinat	מֵעֵדוּת שֶׁקֶר. מִשִׂנְאַת
Habriyot. Mei'alilah. Mimitah	הַבְּרִיּוֹת. מֵעֲלִילָה. מִמִּיתָה
Meshunah. Mei'chalayim Ra'im.	מְשֻׁנָּה. מֵחֲלָאִים רָעִים.
Mimikrim Ra'im.] Midin Kasheh.	מִמִּקְרִים רָעִים.] מִדִּין קָשֶׁה.
Umiba'al Din Kasheh. Bein	וּמִבַּעַל דִּין קָשֶׁה. בֵּין
Shehu Ven-Berit. Uvein She'eino	שֶׁהוּא בֶן־בְּרִית. וּבֵין שֶׁאֵינוֹ
Ven-Berit. [Umidinah Shel	בֶן־בְּרִית. [וּמִדִּינָה שֶׁל
Gehinam.]	גֵּיהִנָּם]:

May it be Your will, Hashem, my God and God of my fathers, to deliver us this day and every day from the shameless and from insolence, from the wicked, from an evil man, [from an evil woman,] from the evil inclination, from an evil friend, from an evil companion, from a bad mishap, from an evil eye, from evil speech, [from informers, from false witness, from the hatred of others, from libel, from an un-natural death, from severe illnesses, from harmful occurences,] from a harsh judgment, and from an harsh litigant, whether he is a son of the covenant or whether he is not a son of the covenant [and from the judgment of Gehinnom].

Blessings of the Torah

Baruch Attah Adonai Eloheinu	בָּרוּךְ אַתָּה יְהֹוָה אֱלֹהֵינוּ
Melech Ha'olam Asher	מֶלֶךְ הָעוֹלָם. אֲשֶׁר
Kideshanu Bemitzvotav	קִדְּשָׁנוּ בְּמִצְוֹתָיו
Vetzivanu Al Divrei Torah.	וְצִוָּנוּ עַל דִּבְרֵי תוֹרָה:

Blessed are You, Hashem our God, King of the universe, Who has sanctified us with His commandments, and commanded us concerning the words of Torah.

Veha'arev Na. Adonai Eloheinu.	וְהַעֲרֶב נָא. יְהֹוָה אֱלֹהֵינוּ.
Et-Divrei Toratecha Befinu	אֶת־דִּבְרֵי תוֹרָתְךָ בְּפִינוּ
Uvefifiyot Ammecha Beit	וּבְפִיפִיּוֹת עַמְּךָ בֵּית
Yisra'el. Venihyeh Anachnu	יִשְׂרָאֵל. וְנִהְיֶה אֲנַחְנוּ
Vetze'etza'einu. Vetze'etza'ei	וְצֶאֱצָאֵינוּ. וְצֶאֱצָאֵי
Tze'etza'einu. [Vetze'etza'ei	צֶאֱצָאֵינוּ. [וְצֶאֱצָאֵי
Ammecha Beit Yisrael.] Kulanu	עַמְּךָ בֵּית יִשְׂרָאֵל.] כֻּלָּנוּ
Yodei Shemecha. Velomedei	יוֹדְעֵי שְׁמֶךָ. וְלוֹמְדֵי
Toratecha Lishmah. Baruch	תוֹרָתְךָ לִשְׁמָה. בָּרוּךְ
Attah Adonai Hamlamed Torah	אַתָּה יְהֹוָה הַמְלַמֵּד תּוֹרָה
Le'ammo Yisra'el.	לְעַמּוֹ יִשְׂרָאֵל:

Hashem our God, make these teachings of Your Torah pleasant in our mouth and in the mouth of all Your people the household of Yisrael, that we, our children and children's children, [and the children of Your nation, the House of Yisrael,] may all know You and learn Your Torah for the love of it. Blessed are You, Hashem, Teacher of the Torah to Yisrael Your people.

Baruch Attah Adonai Eloheinu	בָּרוּךְ אַתָּה יְהֹוָה אֱלֹהֵינוּ
Melech Ha'olam Asher Bachar	מֶלֶךְ הָעוֹלָם. אֲשֶׁר בָּחַר
Banu Mikol-Ha'ammim Venatan	בָּנוּ מִכָּל־הָעַמִּים וְנָתַן
Lanu Et-Torato. Baruch Attah	לָנוּ אֶת־תּוֹרָתוֹ. בָּרוּךְ אַתָּה
Adonai Noten Hatorah.	יְהֹוָה נוֹתֵן הַתּוֹרָה:

Blessed are You, Hashem our God, King of the universe, Who has chosen us from all the nations and gave us His Torah. Blessed are You, Hashem, Giver of the Torah.

Priestly Blessing (Numbers 6:22-27)

Vaydaber Adonai El-Mosheh	וַיְדַבֵּר יְהֹוָה אֶל־מֹשֶׁה
Lemor. Daber El-'Aharon Ve'el-	לֵּאמֹר: דַּבֵּר אֶל־אַהֲרֹן וְאֶל־
Banav Lemor. Koh Tevarechu Et-	בָּנָיו לֵאמֹר כֹּה תְבָרְכוּ אֶת־
Benei Yisra'el; Amor Lahem.	בְּנֵי יִשְׂרָאֵל אָמוֹר לָהֶם:
Yevarechecha Adonai	יְבָרֶכְךָ יְהֹוָה
Veyishmerecha. Ya'er Adonai	וְיִשְׁמְרֶךָ: יָאֵר יְהֹוָה	
Panav Eleicha Vichuneka. Yissa	פָּנָיו אֵלֶיךָ וִיחֻנֶּךָּ: יִשָּׂא
Adonai Panav Eleicha. Veyasem	יְהֹוָה	פָּנָיו אֵלֶיךָ וְיָשֵׂם
Lecha Shalom.	לְךָ שָׁלוֹם:
Vesamu Et-Shemi Al-Benei	וְשָׂמוּ אֶת־שְׁמִי עַל־בְּנֵי
Yisra'el; Va'ani Avarechem.	יִשְׂרָאֵל וַאֲנִי אֲבָרֲכֵם:

And Hashem spoke to Moshe, saying: Speak to Aharon and his sons, saying: So will you bless the children of Yisrael. Say to them:

"Hashem bless you and keep you. Hashem make His countenance shine upon you, and be gracious to you. Hashem lift up His countenance upon you and give you peace."

And they will set My name upon the Children of Yisrael, and I will bless them.

Patach Eliyahu

Some recite Patach Eliyahu before prayer for reception of prayer.

וִיהִי | נֹעַם אֲדֹנָי אֱלֹהֵינוּ עָלֵינוּ וּמַעֲשֵׂה יָדֵינוּ כּוֹנְנָה עָלֵינוּ וּמַעֲשֵׂה יָדֵינוּ כּוֹנְנֵהוּ:

Vihi No'am Adonai Eloheinu. Aleinu Uma'aseh Yadeinu Konenah Aleinu;
Uma'aseh Yadeinu. Konenehu.

And may the graciousness of Hashem our God be on us; Establish also upon us the
work of our hands; and the work of our hands, establish it.

Tikunei Zohar 17a

פָּתַח אֵלִיָּהוּ הַנָּבִיא זָכוּר לְטוֹב וְאָמַר רִבּוֹן עָלְמִין דְּאַנְתְּ הוּא חָד וְלָא
בְּחֻשְׁבָּן. אַנְתְּ הוּא עִלָּאָה עַל כָּל עִלָּאִין סְתִימָא עַל כָּל סְתִימִין. לֵית
מַחֲשָׁבָה תְּפִיסָא בָּךְ כְּלָל: אַנְתְּ הוּא דְּאַפַּקְתְּ עֶשֶׂר תִּקּוּנִין וְקָרֵינָן לוֹן עֶשֶׂר
סְפִירָן. לְאַנְהָגָא בְהוֹן עָלְמִין סְתִימִין דְּלָא אִתְגַּלְיָן וְעָלְמִין דְּאִתְגַּלְיָן. וּבְהוֹן
אִתְכַּסִּיאַת מִבְּנֵי נָשָׁא. וְאַנְתְּ הוּא דְּקָשִׁיר לוֹן וּמְיַחֵד לוֹן: וּבְגִין דְּאַנְתְּ מִלְּגָאו.
כָּל מָאן דְּאַפְרִישׁ חַד מִן חַבְרֵיהּ מֵאִלֵּין עֶשֶׂר אִתְחֲשִׁיב לֵיהּ כְּאִלּוּ אַפְרִישׁ
בָּךְ:

Patach Eliyahu Hanavi Zachur Letov Ve'amar. Ribon Alemin De'ant Hu Chad Vela
Bechushban. Ant Hu Illa'ah Al-Kol-'Illa'in Setima Al-Kol-Setimin. Leit Machashavah
Tefisa Vach Kelal. Ant Hu De'apakt Eser Tikunin Vekareinan Lon Eser Sefiran.
Le'anhaga Vehon Alemin Setimin Dela Itgalyan Ve'alemin De'itgalyan. Uvehon
Itkassi'at Mibenei Nasha. Ve'ant Hu Dekashir Lon Umeyached Lon. Uvegin De'ant
Millegav. Kol-Man De'afrish Chad Min Chavreih Me'ilein Eser Itchashiv Leih Ke'ilu
Afrish Bach.

וְאִלֵּין עֶשֶׂר סְפִירָן אִנּוּן אָזְלִין כְּסִדְרָן. חַד אָרִיךְ וְחַד קָצֵר וְחַד בֵּינוֹנִי: וְאַנְתְּ
הוּא דְּאַנְהִיג לוֹן. וְלֵית מָאן דְּאַנְהִיג לָךְ. לָא לְעֵלָּא וְלָא לְתַתָּא וְלָא מִכָּל
סִטְרָא. לְבוּשִׁין תַּקַּנְתְּ לוֹן דְּמִנַּיְהוּ פָּרְחִין נִשְׁמָתִין לִבְנֵי נָשָׁא: וְכַמָּה גוּפִין
תַּקַּנְתְּ לוֹן דְּאִתְקְרִיאוּ גוּפָא לְגַבֵּי לְבוּשִׁין דִּמְכַסְיָן עֲלֵיהוֹן: וְאִתְקְרִיאוּ בְּתִקּוּנָא
דָא. חֶסֶד דְּרוֹעָא יְמִינָא. גְּבוּרָה דְּרוֹעָא שְׂמָאלָא. תִּפְאֶרֶת גּוּפָא. נֶצַח וְהוֹד
תְּרֵין שׁוֹקִין. יְסוֹד סִיּוּמָא דְּגוּפָא אוֹת בְּרִית קוֹדֶשׁ. מַלְכוּת פֶּה תּוֹרָה שֶׁבְּעַל
פֶּה קָרֵינָן לָהּ. חָכְמָה מוֹחָא אִיהִי מַחֲשָׁבָה מִלְּגָאו. בִּינָה לִבָּא וּבָהּ הַלֵּב
מֵבִין. וְעַל אִלֵּין תְּרֵין כְּתִיב הַנִּסְתָּרֹת לַיהוָֹה אֱלֹהֵינוּ. כֶּתֶר עֶלְיוֹן אִיהוּ כֶּתֶר
מַלְכוּת. וְעָלֵיהּ אִתְמַר מַגִּיד מֵרֵאשִׁית אַחֲרִית. וְאִיהוּ קַרְקַפְתָּא דִּתְפִלֵּי.

מִלְגָאו אִיהוּ יוּ"ד ה"א וא"ו ה"א דְּאִיהוּ אֹרַח אֲצִילוּת. אִיהוּ שַׁקְיוּ דְּאִילָנָא
בִּדְרוֹעוֹי וְעַנְפּוֹי. כְּמַיָא דְּאַשְׁקֵי לְאִילָנָא וְאִתְרַבֵּי בְּהַהוּא שַׁקְיוּ:

Ve'ilein Eser Sefiran Inun Azelin Kesidran. Chad Arich Vechad Katzer Vechad
Beinoni. Ve'ant Hu De'anhig Lon. Veleit Man De'anhig Lach. La Le'ella Vela Letatta
Vela Mikol-Sitra. Levushin Takkant Lon Deminayhu Farechin Nishmatin Livnei
Nasha. Vechamah Gufin Takkant Lon De'itkeri'u Gufa Legabei Levushin
Dimchasyan Aleihon. Ve'itkeri'u Betikuna Da. Chesed Dero'a Yemina. Gevurah
Dero'a Semala. Tif'eret Gufa. Netzach Vehod Terein Shokin. Yesod Siyuma Degufa
Ot Berit Kodesh. Malchut Peh Torah Shebe'al-Peh Kareinon Lah. Chochmah Mocha
Ihi Machashavah Millegav. Binah Liba Uvah Hallev Mevin. Ve'al Ilein Terein Ketiv
Hanistarot. L'Adonai Eloheinu;. Keter Elyon Ihu Keter Malchut. Ve'aleih Itmar
Maggid Mereshit Acharit. Ve'ihu Karkafta Ditfillei. Millegav Ihu Yo"D He" Va"V He"
De'ihu Orach Atzilut. Ihu Shakyu De'ilana Bidro'oy Ve'anpoy. Kemaya De'ashkei
Le'ilana Ve'itrabei Behahu Shakyu.

רִבּוֹן עָלְמִין אַנְתְּ הוּא עִלַּת הָעִלּוֹת וְסִבַּת הַסִּבּוֹת דְּאַשְׁקֵי לְאִילָנָא בְּהַהוּא
נְבִיעוּ. וְהַהוּא נְבִיעוּ אִיהוּ כְּנִשְׁמְתָא לְגוּפָא דְּאִיהִי חַיִּים לְגוּפָא: וּבָךְ לֵית
דִּמְיוֹן וְלֵית דִּיּוּקְנָא (דְּגוּפָא) מִכָּל מַה דִּלְגָאו וּלְבַר. וּבָרָאתָ שְׁמַיָא וְאַרְעָא.
וְאַפֵּקְתְּ מִנְּהוֹן שִׁמְשָׁא וְסִיהֲרָא וְכוֹכְבַיָא וּמַזָּלֵי. וּבְאַרְעָא אִילָנִין וּדְשָׁאִין
וְגִנְתָּא דְּעֵדֶן וְעִשְׂבִּין וְחֵיוָן וְעוֹפִין וְנוּנִין וּבְעִירִין וּבְנֵי נָשָׁא. לְאִשְׁתְּמוֹדְעָא בְּהוֹן
עִלָּאִין וְאֵיךְ יִתְנַהֲגוּן בְּהוֹן עִלָּאִין וְתַתָּאִין. וְאֵיךְ אִשְׁתְּמוֹדְעָן מֵעִלָּאֵי וְתַתָּאֵי
וְלֵית דְּיָדַע בָּךְ כְּלָל. וּבַר מִנָּךְ לֵית יִחוּדָא בְּעִלָּאֵי וְתַתָּאֵי. וְאַנְתְּ אִשְׁתְּמוֹדַע
אָדוֹן עַל כֹּלָּא: וְכָל סְפִירָן כָּל חַד אִית לֵיהּ שֵׁם יְדִיעַ. וּבְהוֹן אִתְקְרִיאוּ
מַלְאָכַיָא. וְאַנְתְּ לֵית לָךְ שֵׁם יְדִיעַ. דְּאַנְתְּ הוּא מְמַלֵּא כָּל שְׁמָהָן וְאַנְתְּ הוּא
שְׁלִימוּ דְּכֻלְּהוּ: וְכַד אַנְתְּ תִּסְתַּלַּק מִנְּהוֹן. אִשְׁתָּאֲרוּ כֻּלְּהוּ שְׁמָהָן כְּגוּפָא בְּלָא
נִשְׁמְתָא: אַנְתְּ הוּא חַכִּים וְלָאו בְּחָכְמָה יְדִיעָא. אַנְתְּ הוּא מֵבִין וְלָאו מִבִּינָה
יְדִיעָא. לֵית לָךְ אֲתַר יְדִיעָא. אֶלָּא לְאִשְׁתְּמוֹדְעָא תָּקְפָּךְ וְחֵילָךְ לִבְנֵי נָשָׁא.
וּלְאַחֲזָאָה לוֹן אֵיךְ אִתְנְהִיג עָלְמָא בְּדִינָא וּבְרַחֲמֵי דְּאִנּוּן צֶדֶק וּמִשְׁפָּט כְּפוּם
עוֹבָדֵיהוֹן דִּבְנֵי נָשָׁא: דִּין אִיהוּ גְּבוּרָה. מִשְׁפָּט עַמּוּדָא דְּאֶמְצָעִיתָא. צֶדֶק
מַלְכוּתָא קַדִּישָׁא. מֹאזְנֵי צֶדֶק תְּרֵין סָמְכֵי קְשׁוֹט. הִין צֶדֶק אוֹת בְּרִית. כֹּלָּא
לְאַחֲזָאָה אֵיךְ אִתְנְהִיג עָלְמָא: אֲבָל לָאו דְּאִית לָךְ צֶדֶק יְדִיעָא דְּאִיהוּ דִּין.
וְלָאו מִשְׁפָּט יְדִיעָא דְּאִיהוּ רַחֲמֵי. וְלָאו מִכָּל אִלֵּין מִדּוֹת כְּלָל: קוּם רַבִּי
שִׁמְעוֹן וְיִתְחַדְּשׁוּן מִלִּין עַל יָדָךְ. דְּהָא רְשׁוּתָא אִית לָךְ לְגַלָּאָה רָזִין טְמִירִין
עַל יָדָךְ. מַה דְּלָא אִתְיְהֵב רְשׁוּ לְגַלָּאָה לְשׁוּם בַּר נָשׁ עַד כְּעַן:

Ribon Alemin Ant Hu Ilat Ha'ilot Vesibat Hassibot De'ashkei Le'ilana Behahu
Nevi'u. Vehahu Nevi'u Ihu Kenishmeta Legufa De'ihi Chayim Legufa. Uvach Leit
Dimyon Veleit Diyukena (Degufa) Mikol Mah Dilgav Ulevar. Uvarata Shemaya
Ve'ar'a. Ve'apakt Minehon Shimsha Vesihara Vechochevaya Umazalei. Uve'ar'a

Ilanin Udesha'in Vegineta De'eden Ve'isbin Vecheivan Ve'ofin Venunin Uve'irin
Uvenei Nasha. Le'ishtemode'a Vehon Illa'in Ve'eich Yitnahagun Behon Illa'in
Vetatta'in. Ve'eich Ishtemode'an Me'illa'ei Vetatta'ei Veleit Deyada Bach Kelal.
Uvar Minach Leit Yichuda Be'illa'ei Vetatta'ei. Ve'ant Ishtemoda Adon Al-Kolla.
Vechol-Sefiran Kol-Chad It Leih Shem Yedia. Uvehon Itkeri'u Mal'achaya. Ve'ant
Leit Lach Shem Yedia. De'ant Hu Memallei Kol Shemahan Ve'ant Hu Shelimu
Dechulehu. Vechad Ant Tistallak Minehon. Ishte'aru Kullehu Shemahan Kegufa Vela
Nishmata. Ant Hu Chakkim Velav Bechochmah Yedi'a. Ant Hu Mevin Velav
Mibinah Yedi'a. Leit Lach Atar Yedi'a. Ella Le'ishtemode'a Tukfach Vecheilach Livnei
Nasha. Ule'achza'ah Lon Eich Itnehig Alema Bedina Uverachamei De'inun Tzedek
Umishpat Kefum Ovadeihon Divnei Nasha. Din Ihu Gevurah. Mishpat Ammuda
De'emtza'ita. Tzedek Malchuta Kaddisha. Mozenei Tzedek Terein Samchei Keshot.
Hin Tzedek Ot Berit. Kolla Le'achza'ah Eich Itnehig Alema. Aval Lav De'it Lach
Tzedek Yedi'a De'ihu Din. Velav Mishpat Yedi'a De'ihu Rachamei. Velav Mikol
'Ilein Middot Kelal. Kum Ribi Shim'on Veyitchadeshun Millin Al Yedach. Deha
Reshuta It Lach Legalla'ah Razin Temirin Al Yedach. Mah Dela Ityehiv Reshu
Legalla'ah Lasum Bar-Nash Ad Ke'An.

קָם רַבִּי שִׁמְעוֹן פָּתַח וְאָמַר. לְךָ יְהוָה הַגְּדֻלָּה וְהַגְּבוּרָה וְהַתִּפְאֶרֶת וְהַנֵּצַח
וְהַהוֹד כִּי כֹל בַּשָּׁמַיִם וּבָאָרֶץ לְךָ יְהוָה הַמַּמְלָכָה וְהַמִּתְנַשֵּׂא לְכֹל לְרֹאשׁ.
עִלָּאִין שְׁמָעוּ אִינוּן דְּמִיכִין דְּחֶבְרוֹן. וְרַעְיָא מְהֵימְנָא אִתְּעָרוּ מִשְּׁנַתְכוֹן. הָקִיצוּ
וְרַנְּנוּ שׁוֹכְנֵי עָפָר. אִלֵּין אִינוּן צַדִּיקַיָּא דְּאִינוּן מִסִּטְרָא דְּהַהִיא דְּאִתְמַר בָּהּ
אֲנִי יְשֵׁנָה וְלִבִּי עֵר. וְלָאו אִינוּן מֵתִים. וּבְגִין דָּא אִתְמַר בְּהוֹן הָקִיצוּ וְרַנְּנוּ
וכו'. רַעְיָא מְהֵימְנָא. אַנְתְּ וַאֲבָהָן הָקִיצוּ וְרַנְּנוּ לְאִתְעָרוּתָא דִּשְׁכִינְתָּא. דְּאִיהִי
יְשֵׁנָה בְּגָלוּתָא. דְּעַד כְּעַן צַדִּיקַיָּא כֻּלְּהוּ דְמִיכִין וְשִׁנְתָּא בְּחוֹרֵיהוֹן: מִיַּד יְהִיבַת
שְׁכִינְתָּא תְּלָת קָלִין לְגַבֵּי רַעְיָא מְהֵימְנָא. וְיֵימָא לֵיהּ קוּם רַעְיָא מְהֵימְנָא.
דְּהָא עֲלָךְ אִתְמַר קוֹל דּוֹדִי דוֹפֵק לְגַבָּאי בְּאַרְבַּע אַתְוָן דִּילֵיהּ. וְיֵימָא בְּהוֹן.
פִּתְחִי לִי אֲחֹתִי רַעְיָתִי יוֹנָתִי תַמָּתִי. דְּהָא תַּם עֲוֹנֵךְ בַּת צִיּוֹן. לֹא יוֹסִיף
לְהַגְלוֹתֵךְ: שֶׁרֹאשִׁי נִמְלָא טָל. מַאי נִמְלָא טָל. אֶלָּא אָמַר קוּדְשָׁא בְּרִיךְ הוּא.
אַנְתְּ חָשַׁבְתְּ דְּמִיּוֹמָא דְאִתְחָרַב בֵּי מַקְדְּשָׁא דְעָאלְנָא בְּבֵיתָא דִילִי. וְעָאלְנָא
בִּישׁוּבָא. לָאו הָכִי. דְּלָא עָאלְנָא כָּל זִמְנָא דְאַנְתְּ בְּגָלוּתָא. הֲרֵי לְךָ סִימָנָא.
שֶׁרֹאשִׁי נִמְלָא טָל ה"א שְׁכִינְתָּא בְּגָלוּתָא. שְׁלִימוּ דִילָהּ וְחַיִּים דִּילָהּ אִיהוּ
טַ"ל. וְדָא אִיהוּ יוֹ"ד ה"א וא"ו וה"א אִיהִי שְׁכִינְתָּא דְּלָא מֵחֶשְׁבָּן טַ"ל. אֶלָּא
יוֹ"ד ה"א וא"ו. דְּסַלְּקִיוּ אַתְוָן לְחֶשְׁבָּן טַ"ל. דְּאִיהִי מַלְיָא לִשְׁכִינְתָּא מִנְּבִיעוּ
דְּכָל מְקוֹרִין עִלָּאִין. מִיַּד קָם רַעְיָא מְהֵימְנָא. וַאֲבָהָן קַדִּישִׁין עִמֵּיהּ. עַד כָּאן
רָזָא דְיִחוּדָא. בָּרוּךְ יְהוָה לְעוֹלָם אָמֵן וְאָמֵן:

Kam Rabbi Shim'on Patach Ve'amar. Lecha Adonai Hagedullah Vehagevurah
Vehatif'eret Vehanetzach Vehahod Ki Chol Bashamayim Uva'aretz Lecha Adonai
Hamamlachah Vehamitnasse Lechol Lerosh. Illa'in Shim'u Inun Demichin
Dechevron. Vera'ya Meheimna Itte'aru Mishenatchon. Hakitzu Veranenu Shochenei

Afar. Ilein Inun Tzaddikaya De'inun Missitra Dehahi De'itmar Bah Ani Yeshenah
Velibi Er. Velav Inun Meitim. Uvegin Da Itmar Behon Hakitzu Veranenu Vechu'.
Ra'ya Meheimna. Ant Va'avahan Hakitzu Veranenu Le'itte'aruta Dishchinta. De'ihi
Yeshenah Begaluta. De'ad Ke'an Tzaddikaya Kullehu Demichin Veshinta
Bechoreihon: Miyad Yehivat Shechinta Telat Kalin Legabei Ra'ya Meheimna.
Veyeima Leih Kum Ra'ya Meheimna, Deha Alach Itmar Kol Dodi Dofek Legaba
Be'arba Atvan Dileih. Veyeima Behon. Pitchi Li Achoti Ra'yati Yonati Tammati.
Deha Tam Avonech Bat Tziyon. Lo Yosif Lehaglotech: Sheroshi Nimla Tal. Ma Nimla
Tal. Ella Amar Kudesha Berich Hu. Ant Chashavt Demiyoma De'itcharav Bei
Makdesha De'alna Beveita Dili. Ve'alna Veyishuva. Lav Hachi. Dela Alna Kol
Zimna De'ant Begaluta. Harei Lecha Simana. Sheroshi Nimla Tal He" Shechinta
Begaluta. Shelimu Dilah Vechayim Dilah Ihu Ta"L. Veda Ihu Yo"D He" Va"V VeHe"
Ihi Shechinta Dela Mechushban Ta"L. Ella Yo"D He" Va"V. Disliku Atvan
Lechushban Ta"L. De'ihi Malya Lishchinta Minevi'u Dechol Mekorin Illa'in. Miyad
Kam Ra'ya Meheimna. Va'avahan Kaddishin Immeih. Ad Kan Raza Deyichuda.
Baruch Adonai Le'olam Amen Ve'Amen:

יְהֵא רַעֲוָא מִן קֳדָם עַתִּיקָא קַדִּישָׁא דְּכָל קַדִּישִׁין טְמִירָא דְּכָל טְמִירִין סְתִימָא
דְּכֹלָּא. דְּיִתְמְשָׁךְ טַלָּא עִלָּאָה מִנֵּיהּ לְמַלְיָא רֵישֵׁיהּ דִּזְעֵיר אַנְפִּין. וּלְהַטִּיל
לַחֲקַל תַּפּוּחִין קַדִּישִׁין בִּנְהִירוּ דְּאַנְפִּין בְּרַעֲוָא וּבְחֶדְוָתָא דְּכֹלָּא. וְיִתְמְשָׁךְ מִן
קֳדָם עַתִּיקָא דְּכָל קַדִּישִׁין טְמִירָא דְּכָל טְמִירִין סְתִימָא דְּכֹלָּא רְעוּתָא
וְרַחֲמֵי חִנָּא וְחִסְדָּא בִּנְהִירוּ עִלָּאָה בִּרְעוּתָא וְחֶדְוָא עָלַי וְעַל כָּל בְּנֵי בֵיתִי וְעַל
כָּל הַנִּלְוִים אֵלַי וְעַל כָּל יִשְׂרָאֵל עַמֵּיהּ. וְיִפְרְקִינָן מִכָּל עַקְתִין בִּישִׁין דְּיֵיתוּן
לְעָלְמָא וְיַזְמִין וְיִתְיְהִיב לָנָא וּלְכָל נַפְשָׁתָנָא חִנָּא וְחִסְדָּא חַיֵּי אֲרִיכֵי וּמְזוֹנֵי
רְוִיחֵי וְרַחֲמֵי מִן קֳדָמֵיהּ. אָמֵן כֵּן יְהִי רָצוֹן אָמֵן וְאָמֵן:

Yehei Ra'ava Min Kodam Atika Kaddisha Dechal Kaddishin Temira Dechol Temirin
Setima Decholla Deyitmeshach Talla Illa'ah Mineih Lemalya Reisheih Diz'eir
Anpin. Ulehatil Lachakal Tappuchin Kaddishin Binhiru De'anpin Bera'ava
Uvechedvata Decholla. Veyitmeshach Min Kodam Atika Kaddisha Dechal-
Kaddishin Temira Dechal-Temirin Setima Dechola Re'uta Verachamei China
Vechisda Binhiru Illa'ah Bir'uta Vechedva Alai Ve'al-Kol-Benei Veiti Ve'al Kol
Hanilvim Elai Ve'al-Kol-Yisrael Ammeih. Veyifrekinan Mikol-'Aktin Bishin Deyeitun
Le'alema Veyazmin Veyityehiv Lana Ulechol-Nafshatana China Vechisda Vechayei
Arichei Umezonei Revichei Verachamei Min Kodameih. Amen Ken Yehi Ratzon
Amen Ve'amen.

Adon Olam

אֲדוֹן עוֹלָם אֲשֶׁר מָלַךְ. בְּטֶרֶם כָּל יְצִיר נִבְרָא:

Adon Olam Asher Malach. Beterem Kol Yetzir Nivra.

Lord over all, Who has ruled forever. Even before first Creation's
wondrous form was framed.

לְעֵת נַעֲשָׂה בְחֶפְצוֹ כֹּל. אֲזַי מֶלֶךְ שְׁמוֹ נִקְרָא:

Le'et Na'asah Vecheftzo Chol. Azai Melech Shemo Nikra.

When by His Divine will all things were made; Then, Almighty King,
was His name proclaimed.

וְאַחֲרֵי כִּכְלוֹת הַכֹּל. לְבַדּוֹ יִמְלֹךְ נוֹרָא:

Ve'acharei Kichlot Hakol. Levado Yimloch Nora.

And after all will cease. In awesome greatness, He alone will reign.

וְהוּא הָיָה וְהוּא הֹוֶה. וְהוּא יִהְיֶה בְּתִפְאָרָה:

Vehu Hayah Vehu Hoveh. Vehu Yihyeh Betif'arah.

Who was, Who is, and Who will forever be, in splendor.

וְהוּא אֶחָד וְאֵין שֵׁנִי. לְהַמְשִׁילוֹ וּלְהַחְבִּירָה:

Vehu Echad Ve'ein Sheni. Lehamshilo Ulehachbirah.

He is One, unequalled, and beyond compare. Without division or
associate.

בְּלִי רֵאשִׁית בְּלִי תַכְלִית. וְלוֹ הָעֹז וְהַמִּשְׂרָה:

Beli Reshit Beli Tachlit. Velo Ha'ohz Vehamisrah.

He is without beginning, without end; He reigns in power.

בְּלִי עֵרֶךְ בְּלִי דִמְיוֹן. בְּלִי שִׁנּוּי וּתְמוּרָה:

Beli Erech Beli Dimyon. Beli Shinui Ut'murah.

To him, no like or equal can ever be; Without change or substitute,
He remains.

בְּלִי חִבּוּר בְּלִי פֵּרוּד. גְּדוֹל כֹּחַ וּגְבוּרָה:

Beli Chibur Beli Pirud. Gedol Koach Ug'vurah.

Without divisibleness or attachment. He supremely reigns in highest
might and power.

וְהוּא אֵלִי וְחַי גּוֹאֲלִי. וְצוּר חֶבְלִי בְּעֵת צָרָה:

Vehu Eli Vechai Go'ali. Vetzur Chevli B'yom Tzarah.

And He is my God and my living Redeemer. My sheltering Rock on
the day of misfortune.

וְהוּא נִסִּי וּמָנוּס. מְנָת כּוֹסִי בְּיוֹם אֶקְרָא:

Vehu Nissi Umanusi. Menat Kosi B'yom Ekra.

My standard, refuge, portion, true. The Portion of my cup on the
day that I call.

וְהוּא רוֹפֵא וְהוּא מַרְפֵּא. וְהוּא צוֹפֶה וְהוּא עֶזְרָה:

Vehu Rofei Vehu Marpe. Vehu Tzofeh Vehu Ezrah.

He is a Healer and a cure; He is a Watchman and a Helper.

בְּיָדוֹ אַפְקִיד רוּחִי. בְּעֵת אִישַׁן וְאָעִירָה:

Beyado Afkid Ruchi. Be'et Ishan Ve'a'irah.

Into His hands I consign my spirit. While wrapped in sleep. and I will
awake again.

וְעִם רוּחִי גְּוִיָּתִי. אֲדֹנָי לִי וְלֹא אִירָא:

Ve'im Ruchi Geviyati. Adonai Li Velo Ira.

And with my soul, my body I resign; Hashem is with me, and I will
not fear .

בְּמִקְדָּשׁוֹ תָּגֵל נַפְשִׁי. מְשִׁיחֵנוּ יִשְׁלַח מְהֵרָה:

Bemikdasho Tagel Nafshi. Meshicheinu Yishlach Meheirah.

In His Temple, my soul will delight; may He send our Messiah soon.

וְאָז נָשִׁיר בְּבֵית קָדְשִׁי. אָמֵן אָמֵן שֵׁם הַנּוֹרָא:

Ve'az Nashir Beveit Kodshi. Amen. Amen. Shem Hanora.

And then we'll sing in my Holy House. Amen, Amen, to the Awe-
inspring Name.

Seder Tzitzit / Order of Tzitzit

One should wrap himself in a fringed garment, and recite the blessing while standing. Before reciting the blessing, one should examine the threads of the tzitzit (fringes) to see if they are lawfully fit, and he must separate the threads from one another (not on Shabbat). He should recite the blessing: "lehitateif betzitzit" (On the tallit katan (small tallit), it is customary to say the blessing: "al mitzvat tzitzit" upon awakening). If the tallit fell off entirely from a person, he must say the blessing again. (If one took it off with the intention of putting it on again, while the small tallit was still left on his body, he does not need to say the blessing again). Tallit Katans that are customarily worn, even though they are not wrapped, fulfill our obligation for fringes. And it is good that one places it over one's head, the long way, and wrap it. He should stand this way wrapped for at least the amount of time it would take to walk four cubits. After this he can pull it over his head and wear it normally. One should return two of the fringes in front, and two behind. On a tallit katan, one can bless "lehitateif betzitzit" even which does not wrap, but only worn. (SA, OC 8)

Some say before:

לְשֵׁם יִחוּד קוּדְשָׁא בְּרִיךְ הוּא וּשְׁכִינְתֵּיה. בִּדְחִילוּ וּרְחִימוּ. וּרְחִימוּ וּדְחִילוּ.
לְיַחֲדָא שֵׁם יוֹ״ד קֵ״י בְּוָא״ו קֵ״י בְּיִחוּדָא שְׁלִים (יהוה) בְּשֵׁם כָּל יִשְׂרָאֵל.
הֲרֵינִי מוּכָן לִלְבּשׁ טַלִּית מְצִיצַת כְּהִלְכָתָהּ כְּמוֹ שֶׁצִוָנוּ יהוה אֱלֹהֵינוּ בְּתוֹרָתוֹ
הַקְּדוֹשָׁה וְעָשׂוּ לָהֶם צִיצַת עַל כַּנְפֵי בִגְדֵיהֶם. כְּדֵי לַעֲשׂוֹת נַחַת רוּחַ לְיוֹצְרִי
וְלַעֲשׂוֹת רְצוֹן בּוֹרְאָ. וַהֲרֵינִי מְכוּוָן לְבָרֵךְ עֲטִיפַת הַטַלִּית כְּתִקּוּן רַבּוֹתֵינוּ
זִכְרוֹנָם לִבְרָכָה. וַהֲרֵינִי מְכוּוָן לִפְטֹר בְּבְרָכָה זוֹ גַּם טַלִּית הַקָּטָן שֶׁעָלַי. וִיהִי
נֹעַם אֲדֹנָי אֱלֹהֵינוּ עָלֵינוּ וּמַעֲשֵׂה יָדֵינוּ כּוֹנְנָה עָלֵינוּ וּמַעֲשֵׂה יָדֵינוּ כּוֹנְנֵהוּ:

Some also have a custom of saying before:

בָּרְכִי נַפְשִׁי אֶת־יְהֹוָה יְהֹוָה אֱלֹהַי גָּדַלְתָּ מְּאֹדהוֹד וְהָדָר לָבָשְׁתָּ: עֹטֶה־אוֹר
כַּשַּׂלְמָה נוֹטֶה שָׁמַיִם כַּיְרִיעָה:

Barchi Nafshi Et Adonai Adonai Elohai Gadalta Me'odhod Vehadar Lavasheta. Oteh
Or Kassalmah Noteh Shamayim Kayeri'ah.

Bless Hashem, Oh my soul. Hashem my God, You are very great; You are clothed with glory and majesty. Who covers Yourself with light as with a garment, who stretches out the heavens like a curtain.

Baruch Attah Adonai Eloheinu	בָּרוּךְ אַתָּה יְהֹוָה אֱלֹהֵינוּ
Melech Ha'olam Asher	מֶלֶךְ הָעוֹלָם. אֲשֶׁר
Kideshanu Bemitzvotav	קִדְּשָׁנוּ בְּמִצְוֹתָיו
Vetzivanu Lehitateif Betzitzit.	וְצִוָּנוּ לְהִתְעַטֵּף בְּצִיצִית:

Blessed are You. Hashem our God, King of the Universe, that has sanctified us with His commandments and commanded us to enwrap ourselves in tzitzit.

Some have a custom of saying afterwards:

מַה־יָּקָר חַסְדְּךָ אֱלֹהִים וּבְנֵי אָדָם בְּצֵל כְּנָפֶיךָ יֶחֱסָיוּן: יִרְוְיֻן מִדֶּשֶׁן בֵּיתֶךָ וְנַחַל עֲדָנֶיךָ תַשְׁקֵם: כִּי־עִמְּךָ מְקוֹר חַיִּים בְּאוֹרְךָ נִרְאֶה־אוֹר: מְשֹׁךְ חַסְדְּךָ לְיֹדְעֶיךָ וְצִדְקָתְךָ לְיִשְׁרֵי־לֵב:

Mah Yakar Chasdecha Elohim Uvenei Adam Betzel Kenafeicha Yechesayun. Yirveyun Mideshen Beitecha Venachal Adaneicha Tashkem. Ki Imecha Mekor Chayim Be'orecha Nir'eh Or. Meshoch Chasdecha Leyodeicha Vetzidkatecha Leyishrei Lev.

How precious is Your lovingkindness, God. And the children of men take refuge in the shadow of Your wings. They are abundantly satisfied with the fatness of Your House; And You make them drink of the river of Your pleasures. For with You is the fountain of life; In Your light we see light. Continue Your lovingkindness to them that know You; And Your righteousness to the upright in heart. (Ps. 56:8-9, 11-12)

Arriving at the Synagogue

When arriving at the Synagogue one bows at the entrance and recites:

Va'ani Berov Chasdecha Avo	וַאֲנִי בְּרֹב חַסְדְּךָ אָבוֹא
Veitecha Eshtachaveh El-	בֵיתֶךָ אֶשְׁתַּחֲוֶה אֶל־
Heichal-Kodshecha	הֵיכַל־קָדְשְׁךָ
Beyir'atecha.	בְּיִרְאָתֶךָ:

As for me, through Your abundant kindness, I will enter Your House; I will prostrate myself toward Your Holy Sanctuary in awe of You.
(Psalms. 5:8)

One then continues to walk and recites the verses:

Adonai Tzeva'ot Imanu; Misgav-	יְהֹוָה צְבָאוֹת עִמָּנוּ מִשְׂגָּב־
Lanu Elohei Ya'akov Selah.	לָנוּ אֱלֹהֵי יַעֲקֹב סֶלָה:

Hashem of hosts is with us; the God of Yaakov is our high tower.
Selah. (Psalms 46:8)

Adonai Tzeva'ot; Ashrei Adam.

Boteach Bach.

יְהֹוָה צְבָאוֹת אַשְׁרֵי אָדָם
בֹּטֵחַ בָּךְ:

Hashem of hosts, happy is the man who trusts in You. (Psalms 84:13)

Adonai Hoshi'ah; Hamelech.

Ya'aneinu Veyom-Kare'enu.

יְהֹוָה הוֹשִׁיעָה הַמֶּלֶךְ
יַעֲנֵנוּ בְיוֹם־קָרְאֵנוּ:

Save, Hashem. May the King answer us on the day that we call. (Psalms 20:10)

Tefillat Chanah / The Prayer of Chanah

וַתִּתְפַּלֵּל חַנָּה וַתֹּאמַר עָלַץ לִבִּי בַּיהֹוָה רָמָה קַרְנִי בַּיהֹוָה רָחַב פִּי
עַל־אוֹיְבַי כִּי שָׂמַחְתִּי בִּישׁוּעָתֶךָ: אֵין־קָדוֹשׁ כַּיהֹוָה כִּי אֵין בִּלְתֶּךָ
וְאֵין צוּר כֵּאלֹהֵינוּ: אַל־תַּרְבּוּ תְדַבְּרוּ גְּבֹהָה גְבֹהָה יֵצֵא עָתָק
מִפִּיכֶם כִּי אֵל דֵּעוֹת יְהֹוָה וְלֹא (וְלוֹ) נִתְכְּנוּ עֲלִלוֹת: קֶשֶׁת גִּבֹּרִים
חַתִּים וְנִכְשָׁלִים אָזְרוּ חָיִל: שְׂבֵעִים בַּלֶּחֶם נִשְׂכָּרוּ וּרְעֵבִים חָדֵלּוּ
עַד־עֲקָרָה יָלְדָה שִׁבְעָה וְרַבַּת בָּנִים אֻמְלָלָה: יְהֹוָה מֵמִית וּמְחַיֶּה
מוֹרִיד שְׁאוֹל וַיָּעַל: יְהֹוָה מוֹרִישׁ וּמַעֲשִׁיר מַשְׁפִּיל אַף־מְרוֹמֵם:
מֵקִים מֵעָפָר דָּל מֵאַשְׁפֹּת יָרִים אֶבְיוֹן לְהוֹשִׁיב עִם־נְדִיבִים וְכִסֵּא
כָבוֹד יַנְחִלֵם כִּי לַיהֹוָה מְצֻקֵי אֶרֶץ וַיָּשֶׁת עֲלֵיהֶם תֵּבֵל: רַגְלֵי חֲסִידָו
יִשְׁמֹר וּרְשָׁעִים בַּחֹשֶׁךְ יִדָּמּוּ כִּי־לֹא בְכֹחַ יִגְבַּר־אִישׁ: יְהֹוָה יֵחַתּוּ
מְרִיבָו עָלָו בַּשָּׁמַיִם יַרְעֵם יְהֹוָה יָדִין אַפְסֵי־אָרֶץ וְיִתֶּן־עֹז לְמַלְכּוֹ
וְיָרֵם קֶרֶן מְשִׁיחוֹ:

Vatitpallel Chanah Vatomar Alatz Libi Badonai Ramah Karni Badonai Rachav Pi Al Oyevai Ki Samachti Bishu'atecha. Ein Kadosh Ka'Adonai Ki Ein Biltecha Ve'ein Tzur Keloheinu. Al Tarbu Tedaberu Gevohah Gevohah Yetze Atak Mipichem Ki El De'ot Adonai Velo Nitkenu Alilot. Keshet Giborim Chatim Venichshalim Azeru Chayil. Seve'im Ballechem Niskaru Ure'evim Chadelu Ad Akarah Yaledah Shiv'ah Verabbat Banim Umlalah. Adonai Memit Umechayeh Morid She'ol Vaya'al. Adonai Morish Uma'ashir Mashpil Af Meromem. Mekim Me'afar Dal Me'ashpot Yarim Evyon Lehoshiv Im Nedivim Vechisse Chavod Yanchilem Ki L'Adonai Metzukei Eretz Vayashet Aleihem Tevel. Raglei Chasidav Yishmor Uresha'im Bachoshech Yiddammu Ki Lo Vechoach Yigbar Ish. Adonai Yechatu Merivav Alav Bashamayim Yar'em Adonai Yadin Afsei Aretz Veyiten Oz Lemalko Veyarem Keren Meshicho.

And Chanah prayed, and said: my heart exults in Hashem, my horn is exalted in Hashem; my mouth is enlarged over my enemies; because I rejoice in Your salvation. There is none as holy as Hashem, for there is none beside You; neither is there any rock like our God. Do not multiply exceedingly proud speech; do not let arrogance come out of your mouth; for Hashem is a God of knowledge, and by Him actions are weighed. The bows of the mighty men are broken, and they that stumbled are girded with strength. They that were full have hired out themselves for bread; and they that were hungry have ceased; while the barren has borne seven, she that had many children has languished. Hashem kills, and makes alive; He brings down to the grave, and brings up. Hashem makes poor, and makes rich; He brings low, He also lifts up. He raises up the poor out of the dust, He raises up the needy from the dung-hill, to make them sit with princes, and inherit the throne of glory; for the pillars of the earth are Hashem's, and He has set the world on them. He will keep the feet of His holy ones, but the wicked will be put to silence in darkness; for not by strength will man prevail. They that strive with Hashem will be broken to pieces; against them He will thunder in heaven; Hashem will judge the ends of the earth; and He will give strength to His king, and exalt the horn of His anointed. (I Samuel 2:1-10)

אָתוֹהִי כְּמָה רַבְרְבִין וְתִמְהוֹהִי כְּמָה תַקִּיפִין מַלְכוּתֵהּ מַלְכוּת עָלַם
וְשָׁלְטָנֵהּ עִם־דָּר וְדָר: וַאֲנַחְנוּ עַמְּךָ | וְצֹאן מַרְעִיתֶךָ נוֹדֶה לְּךָ לְעוֹלָם
לְדוֹר וָדֹר נְסַפֵּר תְּהִלָּתֶךָ: עֶרֶב וָבֹקֶר וְצָהֳרַיִם אָשִׂיחָה וְאֶהֱמֶה
וַיִּשְׁמַע קוֹלִי: בְּרָן־יַחַד כּוֹכְבֵי בֹקֶר וַיָּרִיעוּ כָּל־בְּנֵי אֱלֹהִים:
לֹא־אִירָא מֵרִבְבוֹת עָם אֲשֶׁר סָבִיב שָׁתוּ עָלָי: וַאֲנִי בַּיהוָה אֲצַפֶּה
אוֹחִילָה לֵאלֹהֵי יִשְׁעִי יִשְׁמָעֵנִי אֱלֹהָי:

Atohi Kemah Ravrevin Vetimhohi Kemah Takifin Malchuteh Malchut
Alam Vesholtaneh Im Dar Vedar: Va'anachnu Ammecha Vetzon
Mar'itecha Nodeh Lecha Le'olam Ledor Vador Nesapeir
Tehillatecha: Erev Vavoker Vetzaharayim Asichah Ve'ehemeh
Vayishma Koli: Beron Yachad Kochevei Voker Vayari'u Kol Benei
Elohim: Lo Ira Merivot Am Asher Saviv Shatu Alai: Va'ani Badonai
Atzapeh Ochilah Lelohei Yish'i Yishma'eni Elohai:

How great are His signs. And how mighty are His wonders. His
kingdom is an everlasting kingdom, And His dominion is from
generation to generation. So we that are Your people and the flock
of Your pasture will give You thanks forever; we will tell of Your
praise to all generations. Evening, and morning, and at noon, I will
complain, and moan; and He has heard my voice. When the
morning stars sang together, And all the sons of God shouted for
joy. I am not afraid of ten thousands of people, that have set
themselves against me all around. 'But as for me, I will look to
Hashem; I will wait for the God of my salvation; My God will hear
me. (Daniel 3:33, Psalms 79:13, Psalms 55:18, Job 38:7, Psalms 3:7, Micah 7:7)

Some say before:

לְשֵׁם יִחוּד קוּדְשָׁא בְּרִיךְ הוּא וּשְׁכִינְתֵּיהּ. בִּדְחִילוּ וּרְחִימוּ. וּרְחִימוּ וּדְחִילוּ.
לְיַחֲדָא שֵׁם יוֹ"ד קֵ"י בְּוָא"ו קֵ"י בְּיִחוּדָא שְׁלִים (יהוה) בְּשֵׁם כָּל יִשְׂרָאֵל.
הנה אנחנו באים להתפלל תפלת שחרית. שתקן אברהם אבינו עליו
השלום. עם כל המצות הכלולות בה לתקן את שורשה במקום עליון.
לעשות נחת רוח ליוצרנו ולעשות רצון בוראנו. וִיהִי נֹעַם אֲדֹנָי אֱלֹהֵינוּ עָלֵינוּ
וּמַעֲשֵׂה יָדֵינוּ כּוֹנְנָה עָלֵינוּ וּמַעֲשֵׂה יָדֵינוּ כּוֹנְנֵהוּ:

Vahareini Mekabel Alai Mitzvat	וַהֲרֵינִי מְקַבֵּל עָלַי מִצְוַת
Aseh Shel Ve'ahavta Lere'acha	עֲשֵׂה שֶׁל וְאָהַבְתָּ לְרֵעֲךָ
Kamocha. Vahareini Ohev Kol	כָּמוֹךָ. וַהֲרֵינִי אוֹהֵב כָּל
Echad Mibenei Yisra'el Kenafshi	אֶחָד מִבְּנֵי יִשְׂרָאֵל כְּנַפְשִׁי
Ume'odi. Vahareini Mezammen	וּמְאוֹדִי. וַהֲרֵינִי מְזַמֵּן
Peh Shelli Lehitpallel Lifnei	פֶּה שֶׁלִּי לְהִתְפַּלֵּל לִפְנֵי
Melech Malchei Hamelachim.	מֶלֶךְ מַלְכֵי הַמְּלָכִים.
Hakadosh Baruch Hu:	הַקָּדוֹשׁ בָּרוּךְ הוּא:

I hereby accept upon myself the mitzvah of "and you shall love your neighbor as yourself". And I hereby love all of the Children of Yisrael as my soul and with all of my strength. And I hereby prepare my mouth to pray before the Ruler over king of kings, the Holy, Blessed is He.

The Akedah / The Binding of Yitzchak

Eloheinu Velohei Avoteinu.	אֱלֹהֵינוּ וֵאלֹהֵי אֲבוֹתֵינוּ.
Zochrenu Bezichron Tov	זָכְרֵנוּ בְּזִכְרוֹן טוֹב
Milfaneicha. Ufokdenu Bifkudat	מִלְּפָנֶיךָ. וּפָקְדֵנוּ בִּפְקֻדַּת
Yeshu'ah Verachamim Mishemei	יְשׁוּעָה וְרַחֲמִים מִשְּׁמֵי
Shemei Kedem. Uzechor-Lanu	שְׁמֵי קֶדֶם. וּזְכֹר־לָנוּ
Adonai Eloheinu Ahavat	יְהֹוָה אֱלֹהֵינוּ אַהֲבַת
Hakadmonim Avraham Yitzchak	הַקַּדְמוֹנִים אַבְרָהָם יִצְחָק
Veyisra'el Avadeicha. Et Haberit	וְיִשְׂרָאֵל עֲבָדֶיךָ. אֶת הַבְּרִית וְאֶת
Ve'et Hachesed Ve'et	הַחֶסֶד וְאֶת
Hashevu'ah Shenishba'ta	הַשְּׁבוּעָה שֶׁנִּשְׁבַּעְתָּ
Le'avraham Avinu Behar	לְאַבְרָהָם אָבִינוּ בְּהַר

Hamoriyah. Ve'et Ha'akedah	הַמּוֹרִיָּה. וְאֶת הָעֲקֵדָה
She'akad Et Yitzchak Beno Al-	שֶׁעָקַד אֶת יִצְחָק בְּנוֹ עַל־
Gabei Hamizbe'ach Kakatuv	גַּבֵּי הַמִּזְבֵּחַ כַּכָּתוּב
Betoratach:	בְּתוֹרָתֶךָ:

Our God and God of our fathers, remember us favorably and visit us with mercy and salvation from the eternal high heavens. Remember in our favor, Hashem our God, the love of our ancestors Avraham, Yitzchak and Yisrael Your servants. Remember the covenant, the kindness, and the oath which You swore to our father Avraham on Mount Moriah, and the binding of Yitzchak his son on the altar, as it is written in Your Torah:

Genesis 22:1-19

וַיְהִי אַחַר הַדְּבָרִים הָאֵלֶּה וְהָאֱלֹהִים נִסָּה אֶת־אַבְרָהָם וַיֹּאמֶר אֵלָיו אַבְרָהָם וַיֹּאמֶר הִנֵּנִי: וַיֹּאמֶר קַח־נָא אֶת־בִּנְךָ אֶת־יְחִידְךָ אֲשֶׁר־אָהַבְתָּ אֶת־יִצְחָק וְלֶךְ־לְךָ אֶל־אֶרֶץ הַמֹּרִיָּה וְהַעֲלֵהוּ שָׁם לְעֹלָה עַל אַחַד הֶהָרִים אֲשֶׁר אֹמַר אֵלֶיךָ: וַיַּשְׁכֵּם אַבְרָהָם בַּבֹּקֶר וַיַּחֲבֹשׁ אֶת־חֲמֹרוֹ וַיִּקַּח אֶת־שְׁנֵי נְעָרָיו אִתּוֹ וְאֵת יִצְחָק בְּנוֹ וַיְבַקַּע עֲצֵי עֹלָה וַיָּקָם וַיֵּלֶךְ אֶל־הַמָּקוֹם אֲשֶׁר־אָמַר־לוֹ הָאֱלֹהִים: בַּיּוֹם הַשְּׁלִישִׁי וַיִּשָּׂא אַבְרָהָם אֶת־עֵינָיו וַיַּרְא אֶת־הַמָּקוֹם מֵרָחֹק: וַיֹּאמֶר אַבְרָהָם אֶל־נְעָרָיו שְׁבוּ־לָכֶם פֹּה עִם־הַחֲמוֹר וַאֲנִי וְהַנַּעַר נֵלְכָה עַד־כֹּה וְנִשְׁתַּחֲוֶה וְנָשׁוּבָה אֲלֵיכֶם: וַיִּקַּח אַבְרָהָם אֶת־עֲצֵי הָעֹלָה וַיָּשֶׂם עַל־יִצְחָק בְּנוֹ וַיִּקַּח בְּיָדוֹ אֶת־הָאֵשׁ וְאֶת־הַמַּאֲכֶלֶת וַיֵּלְכוּ שְׁנֵיהֶם יַחְדָּו: וַיֹּאמֶר יִצְחָק אֶל־אַבְרָהָם אָבִיו וַיֹּאמֶר אָבִי וַיֹּאמֶר הִנֶּנִּי בְנִי וַיֹּאמֶר הִנֵּה הָאֵשׁ וְהָעֵצִים וְאַיֵּה הַשֶּׂה לְעֹלָה: וַיֹּאמֶר אַבְרָהָם אֱלֹהִים יִרְאֶה־לּוֹ הַשֶּׂה לְעֹלָה בְּנִי וַיֵּלְכוּ שְׁנֵיהֶם יַחְדָּו: וַיָּבֹאוּ אֶל־הַמָּקוֹם אֲשֶׁר אָמַר־לוֹ הָאֱלֹהִים וַיִּבֶן שָׁם אַבְרָהָם אֶת־הַמִּזְבֵּחַ וַיַּעֲרֹךְ אֶת־הָעֵצִים וַיַּעֲקֹד אֶת־יִצְחָק בְּנוֹ וַיָּשֶׂם אֹתוֹ

עַל־הַמִּזְבֵּחַ מִמַּעַל לָעֵצִים: וַיִּשְׁלַח אַבְרָהָם אֶת־יָדוֹ וַיִּקַּח
אֶת־הַמַּאֲכֶלֶת לִשְׁחֹט אֶת־בְּנוֹ: וַיִּקְרָא אֵלָיו מַלְאַךְ יְהֹוָה מִן־הַשָּׁמַיִם
וַיֹּאמֶר אַבְרָהָם | אַבְרָהָם וַיֹּאמֶר הִנֵּנִי: וַיֹּאמֶר אַל־תִּשְׁלַח יָדְךָ
אֶל־הַנַּעַר וְאַל־תַּעַשׂ לוֹ מְאוּמָה כִּי | עַתָּה יָדַעְתִּי כִּי־יְרֵא אֱלֹהִים
אַתָּה וְלֹא חָשַׂכְתָּ אֶת־בִּנְךָ אֶת־יְחִידְךָ מִמֶּנִּי: וַיִּשָּׂא אַבְרָהָם
אֶת־עֵינָיו וַיַּרְא וְהִנֵּה־אַיִל אַחַר נֶאֱחַז בַּסְּבַךְ בְּקַרְנָיו וַיֵּלֶךְ אַבְרָהָם
וַיִּקַּח אֶת־הָאַיִל וַיַּעֲלֵהוּ לְעֹלָה תַּחַת בְּנוֹ: וַיִּקְרָא אַבְרָהָם
שֵׁם־הַמָּקוֹם הַהוּא יְהֹוָה | יִרְאֶה אֲשֶׁר יֵאָמֵר הַיּוֹם בְּהַר יְהֹוָה יֵרָאֶה:
וַיִּקְרָא מַלְאַךְ יְהֹוָה אֶל־אַבְרָהָם שֵׁנִית מִן־הַשָּׁמָיִם: וַיֹּאמֶר בִּי
נִשְׁבַּעְתִּי נְאֻם־יְהֹוָה כִּי יַעַן אֲשֶׁר עָשִׂיתָ אֶת־הַדָּבָר הַזֶּה וְלֹא חָשַׂכְתָּ
אֶת־בִּנְךָ אֶת־יְחִידֶךָ: כִּי־בָרֵךְ אֲבָרֶכְךָ וְהַרְבָּה אַרְבֶּה אֶת־זַרְעֲךָ
כְּכוֹכְבֵי הַשָּׁמַיִם וְכַחוֹל אֲשֶׁר עַל־שְׂפַת הַיָּם וְיִרַשׁ זַרְעֲךָ אֵת שַׁעַר
אֹיְבָיו: וְהִתְבָּרֲכוּ בְזַרְעֲךָ כֹּל גּוֹיֵי הָאָרֶץ עֵקֶב אֲשֶׁר שָׁמַעְתָּ בְּקֹלִי:
וַיָּשָׁב אַבְרָהָם אֶל־נְעָרָיו וַיָּקֻמוּ וַיֵּלְכוּ יַחְדָּו אֶל־בְּאֵר שָׁבַע וַיֵּשֶׁב
אַבְרָהָם בִּבְאֵר שָׁבַע:

Vayhi. Achar Hadevarim Ha'eleh. Veha'elohim. Nissah Et-'Avraham;
Vayomer Elav. Avraham Vayomer Hineni. Vayomer Kach-Na Et-
Bincha Et-Yechidecha Asher-'Ahavta Et-Yitzchak. Velech-Lecha.
El-'Eretz Hamoriyah; Veha'alehu Sham Le'olah. Al Achad Heharim.
Asher Omar Eleicha. Vayashkem Avraham Baboker. Vayachavosh Et-
Chamoro. Vayikach Et-Shenei Ne'arav Ito. Ve'et Yitzchak Beno;
Vayvakka Atzei Olah. Vayakom Vayelech. El-Hamakom
Asher-'Amar-Lo Ha'elohim. Bayom Hashelishi. Vayissa Avraham
Et-'Einav Vayar Et-Hamakom Merachok. Vayomer Avraham El-
Ne'arav. Shevu-Lachem Poh Im-Hachamor. Va'ani Vehana'ar.
Nelechah Ad-Koh; Venishtachaveh Venashuvah Aleichem. Vayikach
Avraham Et-'Atzei Ha'olah. Vayasem Al-Yitzchak Beno. Vayikach
Beyado. Et-Ha'esh Ve'et-Hama'achelet; Vayelechu Sheneihem
Yachdav. Vayomer Yitzchak El-'Avraham Aviv Vayomer Avi. Vayomer
Hineni Veni; Vayomer. Hineh Ha'esh Veha'etzim. Ve'ayeh Hasseh
Le'olah. Vayomer Avraham. Elohim Yir'eh-Lo Hasseh Le'olah Beni;
Vayelechu Sheneihem Yachdav. Vayavo'u. El-Hamakom Asher Amar-
Lo Ha'elohim Vayiven Sham Avraham Et-Hamizbe'ach. Vaya'aroch

Et-Ha'etzim; Vaya'akod Et-Yitzchak Beno. Vayasem Oto Al-
Hamizbe'ach. Mima'al La'etzim. Vayishlach Avraham Et-Yado.
Vayikach Et-Hama'achelet; Lishchot Et-Beno. Vayikra Elav Mal'ach
Hashem Min-Hashamayim. Vayomer Avraham 'Avraham; Vayomer
Hineni. Vayomer. Al-Tishlach Yadecha El-Hana'ar. Ve'al-Ta'as Lo
Me'umah; Ki Attah Yada'ti. Ki-Yerei Elohim Attah. Velo Chasachta
Et-Bincha Et-Yechidecha Mimeni. Vayissa Avraham Et-'Einav. Vayar
Vehineh-'Ayil. Achar Ne'echaz Bassevach Bekarnav; Vayelech
Avraham Vayikach Et-Ha'ayil. Vaya'alehu Le'olah Tachat Beno.
Vayikra Avraham Shem-Hamakom Hahu Hashem Yir'eh; Asher
Ye'amer Hayom. Behar Hashem Yera'eh. Vayikra Mal'ach Hashem
El-'Avraham; Shenit Min-Hashamayim. Vayomer Bi Nishba'ti
Ne'um-Hashem Ki. Ya'an Asher Asita Et-Hadavar Hazeh. Velo
Chasachta Et-Bincha Et-Yechidecha. Ki-Varech Avarechcha.
Veharbah Arbeh Et-Zar'acha Kechochevei Hashamayim. Vechachol
Asher Al-Sefat Hayam; Veyirash Zar'acha. Et Sha'ar Oyevav.
Vehitbarechu Vezar'acha. Kol Goyei Ha'aretz; Ekev Asher Shama'ta
Bekoli. Vayashov Avraham El-Ne'arav. Vayakumu Vayelechu Yachdav
El-Be'er Shava'; Vayeshev Avraham Biv'er Shava.

1 And it came to pass after these things, that God did test Avraham,
and said to him: 'Avraham'; and he said: 'Here I am.' 2 And He said:
'Take now your son, your only son, whom you love, Yitzchak, and
get into the land of Moriah; and offer him there for a burnt-offering
upon one of the mountains which I will tell you of.' 3 And Avraham
arose early in the morning, and saddled his donkey, and took two of
his young men with him, and Yitzchak his son; and he split the wood
for the burnt-offering, and rose up, and went to the place of which
God had told him. 4 On the third day Avraham lifted up his eyes,
and saw the place from far off. 5 And Avraham said to his young
men: 'Abide here with the donkey, and I and the lad will go over; and
we will worship, and come back to you.' 6 And Avraham took the
wood of the burnt-offering, and laid it on Yitzchak his son; and he
took in his hand the fire(stone) and the knife; and they went
together. 7 And Yitzchak spoke to Avraham his father, and said: 'My
father.' And he said: 'Here I am, my son.' And he said: 'Behold the
fire and the wood; but where is the lamb for a burnt-offering?' 8 And
Avraham said: 'God will provide Himself the lamb for a burnt-

offering, my son.' So they went together. 9 And they came to the
place which God had told him of; and Avraham built the altar there,
and laid the wood in order, and bound Yitzchak his son, and laid
him on the altar, on the wood. 10 And Avraham stretched forth his
hand, and took the knife to slay his son. 11 And the angel of Hashem
called to him from out of heaven, and said: 'Avraham, Avraham.' And
he said: 'Here I am.' 12 And he said: 'Do not lay your hand on the lad,
neither do anything to him; for now I know that you are a God-
fearing man, seeing you have not withheld your son, your only son,
from Me.' 13 And Avraham lifted up his eyes, and looked, and behold
behind him a ram caught in the thicket by his horns. And Avraham
went and took the ram, and offered him up for a burnt-offering
instead of his son. 14 And Avraham called the name of that place
Hashem-Yireh; as it is said to this day: 'In the mount where Hashem
is seen.' 15 And the angel of Hashem called to Avraham a second
time out of heaven, 16 and said: 'By Myself have I sworn, says
Hashem, because you have done this, and have not withheld your
son, your only son, 17 that in blessing I will bless you, and in
multiplying I will multiply your seed as the stars of the heaven, and
as the sand which is on the seashore; and your seed will possess the
gate of his enemies; 18 and in your seed will all the nations of the
earth be blessed; because you have listened to My voice.' 19 So
Avraham returned to his young men, and they rose up and went
together to Be'er-shava; and Avraham dwelt at Be'er-shava.

It is a custom of some to recite the following verse: Leviticus 1:11

וְשָׁחַט אֹתוֹ עַל יֶרֶךְ הַמִּזְבֵּחַ צָפֹנָה לִפְנֵי יְהֹוָה וְזָרְקוּ בְּנֵי אַהֲרֹן הַכֹּהֲנִים
אֶת־דָּמוֹ עַל־הַמִּזְבֵּחַ סָבִיב:

Veshachat Oto Al Yerech Hamizbe'ach Tzafonah Lifnei Adonai Vezareku Benei
Aharon Hakohanim Et-Damo Al-Hamizbe'ach Saviv.

And he will slaughter it on the side of the altar northward before Hashem; and
Aharon's sons, the priests, will dash its blood against the altar all around.

Yehi Ratzon Milfaneicha Adonai	יְהִי רָצוֹן מִלְּפָנֶיךָ יְהֹוָה
Eloheinu Velohei Avoteinu.	אֱלֹהֵינוּ וֵאלֹהֵי אֲבוֹתֵינוּ.
Shetitmallei Rachamim Aleinu.	שֶׁתִּתְמַלֵּא רַחֲמִים עָלֵינוּ.
Uvechein Berov Rachameicha	וּבְכֵן בְּרוֹב רַחֲמֶיךָ
Tizkor Lanu Akedato Shel	תִּזְכּוֹר לָנוּ עֲקֵדָתוֹ שֶׁל
Yitzchak Avinu Ben Avraham	יִצְחָק אָבִינוּ בֶּן אַבְרָהָם
Avinu Alav Hashalom. Ke'ilu Efro	אָבִינוּ עָלָיו הַשָּׁלוֹם. כְּאִלּוּ אֶפְרוֹ
Tzavur Umunach Al Gabei	צָבוּר וּמֻנָּח עַל גַּבֵּי
Hamizbe'ach. Vetabbit Be'efro	הַמִּזְבֵּחַ. וְתַבִּיט בְּאֶפְרוֹ
Lerachem Aleinu. Ulevatel	לְרַחֵם עָלֵינוּ. וּלְבַטֵּל
Me'aleinu Kol Gezeirot Kashot	מֵעָלֵינוּ כָּל גְּזֵירוֹת קָשׁוֹת
Vera'ot. Utezakenu Lashuv	וְרָעוֹת. וּתְזַכֵּנוּ לָשׁוּב
Bitshuvah Shelemah Lefaneicha.	בִּתְשׁוּבָה שְׁלֵמָה לְפָנֶיךָ.
Vetatzilenu Miyetzer Hara	וְתַצִּילֵנוּ מִיֵּצֶר הָרָע
Umikal Chet Ve'avon. Veta'arich	וּמִכָּל חֵטְא וְעָוֹן. וְתַאֲרִיךְ
Yameinu Battov Ushenoteinu	יָמֵינוּ בַּטּוֹב וּשְׁנוֹתֵינוּ
Bane'imim.	בַּנְּעִימִים:

May it be Your will Hashem our God and God of our fathers, that You have with mercy on us, and in the greatness of Your mercy that You would remember the Binding of Yitzchak our father, son of Avraham our father, peace be upon him, as if we had accumulated and laid on our back on the altar. And You will look upon the ashes of pity for mercy upon us, and to cut off from us all harsh and evil decrees. May we merit to return in complete teshuvah (repentance) before You, and save us from the evil inclination and from all sin and transgression, and prolong our days in goodness and our years in pleasantness.

רִבּוֹנוֹ שֶׁל עוֹלָם. כְּמוֹ שֶׁכָּבַשׁ אַבְרָהָם אָבִינוּ אֶת רַחֲמָיו לַעֲשׂוֹת
רְצוֹנְךָ בְּלֵבָב שָׁלֵם. כֵּן יִכְבְּשׁוּ רַחֲמֶיךָ אֶת כַּעַסֶךָ. וְיִגְלוּ רַחֲמֶיךָ עַל
מִדּוֹתֶיךָ. וְתִתְנַהֵג עִמָּנוּ יְהֹוָה אֱלֹהֵינוּ בְּמִדַּת הַחֶסֶד וּבְמִדַּת
הָרַחֲמִים. וְתִכָּנֵס לָנוּ לִפְנִים מִשּׁוּרַת הַדִּין. וּבְטוּבְךָ הַגָּדוֹל יָשׁוּב
חֲרוֹן אַפֶּךָ. מֵעַמְּךָ וּמֵעִירְךָ וּמֵאַרְצְךָ וּמִנַּחֲלָתֶךָ. וְקַיֶּם לָנוּ יְהֹוָה
אֱלֹהֵינוּ אֶת הַדָּבָר שֶׁהִבְטַחְתָּנוּ בְּתוֹרָתֶךָ עַל יְדֵי מֹשֶׁה עַבְדְּךָ
כָּאָמוּר: וְזָכַרְתִּי אֶת־בְּרִיתִי יַעֲקוֹב וְאַף אֶת־בְּרִיתִי יִצְחָק וְאַף
אֶת־בְּרִיתִי אַבְרָהָם אֶזְכֹּר וְהָאָרֶץ אֶזְכֹּר: וְנֶאֱמַר: וְאַף־גַּם־זֹאת
בִּהְיוֹתָם בְּאֶרֶץ אֹיְבֵיהֶם לֹא־מְאַסְתִּים וְלֹא־גְעַלְתִּים לְכַלֹּתָם לְהָפֵר
בְּרִיתִי אִתָּם כִּי אֲנִי יְהֹוָה אֱלֹהֵיהֶם: וְזָכַרְתִּי לָהֶם בְּרִית רִאשֹׁנִים
אֲשֶׁר הוֹצֵאתִי־אֹתָם מֵאֶרֶץ מִצְרַיִם לְעֵינֵי הַגּוֹיִם לִהְיוֹת לָהֶם
לֵאלֹהִים אֲנִי יְהֹוָה: וְנֶאֱמַר: וְשָׁב יְהֹוָה אֱלֹהֶיךָ אֶת־שְׁבוּתְךָ וְרִחֲמֶךָ
וְשָׁב וְקִבֶּצְךָ מִכָּל־הָעַמִּים אֲשֶׁר הֱפִיצְךָ יְהֹוָה אֱלֹהֶיךָ שָׁמָּה:
אִם־יִהְיֶה נִדַּחֲךָ בִּקְצֵה הַשָּׁמָיִם מִשָּׁם יְקַבֶּצְךָ יְהֹוָה אֱלֹהֶיךָ וּמִשָּׁם
יִקָּחֶךָ: וֶהֱבִיאֲךָ יְהֹוָה אֱלֹהֶיךָ אֶל־הָאָרֶץ אֲשֶׁר־יָרְשׁוּ אֲבֹתֶיךָ וִירִשְׁתָּהּ
וְהֵיטִבְךָ וְהִרְבְּךָ מֵאֲבֹתֶיךָ: וְנֶאֱמַר עַל יְדֵי נְבִיאֶךָ: יְהֹוָה חָנֵּנוּ לְךָ
קִוִּינוּ הֱיֵה זְרֹעָם לַבְּקָרִים אַף־יְשׁוּעָתֵנוּ בְּעֵת צָרָה: וְנֶאֱמַר:
וְעֵת־צָרָה הִיא לְיַעֲקֹב וּמִמֶּנָּה יִוָּשֵׁעַ: וְנֶאֱמַר: בְּכָל־צָרָתָם לֹא (לוֹ)
צָר וּמַלְאַךְ פָּנָיו הוֹשִׁיעָם בְּאַהֲבָתוֹ וּבְחֶמְלָתוֹ הוּא גְאָלָם וַיְנַטְּלֵם
וַיְנַשְּׂאֵם כָּל־יְמֵי עוֹלָם: וְנֶאֱמַר:

Ribono Shel Olam. Kemo Shekavash Avraham Avinu Et Rachamav
La'asot Retzonecha Belevav Shalem. Ken Yichbeshu Rachameicha Et
Ka'asecha. Veyigolu Rachameicha Al Middoteicha. Vetitnaheg
Imanu Adonai Eloheinu Bemidat Hachesed Uvemidat Harachamim.
Vetikanes Lanu Lifnim Mishurat Hadin. Uvetuvecha Hagadol Yashuv
Charon Appach. Me'amach Ume'irach Ume'artzach
Uminachalatach. Vekayem Lanu Adonai Eloheinu Et Hadavar
Shehivtachtanu Betoratach Al Yedei Mosheh Avdach Ka'amur.
Vezacharti Et-Beriti Ya'akov; Ve'af Et-Beriti Yitzchak Ve'af Et-Beriti
Avraham Ezkor Veha'aretz Ezkor. Vene'emar. Ve'af-Gam-Zot

Bihyotam Be'eretz Oyeveihem. Lo-Me'astim Velo-Ge'altim
Lechalotam. Lehafer Beriti Ittam; Ki Ani Adonai Eloheihem.
Vezacharti Lahem Berit Rishonim; Asher Hotzeti-'Otam Me'eretz
Mitzrayim Le'einei Hagoyim. Lihyot Lahem Lelohim Ani Adonai.
Vene'emar. Veshav Adonai Eloheicha Et-Shevutecha Verichamecha;
Veshav. Vekibetzcha Mikol-Ha'ammim. Asher Hefitzecha Adonai
Eloheicha Shamah. Im-Yihyeh Niddachacha Biktzeh Hashamayim;
Misham. Yekabetzcha Adonai Eloheicha. Umisham Yikachecha.
Vehevi'acha Adonai Eloheicha. El-Ha'aretz Asher-Yareshu Avoteicha
Virishtah; Veheitivcha Vehirbecha Me'avoteicha. Vene'emar Al Yedei
Nevi'echa. Adonai Chonenu Lecha Kivinu; Heyeh Zero'am
Labekarim. Af-Yeshu'atenu Be'et Tzarah. Vene'emar. Ve'et-Tzarah Hi
Leya'akov. Umimenah Yivashea. Vene'emar. Bechol-Tzaratam Lo
Tzar. Umal'ach Panav Hoshi'am. Be'ahavato Uvechemlato Hu
Ge'alam; Vaynattelem Vaynasse'em Chol-Yemei Olam. Vene'emar.

Sovereign of the universe, Avraham mastered his compassion for his
only son in order to perform Your will with a whole heart; so in like
measure may Your mercy prevail over stern justice. Let mercy
temper justice. Deal with us, Hashem our God, with Your attributes
of mercy and kindness beyond the measure of what we deserve. In
Your great goodness may the flame of Your displeasure turn away
from Your people, from Tziyon Your city, from Your land and Your
heritage. Fulfill to us, Hashem our God, the promise You have
assured us in Your Torah through Your servant Moshe in the words,
"I will remember My covenant with Yaakov and also My covenant
with Yitzchak, and also My covenant with Avraham I will remember,
and the land I will remember." This too have You said, "Yet with all,
when they will be in the land of their enemies I will not repudiate or
reject them to destroy them utterly and to break My covenant with
them, for I am Hashem their God. But for their sakes I will
remember the covenant with their ancestors whom I brought forth
out of the land of Egypt in the sight of the nations, to be their God;
I am Hashem." (Deut. 30:3-5) Even so it is said in Your Torah: "Hashem
your God will bring you back out of captivity and have compassion
on you, and will again gather you from all the nations where
Hashem your God has scattered you. If your dispersed are at the

farthest horizon, then will Hashem your God gather you, and then He will bring you. And Hashem your God will bring you into the land which your fathers possessed, and you will possess it, and He will do you good and multiply you above your fathers." Further it is said by Your prophets: "Hashem be gracious to us, we have waited for You. Be our strength every morning, our saving power also in time of trouble. It is a time of trouble for Yaakov, but he will be saved from it. In all their affliction He was afflicted, and the angel of His presence saved them; in His love and in His pity, He redeemed them and bare them and carried them all the days of old.

מִי־אֵל כָּמוֹךָ אל נֹשֵׂא עָוֹן רחום וְעֹבֵר עַל־פֶּשַׁע וחנון לִשְׁאֵרִית נַחֲלָתוֹ ארך לֹא־הֶחֱזִיק לָעַד אַפּוֹ אפים כִּי־חָפֵץ חֶסֶד הוּא ורב חסד יָשׁוּב יְרַחֲמֵנוּ ואמת יִכְבֹּשׁ עֲוֹנֹתֵינוּ נצר חסד וְתַשְׁלִיךְ בִּמְצֻלוֹת יָם כָּל־חַטֹּאותָם לאלפים תִּתֵּן אֱמֶת לְיַעֲקֹב נושא עון חֶסֶד לְאַבְרָהָם ופשע אֲשֶׁר־נִשְׁבַּעְתָּ לַאֲבֹתֵינוּ וחטאה מִימֵי קֶדֶם ונקה וְנֶאֱמַר: וַהֲבִיאוֹתִים אֶל־הַר קָדְשִׁי וְשִׂמַּחְתִּים בְּבֵית תְּפִלָּתִי עוֹלֹתֵיהֶם וְזִבְחֵיהֶם לְרָצוֹן עַל־מִזְבְּחִי כִּי בֵיתִי בֵּית־תְּפִלָּה יִקָּרֵא לְכָל־הָעַמִּים:

Mi El Kamocha (El) Nose Avon (Rachum) Ve'over Al Pesha (Vechanun) Lish'erit Nachalato (Erek) Lo Hechezik La'ad Appo (Apayim) Ki Chafetz Chesed Hu (Verav Chesed): Yashuv Yerachamenu (V'emet) Yichbosh Avonoteinu (Notzer Chesed) Vetashlich Bimtzulot Yam Kol Chatovtam (Alafim): Titen Emet Leya'akov (Noseh Avon) Chesed Le'avraham (Vafesha) Asher Nishba'ta La'avoteinu (Vechata'ah) Mimei Kedem (Venakeh): Vene'emar: Vahavi'otim El Har Kodshi Vesimachtim Beveit Tefillati Oloteihem Vezivcheihem Leratzon Al Mizbechi Ki Veiti Beit Tefillah Yikare Lechol Ha'ammim:

Who is like You, a God pardoning iniquity and passing over the transgression of the remnant of His heritage, Who does not hold His anger forever, because He delights in mercy? He will again have compassion upon us, He will overcome our iniquities, even, cast all our sins into the depths of the sea." Cast all our sins and all the sins of Your people the House of Yisrael where they will be recalled or remembered no more or burden the heart. "You will show to Yaakov the faithfulness, and to Avraham the mercy, which You have sworn to our fathers from days of old." And it is said: "I will bring them to My holy mountain and make them rejoice in My house of prayer; their offerings and their sacrifices will be accepted upon My altar, for My House will be called a house of prayer for all peoples."

Elu Devarim
Mishnah Peah 1:1; Talmud Shabbat 127a, Kiddushin 39b

אֵלּוּ דְבָרִים שֶׁאֵין לָהֶם שִׁעוּר: הַפֵּאָה. וְהַבִּכּוּרִים. וְהָרֵאָיוֹן.
וּגְמִילוּת חֲסָדִים. וְתַלְמוּד תּוֹרָה: אֵלּוּ דְבָרִים שֶׁאָדָם עוֹשֶׂה אוֹת
וְאוֹכֵל פֵּרוֹתֵיהֶם בָּעוֹלָם הַזֶּה. וְהַקֶּרֶן קַיֶּמֶת לָעוֹלָם הַבָּא: וְאֵלּוּ הֵן:
כִּבּוּד אָב וָאֵם. וּגְמִילוּת חֲסָדִים. וּבִקּוּר חוֹלִים. וְהַכְנָסַת אוֹרְחִים.
וְהַשְׁכָּמַת בֵּית הַכְּנֶסֶת. וַהֲבָאַת שָׁלוֹם בֵּין אָדָם לַחֲבֵרוֹ וּבֵין אִישׁ
לְאִשְׁתּוֹ וְתַלְמוּד תּוֹרָה כְּנֶגֶד כֻּלָּם.

Elu Devarim She'ein Lahem Shi'ur. Hape'ah. Vehabikurim.
Vehare'ayon. Ugemilut Chasadim. Vetalmud Torah. Elu Devarim
She'adam Oseh Ot Ve'ochel Peroteihem Ba'olam Hazeh. Vehakeren
Kayemet La'olam Haba. Ve'elu Hen. Kibud Av Va'em. Ugemilut
Chasadim. Uvikkur Cholim. Vehachnasat Orechim. Vehashkamat
Beit Hakeneset. Vahava'at Shalom Bein Adam Lachavero Uvein Ish
Le'ishto Vetalmud Torah Keneged Kulam.

These are the things for which no limit is prescribed: the corner of the field, the first-fruits, the pilgrimage offerings, the practice of kindness, and the study of the Torah. These are the things the fruits of which a man enjoys in this world, while the principal remains for him in the world to come, namely: honoring father and mother, practice of kindness, early attendance at the schoolhouse morning and evening, hospitality to strangers, visiting the sick, dowering the bride, attending the dead to the grave, devotion in prayer, and making peace between man and his friend; but the study of the Torah equals them all.

Le'olam Yehei Adam

לְעוֹלָם יְהֵא אָדָם יְרֵא שָׁמַיִם בַּסֵּתֶר כְּבַגָּלוּי. וּמוֹדֶה עַל הָאֱמֶת. וְדוֹבֵר אֱמֶת בִּלְבָבוֹ. וְיַשְׁכִּים וְיֹאמַר: רִבּוֹן הָעוֹלָמִים וַאֲדוֹנֵי הָאֲדוֹנִים. לֹא עַל צִדְקוֹתֵינוּ אֲנַחְנוּ מַפִּילִים תַּחֲנוּנֵינוּ לְפָנֶיךָ כִּי עַל רַחֲמֶיךָ הָרַבִּים: אֲדֹנָי שְׁמָעָה אֲדֹנָי סְלָחָה אֲדֹנָי הַקְשִׁיבָה וַעֲשֵׂה אַל־תְּאַחַר לְמַעַנְךָ אֱלֹהַי כִּי־שִׁמְךָ נִקְרָא עַל־עִירְךָ וְעַל־עַמֶּךָ: מָה אֲנַחְנוּ. מֶה חַיֵּינוּ. מֶה חַסְדֵּנוּ. מַה־צִּדְקוֹתֵינוּ. מַה־כֹּחֵנוּ. מַה־גְּבוּרָתֵנוּ. מַה נֹּאמַר לְפָנֶיךָ יְהֹוָה אֱלֹהֵינוּ וֵאלֹהֵי אֲבוֹתֵינוּ. הֲלֹא כָל־הַגִּבּוֹרִים כְּאַיִן לְפָנֶיךָ. וְאַנְשֵׁי הַשֵּׁם כְּלֹא הָיוּ. וַחֲכָמִים כִּבְלִי מַדָּע. וּנְבוֹנִים כִּבְלִי הַשְׂכֵּל. כִּי כָל־מַעֲשֵׂינוּ תֹהוּ. וִימֵי חַיֵּינוּ הֶבֶל לְפָנֶיךָ. וּמוֹתַר הָאָדָם מִן־הַבְּהֵמָה אָיִן כִּי הַכֹּל הָבֶל: לְבַד הַנְּשָׁמָה הַטְּהוֹרָה שֶׁהִיא עֲתִידָה לִתֵּן דִּין וְחֶשְׁבּוֹן לִפְנֵי כִסֵּא כְבוֹדֶךָ. וְכָל־הַגּוֹיִם כְּאַיִן נֶגְדֶּךָ. שֶׁנֶּאֱמַר: הֵן גּוֹיִם כְּמַר מִדְּלִי וּכְשַׁחַק מֹאזְנַיִם נֶחְשָׁבוּ הֵן אִיִּים כַּדַּק יִטּוֹל: אֲבָל אֲנַחְנוּ עַמְּךָ בְּנֵי בְרִיתֶךָ. בְּנֵי אַבְרָהָם אֹהַבְךָ שֶׁנִּשְׁבַּעְתָּ־לּוֹ בְּהַר הַמּוֹרִיָה. זֶרַע יִצְחָק עֲקֵדֶךָ שֶׁנֶּעֱקַד עַל־גַּבֵּי הַמִּזְבֵּחַ. עֲדַת יַעֲקֹב בִּנְךָ בְּכוֹרֶךָ. שֶׁמֵּאַהֲבָתְךָ שֶׁאָהַבְתָּ אוֹתוֹ. וּמִשִּׂמְחָתְךָ שֶׁשָּׂמַחְתָּ־בּוֹ. קָרָאתָ אוֹתוֹ יִשְׂרָאֵל וִישֻׁרוּן:

Le'olam Yehei Adam Yerei Shamayim Basseter Kevagalui. Umodeh Al Ha'emet. Vedover Emet Bilvavo. Veyashkim Veyomar. Ribon Ha'olamim Va' Adonei Ha' Adonim. Lo Al Tzidkoteinu Anachnu Mapilim Tachanuneinu Lefaneicha Ki Al Rachameicha Harabim. Adonai Shema'ah Adonai Selachah. Adonai Hakshivah Va'aseh Al-Te'achar; Lema'ancha Elohai. Ki-Shimcha Nikra. Al-'Irecha Ve'al-'Ammecha. Mah Anachnu. Mah Chayeinu. Mah Chasdenu. Mah-Tzidkoteinu. Mah-Kocheinu. Mah-Gevuratenu. Mah Nomar

Lefaneicha Adonai Eloheinu Velohei Avoteinu. Halo Kol-Hagiborim
Ke'ayin Lefaneicha. Ve'anshei Adonai Kelo Hayu. Vachachamim
Kivli Madda'. Unevonim Kivli Haskel. Ki Chol-Ma'aseinu Tohu.
Vimei Chayeinu Hevel Lefaneicha. Umotar Ha'adam Min-
Habehemah Ayin. Ki Hakol Havel. Levad Haneshamah Hatehorah
Shehi Atidah Litten Din Vecheshbon Lifnei Chisei Chevodecha.
Vechol-Hagoyim Ke'ayin Negdecha. Shene'emar. Hen Goyim
Kemar Mideli. Ucheshachak Mozenayim Nechshavu; Hen Iyim
Kadak Yitol. Aval Anachnu Ammecha Benei Veritecha. Benei
Avraham Ohavecha Shenishba'ta-Lo Behar Hamoriyah. Zera
Yitzchak Akedecha Shene'ekad Al-Gabei Hamizbe'ach. Adat
Ya'akov Bincha Vechorecha. Sheme'ahavatecha She'ahavta Oto.
Umisimchatecha Shessamachta-Bo. Karata Oto Yisra'el Vishurun.

Man should ever be God-fearing in private as well as in public. He
should acknowledge the truth, and speak the truth in his heart. Let
him rise early and say: Master of all worlds, It is not on account of
our own righteousness that we offer our supplications before You,
but on account of Your great compassion. What are we? What is
our life? What is our goodness? What is our virtue? What our help?
What our strength? What our might? What can we say to You,
Hashem our God and God of our fathers? Indeed, all the heroes are
as nothing in Your sight, the men of renown as though they never
existed, the wise as though they were without knowledge, the
intelligent as though they lacked insight; most of their actions are
worthless in Your sight, their entire life is a fleeting breath. Man is
not far above beast, for all is vanity. Except the pure soul, which is
destined to give a strict account before Your glorious Throne.
Before You all the nations are as nothing, as it is written: "The
nations are a mere drop in the bucket, no more than dust upon the
scales. Behold, the isles are like the flying dust." However, we are
Your people, Your children of the covenant, the children of Avraham
Your friend, to whom You made a promise on Mount Moriah; we are
the descendants of his only son Yitzchak, who was bound on the
altar; we are the community of Yaakov Your first-born, who You
named Yisrael and Yeshurun because of Your love for him and Your
delight in him.

Lefichach Anachnu Chayavim	לְפִיכָךְ אֲנַחְנוּ חַיָּבִים
Lehodot Lach. Uleshabechach	לְהוֹדוֹת לָךְ. וּלְשַׁבֵּחָךְ
Ulefa'arach Uleromemach.	וּלְפָאֶרְךָ וּלְרוֹמְמָךְ.
Velitten Shir Shevach Vehoda'ah	וְלִתֵּן שִׁיר שֶׁבַח וְהוֹדָאָה
Leshimcha Hagadol Bechol Yom	לְשִׁמְךָ הַגָּדוֹל בְּכָל יוֹם
Tamid. Ashreinu. Mah Tov	תָּמִיד. אַשְׁרֵינוּ. מַה טוֹב
Chelkeinu. Umah Na'im	חֶלְקֵינוּ. וּמַה נָּעִים
Goraleinu. Umah Yafah Me'od	גּוֹרָלֵנוּ. וּמַה יָּפָה מְאוֹד
Yerushateinu. Ashreinu	יְרוּשָׁתֵינוּ. אַשְׁרֵינוּ
Keshe'anachnu Mashkimim	כְּשֶׁאֲנַחְנוּ מַשְׁכִּימִים
Uma'arivim Bevatei Kenesiyot	וּמַעֲרִיבִים בְּבָתֵּי כְנֵסִיּוֹת
Uvevatei Midrashot	וּבְבָתֵּי מִדְרָשׁוֹת
Umeyachadim Shimcha Bechol	וּמְיַחֲדִים שִׁמְךָ בְּכָל
Yom Tamid Omerim Pa'amayim	יוֹם תָּמִיד אוֹמְרִים פַּעֲמַיִם
Be'ahavah.	בְּאַהֲבָה:

Therefore, it is our duty to give thanks to You, to praise and glorify You, to bless and sanctify Your name, and to offer many thanksgivings to You. Happy are we. How good is our destiny, how pleasant our lot, how beautiful our heritage. Happy are we when morning and evening we gather in the synagogues and houses of learning, forever acclaiming the unity of Your name and eagerly proclaiming twice every day:

שְׁמַע יִשְׂרָאֵל יְהֹוָה אֱלֹהֵינוּ יְהֹוָה | אֶחָד:

Shema Yisrael; Adonai Eloheinu Adonai Echad.

"Hear, O Yisrael, Hashem is our God, Hashem is One."

whisper silently:

בָּרוּךְ שֵׁם כְּבוֹד מַלְכוּתוֹ לְעוֹלָם וָעֶד:

Baruch Shem Kevod Malchuto Le'olam Va'ed.

Blessed is His name and glorious kingdom forever and ever.

Attah Hu Echad Kodem	אַתָּה הוּא אֶחָד קוֹדֶם
Shebarata Ha'olam. Ve'attah Hu	שֶׁבָּרָאתָ הָעוֹלָם. וְאַתָּה הוּא
Echad Le'achar Shebarata	אֶחָד לְאַחַר שֶׁבָּרָאתָ
Ha'olam. Attah Hu El Ba'olam	הָעוֹלָם. אַתָּה הוּא אֵל בָּעוֹלָם
Hazeh. Ve'attah Hu El Ba'olam	הַזֶּה. וְאַתָּה הוּא אֵל בָּעוֹלָם
Haba. Ve'attah-Hu;	הַבָּא. וְאַתָּה־הוּא
Ushenoteicha. Lo Yitamu.	וּשְׁנוֹתֶיךָ לֹא יִתָּמּוּ:
Kadesh Shemach Be'olamach	קַדֵּשׁ שְׁמָךְ בְּעוֹלָמָךְ
Al-'Am Mekadeshei Shemecha.	עַל־עַם מְקַדְּשֵׁי שְׁמֶךָ.
Uvishu'atecha Malkeinu Tarum	וּבִישׁוּעָתְךָ מַלְכֵּנוּ תָּרוּם
Vetagbiah Karnenu. Vetoshi'enu	וְתַגְבִּיהַּ קַרְנֵנוּ. וְתוֹשִׁיעֵנוּ
Bekarov Lema'an Shemecha.	בְּקָרוֹב לְמַעַן שְׁמֶךָ.
Baruch Hamkadesh Shemo	בָּרוּךְ הַמְקַדֵּשׁ שְׁמוֹ
Barabim.	בָּרַבִּים:

Before Your world's creation, You were One; and since creation You are One. You are God in this world; You will be God in the world to come. "You are immutable. Your years have no end." Sanctify Your name in this Your world through Yisrael, a people sanctifying Your name. Raise up and uphold our strength through Your saving power, and save us speedily for Your name's sake. Blessed is the one who sanctifies Your name before mankind.

Attah Hu Adonai Ha'elohim	אַתָּה הוּא יְהֹוָה הָאֱלֹהִים
Bashamayim Mima'al Ve'al-	בַּשָּׁמַיִם מִמַּעַל וְעַל־
Ha'aretz Mitachat. Bishmei	הָאָרֶץ מִתַּחַת. בִּשְׁמֵי
Hashamayim Ha'elyonim	הַשָּׁמַיִם הָעֶלְיוֹנִים
Vehatachtonim. Attah Hu Rishon	וְהַתַּחְתּוֹנִים. אַתָּה הוּא רִאשׁוֹן

Ve'attah Hu Acharon	וְאַתָּה הוּא אַחֲרוֹן
Umibal'adeicha Ein Elohim.	וּמִבַּלְעָדֶיךָ אֵין אֱלֹהִים.
Kabetz Nefutzot Koveicha	קַבֵּץ נְפוּצוֹת קֹוֶיךָ
Me'arba Kanfot Ha'aretz. Yakiru	מֵאַרְבַּע כַּנְפוֹת הָאָרֶץ. יַכִּירוּ
Veyede'u Kol Ba'ei Olam Ki	וְיֵדְעוּ כָּל בָּאֵי עוֹלָם כִּי
Attah Hu Ha'elohim Levadecha	אַתָּה הוּא הָאֱלֹהִים לְבַדְּךָ
Lechol Mamlechot Ha'aretz.	לְכָל מַמְלְכוֹת הָאָרֶץ.
Attah Asita Et Hashamayim Ve'et	אַתָּה עָשִׂיתָ אֶת הַשָּׁמַיִם וְאֶת
Ha'aretz. Et Hayam Ve'et Kol	הָאָרֶץ. אֶת הַיָּם וְאֶת כָּל
Asher Bam. Umi Bechol Ma'aseh	אֲשֶׁר בָּם. וּמִי בְּכָל מַעֲשֵׂה
Yadeicha Ba'elyonim	יָדֶיךָ בָּעֶלְיוֹנִים
Uvatachtonim Sheyomar Lach	וּבַתַּחְתּוֹנִים שֶׁיֹּאמַר לָךְ
Mah-Ta'aseh Umah-Tif'al. Avinu	מַה־תַּעֲשֶׂה וּמַה־תִּפְעָל. אָבִינוּ
Shebashamayim Chai Vekayam.	שֶׁבַּשָּׁמַיִם חַי וְקַיָּם.
Aseh Imanu Chesed Ba'avur	עֲשֵׂה עִמָּנוּ חֶסֶד בַּעֲבוּר
Kevod Shimcha Hagadol	כְּבוֹד שִׁמְךָ הַגָּדוֹל
Hagibor Vehanorah Shenikra	הַגִּבּוֹר וְהַנּוֹרָא שֶׁנִּקְרָא
Aleinu. Vekayem Lanu Adonai	עָלֵינוּ. וְקַיֶּם לָנוּ יְהֹוָה
Eloheinu Et Hadavar	אֱלֹהֵינוּ אֶת הַדָּבָר
Shehivtachtanu Al Yedei	שֶׁהִבְטַחְתָּנוּ עַל יְדֵי
Tzefanyah Chozach Ka'amur.	צְפַנְיָה חוֹזָךְ כָּאָמוּר:
Ba'et Hahi Avi Etchem. Uva'et	בָּעֵת הַהִיא אָבִיא אֶתְכֶם וּבָעֵת
Kabetzi Etchem; Ki-'Etten Etchem	קַבְּצִי אֶתְכֶם כִּי־אֶתֵּן אֶתְכֶם
Leshem Velit'hillah. Bechol	לְשֵׁם וְלִתְהִלָּה בְּכֹל
Ammei Ha'aretz. Beshuvi Et-	עַמֵּי הָאָרֶץ בְּשׁוּבִי אֶת־
Shevuteichem Le'eineichem	שְׁבוּתֵיכֶם לְעֵינֵיכֶם

Amar Adonai.   אָמַר יְהֹוָה:

You, Hashem our God, are in heaven and on earth and in the highest heavens. Truly, You are the first and You are the last; besides You there is no God. Gather the dispersed who yearn for You from the four corners of the earth. Let all mankind realize and know that You alone are God supreme over all the kingdoms of the earth. You have made the heavens, the earth, the sea, and all that is in them. Who is there among all the works of Your hands, among the heavenly or the earthly creatures, that can say to You, "What will You do?" Our Father Who is in heaven, Eternal One, deal kindly with us for the sake of Your great name by which we are called; fulfill for us, Hashem our God, that which is written: "At that time I will bring you home; at that time I will gather you; indeed, I will grant you fame and praise among all the peoples of the earth, when I bring back your captivity before your own eyes, says Hashem."

Korbanot / Offerings

Some say it is good to stand, like the Kohanim who stood while the offerings were made. Some say only Kohanim should stand, while some say that one should stand during Shacharit, but sit during the korbanot of Mincha. Many say it is not necessary to stand. (Kaf HaChayim 1:33, Magen Avraham 48:1, Sha'arei Teshuva 48:1) Some omit this first part "Yehi Ratzon" on Shabbat and Festivals.

Yehi Ratzon Milfaneicha Adonai	יְהִי רָצוֹן מִלְּפָנֶיךָ יְהֹוָה
Eloheinu Velohei Avoteinu	אֱלֹהֵינוּ וֵאלֹהֵי אֲבוֹתֵינוּ
Sheterachem Aleinu. Vetimchol	שֶׁתְּרַחֵם עָלֵינוּ. וְתִמְחוֹל
Lanu Et Kol Chat'oteinu.	לָנוּ אֶת כָּל חַטֹּאותֵינוּ.
Utechapeir Lanu Et-	וּתְכַפֶּר לָנוּ אֶת־
Kol-'Avonoteinu. Vetimchol	כָּל־עֲונוֹתֵינוּ. וְתִמְחוֹל
Vetislach Lechol Pesha'einu.	וְתִסְלַח לְכָל פְּשָׁעֵינוּ.
Vetivneh Beit Hamikdash	וְתִבְנֶה בֵּית הַמִּקְדָּשׁ
Bimheirah Veyameinu. Venakriv	בִּמְהֵרָה בְיָמֵינוּ. וְנַקְרִיב
Lefaneicha Korban Hatamid	לְפָנֶיךָ קָרְבַּן הַתָּמִיד שֶׁיְּכַפֵּר
Sheyechapeir Ba'adeinu. Kemo	בַּעֲדֵינוּ. כְּמוֹ שֶׁכָּתַבְתָּ עָלֵינוּ
Shekatavta Aleinu Betoratach Al	בְּתוֹרָתָךְ עַל יְדֵי מֹשֶׁה עַבְדָּךְ
Yedei Mosheh Avdach Ka'amur.	כָּאָמוּר:

May it be Your will, Hashem our God, God of our fathers, to have mercy on us, and to forgive us all of our sins, and atone for us and all of our transgressions, and to forgive and pardon all of our willful sins. May the Beit HaMikdash speedily be rebuilt in our days, that we may bring before You our Tamid that will atone for us as written for us in Your Torah through Moshe Your servant; as it says:

Tamid / Eternal Offering: Numbers 28:1-8

וַיְדַבֵּר יְהֹוָה אֶל־מֹשֶׁה לֵּאמֹר: צַו אֶת־בְּנֵי יִשְׂרָאֵל וְאָמַרְתָּ אֲלֵהֶם
אֶת־קָרְבָּנִי לַחְמִי לְאִשַּׁי רֵיחַ נִיחֹחִי תִּשְׁמְרוּ לְהַקְרִיב לִי בְּמוֹעֲדוֹ:

וְאָמַרְתָּ לָהֶם זֶה הָאִשֶּׁה אֲשֶׁר תַּקְרִיבוּ לַיהֹוָה כְּבָשִׂים בְּנֵי־שָׁנָה
תְמִימִם שְׁנַיִם לַיּוֹם עֹלָה תָמִיד: אֶת־הַכֶּבֶשׂ אֶחָד תַּעֲשֶׂה בַבֹּקֶר
וְאֵת הַכֶּבֶשׂ הַשֵּׁנִי תַּעֲשֶׂה בֵּין הָעַרְבָּיִם: וַעֲשִׂירִית הָאֵיפָה סֹלֶת
לְמִנְחָה בְּלוּלָה בְּשֶׁמֶן כָּתִית רְבִיעִת הַהִין: עֹלַת תָּמִיד הָעֲשֻׂיָה
בְּהַר סִינַי לְרֵיחַ נִיחֹחַ אִשֶּׁה לַיהֹוָה: וְנִסְכּוֹ רְבִיעִת הַהִין לַכֶּבֶשׂ
הָאֶחָד בַּקֹּדֶשׁ הַסֵּךְ נֶסֶךְ שֵׁכָר לַיהֹוָה: וְאֵת הַכֶּבֶשׂ הַשֵּׁנִי תַּעֲשֶׂה
בֵּין הָעַרְבָּיִם כְּמִנְחַת הַבֹּקֶר וּכְנִסְכּוֹ תַּעֲשֶׂה אִשֵּׁה רֵיחַ נִיחֹחַ
לַיהֹוָה:

Vaydaber Adonai El-Mosheh Lemor. Tzav Et-Benei Yisra'el.
Ve'amarta Aleihem; Et-Korbani Lachmi Le'ishai. Reiach Nichochi.
Tishmeru Lehakriv Li Bemo'ado. Ve'amarta Lahem. Zeh Ha'isheh.
Asher Takrivu L'Adonai Kevasim Benei-Shanah Temimim Shenayim
Layom Olah Tamid. Et-Hakeves Echad Ta'aseh Vaboker; Ve'et
Hakeves Hasheni. Ta'aseh Bein Ha'arbayim. Va'asirit Ha'eifah Solet
Leminchah; Belulah Beshemen Katit Revi'it Hahin. Olat Tamid;
Ha'asuyah Behar Sinai. Lereiach Nichoach. Isheh L'Adonai Venisko
Revi'it Hahin. Lakeves Ha'echad; Bakodesh. Hassech Nesech
Shechar L'Adonai Ve'et Hakeves Hasheni. Ta'aseh Bein Ha'arbayim;
Keminchat Haboker Uchenisko Ta'aseh. Isheh Reiach Nichoach
L'Adonai.

And Hashem spoke to Moshe, saying, Command the children of
Yisrael and say to them, My offering, My bread for My fire-offerings,
you will observe to offer for a sweet savor to Me in its due season.
Say also to them, this is the fire-offering which you will bring to
Hashem: lambs of the first year without blemish, two each day as a
continual burnt-offering. The one lamb you will prepare in the
morning, and the other lamb you will prepare at dusk, with the tenth
of an ephah of fine flour for a meal-offering, mingled with a fourth
of a hin of the purest oil. This is a continual burnt-offering as it was
prepared at Mount Sinai, a fire-offering for a sweet savor to
Hashem. And the drink-offering with it will be a fourth of a hin for
the one lamb. You will pour out the pure wine to Hashem in the holy
place as a drink-offering. The second lamb you will offer at dusk,

preparing it as the morning meal offering and as its drink-offering
of a sweet savor to Hashem.

On Shabbat, some add:

וּבְיוֹם֙ הַשַּׁבָּ֔ת שְׁנֵֽי־כְבָשִׂ֥ים בְּנֵֽי־שָׁנָ֖ה תְּמִימִ֑ם וּשְׁנֵ֣י עֶשְׂרֹנִ֗ים סֹ֤לֶת מִנְחָה֙
בְּלוּלָ֣ה בַשֶּׁ֔מֶן וְנִסְכּֽוֹ׃ עֹלַ֥ת שַׁבַּ֖ת בְּשַׁבַּתּ֑וֹ עַל־עֹלַ֥ת הַתָּמִ֖יד וְנִסְכָּֽהּ׃

Uveyom Hashabbat Shenei Chevasim Benei Shanah Temimim Ushenei Esronim
Solet Minchah Belulah Vashemen Venisko. Olat Shabbat Beshabbato Al Olat
Hatamid Veniskah.

And on the Shabbat day two male lambs of the first year without blemish, and two
tenth parts of an ephah of fine flour for a meal-offering, mingled with oil, and the
drink-offering of it. This is the burnt-offering of every Shabbat, beside the
continual burnt-offering, and the drink-offering of it. (Num. 28:9-10)

On Rosh Chodesh, some add:

וּבְרָאשֵׁי֙ חָדְשֵׁיכֶ֔ם תַּקְרִ֥יבוּ עֹלָ֖ה לַיהֹוָ֑ה פָּרִ֨ים בְּנֵֽי־בָקָ֤ר שְׁנַ֙יִם֙ וְאַ֣יִל אֶחָ֔ד
כְּבָשִׂ֧ים בְּנֵֽי־שָׁנָ֛ה שִׁבְעָ֖ה תְּמִימִֽם׃ וּשְׁלֹשָׁ֣ה עֶשְׂרֹנִ֗ים סֹ֤לֶת מִנְחָה֙ בְּלוּלָ֣ה
בַשֶּׁ֔מֶן לַפָּ֖ר הָֽאֶחָ֑ד וּשְׁנֵ֣י עֶשְׂרֹנִ֗ים סֹ֤לֶת מִנְחָה֙ בְּלוּלָ֣ה בַשֶּׁ֔מֶן לָאַ֖יִל הָֽאֶחָֽד׃
וְעִשָּׂרֹ֣ן עִשָּׂר֗וֹן סֹ֤לֶת מִנְחָה֙ בְּלוּלָ֣ה בַשֶּׁ֔מֶן לַכֶּ֖בֶשׂ הָֽאֶחָ֑ד עֹלָה֙ רֵ֣יחַ נִיחֹ֔חַ אִשֶּׁ֖ה
לַֽיהֹוָֽה׃ וְנִסְכֵּיהֶ֗ם חֲצִ֤י הַהִין֙ יִֽהְיֶ֣ה לַפָּ֔ר וּשְׁלִישִׁ֧ת הַהִ֛ין לָאַ֖יִל וּרְבִיעִ֥ת הַהִ֛ין
לַכֶּ֖בֶשׂ יָ֑יִן זֹ֣את עֹלַ֥ת חֹ֙דֶשׁ֙ בְּחָדְשׁ֔וֹ לְחָדְשֵׁ֖י הַשָּׁנָֽה׃ וּשְׂעִ֨יר עִזִּ֥ים אֶחָ֛ד לְחַטָּ֖את
לַֽיהֹוָ֑ה עַל־עֹלַ֥ת הַתָּמִ֖יד יֵעָשֶׂ֥ה וְנִסְכּֽוֹ׃

Uveroshei Chodsheichem Takrivu Olah L'Adonai Parim Benei Vakar Shenayim
Ve'ayil Echad Kevasim Benei Shanah Shiv'ah Temimim. Usheloshah Esronim Solet
Minchah Belulah Vashemen Lappar Ha'echad Ushenei Esronim Solet Minchah
Belulah Vashemen La'ayil Ha'echad. Ve'issaron Issaron Solet Minchah Belulah
Vashemen Lakeves Ha'echad Olah Reiach Nichoach Isheh L'Adonai. Veniskeihem
Chatzi Hahin Yihyeh Lappar Ushelishit Hahin La'ayil Urevi'it Hahin Lakeves Yayin
Zot Olat Chodesh Bechodsho Lechodshei Hashanah. Use'ir Izim Echad Lechatat
L'Adonai Al Olat Hatamid Ye'aseh Venisko.

And on your new moons you will present a burnt-offering to Hashem: two young
bulls, and one ram, seven male lambs of the first year without blemish; and three-
tenth parts of an ephah of fine flour for a meal-offering, mingled with oil, for each
bull; and two tenth parts of fine flour for a meal-offering, mingled with oil, for the
one ram; and a several tenth part of fine flour mingled with oil for a meal-offering
to every lamb; for a burnt-offering of a sweet savor, an offering made by fire to
Hashem. And their drink-offerings will be half a hin of wine for a bull, and the third
part of a hin for the ram, and the fourth part of a hin for a lamb. This is the burnt-
offering of every new moon throughout the months of the year. And one male goat

for a sin-offering to Hashem; it will be offered beside the continual burnt-offering, and the drink-offering of it. (Num. 28:11-15)

Ketoret / Incense Offering

Attah Hu Adonai Eloheinu.	אַתָּה הוּא יְהֹוָה אֱלֹהֵינוּ.
Shehiktiru Avoteinu Lefaneicha	שֶׁהִקְטִירוּ אֲבוֹתֵינוּ לְפָנֶיךָ
Et Ketoret Hasamim. Bizman	אֶת קְטֹרֶת הַסַּמִּים. בִּזְמַן
Shebeit Hamikdash Kayam.	שֶׁבֵּית הַמִּקְדָּשׁ קַיָּם.
Ka'asher Tzivita Otam Al-Yad	כַּאֲשֶׁר צִוִּיתָ אוֹתָם עַל־יַד
Mosheh Nevi'ach. Kakatuv	מֹשֶׁה נְבִיאָךְ. כַּכָּתוּב
Betoratach:	בְּתוֹרָתָךְ:

You are Hashem, our God, before Whom our ancestors burned the offering of incense in the days of the Beit HaMikdash. For You commanded them through Moshe, Your prophet, as it is written in Your Torah:

Exodus 30:34-36, 7-8

וַיֹּאמֶר יְהֹוָה אֶל־מֹשֶׁה קַח־לְךָ סַמִּים נָטָף | וּשְׁחֵלֶת וְחֶלְבְּנָה
סַמִּים וּלְבֹנָה זַכָּה בַּד בְּבַד יִהְיֶה: וְעָשִׂיתָ אֹתָהּ קְטֹרֶת רֹקַח מַעֲשֵׂה
רוֹקֵחַ מְמֻלָּח טָהוֹר קֹדֶשׁ: וְשָׁחַקְתָּ מִמֶּנָּה הָדֵק וְנָתַתָּה מִמֶּנָּה לִפְנֵי
הָעֵדֻת בְּאֹהֶל מוֹעֵד אֲשֶׁר אִוָּעֵד לְךָ שָׁמָּה קֹדֶשׁ קָדָשִׁים תִּהְיֶה
לָכֶם: וְנֶאֱמַר וְהִקְטִיר עָלָיו אַהֲרֹן קְטֹרֶת סַמִּים בַּבֹּקֶר בַּבֹּקֶר
בְּהֵיטִיבוֹ אֶת־הַנֵּרֹת יַקְטִירֶנָּה: וּבְהַעֲלֹת אַהֲרֹן אֶת־הַנֵּרֹת בֵּין
הָעַרְבַּיִם יַקְטִירֶנָּה קְטֹרֶת תָּמִיד לִפְנֵי יְהֹוָה לְדֹרֹתֵיכֶם:

Vayomer Adonai El-Mosheh Kach-Lecha Samim. Nataf Ushchelet Vechelbenah. Samim Ulevonah Zakah; Bad Bevad Yihyeh. Ve'asita Otah Ketoret. Rokach Ma'aseh Rokeach; Memulach Tahor Kodesh. Veshachakta Mimenah Hadek Venatatah Mimenah Lifnei Ha'eidut Be'ohel Mo'ed. Asher Iva'eid Lecha Shamah; Kodesh Kodashim

Tihyeh Lachem. Vene'emar Vehiktir Alav Aharon Ketoret Samim; Baboker Baboker. Beheitivo Et-Hanerot Yaktirenah. Uveha'alot Aharon Et-Hanerot Bein Ha'arbayim Yaktirenah; Ketoret Tamid Lifnei Adonai Ledoroteichem.

And Hashem said to Moshe, 'Take sweet spices, oil of myrrh, onycha and galbanum, together with clear frankincense, a like weight of each of these sweet spices. And you will make from there incense, a perfume pure and holy, compounded by the perfumer, salted together. And you will crush some of it very fine, and put some of it before the Ark of testimony in the Ohel Moed where I will meet with you; it will be most holy to you. Further it is said in the Torah: "And Aharon will burn the incense of sweet spices on the altar of incense, every morning when he dresses the lamps he will burn it. And at dusk when Aharon lights the lamps he will again burn incense, a perpetual incense before Hashem throughout your generations."

Talmud: Keritot 6a

תָּנוּ רַבָּנָן: פִּטּוּם הַקְּטֹרֶת כֵּיצַד: שְׁלֹשׁ מֵאוֹת וְשִׁשִּׁים וּשְׁמוֹנָה מָנִים הָיוּ בָהּ. שְׁלֹשׁ מֵאוֹת וְשִׁשִּׁים וַחֲמִשָּׁה כְּמִנְיַן יְמוֹת הַחַמָּה. מָנֶה בְּכָל-יוֹם. מַחֲצִיתוֹ בַּבֹּקֶר וּמַחֲצִיתוֹ בָּעֶרֶב. וּשְׁלֹשָׁה מָנִים יְתֵרִים. שֶׁמֵּהֶם מַכְנִיס כֹּהֵן גָּדוֹל. וְנוֹטֵל מֵהֶם מְלֹא חָפְנָיו בְּיוֹם הַכִּפּוּרִים. וּמַחֲזִירָן לְמַכְתֶּשֶׁת בְּעֶרֶב יוֹם הַכִּפּוּרִים. כְּדֵי לְקַיֵּם מִצְוַת דַּקָּה מִן הַדַּקָּה. וְאַחַד-עָשָׂר סַמָּנִים הָיוּ בָהּ. וְאֵלּוּ הֵן:

Tanu Rabbanan. Pitum Haketoret Keitzad: Shelosh Me'ot Veshishim Ushemonah Manim Hayu Vah. Shelosh Me'ot Veshishim Vachamishah Keminyan Yemot Hachamah. Maneh Bechol-Yom. Machatzito Baboker Umachatzito Ba'erev. Usheloshah Manim Yeterim. Shemehem Machnis Kohen Gadol. Venotel Mehem Melo Chafenav Beyom Hakippurim. Umachaziron Lemachteshet Be'erev Yom Hakippurim. Kedei Lekayem Mitzvat Dakah Min Hadakah. Ve'achad-'Asar Samanim Hayu Vah. Ve'elu Hen.

The rabbis have taught how the compounding of the incense was done. In measure the incense contained three hundred and sixty-eight manim, three hundred and sixty-five being one for each day of the year, the remaining three being for the high pin to take his hands full on the Yom Kippur. These last will again ground in a mortar on the eve of Yom Kippur so as to fulfill the command, "take of the finest beaten incense." and these are them:

א הַצֳּרִי ב וְהַצִּפֹּרֶן ג וְהַחֶלְבְּנָה ד וְהַלְּבוֹנָה. מִשְׁקַל שִׁבְעִים שִׁבְעִים
מָנֶה. ה מוֹר. ו וּקְצִיעָה ז וְשִׁבֹּלֶת נֵרְדְּ ח וְכַרְכֹּם. מִשְׁקַל שִׁשָּׁה
עָשָׂר שִׁשָּׁה עָשָׂר מָנֶה. ט קֹשְׁטְ שְׁנֵים עָשָׂר. י קִלּוּפָה שְׁלֹשָׁה. יא
קִנָּמוֹן תִּשְׁעָה. בּוֹרִית־כַּרְשִׁינָה תִּשְׁעָה קַבִּין. יֵין קַפְרִיסִין סְאִין תְּלָת
וְקַבִּין תְּלָתָא. וְאִם לֹא מָצָא יֵין קַפְרִיסִין. מֵבִיא חֲמַר חִיוָר עַתִּיק.
מֶלַח סְדוֹמִית. רוֹבַע. מַעֲלֶה עָשָׁן. כָּל־שֶׁהוּא. רִבִּי נָתָן הַבַּבְלִי
אוֹמֵר: אַף כִּפַּת הַיַּרְדֵּן כָּל־שֶׁהִיא. אִם נָתַן בָּהּ דְּבַשׁ פְּסָלָהּ. וְאִם
חִסֵּר אַחַת מִכָּל־סַמְמָנֶיהָ. חַיָּיב מִיתָה:

Hatzori Vehatziporen Vehachelbenah Vehallevonah. Mishkal Shiv'im Shiv'im Maneh. Mor. Uketzi'ah Veshibolet Nered Vecharkom. Mishkal Shishah Asar Shishah Asar Maneh. Koshet Sheneim Asar. Kilufah Sheloshah. Kinamon Tish'ah. Borit-Karshinah Tish'ah Kabin. Yein Kafrisin Se'in Telat Vekabin Telata. Ve'im Lo Matza Yein Kafrisin. Mevi Chamar Chivar Atik. Melach Sedomit. Rova. Ma'aleh Ashan. Kol-Shehu. Ribi Natan Habavli Omer. Af Kippat Hayarden Kol-Shehi. Im Natan Bah Devash Pesalah. Ve'im Chisser Achat Mikol-Samemaneiha. Chayaiv Mitah.

The incense was compounded of eleven different spices: seventy manim each of balm, onycha, galbanum, and frankincense; sixteen manim each of myrrh, cassia, spikenard, and saffron; twelve manim of costus; three manim of aromatic bark; nine manim of cinnamon; nine kabs of lye of Carsina; three seahs and three kabs of Cyprus wine, though if Cyprus wine could not be had, strong white wine might be substituted for it; the fourth of a kab of salt of Sedom, and a small quantity of a herb which caused the smoke to ascend straight. Rabbi Nathan of Bavel said there was added also a small quantity of kippat of the Yarden. If honey was mixed with the incense, the incense became unfit for sacred use, while the one who omitted any of the ingredients was deemed guilty of mortal error.

רַבָּן שִׁמְעוֹן בֶּן־גַּמְלִיאֵל אוֹמֵר: הַצֳּרִי אֵינוֹ אֶלָּא שְׂרָף. הַנּוֹטֵף מֵעֲצֵי הַקְּטָף. בּוֹרִית כַּרְשִׁינָה. לְמָה הִיא בָאָה: כְּדֵי לְשַׁפּוֹת בָּהּ אֶת־הַצִּפֹּרֶן. כְּדֵי שֶׁתְּהֵא נָאָה. יֵין קַפְרִיסִין. לְמָה הוּא בָא: כְּדֵי לִשְׁרוֹת בּוֹ אֶת־הַצִּפֹּרֶן כְּדֵי שֶׁתְּהֵא עַזָּה. וַהֲלֹא מֵי רַגְלַיִם יָפִין לָהּ: אֶלָּא שֶׁאֵין מַכְנִיסִין מֵי רַגְלַיִם בַּמִּקְדָּשׁ. מִפְּנֵי הַכָּבוֹד:

Rabban Shim'on Ben-Gamli'el Omer. Hatzori Eino Ella Sheraf.
Hanotef Me'atzei Haketaf. Borit Karshinah. Lemah Hi Va'ah: Kedei
Leshapot Bah Et-Hatziporen. Kedei Shetehei Na'ah. Yein Kafrisin.
Lemah Hu Va: Kedei Lishrot Bo Et-Hatziporen Kedei Shetehei Azah.
Vahalo Mei Raglayim Yafin Lah: Ella She'ein Machnisin Mei
Raglayim Bamikdash. Mipenei Hakavod.

Rabban Shimon, son of Gamliel, said that the balm required is that exuding from the balsam tree. Why did they use lye of Carsina? To refine the appearance of the onycha. What was the purpose of the Cyprus wine? To steep the onycha in it so as to harden it. Though mei raglayim might have been adapted for that purpose, it was not used because it was not decent to bring it into the Temple.

תַּנְיָא רִבִּי נָתָן אוֹמֵר: כְּשֶׁהוּא שׁוֹחֵק. אוֹמֵר: הָדֵק הֵיטֵב. הֵיטֵב הָדֵק. מִפְּנֵי שֶׁהַקּוֹל יָפֶה לַבְּשָׂמִים. פִּטְּמָהּ לַחֲצָאִין. כְּשֵׁרָה. לְשָׁלִישׁ וּלְרָבִיעַ. לֹא שָׁמַעְנוּ. אָמַר רִבִּי יְהוּדָה: זֶה הַכְּלָל. אִם כְּמִדָּתָהּ. כְּשֵׁרָה לַחֲצָאִין. וְאִם חִסֵּר אַחַת מִכָּל־סַמְמָנֶיהָ. חַיָּב מִיתָה:

Tanya Ribi Natan Omer. Keshehu Shochek. Omer. Hadek Heitev.
Heitev Hadek. Mipenei Shehakol Yafeh Labesamim. Pittemah
Lachatza'in. Kesherah. Leshalish Uleravia'. Lo Shama'nu. Amar Ribi

Yehudah. Zeh Hakelal. Im Kemidatah. Kesherah Lachatza'in. Ve'im
Chisser Achat Mikol-Samemaneiha. Chayaiv Mitah.

It is taught: Rabbi Natan said that when the priest ground the
incense the one superintending would say, "Grind it very fine, very
fine grind it," because the sound of the human voice is encouraging
in the making of spices. If he had compounded only one hundred
and eighty-four manim (half the required quantity), it was valid, but
there is no tradition as to its permissibility if it was compounded in
one-third or one-quarter proportions of the required quantity.
Rabbi Yehudah said that the general principle is that if it was made
with its ingredients in their correct proportions, it was permissible
in half the quantity; but if one omitted any of the ingredients he was
deemed guilty of mortal error.

תָּנֵי בַר־קַפָּרָא: אַחַת לְשִׁשִּׁים אוֹ לְשִׁבְעִים שָׁנָה. הָיְתָה בָאָה שֶׁל
שִׁירַיִם לַחֲצָאִין. וְעוֹד תָּנֵי בַר־קַפָּרָא: אִלּוּ הָיָה נוֹתֵן בָּהּ קוֹרְטוֹב
שֶׁל דְּבַשׁ. אֵין אָדָם יָכוֹל לַעֲמֹד מִפְּנֵי רֵיחָהּ. וְלָמָּה אֵין מְעָרְבִין
בָּהּ דְּבַשׁ. מִפְּנֵי שֶׁהַתּוֹרָה אָמְרָה: כִּי כָל־שְׂאֹר וְכָל־דְּבַשׁ
לֹא־תַקְטִירוּ מִמֶּנּוּ אִשֶּׁה לַיהֹוָה:

Tanei Var-Kappara. Achat Leshishim O Leshiv'im Shanah. Hayetah
Va'ah Shel Shirayim Lachatza'in. Ve'od Tanei Var-Kappara. Ilu Hayah
Noten Bah Karetov Shel Devash. Ein Adam Yachol La'amod Mipenei
Reichah. Velamah Ein Me'arevin Bah Devash Mipenei Shehatorah
Amerah. Ki Chol-Se'or Vechol-Devash. Lo-Taktiru Mimenu Isheh
L'Adonai.

Bar Kappara taught that once in sixty or seventy years it happened
that, left over, there was over a total of half the required amount
accumulated from the three manim of incense from which the high
priest took his hands full on Yom Kippur. Further Bar Kappara
taught that had one mixed into the incense the smallest quantity of
honey, no one could have stood its scent. Why did they not mix
honey with it? Because the Torah states that, "No leaven, or any
honey, will you burn as an offering made by fire to Hashem."

יְהוָֹה צְבָאוֹת עִמָּנוּ מִשְׂגָּב־לָנוּ אֱלֹהֵי יַעֲקֹב סֶלָה: יְהוָֹה צְבָאוֹת
אַשְׁרֵי אָדָם בֹּטֵחַ בָּךְ: יְהוָֹה הוֹשִׁיעָה הַמֶּלֶךְ יַעֲנֵנוּ בְיוֹם־קָרְאֵנוּ:
וְעָרְבָה לַיהוָֹה מִנְחַת יְהוּדָה וִירוּשָׁלָם כִּימֵי עוֹלָם וּכְשָׁנִים קַדְמֹנִיֹּת:

Adonai Tzeva'ot Imanu; Misgav-Lanu Elohei Ya'akov Selah. Adonai
Tzeva'ot; Ashrei Adam. Boteach Bach. Adonai Hoshi'ah; Hamelech.
Ya'aneinu Veyom-Kor'enu. Ve'arevah L'Adonai Minchat Yehudah
Virushalayim Kimei Olam. Ucheshanim Kadmoniyot.

Hashem of hosts is with us; The God of Yaakov is our high tower.
Selah. Hashem of hosts, happy is the man who trusts in You. Save,
Hashem; Let the King answer us in the day that we call. Then will
the offering of Yehudah and Yerushalayim be pleasant to Hashem,
as in the days of old, and as in ancient years. (Psalms 46:12, 84:13, 20:10,
Malachi 3:4)

Ana Bechoach

אָנָּא בְכֹחַ. גְּדוּלַת יְמִינְךָ. תַּתִּיר צְרוּרָה:

Ana Bechoach. Gedulat Yeminecha. Tatir Tzerurah.
By the great power of Your right hand, Oh set the captive free.

קַבֵּל רִנַּת. עַמְּךָ שַׂגְּבֵנוּ. טַהֲרֵנוּ נוֹרָא:

Kabel Rinat. Ammecha Sagveinu. Tahareinu Nora.
God of awe, accept Your people's prayer; strengthen us, cleanse us.

נָא גִבּוֹר. דּוֹרְשֵׁי יִחוּדֶךָ. כְּבָבַת שָׁמְרֵם:

Na Gibor. Doreshei Yichudecha. Kevavat Shamerem.
Almighty God, guard as the apple of the eye those who seek You.

בָּרְכֵם טַהֲרֵם. רַחֲמֵי צִדְקָתֶךָ. תָּמִיד גָּמְלֵם:

Barechem Taharem. Rachamei Tzidkatecha. Tamid Gamelem.
Bless them, cleanse them, pity them; forever grant them Your truth.

חֲסִין קָדוֹשׁ. בְּרֹב טוּבְךָ. נַהֵל עֲדָתֶךָ:

Chasin Kadosh. Berov Tuvecha. Nahel Adatecha.

Almighty and holy, in Your abundant goodness, guide Your people.

יָחִיד גֵּאֶה. לְעַמְּךָ פְנֵה. זוֹכְרֵי קְדֻשָּׁתֶךָ:

Yachid Ge'eh. Le'ammecha Feneh. Zocherei Kedushatecha.

Supreme God, turn to Your people who are mindful of Your holiness.

שַׁוְעָתֵנוּ קַבֵּל. וּשְׁמַע צַעֲקָתֵנוּ. יוֹדֵעַ תַּעֲלוּמוֹת:

Shav'ateinu Kabel. Ushema Tza'akateinu. Yodea Ta'alumot.

Accept our prayer, hear our cry, You Who knows secret thoughts.

And say silently:

בָּרוּךְ, שֵׁם כְּבוֹד מַלְכוּתוֹ, לְעוֹלָם וָעֶד:

Baruch, Shem Kevod Malchuto, Le'olam Va'ed.

Blessed is the Name of His glorious kingdom forever and ever.

Ribon Ha'olamim. Attah	רִבּוֹן הָעוֹלָמִים. אַתָּה
Tzivitanu Lehakriv Korban	צִוִּיתָנוּ לְהַקְרִיב קָרְבַּן
Hatamid Bemo'ado. Velihyot	הַתָּמִיד בְּמוֹעֲדוֹ. וְלִהְיוֹת
Kohanim Ba'avodatam.	כֹּהֲנִים בַּעֲבוֹדָתָם.
Uleviyim Beduchanam.	וּלְוִיִּם בְּדוּכָנָם.
Veyisra'el Bema'amadam.	וְיִשְׂרָאֵל בְּמַעֲמָדָם.
Ve'attah Ba'avonoteinu Charav	וְעַתָּה בַּעֲווֹנוֹתֵינוּ חָרַב
Beit Hamikdash Uvuttal	בֵּית הַמִּקְדָּשׁ וּבֻטַּל
Hatamid. Ve'ein Lanu Lo Kohen	הַתָּמִיד. וְאֵין לָנוּ לֹא כֹּהֵן
Ba'avodato Velo Levi	בַּעֲבוֹדָתוֹ וְלֹא לֵוִי
Beduchano. Velo Yisra'el	בְּדוּכָנוֹ. וְלֹא יִשְׂרָאֵל
Bema'amado. Ve'attah Amarta.	בְּמַעֲמָדוֹ. וְאַתָּה אָמַרְתָּ:
Uneshalemah Farim Sefateinu.	וּנְשַׁלְּמָה פָרִים שְׂפָתֵינוּ:

Sovereign of the universe, You commanded us to offer the daily offering at its appointed time, with the the Kohanim at their service, the Levi'im on their platform, and Yisrael in their delegations. Now through our sins our Beit Hamikdash is laid waste, its daily offerings are abolished, and we have neither a Kohen at his service, nor Levi on his platform, or Yisrael delegation. But You have said (through Your prophet Hoshea), that we may substitute (the prayer of) our lips for (the sacrifice of) bulls. (Hoshea 14:3)

Lachein Yehi Ratzon	לָכֵן יְהִי רָצוֹן
Milfaneicha Adonai Eloheinu	מִלְפָנֶיךָ יְהוָה אֱלֹהֵינוּ
Velohei Avoteinu. Sheyehei	וֵאלֹהֵי אֲבוֹתֵינוּ. שֶׁיְהֵא
Siach Siftoteinu Zeh Chashuv	שִׂיחַ שִׂפְתוֹתֵינוּ זֶה חָשׁוּב
Umekubbal Umerutzeh	וּמְקֻבָּל וּמְרוּצֶה
Lefaneicha Ke'ilu Hikravnu	לְפָנֶיךָ כְּאִלּוּ הִקְרַבְנוּ
Korban Hatamid Bemo'ado	קָרְבַּן הַתָּמִיד בְּמוֹעֲדוֹ
Ve'amadnu Al Ma'amado.	וְעָמַדְנוּ עַל מַעֲמָדוֹ.
Kemo Shene'emar.	כְּמוֹ שֶׁנֶּאֱמַר:
Uneshalemah Farim Sefateinu.	וּנְשַׁלְמָה פָרִים שְׂפָתֵינוּ:
Vene'emar. Veshachat Oto Al	וְנֶאֱמַר: וְשָׁחַט אֹתוֹ עַל
Yerech Hamizbe'ach Tzafonah	יֶרֶךְ הַמִּזְבֵּחַ צָפֹנָה
Lifnei Adonai Vezareku Benei	לִפְנֵי יְהוָה וְזָרְקוּ בְּנֵי
Aharon Hakohanim Et-Damo	אַהֲרֹן הַכֹּהֲנִים אֶת־דָּמוֹ
Al-Hamizbe'ach Saviv.	עַל־הַמִּזְבֵּחַ סָבִיב:
Vene'emar. Zot Hatorah.	וְנֶאֱמַר: זֹאת הַתּוֹרָה
La'olah Lamminchah. Velachatat	לָעֹלָה לַמִּנְחָה וְלַחַטָּאת
Vela'asham; Velammilu'im.	וְלָאָשָׁם וְלַמִּלּוּאִים
Ulezevach Hashelamim.	וּלְזֶבַח הַשְּׁלָמִים:

Therefore, let it be Your will, Hashem our God and God of our fathers, that the prayer of our lips be accepted before You in favor and accounted as if we had offered the daily Temple sacrifice at its appointed time in the presence of our delegation, for the fulfillment of the ancient words of the Torah, "He will offer the lamb at the side of the altar northward, before Hashem; and Aharon's sons as priests will sprinkle its blood upon the altar." Further the Torah says, "This is the law of the burnt-offering, the meal-offering, the sin-offering, the trespass-offering, the consecration and the sacrifice of the peace-offerings."

Eizehu Mekoman
Mishnah Zevachim, Chap. 5

It was established that one should recite the teaching of "Eizehu Mekoman" and the baraita of Rabbi Yishmael after the section of the daily offering in order that every person would attain merit everyday by learning Bible, Mishnah and Gemara (Talmud). The baraita of Rabbi Yishmael is in place of Gemara since midrash is like Gemara. (SA, OC 50)

אֵיזֶהוּ מְקוֹמָן שֶׁל זְבָחִים. קָדְשֵׁי קָדָשִׁים שְׁחִיטָתָן בַּצָּפוֹן. פַּר
וְשָׂעִיר שֶׁל יוֹם הַכִּפּוּרִים שְׁחִיטָתָן בַּצָּפוֹן. וְקִבּוּל דָּמָן בִּכְלֵי שָׁרֵת
בַּצָּפוֹן. וְדָמָן טָעוּן הַזָּיָה עַל בֵּין הַבַּדִּים וְעַל הַפָּרֹכֶת וְעַל מִזְבַּח
הַזָּהָב. מַתָּנָה אַחַת מֵהֶן מְעַכֶּבֶת. שְׁיָרֵי הַדָּם הָיָה שׁוֹפֵךְ עַל יְסוֹד
מַעֲרָבִי שֶׁל מִזְבֵּחַ הַחִיצוֹן. אִם לֹא נָתַן. לֹא עִכֵּב:

Eizehu Mekoman Shel Zevachim. Kodshi Kadashim Shechitatan Batzafon. Par Vesa'ir Shel Yom Hakippurim Shechitatan Batzafon. Vekibul Daman Bichlei Sharet Batzafon. Vedaman Ta'un Hazayah Al Bein Habadim Ve'al Haparochet Ve'al Mizbach Hazahav. Matanah Achat Mehen Me'akevet. Shiyrei Hadam Hayah Shofech Al Yesod Ma'aravi Shel Mizbe'ach Hachitzon. Im Lo Natan. Lo Ikev:

1. Which were the places of sacrifice in the Temple? The most holy offerings were slaughtered on the north side of the altar, as were also the bull and the male-goat for Yom Kippur. Their blood was received there in a vessel of service to be sprinkled between the

staves of the Ark before the veil of the Holy of Holies and upon the
golden altar. The omission of a sprinkling invalidated the
atonement ceremonial. The priest poured out the remaining blood
on the western base of the outer altar, but if he omitted to do so the
atonement ceremony was not invalidated.

פָּרִים הַנִּשְׂרָפִים וּשְׂעִירִים הַנִּשְׂרָפִים שְׁחִיטָתָן בַּצָּפוֹן. וְקִבּוּל דָּמָן
בִּכְלֵי שָׁרֵת בַּצָּפוֹן. וְדָמָן טָעוּן הַזָּיָה עַל הַפָּרֹכֶת וְעַל מִזְבַּח הַזָּהָב.
מַתָּנָה אַחַת מֵהֶן מְעַכֶּבֶת. שְׁיָרֵי הַדָּם הָיָה שׁוֹפֵךְ עַל יְסוֹד מַעֲרָבִי
שֶׁל מִזְבַּח הַחִיצוֹן. אִם לֹא נָתַן. לֹא עִכֵּב. אֵלּוּ וְאֵלּוּ נִשְׂרָפִין בְּבֵית
הַדָּשֶׁן:

Parim Hanisrafim Use'irim Hanisrafim Shechitatan Batzafon. Vekibul
Daman Bichlei Sharet Batzafon. Vedaman Ta'un Hazayah Al
Haparochet Ve'al Mizbach Hazahav. Matanah Achat Mehen
Me'akevet. Shiyrei Hadam Hayah Shofech Al Yesod Ma'aravi Shel
Mizbach Hachitzon. Im Lo Natan. Lo Ikev. Elu Ve'elu Nisrafin Beveit
Hadashen.

2. The bulls and the male-goats which were to be entirely burnt were
slaughtered on the north side of the altar, and their blood was
received there in a vessel of service to be sprinkled before the veil
and upon the golden altar. The omission of a sprinkling invalidated
the atonement ceremonial. The priest poured out the remaining
blood at the western base of the outer altar; but if he omitted to do
so the atonement ceremony was not invalidated. These as well as
the preceding offerings were burnt in the repository of ashes.

חַטֹּאת הַצִּבּוּר וְהַיָּחִיד. אֵלּוּ הֵן חַטֹּאת הַצִּבּוּר. שְׂעִירֵי רָאשֵׁי
חֳדָשִׁים וְשֶׁל מוֹעֲדוֹת. שְׁחִיטָתָן בַּצָּפוֹן. וְקִבּוּל דָּמָן בִּכְלֵי שָׁרֵת
בַּצָּפוֹן. וְדָמָן טָעוּן אַרְבַּע מַתָּנוֹת עַל אַרְבַּע קְרָנוֹת. כֵּיצַד. עָלָה
בַכֶּבֶשׁ וּפָנָה לַסּוֹבֵב. וּבָא לוֹ לְקֶרֶן דְּרוֹמִית מִזְרָחִית. מִזְרָחִית
צְפוֹנִית. צְפוֹנִית מַעֲרָבִית. מַעֲרָבִית דְּרוֹמִית. שְׁיָרֵי הַדָּם הָיָה שׁוֹפֵךְ

עַל יְסוֹד דְּרוֹמִי. וְנֶאֱכָלִין לִפְנִים מִן הַקְּלָעִים לְזִכְרֵי כְהֻנָּה בְּכָל
מַאֲכָל לְיוֹם וָלַיְלָה עַד חֲצוֹת:

Chatot Hatzibur Vehayachid. Elu Hen Chatot Hatzibur. Se'irei
Roshei Chodashim Veshel Mo'adot. Shechitatan Batzafon. Vekibul
Daman Bichlei Sharet Batzafon. Vedaman Ta'un Arba Matanot Al
Arba Keranot. Keitzad. Alah Vakevesh Ufanah Lassovev. Uva Lo
Lekeren Deromit Mizrachit. Mizrachit Tzefonit. Tzefonit Ma'aravit.
Ma'aravit Deromit. Sheyarei Hadam Hayah Shofech Al Yesod
Deromi. Vene'echalin Lifanim Min Hakkela'im Lezichrei Chehunah
Bechol Ma'achal Leyom Valaylah Ad Chatzot.

3. As for the sin-offerings of the whole congregation and of an
individual, the male-goats offered on Rosh Chodesh and on
festivals are the sin-offerings of the whole congregation. These
were slaughtered on the north side of the altar and their blood was
received there in a ritual vessel. It was required to make four
sprinklings of that blood, once upon each of the four corners of the
altar. How was this done? The priest went up the ascent to the altar
and went around its ledge successively to its southeast, northeast,
northwest and southwest corners. He poured out the remaining
blood at the south side of the base of the outer altar. These
sacrifices, prepared for food after any manner, were eaten within
the hangings of the court only by the males of the priesthood
during that day and evening until midnight.

הָעוֹלָה. קֹדֶשׁ קָדָשִׁים. שְׁחִיטָתָהּ בַּצָּפוֹן. וְקִבּוּל דָּמָהּ בִּכְלֵי שָׁרֵת
בַּצָּפוֹן. וְדָמָהּ טָעוּן שְׁתֵּי מַתָּנוֹת שֶׁהֵן אַרְבַּע. וּטְעוּנָה הֶפְשֵׁט וְנִתּוּחַ
וְכָלִיל לָאִשִּׁים:

Ha'olah. Kodesh Kadashim. Shechitatah Batzafon. Vekibul Damah
Bichlei Sharet Batzafon. Vedamah Ta'un Shetei Matanot Shehen
Arba'. Ute'unah Hefshet Venittuach Vechalil La'ishim

4. The burnt-offering was classed among the most holy of the
offerings. It was slain on the north side of the altar and its blood
was there received in a ritual vessel. It was required to make two
doubled sprinklings of that blood so as to constitute four. That

offering had to be flayed and dismembered and wholly consumed
by fire.

זִבְחֵי שַׁלְמֵי צִבּוּר וַאֲשָׁמוֹת. אֵלּוּ הֵן אֲשָׁמוֹת. אָשָׁם גְּזֵלוֹת. אָשָׁם
מְעִילוֹת. אָשָׁם שִׁפְחָה חֲרוּפָה. אָשָׁם נָזִיר. אָשָׁם מְצוֹרָע. אָשָׁם
תָּלוּי. שְׁחִיטָתָן בַּצָּפוֹן. וְקִבּוּל דָּמָן בִּכְלִי שָׁרֵת בַּצָּפוֹן. וְדָמָן טָעוּן
שְׁתֵּי מַתָּנוֹת שֶׁהֵן אַרְבַּע. וְנֶאֱכָלִין לִפְנִים מִן הַקְּלָעִים לְזִכְרֵי כְהֻנָּה
בְּכָל מַאֲכָל לְיוֹם וָלַיְלָה עַד חֲצוֹת:

Zivchei Shalmei Tzibur Va'ashamot. Elu Hen Ashamot. Asham
Gezelot. Asham Me'ilot. Asham Shifchah Charufah. Asham Nazir.
Asham Metzora'. Asham Talui. Shechitatan Batzafon. Vekibul
Daman Bichli Sharet Batzafon. Vedaman Ta'un Shetei Matanot
Shehen Arba'. Vene'echalin Lefanim Min Hakkela'im Lezichrei
Chehunah Bechol Ma'achal Leyom Valaylah Ad Chatzot

5. As to the peace-offerings of the whole congregation and the
trespass-offerings, the following are the trespass-offerings: for
robbery, for the profane appropriation of sanctified things, for
violating a bethrothed handmaid, that which was brought by the
nazirite who had become defiled by a dead body, by the leper at his
cleansing, and that brought for the sin-offering about which there
was a doubt whether it should be atoned for by a sin-offering. All
these were slaughtered on the north side of the altar and the blood
was received there in a ritual vessel. It was required to make two
doubled sprinklings of that blood so as to constitute four. These
sacrifices, prepared for food after any manner, were eaten only
within the hangings of the court by the males of the priesthood
during that day and evening until midnight.

הַתּוֹדָה וְאֵיל נָזִיר. קָדָשִׁים קַלִּים. שְׁחִיטָתָן בְּכָל מָקוֹם בָּעֲזָרָה.
וְדָמָן טָעוּן שְׁתֵּי מַתָּנוֹת שֶׁהֵן אַרְבַּע. וְנֶאֱכָלִין בְּכָל הָעִיר. לְכָל
אָדָם. בְּכָל מַאֲכָל. לְיוֹם וָלַיְלָה עַד חֲצוֹת. הַמּוּרָם מֵהֶם כַּיּוֹצֵא
בָהֶם. אֶלָּא שֶׁהַמּוּרָם נֶאֱכָל לַכֹּהֲנִים לִנְשֵׁיהֶם וְלִבְנֵיהֶם וּלְעַבְדֵיהֶם:

Hatodah Ve'eil Nazir. Kadashim Kallim. Shechitatan Bechol Makom Ba'azarah. Vedaman Ta'un Shetei Matanot Shehen Arba'. Vene'echalin Bechol Ha'ir. Lechol Adam. Bechol Ma'achal. Leyom Valaylah Ad Chatzot. Hamuram Mehem Kayotzei Vahem. Ella Shehamuram Ne'echal Lakohanim Linsheihem Velivneihem Ule'avdeihem.

6. The thanksgiving-offering of individuals and the ram offered by the nazirite at the close of his vow were of a minor degree of holiness. These might be killed in any part of the court of the Temple. It was required to make two doubled sprinklings of their blood so as to constitute four. They might be eaten prepared for food after any manner, in any part of the city by any person during the whole of that day and evening until midnight. The same rules were observed with the portions of them appertaining to the priests, except that these might be eaten only by the priests, their wives, their children and their servants.

שְׁלָמִים. קָדָשִׁים קַלִּים. שְׁחִיטָתָן בְּכָל מָקוֹם בָּעֲזָרָה. וְדָמָן טָעוּן שְׁתֵּי מַתָּנוֹת שֶׁהֵן אַרְבַּע. וְנֶאֱכָלִין בְּכָל הָעִיר לְכָל אָדָם בְּכָל מַאֲכָל לִשְׁנֵי יָמִים וְלַיְלָה אֶחָד. הַמּוּרָם מֵהֶם כַּיּוֹצֵא בָהֶם. אֶלָּא שֶׁהַמּוּרָם נֶאֱכָל לַכֹּהֲנִים. לִנְשֵׁיהֶם וְלִבְנֵיהֶם וּלְעַבְדֵיהֶם:

Shelamim. Kadashim Kallim. Shechitatan Bechol Makom Ba'azarah. Vedaman Ta'un Shetei Matanot Shehen Arba'. Vene'echalin Bechol Ha'ir Lechol Adam Bechol Ma'achal Lishnei Yamim Valaylah Echad. Hamuram Mehem Kayotzei Bahem. Ella Shehamuram Ne'echal Lakohanim. Linsheihem Velivneihem Ule'avdeihem.

7. The peace-offerings also were holy in a minor degree of holiness. These might be killed in any part of the court of the Temple, and It was required to make two doubled sprinklings of their blood so as to constitute four. They might be eaten prepared for food after any manner, in any part of the city by any person during two days and the intervening night. The same rules were observed with the portions of them appertaining to the priests, except that these

might be eaten only by the priests, their wives, their children and their servants.

הַבְּכוֹר וְהַמַּעֲשֵׂר וְהַפֶּסַח. קָדָשִׁים קַלִּים. שְׁחִיטָתָן בְּכָל מָקוֹם בָּעֲזָרָה. וְדָמָן טָעוּן מַתָּנָה אֶחָת. וּבִלְבַד שֶׁיִּתֵּן כְּנֶגֶד הַיְסוֹד. שִׁנָּה בַּאֲכִילָתָן. הַבְּכוֹר נֶאֱכָל לַכֹּהֲנִים. וְהַמַּעֲשֵׂר לְכָל אָדָם. וְנֶאֱכָלִין בְּכָל הָעִיר לְכָל אָדָם בְּכָל מַאֲכָל לִשְׁנֵי יָמִים וְלַיְלָה אֶחָד. הַפֶּסַח אֵינוֹ נֶאֱכָל אֶלָּא בַלַּיְלָה. וְאֵינוֹ נֶאֱכָל אֶלָּא עַד חֲצוֹת. וְאֵינוֹ נֶאֱכָל אֶלָּא לִמְנוּיָיו. וְאֵינוֹ נֶאֱכָל אֶלָּא צָלִי:

Habechor Vehama'aser Vehapesach. Kadashim Kallim. Shechitatan Bechol Makom Ba'azarah. Vedaman Ta'un Matanah Achat. Uvilvad Sheyiten Keneged Haysod. Shinah Va'achilatan. Habechor Ne'echal Lakohanim. Vehama'aser Lechol Adam. Vene'echalin Bechol Ha'ir Lechol Adam Bechol Ma'achal Lishnei Yamim Valaylah Echad. Hapesach Eino Ne'echal Ella Vallaylah. Ve'eino Ne'echal Ella Ad Chatzot. Ve'eino Ne'echal Ella Limnuyav. Ve'eino Ne'echal Ella Tzali.

8. The first-born of beasts, the tithe of cattle, and the Pesach lamb were also holy in a minor degree. These might be killed in any part of the court of the Temple. Only one sprinkling of their blood was required, but that had to be done towards the base of the altar. In the eating of them, however, the following distinction was made: the first-born animal was eaten by the priests only, but the tithe could be eaten by anyone. Both the first-born animal and the tithe might be eaten prepared for food after any manner, in any part of the city during two days and the intervening night, whereas the Pesach lamb had to be eaten on that night only and not later than midnight. Neither may it be eaten except by those of a previously constituted group, or prepared in any way other than roasted.

Baraita of Rabbi Yishmael

Sifra: Ch. 1 - Preface to Torat Kohanim

רִבִּי יִשְׁמָעֵאל אוֹמֵר: בִּשְׁלֹשׁ עֶשְׂרֵה מִדּוֹת הַתּוֹרָה נִדְרֶשֶׁת: מִקַּל
וָחֹמֶר. מִגְּזֵרָה שָׁוֶה. מִבִּנְיַן אָב וְכָתוּב אֶחָד. וּמִבִּנְיַן אָב וּשְׁנֵי
כְתוּבִים. מִכְּלָל וּפְרָט. מִפְּרָט וּכְלָל. כְּלָל וּפְרָט וּכְלָל. אֵי אַתָּה דָן
אֶלָּא כְּעֵין הַפְּרָט. מִכְּלָל שֶׁהוּא צָרִיךְ לִפְרָט. וּמִפְּרָט שֶׁהוּא צָרִיךְ
לִכְלָל. וְכָל דָּבָר שֶׁהָיָה בִכְלָל וְיָצָא מִן הַכְּלָל לְלַמֵּד. לֹא לְלַמֵּד
עַל עַצְמוֹ יָצָא. אֶלָּא לְלַמֵּד עַל הַכְּלָל כֻּלּוֹ יָצָא. וְכָל דָּבָר שֶׁהָיָה
בִכְלָל. וְיָצָא לִטְעוֹן טָעוֹן אַחֵר שֶׁהוּא כְעִנְיָנוֹ. יָצָא לְהָקֵל וְלֹא
לְהַחְמִיר. וְכָל דָּבָר שֶׁהָיָה בִכְלָל. וְיָצָא לִטְעֹן טָעוֹן אַחֵר שֶׁלֹּא
כְעִנְיָנוֹ. יָצָא לְהָקֵל וּלְהַחְמִיר. וְכָל דָּבָר שֶׁהָיָה בִכְלָל. וְיָצָא לִדּוֹן
בְּדָבָר חָדָשׁ. אֵי אַתָּה יָכוֹל לְהַחֲזִירוֹ לִכְלָלוֹ עַד שֶׁיַּחֲזִירֶנּוּ הַכָּתוּב
לִכְלָלוֹ בְּפֵירוּשׁ. וְדָבָר הַלָּמֵד מֵעִנְיָנוֹ. וְדָבָר הַלָּמֵד מִסּוֹפוֹ. וְכֵן שְׁנֵי
כְתוּבִים הַמַּכְחִישִׁים זֶה אֶת זֶה. עַד שֶׁיָּבֹא הַכָּתוּב הַשְּׁלִישִׁי וְיַכְרִיעַ
בֵּנֵיהֶם:

Ribi Yishma'el Omer. Bishlosh Esreh Middot Hatorah Nidreshet:
Mikal Vachomer. Migezerah Shaveh. Mibinyan Av Vechatuv Echad.
Umibinyan Av Ushenei Chetuvim. Mikelal Uferat. Miperat Uchelal.
Kelal Uferat Uchelal. Ei Attah Dan Ella Ke'ein Haperat. Mikelal
Shehu Tzarich Lifrat. Umiperat Shehu Tzarich Lichlal. Vechol Davar
Shehayah Vichlal Veyatza Min Hakelal Lelamed. Lo Lelamed Al
Atzmo Yatza. Ella Lelamed Al Hakelal Kulo Yatza. Vechol Davar
Shehayah Vichlal. Veyatza Lit'on Ta'un Acher Shehu Che'inyano.
Yatza Lehakel Velo Lehachmir. Vechol Davar Shehayah Bichlal.
Veyatza Lit'on Ta'un Acher Shelo Che'inyano. Yatza Lehakel
Ulehachmir. Vechol Davar Shehayah Bichlal. Veyatza Liddon
Bedavar Chadash. Ei Attah Yachol Lehachaziro Lichlalo Ad
Sheyachazirenu Hakatuv Lichlalo Vefeirush. Vedavar Halamed
Me'inyano. Vedavar Halamed Missofo. Vechan Shenei Chetuvim
Hamachchishim Zeh Et Zeh. Ad Sheyavo Hakatuv Hashelishi
Veyachria Beneihem.

Rabbi Yishmael says the Torah may be expounded by these thirteen
principles of logic:

1. Inference from minor to major, or from major to minor. **2.** Inference from similarity of phrases in texts. **3.** A comprehensive principle derived from one text, or from two related texts. **4.** A general proposition followed by a specifying particular. **5.** A particular term followed by a general proposition. **6.** A general law limited by a specific application and then treated again in general terms must be interpreted according to the tenor of the specific limitation. **7.** A general proposition requiring a particular or specific term to explain it, and conversely, a particular term requiring a general one to complement it. **8.** When a subject included in a general proposition is afterwards particularly excepted to give information concerning it, the exception is made not for that one instance alone, but to apply to the general proposition as a whole. **9.** Whenever anything is first included in a general proposition and is then excepted to prove another similar proposition, this specifying alleviates and does not aggravate the law's restriction. **10.** But when anything is first included in a general proposition and is then excepted to state a case that is not a similar proposition, such specifying alleviates in some respects and in others aggravates the law's restriction. **11.** Anything included in a general proposition and afterwards excepted to determine a new matter can not be applied to the general proposition unless this be expressly done in the text. **12.** An interpretation may be deduced from the text or from subsequent terms of the text. **13.** In like manner when two texts contradict each other we follow the second, until a third text is found which reconciles the contradiction.

יְהוּדָה בֶּן תֵּימָא אוֹמֵר. הֱוֵי עַז כַּנָּמֵר. וְקַל כַּנֶּשֶׁר. וְרָץ כַּצְּבִי. וְגִבּוֹר כָּאֲרִי לַעֲשׂוֹת רְצוֹן אָבִיךְ שֶׁבַּשָּׁמָיִם. הוּא הָיָה אוֹמֵר. עַז פָּנִים לְגֵיהִנָּם. וּבוֹשֶׁת פָּנִים לְגַן עֵדֶן:

Yehudah Ben Teima Omer. Hevei Az Kanamer. Vekal Kanesher. Veratz Katzevi. Vegibor Ka'ari La'asot Retzon Avicha Shebashamayim. Hu Hayah Omer. Az Panim Laggeihinam. Uvoshet Panim Legan Eden.

Yehudah ben Teimah used to say, be as strong as the leopard, as swift as the eagle, as nimble as the gazelle, and as mighty as the lion to do the will of Your Father in Heaven. He used also to say, the arrogant are (destined) for Gehinnom, but the shame-faced are (destined) for Gan Eden. **(Mishnah, Pirkei Avot 5:23, some 20)**

יְהִי רָצוֹן מִלְפָנֶיךָ יְהֹוָה אֱלֹהֵינוּ וֵאלֹהֵי אֲבוֹתֵינוּ. שֶׁתִּבְנֶה בֵּית הַמִּקְדָּשׁ בִּמְהֵרָה בְיָמֵינוּ. וְתֵן חֶלְקֵנוּ בְּתוֹרָתֶךָ. לַעֲשׂוֹת חֻקֵּי רְצוֹנֶךָ. וּלְעָבְדְּךָ בְּלֵבָב שָׁלֵם:

Yehi Ratzon Milfaneicha Adonai Eloheinu Velohei Avoteinu. Shetivneh Beit Hamikdash Bimheirah Veyameinu. Veten Chelkenu Betoratach. La'asot Chukkei Retzonach. Ule'avedach Belevav Shalem:

May it be Your will, Hashem our God, God of our fathers, that the Beit Hamikdash be speedily rebuilt in our days. Set our portion in Your Torah so that we may know to perform Your will and serve You wholeheartedly.

Kaddish Al-Yisrael

Kaddish is only recited in a minyan (ten men). אמן denotes when the congregation responds "Amen" together out loud. According to the Shulchan Arukh, the congregation says "Yehei Shemeh Rabba" to "Yitbarach" out loud together without interruption, and also that one should respond "Amen" after "Yitbarach." (SA, OC 55,56) This is not the common custom today. Though many are accustomed to answering according to their own custom, it is advised to respond in the custom of the one reciting to avoid not fragmenting into smaller groups. ("Lo Titgodedu" - BT, Yevamot 13b / SA, OC 493, Rema / MT, Avodah Zara 12:15)

יִתְגַּדַּל וְיִתְקַדַּשׁ שְׁמֵהּ רַבָּא. אמן בְּעָלְמָא דִּי בְרָא. כִרְעוּתֵהּ. וְיַמְלִיךְ מַלְכוּתֵהּ. וְיַצְמַח פֻּרְקָנֵהּ. וִיקָרֵב מְשִׁיחֵהּ. אמן בְּחַיֵּיכוֹן וּבְיוֹמֵיכוֹן

וּבְחַיֵּי דְכָל בֵּית יִשְׂרָאֵל. בַּעֲגָלָא וּבִזְמַן קָרִיב. וְאִמְרוּ אָמֵן. אמן יְהֵא
שְׁמֵיהּ רַבָּא מְבָרַךְ לְעָלַם וּלְעָלְמֵי עָלְמַיָּא יִתְבָּרַךְ. וְיִשְׁתַּבַּח.
וְיִתְפָּאַר. וְיִתְרוֹמַם. וְיִתְנַשֵּׂא. וְיִתְהַדָּר. וְיִתְעַלֶּה. וְיִתְהַלָּל שְׁמֵהּ
דְקֻדְשָׁא. בְּרִיךְ הוּא. אמן לְעֵלָּא מִן כָּל בִּרְכָתָא שִׁירָתָא. תֻּשְׁבְּחָתָא
וְנֶחֱמָתָא. דַּאֲמִירָן בְּעָלְמָא. וְאִמְרוּ אָמֵן. אמן

Yitgadal Veyitkadash Shemeh Rabba. **Amen** Be'alema Di Vera.
Kir'uteh. Veyamlich Malchuteh. Veyatzmach Purkaneh. Vikarev
Meshicheh. **Amen** Bechayeichon Uveyomeichon Uvechayei Dechal-
Beit Yisra'el. Ba'agala Uvizman Kariv. Ve'imru Amen. **Amen** Yehei
Shemeh Rabba Mevarach Le'alam Ule'alemei Alemaya Yitbarach.
Veyishtabach. Veyitpa'ar. Veyitromam. Veyitnasse. Veyit'hadar.
Veyit'aleh. Veyit'hallal Shemeh Dekudsha. Berich Hu. **Amen** Le'ella
Min Kol Birchata Shirata. Tushbechata Venechemata. Da'amiran
Be'alema. Ve'imru Amen. **Amen**

Glorified and sanctified be God's great name **Amen** throughout the
world which He has created according to His will. May He establish
His kingdom, hastening His salvation and the coming of His
Messiah, **Amen**, in your lifetime and during your days, and within the
life of the entire House of Yisrael, speedily and soon; and say, Amen.
Amen May His great name be blessed forever and to all eternity.
Blessed and praised, glorified and exalted, extolled and honored,
adored and lauded is the name of the Holy One, blessed is He, **Amen**
Beyond all the blessings and hymns, praises and consolations that
are ever spoken in the world; and say, Amen. **Amen**

עַל יִשְׂרָאֵל וְעַל רַבָּנָן. וְעַל תַּלְמִידֵיהוֹן וְעַל כָּל תַּלְמִידֵי תַלְמִידֵיהוֹן.
דְּעָסְקִין בְּאוֹרַיְתָא קַדִּשְׁתָּא. דִּי בְאַתְרָא הָדֵין וְדִי בְכָל אֲתַר וַאֲתַר.
יְהֵא לָנָא וּלְהוֹן וּלְכוֹן חִנָּא וְחִסְדָּא וְרַחֲמֵי. מִן קֳדָם מָארֵי שְׁמַיָּא
וְאַרְעָא וְאִמְרוּ אָמֵן. אמן

Al Yisra'el Ve'al Rabbanan. Ve'al Talmideihon Ve'al Kol Talmidei
Talmideihon. De'asekin Be'orayta Kaddishta. Di Ve'atra Hadein Vedi
Vechal Atar Va'atar. Yehei Lana Ulehon Ulechon China Vechisda
Verachamei. Min Kodam Marei Shemaya Ve'ar'a Ve'imru Amen. **Amen**

May we of Yisrael together with our rabbis, their disciples and pupils, and all who engage in the study of holy Torah here and everywhere, find gracious favor and mercy from their Father Who is in heaven; and say, Amen. ^{Amen}

יְהֵא שְׁלָמָא רַבָּא מִן שְׁמַיָּא. חַיִּים וְשָׂבָע וִישׁוּעָה וְנֶחָמָה. וְשֵׁיזָבָא וּרְפוּאָה וּגְאוּלָה וּסְלִיחָה וְכַפָּרָה וְרֶוַח וְהַצָּלָה לָנוּ וּלְכָל עַמּוֹ יִשְׂרָאֵל. וְאִמְרוּ אָמֵן. אמן

Yehei Shelama Rabba Min Shemaya. Chayim Vesava Vishu'ah Venechamah. Vesheizava Urefu'ah Uge'ulah Uselichah Vechapparah Verevach Vehatzalah Lanu Ulechol Ammo Yisra'el. Ve'imru Amen. ^{Amen}

May abundant peace descend from heaven, with life and plenty, salvation, solace, liberation, healing and redemption, and forgiveness and atonement, enlargement and freedom, for us and all of God's people Yisrael; and say, Amen. ^{Amen}

> One bows and takes three steps backwards, while still bowing. After three steps, while still bowing and before erecting, while saying, "Oseh Shalom Bimromav", turn one's face to the left, "Hu [Berachamav] Ya'aseh Shalom Aleinu", turn one's face to the right; then bow forward like a servant leaving his master. (SA, OC 123:1)

עוֹשֶׂה שָׁלוֹם בִּמְרוֹמָיו. הוּא בְּרַחֲמָיו יַעֲשֶׂה שָׁלוֹם עָלֵינוּ. וְעַל כָּל־עַמּוֹ יִשְׂרָאֵל. וְאִמְרוּ אָמֵן:

Oseh Shalom Bimromav. Hu Berachamav Ya'aseh Shalom Aleinu. Ve'al Kol-'Ammo Yisra'el. Ve'imru Amen.

Creator of peace in His high places, may He in His mercy create peace for us and for all Yisrael, and say Amen.

Hodu
Chronicles 16:8-36

הוֹדוּ לַיהֹוָה קִרְאוּ בִשְׁמוֹ הוֹדִיעוּ בָעַמִּים עֲלִילֹתָיו: שִׁירוּ לוֹ זַמְּרוּ־לוֹ שִׂיחוּ בְּכָל־נִפְלְאֹתָיו: הִתְהַלְלוּ בְּשֵׁם קָדְשׁוֹ יִשְׂמַח לֵב

מְבַקְשֵׁי יְהֹוָה: דִּרְשׁוּ יְהֹוָה וְעֻזּוֹ בַּקְּשׁוּ פָנָיו תָּמִיד: זִכְרוּ נִפְלְאֹתָיו
אֲשֶׁר עָשָׂה מֹפְתָיו וּמִשְׁפְּטֵי־פִיהוּ: זֶרַע יִשְׂרָאֵל עַבְדּוֹ בְּנֵי יַעֲקֹב
בְּחִירָיו: הוּא יְהֹוָה אֱלֹהֵינוּ בְּכָל־הָאָרֶץ מִשְׁפָּטָיו: זִכְרוּ לְעוֹלָם
בְּרִיתוֹ דָּבָר צִוָּה לְאֶלֶף דּוֹר: אֲשֶׁר כָּרַת אֶת־אַבְרָהָם וּשְׁבוּעָתוֹ
לְיִצְחָק: וַיַּעֲמִידֶהָ לְיַעֲקֹב לְחֹק לְיִשְׂרָאֵל בְּרִית עוֹלָם: לֵאמֹר לְךָ
אֶתֵּן אֶרֶץ־כְּנָעַן חֶבֶל נַחֲלַתְכֶם: בִּהְיוֹתְכֶם מְתֵי מִסְפָּר כִּמְעַט וְגָרִים
בָּהּ: וַיִּתְהַלְּכוּ מִגּוֹי אֶל־גּוֹי וּמִמַּמְלָכָה אֶל־עַם אַחֵר: לֹא־הִנִּיחַ
לְאִישׁ לְעָשְׁקָם וַיּוֹכַח עֲלֵיהֶם מְלָכִים: אַל־תִּגְּעוּ בִמְשִׁיחָי וּבִנְבִיאַי
אַל־תָּרֵעוּ:

Hodu L'Adonai Kir'u Vishmo Hodi'u Va'ammim Alilotav. Shiru Lo
Zameru Lo Sichu Bechol Nifle'otav. Hithallelu Beshem Kodsho
Yismach Lev Mevakshei Adonai. Dirshu Adonai Ve'uzo Bakeshu
Fanav Tamid. Zichru Nifle'otav Asher Asah Mofetav Umishpetei
Fihu. Zera Yisra'el Avdo Benei Ya'akov Bechirav: Hu Adonai
Eloheinu Bechol Ha'aretz Mishpatav. Zichru Le'olam Berito Davar
Tzivah Le'elef Dor. Asher Karat Et Avraham Ushevu'ato Leyitzchak.
Vaya'amideha Leya'akov Lechok Leyisra'el Berit Olam. Lemor Lecha
Etten Eretz Kena'an Chevel Nachalatchem. Bihyotechem Metei
Mispar Kim'at Vegarim Bah. Vayithallechu Migoy El Goy
Umimamlachah El Am Acher. Lo Hiniach Le'ish Le'oshkam
Vayochach Aleihem Melachim. Al She'Adonai Bimshichai Uvinvi'ai
Al Tare'u.

Give thanks to Hashem, call on His name; make known His deeds
among the peoples. Sing to Him, sing praises to Him; speak of all
His wonders. Take pride in His holy name; let the heart of those
who seek Hashem rejoice. Inquire of Hashem and His might; seek
His presence continually. Remember the wonders He has done, His
marvels, and the judgments He decreed, descendants of Yisrael -
His servant, children of Yaakov, His chosen. He is Hashem our God;
His judgments are over all the earth. Remember His covenant
forever, the word which He pledged for a thousand generations, the
covenant He made with Avraham, and His oath to Yitzchak. He
confirmed the same to Yaakov as a statute, to Yisrael as an

everlasting covenant, saying: "To you I give the land of Canaan as the portion of your possession." While they were but a few men, very few and strangers in it, when they went about from nation to nation and from realm to realm, He permitted no man to oppress them, and warned kings concerning them: "Do not touch my anointed, and do not harm my prophets."

שִׁירוּ לַיהוָה כָּל־הָאָרֶץ בַּשְּׂרוּ מִיּוֹם־אֶל־יוֹם יְשׁוּעָתוֹ: סַפְּרוּ בַגּוֹיִם אֶת־כְּבוֹדוֹ בְּכָל־הָעַמִּים נִפְלְאוֹתָיו: כִּי גָדוֹל יְהוָה וּמְהֻלָּל מְאֹד וְנוֹרָא הוּא עַל־כָּל־אֱלֹהִים: כִּי כָּל־אֱלֹהֵי הָעַמִּים אֱלִילִים יפסיק מעט וַיהוָה שָׁמַיִם עָשָׂה: הוֹד וְהָדָר לְפָנָיו עֹז וְחֶדְוָה בִּמְקֹמוֹ: הָבוּ לַיהוָה מִשְׁפְּחוֹת עַמִּים הָבוּ לַיהוָה כָּבוֹד וָעֹז: הָבוּ לַיהוָה כְּבוֹד שְׁמוֹ שְׂאוּ מִנְחָה וּבֹאוּ לְפָנָיו הִשְׁתַּחֲווּ לַיהוָה בְּהַדְרַת־קֹדֶשׁ: חִילוּ מִלְּפָנָיו כָּל־הָאָרֶץ אַף־תִּכּוֹן תֵּבֵל בַּל־תִּמּוֹט: יִשְׂמְחוּ הַשָּׁמַיִם וְתָגֵל הָאָרֶץ וְיֹאמְרוּ בַגּוֹיִם יְהוָה מָלָךְ: יִרְעַם הַיָּם וּמְלֹאוֹ יַעֲלֹץ הַשָּׂדֶה וְכָל־אֲשֶׁר־בּוֹ: אָז יְרַנְּנוּ עֲצֵי הַיָּעַר מִלִּפְנֵי יְהוָה כִּי־בָא לִשְׁפּוֹט אֶת־הָאָרֶץ: הוֹדוּ לַיהוָה כִּי טוֹב כִּי לְעוֹלָם חַסְדּוֹ: וְאִמְרוּ הוֹשִׁיעֵנוּ אֱלֹהֵי יִשְׁעֵנוּ וְקַבְּצֵנוּ וְהַצִּילֵנוּ מִן־הַגּוֹיִם לְהֹדוֹת לְשֵׁם קָדְשֶׁךָ לְהִשְׁתַּבֵּחַ בִּתְהִלָּתֶךָ: בָּרוּךְ יְהוָה אֱלֹהֵי יִשְׂרָאֵל מִן־הָעוֹלָם וְעַד הָעֹלָם וַיֹּאמְרוּ כָל־הָעָם אָמֵן וְהַלֵּל לַיהוָה:

Shiru L'Adonai Chol-Ha'aretz. Baseru Miyom-'El-Yom Yeshu'ato. Saperu Vagoyim Et-Kevodo. Bechol-Ha'ammim Nifle'otav. Ki Gadol Adonai Umehulal Me'od. Venora Hu Al-Chol-'Elohim. Ki Chol-'Elohei Ha'ammim Elilim. [pause slightly] Va'Adonai Shamayim Asah. Hod Vehadar Lefanav. Oz Vechedvah Bimkomo. Havu L'Adonai Mishpechot Ammim. Havu L'Adonai Kavod Va'oz. Havu L'Adonai Kevod Shemo; Se'u Minchah Uvo'u Lefanav. Hishtachavu L'Adonai Behadrat-Kodesh. Chilu Millefanav Chol-Ha'aretz. Af-Tikon Tevel Bal-Timot. Yismechu Hashamayim Vetagel Ha'aretz. Veyomeru Vagoyim Adonai Malach. Yir'am Hayam Umelo'o. Ya'alotz Hassadeh Vechol-'Asher-Bo. Az Yeranenu Atzei Haya'ar; Millifnei Adonai Ki-Va Lishpot Et-Ha'aretz. Hodu L'Adonai Ki Tov. Ki Le'olam

Chasdo. Ve'imru Hoshi'enu Elohei Yish'enu, Vekabetzenu
Vehatzileinu Min-Hagoyim; Lehodot Leshem Kodshecha.
Lehishtabe'ach Bit'hilatecha. Baruch Adonai Elohei Yisra'el. Min-
Ha'olam Ve'ad Ha'olam; Vayomeru Chol-Ha'am Amen. Vehallel
L'Adonai.

Sing to Hashem, all the earth; proclaim His salvation day after day.
Recount His glory among the nations, and His wonders among all
the peoples. For great is Hashem and most worthy of praise; He is
to be feared above all gods. For all the gods of the peoples are mere
idols, but [pause slightly] Hashem made the heavens. Majesty and beauty
are in His presence; strength and joy are in His Sanctuary. Ascribe to
Hashem, families of peoples, ascribe to Hashem glory and strength.
Give to Hashem the honor due to His name; bring an offering and
come before him; worship Hashem in holy array. Tremble before
Him, all the earth; indeed, the world is firm that it cannot be shaken.
Let the heavens rejoice, let the earth rejoice, and let them say
among the nations: "Hashem is King!" Let the sea and its fullness
roar; let the field and all that is within rejoice. Then let the trees of
the forest sing before Hashem, Who comes to rule the world. Praise
Hashem, for He is good; for His kindness endures forever. And say:
"Save us, God of our salvation, gather us and deliver us from the
nations, to give thanks to Your holy name, to glory in Your praise."
Blessed is Hashem, the God of Yisrael, from eternity to eternity.
Then all the people said "Amen" and praised Hashem.

רוֹמְמוּ יְהֹוָה אֱלֹהֵינוּ וְהִשְׁתַּחֲווּ לַהֲדֹם רַגְלָיו קָדוֹשׁ הוּא: רוֹמְמוּ
יְהֹוָה אֱלֹהֵינוּ וְהִשְׁתַּחֲווּ לְהַר קָדְשׁוֹ כִּי־קָדוֹשׁ יְהֹוָה אֱלֹהֵינוּ: וְהוּא
רַחוּם יְכַפֵּר עָוֹן וְלֹא יַשְׁחִית וְהִרְבָּה לְהָשִׁיב אַפּוֹ וְלֹא יָעִיר כָּל
חֲמָתוֹ: אַתָּה יְהֹוָה לֹא־תִכְלָא רַחֲמֶיךָ מִמֶּנִּי חַסְדְּךָ וַאֲמִתְּךָ תָּמִיד
יִצְּרוּנִי: זְכֹר־רַחֲמֶיךָ יְהֹוָה וַחֲסָדֶיךָ כִּי מֵעוֹלָם הֵמָּה: תְּנוּ עֹז
לֵאלֹהִים עַל־יִשְׂרָאֵל גַּאֲוָתוֹ וְעֻזּוֹ בַּשְּׁחָקִים: נוֹרָא אֱלֹהִים מִמִּקְדָּשֶׁיךָ
אֵל יִשְׂרָאֵל הוּא נֹתֵן עֹז וְתַעֲצֻמוֹת לָעָם בָּרוּךְ אֱלֹהִים:

Romemu Adonai Eloheinu. Vehishtachavu Lahadom Raglav. Kadosh
Hu. Romemu Adonai Eloheinu. Vehishtachavu Lehar Kodsho; Ki-
Kadosh. Adonai Eloheinu. Vehu Rachum Yechapeir Avon Velo
Yashchit Vehirbah Lehashiv Appo Velo Ya'ir Kol Chamato. Attah
Adonai Lo-Tichla Rachameicha Mimeni; Chasdecha Va'amitecha.
Tamid Yitzeruni. Zechor-Rachameicha Adonai Vachasadeicha; Ki
Me'olam Hemah. Tenu Oz. Lelohim Al-Yisra'el Ga'avato; Ve'uzo.
Bashechakim. Nora Elohim. Mimikdasheicha El Yisra'el. Hu Noten
Oz Veta'atzumot La'am. Baruch Elohim.

Exalt Hashem our God, and worship at His footstool—holy is He.
Exalt Hashem our God, and worship at His holy mountain, for holy
is Hashem our God. He, being merciful, forgives iniquity, and does
not destroy; frequently He turns His anger away, and does not stir
up all His wrath. You, Hashem, will not hold back Your mercy from
me; Your kindness and Your faithfulness will always protect me.
Remember Your mercy, Hashem, and Your kindness, for they have
been since eternity. Give honor to God, Whose majesty is over
Yisrael, whose glory is in the skies. Feared are You, Hashem, from
Your Sanctuary; the God of Yisrael gives strength and power to His
people. Blessed is God.

El-Nekamot

אֵל־נְקָמוֹת יְהֹוָה אֵל נְקָמוֹת הוֹפִיעַ: הִנָּשֵׂא שֹׁפֵט הָאָרֶץ הָשֵׁב
גְּמוּל עַל־גֵּאִים: לַיהֹוָה הַיְשׁוּעָה עַל־עַמְּךָ בִרְכָתֶךָ סֶּלָה: יְהֹוָה
צְבָאוֹת עִמָּנוּ מִשְׂגָּב־לָנוּ אֱלֹהֵי יַעֲקֹב סֶלָה: יְהֹוָה צְבָאוֹת אַשְׁרֵי
אָדָם בֹּטֵחַ בָּךְ: יְהֹוָה הוֹשִׁיעָה הַמֶּלֶךְ יַעֲנֵנוּ בְיוֹם־קָרְאֵנוּ: הוֹשִׁיעָה |
אֶת־עַמֶּךָ וּבָרֵךְ אֶת־נַחֲלָתֶךָ וּרְעֵם וְנַשְּׂאֵם עַד־הָעוֹלָם: נַפְשֵׁנוּ חִכְּתָה
לַיהֹוָה עֶזְרֵנוּ וּמָגִנֵּנוּ הוּא: כִּי־בוֹ יִשְׂמַח לִבֵּנוּ כִּי בְשֵׁם קָדְשׁוֹ
בָטָחְנוּ: יְהִי־חַסְדְּךָ יְהֹוָה עָלֵינוּ כַּאֲשֶׁר יִחַלְנוּ לָךְ: הַרְאֵנוּ יְהֹוָה
חַסְדֶּךָ וְיֶשְׁעֲךָ תִּתֶּן־לָנוּ: קוּמָה עֶזְרָתָה לָּנוּ וּפְדֵנוּ לְמַעַן חַסְדֶּךָ:
אָנֹכִי | יְהֹוָה אֱלֹהֶיךָ הַמַּעַלְךָ מֵאֶרֶץ מִצְרָיִם הַרְחֶב־פִּיךָ וַאֲמַלְאֵהוּ:

אַשְׁרֵי הָעָם שֶׁכָּכָה לּוֹ אַשְׁרֵי הָעָם שֶׁיהֹוָה אֱלֹהָיו: וַאֲנִי | בְּחַסְדְּךָ
בָטַחְתִּי יָגֵל לִבִּי בִּישׁוּעָתֶךָ אָשִׁירָה לַיהֹוָה כִּי גָמַל עָלָי:

El-Nekamot Adonai El Nekamot Hofia. Hinasei Shofet Ha'aretz;
Hasheiv Gemul. Al-Ge'im. L'Adonai Hayshu'ah; Al-'Ammecha
Virchatecha Selah. Adonai Tzeva'ot Imanu; Misgav-Lanu Elohei
Ya'akov Selah. Adonai Tzeva'ot; Ashrei Adam. Boteach Bach.
Adonai Hoshi'ah; Hamelech. Ya'aneinu Veyom-Kor'enu. Hoshi'ah
Et-'Ammecha. Uvarech Et-Nachalatecha; Ure'em Venasse'em. Ad-
Ha'olam. Nafshenu Chiketah L'Adonai Ezrenu Umaginenu Hu. Ki-
Vo Yismach Libenu; Ki Veshem Kodsho Vatachenu. Yehi-Chasdecha
Adonai Aleinu; Ka'asher. Yichalnu Lach. Har'enu Adonai
Chasdecha; Veyesh'acha. Titen-Lanu. Kumah Ezratah Lanu;
Ufedenu. Lema'an Chasdecha. Anochi Adonai Eloheicha.
Hama'alcha Me'eretz Mitzrayim; Harchev-Picha Va'amal'ehu.
Ashrei Ha'am Shekachah Lo; Ashrei Ha'am. She'Adonai Elohav.
Va'ani Bechasdecha Vatachti Yagel Libi. Bishu'atecha Ashirah
L'Adonai Ki Gamal Alai:

God of vengeance, Hashem, God of vengeance, appear. Arise,
Judge of the world, and render to the arrogant what they deserve.
Salvation belongs to Hashem; May Your blessing be upon Your
people. Hashem of hosts is with us; the God of Yaakov is our
Stronghold. Hashem of hosts, happy is the man who trusts in You.
Hashem, save us; may the King answer us when we call. Save Your
people and bless Your heritage; tend them and sustain them forever.
Our soul waits for Hashem; He is our help and our shield. Indeed,
our heart rejoices in Him, for in His holy name we trust. May Your
kindness, Hashem, rest on us, as our hope rests in You. Show us
Your kindness, Hashem, and grant us Your salvation. Arise for our
help, and set us free for Your goodness' sake. I am Hashem your
God, Who brought you up from the land of Mitzrayim; open your
mouth and I will fill it. Happy is the people that is so situated; happy
is the people whose God is Hashem. I have trusted in Your kindness;
may my heart rejoice in Your salvation. I will sing to Hashem,
because He has treated me kindly.

Aromimchah

Psalms 30:2-13

אֲרוֹמִמְךָ יְהֹוָה כִּי דִלִּיתָנִי וְלֹא־שִׂמַּחְתָּ אֹיְבַי לִי: יְהֹוָה אֱלֹהַי שִׁוַּעְתִּי
אֵלֶיךָ וַתִּרְפָּאֵנִי: יְהֹוָה הֶעֱלִיתָ מִן־שְׁאוֹל נַפְשִׁי חִיִּיתַנִי מיורדי
(מִיָּרְדִי)־בוֹר: זַמְּרוּ לַיהֹוָה חֲסִידָיו וְהוֹדוּ לְזֵכֶר קָדְשׁוֹ: כִּי רֶגַע |
בְּאַפּוֹ חַיִּים בִּרְצוֹנוֹ בָּעֶרֶב יָלִין בֶּכִי וְלַבֹּקֶר רִנָּה: וַאֲנִי אָמַרְתִּי
בְשַׁלְוִי בַּל־אֶמּוֹט לְעוֹלָם: יְהֹוָה בִּרְצוֹנְךָ הֶעֱמַדְתָּה לְהַרְרִי עֹז
הִסְתַּרְתָּ פָנֶיךָ הָיִיתִי נִבְהָל: אֵלֶיךָ יְהֹוָה אֶקְרָא וְאֶל־אֲדֹנָי אֶתְחַנָּן:
מַה־בֶּצַע בְּדָמִי בְּרִדְתִּי אֶל שָׁחַת הֲיוֹדְךָ עָפָר הֲיַגִּיד אֲמִתֶּךָ:
שְׁמַע־יְהֹוָה וְחָנֵּנִי יְהֹוָה הֱיֵה־עֹזֵר לִי: הָפַכְתָּ מִסְפְּדִי לְמָחוֹל לִי
פִּתַּחְתָּ שַׂקִּי וַתְּאַזְּרֵנִי שִׂמְחָה: לְמַעַן | יְזַמֶּרְךָ כָבוֹד וְלֹא יִדֹּם. יְהֹוָה
אֱלֹהַי לְעוֹלָם אוֹדֶךָ:

Aromimcha Adonai Ki Dillitani; Velo-Simachta Oyevai Li. Adonai
Elohai; Shiva'ti Eleicha. Vatirpa'eni. Adonai He'elita Min-She'ol
Nafshi; Chiyitani. Miyordi-Vor. Zameru L'Adonai Chasidav; Vehodu.
Lezecher Kodsho. Ki Rega' Be'appo Chayim Birtzono Ba'erev Yalin
Bechi. Velaboker Rinah. Va'ani Amarti Veshalvi; Bal-'Emot Le'olam.
Adonai Birtzonecha He'emadtah Lehareri Oz Histarta Faneicha.
Hayiti Nivhal. Eleicha Adonai Ekra; Ve'el-'Adonai. Etchanan. Mah-
Betza Bedami Beridti El Shachat Hayodecha Afar; Hayagid
Amitecha. Shema'-Adonai Vechoneni; Adonai Heyeh-'Ozeir Li.
Hafachta Mispedi Lemachol Li Pittachta Sakki; Vate'azereini
Simchah. Lema'an Yezamercha Chavod Velo Yidom; Adonai Elohai.
Le'olam Odeka.

I extol You, Hashem, for You have lifted me up, and have not let my
foes rejoice over me. Hashem my God, I cried to You, and You
healed me. Hashem, You have lifted me up from the grave; You have
let me live, that I should not go down to the grave. Sing to Hashem,
you who are godly, and give thanks to His holy name. For His anger
only lasts a moment, but His favor lasts a lifetime; weeping may
lodge with us at evening, but in the morning there are shouts of joy. I
thought in my security I never would be shaken. Hashem, by Your
favor You have established my mountain as a stronghold; but when

Your favor was withdrawn, I was dismayed. To You, Hashem, I called; I appealed to my God: "What profit would my death be, if I went down to the grave? Will the dust praise You? Will it declare Your faithfulness? Hear, Hashem, and be gracious to me; Hashem, be my helper." You have changed my mourning into dancing; You have stripped my sackcloth and girded me with joy; so that my soul may praise You, and not be silent. Hashem my God, I will thank You forever.

Stand for Adonai Melech until after saying the words "Ushemo Echad". (Kaf HaChayim 50:8)

Adonai Melech / Hashem is King

On the Days of Awe (Rosh Hashanah to Yom Kippur) and on Hoshanah Rabbah one chants this twice:

יְהֹוָה הוּא הָאֱלֹהִים:

Adonai Hu Ha'Elohim.
Hashem, He is God.

Adonai Melech. Adonai Malach Adonai Yimloch Le'olam Va'ed.

יְהֹוָה מֶלֶךְ. יְהֹוָה מָלָךְ יְהֹוָה | יִמְלֹךְ לְעֹלָם וָעֶד:

Hashem is King, Hashem was King, Hashem will be King forever and ever.

Adonai Melech. Adonai Malach Adonai Yimloch Le'olam Va'ed.

יְהֹוָה מֶלֶךְ. יְהֹוָה מָלָךְ יְהֹוָה | יִמְלֹךְ לְעֹלָם וָעֶד:

Hashem is King, Hashem was King, Hashem will be King forever and ever.

וְהָיָה יְהֹוָה לְמֶלֶךְ עַל־כָּל־הָאָרֶץ בַּיּוֹם הַהוּא יִהְיֶה יְהֹוָה אֶחָד וּשְׁמוֹ אֶחָד:

Vehayah Adonai Lemelech Al-Chol-Ha'aretz; Bayom Hahu. Yihyeh Adonai Echad Ushemo Echad.

"Hashem will be King over all the earth; and on that day Hashem will be One and His name One." (Zech. 14:9)

Stand until here.

הוֹשִׁיעֵנוּ | יְהֹוָה אֱלֹהֵינוּ וְקַבְּצֵנוּ מִן־הַגּוֹיִם לְהֹדוֹת לְשֵׁם קָדְשֶׁךָ לְהִשְׁתַּבֵּחַ בִּתְהִלָּתֶךָ: בָּרוּךְ יְהֹוָה אֱלֹהֵי יִשְׂרָאֵל מִן־הָעוֹלָם | וְעַד הָעוֹלָם וְאָמַר כָּל־הָעָם אָמֵן הַלְלוּיָהּ: כֹּל הַנְּשָׁמָה תְּהַלֵּל יָהּ הַלְלוּיָהּ:

Hoshi'enu Adonai Eloheinu. Vekabetzeinu Min-Hagoyim Lehodot
Leshem Kodshecha; Lehishtabe'ach. Bit'hilatecha. Baruch Adonai
Elohei Yisra'el Min-Ha'olam Ve'ad Ha'olam. Ve'amar Chol-Ha'am
Amen. Halleluyah. Kol Haneshamah Tehallel Yah. Halleluyah.

Save us, Hashem our God, and gather us from among the nations to
praise Your holy name and triumph in Your praise. Blessed is
Hashem God of Yisrael from everlasting to everlasting, and let all
the people say Amen, Halleluyah. (Psalms 106:47-48) Let every breath
praise Hashem, Halleluyah. (Psalms 150:6)

Psalms for Shabbat

Psalms 19

לַמְנַצֵּחַ מִזְמוֹר לְדָוִד: הַשָּׁמַיִם מְסַפְּרִים כְּבוֹד־אֵל וּמַעֲשֵׂה יָדָיו
מַגִּיד הָרָקִיעַ: יוֹם לְיוֹם יַבִּיעַ אֹמֶר וְלַיְלָה לְּלַיְלָה יְחַוֶּה־דָּעַת:
אֵין־אֹמֶר וְאֵין דְּבָרִים בְּלִי נִשְׁמָע קוֹלָם: בְּכָל־הָאָרֶץ | יָצָא קַוָּם
וּבִקְצֵה תֵבֵל מִלֵּיהֶם לַשֶּׁמֶשׁ שָׂם־אֹהֶל בָּהֶם: וְהוּא כְּחָתָן יֹצֵא
מֵחֻפָּתוֹ יָשִׂישׂ כְּגִבּוֹר לָרוּץ אֹרַח: מִקְצֵה הַשָּׁמַיִם | מוֹצָאוֹ וּתְקוּפָתוֹ
עַל־קְצוֹתָם וְאֵין נִסְתָּר מֵחַמָּתוֹ: תּוֹרַת יְהֹוָה תְּמִימָה מְשִׁיבַת נָפֶשׁ
עֵדוּת יְהֹוָה נֶאֱמָנָה מַחְכִּימַת פֶּתִי: פִּקּוּדֵי יְהֹוָה יְשָׁרִים מְשַׂמְּחֵי־לֵב
מִצְוַת יְהֹוָה בָּרָה מְאִירַת עֵינָיִם: יִרְאַת יְהֹוָה | טְהוֹרָה עוֹמֶדֶת לָעַד
מִשְׁפְּטֵי־יְהֹוָה אֱמֶת צָדְקוּ יַחְדָּו: הַנֶּחֱמָדִים מִזָּהָב וּמִפַּז רָב
וּמְתוּקִים מִדְּבַשׁ וְנֹפֶת צוּפִים: גַּם־עַבְדְּךָ נִזְהָר בָּהֶם בְּשָׁמְרָם עֵקֶב
רָב: שְׁגִיאוֹת מִי־יָבִין מִנִּסְתָּרוֹת נַקֵּנִי: גַּם מִזֵּדִים | חֲשֹׂךְ עַבְדֶּךָ
אַל־יִמְשְׁלוּ־בִי אָז אֵיתָם וְנִקֵּיתִי מִפֶּשַׁע רָב: יִהְיוּ לְרָצוֹן | אִמְרֵי־פִי
וְהֶגְיוֹן לִבִּי לְפָנֶיךָ יְהֹוָה צוּרִי וְגֹאֲלִי:

Lamnatzeach. Mizmor Ledavid. Hashamayim. Mesaperim Kevod-'El;
Uma'aseh Yadav. Maggid Harakia. Yom Leyom Yabbia Omer;
Velaylah Lelaylah. Yechaveh-Da'at. Ein-'Omer Ve'ein Devarim; Beli.
Nishma Kolam. Bechol-Ha'aretz Yatza Kavam. Uviktzeh Tevel
Milleihem; Lashemesh. Sam-'Ohel Bahem. Vehu. Kechaton Yotzei
Mechuppato; Yasis Kegibor. Larutz Orach. Miktzeh Hashamayim
Motza'o. Utekufato Al-Ketzotam; Ve'ein Nistar. Mechamato. Torat
Adonai Temimah Meshivat Nafesh; Edut Adonai Ne'emanah.
Machkimat Peti. Pikudei Adonai Yesharim Mesamechei-Lev; Mitzvat
Hashem Barah. Me'irat Einayim. Yir'at Hashem Tehorah Omedet
La'ad Mishpetei-Hashem Emet; Tzadeku Yachdav. Hanechemadim.
Mizahov Umipaz Rav; Umetukim Midevash. Venofet Tzufim.
Gam-'Avdecha Nizhar Bahem; Beshomram. Ekev Rav. Shegi'ot Mi-
Yavin; Ministarot Nakkeni. Gam Mizeidim Chasoch Avdecha. Al-
Yimshelu-Vi Az Eitam; Venikkeiti. Mippesha Rav. Yihyu Leratzon
Imrei-Fi Vehegyon Libi Lefaneicha; Adonai Tzuri Vego'ali.

For the Leader. A Psalm of David. The heavens declare the glory of God, and the firmament shows the work of His hands; Day to day utters speech, and night to night reveals knowledge; There is no speech, there are no words, neither is their voice heard. Their line is gone out through all the earth, and their words to the end of the world. In them He has set a tent for the sun, Which is as a bridegroom coming out of his chamber, and rejoices as a strong man to run his course. His going out is from the end of the heaven, and his circuit to the ends of it; and there is nothing hidden from the heat of it. The Torah of Hashem is perfect, restoring the soul; the testimony of Hashem is sure, making wise the simple. The precepts of Hashem are right, rejoicing the heart; the commandment of Hashem is pure, enlightening the eyes. The fear of Hashem is clean, enduring forever; the ordinances of Hashem are true, they are righteous altogether; More to be desired are they than gold, even than much fine gold; sweeter also than honey and the honeycomb. Also by them is Your servant warned; in keeping of them there is great reward. Who can discern his errors? Cleanse me from hidden faults. Keep back Your servant from presumptuous sins, that they may not have dominion over me; then I will be faultless, and I will be clear from great transgression. Let the words of my mouth and the meditation of my heart be acceptable before You, Hashem, my Rock, and my Redeemer.

Psalms 33

רַנְּנוּ צַדִּיקִים בַּיהוָה לַיְשָׁרִים נָאוָה תְהִלָּה: הוֹדוּ לַיהוָה בְּכִנּוֹר בְּנֵבֶל עָשׂוֹר זַמְּרוּ־לוֹ: שִׁירוּ־לוֹ שִׁיר חָדָשׁ הֵיטִיבוּ נַגֵּן בִּתְרוּעָה: כִּי־יָשָׁר דְּבַר־יְהוָה וְכָל־מַעֲשֵׂהוּ בֶּאֱמוּנָה: אֹהֵב צְדָקָה וּמִשְׁפָּט חֶסֶד יְהוָה מָלְאָה הָאָרֶץ: בִּדְבַר יְהוָה שָׁמַיִם נַעֲשׂוּ וּבְרוּחַ פִּיו כָּל־צְבָאָם: כֹּנֵס כַּנֵּד מֵי הַיָּם נֹתֵן בְּאֹצָרוֹת תְּהוֹמוֹת: יִירְאוּ מֵיְהוָה

כָּל־הָאָרֶץ מִמֶּנּוּ יָגוּרוּ כָּל־יֹשְׁבֵי תֵבֵל: כִּי הוּא אָמַר וַיֶּהִי הוּא־צִוָּה
וַיַּעֲמֹד: יְהֹוָה הֵפִיר עֲצַת־גּוֹיִם הֵנִיא מַחְשְׁבוֹת עַמִּים: עֲצַת יְהֹוָה
לְעוֹלָם תַּעֲמֹד מַחְשְׁבוֹת לִבּוֹ לְדֹר וָדֹר: אַשְׁרֵי הַגּוֹי אֲשֶׁר־יְהֹוָה
אֱלֹהָיו הָעָם | בָּחַר לְנַחֲלָה לוֹ: מִשָּׁמַיִם הִבִּיט יְהֹוָה רָאָה
אֶת־כָּל־בְּנֵי הָאָדָם: מִמְּכוֹן־שִׁבְתּוֹ הִשְׁגִּיחַ אֶל כָּל־יֹשְׁבֵי הָאָרֶץ:
הַיֹּצֵר יַחַד לִבָּם הַמֵּבִין אֶל־כָּל־מַעֲשֵׂיהֶם: אֵין־הַמֶּלֶךְ נוֹשָׁע
בְּרָב־חָיִל גִּבּוֹר לֹא־יִנָּצֵל בְּרָב־כֹּחַ: שֶׁקֶר הַסּוּס לִתְשׁוּעָה וּבְרֹב
חֵילוֹ לֹא יְמַלֵּט: הִנֵּה עֵין יְהֹוָה אֶל־יְרֵאָיו לַמְיַחֲלִים לְחַסְדּוֹ: לְהַצִּיל
מִמָּוֶת נַפְשָׁם וּלְחַיּוֹתָם בָּרָעָב: נַפְשֵׁנוּ חִכְּתָה לַיהֹוָה עֶזְרֵנוּ וּמָגִנֵּנוּ
הוּא: כִּי־בוֹ יִשְׂמַח לִבֵּנוּ כִּי בְשֵׁם קָדְשׁוֹ בָטָחְנוּ: יְהִי־חַסְדְּךָ יְהֹוָה
עָלֵינוּ כַּאֲשֶׁר יִחַלְנוּ לָךְ:

Ranenu Tzaddikim B'Adonai; Laisharim. Navah Tehilah. Hodu
L'Adonai Bechinor; Benevel Asor. Zameru-Lo. Shiru-Lo Shir
Chadash; Heitivu Naggen. Bitru'ah. Ki-Yashar Devar-Hashem
Vechol-Ma'asehu. Be'emunah. Ohev Tzedakah Umishpat; Chesed
Hashem Male'ah Ha'aretz. Bidvar Adonai Shamayim Na'asu;
Uveruach Piv Chol-Tzeva'am. Kones Kaned Mei Hayam; Noten
Be'otzarot Tehomot. Yire'u Me'Adonai Chol-Ha'aretz; Mimenu
Yaguru. Chol-Yoshevei Tevel. Ki Hu Amar Vayehi; Hu-Tzivah.
Vaya'amod. Adonai Hefir Atzat-Goyim; Heni. Machshevot Ammim.
Atzat Adonai Le'olam Ta'amod; Machshevot Libo. Ledor Vador.
Ashrei Hagoy Asher-Adonai Elohav; Ha'am Bachar Lenachalah Lo.
Mishamayim Hibit Adonai Ra'ah. Et-Chol-Benei Ha'adam.
Mimechon-Shivto Hishgiach; El Chol-Yoshevei Ha'aretz. Hayotzer
Yachad Libam; Hamevin. El-Chol-Ma'aseihem. Ein-Hamelech
Nosha Berov-Chayil; Gibor. Lo-Yinatzel Berov-Koach. Sheker
Hassus Litshu'ah; Uverov Cheilo. Lo Yemallet. Hineh Ein Adonai El-
Yere'av; Lamyachalim Lechasdo. Lehatzil Mimavet Nafsham;
Ulechayotam. Bara'av. Nafshenu Chiketah L'Adonai Ezrenu
Umaginenu Hu. Ki-Vo Yismach Libenu; Ki Veshem Kodsho
Vatachenu. Yehi-Chasdecha Adonai Aleinu; Ka'asher. Yichalnu Lach.

Rejoice in Hashem, you righteous, Praise is suitable for the upright.
Give thanks to Hashem with harp, Sing praises to Him with the
psaltery of ten strings. Sing to Him a new song; Play skillfully amid

shouts of joy. For the word of Hashem is upright; And all His work is done in faithfulness. He loves righteousness and justice; The earth is full of the lovingkindness of Hashem. By the word of Hashem the heavens were made; And all the host of them by the breath of His mouth. He gathers the waters of the sea together as a heap; He lays up the deeps in storehouses. Let all the earth fear Hashem; Let all the inhabitants of the world stand in awe of Him. For He spoke, and it was; He commanded, and it stood. Hashem brings the counsel of the nations to nothing; He makes the thoughts of the peoples of no effect. The counsel of Hashem stands forever, The thoughts of His heart to all generations. Happy is the nation whose God is Hashem; The people whom He has chosen for His own inheritance. Hashem looked from heaven; He beholds all the sons of men; From the place of His Habitation He looks intently on all the inhabitants of the earth; He that fashions the hearts of them all, That considers all their deeds. A king is not saved by the multitude of a host; A mighty man is not delivered by great strength. A horse is a vain thing for safety; Neither does it afford escape by its great strength. Behold, the eye of Hashem is toward them that fear Him, Toward them that wait for His mercy; To deliver their soul from death, And to keep them alive in famine. Our soul has waited for Hashem; He is our help and our shield. For in Him our heart rejoices, Because we have trusted in His holy name. Let Your mercy, Hashem, be upon us, According as we have waited for You.

Psalms 34

לְדָוִד בְּשַׁנּוֹתוֹ אֶת־טַעְמוֹ לִפְנֵי אֲבִימֶלֶךְ וַיְגָרֲשֵׁהוּ וַיֵּלַךְ: אֲבָרֲכָה אֶת־יְהֹוָה בְּכָל־עֵת תָּמִיד תְּהִלָּתוֹ בְּפִי: בַּיהֹוָה תִּתְהַלֵּל נַפְשִׁי יִשְׁמְעוּ עֲנָוִים וְיִשְׂמָחוּ: גַּדְּלוּ לַיהֹוָה אִתִּי וּנְרוֹמְמָה שְׁמוֹ יַחְדָּו: דָּרַשְׁתִּי אֶת־יְהֹוָה וְעָנָנִי וּמִכָּל־מְגוּרוֹתַי הִצִּילָנִי: הִבִּיטוּ אֵלָיו וְנָהָרוּ וּפְנֵיהֶם

אַל־יֶחְפָּרוּ: זֶה עָנִי קָרָא וַיהֹוָה שָׁמֵעַ וּמִכָּל־צָרוֹתָיו הוֹשִׁיעוֹ: חֹנֶה
מַלְאַךְ־יְהֹוָה סָבִיב לִירֵאָיו וַיְחַלְּצֵם: טַעֲמוּ וּרְאוּ כִּי־טוֹב יְהֹוָה אַשְׁרֵי
הַגֶּבֶר יֶחֱסֶה־בּוֹ: יְראוּ אֶת־יְהֹוָה קְדֹשָׁיו כִּי־אֵין מַחְסוֹר לִירֵאָיו:
כְּפִירִים רָשׁוּ וְרָעֵבוּ וְדֹרְשֵׁי יְהֹוָה לֹא־יַחְסְרוּ כָל־טוֹב: לְכוּ־בָנִים
שִׁמְעוּ־לִי יִרְאַת יְהֹוָה אֲלַמֶּדְכֶם: מִי־הָאִישׁ הֶחָפֵץ חַיִּים אֹהֵב יָמִים
לִרְאוֹת טוֹב: נְצֹר לְשׁוֹנְךָ מֵרָע וּשְׂפָתֶיךָ מִדַּבֵּר מִרְמָה: סוּר מֵרָע
וַעֲשֵׂה־טוֹב בַּקֵּשׁ שָׁלוֹם וְרָדְפֵהוּ: עֵינֵי יְהֹוָה אֶל־צַדִּיקִים וְאָזְנָיו
אֶל־שַׁוְעָתָם: פְּנֵי יְהֹוָה בְּעֹשֵׂי רָע לְהַכְרִית מֵאֶרֶץ זִכְרָם: צָעֲקוּ
וַיהֹוָה שָׁמֵעַ וּמִכָּל־צָרוֹתָם הִצִּילָם: קָרוֹב יְהֹוָה לְנִשְׁבְּרֵי־לֵב
וְאֶת־דַּכְּאֵי־רוּחַ יוֹשִׁיעַ: רַבּוֹת רָעוֹת צַדִּיק וּמִכֻּלָּם יַצִּילֶנּוּ יְהֹוָה:
שֹׁמֵר כָּל־עַצְמוֹתָיו אַחַת מֵהֵנָּה לֹא נִשְׁבָּרָה: תְּמוֹתֵת רָשָׁע רָעָה
וְשֹׂנְאֵי צַדִּיק יֶאְשָׁמוּ: פֹּדֶה יְהֹוָה נֶפֶשׁ עֲבָדָיו וְלֹא יֶאְשְׁמוּ
כָּל־הַחֹסִים בּוֹ:

Ledavid. Beshanoto Et-Ta'mo Lifnei Avimelech; Vaygareshehu.
Vayelach. Avarechah Et-Adonai Bechol-'Et; Tamid. Tehilato Befi.
Ba'Adonai Tit'hallel Nafshi; Yishme'u Anavim Veyismachu. Gadelu
L'Adonai Iti; Uneromemah Shemo Yachdav. Darashti Et-Adonai
Ve'anani; Umikol-Megurotai. Hitzilani. Hibitu Elav Venaharu;
Ufeneihem. Al-Yechparu. Zeh Ani Kara Va'Adonai Shamea';
Umikol-Tzarotav. Hoshi'o. Choneh Mal'ach-Adonai Saviv Lire'av.
Vaychalletzem. Ta'amu Ure'u Ki-Tov Adonai Ashrei Hagever.
Yecheseh-Bo. Yer'u Et-Adonai Kedoshav; Ki-'Ein Machsor. Lire'av.
Kefirim Rashu Vera'evu; Vedoreshei Adonai Lo-Yachseru Chol-Tov.
Lechu-Vanim Shim'u-Li; Yir'at Hashem Alamedchem. Mi-Ha'ish
Hechafetz Chayim; Ohev Yamim. Lir'ot Tov. Netzor Leshonecha
Mera'; Usefateicha. Midaber Mirmah. Sur Mero Va'aseh-Tov; Bakesh
Shalom Verodfehu. Einei Adonai El-Tzaddikim; Ve'oznav. El-
Shav'atam. Penei Adonai Be'osei Ra'; Lehachrit Me'eretz Zichram.
Tza'aku Va'Adonai Shamea'; Umikol-Tzarotam. Hitzilam. Karov
Hashem Lenishberei-Lev; Ve'et-Dake'ei-Ruach Yoshia. Rabot Ra'ot
Tzaddik; Umikulam. Yatzilenu Adonai Shomer Chol-'Atzmotav;
Achat Mehenah. Lo Nishbarah. Temotet Rasha Ra'ah; Vesone'ei
Tzaddik Ye'shamu. Podeh Adonai Nefesh Avadav; Velo Ye'shemu.
Chol-Hachosim Bo.

(A Psalm) of David; when he changed his demeanor before Avimelech, who drove him away, and he departed. I will bless Hashem at all times; His praise will continually be in my mouth. My soul will glory in Hashem; The humble will hear of it, and be glad. Magnify Hashem with me, And let us exalt His name together. I sought Hashem, and He answered me, And delivered me from all my fears. They looked to Him, and were radiant; And their faces will never be ashamed. This poor man cried, and Hashem heard, And saved him out of all his troubles. The angel of Hashem encamps around them that fear Him, And delivers them. Consider and see that Hashem is good; Happy is the man that takes refuge in Him. Fear Hashem, His holy ones; For there is no lack to them that fear Him. The young lions do lack, and suffer hunger; But they that seek Hashem do not lack any good thing. Come, you children, heed me; I will teach you the fear of Hashem. Who is the man that desires life, and loves days, That he may see good there in? Keep your tongue from evil, And your lips from speaking guile. Depart from evil, and do good; Seek peace, and pursue it. The eyes of Hashem are toward the righteous, And His ears are open unto their cry. The face of Hashem is against them that do evil, To cut off the remembrance of them from the earth. They cried, and Hashem heard, And delivered them out of all their troubles. Hashem is near to them that are of a broken heart, And saves such as are of a contrite spirit. Many are the ills of the righteous, But Hashem delivers him out of them all. He keeps all his bones; Not one of them is broken. Evil will kill the wicked; And they that hate the righteous will be held guilty. Hashem redeems the soul of His servants; And none of them that take refuge in Him will be desolate.

Psalms 90

תְּפִלָּה לְמֹשֶׁה אִישׁ־הָאֱלֹהִים אֲדֹנָי מָעוֹן אַתָּה הָיִיתָ לָּנוּ בְּדֹר וָדֹר:

בְּטֶרֶם | הָרִים יֻלָּדוּ וַתְּחוֹלֵל אֶרֶץ וְתֵבֵל וּמֵעוֹלָם עַד־עוֹלָם אַתָּה
אֵל: תָּשֵׁב אֱנוֹשׁ עַד־דַּכָּא וַתֹּאמֶר שׁוּבוּ בְנֵי־אָדָם: כִּי אֶלֶף שָׁנִים
בְּעֵינֶיךָ כְּיוֹם אֶתְמוֹל כִּי יַעֲבֹר וְאַשְׁמוּרָה בַלָּיְלָה: זְרַמְתָּם שֵׁנָה יִהְיוּ
בַּבֹּקֶר כֶּחָצִיר יַחֲלֹף: בַּבֹּקֶר יָצִיץ וְחָלָף לָעֶרֶב יְמוֹלֵל וְיָבֵשׁ:
כִּי־כָלִינוּ בְאַפֶּךָ וּבַחֲמָתְךָ נִבְהָלְנוּ: שַׁתָּ עֲוֹנֹתֵינוּ לְנֶגְדֶּךָ עֲלֻמֵנוּ
לִמְאוֹר פָּנֶיךָ: כִּי כָל־יָמֵינוּ פָּנוּ בְעֶבְרָתֶךָ כִּלִּינוּ שָׁנֵינוּ כְמוֹ־הֶגֶה:
יְמֵי־שְׁנוֹתֵינוּ בָהֶם שִׁבְעִים שָׁנָה וְאִם בִּגְבוּרֹת | שְׁמוֹנִים שָׁנָה
וְרָהְבָּם עָמָל וָאָוֶן כִּי־גָז חִישׁ וַנָּעֻפָה: מִי־יוֹדֵעַ עֹז אַפֶּךָ וּכְיִרְאָתְךָ
עֶבְרָתֶךָ: לִמְנוֹת יָמֵינוּ כֵּן הוֹדַע וְנָבִא לְבַב חָכְמָה: שׁוּבָה יְהֹוָה
עַד־מָתָי וְהִנָּחֵם עַל־עֲבָדֶיךָ: שַׂבְּעֵנוּ בַבֹּקֶר חַסְדֶּךָ וּנְרַנְּנָה וְנִשְׂמְחָה
בְּכָל־יָמֵינוּ: שַׂמְּחֵנוּ כִּימוֹת עִנִּיתָנוּ שְׁנוֹת רָאִינוּ רָעָה: יֵרָאֶה
אֶל־עֲבָדֶיךָ פָעֳלֶךָ וַהֲדָרְךָ עַל־בְּנֵיהֶם: וִיהִי | נֹעַם אֲדֹנָי אֱלֹהֵינוּ עָלֵינוּ
וּמַעֲשֵׂה יָדֵינוּ כּוֹנְנָה עָלֵינוּ וּמַעֲשֵׂה יָדֵינוּ כּוֹנְנֵהוּ:

Tefillah Lemosheh Ish-Ha' Elohim Adonai. Ma'on Attah Hayita Lanu.
Bedor Vador. Beterem Harim Yulladu. Vatecholel Eretz Vetevel;
Ume'olam Ad-'Olam. Attah El. Tashev Enosh Ad-Daka; Vatomer.
Shuvu Venei-'Adam. Ki Elef Shanim Be'eineicha. Keyom Etmol Ki
Ya'avor; Ve'ashmurah Valailah. Zeramtom Shenah Yihyu; Baboker.
Kechatzir Yachalof. Baboker Yatzitz Vechalaf; La'erev. Yemolel
Veyavesh. Ki-Chalinu Ve'apecha; Uvachamatecha Nivhalenu. Shata
Avonoteinu Lenegdecha; Alumenu. Lim'or Paneicha. Ki Chol-
Yameinu Panu Ve'evratecha; Killinu Shaneinu Chemo-Hegeh. Yemei-
Shenoteinu Vahem Shiv'im Shanah Ve'im Bigvurot Shemonim
Shanah. Verohbom Amal Va'aven; Ki-Gaz Chish Vana'ufah. Mi-
Yodea Oz Apecha; Ucheyir'atecha. Evratecha. Limnot Yameinu Ken
Hoda'; Venavi. Levav Chochmah. Shuvah Hashem Ad-Matai;
Vehinachem. Al-'Avadeicha. Sabe'einu Vaboker Chasdecha;
Uneranenah Venismechah. Bechol-Yameinu. Samecheinu Kimot
Initanu; Shenot. Ra'inu Ra'ah. Yera'eh El-'Avadeicha Fo'olecha;
Vahadarecha. Al-Beneihem. Vihi No'am Adonai Eloheinu. Aleinu
Uma'aseh Yadeinu Konenah Aleinu; Uma'aseh Yadeinu. Konenehu.

A Prayer of Moshe, the man of God. Hashem, You have been our
dwelling-place in all generations. Before the mountains were

brought out, Or ever You had formed the earth and the world, even from everlasting to everlasting, You are God. You turn man to contrition; And say: 'Return, you children of men.' For a thousand years in Your sight are as yesterday when it is past, And as a watch in the night. You carry them away as with a flood; they are as a sleep; In the morning they are like grass which grows up. In the morning it flourishes, and grows up; In the evening it is cut down, and withers. For we are consumed in Your anger, And by Your wrath we are terrified. You have set our iniquities before You, Our secret sins in the light of Your countenance. For all our days are passed away in Your wrath; We bring our years to an end as a tale that is told. The days of our years are seventy, or even by reason of strength, eighty years; Yet, their pride is but travail and vanity; For it is speedily gone, and we fly away. Who knows the power of Your anger, And Your wrath according to the fear that is due to You? So teach us to number our days, That we may get us a heart of wisdom. Return, Hashem; how long? And may You repent concerning Your servants. Satisfy us in the morning with Your mercy; That we may rejoice and be glad all our days. Make us glad according to the days which You have afflicted us, According to the years which we have seen evil. Let Your work appear to Your servants, And Your glory upon their children. And may the graciousness of Hashem our God be on us; Establish also upon us the work of our hands; and the work of our hands, establish it.

Psalms 91

יֹשֵׁב בְּסֵתֶר עֶלְיוֹן בְּצֵל שַׁדַּי יִתְלוֹנָן: אֹמַר לַיהוָה מַחְסִי וּמְצוּדָתִי אֱלֹהַי אֶבְטַח־בּוֹ: כִּי הוּא יַצִּילְךָ מִפַּח יָקוּשׁ מִדֶּבֶר הַוּוֹת: בְּאֶבְרָתוֹ | יָסֶךְ לָךְ וְתַחַת־כְּנָפָיו תֶּחְסֶה צִנָּה וְסֹחֵרָה אֲמִתּוֹ: לֹא־תִירָא מִפַּחַד לָיְלָה מֵחֵץ יָעוּף יוֹמָם: מִדֶּבֶר בָּאֹפֶל יַהֲלֹךְ מִקֶּטֶב יָשׁוּד צָהֳרָיִם:

יִפֹּל מִצִּדְּךָ | אֶלֶף וּרְבָבָה מִימִינֶךָ אֵלֶיךָ לֹא יִגָּשׁ: רַק בְּעֵינֶיךָ תַבִּיט
וְשִׁלֻּמַת רְשָׁעִים תִּרְאֶה: כִּי־אַתָּה יְהֹוָה מַחְסִי עֶלְיוֹן שַׂמְתָּ מְעוֹנֶךָ:
לֹא־תְאֻנֶּה אֵלֶיךָ רָעָה וְנֶגַע לֹא־יִקְרַב בְּאָהֳלֶךָ: כִּי מַלְאָכָיו יְצַוֶּה־לָּךְ
לִשְׁמָרְךָ בְּכָל־דְּרָכֶיךָ: עַל־כַּפַּיִם יִשָּׂאוּנְךָ פֶּן־תִּגֹּף בָּאֶבֶן רַגְלֶךָ:
עַל־שַׁחַל וָפֶתֶן תִּדְרֹךְ תִּרְמֹס כְּפִיר וְתַנִּין: כִּי בִי חָשַׁק וַאֲפַלְּטֵהוּ
אֲשַׂגְּבֵהוּ כִּי־יָדַע שְׁמִי: יִקְרָאֵנִי | וְאֶעֱנֵהוּ עִמּוֹ־אָנֹכִי בְצָרָה אֲחַלְּצֵהוּ
וַאֲכַבְּדֵהוּ: אֹרֶךְ יָמִים אַשְׂבִּיעֵהוּ וְאַרְאֵהוּ בִּישׁוּעָתִי:

Yoshev Beseter Elyon; Betzel Shaddai. Yitlonan. Omar. L'Adonai
Machsi Umetzudati; Elohai. Evtach-Bo. Ki Hu Yatzilecha Mippach
Yakush. Midever Havot. Be'evrato Yasech Lach Vetachat-Kenafav
Techseh; Tzinah Vesocherah Amito. Lo-Tira Mipachad Lailah;
Mechetz. Ya'uf Yomam. Midever Ba'ofel Yahaloch; Miketev. Yashud
Tzohorayim. Yippol Mitzidecha Elef. Urevavah Miminecha; Eleicha.
Lo Yigash. Rak Be'eineicha Tabbit; Veshilumat Resha'im Tir'eh.
Ki-'Attah Adonai Machsi; Elyon. Samta Me'onecha. Lo-Te'uneh
Eleicha Ra'ah; Venega'. Lo-Yikrav Be'oholecha. Ki Mal'achav
Yetzaveh-Lach; Lishmorcha. Bechol-Deracheicha. Al-Kapayim
Yissa'unecha; Pen-Tiggof Ba'even Raglecha. Al-Shachal Vafeten
Tidroch; Tirmos Kefir Vetanin. Ki Vi Chashak Va'afalletehu;
Asagevehu. Ki-Yada Shemi. Yikra'eni Ve'e'enehu. Immo-'Anochi
Vetzarah; Achalletzehu. Va'achabedehu. Orech Yamim Asbi'ehu;
Ve'ar'ehu. Bishu'ati.

You that dwells in the shadow of the Most High, And abides in the
shadow of the Almighty; I will say of Hashem, Who is my refuge and
my fortress, My God, in Whom I trust, That He will deliver you from
the snare of the fowler, And from the harmful pestilence. He will
cover you with His wings, And under His wings you will take refuge;
His truth is a shield and a buckler. You will not be afraid of the terror
by night, or of the arrow that flies by day; Of the pestilence that
walks in darkness, or of the destruction that wastes at noon. A
thousand may fall at Your side, And ten thousand at Your right
hand; It will not come near you. Only with your eyes you will behold,
And see the recompense of the wicked. For you have made Hashem
your Habitation, Even the Most High, Who is my refuge. No evil will

happen to you, Neither will any plague come near to your tent. For He will give His angels charge over you, To keep you in all your ways. They will bear you upon their hands, Lest you dash your foot against a stone. You will tread upon the lion and asp; The young lion and the serpent you will trample under feet. Because he has set his love upon Me, therefore I will deliver him; I will set him on high, because he has known My name. He will call on Me, and I will answer him; I will be with him in trouble; I will rescue him, and bring him to honor. With long life I will satisfy him, And make Him behold My salvation.

Here during Yom Tov, one says a Psalm of the day for the corresponding Yom Tov: not located in this siddur. Refer to Yom Tov / Shalosh Regalim Siddur.

Psalms 98

מִזְמֹוֹר שִׁירוּ לַיהֹוָֹה | שִׁיר חָדָשׁ כִּי־נִפְלָאוֹת עָשָׂה הוֹשִׁיעָה־לּוֹ יְמִינוֹ וּזְרֹוֹעַ קָדְשֹׁוֹ: הוֹדִיעַ יְהֹוָה יְשׁוּעָתֹוֹ לְעֵינֵי הַגּוֹיִם גִּלָּה צִדְקָתֹוֹ: זָכַר חַסְדֹּוֹ | וֶאֱמוּנָתֹוֹ לְבֵית יִשְׂרָאֵל רָאוּ כָל־אַפְסֵי־אָרֶץ אֵת יְשׁוּעַת אֱלֹהֵינוּ: הָרִיעוּ לַיהֹוָה כָּל־הָאָרֶץ פִּצְחוּ וְרַנְּנוּ וְזַמֵּרוּ: זַמְּרוּ לַיהֹוָה בְּכִנֹּוֹר וְקֹוֹל זִמְרָה: בַּחֲצֹצְרֹוֹת וְקֹוֹל שׁוֹפָר הָרִיעוּ לִפְנֵי | הַמֶּלֶךְ יְהֹוָה: יִרְעַם הַיָּם וּמְלֹאֹו תֵּבֵל וְיֹשְׁבֵי בָהּ: נְהָרֹוֹת יִמְחֲאוּ־כָף יַחַד הָרִים יְרַנֵּנוּ: לִפְנֵי יְהֹוָה כִּי בָא לִשְׁפֹּט הָאָרֶץ יִשְׁפֹּט־תֵּבֵל בְּצֶדֶק וְעַמִּים בְּמֵישָׁרִים:

Mizmor Shiru L'Adonai Shir Chadash Ki-Nifla'ot Asah; Hoshi'ah-Lo Yemino. Uzeroa Kodsho. Hodia Adonai Yeshu'ato; Le'einei Hagoyim. Gillah Tzidkato. Zachar Chasdo Ve'emunato Leveit Yisra'el Ra'u Chol-'Afsei-'Aretz; Et Yeshu'at Eloheinu. Hari'u L'Adonai Chol-Ha'aretz; Pitzchu Veranenu Vezameru. Zameru L'Adonai Bechinor; Bechinor. Vekol Zimrah. Bachatzotzerot Vekol Shofar; Hari'u. Lifnei Hamelech Adonai Yir'am Hayom Umelo'o; Tevel. Veyoshevei Vah. Neharot Yimcha'u-Chaf; Yachad Harim Yeranenu. Lifnei Adonai Ki Va Lishpot Ha'aretz Yishpot-Tevel Betzedek; Ve'ammim. Bemeisharim.

A Psalm. Sing to Hashem a new song; For He has done marvelous things; His right hand, and His holy arm, has worked salvation for Him. Hashem has made His salvation known; His righteousness He revealed in the sight of the nations. He has remembered His mercy and His faithfulness toward the House of Yisrael; All the ends of the earth have seen the salvation of our God. Shout to Hashem, all the earth; Break out and sing for joy, yes, sing praises. Sing praises to Hashem with the harp; With the harp and the voice of melody. With trumpets and sound of the horn shout before the King, Hashem. Let the sea roar, and the fullness of it; The world, and they that dwell there in; Let the floods clap their hands; Let the mountains sing for joy together; Before Hashem, for He has come to judge the earth; He will judge the world with righteousness, And the peoples with equity.

Psalms 121

שִׁיר לַמַּעֲלוֹת אֶשָּׂא עֵינַי אֶל־הֶהָרִים מֵאַיִן יָבֹא עֶזְרִי: עֶזְרִי מֵעִם
יְהוָה עֹשֵׂה שָׁמַיִם וָאָרֶץ: אַל־יִתֵּן לַמּוֹט רַגְלֶךָ אַל־יָנוּם שֹׁמְרֶךָ: הִנֵּה
לֹא־יָנוּם וְלֹא יִישָׁן שׁוֹמֵר יִשְׂרָאֵל: יְהוָה שֹׁמְרֶךָ יְהוָה צִלְּךָ עַל־יַד
יְמִינֶךָ: יוֹמָם הַשֶּׁמֶשׁ לֹא־יַכֶּכָּה וְיָרֵחַ בַּלָּיְלָה: יְהוָה יִשְׁמָרְךָ מִכָּל־רָע
יִשְׁמֹר אֶת־נַפְשֶׁךָ: יְהוָה יִשְׁמָר־צֵאתְךָ וּבוֹאֶךָ מֵעַתָּה וְעַד־עוֹלָם:

Shir. Lama'alot Essa Einai El-Heharim; Me'ayin. Yavo Ezri. Ezri
Me'im Adonai Oseh. Shamayim Va'aretz. Al-Yiten Lamot Raglecha;
Al-Yanum. Shomerecha. Hineh Lo-Yanum Velo Yishan; Shomer.
Yisra'el. Adonai Shomerecha; Hashem Tzillecha. Al-Yad Yeminecha.
Yomam. Hashemesh Lo-Yakekah. Veyareach Balailah. Adonai
Yishmorcha Mikol-Ra'; Yishmor. Et-Nafshecha. Adonai Yishmor-
Tzetecha Uvo'echa; Me'attah. Ve'ad-'Olam.

A Song of Ascents. I will lift up my eyes to the mountains: From where will my help come? My help comes from Hashem, Who made heaven and earth. He will not suffer Your foot to be moved; He that keeps You will not slumber. Behold, He that keeps Yisrael neither slumbers or sleeps. Hashem is your Guardian; Hashem is Your shade on Your right hand. The sun will not harm you by day, or the moon by night. Hashem will keep you from all evil; He will keep your soul. Hashem will guard your going out and your coming in, From this time and forever.

Psalms 122

שִׁיר הַמַּעֲלוֹת לְדָוִד שָׂמַחְתִּי בְּאֹמְרִים לִי בֵּית יְהוָה נֵלֵךְ: עֹמְדוֹת הָיוּ רַגְלֵינוּ בִּשְׁעָרַיִךְ יְרוּשָׁלָ͏ִם: יְרוּשָׁלַ͏ִם הַבְּנוּיָה כְּעִיר שֶׁחֻבְּרָה־לָּהּ יַחְדָּו: שֶׁשָּׁם עָלוּ שְׁבָטִים שִׁבְטֵי־יָהּ עֵדוּת לְיִשְׂרָאֵל לְהֹדוֹת לְשֵׁם יְהוָה: כִּי שָׁמָּה | יָשְׁבוּ כִסְאוֹת לְמִשְׁפָּט כִּסְאוֹת לְבֵית דָּוִד: שַׁאֲלוּ שְׁלוֹם יְרוּשָׁלָ͏ִם יִשְׁלָיוּ אֹהֲבָיִךְ: יְהִי־שָׁלוֹם בְּחֵילֵךְ שַׁלְוָה בְּאַרְמְנוֹתָיִךְ: לְמַעַן אַחַי וְרֵעָי אֲדַבְּרָה־נָּא שָׁלוֹם בָּךְ: לְמַעַן בֵּית־יְהוָה אֱלֹהֵינוּ אֲבַקְשָׁה טוֹב לָךְ:

Shir Hama'alot Ledavid Samachti Be'omerim Li Beit Adonai Nelech. Omedot Hayu Ragleinu Bish'arayich Yerushalayim. Yerushalayim Habenuyah Ke'ir Shechuberah Lah Yachdav. Shesham Alu Shevatim Shivtei Yah Edut Leyisra'el Lehodot Leshem Adonai. Ki Shamah Yashevu Chis'ot Lemishpat Kis'ot Leveit David. Sha'alu Shelom Yerushalayim Yishlayu Ohavayich. Yehi Shalom Becheilech Shalvah Be'armenotayich. Lema'an Achai Vere'ai Adaberah Na Shalom Bach. Lema'an Beit Adonai Eloheinu Avakshah Tov Lach.

A Song of Ascents; of David. I rejoiced when they said to me: 'Let us go to the House of Hashem.' Our feet are standing within your gates, Yerushalayim; Yerushalayim, that is built as a city that is compact together; Where the tribes went up, even the tribes of Hashem, as a testimony to Yisrael, to give thanks to the name of Hashem. For there were set thrones for judgment, the thrones of the House of David. Pray for the peace of Yerushalayim; May they that love You prosper. Peace be within your walls, and prosperity within your palaces. For my brothers and companions' sakes, I will now say: 'Peace be within you.' For the sake of the House of Hashem our God I will seek your good.

Psalms 123

שִׁיר הַמַּעֲלוֹת אֵלֶיךָ נָשָׂאתִי אֶת־עֵינַי הַיֹּשְׁבִי בַּשָּׁמָיִם: הִנֵּה כְעֵינֵי
עֲבָדִים אֶל־יַד אֲדוֹנֵיהֶם כְּעֵינֵי שִׁפְחָה אֶל־יַד גְּבִרְתָּהּ כֵּן עֵינֵינוּ
אֶל־יְהֹוָה אֱלֹהֵינוּ עַד שֶׁיְּחָנֵּנוּ: חָנֵּנוּ יְהֹוָה חָנֵּנוּ כִּי־רַב שָׂבַעְנוּ בוּז:
רַבַּת שָׂבְעָה־לָּהּ נַפְשֵׁנוּ הַלַּעַג הַשַּׁאֲנַנִּים הַבּוּז לִגְאֵיוֹנִים:

Shir Hama'alot Eleicha Nasati Et Einai Hayoshevi Bashamayim.
Hineh Che'einei Avadim El Yad Adoneihem Ke'einei Shifchah El Yad
Gevirtah Ken Eineinu El Adonai Eloheinu Ad Sheyechonenu.
Chonenu Adonai Chonenu Ki Rav Sava'nu Vuz. Rabbat Save'ah Lah
Nafshenu Halla'ag Hasha'ananim Habbuz Lig'eyonim.

A Song of Ascents. To You I lift up my eyes, You that is enthroned in the heavens. Behold, as the eyes of servants to the hand of their master, As the eyes of a maiden to the hand of her mistress; So our eyes look to Hashem our God, until He is gracious to us. Be gracious to us, Hashem, be gracious to us; For we are fully sated with contempt. Our soul is full sated with the scorning of those that are at ease, And with the contempt of the proud oppressors.

Psalms 124

שִׁיר הַמַּעֲלוֹת לְדָוִד לוּלֵי יְהֹוָה שֶׁהָיָה לָנוּ יֹאמַר־נָא יִשְׂרָאֵל: לוּלֵי
יְהֹוָה שֶׁהָיָה לָנוּ בְּקוּם עָלֵינוּ אָדָם: אֲזַי חַיִּים בְּלָעוּנוּ בַּחֲרוֹת אַפָּם
בָּנוּ: אֲזַי הַמַּיִם שְׁטָפוּנוּ נַחְלָה עָבַר עַל־נַפְשֵׁנוּ: אֲזַי עָבַר עַל־נַפְשֵׁנוּ
הַמַּיִם הַזֵּידוֹנִים: בָּרוּךְ יְהֹוָה שֶׁלֹּא נְתָנָנוּ טֶרֶף לְשִׁנֵּיהֶם: נַפְשֵׁנוּ
כְּצִפּוֹר נִמְלְטָה מִפַּח יוֹקְשִׁים הַפַּח נִשְׁבָּר וַאֲנַחְנוּ נִמְלָטְנוּ: עֶזְרֵנוּ
בְּשֵׁם יְהֹוָה עֹשֵׂה שָׁמַיִם וָאָרֶץ:

Shir Hama'alot. LeDavid Lulei Adonai Shehayah Lanu; Yomar-Na
Yisra'el. Lulei Adonai Shehayah Lanu; Bekum Aleinu Adam. Azai
Chayim Bela'unu; Bacharot Appam Banu. Azai Hamayim Shetafunu;
Nachlah Avar Al-Nafshenu. Azai Avar Al-Nafshenu; Hamayim.
Hazeidonim. Baruch Adonai Shelo Netananu Teref Leshineihem.

Nafshenu. Ketzipor Nimletah Mippach Yokeshim Happach Nishbar.
Va'anachnu Nimlatenu. Ezrenu Beshem Adonai Oseh. Shamayim
Va'aretz.

A Song of Ascents; of David. 'If it had not been Hashem Who was
for us', Let Yisrael now say; 'If it had not been Hashem Who was for
us, When men rose up against us, Then they would have swallowed
us up alive, when their wrath was kindled against us; Then the
waters would have overwhelmed us, the stream would have gone
over our soul; Then the proud waters would have gone over our
soul.' Blessed is Hashem, Who has not given us as prey to their
teeth. Our soul is escaped as a bird out of the snare of the fowlers;
The snare is broken, and we escaped. Our help is in the name of
Hashem, Who made heaven and earth.

Psalms 135

הַלְלוּיָהּ | הַלְלוּ אֶת־שֵׁם יְהֹוָה הַלְלוּ עַבְדֵי יְהֹוָה: שֶׁעֹמְדִים בְּבֵית
יְהֹוָה בְּחַצְרוֹת בֵּית אֱלֹהֵינוּ: הַלְלוּיָהּ כִּי־טוֹב יְהֹוָה זַמְּרוּ לִשְׁמוֹ כִּי
נָעִים: כִּי־יַעֲקֹב בָּחַר לוֹ יָהּ יִשְׂרָאֵל לִסְגֻלָּתוֹ: כִּי אֲנִי יָדַעְתִּי כִּי־גָדוֹל
יְהֹוָה וַאֲדֹנֵינוּ מִכָּל־אֱלֹהִים: כֹּל אֲשֶׁר־חָפֵץ יְהֹוָה עָשָׂה בַּשָּׁמַיִם
וּבָאָרֶץ בַּיַּמִּים וְכָל־תְּהוֹמוֹת: מַעֲלֶה נְשִׂאִים מִקְצֵה הָאָרֶץ בְּרָקִים
לַמָּטָר עָשָׂה מוֹצֵא־רוּחַ מֵאוֹצְרוֹתָיו: שֶׁהִכָּה בְּכוֹרֵי מִצְרָיִם מֵאָדָם
עַד־בְּהֵמָה: שָׁלַח | אֹתוֹת וּמֹפְתִים בְּתוֹכֵכִי מִצְרָיִם בְּפַרְעֹה
וּבְכָל־עֲבָדָיו: שֶׁהִכָּה גּוֹיִם רַבִּים וְהָרַג מְלָכִים עֲצוּמִים: לְסִיחוֹן |
מֶלֶךְ הָאֱמֹרִי וּלְעוֹג מֶלֶךְ הַבָּשָׁן וּלְכֹל מַמְלְכוֹת כְּנָעַן: וְנָתַן אַרְצָם
נַחֲלָה נַחֲלָה לְיִשְׂרָאֵל עַמּוֹ: יְהֹוָה שִׁמְךָ לְעוֹלָם יְהֹוָה זִכְרְךָ
לְדֹר־וָדֹר: כִּי־יָדִין יְהֹוָה עַמּוֹ וְעַל־עֲבָדָיו יִתְנֶחָם: עֲצַבֵּי הַגּוֹיִם כֶּסֶף
וְזָהָב מַעֲשֵׂה יְדֵי אָדָם: פֶּה־לָהֶם וְלֹא יְדַבֵּרוּ עֵינַיִם לָהֶם וְלֹא יִרְאוּ:
אָזְנַיִם לָהֶם וְלֹא יַאֲזִינוּ אַף אֵין־יֶשׁ־רוּחַ בְּפִיהֶם: כְּמוֹהֶם יִהְיוּ

עֹשֵׂיהֶם כֹּל אֲשֶׁר־בֹּטֵחַ בָּהֶם: בֵּית יִשְׂרָאֵל בָּרְכוּ אֶת־יְהֹוָה בֵּית
אַהֲרֹן בָּרְכוּ אֶת־יְהֹוָה: בֵּית הַלֵּוִי בָּרְכוּ אֶת־יְהֹוָה יִרְאֵי יְהֹוָה בָּרְכוּ
אֶת־יְהֹוָה: בָּרוּךְ יְהֹוָה | מִצִּיּוֹן שֹׁכֵן יְרוּשָׁלָם הַלְלוּיָהּ:

Halleluyah Hallelu Et Shem Adonai Hallelu Avdei Adonai.
She'omedim Beveit Adonai Bechatzrot Beit Eloheinu. Hallelu Yah Ki
Tov Adonai Zameru Lishmo Ki Na'im. Ki Ya'akov Bachar Lo Yah
Yisra'el Lisgulato. Ki Ani Yada'ti Ki Gadol Adonai Va'adoneinu Mikol
Elohim. Kol Asher Chafetz Adonai Asah Bashamayim Uva'aretz
Bayamim Vechol Tehomot. Ma'aleh Nesi'im Miktzeh Ha'aretz
Berakim Lammatar Asah Motze Ruach Me'otzerotav. Shehikah
Bechorei Mitzrayim Me'adam Ad Behemah. Shalach Otot Umofetim
Betochechi Mitzrayim Befar'oh Uvechol Avadav. Shehikah Goyim
Rabim Veharag Melachim Atzumim. Lesichon Melech Ha'emori
Ule'og Melech Habashan Ulechol Mamlechot Kena'an. Venatan
Artzam Nachalah Nachalah Leyisra'el Ammo. Adonai Shimcha
Le'olam Adonai Zichrecha Ledor Vador. Ki Yadin Adonai Ammo
Ve'al Avadav Yitnecham. Atzabei Hagoyim Kesef Vezahav Ma'aseh
Yedei Adam. Peh Lahem Velo Yedaberu Einayim Lahem Velo Yir'u.
Oznayim Lahem Velo Ya'azinu Af Ein Yesh Ruach Befihem.
Kemohem Yihyu Oseihem Kol Asher Boteach Bahem. Beit Yisra'el
Barachu Et Adonai Beit Aharon Barachu Et Adonai. Beit Hallevi
Barachu Et Adonai Yir'ei Adonai Barachu Et Adonai. Baruch Adonai
Mitziyon Shochein Yerushalayim Halleluyah.

Halleluyah. Praise the name of Hashem; Give praise, servants of
Hashem, You that stand in the House of Hashem, In the courts of
the house of our God. Praise Hashem, for Hashem is good; Sing
praises to His name, for it is pleasant. For Hashem has chosen
Yaakov for Himself, And Yisrael for His own treasure. For I know
that Hashem is great, And that our Lord is above all powers.
Whatever Hashem pleased, that He has done, In heaven and in
earth, in the seas and in all deeps; Who causes the vapors to ascend
from the ends of the earth; He makes lightnings for the rain; He
brings the wind from out of His treasuries. Who struck the first-
born of Mitzrayim, Both of man and beast. He sent signs and
wonders into the midst of you, Mitzrayim, on Pharaoh, and on all
his servants. Who struck many nations, And slew mighty kings:

Sichon king of the Amorites, And Og king of Bashan, And all the kingdoms of Canaan; And gave their land for a heritage, a heritage to Yisrael His people. Hashem, Your name endures forever; Your memorial, Hashem, throughout all generations. For Hashem will judge His people, And relent concerning His servants. The idols of the nations are silver and gold, The work of men's hands. They have mouths, but they do not speak; They have eyes, but they do not see; They have ears, but they do not hear; Neither is there any breath in their mouths. They that make them will be like them; Yes, everyone that trusts in them. House of Yisrael, bless Hashem; House of Aharon, bless Hashem; House of Levi, bless Hashem; You that fear Hashem, bless Hashem. Blessed is Hashem out of Tziyon, Who dwells at Yerushalayim. Halleluyah.

Psalms 136

הוֹדוּ לַיהוָה כִּי־טוֹב כִּי לְעוֹלָם חַסְדּוֹ:

Hodu L'Adonai Ki Tov Ki Le'olam Chasdo.

Give thanks to Hashem, for He is good, For His mercy endures forever.

הוֹדוּ לֵאלֹהֵי הָאֱלֹהִים כִּי לְעוֹלָם חַסְדּוֹ:

Hodu Lelohei Ha'elohim Ki Le'olam Chasdo.

Give thanks to the God of gods, For His mercy endures forever.

הוֹדוּ לַאֲדֹנֵי הָאֲדֹנִים כִּי לְעֹלָם חַסְדּוֹ:

Hodu La'adonei Ha'adonim Ki Le'olam Chasdo.

Give thanks to the Lord of lords, For His mercy endures forever.

לְעֹשֵׂה נִפְלָאוֹת גְּדֹלוֹת לְבַדּוֹ כִּי לְעוֹלָם חַסְדּוֹ:

Le'oseh Nifla'ot Gedolot Levado Ki Le'olam Chasdo.

To Him Who alone does great wonders, For His mercy endures forever.

לְעֹשֵׂה הַשָּׁמַיִם בִּתְבוּנָה כִּי לְעוֹלָם חַסְדּוֹ:

Le'oseh Hashamayim Bitvunah Ki Le'olam Chasdo.

To Him that by understanding made the heavens, For His mercy endures forever.

לְרֹקַע הָאָרֶץ עַל־הַמָּיִם כִּי לְעוֹלָם חַסְדּוֹ:

Leroka Ha'aretz Al Hamayim Ki Le'olam Chasdo.

To Him that spread out the earth above the waters, For His mercy endures forever.

לְעֹשֵׂה אוֹרִים גְּדֹלִים כִּי לְעוֹלָם חַסְדּוֹ:

Le'oseh Orim Gedolim Ki Le'olam Chasdo.

To Him that made great lights, For His mercy endures forever.

אֶת־הַשֶּׁמֶשׁ לְמֶמְשֶׁלֶת בַּיּוֹם כִּי לְעוֹלָם חַסְדּוֹ:

Et Hashemesh Lememshelet Bayom Ki Le'olam Chasdo.

The sun to rule by day, For His mercy endures forever.

אֶת־הַיָּרֵחַ וְכוֹכָבִים לְמֶמְשְׁלוֹת בַּלַּיְלָה כִּי לְעוֹלָם חַסְדּוֹ:

Et Hayareach Vechochavim Lememshelot Balailah Ki Le'olam Chasdo.

The moon and stars to rule by night, For His mercy endures forever.

לְמַכֵּה מִצְרַיִם בִּבְכוֹרֵיהֶם כִּי לְעוֹלָם חַסְדּוֹ:

Lemakeh Mitzrayim Bivchoreihem Ki Le'olam Chasdo.

To Him that struck Mitzrayim in their first-born, For His mercy endures forever.

וַיּוֹצֵא יִשְׂרָאֵל מִתּוֹכָם כִּי לְעוֹלָם חַסְדּוֹ:

Vayotze Yisra'el Mitocham Ki Le'olam Chasdo.

And brought out Yisrael from among them, For His mercy endures forever.

בְּיָד חֲזָקָה וּבִזְרוֹעַ נְטוּיָה כִּי לְעוֹלָם חַסְדּוֹ:

Beyad Chazakah Uvizroa' Netuyah Ki Le'olam Chasdo.

With a strong hand, and with an outstretched arm, For His mercy endures forever.

לְגֹזֵר יַם־סוּף לִגְזָרִים כִּי לְעוֹלָם חַסְדּוֹ:

Legozeir Yam Suf Ligzarim Ki Le'olam Chasdo.

To Him Who divided the Sea of Reeds in two, For His mercy endures forever.

וְהֶעֱבִיר יִשְׂרָאֵל בְּתוֹכוֹ כִּי לְעוֹלָם חַסְדּוֹ:

Vehe'evir Yisra'el Betocho Ki Le'olam Chasdo.

And made Yisrael to pass through the midst of it, For His mercy endures forever.

וְנִעֵר פַּרְעֹה וְחֵילוֹ בְיַם־סוּף כִּי לְעוֹלָם חַסְדּוֹ:

Veni'er Par'oh Vecheilo Veyam Suf Ki Le'olam Chasdo.

But overthrew Pharaoh and his army in the Sea of Reeds, For His mercy endures forever.

לְמוֹלִיךְ עַמּוֹ בַּמִּדְבָּר כִּי לְעוֹלָם חַסְדּוֹ:

Lemolich Ammo Bamidbar Ki Le'olam Chasdo.

To Him that led His people through the wilderness, For His mercy endures forever.

לְמַכֵּה מְלָכִים גְּדֹלִים כִּי לְעוֹלָם חַסְדּוֹ:

Lemakeh Melachim Gedolim Ki Le'olam Chasdo.

To Him that struck great kings; For His mercy endures forever.

וַיַּהֲרֹג מְלָכִים אַדִּירִים כִּי לְעוֹלָם חַסְדּוֹ:

Vayaharog Melachim Adirim Ki Le'olam Chasdo.

And slew mighty kings, For His mercy endures forever.

לְסִיחוֹן מֶלֶךְ הָאֱמֹרִי כִּי לְעוֹלָם חַסְדּוֹ:

Lesichon Melech Ha'emori Ki Le'olam Chasdo.

Sichon king of the Amorites, For His mercy endures forever.

וּלְעוֹג מֶלֶךְ הַבָּשָׁן כִּי לְעוֹלָם חַסְדּוֹ:

Ule'og Melech Habashan Ki Le'olam Chasdo.

And Og king of Bashan, For His mercy endures forever.

וְנָתַן אַרְצָם לְנַחֲלָה כִּי לְעוֹלָם חַסְדּוֹ:

Venatan Artzam Lenachalah Ki Le'olam Chasdo.

And gave their land for a heritage, For His mercy endures forever.

נַחֲלָה לְיִשְׂרָאֵל עַבְדּוֹ כִּי לְעוֹלָם חַסְדּוֹ:

Nachalah Leyisra'el Avdo Ki Le'olam Chasdo.

Even a heritage to Yisrael His servant, For His mercy endures forever.

שֶׁבְּשִׁפְלֵנוּ זָכַר לָנוּ כִּי לְעוֹלָם חַסְדּוֹ:

Shebeshiflenu Zachar Lanu Ki Le'olam Chasdo.

Who remembered us in our low estate, For His mercy endures forever.

וַיִּפְרְקֵנוּ מִצָּרֵינוּ כִּי לְעוֹלָם חַסְדּוֹ:

Vayifrekenu Mitzareinu Ki Le'olam Chasdo.

And has delivered us from our adversaries, For His mercy endures forever.

נֹתֵן לֶחֶם לְכָל־בָּשָׂר כִּי לְעוֹלָם חַסְדּוֹ:

Noten Lechem Lechol Basar Ki Le'olam Chasdo.

Who gives food to all flesh, For His mercy endures forever.

הוֹדוּ לְאֵל הַשָּׁמָיִם כִּי לְעוֹלָם חַסְדּוֹ:

Hodu Le'el Hashamayim Ki Le'olam Chasdo.

Give thanks to the God of Heaven, For His mercy endures forever.

LAWS OF PESUKEI DEZIMRAH

If one finished Baruch She'amar prior to the prayer leader he should say Amen after the leader finishes. After Yishtabach one may say Amen after his own blessing. One must be cautious to refrain from talking from the moment he begins Baruch She'amar until after he concludes the Shemoneh Esrei. (The Amidah). In between these psalms one may ask [of the welfare of another] out of respect [and may reply greetings to any person. And in the middle of [one of] the psalms he may ask [of the welfare of another] out of fear and he may reply out of respect. We should not say these psalms in a hurry, but rather at a pleasant pace. One should not say the blessing on the wrapping of the tzitzit [i.e. tallit] between Pesukei DeZimrah and Yishtabach, rather, he should say it between Yishtabach and Yotzer Ohr. (SA, OC 52,55)

Pesukei DeZimrah / Verses of Praise

If one comes to synagogue and finds the congregation at the end of Pesukei Dezimrah, he should say all of Baruch She'amar, Ashrei, Ps. 148, Ps. 150, Yishtabach, and afterwards Yotzer Ohr, and the Shema and its blessings, and then pray with the congregation. And if he doesn't have much time, he should also skip Ps. 148. And if the congregation has already started with Yotzer and one does not have time to recite Pesukei Dezimrah even with skipping, he should recite the Shema and its blessings with the congregation and pray with them (the Amidah), and afterwards recite all of Pesukei D'zimrah without a blessing before or after. (SA, OC 52)

Some say:

כִּי גָבַר עָלֵינוּ | חַסְדֹּו וֶאֱמֶת־יְהֹוָה לְעוֹלָם הַלְלוּיָהּ: בָּרוּךְ הַמַּנְחִיל מְנוּחָה לְעַמּוֹ יִשְׂרָאֵל בְּיוֹם שַׁבַּת קֹדֶשׁ:

Ki Gavar Aleinu Chasdo. Ve'emet-Adonai Le'olam. Halleluyah. Baruch Hamanchil Menuchah Le'ammo Yisra'el Beyom Shabbat Kodesh.

For great is His mercy towards us; And the truth of Hashem endures forever. Halleluyah. **Psalms 117:2** Blessed is the Giver of rest to His people Yisrael on the holy day of Shabbat.

Baruch She'amar

One must be careful to refrain from talking from the beginning of Baruch She'amar until after he concludes the Amidah. (SA, OC 51) Some grasp the front two tzitzit while saying this prayer.

Stand and recite:

Baruch She'amar Vehayah	בָּרוּךְ שֶׁאָמַר וְהָיָה
Ha'olam. Baruch Hu. Baruch	הָעוֹלָם. בָּרוּךְ הוּא. בָּרוּךְ
Omer Ve'oseh. Baruch Gozeir	אוֹמֵר וְעוֹשֶׂה. בָּרוּךְ גּוֹזֵר
Umekayem. Baruch Oseh	וּמְקַיֵּם. בָּרוּךְ עוֹשֶׂה
Vereshit. Baruch Merachem Al	בְרֵאשִׁית. בָּרוּךְ מְרַחֵם עַל
Ha'aretz. Baruch Merachem Al	הָאָרֶץ. בָּרוּךְ מְרַחֵם עַל
Haberiyot. Baruch Meshalem	הַבְּרִיּוֹת. בָּרוּךְ מְשַׁלֵּם
Sachar Tov Lire'av. Baruch Chai	שָׂכָר טוֹב לִירֵאָיו. בָּרוּךְ חַי
La'ad Vekayam Lanetzach.	לָעַד וְקַיָּם לָנֶצַח.
Baruch Podeh Umatzil. Baruch	בָּרוּךְ פּוֹדֶה וּמַצִּיל. בָּרוּךְ
Shemo. Baruch Attah Adonai	שְׁמוֹ. בָּרוּךְ אַתָּה יְהֹוָה

Eloheinu Melech Ha'olam Ha'el.	אֱלֹהֵינוּ מֶלֶךְ הָעוֹלָם. הָאֵל.
Av Harachaman. Hamhulal	אָב הָרַחֲמָן. הַמְהֻלָּל
Befeh Ammo. Meshubach	בְּפֶה עַמּוֹ. מְשֻׁבָּח
Umefo'ar Bilshon Chasidav	וּמְפֹאָר בִּלְשׁוֹן חֲסִידָיו
Va'avadav. Uveshirei David	וַעֲבָדָיו. וּבְשִׁירֵי דָוִד
Avdach Nehalelach Adonai	עַבְדְּךָ נְהַלֶלְךָ יְהֹוָה
Eloheinu Bishvachot Uvizmirot.	אֱלֹהֵינוּ בִּשְׁבָחוֹת וּבִזְמִירוֹת.
Unegadelach Uneshabechach	וּנְגַדֶּלְךָ וּנְשַׁבֵּחָךָ
Unefa'arach Venamlichach.	וּנְפָאֶרְךָ וְנַמְלִיכָךְ.
Venazkir Shimcha Malkeinu	וְנַזְכִּיר שִׁמְךָ מַלְכֵּנוּ
Eloheinu. Yachid Chai	אֱלֹהֵינוּ. יָחִיד חַי
Ha'olamim. Melech Meshubach	הָעוֹלָמִים. מֶלֶךְ מְשֻׁבָּח
Umefo'ar Adei Ad Shemo	וּמְפֹאָר עֲדֵי עַד שְׁמוֹ
Hagadol. Baruch Attah Adonai	הַגָּדוֹל. בָּרוּךְ אַתָּה יְהֹוָה
Melech Mehulal Batishbachot.	מֶלֶךְ מְהֻלָּל בַּתִּשְׁבָּחוֹת:

Blessed is He Who spoke, and the world came into being; blessed is He. Blessed is He Who says and performs. Blessed is He Who decrees and fulfills. Blessed is He Who created the universe. Blessed is He Who has mercy on the world. Blessed is He Who has mercy on all creatures. Blessed is He Who grants a good reward to those who revere Him. Blessed is He Who lives forever and exists eternally. Blessed is He Who redeems and saves; blessed is His name. Blessed are You, Hashem our God, King of the universe, Oh God, merciful Father, Who is praised by the mouth of His people, lauded and glorified by the tongue of His faithful servants. With the songs, hymns and psalms, of Your servant David will we praise You, Hashem our God; we will exalt, extol, glorify, and proclaim You King; we will call upon Your name, our King, our God. You Who are One, the life of the universe, Oh King, praised and glorified is Your great name forever and ever. Blessed are You, Hashem, King extolled with hymns of praise.

If holding tzitzit, kiss and release them. If the person finished with the blessing that he said before the Chazan finishes, he should hurry to say the following Psalm immediately, and when the Chazan finishes will answer, Amen. One may now sit.

On Yom Tov that lands on a weekday, some skip the first verse:

Psalms 92

מִזְמוֹר שִׁיר לְיוֹם הַשַּׁבָּת: טוֹב לְהֹדוֹת לַיהוָה וּלְזַמֵּר לְשִׁמְךָ עֶלְיוֹן:
לְהַגִּיד בַּבֹּקֶר חַסְדֶּךָ וֶאֱמוּנָתְךָ בַּלֵּילוֹת: עֲלֵי־עָשׂוֹר וַעֲלֵי־נָבֶל עֲלֵי
הִגָּיוֹן בְּכִנּוֹר: כִּי שִׂמַּחְתַּנִי יְהוָה בְּפָעֳלֶךָ בְּמַעֲשֵׂי יָדֶיךָ אֲרַנֵּן:
מַה־גָּדְלוּ מַעֲשֶׂיךָ יְהוָה מְאֹד עָמְקוּ מַחְשְׁבֹתֶיךָ: אִישׁ־בַּעַר לֹא יֵדָע
וּכְסִיל לֹא־יָבִין אֶת־זֹאת: בִּפְרֹחַ רְשָׁעִים | כְּמוֹ עֵשֶׂב וַיָּצִיצוּ
כָּל־פֹּעֲלֵי אָוֶן לְהִשָּׁמְדָם עֲדֵי־עַד: וְאַתָּה מָרוֹם לְעֹלָם יְהוָה: כִּי הִנֵּה
אֹיְבֶיךָ | יְהוָה כִּי־הִנֵּה אֹיְבֶיךָ יֹאבֵדוּ יִתְפָּרְדוּ כָּל־פֹּעֲלֵי אָוֶן: וַתָּרֶם
כִּרְאֵים קַרְנִי בַּלֹּתִי בְּשֶׁמֶן רַעֲנָן: וַתַּבֵּט עֵינִי בְּשׁוּרָי בַּקָּמִים עָלַי
מְרֵעִים תִּשְׁמַעְנָה אָזְנָי: צַדִּיק כַּתָּמָר יִפְרָח כְּאֶרֶז בַּלְּבָנוֹן יִשְׂגֶּה:
שְׁתוּלִים בְּבֵית יְהוָה בְּחַצְרוֹת אֱלֹהֵינוּ יַפְרִיחוּ: עוֹד יְנוּבוּן בְּשֵׂיבָה
דְּשֵׁנִים וְרַעֲנַנִּים יִהְיוּ: לְהַגִּיד כִּי־יָשָׁר יְהוָה צוּרִי וְלֹא־עַלְתָה
(עוֹלָתָה) בּוֹ:

Mizmor Shir. Leyom Hashabbat. Tov. Lehodot L'Adonai Ulezamer Leshimcha Elyon. Lehagid Baboker Chasdecha; Ve'emunatecha. Balleilot. Alei-'Asor Va'alei-Navel; Alei Higayon Bechinor. Ki Simachtani Adonai Befo'olecha; Bema'asei Yadeicha Aranen. Mah-Gadelu Ma'aseicha Adonai Me'od. Ameku Machshevoteicha. Ish-Ba'ar Lo Yeda'; Uchesil. Lo-Yavin Et-Zot. Bifroach Resha'im Kemo Esev. Vayatzitzu Chol-Po'alei Aven; Lehishamedam Adei-'Ad. Ve'attah Marom. Le'olam Adonai Ki Hineh Oyeveicha Adonai Ki-Hineh Oyeveicha Yovedu; Yitparedu. Chol-Po'alei Aven. Vatarem Kir'eim Karni; Baloti. Beshemen Ra'anan. Vatabet Eini. Beshurai Bakamim Alai Mere'im. Tishma'nah Oznai. Tzaddik Kattamar

Yifrach; Ke'erez Ballevanon Yisgeh. Shetulim Beveit Adonai
Bechatzrot Eloheinu Yafrichu. Od Yenuvun Beseivah; Deshenim
Vera'ananim Yihyu. Lehagid Ki-Yashar Adonai Tzuri. Velo-Avlatah
Bo.

A Psalm, a Song. For the Shabbat day. It is a good thing to give
thanks to Hashem, And to sing praises to Your name, Most High; To
declare Your lovingkindness in the morning, And Your faithfulness
in the night seasons, With an instrument of ten strings, and with the
psaltery; With a solemn sound on the harp. For You, Hashem, have
made me glad through Your work; I will rejoice in the works of Your
hands. How great are Your works, Hashem. Your thoughts are very
deep. A brutish man doesn't know, Neither does a fool understand
this. When the wicked spring up as the grass, And when all the
workers of iniquity flourish; It is that they may be destroyed forever.
But You, Hashem, are on high forever. For, behold, Your enemies,
Hashem, For, behold, Your enemies will perish: All the workers of
iniquity will be scattered. But my horn You have exalted like the
horn of the wild-ox; I am anointed with rich oil. My eye has also
gazed on them that lie in wait for me, My ears have heard my desire
of the evil-doers that rise up against me. The righteous will flourish
like the palm-tree; He will grow like a cedar in Levanon. Planted in
the House of Hashem, They will flourish in the courts of our God.
They will still bring forth fruit in old age; They will be full of sap and
richness; To declare that Hashem is upright, My Rock, in Whom
there is no unrighteousness.

Psalms 93

יְהֹוָה מָלָךְ גֵּאוּת לָבֵשׁ לָבֵשׁ יְהֹוָה עֹז הִתְאַזָּר אַף־תִּכּוֹן תֵּבֵל
בַּל־תִּמּוֹט: נָכוֹן כִּסְאֲךָ מֵאָז מֵעוֹלָם אָתָּה: נָשְׂאוּ נְהָרוֹת | יְהֹוָה
נָשְׂאוּ נְהָרוֹת קוֹלָם יִשְׂאוּ נְהָרוֹת דָּכְיָם: מִקֹּלוֹת | מַיִם רַבִּים אַדִּירִים
מִשְׁבְּרֵי־יָם אַדִּיר בַּמָּרוֹם יְהֹוָה: עֵדֹתֶיךָ | נֶאֶמְנוּ מְאֹד לְבֵיתְךָ
נַאֲוָה־קֹדֶשׁ יְהֹוָה לְאֹרֶךְ יָמִים:

Adonai Maloch Ge'ut Lavesh Lavesh Adonai Oz Hit'azar; Af-Tikon
Tevel. Bal-Timot. Nachon Kis'acha Me'az; Me'olam Attah. Nase'u
Neharot Adonai Nase'u Neharot Kolam; Yis'u Neharot Dochyam.
Mikolot Mayim Rabim. Adirim Mishberei-Yam; Adir Bamarom
Adonai Edoteicha Ne'emnu Me'od. Leveitecha Na'avah-Kodesh;
Adonai Le'orech Yamim.

Hashem reigns; He is clothed in majesty; Hashem is clothed, He has
girded Himself with strength; The world is established, that it
cannot be moved. Your Throne is established from old; You are
from everlasting. The floods have lifted up, Hashem, the floods have
lifted up their voice; the floods lift up their roaring. Above the voices
of many waters, the mighty breakers of the sea, Hashem on high is
mighty. Your testimonies are very sure, holiness suits Your House,
Hashem, forever.

Yehi Chevod

יְהִי כְבוֹד יְהֹוָה לְעוֹלָם יִשְׂמַח יְהֹוָה בְּמַעֲשָׂיו: ר יְהִי שֵׁם יְהֹוָה
מְבֹרָךְ מֵעַתָּה וְעַד־עוֹלָם: · מִמִּזְרַח־שֶׁמֶשׁ עַד־מְבוֹאוֹ מְהֻלָּל שֵׁם
יְהֹוָה: ש רָם עַל־כָּל־גּוֹיִם | יְהֹוָה עַל הַשָּׁמַיִם כְּבוֹדוֹ: · יְהֹוָה שִׁמְךָ
לְעוֹלָם יְהֹוָה זִכְרְךָ לְדֹר־וָדֹר: ר יְהֹוָה בַּשָּׁמַיִם הֵכִין כִּסְאוֹ וּמַלְכוּתוֹ
בַּכֹּל מָשָׁלָה: ר יִשְׂמְחוּ הַשָּׁמַיִם וְתָגֵל הָאָרֶץ וְיֹאמְרוּ בַגּוֹיִם יְהֹוָה
מָלָךְ: ש יְהֹוָה מֶלֶךְ. יְהֹוָה מָלָךְ. יְהֹוָה | יִמְלֹךְ לְעֹלָם וָעֶד: · יְהֹוָה
מֶלֶךְ עוֹלָם וָעֶד אָבְדוּ גוֹיִם מֵאַרְצוֹ: ר יְהֹוָה הֵפִיר עֲצַת־גּוֹיִם הֵנִיא
מַחְשְׁבוֹת עַמִּים: · רַבּוֹת מַחֲשָׁבוֹת בְּלֶב־אִישׁ וַעֲצַת יְהֹוָה הִיא
תָקוּם: ש עֲצַת יְהֹוָה לְעוֹלָם תַּעֲמֹד מַחְשְׁבוֹת לִבּוֹ לְדֹר וָדֹר: · כִּי
הוּא אָמַר וַיֶּהִי הוּא־צִוָּה וַיַּעֲמֹד: ש כִּי־בָחַר יְהֹוָה בְּצִיּוֹן אִוָּהּ
לְמוֹשָׁב לוֹ: ר כִּי־יַעֲקֹב בָּחַר לוֹ יָהּ יִשְׂרָאֵל לִסְגֻלָּתוֹ: · כִּי | לֹא־יִטֹּשׁ
יְהֹוָה עַמּוֹ וְנַחֲלָתוֹ לֹא יַעֲזֹב: ר וְהוּא רַחוּם | יְכַפֵּר עָוֹן וְלֹא־יַשְׁחִית
וְהִרְבָּה לְהָשִׁיב אַפּוֹ וְלֹא־יָעִיר כָּל־חֲמָתוֹ: ש יְהֹוָה הוֹשִׁיעָה הַמֶּלֶךְ
יַעֲנֵנוּ בְיוֹם־קָרְאֵנוּ:

Yehi Chevod Adonai Le'olam; Yismach Adonai Bema'asav. Yehi
Shem Adonai Mevorach; Me'attah. Ve'ad-'Olam. Mimizrach-
Shemesh Ad-Mevo'o; Mehulal. Shem Adonai. Ram Al-Kol-Goyim
Adonai Al Hashamayim Kevodo. Adonai Shimcha Le'olam; Adonai
Zichrecha Ledor-Vador. Adonai Bashamayim Hechin Kis'o;
Umalchuto. Bakol Mashalah. Yismechu Hashamayim Vetagel
Ha'aretz. Veyomeru Vagoyim Adonai Malach. Adonai Melech.
Adonai Malach. Adonai Yimloch Le'olam Va'ed. Adonai Melech
Olam Va'ed; Avedu Goyim. Me'artzo. Adonai Hefir Atzat-Goyim;
Heni. Machshevot Ammim. Rabot Machashavot Belev-'Ish; Va'atzat
Adonai Hi Takum. Atzat Adonai Le'olam Ta'amod; Machshevot Libo.
Ledor Vador. Ki Hu Amar Vayehi; Hu-Tzivah. Vaya'amod. Ki-Vachar
Adonai Betziyon; Ivah. Lemoshav Lo. Ki-Ya'akov. Bachar Lo Yah;
Yisra'el. Lisgulato. Ki Lo-Yitosh Adonai Ammo; Venachalato. Lo
Ya'azov. Vehu Rachum Yechapeir Avon Velo-Yashchit Vehirbah
Lehashiv Appo; Velo-Ya'ir. Chol-Chamato. Adonai Hoshi'ah;
Hamelech. Ya'aneinu Veyom-Kor'enu.

May the glory of Hashem endure forever; let Hashem rejoice in His
works. Blessed is the name of Hashem From this time forth and
forever. From the rising of the sun to the going down of it, Hashem's
name is to be praised. Hashem is high above all nations, His glory is
above the heavens. Hashem, Your name endures forever; Your
memorial, Hashem, throughout all generations. Hashem has
established His Throne in the heavens; And His kingdom rules over
all. Let the heavens rejoice and the earth rejoice; let them declare
among the nations, "Hashem is King!". Hashem will reign forever
and ever. Hashem is King forever and ever; The nations are perished
out of His land. Hashem brings the counsel of the nations to
nothing; He makes the thoughts of the peoples of no effect. Many
designs are in a man's mind, But it is Hashem's plan that is
accomplished. The counsel of Hashem stands forever, The
thoughts of His heart to all generations. For He spoke, and it was;
He commanded, and it stood. For Hashem has chosen Tziyon; He
has desired it for His Habitation: For Hashem has chosen Yaakov
for Himself, And Yisrael for His own treasure. For Hashem will not
cast off His people, Neither will He forsake His inheritance. But He,

being full of compassion, forgives iniquity, and does not destroy;
Many times He turns His anger away, And does not stir up all of His
wrath. Save, Hashem; Let the King answer us in the day that we call.
Psalms 104:31, 113:2-4, 135:13, 103:19, 1 Chron. 16:31, Ex. 15:18, Psalms 10:16, 33:10, Prov. 19:21,
Psalms 33:11, 33:9, 132:13, 135:4, 94:14, 78:38, 20:10

Ashrei

When saying the verse "Potei'ach Et Yadecha" one should focus one's heart. If one did not focus he
must return and repeat. (SA, OC 51:7) It is customary to open your hands toward Heaven as a
symbol of our acceptance of the abundance Hashem bestows upon us from Heaven. (BTH, Ex.
9:29, 1 Kings 8:54).

אַשְׁרֵי יוֹשְׁבֵי בֵיתֶךָ עוֹד יְהַלְלוּךָ סֶּלָה: אַשְׁרֵי הָעָם שֶׁכָּכָה לּוֹ אַשְׁרֵי
הָעָם שֶׁיְהֹוָה אֱלֹהָיו:

Ashrei Yoshevei Veitecha; Od. Yehalelucha Selah. Ashrei Ha'am
Shekachah Lo; Ashrei Ha'am. She'Adonai Elohav.

Happy are those who dwell in Your House; they are ever praising
You. Happy are the people that is so situated; happy are the people
whose God is Hashem. (Psalms 84:5, 144:15)

Psalms 145

תְּהִלָּה לְדָוִד אֲרוֹמִמְךָ אֱלוֹהַי הַמֶּלֶךְ וַאֲבָרְכָה שִׁמְךָ לְעוֹלָם וָעֶד:
בְּכָל־יוֹם אֲבָרְכֶךָ וַאֲהַלְלָה שִׁמְךָ לְעוֹלָם וָעֶד: גָּדוֹל יְהֹוָה וּמְהֻלָּל
מְאֹד וְלִגְדֻלָּתוֹ אֵין חֵקֶר: דּוֹר לְדוֹר יְשַׁבַּח מַעֲשֶׂיךָ וּגְבוּרֹתֶיךָ יַגִּידוּ:
הֲדַר כְּבוֹד הוֹדֶךָ וְדִבְרֵי נִפְלְאֹתֶיךָ אָשִׂיחָה: וֶעֱזוּז נוֹרְאֹתֶיךָ יֹאמֵרוּ
וּגְדֻלָּתְךָ אֲסַפְּרֶנָּה: זֵכֶר רַב־טוּבְךָ יַבִּיעוּ וְצִדְקָתְךָ יְרַנֵּנוּ: חַנּוּן וְרַחוּם
יְהֹוָה אֶרֶךְ אַפַּיִם וּגְדָל־חָסֶד: טוֹב־יְהֹוָה לַכֹּל וְרַחֲמָיו עַל־כָּל־מַעֲשָׂיו:
יוֹדוּךָ יְהֹוָה כָּל־מַעֲשֶׂיךָ וַחֲסִידֶיךָ יְבָרְכוּכָה: כְּבוֹד מַלְכוּתְךָ יֹאמֵרוּ
וּגְבוּרָתְךָ יְדַבֵּרוּ: לְהוֹדִיעַ | לִבְנֵי הָאָדָם גְּבוּרֹתָיו וּכְבוֹד הֲדַר
מַלְכוּתוֹ: מַלְכוּתְךָ מַלְכוּת כָּל־עֹלָמִים וּמֶמְשַׁלְתְּךָ בְּכָל־דּוֹר וָדֹר:
סוֹמֵךְ יְהֹוָה לְכָל־הַנֹּפְלִים וְזוֹקֵף לְכָל־הַכְּפוּפִים: עֵינֵי־כֹל אֵלֶיךָ

פּוֹתֵחַ אֶת־יָדֶךָ יְשַׁבֵּרוּ וְאַתָּה נוֹתֵן־לָהֶם אֶת־אָכְלָם בְּעִתּוֹ:
וּמַשְׂבִּיעַ לְכָל־חַי רָצוֹן: צַדִּיק יְהוָה בְּכָל־דְּרָכָיו וְחָסִיד
בְּכָל־מַעֲשָׂיו: קָרוֹב יְהוָה לְכָל־קֹרְאָיו לְכֹל אֲשֶׁר יִקְרָאֻהוּ בֶאֱמֶת:
רְצוֹן־יְרֵאָיו יַעֲשֶׂה וְאֶת־שַׁוְעָתָם יִשְׁמַע וְיוֹשִׁיעֵם: שׁוֹמֵר יְהוָה
אֶת־כָּל־אֹהֲבָיו וְאֵת כָּל־הָרְשָׁעִים יַשְׁמִיד: תְּהִלַּת יְהוָה יְדַבֶּר־פִּי
וִיבָרֵךְ כָּל־בָּשָׂר שֵׁם קָדְשׁוֹ לְעוֹלָם וָעֶד: וַאֲנַחְנוּ | נְבָרֵךְ יָהּ מֵעַתָּה
וְעַד־עוֹלָם הַלְלוּיָהּ:

Tehilah. Ledavid Aromimcha Elohai Hamelech; Va'avarechah
Shimcha. Le'olam Va'ed. Bechol-Yom Avarecheka; Va'ahalelah
Shimcha. Le'olam Va'ed. Gadol Adonai Umehulal Me'od;
Veligdulato. Ein Cheiker. Dor Ledor Yeshabach Ma'aseicha;
Ugevuroteicha Yagidu. Hadar Kevod Hodecha; Vedivrei
Nifle'oteicha Asichah. Ve'ezuz Nore'oteicha Yomeru; Ug'dulatecha
Asap'renah. Zecher Rav-Tuvecha Yabi'u; Vetzidkatecha Yeranenu.
Chanun Verachum Adonai Erech Apayim. Ugedol-Chased. Tov-
Adonai Lakol; Verachamav. Al-Chol-Ma'asav. Yoducha Adonai Chol-
Ma'aseicha; Vachasideicha. Yevarechuchah. Kevod Malchutecha
Yomeru; Ugevuratecha Yedaberu. Lehodia Livnei Ha'adam
Gevurotav; Uchevod. Hadar Malchuto. Malchutecha. Malchut
Chol-'Olamim; Umemshaltecha. Bechol-Dor Vador. Somech Adonai
Lechol-Hanofelim; Vezokeif. Lechol-Hakefufim. Einei-Chol Eleicha
Yesaberu; Ve'attah Noten-Lahem Et-'Ochlam Be'ito. **Potei'ach Et-
Yadecha; Umasbia Lechol-Chai Ratzon.** Tzaddik Adonai Bechol-
Derachav; Vechasid. Bechol-Ma'asav. Karov Adonai Lechol-Kore'av;
Lechol Asher Yikra'uhu Ve'emet. Retzon-Yere'av Ya'aseh; Ve'et-
Shav'atam Yishma'. Veyoshi'em. Shomer Adonai Et-Chol-'Ohavav;
Ve'et Chol-Haresha'im Yashmid. Tehillat Adonai Yedaber Pi Vivarech
Chol-Basar Shem Kodsho. Le'olam Va'ed. Va'anachnu Nevarech Yah.
Me'attah Ve'ad-'Olam. Halleluyah.

A Psalm of praise; of David. **א** I will extol You, my God, Oh King; And
I will bless Your name forever and ever. **ב** Every day I will bless You;
And I will praise Your name forever and ever. **ג** Great is Hashem, and
highly to be praised; And His greatness is unsearchable. **ד** One
generation will applaud Your works to another, And will declare
Your mighty acts. **ה** The glorious splendor of Your majesty, And
Your wondrous works, I will rehearse. **ו** And men will speak of the

might of Your tremendous acts; And I will tell of Your greatness. ר
They will utter the fame of Your great goodness, And will sing of
Your righteousness. ח Hashem is gracious, and full of compassion;
Slow to anger, and of great mercy. ט Hashem is good to all; And His
tender mercies are over all His works. י All Your works will praise
You, Hashem; And Your holy-ones will bless You. כ They will speak
of the glory of Your kingdom, And talk of Your might; ל To make
known to the sons of men His mighty acts, And the glory of the
beauty of His kingdom. מ Your kingdom is a kingdom for all ages,
And Your dominion endures throughout all generations. ס Hashem
upholds all that fall, And raises up all those that are bowed down. ע
The eyes of all wait for You, And You give them their food in due
season. פ **You open Your hand, And satisfy every living thing
with favor.** צ Hashem is righteous in all His ways, And gracious in all
His works. ק Hashem is near to all them that call upon Him, To all
that call upon Him in truth. ר He will fulfill the desire of those that
fear Him; He also will hear their cry, and will save them. ש Hashem
preserves all them that love Him; But all the wicked will He destroy.
ת My mouth will speak the praise of Hashem; And let all flesh bless
His holy name forever and ever.

Psalms 146

הַלְלוּיָהּ הַלְלִי נַפְשִׁי אֶת־יְהֹוָה: אֲהַלְלָה יְהֹוָה בְּחַיָּי אֲזַמְּרָה לֵאלֹהַי
בְּעוֹדִי: אַל־תִּבְטְחוּ בִנְדִיבִים בְּבֶן־אָדָם | שֶׁאֵין לוֹ תְשׁוּעָה: תֵּצֵא
רוּחוֹ יָשֻׁב לְאַדְמָתוֹ בַּיּוֹם הַהוּא אָבְדוּ עֶשְׁתֹּנֹתָיו: אַשְׁרֵי שֶׁאֵל יַעֲקֹב
בְּעֶזְרוֹ שִׂבְרוֹ עַל־יְהֹוָה אֱלֹהָיו: עֹשֶׂה | שָׁמַיִם וָאָרֶץ אֶת־הַיָּם
וְאֶת־כָּל־אֲשֶׁר־בָּם הַשֹּׁמֵר אֱמֶת לְעוֹלָם: עֹשֶׂה מִשְׁפָּט | לָעֲשׁוּקִים
נֹתֵן לֶחֶם לָרְעֵבִים יְהֹוָה מַתִּיר אֲסוּרִים: יְהֹוָה | פֹּקֵחַ עִוְרִים יְהֹוָה
זֹקֵף כְּפוּפִים יְהֹוָה אֹהֵב צַדִּיקִים: יְהֹוָה | שֹׁמֵר אֶת־גֵּרִים יָתוֹם

וְאַלְמָנָה יְעוֹדֵד וְדֶרֶךְ רְשָׁעִים יְעַוֵּת: יִמְלֹךְ יְהוָֹה | לְעוֹלָם אֱלֹהַיִךְ צִיּוֹן
לְדֹר וָדֹר הַלְלוּיָהּ:

Halleluyah Haleli Nafshi. Et-Adonai Ahalelah Adonai Bechayai;
Azemerah Lelohai Be'odi. Al-Tivtechu Vindivim; Beven-'Adam
She'ein Lo Teshu'ah. Tetzei Rucho Yashuv Le'admato; Bayom Hahu.
Avedu Eshtonotav. Ashrei. She'el Ya'akov Be'ezro; Sivro. Al-Adonai
Elohav. Oseh Shamayim Va'aretz. Et-Hayam Ve'et-Chol-'Asher-Bam;
Hashomer Emet Le'olam. Oseh Mishpat La'ashukim. Noten Lechem
Lare'evim; Adonai Matir Asurim. Adonai Pokei'ach Ivrim. Adonai
Zokeif Kefufim; Adonai Ohev Tzaddikim. Adonai Shomer Et-Gerim.
Yatom Ve'almanah Ye'oded; Vederech Resha'im Ye'avet. Yimloch
Adonai Le'olam. Elohayich Tziyon Ledor Vador. Halleluyah.

Halleluyah. Praise Hashem, my soul. I will praise Hashem while I live;
I will sing praises to my God while I have my being. Do not put your
trust in princes, Or in the son of man, in whom there is no help. His
breath goes out, he returns to his dust; In that very day his thoughts
perish. Happy is he whose help is the God of Yaakov, Whose hope
is in Hashem his God, Who made heaven and earth, The sea, and all
that in them is; Who keeps truth forever; Who executes justice for
the oppressed; Who gives bread to the hungry. Hashem releases the
prisoners; Hashem opens the eyes of the blind; Hashem raises up
them that are bowed down; Hashem loves the righteous; Hashem
preserves the strangers; He upholds the fatherless and the widow;
But the way of the wicked He makes crooked. Hashem will reign
forever, Your God, Oh Tziyon, to all generations. Halleluyah.

Psalms 147

הַלְלוּיָהּ | כִּי־טוֹב זַמְּרָה אֱלֹהֵינוּ כִּי־נָעִים נָאוָה תְהִלָּה: בּוֹנֵה
יְרוּשָׁלַםִ יְהוָה נִדְחֵי יִשְׂרָאֵל יְכַנֵּס: הָרֹפֵא לִשְׁבוּרֵי לֵב וּמְחַבֵּשׁ
לְעַצְּבוֹתָם: מוֹנֶה מִסְפָּר לַכּוֹכָבִים לְכֻלָּם שֵׁמוֹת יִקְרָא: גָּדוֹל אֲדוֹנֵינוּ
וְרַב־כֹּחַ לִתְבוּנָתוֹ אֵין מִסְפָּר: מְעוֹדֵד עֲנָוִים יְהוָה מַשְׁפִּיל רְשָׁעִים
עֲדֵי־אָרֶץ: עֱנוּ לַיהוָה בְּתוֹדָה זַמְּרוּ לֵאלֹהֵינוּ בְכִנּוֹר: הַמְכַסֶּה שָׁמַיִם

| בֶּעָבִים הַמֵּכִין לָאָרֶץ מָטָר הַמַּצְמִיחַ הָרִים חָצִיר: נוֹתֵן לִבְהֵמָה
לַחְמָהּ לִבְנֵי עֹרֵב אֲשֶׁר יִקְרָאוּ: לֹא בִגְבוּרַת הַסּוּס יֶחְפָּץ
לֹא־בְשׁוֹקֵי הָאִישׁ יִרְצֶה: רוֹצֶה יְהוָה אֶת־יְרֵאָיו אֶת־הַמְיַחֲלִים
לְחַסְדּוֹ: שַׁבְּחִי יְרוּשָׁלַם אֶת־יְהוָה הַלְלִי אֱלֹהַיִךְ צִיּוֹן: כִּי־חִזַּק בְּרִיחֵי
שְׁעָרָיִךְ בֵּרַךְ בָּנַיִךְ בְּקִרְבֵּךְ: הַשָּׂם־גְּבוּלֵךְ שָׁלוֹם חֵלֶב חִטִּים יַשְׂבִּיעֵךְ:
הַשֹּׁלֵחַ אִמְרָתוֹ אָרֶץ עַד־מְהֵרָה יָרוּץ דְּבָרוֹ: הַנֹּתֵן שֶׁלֶג כַּצָּמֶר כְּפוֹר
כָּאֵפֶר יְפַזֵּר: מַשְׁלִיךְ קַרְחוֹ כְפִתִּים לִפְנֵי קָרָתוֹ מִי יַעֲמֹד: יִשְׁלַח
דְּבָרוֹ וְיַמְסֵם יַשֵּׁב רוּחוֹ יִזְּלוּ־מָיִם: מַגִּיד דְּבָרָיו לְיַעֲקֹב חֻקָּיו
וּמִשְׁפָּטָיו לְיִשְׂרָאֵל: לֹא עָשָׂה כֵן | לְכָל־גּוֹי וּמִשְׁפָּטִים בַּל־יְדָעוּם
הַלְלוּיָהּ:

Halleluyah; Ki-Tov Zemerah Eloheinu; Ki-Na'im. Navah Tehilah.
Boneh Yerushalami Adonai Nidchei Yisra'el Yechanes. Harofei
Lishvurei Lev; Umechabesh. Le'atzevotam. Moneh Mispor
Lakkochavim; Lechulam. Shemot Yikra. Gadol Adoneinu Verav-
Koach; Litvunato. Ein Mispar. Me'oded Anavim Adonai Mashpil
Resha'im Adei-'Aretz. Enu L'Adonai Betodah; Zameru Leloheinu
Vechinor. Hamchaseh Shamayim Be'avim. Ha'meichin La'aretz
Matar; Hamatzmiach Harim Chatzir. Noten Livhemah Lachmah;
Livnei Orev. Asher Yikra'u. Lo Vigvurat Hassus Yechpatz; Lo-
Veshokei Ha'ish Yirtzeh. Rotzeh Adonai Et-Yere'av; Et-Hamyachalim
Lechasdo. Shabechi Yerushalayim Et-Adonai Haleli Elohayich
Tziyon. Ki-Chizak Berichei She'arayich; Berach Banayich Bekirbech.
Hassam-Gevulech Shalom; Chelev Chitim. Yasbi'ech. Hasholeach
Imrato Aretz; Ad-Meheirah. Yarutz Devaro. Hanotein Sheleg
Katzamer; Kefor. Ka'efer Yefazer. Mashlich Karcho Chefitim; Lifnei
Karato. Mi Ya'amod. Yishlach Devaro Veyamsem; Yashev Rucho.
Yizelu-Mayim. Maggid Devarav Leya'akov; Chukkav Umishpatav.
Leyisra'el. Lo Asah Chein Lechol-Goy. Umishpatim Bal-Yeda'um.
Halleluyah.

Halleluyah; For it is good to sing praises to our God; For it is
pleasant, and praise is suitable. Hashem builds up Yerushalayim, He
gathers together the dispersed of Yisrael; Who heals the broken in
heart, And binds up their wounds. He counts the number of the
stars; He gives them all their names. Great is our Hashem, and

mighty in power; His understanding is infinite. Hashem upholds the humble; He brings the wicked down to the ground. Sing to Hashem with thanksgiving, Sing praises upon the harp to our God; Who covers the heaven with clouds, Who prepares rain for the earth, Who makes the mountains to spring with grass. He gives to the beast his food, And to the young ravens which cry. He doesn't delight in the strength of the horse; He takes no pleasure in the legs of a man. Hashem takes pleasure in them that fear Him, In those that wait for His mercy. Glorify Hashem, Oh Yerushalayim; Praise your God, Oh Tziyon. For He has made strong the bars of your gates; He has blessed your children within you. He makes your borders peace; He gives you in plenty the fat of wheat. He sends out His commandment on earth; His word runs very swiftly. He gives snow like wool; He scatters the hoar-frost like ashes. He casts out His ice like crumbs; Who can stand before His cold? He sends out His word, and melts them; He causes His wind to blow, and the waters flow. He declares His word to Yaakov, His statutes and His ordinances to Yisrael. He has not dealt so with any nation; And as for His ordinances, they have not known them. Halleluyah.

Psalms 148

הַלְלוּיָהּ | הַלְלוּ אֶת־יְהֹוָה מִן־הַשָּׁמַיִם הַלְלוּהוּ בַּמְּרוֹמִים: הַלְלוּהוּ כָל־מַלְאָכָיו הַלְלוּהוּ כָּל־צְבָאָו: הַלְלוּהוּ שֶׁמֶשׁ וְיָרֵחַ הַלְלוּהוּ כָּל־כּוֹכְבֵי אוֹר: הַלְלוּהוּ שְׁמֵי הַשָּׁמָיִם וְהַמַּיִם אֲשֶׁר | מֵעַל הַשָּׁמָיִם: יְהַלְלוּ אֶת־שֵׁם יְהֹוָה כִּי הוּא צִוָּה וְנִבְרָאוּ: וַיַּעֲמִידֵם לָעַד לְעוֹלָם חָק־נָתַן וְלֹא יַעֲבוֹר: הַלְלוּ אֶת־יְהֹוָה מִן־הָאָרֶץ תַּנִּינִים וְכָל־תְּהֹמוֹת: אֵשׁ וּבָרָד שֶׁלֶג וְקִיטוֹר רוּחַ סְעָרָה עֹשָׂה דְבָרוֹ: הֶהָרִים וְכָל־גְּבָעוֹת עֵץ פְּרִי וְכָל־אֲרָזִים: הַחַיָּה וְכָל־בְּהֵמָה רֶמֶשׂ וְצִפּוֹר כָּנָף: מַלְכֵי־אֶרֶץ וְכָל־לְאֻמִּים שָׂרִים וְכָל־שֹׁפְטֵי אָרֶץ: בַּחוּרִים

וְגַם־בְּתוּלוֹת זְקֵנִים עִם־נְעָרִים: יְהַלְלוּ׀ אֶת־שֵׁם יְהֹוָה כִּי־נִשְׂגָּב שְׁמוֹ
לְבַדּוֹ הוֹדוֹ עַל־אֶרֶץ וְשָׁמָיִם: וַיָּרֶם קֶרֶן׀ לְעַמּוֹ תְּהִלָּה לְכָל־חֲסִידָיו
לִבְנֵי יִשְׂרָאֵל עַם קְרֹבוֹ הַלְלוּיָהּ:

Halleluyah Halelu Et-Adonai Min-Hashamayim; Halleluhu.
Bameromim. Halleluhu Chol-Mal'achav; Halleluhu. Chol-Tzeva'av.
Halleluhu Shemesh Veyareach; Halleluhu. Chol-Kochevei Or.
Halleluhu Shemei Hashamayim; Vehamayim. Asher Me'al
Hashamayim. Yehalelu Et-Shem Adonai Ki Hu Tzivah Venivra'u.
Vaya'amidem La'ad Le'olam; Chok-Natan. Velo Ya'avor. Halelu Et-
Adonai Min-Ha'aretz; Taninim. Vechol-Tehomot. Esh Uvarod Sheleg
Vekitor; Ruach Se'arah. Osah Devaro. Heharim Vechol-Geva'ot; Etz
Peri. Vechol-'Arazim. Hachayah Vechol-Behemah; Remes Vetzipor
Kanaf. Malchei-'Eretz Vechol-Le'ummim; Sarim. Vechol-Shofetei
Aretz. Bachurim Vegam-Betulot; Zekenim. Im-Ne'arim. Yehalelu Et-
Shem Adonai Ki-Nisgav Shemo Levado; Hodo. Al-'Eretz
Veshamayim. Vayarem Keren Le'ammo Tehilah Lechol-Chasidav.
Livnei Yisra'el Am Kerovo. Halleluyah.

Halleluyah. Praise Hashem from the heavens; Praise Him in the heights. Praise Him, all His angels; Praise Him, all His hosts. Praise Him, sun and moon; Praise Him, all stars of light. Praise Him, heavens of heavens, And waters that are above the heavens. Let them praise the name of Hashem; For He commanded, and they were created. He also established them forever and ever; He made a decree which will not be transgressed. Praise Hashem from the earth, Sea-monsters, and all deeps; Fire and hail, snow and vapor, Stormy wind, fulfilling His word; Mountains and all hills, Fruitful trees and all cedars; Beasts and all cattle, Creeping things and winged fowl; Kings of the earth and all peoples, Princes and all judges of the earth; Both young men and maidens, Old men and children; Let them praise the name of Hashem, For His name alone is exalted; His glory is above the earth and heaven. And He has lifted up a horn for His people, A praise for all His holy-ones, Even for the children of Yisrael, a people near to Him. Halleluyah.

Psalms 149

הַלְלוּיָהּ | שִׁירוּ לַיהוָה שִׁיר חָדָשׁ תְּהִלָּתוֹ בִּקְהַל חֲסִידִים: יִשְׂמַח
יִשְׂרָאֵל בְּעֹשָׂיו בְּנֵי־צִיּוֹן יָגִילוּ בְמַלְכָּם: יְהַלְלוּ שְׁמוֹ בְמָחוֹל בְּתֹף
וְכִנּוֹר יְזַמְּרוּ־לוֹ: כִּי־רוֹצֶה יְהוָה בְּעַמּוֹ יְפָאֵר עֲנָוִים בִּישׁוּעָה: יַעְלְזוּ
חֲסִידִים בְּכָבוֹד יְרַנְּנוּ עַל־מִשְׁכְּבוֹתָם: רוֹמְמוֹת אֵל בִּגְרוֹנָם וְחֶרֶב
פִּיפִיּוֹת בְּיָדָם: לַעֲשׂוֹת נְקָמָה בַּגּוֹיִם תּוֹכֵחוֹת בַּלְאֻמִּים: לֶאְסֹר
מַלְכֵיהֶם בְּזִקִּים וְנִכְבְּדֵיהֶם בְּכַבְלֵי בַרְזֶל: לַעֲשׂוֹת בָּהֶם | מִשְׁפָּט
כָּתוּב הָדָר הוּא לְכָל־חֲסִידָיו הַלְלוּיָהּ:

Halleluyah. Shiru L'adonai Shir Chadash; Tehilato. Bik'hal
Chasidim. Yismach Yisra'el Be'osav; Benei-Tziyon. Yagilu Vemalkam.
Yehalelu Shemo Vemachol; Betof Vechinor. Yezameru-Lo. Ki-Rotzeh
Adonai Be'ammo; Yefa'er Anavim. Bishu'ah. Ya'lezu Chasidim
Bechavod; Yeranenu. Al-Mishkevotam. Romemot El Bigronam;
Vecherev Pifiyot Beyadam. La'asot Nekamah Bagoyim; Tochechot.
Bal'ummim. Le'sor Malcheihem Bezikkim; Venichbedeihem.
Bechavlei Varzel. La'asot Bahem Mishpat Katuv. Hadar Hu Lechol-
Chasidav. Halleluyah.

Halleluyah. Sing to Hashem a new song, And His praise in the
assembly of the holy-ones. Let Yisrael rejoice in his Maker; Let the
children of Tziyon be joyful in their King. Let them praise His name
in the dance; Let them sing praises to Him with the timbrel and
harp. For Hashem takes pleasure in His people; He adorns the
humble with salvation. Let the holy-ones exult in glory; Let them
sing for joy upon their beds. Let the high praises of God be in their
mouth, And a two-edged sword in their hand; To execute
vengeance on the nations, And chastisements on the peoples; To
bind their kings with chains, And their nobles with shackles of iron;
To execute on them the written judgment; He is the glory of all His
holy-ones. Halleluyah.

Psalms 150

הַלְלוּיָהּ | הַלְלוּ־אֵל בְּקָדְשׁוֹ הַלְלוּהוּ בִּרְקִיעַ עֻזּוֹ: הַלְלוּהוּ
בִגְבוּרֹתָיו הַלְלוּהוּ כְּרֹב גֻּדְלוֹ: הַלְלוּהוּ בְּתֵקַע שׁוֹפָר הַלְלוּהוּ בְּנֵבֶל
וְכִנּוֹר: הַלְלוּהוּ בְּתֹף וּמָחוֹל הַלְלוּהוּ בְּמִנִּים וְעֻגָב: הַלְלוּהוּ
בְצִלְצְלֵי־שָׁמַע הַלְלוּהוּ בְּצִלְצְלֵי תְרוּעָה: כֹּל הַנְּשָׁמָה תְּהַלֵּל יָהּ
הַלְלוּיָהּ: כֹּל הַנְּשָׁמָה תְּהַלֵּל יָהּ הַלְלוּיָהּ:

Halleluyah Halelu-'El Bekod'sho; Halleluhu. Birkia Uzo. Halleluhu
Vigvurotav; Halleluhu. Kerov Gudlo. Halleluhu Beteka Shofar;
Halleluhu. Benevel Vechinor. Halleluhu Betof Umachol; Halleluhu.
Beminim Ve'ugav. Halleluhu Vetziltzelei-Shama'; Halleluhu.
Betziltzelei Teru'ah. Kol Haneshamah Tehallel Yah. Halleluyah. Kol
Haneshamah Tehallel Yah. Halleluyah.

Halleluyah. Praise God in His Sanctuary; Praise Him in the
firmament of His power. Praise Him for His mighty acts; Praise Him
according to His abundant greatness. Praise Him with the blast of
the shofar; Praise Him with the psaltery and harp. Praise Him with
the timbrel and dance; Praise Him with stringed instruments and
the pipe. Praise Him with the loud-sounding cymbals; Praise Him
with the clanging cymbals. Let everything that has breath praise
Hashem. Halleluyah.

בָּרוּךְ יְהֹוָה לְעוֹלָם אָמֵן | וְאָמֵן: בָּרוּךְ יְהֹוָה | מִצִּיּוֹן שֹׁכֵן יְרוּשָׁלָם
הַלְלוּיָהּ: בָּרוּךְ | יְהֹוָה אֱלֹהִים אֱלֹהֵי יִשְׂרָאֵל עֹשֵׂה נִפְלָאוֹת לְבַדּוֹ:
וּבָרוּךְ | שֵׁם כְּבוֹדוֹ לְעוֹלָם וְיִמָּלֵא כְבוֹדוֹ אֶת־כָּל הָאָרֶץ אָמֵן |
וְאָמֵן:

Baruch Adonai Le'olam. Amen Ve'amen. Baruch Adonai Mitziyon.
Shochein Yerushalayim Halleluyah. Baruch Adonai Elohim Elohei
Yisra'el; Oseh Nifla'ot Levado. Uvaruch Shem Kevodo. Le'olam
Veyimmalei Chevodo Et-Kol Ha'aretz. Amen Ve'amen.

Blessed is Hashem forever more. Amen, and Amen. Blessed is
Hashem from Tziyon, Who dwells at Yerushalayim. Halleluyah.

Blessed is Hashem-Elohim, the God of Yisrael, Who only does wondrous things; And blessed is His glorious name forever; And let the whole earth be filled with His glory. Amen, and Amen. (Psalms 89:53,135:21, 72:18-19)

Vayvarech David
I Chronicles 29:10-13

One should stand and recite:

וַיְבָרֶךְ דָּוִיד אֶת־יְהֹוָה לְעֵינֵי כָּל־הַקָּהָל וַיֹּאמֶר דָּוִיד בָּרוּךְ אַתָּה יְהֹוָה

אֱלֹהֵי יִשְׂרָאֵל אָבִינוּ מֵעוֹלָם וְעַד־עוֹלָם: לְךָ יְהֹוָה הַגְּדֻלָּה וְהַגְּבוּרָה

וְהַתִּפְאֶרֶת וְהַנֵּצַח וְהַהוֹד כִּי־כֹל בַּשָּׁמַיִם וּבָאָרֶץ לְךָ יְהֹוָה הַמַּמְלָכָה

וְהַמִּתְנַשֵּׂא לְכֹל לְרֹאשׁ: וְהָעֹשֶׁר וְהַכָּבוֹד מִלְּפָנֶיךָ וְאַתָּה מוֹשֵׁל בַּכֹּל

וּבְיָדְךָ כֹּחַ וּגְבוּרָה וּבְיָדְךָ לְגַדֵּל וּלְחַזֵּק לַכֹּל: וְעַתָּה אֱלֹהֵינוּ מוֹדִים

אֲנַחְנוּ לָךְ וּמְהַלְלִים לְשֵׁם תִּפְאַרְתֶּךָ:

Vayvarech David Et-Adonai Le'einei Chol-Hakahal; Vayomer David.
Baruch Attah Adonai Elohei Yisra'el Avinu. Me'olam Ve'ad-'Olam.
Lecha Adonai Hagedullah Vehagevurah Vehatif'eret Vehanetzach
Vehahod. Ki-Chol Bashamayim Uva'aretz; Lecha Adonai
Hamamlachah. Vehamitnasei Lechol Lerosh. Veha'osher Vehakavod
Milfaneicha. Ve'attah Moshel Bakol. Uveyadecha Koach Ugevurah;
Uveyadecha. Legadel Ulechazek Lakol. Ve'attah Eloheinu. Modim
Anachnu Lach; Umehalelim Leshem Tif'artecha.

And David blessed Hashem before all the congregation; and David said: 'Blessed are You, Hashem, the God of Yisrael our father, forever and ever. Yours, Hashem, is the greatness, and the power, and the glory, and the victory, and the majesty; for all that is in the heaven and in the earth is Yours; Yours is the kingdom, Hashem, and You are exalted as head above all. Both riches and honor come from You, and You rule over all; and in Your hand is power and might; and it is in Your hand to make great, and to give strength to all. Now, our God, we thank You, and praise Your glorious name.

Nehemiah 9:5-11

וִיבָרְכוּ֙ שֵׁ֣ם כְּבוֹדֶ֔ךָ וּמְרוֹמַ֥ם עַל־כָּל־בְּרָכָ֖ה וּתְהִלָּֽה: אַתָּה־ה֣וּא יְהוָה֮
לְבַדֶּךָ֒ את (אַתָּ֣ה) עָשִׂ֣יתָ אֶת־הַשָּׁמַ֗יִם֙ שְׁמֵ֤י הַשָּׁמַ֨יִם֙ וְכָל־צְבָאָ֔ם
הָאָ֜רֶץ וְכָל־אֲשֶׁ֣ר עָלֶ֗יהָ הַיַּמִּים֙ וְכָל־אֲשֶׁ֣ר בָּהֶ֔ם וְאַתָּ֖ה מְחַיֶּ֣ה
אֶת־כֻּלָּ֑ם וּצְבָ֥א הַשָּׁמַ֖יִם לְךָ֥ מִשְׁתַּחֲוִֽים: אַתָּה־הוּא֙ יְהוָ֣ה הָאֱלֹהִ֔ים
אֲשֶׁ֤ר בָּחַ֨רְתָּ֙ בְּאַבְרָ֔ם וְהוֹצֵאת֖וֹ מֵא֣וּר כַּשְׂדִּ֑ים וְשַׂ֥מְתָּ שְּׁמ֖וֹ אַבְרָהָֽם:
וּמָצָ֣אתָ אֶת־לְבָבוֹ֮ נֶאֱמָ֣ן לְפָנֶיךָ֒ וְכָר֨וֹת עִמּ֜וֹ הַבְּרִ֗ית לָתֵ֡ת אֶת־אֶ֣רֶץ
הַכְּנַעֲנִ֣י הַחִתִּ֣י הָאֱמֹרִ֣י וְהַפְּרִזִּ֣י וְהַיְבוּסִ֣י וְהַגִּרְגָּשִׁ֗י לָתֵ֣ת לְזַרְע֑וֹ וַתָּ֨קֶם֙
אֶת־דְּבָרֶ֔יךָ כִּ֥י צַדִּ֖יק אָֽתָּה: וַתֵּ֛רֶא אֶת־עֳנִ֥י אֲבֹתֵ֖ינוּ בְּמִצְרָ֑יִם
וְאֶת־זַעֲקָתָ֥ם שָׁמַ֖עְתָּ עַל־יַם־סֽוּף: וַ֠תִּתֵּן אֹתֹ֨ת וּמֹֽפְתִ֜ים בְּפַרְעֹ֤ה
וּבְכָל־עֲבָדָיו֙ וּבְכָל־עַ֣ם אַרְצ֔וֹ כִּ֣י יָדַ֔עְתָּ כִּ֥י הֵזִ֖ידוּ עֲלֵיהֶ֑ם וַתַּֽעַשׂ־לְךָ֥
שֵׁ֖ם כְּהַיּ֣וֹם הַזֶּֽה: וְהַיָּם֙ בָּקַ֣עְתָּ לִפְנֵיהֶ֔ם וַיַּֽעַבְר֥וּ בְתֽוֹךְ־הַיָּ֖ם בַּיַּבָּשָׁ֑ה
וְאֶת־רֹֽדְפֵיהֶ֗ם הִשְׁלַ֧כְתָּ בִמְצוֹלֹ֛ת כְּמוֹ־אֶ֖בֶן בְּמַ֥יִם עַזִּֽים:

Vivarechu Shem Kevodecha. Umeromam Al-Chol-Berachah
Utehilah. Attah-Hu Adonai Levadecha Et-Attah Asita Et-Hashamayim
Shemei Hashamayim Vechol-Tzeva'am. Ha'aretz Vechol-'Asher
Aleiha Hayamim Vechol-'Asher Bahem. Ve'attah Mechayeh Et-
Kulam; Utzeva Hashamayim Lecha Mishtachavim. Attah-Hu Adonai
Ha'elohim. Asher Bacharta Be'avram. Vehotzeto Me'ur Kasdim;
Vesamta Shemo Avraham. Umatzata Et-Levavo Ne'eman Lefaneicha
Vecharot Imo Haberit. Latet Et-'Eretz Hakena'ani Hachiti Ha'emori
Vehaperizi Vehayvusi Vehagirgashi Latet Lezar'o; Vatakem Et-
Devareicha. Ki Tzaddik Attah. Vaterei Et-'Oni Avoteinu Bemitzrayim;
Ve'et-Za'akatam Shama'ta Al-Yam-Suf. Vatiten Otot Umofetim
Befar'oh Uvechol-'Avadav Uvechol-'Am Artzo. Ki Yada'ta. Ki
Hezidu Aleihem; Vata'as-Lecha Shem Kehayom Hazeh. Vehayam
Baka'ta Lifneihem. Vaya'avru Vetoch-Hayam Bayabashah; Ve'et-
Rodefeihem Hishlachta Vimtzolot Kemo-'Even Bemayim Azim.

Blessed is Your glorious Name, that is exalted above all blessing and
praise. You are Hashem, even You alone; You have made heaven, the
heaven of heavens, with all their host, the earth and all things that
are on it, the seas and all that is in them, and You preserve them all;
and the host of heaven worship You. You are Hashem the God,

Who chose Avram, and brought him out out from Ur of Kasdim, and gave him the name of Avraham; and found his heart faithful before You, and made a covenant with him to give the land of the Canaani, the Hitti, the Emori, and the Perizi, and the Yevusi, and the Girgashi, even to give it to his seed, and have performed Your words; for You are righteous; And You saw the affliction of our fathers in Mitzrayim, and heard their cry by the Sea of Reeds; and did show signs and wonders on Pharaoh, and on all his servants, and on all the people of his land; for You knew that they dealt proudly against them; and gave You a name, as it is this day. And You divided the sea before them, so that they went through the midst of the sea on the dry land; and You cast their pursuers into the depths, as a stone into the mighty waters.

Shirat Hayam / Song at the Sea
Exodus 14:30-31

וַיּוֹשַׁע יְהֹוָה בַּיּוֹם הַהוּא אֶת־יִשְׂרָאֵל מִיַּד מִצְרָיִם וַיַּרְא יִשְׂרָאֵל אֶת־מִצְרַיִם מֵת עַל־שְׂפַת הַיָּם: וַיַּרְא יִשְׂרָאֵל אֶת־הַיָּד הַגְּדֹלָה אֲשֶׁר עָשָׂה יְהֹוָה בְּמִצְרַיִם וַיִּירְאוּ הָעָם אֶת־יְהֹוָה וַיַּאֲמִינוּ בַּיהֹוָה וּבְמֹשֶׁה עַבְדּוֹ:

Vayosha Adonai Bayom Hahu Et-Yisra'el Miyad Mitzrayim; Vayar Yisra'el Et-Mitzrayim. Met Al-Sefat Hayam. Vayar Yisra'el Et-Hayad Hagedolah. Asher Asah Adonai Bemitzrayim. Vayire'u Ha'am Et-Adonai Vaya'aminu B'Adonai. Uvemosheh Avdo.

And Hashem saved Yisrael on that day out of the hand of Mitzrayim; and Yisrael saw Mitzrayim dead upon the sea-shore. And Yisrael saw the great work which Hashem performed on Mitzrayim, and the people feared Hashem; and they believed in Hashem, and in His servant Moshe.

Exodus 15:1-18

אָז יָשִׁיר־מֹשֶׁה וּבְנֵי יִשְׂרָאֵל אֶת־הַשִּׁירָה הַזֹּאת לַיהֹוָה וַיֹּאמְרוּ
לֵאמֹר אָשִׁירָה לַיהֹוָה כִּי־גָאֹה גָּאָה סוּס וְרֹכְבוֹ רָמָה בַיָּם: עָזִּי
וְזִמְרָת יָהּ וַיְהִי־לִי לִישׁוּעָה זֶה אֵלִי וְאַנְוֵהוּ אֱלֹהֵי אָבִי וַאֲרֹמְמֶנְהוּ:
יְהֹוָה אִישׁ מִלְחָמָה יְהֹוָה שְׁמוֹ: מַרְכְּבֹת פַּרְעֹה וְחֵילוֹ יָרָה בַיָּם
וּמִבְחַר שָׁלִשָׁיו טֻבְּעוּ בְיַם־סוּף: תְּהֹמֹת יְכַסְיֻמוּ יָרְדוּ בִמְצוֹלֹת
כְּמוֹ־אָבֶן: יְמִינְךָ יְהֹוָה נֶאְדָּרִי בַּכֹּחַ יְמִינְךָ יְהֹוָה תִּרְעַץ אוֹיֵב: וּבְרֹב
גְּאוֹנְךָ תַּהֲרֹס קָמֶיךָ תְּשַׁלַּח חֲרֹנְךָ יֹאכְלֵמוֹ כַּקַּשׁ: וּבְרוּחַ אַפֶּיךָ
נֶעֶרְמוּ מַיִם נִצְּבוּ כְמוֹ־נֵד נֹזְלִים קָפְאוּ תְהֹמֹת בְּלֶב־יָם: אָמַר אוֹיֵב
אֶרְדֹּף אַשִּׂיג אֲחַלֵּק שָׁלָל תִּמְלָאֵמוֹ נַפְשִׁי אָרִיק חַרְבִּי תּוֹרִישֵׁמוֹ יָדִי:
נָשַׁפְתָּ בְרוּחֲךָ כִּסָּמוֹ יָם צָלְלוּ כַּעוֹפֶרֶת בְּמַיִם אַדִּירִים: מִי־כָמֹכָה
בָּאֵלִם יְהֹוָה מִי כָּמֹכָה נֶאְדָּר בַּקֹּדֶשׁ נוֹרָא תְהִלֹּת עֹשֵׂה פֶלֶא: נָטִיתָ
יְמִינְךָ תִּבְלָעֵמוֹ אָרֶץ: נָחִיתָ בְחַסְדְּךָ עַם־זוּ גָּאָלְתָּ נֵהַלְתָּ בְעָזְּךָ
אֶל־נְוֵה קָדְשֶׁךָ: שָׁמְעוּ עַמִּים יִרְגָּזוּן חִיל אָחַז יֹשְׁבֵי פְּלָשֶׁת: אָז
נִבְהֲלוּ אַלּוּפֵי אֱדוֹם אֵילֵי מוֹאָב יֹאחֲזֵמוֹ רָעַד נָמֹגוּ כֹּל יֹשְׁבֵי כְנָעַן:
תִּפֹּל עֲלֵיהֶם אֵימָתָה וָפַחַד בִּגְדֹל זְרוֹעֲךָ יִדְּמוּ כָּאָבֶן עַד־יַעֲבֹר עַמְּךָ
יְהֹוָה עַד־יַעֲבֹר עַם־זוּ קָנִיתָ: תְּבִאֵמוֹ וְתִטָּעֵמוֹ בְּהַר נַחֲלָתְךָ מָכוֹן
לְשִׁבְתְּךָ פָּעַלְתָּ יְהֹוָה מִקְּדָשׁ אֲדֹנָי כּוֹנְנוּ יָדֶיךָ: יְהֹוָה | יִמְלֹךְ לְעֹלָם
וָעֶד: יְהֹוָה | יִמְלֹךְ לְעֹלָם וָעֶד: יְהֹוָה מַלְכוּתֵהּ קָאִים לְעָלַם וּלְעָלְמֵי
עָלְמַיָּא: כִּי בָא סוּס פַּרְעֹה בְּרִכְבּוֹ וּבְפָרָשָׁיו בַּיָּם וַיָּשֶׁב יְהֹוָה עֲלֵהֶם
אֶת־מֵי הַיָּם וּבְנֵי יִשְׂרָאֵל הָלְכוּ בַיַּבָּשָׁה בְּתוֹךְ הַיָּם:

Az Yashir-Mosheh Uvenei Yisra'el Et-Hashirah Hazot L'Adonai
Vayomeru Lemor; Ashirah L'Adonai Ki-Ga'oh Ga'ah. Sus Verochevo
Ramah Vayam. Ozi Vezimrat Yah. Vayhi-Li Lishu'ah; Zeh Eli
Ve'anvehu. Elohei Avi Va'aromemenhu. Adonai Ish Milchamah;
Adonai Shemo. Markevot Par'oh Vecheilo Yarah Vayam; Umivchar
Shalishav Tube'u Veyam-Suf. Tehomot Yechasyumu; Yaredu Vimtzolot
Kemo-'Aven. Yeminecha Adonai Ne'dari Bakoach; Yeminecha
Adonai Tir'atz Oyev. Uverov Ge'onecha Taharos Kameicha;
Teshallach Charonecha. Yochelemo Kakash. Uveruach Appeicha

Ne'ermu Mayim. Nitzevu Chemo-Ned Nozelim; Kafe'u Tehomot
Belev-Yam. Amar Oyev Erdof Assig Achallek Shalal; Timla'emo
Nafshi. Arik Charbi. Torishemo Yadi. Nashafta Veruchacha Kisamo
Yam; Tzalelu Ka'oferet. Bemayim Adirim. Mi-Chamochah Ba'elim
Adonai Mi Kamochah Ne'dar Bakodesh; Nora Tehillot Oseh Fele.
Natita Yeminecha. Tivla'emo Aretz. Nachita Vechasdecha Am-Zu
Ga'aleta; Nehalta Ve'ozecha El-Neveh Kodshecha. Shame'u Ammim
Yirgazun; Chil Achaz. Yoshevei Pelashet. Az Nivhalu Alufei Edom.
Eilei Mo'av. Yochazemo Ra'ad; Namogu Kol Yoshevei Chena'an.
Tipol Aleihem Eimatah Vafachad. Bigdol Zero'acha Yidemu Ka'aven;
Ad-Ya'avor Ammecha Adonai Ad-Ya'avor Am-Zu Kanita. Tevi'emo.
Vetita'emo Behar Nachalatecha. Machon Leshivtecha Pa'alta Adonai
Mikkedash Adonai Konenu Yadeicha. Adonai Yimloch Le'olam
Va'ed. Adonai Yimloch Le'olam Va'ed. Adonai Malchuteh Ka'im
Le'alam Ule'alemei Alemaya. Ki Va Sus Par'oh Berichbo
Uvefarashav Bayam. Vayashev Adonai Aleihem Et-Mei Hayam;
Uvenei Yisra'el Halechu Vayabashah Betoch Hayam.

Then Moshe and the children of Yisrael sang this song to Hashem,
and spoke, saying: I will sing to Hashem, for He is highly exalted;
The horse and his rider He has thrown into the sea. Hashem is my
strength and song, And He has become my salvation; This is my
God, and I will glorify Him; My father's God, and I will exalt Him.
Hashem is a man of war, Hashem is His name. Pharaoh's chariots
and his host He has cast into the sea, And His chosen captains are
sunk in the Sea of Reeds. The deeps cover them—They went down
into the depths like a stone. Your right hand, Hashem, glorious in
power, Your right hand, Hashem, shatters the enemy. And in Your
abundant excellency You overthrow those that rise up against You;
You send out Your wrath, it consumes them like straw. And with the
breath of Your nostrils the waters were piled up. The waters stood
upright as a wall; The flowing water froze in the heart of the sea.
The enemy said: 'I will pursue, I will overtake, I will divide the spoil;
My lust will be satisfied on them; I will draw my sword, my hand will
destroy them.' You blew with Your wind, the sea covered them; They
sank like lead in mighty waters. Who is like You, Hashem, among the
gods, Who is like You, glorified in holiness, You are awesome in

praise, working wonders. You stretched out Your right hand—The earth swallowed them. In Your love You led the people that You have redeemed; You have guided them in Your strength to Your holy Habitation. The nations have heard, they tremble; Pains have taken hold on the inhabitants of Philistia. Then the chiefs of Edom were afraid; The mighty men of Moav, trembling took hold of them; All the inhabitants of Canaan have melted away. Terror and dread falls upon them; By the greatness of Your arm they are as still as a stone; Until Your people pass over, Hashem, Until the people pass over that You have acquired. You will bring them in, and plant them in the mountain of Your inheritance, The place, Hashem, which You have made for You to dwell in, The Sanctuary, Hashem, which Your hands have established. Hashem will reign forever and ever.

כִּי לַיהוָה הַמְּלוּכָה וּמֹשֵׁל בַּגּוֹיִם: וְעָלוּ מוֹשִׁעִים בְּהַר צִיּוֹן לִשְׁפֹּט אֶת־הַר עֵשָׂו וְהָיְתָה לַיהוָה הַמְּלוּכָה: וְהָיָה יְהוָה לְמֶלֶךְ עַל־כָּל־הָאָרֶץ בַּיּוֹם הַהוּא יִהְיֶה יְהוָה אֶחָד וּשְׁמוֹ אֶחָד:

Ki L'Adonai Hameluchah; Umoshel. Bagoyim. Ve'alu Moshi'im Behar Tziyon. Lishpot Et-Har Esav; Vehayetah L'Adonai Hameluchah. Vehayah Adonai Lemelech Al-Chol-Ha'aretz; Bayom Hahu. Yihyeh Adonai Echad Ushemo Echad.

For dominion is Hashem's and He governs the nations. Saviors will go up Mount Tziyon to judge the Mount of Esav, and sovereignty will be Hashem's. Hashem will be King over all the earth; and on that day Hashem will be One and His name One. (Ps. 22:29, Obadiah 1:21, Zech. 14:9)

Continue with Nishmat Kol Chai.

Nishmat Kol Chai

Nishmat Kol Chai Tevarech Et	נִשְׁמַת כָּל חַי תְּבָרֵךְ אֶת
Shimcha Adonai Eloheinu.	שִׁמְךָ יְהֹוָה אֱלֹהֵינוּ.
Veruach Kol Basar Tefa'er	וְרוּחַ כָּל בָּשָׂר תְּפָאֵר
Uteromem Zichrecha Malkeinu	וּתְרוֹמֵם זִכְרְךָ מַלְכֵּנוּ
Tamid. Min Ha'olam Ve'ad	תָּמִיד: מִן הָעוֹלָם וְעַד
Ha'olam Attah El.	הָעוֹלָם אַתָּה אֵל.
Umibal'adeicha Ein Lanu	וּמִבַּלְעָדֶיךָ אֵין לָנוּ
Melech Go'el Umoshia'. Podeh	מֶלֶךְ גּוֹאֵל וּמוֹשִׁיעַ. פּוֹדֶה
Umatzil. Ve'oneh Umerachem.	וּמַצִּיל וְעוֹנֶה וּמְרַחֵם
Bechol Et Tzarah Vetzukah. Ein	בְּכָל עֵת צָרָה וְצוּקָה. אֵין
Lanu Melech Ozeir Vesomech	לָנוּ מֶלֶךְ עוֹזֵר וְסוֹמֵךְ
Ella Attah:	אֶלָּא אָתָּה:

The soul of every living being will bless Your name, Hashem our God, and the spirit of all flesh will glorify and exalt Your memorial, our King, continually. From eternity to eternity You are God; and besides You, we have no King Who redeems and saves, sets free and delivers, Who supports and has mercy in all times of trouble and distress. We have no King Who helps and supports but You.

Elohei Harishonim	אֱלֹהֵי הָרִאשׁוֹנִים
Veha'acharonim. Eloah Kol	וְהָאַחֲרוֹנִים. אֱלוֹהַּ כָּל־
Beriyot. Adon Kol Toladot.	בְּרִיּוֹת. אֲדוֹן כָּל־תּוֹלָדוֹת.
Hamehulal Bechol Hatishbachot.	הַמְהֻלָּל בְּכָל־הַתִּשְׁבָּחוֹת.
Hamenaheg Olamo Bechesed.	הַמְנַהֵג עוֹלָמוֹ בְּחֶסֶד.
Uveriyotav Berachamim.	וּבְרִיּוֹתָיו בְּרַחֲמִים.
v'Adonai Elohim Emet. Lo Yanum	וַיהֹוָה אֱלֹהִים אֱמֶת. לֹא יָנוּם
Velo Yishan. Hame'orer	וְלֹא יִישָׁן. הַמְעוֹרֵר

Yeshenim Vehamekitz Nirdamim.	יְשֵׁנִים וְהַמֵּקִיץ נִרְדָּמִים.
Mechayeh Meitim Verofe	מְחַיֶּה מֵתִים וְרוֹפֵא
Cholim. Pokei'ach Ivrim Vezokeif	חוֹלִים. פּוֹקֵחַ עִוְרִים וְזוֹקֵף
Kefufim. Hamesiach Illemim	כְּפוּפִים. הַמֵּשִׂיחַ אִלְּמִים
Vehamefa'aneach Ne'elamim.	וְהַמְפַעֲנֵחַ נֶעֱלָמִים.
Ulecha Levadecha Anachnu	וּלְךָ לְבַדְּךָ אֲנַחְנוּ
Modim:	מוֹדִים:

God of the first and of the last, the God of all creatures, the Lord of all generations Who is praised with all praises, and guides His world in kindness and His creatures in mercy. And Hashem-Elohim is true, He does not slumber or sleep; He arouses the sleepers and awakens the slumberers; He gives life to the dead, and heals the sick, gives sight to the blind, straightens the bent, gives speech to the mute, and reveals the concealed. To You alone we give thanks.

Ve'ilu Finu Male Shirah Chayam.	וְאִלּוּ פִינוּ מָלֵא שִׁירָה כַיָּם.
Uleshonenu Rinah Kahamon	וּלְשׁוֹנֵנוּ רִנָּה כַּהֲמוֹן
Gallav. Vesiftoteinu Shevach	גַּלָּיו. וְשִׂפְתוֹתֵינוּ שֶׁבַח
Kemerchavei Rakia'. Ve'eineinu	כְּמֶרְחֲבֵי רָקִיעַ. וְעֵינֵינוּ
Me'irot Kashemesh	מְאִירוֹת כַּשֶּׁמֶשׁ
Vechayareach. Veyadeinu Ferusot	וְכַיָּרֵחַ. וְיָדֵינוּ פְרוּשׂוֹת
Kenishrei Shamayim. Veragleinu	כְּנִשְׁרֵי שָׁמָיִם. וְרַגְלֵינוּ
Kalot Ka'ayalot. Ein Anachnu	קַלּוֹת כָּאַיָּלוֹת. אֵין אֲנַחְנוּ
Maspikin Lehodot Lecha Adonai	מַסְפִּיקִין לְהוֹדוֹת לְךָ יְהוָה
Eloheinu. Ulevarech Et Shimcha	אֱלֹהֵינוּ. וּלְבָרֵךְ אֶת־שִׁמְךָ
Malkenu. Al Achat Me'elef Alfei	מַלְכֵּנוּ. עַל־אַחַת מֵאֶלֶף אַלְפֵי
Alafim. Verov Ribei Rivavot	אֲלָפִים. וְרוֹב רִבֵּי רְבָבוֹת
Pe'amim. Hatovot Nissim	פְּעָמִים. הַטּוֹבוֹת נִסִּים

Venifla'ot She'asita Imanu Ve'im	וְנִפְלָאוֹת שֶׁעָשִׂיתָ עִמָּנוּ וְעִם
Avoteinu. Millefanim	אֲבוֹתֵינוּ. מִלְּפָנִים
Mimitzrayim Ge'altanu Adonai	מִמִּצְרַיִם גְּאַלְתָּנוּ יְהֹוָה
Eloheinu. Mibeit Avadim	אֱלֹהֵינוּ. מִבֵּית עֲבָדִים
Peditanu. Bera'av Zantanu	פְּדִיתָנוּ. בְּרָעָב זַנְתָּנוּ
Uvesava Kilkaltanu. Mecherev	וּבְשָׂבָע כִּלְכַּלְתָּנוּ. מֵחֶרֶב
Hitzaltanu. Midever Milatanu.	הִצַּלְתָּנוּ. מִדֶּבֶר מִלַּטְתָּנוּ.
Umechola'im Ra'im Verabim	וּמֵחֳלָאִים רָעִים וְרַבִּים
Dillitanu. Ad Henah Azarunu	דִּלִּיתָנוּ. עַד הֵנָּה עֲזָרוּנוּ
Rachameicha. Velo Azavunu	רַחֲמֶיךָ. וְלֹא עֲזָבוּנוּ
Chasadeicha. Al Ken Evarim	חֲסָדֶיךָ. עַל כֵּן אֵבָרִים
Sheppillagta Banu. Veruach	שֶׁפִּלַּגְתָּ בָּנוּ. וְרוּחַ
Uneshamah Shenafachta	וּנְשָׁמָה שֶׁנָּפַחְתָּ
Be'apeinu. Velashon Asher Samta	בְּאַפֵּינוּ. וְלָשׁוֹן אֲשֶׁר שַׂמְתָּ
Befinu. Hen Hem Yodu	בְּפִינוּ. הֵן הֵם יוֹדוּ
Vivarechu Vishabechu Vifa'aru	וִיבָרְכוּ וִישַׁבְּחוּ וִיפָאֲרוּ
Vishoreru Et Shimcha Malkenu	וִישׁוֹרְרוּ אֶת־שִׁמְךָ מַלְכֵּנוּ
Tamid. Ki Chol Peh Lecha Yodeh.	תָּמִיד. כִּי כָל־פֶּה לְךָ יוֹדֶה.
Vechol Lashon Lecha	וְכָל־לָשׁוֹן לְךָ
Teshabei'ach. Vechol Ayin Lecha	תְשַׁבֵּחַ. וְכָל־עַיִן לְךָ
Tetzapeh. Vechol Berech Lecha	תְצַפֶּה. וְכָל־בֶּרֶךְ לְךָ
Tichra. Vechol Komah Lefaneicha	תִכְרַע. וְכָל־קוֹמָה לְפָנֶיךָ
Tishtachaveh. Vehallevavot	תִשְׁתַּחֲוֶה. וְהַלְּבָבוֹת
Yira'ucha. Vehakerev	יִירָאוּךָ. וְהַקֶּרֶב
Vehakkelayot Yezameru	וְהַכְּלָיוֹת יְזַמֵּרוּ
Lishmecha. Kadavar Shene'emar	לִשְׁמֶךָ. כַּדָּבָר שֶׁנֶּאֱמַר

Kal Atzmotai Tomarnah Adonai	כָּל-עַצְמוֹתַי תֹּאמַרְנָה יְהוָה
Mi Chamocha Matzil Ani	מִי כָמוֹךָ מַצִּיל עָנִי
Mechazak Mimenu Ve'ani	מֵחָזָק מִמֶּנּוּ וְעָנִי
Ve'evyon Migozelo:	וְאֶבְיוֹן מִגֹּזְלוֹ:

And though our mouths were full of song as the sea, and our tongues of exultation as the multitude of its waves, and our lips full of praise as the wide-extended firmament; and though our eyes shine with light like the sun and the moon and our hands were spread out like the eagles of the sky, and our feet were as swift as a deer's, we still would be unable to sufficiently thank You, Hashem our God, and to bless Your name for one thousandth or one ten thousandth part and myriad of myriads of the favors, miracles and wonders which You have performed for our fathers and for us. You redeemed us from Mitzrayim, Hashem our God, and redeemed us from the house of bondage; in famine You fed us, and sustained us in abundance; from the sword You rescued us, from pestilence You saved us, and from severe and numerous diseases You rescued us. Until now, Your mercy has helped us, and Your loving kindness has not left us. Then the limbs which You have set on us, and the spirit and soul which You have breathed into our nostrils, and the tongue that you have placed in our mouths shall thank, bless, praise, glorify, and sing about Your name, our King, forever. For every mouth will give thanks to You, and every tongue will swear to You; and every eye will look to You, and every knee will kneel to You, and all the upright will bow before You, and all hearts will fear You, and all the inward parts and reins will sing to Your name, as it says, 'All my bones will say, Hashem, who is like You?' "Who delivers the poor from one too strong for him; the poor and needy from him who robs him." (Ps. 35:10)

Shav'at Aniyim Attah Tishma.	שַׁוְעַת עֲנִיִּים אַתָּה תִשְׁמַע.
Tza'akat Haddal Takshiv	צַעֲקַת הַדַּל תַּקְשִׁיב

Vetoshia¹. Vechatuv Ranenu	וְתוֹשִׁיעַ. וְכָתוּב רַנְּנוּ
Tzaddikim Badonai Layesharim	צַדִּיקִים בַּיהוָה לַיְשָׁרִים
Navah Tehillah:	נָאוָה תְהִלָּה:

You hear the cry of the poor, and regard the cry of the destitute and save them. And it is written, "Rejoice in Hashem, you righteous, praise is suitable for the upright." (Ps. 33:1)

Befi Yesharim Titromam.	בְּפִי יְשָׁרִים תִּתְרוֹמָם.
Uvesiftei Tzaddikim Titbarach.	וּבְשִׂפְתֵי צַדִּיקִים תִּתְבָּרַךְ.
Uvilshon Chasidim Titkadash.	וּבִלְשׁוֹן חֲסִידִים תִּתְקַדָּשׁ.
Uvekerev Kedoshim Tithallal:	וּבְקֶרֶב קְדוֹשִׁים תִּתְהַלָּל:

By the mouth of the upright will You be exalted, by the lips of the righteous You will be blessed, by the tongue of the pious You will be sanctified, and in the midst of the holy-ones You will be praised;

Bemikhalot Rivot Ammecha Beit	בְּמִקְהֲלוֹת רִבְבוֹת עַמְּךָ בֵּית
Yisra'el. Shekken Chovat Kol	יִשְׂרָאֵל. שֶׁכֵּן חוֹבַת כָּל־
Hayetzurim Lefaneicha Adonai	הַיְצוּרִים לְפָנֶיךָ יְהוָה
Eloheinu Velohei Avoteinu.	אֱלֹהֵינוּ וֵאלֹהֵי אֲבוֹתֵינוּ.
Lehodot. Lehallel. Leshabei'ach.	לְהוֹדוֹת. לְהַלֵּל. לְשַׁבֵּחַ.
Lefa'er. Leromem. Lehader	לְפָאֵר. לְרוֹמֵם. לְהַדֵּר
Ulenatzeach. Al Kol Divrei	וּלְנַצֵּחַ. עַל כָּל־דִּבְרֵי
Shirot Vetishbechot David Ben	שִׁירוֹת וְתִשְׁבְּחוֹת דָּוִד בֶּן־
Yishai Avdecha Meshichecha.	יִשַׁי עַבְדְּךָ מְשִׁיחֶךָ.
Uvechen:	וּבְכֵן:

In the assemblies of the myriads of Your people, the House of Yisrael; for this is the duty of every creature towards You, Hashem our God, and the God of our fathers, to give thanks, to praise, extol, glorify, exalt, ascribe honor and victory, beyond all the words of song and praises of David, the son of Yishai, Your servant and Your anointed. And so:

Yishtabach

One should not say Yishtabach unless he has said Baruch She'amar and some of Pesukei De'zimrah. The leader should say Yishtabach while standing. (SA, OC 53)

Remain standing and say:

Yishtabach Shimcha La'ad	יִשְׁתַּבַּח שִׁמְךָ לָעַד
Malkeinu. Ha'el Hamelech	מַלְכֵּנוּ. הָאֵל הַמֶּלֶךְ
Hagadol Vehakadosh.	הַגָּדוֹל וְהַקָּדוֹשׁ.
Bashamayim Uva'aretz. Ki	בַּשָּׁמַיִם וּבָאָרֶץ. כִּי
Lecha Na'eh Adonai Eloheinu	לְךָ נָאֶה יְהֹוָה אֱלֹהֵינוּ
Velohei Avoteinu Le'olam Va'ed.	וֵאלֹהֵי אֲבוֹתֵינוּ לְעוֹלָם וָעֶד.
א Shir. ב Ushevachah. ג Hallel. ד	א שִׁיר. ב וּשְׁבָחָה. ג הַלֵּל. ד
Vezimrah. ה Oz. ו Umemshalah.	וְזִמְרָה. ה עֹז. ו וּמֶמְשָׁלָה.
ז Netzach. ח Gedullah. ט	ז נֶצַח. ח גְּדֻלָּה. ט
Gevurah. י Tehilah. יא Vetif'eret.	גְּבוּרָה. י תְּהִלָּה. יא וְתִפְאֶרֶת.
יב Kedushah. יג Umalchut.	יב קְדֻשָּׁה. יג וּמַלְכוּת.
Berachot Vehoda'ot. Leshimcha	בְּרָכוֹת וְהוֹדָאוֹת. לְשִׁמְךָ
Hagadol Vehakadosh.	הַגָּדוֹל וְהַקָּדוֹשׁ.
Ume'olam Ve'ad Olam Attah El.	וּמֵעוֹלָם וְעַד עוֹלָם אַתָּה אֵל.
Baruch Attah Adonai Melech	בָּרוּךְ אַתָּה יְהֹוָה מֶלֶךְ
Gadol Umehulal Batishbachot.	גָּדוֹל וּמְהֻלָּל בַּתִּשְׁבָּחוֹת.
El Hahoda'ot. Adon Hanifla'ot.	אֵל הַהוֹדָאוֹת. אֲדוֹן הַנִּפְלָאוֹת.
Borei Kol-Haneshamot. Ribon	בּוֹרֵא כָּל־הַנְּשָׁמוֹת. רִבּוֹן
Kol-Hama'asim. Habocher	כָּל־הַמַּעֲשִׂים. הַבּוֹחֵר
Beshirei Zimrah. Melech El Chai	בְּשִׁירֵי זִמְרָה. מֶלֶךְ אֵל חַי
Ha'Olamim. Amen.	הָעוֹלָמִים. אָמֵן.

May Your name be praised forever, God, the King, the great and holy in heaven and on earth; for to You, Hashem our God and the God of our fathers, forever pertain 1. song 2. and praise, 3. lauding and 4. hymn, 5. strength and 6. dominion, 7. victory, 8. greatness, 9. might, 10. adoration and 11. glory, 12. holiness and 13. majesty. Blessings and thanksgivings to Your great and holy name. From eternity to eternity You are God. Blessed are You, Hashem, King, great and adored with praises, God of thanksgivings, Lord of the wonders. Creator of all souls, and Sovereign of all works, Who chooses musical songs of praise; King, God, Who lives eternally. Amen.

On Shabbat Shuvah (Shabbat during the Ten Days of Repentance between Rosh Hashanah and Yom Kippur) say:

Psalms 130

שִׁיר הַמַּעֲלוֹת מִמַּעֲמַקִּים קְרָאתִיךָ יְהֹוָה: אֲדֹנָי שִׁמְעָה בְקוֹלִי תִּהְיֶינָה אָזְנֶיךָ קַשֻּׁבוֹת לְקוֹל תַּחֲנוּנָי: אִם־עֲוֹנוֹת תִּשְׁמָר־יָהּ אֲדֹנָי מִי יַעֲמֹד: כִּי־עִמְּךָ הַסְּלִיחָה לְמַעַן תִּוָּרֵא: קִוִּיתִי יְהֹוָה קִוְּתָה נַפְשִׁי וְלִדְבָרוֹ הוֹחָלְתִּי: נַפְשִׁי לַאדֹנָי מִשֹּׁמְרִים לַבֹּקֶר שֹׁמְרִים לַבֹּקֶר: יַחֵל יִשְׂרָאֵל אֶל־יְהֹוָה כִּי־עִם־יְהֹוָה הַחֶסֶד וְהַרְבֵּה עִמּוֹ פְדוּת: וְהוּא יִפְדֶּה אֶת־יִשְׂרָאֵל מִכֹּל עֲוֹנֹתָיו:

Shir Hama'alot; Mima'amakim Keraticha Adonai: Adonai Shim'ah Vekoli Tihyeinah Ozneicha Kashuvot; Lekol. Tachanunai. Im-Avonot Tishmor-Yah; Adonai. Mi Ya'amod. Ki-'Imecha Haselichah; Lema'an. Tivare. Kiviti Adonai Kivetah Nafshi; Velidvaro Hochaleti. Nafshi L'Adonai; Mishomerim Laboker. Shomerim Laboker. Yachel Yisra'el. El-Adonai Ki-'Im-Adonai Hachesed; Veharbeh Imo Fedut. Vehu Yifdeh Et-Yisra'el; Mikol Avonotav.

A Song of Ascents. Out of the depths have I called You, Hashem. Hashem, listen to my voice; let Your ears be attentive to the voice of my supplications. If You, Hashem, should mark iniquities, Hashem, who could stand? For with You there is forgiveness, that You may be feared. I wait for Hashem, my soul waits, and in His word do I hope. My soul waits for Hashem, more than watchmen for the morning; yes, more than watchmen for the morning. Oh Yisrael, hope in Hashem; for with Hashem there is mercy, and with Him is abundant redemption. And He will redeem Yisrael from all his iniquities.

Hatzi-Kaddish / Half Kaddish

Kaddish is only recited in a minyan (ten men). אמן denotes when the congregation responds "Amen" together out loud. According to the Shulchan Arukh, the congregation says "Yehei Shemeh Rabba" to "Yitbarach" out loud together without interruption, and also that one should respond "Amen" after "Yitbarach." (SA, OC 55,56) This is not the common custom today. Though many are accustomed to answering according to their own custom, it is advised to respond in the custom of the one reciting to avoid not fragmenting into smaller groups. ("Lo Titgodedu" - BT, Yevamot 13b / SA, OC 493, Rema / MT, Avodah Zara 12:15)

יִתְגַּדַּל וְיִתְקַדַּשׁ שְׁמֵהּ רַבָּא. אמן בְּעָלְמָא דִּי בְרָא. כִּרְעוּתֵהּ. וְיַמְלִיךְ מַלְכוּתֵהּ. וְיַצְמַח פֻּרְקָנֵהּ. וִיקָרֵב מְשִׁיחֵהּ. אמן בְּחַיֵּיכוֹן וּבְיוֹמֵיכוֹן וּבְחַיֵּי דְכָל בֵּית יִשְׂרָאֵל. בַּעֲגָלָא וּבִזְמַן קָרִיב. וְאִמְרוּ אָמֵן. אמן יְהֵא שְׁמֵיהּ רַבָּא מְבָרַךְ לְעָלַם וּלְעָלְמֵי עָלְמַיָּא יִתְבָּרַךְ. וְיִשְׁתַּבַּח. וְיִתְפָּאַר. וְיִתְרוֹמַם. וְיִתְנַשֵּׂא. וְיִתְהַדָּר. וְיִתְעַלֶּה. וְיִתְהַלָּל שְׁמֵהּ דְּקֻדְשָׁא. בְּרִיךְ הוּא. אמן לְעֵלָּא מִן כָּל בִּרְכָתָא שִׁירָתָא. תֻּשְׁבְּחָתָא וְנֶחֱמָתָא. דַּאֲמִירָן בְּעָלְמָא. וְאִמְרוּ אָמֵן. אמן

Yitgadal Veyitkadash Shemeh Rabba. Amen Be'alema Di Vera. Kir'uteh. Veyamlich Malchuteh. Veyatzmach Purkaneh. Vikarev Meshicheh. Amen Bechayeichon Uveyomeichon Uvechayei Dechal-Beit Yisra'el. Ba'agala Uvizman Kariv. Ve'imru Amen. Amen Yehei Shemeh Rabba Mevarach Le'alam Ule'alemei Alemaya Yitbarach. Veyishtabach. Veyitpa'ar. Veyitromam. Veyitnasse. Veyit'hadar. Veyit'aleh. Veyit'hallal Shemeh Dekudsha. Berich Hu. Amen Le'ella Min Kol Birchata Shirata. Tushbechata Venechemata. Da'amiran Be'alema. Ve'imru Amen. Amen

Glorified and sanctified be God's great name Amen throughout the world which He has created according to His will. May He establish His kingdom, hastening His salvation and the coming of His

Messiah, Amen, in your lifetime and during your days, and within the life of the entire House of Yisrael, speedily and soon; and say, Amen. Amen May His great name be blessed forever and to all eternity. Blessed and praised, glorified and exalted, extolled and honored, adored and lauded is the name of the Holy One, blessed is He, Amen Beyond all the blessings and hymns, praises and consolations that are ever spoken in the world; and say, Amen. Amen

Barechu / Call to Prayer

Barechu / Call to Prayer is made only if there is a minyan (10 men).

The Chazan bows and says:

בָּרְכוּ אֶת יְהֹוָה הַמְבֹרָךְ:

Barechu Et Adonai Hamevorach.

Bless Hashem, the blessed One.

The kahal / congregation answers:

בָּרוּךְ יְהֹוָה הַמְבֹרָךְ לְעוֹלָם וָעֶד:

Baruch Adonai Hamevorach Le'olam Va'ed.

Blessed is Hashem Who is blessed for all eternity.

The Chazan says:

בָּרוּךְ יְהֹוָה הַמְבֹרָךְ לְעוֹלָם וָעֶד:

Baruch Adonai Hamevorach Le'olam Va'ed.

Blessed is Hashem Who is blessed for all eternity.

LAWS OF KERIYAT SHEMA / THE RECITATION OF SHEMA

The time for reciting the Shema in the morning, is from the time when, at a distance of four cubits, one is able to recognize a person with whom he is slightly acquainted; and ends with the third hour of the day, which is one fourth of the day. If one has an accident, or he is on the road, he may recite it at daybreak. If one will be traveling later in a place where they will not be able to concentrate even for the first section until "upon your heart" or members of their caravan are going quickly and won't wait for one at all, then one can recite it with its blessings from Olot Shachar (about 72 minutes before sunrise). The latest time of reciting Shema is the end of the third hour (from sunrise, about 3.5 modern hrs). (SA, OC 58)

Kriyat Shema Uvirchotei'a / The Recital of Shema and Blessings

Yotzer Ohr

Baruch Attah Adonai Eloheinu	בָּרוּךְ אַתָּה יְהֹוָה אֱלֹהֵינוּ
Melech Ha'olam Yotzer Ohr	מֶלֶךְ הָעוֹלָם. יוֹצֵר אוֹר
Uvorei Choshech. Oseh Shalom	וּבוֹרֵא חֹשֶׁךְ. עֹשֶׂה שָׁלוֹם
Uvorei Et Hakol. Hakol Yoducha.	וּבוֹרֵא אֶת הַכֹּל. הַכֹּל יוֹדוּךָ.
Vehakol Yeshabechucha. Vehakol	וְהַכֹּל יְשַׁבְּחוּךָ. וְהַכֹּל
Yomeru Ein Kadosh K'Adonai.	יֹאמְרוּ אֵין קָדוֹשׁ כַּיהֹוָה .
Hakol Yeromemucha Selah.	הַכֹּל יְרוֹמְמוּךָ סֶּלָה.
Yotzer Hakol. Ha' El Hapotei'ach	יוֹצֵר הַכֹּל. הָאֵל הַפּוֹתֵחַ
Bechol Yom Daltot Sha'arei	בְּכָל יוֹם דַּלְתוֹת שַׁעֲרֵי
Mizrach. Uvokea Challonei	מִזְרָח. וּבוֹקֵעַ חַלּוֹנֵי
Rakia'. Motzi Chamah	רָקִיעַ. מוֹצִיא חַמָּה
Mimekomah Ulevanah	מִמְּקוֹמָהּ וּלְבָנָה
Mimechon Shivtah. Ume'ir	מִמְּכוֹן שִׁבְתָּהּ. וּמֵאִיר
La'olam Kulo Uleyoshevav.	לְעוֹלָם כֻּלּוֹ וּלְיוֹשְׁבָיו.
Shebara Bemidat Harachamim.	שֶׁבָּרָא בְּמִדַּת הָרַחֲמִים.
Hame'ir La'aretz Veladarim	הַמֵּאִיר לָאָרֶץ וְלַדָּרִים
Aleiha Berachamim. Uvetuvo	עָלֶיהָ בְּרַחֲמִים. וּבְטוּבוֹ
Mechadesh Bechol Yom Tamid	מְחַדֵּשׁ בְּכָל יוֹם תָּמִיד
Ma'aseh Bereshit. Mah Rabbu	מַעֲשֵׂה בְרֵאשִׁית. מָה רַבּוּ
Ma'aseicha Adonai Kulam	מַעֲשֶׂיךָ יְהֹוָה כֻּלָּם
Bechochmah Asita. Male'ah	בְּחָכְמָה עָשִׂיתָ. מָלְאָה
Ha'aretz Kinyanecha. Hamelech	הָאָרֶץ קִנְיָנֶךָ. הַמֶּלֶךְ
Hameromam Levado Me'az.	הַמְרוֹמָם לְבַדּוֹ מֵאָז.

Hameshubach Vehamefo'ar

Vehamitnasei Mimot Olam.

הַמְשֻׁבָּח וְהַמְפוֹאָר

וְהַמִּתְנַשֵּׂא מִימוֹת עוֹלָם.

Blessed are You, Hashem, our God, King of the universe, Who forms light, and creates darkness; makes peace, and creates all things. All will thank You, and all will praise You, and all will declare, there is none holy like Hashem. All will extol You forever, Who forms all things. God, Who daily opens the doors of the gates of the east, Who breaks open the windows of the firmament, brings out the sun from its place, and the moon from the place of its abode, and lights up the whole world and its inhabitants who You created, with the attribute of mercy. You give light to the earth and to those who dwell there in with mercy, and in Your goodness every day constantly renews the work of creation. How great are Your works, Hashem. In wisdom You made them all; the earth is full of Your possessions. You are the only King Who is praised ever since creation; praised, glorified, and exalted from days of old.

Elohei Olam. Berachameicha

אֱלֹהֵי עוֹלָם. בְּרַחֲמֶיךָ

Harabim Rachem Aleinu. Adon

הָרַבִּים רַחֵם עָלֵינוּ. אֲדוֹן

Uzenu. Tzur Misgabenu. Magen

עֻזֵּנוּ. צוּר מִשְׂגַּבֵּנוּ. מָגֵן

Yish'enu. Misgav Ba'adenu. Ein

יִשְׁעֵנוּ. מִשְׂגָּב בַּעֲדֵנוּ. אֵין

Aroch Lach Ve'ein Zulatach.

עֲרוֹךְ לָךְ וְאֵין זוּלָתָךְ.

Efes Biltach. Umi Domeh Lach.

אֶפֶס בִּלְתָּךְ. וּמִי דוֹמֶה לָּךְ.

Ein Aroch Lach Adonai Eloheinu

אֵין עֲרוֹךְ לָךְ יְהֹוָה אֱלֹהֵינוּ

Ba'olam Hazeh. Ve'ein Zulatach

בָּעוֹלָם הַזֶּה. וְאֵין זוּלָתָךְ

Malkeinu Lechayei Ha'olam

מַלְכֵּנוּ לְחַיֵּי הָעוֹלָם

Haba. Efes Biltach Go'alenu

הַבָּא. אֶפֶס בִּלְתָּךְ גּוֹאֲלֵנוּ

Limot Hamashiach. Umi

לִימוֹת הַמָּשִׁיחַ. וּמִי

Domeh Lach Moshi'enu

דוֹמֶה לָךְ מוֹשִׁיעֵנוּ

Litchiyat Hameitim.

לִתְחִיַּת הַמֵּתִים.

Everlasting God, in the abundance of Your mercy have compassion
on us. Lord of our strength. Rock of our fortress. Shield of our
salvation. Be a defense for us. There is none to compare with You;
nor is there anyone beside You: there is none but You; and who is
like You? There is none to be compared with You, Hashem our God,
in this world: nor is there anyone beside You, our King in the life of
the world to come. There is none but You, our Redeemer, for the
days of the Messiah: and who will be like You, our Savior, at the
resurrection of the dead?

El Adon

El Adon Al Kol Hama'asim.	אֵל אָדוֹן עַל כָּל הַמַּעֲשִׂים.
Baruch Umevorach Befi Chol	בָּרוּךְ וּמְבֹרָךְ בְּפִי כָל
Haneshamah. Gadelu Vetuvo	הַנְּשָׁמָה: גָּדְלוֹ וְטוּבוֹ
Malei Olam. Da'at Utevunah	מָלֵא עוֹלָם. דַּעַת וּתְבוּנָה
Sovim Hodo. Hamitga'eh Al	סוֹבְבִים הוֹדוֹ: הַמִּתְגָּאֶה עַל
Chayot Hakodesh. Venehdar	חַיּוֹת הַקֹּדֶשׁ. וְנֶהְדָּר
Bechavod Al Hamerkavah.	בְּכָבוֹד עַל הַמֶּרְכָּבָה:
Zechut Umishor Lifnei Chis'o.	זְכוּת וּמִישׁוֹר לִפְנֵי כִסְאוֹ.
Chesed Verachamim Malei	חֶסֶד וְרַחֲמִים מָלֵא
Chevodo. Tovim Me'orot	כְבוֹדוֹ: טוֹבִים מְאוֹרוֹת
Shebera'am Eloheinu. Yetzaram	שֶׁבְּרָאָם אֱלֹהֵינוּ. יְצָרָם
Beda'at Bevinah Uvehaskel.	בְּדַעַת בְּבִינָה וּבְהַשְׂכֵּל:
Koach Ugevurah Natan Bahem.	כֹּחַ וּגְבוּרָה נָתַן בָּהֶם.
Lihyot Moshelim Bekerev Tevel.	לִהְיוֹת מוֹשְׁלִים בְּקֶרֶב תֵּבֵל:
Mele'im Ziv Umefikim Nogah.	מְלֵאִים זִיו וּמְפִיקִים נֹגַהּ.
Na'eh Zivam Bechol Ha'olam.	נָאֶה זִיוָם בְּכָל הָעוֹלָם:

Semechim Betzetam Sasim	שְׂמֵחִים בְּצֵאתָם שָׂשִׂים
Bvo'am. Osim Be'eimah Retzon	בְּבֹאָם. עוֹשִׂים בְּאֵימָה רְצוֹן
Koneihem. Pe'er Vechavod	קוֹנֵיהֶם: פְּאֵר וְכָבוֹד
Notenim Lishmo. Tzoholah	נוֹתְנִים לִשְׁמוֹ. צָהֳלָה
Verinah Lezecher Malchuto.	וְרִנָּה לְזֵכֶר מַלְכוּתוֹ:
Kara Lashemesh Vayizrach Or.	קָרָא לַשֶּׁמֶשׁ וַיִּזְרַח אוֹר.
Ra'ah Vehitkin Tzurat Halevanah.	רָאָה וְהִתְקִין צוּרַת הַלְּבָנָה:
Shevach Notenim Lo Kol Tzeva	שֶׁבַח נוֹתְנִים לוֹ כָּל צְבָא
Marom. Tif'eret Ugedullah.	מָרוֹם. תִּפְאֶרֶת וּגְדֻלָּה.
Serafim Vechayot Ve'ofanei	שְׂרָפִים וְחַיּוֹת וְאוֹפַנֵּי
Hakodesh.	הַקֹּדֶשׁ:

God is the Lord of all creation; Blessed and praised is He by every soul. His greatness and goodness fill the universe; Knowledge and understanding surround His majesty. He is exalted above the holy Chayot, and adorned in glory above the Chariot. Merit and justice stand before His Throne; Kindness and mercy fill His glory. Good are the luminaries which our God has created; He made them with knowledge, understanding and insight; He placed in them strength and might to have dominion over the world. Full of splendor, they radiate brightness; Beautiful is their brilliance throughout the world. They rejoice in their rising and are glad in their setting, performing with reverence the will of their Creator. They give glory and honor to His name, And joy and song to commemorate His Kingdom. He called to the sun, and it shined with light; He saw fit to regulate the form of the moon. All the hosts of heaven give Him praise; the Seraphim, and holy Chayot and Ophanim render glory and grandeur.

On a Yom Tov, that is not Shabbat, skip La'El Asher Shavat:

La'El Asher Shavat

La'el Asher Shavat Mikol	לָאֵל אֲשֶׁר שָׁבַת מִכָּל
Hama'asim. Uvayom Hashevi'i	הַמַּעֲשִׂים. וּבַיּוֹם הַשְּׁבִיעִי
Nit'allah Veyashav Al Kissei	נִתְעַלָּה וְיָשַׁב עַל כִּסֵּא
Chevodo. Tif'eret Atah Leyom	כְבוֹדוֹ. תִּפְאֶרֶת עָטָה לְיוֹם
Hamenuchah. Oneg Kara	הַמְּנוּחָה. עֹנֶג קָרָא
Leyom Hashabbat. Zeh Shir	לְיוֹם הַשַּׁבָּת. זֶה שִׁיר
Shevach Shel Yom Hashevi'i.	שֶׁבַח שֶׁל יוֹם הַשְּׁבִיעִי.
Shebo Shavat El Mikol	שֶׁבּוֹ שָׁבַת אֵל מִכָּל
Melachto. Veyom Hashevi'i	מְלַאכְתּוֹ. וְיוֹם הַשְּׁבִיעִי
Meshabei'ach Ve'omer Mizmor	מְשַׁבֵּחַ וְאוֹמֵר מִזְמוֹר
Shir. Leyom Hashabbat.	שִׁיר לְיוֹם הַשַּׁבָּת:
Lefichach Yefa'aru La'el Kol	לְפִיכָךְ יְפָאֲרוּ לָאֵל כָּל
Tzurav. Shevach Vikar	יְצוּרָיו. שֶׁבַח וִיקָר
Ugedullah Vechavod Yitenu	וּגְדֻלָּה וְכָבוֹד יִתְּנוּ
Lamelech Yotzer Kol. Hamanchil	לַמֶּלֶךְ יוֹצֵר כֹּל. הַמַּנְחִיל
Menuchah Le'ammo Yisra'el	מְנוּחָה לְעַמּוֹ יִשְׂרָאֵל
Beyom Shabbat Kodesh.	בְּיוֹם שַׁבַּת קֹדֶשׁ:

To God (they will give praise) Who rested from all of His works on the seventh day and enthroned Himself and sat on His Throne of glory. With splendor He fixed the day of rest, calling the Shabbat a day of delight; This song of praise of the seventh day, for on it God rested from all His work, and the Seventh day praises and says, "A psalm, a song of the Shabbat day." For this let all the work of His hands glorify God, ascribing praise, honor and greatness and glory to the King, Former of all, Who grants rest to His people, Yisrael, on the holy day of Shabbat.

On all other days, continue here:

Shimcha Adonai Eloheinu	שִׁמְךָ יְהֹוָה אֱלֹהֵינוּ
Yitkadash. Vezichrecha Yitpa'ar	יִתְקַדָּשׁ. וְזִכְרְךָ יִתְפָּאַר
Malkeinu. Bashamayim Mima'al	מַלְכֵּנוּ. בַּשָּׁמַיִם מִמַּעַל
Ve'al Ha'aretz Mitachat. Al Kol	וְעַל הָאָרֶץ מִתָּחַת. עַל כָּל
Shevach Ma'aseh Yadeicha.	שֶׁבַח מַעֲשֵׂה יָדֶיךָ.
Ve'al Me'orei Or Sheyatzarta.	וְעַל מְאוֹרֵי אוֹר שֶׁיָּצַרְתָּ.
Hemah Yefa'arucha Selah.	הֵמָּה יְפָאֲרוּךְ סֶלָה.

Your name, Hashem our God, will be sanctified, and Your memorial, our King, will be glorified in the heavens above, and on the earth beneath, for all the praiseworthy work of Your hands, and for the luminaries which You have formed. They will glorify You forever.

Titbarach Lanetzach

Titbarach Lanetzach Tzurenu	תִּתְבָּרַךְ לָנֶצַח צוּרֵנוּ
Malkeinu Vego'alenu Borei	מַלְכֵּנוּ וְגוֹאֲלֵנוּ בּוֹרֵא
Kedoshim. Yishtabach Shimcha	קְדוֹשִׁים. יִשְׁתַּבַּח שִׁמְךָ
La'ad Malkeinu Yotzer	לָעַד מַלְכֵּנוּ יוֹצֵר
Mesharetim. Va'asher	מְשָׁרְתִים. וַאֲשֶׁר
Mesharetav Kulam Omedim	מְשָׁרְתָיו כֻּלָּם עוֹמְדִים
Berum Olam Umashmi'im	בְּרוּם עוֹלָם וּמַשְׁמִיעִים
Beyir'ah Yachad Bekol Divrei	בְּיִרְאָה יַחַד בְּקוֹל דִּבְרֵי
Elohim Chayim Umelech Olam.	אֱלֹהִים חַיִּים וּמֶלֶךְ עוֹלָם.
Kulam Ahuvim. Kulam Berurim.	כֻּלָּם אֲהוּבִים. כֻּלָּם בְּרוּרִים.
Kulam Giborim. Kulam	כֻּלָּם גִּבּוֹרִים. כֻּלָּם
Kedoshim. Kulam Osim	קְדוֹשִׁים. כֻּלָּם עוֹשִׂים
Be'eimah Uveyir'ah Ratzon	בְּאֵימָה וּבְיִרְאָה רָצוֹן

Koneihem. Vechulam Potechim	קוֹנֵיהֶם. וְכֻלָּם פּוֹתְחִים
Et Pihem Bikdushah Uvetaharah.	אֶת פִּיהֶם בִּקְדוּשָׁה וּבְטָהֳרָה.
Beshirah Uvezimrah.	בְּשִׁירָה וּבְזִמְרָה.
Umevarechin Umeshabechin	וּמְבָרְכִין וּמְשַׁבְּחִין
Umefa'arin Umakdishin	וּמְפָאֲרִין וּמַקְדִּישִׁין
Uma'aritzin Umamlichin Et	וּמַעֲרִיצִין וּמַמְלִיכִין אֶת
Shem Ha'el Hamelech Hagadol	שֵׁם הָאֵל הַמֶּלֶךְ הַגָּדוֹל
Hagibor Vehanorah Kadosh Hu.	הַגִּבּוֹר וְהַנּוֹרָא קָדוֹשׁ הוּא.
Vechulam Mekabelim Aleihem	וְכֻלָּם מְקַבְּלִים עֲלֵיהֶם
Ol Malchut Shamayim Zeh	עֹל מַלְכוּת שָׁמַיִם זֶה
Mizeh. Venotenim Reshut Zeh	מִזֶּה. וְנוֹתְנִים רְשׁוּת זֶה
Lazeh Lehakdish Leyotzeram	לָזֶה לְהַקְדִּישׁ לְיוֹצְרָם
Benachat Ruach Besafah Berurah	בְּנַחַת רוּחַ בְּשָׂפָה בְרוּרָה
Uvin'imah Kedushah. Kulam	וּבִנְעִימָה קְדוּשָׁה. כֻּלָּם
Ke'echad Onim Be'eimah.	כְּאֶחָד עוֹנִים בְּאֵימָה.
Ve'omerim Beyir'ah.	וְאוֹמְרִים בְּיִרְאָה:

Be forever blessed, our Rock, our King and Redeemer, Creator of holy-beings; may Your name be praised forever, our King, Creator of ministering angels, all of whom stand in the heights of the universe and reverently proclaim in unison, aloud, the words of the living God and everlasting King. All of them are beloved, all of them are pure, all of them are mighty, all of them are holy; they all perform with awe and reverence the will of their Creator; they all open their mouth with holiness and purity, with song and melody, while they bless and praise, glorify, sanctify and revere and acclaim the kingship of the name of God, the great, mighty and awesome King; holy is He. They all accept the yoke of the kingdom of heaven, one from the other, graciously granting permission to one another to sanctify their Creator. In serene spirit, with pure speech they all acclaim as one with reverence, and say with fear:

This "Kedusha" is said being seated. If one is standing, he now sits.

קָדוֹשׁ | קָדוֹשׁ קָדוֹשׁ יְהֹוָה צְבָאוֹת מְלֹא כָל־הָאָרֶץ כְּבוֹדוֹ:
וְהָאוֹפַנִּים וְחַיּוֹת הַקֹּדֶשׁ בְּרַעַשׁ גָּדוֹל מִתְנַשְּׂאִים לְעֻמַּת הַשְּׂרָפִים.
לְעֻמָּתָם מְשַׁבְּחִים וְאוֹמְרִים: בָּרוּךְ כְּבוֹד־יְהֹוָה מִמְּקוֹמוֹ:

Kadosh Kadosh Kadosh Adonai Tzeva'ot; Melo Chol-Ha'aretz Kevodo. Veha'ofanim Vechayot Hakodesh Bera'ash Gadol Mitnasse'im Le'ummat Hasrafim. Le'ummatam Meshabechim Ve'omerim. **Baruch Kevod-Adonai Mimekomo.**

Holy, holy, holy is Hashem of hosts; The whole earth is full of His glory. Then the Ophanim and the holy Chayot, rising with a great sound toward the Seraphim, facing them they respond with praise and say: **Blessed is the glory of Hashem from His Abode.**

La'El Baruch

La'el Baruch. Ne'imot Yitenu.	לָאֵל בָּרוּךְ. נְעִימוֹת יִתֵּנוּ.
Lamelech El Chai Vekayam.	לַמֶּלֶךְ אֵל חַי וְקַיָּם.
Zemirot Yomeru Vetishbachot	זְמִירוֹת יֹאמְרוּ וְתִשְׁבָּחוֹת
Yashmi'u. Ki Hu Levado Marom	יַשְׁמִיעוּ. כִּי הוּא לְבַדּוֹ מָרוֹם
Vekadosh. Po'el Gevurot. Oseh	וְקָדוֹשׁ. פּוֹעֵל גְּבוּרוֹת. עוֹשֶׂה
Chadashot. Ba'al Milchamot.	חֲדָשׁוֹת. בַּעַל מִלְחָמוֹת.
Zorea Tzedakot. Matzmiach	זוֹרֵעַ צְדָקוֹת. מַצְמִיחַ
Yeshu'ot. Borei Refu'ot. Nora	יְשׁוּעוֹת. בּוֹרֵא רְפוּאוֹת. נוֹרָא
Tehillot. Adon Hanifla'ot.	תְּהִלּוֹת. אֲדוֹן הַנִּפְלָאוֹת.
Hamchadesh Betuvo Bechol Yom	הַמְחַדֵּשׁ בְּטוּבוֹ בְּכָל יוֹם
Tamid Ma'aseh Vereshit Ka'amur.	תָּמִיד מַעֲשֵׂה בְרֵאשִׁית כָּאָמוּר:

Le'oseh Orim Gedolim; Ki	לְעֹשֵׂה אוֹרִים גְּדֹלִים כִּי
Le'olam Chasdo. Baruch Attah	לְעוֹלָם חַסְדּוֹ: בָּרוּךְ אַתָּה
Adonai Yotzer Hame'orot.	יְהֹוָה יוֹצֵר הַמְּאוֹרוֹת:

To the blessed God they offer melodies; to the King, the living and living God, they utter hymns and praises. They proclaim: He alone, exalted and holy, does mighty acts and creates new things; He is a Master of wars Who sows justice, produces salvations, and creates healing. Awesome in praise, Lord of wonders, in His goodness He renews the work of Creation every day, constantly, as it is said: "To the Maker of great lights; for His kindness endures forever." Blessed are You, Hashem, Former of the lights.

Ahavat Olam

Ahavat Olam Ahavtanu Adonai	אַהֲבַת עוֹלָם אֲהַבְתָּנוּ יְהֹוָה
Eloheinu. Chemlah Gedolah	אֱלֹהֵינוּ. חֶמְלָה גְּדוֹלָה
Viterah Chamalta Aleinu. Avinu	וִיתֵרָה חָמַלְתָּ עָלֵינוּ. אָבִינוּ
Malkeinu. Ba'avur Shimcha	מַלְכֵּנוּ. בַּעֲבוּר שִׁמְךָ
Hagadol Uva'avur Avoteinu	הַגָּדוֹל וּבַעֲבוּר אֲבוֹתֵינוּ
Shebatechu Bach Vat'lam'deimo	שֶׁבָּטְחוּ בָךְ וַתְּלַמְּדֵמוֹ
Chukkei Chayim La'asot	חֻקֵּי חַיִּים לַעֲשׂוֹת
Retzonecha Belevav Shalem. Ken	רְצוֹנְךָ בְּלֵבָב שָׁלֵם. כֵּן
Techanenu Avinu. Av	תְּחָנֵּנוּ אָבִינוּ. אָב
Harachaman Hamrachem.	הָרַחֲמָן הַמְרַחֵם.
Rachem Na Aleinu. Veten	רַחֵם נָא עָלֵינוּ. וְתֵן
Belibeinu Vinah Lehavin.	בְּלִבֵּנוּ בִינָה לְהָבִין.
Lehaskil. Lishmoa'. Lilmod	לְהַשְׂכִּיל. לִשְׁמֹעַ. לִלְמֹד

Ulelamed. Lishmor Vela'asot

וּלְלַמֵּד. לִשְׁמֹר וְלַעֲשׂוֹת

Ulekayem Et-Kol-Divrei Talmud

וּלְקַיֵּם אֶת־כָּל־דִּבְרֵי תַּלְמוּד

Toratecha Be'ahavah.

תּוֹרָתְךָ בְּאַהֲבָה:

With love everlasting You have loved us, Hashem our God; You have lavished on us tenderness, great and abundant. Our Father and Ruler, to our fathers who trusted in You, You taught the statutes of life that they should do Your will with a perfect heart. So also for Your great sake and for their sake be gracious to us, our Father, all-merciful Father. Have pity on us, You Who are merciful. Give to our heart understanding to understand, to comprehend, to hear, to learn and to teach, to guard and perform and to fulfill all the words of Your teaching of Torah, with love.

Veha'er Eineinu Betoratecha

וְהָאֵר עֵינֵינוּ בְּתוֹרָתֶךָ

Vedabek Libenu

וְדַבֵּק לִבֵּנוּ

Vemitzvoteicha. Veyached

בְּמִצְוֹתֶיךָ. וְיַחֵד

Levavenu Le'ahavah Uleyir'ah

לְבָבֵנוּ לְאַהֲבָה וּלְיִרְאָה

Et-Shemecha. Lo Nevosh Velo

אֶת־שְׁמֶךָ. לֹא נֵבוֹשׁ וְלֹא

Nikalem Velo Nikashel Le'olam

נִכָּלֵם וְלֹא נִכָּשֵׁל לְעוֹלָם

Va'ed. Ki Veshem Kodshecha

וָעֶד. כִּי בְשֵׁם קָדְשְׁךָ

Hagadol Hagibor Vehanorah

הַגָּדוֹל הַגִּבּוֹר וְהַנּוֹרָא

Batachenu. Nagilah

בָּטָחְנוּ. נָגִילָה

Venismechah Bishu'atecha.

וְנִשְׂמְחָה בִּישׁוּעָתֶךָ.

Verachameicha Adonai

וְרַחֲמֶיךָ יְהֹוָה

Eloheinu Vachasadeicha

אֱלֹהֵינוּ וַחֲסָדֶיךָ

Harabim. Al Ya'azvunu Netzach

הָרַבִּים. אַל יַעַזְבוּנוּ נֶצַח

Selah Va'ed.

סֶלָה וָעֶד:

Enlighten our eyes through Your Torah. Make our heart cleave to Your commandments, and unify our hearts to love and reverence

Your name, that we never be brought to shame or confusion or stumbling for we put our trust in Your great power and awesome name. Let us be glad and rejoice in Your salvation. Hashem our God, and may Your manifold loving kindnesses never leave us.

([*] denotes gathering all four tzitzit on Tallit corners together in one's left hand.)

Maher Vehavei Aleinu Berachah	מַהֵר וְהָבֵא עָלֵינוּ בְּרָכָה
Veshalom Meheirah *Me'arba	וְשָׁלוֹם מְהֵרָה *מֵאַרְבַּע
Kanfot Kol-Ha'aretz. Ushevor	כַּנְפוֹת כָּל־הָאָרֶץ. וּשְׁבֹר
Ol Hagoyim Me'al Tzavarenu.	עֹל הַגּוֹיִם מֵעַל צַוָּארֵנוּ.
Veholicheinu Meheirah	וְהוֹלִיכֵנוּ מְהֵרָה
Komemiyut Le'artzenu. Ki El	קוֹמְמִיּוּת לְאַרְצֵנוּ. כִּי אֵל
Po'el Yeshu'ot Attah. Uvanu	פּוֹעֵל יְשׁוּעוֹת אַתָּה. וּבָנוּ
Vacharta Mikol Am Velashon.	בָחַרְתָּ מִכָּל עַם וְלָשׁוֹן.
Vekeravtanu Malkeinu	וְקֵרַבְתָּנוּ מַלְכֵּנוּ
Leshimcha Hagadol Be'ahavah.	לְשִׁמְךָ הַגָּדוֹל בְּאַהֲבָה.
Lehodot Lach Uleyachedcha	לְהוֹדוֹת לָךְ וּלְיַחֶדְךָ
Leyir'ah Ule'ahavah Et-Shimcha.	לְיִרְאָה וּלְאַהֲבָה אֶת־שְׁמֶךָ.
Baruch Attah Adonai	בָּרוּךְ אַתָּה יְהֹוָה
Habbocher Be'ammo Yisra'el	הַבּוֹחֵר בְּעַמּוֹ יִשְׂרָאֵל
Be'ahavah.	בְּאַהֲבָה:

Hasten to bring upon us blessing and peace quickly *from the four corners of the earth. Break the alien yoke from our necks, and speedily lead us upright to our land. For You are God Who works deliverance, and You, Divine King, have chosen us from all other peoples and tongues and in love drawn us near to Your great name, to give You thanks, proclaim Your unity and fear and love Your name. Blessed are You, Hashem, Who chooses His people Yisrael in love.

LAWS OF RECITING THE SHEMA

One who recites the Shema, but did not have intention during the first verse, 'Shema Yisrael', one did not fulfill their obligation. As for the rest, if they read during the specified time and did not have intention, they have fulfilled their obligation. One should recite the Shema with intention, awe, fear, shaking and trembling. The verse states: "Which I have commanded you today," (Deut. 6:6) which teaches that every day it should appear in your eyes as if it was new, and not like someone who already heard it many times and it is not precious to him. The custom is to place one's hands over their face during the recitation of the first verse in order that one will not look at something else that will prevent him from directing his heart. (SA, OC 59-61) The Shema should be recited with the notes as they are in the Torah; (but no one is particular about this). One may read the Shema while walking, sitting, reclining or riding, providing he does not lie with his face downward or laying on his back with his face upward. When reading the Shema while walking, one must stand still when reading the first verse. If one recited the Recitation of the Shema on one's own and entered the synagogue and found the congregation reciting the Recitation of the Shema, it is best that one should recite the entire Recitation of the Shema along with them. If one forgot to put on tzitzit or tefillin, one can interrupt between sections [of Shema or it's blessings] and don them, and one can make a blessing over them. If one forgot to put on the tallit or the tefillin, he may pause between the chapters of the Shema and put them on. (And concerning the tallit, it is customary not to say the blessing till after the prayers.) It is prohibited to recite in a place where there is excrement, urine, manure, or a swine, or in any filthy place (garbage with bad smell, etc.), or in front of a naked person. (But it is permissible if the naked person is a minor). If a receptacle was placed over the above mentioned unclean things, one may read there. (SA, OC 65,66, 75-76)

The Shema

Deuteronomy 6:4-9

One covers their eyes and says:

שְׁמַע יִשְׂרָאֵל יְהֹוָה אֱלֹהֵינוּ יְהֹוָה|אֶחָד:

Shema Yisrael; Adonai Eloheinu Adonai Echad.
"Hear, O Yisrael, Hashem is our God, Hashem is One."

Whisper silently:

בָּרוּךְ שֵׁם כְּבוֹד מַלְכוּתוֹ לְעוֹלָם וָעֶד:
Baruch Shem Kevod Malchuto Le'olam Va'ed.
Blessed is His name and glorious kingdom forever and ever.

Ve'ahavta

וְאָהַבְתָּ אֵת יְהֹוָה אֱלֹהֶיךָ בְּכָל־לְבָבְךָ וּבְכָל־נַפְשְׁךָ וּבְכָל־מְאֹדֶךָ:
וְהָיוּ הַדְּבָרִים הָאֵלֶּה אֲשֶׁר אָנֹכִי מְצַוְּךָ הַיּוֹם עַל־לְבָבֶךָ: וְשִׁנַּנְתָּם

לְבָנֶיךָ וְדִבַּרְתָּ בָּם בְּשִׁבְתְּךָ בְּבֵיתֶךָ וּבְלֶכְתְּךָ בַדֶּרֶךְ וּבְשָׁכְבְּךָ
וּבְקוּמֶךָ: וּקְשַׁרְתָּם לְאוֹת עַל־יָדֶךָ וְהָיוּ לְטֹטָפֹת בֵּין עֵינֶיךָ: וּכְתַבְתָּם
עַל־מְזֻזוֹת בֵּיתֶךָ וּבִשְׁעָרֶיךָ:

Ve'ahavta Et Adonai Eloheicha; Bechol-Levavecha Uvechol-
Nafshecha Uvechol-Me'odecha. Vehayu Hadevarim Ha'eleh. Asher
Anochi Metzavecha Hayom Al-Levavecha. Veshinantam Levaneicha.
Vedibarta Bam; Beshivtecha Beveitecha Uvelechtecha Vaderech.
Uveshochbecha Uvekumecha. Ukeshartam Le'ot Al-Yadecha;
Vehayu Letotafot Bein Eineicha. Uchetavtam Al-Mezuzot Beitecha
Uvish'areicha.

And you will love Hashem your God with all your heart, and with all
your soul, and with all your might. And these words, which I
command you this day, will be upon your heart; and you will teach
them diligently to your children, and will talk of them when you sit
in your house, and when you walk by the way, and when you lie
down, and when you rise up. And you will bind them for a sign on
your hand, and they will be for frontlets between your eyes. And you
will write them on the doorposts of your house, and on your gates.

Vehayah Im-Shamoa

וְהָיָה אִם־שָׁמֹעַ תִּשְׁמְעוּ אֶל־מִצְוֹתַי אֲשֶׁר אָנֹכִי מְצַוֶּה אֶתְכֶם הַיּוֹם
לְאַהֲבָה אֶת־יְהֹוָה אֱלֹהֵיכֶם וּלְעָבְדוֹ בְּכָל־לְבַבְכֶם וּבְכָל־נַפְשְׁכֶם:
וְנָתַתִּי מְטַר־אַרְצְכֶם בְּעִתּוֹ יוֹרֶה וּמַלְקוֹשׁ וְאָסַפְתָּ דְגָנֶךָ וְתִירשְׁךָ
וְיִצְהָרֶךָ: וְנָתַתִּי עֵשֶׂב בְּשָׂדְךָ לִבְהֶמְתֶּךָ וְאָכַלְתָּ וְשָׂבָעְתָּ: הִשָּׁמְרוּ
לָכֶם פֶּן יִפְתֶּה לְבַבְכֶם וְסַרְתֶּם וַעֲבַדְתֶּם אֱלֹהִים אֲחֵרִים
וְהִשְׁתַּחֲוִיתֶם לָהֶם: וְחָרָה אַף־יְהֹוָה בָּכֶם וְעָצַר אֶת־הַשָּׁמַיִם
וְלֹא־יִהְיֶה מָטָר וְהָאֲדָמָה לֹא תִתֵּן אֶת־יְבוּלָהּ וַאֲבַדְתֶּם מְהֵרָה מֵעַל
הָאָרֶץ הַטֹּבָה אֲשֶׁר יְהֹוָה נֹתֵן לָכֶם: וְשַׂמְתֶּם אֶת־דְּבָרַי אֵלֶּה
עַל־לְבַבְכֶם וְעַל־נַפְשְׁכֶם וּקְשַׁרְתֶּם אֹתָם לְאוֹת עַל־יֶדְכֶם וְהָיוּ

לְטוֹטָפֹת בֵּין עֵינֵיכֶם. וְלִמַּדְתֶּם אֹתָם אֶת־בְּנֵיכֶם לְדַבֵּר בָּם בְּשִׁבְתְּךָ
בְּבֵיתֶךָ וּבְלֶכְתְּךָ בַדֶּרֶךְ וּבְשָׁכְבְּךָ וּבְקוּמֶךָ: וּכְתַבְתָּם עַל־מְזוּזוֹת בֵּיתֶךָ
וּבִשְׁעָרֶיךָ: לְמַעַן יִרְבּוּ יְמֵיכֶם וִימֵי בְנֵיכֶם עַל הָאֲדָמָה אֲשֶׁר נִשְׁבַּע
יהוה לַאֲבֹתֵיכֶם לָתֵת לָהֶם כִּימֵי הַשָּׁמַיִם עַל־הָאָרֶץ:

Vehayah Im-Shmoa Tishme'u El-Mitzvotai. Asher Anochi Metzaveh
Etchem Hayom; Le'ahavah Et-Adonai Eloheichem Ule'avdo. Bechol-
Levavchem Uvechol-Nafshechem. Venatati Metar-'Artzechem Be'ito
Yoreh Umalkosh; Ve'asafta Deganecha. Vetiroshecha Veyitzharecha.
Venatati Esev Besadecha Livhemtecha; Ve'achalta Vesava'eta.
Hishameru Lachem. Pen Yifteh Levavchem; Vesartem. Va'avadtem
Elohim Acherim. Vehishtachavitem Lahem. Vecharah Af-Adonai
Bachem. Ve'atzar Et-Hashamayim Velo-Yihyeh Matar. Veha'adamah.
Lo Titen Et-Yevulah; Va'avadtem Meheirah. Me'al Ha'aretz Hatovah.
Asher Adonai Noten Lachem. Vesamtem Et-Devarai Eleh. Al-
Levavchem Ve'al-Nafshechem; Ukeshartem Otam Le'ot Al-Yedchem.
Vehayu Letotafot Bein Eineichem. Velimadtem Otam Et-Beneichem
Ledaber Bam; Beshivtecha Beveitecha Uvelechtecha Vaderech.
Uveshochbecha Uvekumecha. Uchetavtam Al-Mezuzot Beitecha
Uvish'areicha. Lema'an Yirbu Yemeichem Vimei Veneichem. Al
Ha'adamah. Asher Nishba Adonai La'avoteichem Latet Lahem;
Kimei Hashamayim Al-Ha'aretz.

And it will come to pass, if you will observe My commandments
which I command you this day, to love Hashem your God, and to
serve Him with all your heart and with all your soul, that I will give
the rain of your land in its season, the former rain and the latter
rain, that you may gather in your corn, and your wine, and your oil.
And I will give grass in your fields for your cattle, and you will eat
and be satisfied. Be cautious, in case your heart is deceived, and you
turn aside, and serve other gods, and worship them; and the anger
of Hashem is kindled against you, and He shut up the heaven, so
that there will be no rain, and the ground will not yield her fruit; and
you perish quickly from off the good land which Hashem gives you.
Therefore you will lay up these words in your heart and in your soul;
and you will bind them for a sign upon your hand, and they will be
for frontlets between your eyes. And you will teach them to your

children, talking of them, when you sit in your house, and when you walk by the way, and when you lie down, and when you rise up. And you will write them on the doorposts of your house, and on your gates; that your days may be multiplied, and the days of your children, upon the land which Hashem swore to your fathers to give them, as the days of the heavens above the earth. (Deuteronomy 11:13-21)

Numbers 15:37-41

Below [*] denotes when to kiss your tzitzit, on "ure'item otoh" gaze at the tzitziyot in hand (SA, OC 24,4), on "ve'acharei eineichem" some pass them in front of their eyes and kiss them. (BI"H).

וַיֹּאמֶר יְהֹוָה אֶל־מֹשֶׁה לֵּאמֹר: דַּבֵּר אֶל־בְּנֵי יִשְׂרָאֵל וְאָמַרְתָּ אֲלֵהֶם
וְעָשׂוּ לָהֶם *צִיצִת עַל־כַּנְפֵי בִגְדֵיהֶם לְדֹרֹתָם וְנָתְנוּ עַל־*צִיצִת
הַכָּנָף פְּתִיל תְּכֵלֶת: וְהָיָה לָכֶם *לְצִיצִת *וּרְאִיתֶם אֹתוֹ וּזְכַרְתֶּם
אֶת־כָּל־מִצְוֹת יְהֹוָה וַעֲשִׂיתֶם אֹתָם וְלֹא־תָתוּרוּ אַחֲרֵי לְבַבְכֶם וְאַחֲרֵי
עֵינֵיכֶם אֲשֶׁר־אַתֶּם זֹנִים אַחֲרֵיהֶם: לְמַעַן תִּזְכְּרוּ וַעֲשִׂיתֶם
אֶת־כָּל־מִצְוֹתָי וִהְיִיתֶם קְדֹשִׁים לֵאלֹהֵיכֶם: אֲנִי יְהֹוָה אֱלֹהֵיכֶם אֲשֶׁר
הוֹצֵאתִי אֶתְכֶם מֵאֶרֶץ מִצְרַיִם לִהְיוֹת לָכֶם לֵאלֹהִים אֲנִי יְהֹוָה
אֱלֹהֵיכֶם: אֱמֶת.

Vayomer Adonai El-Mosheh Lemor. Daber El-Benei Yisra'el
Ve'amarta Aleihem. Ve'asu Lahem *Tzitzit Al-Kanfei Vigdeihem
Ledorotam; Venatenu Al-*Tzitzit Hakanaf Petil Techelet. Vehayah
Lachem *Letzitzit *Ure'Item Oto Uzechartem Et-Chol-Mitzvot
Adonai Va'asitem Otam; Velo-Taturu Acharei Levavchem Ve'acharei
Eineichem. Asher-'Attem Zonim Achareihem. Lema'an Tizkeru.
Va'asitem Et-Chol-Mitzvotai; Vihyitem Kedoshim Leloheichem. Ani
Adonai Eloheichem. Asher Hotzeti Etchem Me'eretz Mitzrayim.
Lihyot Lachem Lelohim; Ani Adonai Eloheichem. Emet.

And Hashem spoke to Moshe, saying: Speak to the children of Yisrael, and command them to make *tzitzit on the corners of their garments throughout their generations, and that they put a thread of tekhelet with the *tzitzit of each corner. And they will be to you for *tzitzit, that *you may look upon them, and remember all the commandments of Hashem, and do them; and that you do not go about after your own heart and your own eyes, after which you go whoring; that you may remember and do all My commandments, and be holy to your God. I am Hashem your God, Who brought you out of the land of Mitzrayim, to be your God: I am Hashem your God. It is true.

יְהֹוָה אֱלֹהֵיכֶם אֱמֶת:

Adonai Eloheichem Emet.

Hashem, your God, is true.

Veyatziv

Veyatziv. Venachon. Vekayam.	וְיַצִּיב. וְנָכוֹן. וְקַיָּם.
Veyashar. Vene'eman. Ve'ahuv.	וְיָשָׁר. וְנֶאֱמָן. וְאָהוּב.
Vechaviv. Venechmad. Vena'im.	וְחָבִיב. וְנֶחְמָד. וְנָעִים.
Venora. Ve'adir. Umetukan.	וְנוֹרָא. וְאַדִּיר. וּמְתוּקָן.
Umekubbal. Vetov. Veyafeh.	וּמְקֻבָּל. וְטוֹב. וְיָפֶה.
Hadavar Hazeh Aleinu Le'olam	הַדָּבָר הַזֶּה עָלֵינוּ לְעוֹלָם
Va'ed.	וָעֶד.

And firm, and established, and constant, and upright, and faithful, and beloved, and cherished, and delightful, and nice, and awesome, and powerful, and correct, and acceptable is this good and beautiful matter to us for all time.

Below [*] denotes kissing, passing before your eyes and letting go of your tzitziyot at "La'ad" [forever].

Emet. Elohei Olam Malkeinu	אֱמֶת. אֱלֹהֵי עוֹלָם מַלְכֵּנוּ
Tzur Ya'akov Magen Yish'enu.	צוּר יַעֲקֹב מָגֵן יִשְׁעֵנוּ.

Ledor Vador Hu Kayam. Ushemo	לְדוֹר וָדוֹר הוּא קַיָּם. וּשְׁמוֹ
Kayam. Vechis'o Nachon.	קַיָּם. וְכִסְאוֹ נָכוֹן.
Umalchuto Ve'emunato La'ad	וּמַלְכוּתוֹ וֶאֱמוּנָתוֹ לָעַד
Kayemet. Udevarav Chayim	קַיֶּמֶת. וּדְבָרָיו חַיִּים
Vekayamim. Vene'emanim	וְקַיָּמִים. וְנֶאֱמָנִים
Venechemadim *La'ad	וְנֶחֱמָדִים *לָעַד
Ule'olemei Olamim. Al	וּלְעוֹלְמֵי עוֹלָמִים. עַל
Avoteinu. Aleinu Ve'al Baneinu	אֲבוֹתֵינוּ. עָלֵינוּ וְעַל בָּנֵינוּ
Ve'al Doroteinu Ve'al Kol Dorot	וְעַל דּוֹרוֹתֵינוּ וְעַל כָּל דּוֹרוֹת
Zera Yisra'el Avadeicha. Al	זֶרַע יִשְׂרָאֵל עֲבָדֶיךָ. עַל
Harishonim Ve'al Ha'acharonim	הָרִאשׁוֹנִים וְעַל הָאַחֲרוֹנִים
Davar Tov Vekayam Be'emet	דָּבָר טוֹב וְקַיָּם בֶּאֱמֶת
Ve'emunah Chok Velo Ya'avor.	וֶאֱמוּנָה חוֹק וְלֹא יַעֲבוֹר.
Emet She'attah Hu Adonai	אֱמֶת שָׁאַתָּה הוּא יְהֹוָה
Eloheinu Velohei Avoteinu.	אֱלֹהֵינוּ וֵאלֹהֵי אֲבוֹתֵינוּ.
Malkeinu Melech Avoteinu.	מַלְכֵּנוּ מֶלֶךְ אֲבוֹתֵינוּ.
Go'alenu Go'el Avoteinu.	גּוֹאֲלֵנוּ גּוֹאֵל אֲבוֹתֵינוּ.
Yotzreinu Tzur Yeshu'ateinu.	יוֹצְרֵנוּ צוּר יְשׁוּעָתֵנוּ.
Podenu Umatzilenu Me'olam Hu	פּוֹדֵנוּ וּמַצִּילֵנוּ מֵעוֹלָם הוּא
Shemecha. Ve'ein Lanu Od	שְׁמֶךָ. וְאֵין לָנוּ עוֹד אֱלֹהִים
Elohim Zulatecha Selah.	זוּלָתְךָ סֶלָה:

It is true that the eternal God our Ruler, the Rock of Yaakov, our saving Shield, exists eternally generation to generation, without end. He is eternal; His Throne is established, and His rule abides unchanging *forever. His teachings are eternally living, and unchanging, and faithful, and delightful for all time for our forefathers as well as for us, our children and descendants and all generations of the seed of Yisrael, Your servants. On the first and the later generations it is good and enduring. In truth and faith, it is a law that will not pass away. It is true that You are Hashem our God and God of our fathers, our divine Ruler and Ruler of our fathers, our Redeemer and Redeemer of our fathers. From old You have been our Rock, the Rock of our salvation and our saving Deliverer, and we have no other God besides You.

Ezrat Avoteinu

Ezrat Avoteinu Attah Hu	עֶזְרַת אֲבוֹתֵינוּ אַתָּה הוּא
Me'olam. Magen Umoshia	מֵעוֹלָם. מָגֵן וּמוֹשִׁיעַ
Lahem Velivneihem Achareihem	לָהֶם וְלִבְנֵיהֶם אַחֲרֵיהֶם
Bechol Dor Vador. Berum Olam	בְּכָל דּוֹר וָדוֹר. בְּרוּם עוֹלָם
Moshavecha. Umishpateicha.	מוֹשָׁבֶךָ. וּמִשְׁפָּטֶיךָ.
Vetzidkatecha Ad Afsei Aretz.	וְצִדְקָתְךָ עַד אַפְסֵי אָרֶץ.
Emet Ashrei Ish Sheyishma	אֱמֶת אַשְׁרֵי אִישׁ שֶׁיִּשְׁמַע
Lemitzvoteicha Vetoratecha	לְמִצְוֹתֶיךָ וְתוֹרָתְךָ
Udevarecha Yasim Al Libo. Emet	וּדְבָרְךָ יָשִׂים עַל לִבּוֹ. אֱמֶת
She'attah Hu Adon Le'ammecha	שָׁאַתָּה הוּא אָדוֹן לְעַמֶּךָ
Umelech Gibor Lariv Rivam	וּמֶלֶךְ גִּבּוֹר לָרִיב רִיבָם
Le'avot Uvanim. Emet Attah Hu	לְאָבוֹת וּבָנִים. אֱמֶת אַתָּה הוּא
Rishon Ve'attah Hu Acharon	רִאשׁוֹן וְאַתָּה הוּא אַחֲרוֹן
Umibal'adeicha Ein Lanu	וּמִבַּלְעָדֶיךָ אֵין לָנוּ
Melech Go'el Umoshia.	מֶלֶךְ גּוֹאֵל וּמוֹשִׁיעַ.

From ancient times, You have been the help of our fathers, a Shield and a Savior for them and their children after them in every generation. Your dwelling is in the heights of the universe, yet Your righteousness and justice are to the ends of the earth. It is true that happy is the man who listens to Your commandments, who sets

Your Torah and Your Word in his heart. It is true that You are the Lord of Your people, Their mighty King to fight their cause in every generation. It is true that You are the First and You are the Last, and besides You we have no king, redeemer and savior.

Emet Mimitzrayim Ge'altanu	אֱמֶת מִמִּצְרַיִם גְּאַלְתָּנוּ
Adonai Eloheinu. Mibeit	יְהֹוָה אֱלֹהֵינוּ. מִבֵּית
Avadim Peditanu. Kol	עֲבָדִים פְּדִיתָנוּ. כָּל
Bechoreihem Haragta.	בְּכוֹרֵיהֶם הָרָגְתָּ.
Uvechorecha Yisra'el Ga'alta.	וּבְכוֹרְךָ יִשְׂרָאֵל גָּאָלְתָּ.
Veyam-Suf Lahem Baka'ta.	וְיַם־סוּף לָהֶם בָּקַעְתָּ.
Vezeidim Tiba'ta. Vididim Averu	וְזֵדִים טִבַּעְתָּ. וִידִידִים עָבְרוּ
Yam. Vaychasu Mayim	יָם. וַיְכַסּוּ מַיִם
Tzareihem Echad Mehem Lo	צָרֵיהֶם אֶחָד מֵהֶם לֹא
Notar. Al Zot Shibechu Ahuvim.	נוֹתָר. עַל זֹאת שִׁבְּחוּ אֲהוּבִים.
Veromemu La'el. Venatenu	וְרוֹמְמוּ לָאֵל. וְנָתְנוּ
Yedidim Zemirot Shirot	יְדִידִים זְמִירוֹת שִׁירוֹת
Vetishbachot Berachot	וְתִשְׁבָּחוֹת בְּרָכוֹת
Vehoda'ot LaMelech El Chai	וְהוֹדָאוֹת לַמֶּלֶךְ אֵל חַי
Vekayam. Ram Venissa. Gadol	וְקַיָּם. רָם וְנִשָּׂא. גָּדוֹל
Venora. Mashpil Ge'im Adei	וְנוֹרָא. מַשְׁפִּיל גֵּאִים עֲדֵי
Aretz. Magbiah Shefalim Ad	אָרֶץ. מַגְבִּיהַּ שְׁפָלִים עַד
Marom. Motzi Asirim. Podeh	מָרוֹם. מוֹצִיא אֲסִירִים. פּוֹדֶה
Anavim. Ozeir Dallim. Ha'oneh	עֲנָוִים. עוֹזֵר דַּלִּים. הָעוֹנֶה
Le'ammo Yisra'el Be'et	לְעַמּוֹ יִשְׂרָאֵל בְּעֵת
Shave'am Elav.	שַׁוְּעָם אֵלָיו.

It is true that You, Hashem our God, have redeemed us from Mitzrayim and rescued us from the house of bondage, slaying all the firstborn of Mitzrayim and redeeming Your firstborn, Yisrael. For them You parted the Sea of Reeds and drowned the arrogant. The beloved passed through the sea, but "the waters covered their enemies, not one of them remained." On this, His cherished ones sang exalting praises to God. The beloved offered hymns, songs, and praises, blessings and thanksgiving to the divine Ruler Who is the ever-living God. He Who is supremely exalted, all-powerful, and awe-inspiring, brings down the proud to earth, raises the lowly, frees the bound, rescues the humble, helps the poor, and answers His people Yisrael when they cry to Him.

One now stands in preparation for the Amidah.

Tehilot La'el Elyon Go'alam.	תְּהִלוֹת לָאֵל עֶלְיוֹן גּוֹאֲלָם.
Baruch Hu Umevorach. Mosheh	בָּרוּךְ הוּא וּמְבוֹרָךְ. מֹשֶׁה
Uvenei Yisra'el Lecha Anu	וּבְנֵי יִשְׂרָאֵל לְךָ עָנוּ
Shirah Vesimchah Rabah.	שִׁירָה בְּשִׂמְחָה רַבָּה.
Ve'ameru Chulam. Mi-	וְאָמְרוּ כֻלָּם: מִי־
Chamochah Ba'elim Adonai Mi	כָמֹכָה בָּאֵלִם יְהֹוָה מִי
Kamochah Ne'dar Bakodesh;	כָּמֹכָה נֶאְדָּר בַּקֹּדֶשׁ
Nora Tehillot Oseh Fele. Shirah	נוֹרָא תְהִלֹּת עֹשֵׂה פֶלֶא: שִׁירָה
Chadashah Shibechu Ge'ulim	חֲדָשָׁה שִׁבְּחוּ גְאוּלִים
Leshimcha Hagadol Al Sefat	לְשִׁמְךָ הַגָּדוֹל עַל שְׂפַת
Hayam. Yachad Chulam Hodu	הַיָּם. יַחַד כֻּלָּם הוֹדוּ
Vehimlichu Ve'ameru. Adonai	וְהִמְלִיכוּ וְאָמְרוּ: יְהֹוָה │
Yimloch Le'olam Va'ed.	יִמְלֹךְ לְעֹלָם וָעֶד:
Vene'emar. Go'alenu Adonai	וְנֶאֱמַר: גֹּאֲלֵנוּ יְהֹוָה
Tzeva'ot Shemo; Kedosh	צְבָאוֹת שְׁמוֹ קְדוֹשׁ
Yisra'el. Baruch Attah Adonai	יִשְׂרָאֵל: בָּרוּךְ אַתָּה יְהֹוָה
Ga'al Yisra'el.	גָּאַל יִשְׂרָאֵל:

Praises to the Supreme God, their Redeemer, blessed is He. To You Moshe and all the children of Yisrael proclaimed a song with great joy, "Who is like You, Hashem, among the gods, Who is like You, glorified in holiness, You are awesome in praises, working wonders." The redeemed ones sang a new song of praise to Your great name on the sea shore. Together they thanked You, proclaiming Your kingly power, and said, "Hashem will reign forever and ever." So also it is said: "Our Redeemer, Hashem of hosts is His name, The Holy One of Yisrael." Blessed are You, Hashem, Redeemer of Yisrael.

LAWS OF AMIDAH / SHACHARIT

The time for the Amidah: its command is that it should begin with the blossoming of the sun, as it is written, "They will revere You while the sun endures." (Ps. 72:5). And its time continues until the end of four hours which is a third of the daytime. And if one erred or transgressed and prayed after the fourth hour until noon, even though one does not have the reward as praying at its proper time, there is still a reward of prayer. A person should make an effort to pray in the synagogue with a congregation, and if he is unable to due to an extenuating circumstance that he is not able to come to the synagogue, he should intend to pray at the time that the congregation is praying. When one stands [praying] with the congregation, it is forbidden to advance one's prayer [ahead of] the prayer of the congregation, unless the time [for prayer] is passing. (SA, OC 89, 90) When one gets up to pray if he is standing outside the Land of Yisrael, he should turn his face toward the Land of Yisrael and focus also on Yerushalayim and the Temple and the Holy of Holies. One who is not able to determine the directions, [should] direct one's heart to their Father in Heaven. One should consider oneself as if one is standing in the Beit Hamikdash, and in one's heart, one should be directed upward towards Heaven. One who prays needs to intend in their heart the meaning of the words which are coming out of their mouth. They should think as if the Divine Presence is before them, and remove all distracting thoughts from themselves, until their thoughts and intention are pure in their prayer. (SA, OC 94, 95, 98) These are the blessings at which we bow: in Avot, at the beginning and at the end; in Modim, at the beginning and at the end. And if you come to bow at the end of every blessing or at the beginning, we teach him to not bow but in the middle, one can bow. One needs to bend until all the vertebrae in his spine are bent. His head should stay straight and submissive. One should not bow too much until his mouth is opposite his belt. If he is sick or old and cannot bow, he should humble his head, that is enough. Bow at "Baruch" and stand up at Hashem's name. (SA, OC 113,114) One should position one's feet next to each other as though they are one, in order to imitate angels, as it written regarding them: "their feet are a straight foot" (Ez. 1:7), which is to say their feet appeared as one foot. One should take three steps forward in the way of coming close and approaching a matter that must be done. (SA, OC 95, Rema) If he wants to add in each of the middle blessings, something like that blessing, he may add. How so? If there was a sick person he was asking for mercy over, in the blessing "heal us." If he needs to earn a living, he would ask in the blessing over the years. And in "who hears prayer" he can ask for any of his needs, which includes all requests. (Hagah: And when he adds, he should first recite the blessing and then add, but he should not add and then begin the blessing [Tur 567]). And according to Rabbeinu Yona, when he adds to the blessing something like the blessing, if he is adding something on behalf of all of Yisrael, he would say it in plural language and not singular language, and he should add at the end of the blessing and not the middle. And if he is asking for his own needs, like, there is a sick person in his home or he needs to earn a living, he may ask even in the middle of a blessing, as long as he does so in the singular and not the plural. And during the blessing, "who hears prayer" and also at the end of prayer he may ask in either plural or singular, whether this is for his own needs or those of the many. (SA, OC 119:1)

Amidah / Shemoneh Esrei - Shacharit

Take three steps forward and say:

Adonai Sefatai Tiftach; Ufi. Yagid

אֲדֹנָי שְׂפָתַי תִּפְתָּח וּפִי יַגִּיד

Tehilatecha.

תְּהִלָּתֶךָ:

Hashem, open my lips, that my mouth may declare Your praise.

Avot / Fathers

Bow at "Baruch Attah" / "Blessed are You". Raise up at Adonai / Hashem.

Baruch Attah Adonai Eloheinu

בָּרוּךְ אַתָּה יְהֹוָה אֱלֹהֵינוּ

Velohei Avoteinu. Elohei

וֵאלֹהֵי אֲבוֹתֵינוּ. אֱלֹהֵי

Avraham. Elohei Yitzchak.

אַבְרָהָם. אֱלֹהֵי יִצְחָק.

Velohei Ya'akov. Ha'el Hagadol

וֵאלֹהֵי יַעֲקֹב. הָאֵל הַגָּדוֹל

Hagibor Vehanorah. El Elyon.

הַגִּבּוֹר וְהַנּוֹרָא. אֵל עֶלְיוֹן.

Gomel Chasadim Tovim. Koneh

גּוֹמֵל חֲסָדִים טוֹבִים. קוֹנֵה

Hakol. Vezocher Chasdei Avot.

הַכֹּל. וְזוֹכֵר חַסְדֵּי אָבוֹת.

Umevi Go'el Livnei Veneihem

וּמֵבִיא גוֹאֵל לִבְנֵי בְנֵיהֶם

Lema'an Shemo Be'ahavah.

לְמַעַן שְׁמוֹ בְּאַהֲבָה:

Blessed are You, Hashem our God and God of our fathers, God of Avraham, God of Yitzchak and God of Yaakov; the great, mighty and revered God, most high God, Who bestows lovingkindness. Master of all things; Who remembers the kindnesses of our fathers, and Who will bring a redeemer to their children's children for the sake of His name in love.

During the 10 days of repentance (Rosh Hashanah to Yom Kippur) add:

Zochrenu Lechayim. Melech Chafetz

זָכְרֵנוּ לְחַיִּים. מֶלֶךְ חָפֵץ

Bachayim. Katevenu Besefer Chayim.

בַּחַיִּים. כָּתְבֵנוּ בְּסֵפֶר חַיִּים.

Lema'anach Elohim Chayim.

לְמַעַנְךָ אֱלֹהִים חַיִּים.

Remember us to life, King Who delights in life; inscribe us in the book of life for Your sake, Oh living God.

Bow at "Baruch Attah" / Blessed are You. Raise up at Adonai / Hashem.

Melech Ozeir Umoshia   מֶלֶךְ עוֹזֵר וּמוֹשִׁיעַ

Umagen. Baruch Attah Adonai   וּמָגֵן: בָּרוּךְ אַתָּה יְהֹוָה

Magen Avraham.   מָגֵן אַבְרָהָם:

King, Supporter, and Savior and Shield. Blessed are You, Hashem, Shield of Avraham.

Gevurot / Powers

We [in Yisrael] begin to say "Mashiv Haruach" in the second blessing of the Amidah from the Musaf [Additional] Service of the last day of Sukkot, and conclude at the Musaf [Additional] Service of the first day of Pesach. On the first day of Pesach the congregation still says it in the Musaf Service, but the Reader stops saying it then. In lands outside of Yisrael, [in the Birkhat HaShanim / Blessing for the Years,] we begin to pray for rain in the Arvit (Evening) Service of the sixtieth day after the New Moon of Tishrei, and in Yisrael we begin to say it in the evening of the seventh day of Cheshvan, and it is said until the Afternoon Service on the day preceding the first day of Passover. If one prayed for rain in the summer, or if one omitted to pray for it in the winter, he must repeat the Amidah again. If one said "Morid Hageshem" in the summer time, he must repeat again from the beginning of the blessing. If he already concluded the blessing, he must read the entire Amidah again. Likewise in the winter, if he omitted it, he must begin all over again. (SA, OC 117)

Attah Gibor Le'olam Adonai.   אַתָּה גִבּוֹר לְעוֹלָם אֲדֹנָי.

Mechayeh Meitim Attah. Rav   מְחַיֶּה מֵתִים אַתָּה. רַב

Lehoshia.   לְהוֹשִׁיעַ.

You, Hashem, are mighty forever; You revive the dead; You are powerful to save.

B'ketz: Morid Hatal.   בקיץ: מוֹרִיד הַטָּל.

B'choref: Mashiv Haruach Umorid   בחורף: מַשִּׁיב הָרוּחַ וּמוֹרִיד

Hageshem.   הַגֶּשֶׁם.

In summer: You cause the dew to fall.

In winter: You cause the wind to blow and the rain to fall.

Mechalkel Chayim Bechesed.   מְכַלְכֵּל חַיִּים בְּחֶסֶד.

Mechayeh Meitim Berachamim   מְחַיֶּה מֵתִים בְּרַחֲמִים

Rabim. Somech Nofelim. Verofei	רַבִּים. סוֹמֵךְ נוֹפְלִים. וְרוֹפֵא
Cholim. Umatir Asurim.	חוֹלִים. וּמַתִּיר אֲסוּרִים.
Umekayem Emunato Lishenei	וּמְקַיֵּם אֱמוּנָתוֹ לִישֵׁנֵי
Afar. Mi Chamocha Ba'al	עָפָר. מִי כָמוֹךָ בַּעַל
Gevurot. Umi Domeh Lach.	גְּבוּרוֹת. וּמִי דוֹמֶה לָּךְ.
Melech Memit Umechayeh	מֶלֶךְ מֵמִית וּמְחַיֶּה
Umatzmiach Yeshu'ah.	וּמַצְמִיחַ יְשׁוּעָה.

You sustain the living with kindness, and revive the dead with great mercy; You support all who fall, and heal the sick; You set the captives free, and keep faith with those who sleep in the dust. Who is like You, Master of power? Who resembles You, Oh King? You bring death and restore life, and cause salvation to flourish.

During the 10 days of repentance (Rosh Hashanah to Yom Kippur) add:

Mi Chamocha Av Harachaman. Zocher	מִי כָמוֹךָ אָב הָרַחֲמָן. זוֹכֵר
Yetzurav Berachamim Lechayim.	יְצוּרָיו בְּרַחֲמִים לְחַיִּים.

Who is like You, merciful Father? In mercy You remember Your creatures to life.

Vene'eman Attah Lehachayot	וְנֶאֱמָן אַתָּה לְהַחֲיוֹת
Meitim. Baruch Attah Adonai	מֵתִים: בָּרוּךְ אַתָּה יְהֹוָה
Mechayeh Hameitim.	מְחַיֵּה הַמֵּתִים:

And You are faithful to revive the dead. Blessed are You, Hashem, Who revives the dead.

Kedusha

> Kedusha is said only in a minyan (10 men). If one is not available, skip to "Kedushat Hashem". It is proper to position one's feet together at the time one is reciting Kedushah with the prayer-leader.

Nakdishach Vena'aritzach.	נַקְדִּישָׁךְ וְנַעֲרִיצָךְ.
Keno'am Siach Sod Sarfei	כְּנֹעַם שִׂיחַ סוֹד שַׂרְפֵי
Kodesh. Hamshaleshim Lecha	קֹדֶשׁ. הַמְשַׁלְּשִׁים לְךָ

Kedushah. Vechein Katuv Al Yad	קְדֻשָּׁה. וְכֵן כָּתוּב עַל יַד
Nevi'ach. Vekara Zeh El-Zeh	נְבִיאָךְ: וְקָרָא זֶה אֶל־זֶה
Ve'amar. **Kadosh Kadosh Kadosh**	וְאָמַר **קָדוֹשׁ	קָדוֹשׁ קָדוֹשׁ**
Adonai Tzeva'ot; Melo Chol-	**יְהוָה צְבָאוֹת מְלֹא כָל־**
Ha'aretz Kevodo. Le'ummatam	**הָאָרֶץ כְּבוֹדוֹ:** לְעֻמָּתָם
Meshabechim Ve'omerim.	מְשַׁבְּחִים וְאוֹמְרִים:
Baruch Kevod-Adonai	**בָּרוּךְ כְּבוֹד־יְהוָה**
Mimekomo. Uvedivrei	**מִמְּקוֹמוֹ:** וּבְדִבְרֵי
Kodshecha Katuv Lemor.	קָדְשָׁךְ כָּתוּב לֵאמֹר: יִמְלֹךְ
Yimloch Adonai Le'olam.	**יְהוָה	לְעוֹלָם אֱלֹהַיִךְ**
Elohayich Tziyon Ledor Vador.	**צִיּוֹן לְדֹר וָדֹר**
Halleluyah.	**הַלְלוּיָהּ:**

We sanctify and revere You in the sweet words of the assembly of holy Seraphim who three times acclaim Your holiness, as it is written by Your prophet: "They keep calling to one another: **'Holy, holy, holy is Hashem of hosts; The whole earth is full of His glory."** Angels respond with praise and say: **"Blessed is the glory of Hashem from His Abode."** And in Your holy scriptures it is written: **"Hashem will reign forever, your God, Tziyon, from generation to generation. Halleluyah."**

Kedushat HaShem / Holiness of the Name

Attah Kadosh Veshimcha	אַתָּה קָדוֹשׁ וְשִׁמְךָ
Kadosh. Ukedoshim Bechol-	קָדוֹשׁ. וּקְדוֹשִׁים בְּכָל־
Yom Yehalelucha Selah. Baruch	יוֹם יְהַלְלוּךָ סֶּלָה: בָּרוּךְ
Attah Adonai Ha' El Hakadosh.	אַתָּה יְהוָה הָאֵל הַקָּדוֹשׁ:

You are holy and Your name is holy, and the holy-ones will praise You every day, selah. Blessed are You, Hashem, The Holy God.

During the 10 days of repentance (Rosh Hashanah to Yom Kippur) say:

Hamelech Hakadosh.   הַמֶּלֶךְ הַקָּדוֹשׁ:

The Holy King.

If one is unsure or forgot if they said, repeat the Amidah. If it was immediately said after, it is fulfilled.

Kedushat HaYom / Holiness of the Day

Yismach Mosheh Bematenat	יִשְׂמַח מֹשֶׁה בְּמַתְּנַת
Chelko. Ki Eved Ne'eman	חֶלְקוֹ. כִּי עֶבֶד נֶאֱמָן
Karata Lo. Kelil Tif'eret	קָרָאתָ לּוֹ. כְּלִיל תִּפְאֶרֶת
Berosho Natata. Be'amedo	בְּרֹאשׁוֹ נָתַתָּ. בְּעָמְדוֹ
Lefaneicha Al-Har Sinai. Shenei	לְפָנֶיךָ עַל־הַר סִינַי. שְׁנֵי
Luchot Avanim Horid Beyado.	לוּחוֹת אֲבָנִים הוֹרִיד בְּיָדוֹ.
Vechatuv Bahem Shemirat	וְכָתוּב בָּהֶם שְׁמִירַת
Shabbat. Vechein Katuv	שַׁבָּת. וְכֵן כָּתוּב
Betoratach.	בְּתוֹרָתֶךְ:

Moshe rejoiced with the gift of his portion, for You called him a faithful servant. A crown of glory You set on his head when he stood before You on Mount Sinai. Two tablets of stone he brought down in his hand and inscribed upon them was the keeping of Shabbat as it is written in Your Torah:

וְשָׁמְרוּ בְנֵי־יִשְׂרָאֵל אֶת־הַשַּׁבָּת לַעֲשׂוֹת אֶת־הַשַּׁבָּת לְדֹרֹתָם בְּרִית עוֹלָם: בֵּינִי וּבֵין בְּנֵי יִשְׂרָאֵל אוֹת הִוא לְעֹלָם כִּי־שֵׁשֶׁת יָמִים עָשָׂה יְהוָה אֶת־הַשָּׁמַיִם וְאֶת־הָאָרֶץ וּבַיּוֹם הַשְּׁבִיעִי שָׁבַת וַיִּנָּפַשׁ:

Veshameru Venei-Yisra'el Et-Hashabbat; La'asot Et-Ha Shabbat Ledorotam Berit Olam. Beini Uvein Benei Yisra'el. Ot Hi Le'olam; Ki-Sheshet Yamim. Asah Adonai Et-Hashamayim Ve'et-Ha'aretz. Uvayom Hashevi'i. Shavat Vayinafash.

The children of Yisrael will keep the Shabbat, to observe the Shabbat throughout their generations, for a perpetual covenant. It is a sign between Me and the children of Yisrael forever; for in six days Hashem made heaven and earth, and on the seventh day He ceased from His work and rested. (Ex. 31:16-17)

Velo Netatto Adonai Eloheinu	וְלֹא נְתַתּוֹ יְהֹוָה אֱלֹהֵינוּ
Legoyei Ha'aratzot. Velo	לְגוֹיֵי הָאֲרָצוֹת. וְלֹא
Hinchalto Malkeinu Le'ovedei	הִנְחַלְתּוֹ מַלְכֵּנוּ לְעוֹבְדֵי
Elilim. Gam Bimnuchato Lo	אֱלִילִים. גַּם בִּמְנוּחָתוֹ לֹא
Yishkenu Arelim. Ki	יִשְׁכְּנוּ עֲרֵלִים. כִּי
Le'ammecha Yisra'el Netatto	לְעַמְּךָ יִשְׂרָאֵל נְתַתּוֹ
Be'ahavah. Lezera Ya'akov	בְּאַהֲבָה. לְזֶרַע יַעֲקֹב
Asher Bam Bachar'ta.	אֲשֶׁר בָּם בָּחָרְתָּ:

And You did not give it, Hashem our God, to the nations of the lands; neither did You give it as an inheritance, our King, to those who worship idols; also in it's rest, the uncircumcised will not dwell; for You have bestowed it to Your people, Yisrael, with love, to the seed of Yaakov, whom You have chosen.

Yismechu Vemalchutach	יִשְׂמְחוּ בְמַלְכוּתָךְ
Shomerei Shabbat Vekore'ei	שׁוֹמְרֵי שַׁבָּת וְקוֹרְאֵי
Oneg. Am Mekadeshei Shevi'i.	עֹנֶג. עַם מְקַדְּשֵׁי שְׁבִיעִי.
Kulam Yisbe'u Veyit'anegu	כֻּלָּם יִשְׂבְּעוּ וְיִתְעַנְּגוּ
Mituvach. Vehashevi'i Ratzita	מִטּוּבָךְ. וְהַשְּׁבִיעִי רָצִיתָ
Bo Vekidashto. Chemdat Yamim	בּוֹ וְקִדַּשְׁתּוֹ. חֶמְדַּת יָמִים
Oto Karata.	אוֹתוֹ קָרָאתָ:

They will rejoice in Your rule, those who keep Shabbat and call it a delight. A people who sanctify the seventh day, they will all be satisfied and delight in Your goodness. And the seventh, You desired it, and sanctified it, declaring it "the desired of days".

Eloheinu Velohei Avoteinu.	אֱלֹהֵינוּ וֵאלֹהֵי אֲבוֹתֵינוּ.
Retzeh Na Bimnuchatenu.	רְצֵה נָא בִּמְנוּחָתֵנוּ.
Kadeshenu Bemitzvoteicha. Sim	קַדְּשֵׁנוּ בְּמִצְוֹתֶיךָ. שִׂים
Chelkenu Betoratach. Sabe'einu	חֶלְקֵנוּ בְּתוֹרָתֶךָ. שַׂבְּעֵנוּ
Mituvach. Same'ach Nafshenu	מִטּוּבֶךָ. שַׂמֵּחַ נַפְשֵׁנוּ
Bishu'atach. Vetaher Libenu	בִּישׁוּעָתֶךָ. וְטַהֵר לִבֵּנוּ
Le'avdecha Ve'emet.	לְעָבְדְּךָ בֶּאֱמֶת.
Vehanchilenu Adonai Eloheinu	וְהַנְחִילֵנוּ יְהֹוָה אֱלֹהֵינוּ
Be'ahavah Uveratzon Shabbat	בְּאַהֲבָה וּבְרָצוֹן שַׁבַּת
Kodshecha. Veyanuchu Vo Kol-	קָדְשֶׁךָ. וְיָנוּחוּ בוֹ כָּל־
Yisra'el Mekadeshei Shemecha.	יִשְׂרָאֵל מְקַדְּשֵׁי שְׁמֶךָ.
Baruch Attah Adonai Mekadesh	בָּרוּךְ אַתָּה יְהֹוָה מְקַדֵּשׁ
Hashabbat.	הַשַּׁבָּת.

Our God, God of our fathers, be pleased with our rest. Sanctify us through Your commandments and grant our portion in Your Torah. Content us with Your goodness. Rejoice our soul with Your salvation. And make our heart pure to serve You in truth. Cause us to inherit, Hashem our God, Your holy Shabbat with love and favor: and grant rest on it to all Yisrael, who sanctify Your name. Blessed are You, Hashem Who sanctifies the Shabbat.

Avodah / Temple Service

Retzeh Adonai Eloheinu	רְצֵה יְהֹוָה אֱלֹהֵינוּ
Be'ammecha Yisra'el Velitfilatam	בְּעַמְּךָ יִשְׂרָאֵל וְלִתְפִלָּתָם
She'eh. Vehasheiv Ha'avodah	שְׁעֵה. וְהָשֵׁב הָעֲבוֹדָה
Lidvir Beitecha. Ve'ishei Yisra'el	לִדְבִיר בֵּיתֶךָ. וְאִשֵּׁי יִשְׂרָאֵל
Utefilatam. Meheirah Be'ahavah	וּתְפִלָּתָם. מְהֵרָה בְּאַהֲבָה
Tekabel Beratzon. Utehi	תְּקַבֵּל בְּרָצוֹן. וּתְהִי
Leratzon Tamid Avodat Yisra'el	לְרָצוֹן תָּמִיד עֲבוֹדַת יִשְׂרָאֵל
Ammecha.	עַמֶּךָ:

Be favorable, Hashem our God, on Your people Yisrael and regard their prayers. And the service to the Sanctuary of Your House, and the fire offerings of Yisrael, and their prayers accept soon with love. And may the service of Your people, Yisrael, always be favorable.

On Rosh Chodesh and Chol HaMoed Passover and Sukkot say:

Ya'aleh Veyavo

אֱלֹהֵינוּ וֵאלֹהֵי אֲבוֹתֵינוּ. יַעֲלֶה וְיָבֹא. וְיַגִּיעַ וְיֵרָאֶה. וְיֵרָצֶה וְיִשָּׁמַע. וְיִפָּקֵד וְיִזָּכֵר. זִכְרוֹנֵנוּ וְזִכְרוֹן אֲבוֹתֵינוּ. זִכְרוֹן יְרוּשָׁלַיִם עִירָךְ. וְזִכְרוֹן מָשִׁיחַ בֶּן־דָּוִד עַבְדָּךְ. וְזִכְרוֹן כָּל־עַמְּךָ בֵּית יִשְׂרָאֵל לְפָנֶיךָ. לִפְלֵיטָה. לְטוֹבָה. לְחֵן. לְחֶסֶד וּלְרַחֲמִים. לְחַיִּים טוֹבִים וּלְשָׁלוֹם. בְּיוֹם:

Eloheinu Velohei Avoteinu. Ya'aleh Veyavo. Veyagia Veyera'eh. Veyeratzeh Veyishama'. Veyipaked Veyizacher. Zichronenu Vezichron Avoteinu. Zichron Yerushalayim Irach. Vezichron Mashiach Ben-David Avdach. Vezichron Kol-'Ammecha Beit Yisra'el Lefaneicha. Lifleitah. Letovah. Lechein. Lechesed Ulerachamim. Lechayim Tovim Uleshalom. Beyom:

Our God, and God of our fathers, may it rise, and come, arrive, appear, find favor, and be heard, and be considered, and be remembered our remembrance and the remembrance of our fathers, Yerushalayim Your city, the remembrance of Messiah ben David Your servant, and the remembrance of all Your people of the House of Yisrael before You for deliverance, for good favor, for kindness and mercy, for good life and for peace. On this day of:

On Rosh Chodesh:

רֹאשׁ חֹדֶשׁ הַזֶּה.

Rosh Chodesh Hazeh.
Rosh Chodesh (New Moon).

On Pesach:

חַג הַמַּצוֹת הַזֶּה. בְּיוֹם מִקְרָא קֹדֶשׁ הַזֶּה.

Chag Hamatzot Hazeh. Beyom Mikra Kodesh Hazeh.
The Festival of Matzot. on this day of holy convocation.

On Sukkot:

חַג הַסֻּכּוֹת הַזֶּה. בְּיוֹם מִקְרָא קֹדֶשׁ הַזֶּה.

Chag Hasukkot Hazeh. Beyom Mikra Kodesh Hazeh.
The Festival of Sukkot. on this day of holy convocation.

לְרַחֵם בּוֹ עָלֵינוּ וּלְהוֹשִׁיעֵנוּ. זָכְרֵנוּ יְהוָה אֱלֹהֵינוּ בּוֹ לְטוֹבָה. וּפָקְדֵנוּ בּוֹ
לִבְרָכָה. וְהוֹשִׁיעֵנוּ בּוֹ לְחַיִּים טוֹבִים. בִּדְבַר יְשׁוּעָה וְרַחֲמִים. חוּס וְחָנֵּנוּ.
וַחֲמוֹל וְרַחֵם עָלֵינוּ. וְהוֹשִׁיעֵנוּ כִּי אֵלֶיךָ עֵינֵינוּ. כִּי אֵל מֶלֶךְ חַנּוּן וְרַחוּם אָתָּה:

Lerachem Bo Aleinu Ulehoshi'enu. Zochrenu Adonai Eloheinu Bo Letovah.
Ufokdenu Vo Livrachah. Vehoshi'enu Vo Lechayim Tovim. Bidvar Yeshu'ah
Verachamim. Chus Vechanenu. Vachamol Verachem Aleinu. Vehoshi'enu Ki Eleicha
Eineinu. Ki El Melech Chanun Verachum Attah.

to have mercy upon us and save us. Remember us, Hashem our God, on it for good.
Be mindful of us on it for blessing and save us on it for a life of good. With the
promise of salvation and mercy, show us pity, and be gracious to us and have
compassion and mercy on us and save us. For our eyes are lifted towards You, for
You, God, are a gracious and merciful King.

Attah Berachameicha Harabim.	וְאַתָּה בְּרַחֲמֶיךָ הָרַבִּים.
Tachpotz Banu Vetirtzenu.	תַּחְפֹּץ בָּנוּ וְתִרְצֵנוּ.
Vetechezeinah Eineinu	וְתֶחֱזֶינָה עֵינֵינוּ
Beshuvecha Letziyon	בְּשׁוּבְךָ לְצִיּוֹן
Berachamim. Baruch Attah	בְּרַחֲמִים: בָּרוּךְ אַתָּה
Adonai Hamachazir Shechinato	יְהוָה הַמַּחֲזִיר שְׁכִינָתוֹ
Letziyon.	לְצִיּוֹן.

And You, in Your abundant mercy, delight in us, and be favorable to
us, so that our eyes may witness Your return to Tziyon with mercy.
Blessed are You, Hashem Who returns His Presence to Tziyon.

SHABBAT SHACHARIT - THE AMIDAH

Hoda'ah (Modim) / Thanksgiving

On Saying "Modim" / "We are Thankful" One Bows and begins to rise after "Adonai" / "Hashem".

Modim Anachnu Lach.	מוֹדִים אֲנַחְנוּ לָךְ.
She'attah Hu Adonai Eloheinu	שָׁאַתָּה הוּא יְהֹוָה אֱלֹהֵינוּ
Velohei Avoteinu Le'olam Va'ed.	וֵאלֹהֵי אֲבוֹתֵינוּ לְעוֹלָם וָעֶד.
Tzurenu Tzur Chayeinu	צוּרֵנוּ צוּר חַיֵּינוּ
Umagen Yish'enu Attah Hu.	וּמָגֵן יִשְׁעֵנוּ אַתָּה הוּא.
Ledor Vador Nodeh Lecha	לְדוֹר וָדוֹר נוֹדֶה לְךָ
Unsapeir Tehilatecha. Al	וּנְסַפֵּר תְּהִלָּתֶךָ. עַל
Chayeinu Hamesurim	חַיֵּינוּ הַמְּסוּרִים
Beyadecha. Ve'al Nishmoteinu	בְּיָדֶךָ. וְעַל נִשְׁמוֹתֵינוּ
Hapekudot Lach. Ve'al Niseicha	הַפְּקוּדוֹת לָךְ. וְעַל נִסֶּיךָ
Shebechol-Yom Imanu. Ve'al	שֶׁבְּכָל־יוֹם עִמָּנוּ. וְעַל
Nifle'oteicha Vetovoteicha	נִפְלְאוֹתֶיךָ וְטוֹבוֹתֶיךָ
Shebechol-'Et. Erev Vavoker	שֶׁבְּכָל־עֵת. עֶרֶב וָבֹקֶר
Vetzaharayim. Hatov. Ki Lo	וְצָהֳרָיִם. הַטּוֹב. כִּי לֹא
Chalu Rachameicha.	כָלוּ רַחֲמֶיךָ.
Hamerachem. Ki Lo Tamu	הַמְרַחֵם. כִּי לֹא תַמּוּ
Chasadeicha. Ki Me'olam	חֲסָדֶיךָ. כִּי מֵעוֹלָם
Kivinu Lach.	קִוִּינוּ לָךְ:

We are thankful to You, Hashem our God and the God of our fathers, forever. You are our strength and Rock of our life and the Shield of our salvation. In every generation we will thank You and recount Your praise for our lives which are given into Your hand, for our souls which are placed in Your care, and for Your miracles which are daily with us, and for Your wonders and goodness—evening, morning and noon. The Beneficent One, for Your mercies never end, Merciful One, for Your kindness has never ceased, for we have always placed our hope in You.

Modim Derabbanan

During the repetition, this is to be recited softly while the Chazan reads the Modim. Still bow at Modim as before.

מוֹדִים אֲנַחְנוּ לָךְ. שָׁאַתָּה הוּא יְהוָה אֱלֹהֵינוּ וֵאלֹהֵי אֲבוֹתֵינוּ. אֱלֹהֵי כָל בָּשָׂר. יוֹצְרֵנוּ יוֹצֵר בְּרֵאשִׁית. בְּרָכוֹת וְהוֹדָאוֹת לְשִׁמְךָ הַגָּדוֹל וְהַקָּדוֹשׁ. עַל שֶׁהֶחֱיִיתָנוּ וְקִיַּמְתָּנוּ. כֵּן תְּחַיֵּנוּ וּתְחָנֵּנוּ וְתֶאֱסוֹף גָּלְיוֹתֵינוּ לְחַצְרוֹת קָדְשֶׁךָ. לִשְׁמֹר חֻקֶּיךָ וְלַעֲשׂוֹת רְצוֹנֶךָ וּלְעָבְדְּךָ בְּלֵבָב שָׁלֵם. עַל שֶׁאֲנַחְנוּ מוֹדִים לָךְ. בָּרוּךְ אֵל הַהוֹדָאוֹת.

Modim Anachnu Lach. She'attah Hu Adonai Eloheinu Velohei Avoteinu. Elohei Chol Basar. Yotzreinu Yotzer Bereshit. Berachot Vehoda'ot Leshimcha Hagadol Vehakadosh. Al Shehecheyitanu Vekiyamtanu. Ken Techayeinu Utechanenu Vete'esof Galyoteinu Lechatzrot Kodshecha. Lishmor Chukkeicha Vela'asot Retzonecha Ule'avedecha Velevav Shalem. Al She'anachnu Modim Lach. Baruch El Hahoda'ot.

We are thankful to You, Hashem our God and the God of our fathers. God of all flesh, our Creator and Former of Creation, blessings and thanks to Your great and holy name, for You have kept us alive and sustained us; may You always grant us life and be gracious to us. And gather our exiles to Your holy courtyards to observe Your statutes, and to do Your will, and to serve You with a perfect heart. For this we thank You. Blessed is God of thanksgivings.

Al HaNissim

On Purim and Hanukkah an extra prayer is added here:

עַל הַנִּסִּים וְעַל הַפֻּרְקָן וְעַל הַגְּבוּרוֹת וְעַל הַתְּשׁוּעוֹת וְעַל הַנִּפְלָאוֹת וְעַל הַנֶּחָמוֹת שֶׁעָשִׂיתָ לַאֲבוֹתֵינוּ בַּיָּמִים הָהֵם בַּזְּמַן הַזֶּה:

Al Hanissim Ve'al Hapurkan Ve'al Hagevurot Ve'al Hateshu'ot Ve'al Hanifla'ot Ve'al Hanechamot She'asita La'avoteinu Bayamim Hahem Bazman Hazeh.

For the miracles, and for the triumphant liberation, and the mighty works, and for the deliverances, and for the wonders, and for the consolations which You have done for our fathers in those days at this season:

On Hanukkah:

בִּימֵי מַתִּתְיָה בֶן־יוֹחָנָן כֹּהֵן גָּדוֹל. חַשְׁמוֹנָאִי וּבָנָיו כְּשֶׁעָמְדָה מַלְכוּת יָוָן הָרְשָׁעָה עַל עַמְּךָ יִשְׂרָאֵל. לְשַׁכְּחָם תּוֹרָתֶךָ וּלְהַעֲבִירָם מֵחֻקֵּי רְצוֹנֶךָ. וְאַתָּה בְּרַחֲמֶיךָ הָרַבִּים עָמַדְתָּ לָהֶם בְּעֵת צָרָתָם. רַבְתָּ אֶת רִיבָם. דַּנְתָּ אֶת דִּינָם. נָקַמְתָּ אֶת נִקְמָתָם. מָסַרְתָּ גִבּוֹרִים בְּיַד חַלָּשִׁים. וְרַבִּים בְּיַד מְעַטִּים. וּרְשָׁעִים

בְּיַד צַדִּיקִים. וּטְמֵאִים בְּיַד טְהוֹרִים. וְזֵדִים בְּיַד עוֹסְקֵי תוֹרָתֶךָ. לְךָ עָשִׂיתָ שֵׁם
גָּדוֹל וְקָדוֹשׁ בְּעוֹלָמֶךָ. וּלְעַמְּךָ יִשְׂרָאֵל עָשִׂיתָ תְּשׁוּעָה גְדוֹלָה וּפֻרְקָן כְּהַיּוֹם
הַזֶּה. וְאַחַר כָּךְ בָּאוּ בָנֶיךָ לִדְבִיר בֵּיתֶךָ. וּפִנּוּ אֶת־הֵיכָלֶךָ. וְטִהֲרוּ אֶת־מִקְדָּשֶׁךָ.
וְהִדְלִיקוּ נֵרוֹת בְּחַצְרוֹת קָדְשֶׁךָ. וְקָבְעוּ שְׁמוֹנַת יְמֵי חֲנֻכָּה אֵלּוּ בְּהַלֵּל
וּבְהוֹדָאָה. וְעָשִׂיתָ עִמָּהֶם נִסִּים וְנִפְלָאוֹת וְנוֹדֶה לְשִׁמְךָ הַגָּדוֹל סֶלָה:

Bimei Mattityah Ven-Yochanan Kohen Gadol. Chashmona'i Uvanav Keshe'amedah
Malchut Yavan Haresha'ah Al Ammecha Yisra'el. Leshakecham Toratach
Uleha'aviram Mechukkei Retzonach. Ve'attah Berachameicha Harabim Amadta
Lahem Be'et Tzaratam. Ravta Et Rivam. Danta Et Dinam. Nakamta Et Nikmatam.
Masarta Giborim Beyad Chalashim. Verabim Beyad Me'atim. Uresha'im Beyad
Tzaddikim. Uteme'im Beyad Tehorim. Vezeidim Beyad Osekei Toratecha. Lecha
Asita Shem Gadol Vekadosh Be'olamach. Ule'ammecha Yisra'el Asita Teshu'ah
Gedolah Ufurkan Kehayom Hazeh. Ve'achar Kach Ba'u Vaneicha Lidvir Beitecha.
Ufinu Et-Heichalecha. Vetiharu Et-Mikdashecha. Vehidliku Nerot Bechatzrot
Kodshecha. Vekave'u Shemonat Yemei Chanukkah Elu Behallel Uvehoda'ah.
Ve'asita Imahem Nissim Venifla'ot Venodeh Leshimcha Hagadol Selah.

Then in the days of Mattityahu ben-Yochanan, High Priest, the Hasmonean and his
sons, when the cruel Greek power rose up against Your people, Yisrael, to make
them forget Your Torah and transgress the statutes of Your will. And You, in Your
great compassion, stood up for them in time of their trial to plead their cause and
defend their judgment. Giving out retribution, delivered the strong into the hand
of the weak, and the many into the hand of the few, and the wicked into the hand of
the upright, and the impure into the hand of the pure, and tyrants into the hand of
the devotees of Your Torah. You made for Yourself a great and holy name in Your
world. And for Your people, Yisrael, You performed a great salvation and
liberation as this very day. Then Your children came to the Sanctuary of Your
House, cleared Your Temple, cleansed Your Sanctuary and kindled lights in Your
courtyards, and they instituted these eight days of Hanukkah for praise and
thanksgiving. And You did miracles and wonders for them, and we give thanks to
Your great name, selah.

On Purim:

בִּימֵי מָרְדְּכַי וְאֶסְתֵּר בְּשׁוּשַׁן הַבִּירָה. כְּשֶׁעָמַד עֲלֵיהֶם הָמָן הָרָשָׁע. בִּקֵּשׁ
לְהַשְׁמִיד לַהֲרֹג וּלְאַבֵּד אֶת־כָּל־הַיְּהוּדִים מִנַּעַר וְעַד זָקֵן טַף וְנָשִׁים בְּיוֹם אֶחָד.
בִּשְׁלֹשָׁה עָשָׂר לְחֹדֶשׁ שְׁנֵים עָשָׂר. הוּא חֹדֶשׁ אֲדָר. וּשְׁלָלָם לָבוֹז. וְאַתָּה
בְּרַחֲמֶיךָ הָרַבִּים הֵפַרְתָּ אֶת־עֲצָתוֹ וְקִלְקַלְתָּ אֶת־מַחֲשַׁבְתּוֹ. וַהֲשֵׁבוֹתָ לּוֹ גְּמוּלוֹ
בְּרֹאשׁוֹ. וְתָלוּ אוֹתוֹ וְאֶת־בָּנָיו עַל הָעֵץ. וְעָשִׂיתָ עִמָּהֶם נֵס וָפֶלֶא וְנוֹדֶה לְשִׁמְךָ
הַגָּדוֹל סֶלָה:

Bimei Mordechai Ve'ester Beshushan Habirah. Keshe'amad Aleihem Haman
Harasha. Bikesh Lehashmid Laharog Ule'abed Et-Kol-Hayehudim Mina'ar Ve'ad

Zaken Taf Venashim Beyom Echad. Bishloshah Asar Lechodesh Sheneim Asar. Hu
Chodesh Adar. Ushelalam Lavoz. Ve'attah Berachameicha Harabim Hefarta
Et-'Atzato Vekilkalta Et-Machashavto. Vahasheivota Lo Gemulo Verosho. Vetalu Oto
Ve'et-Banav Al Ha'etz. Ve'asita Imahem Nes Vafelei Venodeh Leshimcha Hagadol
Selah.

In the days of Mordechai and Ester in Shushan, the capital, the wicked Haman rose
up and sought to destroy, slay and utterly annihilate all of the Yehudim, both young
and old, women and children, on one day, on the thirteenth day of the twelfth
month, which is the month of Adar, and to plunder their possessions. But You in
Your great mercy You broke his plan and spoiled his designs, causing them to recoil
on his own head, and they hanged him and his sons on the gallows. And You did
miracles and wonders for them, and we give thanks to Your great name, selah.

Ve'al Kulam Yitbarach.	וְעַל כֻּלָּם יִתְבָּרַךְ.
Veyitromam. Veyitnasse. Tamid.	וְיִתְרוֹמַם. וְיִתְנַשֵּׂא. תָּמִיד.
Shimcha Malkeinu. Le'olam	שִׁמְךָ מַלְכֵּנוּ. לְעוֹלָם
Va'ed. Vechol-Hachayim	וָעֶד. וְכָל־הַחַיִּים
Yoducha Selah.	יוֹדוּךָ סֶּלָה:

For all these acts, may Your name, our King, be blessed, extolled
and exalted forever. And all of the living will thank You, selah.

During the 10 days of repentance (Rosh Hashanah to Yom Kippur) say:

Uchetov Lechayim Tovim Kol Benei	וּכְתֹב לְחַיִּים טוֹבִים כָּל בְּנֵי
Veritecha.	בְרִיתֶךָ.

Inscribe all of Your people of the covenant for a happy life.

Bow at "Baruch Attah" / "Blessed are You". Raise up at Adonai / Hashem.

Vihalelu Vivarechu Et-Shimcha	וִיהַלְלוּ וִיבָרְכוּ אֶת־שִׁמְךָ
Hagadol Be'emet Le'olam Ki	הַגָּדוֹל בֶּאֱמֶת לְעוֹלָם כִּי
Tov. Ha'el Yeshu'ateinu	טוֹב. הָאֵל יְשׁוּעָתֵנוּ
Ve'ezrateinu Selah. Ha'el Hatov.	וְעֶזְרָתֵנוּ סֶלָה. הָאֵל הַטּוֹב:
Baruch Attah Adonai Hatov	בָּרוּךְ אַתָּה יְהֹוָה הַטּוֹב
Shimcha Ulecha Na'eh	שִׁמְךָ וּלְךָ נָאֶה
Lehodot.	לְהוֹדוֹת:

And they will praise and bless Your great and good name sincerely, forever. For You are good, the God of our salvation and our help forever, the Good God. Blessed are You, Hashem, Your name is good and to You it is good to give thanks.

Birkhat Kohanim / The Priestly Blessing

If there is more than one Kohen present, start here. If there is not, start with Eloheinu Velohei Avoteinu below:

Some say:

לְשֵׁם יְחוּד קוּדְשָׁא בְּרִיךְ הוּא וּשְׁכִינְתֵּיה. בִּדְחִילוּ וּרְחִימוּ. וּרְחִימוּ וּדְחִילוּ. לְיַחֲדָא שֵׁם יוֹ"ד קֵ"י בְּוָא"ו קֵ"י בְּיְחוּדָא שְׁלִים (יהוה) בְּשֵׁם כָּל יִשְׂרָאֵל. הִנֵּה אָנֹכִי מוּכָן וּמְזוּמָן לְקַיֵּים מִצְוַת עֲשֵׂה לְבָרֵךְ אֶת יִשְׂרָאֵל בִּרְכַּת כֹּהֲנִים בִּנְשִׂיאוּת כַּפִּים לַעֲשׂוֹת נַחַת רוּחַ לְיוֹצְרֵנוּ וּלְהַמְשִׁיךְ שֶׁפַע וּבְרָכָה לְכָל הָעוֹלָמוֹת הַקְּדוֹשִׁים. וִיהִי נֹעַם אֲדֹנָי אֱלֹהֵינוּ עָלֵינוּ וּמַעֲשֵׂה יָדֵינוּ כּוֹנְנָה עָלֵינוּ וּמַעֲשֵׂה יָדֵינוּ כּוֹנְנֵהוּ:

The Kohanim stand on the pulpit after Modim Derabbanan and say:

יְהִי רָצוֹן מִלְּפָנֶיךָ יְהֹוָה אֱלֹהֵינוּ וֵאלֹהֵי אֲבוֹתֵינוּ שֶׁתִּהְיֶה בְּרָכָה זוֹ שֶׁצִּוִּיתָנוּ לְבָרֵךְ אֶת־עַמְּךָ יִשְׂרָאֵל בְּרָכָה שְׁלֵמָה וְלֹא יִהְיֶה בָהּ מִכְשׁוֹל וְעָוֹן מֵעַתָּה וְעַד עוֹלָם:

Yehi Ratzon Milfaneicha Adonai Eloheinu Velohei Avoteinu Shetihyeh Berachah Zo Shetzivitanu Levarech Et-'Ammecha Yisra'el Berachah Shelemah Velo Yihyeh Vah Michshol Ve'avon Me'attah Ve'ad Olam.

May it be Your Will, Hashem our God, that this blessing which You have commanded us to bless Your people Yisrael with will be a perfect blessing. May there not be in it any stumbling or perverseness from now and forever.

Then they say the blessing. If there is more than one Cohen, the leader calls them, "Kohanim!".

בָּרוּךְ אַתָּה יְהֹוָה אֱלֹהֵינוּ מֶלֶךְ הָעוֹלָם. אֲשֶׁר קִדְּשָׁנוּ בִּקְדֻשָּׁתוֹ שֶׁל־אַהֲרֹן. וְצִוָּנוּ לְבָרֵךְ אֶת־עַמּוֹ יִשְׂרָאֵל בְּאַהֲבָה:

Baruch Attah Adonai Eloheinu Melech Ha'olam Asher Kideshanu Bikdushato Shel-Aharon. Vetzivanu Levarech Et-'Ammo Yisra'el Be'ahavah. Amen.

Blessed are You Hashem our God, King of the universe, Who has sanctified us with
the sanctification of Aharon and commanded us to bless His people, Yisrael, with
love.

The congregation answers:

אָמֵן:

Amen.

And the Chazan and the Kohanim say after him exactly:

Yevarechecha Adonai Veyishmerecha.

יְבָרֶכְךָ יְהֹוָה וְיִשְׁמְרֶךָ:

And answer: Amen

ועונים: אָמֵן:

Hashem bless you and keep you. **And answer:** Amen

Ya'er Adonai Panav Eleicha Vichuneka.

יָאֵר יְהֹוָה | פָּנָיו אֵלֶיךָ וִיחֻנֶּךָּ:

And Answer: Amen

ועונים: אָמֵן:

Hashem make His countenance shine upon you, and be gracious to you. **And answer:**
Amen

Yissa Adonai Panav Eleicha. Veyasem

יִשָּׂא יְהֹוָה | פָּנָיו אֵלֶיךָ וְיָשֵׂם

Lecha Shalom. **And answer:** Amen

לְךָ שָׁלוֹם: ועונים: אָמֵן:

Hashem lift up His countenance towards you and give you peace. **And answer:** Amen

When the Chazan begins the Sim Shalom below, the Kohanim face toward the Ark and say:

רִבּוֹן הָעוֹלָמִים עָשִׂינוּ מַה שֶּׁגָּזַרְתָּ עָלֵינוּ. עֲשֵׂה אַתָּה מַה שֶּׁהִבְטַחְתָּנוּ.
הַשְׁקִיפָה מִמְּעוֹן קָדְשְׁךָ מִן־הַשָּׁמַיִם וּבָרֵךְ אֶת־עַמְּךָ אֶת־יִשְׂרָאֵל:

Ribon Ha'olamim Asinu Mah Shegazarta Aleinu. Aseh Attah Mah-Shehivtachetanu.
Hashkifah Mime'on Kodshecha Min-Hashamayim. Uvarech Et-'Ammecha Et-
Yisra'el.

Sovereign of the universe, We have done what You have decreed for us, You have
done as You promised. "Look down from Your holy Habitation, from heaven, and
bless Your people Yisrael." (Deut. 26:15)

Eloheinu Velohei Avoteinu

If there are no Kohanim, the Chazan recites a substitute blessing:

Eloheinu Velohei Avoteinu.

אֱלֹהֵינוּ וֵאלֹהֵי אֲבוֹתֵינוּ.

Barecheinu Baberachah

בָּרְכֵנוּ בַּבְּרָכָה

Hamshuleshet Batorah	הַמְשֻׁלֶּשֶׁת בַּתּוֹרָה
Haketuvah Al Yedei Mosheh	הַכְּתוּבָה עַל יְדֵי מֹשֶׁה
Avdach. Ha'amurah Mipi Aharon	עַבְדָּךְ. הָאֲמוּרָה מִפִּי אַהֲרֹן
Uvanav Hakohanim Im	וּבָנָיו הַכֹּהֲנִים עַם
Kedosheicha Ka'amur.	קְדוֹשֶׁיךָ כָּאָמוּר:

Our God, God of our fathers, bless us with the threefold blessing written in the Torah by Your servant Moshe, and spoken by the mouth of Aharon and his descendants Your consecrated Kohanim:

Yevarechecha Adonai	יְבָרֶכְךָ יְהֹוָה
Veyishmerecha. And answer: Ken	וְיִשְׁמְרֶךָ: ועונים: כֵּן
Yehi Ratzon.	יְהִי רָצוֹן:

Hashem bless you and keep you. And answer: May this be His will.

Ya'er Adonai Panav Eleicha	יָאֵר יְהֹוָה ׀ פָּנָיו אֵלֶיךָ
Vichuneka. And answer: Ken Yehi	וִיחֻנֶּךָּ: ועונים: כֵּן יְהִי
Ratzon.	רָצוֹן:

Hashem make His countenance shine upon you, and be gracious to you. And answer: May this be His will.

Yissa Adonai Panav Eleicha.	יִשָּׂא יְהֹוָה ׀ פָּנָיו אֵלֶיךָ
Veyasem Lecha Shalom.	וְיָשֵׂם לְךָ שָׁלוֹם:
And answer: Ken Yehi Ratzon.	ועונים: כֵּן יְהִי רָצוֹן:

Hashem lift up His countenance towards you and give you peace. And answer: May this be His will.

Vesamu Et-Shemi Al-Benei	וְשָׂמוּ אֶת־שְׁמִי עַל־בְּנֵי
Yisra'el; Va'ani Avarechem.	יִשְׂרָאֵל וַאֲנִי אֲבָרֲכֵם:

And they will set My name upon the Children of Yisra'el, and I will bless them.

Sim Shalom / Grant Peace

Sim Shalom Tovah Uverachah.	שִׂים שָׁלוֹם טוֹבָה וּבְרָכָה.
Chayim Chein Vachesed	חַיִּים חֵן וָחֶסֶד
Verachamim. Aleinu Ve'al Kol-	וְרַחֲמִים. עָלֵינוּ וְעַל כָּל־
Yisra'el Ammecha. Uvarecheinu	יִשְׂרָאֵל עַמֶּךָ. וּבָרְכֵנוּ
Avinu Kulanu Ke'echad Be'or	אָבִינוּ כֻּלָּנוּ כְּאֶחָד בְּאוֹר
Paneicha. Ki Ve'or Paneicha	פָּנֶיךָ. כִּי בְאוֹר פָּנֶיךָ
Natata Lanu Adonai Eloheinu	נָתַתָּ לָנוּ יְהוָה אֱלֹהֵינוּ
Torah Vechayim. Ahavah	תּוֹרָה וְחַיִּים. אַהֲבָה
Vachesed. Tzedakah	וָחֶסֶד. צְדָקָה
Verachamim. Berachah	וְרַחֲמִים. בְּרָכָה
Veshalom. Vetov Be'eineicha	וְשָׁלוֹם. וְטוֹב בְּעֵינֶיךָ
Levarecheinu Ulevarech Et-	לְבָרְכֵנוּ וּלְבָרֵךְ אֶת־
Kol-'Ammecha Yisra'el. Berov	כָּל־עַמְּךָ יִשְׂרָאֵל. בְּרֹב
Oz Veshalom.	עֹז וְשָׁלוֹם:

Grant peace, goodness and blessing, a life of grace, and kindness and mercy, to us and to all Yisrael, Your people. And bless us, our Father, all as one with the light of Your countenance; for with the light of Your countenance You have given us, Hashem our God, a Torah and life, love and kindness, righteousness and mercy, blessing and peace. May it be good in Your eyes to bless us and bless all of Your people, Yisrael, with abundant strength and peace.

During the 10 days of repentance (Rosh Hashanah to Yom Kippur) say:

Uvesefer Chayim. Berachah Veshalom.	וּבְסֵפֶר חַיִּים. בְּרָכָה וְשָׁלוֹם.
Ufarnasah Tovah Vishu'ah Venechamah.	וּפַרְנָסָה טוֹבָה וִישׁוּעָה וְנֶחָמָה.
Ugezerot Tovot. Nizacher Venikkatev	וּגְזֵרוֹת טוֹבוֹת. נִזָּכֵר וְנִכָּתֵב
Lefaneicha. Anachnu Vechol Ammecha	לְפָנֶיךָ. אֲנַחְנוּ וְכָל עַמְּךָ
Beit Yisra'el. Lechayim Tovim	בֵּית יִשְׂרָאֵל. לְחַיִּים טוֹבִים

Uleshalom.   וּלְשָׁלוֹם.

May we and all Yisrael Your people be remembered and inscribed before You in the
book of life and blessing, peace and prosperity, for a happy life and for peace.

Baruch Attah Adonai   בָּרוּךְ אַתָּה יהוווהו

Hamevarech Et Ammo Yisra'el   הַמְבָרֵךְ אֶת עַמּוֹ יִשְׂרָאֵל

Bashalom. Amen.   בַּשָּׁלוֹם. אָמֵן:

Blessed are You, Hashem, Who blesses His people Yisrael with
peace. Amen.

Yihyu Leratzon Imrei-Fi Vehegyon Libi   יִהְיוּ לְרָצוֹן | אִמְרֵי־פִי וְהֶגְיוֹן לִבִּי

Lefaneicha; Adonai Tzuri Vego'ali.   לְפָנֶיךָ יְהֹוָה צוּרִי וְגֹאֲלִי:

May the words of my mouth and the meditation of my heart find favor before You,
Hashem my Rock and my Redeemer.

The chazan's repetition ends here; personal / individual continue:

Elohai. Netzor Leshoni Meira   אֱלֹהַי. נְצֹר לְשׁוֹנִי מֵרָע

Vesiftotai Midaber Mirmah.   וּשְׂפָתוֹתַי מִדַּבֵּר מִרְמָה.

Velimkalelai Nafshi Tidom.   וְלִמְקַלְלַי נַפְשִׁי תִדֹּם.

Venafshi Ke'afar Lakol Tihyeh.   וְנַפְשִׁי כֶּעָפָר לַכֹּל תִּהְיֶה.

Petach Libi Betoratecha.   פְּתַח לִבִּי בְּתוֹרָתֶךָ.

Ve'acharei Mitzvoteicha Tirdof   וְאַחֲרֵי מִצְוֹתֶיךָ תִּרְדֹּף

Nafshi. Vechol-Hakamim Alai   נַפְשִׁי. וְכָל־הַקָּמִים עָלַי

Lera'ah. Meheirah Hafer Atzatam   לְרָעָה. מְהֵרָה הָפֵר עֲצָתָם

Vekalkel Machshevotam. Aseh   וְקַלְקֵל מַחְשְׁבוֹתָם. עֲשֵׂה

Lema'an Shemach. Aseh   לְמַעַן שְׁמֶךָ. עֲשֵׂה

Lema'an Yeminach. Aseh	לְמַעַן יְמִינָךְ. עֲשֵׂה
Lema'an Toratach. Aseh Lema'an	לְמַעַן תּוֹרָתָךְ. עֲשֵׂה לְמַעַן
Kedushatach. Lema'an	קְדֻשָּׁתָךְ. לְמַעַן
Yechaletzun Yedideicha;	יֵחָלְצוּן יְדִידֶיךָ
Hoshi'ah Yeminecha Va'aneni.	הוֹשִׁיעָה יְמִינְךָ וַעֲנֵנִי:

My God, guard my tongue from evil, and my lips from speaking deceit. And to those who curse me may my soul be silent; and may my soul be like the dust to all. Open my heart to Your Torah, that my soul may follow after Your commandments. And all that rise to do evil against me, speedily nullify their plan, and spoil their thoughts. Do it for the sake of Your name; do it for the sake of Your right hand; do it for the sake of Your Torah, do it for the sake of Your holiness. That Your beloved may be rescued, save with Your right hand and answer me. (Ps. 60:7)

Yihyu Leratzon Imrei-Fi Vehegyon Libi	יִהְיוּ לְרָצוֹן אִמְרֵי־פִי וְהֶגְיוֹן לִבִּי
Lefaneicha; Adonai Tzuri Vego'ali.	לְפָנֶיךָ יְהֹוָה צוּרִי וְגֹאֲלִי:

May the words of my mouth and the meditation of my heart find favor before You, Hashem my Rock and my Redeemer.

Oseh Shalom

One bows and takes three steps backwards, while still bowing. After three steps, while still bowing and before erecting, while saying, "Oseh Shalom Bimromav", turn one's face to the left, "Hu [Berachamav] Ya'aseh Shalom Aleinu", turn one's face to the right; [face forward and] then bow forward like a servant leaving his master. (SA, OC 123:1)

Oseh Shalom On the 10 Days of	עוֹשֶׂה שָׁלוֹם
Repentance: (Hashalom) Bimromav, Hu	בעשי"ת (הַשָּׁלוֹם) בִּמְרוֹמָיו. הוּא
Berachamav Ya'aseh Shalom	בְּרַחֲמָיו יַעֲשֶׂה שָׁלוֹם
Aleinu, Ve'al Kol-'Ammo Yisra'el,	עָלֵינוּ. וְעַל כָּל־עַמּוֹ יִשְׂרָאֵל.
Ve'imru Amen.	וְאִמְרוּ אָמֵן:

Creator of On the 10 Days of Repentance: (the) peace in His high places, may He in His mercy create peace for us and for all Yisrael, and say Amen.

Yehi Ratzon Milfaneicha Adonai	יְהִי רָצוֹן מִלְּפָנֶיךָ יְהֹוָה
Eloheinu Velohei Avoteinu. Shetivneh	אֱלֹהֵינוּ וֵאלֹהֵי אֲבוֹתֵינוּ. שֶׁתִּבְנֶה
Beit Hamikdash Bimheirah Veyameinu.	בֵּית הַמִּקְדָּשׁ בִּמְהֵרָה בְיָמֵינוּ.
Veten Chelkenu Vetoratach La'asot	וְתֵן חֶלְקֵנוּ בְּתוֹרָתֶךָ לַעֲשׂוֹת
Chukkei. Retzonach Ule'avedach	חֻקֵּי רְצוֹנָךְ וּלְעָבְדָךְ
Belevav Shalem.	בְּלֵבָב שָׁלֵם:

May it be Your will, Hashem our God and God of our fathers, that the Beit HaMikdash be speedily rebuilt in our days, and grant us a share in Your Torah so we may fulfill the statutes of Your will and serve You with a whole heart.

This is the end of the individual Amidah. Stay standing until the leader's repetition of the Amidah, then take three steps forward. When the leader repeats the prayers, the community must be quiet, and to focus (have intention) on the blessings from the leader and respond "amen". And if there are not nine people with intention for his blessings, this is similar to a blessing in vain. Therefore, each person should make himself as if there are not nine others, and he will have intention for the blessings of the Chazan. On every blessing that a man hears in any place he should say, "Baruch Hu Uvaruch Shemo" (Blessed is He and blessed is His Name.) (SA, OC 124:4)

On Rosh Hodesh, Chol HaMoed and Hanukkah, say Hallel here. On Shabbat continue with Yehi Shem.

Avinu Malkeinu / Our Father and King

Said only during the 10 days of repentance (Rosh Hashanah to Yom Kippur), after the chazan's repetition:

אָבִינוּ מַלְכֵּנוּ אֵין לָנוּ מֶלֶךְ אֶלָּא אָתָּה:

Avinu Malkeinu Ein Lanu Melech Ella Attah.

Our Father and King, we have no King but You.

אָבִינוּ מַלְכֵּנוּ עֲשֵׂה עִמָּנוּ לְמַעַן שְׁמֶךָ:

Avinu Malkeinu Aseh Imanu Lema'an Shemecha.

Our Father and King, deal with us for Your Name's sake.

אָבִינוּ מַלְכֵּנוּ חַדֵּשׁ עָלֵינוּ שָׁנָה טוֹבָה:

Avinu Malkeinu Chadesh Aleinu Shanah Tovah.

Our Father and King, bring us a new year of good.

אָבִינוּ מַלְכֵּנוּ בַּטֵּל מֵעָלֵינוּ כָּל־גְּזֵרוֹת קָשׁוֹת וְרָעוֹת:

Avinu Malkeinu Battel Me'aleinu Kol-Gezerot Kashot Vera'ot.

Our Father and King, annul all hurtful and evil decrees against us.

אָבִינוּ מַלְכֵּנוּ בַּטֵּל מַחְשְׁבוֹת שׂוֹנְאֵינוּ:

Avinu Malkeinu Battel Machshevot Sone'einu.

Our Father and King, annul the devices of those who hate us.

אָבִינוּ מַלְכֵּנוּ הָפֵר עֲצַת אוֹיְבֵינוּ:

Avinu Malkeinu Hafer Atzat Oyeveinu.

Our Father and King, bring to nothing the hostile design of our enemies.

אָבִינוּ מַלְכֵּנוּ כַּלֵּה כָּל צַר וּמַשְׂטִין מֵעָלֵינוּ:

Avinu Malkeinu Kaleh Kol Tzar Umastin Me'aleinu.

Our Father and King, ward off from us all pain and accusation from us.

אָבִינוּ מַלְכֵּנוּ כַּלֵּה דֶּבֶר וְחֶרֶב וְרָעָב וּשְׁבִי וּבִזָּה וּמַשְׁחִית וּמַגֵּפָה וְיֵצֶר הָרָע וְחוֹלָאִים רָעִים מִבְּנֵי בְרִיתֶךָ:

Avinu Malkeinu Kaleh Dever Vecherev Vera'ah Vera'av Ushevi
Uvizah Umashchit Umagefah Veyetzer Hara Vechola'im Ra'im
Mibenei Veritecha.

Our Father and King, ward off pestilence, sword, famine, captivity,
disaster, destruction from the children of Your covenant.

אָבִינוּ מַלְכֵּנוּ שְׁלַח רְפוּאָה שְׁלֵמָה לְכָל חוֹלֵי עַמֶּךְ:

Avinu Malkeinu Shelach Refu'ah Shelemah Lechol Cholei
Ammecha.

Our Father and King, restore to perfect health the sick of Your
people.

אָבִינוּ מַלְכֵּנוּ מְנַע מַגֵּפָה מִנַּחֲלָתֶךְ:

Avinu Malkeinu Mena Magefah Minachalatecha.

Our Father and King, hold back pestilence from Your heritage.

אָבִינוּ מַלְכֵּנוּ זָכוּר כִּי עָפָר אֲנָחְנוּ:

Avinu Malkeinu Zachur Ki Afar Anach'nu.

Our Father and King, remember that we are but dust.

אָבִינוּ מַלְכֵּנוּ קְרַע רוֹעַ גְּזַר דִּינֵנוּ:

Avinu Malkeinu Kera Roa Gezar Dinenu.

Our Father and King, repeal the evil decreed against us.

אָבִינוּ מַלְכֵּנוּ כָּתְבֵנוּ בְּסֵפֶר חַיִּים טוֹבִים:

Avinu Malkeinu Katevenu Besefer Chayim Tovim.

Our Father and King, inscribe us for good in the Book of Life.

אָבִינוּ מַלְכֵּנוּ כָּתְבֵנוּ בְּסֵפֶר צַדִּיקִים וַחֲסִידִים:

Avinu Malkeinu Katevenu Besefer Tzaddikim Vachasidim.

Our Father and King, inscribe us in the Book of the Righteous and
the Pious.

אָבִינוּ מַלְכֵּנוּ כָּתְבֵנוּ בְּסֵפֶר יְשָׁרִים וּתְמִימִים:

Avinu Malkeinu Katevenu Besefer Yesharim Utemimim.

Our Father, Our King, inscribe us in the Book of the Straight and
Simple.

אָבִינוּ מַלְכֵּנוּ כָּתְבֵנוּ בְּסֵפֶר פַּרְנָסָה וְכַלְכָּלָה טוֹבָה:

Avinu Malkeinu Katevenu Besefer Parnasah Vechalkalah Tovah.

Our Father, Our King, inscribe us in the Book of Good Income and Sustenance.

אָבִינוּ מַלְכֵּנוּ כָּתְבֵנוּ בְּסֵפֶר מְחִילָה וּסְלִיחָה וְכַפָּרה:

Avinu Malkeinu Katevenu Besefer Mechilah Uselichah Vechapparah.

Our Father and King, inscribe us in the Book of Pardon and Atonement.

אָבִינוּ מַלְכֵּנוּ כָּתְבֵנוּ בְּסֵפֶר גְּאֻלָּה וִישׁוּעָה:

Avinu Malkeinu Katevenu Besefer Ge'ulah Vishu'ah.

Our Father and King, inscribe us in the Book of Redemption and Deliverance.

אָבִינוּ מַלְכֵּנוּ זָכְרֵנוּ בְּזִכְרוֹן טוֹב מִלְּפָנֶיךָ:

Avinu Malkeinu Zochrenu Bezichron Tov Milfaneicha.

Our Father and King, remember us for good before You.

אָבִינוּ מַלְכֵּנוּ הַצְמַח לָנוּ יְשׁוּעָה בְּקָרוֹב:

Avinu Malkeinu Hatzmach Lanu Yeshu'ah Bekarov.

Our Father and King, make our salvation soon to spring forth.

אָבִינוּ מַלְכֵּנוּ הָרֵם קֶרֶן יִשְׂרָאֵל עַמֶּךָ:

Avinu Malkeinu Harem Keren Yisra'el Ammecha.

Our Father and King, raise up the strength of Your people Yisrael.

אָבִינוּ מַלְכֵּנוּ וְהָרֵם קֶרֶן מְשִׁיחֶךָ:

Avinu Malkeinu Veharem Keren Meshichecha.

Our Father and King, raise up the strength of Your anointed (Messiah).

אָבִינוּ מַלְכֵּנוּ חָנֵּנוּ וַעֲנֵנוּ:

Avinu Malkeinu Chonenu Va'aneinu.

Our Father and King, have grace on us and answer us.

אָבִינוּ מַלְכֵּנוּ הַחֲזִירֵנוּ בִּתְשׁוּבָה שְׁלֵמָה לְפָנֶיךָ:

Avinu Malkeinu Hachazirenu Bitshuvah Shelemah Lefaneicha.
Our Father and King, bring us back through perfect repentance before You.

אָבִינוּ מַלְכֵּנוּ שְׁמַע קוֹלֵנוּ חוּס וְרַחֵם עָלֵינוּ:

Avinu Malkeinu Shema Koleinu Chus Verachem Aleinu.
Our Father and King, hear our voice, take pity on us and be merciful to us.

אָבִינוּ מַלְכֵּנוּ עֲשֵׂה לְמַעַנְךָ אִם לֹא לְמַעֲנֵנוּ:

Avinu Malkeinu Aseh Lema'anach Im Lo Lema'aneinu.
Our Father and King, grant our prayer, if not because of our merit, then for Your own sake.

אָבִינוּ מַלְכֵּנוּ קַבֵּל בְּרַחֲמִים וּבְרָצוֹן אֶת תְּפִלָּתֵנוּ:

Avinu Malkeinu Kabel Berachamim Uveratzon Et Tefillateinu.
Our Father and King, accept our prayer with merciful favor.

אָבִינוּ מַלְכֵּנוּ אַל תְּשִׁיבֵנוּ רֵיקָם מִלְפָנֶיךָ:

Avinu Malkeinu Al Teshivenu Reikam Milfaneicha.
Our Father and King, turn us not away empty from Your presence.

Said on all days Tachanun is not recited:

Yehi Shem

יְהִי שֵׁם יְהֹוָה מְבֹרָךְ מֵעַתָּה וְעַד־עוֹלָם: מִמִּזְרַח־שֶׁמֶשׁ עַד־מְבוֹאוֹ מְהֻלָּל שֵׁם יְהֹוָה: רָם עַל־כָּל־גּוֹיִם | יְהֹוָה עַל הַשָּׁמַיִם כְּבוֹדוֹ: יְהֹוָה אֲדֹנֵינוּ מָה־אַדִּיר שִׁמְךָ בְּכָל־הָאָרֶץ:

Yehi Shem Adonai Mevorach; Me'attah. Ve'ad-'Olam. Mimizrach-Shemesh Ad-Mevo'o; Mehulal. Shem Adonai Ram Al-Chol-Goyim Adonai Al Hashamayim Kevodo. Adonai Adoneinu; Mah-'Adir Shimcha. Bechol-Ha'aretz.

Blessed is the name of Hashem from this time forward and forever. From the rising of the sun to it's going down, Hashem's name is to be praised. Hashem, our Lord, How glorious is Your name in all of the earth. (Psalms 113:2-4, 8:2)

Kaddish Titkabbal

Kaddish is only recited in a minyan (ten men). אמן denotes when the congregation responds "Amen" together out loud. According to the Shulchan Arukh, the congregation says "Yehei Shemeh Rabba" to "Yitbarach" out loud together without interruption, and also that one should respond "Amen" after "Yitbarach." (SA, OC 55,56) This is not the common custom today. Though many are accustomed to answering according to their own custom, it is advised to respond in the custom of the one reciting to avoid not fragmenting into smaller groups. ("Lo Titgodedu" - BT, Yevamot 13b / SA, OC 493, Rema / MT, Avodah Zara 12:15)

יִתְגַּדַּל וְיִתְקַדַּשׁ שְׁמֵהּ רַבָּא. אָמֵן בְּעָלְמָא דִּי בְרָא. כִרְעוּתֵהּ. וְיַמְלִיךְ מַלְכוּתֵהּ.
וְיַצְמַח פֻּרְקָנֵהּ. וִיקָרֵב מְשִׁיחֵהּ. אָמֵן בְּחַיֵּיכוֹן וּבְיוֹמֵיכוֹן וּבְחַיֵּי דְכָל בֵּית
יִשְׂרָאֵל. בַּעֲגָלָא וּבִזְמַן קָרִיב. וְאִמְרוּ אָמֵן. אָמֵן יְהֵא שְׁמֵהּ רַבָּא מְבָרַךְ לְעָלַם
וּלְעָלְמֵי עָלְמַיָּא יִתְבָּרַךְ. וְיִשְׁתַּבַּח. וְיִתְפָּאַר. וְיִתְרוֹמַם. וְיִתְנַשֵּׂא. וְיִתְהַדָּר.
וְיִתְעַלֶּה. וְיִתְהַלָּל שְׁמֵהּ דְּקֻדְשָׁא. בְּרִיךְ הוּא. אָמֵן לְעֵלָּא מִן כָּל בִּרְכָתָא
שִׁירָתָא. תֻּשְׁבְּחָתָא וְנֶחֱמָתָא. דַּאֲמִירָן בְּעָלְמָא. וְאִמְרוּ אָמֵן. אָמֵן

Yitgadal Veyitkadash Shemeh Rabba. Amen Be'alema Di Vera. Kir'uteh. Veyamlich Malchuteh. Veyatzmach Purkaneh. Vikarev Meshicheh. Amen Bechayeichon Uveyomeichon Uvechayei Dechal-Beit Yisra'el. Ba'agala Uvizman Kariv. Ve'imru Amen. Amen Yehei Shemeh Rabba Mevarach Le'alam Ule'alemei Alemaya Yitbarach. Veyishtabach. Veyitpa'ar. Veyitromam. Veyitnasse. Veyit'hadar. Veyit'aleh. Veyit'hallal Shemeh Dekudsha. Berich Hu. Amen Le'ella Min Kol Birchata Shirata. Tushbechata Venechemata. Da'amiran Be'alema. Ve'imru Amen. Amen

Glorified and sanctified be God's great name Amen throughout the world which He has created according to His will. May He establish His kingdom, hastening His salvation and the coming of His Messiah, Amen, in your lifetime and during your days, and within the life of the entire House of Yisrael, speedily and soon; and say, Amen. Amen May His great name be blessed forever and to all eternity. Blessed and praised, glorified and exalted, extolled and honored, adored and lauded is the name of the Holy One, blessed is He, Amen Beyond all the blessings and hymns, praises and consolations that are ever spoken in the world; and say, Amen. Amen

תִּתְקַבַּל צְלוֹתָנָא וּבָעוּתָנָא. עִם צְלוֹתְהוֹן וּבָעוּתְהוֹן דְּכָל בֵּית יִשְׂרָאֵל. קֳדָם
אֲבוּנָא דְּבִשְׁמַיָּא וְאַרְעָא. וְאִמְרוּ אָמֵן. אָמֵן

Titkabbal Tzelotana Uva'utana. Im Tzelotehon Uva'utehon Dechol Beit Yisra'el. Kodam Avuna Devishmaya Ve'ar'a. Ve'imru Amen. Amen

May the prayer and supplication of the whole House of Yisrael be accepted before their Father in heaven, and say, Amen. Amen

יְהֵא שְׁלָמָא רַבָּא מִן שְׁמַיָּא. חַיִּים וְשָׂבָע וִישׁוּעָה וְנֶחָמָה. וְשֵׁיזָבָא וּרְפוּאָה
וּגְאוּלָה וּסְלִיחָה וְכַפָּרָה וְרֶוַח וְהַצָּלָה לָנוּ וּלְכָל עַמּוֹ יִשְׂרָאֵל. וְאִמְרוּ אָמֵן. אָמֵן

Yehei Shelama Rabba Min Shemaya. Chayim Vesava Vishu'ah Venechamah. Vesheizava Urefu'ah Uge'ulah Uselichah Vechapparah Verevach Vehatzalah Lanu Ulechol Ammo Yisra'el. Ve'imru Amen. Amen

May abundant peace descend from heaven, with life and plenty, salvation, solace, liberation, healing and redemption, and forgiveness and atonement, enlargement and freedom, for us and all of God's people Yisrael; and say, Amen. ^{Amen}

> One bows and takes three steps backwards, while still bowing. After three steps, while still bowing and before erecting, while saying, "Oseh Shalom Bimromav", turn one's face to the left, "Hu [Berachamav] Ya'aseh Shalom Aleinu", turn one's face to the right; then bow forward like a servant leaving his master. (SA, OC 123:1)

עוֹשֶׂה שָׁלוֹם בעשי״ת (הַשָּׁלוֹם) בִּמְרוֹמָיו. הוּא בְּרַחֲמָיו יַעֲשֶׂה שָׁלוֹם עָלֵינוּ. וְעַל כָּל־עַמּוֹ יִשְׂרָאֵל. וְאִמְרוּ אָמֵן:

Oseh Shalom **On the 10 days of repentance:** (Hashalom) Bimromav, Hu Berachamav Ya'aseh Shalom Aleinu, Ve'al Kol-'Ammo Yisra'el, Ve'imru Amen.

Creator of **On the 10 days of repentance:** (the) peace in His high places, may He in His mercy create peace for us and for all Yisrael, and say Amen.

> **THE TORAH READING FOR SHABBAT-ROSH CHODESH IS ON PAGE 650.**

Kriyat HaTorah / The Torah Reading

The Ark is opened and the following is read. On Rosh Chodesh the first two lines are skipped:

אַתָּה הָרְאֵתָ לָדַעַת כִּי יְהוָה הוּא הָאֱלֹהִים אֵין עוֹד מִלְּבַדּוֹ:
אֵין־כָּמוֹךָ בָאֱלֹהִים | אֲדֹנָי וְאֵין כְּמַעֲשֶׂיךָ:

Attah Hor'eta Lada'at Ki Adonai Hu Ha'elohim Ein Od Millevado.
Ein Kamocha Va'elohim Adonai Ve'ein Kema'aseicha.

To You it was shown, that You might know that Hashem, He is God;
there is no one else beside Him. There is no one like You among the
gods, Hashem, And there are no works like Yours. (Ps. 115:2-4, 8:2, Deut.
4:35, Ps. 86:8)

יְהִי יְהוָה אֱלֹהֵינוּ עִמָּנוּ כַּאֲשֶׁר הָיָה עִם־אֲבֹתֵינוּ אַל־יַעַזְבֵנוּ
וְאַל־יִטְּשֵׁנוּ: הוֹשִׁיעָה | אֶת־עַמֶּךָ וּבָרֵךְ אֶת־נַחֲלָתֶךָ וּרְעֵם וְנַשְּׂאֵם
עַד־הָעוֹלָם:

Yehi Adonai Eloheinu Imanu Ka'asher Hayah Im Avoteinu Al
Ya'azvenu Ve'al Yiteshnu. Hoshi'ah Et Ammecha Uvarech Et
Nachalatecha Ure'em Venasse'em Ad Ha'olam.

May Hashem our God be with us, as He was with our fathers; may
He not leave us, or forsake us. Save Your people, and bless Your
inheritance; And tend them, and carry them forever. (I Kings 8:57, Ps. 28:9)

וַיְהִי בִּנְסֹעַ הָאָרֹן וַיֹּאמֶר מֹשֶׁה קוּמָה | יְהוָה וְיָפֻצוּ אֹיְבֶיךָ וְיָנֻסוּ
מְשַׂנְאֶיךָ מִפָּנֶיךָ: קוּמָה יְהוָה לִמְנוּחָתֶךָ אַתָּה וַאֲרוֹן עֻזֶּךָ: כֹּהֲנֶיךָ
יִלְבְּשׁוּ־צֶדֶק וַחֲסִידֶיךָ יְרַנֵּנוּ: בַּעֲבוּר דָּוִד עַבְדֶּךָ אַל־תָּשֵׁב פְּנֵי
מְשִׁיחֶךָ:

Vayhi Binsoa' Ha'aron Vayomer Mosheh Kumah Adonai Veyafutzu
Oyeveicha Veyanusu Mesan'eicha Mippaneicha. Kumah Adonai
Limnuchatecha Attah Va'aron Uzecha. Kohaneicha Yilbeshu Tzedek
Vachasideicha Yeranenu. Ba'avur David Avdecha Al Tashev Penei
Meshichecha.

And it came to pass, when the ark set out, that Moshe said: 'Rise up,
Hashem, and let Your enemies be scattered; and let them that hate

You flee from before You.' Arise, Hashem, to Your resting-place; You, and the ark of Your strength. Let Your priests be clothed with righteousness; And let Your saints shout for joy. For Your servant David's sake do not turn away the face of Your anointed. (Num. 10:35, Ps. 132:8-10)

Opening of the Ark

Some say Berich Shemei, which is written in the Zohar of Parashat Vayakel:

בְּרִיךְ שְׁמֵהּ דְּמָארֵי עָלְמָא בְּרִיךְ כִּתְרָךְ וְאַתְרָךְ. יְהֵא רְעוּתָךְ. עִם
עַמָּךְ יִשְׂרָאֵל לְעָלַם. וּפוּרְקַן יְמִינָךְ אַחֲזֵי לְעַמָּךְ בְּבֵית מִקְדָּשָׁךְ.
לְאַמְטוּיֵי לָנָא מִטּוּב נְהוֹרָךְ. וּלְקַבֵּל צְלוֹתָנָא בְּרַחֲמִין. יְהֵא רַעֲוָא
קֳדָמָךְ דְּתוֹרִיךְ לָן חַיִּין בְּטִיבוּ. וְלֶהֱוֵי אֲנָא עַבְדָּךְ פְּקִידָא בְּגוֹ
צַדִּיקַיָּא. לְמִרְחַם עֲלַי וּלְמִנְטַר יָתִי וְיַת כָּל דִּי לִי וְדִי לְעַמָּךְ יִשְׂרָאֵל.
אַנְתְּ הוּא זָן לְכֹלָּא וּמְפַרְנֵס לְכֹלָּא. אַנְתְּ הוּא שַׁלִּיט עַל כֹּלָּא אַנְתְּ
הוּא דְשַׁלִּיט עַל מַלְכַיָּא וּמַלְכוּתָא דִּילָךְ הִיא. אֲנָא עַבְדָּא דְקוּדְשָׁא
בְּרִיךְ הוּא דְסָגִידְנָא קַמֵּהּ וּמִן קַמֵּי דִּיקַר אוֹרַיְתֵהּ בְּכָל־עִידָן וְעִידָן.
לָא עַל אֱנָשׁ רָחִיצְנָא. וְלָא עַל בַּר אֱלָהִין סָמִיכְנָא. אֶלָּא בֶּאֱלָהָא
דִשְׁמַיָּא דְּהוּא אֱלָהָא דִקְשׁוֹט. וְאוֹרַיְתֵהּ קְשׁוֹט. וּנְבִיאוֹהִי קְשׁוֹט.
וּמַסְגֵּי לְמֶעְבַּד טַבְוָן וּקְשׁוֹט. בֵּיהּ אֲנָא רָחִיץ וְלִשְׁמֵהּ יַקִּירָא
קַדִּישָׁא אֲנָא אָמַר תֻּשְׁבְּחָן. יְהֵא רַעֲוָא קֳדָמָךְ דְּתִפְתַּח לִבִּי
בְּאוֹרַיְתָךְ. (וְתֵיהַב לִי בְּנִין דִּכְרִין דְּעָבְדִין רְעוּתָךְ). וְתַשְׁלִים מִשְׁאֲלִין
דְּלִבַּאי וְלִבָּא דְכָל־עַמָּךְ יִשְׂרָאֵל לְטַב וּלְחַיִּין וְלִשְׁלָם אָמֵן:

Berich Shemeh Demarei Alema Berich Kitrach Ve'atrach. Yehe
Re'utach. Im Amach Yisra'el Le'alam. Ufurekan Yeminach Achzei
Le'amach Beveit Mikdashach. Le'amtuyei Lana Mituv Nehorach.
Ulekabel Tzelotana Berachamin. Yehe Ra'ava Kodamach Detorich
Lan Chayin Betivu. Velehevei Ana Avdach Pekida Bego Tzaddikaya.
Lemircham Alai Ulemintar Yati Veyat Kol Di Li Vedi Le'amach
Yisra'el. Ant Hu Zan Lechola Umefarnes Lechola. Ant Hu Shallit Al
Kola Ant Hu Deshallit Al Malchaya Umalchuta Dilach Hi. Ana Avda
Dekudesha Berich Hu Desagidna Kameh Umin Kamei Dikar

Orayteh Bechl Idan Ve'idan. La Al Enash Rachitzna. Vela Al Bar
Elahin Samichna. Ella Ve'elaha Dishmaya Dehu Elaha Dikshot.
Ve'orayteh Keshot. Unevi'ohi Keshot. Umasgei Leme'bad Tavan
Ukeshot. Beih Ana Rachitz Velishmeh Yakira Kaddisha Ana Emar
Tushbechan. Yehe Ra'ava Kodamach Detiftach Libi Be'oraytach.
(Vetihav Li Benin Dichrin De'avedin Re'utach). Vetashlim Mish'alin
Deliba Veliba Dechol Amach Yisra'el Letav Ulechayin Velishlam
Amen:

Blessed is the name of the Lord of the universe. Blessed is Your
crown and Your dominion. May Your goodwill always abide with
Your people Yisrael. Reveal Your saving power to Your people in
Your Sanctuary; bestow on us the good gift of Your light, and accept
our prayer in mercy. May it be Your will to prolong our life in
happiness. Let me also be counted among the righteous, so that
You may have compassion on me and shelter me and mine and all
that belong to Your people Yisrael. You are He Who nourishes and
sustains all; You are He Who rules over all; You are He Who rules
over kings, for dominion is Yours. I am the servant of the Holy One,
blessed is He, before Whom and before Whose glorious Torah I
bow at all times. I do not put my trust in man, or rely on any angel,
but only in the God of Heaven Who is the God of truth, Whose
Torah is truth and Whose Prophets are truth, and Who performs
many deeds of goodness and truth. In Him I put my trust, and to His
holy and glorious name I declare praises. May it be Your will to open
my heart to Your Torah, and to fulfill the wishes of my heart and of
the heart of all of Your people Yisrael for happiness, life and peace.

Take out the Torah scroll and say:

בָּרוּךְ הַמָּקוֹם שֶׁנָּתַן תּוֹרָה לְעַמּוֹ יִשְׂרָאֵל. בָּרוּךְ הוּא: אַשְׁרֵי הָעָם
שֶׁכָּכָה לּוֹ אַשְׁרֵי הָעָם שֶׁיהוה אֱלֹהָיו:

Baruch Hamakom Shenatan Torah Le'ammo Yisra'el. Baruch Hu.
Ashrei Ha'am Shekachah Lo; Ashrei Ha'am. She'Adonai Elohav.

Blessed is the universal Lord Who has given the Torah to His people Yisrael, blessed is He. "Happy are the people whose lot is so, happy are the people whose God is Hashem."

Reader takes the Torah out to platform and the Chazan says in unison with congregation:

גַּדְּלוּ לַיהֹוָה אִתִּי וּנְרוֹמְמָה שְׁמוֹ יַחְדָּו:

Gadelu L'Adonai Iti; Uneromemah Shemo Yachdav.

Exalt Hashem with me, And let us glorify His name in unison. (Psalms 34:4)

רוֹמְמוּ יְהֹוָה אֱלֹהֵינוּ וְהִשְׁתַּחֲווּ לַהֲדֹם רַגְלָיו קָדוֹשׁ הוּא: רוֹמְמוּ
יְהֹוָה אֱלֹהֵינוּ וְהִשְׁתַּחֲווּ לְהַר קָדְשׁוֹ כִּי־קָדוֹשׁ יְהֹוָה אֱלֹהֵינוּ:
אֵין־קָדוֹשׁ כַּיהֹוָה כִּי אֵין בִּלְתֶּךָ וְאֵין צוּר כֵּאלֹהֵינוּ: כִּי מִי אֱלוֹהַּ
מִבַּלְעֲדֵי יְהֹוָה וּמִי צוּר זוּלָתִי אֱלֹהֵינוּ: תּוֹרָה צִוָּה־לָנוּ מֹשֶׁה
מוֹרָשָׁה קְהִלַּת יַעֲקֹב: עֵץ־חַיִּים הִיא לַמַּחֲזִיקִים בָּהּ וְתֹמְכֶיהָ
מְאֻשָּׁר: דְּרָכֶיהָ דַרְכֵי־נֹעַם וְכָל־נְתִיבוֹתֶיהָ שָׁלוֹם: שָׁלוֹם רָב לְאֹהֲבֵי
תוֹרָתֶךָ וְאֵין־לָמוֹ מִכְשׁוֹל: יְהֹוָה עֹז לְעַמּוֹ יִתֵּן יְהֹוָה | יְבָרֵךְ אֶת־עַמּוֹ
בַשָּׁלוֹם:

Romemu Adonai Eloheinu. Vehishtachavu Lahadom Raglav. Kadosh Hu. Romemu Adonai Eloheinu. Vehishtachavu Lehar Kodsho; Ki-Kadosh. Adonai Eloheinu. Ein-Kadosh K'Adonai Ki Ein Biltecha; Ve'ein Tzur Keloheinu. Ki Mi Eloah Mibal'adei Adonai Umi Tzur. Zulati Eloheinu Torah Tzivah-Lanu Mosheh; Morashah Kehilat Ya'akov. Etz-Chayim Hi Lamachazikim Bah; Vetomecheiha Me'ushar. Deracheiha Darchei-No'am; Vechol-Netivoteiha Shalom. Shalom Rav Le'ohavei Toratecha; Ve'ein-Lamo Michshol. Adonai Oz Le'ammo Yiten; Adonai Yevarech Et-'Ammo Vashalom.

Exalt Hashem our God, And worship at His footstool, For He is holy. Exalt Hashem our God, And worship at His holy mountain, For Hashem our God is holy. There is none other as holy as Hashem, For there is none besides Him, or Rock like our God. For who is God except Hashem, Or who is the Rock besides our God? A Torah Moshe commanded us, A heritage for the congregation of

Yaakov. It is a tree of life for those who lay hold of it, And happy are those who cling to it. Its ways are ways of pleasantness, And all its pathways peace. Great peace have those who love Your Torah, And for them there is no stumbling. Hashem will give strength to His people. Hashem will bless His people with peace.

כִּי שֵׁם יְהֹוָה אֶקְרָא הָבוּ גֹדֶל לֵאלֹהֵינוּ: הַכֹּל תְּנוּ עֹז לֵאלֹהִים, וּתְנוּ כָבוֹד לַתּוֹרָה:

Ki Shem Adonai Ekra Havu Godel Leloheinu. Hakol Tenu Oz Lelohim, Utenu Chavod Latorah:

For I will proclaim the name of Hashem; Ascribe greatness to our God. Let all give might to God and give honor to the Torah. (Deut. 32:3, Psalms 68:35, 62:12)

Hagbahah / Lifting of the Torah

The lifting of the Sefer Torah. As it is raised and turned the congregation says:

Deuteronomy 4:44, 33:4

Vezot Hatorah; Asher-Sam	וְזֹאת הַתּוֹרָה אֲשֶׁר־שָׂם
Mosheh. Lifnei Benei Yisra'el.	מֹשֶׁה לִפְנֵי בְּנֵי יִשְׂרָאֵל:
Torah Tzivah-Lanu Mosheh;	תּוֹרָה צִוָּה־לָנוּ מֹשֶׁה
Morashah Kehilat Ya'akov. Ha'	מוֹרָשָׁה קְהִלַּת יַעֲקֹב: הָאֵל
El Tamim Darko Imrat-Adonai	תָּמִים דַּרְכּוֹ אִמְרַת־יְהֹוָה
Tzerufah; Magen Hu. Lechol	צְרוּפָה מָגֵן הוּא לְכֹל	
Hachosim Bo.	הַחֹסִים בּוֹ:

"And this is the Torah which Moshe placed before the children of Yisrael. The Torah which Moshe commanded us, the heritage for the congregation of Yaakov." "The way of God is perfect; the word of Hashem is tried; He is a Shield to all those who trust in Him."

> The first section of the Parashah (weekly portion of the Torah) of the following Shabbat is then read from the Torah. Three men, representing respectively the priesthood (Kohen), the Levites (Levi) and all Yisrael, are successively called to the Torah for its reading. As each approaches the Torah, he says:

In some kehilot (congregations), the Oleh / Reader says:

Adonai Imachem.

יְהֹוָה עִמָּכֶם:

Hashem be with you.

The kahal / congregation:

Yevarechekha Adonai.

יְבָרֶכְךָ יְהֹוָה:

May Hashem bless You.

The Oleh / Reader:

Barechu Et Adonai Hamevorach.

בָּרְכוּ אֶת יְהֹוָה הַמְבֹרָךְ:

Bless Hashem, Who is forever blessed.

The kahal / congregation:

Baruch Adonai Hamevorach
Le'olam Va'ed.

בָּרוּךְ יְהֹוָה הַמְבֹרָךְ
לְעוֹלָם וָעֶד:

Blessed is Hashem Who is blessed for all eternity.

The Oleh and Chazan:

Baruch Adonai Hamevorach
Le'olam Va'ed.

בָּרוּךְ יְהֹוָה הַמְבֹרָךְ
לְעוֹלָם וָעֶד:

Blessed is Hashem Who is blessed for all eternity.

Baruch Attah Adonai Eloheinu
Melech Ha'olam Asher Bachar
Banu Mikol Ha'ammim Venatan
Lanu Et Torato. Baruch Attah
Adonai Noten Hatorah.

בָּרוּךְ אַתָּה יְהֹוָה אֱלֹהֵינוּ
מֶלֶךְ הָעוֹלָם. אֲשֶׁר בָּחַר
בָּנוּ מִכָּל הָעַמִּים וְנָתַן
לָנוּ אֶת תּוֹרָתוֹ. בָּרוּךְ אַתָּה
יְהֹוָה נוֹתֵן הַתּוֹרָה:

Blessed are You, Hashem our God, King of the universe, You have chosen us from all peoples and given us Your Torah. Blessed are You, Hashem, Giver of the Torah.

> There is no need for the assembly to stand up during the reading of the Torah. (SA, OC 146:4)

After reading from the Torah, the reader holds the Sefer Torah and blesses (SA, OC 139:11):

Baruch Attah Adonai Eloheinu	בָּרוּךְ אַתָּה יְהֹוָה אֱלֹהֵינוּ
Melech Ha'olam Asher Natan	מֶלֶךְ הָעוֹלָם. אֲשֶׁר נָתַן
Lanu Et Torato Torat Emet.	לָנוּ אֶת תּוֹרָתוֹ תּוֹרַת אֱמֶת.
Vechayei Olam Nata	וְחַיֵּי עוֹלָם נָטַע
Betocheinu. Baruch Attah	בְּתוֹכֵנוּ. בָּרוּךְ אַתָּה
Adonai Noten Hatorah.	יְהֹוָה נוֹתֵן הַתּוֹרָה:

Blessed are You, Hashem our God, King of the universe, You have given us Your Torah of truth, and have planted among us eternal life. Blessed are You, Hashem, Giver of the Torah.

And say Hatzi-Kaddish:

> Kaddish is only recited in a minyan (ten men). אמן denotes when the congregation responds "Amen" together out loud. According to the Shulchan Arukh, the congregation says "Yehei Shemeh Rabba" to "Yitbarach" out loud together without interruption, and also that one should respond "Amen" after "Yitbarach." (SA, OC 55,56) This is not the common custom today. Though many are accustomed to answering according to their own custom, it is advised to respond in the custom of the one reciting to avoid not fragmenting into smaller groups. ("Lo Titgodedu" - BT, Yevamot 13b / SA, OC 493, Rema / MT, Avodah Zara 12:15)

יִתְגַּדַּל וְיִתְקַדַּשׁ שְׁמֵהּ רַבָּא. אמן בְּעָלְמָא דִּי בְרָא. כִרְעוּתֵהּ. וְיַמְלִיךְ מַלְכוּתֵהּ.
וְיַצְמַח פֻּרְקָנֵהּ. וִיקָרֵב מְשִׁיחֵהּ. אמן בְּחַיֵּיכוֹן וּבְיוֹמֵיכוֹן וּבְחַיֵּי דְכָל בֵּית
יִשְׂרָאֵל. בַּעֲגָלָא וּבִזְמַן קָרִיב. וְאִמְרוּ אָמֵן. אמן יְהֵא שְׁמֵהּ רַבָּא מְבָרַךְ לְעָלַם
וּלְעָלְמֵי עָלְמַיָּא יִתְבָּרַךְ. וְיִשְׁתַּבַּח. וְיִתְפָּאַר. וְיִתְרוֹמַם. וְיִתְנַשֵּׂא. וְיִתְהַדָּר.
וְיִתְעַלֶּה. וְיִתְהַלָּל שְׁמֵהּ דְּקֻדְשָׁא. בְּרִיךְ הוּא. אמן לְעֵלָּא מִן כָּל בִּרְכָתָא
שִׁירָתָא. תֻּשְׁבְּחָתָא וְנֶחֱמָתָא. דַּאֲמִירָן בְּעָלְמָא. וְאִמְרוּ אָמֵן. אמן

Yitgadal Veyitkadash Shemeh Rabba. ᴬᵐᵉⁿ Be'alema Di Vera. Kir'uteh. Veyamlich Malchuteh. Veyatzmach Purkaneh. Vikarev Meshicheh. ᴬᵐᵉⁿ Bechayeichon Uveyomeichon Uvechayei Dechal-Beit Yisra'el. Ba'agala Uvizman Kariv. Ve'imru Amen. ᴬᵐᵉⁿ Yehei Shemeh Rabba Mevarach Le'alam Ule'alemei Alemaya Yitbarach. Veyishtabach. Veyitpa'ar. Veyitromam. Veyitnasse. Veyit'hadar. Veyit'aleh. Veyit'hallal Shemeh Dekudsha. Berich Hu. ᴬᵐᵉⁿ Le'ella Min Kol Birchata Shirata. Tushbechata Venechemata. Da'amiran Be'alema. Ve'imru Amen. ᴬᵐᵉⁿ

Glorified and sanctified be God's great name ᴬᵐᵉⁿ throughout the world which He has created according to His will. May He establish His kingdom, hastening His salvation and the coming of His Messiah, ᴬᵐᵉⁿ, in your lifetime and during your days, and within the life of the entire House of Yisrael, speedily and soon; and say, Amen. ᴬᵐᵉⁿ May His great name be blessed forever and to all eternity. Blessed and praised, glorified and exalted, extolled and honored, adored and lauded is the name of the Holy One, blessed is He, ᴬᵐᵉⁿ Beyond all the blessings and hymns, praises and consolations that are ever spoken in the world; and say, Amen. ᴬᵐᵉⁿ

Birkhat HaGomel / The Thanksgiving Blessing

After the last Torah reading, recite. It is necessary to bless in front of ten men (minyan).

Before the blessing say:

Odeh Adonai Bechol-Levav;

Besod Yesharim Ve'edah.

אוֹדֶה יְהוָה בְּכָל־לֵבָב

בְּסוֹד יְשָׁרִים וְעֵדָה:

I will give thanks to Hashem with my whole heart. In the council of the upright, and in the congregation.

And bless:

Baruch Attah Adonai Eloheinu

Melech Ha'olam Hagomel

Lechayavim Tovot. Sheggemalani

Kol-Tuv.

בָּרוּךְ אַתָּה יְהוָה אֱלֹהֵינוּ

מֶלֶךְ הָעוֹלָם. הַגּוֹמֵל

לְחַיָּבִים טוֹבוֹת. שֶׁגְּמָלַנִי

כָּל־טוּב:

Blessed are You Hashem, our God, King of the Universe, Who rewards the undeserving with good, and has rewarded me with every kindness.

And the kahal / congregation answers:

Amen. Ha' El Sheggemalecha	אָמֵן. הָאֵל שֶׁגְּמָלְךָ
Kol-Tuv. Hu Yigmalecha Kol-Tuv	כָּל־טוּב. הוּא יִגְמָלְךָ כָּל־טוּב
Selah.	סֶלָה:

Amen. May the God Who has rewarded you every kindness, forever reward you with every kindness.

Misheberakh - Shabbat

Blessing for the Congregation:

יְהִי שֵׁם יְהֹוָה מְבֹרָךְ מֵעַתָּה וְעַד עוֹלָם:

Yehi Shem Adonai Mevorach Me'attah Ve'ad Olam:

Blessed is the name of Hashem from this time on and forever. **(Psalms 113:2)**

מִי שֶׁבֵּרַךְ אֲבוֹתֵינוּ אַבְרָהָם יִצְחָק וְיַעֲקֹב וּמֹשֶׁה וְאַהֲרֹן וְדָוִד וּשְׁלֹמֹה. וְכָל הַקְּהִלּוֹת הַקְּדוֹשׁוֹת וְהַטְּהוֹרוֹת. הוּא יְבָרֵךְ אֶת כָּל הַקָּהָל הַקָּדוֹשׁ הַזֶּה. גְּדוֹלִים וּקְטַנִּים. הֵם וּנְשֵׁיהֶם וּבְנֵיהֶם וְתַלְמִידֵיהֶם. וְכָל־אֲשֶׁר לָהֶם. מַלְכָּא דְעָלְמָא הוּא יְבָרֵךְ יַתְכוֹן. וִיזַכֶּה יַתְכוֹן. וְיִשְׁמַע בְּקָל צְלוֹתְכוֹן. תִּתְפָּרְקוּן וְתִשְׁתֵּזְבוּן מִכָּל צָרָה וְעָקְתָּא. וִיהֵא מֵימְרָא דַּיהֹוָה בְּסַעְדְּכֶם. וְיָגֵן בַּעֲדְכֶם. וְיִפְרוֹשׂ סֻכַּת שְׁלוֹמוֹ עֲלֵיכֶם. וְיִטַּע בֵּינֵיכֶם אַהֲבָה וְאַחְוָה. שָׁלוֹם וְרֵעוּת. וִיסַלֵּק שִׂנְאַת חִנָּם מִבֵּינֵיכֶם. וְיִשְׁבּוֹר עֹל הַגּוֹיִם מֵעַל צַוְּארֵיכֶם. וִיקַיֵּם בָּכֶם מִקְרָא שֶׁכָּתוּב יְהֹוָה אֱלֹהֵי אֲבוֹתֵכֶם יֹסֵף עֲלֵיכֶם כָּכֶם אֶלֶף פְּעָמִים וִיבָרֵךְ אֶתְכֶם כַּאֲשֶׁר דִּבֶּר לָכֶם: בשבת תשובה: (וְיִכְתָּבְכֶם הָאֵל בְּסֵפֶר חַיִּים טוֹבִים.) וְכֵן יְהִי רָצוֹן וְנֹאמַר אָמֵן:

Mi Sheberach Avoteinu Avraham Yitzchak Veya'akov Umosheh
Ve'aharon Vedavid Ushelomoh. Vechol Hakehilot Hakkedoshot
Vehatehorot. Hu Yevarech Et Kol Hakahal Hakadosh Hazeh.
Gedolim Uketanim. Hem Unesheihem Uveneihem Vetalmideihem.
Vechol Asher Lahem. Malka De'alema Hu Yevarech Yatchon.
Vizakeh Yatchon. Veyishma Bekal Tzelotechon. Titparekun
Vetishtezevun Mikol Tzarah Ve'akta. Vihe Meimra D'Adonai
Besa'dechem. Veyagen Ba'adchem. Veyifros Sukkat Shelomo
Aleichem. Veyitta Beineichem Ahavah Ve'achvah. Shalom Vere'ut.
Visallek Sin'at Chinam Mibeineichem. Veyishbor Ol Hagoyim Me'al
Tzavareichem. Vikayem Bachem Mikra Shekatuv Adonai Elohei
Avotechem Yosef Aleichem Kachem Elef Pe'amim Vivarech Etchem
Ka'asher Diber Lachem. On Shabbat in the Penitential Days add: (Veyichtavechem
Ha'el Besefer Chayim Tovim.) Vechein Yehi Ratzon Venomar Amen:

May He Who blessed our fathers Avraham, Yitzchak and Yaakov,
Moshe and Aharon. David and Shlomo, and all of the holy and pure
congregations; bless this holy congregation, both great and small;
them, their children, their wives, and their disciples, and all that
belongs to them. May the supreme King of the universe bless you
and purify you, and attend to the voice of your supplication; may He
redeem and deliver you from all manner of trouble and distress.
May the word of Hashem support and shield you; and may He
spread His tent of peace over you, and plant among you brotherly
love, peace, and friendship. May He remove from among you all
manner of baseless enmity, and break the yoke of the nations from
off your neck; and fulfill in you what is written, "May Hashem, God
of your fathers make you a thousand times as many as you are, and
bless you as He has promised you.' On Shabbat in the Penitential Days add: (And
may He inscribe you in the book of life.) And may this be the will of God,
and let us say, Amen.

Continue with the Blessing for the sick of the Congregation.

Blessing for the sick of the Congregation:

מִי שֶׁבֵּרַךְ אֲבוֹתֵינוּ וְאִמוֹתֵינוּ. אַבְרָהָם יִצְחָק וְיַעֲקֹב. שָׂרָה. רִבְקָה. רָחֵל וְלֵאָה. הוּא יְבָרֵךְ אֶת הַחוֹלִים:

פְּלוֹנִי בֶּן/בַּת פְּלוֹנִי

הַקָּדוֹשׁ בָּרוּךְ הוּא יְמַלֵּא רַחֲמִים עֲלֵיהֶם לְהַחֲלִימָם וּלְרַפְּאוֹתָם וּלְהַחֲזִיקָם וּלְהַחֲיוֹתָם. וְיִשְׁלַח לָהֶם מְהֵרָה רְפוּאָה שְׁלֵמָה מִן הַשָּׁמַיִם בִּרְמַ"ח אֵבָרָיו. וּשְׁסָ"ה גִידָיו. בְּתוֹךְ שְׁאָר חוֹלֵי יִשְׂרָאֵל. רְפוּאַת הַנֶּפֶשׁ וּרְפוּאַת הַגּוּף. הַשְׁתָּא בַּעֲגָלָא וּבִזְמַן קָרִיב. וְנֹמַר אָמֵן:

Mi Sheberach Avoteinu Ve'imoteinu. Avraham Yitzchak Veya'akov. Sarah. Rivkah. Rachel Vele'ah. Hu Yevarech Et Hacholim:

Peloni Ben/Bat Peloni

Hakadosh Baruch Hu Rachamim Aleihem Lehachalimam Ulerappe'otam Ulehachazikam Ulhachayotam. Veyishlach Lahem Meheirah Refu'ah Shelemah Min Hashamayim 248 Eivarav. 365 Gidav. Betoch She'ar Cholei Yisra'el. Refu'at Hanefesh Urefu'at Haguf. Hashta Ba'agala Uvizman Kariv. Venomar Amen:

He Who blessed our patriarchs and matriarchs: Avraham, Yitzchak, and Yaakov, Sarah, Rivkah, Rachel and Leah, may He bless the sick:

_____ ben (son of)/bat (daughter of) _____

May the Holy One, blessed is He, be filled with compassion upon them, to give them health, and to heal them, and to strengthen them, and to preserve them alive. And may He send them speedily a perfect healing from heaven in their 248 members and their 365 sinews among the other sick of Yisrael, a healing of the soul and a healing of the body. May this occur at once, speedily and without delay and let us say, Amen.

Continue with the Reading of the Haftorah.

Kriyat Haftarah / The Haftarah Reading

Baruch Attah Adonai Eloheinu	בָּרוּךְ אַתָּה יְהֹוָה אֱלֹהֵינוּ
Melech Ha'olam Asher Bachar	מֶלֶךְ הָעוֹלָם. אֲשֶׁר בָּחַר
Binvi'im Tovim Veratzah	בִּנְבִיאִים טוֹבִים וְרָצָה
Vedivreihem Hane'emarim	בְדִבְרֵיהֶם הַנֶּאֱמָרִים
Be'emet. Baruch Attah Adonai	בֶאֱמֶת. בָּרוּךְ אַתָּה יְהֹוָה
Habbocher Batorah Uvemosheh	הַבּוֹחֵר בַּתּוֹרָה וּבְמֹשֶׁה
Avdo. Uveyisra'el Ammo	עַבְדּוֹ. וּבְיִשְׂרָאֵל עַמּוֹ
Uvinvi'ei Ha'emet Vehatzedek:	וּבִנְבִיאֵי הָאֱמֶת וְהַצֶּדֶק:

Blessed are You, Hashem our God, King of the universe, Who chose Your faithful prophets and find delight in their words uttered in truth. Blessed are You, Hashem Who has chosen the Torah, Your servant Moshe, Your people Yisrael and Your prophets of truth and righteousness.

After the recitation of the Haftarah say:

גָּאֲלֵנוּ יְהֹוָה צְבָאוֹת שְׁמוֹ קְדוֹשׁ יִשְׂרָאֵל:

Go'alenu Adonai Tzeva'ot Shemo; Kedosh Yisra'el.

Our Redeemer, Hashem of hosts is His name, the Holy One of Yisrael. (Isaiah 47:4)

And then bless:

Baruch Attah Adonai Eloheinu	בָּרוּךְ אַתָּה יְהֹוָה אֱלֹהֵינוּ
Melech Ha'olam Tzur Kol-	מֶלֶךְ הָעוֹלָם. צוּר כָּל־
Ha'olamim. Tzaddik Bechol-	הָעוֹלָמִים. צַדִּיק בְּכָל־
Haddorot. Ha'el Hane'eman	הַדּוֹרוֹת. הָאֵל הַנֶּאֱמָן
Ha'omer Ve'oseh. Hamdaber	הָאוֹמֵר וְעֹשֶׂה. הַמְדַבֵּר

Umekayem. Shekol-Devarav	וּמְקַיֵּם. שֶׁכָּל־דְּבָרָיו
Emet Vatzedek. Ne'eman. Attah	אֱמֶת וָצֶדֶק. נֶאֱמָן. אַתָּה
Hu Adonai Eloheinu.	הוּא יְהֹוָה אֱלֹהֵינוּ.
Vene'emanim Devareicha.	וְנֶאֱמָנִים דְּבָרֶיךָ.
Vedavar Echad Midevareicha	וְדָבָר אֶחָד מִדְּבָרֶיךָ
Achor Lo Yashuv Reikam. Ki El	אָחוֹר לֹא יָשׁוּב רֵיקָם. כִּי אֵל
Melech Ne'eman Verachaman	מֶלֶךְ נֶאֱמָן וְרַחֲמָן
Attah. Baruch Attah Adonai	אַתָּה. בָּרוּךְ אַתָּה יְהֹוָה
Ha'el Hane'eman Bechol-	הָאֵל הַנֶּאֱמָן בְּכָל־
Devarav.	דְּבָרָיו:

Blessed are You, Hashem our God, King of the universe, Rock of all ages, true in all generations. God Who keeps faith, Who promises and performs, Who speaks and fulfills, all Your words are true and right. Faithful are You, Hashem our God, and trustworthy are Your promises; not even one of Your words will return unfulfilled. For You are God, the King Who keeps faith. Blessed are You, Hashem, The God faithful in all Your words.

Rachem Al Tziyon Ki Hi Beit	רַחֵם עַל צִיּוֹן כִּי הִיא בֵּית
Chayeinu. Vela'aluvat Nefesh	חַיֵּינוּ. וְלַעֲלוּבַת נֶפֶשׁ
Toshia Bimheirah Veyameinu.	תּוֹשִׁיעַ בִּמְהֵרָה בְיָמֵינוּ.
Baruch Attah Adonai	בָּרוּךְ אַתָּה יְהֹוָה
Mesame'ach Tziyon Bevaneiha.	מְשַׂמֵּחַ צִיּוֹן בְּבָנֶיהָ:

Have pity on Tziyon, for it is the home of our life, and soon in our own time save Your city afflicted of soul. Blessed are You, Hashem Who makes Tziyon rejoice in her children.

Samecheinu Adonai Eloheinu.	שַׂמְּחֵנוּ יְהֹוָה אֱלֹהֵינוּ.
Be'eliyahu Hanavi Avdach.	בְּאֵלִיָּהוּ הַנָּבִיא עַבְדָּךְ.
Uvemalchut Beit David	וּבְמַלְכוּת בֵּית דָּוִד
Meshichach. Bimheirah Yavo	מְשִׁיחָךְ. בִּמְהֵרָה יָבֹא
Veyagel Libenu. Al Kis'o Lo	וְיָגֵל לִבֵּנוּ. עַל כִּסְאוֹ לֹא
Yeshev Zar. Velo Yinchalu Od	יֵשֵׁב זָר. וְלֹא יִנְחֲלוּ עוֹד
Acherim Et Kevodo. Ki Veshem	אֲחֵרִים אֶת כְּבוֹדוֹ. כִּי בְשֵׁם
Kodshecha Nishba'ta Lo. Shelo	קָדְשְׁךָ נִשְׁבַּעְתָּ לּוֹ. שֶׁלֹּא
Yichbeh Nero Le'olam Va'ed.	יִכְבֶּה נֵרוֹ לְעוֹלָם וָעֶד.
Baruch Attah Adonai Magen	בָּרוּךְ אַתָּה יְהֹוָה מָגֵן
David.	דָּוִד:

Hashem, our God, cause us to rejoice in the coming of Your servant Eliyahu, the prophet, and in the kingdom of the House of David, Your anointed. May he come speedily, and gladden our hearts. Do not suffer a stranger to sit on his throne, or any other to inherit his glory; for by Your holy name have You sworn to him that his lamp will never be extinguished. Blessed are You, Hashem, the Shield of David.

Al Hatorah. Ve'al Ha'avodah.	עַל הַתּוֹרָה. וְעַל הָעֲבוֹדָה.
Ve'al Hanevi'im. Ve'al Yom	וְעַל הַנְּבִיאִים. וְעַל יוֹם
Hashabbat Hazeh Shenatata	הַשַּׁבָּת הַזֶּה שֶׁנָּתַתָּ
Lanu Adonai Eloheinu Likdushah	לָנוּ יְהֹוָה אֱלֹהֵינוּ לִקְדֻשָּׁה
Velimnuchah Lechavod	וְלִמְנוּחָה לְכָבוֹד
Uletif'aret. Al Hakol Adonai	וּלְתִפְאָרֶת. עַל הַכֹּל יְהֹוָה
Eloheinu Anachnu Modim Lach	אֱלֹהֵינוּ אֲנַחְנוּ מוֹדִים לָךְ
Umevarechim Otach. Yitbarach	וּמְבָרְכִים אוֹתָךְ. יִתְבָּרַךְ

Shimcha Befi Kol-Chai Tamid

Le'olam Va'ed. Baruch Attah

Adonai Mekadesh Hashabbat.

Amen.

שִׁמְךָ בְּפִי כָּל־חַי תָּמִיד
לְעוֹלָם וָעֶד. בָּרוּךְ אַתָּה
יְהֹוָה מְקַדֵּשׁ הַשַּׁבָּת.
אָמֵן.

For the sake of the Torah, the worship, and the prophets, and this Shabbat-day, which You have given us, for a day of sanctification, rest, glory, and honor; for all which, Hashem our God, we thank and praise You; blessed is Your name in the mouth of every living creature, continually, and forever. Blessed are You, Hashem, Who sanctifies the Shabbat.

On Yom Tov say:

עַל הַתּוֹרָה וְעַל הָעֲבוֹדָה וְעַל הַנְּבִיאִים בשבת: (וְעַל יוֹם הַשַּׁבָּת הַזֶּה). וְעַל יוֹם:

Al Hatorah Ve'al Ha'avodah Ve'al Hanevi'im **On Shabbat:** (Ve'al Yom Hashabbat Hazeh). Ve'al Yom:

We thank You for the Torah, for the worship, for the Prophets **On Shabbat:** (for this Shabbat day) and for this day of:

On Pesach:

חַג הַמַּצּוֹת הַזֶּה:

Chag Hamatzot Hazeh:

The Festival of Matzot,

On Shavuot:

חַג הַשָּׁבוּעוֹת:

Chag Hashavu'ot:

The Festival of Shavuot,

On Sukkot:

חַג הַסֻּכּוֹת:

Chag Hasukkot:

The Festival of Sukkot,

On Shemini Atzeret:

שְׁמִינִי חַג עֲצֶרֶת:

Shemini Chag Atzeret:

The Festival of Shemini Atzeret,

הַזֶּה. שֶׁנָּתַתָּ לָנוּ יְהֹוָה אֱלֹהֵינוּ בשבת: (לִקְדֻשָּׁה וְלִמְנוּחָה) לְשָׂשׂוֹן וּלְשִׂמְחָה. לְכָבוֹד וּלְתִפְאָרֶת. עַל הַכֹּל. יְהֹוָה אֱלֹהֵינוּ אֲנַחְנוּ מוֹדִים לָךְ וּמְבָרְכִים אוֹתָךְ. יִתְבָּרַךְ שִׁמְךָ בְּפִי כָּל חַי תָּמִיד לְעוֹלָם וָעֶד. בָּרוּךְ אַתָּה יְהֹוָה מְקַדֵּשׁ בשבת: (הַשַּׁבָּת וְ)יִשְׂרָאֵל וְהַזְּמַנִּים:

Hazeh. Shenatatta Lanu Adonai Eloheinu On Shabbat: (Likdushah Velimnuchah) Lesason Ulesimchah. Lechavod Uletif'aret. Al Hakol. Adonai Eloheinu Anachnu Modim Lach Umevarechim Otach. Yitbarach Shimcha Befi Kol Chai Tamid Le'olam Va'ed. Baruch Attah Adonai Mekadesh On Shabbat: (Hashabbat Ve) Yisra'el Vehazmanim:

which You have given us, Hashem our God, On Shabbat: (for holiness and rest), for joy and gladness, for glory and beauty. We thank and bless You, Hashem our God, for all things; may Your name forever be blessed by every living being. Blessed are You, Hashem, Who sanctifies On Shabbat: (Shabbat and) Yisrael and the seasons.

Birkhat HaChodesh / Blessing of the New Month

On the Shabbat before Rosh Chodesh, except for Rosh Chodesh Tishrei and Rosh Chodesh Av, a new rosh/head is announced.

Yehi Ratzon Millifnei Elohei — יְהִי רָצוֹן מִלִּפְנֵי אֱלֹהֵי

Hashamayim Lechonen Et Beit — הַשָּׁמַיִם לְכוֹנֵן אֶת בֵּית

Chayeinu Ulehashiv Shechinato — חַיֵּינוּ וּלְהָשִׁיב שְׁכִינָתוֹ

Letocho Bimheirah Beyameinu. — לְתוֹכוֹ בִּמְהֵרָה בְּיָמֵינוּ.

Ve'imru Amen: — וְאִמְרוּ אָמֵן:

May it be the will of the God of Heaven to establish the House of our life, and speedily in our days to restore His Divine Presence there to it; and say, Amen.

Yehi Ratzon Millifnei Elohei — יְהִי רָצוֹן מִלִּפְנֵי אֱלֹהֵי

Hashamayim. Lerachem Al — הַשָּׁמַיִם. לְרַחֵם עַל

Peleitatenu. Vela'atzor — פְּלֵיטָתֵנוּ. וְלַעֲצוֹר

Hamagefah. Vehamashchit. — הַמַּגֵּפָה. וְהַמַּשְׁחִית.

Vehacherev. Vehara'av. — וְהַחֶרֶב. וְהָרָעָב.

Vehashevi. Vehabizah. Me'aleinu	וְהַשֶּׁבִי. וְהַבִּזָּה. מֵעָלֵינוּ
Ume'al Ammo Yisra'el. Ve'imru	וּמֵעַל עַמּוֹ יִשְׂרָאֵל. וְאִמְרוּ
Amen:	אָמֵן:

May it be the will of the God of Heaven to have compassion on the remnant of us which have escaped; and to withhold pestilence, destruction, sword, famine, captivity, and spoil from us, and from all His people Yisrael, and say, Amen.

Yehi Ratzon Millifnei Elohei	יְהִי רָצוֹן מִלִּפְנֵי אֱלֹהֵי
Hashamayim Lekayem Lanu	הַשָּׁמַיִם לְקַיֵּם לָנוּ אֶת
Kol Chachmei Yisra'el. Hem	כָּל־חַכְמֵי יִשְׂרָאֵל. הֵם
Unesheihem Uveneihem	וּנְשֵׁיהֶם וּבְנֵיהֶם
Vetalmideihem. Bechol	וְתַלְמִידֵיהֶם. בְּכָל־
Mekomot Moshevoteihem.	מְקוֹמוֹת מוֹשְׁבוֹתֵיהֶם.
Ve'imru Amen:	וְאִמְרוּ אָמֵן:

May it be the will of the God of Heaven to preserve for us all the wise men of Yisrael, them, their children, wives, and disciples, in all the places of their residence, and say, Amen.

Yehi Ratzon Millifnei Elohei	יְהִי רָצוֹן מִלִּפְנֵי אֱלֹהֵי
Hashamayim. Shenishma	הַשָּׁמַיִם. שֶׁנִּשְׁמַע
Venitbaser Besorot Tovot.	וְנִתְבַּשֵּׂר בְּשׂוֹרוֹת טוֹבוֹת.
Besorot Yeshu'ot Venechamot.	בְּשׂוֹרוֹת יְשׁוּעוֹת וְנֶחָמוֹת.
Me'arba Kanfot Ha'aretz.	מֵאַרְבַּע כַּנְפוֹת הָאָרֶץ.
Ve'imru Amen:	וְאִמְרוּ אָמֵן:

May it be the will of the God of heaven that we may hear and be informed of good news, even the good news of salvation and consolation, from all the four corners of the earth, and say, Amen.

Mi She'asah Nissim La'avoteinu	מִי שֶׁעָשָׂה נִסִּים לַאֲבוֹתֵינוּ
Umimitzrayim Ge'alam. Hu	וּמִמִּצְרַיִם גְּאָלָם. הוּא
Yig'al Otanu Veyashiv Banim	יִגְאַל אוֹתָנוּ וְיָשִׁיב בָּנִים
Ligvulam. Besiman Tov Yehe	לִגְבוּלָם. בְּסִימָן טוֹב יְהֵא
Lanu Rosh Chodesh Peloni	לָנוּ רֹאשׁ חֹדֶשׁ פלוני
Beyom Peloni Ve'peloni (Chiddusheih	בְּיוֹם פלוני (ופלוני) (חִדּוּשֵׁיהּ
Beyom Peloni Ukevu'eih Uminyaneih	בְּיוֹם פְּלוֹנִי וּקְבוּעֵיהּ וּמִנְיָנֵיהּ
Beyom Peloni). Yechadeshehu	בְּיוֹם פְּלוֹנִי). יְחַדְּשֵׁהוּ
Hakadosh Baruch Hu Aleinu	הַקָּדוֹשׁ בָּרוּךְ הוּא עָלֵינוּ
Ve'al Ammo Yisra'el Bechol	וְעַל עַמּוֹ יִשְׂרָאֵל בְּכָל־
Makom Shehem. Letovah	מָקוֹם שֶׁהֵם. לְטוֹבָה
Velivrachah. Lesason	וְלִבְרָכָה. לְשָׂשׂוֹן
Ulesimchah. Lishu'ah	וּלְשִׂמְחָה. לִישׁוּעָה
Ulenechamah. Lefarnasah	וּלְנֶחָמָה. לְפַרְנָסָה
Ulechalkalah Tovah. Lishmu'ot	וּלְכַלְכָּלָה טוֹבָה. לִשְׁמוּעוֹת
Tovot. Velivsorot Tovot. B'choref:	טוֹבוֹת. וְלִבְשׂוֹרוֹת טוֹבוֹת. בחורף:
(Veligshamim Be'ittam.) B'ketz: (Uletalle	(וְלִגְשָׁמִים בְּעִתָּם.) בקיץ: (וּלְטַלְלֵי
Verachah.) Velirfu'ah Shelemah.	בְרָכָה.) וְלִרְפוּאָה שְׁלֵמָה.
Velig'ullah Kerovah. Ve'imru	וְלִגְאֻלָּה קְרוֹבָה. וְאִמְרוּ
Amen:	אָמֵן:

May He Who performed miracles for our fathers, and redeemed them from Mitzrayim, redeem us, and cause His children to return to their own territory: With a good sign may there be for us Rosh Chodesh name of the month, on the day of the week day (and day of the

<u>week),</u> (the renewal is on the day of the week day and its fixing and ordination is on <u>the day of the week day).</u> May the Holy One, blessed is He, renew it for us, and His people Yisrael, wherever situated for good and blessing, joy, and gladness, salvation and consolation; for sustenance and maintenance, good reports and good news; **In winter:** (for rains in their due season,) **In summer:** (and for the dew of blessing,) for a perfect cure, and speedy redemption; and say, Amen.

Prayer for the Government

Hanotein Teshu'ah	הַנּוֹתֵן תְּשׁוּעָה
Lammelachim. Umemshalah	לַמְּלָכִים. וּמֶמְשָׁלָה
Lansichim. Umalchuto Malchut	לַנְּסִיכִים. וּמַלְכוּתוֹ מַלְכוּת
Kol Olamim. Hapotzeh Et David	כָּל־עוֹלָמִים. הַפּוֹצֶה אֶת־דָּוִד
Avdo Mecherev Ra'ah.	עַבְדּוֹ מֵחֶרֶב רָעָה.
Hanotein Bayam Darech.	הַנּוֹתֵן בַּיָּם דָּרֶךְ.
Uvemayim Azim Netivah. Hu	וּבְמַיִם עַזִּים נְתִיבָה. הוּא
Yevarech. Veyishmor. Veyintzor.	יְבָרֵךְ. וְיִשְׁמֹר. וְיִנְצֹר.
Veya'azor. Virovmem. Vigadel.	וְיַעֲזֹר. וִירוֹמֵם. וִיגַדֵּל.
Vinashe Lema'lah Lema'lah Et:	וִינַשֵּׂא לְמַעְלָה לְמַעְלָה אֶת־:

May He Who dispenses assistance to kings, and dominion to princes; Whose kingdom is an everlasting kingdom; Who delivered His servant David from the destructive sword; Who makes a way in the sea, and a path in the mighty waters; bless, preserve, guard, assist, exalt, and raise to a high eminence:

Nesi Artzot Haberit Umishnehu	נְשִׂיא אַרְצוֹת הַבְּרִית וּמִשְׁנֵהוּ
Ve'et Kol Sarei Ha'aretz Hazot.	וְאֶת כָּל שָׂרֵי הָאָרֶץ הַזֹּאת.

The President and the Vice-President and all of the officers of this land.

Melech Malchei Hamelachim.	מֶלֶךְ מַלְכֵי הַמְּלָכִים.
Berachamav Yishmerem	בְּרַחֲמָיו יִשְׁמְרֵם
Vichayeim. Umikol-Tzarah	וִיחַיֵּים. וּמִכָּל-צָרָה
Vanezek Yatzilem: Melech	וָנֶזֶק יַצִּילֵם: מֶלֶךְ
Malchei Hamelachim.	מַלְכֵי הַמְּלָכִים.
Berachamav Yiten Belibam	בְּרַחֲמָיו יִתֵּן בְּלִבָּם
Uvelev Kol Yo'atzeihem Vesarav	וּבְלֵב כָּל-יוֹעֲצֵיהֶם וְשָׂרָיו
Rachamanut. La'asot Tovah	רַחֲמָנוּת. לַעֲשׂוֹת טוֹבָה
Imanu. Ve'im Kol Yisra'el	עִמָּנוּ. וְעִם כָּל-יִשְׂרָאֵל
Acheinu: Bimeihem	אַחֵינוּ: בִּימֵיהֶם
Uveyameinu Tivasha Yehudah.	וּבְיָמֵינוּ תִּוָּשַׁע יְהוּדָה.
Veyisra'el Yishkon Lavetach.	וְיִשְׂרָאֵל יִשְׁכֹּן לָבֶטַח.
Uva Letziyon Go'el. Vechen	וּבָא לְצִיּוֹן גּוֹאֵל. וְכֵן
Yehi Ratzon Venomar Amen.	יְהִי רָצוֹן וְנֹאמַר אָמֵן.

May the Supreme King of kings, through His infinite mercy preserve them, and grant them life, and deliver them from all manner of trouble and injury. May the Supreme King of kings, through His infinite mercy, inspire the heart of them and all of their counselors and officers with benevolence towards us, and all Yisrael our brothers. In their days and in ours may Yehudah be saved, and Yisrael dwell securely; and may the Redeemer come to Tziyon. May this be the will of God, and let us say. Amen.

Hachrazat Ta'anit Tzibur / Announcement of Public Fast

On the Shabbat before the fast of the 17th of Tammuz and the 10th of Tevet, the cantor declares
and there is no proclamation of the fast of the Tisha B' Av and Yom Kippur and the fast of Esther.
(SA, OC 550:4)

Acheinu Beit Yisra'el Shema'u.	אַחֵינוּ בֵּית יִשְׂרָאֵל שְׁמָעוּ.
Tzom On 17th of Tammuz: (Harevi'i) On	צוֹם לי"ז בתמוז: (הָרְבִיעִי)
10th of Tevet: (Ha'asiri) Yihyeh Yom	לעשרה בטבת: (הָעֲשִׂירִי) יִהְיֶה יוֹם
___. Yahafoch Oto Hakadosh	(___). יַהֲפֹךְ אוֹתוֹ הַקָּדוֹשׁ
Baruch Hu Lesason	בָּרוּךְ הוּא לְשָׂשׂוֹן
Ulesimchah. Kedichtiv Koh-	וּלְשִׂמְחָה. כְּדִכְתִיב כֹּה־
Amar Adonai Tzeva'ot Tzom	אָמַר יְהוָה צְבָאוֹת צוֹם
Harevi'i Vetzom Hachamishi	הָרְבִיעִי וְצוֹם הַחֲמִישִׁי
Vetzom Hashevi'i Vetzom	וְצוֹם הַשְּׁבִיעִי וְצוֹם
Ha'asiri Yihyeh Leveit Yehudah	הָעֲשִׂירִי יִהְיֶה לְבֵית־יְהוּדָה
Lesason Ulesimchah	לְשָׂשׂוֹן וּלְשִׂמְחָה
Ulemo'adim Tovim Veha'emet	וּלְמֹעֲדִים טוֹבִים וְהָאֱמֶת
Vehashalom Ehavu.	וְהַשָּׁלוֹם אֱהָבוּ:

Our brothers, the House of Yisrael, be informed that the fast of On
the 17th of Tammuz: (the fourth month) On the 10th of Tevet: (the tenth month) will be
on ___. May the Holy Blessed One turn it into joy and gladness; as it
is written, "So says Hashem of hosts: The fast of the fourth month,
and the fast of the fifth, and the fast of the seventh, and the fast of
the tenth, will be to the house of Yehudah joy and gladness, and
cheerful seasons; so love truth and peace." (Zech. 8:19)

Continue with Ashrei.

יְהִי־חַסְדְּךָ יְהוָה עָלֵינוּ כַּאֲשֶׁר יִחַלְנוּ לָךְ:

Yehi Chasdecha Adonai Aleinu Ka'asher Yichalnu Lach.

Let Your mercy, Hashem, be upon us, according as we have waited for You. (Psalms 33:22)

Ashrei

When saying the verse "Potei'ach Et Yadecha" one should focus one's heart. If one did not focus he must return and repeat. (SA, OC 51:7) It is customary to open your hands toward Heaven as a symbol of our acceptance of the abundance Hashem bestows upon us from Heaven. (BTH, Ex. 9:29, I Kings 8:54).

אַשְׁרֵי יוֹשְׁבֵי בֵיתֶךָ עוֹד יְהַלְלוּךָ סֶּלָה: אַשְׁרֵי הָעָם שֶׁכָּכָה לּוֹ אַשְׁרֵי הָעָם שֶׁיְהוָה אֱלֹהָיו:

Ashrei Yoshevei Veitecha; Od. Yehalelucha Selah. Ashrei Ha'am Shekachah Lo; Ashrei Ha'am. She'Adonai Elohav.

Happy are those who dwell in Your House; they are ever praising You. Happy are the people that is so situated; happy are the people whose God is Hashem. (Psalms 84:5, 144:15)

Psalms 145

תְּהִלָּה לְדָוִד אֲרוֹמִמְךָ אֱלוֹהַי הַמֶּלֶךְ וַאֲבָרְכָה שִׁמְךָ לְעוֹלָם וָעֶד:
בְּכָל־יוֹם אֲבָרְכֶךָ וַאֲהַלְלָה שִׁמְךָ לְעוֹלָם וָעֶד: גָּדוֹל יְהוָה וּמְהֻלָּל
מְאֹד וְלִגְדֻלָּתוֹ אֵין חֵקֶר: דּוֹר לְדוֹר יְשַׁבַּח מַעֲשֶׂיךָ וּגְבוּרֹתֶיךָ יַגִּידוּ:
הֲדַר כְּבוֹד הוֹדֶךָ וְדִבְרֵי נִפְלְאֹתֶיךָ אָשִׂיחָה: וֶעֱזוּז נוֹרְאֹתֶיךָ יֹאמֵרוּ
וּגְדֻלָּתְךָ אֲסַפְּרֶנָּה: זֵכֶר רַב־טוּבְךָ יַבִּיעוּ וְצִדְקָתְךָ יְרַנֵּנוּ: חַנּוּן וְרַחוּם
יְהוָה אֶרֶךְ אַפַּיִם וּגְדָל־חָסֶד: טוֹב־יְהוָה לַכֹּל וְרַחֲמָיו עַל־כָּל־מַעֲשָׂיו:
יוֹדוּךָ יְהוָה כָּל־מַעֲשֶׂיךָ וַחֲסִידֶיךָ יְבָרְכוּכָה: כְּבוֹד מַלְכוּתְךָ יֹאמֵרוּ
וּגְבוּרָתְךָ יְדַבֵּרוּ: לְהוֹדִיעַ | לִבְנֵי הָאָדָם גְּבוּרֹתָיו וּכְבוֹד הֲדַר
מַלְכוּתוֹ: מַלְכוּתְךָ מַלְכוּת כָּל־עֹלָמִים וּמֶמְשַׁלְתְּךָ בְּכָל־דּוֹר וָדֹר:
סוֹמֵךְ יְהוָה לְכָל־הַנֹּפְלִים וְזוֹקֵף לְכָל־הַכְּפוּפִים: עֵינֵי־כֹל אֵלֶיךָ
יְשַׂבֵּרוּ וְאַתָּה נוֹתֵן־לָהֶם אֶת־אָכְלָם בְּעִתּוֹ: **פּוֹתֵחַ אֶת־יָדֶךָ**

וּמַשְׂבִּיעַ לְכָל־חַי רָצוֹן: צַדִּיק יְהוָה בְּכָל־דְּרָכָיו וְחָסִיד
בְּכָל־מַעֲשָׂיו: קָרוֹב יְהוָה לְכָל־קֹרְאָיו לְכֹל אֲשֶׁר יִקְרָאֻהוּ בֶאֱמֶת:
רְצוֹן־יְרֵאָיו יַעֲשֶׂה וְאֶת־שַׁוְעָתָם יִשְׁמַע וְיוֹשִׁיעֵם: שׁוֹמֵר יְהוָה
אֶת־כָּל־אֹהֲבָיו וְאֵת כָּל־הָרְשָׁעִים יַשְׁמִיד: תְּהִלַּת יְהוָה יְדַבֶּר פִּי
וִיבָרֵךְ כָּל־בָּשָׂר שֵׁם קָדְשׁוֹ לְעוֹלָם וָעֶד: וַאֲנַחְנוּ | נְבָרֵךְ יָהּ מֵעַתָּה
וְעַד־עוֹלָם הַלְלוּיָהּ:

Tehilah. Ledavid Aromimcha Elohai Hamelech; Va'avarechah
Shimcha. Le'olam Va'ed. Bechol-Yom Avarecheka; Va'ahalelah
Shimcha. Le'olam Va'ed. Gadol Adonai Umehulal Me'od;
Veligdulato. Ein Cheiker. Dor Ledor Yeshabach Ma'aseicha;
Ugevuroteicha Yagidu. Hadar Kevod Hodecha; Vedivrei
Nifle'oteicha Asichah. Ve'ezuz Nore'oteicha Yomeru; Ug'dulatecha
Asap'renah. Zecher Rav-Tuvecha Yabi'u; Vetzidkatecha Yeranenu.
Chanun Verachum Adonai Erech Apayim. Ugedol-Chased. Tov-
Adonai Lakol; Verachamav. Al-Chol-Ma'asav. Yoducha Adonai Chol-
Ma'aseicha; Vachasideicha. Yevarechuchah. Kevod Malchutecha
Yomeru; Ugevuratecha Yedaberu. Lehodia Livnei Ha'adam
Gevurotav; Uchevod. Hadar Malchuto. Malchutecha. Malchut
Chol-'Olamim; Umemshaltecha. Bechol-Dor Vador. Somech Adonai
Lechol-Hanofelim; Vezokeif. Lechol-Hakefufim. Einei-Chol Eleicha
Yesaberu; Ve'attah Noten-Lahem Et-'Ochlam Be'ito. **Potei'ach Et-
Yadecha; Umasbia Lechol-Chai Ratzon.** Tzaddik Adonai Bechol-
Derachav; Vechasid. Bechol-Ma'asav. Karov Adonai Lechol-Kore'av;
Lechol Asher Yikra'uhu Ve'emet. Retzon-Yere'av Ya'aseh; Ve'et-
Shav'atam Yishma'. Veyoshi'em. Shomer Adonai Et-Chol-'Ohavav;
Ve'et Chol-Haresha'im Yashmid. Tehillat Adonai Yedaber Pi Vivarech
Chol-Basar Shem Kodsho. Le'olam Va'ed. Va'anachnu Nevarech Yah.
Me'attah Ve'ad-'Olam. Halleluyah.

A Psalm of praise; of David. א I will extol You, my God, Oh King; And
I will bless Your name forever and ever. ב Every day I will bless You;
And I will praise Your name forever and ever. ג Great is Hashem, and
highly to be praised; And His greatness is unsearchable. ד One
generation will applaud Your works to another, And will declare
Your mighty acts. ה The glorious splendor of Your majesty, And
Your wondrous works, I will rehearse. ו And men will speak of the
might of Your tremendous acts; And I will tell of Your greatness. ז

They will utter the fame of Your great goodness, And will sing of
Your righteousness. ח Hashem is gracious, and full of compassion;
Slow to anger, and of great mercy. ט Hashem is good to all; And His
tender mercies are over all His works. י All Your works will praise
You, Hashem; And Your holy-ones will bless You. כ They will speak
of the glory of Your kingdom, And talk of Your might; ל To make
known to the sons of men His mighty acts, And the glory of the
beauty of His kingdom. מ Your kingdom is a kingdom for all ages,
And Your dominion endures throughout all generations. ס Hashem
upholds all that fall, And raises up all those that are bowed down. ע
The eyes of all wait for You, And You give them their food in due
season. פ **You open Your hand, And satisfy every living thing
with favor.** צ Hashem is righteous in all His ways, And gracious in all
His works. ק Hashem is near to all them that call upon Him, To all
that call upon Him in truth. ר He will fulfill the desire of those that
fear Him; He also will hear their cry, and will save them. ש Hashem
preserves all them that love Him; But all the wicked will He destroy.
ת My mouth will speak the praise of Hashem; And let all flesh bless
His holy name forever and ever.

Many recite before returning the Torah scroll. On a Yom Tov, the first verse following is skipped.

בָּרוּךְ יְהֹוָה אֲשֶׁר נָתַן מְנוּחָה לְעַמּוֹ יִשְׂרָאֵל כְּכֹל אֲשֶׁר דִּבֵּר
לֹא־נָפַל דָּבָר אֶחָד מִכֹּל דְּבָרוֹ הַטּוֹב אֲשֶׁר דִּבֶּר בְּיַד מֹשֶׁה עַבְדּוֹ:
יְהִי יְהֹוָה אֱלֹהֵינוּ עִמָּנוּ כַּאֲשֶׁר הָיָה עִם־אֲבֹתֵינוּ אַל־יַעַזְבֵנוּ
וְאַל־יִטְּשֵׁנוּ: לְהַטּוֹת לְבָבֵנוּ אֵלָיו לָלֶכֶת בְּכָל־דְּרָכָיו וְלִשְׁמֹר מִצְוֹתָיו
וְחֻקָּיו וּמִשְׁפָּטָיו אֲשֶׁר צִוָּה אֶת־אֲבֹתֵינוּ: וְיִהְיוּ דְבָרַי אֵלֶּה אֲשֶׁר
הִתְחַנַּנְתִּי לִפְנֵי יְהֹוָה קְרֹבִים אֶל־יְהֹוָה אֱלֹהֵינוּ יוֹמָם וָלַיְלָה לַעֲשׂוֹת |
מִשְׁפַּט עַבְדּוֹ וּמִשְׁפַּט עַמּוֹ יִשְׂרָאֵל דְּבַר־יוֹם בְּיוֹמוֹ: לְמַעַן דַּעַת
כָּל־עַמֵּי הָאָרֶץ כִּי יְהֹוָה הוּא הָאֱלֹהִים אֵין עוֹד: לֹא־יָמוּשׁ סֵפֶר
הַתּוֹרָה הַזֶּה מִפִּיךָ וְהָגִיתָ בּוֹ יוֹמָם וָלַיְלָה לְמַעַן תִּשְׁמֹר לַעֲשׂוֹת

כְּכָל־הַכָּתוּב בּוֹ כִּי־אָז תַּצְלִיחַ אֶת־דְּרָכֶךָ וְאָז תַּשְׂכִּיל: הֲלוֹא צִוִּיתִיךָ
חֲזַק וֶאֱמָץ אַל־תַּעֲרֹץ וְאַל־תֵּחָת כִּי עִמְּךָ יְהֹוָה אֱלֹהֶיךָ בְּכָל אֲשֶׁר
תֵּלֵךְ:

Baruch Adonai Asher Natan Menuchah Le'ammo Yisra'el Kechol
Asher Diber Lo Nafal Davar Echad Mikol Devaro Hatov Asher Diber
Beyad Mosheh Avdo. Yehi Adonai Eloheinu Imanu Ka'asher Hayah
Im Avoteinu Al Ya'azvenu Ve'al Yiteshenu. Lehatot Levavenu Elav
Lalechet Bechol Derachav Velishmor Mitzvotav Vechukkav
Umishpatav Asher Tzivah Et Avoteinu. Veyihyu Devarai Eleh Asher
Hitchananti Lifnei Adonai Kerovim El Adonai Eloheinu Yomam
Valailah La'asot Mishpat Avdo Umishpat Ammo Yisra'el Devar Yom
Beyomo. Lema'an Da'at Kol Ammei Ha'aretz Ki Adonai Hu
Ha'elohim Ein Od. Lo Yamush Sefer Hatorah Hazeh Mipicha
Vehagita Bo Yomam Valaylah Lema'an Tishmor La'asot Kechol
Hakatuv Bo Ki Az Tatzliach Et Derachecha Ve'az Taskil. Halo
Tziviticha Chazak Ve'ematz Al Ta'arotz Ve'al Techat Ki Imecha
Adonai Eloheicha Bechol Asher Telech.

Blessed is Hashem, that has given rest to His people Yisrael,
according to all that He promised; one word has not failed of all His
good promise, which He promised by the hand of Moshe His
servant. May Hashem our God be with us, as He was with our
fathers; let Him not leave us, or forsake us; that He may incline our
hearts to Him, to walk in all His ways, and to keep His
commandments, and His statutes, and His ordinances, which He
commanded our fathers. And let these my words, which I have made
supplication before Hashem, be near to Hashem our God day and
night, that He maintain the cause of His servant, and the cause of
His people Yisrael, as every day will require; that all the peoples of
the earth may know that Hashem, He is God; there is none else. (1
Kings 8:56-60) This book of the Torah will not depart out of your
mouth, but you will meditate in it day and night, that you may
observe to do according to all that is written in it; for then you will
make your ways prosperous, and then you will have good success.
Have I not commanded you? Be strong and of good courage; do not

be afraid, neither be dismayed: for Hashem your God is with you wherever you go. (Joshua 1:8-9)

יִמְלֹךְ יְהֹוָה | לְעוֹלָם אֱלֹהַיִךְ צִיּוֹן לְדֹר וָדֹר הַלְלוּיָהּ: ב׳ פעמים

Yimloch Adonai Le'olam Elohayich Tziyon Ledor Vador Halleluyah.

"Hashem will reign forever; your God, Tziyon to all generations. Halleluyah. " (Psalms 147:10) repeat 2x

Return the Torah scroll to its place and say the Psalm:

Psalms 29

מִזְמוֹר לְדָוִד הָבוּ לַיהוָה בְּנֵי אֵלִים הָבוּ לַיהֹוָה כָּבוֹד וָעֹז: הָבוּ
לַיהוָה כְּבוֹד שְׁמוֹ הִשְׁתַּחֲווּ לַיהֹוָה בְּהַדְרַת־קֹדֶשׁ: קוֹל יְהֹוָה
עַל־הַמָּיִם אֵל־הַכָּבוֹד הִרְעִים יְהֹוָה עַל־מַיִם רַבִּים: קוֹל־יְהֹוָה בַּכֹּחַ
קוֹל יְהֹוָה בֶּהָדָר: קוֹל יְהֹוָה שֹׁבֵר אֲרָזִים וַיְשַׁבֵּר יְהֹוָה אֶת־אַרְזֵי
הַלְּבָנוֹן: וַיַּרְקִידֵם כְּמוֹ־עֵגֶל לְבָנוֹן וְשִׂרְיֹן כְּמוֹ בֶן־רְאֵמִים: קוֹל־יְהֹוָה
חֹצֵב לַהֲבוֹת אֵשׁ: קוֹל יְהוֹוָהוּ יָחִיל מִדְבָּר יָחִיל יְהֹוָה מִדְבַּר
קָדֵשׁ: קוֹל יְהֹוָה | יְחוֹלֵל אַיָּלוֹת וַיֶּחֱשֹׂף יְעָרוֹת וּבְהֵיכָלוֹ כֻּלּוֹ אֹמֵר
כָּבוֹד: יְהֹוָה לַמַּבּוּל יָשָׁב וַיֵּשֶׁב יְהֹוָה מֶלֶךְ לְעוֹלָם: יְהֹוָה עֹז לְעַמּוֹ
יִתֵּן יְהֹוָה | יְבָרֵךְ אֶת־עַמּוֹ בַשָּׁלוֹם:

Mizmor. LeDavid Havu L'Adonai Benei Elim; Havu L'Adonai Kavod Va'oz. Havu L'Adonai Kevod Shemo; Hishtachavu L'Adonai Behadrat-Kodesh. Kol Adonai Al-Hamayim El-Hakavod Hir'im; Adonai Al-Mayim Rabim. Kol-Adonai Bakoach; Kol Adonai Behadar. Kol Adonai Shoveir Arazim; Vayshaber Adonai Et-'Arzei Hallevanon. Vayarkidem Kemo-'Egel; Levanon Vesiryon. Kemo Ven-Re'emim. Kol-Adonai Chotzev. Lahavot Esh. Kol Adonai Yachil Midbar; Yachil Adonai Midbar Kadesh. Kol Adonai Yecholel Ayalot Vayechesof Ye'arot Uveheichalo; Kulo. Omer Kavod. Adonai Lammabbul Yashav; Vayeshev Adonai Melech Le'olam. Adonai Oz Le'ammo Yiten; Adonai Yevarech Et-'Ammo Vashalom.

A Psalm of David. Ascribe to Hashem, sons of might, Ascribe to Hashem glory and strength. Ascribe to Hashem the glory due to His

name; Worship Hashem in the beauty of holiness. The voice of
Hashem is upon the waters; The God of glory thunders, Even
Hashem upon many waters. The voice of Hashem is powerful; The
voice of Hashem is full of majesty. The voice of Hashem breaks the
cedars; yes, Hashem breaks in pieces the cedars of Levanon. He
makes them also to skip like a calf; Levanon and Sirion like a young
wild-ox. The voice of Hashem hews out flames of fire. The voice of
Hashem shakes the wilderness; Hashem shakes the wilderness of
Kadesh. The voice of Hashem makes the hinds to calve, And strips
the forests bare; And in His Temple all say: 'Glory.' Hashem sat
enthroned at the flood; Hashem sits as King forever. Hashem will
give strength to His people; Hashem will bless His people with
peace.

When the Torah scroll is brought into the ark, the chazan says:

שׁוּבָה לִמְעוֹנֶךָ וּשְׁכוֹן בְּבֵית מַאֲוַיֶּךָ. כִּי כָל־פֶּה וְכָל־לָשׁוֹן יִתְּנוּ הוֹד
וְהָדָר לְמַלְכוּתֶךָ: וּבְנֻחֹה יֹאמַר שׁוּבָה יְהֹוָה רִבְבוֹת אַלְפֵי יִשְׂרָאֵל:
הֲשִׁיבֵנוּ יְהֹוָה | אֵלֶיךָ וְנָשׁוּב (וְנָשׁוּבָה) חַדֵּשׁ יָמֵינוּ כְּקֶדֶם:

Shuvah Lim'onach Ushechon Beveit Ma'avayach. Ki Chol Peh
Vechol Lashon Yitenu Hod Vehadar Lemalchutach: Uvenuchoh
Yomar Shuvah Adonai Rivot Alfei Yisra'el. Hashiveinu Adonai
Eleicha Venashuvah Chadesh Yameinu Kekedem.

Return to Your dwelling, and reside in Your Temple; for every mouth
and tongue will ascribe honor and glory to Your kingdom. "And
when the Ark rested, he said: 'Return, Hashem, to the ten thousands
of the families of Yisrael. Turn us to You, Hashem, and we will
return; Renew our days as of old. (Numbers 10:36, Lam. 5:21)

Say Hatzi-Kaddish:

Kaddish is only recited in a minyan (ten men). אמן denotes when the congregation responds "Amen" together out loud. According to the Shulchan Arukh, the congregation says "Yehei Shemeh Rabba" to "Yitbarach" out loud together without interruption, and also that one should respond "Amen" after "Yitbarach." (SA, OC 55,56) This is not the common custom today. Though many are accustomed to answering according to their own custom, it is advised to respond in the custom of the one reciting to avoid not fragmenting into smaller groups. ("Lo Titgodedu" - BT, Yevamot 13b / SA, OC 493, Rema / MT, Avodah Zara 12:15)

יִתְגַּדַּל וְיִתְקַדַּשׁ שְׁמֵהּ רַבָּא. אמן בְּעָלְמָא דִּי בְרָא. כִרְעוּתֵהּ. וְיַמְלִיךְ מַלְכוּתֵהּ.
וְיַצְמַח פֻּרְקָנֵהּ. וִיקָרֵב מְשִׁיחֵהּ. אמן בְּחַיֵּיכוֹן וּבְיוֹמֵיכוֹן וּבְחַיֵּי דְכָל בֵּית
יִשְׂרָאֵל. בַּעֲגָלָא וּבִזְמַן קָרִיב. וְאִמְרוּ אָמֵן. אמן יְהֵא שְׁמֵהּ רַבָּא מְבָרַךְ לְעָלַם
וּלְעָלְמֵי עָלְמַיָּא יִתְבָּרַךְ. וְיִשְׁתַּבַּח. וְיִתְפָּאַר. וְיִתְרוֹמַם. וְיִתְנַשֵּׂא. וְיִתְהַדָּר.
וְיִתְעַלֶּה. וְיִתְהַלָּל שְׁמֵהּ דְּקֻדְשָׁא. בְּרִיךְ הוּא. אמן לְעֵלָּא מִן כָּל בִּרְכָתָא
שִׁירָתָא. תֻּשְׁבְּחָתָא וְנֶחֱמָתָא. דַּאֲמִירָן בְּעָלְמָא. וְאִמְרוּ אָמֵן. אמן

Yitgadal Veyitkadash Shemeh Rabba. ^{Amen} Be'alema Di Vera. Kir'uteh. Veyamlich Malchuteh. Veyatzmach Purkaneh. Vikarev Meshicheh. ^{Amen} Bechayeichon Uveyomeichon Uvechayei Dechal-Beit Yisra'el. Ba'agala Uvizman Kariv. Ve'imru Amen. ^{Amen} Yehei Shemeh Rabba Mevarach Le'alam Ule'alemei Alemaya Yitbarach. Veyishtabach. Veyitpa'ar. Veyitromam. Veyitnasse. Veyit'hadar. Veyit'aleh. Veyit'hallal Shemeh Dekudsha. Berich Hu. ^{Amen} Le'ella Min Kol Birchata Shirata. Tushbechata Venechemata. Da'amiran Be'alema. Ve'imru Amen. ^{Amen}

Glorified and sanctified be God's great name ^{Amen} throughout the world which He has created according to His will. May He establish His kingdom, hastening His salvation and the coming of His Messiah, ^{Amen}, in your lifetime and during your days, and within the life of the entire House of Yisrael, speedily and soon; and say, Amen. ^{Amen} May His great name be blessed forever and to all eternity. Blessed and praised, glorified and exalted, extolled and honored, adored and lauded is the name of the Holy One, blessed is He, ^{Amen} Beyond all the blessings and hymns, praises and consolations that are ever spoken in the world; and say, Amen. ^{Amen}

MUSAF FOR SHABBAT-ROSH CHODESH IS ON PAGE 652.

MUSAF / ADDITIONAL SERVICE

Take three steps forward and say:

Adonai Sefatai Tiftach; Ufi. Yagid

Tehilatecha.

אֲדֹנָי שְׂפָתַי תִּפְתָּח וּפִי יַגִּיד

תְּהִלָּתֶךָ:

Hashem, open my lips, that my mouth may declare Your praise.

Avot / Fathers

Bow at "Baruch Attah" / "Blessed are You". Raise up at Adonai / Hashem.

Baruch Attah Adonai Eloheinu

בָּרוּךְ אַתָּה יְהֹוָה אֱלֹהֵינוּ

Velohei Avoteinu. Elohei

וֵאלֹהֵי אֲבוֹתֵינוּ. אֱלֹהֵי

Avraham. Elohei Yitzchak.

אַבְרָהָם. אֱלֹהֵי יִצְחָק.

Velohei Ya'akov. Ha'el Hagadol

וֵאלֹהֵי יַעֲקֹב. הָאֵל הַגָּדוֹל

Hagibor Vehanorah. El Elyon.

הַגִּבּוֹר וְהַנּוֹרָא. אֵל עֶלְיוֹן.

Gomel Chasadim Tovim. Koneh

גּוֹמֵל חֲסָדִים טוֹבִים. קוֹנֵה

Hakol. Vezocher Chasdei Avot.

הַכֹּל. וְזוֹכֵר חַסְדֵּי אָבוֹת.

Umevi Go'el Livnei Veneihem

וּמֵבִיא גוֹאֵל לִבְנֵי בְנֵיהֶם

Lema'an Shemo Be'ahavah.

לְמַעַן שְׁמוֹ בְּאַהֲבָה:

Blessed are You, Hashem our God and God of our fathers, God of Avraham, God of Yitzchak and God of Yaakov; the great, mighty and revered God, most high God, Who bestows lovingkindness. Master of all things; Who remembers the kindnesses of our fathers, and Who will bring a redeemer to their children's children for the sake of His name in love.

During the 10 days of repentance (Rosh Hashanah to Yom Kippur) add:

Zochrenu Lechayim. Melech Chafetz

זָכְרֵנוּ לְחַיִּים. מֶלֶךְ חָפֵץ

Bachayim. Katevenu Besefer Chayim.

בַּחַיִּים. כָּתְבֵנוּ בְּסֵפֶר חַיִּים.

Lema'anach Elohim Chayim.

לְמַעַנְךָ אֱלֹהִים חַיִּים.

Remember us to life, King Who delights in life; inscribe us in the book of life for Your sake, Oh living God.

Bow at "Baruch Attah" / Blessed are You. Raise up at Adonai / Hashem.

Melech Ozeir Umoshia

מֶלֶךְ עוֹזֵר וּמוֹשִׁיעַ

Umagen. Baruch Attah Adonai

וּמָגֵן: בָּרוּךְ אַתָּה יְהֹוָה

Magen Avraham.

מָגֵן אַבְרָהָם:

King, Supporter, and Savior and Shield. Blessed are You, Hashem, Shield of Avraham.

Gevurot / Powers

We [in Yisrael] begin to say "Mashiv Haruach" in the second blessing of the Amidah from the Musaf [Additional] Service of the last day of Sukkot, and conclude at the Musaf [Additional] Service of the first day of Pesach. On the first day of Pesach the congregation still says it in the Musaf Service, but the Reader stops saying it then. In lands outside of Yisrael, [in the Birkhat HaShanim / Blessing for the Years,] we begin to pray for rain in the Arvit (Evening) Service of the sixtieth day after the New Moon of Tishrei, and in Yisrael we begin to say it in the evening of the seventh day of Cheshvan, and it is said until the Afternoon Service on the day preceding the first day of Passover. If one prayed for rain in the summer, or if one omitted to pray for it in the winter, he must repeat the Amidah again. If one said "Morid Hageshem" in the summer time, he must repeat again from the beginning of the blessing. If he already concluded the blessing, he must read the entire Amidah again. Likewise in the winter, if he omitted it, he must begin all over again. (SA, OC 117)

Attah Gibor Le'olam Adonai.

אַתָּה גִבּוֹר לְעוֹלָם אֲדֹנָי.

Mechayeh Meitim Attah. Rav

מְחַיֶּה מֵתִים אַתָּה. רַב

Lehoshia.

לְהוֹשִׁיעַ.

You, Hashem, are mighty forever; You revive the dead; You are powerful to save.

B'ketz: Morid Hatal.

בקיץ: מוֹרִיד הַטָּל.

B'choref: Mashiv Haruach Umorid Hageshem.

בחורף: מַשִּׁיב הָרוּחַ וּמוֹרִיד הַגָּשֶׁם.

In summer: You cause the dew to fall.

In winter: You cause the wind to blow and the rain to fall.

Mechalkel Chayim Bechesed.

מְכַלְכֵּל חַיִּים בְּחֶסֶד.

Mechayeh Meitim Berachamim

מְחַיֶּה מֵתִים בְּרַחֲמִים

Rabim. Somech Nofelim. Verofei	רַבִּים. סוֹמֵךְ נוֹפְלִים. וְרוֹפֵא
Cholim. Umatir Asurim.	חוֹלִים. וּמַתִּיר אֲסוּרִים.
Umekayem Emunato Lishenei	וּמְקַיֵּם אֱמוּנָתוֹ לִישֵׁנֵי
Afar. Mi Chamocha Ba'al	עָפָר. מִי כָמוֹךָ בַּעַל
Gevurot. Umi Domeh Lach.	גְּבוּרוֹת. וּמִי דוֹמֶה לָּךְ.
Melech Memit Umechayeh	מֶלֶךְ מֵמִית וּמְחַיֶּה
Umatzmiach Yeshu'ah.	וּמַצְמִיחַ יְשׁוּעָה.

You sustain the living with kindness, and revive the dead with great mercy; You support all who fall, and heal the sick; You set the captives free, and keep faith with those who sleep in the dust. Who is like You, Master of power? Who resembles You, Oh King? You bring death and restore life, and cause salvation to flourish.

During the 10 days of repentance (Rosh Hashanah to Yom Kippur) add:

Mi Chamocha Av Harachaman. Zocher	מִי כָמוֹךָ אָב הָרַחֲמָן. זוֹכֵר
Yetzurav Berachamim Lechayim.	יְצוּרָיו בְּרַחֲמִים לְחַיִּים.

Who is like You, merciful Father? In mercy You remember Your creatures to life.

Vene'eman Attah Lehachayot	וְנֶאֱמָן אַתָּה לְהַחֲיוֹת
Meitim. Baruch Attah Adonai	מֵתִים: בָּרוּךְ אַתָּה יְהֹוָה
Mechayeh Hameitim.	מְחַיֵּה הַמֵּתִים:

And You are faithful to revive the dead. Blessed are You, Hashem, Who revives the dead.

Kedusha

Kedusha is said only in a minyan (10 men). If one is not available, skip to "Holiness". It is proper to position one's feet together at the time one is reciting Kedushah with the prayer-leader.

Keter Yitenu Lecha. Adonai	כֶּתֶר יִתְּנוּ לְךָ. יְהֹוָה
Eloheinu. Mal'achim Hamonei	אֱלֹהֵינוּ. מַלְאָכִים הֲמוֹנֵי

Ma'lah. Im Ammecha Yisra'el	מַעְלָה. עִם עַמְּךָ יִשְׂרָאֵל
Kevutzei Mattah. Yachad Kulam	קְבוּצֵי מַטָּה. יַחַד כֻּלָּם
Kedushah Lecha Yeshalleshu.	קְדֻשָּׁה לְךָ יְשַׁלֵּשׁוּ.
Kadavar Ha'amur Al Yad	כַּדָּבָר הָאָמוּר עַל יַד
Nevi'ach Vekara Zeh El Zeh	נְבִיאָךְ וְקָרָא זֶה אֶל־זֶה
Ve'amar **Kadosh Kadosh Kadosh**	וְאָמַר **קָדוֹשׁ	קָדוֹשׁ קָדוֹשׁ**
Adonai Tzeva'ot Melo Chol	**יְהֹוָה צְבָאוֹת מְלֹא כָל־**
Ha'aretz Kevodo. Kevodo Male	**הָאָרֶץ כְּבוֹדוֹ:** כְּבוֹדוֹ מָלֵא
Olam. Umesharetav Sho'alim	עוֹלָם. וּמְשָׁרְתָיו שׁוֹאֲלִים
Ayeh Mekom Kevodo	אַיֵּה מְקוֹם כְּבוֹדוֹ
Leha'aritzo: Le'ummatam	לְהַעֲרִיצוֹ: לְעֻמָּתָם
Meshabechim Ve'omerim **Baruch**	מְשַׁבְּחִים וְאוֹמְרִים **בָּרוּךְ**
Kevod Adonai Mimekomo.	**כְּבוֹד־יְהֹוָה מִמְּקוֹמוֹ:**
Mimekomo Hu Yifen	מִמְּקוֹמוֹ הוּא יִפֶן
Berachamav Le'ammo	בְּרַחֲמָיו לְעַמּוֹ
Hameyachadim Shemo Erev	הַמְיַחֲדִים שְׁמוֹ עֶרֶב
Vavoker. Bechol Yom Tamid	וָבֹקֶר. בְּכָל יוֹם תָּמִיד
Omerim Pa'amayim Be'ahavah	אוֹמְרִים פַּעֲמַיִם בְּאַהֲבָה
Shema Yisra'el Adonai Eloheinu	**שְׁמַע יִשְׂרָאֵל יְהֹוָה אֱלֹהֵינוּ**
Adonai Echad. Hu Eloheinu. Hu	**יְהֹוָה	אֶחָד:** הוּא אֱלֹהֵינוּ. הוּא
Avinu. Hu Malkeinu. Hu	אָבִינוּ. הוּא מַלְכֵּנוּ. הוּא
Moshi'enu. Hu Yoshi'enu	מוֹשִׁיעֵנוּ. הוּא יוֹשִׁיעֵנוּ
Veyig'alenu Shenit.	וְיִגְאָלֵנוּ שֵׁנִית.
Veyashmi'enu Berachamav	וְיַשְׁמִיעֵנוּ בְּרַחֲמָיו
Le'einei Kol Chai Lemor. Hen	לְעֵינֵי כָּל חַי לֵאמֹר. הֵן
Ga'alti Etchem Acharit Kereshit	גָּאַלְתִּי אֶתְכֶם אַחֲרִית כְּרֵאשִׁית

Lihyot Lachem Lelohim. **Ani**   לִהְיוֹת לָכֶם לֵאלֹהִים. אֲנִי

Adonai Eloheichem: Uvedivrei   יְהֹוָה אֱלֹהֵיכֶם: וּבְדִבְרֵי

Kodshecha Katuv Lemor **Yimloch**   קָדְשְׁךָ כָּתוּב לֵאמֹר יִמְלֹךְ

Adonai Le'olam Elohayich   יְהֹוָה | לְעוֹלָם אֱלֹהַיִךְ

Tziyon Ledor Vador Halleluyah: צִיּוֹן לְדֹר וָדֹר הַלְלוּיָהּ:

To You, Hashem our God, will the heavenly host of angels above, with Your people Yisrael assembled beneath, give a crown; all with one accord will thrice proclaim the holy praise to You, according to the word spoken by Your prophet, "And one cried to another, and said, **"Holy, holy, holy is Hashem of hosts, the whole earth is full of His glory."** His glory fills the world, and His ministering angels enquire. Where is the place of His glory that they may worship him with awe? While those angels turning towards each other continue praising and saying: **"Blessed is the glory of Hashem from His place."** From His place may He turn to His people with mercy, who evening and morning daily proclaim the unity of His name, by repeating twice every day with love, **"Hear, O Yisrael. Hashem is our God, Hashem is One."** He is our God, He is our Father, He is our King, He is our Savior; He will save and redeem us a second time, and through His infinite mercy will let us hear (when He will proclaim) in the presence of all living, Behold, I have now redeemed you in the latter times, as at the beginning, to be your God. **"I am Hashem your God."** And in Your holy Word it is written, saying, **"Hashem will reign forever your God, Tziyon, to all generations. Halleluyah."**

Kedushat HaShem / Holiness of the Name

Attah Kadosh Veshimcha   אַתָּה קָדוֹשׁ וְשִׁמְךָ

Kadosh. Ukedoshim Bechol-Yom   קָדוֹשׁ. וּקְדוֹשִׁים בְּכָל־יוֹם

Yehalelucha Selah. Baruch Attah   יְהַלְלוּךָ סֶּלָה: בָּרוּךְ אַתָּה

Adonai Ha' El Hakadosh.   יְהֹוָה הָאֵל הַקָּדוֹשׁ:

You are holy and Your name is holy, and the holy-ones will praise You every day, selah. Blessed are You, Hashem, The Holy God.

During the 10 days of repentance (Rosh Hashanah to Yom Kippur) say:

Hamelech Hakadosh.   הַמֶּלֶךְ הַקָּדוֹשׁ:

The Holy King.

If one is unsure or forgot if they said, repeat the Amidah. If it was immediately said after, it is fulfilled.

Kedushat HaYom / Holiness of the Day

Tikanta Shabbat. Ratzita	תִּכַּנְתָּ שַׁבָּת. רָצִיתָ
Karebnoteiha. Tzivita	קָרְבְּנוֹתֶיהָ. צִוִּיתָ
Feirusheiha Im Siddurei	פֵּירוּשֶׁיהָ עִם סִדּוּרֵי
Nesacheiha. Me'anegeiha	נְסָכֶיהָ. מְעַנְּגֶיהָ
Le'olam Kavod Yinchalu.	לְעוֹלָם כָּבוֹד יִנְחָלוּ.
To'ameiha Chayim Zachu.	טוֹעֲמֶיהָ חַיִּים זָכוּ.
Vegam Ha'ohavim Devareiha	וְגַם הָאוֹהֲבִים דְּבָרֶיהָ
Gedullah Vacharu. Az Missinai	גְּדֻלָּה בָחָרוּ. אָז מִסִּינַי
Nitztavu Tzivuyei Fe'aleiha	נִצְטַוּוּ צִוּוּיֵי פְּעָלֶיהָ
Kara'ui.	כָּרָאוּי:

You have instituted Shabbat and favored its offerings. You prescribed its duties with the orders of its libations. Those who delight in it forever will inherit glory; those who enjoy its goodness will merit eternal life; those who love its matters have chosen greatness. Then, from Sinai, they were commanded how to appropriately observe it.

Yehi Ratzon Milfaneicha Adonai	יְהִי רָצוֹן מִלְּפָנֶיךָ יְהֹוָה
Eloheinu Velohei Avoteinu.	אֱלֹהֵינוּ וֵאלֹהֵי אֲבוֹתֵינוּ.
Sheta'alenu Vesimchah	שֶׁתַּעֲלֵנוּ בְשִׂמְחָה
Le'artzenu Vetita'enu Bigvulenu.	לְאַרְצֵנוּ וְתִטָּעֵנוּ בִּגְבוּלֵנוּ.
Vesham Na'aseh Lefaneicha Et	וְשָׁם נַעֲשֶׂה לְפָנֶיךָ אֶת
Karbenot Chovoteinu Temidim	קָרְבְּנוֹת חוֹבוֹתֵינוּ תְּמִידִים
Kesidram Umusafim	כְּסִדְרָם וּמוּסָפִים
Kehilchatam. Et Musaf Yom	כְּהִלְכָתָם. אֶת מוּסַף יוֹם
Hashabbat Hazeh Na'aseh	הַשַּׁבָּת הַזֶּה נַעֲשֶׂה
Venakriv Lefaneicha Be'ahavah.	וְנַקְרִיב לְפָנֶיךָ בְּאַהֲבָה.
Kemitzvat Retzonach. Kemo	כְּמִצְוַת רְצוֹנָךְ. כְּמוֹ
Shekatavta Aleinu Betoratach. Al	שֶׁכָּתַבְתָּ עָלֵינוּ בְּתוֹרָתָךְ. עַל
Yedei Mosheh Avdach. Ka'amur:	יְדֵי מֹשֶׁה עַבְדָּךְ. כָּאָמוּר:

May it be Your will, Hashem our God and God of our fathers, to bring us up with joy to our land, and to plant us in our own territory; and there we will perform in Your presence, the eternal offerings of our duty; the continual offerings according to their order and the Musaf (additional) offerings according to their laws. The Musaf offering of this Shabbat-day we will offer before You with love according to the commands of Your will, as You have written concerning us in Your Torah, by the hand of Moshe, Your servant; as it is said:

וּבְיוֹם הַשַּׁבָּת שְׁנֵי־כְבָשִׂים בְּנֵי־שָׁנָה תְּמִימִם וּשְׁנֵי עֶשְׂרֹנִים סֹלֶת מִנְחָה בְּלוּלָה בַשֶּׁמֶן וְנִסְכּוֹ: עֹלַת שַׁבַּת בְּשַׁבַּתּוֹ עַל־עֹלַת הַתָּמִיד וְנִסְכָּהּ:

Uveyom Hashabbat. Shenei-Chevasim Benei-Shanah Temimim; Ushenei Esronim. Solet Minchah Belulah Vashemen Venisko. Olat Shabbat BeShabbato; Al-'Olat HaTamid Veniskah.

And on the Shabbat day two male lambs of the first year without blemish, and two tenth parts of an ephah of fine flour for a meal-offering, mingled with oil, and the drink-offering accordingly. This is the burnt-offering of every Shabbat, in addition to the continual burnt-offering, and the drink-offering. (Numbers 28:9-10)

Yismechu Vemalchutach	יִשְׂמְחוּ בְמַלְכוּתְךָ
Shomerei Shabbat Vekore'ei	שׁוֹמְרֵי שַׁבָּת וְקוֹרְאֵי
Oneg. Am Mekaddeshei Shevi'i.	עֹנֶג. עַם מְקַדְּשֵׁי שְׁבִיעִי.
Kullam Yisbe'u Veyit'annegu	כֻּלָּם יִשְׂבְּעוּ וְיִתְעַנְּגוּ
Mittuvach. Vehashevi'i Ratzita	מִטּוּבָךְ. וְהַשְּׁבִיעִי רָצִיתָ
Bo Vekiddashto. Chemdat	בּוֹ וְקִדַּשְׁתּוֹ. חֶמְדַּת
Yamim Oto Karata. Zecher	יָמִים אוֹתוֹ קָרָאתָ. זֵכֶר
Lema'aseh Vereshit:	לְמַעֲשֵׂה בְרֵאשִׁית:

Those who keep the Shabbat and call it a delight will rejoice in Your Kingship. All of Your people who sanctify the seventh day will find satisfaction and be delighted in Your goodness. For it is a day which You wanted and sanctified it, calling it the most desirable of all days, a memory of the work of Creation.

Eloheinu Velohei Avoteinu.	אֱלֹהֵינוּ וֵאלֹהֵי אֲבוֹתֵינוּ.
Retzeh Na Bimnuchatenu.	רְצֵה נָא בִמְנוּחָתֵנוּ.
Kadeshenu Bemitzvoteicha. Sim	קַדְּשֵׁנוּ בְּמִצְוֹתֶיךָ. שִׂים
Chelkenu Betoratach. Sabe'einu	חֶלְקֵנוּ בְּתוֹרָתֶךָ. שַׂבְּעֵנוּ
Mituvach. Same'ach Nafshenu	מִטּוּבָךְ. שַׂמֵּחַ נַפְשֵׁנוּ
Bishu'atach. Vetaher Libenu	בִּישׁוּעָתֶךָ. וְטַהֵר לִבֵּנוּ
Le'avdecha Ve'emet.	לְעָבְדְּךָ בֶּאֱמֶת.

Vehanchilenu Adonai Eloheinu	וְהַנְחִילֵנוּ יְהֹוָה אֱלֹהֵינוּ
Be'ahavah Uveratzon Shabbat	בְּאַהֲבָה וּבְרָצוֹן שַׁבַּת
Kodshecha. Veyanuchu Vo Kol-	קָדְשֶׁךָ. וְיָנוּחוּ בוֹ כָּל
Yisra'el Mekadeshei Shemecha.	יִשְׂרָאֵל מְקַדְּשֵׁי שְׁמֶךָ.
Baruch Attah Adonai Mekadesh	בָּרוּךְ אַתָּה יְהֹוָה מְקַדֵּשׁ
Hashabbat.	הַשַּׁבָּת:

Our God, God of our fathers, be pleased with our rest. Sanctify us through Your commandments and grant our portion in Your Torah. Content us with Your goodness. Rejoice our soul with Your salvation. And make our heart pure to serve You in truth. Cause us to inherit, Hashem our God, Your holy Shabbat with love and favor; and grant rest on it to all Yisrael who sanctify Your name. Blessed are You, Hashem Who sanctifies the Shabbat.

Avodah / Temple Service

Retzeh Adonai Eloheinu	רְצֵה יְהֹוָה אֱלֹהֵינוּ
Be'ammecha Yisra'el Velitfilatam	בְּעַמְּךָ יִשְׂרָאֵל וְלִתְפִלָּתָם
She'eh. Vehasheiv Ha'avodah	שְׁעֵה. וְהָשֵׁב הָעֲבוֹדָה
Lidvir Beitecha. Ve'ishei Yisra'el	לִדְבִיר בֵּיתֶךָ. וְאִשֵּׁי יִשְׂרָאֵל
Utefilatam. Meheirah Be'ahavah	וּתְפִלָּתָם. מְהֵרָה בְּאַהֲבָה
Tekabel Beratzon. Utehi Leratzon	תְקַבֵּל בְּרָצוֹן. וּתְהִי לְרָצוֹן
Tamid Avodat Yisra'el Ammecha.	תָּמִיד עֲבוֹדַת יִשְׂרָאֵל עַמֶּךָ.
Ve'attah Berachameicha	וְאַתָּה בְּרַחֲמֶיךָ
Harabim. Tachpotz Banu	הָרַבִּים. תַּחְפֹּץ בָּנוּ
Vetirtzenu. Vetechezeinah	וְתִרְצֵנוּ. וְתֶחֱזֶינָה

Eineinu Beshuvecha Letziyon	עֵינֵינוּ בְּשׁוּבְךָ לְצִיּוֹן
Berachamim. Baruch Attah	בְּרַחֲמִים. בָּרוּךְ אַתָּה
Adonai Hamachazir Shechinato	יְהֹוָה הַמַּחֲזִיר שְׁכִינָתוֹ
Letziyon:	לְצִיּוֹן:

Be favorable, Hashem our God, on Your people Yisrael and regard their prayers. And the service to the Sanctuary of Your House, and the fire offerings of Yisrael, and their prayers accept soon with love. And You, in Your abundant mercy, delight in us, and be favorable to us, so that our eyes may witness Your return to Tziyon with mercy. Blessed are You, Hashem Who returns His Presence to Tziyon.

Hoda'ah (Modim) / Thanksgiving

On Saying "Modim" / "We are Thankful" One Bows and begins to rise after "Adonai" / "Hashem".

Modim Anachnu Lach. She'attah	מוֹדִים אֲנַחְנוּ לָךְ. שָׁאַתָּה
Hu Adonai Eloheinu Velohei	הוּא יְהֹוָה אֱלֹהֵינוּ וֵאלֹהֵי
Avoteinu Le'olam Va'ed. Tzurenu	אֲבוֹתֵינוּ לְעוֹלָם וָעֶד. צוּרֵנוּ
Tzur Chayeinu Umagen Yish'enu	צוּר חַיֵּינוּ וּמָגֵן יִשְׁעֵנוּ
Attah Hu. Ledor Vador Nodeh	אַתָּה הוּא. לְדוֹר וָדוֹר נוֹדֶה
Lecha Unsapeir Tehilatecha. Al	לְךָ וּנְסַפֵּר תְּהִלָּתֶךָ. עַל
Chayeinu Hamesurim	חַיֵּינוּ הַמְּסוּרִים
Beyadecha. Ve'al Nishmoteinu	בְּיָדֶךָ. וְעַל נִשְׁמוֹתֵינוּ
Hapekudot Lach. Ve'al Niseicha	הַפְּקוּדוֹת לָךְ. וְעַל נִסֶּיךָ
Shebechol-Yom Imanu. Ve'al	שֶׁבְּכָל־יוֹם עִמָּנוּ. וְעַל
Nifle'oteicha Vetovoteicha	נִפְלְאוֹתֶיךָ וְטוֹבוֹתֶיךָ
Shebechol-'Et. Erev Vavoker	שֶׁבְּכָל־עֵת. עֶרֶב וָבֹקֶר
Vetzaharayim. Hatov. Ki Lo	וְצָהֳרָיִם. הַטּוֹב. כִּי לֹא

Chalu Rachameicha.

כָּלוּ רַחֲמֶיךָ.

Hamerachem. Ki Lo Tamu

הַמְּרַחֵם. כִּי לֹא תַמּוּ

Chasadeicha. Ki Me'olam Kivinu

חֲסָדֶיךָ. כִּי מֵעוֹלָם קִוִּינוּ

Lach.

לָךְ:

We are thankful to You, Hashem our God and the God of our fathers, forever. You are our strength and Rock of our life and the Shield of our salvation. In every generation we will thank You and recount Your praise for our lives which are given into Your hand, for our souls which are placed in Your care, and for Your miracles which are daily with us, and for Your wonders and goodness—evening, morning and noon. The Beneficent One, for Your mercies never end, Merciful One, for Your kindness has never ceased, for we have always placed our hope in You.

Modim Derabbanan

During the repetition, this is to be recited softly while the Chazan reads the Modim. Still bow at Modim as before.

מוֹדִים אֲנַחְנוּ לָךְ. שָׁאַתָּה הוּא יְהֹוָה אֱלֹהֵינוּ וֵאלֹהֵי אֲבוֹתֵינוּ. אֱלֹהֵי כָל בָּשָׂר. יוֹצְרֵנוּ יוֹצֵר בְּרֵאשִׁית. בְּרָכוֹת וְהוֹדָאוֹת לְשִׁמְךָ הַגָּדוֹל וְהַקָּדוֹשׁ. עַל שֶׁהֶחֱיִיתָנוּ וְקִיַּמְתָּנוּ. כֵּן תְּחַיֵּנוּ וּתְחָנֵּנוּ וְתֶאֱסוֹף גָּלְיוֹתֵינוּ לְחַצְרוֹת קָדְשֶׁךָ. לִשְׁמֹר חֻקֶּיךָ וְלַעֲשׂוֹת רְצוֹנֶךָ וּלְעָבְדְּךָ בְּלֵבָב שָׁלֵם. עַל שֶׁאֲנַחְנוּ מוֹדִים לָךְ. בָּרוּךְ אֵל הַהוֹדָאוֹת.

Modim Anachnu Lach. She'attah Hu Adonai Eloheinu Velohei Avoteinu. Elohei Chol Basar. Yotzreinu Yotzer Bereshit. Berachot Vehoda'ot Leshimcha Hagadol Vehakadosh. Al Shehecheyitanu Vekiyamtanu. Ken Techayeinu Utechanenu Vete'esof Galyoteinu Lechatzrot Kodshecha. Lishmor Chukkeicha Vela'asot Retzonecha Ule'avedecha Velevav Shalem. Al She'anachnu Modim Lach. Baruch El Hahoda'ot.

We are thankful to You, Hashem our God and the God of our fathers. God of all flesh, our Creator and Former of Creation, blessings and thanks to Your great and holy name, for You have kept us alive and sustained us; may You always grant us life and be gracious to us. And gather our exiles to Your holy courtyards to observe Your statutes, and to do Your will, and to serve You with a perfect heart. For this we thank You. Blessed is God of thanksgivings.

Al HaNissim

On Purim and Hanukkah an extra prayer is added here:

עַל הַנִּסִים וְעַל הַפֻּרְקָן וְעַל הַגְּבוּרוֹת וְעַל הַתְּשׁוּעוֹת וְעַל הַנִּפְלָאוֹת וְעַל
הַנֶּחָמוֹת שֶׁעָשִׂיתָ לַאֲבוֹתֵינוּ בַּיָּמִים הָהֵם בַּזְּמַן הַזֶּה:

Al Hanissim Ve'al Hapurkan Ve'al Hagevurot Ve'al Hateshu'ot Ve'al Hanifla'ot Ve'al
Hanechamot She'asita La'avoteinu Bayamim Hahem Bazman Hazeh.

For the miracles, and for the triumphant liberation, and the mighty works, and for
the deliverances, and for the wonders, and for the consolations which You have
done for our fathers in those days at this season:

On Hanukkah:

בִּימֵי מַתִּתְיָה בֶן־יוֹחָנָן כֹּהֵן גָּדוֹל. חַשְׁמוֹנָאִי וּבָנָיו כְּשֶׁעָמְדָה מַלְכוּת יָוָן
הָרְשָׁעָה עַל עַמְּךָ יִשְׂרָאֵל. לְשַׁכְּחָם תּוֹרָתָךְ וּלְהַעֲבִירָם מֵחֻקֵּי רְצוֹנָךְ. וְאַתָּה
בְּרַחֲמֶיךָ הָרַבִּים עָמַדְתָּ לָהֶם בְּעֵת צָרָתָם. רַבְתָּ אֶת רִיבָם. דַּנְתָּ אֶת דִּינָם.
נָקַמְתָּ אֶת נִקְמָתָם. מָסַרְתָּ גִבּוֹרִים בְּיַד חַלָּשִׁים. וְרַבִּים בְּיַד מְעַטִּים. וּרְשָׁעִים
בְּיַד צַדִּיקִים. וּטְמֵאִים בְּיַד טְהוֹרִים. וְזֵדִים בְּיַד עוֹסְקֵי תוֹרָתֶךָ. לְךָ עָשִׂיתָ שֵׁם
גָּדוֹל וְקָדוֹשׁ בְּעוֹלָמָךְ. וּלְעַמְּךָ יִשְׂרָאֵל עָשִׂיתָ תְּשׁוּעָה גְדוֹלָה וּפֻרְקָן כְּהַיּוֹם
הַזֶּה. וְאַחַר כָּךְ בָּאוּ בָנֶיךָ לִדְבִיר בֵּיתֶךָ. וּפִנּוּ אֶת־הֵיכָלֶךָ. וְטִהֲרוּ אֶת־מִקְדָּשֶׁךָ.
וְהִדְלִיקוּ נֵרוֹת בְּחַצְרוֹת קָדְשֶׁךָ. וְקָבְעוּ שְׁמוֹנַת יְמֵי חֲנֻכָּה אֵלּוּ בְּהַלֵּל
וּבְהוֹדָאָה. וְעָשִׂיתָ עִמָּהֶם נִסִים וְנִפְלָאוֹת וְנוֹדֶה לְשִׁמְךָ הַגָּדוֹל סֶלָה:

Bimei Mattityah Ven-Yochanan Kohen Gadol. Chashmona'i Uvanav Keshe'amedah
Malchut Yavan Haresha'ah Al Ammecha Yisra'el. Leshakecham Toratach
Uleha'aviram Mechukkei Retzonach. Ve'attah Berachameicha Harabim Amadta
Lahem Be'et Tzaratam. Ravta Et Rivam. Danta Et Dinam. Nakamta Et Nikmatam.
Masarta Giborim Beyad Chalashim. Verabim Beyad Me'atim. Uresha'im Beyad
Tzaddikim. Uteme'im Beyad Tehorim. Vezeidim Beyad Osekei Toratecha. Lecha
Asita Shem Gadol Vekadosh Be'olamach. Ule'ammecha Yisra'el Asita Teshu'ah
Gedolah Ufurkan Kehayom Hazeh. Ve'achar Kach Ba'u Vaneicha Lidvir Beitecha.
Ufinu Et-Heichalecha. Vetiharu Et-Mikdashecha. Vehidliku Nerot Bechatzrot
Kodshecha. Vekave'u Shemonat Yemei Chanukkah Elu Behallel Uvehoda'ah.
Ve'asita Imahem Nissim Venifla'ot Venodeh Leshimcha Hagadol Selah.

Then in the days of Mattityahu ben-Yochanan, High Priest, the Hasmonean and his
sons, when the cruel Greek power rose up against Your people, Yisrael, to make
them forget Your Torah and transgress the statutes of Your will. And You, in Your
great compassion, stood up for them in time of their trial to plead their cause and
defend their judgment. Giving out retribution, delivered the strong into the hand
of the weak, and the many into the hand of the few, and the wicked into the hand of
the upright, and the impure into the hand of the pure, and tyrants into the hand of
the devotees of Your Torah. You made for Yourself a great and holy name in Your

world. And for Your people, Yisrael, You performed a great salvation and liberation as this very day. Then Your children came to the Sanctuary of Your House, cleared Your Temple, cleansed Your Sanctuary and kindled lights in Your courtyards, and they instituted these eight days of Hanukkah for praise and thanksgiving. And You did miracles and wonders for them, and we give thanks to Your great name, selah.

On Purim:

בִּימֵי מָרְדְּכַי וְאֶסְתֵּר בְּשׁוּשַׁן הַבִּירָה. כְּשֶׁעָמַד עֲלֵיהֶם הָמָן הָרָשָׁע. בִּקֵּשׁ לְהַשְׁמִיד לַהֲרֹג וּלְאַבֵּד אֶת־כָּל־הַיְּהוּדִים מִנַּעַר וְעַד זָקֵן טַף וְנָשִׁים בְּיוֹם אֶחָד. בִּשְׁלֹשָׁה עָשָׂר לְחֹדֶשׁ שְׁנֵים עָשָׂר. הוּא חֹדֶשׁ אֲדָר. וּשְׁלָלָם לָבוֹז. וְאַתָּה בְּרַחֲמֶיךָ הָרַבִּים הֵפַרְתָּ אֶת־עֲצָתוֹ וְקִלְקַלְתָּ אֶת־מַחֲשַׁבְתּוֹ. וַהֲשֵׁבוֹתָ לּוֹ גְּמוּלוֹ בְּרֹאשׁוֹ. וְתָלוּ אוֹתוֹ וְאֶת־בָּנָיו עַל הָעֵץ. וְעָשִׂיתָ עִמָּהֶם נֵס וָפֶלֶא וְנוֹדֶה לְשִׁמְךָ הַגָּדוֹל סֶלָה:

Bimei Mordechai Ve'ester Beshushan Habirah. Keshe'amad Aleihem Haman Harasha. Bikesh Lehashmid Laharog Ule'abed Et-Kol-Hayehudim Mina'ar Ve'ad Zaken Taf Venashim Beyom Echad. Bishloshah Asar Lechodesh Sheneim Asar. Hu Chodesh Adar. Ushelalam Lavoz. Ve'attah Berachameicha Harabim Hefarta Et-'Atzato Vekilkalta Et-Machashavto. Vahasheivota Lo Gemulo Verosho. Vetalu Oto Ve'et-Banav Al Ha'etz. Ve'asita Imahem Nes Vafelei Venodeh Leshimcha Hagadol Selah.

In the days of Mordechai and Ester in Shushan, the capital, the wicked Haman rose up and sought to destroy, slay and utterly annihilate all of the Yehudim, both young and old, women and children, on one day, on the thirteenth day of the twelfth month, which is the month of Adar, and to plunder their possessions. But You in Your great mercy You broke his plan and spoiled his designs, causing them to recoil on his own head, and they hanged him and his sons on the gallows. And You did miracles and wonders for them, and we give thanks to Your great name, selah.

Ve'al Kulam Yitbarach.	וְעַל כֻּלָּם יִתְבָּרַךְ.
Veyitromam. Veyitnasse. Tamid.	וְיִתְרוֹמַם. וְיִתְנַשֵּׂא. תָּמִיד.
Shimcha Malkeinu. Le'olam	שִׁמְךָ מַלְכֵּנוּ. לְעוֹלָם
Va'ed. Vechol-Hachayim	וָעֶד. וְכָל־הַחַיִּים
Yoducha Selah.	יוֹדוּךָ סֶלָה:

For all these acts, may Your name, our King, be blessed, extolled and exalted forever. And all of the living will thank You, selah.

During the 10 days of repentance (Rosh Hashanah to Yom Kippur) say:

Uchetov Lechayim Tovim Kol Benei

Veritecha.

וּכְתֹב לְחַיִּים טוֹבִים כָּל בְּנֵי

בְרִיתֶךָ.

Inscribe all of Your people of the covenant for a happy life.

Bow at "Baruch Attah" / "Blessed are You". Raise up at Adonai / Hashem.

Vihalelu Vivarechu Et-Shimcha

וִיהַלְלוּ וִיבָרְכוּ אֶת־שִׁמְךָ

Hagadol Be'emet Le'olam Ki

הַגָּדוֹל בֶּאֱמֶת לְעוֹלָם כִּי

Tov. Ha'el Yeshu'ateinu

טוֹב. הָאֵל יְשׁוּעָתֵנוּ

Ve'ezrateinu Selah. Ha'el Hatov.

וְעֶזְרָתֵנוּ סֶלָה. הָאֵל הַטּוֹב:

Baruch Attah Adonai Hatov

בָּרוּךְ אַתָּה יְהֹוָה הַטּוֹב

Shimcha Ulecha Na'eh

שִׁמְךָ וּלְךָ נָאֶה

Lehodot.

לְהוֹדוֹת:

And they will praise and bless Your great and good name sincerely, forever. For You are good, the God of our salvation and our help forever, the Good God. Blessed are You, Hashem, Your name is good and to You it is good to give thanks.

Birkhat Kohanim / The Priestly Blessing

If there is more than one Kohen present, start here. If there is not, start with Eloheinu Velohei Avoteinu below:

Some say:

לְשֵׁם יִחוּד קוּדְשָׁא בְּרִיךְ הוּא וּשְׁכִינְתֵּיהּ. בִּדְחִילוּ וּרְחִימוּ. וּרְחִימוּ וּדְחִילוּ. לְיַחֲדָא שֵׁם יוֹ"ד קֵ"י בְּוָא"ו קֵ"י בְּיִחוּדָא שְׁלִים (יהוה) בְּשֵׁם כָּל יִשְׂרָאֵל. הִנֵּה אָנֹכִי מוּכָן וּמְזוּמָן לְקַיֵּים מִצְוַת עֲשֵׂה לְבָרֵךְ אֶת יִשְׂרָאֵל בִּרְכַּת כֹּהֲנִים בִּנְשִׂיאוּת כַּפַּיִם לַעֲשׂוֹת נַחַת רוּחַ לְיוֹצְרֵנוּ וּלְהַמְשִׁיךְ שֶׁפַע וּבְרָכָה לְכָל הָעוֹלָמוֹת הַקְּדוֹשִׁים. וִיהִי נֹעַם אֲדֹנָי אֱלֹהֵינוּ עָלֵינוּ וּמַעֲשֵׂה יָדֵינוּ כּוֹנְנָה עָלֵינוּ וּמַעֲשֵׂה יָדֵינוּ כּוֹנְנֵהוּ:

The Kohanim stand on the pulpit after Modim Derabbanan and say:

יְהִי רָצוֹן מִלְּפָנֶיךָ יְהֹוָה אֱלֹהֵינוּ וֵאלֹהֵי אֲבוֹתֵינוּ שֶׁתִּהְיֶה בְּרָכָה זוֹ שֶׁצִּוִּיתָנוּ לְבָרֵךְ אֶת־עַמְּךָ יִשְׂרָאֵל בְּרָכָה שְׁלֵמָה וְלֹא יִהְיֶה בָהּ מִכְשׁוֹל וְעָוֹן מֵעַתָּה וְעַד עוֹלָם:

Yehi Ratzon Milfaneicha Adonai Eloheinu Velohei Avoteinu Shetihyeh Berachah Zo Shetzivitanu Levarech Et-'Ammecha Yisra'el Berachah Shelemah Velo Yihyeh Vah Michshol Ve'avon Me'attah Ve'ad Olam.

May it be Your Will, Hashem our God, that this blessing which You have commanded us to bless Your people Yisrael with will be a perfect blessing. May there not be in it any stumbling or perverseness from now and forever.

Then they say the blessing. If there is more than one Kohen, the leader calls them, "Kohanim!".

בָּרוּךְ אַתָּה יְהֹוָה אֱלֹהֵינוּ מֶלֶךְ הָעוֹלָם. אֲשֶׁר קִדְּשָׁנוּ בִּקְדֻשָּׁתוֹ שֶׁל־אַהֲרֹן. וְצִוָּנוּ לְבָרֵךְ אֶת־עַמּוֹ יִשְׂרָאֵל בְּאַהֲבָה:

Baruch Attah Adonai Eloheinu Melech Ha'olam Asher Kideshanu Bikdushato Shel-Aharon. Vetzivanu Levarech Et-'Ammo Yisra'el Be'ahavah. Amen.

Blessed are You Hashem our God, King of the universe, Who has sanctified us with the sanctification of Aharon and commanded us to bless His people, Yisrael, with love.

The congregation answers:

אָמֵן:
Amen.

And the Chazan and the Kohanim say after him exactly:

יְבָרֶכְךָ יְהֹוָה וְיִשְׁמְרֶךָ: ועונים: אָמֵן:

Yevarechecha Adonai Veyishmerecha. And answer: Amen

Hashem bless you and keep you. And answer: Amen

יָאֵר יְהֹוָה | פָּנָיו אֵלֶיךָ וִיחֻנֶּךָ: ועונים: אָמֵן:

Ya'er Adonai Panav Eleicha Vichuneka. And answer: Amen

Hashem make His countenance shine upon you, and be gracious to you. And answer: Amen

יִשָּׂא יְהֹוָה | פָּנָיו אֵלֶיךָ וְיָשֵׂם לְךָ שָׁלוֹם: ועונים: אָמֵן:

Yissa Adonai Panav Eleicha. Veyasem Lecha Shalom. And answer: Amen

Hashem lift up His countenance towards you and give you peace.
And answer: Amen

When the Chazan begins the Sim Shalom below, the Kohanim face toward the Ark and say:

רִבּוֹן הָעוֹלָמִים עָשִׂינוּ מַה שֶׁגָּזַרְתָּ עָלֵינוּ. עֲשֵׂה אַתָּה מַה שֶׁהִבְטַחְתָּנוּ.
הַשְׁקִיפָה מִמְּעוֹן קָדְשְׁךָ מִן־הַשָּׁמַיִם וּבָרֵךְ אֶת־עַמְּךָ אֶת־יִשְׂרָאֵל:

Ribon Ha'olamim Asinu Mah Shegazarta Aleinu. Aseh Attah Mah-Shehivtachetanu.
Hashkifah Mime'on Kodshecha Min-Hashamayim. Uvarech Et-'Ammecha Et-
Yisra'el.

Sovereign of the universe, We have done what You have decreed for us, You have
done as You promised. "Look down from Your holy Habitation, from heaven, and
bless Your people Yisrael." (Deut. 26:15)

Eloheinu Velohei Avoteinu

If there are no Kohanim, the Chazan recites a substitute blessing:

אֱלֹהֵינוּ וֵאלֹהֵי אֲבוֹתֵינוּ. בָּרְכֵנוּ בַבְּרָכָה הַמְשֻׁלֶּשֶׁת בַּתּוֹרָה
הַכְּתוּבָה עַל יְדֵי מֹשֶׁה עַבְדָּךְ. הָאֲמוּרָה מִפִּי אַהֲרֹן וּבָנָיו הַכֹּהֲנִים
עַם קְדוֹשֶׁיךָ כָּאָמוּר:

Eloheinu Velohei Avoteinu. Barecheinu Baberachah Hamshuleshet
Batorah Haketuvah Al Yedei Mosheh Avdach. Ha'amurah Mipi
Aharon Uvanav Hakohanim Im Kedosheicha Ka'amur.

Our God, God of our fathers, bless us with the threefold blessing
written in the Torah by Your servant Moshe, and spoken by the
mouth of Aharon and his descendants Your consecrated Kohanim:

יְבָרֶכְךָ יְהֹוָה וְיִשְׁמְרֶךָ: ועונים: כֵּן יְהִי רָצוֹן:

Yevarechecha Adonai Veyishmerecha. And answer: Ken Yehi Ratzon.

Hashem bless you and keep you. And answer: May this be His will.

יָאֵר יְהֹוָה | פָּנָיו אֵלֶיךָ וִיחֻנֶּךָּ: ועונים: כֵּן יְהִי רָצוֹן:

Ya'er Adonai Panav Eleicha Vichuneka. And answer: Ken Yehi Ratzon.

Hashem make His countenance shine upon you, and be gracious to
you. And answer: May this be His will.

יִשָּׂא יְהֹוָה ׀ פָּנָיו אֵלֶיךָ וְיָשֵׂם לְךָ שָׁלוֹם: וَעونים: כֵּן יְהִי רָצוֹן:

Yissa Adonai Panav Eleicha. Veyasem Lecha Shalom. **And answer:** Ken Yehi Ratzon.

Hashem lift up His countenance towards you and give you peace. **And answer:** May this be His will.

וְשָׂמוּ אֶת־שְׁמִי עַל־בְּנֵי יִשְׂרָאֵל וַאֲנִי אֲבָרְכֵם:

Vesamu Et-Shemi Al-Benei Yisra'el; Va'ani Avarechem.

And they will set My name upon the Children of Yisrael, and I will bless them.

Sim Shalom / Grant Peace

Sim Shalom Tovah Uverachah.	שִׂים שָׁלוֹם טוֹבָה וּבְרָכָה.
Chayim Chein Vachesed	חַיִּים חֵן וָחֶסֶד
Verachamim. Aleinu Ve'al Kol-	וְרַחֲמִים. עָלֵינוּ וְעַל כָּל־
Yisra'el Ammecha. Uvarecheinu	יִשְׂרָאֵל עַמֶּךָ. וּבָרְכֵנוּ
Avinu Kulanu Ke'echad Be'or	אָבִינוּ כֻּלָּנוּ כְּאֶחָד בְּאוֹר
Paneicha. Ki Ve'or Paneicha	פָּנֶיךָ. כִּי בְאוֹר פָּנֶיךָ
Natata Lanu Adonai Eloheinu	נָתַתָּ לָּנוּ יְהֹוָה אֱלֹהֵינוּ
Torah Vechayim. Ahavah	תּוֹרָה וְחַיִּים. אַהֲבָה
Vachesed. Tzedakah	וָחֶסֶד. צְדָקָה
Verachamim. Berachah	וְרַחֲמִים. בְּרָכָה
Veshalom. Vetov Be'eineicha	וְשָׁלוֹם. וְטוֹב בְּעֵינֶיךָ
Levarecheinu Ulevarech Et-	לְבָרְכֵנוּ וּלְבָרֵךְ אֶת־
Kol-'Ammecha Yisra'el. Berov	כָּל־עַמְּךָ יִשְׂרָאֵל. בְּרֹב
Oz Veshalom.	עֹז וְשָׁלוֹם:

Grant peace, goodness and blessing, a life of grace, and kindness and mercy, to us and to all Yisrael, Your people. And bless us, our Father, all as one with the light of Your countenance; for with the light of Your countenance You have given us, Hashem our God, a Torah and life, love and kindness, righteousness and mercy, blessing and peace. May it be good in Your eyes to bless us and bless all of Your people, Yisrael, with abundant strength and peace.

During the 10 days of repentance (Rosh Hashanah to Yom Kippur) say:

Uvesefer Chayim. Berachah Veshalom.	וּבְסֵפֶר חַיִּים. בְּרָכָה וְשָׁלוֹם.
Ufarnasah Tovah Vishu'ah	וּפַרְנָסָה טוֹבָה וִישׁוּעָה
Venechamah. Ugezerot Tovot. Nizacher	וְנֶחָמָה. וּגְזֵרוֹת טוֹבוֹת. נִזָּכֵר
Venikkatev Lefaneicha. Anachnu	וְנִכָּתֵב לְפָנֶיךָ. אֲנַחְנוּ
Vechol Ammecha Beit Yisra'el.	וְכָל עַמְּךָ בֵּית יִשְׂרָאֵל.
Lechayim Tovim Uleshalom.	לְחַיִּים טוֹבִים וּלְשָׁלוֹם.

May we and all Yisrael Your people be remembered and inscribed before You in the book of life and blessing, peace and prosperity, for a happy life and for peace.

Baruch Attah Adonai	בָּרוּךְ אַתָּה יהוה
Hamevarech Et Ammo Yisra'el	הַמְבָרֵךְ אֶת עַמּוֹ יִשְׂרָאֵל
Bashalom. Amen.	בַּשָּׁלוֹם. אָמֵן:

Blessed are You, Hashem, Who blesses His people Yisrael with peace. Amen.

Yihyu Leratzon Imrei-Fi Vehegyon Libi	יִהְיוּ לְרָצוֹן אִמְרֵי־פִי וְהֶגְיוֹן לִבִּי
Lefaneicha; Adonai Tzuri Vego'ali.	לְפָנֶיךָ יְהֹוָה צוּרִי וְגֹאֲלִי:

May the words of my mouth and the meditation of my heart find favor before You, Hashem my Rock and my Redeemer.

The chazan's repetition ends here; personal / individual continue:

Elohai. Netzor Leshoni Meira	אֱלֹהַי. נְצֹר לְשׁוֹנִי מֵרָע
Vesiftotai Midaber Mirmah.	וְשִׂפְתוֹתַי מִדַּבֵּר מִרְמָה.
Velimkalelai Nafshi Tidom.	וְלִמְקַלְלַי נַפְשִׁי תִדֹּם.
Venafshi Ke'afar Lakol Tihyeh.	וְנַפְשִׁי כֶּעָפָר לַכֹּל תִּהְיֶה.
Petach Libi Betoratecha.	פְּתַח לִבִּי בְּתוֹרָתֶךָ.
Ve'acharei Mitzvoteicha Tirdof	וְאַחֲרֵי מִצְוֹתֶיךָ תִּרְדּוֹף
Nafshi. Vechol-Hakamim Alai	נַפְשִׁי. וְכָל־הַקָּמִים עָלַי
Lera'ah. Meheirah Hafer	לְרָעָה. מְהֵרָה הָפֵר
Atzatam Vekalkel	עֲצָתָם וְקַלְקֵל
Machshevotam. Aseh Lema'an	מַחֲשְׁבוֹתָם. עֲשֵׂה לְמַעַן
Shemach. Aseh Lema'an	שְׁמֶךָ. עֲשֵׂה לְמַעַן
Yeminach. Aseh Lema'an	יְמִינֶךָ. עֲשֵׂה לְמַעַן
Toratach. Aseh Lema'an	תּוֹרָתֶךָ. עֲשֵׂה לְמַעַן
Kedushatach. Lema'an	קְדֻשָּׁתֶךָ. לְמַעַן
Yechaletzun Yedideicha;	יֵחָלְצוּן יְדִידֶיךָ
Hoshi'ah Yeminecha Va'aneni.	הוֹשִׁיעָה יְמִינְךָ וַעֲנֵנִי:

My God, guard my tongue from evil, and my lips from speaking deceit. And to those who curse me may my soul be silent; and may my soul be like the dust to all. Open my heart to Your Torah, that my soul may follow after Your commandments. And all that rise to do evil against me, speedily nullify their plan, and spoil their thoughts. Do it for the sake of Your name; do it for the sake of Your right hand; do it for the sake of Your Torah, do it for the sake of Your holiness. That Your beloved may be rescued, save with Your right hand and answer me. (Ps. 60:7)

Yihyu Leratzon Imrei-Fi Vehegyon Libi	יִהְיוּ לְרָצוֹן אִמְרֵי־פִי וְהֶגְיוֹן לִבִּי
Lefaneicha; Adonai Tzuri Vego'ali.	לְפָנֶיךָ יְהֹוָה צוּרִי וְגֹאֲלִי:

May the words of my mouth and the meditation of my heart find favor before You, Hashem my Rock and my Redeemer.

Oseh Shalom

One bows and takes three steps backwards, while still bowing. After three steps, while still bowing and before erecting, while saying, "Oseh Shalom Bimromav", turn one's face to the left, "Hu [Berachamav] Ya'aseh Shalom Aleinu", turn one's face to the right; [face forward and] then bow forward like a servant leaving his master. (SA, OC 123:1)

Oseh Shalom **On the 10 Days of**

Repentance: (Hashalom) Bimromav,

Hu Berachamav Ya'aseh Shalom

Aleinu, Ve'al Kol-'Ammo

Yisra'el, Ve'imru Amen.

עוֹשֶׂה שָׁלוֹם

בעשיי אוי: (הַשָּׁלוֹם) בִּמְרוֹמָיו.

הוּא בְּרַחֲמָיו יַעֲשֶׂה שָׁלוֹם

עָלֵינוּ. וְעַל כָּל־עַמּוֹ

יִשְׂרָאֵל. וְאִמְרוּ אָמֵן:

Creator of **On the 10 Days of Repentance:** (the) peace in His high places, may He in His mercy create peace for us and for all Yisrael, and say Amen.

Yehi Ratzon Milfaneicha Adonai

Eloheinu Velohei Avoteinu. Shetivneh

Beit Hamikdash Bimheirah Veyameinu.

Veten Chelkenu Vetoratach La'asot

Chukkei. Retzonach Ule'avedach

Belevav Shalem.

יְהִי רָצוֹן מִלְּפָנֶיךָ יְהֹוָה

אֱלֹהֵינוּ וֵאלֹהֵי אֲבוֹתֵינוּ. שֶׁתִּבְנֶה

בֵּית הַמִּקְדָּשׁ בִּמְהֵרָה בְיָמֵינוּ.

וְתֵן חֶלְקֵנוּ בְּתוֹרָתָךְ לַעֲשׂוֹת

חֻקֵּי רְצוֹנָךְ וּלְעָבְדָךְ

בְּלֵבָב שָׁלֵם:

May it be Your will, Hashem our God and God of our fathers, that the Beit HaMikdash be speedily rebuilt in our days, and grant us a share in Your Torah so we may fulfill the statutes of Your will and serve You with a whole heart.

Yehi Shem

Yehi Shem Adonai Mevorach; Me'attah.

Ve'ad-'Olam. Mimizrach-Shemesh Ad-

Mevo'o; Mehulal. Shem Adonai Ram

Al-Chol-Goyim Adonai Al Hashamayim

Kevodo. Adonai Adoneinu; Mah-'Adir

Shimcha. Bechol-Ha'aretz.

יְהִי שֵׁם יְהוָה מְבֹרָךְ מֵעַתָּה

וְעַד־עוֹלָם: מִמִּזְרַח־שֶׁמֶשׁ עַד־

מְבוֹאוֹ מְהֻלָּל שֵׁם יְהוָה: רָם

עַל־כָּל־גּוֹיִם | יְהוָה עַל הַשָּׁמַיִם

כְּבוֹדוֹ: יְהוָה אֲדֹנֵינוּ מָה־אַדִּיר

שִׁמְךָ בְּכָל־הָאָרֶץ:

Blessed is the name of Hashem from this time forward and forever. From the rising of the sun to it's going down, Hashem's name is to be praised. Hashem, our Lord, How glorious is Your name in all of the earth. **(Psalms 113:2-4, 8:2)**

Kaddish Titkabbal

> **Kaddish is only recited in a minyan (ten men).** אמ **denotes when the congregation responds "Amen" together out loud. According to the Shulchan Arukh, the congregation says "Yehei Shemeh Rabba" to "Yitbarach" out loud together without interruption, and also that one should respond "Amen" after "Yitbarach." (SA, OC 55,56) This is not the common custom today. Though many are accustomed to answering according to their own custom, it is advised to respond in the custom of the one reciting to avoid not fragmenting into smaller groups. ("Lo Titgodedu" - BT, Yevamot 13b / SA, OC 493, Rema / MT, Avodah Zara 12:15)**

יִתְגַּדַּל וְיִתְקַדַּשׁ שְׁמֵהּ רַבָּא. אמ בְּעָלְמָא דִּי בְרָא. כִּרְעוּתֵהּ. וְיַמְלִיךְ מַלְכוּתֵהּ.
וְיַצְמַח פֻּרְקָנֵהּ. וִיקָרֵב מְשִׁיחֵהּ. אמ בְּחַיֵּיכוֹן וּבְיוֹמֵיכוֹן וּבְחַיֵּי דְכָל בֵּית
יִשְׂרָאֵל. בַּעֲגָלָא וּבִזְמַן קָרִיב. וְאִמְרוּ אָמֵן. אמ יְהֵא שְׁמֵהּ רַבָּא מְבָרַךְ לְעָלַם
וּלְעָלְמֵי עָלְמַיָּא יִתְבָּרַךְ. וְיִשְׁתַּבַּח. וְיִתְפָּאַר. וְיִתְרוֹמַם. וְיִתְנַשֵּׂא. וְיִתְהַדָּר.
וְיִתְעַלֶּה. וְיִתְהַלָּל שְׁמֵהּ דְּקֻדְשָׁא. בְּרִיךְ הוּא. אמ לְעֵלָּא מִן כָּל בִּרְכָתָא
שִׁירָתָא. תֻּשְׁבְּחָתָא וְנֶחֱמָתָא. דַּאֲמִירָן בְּעָלְמָא. וְאִמְרוּ אָמֵן. אמ

Yitgadal Veyitkadash Shemeh Rabba. **Amen** Be'alema Di Vera. Kir'uteh. Veyamlich Malchuteh. Veyatzmach Purkaneh. Vikarev Meshicheh. **Amen** Bechayeichon Uveyomeichon Uvechayei Dechal-Beit Yisra'el. Ba'agala Uvizman Kariv. Ve'imru Amen. **Amen** Yehei Shemeh Rabba Mevarach Le'alam Ule'alemei Alemaya Yitbarach. Veyishtabach. Veyitpa'ar. Veyitromam. Veyitnasse. Veyit'hadar. Veyit'aleh. Veyit'hallal Shemeh Dekudsha. Berich Hu. **Amen** Le'ella Min Kol Birchata Shirata. Tushbechata Venechemata. Da'amiran Be'alema. Ve'imru Amen. **Amen**

Glorified and sanctified be God's great name **Amen** throughout the world which He has created according to His will. May He establish His kingdom, hastening His salvation and the coming of His Messiah, **Amen**, in your lifetime and during your days, and within the life of the entire House of Yisrael, speedily and soon; and say, Amen. **Amen** May His great name be blessed forever and to all eternity. Blessed and praised, glorified and exalted, extolled and honored, adored and lauded be the

name of the Holy One, blessed is He, ^{Amen} Beyond all the blessings and hymns, praises and consolations that are ever spoken in the world; and say, Amen. ^{Amen}

תִּתְקַבַּל צְלוֹתַנָא וּבָעוּתַנָא. עִם צְלוֹתְהוֹן וּבָעוּתְהוֹן דְּכָל בֵּית יִשְׂרָאֵל. קֳדָם
אֲבוּנָא דְּבִשְׁמַיָּא וְאַרְעָא. וְאִמְרוּ אָמֵן. אₘₙ

Titkabbal Tzelotana Uva'utana. Im Tzelotehon Uva'utehon Dechol Beit Yisra'el.
Kodam Avuna Devishmaya Ve'ar'a. Ve'imru Amen. ^{Amen}

May the prayer and supplication of the whole House of Yisrael be accepted before their Father in heaven, and say, Amen. ^{Amen}

יְהֵא שְׁלָמָא רַבָּא מִן שְׁמַיָּא. חַיִּים וְשָׂבָע וִישׁוּעָה וְנֶחָמָה. וְשֵׁיזָבָא וּרְפוּאָה
וּגְאוּלָה וּסְלִיחָה וְכַפָּרָה וְרֶוַח וְהַצָּלָה לָנוּ וּלְכָל עַמּוֹ יִשְׂרָאֵל. וְאִמְרוּ אָמֵן. אₘₙ

Yehei Shelama Rabba Min Shemaya. Chayim Vesava Vishu'ah Venechamah.
Vesheizava Urefu'ah Uge'ulah Uselichah Vechapparah Verevach Vehatzalah Lanu
Ulechol Ammo Yisra'el. Ve'imru Amen. ^{Amen}

May abundant peace descend from heaven, with life and plenty, salvation, solace, liberation, healing and redemption, and forgiveness and atonement, enlargement and freedom, for us and all of God's people Yisrael; and say, Amen. ^{Amen}

One bows and takes three steps backwards, while still bowing. After three steps, while still bowing and before erecting, while saying, "Oseh Shalom Bimromav", turn one's face to the left, "Hu [Berachamav] Ya'aseh Shalom Aleinu", turn one's face to the right; then bow forward like a servant leaving his master. (SA, OC 123:1)

עוֹשֶׂה שָׁלוֹם בעשׂי﬏ אוﬞ: (הַשָּׁלוֹם) בִּמְרוֹמָיו. הוּא בְּרַחֲמָיו יַעֲשֶׂה שָׁלוֹם עָלֵינוּ. וְעַל
כָּל־עַמּוֹ יִשְׂרָאֵל. וְאִמְרוּ אָמֵן:

Oseh Shalom **On the 10 days of repentance:** (Hashalom) Bimromav, Hu Berachamav
Ya'aseh Shalom Aleinu, Ve'al Kol-'Ammo Yisra'el, Ve'imru Amen.

Creator of **On the 10 days of repentance:** (the) peace in His high places, may He in His mercy create peace for us and for all Yisrael, and say Amen.

Mishnah, Tractate Sanhedrin, 10:1

כָּל יִשְׂרָאֵל יֵשׁ לָהֶם חֵלֶק לְעוֹלָם הַבָּא. שֶׁנֶּאֱמַר וְעַמֵּךְ כֻּלָּם צַדִּיקִים. לְעוֹלָם
יִירְשׁוּ אָרֶץ. נֵצֶר מַטָּעַי מַעֲשֵׂה יָדַי לְהִתְפָּאֵר:

Kol Yisra'el Yesh Lahem Chelek La'olam Haba. Shene'emar Ve'ammecha Kulam
Tzaddikim. Le'olam Yiyreshu Aretz. Netzer Matta'ai Ma'aseh Yadai Lhitpa'er.

All Yisrael have a portion in the world to come: for it is said: "Your people also will be all righteous, They will inherit the land forever; The branch of My planting, the work of My hands, in which I glory." (Isaiah 60:21)

Talmud, Tractate Berakhot, 17a

אָמַר רַבִּי יְהוּדָה אַשְׁרֵי מִי שֶׁעֲמָלוֹ בַּתּוֹרָה וְעוֹשֶׂה נַחַת רוּחַ לְיוֹצְרוֹ. גָּדֵל בְּשֵׁם טוֹב. וְנִפְטָר בְּשֵׁם טוֹב מִן הָעוֹלָם. וְעָלָיו אָמַר שְׁלֹמֹה בְּחָכְמָתוֹ טוֹב שֵׁם מִשֶּׁמֶן טוֹב. וְיוֹם הַמָּוֶת מִיּוֹם הִוָּלְדוֹ. לְמֹד תּוֹרָה הַרְבֵּה וְיִתְּנוּ לְךָ שָׂכָר הַרְבֵּה. וְדַע. מַתַּן שְׂכָרָם שֶׁל צַדִּיקִים לֶעָתִיד לָבֹא:

Amar Ribi Yehudah Ashrei Mi She'amalo Batorah Ve'oseh Nachat Ruach Leyotzero. Gadel Beshem Tov. Veniftar Beshem Tov Min Ha'olam. Ve'alav Amar Shlomoh Bechachemato Tov Shem Mishemen Tov. Veyom Hamavet Miyom Hivoldo. Lemod Torah Harbeh Veyittnu Lecha Sachar Harbeh. Veda. Matan Secharam Shel Tzaddikim Le'atid Lavo:

Rabbi Yehudah said, happy is he whose toil is in the Torah. He rejoices the heart of his Maker, spending his days with a good name, and passing on from this life with a good name. To him apply the words Solomon spoke in his wisdom, "A good name is better than precious oil; And the day of death than the day of one's birth." (Ecc. 7:1) Study Torah greatly and great will be your reward; but know that the true reward of the good is reserved for the future life.

Mishnah, Tractate Makkot, 3:16

רַבִּי חֲנַנְיָה בֶּן עֲקַשְׁיָא אוֹמֵר רָצָה הַקָּדוֹשׁ בָּרוּךְ הוּא לְזַכּוֹת אֶת יִשְׂרָאֵל. לְפִיכָךְ הִרְבָּה לָהֶם תּוֹרָה וּמִצְוֹת. שֶׁנֶּאֱמַר יְהוָה חָפֵץ לְמַעַן צִדְקוֹ יַגְדִּיל תּוֹרָה וְיַאְדִּיר:

Rabbi Chananyah Ben Akashya Omer Ratzah Hakadosh Baruch Hu Lezakkot Et Yisra'el. Lefichach Hirbah Lahem Torah Umitzvot. Shene'emar Adonai Chafetz Lema'an Tzidko Yagdil Torah Veya'dir.

Rabbi Chananya son of Akashia stated, The Holy One Blessed is He, being pleased to make Yisrael worthy of enjoying happiness, has enlarged the Torah with many precepts; as it is said, "Hashem was pleased, for His righteousness' sake, To make the Torah great and glorious." (Isaiah 42:21)

Ein Keloheinu

Ein Keloheinu. Ein Kadoneinu.	אֵין כֵּאלֹהֵינוּ. אֵין כַּאדוֹנֵנוּ.
Ein Kemalkeinu. Ein	אֵין כְּמַלְכֵּנוּ. אֵין
Kemoshi'enu.	כְּמוֹשִׁיעֵנוּ:
Mi Keloheinu. Mi Kadoneinu.	מִי כֵאלֹהֵינוּ. מִי כַאדוֹנֵנוּ.
Mi Kemalkeinu. Mi	מִי כְּמַלְכֵּנוּ. מִי
Kemoshi'enu.	כְּמוֹשִׁיעֵנוּ:
Nodeh Leloheinu. Nodeh	נוֹדֶה לֵאלֹהֵינוּ. נוֹדֶה
Ladoneinu. Nodeh Lemalkeinu.	לַאדוֹנֵנוּ. נוֹדֶה לְמַלְכֵּנוּ.
Nodeh Lemoshi'enu.	נוֹדֶה לְמוֹשִׁיעֵנוּ:
Baruch Eloheinu. Baruch	בָּרוּךְ אֱלֹהֵינוּ. בָּרוּךְ
Adoneinu. Baruch Malkeinu.	אֲדוֹנֵנוּ. בָּרוּךְ מַלְכֵּנוּ.
Baruch Moshi'enu.	בָּרוּךְ מוֹשִׁיעֵנוּ:
Attah Hu Eloheinu. Attah Hu	אַתָּה הוּא אֱלֹהֵינוּ. אַתָּה הוּא
Adoneinu. Attah Hu Malkeinu.	אֲדוֹנֵנוּ. אַתָּה הוּא מַלְכֵּנוּ.
Attah Hu Moshi'enu. Attah	אַתָּה הוּא מוֹשִׁיעֵנוּ: אַתָּה
Toshi'enu. Attah Takum	תוֹשִׁיעֵנוּ. אַתָּה תָקוּם
Terachem Tziyon; Ki-'Et	תְּרַחֵם צִיּוֹן כִּי־עֵת
Lechenenah. Ki-Va Mo'ed.	לְחֶנְנָהּ כִּי־בָא מוֹעֵד:

Who is like our God, Who is like our Lord, Who is like our King, Who is like our Savior?

There is none like our God, There is none like our Lord, There is none like our King, There is none like our Savior.

Let us praise our God, Let us praise our Lord, Let us praise our King, Let us praise our Savior.

Blessed is our God, Blessed is our Lord, Blessed is our King, Blessed is our Savior.

You are our God, You are our Lord, You are our King, You are our

Savior. You will save us. "You will arise and pity Tziyon; For it is time
to show her Your grace, For the appointed time comes."

Ketoret / Incense Offering

אַתָּה הוּא יְהֹוָה אֱלֹהֵינוּ. שֶׁהִקְטִירוּ אֲבוֹתֵינוּ לְפָנֶיךָ אֶת קְטֹרֶת
הַסַּמִּים. בִּזְמַן שֶׁבֵּית הַמִּקְדָּשׁ קַיָּם. כַּאֲשֶׁר צִוִּיתָ אוֹתָם עַל־יַד
מֹשֶׁה נְבִיאָךְ. כַּכָּתוּב בְּתוֹרָתֶךָ:

Attah Hu Adonai Eloheinu. Shehiktiru Avoteinu Lefaneicha Et
Ketoret Hasamim. Bizman Shebeit Hamikdash Kayam. Ka'asher
Tzivita Otam Al-Yad Mosheh Nevi'ach. Kakatuv Betoratach:

You are Hashem, our God, before Whom our ancestors burned the
offering of incense in the days of the Beit HaMikdash. For You
commanded them through Moshe, Your prophet, as it is written in
Your Torah:

Exodus 30:34-36, 7-8

וַיֹּאמֶר יְהֹוָה אֶל־מֹשֶׁה קַח־לְךָ סַמִּים נָטָף | וּשְׁחֵלֶת וְחֶלְבְּנָה סַמִּים
וּלְבֹנָה זַכָּה בַּד בְּבַד יִהְיֶה: וְעָשִׂיתָ אֹתָהּ קְטֹרֶת רֹקַח מַעֲשֵׂה רוֹקֵחַ
מְמֻלָּח טָהוֹר קֹדֶשׁ: וְשָׁחַקְתָּ מִמֶּנָּה הָדֵק וְנָתַתָּה מִמֶּנָּה לִפְנֵי הָעֵדֻת
בְּאֹהֶל מוֹעֵד אֲשֶׁר אִוָּעֵד לְךָ שָׁמָּה קֹדֶשׁ קָדָשִׁים תִּהְיֶה לָכֶם:
וְנֶאֱמַר: וְהִקְטִיר עָלָיו אַהֲרֹן קְטֹרֶת סַמִּים בַּבֹּקֶר בַּבֹּקֶר בְּהֵיטִיבוֹ
אֶת־הַנֵּרֹת יַקְטִירֶנָּה: וּבְהַעֲלֹת אַהֲרֹן אֶת־הַנֵּרֹת בֵּין הָעַרְבַּיִם
יַקְטִירֶנָּה קְטֹרֶת תָּמִיד לִפְנֵי יְהֹוָה לְדֹרֹתֵיכֶם:

Vayomer Adonai El-Mosheh Kach-Lecha Samim. Nataf Ushchelet
Vechelbenah. Samim Ulevonah Zakah; Bad Bevad Yihyeh. Ve'asita
Otah Ketoret. Rokach Ma'aseh Rokeach; Memulach Tahor Kodesh.
Veshachakta Mimenah Hadek Venatatah Mimenah Lifnei Ha'eidut
Be'ohel Mo'ed. Asher Iva'eid Lecha Shamah; Kodesh Kodashim

Tihyeh Lachem. Vene'emar Vehiktir Alav Aharon Ketoret Samim;
Baboker Baboker. Beheitivo Et-Hanerot Yaktirenah. Uveha'alot
Aharon Et-Hanerot Bein Ha'arbayim Yaktirenah; Ketoret Tamid Lifnei
Adonai Ledoroteichem.

And Hashem said to Moshe, 'Take sweet spices, oil of myrrh,
onycha and galbanum, together with clear frankincense, a like
weight of each of these sweet spices. And you will make from there
incense, a perfume pure and holy, compounded by the perfumer,
salted together. And you will crush some of it very fine, and put
some of it before the Ark of testimony in the Ohel Moed where I will
meet with you; it will be most holy to you. Further it is said in the
Torah: "And Aharon will burn the incense of sweet spices on the
altar of incense, every morning when he dresses the lamps he will
burn it. And at dusk when Aharon lights the lamps he will again burn
incense, a perpetual incense before Hashem throughout your
generations."

Talmud: Keritot 6a

תָּנוּ רַבָּנָן: פִּטוּם הַקְטֹרֶת כֵּיצַד: שְׁלֹשׁ מֵאוֹת וְשִׁשִּׁים וּשְׁמוֹנָה מָנִים
הָיוּ בָהּ. שְׁלֹשׁ מֵאוֹת וְשִׁשִּׁים וַחֲמִשָּׁה כְּמִנְיַן יְמוֹת הַחַמָּה. מָנֶה
בְּכָל־יוֹם. מַחֲצִיתוֹ בַּבֹּקֶר וּמַחֲצִיתוֹ בָּעֶרֶב. וּשְׁלֹשָׁה מָנִים יְתֵרִים.
שֶׁמֵּהֶם מַכְנִיס כֹּהֵן גָּדוֹל. וְנוֹטֵל מֵהֶם מְלֹא חָפְנָיו בְּיוֹם הַכִּפּוּרִים.
וּמַחֲזִירָן לְמַכְתֶּשֶׁת בְּעֶרֶב יוֹם הַכִּפּוּרִים. כְּדֵי לְקַיֵּם מִצְוַת דַּקָּה מִן
הַדַּקָּה. וְאַחַד־עָשָׂר סַמָּנִים הָיוּ בָהּ. וְאֵלּוּ הֵן:

Tanu Rabbanan. Pitum Haketoret Keitzad: Shelosh Me'ot Veshishim
Ushemonah Manim Hayu Vah. Shelosh Me'ot Veshishim
Vachamishah Keminyan Yemot Hachamah. Maneh Bechol-Yom.
Machatzito Baboker Umachatzito Ba'erev. Usheloshah Manim
Yeterim. Shemehem Machnis Kohen Gadol. Venotel Mehem Melo
Chafenav Beyom Hakippurim. Umachaziron Lemachteshet Be'erev
Yom Hakippurim. Kedei Lekayem Mitzvat Dakah Min Hadakah.
Ve'achad-'Asar Samanim Hayu Vah. Ve'elu Hen.

The rabbis have taught how the compounding of the incense was done. In measure the incense contained three hundred and sixty-eight manim, three hundred and sixty-five being one for each day of the year, the remaining three being for the high priest to take his hands full on the Yom Kippur. These last were again ground in a mortar on the eve of Yom Kippur so as to fulfill the command, "take of the finest beaten incense." and these are them:

א הַצֳּרִי ב וְהַצִּפֹּרֶן ג וְהַחֶלְבְּנָה ד וְהַלְּבוֹנָה. מִשְׁקַל שִׁבְעִים שִׁבְעִים מָנֶה. ה מוֹר. ו וּקְצִיעָה ז וְשִׁבֹּלֶת נֵרְדְּ ח וְכַרְכֹּם. מִשְׁקַל שִׁשָּׁה עָשָׂר שִׁשָּׁה עָשָׂר מָנֶה. ט קֹשְׁטְ שְׁנֵים עָשָׂר. י קִלּוּפָה שְׁלֹשָׁה. יא קִנָּמוֹן תִּשְׁעָה. בּוֹרִית־כַּרְשִׁינָה תִּשְׁעָה קַבִּין. יֵין קַפְרִיסִין סְאִין תְּלָת וְקַבִּין תְּלָתָא. וְאִם לֹא מָצָא יֵין קַפְרִיסִין. מֵבִיא חֲמַר חִיוָר עַתִּיק. מֶלַח סְדוֹמִית. רוֹבַע. מַעֲלֶה עָשָׁן. כָּל־שֶׁהוּא. רִבִּי נָתָן הַבַּבְלִי אוֹמֵר: אַף כִּפַּת הַיַּרְדֵּן כָּל־שֶׁהִיא. אִם נָתַן בָּהּ דְּבַשׁ פְּסָלָהּ. וְאִם חִסֵּר אַחַת מִכָּל־סַמְמָנֶיהָ. חַיָּב מִיתָה:

Hatzori Vehatziporen Vehachelbenah Vehallevonah. Mishkal Shiv'im Shiv'im Maneh. Mor. Uketzi'ah Veshibolet Nered Vecharkom. Mishkal Shishah Asar Shishah Asar Maneh. Koshet Sheneim Asar. Kilufah Sheloshah. Kinamon Tish'ah. Borit-Karshinah Tish'ah Kabin. Yein Kafrisin Se'in Telat Vekabin Telata. Ve'im Lo Matza Yein Kafrisin. Mevi Chamar Chivar Atik. Melach Sedomit. Rova. Ma'aleh Ashan. Kol-Shehu. Ribi Natan Habavli Omer. Af Kippat Hayarden Kol-Shehi. Im Natan Bah Devash Pesalah. Ve'im Chisser Achat Mikol-Samemaneiha. Chayaiv Mitah.

The incense was compounded of eleven different spices: seventy manim each of balm, onycha, galbanum, and frankincense; sixteen manim each of myrrh, cassia, spikenard, and saffron; twelve manim of costus; three manim of aromatic bark; nine manim of cinnamon; nine kabs of lye of Carsina; three seahs and three kabs of Cyprus wine, though if Cyprus wine could not be had, strong white wine might be substituted for it; the fourth of a kab of salt of Sedom, and a small quantity of a herb which caused the smoke to ascend straight. Rabbi Nathan of Bavel said there was added also a small quantity of kippat of the Yarden. If honey was mixed with the incense, the incense became unfit for sacred use, while the one who omitted any of the ingredients was deemed guilty of mortal error.

רַבָּן שִׁמְעוֹן בֶּן גַּמְלִיאֵל אוֹמֵר: הַצֳּרִי אֵינוֹ אֶלָּא שְׂרָף. הַנּוֹטֵף מֵעֲצֵי הַקְּטָף. בֹּרִית כַּרְשִׁינָה. לְמָה הִיא בָאָה: כְּדֵי לְשַׁפּוֹת בָּהּ אֶת־הַצִּפֹּרֶן. כְּדֵי שֶׁתְּהֵא נָאָה. יֵין קַפְרִיסִין. לְמָה הוּא בָא: כְּדֵי לִשְׁרוֹת בּוֹ אֶת־הַצִּפֹּרֶן כְּדֵי שֶׁתְּהֵא עַזָּה. וַהֲלֹא מֵי רַגְלַיִם יָפִין לָהּ: אֶלָּא שֶׁאֵין מַכְנִיסִין מֵי רַגְלַיִם בַּמִּקְדָּשׁ. מִפְּנֵי הַכָּבוֹד:

Rabban Shim'on Ben-Gamli'el Omer. Hatzori Eino Ella Sheraf.
Hanotef Me'atzei Haketaf. Borit Karshinah. Lemah Hi Va'ah: Kedei
Leshapot Bah Et-Hatziporen. Kedei Shetehei Na'ah. Yein Kafrisin.
Lemah Hu Va: Kedei Lishrot Bo Et-Hatziporen Kedei Shetehei Azah.
Vahalo Mei Raglayim Yafin Lah: Ella She'ein Machnisin Mei
Raglayim Bamikdash. Mipenei Hakavod.

Rabban Shimon, son of Gamliel, said that the balm required is that exuding from the balsam tree. Why did they use lye of Carsina? To refine the appearance of the onycha. What was the purpose of the Cyprus wine? To steep the onycha in it so as to harden it. Though mei raglayim might have been adapted for that purpose, it was not used because it was not decent to bring it into the Temple.

תַּנְיָא רִבִּי נָתָן אוֹמֵר: כְּשֶׁהוּא שׁוֹחֵק. אוֹמֵר: הָדֵק הֵיטֵב. הֵיטֵב הָדֵק. מִפְּנֵי שֶׁהַקּוֹל יָפֶה לַבְּשָׂמִים. פִּטְּמָהּ לַחֲצָאִין. כְּשֵׁרָה. לְשָׁלִישׁ וְלִרְבִיעַ. לֹא שָׁמַעְנוּ. אָמַר רִבִּי יְהוּדָה: זֶה הַכְּלָל. אִם כְּמִדָּתָהּ. כְּשֵׁרָה לַחֲצָאִין. וְאִם חִסֵּר אַחַת מִכָּל־סַמְמָנֶיהָ. חַיָּיב מִיתָה:

Tanya Ribi Natan Omer. Keshehu Shochek. Omer. Hadek Heitev.
Heitev Hadek. Mipenei Shehakol Yafeh Labesamim. Pittemah
Lachatza'in. Kesherah. Leshalish Uleravia'. Lo Shama'nu. Amar Ribi
Yehudah. Zeh Hakelal. Im Kemidatah. Kesherah Lachatza'in. Ve'im
Chisser Achat Mikol-Samemaneiha. Chayaiv Mitah.

It is taught: Rabbi Natan said that when the priest ground the
incense the one superintending would say, "Grind it very fine, very
fine grind it," because the sound of the human voice is encouraging
in the making of spices. If he had compounded only one hundred
and eighty-four manim (half the required quantity), it was valid, but
there is no tradition as to its permissibility if it was compounded in
one-third or one-quarter proportions of the required quantity.
Rabbi Yehudah said that the general principle is that if it was made
with its ingredients in their correct proportions, it was permissible
in half the quantity; but if one omitted any of the ingredients he was
deemed guilty of mortal error.

תָּנֵי בַר־קַפָּרָא: אַחַת לְשִׁשִּׁים אוֹ לְשִׁבְעִים שָׁנָה. הָיְתָה בָאָה שֶׁל
שִׁירַיִם לַחֲצָאִין. וְעוֹד תָּנֵי בַר־קַפָּרָא: אִלּוּ הָיָה נוֹתֵן בָּהּ קָרְטוֹב
שֶׁל דְּבַשׁ. אֵין אָדָם יָכוֹל לַעֲמֹד מִפְּנֵי רֵיחָהּ. וְלָמָּה אֵין מְעָרְבִין
בָּהּ דְּבַשׁ. מִפְּנֵי שֶׁהַתּוֹרָה אָמְרָה: כִּי כָל־שְׂאֹר וְכָל־דְּבַשׁ
לֹא־תַקְטִירוּ מִמֶּנּוּ אִשֶּׁה לַיהֹוָה:

Tanei Var-Kappara. Achat Leshishim O Leshiv'im Shanah. Hayetah
Va'ah Shel Shirayim Lachatza'in. Ve'od Tanei Var-Kappara. Ilu Hayah
Noten Bah Karetov Shel Devash. Ein Adam Yachol La'amod Mipenei
Reichah. Velamah Ein Me'arevin Bah Devash Mipenei Shehatorah
Amerah. Ki Chol-Se'or Vechol-Devash. Lo-Taktiru Mimenu Isheh
L'Adonai.

Bar Kappara taught that once in sixty or seventy years it happened
that, left over, there was over a total of half the required amount
accumulated from the three manim of incense from which the high
priest took his hands full on Yom Kippur. Further Bar Kappara

taught that had one mixed into the incense the smallest quantity of honey, no one could have stood its scent. Why did they not mix honey with it? Because the Torah states that, "No leaven, or any honey, will you burn as an offering made by fire to Hashem."

יְהֹוָה צְבָאוֹת עִמָּנוּ מִשְׂגָּב־לָנוּ אֱלֹהֵי יַעֲקֹב סֶלָה: יְהֹוָה צְבָאוֹת אַשְׁרֵי אָדָם בֹּטֵחַ בָּךְ: יְהֹוָה הוֹשִׁיעָה הַמֶּלֶךְ יַעֲנֵנוּ בְיוֹם־קָרְאֵנוּ: וְעָרְבָה לַיהֹוָה מִנְחַת יְהוּדָה וִירוּשָׁלָיִם כִּימֵי עוֹלָם וּכְשָׁנִים קַדְמֹנִיֹּת:

Adonai Tzeva'ot Imanu; Misgav-Lanu Elohei Ya'akov Selah. Adonai Tzeva'ot; Ashrei Adam. Boteach Bach. Adonai Hoshi'ah; Hamelech. Ya'aneinu Veyom-Kor'enu. Ve'arevah L'Adonai Minchat Yehudah Virushalayim Kimei Olam. Ucheshanim Kadmoniyot.

Hashem of hosts is with us; The God of Yaakov is our high tower. Selah. Hashem of hosts, happy is the man who trusts in You. Save, Hashem; Let the King answer us in the day that we call. Then will the offering of Yehudah and Yerushalayim be pleasant to Hashem, as in the days of old, and as in ancient years. (Psalms 46:12, 84:13, 20:10, Malachi 3:4)

תָּנָא דְבֵי אֵלִיָּהוּ. כָּל־הַשּׁוֹנֶה הֲלָכוֹת בְּכָל־יוֹם. מֻבְטָח לוֹ שֶׁהוּא בֶן־הָעוֹלָם הַבָּא. שֶׁנֶּאֱמַר הֲלִיכוֹת עוֹלָם לוֹ: אַל־תִּקְרֵי הֲלִיכוֹת. אֶלָּא הֲלָכוֹת. אָמַר רַבִּי אֶלְעָזָר אָמַר רַבִּי חֲנִינָא תַּלְמִידֵי חֲכָמִים מַרְבִּים שָׁלוֹם בָּעוֹלָם. שֶׁנֶּאֱמַר וְכָל־בָּנַיִךְ לִמּוּדֵי יְהֹוָה וְרַב שְׁלוֹם בָּנָיִךְ: אַל־תִּקְרֵי בָּנָיִךְ אֶלָּא בּוֹנָיִךְ: יְהִי־שָׁלוֹם בְּחֵילֵךְ שַׁלְוָה בְּאַרְמְנוֹתָיִךְ: לְמַעַן אַחַי וְרֵעָי אֲדַבְּרָה־נָּא שָׁלוֹם בָּךְ: לְמַעַן בֵּית־יְהֹוָה אֱלֹהֵינוּ אֲבַקְשָׁה טוֹב לָךְ: וּרְאֵה־בָנִים לְבָנֶיךָ שָׁלוֹם עַל־יִשְׂרָאֵל: שָׁלוֹם רָב לְאֹהֲבֵי תוֹרָתֶךָ וְאֵין־לָמוֹ מִכְשׁוֹל: יְהֹוָה עֹז לְעַמּוֹ יִתֵּן יְהֹוָה | יְבָרֵךְ אֶת־עַמּוֹ בַשָּׁלוֹם:

Tana Devei Eliyahu. Kol-Hashoneh Halachot Bechol-Yom. Muvtach Lo Shehu Ven-Ha'olam Haba. Shene'emar Halichot Olam Lo. Al-Tikrei Halichot. Ella Halachot. Amar Ribi El'azar Amar Ribi Chanina Talmidei Chachamim Marbim Shalom Ba'olam. Shene'emar Vechol-Banayich Limmudei Adonai Verav Shelom Banayich. Al-Tikrei Vanayich Ella Vonayich. Yehi-Shalom Becheilech; Shalvah. Be'armenotayich. Lema'an Achai Vere'ai; Adaberah-Na Shalom Bach. Lema'an Beit-Adonai Eloheinu; Avakshah Tov Lach. Ure'eh-Vanim Levaneicha; Shalom. Al-Yisra'el. Shalom Rav Le'ohavei Toratecha; Ve'ein-Lamo Michshol. Adonai Oz Le'ammo Yiten; Adonai Yevarech Et-'Ammo Vashalom.

It was taught in the school of Eliyahu, that every one who studies the legal interpretations of the Torah daily, is sure to enjoy the bliss of the world to come; as it is said "his ways are everlasting." Do not read *halichot* "ways," but *halachot* "legal interpretations." Rabbi Elazar in the name of Rabbi Chanina says, that the wise men promote peace in the world: as it is said: "And all your children study the Torah of Hashem: and great will be the peace of your children." Read not *banayich*, "your children," but *bonayich*, "your builders." "May there be peace within your walls, and prosperity within your palaces. For the sake of my brothers and friends, I will now speak of peace within you. For the sake of the House of Hashem our God, I will seek your good. And you will see your children's children, and peace in Yisrael. Those who love Your Torah have abundant peace and none will obstruct them. Hashem will give strength to His people; Hashem will bless His people with peace."

Kaddish Al-Yisrael

Kaddish is only recited in a minyan (ten men). אמן denotes when the congregation responds "Amen" together out loud. According to the Shulchan Arukh, the congregation says "Yehei Shemeh Rabba" to "Yitbarach" out loud together without interruption, and also that one should respond "Amen" after "Yitbarach." (SA, OC 55,56) This is not the common custom today. Though many are accustomed to answering according to their own custom, it is advised to respond in the custom of the one reciting to avoid not fragmenting into smaller groups. ("Lo Titgodedu" - BT, Yevamot 13b / SA, OC 493, Rema / MT, Avodah Zara 12:15)

יִתְגַּדַּל וְיִתְקַדַּשׁ שְׁמֵהּ רַבָּא. אמן בְּעָלְמָא דִּי בְרָא. כִּרְעוּתֵהּ. וְיַמְלִיךְ
מַלְכוּתֵהּ. וְיַצְמַח פֻּרְקָנֵהּ. וִיקָרֵב מְשִׁיחֵהּ. אמן בְּחַיֵּיכוֹן וּבְיוֹמֵיכוֹן
וּבְחַיֵּי דְכָל בֵּית יִשְׂרָאֵל. בַּעֲגָלָא וּבִזְמַן קָרִיב. וְאִמְרוּ אָמֵן. אמן יְהֵא
שְׁמֵיהּ רַבָּא מְבָרַךְ לְעָלַם וּלְעָלְמֵי עָלְמַיָּא יִתְבָּרַךְ. וְיִשְׁתַּבַּח.
וְיִתְפָּאַר. וְיִתְרוֹמַם. וְיִתְנַשֵּׂא. וְיִתְהַדָּר. וְיִתְעַלֶּה. וְיִתְהַלָּל שְׁמֵהּ
דְּקֻדְשָׁא. בְּרִיךְ הוּא. אמן לְעֵלָּא מִן כָּל בִּרְכָתָא שִׁירָתָא. תֻּשְׁבְּחָתָא
וְנֶחֱמָתָא. דַּאֲמִירָן בְּעָלְמָא. וְאִמְרוּ אָמֵן. אמן

Yitgadal Veyitkadash Shemeh Rabba. Amen Be'alema Di Vera.
Kir'uteh. Veyamlich Malchuteh. Veyatzmach Purkaneh. Vikarev
Meshicheh. Amen Bechayeichon Uveyomeichon Uvechayei Dechal-
Beit Yisra'el. Ba'agala Uvizman Kariv. Ve'imru Amen. Amen Yehei
Shemeh Rabba Mevarach Le'alam Ule'alemei Alemaya Yitbarach.
Veyishtabach. Veyitpa'ar. Veyitromam. Veyitnasse. Veyit'hadar.
Veyit'aleh. Veyit'hallal Shemeh Dekudsha. Berich Hu. Amen Le'ella
Min Kol Birchata Shirata. Tushbechata Venechemata. Da'amiran
Be'alema. Ve'imru Amen. Amen

Glorified and sanctified be God's great name Amen throughout the
world which He has created according to His will. May He establish
His kingdom, hastening His salvation and the coming of His
Messiah, Amen, in your lifetime and during your days, and within the
life of the entire House of Yisra'el, speedily and soon; and say, Amen.
Amen May His great name be blessed forever and to all eternity.
Blessed and praised, glorified and exalted, extolled and honored,
adored and lauded is the name of the Holy One, blessed is He, Amen
Beyond all the blessings and hymns, praises and consolations that
are ever spoken in the world; and say, Amen. Amen

עַל יִשְׂרָאֵל וְעַל רַבָּנָן. וְעַל תַּלְמִידֵיהוֹן וְעַל כָּל תַּלְמִידֵי תַלְמִידֵיהוֹן.
דְּעָסְקִין בְּאוֹרַיְתָא קַדִּשְׁתָּא. דִּי בְאַתְרָא הָדֵין וְדִי בְכָל אֲתַר וַאֲתַר.
יְהֵא לָנָא וּלְהוֹן וּלְכוֹן חִנָּא וְחִסְדָּא וְרַחֲמֵי. מִן קֳדָם מָארֵי שְׁמַיָּא
וְאַרְעָא וְאִמְרוּ אָמֵן. אמן

Al Yisra'el Ve'al Rabbanan. Ve'al Talmideihon Ve'al Kol Talmidei
Talmideihon. De'asekin Be'orayta Kaddishta. Di Ve'atra Hadein Vedi

Vechal Atar Va'atar. Yehei Lana Ulehon Ulechon China Vechisda Verachamei. Min Kodam Marei Shemaya Ve'ar'a Ve'imru Amen. ^{Amen}

May we of Yisrael together with our rabbis, their disciples and pupils, and all who engage in the study of holy Torah here and everywhere, find gracious favor and mercy from their Father Who is in heaven; and say, Amen. ^{Amen}

יְהֵא שְׁלָמָא רַבָּא מִן שְׁמַיָּא. חַיִּים וְשָׂבָע וִישׁוּעָה וְנֶחָמָה. וְשֵׁיזָבָא וּרְפוּאָה וּגְאוּלָה וּסְלִיחָה וְכַפָּרָה וְרֶוַח וְהַצָּלָה לָנוּ וּלְכָל עַמּוֹ יִשְׂרָאֵל. וְאִמְרוּ אָמֵן. אמן

Yehei Shelama Rabba Min Shemaya. Chayim Vesava Vishu'ah Venechamah. Vesheizava Urefu'ah Uge'ulah Uselichah Vechapparah Verevach Vehatzalah Lanu Ulechol Ammo Yisra'el. Ve'imru Amen. ^{Amen}

May abundant peace descend from heaven, with life and plenty, salvation, solace, liberation, healing and redemption, and forgiveness and atonement, enlargement and freedom, for us and all of God's people Yisrael; and say, Amen. ^{Amen}

> One bows and takes three steps backwards, while still bowing. After three steps, while still bowing and before erecting, while saying, "Oseh Shalom Bimromav", turn one's face to the left, "Hu [Berachamav] Ya'aseh Shalom Aleinu", turn one's face to the right; then bow forward like a servant leaving his master. (SA, OC 123:1)

עוֹשֶׂה שָׁלוֹם בִּמְרוֹמָיו. הוּא בְּרַחֲמָיו יַעֲשֶׂה שָׁלוֹם עָלֵינוּ. וְעַל כָּל־עַמּוֹ יִשְׂרָאֵל. וְאִמְרוּ אָמֵן:

Oseh Shalom Bimromav. Hu Berachamav Ya'aseh Shalom Aleinu. Ve'al Kol-'Ammo Yisra'el. Ve'imru Amen.

Creator of peace in His high places, may He in His mercy create peace for us and for all Yisrael, and say Amen.

Continue with the Barechu through Adon Olam.

Barechu

Barechu / Call to Prayer is only said with 10 men (minyan).

The Chazan says:

בָּרְכוּ אֶת יְהֹוָה הַמְבֹרָךְ:

Barechu Et Adonai Hamevorach.

Bless Hashem, the blessed One.

The kahal / congregation answers:

בָּרוּךְ יְהֹוָה הַמְבֹרָךְ לְעוֹלָם וָעֶד:

Baruch Adonai Hamevorach Le'olam Va'ed.

Blessed is Hashem Who is blessed for all eternity.

The Chazan says:

בָּרוּךְ יְהֹוָה הַמְבֹרָךְ לְעוֹלָם וָעֶד:

Baruch Adonai Hamevorach Le'olam Va'ed.

Blessed is Hashem Who is blessed for all eternity.

Aleinu

[*] denotes pausing and then bowing when saying "Va'anachnu Mistachavim". Some take Tefillin off after Aleinu.

Aleinu Leshabei'ach La'adon	עָלֵינוּ לְשַׁבֵּחַ לַאֲדוֹן
Hakol. Latet Gedullah Leyotzer	הַכֹּל. לָתֵת גְּדֻלָּה לְיוֹצֵר
Bereshit. Shelo Asanu Kegoyei	בְּרֵאשִׁית. שֶׁלֹּא עָשָׂנוּ כְּגוֹיֵי
Ha'aratzot. Velo Samanu	הָאֲרָצוֹת. וְלֹא שָׂמָנוּ
Kemishpechot Ha'adamah. Shelo	כְּמִשְׁפְּחוֹת הָאֲדָמָה. שֶׁלֹּא
Sam Chelkenu Kahem	שָׂם חֶלְקֵנוּ כָּהֶם
Vegoraleinu Kechal-Hamonam.	וְגוֹרָלֵנוּ כְּכָל־הֲמוֹנָם.
Shehem Mishtachavim Lahevel	שֶׁהֵם מִשְׁתַּחֲוִים לְהֶבֶל
Varik. Umitpallelim El-'El Lo	וָרִיק. וּמִתְפַּלְלִים אֶל־אֵל לֹא

Yoshia. *Va'anachnu	יוֹשִׁיעַ. *וַאֲנַחְנוּ
Mishtachavim Lifnei Melech	מִשְׁתַּחֲוִים לִפְנֵי מֶלֶךְ
Malchei Hamelachim Hakadosh	מַלְכֵי הַמְּלָכִים הַקָּדוֹשׁ
Baruch Hu. Shehu Noteh	בָּרוּךְ הוּא. שֶׁהוּא נוֹטֶה
Shamayim Veyosed Aretz.	שָׁמַיִם וְיוֹסֵד אָרֶץ.
Umoshav Yekaro Bashamayim	וּמוֹשַׁב יְקָרוֹ בַּשָּׁמַיִם
Mima'al. Ushechinat Uzo	מִמַּעַל. וּשְׁכִינַת עֻזּוֹ
Begavehei Meromim. Hu	בְּגָבְהֵי מְרוֹמִים. הוּא
Eloheinu. Ve'ein Od Acher. Emet	אֱלֹהֵינוּ. וְאֵין עוֹד אַחֵר. אֱמֶת
Malkeinu Ve'efes Zulato.	מַלְכֵּנוּ וְאֶפֶס זוּלָתוֹ.
Kakatuv Batorah. Veyada'ta	כַּכָּתוּב בַּתּוֹרָה. וְיָדַעְתָּ
Hayom. Vahasheivota El-	הַיּוֹם. וַהֲשֵׁבֹתָ אֶל־
Levavecha Ki Adonai Hu	לְבָבֶךָ כִּי יְהֹוָה הוּא
Ha'elohim. Bashamayim	הָאֱלֹהִים בַּשָּׁמַיִם
Mima'al. Ve'al-Ha'aretz	מִמַּעַל וְעַל־הָאָרֶץ
Mitachat; Ein Od.	מִתָּחַת אֵין עוֹד:

It is our obligation us to praise the Lord of all. To render greatness to the Former of creation. For He has not made us like the nations of the lands, nor set us to be like the families of the earth. Who has not given our portion like theirs and our lot like their masses that bow down to vanity and emptiness, "And pray to a god that does not save." *'But we bow before the supreme King of kings, the Holy One, blessed is He. Who stretches out the heavens and laid the foundations of the earth and His glorious seat is in the heavens above, and the presence of His might in the most exalted of heights. He is our God, there is no other. In truth our King, there is no one except Him. As it is written in the Torah: "This day know and lay it to your heart, that Hashem, He is God in the heavens above and on the earth beneath. There is no one else."

Al Ken Nekaveh Lach. Adonai	עַל כֵּן נְקַוֶּה לְּךָ. יְהֹוָה
Eloheinu. Lir'ot Meheirah	אֱלֹהֵינוּ. לִרְאוֹת מְהֵרָה
Betif'eret Uzach. Leha'avir	בְּתִפְאֶרֶת עֻזֶּךָ. לְהַעֲבִיר
Gilulim Min Ha'aretz.	גִּלּוּלִים מִן הָאָרֶץ.
Veha'elilim Karot Yikaretun.	וְהָאֱלִילִים כָּרוֹת יִכָּרֵתוּן.
Letakken Olam Bemalchut	לְתַקֵּן עוֹלָם בְּמַלְכוּת
Shaddai. Vechol-Benei Vasar	שַׁדַּי. וְכָל-בְּנֵי בָשָׂר
Yikre'u Vishmecha. Lehafnot	יִקְרְאוּ בִשְׁמֶךָ. לְהַפְנוֹת
Eleicha Kol-Rish'ei Aretz. Yakiru	אֵלֶיךָ כָּל-רִשְׁעֵי אָרֶץ. יַכִּירוּ
Veyede'u Kol-Yoshevei Tevel. Ki	וְיֵדְעוּ כָּל-יוֹשְׁבֵי תֵבֵל. כִּי
Lecha Tichra Kol-Berech. Tishava	לְךָ תִכְרַע כָּל-בֶּרֶךְ. תִּשָּׁבַע
Kol-Lashon. Lefaneicha. Adonai	כָּל-לָשׁוֹן. לְפָנֶיךָ. יְהֹוָה
Eloheinu Yichre'u Veyipolu.	אֱלֹהֵינוּ יִכְרְעוּ וְיִפֹּלוּ.
Velichvod Shimcha Yekar Yitenu.	וְלִכְבוֹד שִׁמְךָ יְקָר יִתֵּנוּ.
Vikabelu Chulam Et-'Ol	וִיקַבְּלוּ כֻלָּם אֶת-עֹל
Malchutecha. Vetimloch Aleihem	מַלְכוּתֶךָ. וְתִמְלוֹךְ עֲלֵיהֶם
Meheirah Le'olam Va'ed. Ki	מְהֵרָה לְעוֹלָם וָעֶד. כִּי
Hamalchut Shelecha Hi.	הַמַּלְכוּת שֶׁלְּךָ הִיא.
Ule'olemei Ad Timloch	וּלְעוֹלְמֵי עַד תִּמְלוֹךְ
Bechavod. Kakatuv Betoratach.	בְּכָבוֹד. כַּכָּתוּב בְּתוֹרָתֶךָ:
Adonai Yimloch Le'olam Va'ed.	יְהֹוָה ׀ יִמְלֹךְ לְעֹלָם וָעֶד:
Vene'emar. Vehayah Adonai	וְנֶאֱמַר. וְהָיָה יְהֹוָה
Lemelech Al-Kol-Ha'aretz;	לְמֶלֶךְ עַל־כָּל־הָאָרֶץ
Bayom Hahu. Yihyeh Adonai	בַּיּוֹם הַהוּא יִהְיֶה יְהֹוָה
Echad Ushemo Echad.	אֶחָד וּשְׁמוֹ אֶחָד:

Therefore we hope in You, Hashem our God, soon to see Your glorious might, to remove idols from the earth and the non-gods will be wholly cut down, to rectify the world with the kingdom of El Shaddai, and all children of flesh will call on Your name and all of the earth's wicked will turn to You. All that dwell on earth will understand and know that to You every knee must bend, and every tongue swear. Before You, Hashem our God, may all kneel and fall and give honor to Your glorious name. And they will all accept the yoke of Your kingdom. And may You speedily rule over them forever. For dominion is Yours, and forever You will reign in glory, as is written in Your Torah, "Hashem will reign forever and ever." For, it is said, "Hashem will be King over all the earth; and on that day Hashem will be One and His name One."

Uvetoratecha Adonai Eloheinu	וּבְתוֹרָתְךָ יְהֹוָה אֱלֹהֵינוּ
Katuv Lemor. Shema Yisra'el;	כָּתוּב לֵאמֹר. שְׁמַע יִשְׂרָאֵל
Adonai Eloheinu Adonai Echad.	יְהֹוָה אֱלֹהֵינוּ יְהֹוָה אֶחָד:

And in Your Torah, Hashem our God, it is written: Hear O Yisrael Hashem our God, Hashem is One.

Some say:

Psalms 92

מִזְמוֹר שִׁיר לְיוֹם הַשַּׁבָּת: טוֹב לְהֹדוֹת לַיהוָה וּלְזַמֵּר לְשִׁמְךָ עֶלְיוֹן: לְהַגִּיד בַּבֹּקֶר חַסְדֶּךָ וֶאֱמוּנָתְךָ בַּלֵּילוֹת: עֲלֵי־עָשׂוֹר וַעֲלֵי־נָבֶל עֲלֵי הִגָּיוֹן בְּכִנּוֹר: כִּי שִׂמַּחְתַּנִי יְהוָה בְּפָעֳלֶךָ בְּמַעֲשֵׂי יָדֶיךָ אֲרַנֵּן: מַה־גָּדְלוּ מַעֲשֶׂיךָ יְהוָה מְאֹד עָמְקוּ מַחְשְׁבֹתֶיךָ: אִישׁ־בַּעַר לֹא יֵדָע וּכְסִיל לֹא־יָבִין אֶת־זֹאת: בִּפְרֹחַ רְשָׁעִים | כְּמוֹ עֵשֶׂב וַיָּצִיצוּ כָּל־פֹּעֲלֵי אָוֶן לְהִשָּׁמְדָם עֲדֵי־עַד: וְאַתָּה מָרוֹם לְעֹלָם יְהוָה: כִּי הִנֵּה אֹיְבֶיךָ | יְהוָה כִּי־הִנֵּה אֹיְבֶיךָ יֹאבֵדוּ יִתְפָּרְדוּ כָּל־פֹּעֲלֵי אָוֶן: וַתָּרֶם כִּרְאֵים קַרְנִי בַּלֹּתִי בְּשֶׁמֶן רַעֲנָן: וַתַּבֵּט עֵינִי בְּשׁוּרָי בַּקָּמִים עָלַי מְרֵעִים תִּשְׁמַעְנָה אָזְנָי: צַדִּיק כַּתָּמָר יִפְרָח כְּאֶרֶז בַּלְּבָנוֹן יִשְׂגֶּה: שְׁתוּלִים בְּבֵית יְהוָה בְּחַצְרוֹת

אֱלֹהֵינוּ יַפְרִיחוּ: עוֹד יְנוּבוּן בְּשֵׂיבָה דְּשֵׁנִים וְרַעֲנַנִּים יִהְיוּ: לְהַגִּיד כִּי־יָשָׁר יְהוָה צוּרִי וְלֹא־(עַוְלָתָה) עלתה בּוֹ:

Mizmor Shir. Leyom Hashabbat. Tov. Lehodot L'Adonai Ulezamer Leshimcha Elyon. Lehagid Baboker Chasdecha; Ve'emunatecha. Balleilot. Alei-'Asor Va'alei-Navel; Alei Higayon Bechinor. Ki Simachtani Adonai Befo'olecha; Bema'asei Yadeicha Aranen. Mah-Gadelu Ma'aseicha Adonai Me'od. Ameku Machshevoteicha. Ish-Ba'ar Lo Yeda'; Uchesil. Lo-Yavin Et-Zot. Bifroach Resha'im Kemo Esev. Vayatzitzu Chol-Po'alei Aven; Lehishamedam Adei-'Ad. Ve'attah Marom. Le'olam Adonai Ki Hineh Oyeveicha Adonai Ki-Hineh Oyeveicha Yovedu; Yitparedu. Chol-Po'alei Aven. Vatarem Kir'eim Karni; Baloti. Beshemen Ra'anan. Vatabet Eini. Beshurai Bakamim Alai Mere'im. Tishma'nah Oznai. Tzaddik Kattamar Yifrach; Ke'erez Ballevanon Yisgeh. Shetulim Beveit Adonai Bechatzrot Eloheinu Yafrichu. Od Yenuvun Beseivah; Deshenim Vera'ananim Yihyu. Lehagid Ki-Yashar Adonai Tzuri. Velo-Avlatah Bo.

A Psalm, a Song. For the Shabbat day. It is a good thing to give thanks to Hashem, And to sing praises to Your name, Most High; To declare Your lovingkindness in the morning, And Your faithfulness in the night seasons, With an instrument of ten strings, and with the psaltery; With a solemn sound on the harp. For You, Hashem, have made me glad through Your work; I will rejoice in the works of Your hands. How great are Your works, Hashem. Your thoughts are very deep. A brutish man doesn't know, Neither does a fool understand this. When the wicked spring up as the grass, And when all the workers of iniquity flourish; It is that they may be destroyed forever. But You, Hashem, are on high forever. For, behold, Your enemies, Hashem, For, behold, Your enemies will perish: All the workers of iniquity will be scattered. But my horn You have exalted like the horn of the wild-ox; I am anointed with rich oil. My eye has also gazed on them that lie in wait for me, My ears have heard my desire of the evil-doers that rise up against me. The righteous will flourish like the palm-tree; He will grow like a cedar in Levanon. Planted in the House of Hashem, They will flourish in the courts of our God. They will still bring forth fruit in old age; They will be full of sap and richness; To declare that Hashem is upright, My Rock, in Whom there is no unrighteousness.

Conclude with the Adon Olam.

Adon Olam

אֲדוֹן עוֹלָם אֲשֶׁר מָלַךְ. בְּטֶרֶם כָּל יְצִיר נִבְרָא:

Adon Olam Asher Malach. Beterem Kol Yetzir Nivra.

Lord over all, Who has ruled forever. Even before first Creation's
wondrous form was framed.

לְעֵת נַעֲשָׂה בְחֶפְצוֹ כֹּל. אֲזַי מֶלֶךְ שְׁמוֹ נִקְרָא:

Le'et Na'asah Vecheftzo Chol. Azai Melech Shemo Nikra.

When by His Divine will all things were made; Then, Almighty King,
was His name proclaimed.

וְאַחֲרֵי כִּכְלוֹת הַכֹּל. לְבַדּוֹ יִמְלֹךְ נוֹרָא:

Ve'acharei Kichlot Hakol. Levado Yimloch Nora.

And after all will cease. In awesome greatness, He alone will reign.

וְהוּא הָיָה וְהוּא הֹוֶה. וְהוּא יִהְיֶה בְּתִפְאָרָה:

Vehu Hayah Vehu Hoveh. Vehu Yihyeh Betif'arah.

Who was, Who is, and Who will forever be, in splendor.

וְהוּא אֶחָד וְאֵין שֵׁנִי. לְהַמְשִׁילוֹ וּלְהַחְבִּירָה:

Vehu Echad Ve'ein Sheni. Lehamshilo Ulehachbirah.

He is One, unequalled, and beyond compare. Without division or
associate.

בְּלִי רֵאשִׁית בְּלִי תַכְלִית. וְלוֹ הָעֹז וְהַמִּשְׂרָה:

Beli Reshit Beli Tachlit. Velo Ha'ohz Vehamisrah.

He is without beginning, without end; He reigns in power.

בְּלִי עֵרֶךְ בְּלִי דִמְיוֹן. בְּלִי שִׁנּוּי וּתְמוּרָה:

Beli Erech Beli Dimyon. Beli Shinui Ut'murah.

To him, no like or equal can ever be; Without change or substitute,
He remains.

בְּלִי חִבּוּר בְּלִי פֵּרוּד. גְּדוֹל כֹּחַ וּגְבוּרָה:

Beli Chibur Beli Pirud. Gedol Koach Ug'vurah.

Without divisibleness or attachment. He supremely reigns in highest might and power.

וְהוּא אֵלִי וְחַי גּוֹאֲלִי. וְצוּר חֶבְלִי בְּיוֹם צָרָה:

Vehu Eli Vechai Go'ali. Vetzur Chevli B'yom Tzarah.

And He is my God and my living Redeemer. My sheltering Rock on the day of misfortune.

וְהוּא נִסִי וּמָנוּס. מְנָת כּוֹסִי בְּיוֹם אֶקְרָא:

Vehu Nissi Umanusi. Menat Kosi B'yom Ekra.

My standard, refuge, portion, true. The Portion of my cup on the day that I call.

וְהוּא רוֹפֵא וְהוּא מַרְפֵּא. וְהוּא צוֹפֶה וְהוּא עֶזְרָה:

Vehu Rofei Vehu Marpe. Vehu Tzofeh Vehu Ezrah.

He is a Healer and a cure; He is a Watchman and a Helper.

בְּיָדוֹ אַפְקִיד רוּחִי. בְּעֵת אִישַׁן וְאָעִירָה:

Beyado Afkid Ruchi. Be'et Ishan Ve'a'irah.

Into His hands I consign my spirit. While wrapped in sleep. and I will awake again.

וְעִם רוּחִי גְּוִיָּתִי. אֲדֹנָי לִי וְלֹא אִירָא:

Ve'im Ruchi Geviyati. Adonai Li Velo Ira.

And with my soul, my body I resign; Hashem is with me, and I will not fear .

בְּמִקְדָּשׁוֹ תָּגֵל נַפְשִׁי. מְשִׁיחֵנוּ יִשְׁלַח מְהֵרָה:

Bemikdasho Tagel Nafshi. Meshicheinu Yishlach Meheirah.

In His Temple, my soul will delight; may He send our Messiah soon.

וְאָז נָשִׁיר בְּבֵית קָדְשִׁי. אָמֵן אָמֵן שֵׁם הַנּוֹרָא:

Ve'az Nashir Beveit Kodshi. Amen. Amen. Shem Hanora.

And then we'll sing in my Holy House. Amen, Amen, to the Awe-inspring Name.

ADDITIONS FOR SHACHARIT

The Thirteen Principles of Faith
As set by Rabbi Moses ben Maimon, i.e. The Ramban

א אֲנִי מַאֲמִין בֶּאֱמוּנָה שְׁלֵמָה. שֶׁהַבּוֹרֵא יִתְבָּרַךְ שְׁמוֹ הוּא בּוֹרֵא וּמַנְהִיג לְכָל הַבְּרוּאִים וְהוּא לְבַדּוֹ עָשָׂה וְעוֹשֶׂה וְיַעֲשֶׂה לְכָל הַמַּעֲשִׂים:

א Ani Ma'amin Be'emunah Shelemah. ShehaBorei Yitbarach Shemo Hu Borei Umanhig Lechol Haberu'im Vehu Levado Asah Ve'oseh Veya'aseh Lechol Hama'asim:

1. I believe, with a perfect faith, that the Creator, blessed is His name, is the Creator and Guide of everything that has been created, and that He alone has made, does make, and will make all things.

ב אֲנִי מַאֲמִין בֶּאֱמוּנָה שְׁלֵמָה. שֶׁהַבּוֹרֵא יִתְבָּרַךְ שְׁמוֹ הוּא יָחִיד וְאֵין יְחִידוּת כָּמוֹהוּ בְּשׁוּם פָּנִים וְהוּא לְבַדּוֹ אֱלֹהֵינוּ. הָיָה הֹוֶה וְיִהְיֶה:

ב Ani Ma'amin Be'emunah Shelemah. Shehaborei Yitbarach Shemo Hu Yachid Ve'ein Yechidut Kamohu Beshum Panim Vehu Levado Eloheinu. Hayah Hoveh Veyihyeh:

2. I believe, with a perfect faith, that the Creator, blessed is His name, is a Unity, and that there is no unity in any manner whatsoever like Him, and that He alone is our God, Who was, is, and ever will be.

ג אֲנִי מַאֲמִין בֶּאֱמוּנָה שְׁלֵמָה שֶׁהַבּוֹרֵא יִתְבָּרַךְ שְׁמוֹ אֵינוֹ גוּף וְלֹא יַשִּׂיגוּהוּ מַשִּׂיגֵי הַגּוּף וְאֵין לוֹ שׁוּם דִּמְיוֹן כְּלָל:

ג Ani Ma'amin Be'emunah Shelemah Shehaborei Yitbarach Shemo Eino Guf Velo Yassiguhu Massigei Haguf Ve'ein Lo Shum Dimyon Kelal:

3. I believe, with a perfect faith, that the Creator, blessed is His name, is incorporeal, and that He is free from all the accidents of matter, and that He has no form whatsoever.

ד אֲנִי מַאֲמִין בֶּאֱמוּנָה שְׁלֵמָה שֶׁהַבּוֹרֵא יִתְבָּרַךְ שְׁמוֹ הוּא רִאשׁוֹן וְהוּא אַחֲרוֹן:

ד Ani Ma'amin Be'emunah Shelemah Shehaborei Yitbarach Shemo Hu Rishon Vehu Acharon:

4. I believe, with a perfect faith, that the Creator, blessed is His name, is the first and the last.

ה אֲנִי מַאֲמִין בֶּאֱמוּנָה שְׁלֵמָה שֶׁהַבּוֹרֵא יִתְבָּרַךְ שְׁמוֹ לוֹ לְבַדּוֹ רָאוּי לְהִתְפַּלֵל. וְאֵין רָאוּי לְהִתְפַּלֵל לְזוּלָתוֹ:

ה Ani Ma'amin Be'emunah Shelemah Shehaborei Yitbarach Shemo Lo Levado Ra'ui Lehitpallel. Ve'ein Ra'ui Lehitpallel Lezulato:

5. I believe, with a perfect faith, that to the Creator, blessed is His name, and to Him alone, it is right to pray, and that it is not right to pray to any being besides Him.

ו אֲנִי מַאֲמִין בֶּאֱמוּנָה שְׁלֵמָה שֶׁכָּל דִּבְרֵי נְבִיאִים אֱמֶת:

ו Ani Ma'amin Be'emunah Shelemah Shekol Divrei Nevi'im Emet:

6. I believe, with a perfect faith, that all the words of the prophets are true.

ז אֲנִי מַאֲמִין בֶּאֱמוּנָה שְׁלֵמָה שֶׁנְּבוּאַת מֹשֶׁה רַבֵּנוּ עָלָיו הַשָּׁלוֹם הָיְתָה אֲמִתִּית וְשֶׁהוּא הָיָה אָב לַנְּבִיאִים לַקּוֹדְמִים לְפָנָיו וְלַבָּאִים אַחֲרָיו:

ז Ani Ma'amin Be'emunah Shelemah Shenevu'at Mosheh Rabeinu Alav Hashalom Hayetah Amitit Veshehu Hayah Av Lanevi'im Lakodemim Lefanav Velaba'im Acharav:

7. I believe, with a perfect faith, that the prophecy of Moshe our teacher, peace be to him, was true, and that he was the chief of the prophets who preceded and of those that succeeded him.

ח אֲנִי מַאֲמִין בֶּאֱמוּנָה שְׁלֵמָה שֶׁכָּל הַתּוֹרָה הַמְצוּיָּה עַתָּה בְּיָדֵינוּ הִיא הַנְּתוּנָה לְמֹשֶׁה רַבֵּנוּ עָלָיו הַשָּׁלוֹם:

ח Ani Ma'amin Be'emunah Shelemah Shekol Hatorah Hametzuyah Attah Veyadeinu Hi Hanetunah Lemosheh Rabeinu Alav Hashalom:

8. I believe, with a perfect faith, that the whole Torah, as now in our possession, is the very same that was given to Moshe our teacher, peace be to him.

ט אֲנִי מַאֲמִין בֶּאֱמוּנָה שְׁלֵמָה שֶׁזֹּאת הַתּוֹרָה לֹא תְהֵא מֻחְלֶפֶת וְלֹא תְהֵא תּוֹרָה אַחֶרֶת מֵאֵת הַבּוֹרֵא יִתְבָּרַךְ שְׁמוֹ:

ט Ani Ma'amin Be'emunah Shelemah Shezot Hatorah Lo Tehei Muchlefet Velo Tehei Torah Acheret Me'et HaBorei Yitbarach Shemo:

9. I believe, with a perfect faith, that this Torah will not be changed, and that there will never be any other Torah given by the Creator, blessed is His name.

י אֲנִי מַאֲמִין בֶּאֱמוּנָה שְׁלֵמָה. שֶׁהַבּוֹרֵא יִתְבָּרַךְ שְׁמוֹ יוֹדֵעַ כָּל מַעֲשֵׂה בְּנֵי אָדָם וְכָל-מַחְשְׁבֹתָם שֶׁנֶּאֱמַר הַיֹּצֵר יַחַד לִבָּם הַמֵּבִין אֶל-כָּל-מַעֲשֵׂיהֶם:

׳ Ani Ma'amin Be'emunah Shelemah. Shehaborei Yitbarach Shemo Yodea' Kol Ma'aseh Venei Adam Vechol-Machshevotam Shene'emar Hayotzer Yachad Libam Hamevin El-Kol-Ma'aseihem:

10. I believe, with a perfect faith, that the Creator, blessed is His name, knows every deed of mankind, and all their thoughts; as it is said, "He that fashions the hearts of them all, understands all of their deeds."

יא אֲנִי מַאֲמִין בֶּאֱמוּנָה שְׁלֵמָה שֶׁהַבּוֹרֵא יִתְבָּרַךְ שְׁמוֹ גּוֹמֵל טוֹב לְשׁוֹמְרֵי מִצְוֹתָיו וּמַעֲנִישׁ לְעוֹבְרֵי מִצְוֹתָיו:

יא Ani Ma'amin Be'emunah Shelemah Shehaborei Yitbarach Shemo Gomel Tov Leshomerei Mitzvotav Uma'anish Le'overei Mitzvotav:

11. I believe, with a perfect faith, that the Creator, blessed is His name, rewards those that keep His commandments, and punishes those that transgress them.

יב אֲנִי מַאֲמִין בֶּאֱמוּנָה שְׁלֵמָה. בְּבִיאַת הַמָּשִׁיחַ. וְאַף עַל פִּי שֶׁיִּתְמַהְמֵהַּ. עִם כָּל-זֶה אֲחַכֶּה-לוֹ בְּכָל יוֹם שֶׁיָּבֹא:

יב Ani Ma'amin Be'emunah Shelemah. Bevi'at Hamashiach. Ve'af Al Pi Sheyitmahmeah. Im Kol-Zeh Achakeh-Lo Bechol Yom Sheyavo:

12. I believe, with a perfect faith, in the coming of the Messiah, and, though he delays, I will daily wait his coming.

יג אֲנִי מַאֲמִין בֶּאֱמוּנָה שְׁלֵמָה. שֶׁתִּהְיֶה תְּחִיַּת הַמֵּתִים בְּעֵת שֶׁיַּעֲלֶה רָצוֹן מֵאֵת הַבּוֹרֵא יִתְבָּרַךְ שְׁמוֹ וְיִתְעַלֶּה זִכְרוֹ לָעַד וּלְנֵצַח נְצָחִים:

יג Ani Ma'amin Be'emunah Shelemah. Shetihyeh Techiyat Hameitim Be'et Sheya'aleh Ratzon Me'et Haborei Yitbarach Shemo Veyit'aleh Zichro La'ad Ulenetzach Netzachim:

13. I believe, with a perfect faith, that there will be the resurrection of the dead at the time when it will please the Creator, blessed is His name, and exalted is His memorial forever and ever.

The Ten Remembrances

לְשֵׁם יְחוּד קוּדְשָׁא בְּרִיךְ הוּא וּשְׁכִינְתֵּיהּ. הֲרֵי אֲנִי מְקַיֵּם מִצְוַת
עֶשֶׂר זְכִירוֹת. שֶׁחַיָּיב כָּל אָדָם לִזְכּוֹר בְּכָל יוֹם. וְאֵלּוּ הֵם:
א יְצִיאַת מִצְרַיִם. ב וְהַשַּׁבָּת. ג וְהַמָּן. ד וּמַעֲשֵׂה עֲמָלֵק. ה וּמַעֲמַד
הַר סִינַי. ו וּמַה שֶׁהִקְצִיפוּ אֲבוֹתֵינוּ לְהַקָּדוֹשׁ בָּרוּךְ הוּא בַּמִּדְבָּר
וּבִפְרָט בָּעֵגֶל. ז וּמַה שֶׁיָּעֲצוּ בָלָק וּבִלְעָם לַעֲשׂוֹת לַאֲבוֹתֵינוּ לְמַעַן
דַּעַת צִדְקוֹת יְהֹוָה. ח וּמַעֲשֵׂה מִרְיָם הַנְּבִיאָה. ט וּמִצְוַת וְזָכַרְתָּ אֶת
יְהֹוָה אֱלֹהֶיךָ כִּי הוּא הַנֹּתֵן לְךָ כֹּחַ לַעֲשׂוֹת חָיִל. י וּזְכִירַת יְרוּשָׁלַיִם
תִּבָּנֶה וְתִכּוֹנֵן בִּמְהֵרָה בְיָמֵינוּ אָמֵן:

Leshem Yichud Kudesha Berich Hu Ushechinteih. Harei Ani
Mekayem Mitzvat Eser Zechirot. Shechayaiv Kol Adam Lizkor
Bechol Yom. Ve'elu Hem:
א Yetzi'at Mitzrayim. ב Vehashabbat. ג Vehaman. ד Uma'aseh Amalek.
ה Uma'amad Har Sinai. ו Umah Shehiktzifu Avoteinu Lehakadosh
Baruch Hu Bamidbar Uvifrat Ba'egel. ז Umah Sheya'atzu Valak
Uvil'am La'asot La'avoteinu Lema'an Da'at Tzidkot Adonai. ח
Uma'aseh Miryam Hanevi'ah. ט Umitzvat Vezacharta Et Adonai
Eloheicha Ki Hu Hanotein Lecha Koach La'asot Chayil. י Uzechirat
Yerushalayim Tibaneh Vetikonen Bimheirah Veyameinu Amen:

For the sake of the unification of the Holy One, blessed is He, with
His Divine Presence. Behold, I fulfill the mitzvah of the Ten
Remembrances. It is obligated for all men to remember every day.
And they are:

¹ The going out from Egypt. ² And the Shabbat. ³ And the Manna. ⁴
And what Amalek did. ⁵ The Giving and receiving of the Torah at
Har Sinai. ⁶ And that our fathers infuriated the Holy One, Blessed is
He, in the wilderness, especially with the Golden Calf. ⁷ And what
Balak and Bilam sought to do to our fathers so that we would know
the righteousness of Hashem. ⁸ The incident concerning Miryam
the prophetess. ⁹ The mitzvah of You will remember Hashem, your
God. For it is He Who gives you power to get wealth. ¹⁰ And the

remembrance of Yerushalayim, may it be rebuilt and established soon and in our days, Amen.

When leaving the synagogue say:

יְהֹוָה נְחֵנִי בְצִדְקָתֶךָ לְמַעַן שׁוֹרְרָי הַיְשַׁר לְפָנַי דַּרְכֶּךָ: וְיַעֲקֹב הָלַךְ לְדַרְכּוֹ וַיִּפְגְּעוּ־בוֹ מַלְאֲכֵי אֱלֹהִים: וַיֹּאמֶר יַעֲקֹב כַּאֲשֶׁר רָאָם מַחֲנֵה אֱלֹהִים זֶה וַיִּקְרָא שֵׁם־הַמָּקוֹם הַהוּא מַחֲנָיִם:

Adonai Necheni Vetzidkatecha Lema'an Shorerai Chayshar Lifnei Deracheicha: Veya'akov Chalach Ledarko Vayifge'u Vo Mal'achei Elohim: Vayomer Ya'akov Ka'asher Ra'am Machaneh Elohim Zeh Vayikra Shem Hamakom Hahu Machanayim.

Hashem, lead me in Your righteousness because of those that lie in wait for me; Make Your way straight before my face. And Yaakov went on his way, and the angels of God met him. And Yaakov said when he saw them: 'This is God's camp.' And he called the name of that place Machanayim. **(Ps. 5:8, Gen. 32:2-3)**

Se'udat Yom Shabbat / The Shabbat Day Meal

Some have the custom (BTH', BT Shabbat 33b:8) of circling, to his right (when he is facing, conter-clockwise) the table with 2 myrtle branches, holding them together, making the appropriate blessing for sweet smelling trees (borei atzei vesamim), smelling them and saying:

זָכוֹר וְשָׁמוֹר בְּדִיבּוּר אֶחָד נֶאֱמְרוּ:

Remember and keep [the Shabbat] were said in one utterance.

And also say:

רֵיחַ נִיחוֹחַ אִשֶּׁה לַיהוה:

A soothing fragrance to Hashem.

Mishnah, Tractate Kelim, 1:6-9

עֶשֶׂר קְדָשׁוֹת הֵן. אֶרֶץ יִשְׂרָאֵל מְקֻדֶּשֶׁת מִכָּל הָאֲרָצוֹת. וּמַה הִיא קְדֻשָּׁתָהּ. שֶׁמְּבִיאִים מִמֶּנָּה הָעֹמֶר וְהַבִּכּוּרִים וּשְׁתֵּי הַלֶּחֶם. מַה שֶּׁאֵין מְבִיאִין כֵּן מִכָּל הָאֲרָצוֹת: עֲיָרוֹת הַמֻּקָּפוֹת חוֹמָה מְקֻדָּשׁוֹת מִמֶּנָּה. שֶׁמְּשַׁלְּחִין מִתּוֹכָן אֶת הַמְּצוֹרָעִים. וּמְסַבְּבִין לְתוֹכָן מֵת עַד שֶׁיִּרְצוּ. יָצָא. אֵין מַחֲזִירִין אוֹתוֹ: לִפְנִים מִן הַחוֹמָה מְקֻדָּשׁ מֵהֶם. שֶׁאוֹכְלִים שָׁם קָדָשִׁים קַלִּים וּמַעֲשֵׂר שֵׁנִי. הַר הַבַּיִת מְקֻדָּשׁ מִמֶּנּוּ. שֶׁאֵין זָבִים וְזָבוֹת נִדּוֹת וְיוֹלְדוֹת נִכְנָסִים לְשָׁם. הַחֵיל מְקֻדָּשׁ מִמֶּנּוּ. שֶׁאֵין גּוֹיִם וּטְמֵאֵי מֵתִים נִכְנָסִים לְשָׁם. עֶזְרַת נָשִׁים מְקֻדֶּשֶׁת מִמֶּנּוּ. שֶׁאֵין טְבוּל יוֹם נִכְנָס לְשָׁם. וְאֵין חַיָּבִים עָלֶיהָ חַטָּאת. עֶזְרַת יִשְׂרָאֵל מְקֻדֶּשֶׁת מִמֶּנָּה. שֶׁאֵין מְחֻסַּר כִּפּוּרִים נִכְנָס לְשָׁם. וְחַיָּבִין עָלֶיהָ חַטָּאת. עֶזְרַת הַכֹּהֲנִים מְקֻדֶּשֶׁת מִמֶּנָּה. שֶׁאֵין יִשְׂרָאֵלִים נִכְנָסִים לְשָׁם אֶלָּא בִּשְׁעַת צָרְכֵיהֶם. לִסְמִיכָה לִשְׁחִיטָה וְלִתְנוּפָה: בֵּין הָאוּלָם וְלַמִּזְבֵּחַ מְקֻדָּשׁ מִמֶּנָּה. שֶׁאֵין בַּעֲלֵי מוּמִין וּפְרוּעֵי רֹאשׁ נִכְנָסִים לְשָׁם. הַהֵיכָל מְקֻדָּשׁ מִמֶּנּוּ. שֶׁאֵין נִכְנָס לְשָׁם שֶׁלֹּא רְחוּץ יָדַיִם וְרַגְלַיִם. קֹדֶשׁ הַקֳּדָשִׁים מְקֻדָּשׁ מֵהֶם. שֶׁאֵין נִכְנָס לְשָׁם אֶלָּא כֹהֵן גָּדוֹל בְּיוֹם הַכִּפּוּרִים בִּשְׁעַת הָעֲבוֹדָה. אָמַר רַבִּי יוֹסֵי. בַּחֲמִשָּׁה דְבָרִים בֵּין הָאוּלָם וְלַמִּזְבֵּחַ שָׁוֶה לַהֵיכָל. שֶׁאֵין בַּעֲלֵי מוּמִין. וּפְרוּעֵי רֹאשׁ. וּשְׁתוּיֵי יַיִן. וְשֶׁלֹּא רְחוּץ יָדַיִם וְרַגְלַיִם נִכְנָסִין לְשָׁם. וּפוֹרְשִׁין מִבֵּין הָאוּלָם וְלַמִּזְבֵּחַ בִּשְׁעַת הַקְטָרָה:

Eser Kedushot Hen. Eretz Yisra'el Mekudeshet Mikol Ha'aratzot. Umah Hi Kedushatah. Shemevi'im Mimenah Ha'omer Vehabikkurim Ushetei Hallechem. Mah She'ein Mevi'in Ken Mikol Ha'aratzot: Ayarot Hamukafot Chomah Mekudashot Mimenah. Shemeshalechin Mitochan Et Hametzora'im. Umesabevin Letochan Met Ad Sheyirtzu. Yatza. Ein Machazirin Oto: Lifnim Min Hachomah

Mekudash Mehem. She'ochelim Sham Kadashim Kallim Uma'aser Sheni. Har Habayit Mekudash Mimenu. She'ein Zavim Vezavot Niddot Veyoledot Nichnasim Lesham. Hacheil Mekudash Mimenu. She'ein Goyim Uteme'ei Meitim Nichnasim Lesham. Azarat Nashim Mekudeshet Mimenu. She'ein Tevul Yom Nichnas Lesham. Ve'ein Chayavim Aleiha Chatat. Azarat Yisra'el Mekudeshet Mimenah. She'ein Mechussar Kippurim Nichnas Lesham. Vechayavin Aleiha Chatat. Azarat Hakohanim Mekudeshet Mimenah. She'ein Yisra'elim Nichnasim Lesham Ella Vish'at Tzarecheihem. Lismichah Lishchitah Velitnufah: Bein Ha'ulam Velamizbe'ach Mekudash Mimenah. She'ein Ba'alei Mumin Uferu'ei Rosh Nichnasim Lesham. Haheichal Mekudash Mimenu. She'ein Nichnas Lesham Shelo Rechutz Yadayim Veraglayim. Kodesh Hakodashim Mekudash Mehem. She'ein Nichnas Lesham Ella Chohen Gadol Beyom Hakippurim Bish'at Ha'avodah. Amar Ribi Yosei. Bachamishah Devarim Bein Ha'ulam Velamizbe'ach Shaveh Laheichal. She'ein Ba'alei Mumin. Uferu'ei Rosh. Ushetuyei Yayin. Veshelo Rechutz Yadayim Veraglayim Nichnasin Lesham. Uforeshin Mibein Ha'ulam Velamizbe'ach Bish'at Haktarah:

There are ten degrees of holiness. The land of Yisrael is holier than any other land. Where in it lies its holiness? In that from it they may bring the Omer, the Firstfruits, and the Two Loaves, which may not be brought from any other land. The walled cities are still more holy, in that they must send out the metzora'im (lepers) from their midst, and they may carry around a corpse there in it wherever they want, but once it is taken out, they may not bring it back. Within the wall (of Yerushalayim) it is more holy than these, because there (only) they may eat the lesser holy things and the Second Tithe. The Temple Mount is still more holy, for no man or woman that has a flux, no menstruant, and no woman after childbirth may enter there in it. The Rampart is still more holy, for no gentile and none that have contracted uncleanness from a corpse may enter there in it. The Court of the Women is still more holy, for no one that had immersed himself the selfsame day [because of uncleanness] may enter there into it, yet no one would then by it become liable for a Sin-offering. The Court of the Yisraelim is still more holy, for no one whose atonement is incomplete may enter there in it, and they would there by it become liable to a Sin-offering. The Court of the Kohanim is still more holy, for Yisraelim may not enter there in except only when they must perform the laying on of hands, slaughtering, and waving. Between the Porch and the Altar is still more holy, for no one that has a blemish or whose hair is unloosed may enter there. The Sanctuary is still more holy, for no one may enter there into it with unwashed hands and feet. The Holy of Holies is still more holy, for no one may enter there in except only the Kohen Gadol (High Priest) on Yom Kippur at the time of the [Temple] service. R. Yosei said: In five things is the space between the Porch and the Altar equal to the Sanctuary: for those that have a blemish may not enter there, or that have drunken wine, or that have unwashed hands and feet, and men must keep far from between the Porch and the Altar at the time of burning the incense.

THE SHABBAT DAY MEAL

422

Mishnah, Tractate Kelim, 2:1

כְּלֵי עֵץ. וּכְלֵי עוֹר. וּכְלֵי עֶצֶם. וּכְלֵי זְכוּכִית. פְּשׁוּטֵיהֶן טְהוֹרִים. וּמְקַבְּלֵיהֶן טְמֵאִים. נִשְׁבָּרוּ. טָהֲרוּ. חָזַר וְעָשָׂה מֵהֶם כֵּלִים. מְקַבְּלִין טֻמְאָה מִכָּאן וּלְהַבָּא. כְּלֵי חֶרֶס וּכְלֵי נֶתֶר. טֻמְאָתָן שָׁוָה. מִטַּמְּאִין וּמְטַמְּאִין בַּאֲוִיר. וּמִטַּמְּאִין מֵאֲחוֹרֵיהֶן. וְאֵינָן מְטַמְּאִין מִגַּבֵּיהֶן. וּשְׁבִירָתָן הִיא טַהֲרָתָן:

Kelei Etz. Uchelei Or. Uchelei Etzem. Uchelei Zechuchit. Peshuteihen Tehorim. Umekabeleihen Teme'im. Nishbaru. Taharu. Chazar Ve'asah Mehem Kelim. Mekabelin Tum'ah Mikkan Ulehabba. Kelei Cheres Uchelei Neter. Tum'atan Shavah. Mittame'in Umetamme'in Ba'avir. Umitame'in Me'achoreihen. Ve'einan Mittame'in Migabeihen. Usheviratan Hi Taharatan:

Utensils of wood, leather, bone, or glass that are flat are not susceptible to uncleanness. If they form a receptacle they are susceptible. After they are broken they become clean, but if again utensils are made of them they once more become susceptible. Earthenware vessels and vessels of alum-crystal are alike in what concerns uncleanness: they contract uncleanness and convey uncleanness through their air-space, and they contract uncleanness [when overturned] from what touches their [concave] bottoms but not from what touches their outer sides; and when they are broken they become insusceptible to uncleanness.

It is customary for some to say Zohar Parashat Yitro (2:88b; 4-10).

ביומא דשבתא. בסעודתא תנינא. כתיב אז תתענג על יהוה. על יהוה ודai. דההיא שעתא אתגליא עתיקא קדישא. וכלהו עלמין בחדותא. ושלימו וחדותא דעתיקא עבדינן. וסעודתא דילה היא ודאי. בסעודתא תליתאה דשבתא. כתיב והאכלתיך נחלת יעקב אביך. דא היא סעודתא דזעיר אנפין. דהוי בשלימותא. וכלהו שתא יומין. מההוא שלימו מתברכן. ובעי בר נש למחדי בסעודתה. ולאשלמא אלין סעודתי. דאנון סעודתי מהימנותא שלימתא. דזרעא קדישא דישראל. די מהימנותא עלאה. דהא דילהון היא. ולא דעמין עובדי עבודה זרה. ובגיני כך אמר. ביני ובין בני ישראל. תא חזי. בסעודתי אלין. אשתמודעון ישראל. דאנון בני מלכא. דאנון מהיכלא דמלכא. דאנון בני מהימנותא. ומאן דפגים חד סעודתא מניהו. אחזי פגימותא לעלא. ואחזי גרמה דלאו מבני מלכא עלאה הוא. דלאו מבני היכלא דמלכא הוא דלאו מזרעא קדישא דישראל הוא. ויהבין עלה חומרא דתלת מלין. דינא דגיהנם וכו'. ותא חזי. בכלהו שאר זמנין וחגין. בעי בר נש לחדי. ולמחדי למסכני. ואי הוא חדי בלחודוי. ולא יהיב

למסכני. עונשה סגי. דהא בלחודוי חדי. ולא יהיב חדו לאחרא. עלה כתיב
וזריתי פרש על פניכם פרש חגיכם. ואי איהו בשבתא חדי. אף על גב דלא
יהיב לאחרא. לא יהבין עלה עונשא. כשאר זמנין וחגין. דכתיב פרש
חגיכם. פרש חגיכם קאמר. ולא פרש שבתכם. וכתיב חדשיכם ומועדיכם
שנאה נפשי. ואלו שבת לא קאמר. ובגיני כך כתיב. ביני ובין בני ישראל.
ומשום דכל מהימנותא אשתכח בשבתא. יהבין ליה לבר נש נשמתא
אחרא. נשמתא עלאה. נשמתא דכל שלימו בה. כדוגמא דעלמא דאתי.
ובגיני כך אקרי שבת. מהו שבת. שמא דקדשא בריך הוא. שמא דאיהו
שלים מכל סטרוי. אמר רבי יוסי. ודאי כך הוא. וי ליה לבר נש. דלא
אשלים חדותא דמלכא קדישא. ומאן חדותא דילה. אלין תלת סעודתי
מהימנותא. סעודתי דאברהם יצחק ויעקב כלילן בהו. וכלהו חידו על חידו
מהימנותא שלימותא. מכל סטרוי. תאנא. בהדין יומא מתעטרן אבהן. וכל
בנין ינקין. מה דלאו הכי בכל שאר חגין וזמנין. בהדין יומא. חיבא דגיהנם
ניחין. בהדין יומא. כל דינין אתכפין. ולא מתערין בעלמא. בהדין יומא
אוריתא מתעטרא בעטרין שלמין. בהדין יומא. חדותא ותפנוקא אשתמע.
במאתן וחמשין עלמין. ברוך יהוה לעולם אמן ואמן:

אַתְקִינוּ אַתְקִינוּ סְעוּדָתָא דִמְהֵימְנוּתָא שְׁלֵימָתָא חֶדְוָתָא דְמַלְכָּא קַדִּישָׁא:
אַתְקִינוּ סְעוּדָתָא דְמַלְכָּא. דָּא הִיא סְעוּדָתָא דְעַתִּיקָא קַדִּישָׁא: (וַחֲקַל תַּפּוּחִין
קַדִּישִׁין וּזְעֵיר אַנְפִּין אַתְיָן לְסַעֲדָא בַּהֲדֵיהּ):

Atkinu Atkinu Se'udata Dimheimnuta Sheleimata Chedvata Demalka Kaddisha:
Atkinu Se'udata Demalka. Da Hi Se'udata De'atika Kaddisha: (Uze'eir Anpin Vachakal
Tappuchin Kaddishin Atyan Lesa'ada Bahadeih:)

Asader L'Seudatah
Yitzhak Luria

אֲסַדֵּר לִסְעוּדָתָא. בְּצַפְרָא דְשַׁבַּתָא. וְאַזְמִין בַּהּ הַשְׁתָּא. עַתִּיקָא קַדִּישָׁא:

Asader Lis'udata. Betzafra Deshabbata. Ve'azmin Bah Hashta. Atika Kaddisha:

נְהוֹרֵיהּ יִשְׁרֵי בָהּ. בְּקִדּוּשָׁא רַבָּא. וּבְחַמְרָא טָבָא. דְּבֵהּ תֶּחְדֵּי נַפְשָׁא:

Nehoreih Yishrei Vah. Bekiddusha Rabba. Uvechamra Tava. Deveh Techdei Nafsha:

יִשַׁדֵּר לָן שׁוּפְרֵהּ. וְנֶחֱזֵי בִיקָרֵיהּ. וְיַחֲזֵי לָן סִתְרֵהּ. דְּאִתְאֲמַר בִּלְחִישָׁא:

Yeshader Lan Shufereh. Venechezei Bikareih. Veyachazei Lan Sitreh. De'it'amar
Bilchisha:

יְגַלֶּה לָן טַעֲמֵי. דְּבִתְרֵיסַר נַהֲמֵי. דְּאִנּוּן אָת בִּישְׁמֵיהּ. כְּפִילָא וּקְלִישָׁא:

Yegaleh Lan Ta'amei. Devitreisar Nahamei. De'inun At Bishmeih. Kefila Ukelisha:

צְרוֹרָא דִלְעֵלָּא. דְּבֵיהּ חַיֵּי כֹלָּא. דְּיִתְרַבֵּי חֵילָא. וְתִסַּק עַד רֵישָׁא:

Tzerora Dil'ella. Deveih Chayei Cholla. Deyitrabei Cheila. Vetissak Ad Reisha:

חֲדוּ חַצְדֵּי חַקְלָא. בְּדִבּוּר וּבְקָלָא. וּמַלִּילוּ מִלָּה. כְּמִתִיקָא וּכְדוּבְשָׁא:

Chadu Chatzdei Chakla. Bedibur Uvekala. Umallilu Millah. Kimtika Ucheduvesha:

קֳדָם רִבּוֹן עָלְמִין. בְּמִלִּין סְתִימִין. תְּגַלּוּן פִּתְגָמִין. וְתֵימְרוּן חִדּוּשָׁא:

Kodam Ribon Alemin. Bemillin Setimin. Tegalun Pitgamin. Veteimrun Chiddusha:

לְעַטֵּר פָּתוֹרָא. בְּרָזָא יַקִּירָא. עֲמִיקָא וּטְמִירָא. וְלָאו מִלְּתָא אַוְשָׁא:

Le'atter Patora. Beraza Yakkira. Amika Utemira. Velav Milleta Avsha:

וְאִלֵּין מִלַּיָּא. יְהוֹן בִּרְקִיעַיָּא. וְתַמָּן מַאן שַׁרְיָא. הֲלָא הַהוּא שִׁמְשָׁא:

Ve'ilein Millaya. Yehon Birki'aya. Vetamman Man Sharya. Hala Hahu Shimsha:

רְבוּ יַתִּיר יִסְגֵּי. לְעֵלָּא מִן דַּרְגֵּהּ. וְיִסַּב בַּת זוּגֵהּ. דְּהֲוַת פְּרִישָׁא:

Revu Yatir Yisgei. Le'ella Min Dargeh. Veyissav Bat Zugeh. Dehavat Perisha:

Zohar 2:207b:10

קידושא דיומא. הא אוקמוה בורא פרי הגפן. ולא יתיר. דהא יומא קאים
לקדשא ליה. מה דלית הכי בליליא. דאנן צריכין לקדשא ליה. בהני מלין.
כמה דאוקימנא. ולא אתקדש האי ליליא. אלא בעמא קדישא לתתא. כד
שריא עליהו ההוא רוחא עלאה. ואנן בעינן לקדשא ליה ברעותא דלבא.
ולכונא דעתא להאי. ויומא איהו קא מקדשא ליה. וישראל מתקדשין
בצלותין ובעותין. ומתקדשין בקדשתיה. דהאי יומא. זכאין ישראל. עמא
קדישא. דאחסינו יומא דא. אחסנת ירותא לעלמין. ברוך יהוה לעולם אמן
ואמן:

Daytime Kiddush - The Shabbat Day Meal

Psalms 23

Mizmor Ledavid; Adonai Ro'i.	מִזְמוֹר לְדָוִד יְהוָה רֹעִי
Lo Echsar. Bin'ot Deshei	לֹא אֶחְסָר: בִּנְאוֹת דֶּשֶׁא
Yarbitzeni; Al Mei Menuchot	יַרְבִּיצֵנִי עַל מֵי מְנֻחוֹת
Yenahaleini. Nafshi Yeshovev;	יְנַהֲלֵנִי: נַפְשִׁי יְשׁוֹבֵב
Yancheini Vema'gelei-Tzedek.	יַנְחֵנִי בְמַעְגְּלֵי־צֶדֶק
Lema'an Shemo. Gam Ki-'Elech	לְמַעַן שְׁמוֹ: גַּם כִּי־אֵלֵךְ
Begei Tzalmavet Lo-'Ira Ra'.	בְּגֵיא צַלְמָוֶת לֹא־אִירָא רָע
Ki-'Attah Immadi; Shivtecha	כִּי־אַתָּה עִמָּדִי שִׁבְטְךָ
Umish'antecha. Hemah	וּמִשְׁעַנְתֶּךָ הֵמָּה
Yenachamuni. Ta'aroch Lefanai	יְנַחֲמֻנִי: תַּעֲרֹךְ לְפָנַי |
Shulchan. Neged Tzorerai;	שֻׁלְחָן נֶגֶד צֹרְרָי
Dishanta Vashemen Roshi. Kosi	דִּשַּׁנְתָּ בַשֶּׁמֶן רֹאשִׁי כּוֹסִי
Revayah Ach Tov Vachesed	רְוָיָה אַךְ | טוֹב וָחֶסֶד
Yirdefuni Chol-Yemei Chayai;	יִרְדְּפוּנִי כָּל־יְמֵי חַיָּי
Veshavti Beveit-Adonai Le'orech	וְשַׁבְתִּי בְּבֵית־יְהוָה לְאֹרֶךְ
Yamim.	יָמִים:

A Psalm of David. Hashem is my Shepherd; I will not want. He makes me to lie down in green pastures; He leads me beside the still waters. He restores my soul; He guides me in straight paths for His name's sake. Even though I walk through the valley of the shadow of death, I will fear no evil, for You are with me; Your rod and Your staff, they comfort me. You prepare a table before me in the presence of my enemies; You have anointed my head with oil; my cup runs over. Surely goodness and mercy will follow me all the days of my life; And I will dwell in the House of Hashem forever.

אִם־תָּשִׁיב אִם־תָּשִׁיב מִשַּׁבָּת רַגְלֶךָ עֲשׂוֹת חֲפָצֶךָ בְּיוֹם קָדְשִׁי
וְקָרָאתָ לַשַּׁבָּת עֹנֶג לִקְדוֹשׁ יְהֹוָה מְכֻבָּד וְכִבַּדְתּוֹ מֵעֲשׂוֹת דְּרָכֶיךָ
מִמְּצוֹא חֶפְצְךָ וְדַבֵּר דָּבָר: אָז תִּתְעַנַּג עַל־יְהֹוָה וְהִרְכַּבְתִּיךָ
עַל־בָּמֳותֵי אָרֶץ וְהַאֲכַלְתִּיךָ נַחֲלַת יַעֲקֹב אָבִיךָ כִּי פִּי יְהֹוָה דִּבֵּר:

Im Tashiv Im Tashiv Mishabbat Raglecha Asot Chafatzecha Beyom
Kodshi Vekarata Lashabbat Oneg Likdosh Adonai Mechubbad
Vechibadto Me'asot Deracheicha Mimetzo Cheftzecha Vedaber
Davar. Az Tit'anag Al Adonai Vehirkavticha Al Bomovtei Aretz
Veha'achalticha Nachalat Ya'akov Avicha Ki Pi Adonai Diber.

If you turn away your foot because of the Shabbat, From pursuing your business on My holy day; And call the Shabbat a delight, And the holy of Hashem honorable; And will honor it, not doing your usual ways, or pursuing your business, or speaking of it; Then you will delight yourself in Hashem, And I will make you to ride on the high places of the earth, And I will feed you with the heritage of Yaakov your father; For the mouth of Hashem has spoken it. (Isaiah 58:13-14)

וְשָׁמְרוּ בְנֵי־יִשְׂרָאֵל אֶת־הַשַּׁבָּת לַעֲשׂוֹת אֶת־הַשַּׁבָּת לְדֹרֹתָם בְּרִית
עוֹלָם: בֵּינִי וּבֵין בְּנֵי יִשְׂרָאֵל אוֹת הִוא לְעֹלָם כִּי־שֵׁשֶׁת יָמִים עָשָׂה
יְהֹוָה אֶת־הַשָּׁמַיִם וְאֶת־הָאָרֶץ וּבַיּוֹם הַשְּׁבִיעִי שָׁבַת וַיִּנָּפַשׁ:

Veshameru Venei-Yisra'el Et-Hashabbat; La'asot Et-Ha Shabbat
Ledorotam Berit Olam. Beini. Uvein Benei Yisra'el. Ot Hi Le'olam;
Ki-Sheshet Yamim. Asah Adonai Et-Hashamayim Ve'et-Ha'aretz.
Uvayom Hashevi'i. Shavat Vayinafash.

The children of Yisrael will keep the Shabbat, to observe the Shabbat throughout their generations, for a perpetual covenant. It is a sign between Me and the children of Yisrael forever; for in six days Hashem made heaven and earth, and on the seventh day He ceased from His work and rested. (Ex. 31:16-17)

Some say:

זָכוֹר אֶת־יוֹם הַשַּׁבָּת לְקַדְּשׁוֹ שֵׁשֶׁת יָמִים תַּעֲבֹד וְעָשִׂיתָ כָּל־מְלַאכְתֶּךָ וְיוֹם
הַשְּׁבִיעִי שַׁבָּת לַיהוָה אֱלֹהֶיךָ לֹא־תַעֲשֶׂה כָל־מְלָאכָה אַתָּה וּבִנְךָ־וּבִתֶּךָ עַבְדְּךָ
וַאֲמָתְךָ וּבְהֶמְתֶּךָ וְגֵרְךָ אֲשֶׁר בִּשְׁעָרֶיךָ כִּי שֵׁשֶׁת־יָמִים עָשָׂה יְהוָה אֶת־הַשָּׁמַיִם
וְאֶת־הָאָרֶץ אֶת־הַיָּם וְאֶת־כָּל־אֲשֶׁר־בָּם וַיָּנַח בַּיּוֹם הַשְּׁבִיעִי:

Zachor Et Yom Hashabbat Lekadesho Sheshet Yamim Ta'avod Ve'asita Kol
Melachtecha Veyom Hashevi'i Shabbat L'Adonai Eloheicha Lo Ta'aseh Chol
Melachah Attah Uvincha Uvitecha Avdecha Va'amatecha Uvehemtecha Vegercha
Asher Bish'areicha Ki Sheshet Yamim Asah Adonai Et Hashamayim Ve'et Ha'aretz Et
Hayam Ve'et Kol Asher Bam Vayanach Bayom Hashevi'i:

Remember the Shabbat day, to keep it holy. Six days you will labor, and do all of
your work; but the seventh day is a Shabbat to Hashem your God, in it you will not
do any manner of work, you, or your son, or your daughter, or your male-servant,
or your maid-servant, or your cattle, or your stranger that is within your gates; for
in six days Hashem made heaven and earth, the sea, and all that in them is, and
rested on the seventh day; (Ex. 20:8-11)

עַל־כֵּן בֵּרַךְ יְהוָה אֶת־יוֹם הַשַּׁבָּת וַיְקַדְּשֵׁהוּ:

Al Ken Berakh Adonai Et-Yom Hashabbat Vaikadshehu.

So Hashem blessed the Shabbat day, and sanctified it. (Ex. 20:11)

The one making the blessing says:

Savri Maranan!   סַבְרִי מָרָנָן:

Gentlemen, with your attention!

And answer:

Le'chayim!   לְחַיִּים:

To life!

Baruch Attah Adonai Eloheinu   בָּרוּךְ אַתָּה יְהוָה. אֱלֹהֵינוּ

Melech Ha'olam Borei Pri   מֶלֶךְ הָעוֹלָם. בּוֹרֵא פְּרִי

Hagefen.   הַגָּפֶן:

Blessed are You, Hashem our God, King of the universe, Who
creates the fruit of the vine.

> At this point, sit and drink.

Netilat Yadayim / Washing of Hands

Wash hands before the meal, according to the ritual (laws are listed in Shabbat Shacharit):

Baruch Attah Adonai Eloheinu Melech

Ha'olam Asher Kideshanu Bemitzvotav

Vetzivanu Al Netilat Yadayim.

בָּרוּךְ אַתָּה יְהֹוָה אֱלֹהֵינוּ מֶלֶךְ
הָעוֹלָם. אֲשֶׁר קִדְּשָׁנוּ בְּמִצְוֹתָיו
וְצִוָּנוּ עַל נְטִילַת יָדָיִם:

Blessed are You, Hashem our God, King of the universe, Who has sanctified us with His commandments, and commanded us concerning the washing of hands.

> Some authorities hold that one does not need to careful of pausing between Netilat and Hamotzi, and there are those who say that one needs to be careful. It is good to be careful. (Rema': The amount of time equivalent to walking 22 cubits [55 ft.] is considered a pause [Tosefot Perek Elu Ne'emarim]). (SA, OC 166) REMA: It is a meritorious act to place salt on the table before breaking the bread.)

He will hold two loaves of bread in his two hands, and the giver will bless. And it is customary to say these verses before the blessing:

עֵינֵי־כֹל אֵלֶיךָ יְשַׂבֵּרוּ וְאַתָּה נוֹתֵן־לָהֶם אֶת־אָכְלָם בְּעִתּוֹ: פּוֹתֵחַ אֶת־יָדֶךָ
וּמַשְׂבִּיעַ לְכָל־חַי רָצוֹן:

Einei-Chol Eleicha Yesaberu; Ve'attah Noten-Lahem Et-'Ochlam Be'ito. Potei'ach Et-Yadecha; Umasbia Lechol-Chai Ratzon.

The eyes of all wait for You, And You give them their food in due season. You open Your hand, and satisfy every living thing with favor. (Ps. 145:15-16)

Baruch Attah Adonai Eloheinu

Melech Ha'olam Hamotzi

Lechem Min Ha'aretz.

בָּרוּךְ אַתָּה יְהֹוָה אֱלֹהֵינוּ
מֶלֶךְ הָעוֹלָם. הַמּוֹצִיא
לֶחֶם מִן הָאָרֶץ:

Blessed are You, Hashem our God, King of the universe Who brings forth bread from the earth.

Take a slice of bread and dip it in salt.

Before the meal some say:

לְשֵׁם יְחוּד קוּדְשָׁא בְּרִיךְ הוּא וּשְׁכִינְתֵּיה. בִּדְחִילוּ וּרְחִימוּ. וּרְחִימוּ וּדְחִילוּ. לְיַחֲדָא שֵׁם יוֹ״ד קֵ״י בְּוָא״ו קֵ״י בְּיִחוּדָא שְׁלִים (יהוה) בְּשֵׁם כָּל יִשְׂרָאֵל. הנה אנכי בא לקיים מצות סעודה שניה שֶׁל שבת קדש המיסת לאברהם חסידא לתקן את שרשה במקום עליון. ובזכותה נצול מדינה שֶׁל גיהנם ויקיים בנו מקרא שכתוב אז תתענג על יהוה והרכבתיך על־במותי ארץ והאכלתיך נחלת יעקב אביך כי פי יהוה דבר. וִיהִי נֹעַם אֲדֹנָי אֱלֹהֵינוּ עָלֵינוּ וּמַעֲשֵׂה יָדֵינוּ כּוֹנְנָה עָלֵינוּ וּמַעֲשֵׂה יָדֵינוּ כּוֹנְנֵהוּ:

SHABBAT MINCHA / SHABBAT AFTERNOON PRAYER

Korbanot / Offerings

Mincha (Afternoon Prayer) can be recited from about 6 and a half hours (about 30 minutes past halachic noontime) until sundown. This first broad time is known as Mincha Gedolah, but ideally Mincha should be recited at Mincha Ketanah, which is about 9.5 halachic hours and completed by sundown. It is preferable to wash hands before the service. If water is available it is not necessary. If one forgot and did not pray Mincha, they should pray Arvit (Evening Prayer) twice and says Ashrei first, which is a payment for the Mincha prayer. (SA, OC 233,234 / MB) According to Chazal (Our Sages of Blessed Memory), one should take care with the Mincha prayer, because Eliyahu was answered during Mincha. (I Kings 18:36, BT' Berachot 6b). This being the busiest time of day for most people, it can be easy to be less attentive. Some also say Patach Eliyahu before this (located in Shacharit Service).

Some say:

לְשֵׁם יְחוּד קוּדְשָׁא בְּרִיךְ הוּא וּשְׁכִינְתֵּיהּ. בִּדְחִילוּ וּרְחִימוּ. וּרְחִימוּ וּדְחִילוּ. לְיַחֲדָא שֵׁם יוֹ"ד קֵ"י בְּוָא"ו קֵ"י בְּיִחוּדָא שְׁלִים (יהוה) בְּשֵׁם כָּל יִשְׂרָאֵל. הִנֵּה אֲנַחְנוּ בָּאִים לְהִתְפַּלֵּל תְּפִלַּת מִנְחָה שֶׁתִּקֵּן יִצְחָק אָבִינוּ עָלָיו הַשָּׁלוֹם. עִם כָּל הַמִּצְוֹת הַכְּלוּלוֹת בָּהּ. לְתַקֵּן אֶת שׁוּרְשָׁהּ בְּמָקוֹם עֶלְיוֹן לַעֲשׂוֹת נַחַת רוּחַ לְיוֹצְרֵנוּ וְלַעֲשׂוֹת רְצוֹן בּוֹרְאֵנוּ. וִיהִי נֹעַם אֲדֹנָי אֱלֹהֵינוּ עָלֵינוּ וּמַעֲשֵׂה יָדֵינוּ כּוֹנְנָה עָלֵינוּ וּמַעֲשֵׂה יָדֵינוּ כּוֹנְנֵהוּ:

Psalms 84

לַמְנַצֵּחַ עַל־הַגִּתִּית לִבְנֵי־קֹרַח מִזְמוֹר: מַה־יְּדִידוֹת מִשְׁכְּנוֹתֶיךָ יְהוָה צְבָאוֹת: נִכְסְפָה וְגַם־כָּלְתָה | נַפְשִׁי לְחַצְרוֹת יְהוָה לִבִּי וּבְשָׂרִי יְרַנְּנוּ אֶל אֵל־חָי: גַּם־צִפּוֹר מָצְאָה בַיִת וּדְרוֹר | קֵן לָהּ אֲשֶׁר־שָׁתָה אֶפְרֹחֶיהָ אֶת־מִזְבְּחוֹתֶיךָ יְהוָה צְבָאוֹת מַלְכִּי וֵאלֹהָי: אַשְׁרֵי יוֹשְׁבֵי בֵיתֶךָ עוֹד יְהַלְלוּךָ סֶּלָה: אַשְׁרֵי אָדָם עוֹז־לוֹ בָךְ מְסִלּוֹת בִּלְבָבָם: עֹבְרֵי | בְּעֵמֶק הַבָּכָא מַעְיָן יְשִׁיתוּהוּ גַּם־בְּרָכוֹת יַעְטֶה מוֹרֶה: יֵלְכוּ מֵחַיִל אֶל־חָיִל יֵרָאֶה אֶל־אֱלֹהִים בְּצִיּוֹן: יְהוָה אֱלֹהִים צְבָאוֹת שִׁמְעָה תְפִלָּתִי הַאֲזִינָה אֱלֹהֵי יַעֲקֹב סֶלָה: מָגִנֵּנוּ רְאֵה אֱלֹהִים וְהַבֵּט פְּנֵי מְשִׁיחֶךָ: כִּי טוֹב־יוֹם בַּחֲצֵרֶיךָ מֵאָלֶף בָּחַרְתִּי הִסְתּוֹפֵף

בְּבֵית אֱלֹהַי מִדּוּר בְּאָהֳלֵי־רֶשַׁע: כִּי שֶׁמֶשׁ | וּמָגֵן יְהֹוָה אֱלֹהִים חֵן
וְכָבוֹד יִתֵּן יְהֹוָה לֹא יִמְנַע־טוֹב לַהֹלְכִים בְּתָמִים: יְהֹוָה צְבָאוֹת
אַשְׁרֵי אָדָם בֹּטֵחַ בָּךְ:

Lamnatzeach Al-Hagitit; Livnei-Korach Mizmor. Mah-Yedidot
Mishkenoteicha. Adonai Tzeva'ot. Nichsefah Vegam-Kaletah Nafshi
Lechatzrot Adonai Libi Uvesari; Yeranenu. El El-Chai. Gam-Tzipor
Matze'ah Vayit Uderor Ken Lah Asher-Shatah Efrocheiha Et-
Mizbechoteicha Adonai Tzeva'ot; Malki. Velohai. Ashrei Yoshevei
Veitecha; Od Yehalelucha Selah. Ashrei Adam Oz-Lo Vach; Mesilot.
Bilvavam. Overei Be'emek Habacha Ma'yan Yeshituhu; Gam-
Berachot. Ya'teh Moreh. Yelechu Mechayil El-Chayil; Yera'eh El-'
Elohim Betziyon. Adonai Elohim Tzeva'ot Shim'ah Tefillati;
Ha'azinah Elohei Ya'akov Selah. Maginenu Re'eh Elohim; Vehabeit.
Penei Meshichecha. Ki Tov-Yom Bachatzereicha. Me'alef Bacharti.
Histofef Beveit Elohai; Midur. Be'oholei-Resha. Ki Shemesh Umagen
Adonai Elohim Chein Vechavod Yiten Adonai Lo Yimna'-Tov
Laholechim Betamim. Adonai Tzeva'ot; Ashrei Adam. Botei'ach
Bach.

For the Leader; upon the Gittit. A Psalm of the sons of Korach. How
lovely are Your tabernacles, Hashem of hosts. My soul yearns, even
pines for the courts of Hashem; my heart and my flesh sing for joy
to the living God. Also, the sparrow has found a house, and the
swallow a nest for herself, where she may lay her young; Your Altars,
Hashem of hosts, My King, and my God—Happy are they that dwell
in Your House, they are ever praising You. Selah. Happy is the man
whose strength is in You; in whose heart are the highways. Passing
through the valley of Baca they make it a place of springs; also, the
early rain clothes it with blessings. They go from strength to
strength, every one of them appears before God in Tziyon. Hashem
God of hosts, hear my prayer; give ear, God of Yaakov, selah.
Behold, God our Shield, and look upon the face of Your anointed.
For a day in Your courts is better than a thousand; I would rather
stand at the threshold of the House of my God, than to dwell in the
tents of wickedness. For Hashem-Elohim is a sun and a shield;
Hashem gives grace and glory; He will withhold no good thing from

those that walk uprightly. Hashem of hosts, happy is the man that trusts in You.

Tamid / Eternal Offering: Numbers 28:1-8

וַיְדַבֵּר יְהֹוָה אֶל־מֹשֶׁה לֵּאמֹר: צַו אֶת־בְּנֵי יִשְׂרָאֵל וְאָמַרְתָּ אֲלֵהֶם
אֶת־קָרְבָּנִי לַחְמִי לְאִשַּׁי רֵיחַ נִיחֹחִי תִּשְׁמְרוּ לְהַקְרִיב לִי בְּמוֹעֲדוֹ:
וְאָמַרְתָּ לָהֶם זֶה הָאִשֶּׁה אֲשֶׁר תַּקְרִיבוּ לַיהֹוָה כְּבָשִׂים בְּנֵי־שָׁנָה
תְמִימֵם שְׁנַיִם לַיּוֹם עֹלָה תָמִיד: אֶת־הַכֶּבֶשׂ אֶחָד תַּעֲשֶׂה בַבֹּקֶר
וְאֵת הַכֶּבֶשׂ הַשֵּׁנִי תַּעֲשֶׂה בֵּין הָעַרְבָּיִם: וַעֲשִׂירִית הָאֵיפָה סֹלֶת
לְמִנְחָה בְּלוּלָה בְּשֶׁמֶן כָּתִית רְבִיעִת הַהִין: עֹלַת תָּמִיד הָעֲשֻׂיָה
בְּהַר סִינַי לְרֵיחַ נִיחֹחַ אִשֶּׁה לַיהֹוָה: וְנִסְכּוֹ רְבִיעִת הַהִין לַכֶּבֶשׂ
הָאֶחָד בַּקֹּדֶשׁ הַסֵּךְ נֶסֶךְ שֵׁכָר לַיהֹוָה: וְאֵת הַכֶּבֶשׂ הַשֵּׁנִי תַּעֲשֶׂה
בֵּין הָעַרְבָּיִם כְּמִנְחַת הַבֹּקֶר וּכְנִסְכּוֹ תַּעֲשֶׂה אִשֶּׁה רֵיחַ נִיחֹחַ
לַיהֹוָה:

Vaydaber Adonai El-Mosheh Lemor. Tzav Et-Benei Yisra'el.
Ve'amarta Aleihem; Et-Korbani Lachmi Le'ishai. Reiach Nichochi.
Tishmeru Lehakriv Li Bemo'ado. Ve'amarta Lahem. Zeh Ha'isheh.
Asher Takrivu L'Adonai Kevasim Benei-Shanah Temimim Shenayim
Layom Olah Tamid. Et-Hakeves Echad Ta'aseh Vaboker; Ve'et
Hakeves Hasheni. Ta'aseh Bein Ha'arbayim. Va'asirit Ha'eifah Solet
Leminchah; Belulah Beshemen Katit Revi'it Hahin. Olat Tamid;
Ha'asuyah Behar Sinai. Lereiach Nichoach. Isheh L'Adonai Venisko
Revi'it Hahin. Lakeves Ha'echad; Bakodesh. Hassech Nesech
Shechar L'Adonai Ve'et Hakeves Hasheni. Ta'aseh Bein Ha'arbayim;
Keminchat Haboker Uchenisko Ta'aseh. Isheh Reiach Nichoach
L'Adonai.

And Hashem spoke to Moshe, saying, Command the children of Yisrael and say to them, My offering, My bread for My fire-offerings, you will observe to offer for a sweet savor to Me in its due season. Say also to them, this is the fire-offering which you will bring to Hashem: lambs of the first year without blemish, two each day as a continual burnt-offering. The one lamb you will prepare in the morning, and the other lamb you will prepare at dusk, with the tenth of an ephah of fine flour for a meal-offering, mingled with a fourth of a hin of the purest oil. This is a continual burnt-offering as it was prepared at Mount Sinai, a fire-offering for a sweet savor to Hashem. And the drink-offering with it will be a fourth of a hin for the one lamb. You will pour out the pure wine to Hashem in the holy place as a drink-offering. The second lamb you will offer at dusk, preparing it as the morning meal offering and as its drink-offering of a sweet savor to Hashem.

On Shabbat, some add:

וּבְיוֹם֙ הַשַּׁבָּ֔ת שְׁנֵֽי־כְבָשִׂ֥ים בְּנֵֽי־שָׁנָ֖ה תְּמִימִ֑ם וּשְׁנֵ֣י עֶשְׂרֹנִ֗ים סֹ֧לֶת מִנְחָ֛ה בְּלוּלָ֥ה בַשֶּׁ֖מֶן וְנִסְכּֽוֹ: עֹלַ֧ת שַׁבַּ֛ת בְּשַׁבַּתּ֖וֹ עַל־עֹלַ֥ת הַתָּמִ֖יד וְנִסְכָּֽהּ:

Uveyom Hashabbat Shenei Chevasim Benei Shanah Temimim Ushenei Esronim Solet Minchah Belulah Vashemen Venisko. Olat Shabbat Beshabbato Al Olat Hatamid Veniskah.

And on the Shabbat day two male lambs of the first year without blemish, and two tenth parts of an ephah of fine flour for a meal-offering, mingled with oil, and the drink-offering of it. This is the burnt-offering of every Shabbat, beside the continual burnt-offering, and the drink-offering of it.

On Rosh Chodesh, some add:

וּבְרָאשֵׁי֙ חָדְשֵׁיכֶ֔ם תַּקְרִ֥יבוּ עֹלָ֖ה לַֽיהוָ֑ה פָּרִ֨ים בְּנֵֽי־בָקָ֤ר שְׁנַ֙יִם֙ וְאַ֣יִל אֶחָ֔ד כְּבָשִׂ֧ים בְּנֵֽי־שָׁנָ֛ה שִׁבְעָ֖ה תְּמִימִֽם: וּשְׁלֹשָׁ֣ה עֶשְׂרֹנִ֗ים סֹ֤לֶת מִנְחָה֙ בְּלוּלָ֣ה בַשֶּׁ֔מֶן לַפָּ֖ר הָֽאֶחָ֑ד וּשְׁנֵ֣י עֶשְׂרֹנִ֗ים סֹ֤לֶת מִנְחָה֙ בְּלוּלָ֣ה בַשֶּׁ֔מֶן לָאַ֖יִל הָֽאֶחָֽד: וְעִשָּׂרֹ֣ן עִשָּׂר֗וֹן סֹ֤לֶת מִנְחָה֙ בְּלוּלָ֣ה בַשֶּׁ֔מֶן לַכֶּ֖בֶשׂ הָֽאֶחָ֑ד עֹלָה֙ רֵ֣יחַ נִיחֹ֔חַ אִשֶּׁ֖ה לַֽיהוָֽה: וְנִסְכֵּיהֶ֗ם חֲצִ֣י הַהִין֮

יִהְיֶה לַפָּר וּשְׁלִישִׁת הַהִין לָאַיִל וּרְבִיעִת הַהִין לַכֶּבֶשׂ יָיִן זֹאת עֹלַת
חֹדֶשׁ בְּחָדְשׁוֹ לְחָדְשֵׁי הַשָּׁנָה: וּשְׂעִיר עִזִּים אֶחָד לְחַטָּאת לַיהֹוָה
עַל־עֹלַת הַתָּמִיד יֵעָשֶׂה וְנִסְכּוֹ:

Uveroshei Chodsheichem Takrivu Olah L'Adonai Parim Benei Vakar
Shenayim Ve'ayil Echad Kevasim Benei Shanah Shiv'ah Temimim.
Usheloshah Esronim Solet Minchah Belulah Vashemen Lappar
Ha'echad Ushenei Esronim Solet Minchah Belulah Vashemen
La'ayil Ha'echad. Ve'issaron Issaron Solet Minchah Belulah
Vashemen Lakeves Ha'echad Olah Reiach Nichoach Isheh
L'Adonai. Veniskeihem Chatzi Hahin Yihyeh Lappar Ushelishit
Hahin La'ayil Urevi'it Hahin Lakeves Yayin Zot Olat Chodesh
Bechodsho Lechodshei Hashanah. Use'ir Izim Echad Lechatat
L'Adonai Al Olat Hatamid Ye'aseh Venisko.

And on your new moons you will present a burnt-offering to
Hashem: two young bulls, and one ram, seven male lambs of the
first year without blemish; and three-tenth parts of an ephah of fine
flour for a meal-offering, mingled with oil, for each bull; and two
tenth parts of fine flour for a meal-offering, mingled with oil, for the
one ram; and a several tenth part of fine flour mingled with oil for a
meal-offering to every lamb; for a burnt-offering of a sweet savor, an
offering made by fire to Hashem. And their drink-offerings will be
half a hin of wine for a bull, and the third part of a hin for the ram,
and the fourth part of a hin for a lamb. This is the burnt-offering of
every new moon throughout the months of the year. And one male
goat for a sin-offering to Hashem; it will be offered beside the
continual burnt-offering, and the drink-offering of it. (Num. 28:11-15)

Ketoret / Incense Offering

אַתָּה הוּא יְהֹוָה אֱלֹהֵינוּ. שֶׁהִקְטִירוּ אֲבוֹתֵינוּ לְפָנֶיךָ אֶת קְטֹרֶת
הַסַּמִּים. בִּזְמַן שֶׁבֵּית הַמִּקְדָּשׁ קַיָּם. כַּאֲשֶׁר צִוִּיתָ אוֹתָם עַל־יַד
מֹשֶׁה נְבִיאָךְ. כַּכָּתוּב בְּתוֹרָתָךְ:

Attah Hu Adonai Eloheinu. Shehiktiru Avoteinu Lefaneicha Et
Ketoret Hasamim. Bizman Shebeit Hamikdash Kayam. Ka'asher
Tzivita Otam Al-Yad Mosheh Nevi'ach. Kakatuv Betoratach:

You are Hashem, our God, before Whom our ancestors burned the
offering of incense in the days of the Beit HaMikdash. For You
commanded them through Moshe, Your prophet, as it is written in
Your Torah:

Exodus 30:34-36, 7-8

וַיֹּאמֶר יְהֹוָה אֶל־מֹשֶׁה קַח־לְךָ סַמִּים נָטָף ׀ וּשְׁחֵלֶת וְחֶלְבְּנָה
סַמִּים וּלְבֹנָה זַכָּה בַּד בְּבַד יִהְיֶה: וְעָשִׂיתָ אֹתָהּ קְטֹרֶת רֹקַח מַעֲשֵׂה
רוֹקֵחַ מְמֻלָּח טָהוֹר קֹדֶשׁ: וְשָׁחַקְתָּ מִמֶּנָּה הָדֵק וְנָתַתָּה מִמֶּנָּה לִפְנֵי
הָעֵדֻת בְּאֹהֶל מוֹעֵד אֲשֶׁר אִוָּעֵד לְךָ שָׁמָּה קֹדֶשׁ קָדָשִׁים תִּהְיֶה
לָכֶם: וְנֶאֱמַר וְהִקְטִיר עָלָיו אַהֲרֹן קְטֹרֶת סַמִּים בַּבֹּקֶר בַּבֹּקֶר
בְּהֵיטִיבוֹ אֶת־הַנֵּרֹת יַקְטִירֶנָּה: וּבְהַעֲלֹת אַהֲרֹן אֶת־הַנֵּרֹת בֵּין
הָעַרְבַּיִם יַקְטִירֶנָּה קְטֹרֶת תָּמִיד לִפְנֵי יְהֹוָה לְדֹרֹתֵיכֶם:

Vayomer Adonai El-Mosheh Kach-Lecha Samim. Nataf Ushchelet
Vechelbenah. Samim Ulevonah Zakah; Bad Bevad Yihyeh. Ve'asita
Otah Ketoret. Rokach Ma'aseh Rokeach; Memulach Tahor Kodesh.
Veshachakta Mimenah Hadek Venatatah Mimenah Lifnei Ha'eidut
Be'ohel Mo'ed. Asher Iva'eid Lecha Shamah; Kodesh Kodashim
Tihyeh Lachem. Vene'emar Vehiktir Alav Aharon Ketoret Samim;
Baboker Baboker. Beheitivo Et-Hanerot Yaktirenah. Uveha'alot
Aharon Et-Hanerot Bein Ha'arbayim Yaktirenah; Ketoret Tamid Lifnei
Adonai Ledoroteichem.

And Hashem said to Moshe, 'Take sweet spices, oil of myrrh,
onycha and galbanum, together with clear frankincense, a like
weight of each of these sweet spices. And you will make from there
incense, a perfume pure and holy, compounded by the perfumer,
salted together. And you will crush some of it very fine, and put
some of it before the Ark of testimony in the Ohel Moed where I will
meet with you; it will be most holy to you. Further it is said in the
Torah: "And Aharon will burn the incense of sweet spices on the
altar of incense, every morning when he dresses the lamps he will

burn it. And at dusk when Aharon lights the lamps he will again burn incense, a perpetual incense before Hashem throughout your generations."

Talmud: Keritot 6a

תָּנוּ רַבָּנָן: פִּטוּם הַקְּטֹרֶת כֵּיצַד: שְׁלֹשׁ מֵאוֹת וְשִׁשִּׁים וּשְׁמוֹנָה מָנִים הָיוּ בָהּ. שְׁלֹשׁ מֵאוֹת וְשִׁשִּׁים וַחֲמִשָּׁה כְּמִנְיַן יְמוֹת הַחַמָּה. מָנֶה בְּכָל־יוֹם. מַחֲצִיתוֹ בַּבֹּקֶר וּמַחֲצִיתוֹ בָּעֶרֶב. וּשְׁלֹשָׁה מָנִים יְתֵרִים. שֶׁמֵּהֶם מַכְנִיס כֹּהֵן גָּדוֹל. וְנוֹטֵל מֵהֶם מְלֹא חָפְנָיו בְּיוֹם הַכִּפּוּרִים. וּמַחֲזִירָן לְמַכְתֶּשֶׁת בְּעֶרֶב יוֹם הַכִּפּוּרִים. כְּדֵי לְקַיֵּם מִצְוַת דַּקָּה מִן הַדַּקָּה. וְאַחַד־עָשָׂר סַמָּנִים הָיוּ בָהּ. וְאֵלּוּ הֵן:

Tanu Rabbanan. Pitum Haketoret Keitzad: Shelosh Me'ot Veshishim Ushemonah Manim Hayu Vah. Shelosh Me'ot Veshishim Vachamishah Keminyan Yemot Hachamah. Maneh Bechol-Yom. Machatzito Baboker Umachatzito Ba'erev. Usheloshah Manim Yeterim. Shemehem Machnis Kohen Gadol. Venotel Mehem Melo Chafenav Beyom Hakippurim. Umachaziron Lemachteshet Be'erev Yom Hakippurim. Kedei Lekayem Mitzvat Dakah Min Hadakah. Ve'achad-'Asar Samanim Hayu Vah. Ve'elu Hen.

The rabbis have taught how the compounding of the incense was done. In measure the incense contained three hundred and sixty-eight manim, three hundred and sixty-five being one for each day of the year, the remaining three being for the high priest to take his hands full on the Yom Kippur. These last were again ground in a mortar on the eve of Yom Kippur so as to fulfill the command, "take of the finest beaten incense." and these are them:

א הַצֳּרִי ב וְהַצִּפֹּרֶן ג וְהַחֶלְבְּנָה ד וְהַלְּבוֹנָה. מִשְׁקַל שִׁבְעִים שִׁבְעִים מָנֶה. ה מוֹר. ו וּקְצִיעָה ז וְשִׁבֹּלֶת נֵרְדְּ ח וְכַרְכֹּם. מִשְׁקַל שִׁשָּׁה עָשָׂר שִׁשָּׁה עָשָׂר מָנֶה. ט קֹשְׁטְ שְׁנֵים עָשָׂר. י קִלּוּפָה שְׁלֹשָׁה. יא קִנָּמוֹן תִּשְׁעָה. בּוֹרִית־כַּרְשִׁינָה תִּשְׁעָה קַבִּין. יֵין קַפְרִיסִין סְאִין תְּלָת וְקַבִּין

תְּלָתָא. וְאִם לֹא מָצָא יֵין קַפְרִיסִין. מֵבִיא חֲמַר חִיוָר עַתִּיק. מֶלַח
סְדוֹמִית. רֹובַע. מַעֲלֶה עָשָׁן. כָּל־שֶׁהוּא. רַבִּי נָתָן הַבַּבְלִי אוֹמֵר: אַף
כִּפַּת הַיַּרְדֵּן כָּל־שֶׁהִיא. אִם נָתַן בָּהּ דְּבַשׁ פְּסָלָהּ. וְאִם חִסֵּר אַחַת
מִכָּל־סַמְמָנֶיהָ. חַיָּב מִיתָה:

Hatzori Vehatziporen Vehachelbenah Vehallevonah. Mishkal
Shiv'im Shiv'im Maneh. Mor. Uketzi'ah Veshibolet Nered
Vecharkom. Mishkal Shishah Asar Shishah Asar Maneh. Koshet
Sheneim Asar. Kilufah Sheloshah. Kinamon Tish'ah. Borit-Karshinah
Tish'ah Kabin. Yein Kafrisin Se'in Telat Vekabin Telata. Ve'im Lo
Matza Yein Kafrisin. Mevi Chamar Chivar Atik. Melach Sedomit.
Rova. Ma'aleh Ashan. Kol-Shehu. Ribi Natan Habavli Omer. Af
Kippat Hayarden Kol-Shehi. Im Natan Bah Devash Pesalah. Ve'im
Chisser Achat Mikol-Samemaneiha. Chayaiv Mitah.

The incense was compounded of eleven different spices: seventy
manim each of balm, onycha, galbanum, and frankincense; sixteen
manim each of myrrh, cassia, spikenard, and saffron; twelve manim
of costus; three manim of aromatic bark; nine manim of cinnamon;
nine kabs of lye of Carsina; three seahs and three kabs of Cyprus
wine, though if Cyprus wine could not be had, strong white wine
might be substituted for it; the fourth of a kab of salt of Sedom, and
a small quantity of a herb which caused the smoke to ascend
straight. Rabbi Nathan of Bavel said there was added also a small
quantity of kippat of the Yarden. If honey was mixed with the
incense, the incense became unfit for sacred use, while the one who
omitted any of the ingredients was deemed guilty of mortal error.

רַבָּן שִׁמְעוֹן בֶּן־גַּמְלִיאֵל אוֹמֵר: הַצֳּרִי אֵינוֹ אֶלָּא שְׂרָף. הַנּוֹטֵף מֵעֲצֵי
הַקְּטָף. בֹּרִית כַּרְשִׁינָה. לְמָה הִיא בָאָה: כְּדֵי לְשַׁפּוֹת בָּהּ
אֶת־הַצִּפֹּרֶן. כְּדֵי שֶׁתְּהֵא נָאָה. יֵין קַפְרִיסִין. לְמָה הוּא בָא: כְּדֵי
לִשְׁרוֹת בּוֹ אֶת־הַצִּפֹּרֶן כְּדֵי שֶׁתְּהֵא עַזָּה. וַהֲלֹא מֵי רַגְלַיִם יָפִין לָהּ:
אֶלָּא שֶׁאֵין מַכְנִיסִין מֵי רַגְלַיִם בַּמִּקְדָּשׁ. מִפְּנֵי הַכָּבוֹד:

Rabban Shim'on Ben-Gamli'el Omer. Hatzori Eino Ella Sheraf.
Hanotef Me'atzei Haketaf. Borit Karshinah. Lemah Hi Va'ah: Kedei
Leshapot Bah Et-Hatziporen. Kedei Shetehei Na'ah. Yein Kafrisin.
Lemah Hu Va: Kedei Lishrot Bo Et-Hatziporen Kedei Shetehei Azah.
Vahalo Mei Raglayim Yafin Lah: Ella She'ein Machnisin Mei
Raglayim Bamikdash. Mipenei Hakavod.

Rabban Shimon, son of Gamliel, said that the balm required is that
exuding from the balsam tree. Why did they use lye of Carsina? To
refine the appearance of the onycha. What was the purpose of the
Cyprus wine? To steep the onycha in it so as to harden it. Though
mei raglayim might have been adapted for that purpose, it was not
used because it was not decent to bring it into the Temple.

תַּנְיָא רִבִּי נָתָן אוֹמֵר: כְּשֶׁהוּא שׁוֹחֵק. אוֹמֵר: הָדֵק הֵיטֵב. הֵיטֵב
הָדֵק. מִפְּנֵי שֶׁהַקּוֹל יָפֶה לַבְּשָׂמִים. פִּטְמָהּ לַחֲצָאִין. כְּשֵׁרָה.
לְשָׁלִישׁ וּלְרָבִיעַ. לֹא שָׁמַעְנוּ. אָמַר רִבִּי יְהוּדָה: זֶה הַכְּלָל. אִם
כְּמִדָּתָהּ. כְּשֵׁרָה לַחֲצָאִין. וְאִם חִסֵּר אַחַת מִכָּל־סַמְמָנֶיהָ. חַיָּב
מִיתָה:

Tanya Ribi Natan Omer. Keshehu Shochek. Omer. Hadek Heitev.
Heitev Hadek. Mipenei Shehakol Yafeh Labesamim. Pittemah
Lachatza'in. Kesherah. Leshalish Uleravia'. Lo Shama'nu. Amar Ribi
Yehudah. Zeh Hakelal. Im Kemidatah. Kesherah Lachatza'in. Ve'im
Chisser Achat Mikol-Samemaneiha. Chayaiv Mitah.

It is taught: Rabbi Natan said that when the priest ground the
incense the one superintending would say, "Grind it very fine, very
fine grind it," because the sound of the human voice is encouraging
in the making of spices. If he had compounded only one hundred
and eighty-four manim (half the required quantity), it was valid, but
there is no tradition as to its permissibility if it was compounded in
one-third or one-quarter proportions of the required quantity.
Rabbi Yehudah said that the general principle is that if it was made
with its ingredients in their correct proportions, it was permissible
in half the quantity; but if one omitted any of the ingredients he was
deemed guilty of mortal error.

תָּנֵי בַר־קַפָּרָא: אַחַת לְשִׁשִּׁים אוֹ לְשִׁבְעִים שָׁנָה. הָיְתָה בָאָה שֶׁל שִׁירַיִם לַחֲצָאִין. וְעוֹד תָּנֵי בַר־קַפָּרָא: אִלּוּ הָיָה נוֹתֵן בָּהּ קוֹרְטוֹב שֶׁל דְּבַשׁ. אֵין אָדָם יָכוֹל לַעֲמֹד מִפְּנֵי רֵיחָהּ. וְלָמָּה אֵין מְעָרְבִין בָּהּ דְּבַשׁ. מִפְּנֵי שֶׁהַתּוֹרָה אָמְרָה: כִּי כָל־שְׂאֹר וְכָל־דְּבַשׁ לֹא־תַקְטִירוּ מִמֶּנּוּ אִשֶּׁה לַיהֹוָה:

Tanei Var-Kappara. Achat Leshishim O Leshiv'im Shanah. Hayetah Va'ah Shel Shirayim Lachatza'in. Ve'od Tanei Var-Kappara. Ilu Hayah Noten Bah Karetov Shel Devash. Ein Adam Yachol La'amod Mipenei Reichah. Velamah Ein Me'arevin Bah Devash. Mipenei Shehatorah Amerah. Ki Chol-Se'or Vechol-Devash. Lo-Taktiru Mimenu Isheh L'Adonai.

Bar Kappara taught that once in sixty or seventy years it happened that, left over, there was over a total of half the required amount accumulated from the three manim of incense from which the high priest took his hands full on Yom Kippur. Further Bar Kappara taught that had one mixed into the incense the smallest quantity of honey, no one could have stood its scent. Why did they not mix honey with it? Because the Torah states that, "No leaven, or any honey, will you burn as an offering made by fire to Hashem."

Ashrei

When saying the verse "Potei'ach Et Yadecha" one should focus one's heart. If one did not focus he must return and repeat. (SA, OC 51:7) It is customary to open your hands toward Heaven as a symbol of our acceptance of the abundance Hashem bestows upon us from Heaven. (BTH, Ex. 9:29, I Kings 8:54).

אַשְׁרֵי יוֹשְׁבֵי בֵיתֶךָ עוֹד יְהַלְלוּךָ סֶּלָה: אַשְׁרֵי הָעָם שֶׁכָּכָה לּוֹ אַשְׁרֵי הָעָם שֶׁיְהֹוָה אֱלֹהָיו:

Ashrei Yoshevei Veitecha; Od. Yehalelucha Selah. Ashrei Ha'am Shekachah Lo; Ashrei Ha'am. She'Adonai Elohav.

Happy are those who dwell in Your House; they are ever praising You. Happy are the people that is so situated; happy are the people whose God is Hashem. (Psalms 84:5, 144:15)

Psalms 145

תְּהִלָּה לְדָוִד אֲרוֹמִמְךָ אֱלוֹהַי הַמֶּלֶךְ וַאֲבָרְכָה שִׁמְךָ לְעוֹלָם וָעֶד:
בְּכָל־יוֹם אֲבָרְכֶךָ וַאֲהַלְלָה שִׁמְךָ לְעוֹלָם וָעֶד: גָּדוֹל יְהֹוָה וּמְהֻלָּל
מְאֹד וְלִגְדֻלָּתוֹ אֵין חֵקֶר: דּוֹר לְדוֹר יְשַׁבַּח מַעֲשֶׂיךָ וּגְבוּרֹתֶיךָ יַגִּידוּ:
הֲדַר כְּבוֹד הוֹדֶךָ וְדִבְרֵי נִפְלְאֹתֶיךָ אָשִׂיחָה: וֶעֱזוּז נוֹרְאֹתֶיךָ יֹאמֵרוּ
וּגְדֻלָּתְךָ אֲסַפְּרֶנָּה: זֵכֶר רַב־טוּבְךָ יַבִּיעוּ וְצִדְקָתְךָ יְרַנֵּנוּ: חַנּוּן וְרַחוּם
יְהֹוָה אֶרֶךְ אַפַּיִם וּגְדָל־חָסֶד: טוֹב־יְהֹוָה לַכֹּל וְרַחֲמָיו עַל־כָּל־מַעֲשָׂיו:
יוֹדוּךָ יְהֹוָה כָּל־מַעֲשֶׂיךָ וַחֲסִידֶיךָ יְבָרְכוּכָה: כְּבוֹד מַלְכוּתְךָ יֹאמֵרוּ
וּגְבוּרָתְךָ יְדַבֵּרוּ: לְהוֹדִיעַ | לִבְנֵי הָאָדָם גְּבוּרֹתָיו וּכְבוֹד הֲדַר
מַלְכוּתוֹ: מַלְכוּתְךָ מַלְכוּת כָּל־עֹלָמִים וּמֶמְשַׁלְתְּךָ בְּכָל־דּוֹר וָדֹר:
סוֹמֵךְ יְהֹוָה לְכָל־הַנֹּפְלִים וְזוֹקֵף לְכָל־הַכְּפוּפִים: עֵינֵי־כֹל אֵלֶיךָ
יְשַׂבֵּרוּ וְאַתָּה נוֹתֵן־לָהֶם אֶת־אָכְלָם בְּעִתּוֹ: **פּוֹתֵחַ אֶת־יָדֶךָ**
וּמַשְׂבִּיעַ לְכָל־חַי רָצוֹן: צַדִּיק יְהֹוָה בְּכָל־דְּרָכָיו וְחָסִיד
בְּכָל־מַעֲשָׂיו: קָרוֹב יְהֹוָה לְכָל־קֹרְאָיו לְכֹל אֲשֶׁר יִקְרָאֻהוּ בֶאֱמֶת:
רְצוֹן־יְרֵאָיו יַעֲשֶׂה וְאֶת־שַׁוְעָתָם יִשְׁמַע וְיוֹשִׁיעֵם: שׁוֹמֵר יְהֹוָה
אֶת־כָּל־אֹהֲבָיו וְאֵת כָּל־הָרְשָׁעִים יַשְׁמִיד: תְּהִלַּת יְהֹוָה יְדַבֶּר פִּי
וִיבָרֵךְ כָּל־בָּשָׂר שֵׁם קָדְשׁוֹ לְעוֹלָם וָעֶד: וַאֲנַחְנוּ | נְבָרֵךְ יָהּ מֵעַתָּה
וְעַד־עוֹלָם הַלְלוּיָהּ:

Tehilah. Ledavid Aromimcha Elohai Hamelech; Va'avarechah
Shimcha. Le'olam Va'ed. Bechol-Yom Avarecheka; Va'ahalelah
Shimcha. Le'olam Va'ed. Gadol Adonai Umehulal Me'od;
Veligdulato. Ein Cheiker. Dor Ledor Yeshabach Ma'aseicha;
Ugevuroteicha Yagidu. Hadar Kevod Hodecha; Vedivrei
Nifle'oteicha Asichah. Ve'ezuz Nore'oteicha Yomeru; Ug'dulatecha
Asap'renah. Zecher Rav-Tuvecha Yabi'u; Vetzidkatecha Yeranenu.
Chanun Verachum Adonai Erech Apayim. Ugedol-Chased. Tov-

Adonai Lakol; Verachamav. Al-Chol-Ma'asav. Yoducha Adonai Chol-
Ma'aseicha; Vachasideicha. Yevarechuchah. Kevod Malchutecha
Yomeru; Ugevuratecha Yedaberu. Lehodia Livnei Ha'adam
Gevurotav; Uchevod. Hadar Malchuto. Malchutecha. Malchut
Chol-'Olamim; Umemshaltecha. Bechol-Dor Vador. Somech Adonai
Lechol-Hanofelim; Vezokeif. Lechol-Hakefufim. Einei-Chol Eleicha
Yesaberu; Ve'attah Noten-Lahem Et-'Ochlam Be'ito. **Potei'ach Et-
Yadecha; Umasbia Lechol-Chai Ratzon.** Tzaddik Adonai Bechol-
Derachav; Vechasid. Bechol-Ma'asav. Karov Adonai Lechol-Kore'av;
Lechol Asher Yikra'uhu Ve'emet. Retzon-Yere'av Ya'aseh; Ve'et-
Shav'atam Yishma'. Veyoshi'em. Shomer Adonai Et-Chol-'Ohavav;
Ve'et Chol-Haresha'im Yashmid. Tehillat Adonai Yedaber Pi Vivarech
Chol-Basar Shem Kodsho. Le'olam Va'ed. Va'anachnu Nevarech Yah.
Me'attah Ve'ad-'Olam. Halleluyah.

A Psalm of praise; of David. א I will extol You, my God, Oh King; And
I will bless Your name forever and ever. ב Every day I will bless You;
And I will praise Your name forever and ever. ג Great is Hashem, and
highly to be praised; And His greatness is unsearchable. ד One
generation will applaud Your works to another, And will declare
Your mighty acts. ה The glorious splendor of Your majesty, And
Your wondrous works, I will rehearse. ו And men will speak of the
might of Your tremendous acts; And I will tell of Your greatness. ז
They will utter the fame of Your great goodness, And will sing of
Your righteousness. ח Hashem is gracious, and full of compassion;
Slow to anger, and of great mercy. ט Hashem is good to all; And His
tender mercies are over all His works. י All Your works will praise
You, Hashem; And Your holy-ones will bless You. כ They will speak
of the glory of Your kingdom, And talk of Your might; ל To make
known to the sons of men His mighty acts, And the glory of the
beauty of His kingdom. מ Your kingdom is a kingdom for all ages,
And Your dominion endures throughout all generations. ס Hashem
upholds all that fall, And raises up all those that are bowed down. ע
The eyes of all wait for You, And You give them their food in due
season. פ **You open Your hand, And satisfy every living thing
with favor.** צ Hashem is righteous in all His ways, And gracious in all
His works. ק Hashem is near to all them that call upon Him, To all

that call upon Him in truth. ר He will fulfill the desire of those that fear Him; He also will hear their cry, and will save them. ש Hashem preserves all them that love Him; But all the wicked will He destroy. ת My mouth will speak the praise of Hashem; And let all flesh bless His holy name forever and ever.

Uva Letziyon

> One should be very careful to say the kedushah of Uva Letziyon with kavanah (intention). (SA, OC 132:1) It is ideal to say this kedusha seated and with a minyan (10 men). If one says this by himself, it should be recited like one would read from the Torah with cantillation.

Uva Letziyon Go'el. Uleshavei	וּבָא לְצִיּוֹן גּוֹאֵל וּלְשָׁבֵי
Fesha Beya'akov; Ne'um Adonai	פֶּשַׁע בְּיַעֲקֹב נְאֻם יְהֹוָה:
Va'ani. Zot Beriti Otam Amar	וַאֲנִי זֹאת בְּרִיתִי אוֹתָם אָמַר
Adonai Ruchi Asher Aleicha.	יְהֹוָה רוּחִי אֲשֶׁר עָלֶיךָ
Udevarai Asher-Samti Beficha;	וּדְבָרַי אֲשֶׁר־שַׂמְתִּי בְּפִיךָ
Lo-Yamushu Mipicha Umipi	לֹא־יָמוּשׁוּ מִפִּיךָ וּמִפִּי
Zar'acha Umipi Zera Zar'acha	זַרְעֲךָ וּמִפִּי זֶרַע זַרְעֲךָ
Amar Adonai Me'attah	אָמַר יְהֹוָה מֵעַתָּה
Ve'ad-'Olam. Ve'attah Kadosh;	וְעַד־עוֹלָם: וְאַתָּה קָדוֹשׁ
Yoshev. Tehillot Yisra'el. Vekara	יוֹשֵׁב תְּהִלּוֹת יִשְׂרָאֵל: וְקָרָא
Zeh El-Zeh Ve'amar. **Kadosh**	זֶה אֶל־זֶה וְאָמַר קָדוֹשׁ |
Kadosh Kadosh Adonai Tzeva'ot;	קָדוֹשׁ קָדוֹשׁ יְהֹוָה צְבָאוֹת
Melo Chol-Ha'aretz Kevodo.	מְלֹא כָל־הָאָרֶץ כְּבוֹדוֹ:
Umekabelin Dein Min Dein	וּמְקַבְּלִין דֵּין מִן דֵּין
Ve'amerin. Kaddish Bishmei	וְאָמְרִין: קַדִּישׁ בִּשְׁמֵי
Meroma Illa'ah Beit Shechineteh.	מְרוֹמָא עִלָּאָה בֵּית שְׁכִינְתֵּהּ.
Kaddish Al Ar'a Ovad	קַדִּישׁ עַל אַרְעָא עוֹבַד
Gevureteh. Kaddish Le'alam	גְּבוּרְתֵּהּ. קַדִּישׁ לְעָלַם

Ule'alemei Alemaya. Adonai	וּלְעָלְמֵי עָלְמַיָּא. יְהֹוָה
Tzeva'ot Malya Chol-'Ar'a Ziv	צְבָאוֹת מַלְיָא כָל-אַרְעָא זִיו
Yekareh. Vatissa'eni Ruach.	יְקָרֵהּ: וַתִּשָּׂאֵנִי רוּחַ
Va'eshma Acharai. Kol Ra'ash	וָאֶשְׁמַע אַחֲרַי קוֹל רַעַשׁ
Gadol; **Baruch Kevod-Adonai**	גָּדוֹל **בָּרוּךְ כְּבוֹד־יְהֹוָה**
Mimekomo. Unetalatni Rucha.	**מִמְּקוֹמוֹ:** וּנְטָלַתְנִי רוּחָא.
Ushema'it Batrai Kal Zia Sagi	וּשְׁמָעִית בַּתְרַי קָל זִיעַ שַׂגִּיא
Dimshabechin Ve'amerin. Berich	דִּמְשַׁבְּחִין וְאָמְרִין: בְּרִיךְ
Yekara Da'Adonai Me'atar Beit	יְקָרָא דַיהֹוָה מֵאֲתַר בֵּית
Shechineteh. **Adonai Yimloch**	שְׁכִינְתֵּהּ: **יְהֹוָה	יִמְלֹךְ**
Le'olam Va'ed. Adonai	**לְעֹלָם וָעֶד:** יְהֹוָה
Malchuteih Ka'im Le'alam	מַלְכוּתֵיהּ קָאִים לְעָלַם
Ule'alemei Alemaya. Adonai	וּלְעָלְמֵי עָלְמַיָּא: יְהֹוָה
Elohei Avraham Yitzchak	אֱלֹהֵי אַבְרָהָם יִצְחָק
Veyisra'el Avoteinu. Shomrah-	וְיִשְׂרָאֵל אֲבֹתֵינוּ שָׁמְרָה־
Zot Le'olam. Leyetzer	זֹאת לְעוֹלָם לְיֵצֶר
Machshevot Levav Ammecha;	מַחְשְׁבוֹת לְבַב עַמֶּךָ
Vehachein Levavam Eleicha.	וְהָכֵן לְבָבָם אֵלֶיךָ:
Vehu Rachum Yechapeir Avon	וְהוּא רַחוּם	יְכַפֵּר עָוֹן
Velo-Yashchit Vehirbah Lehashiv	וְלֹא־יַשְׁחִית וְהִרְבָּה לְהָשִׁיב
Appo; Velo-Ya'ir. Chol-Chamato.	אַפּוֹ וְלֹא־יָעִיר כָּל־חֲמָתוֹ:
Ki-'Attah Adonai Tov Vesalach;	כִּי־אַתָּה אֲדֹנָי טוֹב וְסַלָּח
Verav-Chesed Lechol-Kore'eicha.	וְרַב־חֶסֶד לְכָל־קֹרְאֶיךָ:
Tzidkatecha Tzedek Le'olam;	צִדְקָתְךָ צֶדֶק לְעוֹלָם
Vetoratecha Emet. Titen Emet	וְתוֹרָתְךָ אֱמֶת: תִּתֵּן אֱמֶת
Leya'akov. Chesed Le'avraham;	לְיַעֲקֹב חֶסֶד לְאַבְרָהָם
Asher-Nishba'ta La'avoteinu	אֲשֶׁר־נִשְׁבַּעְתָּ לַאֲבֹתֵינוּ

Mimei Kedem. Baruch Adonai	מִימֵי קֶדֶם: בָּרוּךְ אֲדֹנָי
Yom Yom Ya'amas-Lanu. Ha'el	יוֹם ׀ יוֹם יַעֲמָס־לָנוּ הָאֵל
Yeshu'atenu Selah. Adonai	יְשׁוּעָתֵנוּ סֶלָה: יְהֹוָה
Tzeva'ot Imanu; Misgav-Lanu	צְבָאוֹת עִמָּנוּ מִשְׂגָּב־לָנוּ
Elohei Ya'akov Selah. Adonai	אֱלֹהֵי יַעֲקֹב סֶלָה: יְהֹוָה
Tzeva'ot; Ashrei Adam. Boteach	צְבָאוֹת אַשְׁרֵי אָדָם בֹּטֵחַ
Bach. Adonai Hoshi'ah;	בָּךְ: יְהֹוָה הוֹשִׁיעָה
Hamelech. Ya'aneinu Veyom-	הַמֶּלֶךְ יַעֲנֵנוּ בְיוֹם־
Kor'enu.	קָרְאֵנוּ:

"A redeemer will come to Tziyon and to those in Yaakov who turn from transgression, says Hashem. As for Me, this is My covenant with them, says Hashem: My spirit which is upon you, and My words which I have put in your mouth, will not depart out of your mouth, or out of the mouth of your children, or out of the mouth of your children's children from now on forever, says Hashem. "For You are holy and are enthroned amidst the praises of Yisrael." "The angels called one to another, and said, **"Holy, Holy, Holy is Hashem of hosts, The fullness of all the earth is His glory."** And they receive word from each other and say, Holy in the highest heavens, the abode of His Divine Presence. Holy upon earth the work of His mighty power. Holy forever and to all eternity, is Hashem of hosts. The whole earth is full of His glorious splendor. "Then a spirit lifted me and behind me I heard a mighty sound, **'Blessed is Hashem's glory from His Abode.'"** Then the spirit raised me and I heard behind me a mighty moving sound of those who uttered His praise, proclaiming, 'Blessed is the glory of Hashem from the abiding place of His Divine Presence.' **"Hashem will reign forever and ever."** The rule of Hashem is established forever and ever. "Oh Hashem God of Avraham, Yitzchak and Yisrael, our fathers, forever preserve this as the inward thoughts of the heart of Your people and direct

their hearts toward You. For He being merciful, will forgive iniquity
and not destroy, yes, many times He averts His anger and does not
awaken all of His wrath. For You, Hashem, are good and forgiving,
and abounding in mercy to all who call upon You. Your
righteousness is everlasting righteousness, and Your Torah is truth.
You give truth to Yaakov, kindness to Avraham, As You have sworn
to our fathers from ancient days. Blessed is Hashem, day to day He
bears our burdens, The God of our salvation forever. Hashem of
hosts is with us, The God of Yaakov is our high refuge forever.
Hashem of hosts, Happy is the man who trusts in You. Hashem,
save us, May the King answer us on the day when we call."

Baruch Eloheinu Shebera'anu

Baruch Eloheinu Shebera'anu	בָּרוּךְ אֱלֹהֵינוּ שֶׁבְּרָאָנוּ
Lichvodo. Vehivdilanu Min	לִכְבוֹדוֹ. וְהִבְדִּילָנוּ מִן
Hato'im. Venatan Lanu Torat	הַתּוֹעִים. וְנָתַן לָנוּ תּוֹרַת
Emet. Vechayei Olam Nata	אֱמֶת. וְחַיֵּי עוֹלָם נָטַע
Betocheinu. Hu Yiftach Libenu	בְּתוֹכֵנוּ. הוּא יִפְתַּח לִבֵּנוּ
Betorato. Veyasim Belibeinu	בְּתוֹרָתוֹ. וְיָשִׂים בְּלִבֵּנוּ
Ahavato Veyir'ato La'asot	אַהֲבָתוֹ וְיִרְאָתוֹ לַעֲשׂוֹת
Retzono. Ule'avedo Belevav	רְצוֹנוֹ. וּלְעָבְדוֹ בְּלֵבָב
Shalem. Lo Niga Larik. Velo	שָׁלֵם. לֹא נִיגַע לָרִיק. וְלֹא
Neled Labehalah. Yehi Ratzon	נֵלֵד לַבֶּהָלָה. יְהִי רָצוֹן
Milfaneicha Adonai Eloheinu	מִלְּפָנֶיךָ יְהֹוָה אֱלֹהֵינוּ
Velohei Avoteinu. Shenishmor	וֵאלֹהֵי אֲבוֹתֵינוּ. שֶׁנִּשְׁמוֹר
Chukkeicha Umitzvoteicha	חֻקֶּיךָ וּמִצְוֹתֶיךָ
Ba'olam Hazeh. Venizkeh.	בָּעוֹלָם הַזֶּה. וְנִזְכֶּה.
Venichyeh. Venirash Tovah	וְנִחְיֶה. וְנִירַשׁ טוֹבָה

Uverachah Lechayei Ha'olam	וּבְרָכָה לְחַיֵּי הָעוֹלָם
Haba. Lema'an Yezamercha	הַבָּא: לְמַעַן | יְזַמֶּרְךָ
Chavod Velo Yidom; Adonai	כָבוֹד וְלֹא יִדֹּם יְהֹוָה
Elohai. Le'olam Odeka. Adonai	אֱלֹהַי לְעוֹלָם אוֹדֶךָ: יְהֹוָה
Chafetz Lema'an Tzidko; Yagdil	חָפֵץ לְמַעַן צִדְקוֹ יַגְדִּיל
Torah Veya'dir. Veyivtechu Vecha	תּוֹרָה וְיַאְדִּיר: וְיִבְטְחוּ בְךָ
Yodei Shemecha; Ki Lo-'Azavta	יוֹדְעֵי שְׁמֶךָ כִּי לֹא־עָזַבְתָּ
Doresheicha Adonai. Adonai	דֹרְשֶׁיךָ יְהֹוָה: יְהֹוָה
Adoneinu; Mah-'Adir Shimcha.	אֲדֹנֵינוּ מָה־אַדִּיר שִׁמְךָ
Bechol-Ha'aretz. Chizku	בְּכָל־הָאָרֶץ: חִזְקוּ
Veya'ametz Levavchem; Chol-	וְיַאֲמֵץ לְבַבְכֶם כָּל־
Hamyachalim. L'Adonai.	הַמְיַחֲלִים לַיהֹוָה:

Blessed is our God, Who has created us for His glory, and has separated us from those that go astray, and has given to us the Torah of truth and planted everlasting life in our midst. May He open our hearts to His Torah, and place love and fear of Him within our hearts, to do His will and serve Him with a perfect heart, that we may not labor in vain, or bring forth confusion. May it be Your will, Hashem our God and God of our fathers, that we may keep Your statutes and commandments in this world and may we merit and live and inherit happiness and blessing for the life of the world to come. To the end that my glory may sing to You, and not be silent. Hashem my God, I will give thanks to You forever. It pleased Hashem, for His righteousness' sake, to magnify the Torah and to make it glorious. And those that know Your name will put their trust in You; for You have not forsaken those that seek You, Hashem. Oh Hashem, our Lord, How glorious is Your name in all of the earth. Be strong, and let your heart take courage, all of you that wait for Hashem.

And say Hatzi-Kaddish.

Kaddish is only recited in a minyan (ten men). אמן denotes when the congregation responds "Amen" together out loud. According to the Shulchan Arukh, the congregation says "Yehei Shemeh Rabba" to "Yitbarach" out loud together without interruption, and also that one should respond "Amen" after "Yitbarach." (SA, OC 55,56) This is not the common custom today. Though many are accustomed to answering according to their own custom, it is advised to respond in the custom of the one reciting to avoid not fragmenting into smaller groups. ("Lo Titgodedu" - BT, Yevamot 13b / SA, OC 493, Rema / MT, Avodah Zara 12:15)

יִתְגַּדַּל וְיִתְקַדַּשׁ שְׁמֵהּ רַבָּא. אמן בְּעָלְמָא דִּי בְרָא. כִּרְעוּתֵהּ. וְיַמְלִיךְ מַלְכוּתֵהּ. וְיַצְמַח פֻּרְקָנֵהּ. וִיקָרֵב מְשִׁיחֵהּ. אמן בְּחַיֵּיכוֹן וּבְיוֹמֵיכוֹן וּבְחַיֵּי דְכָל בֵּית יִשְׂרָאֵל. בַּעֲגָלָא וּבִזְמַן קָרִיב. וְאִמְרוּ אָמֵן. אמן יְהֵא שְׁמֵהּ רַבָּא מְבָרַךְ לְעָלַם וּלְעָלְמֵי עָלְמַיָּא יִתְבָּרַךְ. וְיִשְׁתַּבַּח. וְיִתְפָּאַר. וְיִתְרוֹמַם. וְיִתְנַשֵּׂא. וְיִתְהַדָּר. וְיִתְעַלֶּה. וְיִתְהַלָּל שְׁמֵהּ דְּקֻדְשָׁא. בְּרִיךְ הוּא. אמן לְעֵלָּא מִן כָּל בִּרְכָתָא שִׁירָתָא. תֻּשְׁבְּחָתָא וְנֶחֱמָתָא. דַּאֲמִירָן בְּעָלְמָא. וְאִמְרוּ אָמֵן. אמן

Yitgadal Veyitkadash Shemeh Rabba. Amen Be'alema Di Vera. Kir'uteh. Veyamlich Malchuteh. Veyatzmach Purkaneh. Vikarev Meshicheh. Amen Bechayeichon Uveyomeichon Uvechayei Dechal-Beit Yisra'el. Ba'agala Uvizman Kariv. Ve'imru Amen. Amen Yehei Shemeh Rabba Mevarach Le'alam Ule'alemei Alemaya Yitbarach. Veyishtabach. Veyitpa'ar. Veyitromam. Veyitnasse. Veyit'hadar. Veyit'aleh. Veyit'hallal Shemeh Dekudsha. Berich Hu. Amen Le'ella Min Kol Birchata Shirata. Tushbechata Venechemata. Da'amiran Be'alema. Ve'imru Amen. Amen

Glorified and sanctified be God's great name Amen throughout the world which He has created according to His will. May He establish His kingdom, hastening His salvation and the coming of His Messiah, Amen, in your lifetime and during your days, and within the life of the entire House of Yisrael, speedily and soon; and say, Amen. Amen May His great name be blessed forever and to all eternity. Blessed and praised, glorified and exalted, extolled and honored, adored and lauded is the name of the Holy One, blessed is He, Amen Beyond all the blessings and hymns, praises and consolations that are ever spoken in the world; and say, Amen. Amen

Kriyat HaTorah / Torah Reading - Shabbat Mincha

During Shabbat Minchah we take out one Torah and and three persons are called up for the reading of the parasha of the following week. And even when Yom Tov falls on Shabbat we read the next week's parashah and not the one for Yom Tov. (SA, OC 292:1)

Before opening the Ark say:

וַאֲנִי תְפִלָּתִי־לְךָ ׀ יְהֹוָה עֵת רָצוֹן אֱלֹהִים בְּרָב־חַסְדֶּךָ עֲנֵנִי בֶּאֱמֶת יִשְׁעֶךָ: ב׳ פעמים

Va'ani Tefillati-Lekha Adonai Et Ratzon Elohim Berov-Chasdeikha Aneni Be'emet Yishekha.

But as for me, let my prayer be to You, Hashem, in an acceptable time; God, in the abundance of Your mercy, Answer me with the truth of Your salvation. (2 times)

The ark is opened.

Some say:

Berich Shemeh Demarei Alema	בְּרִיךְ שְׁמֵהּ דְּמָארֵי עָלְמָא
Berich Kitrach Ve'atrach. Yehe	בְּרִיךְ כִּתְרָךְ וְאַתְרָךְ. יְהֵא
Re'utach. Im Amach Yisra'el	רְעוּתָךְ. עִם עַמָּךְ יִשְׂרָאֵל
Le'alam. Ufurekan Yeminach	לְעָלַם. וּפוּרְקַן יְמִינָךְ
Achzei Le'amach Beveit	אַחֲזֵי לְעַמָּךְ בְּבֵית
Mikdashach. Le'amtuyei Lana	מִקְדָּשָׁךְ. לְאַמְטוּיֵי לָנָא
Mituv Nehorach. Ulekabel	מִטּוּב נְהוֹרָךְ. וּלְקַבֵּל
Tzelotana Berachamin. Yehe	צְלוֹתָנָא בְּרַחֲמִין. יְהֵא
Ra'ava Kodamach Detorich Lan	רַעֲוָא קֳדָמָךְ דְּתוֹרִיךְ לָן
Chayin Betivu. Velehevei Ana	חַיִּין בְּטִיבוּ. וְלֶהֱוֵי אֲנָא
Avdach Pekida Bego Tzaddikaya.	עַבְדָּךְ פְּקִידָא בְּגוֹ צַדִּיקַיָּא.

Lemircham Alai Ulemintar Yati	לְמִרְחַם עֲלֵי וּלְמִנְטַר יָתִי
Veyat Kol Di Li Vedi Le'amach	וְיַת כָּל דִּי לִי וְדִי לְעַמָּךְ
Yisra'el. Ant Hu Zan Lechola	יִשְׂרָאֵל. אַנְתְּ הוּא זָן לְכֹלָּא
Umefarnes Lechola. Ant Hu	וּמְפַרְנֵס לְכֹלָּא. אַנְתְּ הוּא
Shallit Al Kola Ant Hu	שַׁלִּיט עַל כֹּלָּא אַנְתְּ הוּא
Deshallit Al Malchaya	דְּשַׁלִּיט עַל מַלְכַיָּא
Umalchuta Dilach Hi. Ana Avda	וּמַלְכוּתָא דִּילָךְ הִיא. אֲנָא עַבְדָּא
Dekudesha Berich Hu Desagidna	דְּקֻדְשָׁא בְּרִיךְ הוּא דְּסָגִידְנָא
Kameh Umin Kamei Dikar	קַמֵּה וּמִן קַמֵּי דִּיקַר
Orayteh Bechl Idan Ve'idan. La	אוֹרַיְתֵה בְּכָל־עִדָּן וְעִדָּן. לָא
Al Enash Rachitzna. Vela Al Bar	עַל אֱנָשׁ רָחִיצְנָא. וְלָא עַל בַּר
Elahin Samichna. Ella Ve'elaha	אֱלָהִין סָמִיכְנָא. אֶלָּא בֶּאֱלָהָא
Dishmaya Dehu Elaha Dikshot.	דִּשְׁמַיָּא דְּהוּא אֱלָהָא דִקְשׁוֹט.
Ve'orayteh Keshot. Unevi'ohi	וְאוֹרַיְתֵה קְשׁוֹט. וּנְבִיאוֹהִי
Keshot. Umasgei Leme'bad	קְשׁוֹט. וּמַסְגֵּי לְמֶעְבַּד
Tavan Ukeshot. Beih Ana Rachitz	טַבְוָן וּקְשׁוֹט. בֵּיה אֲנָא רָחִיץ
Velishmeh Yakira Kaddisha Ana	וְלִשְׁמֵה יַקִּירָא קַדִּישָׁא אֲנָא
Emar Tushbechan. Yehe Ra'ava	אֲמַר תֻּשְׁבְּחָן. יְהֵא רַעֲוָא
Kodamach Detiftach Libi	קֳדָמָךְ דְּתִפְתַּח לִבִּי
Be'oraytach. (Vetihav Li Benin	בְּאוֹרַיְתָךְ. (וְתִיהַב לִי בְּנִין
Dichrin De'avedin Re'utach).	דִּכְרִין דְּעָבְדִין רְעוּתָךְ).
Vetashlim Mish'alin Deliba	וְתַשְׁלִים מִשְׁאֲלִין דְּלִבָּאִי
Veliba Dechol Amach Yisra'el	וְלִבָּא דְכָל־עַמָּךְ יִשְׂרָאֵל
Letav Ulechayin Velishlam	לְטַב וּלְחַיִּין וְלִשְׁלָם
Amen:	אָמֵן:

Blessed is the name of the Lord of the universe. Blessed is Your crown and Your dominion. May Your goodwill always abide with

Your people Yisrael. Reveal Your saving power to Your people in
Your Sanctuary; bestow on us the good gift of Your light, and accept
our prayer in mercy. May it be Your will to prolong our life in
happiness. Let me also be counted among the righteous, so that
You may have compassion on me and shelter me and mine and all
that belong to Your people Yisrael. You are He Who nourishes and
sustains all; You are He Who rules over all; You are He Who rules
over kings, for dominion is Yours. I am the servant of the Holy One,
blessed is He, before Whom and before Whose glorious Torah I
bow at all times. I do not put my trust in man, or rely on any angel,
but only in the God of Heaven Who is the God of truth, Whose
Torah is truth and Whose Prophets are truth, and Who performs
many deeds of goodness and truth. In Him I put my trust, and to His
holy and glorious name I declare praises. May it be Your will to open
my heart to Your Torah, and to fulfill the wishes of my heart and of
the heart of all of Your people Yisrael for happiness, life and peace.

Take out the Torah Scroll and say:

בָּרוּךְ הַמָּקוֹם שֶׁנָּתַן תּוֹרָה לְעַמּוֹ יִשְׂרָאֵל. בָּרוּךְ הוּא: אַשְׁרֵי הָעָם
שֶׁכָּכָה לּוֹ. אַשְׁרֵי הָעָם שֶׁיהֹוָה אֱלֹהָיו:

Baruch Hamakom Shenatan Torah Le'ammo Yisra'el. Baruch Hu:
Ashrei Ha'am Shekachah Lo. Ashrei Ha'am She'Adonai Elohav:

Blessed is the place where the Torah was given to His people
Yisrael, blessed is He; Happy are the people that is so situated;
happy are the people whose God is Hashem. (Psalms 144:15)

Leading the Torah to the Ark say:

גַּדְּלוּ לַיהֹוָה אִתִּי וּנְרוֹמְמָה שְׁמוֹ יַחְדָּו: רוֹמְמוּ יְהֹוָה אֱלֹהֵינוּ
וְהִשְׁתַּחֲווּ לַהֲדֹם רַגְלָיו קָדוֹשׁ הוּא: רוֹמְמוּ יְהֹוָה אֱלֹהֵינוּ וְהִשְׁתַּחֲווּ

לְהַר קָדְשׁוֹ כִּי־קָדוֹשׁ יְהֹוָה אֱלֹהֵינוּ:

Gadelu L'Adonai Iti Uneromemah Shemo Yachdav. Romemu Adonai
Eloheinu Vehishtachavu Lahadom Raglav Kadosh Hu. Romemu
Adonai Eloheinu Vehishtachavu Lehar Kodsho Ki Kadosh Adonai
Eloheinu.

Exalt Hashem with me, And let us glorify His name in unison. (Psalms
34:4) Exalt Hashem our God, And worship at His holy hill; For
Hashem our God is holy. (Psalms 99:9)

אֵין־קָדוֹשׁ כַּיהֹוָה כִּי אֵין בִּלְתֶּךָ וְאֵין צוּר כֵּאלֹהֵינוּ: כִּי מִי אֱלוֹהַּ
מִבַּלְעֲדֵי יְהֹוָה וּמִי צוּר זוּלָתִי אֱלֹהֵינוּ: תּוֹרָה צִוָּה־לָנוּ מֹשֶׁה
מוֹרָשָׁה קְהִלַּת יַעֲקֹב: עֵץ־חַיִּים הִיא לַמַּחֲזִיקִים בָּהּ וְתֹמְכֶיהָ
מְאֻשָּׁר: דְּרָכֶיהָ דַרְכֵי־נֹעַם וְכָל־נְתִיבוֹתֶיהָ שָׁלוֹם: שָׁלוֹם רָב לְאֹהֲבֵי
תוֹרָתֶךָ וְאֵין־לָמוֹ מִכְשׁוֹל: יְהֹוָה עֹז לְעַמּוֹ יִתֵּן יְהֹוָה | יְבָרֵךְ אֶת־עַמּוֹ
בַשָּׁלוֹם: כִּי שֵׁם יְהֹוָה אֶקְרָא הָבוּ גֹדֶל לֵאלֹהֵינוּ: הַכֹּל תְּנוּ עֹז
לֵאלֹהִים. וּתְנוּ כָבוֹד לַתּוֹרָה:

Ein-Kadosh K'Adonai Ki Ein Biltecha; Ve'ein Tzur Keloheinu. Ki Mi
Eloah Mibal'adei Adonai Umi Tzur. Zulati Eloheinu Torah Tzivah-
Lanu Mosheh; Morashah Kehilat Ya'akov. Etz-Chayim Hi
Lamachazikim Bah; Vetomecheiha Me'ushar. Deracheiha Darchei-
No'am; Vechol-Netivoteiha Shalom. Shalom Rav Le'ohavei
Toratecha; Ve'ein-Lamo Michshol. Adonai Oz Le'ammo Yiten;
Adonai Yevarech Et-'Ammo Vashalom. Ki Shem Adonai Ekra Havu
Godel L' Eloheinu: Hakol Tenu Oz L' Elohim Utenu Kavod La'
Torah.

There is none other as holy as Hashem, For there is none besides
Him, or Rock like our God. For who is God except Hashem, Or who
is the Rock besides our God? A Torah Moshe commanded us, A
heritage for the congregation of Yaakov. It is a tree of life for those
who lay hold of it, And happy are those who cling to it. Its ways are
ways of pleasantness, And all its pathways peace. Great peace have
those who love Your Torah, And for them there is no stumbling.
Hashem will give strength to His people. Hashem will bless His
people with peace. For I will proclaim the name of Hashem; Ascribe

greatness to our God. For I will proclaim the name of Hashem;
Ascribe greatness to our God. Let all give might to God and give
honor to the Torah. (Deut. 32:3)

Hagbahah / Lifting of the Torah

The lifting of the Sefer Torah. As it is raised and turned the congregation says:

Deuteronomy 4:44, 33:4

Vezot Hatorah; Asher-Sam	וְזֹאת הַתּוֹרָה אֲשֶׁר־שָׂם
Mosheh. Lifnei Benei Yisra'el.	מֹשֶׁה לִפְנֵי בְּנֵי יִשְׂרָאֵל:
Torah Tzivah-Lanu Mosheh;	תּוֹרָה צִוָּה־לָנוּ מֹשֶׁה
Morashah Kehilat Ya'akov.	מוֹרָשָׁה קְהִלַּת יַעֲקֹב:
Ha' El Tamim Darko Imrat-	הָאֵל תָּמִים דַּרְכּוֹ אִמְרַת־
Adonai Tzerufah; Magen Hu.	יְהֹוָה צְרוּפָה מָגֵן הוּא
Lechol Hachosim Bo.	לְכֹל	הַחֹסִים בּוֹ:

"And this is the Torah which Moshe placed before the children of
Yisrael. The Torah which Moshe commanded us, the heritage for
the congregation of Yaakov." "The way of God is perfect; the word
of Hashem is tried; He is a Shield to all those who trust in Him."

Continue with the blessings for the Torah Reading.

In some kehilot (congregations), the Oleh / Reader says:

Adonai Imachem.

יְהֹוָה עִמָּכֶם:

Hashem be with you.

The kahal / congregation:

Yevarechekha Adonai.

יְבָרֶכְךָ יְהֹוָה:

May Hashem bless You.

The Oleh / Reader:

Barechu Et Adonai Hamevorach.

בָּרְכוּ אֶת יְהֹוָה הַמְּבֹרָךְ:

Bless Hashem, Who is forever blessed.

The kahal / congregation:

Baruch Adonai Hamevorach
Le'olam Va'ed.

בָּרוּךְ יְהֹוָה הַמְּבֹרָךְ
לְעוֹלָם וָעֶד:

Blessed is Hashem Who is blessed for all eternity.

The Oleh and Chazan:

Baruch Adonai Hamevorach
Le'olam Va'ed.

בָּרוּךְ יְהֹוָה הַמְּבֹרָךְ
לְעוֹלָם וָעֶד:

Blessed is Hashem Who is blessed for all eternity.

Baruch Attah Adonai Eloheinu
Melech Ha'olam Asher Bachar
Banu Mikol Ha'ammim Venatan
Lanu Et Torato. Baruch Attah
Adonai Noten Hatorah.

בָּרוּךְ אַתָּה יְהֹוָה אֱלֹהֵינוּ
מֶלֶךְ הָעוֹלָם. אֲשֶׁר בָּחַר
בָּנוּ מִכָּל הָעַמִּים וְנָתַן
לָנוּ אֶת תּוֹרָתוֹ. בָּרוּךְ אַתָּה
יְהֹוָה נוֹתֵן הַתּוֹרָה:

Blessed are You, Hashem our God, King of the universe, You have chosen us from all peoples and given us Your Torah. Blessed are You, Hashem, Giver of the Torah.

There is no need for the assembly to stand up during the reading of the Torah. (SA, OC 146:4)

After reading from the Torah, the reader holds the Sefer Torah and blesses (SA, OC 139:11):

Baruch Attah Adonai Eloheinu	בָּרוּךְ אַתָּה יְהֹוָה אֱלֹהֵינוּ
Melech Ha'olam Asher Natan	מֶלֶךְ הָעוֹלָם. אֲשֶׁר נָתַן
Lanu Et Torato Torat Emet.	לָנוּ אֶת תּוֹרָתוֹ תּוֹרַת אֱמֶת.
Vechayei Olam Nata	וְחַיֵּי עוֹלָם נָטַע
Betocheinu. Baruch Attah	בְּתוֹכֵנוּ. בָּרוּךְ אַתָּה
Adonai Noten Hatorah.	יְהֹוָה נוֹתֵן הַתּוֹרָה:

Blessed are You, Hashem our God, King of the universe, You have given us Your Torah of truth, and have planted among us eternal life. Blessed are You, Hashem, Giver of the Torah.

Kaddish is not recited after reading the Torah.

Psalms 92

מִזְמוֹר שִׁיר לְיוֹם הַשַּׁבָּת: טוֹב לְהֹדוֹת לַיהֹוָה וּלְזַמֵּר לְשִׁמְךָ עֶלְיוֹן: לְהַגִּיד בַּבֹּקֶר חַסְדֶּךָ וֶאֱמוּנָתְךָ בַּלֵּילוֹת: עֲלֵי־עָשׂוֹר וַעֲלֵי־נָבֶל עֲלֵי הִגָּיוֹן בְּכִנּוֹר: כִּי שִׂמַּחְתַּנִי יְהֹוָה בְּפָעֳלֶךָ בְּמַעֲשֵׂי יָדֶיךָ אֲרַנֵּן: מַה־גָּדְלוּ מַעֲשֶׂיךָ יְהֹוָה מְאֹד עָמְקוּ מַחְשְׁבֹתֶיךָ: אִישׁ־בַּעַר לֹא יֵדָע וּכְסִיל לֹא־יָבִין אֶת־זֹאת: בִּפְרֹחַ רְשָׁעִים | כְּמוֹ עֵשֶׂב וַיָּצִיצוּ כָּל־פֹּעֲלֵי אָוֶן לְהִשָּׁמְדָם עֲדֵי־עַד: וְאַתָּה מָרוֹם לְעֹלָם יְהֹוָה: כִּי הִנֵּה אֹיְבֶיךָ | יְהֹוָה כִּי־הִנֵּה אֹיְבֶיךָ יֹאבֵדוּ יִתְפָּרְדוּ כָּל־פֹּעֲלֵי אָוֶן: וַתָּרֶם כִּרְאֵים קַרְנִי בַּלֹּתִי בְּשֶׁמֶן רַעֲנָן: וַתַּבֵּט עֵינִי בְּשׁוּרָי בַּקָּמִים עָלַי מְרֵעִים תִּשְׁמַעְנָה אָזְנָי: צַדִּיק כַּתָּמָר יִפְרָח כְּאֶרֶז בַּלְּבָנוֹן יִשְׂגֶּה: שְׁתוּלִים בְּבֵית יְהֹוָה בְּחַצְרוֹת אֱלֹהֵינוּ יַפְרִיחוּ: עוֹד יְנוּבוּן בְּשֵׂיבָה דְּשֵׁנִים וְרַעֲנַנִּים יִהְיוּ: לְהַגִּיד כִּי־יָשָׁר יְהֹוָה צוּרִי וְלֹא־(עֲוֹלָתָה) עַלְתָה בּוֹ:

Mizmor Shir. Leyom Hashabbat. Tov. Lehodot L'Adonai Ulezamer
Leshimcha Elyon. Lehagid Baboker Chasdecha; Ve'emunatecha.
Baleilot. Alei-'Asor Va'alei-Navel; Alei Higayon Bechinor. Ki
Simachtani Adonai Befo'olecha; Bema'asei Yadeicha Aranen. Mah-
Gadelu Ma'aseicha Adonai Me'od. Ameku Machshevoteicha. Ish-
Ba'ar Lo Yeda'; Uchesil. Lo-Yavin Et-Zot. Bifroach Resha'im Kemo
Esev. Vayatzitzu Chol-Po'alei Aven; Lehishamedam Adei-'Ad.
Ve'attah Marom. Le'olam Adonai Ki Hineh Oyeveicha Adonai Ki-
Hineh Oyeveicha Yovedu; Yitparedu. Chol-Po'alei Aven. Vatarem
Kir'eim Karni; Baloti. Beshemen Ra'anan. Vatabet Eini. Beshurai
Bakamim Alai Mere'im. Tishma'nah Oznai. Tzaddik Kattamar
Yifrach; Ke'erez Ballevanon Yisgeh. Shetulim Beveit Adonai
Bechatzrot Eloheinu Yafrichu. Od Yenuvun Beseivah; Deshenim
Vera'ananim Yihyu. Lehagid Ki-Yashar Adonai Tzuri. Velo-Avlatah
Bo.

A Psalm, a Song. For the Shabbat day. It is a good thing to give
thanks to Hashem, And to sing praises to Your name, Most High; To
declare Your lovingkindness in the morning, And Your faithfulness
in the night seasons, With an instrument of ten strings, and with the
psaltery; With a solemn sound on the harp. For You, Hashem, have
made me glad through Your work; I will rejoice in the works of Your
hands. How great are Your works, Hashem. Your thoughts are very
deep. A brutish man doesn't know, Neither does a fool understand
this. When the wicked spring up as the grass, And when all the
workers of iniquity flourish; It is that they may be destroyed forever.
But You, Hashem, are on high forever. For, behold, Your enemies,
Hashem, For, behold, Your enemies will perish: All the workers of
iniquity will be scattered. But my horn You have exalted like the
horn of the wild-ox; I am anointed with rich oil. My eye has also
gazed on them that lie in wait for me, My ears have heard my desire
of the evil-doers that rise up against me. The righteous will flourish
like the palm-tree; He will grow like a cedar in Levanon. Planted in
the House of Hashem, They will flourish in the courts of our God.
They will still bring forth fruit in old age; They will be full of sap and
richness; To declare that Hashem is upright, My Rock, in Whom
there is no unrighteousness.

All stand and return the Torah to its place and say:

יְהַלְלוּ | אֶת־שֵׁם יְהֹוָה כִּי־נִשְׂגָּב שְׁמוֹ לְבַדּוֹ הוֹדוֹ עַל־אֶרֶץ וְשָׁמָיִם:
וַיָּרֶם קֶרֶן | לְעַמּוֹ תְּהִלָּה לְכָל־חֲסִידָיו לִבְנֵי יִשְׂרָאֵל עַם קְרֹבוֹ
הַלְלוּיָהּ: יְהֹוָה הוּא הָאֱלֹהִים. יְהֹוָה הוּא הָאֱלֹהִים בַּשָּׁמַיִם מִמַּעַל
וְעַל־הָאָרֶץ מִתָּחַת אֵין עוֹד: אֵין־כָּמוֹךָ בָאֱלֹהִים | אֲדֹנָי וְאֵין
כְּמַעֲשֶׂיךָ:

Yehalelu Et-Shem Adonai Ki-Nisgav Shemo Levado; Hodo. Al-'Eretz
Veshamayim. Vayarem Keren Le'ammo Tehilah Lechol-Chasidav.
Livnei Yisra'el Am Kerovo. Halleluyah. Adonai Hu Ha'elohim.
Adonai Hu Ha'elohim. Bashamayim Mima'al. Ve'al-Ha'aretz
Mitachat; Ein Od. Ein-Kamocha Va'elohim Adonai. Ve'ein
Kema'aseicha.

"Let them praise the name of Hashem, For exalted is His name
alone; His glory is over the earth and the heavens. He has lifted up
the horn of strength of His people; He is the praise of all His pious
servants, Of the children of Yisrael, the people near to Him.
Halleluyah — Praise Hashem. Hashem, He is God, Hashem, He is
God, In the heavens above and on the earth beneath. There is none
else. There is none like You, Hashem, among the gods, or nothing
like Your works." (Ps. 148:13, 86:8)

Some add:

וּבְנֻחֹה יֹאמַר שׁוּבָה יְהֹוָה רִבְבוֹת אַלְפֵי יִשְׂרָאֵל: הֲשִׁיבֵנוּ יְהֹוָה |
אֵלֶיךָ וְנָשׁוּבָה (וְנָשׁוּבָה) חַדֵּשׁ יָמֵינוּ כְּקֶדֶם: וַיִּירָא וַיֹּאמַר מַה־נּוֹרָא
הַמָּקוֹם הַזֶּה אֵין זֶה כִּי אִם־בֵּית אֱלֹהִים וְזֶה שַׁעַר הַשָּׁמָיִם:

Uvenuchoh Yomar Shuvah Adonai Rivot Alfei Yisra'el. Hashiveinu
Adonai Eleicha Venashuvah. Chadesh Yameinu Kekedem.

And when it rested, he said: 'Return, Hashem, to the ten thousands
of the families of Israel.' "Hashem, turn us again towards You, and
we will return. Renew our days as of old." And he was afraid, and
said: 'How awesome is this place. This is none other than the House
of God, and this is the gate of heaven.' (Num. 10:36, Lam. 5:21, Gen. 28:17)

When the scroll of the Torah has been replaced in the Ark:

כִּי לֶקַח טוֹב נָתַתִּי לָכֶם תּוֹרָתִי אַל־תַּעֲזֹבוּ: תִּכּוֹן תְּפִלָּתִי קְטֹרֶת לְפָנֶיךָ מַשְׂאַת כַּפַּי מִנְחַת־עָרֶב: הַקְשִׁיבָה | לְקוֹל שַׁוְעִי מַלְכִּי וֵאלֹהָי כִּי־אֵלֶיךָ אֶתְפַּלָּל:

Ki Lekach Tov Natati Lachem Torati Al Ta'azovu. Tikon Tefillati Ketoret Lefaneicha Mas'at Kapai Minchat Arev: Hakshivah Lekol Shav'i Malki Velohai Ki Eleicha Etpalal:

For I give you good teaching; Do not forsake my Torah. Let my prayer be set as incense before You, The lifting up of my hands as the evening sacrifice. Attend to the voice of my cry, my King, and my God; For to You do I pray. (Proverbs 4:2, Psalms 141:2, 5:3)

The Chazan Says Hatzi-Kaddish.

Kaddish is only recited in a minyan (ten men). אמן denotes when the congregation responds "Amen" together out loud. According to the Shulchan Arukh, the congregation says "Yehei Shemeh Rabba" to "Yitbarach" out loud together without interruption, and also that one should respond "Amen" after "Yitbarach." (SA, OC 55,56) This is not the common custom today. Though many are accustomed to answering according to their own custom, it is advised to respond in the custom of the one reciting to avoid not fragmenting into smaller groups. ("Lo Titgodedu" - BT, Yevamot 13b / SA, OC 493, Rema / MT, Avodah Zara 12:15)

יִתְגַּדַּל וְיִתְקַדַּשׁ שְׁמֵהּ רַבָּא. אמן בְּעָלְמָא דִּי בְרָא. כִרְעוּתֵהּ. וְיַמְלִיךְ מַלְכוּתֵהּ. וְיַצְמַח פֻּרְקָנֵהּ. וִיקָרֵב מְשִׁיחֵהּ. אמן בְּחַיֵּיכוֹן וּבְיוֹמֵיכוֹן וּבְחַיֵּי דְכָל בֵּית יִשְׂרָאֵל. בַּעֲגָלָא וּבִזְמַן קָרִיב. וְאִמְרוּ אָמֵן. אמן יְהֵא שְׁמֵיהּ רַבָּא מְבָרַךְ לְעָלַם וּלְעָלְמֵי עָלְמַיָּא יִתְבָּרַךְ. וְיִשְׁתַּבַּח. וְיִתְפָּאַר. וְיִתְרוֹמַם. וְיִתְנַשֵּׂא. וְיִתְהַדָּר. וְיִתְעַלֶּה. וְיִתְהַלָּל שְׁמֵהּ דְּקֻדְשָׁא. בְּרִיךְ הוּא. אמן לְעֵלָּא מִן כָּל בִּרְכָתָא שִׁירָתָא. תֻּשְׁבְּחָתָא וְנֶחֱמָתָא. דַּאֲמִירָן בְּעָלְמָא. וְאִמְרוּ אָמֵן. אמן

Yitgadal Veyitkadash Shemeh Rabba. **Amen** Be'alema Di Vera. Kir'uteh. Veyamlich Malchuteh. Veyatzmach Purkaneh. Vikarev Meshicheh. **Amen** Bechayeichon Uveyomeichon Uvechayei Dechal-Beit Yisra'el. Ba'agala Uvizman Kariv. Ve'imru Amen. **Amen** Yehei Shemeh Rabba Mevarach Le'alam Ule'alemei Alemaya Yitbarach.

Veyishtabach. Veyitpa'ar. Veyitromam. Veyitnasse. Veyit'hadar. Veyit'aleh. Veyit'hallal Shemeh Dekudsha. Berich Hu. ᴬᵐᵉⁿ Le'ella Min Kol Birchata Shirata. Tushbechata Venechemata. Da'amiran Be'alema. Ve'imru Amen. ᴬᵐᵉⁿ

Glorified and sanctified be God's great name ᴬᵐᵉⁿ throughout the world which He has created according to His will. May He establish His kingdom, hastening His salvation and the coming of His Messiah, ᴬᵐᵉⁿ, in your lifetime and during your days, and within the life of the entire House of Yisrael, speedily and soon; and say, Amen. ᴬᵐᵉⁿ May His great name be blessed forever and to all eternity. Blessed and praised, glorified and exalted, extolled and honored, adored and lauded is the name of the Holy One, blessed is He, ᴬᵐᵉⁿ Beyond all the blessings and hymns, praises and consolations that are ever spoken in the world; and say, Amen. ᴬᵐᵉⁿ

LAWS OF AMIDAH

When one gets up to pray if he was standing outside the Land of Yisrael, he should turn his face toward the Land of Yisrael and focus also on Yerushalayim and the Temple and the Holy of Holies. One who is not able to determine the directions, [should] direct one's heart to their Father in Heaven. One should consider oneself as if one is standing in the Beit Hamikdash, and in one's heart, one should be directed upward towards Heaven. One who prays needs to intend in their heart the meaning of the words which are coming out of their mouth. They should think as if the Divine Presence is before them, and remove all distracting thoughts from themselves, until their thoughts and intention are pure in their prayer. (SA, OC 94, 95, 98) These are the blessings at which we bow: in Avot, at the beginning and at the end; in Modim, at the beginning and at the end. And if you come to bow at the end of every blessing or at the beginning, we teach him to not bow but in the middle, one can bow. One needs to bend until all the vertebrae in his spine are bent. His head should stay straight and submissive. One should not bow too much until his mouth is opposite his belt. If he is sick or old and cannot bow, he should humble his head, that is enough. Bow at "Baruch" and stand up at Hashem's name. (SA, OC 113,114) One should position one's feet next to each other as though they are one, in order to imitate angels, as it written regarding them: "their feet were a straight foot" (Ez. 1:7), which is to say their feet appeared as one foot. One should take three steps forward in the way of coming close and approaching a matter that must be done. (SA, OC 95, Rema)

Amidah / Shemoneh Esrei - Mincha

Take three steps forward and say:

Adonai Sefatai Tiftach; Ufi. Yagid
Tehilatecha.

אֲדֹנָי שְׂפָתַי תִּפְתָּח וּפִי יַגִּיד
תְּהִלָּתֶךָ:

Hashem, open my lips, that my mouth may declare Your praise.

Avot / Fathers

Bow at "Baruch Attah" / "Blessed are You". Raise up at Adonai / Hashem.

Baruch Attah Adonai Eloheinu

בָּרוּךְ אַתָּה יְהוָֹה אֱלֹהֵינוּ

Velohei Avoteinu. Elohei

וֵאלֹהֵי אֲבוֹתֵינוּ. אֱלֹהֵי

Avraham. Elohei Yitzchak.

אַבְרָהָם. אֱלֹהֵי יִצְחָק.

Velohei Ya'akov. Ha'el Hagadol

וֵאלֹהֵי יַעֲקֹב. הָאֵל הַגָּדוֹל

Hagibor Vehanorah. El Elyon.

הַגִּבּוֹר וְהַנּוֹרָא. אֵל עֶלְיוֹן.

Gomel Chasadim Tovim. Koneh

גּוֹמֵל חֲסָדִים טוֹבִים. קוֹנֵה

Hakol. Vezocher Chasdei Avot.

הַכֹּל. וְזוֹכֵר חַסְדֵּי אָבוֹת.

Umevi Go'el Livnei Veneihem

וּמֵבִיא גוֹאֵל לִבְנֵי בְנֵיהֶם

Lema'an Shemo Be'ahavah.

לְמַעַן שְׁמוֹ בְּאַהֲבָה:

Blessed are You, Hashem our God and God of our fathers, God of Avraham, God of Yitzchak and God of Yaakov; the great, mighty and revered God, most high God, Who bestows lovingkindness. Master of all things; Who remembers the kindnesses of our fathers, and Who will bring a redeemer to their children's children for the sake of His name in love.

During the 10 days of repentance (Rosh Hashanah to Yom Kippur) add:

Zochrenu Lechayim. Melech Chafetz

זָכְרֵנוּ לְחַיִּים. מֶלֶךְ חָפֵץ

Bachayim. Katevenu Besefer Chayim.

בַּחַיִּים. כָּתְבֵנוּ בְּסֵפֶר חַיִּים.

Lema'anach Elohim Chayim.

לְמַעַנְךָ אֱלֹהִים חַיִּים.

Remember us to life, King Who delights in life; inscribe us in the book of life for Your sake, Oh living God.

Bow at "Baruch Attah" / Blessed are You. Raise up at Adonai / Hashem.

Melech Ozeir Umoshia   מֶלֶךְ עוֹזֵר וּמוֹשִׁיעַ

Umagen. Baruch Attah Adonai   וּמָגֵן: בָּרוּךְ אַתָּה יְהֹוָה

Magen Avraham.   מָגֵן אַבְרָהָם:

King, Supporter, and Savior and Shield. Blessed are You, Hashem, Shield of Avraham.

Gevurot / Powers

We [in Yisrael] begin to say "Mashiv Haruach" in the second blessing of the Amidah from the Musaf [Additional] Service of the last day of Sukkot, and conclude at the Musaf [Additional] Service of the first day of Pesach. On the first day of Pesach the congregation still says it in the Musaf Service, but the Reader stops saying it then. In lands outside of Yisrael, [in the Birkhat HaShanim / Blessing for the Years,] we begin to pray for rain in the Arvit (Evening) Service of the sixtieth day after the New Moon of Tishrei, and in Yisrael we begin to say it in the evening of the seventh day of Cheshvan, and it is said until the Afternoon Service on the day preceding the first day of Passover. If one prayed for rain in the summer, or if one omitted to pray for it in the winter, he must repeat the Amidah again. If one said "Morid Hageshem" in the summer time, he must repeat again from the beginning of the blessing. If he already concluded the blessing, he must read the entire Amidah again. Likewise in the winter, if he omitted it, he must begin all over again. (SA, OC 117)

Attah Gibor Le'olam Adonai.   אַתָּה גִבּוֹר לְעוֹלָם אֲדֹנָי.

Mechayeh Meitim Attah. Rav   מְחַיֵּה מֵתִים אַתָּה. רַב

Lehoshia.   לְהוֹשִׁיעַ.

You, Hashem, are mighty forever; You revive the dead; You are powerful to save.

B'ketz: Morid Hatal.   בקיץ: מוֹרִיד הַטָּל.

B'choref: Mashiv Haruach Umorid   בחורף: מַשִּׁיב הָרוּחַ וּמוֹרִיד

Hageshem.   הַגֶּשֶׁם.

In summer: You cause the dew to fall.

In winter: You cause the wind to blow and the rain to fall.

Mechalkel Chayim Bechesed.   מְכַלְכֵּל חַיִּים בְּחֶסֶד.

Mechayeh Meitim Berachamim   מְחַיֵּה מֵתִים בְּרַחֲמִים

Rabim. Somech Nofelim. Verofei	רַבִּים. סוֹמֵךְ נוֹפְלִים. וְרוֹפֵא
Cholim. Umatir Asurim.	חוֹלִים. וּמַתִּיר אֲסוּרִים.
Umekayem Emunato Lishenei	וּמְקַיֵּם אֱמוּנָתוֹ לִישֵׁנֵי
Afar. Mi Chamocha Ba'al	עָפָר. מִי כָמוֹךָ בַּעַל
Gevurot. Umi Domeh Lach.	גְּבוּרוֹת. וּמִי דוֹמֶה לָּךְ.
Melech Memit Umechayeh	מֶלֶךְ מֵמִית וּמְחַיֶּה
Umatzmiach Yeshu'ah.	וּמַצְמִיחַ יְשׁוּעָה.

You sustain the living with kindness, and revive the dead with great mercy; You support all who fall, and heal the sick; You set the captives free, and keep faith with those who sleep in the dust. Who is like You, Master of power? Who resembles You, Oh King? You bring death and restore life, and cause salvation to flourish.

During the 10 days of repentance (Rosh Hashanah to Yom Kippur) add:

| Mi Chamocha Av Harachaman. Zocher | מִי כָמוֹךָ אָב הָרַחֲמָן. זוֹכֵר |
| Yetzurav Berachamim Lechayim. | יְצוּרָיו בְּרַחֲמִים לְחַיִּים. |

Who is like You, merciful Father? In mercy You remember Your creatures to life.

Vene'eman Attah Lehachayot	וְנֶאֱמָן אַתָּה לְהַחֲיוֹת
Meitim. Baruch Attah Adonai	מֵתִים: בָּרוּךְ אַתָּה יְהֹוֶה
Mechayeh Hameitim.	מְחַיֵּה הַמֵּתִים:

And You are faithful to revive the dead. Blessed are You, Hashem, Who revives the dead.

Kedusha

Kedusha is said only in a minyan (10 men). If one is not available, skip to "Kedushat Hashem". It is proper to position one's feet together at the time one is reciting Kedushah with the prayer-leader.

Nakdishach Vena'aritzach.	נַקְדִּישָׁךְ וְנַעֲרִיצָךְ.
Keno'am Siach Sod Sarfei	כְּנְעַם שִׂיחַ סוֹד שַׂרְפֵי
Kodesh. Hamshaleshim Lecha	קֹדֶשׁ. הַמְשַׁלְּשִׁים לְךָ

Kedushah. Vechein Katuv Al Yad	קְדֻשָּׁה. וְכֵן כָּתוּב עַל יַד
Nevi'ach. Vekara Zeh El-Zeh	נְבִיאָךְ: וְקָרָא זֶה אֶל־זֶה
Ve'amar. **Kadosh Kadosh Kadosh**	וְאָמַר קָדוֹשׁ | קָדוֹשׁ קָדוֹשׁ
Adonai Tzeva'ot; Melo Chol-	יְהֹוָה צְבָאוֹת מְלֹא כָל־
Ha'aretz Kevodo. Le'ummatam	הָאָרֶץ כְּבוֹדוֹ: לְעֻמָּתָם
Meshabechim Ve'omerim.	מְשַׁבְּחִים וְאוֹמְרִים:
Baruch Kevod-Adonai	בָּרוּךְ כְּבוֹד־יְהֹוָה
Mimekomo. Uvedivrei	מִמְּקוֹמוֹ: וּבְדִבְרֵי
Kodshecha Katuv Lemor.	קָדְשְׁךָ כָּתוּב לֵאמֹר: יִמְלֹךְ
Yimloch Adonai Le'olam.	יְהֹוָה | לְעוֹלָם אֱלֹהַיִךְ
Elohayich Tziyon Ledor Vador.	צִיּוֹן לְדֹר וָדֹר
Halleluyah.	הַלְלוּיָהּ:

We sanctify and revere You in the sweet words of the assembly of holy Seraphim who three times acclaim Your holiness, as it is written by Your prophet: "They keep calling to one another: '**Holy, holy, holy is Hashem of hosts; The whole earth is full of His glory.**" Angels respond with praise and say: "**Blessed is the glory of Hashem from His Abode.**" And in Your holy scriptures it is written: "**Hashem will reign forever, your God, Tziyon, from generation to generation. Halleluyah.**"

Kedushat HaShem / Holiness of the Name

Attah Kadosh Veshimcha	אַתָּה קָדוֹשׁ וְשִׁמְךָ
Kadosh. Ukedoshim Bechol-	קָדוֹשׁ. וּקְדוֹשִׁים בְּכָל־
Yom Yehalelucha Selah. Baruch	יוֹם יְהַלְלוּךָ סֶּלָה: בָּרוּךְ
Attah Adonai Ha' El Hakadosh.	אַתָּה יְהֹוָה הָאֵל הַקָּדוֹשׁ:

You are holy and Your name is holy, and the holy-ones will praise You every day, selah. Blessed are You, Hashem, The Holy God.

During the 10 days of repentance (Rosh Hashanah to Yom Kippur) say:

Hamelech Hakadosh.　　　　　　　　　　הַמֶּלֶךְ הַקָּדוֹשׁ:

The Holy King.

If one is unsure or forgot if they said, repeat the Amidah. If it was immediately said after, it is fulfilled.

Kedushat HaYom / Holiness of the Day

Attah Echad Veshimcha Echad.	אַתָּה אֶחָד וְשִׁמְךָ אֶחָד.
Umi Che'ammecha Ke'yisrael	וּמִי כְעַמְּךָ כְּיִשְׂרָאֵל
Goy Echad Ba'aretz. Tif'eret	גּוֹי אֶחָד בָּאָרֶץ. תִּפְאֶרֶת
Gedullah. Va'ateret Yeshu'ah.	גְּדֻלָּה. וַעֲטֶרֶת יְשׁוּעָה.
Yom Menuchah Ukedushah	יוֹם מְנוּחָה וּקְדֻשָּׁה
Le'ammecha Natata. Avraham	לְעַמְּךָ נָתָתָּ. אַבְרָהָם
Yagel. Yitzchak Yerannen.	יָגֵל. יִצְחָק יְרַנֵּן.
Ya'akov Uvanav Yanuchu Vo.	יַעֲקֹב וּבָנָיו יָנוּחוּ בוֹ.
Menuchat Ahavah Unedavah.	מְנוּחַת אַהֲבָה וּנְדָבָה.
Menuchat Emet Ve'emunah.	מְנוּחַת אֱמֶת וֶאֱמוּנָה.
Menuchat Shalom Hashket	מְנוּחַת שָׁלוֹם הַשְׁקֵט
Vavetach. Menuchah Shelemah	וָבֶטַח. מְנוּחָה שְׁלֵמָה
She'attah Hu Rotzeh Vah. Yakiru	שֶׁאַתָּה הוּא רוֹצֶה בָּהּ. יַכִּירוּ
Vaneicha Veyede'u Ki Me'itecha	בָנֶיךָ וְיֵדְעוּ כִּי מֵאִתְּךָ
Hi Menuchatam. Ve'al	הִיא מְנוּחָתָם. וְעַל
Menuchatam Yakdishu Et	מְנוּחָתָם יַקְדִּישׁוּ אֶת
Shemecha:	שְׁמֶךָ:

You are One and Your name is One, and who is like Your people Yisrael, a unique nation on earth? A great glory, and a crown of salvation, and a day of rest and holiness You gave. Avraham rejoiced, Yitzchak sang out, Yaakov and his sons would rest on it; a rest of love and generosity, a rest of truth and faith, a rest of peace, and silence and safety. A perfect rest that You want to come. May Your children know and understand that their rest is from You; and in their rest, may they sanctify Your name.

Eloheinu Velohei Avoteinu.	אֱלֹהֵינוּ וֵאלֹהֵי אֲבוֹתֵינוּ.
Retzeh Na Bimnuchatenu.	רְצֵה נָא בִמְנוּחָתֵנוּ.
Kadeshenu Bemitzvoteicha. Sim	קַדְּשֵׁנוּ בְּמִצְוֹתֶיךָ. שִׂים
Chelkenu Betoratach. Sabe'einu	חֶלְקֵנוּ בְּתוֹרָתָךְ. שַׂבְּעֵנוּ
Mituvach. Same'ach Nafshenu	מִטּוּבָךְ. שַׂמֵּחַ נַפְשֵׁנוּ
Bishu'atach. Vetaher Libenu	בִּישׁוּעָתָךְ. וְטַהֵר לִבֵּנוּ
Le'avdecha Ve'emet.	לְעָבְדְּךָ בֶּאֱמֶת.
Vehanchilenu Adonai Eloheinu	וְהַנְחִילֵנוּ יְהֹוָה אֱלֹהֵינוּ
Be'ahavah Uveratzon Shabbat	בְּאַהֲבָה וּבְרָצוֹן שַׁבַּת
Kodshecha. Veyanuchu Vo Kol-	קָדְשֶׁךָ. וְיָנוּחוּ בוֹ כָּל־
Yisra'el Mekadeshei Shemecha.	יִשְׂרָאֵל מְקַדְּשֵׁי שְׁמֶךָ.
Baruch Attah Adonai Mekadesh	בָּרוּךְ אַתָּה יְהֹוָה מְקַדֵּשׁ
Hashabbat.	הַשַּׁבָּת.

Our God, God of our fathers, be pleased with our rest. Sanctify us through Your commandments and grant our portion in Your Torah. Content us with Your goodness. Rejoice our soul with Your salvation. And make our heart pure to serve You in truth. Cause us to inherit, Hashem our God, Your holy Shabbat with love and favor: and grant rest on it to all Yisrael, who sanctify Your name. Blessed are You, Hashem Who sanctifies the Shabbat.

Avodah / Temple Service

Retzeh Adonai Eloheinu	רְצֵה יְהֹוָה אֱלֹהֵינוּ
Be'ammecha Yisra'el Velitfilatam	בְּעַמְּךָ יִשְׂרָאֵל וְלִתְפִלָּתָם
She'eh. Vehasheiv Ha'avodah	שְׁעֵה. וְהָשֵׁב הָעֲבוֹדָה
Lidvir Beitecha. Ve'ishei Yisra'el	לִדְבִיר בֵּיתֶךָ. וְאִשֵּׁי יִשְׂרָאֵל
Utefilatam. Meheirah Be'ahavah	וּתְפִלָּתָם. מְהֵרָה בְּאַהֲבָה
Tekabel Beratzon. Utehi	תְקַבֵּל בְּרָצוֹן. וּתְהִי
Leratzon Tamid Avodat Yisra'el	לְרָצוֹן תָּמִיד עֲבוֹדַת יִשְׂרָאֵל
Ammecha.	עַמֶּךָ:

Be favorable, Hashem our God, on Your people Yisrael and regard their prayers. And the service to the Sanctuary of Your House, and the fire offerings of Yisrael, and their prayers accept soon with love. And may the service of Your people, Yisrael, always be favorable.

On Rosh Chodesh and Chol HaMoed Passover and Sukkot say:

Ya'aleh Veyavo

אֱלֹהֵינוּ וֵאלֹהֵי אֲבוֹתֵינוּ. יַעֲלֶה וְיָבֹא. וְיַגִּיעַ וְיֵרָאֶה. וְיֵרָצֶה וְיִשָּׁמַע. וְיִפָּקֵד וְיִזָּכֵר. זִכְרוֹנֵנוּ וְזִכְרוֹן אֲבוֹתֵינוּ. זִכְרוֹן יְרוּשָׁלַיִם עִירָךְ. וְזִכְרוֹן מָשִׁיחַ בֶּן־דָּוִד עַבְדָּךְ. וְזִכְרוֹן כָּל־עַמְּךָ בֵּית יִשְׂרָאֵל לְפָנֶיךָ. לִפְלֵיטָה. לְטוֹבָה. לְחֵן. לְחֶסֶד וּלְרַחֲמִים. לְחַיִּים טוֹבִים וּלְשָׁלוֹם. בְּיוֹם:

Eloheinu Velohei Avoteinu. Ya'aleh Veyavo. Veyagia Veyera'eh. Veyeratzeh Veyishama'. Veyipaked Veyizacher. Zichronenu Vezichron Avoteinu. Zichron Yerushalayim Irach. Vezichron Mashiach Ben-David Avdach. Vezichron Kol-'Ammecha Beit Yisra'el Lefaneicha. Lifleitah. Letovah. Lechein. Lechesed Ulerachamim. Lechayim Tovim Uleshalom. Beyom:

Our God, and God of our fathers, may it rise, and come, arrive, appear, find favor, and be heard, and be considered, and be remembered our remembrance and the remembrance of our fathers, Yerushalayim Your city, the remembrance of Messiah ben David Your servant, and the remembrance of all Your people of the House of Yisrael before You for deliverance, for good favor, for kindness and mercy, for good life and for peace. On this day of:

On Rosh Chodesh:

רֹאשׁ חֹדֶשׁ הַזֶּה.

Rosh Chodesh Hazeh.

Rosh Chodesh (New Moon).

On Pesach:

חַג הַמַּצוֹת הַזֶּה. בְּיוֹם מִקְרָא קֹדֶשׁ הַזֶּה.

Chag Hamatzot Hazeh. Beyom Mikra Kodesh Hazeh.

The Festival of Matzot. on this day of holy convocation.

On Sukkot:

חַג הַסֻּכּוֹת הַזֶּה. בְּיוֹם מִקְרָא קֹדֶשׁ הַזֶּה.

Chag Hasukkot Hazeh. Beyom Mikra Kodesh Hazeh.

The Festival of Sukkot. on this day of holy convocation.

לְרַחֵם בּוֹ עָלֵינוּ וּלְהוֹשִׁיעֵנוּ. זָכְרֵנוּ יְהֹוָה אֱלֹהֵינוּ בּוֹ לְטוֹבָה. וּפָקְדֵנוּ בּוֹ
לִבְרָכָה. וְהוֹשִׁיעֵנוּ בּוֹ לְחַיִּים טוֹבִים. בִּדְבַר יְשׁוּעָה וְרַחֲמִים. חוּס וְחָנֵּנוּ.
וַחֲמוֹל וְרַחֵם עָלֵינוּ. וְהוֹשִׁיעֵנוּ כִּי אֵלֶיךָ עֵינֵינוּ. כִּי אֵל מֶלֶךְ חַנּוּן וְרַחוּם אָתָּה:

Lerachem Bo Aleinu Ulehoshi'enu. Zochrenu Adonai Eloheinu Bo Letovah.
Ufokdenu Vo Livrachah. Vehoshi'enu Vo Lechayim Tovim. Bidvar Yeshu'ah
Verachamim. Chus Vechanenu. Vachamol Verachem Aleinu. Vehoshi'enu Ki Eleicha
Eineinu. Ki El Melech Chanun Verachum Attah.

to have mercy upon us and save us. Remember us, Hashem our God, on it for good.
Be mindful of us on it for blessing and save us on it for a life of good. With the
promise of salvation and mercy, show us pity, and be gracious to us and have
compassion and mercy on us and save us. For our eyes are lifted towards You, for
You, God, are a gracious and merciful King.

Attah Berachameicha Harabim.	וְאַתָּה בְּרַחֲמֶיךָ הָרַבִּים.
Tachpotz Banu Vetirtzenu.	תַּחְפֹּץ בָּנוּ וְתִרְצֵנוּ.
Vetechezeinah Eineinu	וְתֶחֱזֶינָה עֵינֵינוּ
Beshuvecha Letziyon	בְּשׁוּבְךָ לְצִיּוֹן
Berachamim. Baruch Attah	בְּרַחֲמִים: בָּרוּךְ אַתָּה
Adonai Hamachazir Shechinato	יְהֹוָה הַמַּחֲזִיר שְׁכִינָתוֹ
Letziyon.	לְצִיּוֹן.

And You, in Your abundant mercy, delight in us, and be favorable to us, so that our eyes may witness Your return to Tziyon with mercy. Blessed are You, Hashem Who returns His Presence to Tziyon.

<u>Hoda'ah (Modim) / Thanksgiving</u>

On Saying "Modim" / "We are Thankful" One Bows and begins to rise after "Adonai" / "Hashem".

Modim Anachnu Lach.	מוֹדִים אֲנַחְנוּ לָךְ.
She'attah Hu Adonai Eloheinu	שָׁאַתָּה הוּא יְהֹוָה אֱלֹהֵינוּ
Velohei Avoteinu Le'olam Va'ed.	וֵאלֹהֵי אֲבוֹתֵינוּ לְעוֹלָם וָעֶד.
Tzurenu Tzur Chayeinu	צוּרֵנוּ צוּר חַיֵּינוּ
Umagen Yish'enu Attah Hu.	וּמָגֵן יִשְׁעֵנוּ אַתָּה הוּא.
Ledor Vador Nodeh Lecha	לְדוֹר וָדוֹר נוֹדֶה לְךָ
Unsapeir Tehilatecha. Al	וּנְסַפֵּר תְּהִלָּתֶךָ. עַל
Chayeinu Hamesurim	חַיֵּינוּ הַמְּסוּרִים
Beyadecha. Ve'al Nishmoteinu	בְּיָדֶךָ. וְעַל נִשְׁמוֹתֵינוּ
Hapekudot Lach. Ve'al Niseicha	הַפְּקוּדוֹת לָךְ. וְעַל נִסֶּיךָ
Shebechol-Yom Imanu. Ve'al	שֶׁבְּכָל־יוֹם עִמָּנוּ. וְעַל
Nifle'oteicha Vetovoteicha	נִפְלְאוֹתֶיךָ וְטוֹבוֹתֶיךָ
Shebechol-'Et. Erev Vavoker	שֶׁבְּכָל־עֵת. עֶרֶב וָבֹקֶר
Vetzaharayim. Hatov. Ki Lo	וְצָהֳרָיִם. הַטּוֹב. כִּי לֹא
Chalu Rachameicha.	כָלוּ רַחֲמֶיךָ.
Hamerachem. Ki Lo Tamu	הַמְרַחֵם. כִּי לֹא תַמּוּ
Chasadeicha. Ki Me'olam	חֲסָדֶיךָ. כִּי מֵעוֹלָם
Kivinu Lach.	קִוִּינוּ לָךְ:

We are thankful to You, Hashem our God and the God of our fathers, forever. You are our strength and Rock of our life and the

Shield of our salvation. In every generation we will thank You and recount Your praise for our lives which are given into Your hand, for our souls which are placed in Your care, and for Your miracles which are daily with us, and for Your wonders and goodness—evening, morning and noon. The Beneficent One, for Your mercies never end, Merciful One, for Your kindness has never ceased, for we have always placed our hope in You.

Modim Derabbanan

During the repetition, this is to be recited softly while the Chazan reads the Modim. Still bow at Modim as before.

מוֹדִים אֲנַחְנוּ לָךְ. שָׁאַתָּה הוּא יְהֹוָה אֱלֹהֵינוּ וֵאלֹהֵי אֲבוֹתֵינוּ. אֱלֹהֵי כָל בָּשָׂר. יוֹצְרֵנוּ יוֹצֵר בְּרֵאשִׁית. בְּרָכוֹת וְהוֹדָאוֹת לְשִׁמְךָ הַגָּדוֹל וְהַקָּדוֹשׁ. עַל שֶׁהֶחֱיִיתָנוּ וְקִיַּמְתָּנוּ. כֵּן תְּחַיֵּנוּ וּתְחָנֵּנוּ וְתֶאֱסוֹף גָּלִיּוֹתֵינוּ לְחַצְרוֹת קָדְשֶׁךָ. לִשְׁמֹר חֻקֶּיךָ וְלַעֲשׂוֹת רְצוֹנֶךָ וּלְעָבְדְּךָ בְּלֵבָב שָׁלֵם. עַל שֶׁאֲנַחְנוּ מוֹדִים לָךְ. בָּרוּךְ אֵל הַהוֹדָאוֹת.

Modim Anachnu Lach. She'attah Hu Adonai Eloheinu Velohei Avoteinu. Elohei Chol Basar. Yotzreinu Yotzer Bereshit. Berachot Vehoda'ot Leshimcha Hagadol Vehakadosh. Al Shehecheyitanu Vekiyamtanu. Ken Techayeinu Utechanenu Vete'esof Galyoteinu Lechatzrot Kodshecha. Lishmor Chukkeicha Vela'asot Retzonecha Ule'avedecha Velevav Shalem. Al She'anachnu Modim Lach. Baruch El Hahoda'ot.

We are thankful to You, Hashem our God and the God of our fathers. God of all flesh, our Creator and Former of Creation, blessings and thanks to Your great and holy name, for You have kept us alive and sustained us; may You always grant us life and be gracious to us. And gather our exiles to Your holy courtyards to observe Your statutes, and to do Your will, and to serve You with a perfect heart. For this we thank You. Blessed is God of thanksgivings.

Al HaNissim

On Purim and Hanukkah an extra prayer is added here:

עַל הַנִּסִּים וְעַל הַפֻּרְקָן וְעַל הַגְּבוּרוֹת וְעַל הַתְּשׁוּעוֹת וְעַל הַנִּפְלָאוֹת וְעַל הַנֶּחָמוֹת שֶׁעָשִׂיתָ לַאֲבוֹתֵינוּ בַּיָּמִים הָהֵם בַּזְּמַן הַזֶּה:

Al Hanissim Ve'al Hapurkan Ve'al Hagevurot Ve'al Hateshu'ot Ve'al Hanifla'ot Ve'al Hanechamot She'asita La'avoteinu Bayamim Hahem Bazman Hazeh.

For the miracles, and for the triumphant liberation, and the mighty works, and for the deliverances, and for the wonders, and for the consolations which You have done for our fathers in those days at this season:

On Hanukkah:

בִּימֵי מַתִּתְיָה בֶן־יוֹחָנָן כֹּהֵן גָּדוֹל. חַשְׁמוֹנָאִי וּבָנָיו כְּשֶׁעָמְדָה מַלְכוּת יָוָן
הָרְשָׁעָה עַל עַמְּךָ יִשְׂרָאֵל. לְשַׁכְּחָם תּוֹרָתֶךָ וּלְהַעֲבִירָם מֵחֻקֵּי רְצוֹנֶךָ. וְאַתָּה
בְּרַחֲמֶיךָ הָרַבִּים עָמַדְתָּ לָהֶם בְּעֵת צָרָתָם. רַבְתָּ אֶת רִיבָם. דַּנְתָּ אֶת דִּינָם.
נָקַמְתָּ אֶת נִקְמָתָם. מָסַרְתָּ גִבּוֹרִים בְּיַד חַלָּשִׁים. וְרַבִּים בְּיַד מְעַטִּים. וּרְשָׁעִים
בְּיַד צַדִּיקִים. וּטְמֵאִים בְּיַד טְהוֹרִים. וְזֵדִים בְּיַד עוֹסְקֵי תוֹרָתֶךָ. לְךָ עָשִׂיתָ שֵׁם
גָּדוֹל וְקָדוֹשׁ בְּעוֹלָמֶךָ. וּלְעַמְּךָ יִשְׂרָאֵל עָשִׂיתָ תְּשׁוּעָה גְדוֹלָה וּפֻרְקָן כְּהַיּוֹם
הַזֶּה. וְאַחַר כָּךְ בָּאוּ בָנֶיךָ לִדְבִיר בֵּיתֶךָ. וּפִנּוּ אֶת־הֵיכָלֶךָ. וְטִהֲרוּ אֶת־מִקְדָּשֶׁךָ.
וְהִדְלִיקוּ נֵרוֹת בְּחַצְרוֹת קָדְשֶׁךָ. וְקָבְעוּ שְׁמוֹנַת יְמֵי חֲנֻכָּה אֵלּוּ בְּהַלֵּל
וּבְהוֹדָאָה. וְעָשִׂיתָ עִמָּהֶם נִסִּים וְנִפְלָאוֹת וְנוֹדֶה לְשִׁמְךָ הַגָּדוֹל סֶלָה:

Bimei Mattityah Ven-Yochanan Kohen Gadol. Chashmona'i Uvanav Keshe'amedah
Malchut Yavan Haresha'ah Al Ammecha Yisra'el. Leshakecham Toratach
Uleha'aviram Mechukkei Retzonach. Ve'attah Berachameicha Harabim Amadta
Lahem Be'et Tzaratam. Ravta Et Rivam. Danta Et Dinam. Nakamta Et Nikmatam.
Masarta Giborim Beyad Chalashim. Verabim Beyad Me'atim. Uresha'im Beyad
Tzaddikim. Uteme'im Beyad Tehorim. Vezeidim Beyad Osekei Toratecha. Lecha
Asita Shem Gadol Vekadosh Be'olamach. Ule'ammecha Yisra'el Asita Teshu'ah
Gedolah Ufurkan Kehayom Hazeh. Ve'achar Kach Ba'u Vaneicha Lidvir Beitecha.
Ufinu Et-Heichalecha. Vetiharu Et-Mikdashecha. Vehidliku Nerot Bechatzrot
Kodshecha. Vekave'u Shemonat Yemei Chanukkah Elu Behallel Uvehoda'ah.
Ve'asita Imahem Nissim Venifla'ot Venodeh Leshimcha Hagadol Selah.

Then in the days of Mattityahu ben-Yochanan, High Priest. The Hasmonean and
his sons, when the cruel Greek power rose up against Your people, Yisrael, to make
them forget Your Torah and transgress the statutes of Your will. And You, in Your
great compassion, stood up for them in time of their trial to plead their cause and
defend their judgment. Giving out retribution, delivered the strong into the hand
of the weak, and the many into the hand of the few, and the wicked into the hand of
the upright, and the impure into the hand of the pure, and tyrants into the hand of
the devotees of Your Torah. You made for Yourself a great and holy name in Your
world. And for Your people, Yisrael, You performed a great salvation and
liberation as this very day. Then Your children came to the Sanctuary of Your
House, cleared Your Temple, cleansed Your Sanctuary and kindled lights in Your
courtyards, and they instituted these eight days of Hanukkah for praise and
thanksgiving. And You did miracles and wonders for them, and we give thanks to
Your great name, selah.

On Purim:

בִּימֵי מָרְדְּכַי וְאֶסְתֵּר בְּשׁוּשַׁן הַבִּירָה. כְּשֶׁעָמַד עֲלֵיהֶם הָמָן הָרָשָׁע. בִּקֵּשׁ
לְהַשְׁמִיד לַהֲרֹג וּלְאַבֵּד אֶת־כָּל־הַיְּהוּדִים מִנַּעַר וְעַד זָקֵן טַף וְנָשִׁים בְּיוֹם אֶחָד.

בִּשְׁלֹשָׁה עָשָׂר לְחֹדֶשׁ שְׁנֵים עָשָׂר. הוּא חֹדֶשׁ אֲדָר. וּשְׁלָלָם לָבוֹז. וְאַתָּה בְּרַחֲמֶיךָ הָרַבִּים הֵפַרְתָּ אֶת־עֲצָתוֹ וְקִלְקַלְתָּ אֶת־מַחֲשַׁבְתּוֹ. וַהֲשֵׁבוֹתָ לּוֹ גְּמוּלוֹ בְּרֹאשׁוֹ. וְתָלוּ אוֹתוֹ וְאֶת־בָּנָיו עַל הָעֵץ. וְעָשִׂיתָ עִמָּהֶם נֵס וָפֶלֶא וְנוֹדֶה לְשִׁמְךָ הַגָּדוֹל סֶלָה:

Bimei Mordechai Ve'ester Beshushan Habirah. Keshe'amad Aleihem Haman Harasha. Bikesh Lehashmid Laharog Ule'abed Et-Kol-Hayehudim Mina'ar Ve'ad Zaken Taf Venashim Beyom Echad. Bishloshah Asar Lechodesh Sheneim Asar. Hu Chodesh Adar. Ushelalam Lavoz. Ve'attah Berachameicha Harabim Hefarta Et-'Atzato Vekilkalta Et-Machashavto. Vahasheivota Lo Gemulo Verosho. Vetalu Oto Ve'et-Banav Al Ha'etz. Ve'asita Imahem Nes Vafelei Venodeh Leshimcha Hagadol Selah.

In the days of Mordechai and Ester in Shushan, the capital, the wicked Haman rose up and sought to destroy, slay and utterly annihilate all of the Yehudim, both young and old, women and children, on one day, on the thirteenth day of the twelfth month, which is the month of Adar, and to plunder their possessions. But You in Your great mercy You broke his plan and spoiled his designs, causing them to recoil on his own head, and they hanged him and his sons on the gallows. And You did miracles and wonders for them, and we give thanks to Your great name, selah.

Ve'al Kulam Yitbarach.	וְעַל כֻּלָּם יִתְבָּרַךְ.
Veyitromam. Veyitnasse. Tamid.	וְיִתְרוֹמַם. וְיִתְנַשֵּׂא. תָּמִיד.
Shimcha Malkeinu. Le'olam	שִׁמְךָ מַלְכֵּנוּ. לְעוֹלָם
Va'ed. Vechol-Hachayim	וָעֶד. וְכָל־הַחַיִּים
Yoducha Selah.	יוֹדוּךָ סֶלָה:

For all these acts, may Your name, our King, be blessed, extolled and exalted forever. And all of the living will thank You, selah.

During the 10 days of repentance (Rosh Hashanah to Yom Kippur) say:

Uchetov Lechayim Tovim Kol Benei Veritecha.

וּכְתֹב לְחַיִּים טוֹבִים כָּל בְּנֵי בְרִיתֶךָ.

Inscribe all of Your people of the covenant for a happy life.

Bow at "Baruch Attah" / "Blessed are You". Raise up at Adonai / Hashem.

Vihalelu Vivarechu Et-Shimcha
Hagadol Be'emet Le'olam Ki Tov.

וִיהַלְלוּ וִיבָרְכוּ אֶת־שִׁמְךָ הַגָּדוֹל בֶּאֱמֶת לְעוֹלָם כִּי טוֹב.

Ha'el Yeshu'ateinu Ve'ezrateinu	הָאֵל יְשׁוּעָתֵנוּ וְעֶזְרָתֵנוּ
Selah. Ha'el Hatov. Baruch Attah	סֶלָה. הָאֵל הַטּוֹב: בָּרוּךְ אַתָּה
Adonai Hatov Shimcha Ulecha	יְהֹוָה הַטּוֹב שִׁמְךָ וּלְךָ
Na'eh Lehodot.	נָאֶה לְהוֹדוֹת:

And they will praise and bless Your great and good name sincerely, forever. For You are good, the God of our salvation and our help forever, the Good God. Blessed are You, Hashem, Your name is good and to You it is good to give thanks.

Sim Shalom / Grant Peace

Sim Shalom Tovah Uverachah.	שִׂים שָׁלוֹם טוֹבָה וּבְרָכָה.
Chayim Chein Vachesed	חַיִּים חֵן וָחֶסֶד
Verachamim. Aleinu Ve'al Kol-	וְרַחֲמִים. עָלֵינוּ וְעַל כָּל־
Yisra'el Ammecha. Uvarecheinu	יִשְׂרָאֵל עַמֶּךָ. וּבָרְכֵנוּ
Avinu Kulanu Ke'echad Be'or	אָבִינוּ כֻּלָּנוּ כְּאֶחָד בְּאוֹר
Paneicha. Ki Ve'or Paneicha	פָּנֶיךָ. כִּי בְאוֹר פָּנֶיךָ
Natata Lanu Adonai Eloheinu	נָתַתָּ לָּנוּ יְהֹוָה אֱלֹהֵינוּ
Torah Vechayim. Ahavah	תּוֹרָה וְחַיִּים. אַהֲבָה
Vachesed. Tzedakah	וָחֶסֶד. צְדָקָה
Verachamim. Berachah	וְרַחֲמִים. בְּרָכָה
Veshalom. Vetov Be'eineicha	וְשָׁלוֹם. וְטוֹב בְּעֵינֶיךָ
Levarecheinu Ulevarech Et-	לְבָרְכֵנוּ וּלְבָרֵךְ אֶת־
Kol-'Ammecha Yisra'el. Berov	כָּל־עַמְּךָ יִשְׂרָאֵל. בְּרֹב
Oz Veshalom.	עֹז וְשָׁלוֹם:

Grant peace, goodness and blessing, a life of grace, and kindness and mercy, to us and to all Yisrael, Your people. And bless us, our

Father, all as one with the light of Your countenance; for with the light of Your countenance You have given us, Hashem our God, a Torah and life, love and kindness, righteousness and mercy, blessing and peace. May it be good in Your eyes to bless us and bless all of Your people, Yisrael, with abundant strength and peace.

During the 10 days of repentance (Rosh Hashanah to Yom Kippur) say:

Uvesefer Chayim. Berachah Veshalom.	וּבְסֵפֶר חַיִּים. בְּרָכָה וְשָׁלוֹם.
Ufarnasah Tovah Vishu'ah Venechamah.	וּפַרְנָסָה טוֹבָה וִישׁוּעָה וְנֶחָמָה.
Ugezerot Tovot. Nizacher Venikkatev	וּגְזֵרוֹת טוֹבוֹת. נִזָּכֵר וְנִכָּתֵב
Lefaneicha. Anachnu Vechol Ammecha	לְפָנֶיךָ. אֲנַחְנוּ וְכָל עַמְּךָ
Beit Yisra'el. Lechayim Tovim	בֵּית יִשְׂרָאֵל. לְחַיִּים טוֹבִים
Uleshalom.	וּלְשָׁלוֹם.

May we and all Yisrael Your people be remembered and inscribed before You in the book of life and blessing, peace and prosperity, for a happy life and for peace.

Baruch Attah Adonai	בָּרוּךְ אַתָּה יוהווהו
Hamevarech Et Ammo Yisra'el	הַמְבָרֵךְ אֶת עַמּוֹ יִשְׂרָאֵל
Bashalom. Amen.	בַּשָּׁלוֹם. אָמֵן:

Blessed are You, Hashem, Who blesses His people Yisrael with peace. Amen.

Yihyu Leratzon Imrei-Fi Vehegyon Libi	יִהְיוּ לְרָצוֹן אִמְרֵי־פִי וְהֶגְיוֹן לִבִּי
Lefaneicha; Adonai Tzuri Vego'ali.	לְפָנֶיךָ יְהֹוָה צוּרִי וְגֹאֲלִי:

May the words of my mouth and the meditation of my heart find favor before You, Hashem my Rock and my Redeemer.

The chazan's repetition ends here; personal / individual continue:

Elohai. Netzor Leshoni Meira	אֱלֹהַי. נְצֹר לְשׁוֹנִי מֵרָע
Vesiftotai Midaber Mirmah.	וְשִׂפְתוֹתַי מִדַּבֵּר מִרְמָה.
Velimkalelai Nafshi Tidom.	וְלִמְקַלְלַי נַפְשִׁי תִדֹּם.
Venafshi Ke'afar Lakol Tihyeh.	וְנַפְשִׁי כֶּעָפָר לַכֹּל תִּהְיֶה.
Petach Libi Betoratecha.	פְּתַח לִבִּי בְּתוֹרָתֶךָ.
Ve'acharei Mitzvoteicha Tirdof	וְאַחֲרֵי מִצְוֹתֶיךָ תִּרְדֹּף
Nafshi. Vechol-Hakamim Alai	נַפְשִׁי. וְכָל־הַקָּמִים עָלַי
Lera'ah. Meheirah Hafer Atzatam	לְרָעָה. מְהֵרָה הָפֵר עֲצָתָם
Vekalkel Machshevotam. Aseh	וְקַלְקֵל מַחְשְׁבוֹתָם. עֲשֵׂה
Lema'an Shemach. Aseh	לְמַעַן שְׁמֶךָ. עֲשֵׂה
Lema'an Yeminach. Aseh	לְמַעַן יְמִינָךְ. עֲשֵׂה
Lema'an Toratach. Aseh Lema'an	לְמַעַן תּוֹרָתָךְ. עֲשֵׂה לְמַעַן
Kedushatach. Lema'an	קְדֻשָּׁתָךְ. לְמַעַן
Yechaletzun Yedideicha;	יֵחָלְצוּן יְדִידֶיךָ
Hoshi'ah Yeminecha Va'aneni.	הוֹשִׁיעָה יְמִינְךָ וַעֲנֵנִי:

My God, guard my tongue from evil, and my lips from speaking deceit. And to those who curse me may my soul be silent; and may my soul be like the dust to all. Open my heart to Your Torah, that my soul may follow after Your commandments. And all that rise to do evil against me, speedily nullify their plan, and spoil their thoughts. Do it for the sake of Your name; do it for the sake of Your right hand; do it for the sake of Your Torah, do it for the sake of Your holiness. That Your beloved may be rescued, save with Your right hand and answer me. (Ps. 60:7)

Yihyu Leratzon Imrei-Fi Vehegyon Libi	יִהְיוּ לְרָצוֹן אִמְרֵי־פִי וְהֶגְיוֹן לִבִּי
Lefaneicha; Adonai Tzuri Vego'ali.	לְפָנֶיךָ יְהֹוָה צוּרִי וְגֹאֲלִי:

May the words of my mouth and the meditation of my heart find favor before You, Hashem my Rock and my Redeemer.

Oseh Shalom

One bows and takes three steps backwards, while still bowing. After three steps, while still bowing and before erecting, while saying, "Oseh Shalom Bimromav", turn one's face to the left, "Hu [Berachamav] Ya'aseh Shalom Aleinu", turn one's face to the right; [face forward and] then bow forward like a servant leaving his master. (SA, OC 123:1)

Oseh Shalom On the 10 Days of	עוֹשֶׂה שָׁלוֹם
Repentance: (Hashalom) Bimromav, Hu	בעש״ת אומ׳: (הַשָּׁלוֹם) בִּמְרוֹמָיו. הוּא
Berachamav Ya'aseh Shalom	בְּרַחֲמָיו יַעֲשֶׂה שָׁלוֹם
Aleinu, Ve'al Kol-'Ammo Yisra'el,	עָלֵינוּ. וְעַל כָּל־עַמּוֹ יִשְׂרָאֵל.
Ve'imru Amen.	וְאִמְרוּ אָמֵן:

Creator of On the 10 Days of Repentance: (the) peace in His high places, may He in His mercy create peace for us and for all Yisrael, and say Amen.

Yehi Ratzon Milfaneicha Adonai	יְהִי רָצוֹן מִלְפָנֶיךָ יְהֹוָה
Eloheinu Velohei Avoteinu. Shetivneh	אֱלֹהֵינוּ וֵאלֹהֵי אֲבוֹתֵינוּ. שֶׁתִּבְנֶה
Beit Hamikdash Bimheirah Veyameinu.	בֵּית הַמִּקְדָּשׁ בִּמְהֵרָה בְיָמֵינוּ.
Veten Chelkenu Vetoratach La'asot	וְתֵן חֶלְקֵנוּ בְתוֹרָתָךְ לַעֲשׂוֹת
Chukkei. Retzonach Ule'avedach	חֻקֵּי רְצוֹנָךְ וּלְעָבְדָךְ
Belevav Shalem.	בְּלֵבָב שָׁלֵם:

May it be Your will, Hashem our God and God of our fathers, that the Beit HaMikdash be speedily rebuilt in our days, and grant us a share in Your Torah so we may fulfill the statutes of Your will and serve You with a whole heart.

Yehi Shem

יְהִי שֵׁם יְהֹוָה מְבֹרָךְ מֵעַתָּה וְעַד־עוֹלָם: מִמִּזְרַח־שֶׁמֶשׁ עַד־מְבוֹאוֹ מְהֻלָּל שֵׁם יְהֹוָה: רָם עַל־כָּל־גּוֹיִם | יְהֹוָה עַל הַשָּׁמַיִם כְּבוֹדוֹ: יְהֹוָה אֲדֹנֵינוּ מָה־אַדִּיר שִׁמְךָ בְּכָל־הָאָרֶץ:

Yehi Shem Adonai Mevorach; Me'attah. Ve'ad-'Olam. Mimizrach-Shemesh Ad-Mevo'o; Mehulal. Shem Adonai Ram Al-Chol-Goyim Adonai Al Hashamayim Kevodo. Adonai Adoneinu; Mah-'Adir Shimcha. Bechol-Ha'aretz.

Blessed is the name of Hashem from this time forward and forever. From the rising of the sun to it's going down, Hashem's name is to be praised. Hashem, our Lord, How glorious is Your name in all of the earth. (Psalms 113:2-4, 8:2)

On Shabbat Shuvah, Avinu Malkheinu, is said here:

אָבִינוּ מַלְכֵּנוּ אֵין לָנוּ מֶלֶךְ אֶלָּא אָתָּה:

Avinu Malkeinu Ein Lanu Melech Ella Attah.

Our Father and King, we have no King but You.

אָבִינוּ מַלְכֵּנוּ עֲשֵׂה עִמָּנוּ לְמַעַן שְׁמֶךָ:

Avinu Malkeinu Aseh Imanu Lema'an Shemecha.

Our Father and King, deal with us for Your Name's sake.

אָבִינוּ מַלְכֵּנוּ חַדֵּשׁ עָלֵינוּ שָׁנָה טוֹבָה:

Avinu Malkeinu Chadesh Aleinu Shanah Tovah.

Our Father and King, bring us a new year of good.

אָבִינוּ מַלְכֵּנוּ בַּטֵּל מֵעָלֵינוּ כָּל־גְּזֵרוֹת קָשׁוֹת וְרָעוֹת:

Avinu Malkeinu Battel Me'aleinu Kol-Gezerot Kashot Vera'ot.

Our Father and King, annul all hurtful and evil decrees against us.

אָבִינוּ מַלְכֵּנוּ בַּטֵּל מַחְשְׁבוֹת שׂוֹנְאֵינוּ:

Avinu Malkeinu Battel Machshevot Sone'einu.

Our Father and King, annul the devices of those who hate us.

אָבִינוּ מַלְכֵּנוּ הָפֵר עֲצַת אוֹיְבֵינוּ:

Avinu Malkeinu Hafer Atzat Oyeveinu.

Our Father and King, bring to nothing the hostile design of our enemies.

אָבִינוּ מַלְכֵּנוּ כַּלֵּה כָּל צַר וּמַשְׂטִין מֵעָלֵינוּ:

Avinu Malkeinu Kaleh Kol Tzar Umastin Me'aleinu.

Our Father and King, ward off from us all pain and accusation from us.

אָבִינוּ מַלְכֵּנוּ כַּלֵּה דֶּבֶר וְחֶרֶב וְרָעָב וְרָעָה וּשְׁבִי וּבִזָּה וּמַשְׁחִית
וּמַגֵּפָה וְיֵצֶר הָרָע וְחוֹלָאִים רָעִים מִבְּנֵי בְרִיתֶךָ:

Avinu Malkeinu Kaleh Dever Vecherev Vera'ah Vera'av Ushevi
Uvizah Umashchit Umagefah Veyetzer Hara Vechola'im Ra'im
Mibenei Veritecha.

Our Father and King, ward off pestilence, sword, famine, captivity, disaster, destruction from the children of Your covenant.

אָבִינוּ מַלְכֵּנוּ שְׁלַח רְפוּאָה שְׁלֵמָה לְכָל חוֹלֵי עַמֶּךָ:

Avinu Malkeinu Shelach Refu'ah Shelemah Lechol Cholei
Ammecha.

Our Father and King, restore to perfect health the sick of Your people.

אָבִינוּ מַלְכֵּנוּ מְנַע מַגֵּפָה מִנַּחֲלָתֶךָ:

Avinu Malkeinu Mena Magefah Minachalatecha.

Our Father and King, hold back pestilence from Your heritage.

אָבִינוּ מַלְכֵּנוּ זְכוֹר כִּי עָפָר אֲנָחְנוּ:

Avinu Malkeinu Zachur Ki Afar Anach'nu.

Our Father and King, remember that we are but dust.

אָבִינוּ מַלְכֵּנוּ קְרַע רוֹעַ גְּזַר דִּינֵנוּ:

Avinu Malkeinu Kera Roa Gezar Dinenu.

Our Father and King, repeal the evil decreed against us.

אָבִינוּ מַלְכֵּנוּ כָּתְבֵנוּ בְּסֵפֶר חַיִּים טוֹבִים:

Avinu Malkeinu Katevenu Besefer Chayim Tovim.

Our Father and King, inscribe us for good in the Book of Life.

אָבִינוּ מַלְכֵּנוּ כָּתְבֵנוּ בְּסֵפֶר צַדִּיקִים וַחֲסִידִים:

Avinu Malkeinu Katevenu Besefer Tzaddikim Vachasidim.

Our Father and King, inscribe us in the Book of the Righteous and the Pious.

אָבִינוּ מַלְכֵּנוּ כָּתְבֵנוּ בְּסֵפֶר יְשָׁרִים וּתְמִימִים:

Avinu Malkeinu Katevenu Besefer Yesharim Utemimim.

Our Father, Our King, inscribe us in the Book of the Straight and Simple.

אָבִינוּ מַלְכֵּנוּ כָּתְבֵנוּ בְּסֵפֶר פַּרְנָסָה וְכַלְכָּלָה טוֹבָה:

Avinu Malkeinu Katevenu Besefer Parnasah Vechalkalah Tovah.

Our Father, Our King, inscribe us in the Book of Good Income and Sustenance.

אָבִינוּ מַלְכֵּנוּ כָּתְבֵנוּ בְּסֵפֶר מְחִילָה וּסְלִיחָה וְכַפָּרָה:

Avinu Malkeinu Katevenu Besefer Mechilah Uselichah Vechapparah.

Our Father and King, inscribe us in the Book of Pardon and Atonement.

אָבִינוּ מַלְכֵּנוּ כָּתְבֵנוּ בְּסֵפֶר גְּאֻלָּה וִישׁוּעָה:

Avinu Malkeinu Katevenu Besefer Ge'ulah Vishu'ah.

Our Father and King, inscribe us in the Book of Redemption and Deliverance.

אָבִינוּ מַלְכֵּנוּ זָכְרֵנוּ בְּזִכְרוֹן טוֹב מִלְפָנֶיךָ:

Avinu Malkeinu Zochrenu Bezichron Tov Milfaneicha.

Our Father and King, remember us for good before You.

אָבִינוּ מַלְכֵּנוּ הַצְמַח לָנוּ יְשׁוּעָה בְּקָרוֹב:

Avinu Malkeinu Hatzmach Lanu Yeshu'ah Bekarov.

Our Father and King, make our salvation soon to spring forth.

אָבִינוּ מַלְכֵּנוּ הָרֵם קֶרֶן יִשְׂרָאֵל עַמֶּךָ:

Avinu Malkeinu Harem Keren Yisra'el Ammecha.

Our Father and King, raise up the strength of Your people Yisrael.

אָבִינוּ מַלְכֵּנוּ וְהָרֵם קֶרֶן מְשִׁיחֶךָ:

Avinu Malkeinu Veharem Keren Meshichecha.

Our Father and King, raise up the strength of Your anointed (Messiah).

אָבִינוּ מַלְכֵּנוּ חָנֵּנוּ וַעֲנֵנוּ:

Avinu Malkeinu Chonenu Va'aneinu.

Our Father and King, have grace on us and answer us.

אָבִינוּ מַלְכֵּנוּ הַחֲזִירֵנוּ בִּתְשׁוּבָה שְׁלֵמָה לְפָנֶיךָ:

Avinu Malkeinu Hachazirenu Bitshuvah Shelemah Lefaneicha.

Our Father and King, bring us back through perfect repentance before You.

אָבִינוּ מַלְכֵּנוּ שְׁמַע קוֹלֵנוּ חוּס וְרַחֵם עָלֵינוּ:

Avinu Malkeinu Shema Koleinu Chus Verachem Aleinu.

Our Father and King, hear our voice, take pity on us and be merciful to us.

אָבִינוּ מַלְכֵּנוּ עֲשֵׂה לְמַעַנָךְ אִם לֹא לְמַעֲנֵנוּ:

Avinu Malkeinu Aseh Lema'anach Im Lo Lema'aneinu.

Our Father and King, grant our prayer, if not because of our merit, then for Your own sake.

אָבִינוּ מַלְכֵּנוּ קַבֵּל בְּרַחֲמִים וּבְרָצוֹן אֶת תְּפִלָּתֵנוּ:

Avinu Malkeinu Kabel Berachamim Uveratzon Et Tefillateinu.

Our Father and King, accept our prayer with merciful favor.

אָבִינוּ מַלְכֵּנוּ אַל תְּשִׁיבֵנוּ רֵיקָם מִלְּפָנֶיךָ:

Avinu Malkeinu Al Teshivenu Reikam Milfaneicha.

Our Father and King, turn us not away empty from Your presence.

Continue with Tzidkatecha Tzedek.

Tzidkatecha Tzedek

Say 'Tzidkatecha Tzedek' at Shabbat Mincha unless it is a day on which, if it were a weekday, we would not say Tachanun. (SA, OC 292:2)

צִדְקָתְךָ | כְּהַרְרֵי־אֵל מִשְׁפָּטֶיךָ תְּהוֹם רַבָּה אָדָם וּבְהֵמָה תוֹשִׁיעַ יְהֹוָה: וְצִדְקָתְךָ אֱלֹהִים עַד־מָרוֹם אֲשֶׁר־עָשִׂיתָ גְדֹלוֹת אֱלֹהִים מִי כָמוֹךָ: צִדְקָתְךָ צֶדֶק לְעוֹלָם וְתוֹרָתְךָ אֱמֶת:

Tzidkatecha Keharrei El Mishpateicha Tehom Rabah Adam Uvehemah Toshia' Adonai. Vetzidkatecha Elohim Ad Marom Asher Asita Gedolot Elohim Mi Chamocha. Tzidkatecha Tzedek Le'olam Vetoratecha Emet.

"Your righteousness is like the mighty mountains; Your judgments are like the great deep; Man and beast You preserve, Hashem. Your righteousness also, God, which reaches to high heaven; You Who has done great things, God, Who is like You? Your righteousness is an everlasting righteousness, and Your Torah is truth." (Psalms 36:7. 71:19, 119:142)

On a day when Tachanun is not said on weekday Mincha, do not say Tzidkatecha, but say:

Yehi Shem

יְהִי שֵׁם יְהֹוָה מְבֹרָךְ מֵעַתָּה וְעַד־עוֹלָם: מִמִּזְרַח־שֶׁמֶשׁ עַד־מְבוֹאוֹ מְהֻלָּל שֵׁם יְהֹוָה: רָם עַל־כָּל־גּוֹיִם | יְהֹוָה עַל הַשָּׁמַיִם כְּבוֹדוֹ: יְהֹוָה אֲדֹנֵינוּ מָה־אַדִּיר שִׁמְךָ בְּכָל־הָאָרֶץ:

Yehi Shem Adonai Mevorach; Me'attah. Ve'ad-'Olam. Mimizrach-Shemesh Ad-Mevo'o; Mehulal. Shem Adonai Ram Al-Chol-Goyim Adonai Al Hashamayim Kevodo. Adonai Adoneinu; Mah-'Adir Shimcha. Bechol-Ha'aretz.

Blessed is the name of Hashem from this time forward and forever. From the rising of the sun to it's going down, Hashem's name is to be praised. Hashem, our Lord, How glorious is Your name in all of the earth. (Psalms 113:2-4, 8:2)

And the Chazan says Kaddish Titkabbal:

Kaddish Titkabbal

> Kaddish is only recited in a minyan (ten men). אמן denotes when the congregation responds "Amen"
> together out loud. According to the Shulchan Arukh, the congregation says "Yehei Shemeh Rabba"
> to "Yitbarach" out loud together without interruption, and also that one should respond "Amen"
> after "Yitbarach." (SA, OC 55,56) This is not the common custom today. Though many are
> accustomed to answering according to their own custom, it is advised to respond in the custom of
> the one reciting to avoid not fragmenting into smaller groups. ("Lo Titgodedu" - BT, Yevamot 13b /
> SA, OC 493, Rema / MT, Avodah Zara 12:15)

יִתְגַּדַּל וְיִתְקַדַּשׁ שְׁמֵהּ רַבָּא. אמן בְּעָלְמָא דִּי בְרָא. כִרְעוּתֵהּ. וְיַמְלִיךְ
מַלְכוּתֵהּ. וְיַצְמַח פֻּרְקָנֵהּ. וִיקָרֵב מְשִׁיחֵהּ. אמן בְּחַיֵּיכוֹן וּבְיוֹמֵיכוֹן
וּבְחַיֵּי דְכָל בֵּית יִשְׂרָאֵל. בַּעֲגָלָא וּבִזְמַן קָרִיב. וְאִמְרוּ אָמֵן. אמן יְהֵא
שְׁמֵיהּ רַבָּא מְבָרַךְ לְעָלַם וּלְעָלְמֵי עָלְמַיָּא יִתְבָּרַךְ. וְיִשְׁתַּבַּח.
וְיִתְפָּאַר. וְיִתְרוֹמַם. וְיִתְנַשֵּׂא. וְיִתְהַדָּר. וְיִתְעַלֶּה. וְיִתְהַלָּל שְׁמֵהּ
דְּקֻדְשָׁא. בְּרִיךְ הוּא. אמן לְעֵלָּא מִן כָּל בִּרְכָתָא שִׁירָתָא. תֻּשְׁבְּחָתָא
וְנֶחֱמָתָא. דַּאֲמִירָן בְּעָלְמָא. וְאִמְרוּ אָמֵן. אמן

Yitgadal Veyitkadash Shemeh Rabba. Amen Be'alema Di Vera.
Kir'uteh. Veyamlich Malchuteh. Veyatzmach Purkaneh. Vikarev
Meshicheh. Amen Bechayeichon Uveyomeichon Uvechayei Dechal-
Beit Yisra'el. Ba'agala Uvizman Kariv. Ve'imru Amen. Amen Yehei
Shemeh Rabba Mevarach Le'alam Ule'alemei Alemaya Yitbarach.
Veyishtabach. Veyitpa'ar. Veyitromam. Veyitnasse. Veyit'hadar.
Veyit'aleh. Veyit'hallal Shemeh Dekudsha. Berich Hu. Amen Le'ella
Min Kol Birchata Shirata. Tushbechata Venechemata. Da'amiran
Be'alema. Ve'imru Amen. Amen

Glorified and sanctified be God's great name Amen throughout the
world which He has created according to His will. May He establish
His kingdom, hastening His salvation and the coming of His
Messiah, Amen, in your lifetime and during your days, and within the
life of the entire House of Yisrael, speedily and soon; and say, Amen.
Amen May His great name be blessed forever and to all eternity.
Blessed and praised, glorified and exalted, extolled and honored,
adored and lauded is the name of the Holy One, blessed is He, Amen
Beyond all the blessings and hymns, praises and consolations that
are ever spoken in the world; and say, Amen. Amen

תִּתְקַבַּל צְלוֹתָנָא וּבָעוּתָנָא. עִם צְלוֹתְהוֹן וּבָעוּתְהוֹן דְּכָל בֵּית
יִשְׂרָאֵל. קֳדָם אֲבוּנָא דְּבִשְׁמַיָּא וְאַרְעָא. וְאִמְרוּ אָמֵן. אָמֵן

Titkabbal Tzelotana Uva'utana. Im Tzelotehon Uva'utehon Dechol
Beit Yisra'el. Kodam Avuna Devishmaya Ve'ar'a. Ve'imru Amen. Amen

May the prayer and supplication of the whole House of Yisrael be
accepted before their Father in heaven, and say, Amen. Amen

יְהֵא שְׁלָמָא רַבָּא מִן שְׁמַיָּא. חַיִּים וְשָׂבָע וִישׁוּעָה וְנֶחָמָה. וְשֵׁיזָבָא
וּרְפוּאָה וּגְאוּלָה וּסְלִיחָה וְכַפָּרָה וְרֶוַח וְהַצָּלָה לָנוּ וּלְכָל עַמּוֹ
יִשְׂרָאֵל. וְאִמְרוּ אָמֵן. אָמֵן

Yehei Shelama Rabba Min Shemaya. Chayim Vesava Vishu'ah
Venechamah. Vesheizava Urefu'ah Uge'ulah Uselichah
Vechapparah Verevach Vehatzalah Lanu Ulechol Ammo Yisra'el.
Ve'imru Amen. Amen

May abundant peace descend from heaven, with life and plenty,
salvation, solace, liberation, healing and redemption, and
forgiveness and atonement, enlargement and freedom, for us and
all of God's people Yisrael; and say, Amen. Amen

> One bows and takes three steps backwards, while still bowing. After three steps, while still bowing and before erecting, while saying, "Oseh Shalom Bimromav", turn one's face to the left, "Hu [Berachamav] Ya'aseh Shalom Aleinu", turn one's face to the right; then bow forward like a servant leaving his master. (SA, OC 123:1)

עוֹשֶׂה שָׁלוֹם בעשי״ת: (הַשָּׁלוֹם) בִּמְרוֹמָיו. הוּא בְּרַחֲמָיו יַעֲשֶׂה שָׁלוֹם
עָלֵינוּ. וְעַל כָּל־עַמּוֹ יִשְׂרָאֵל. וְאִמְרוּ אָמֵן:

Oseh Shalom On the 10 Days of Repentance: (Hashalom) Bimromav, Hu
Berachamav Ya'aseh Shalom Aleinu, Ve'al Kol-'Ammo Yisra'el,
Ve'imru Amen.

Creator of On the 10 Days of Repentance: (the) peace in His high places, may
He in His mercy create peace for us and for all Yisrael, and say
Amen.

On Shabbat Chol HaMoed and for some on Shabbat before a Yom Tov, the Psalm for Yom Tov is recited instead of Psalms 111.

Psalms 111

הַלְלוּיָהּ | אוֹדֶה יְהֹוָה בְּכָל־לֵבָב בְּסוֹד יְשָׁרִים וְעֵדָה: גְּדֹלִים מַעֲשֵׂי
יְהֹוָה דְּרוּשִׁים לְכָל־חֶפְצֵיהֶם: הוֹד־וְהָדָר פָּעֳלוֹ וְצִדְקָתוֹ עֹמֶדֶת לָעַד:
זֵכֶר עָשָׂה לְנִפְלְאֹתָיו חַנּוּן וְרַחוּם יְהֹוָה: טֶרֶף נָתַן לִירֵאָיו יִזְכֹּר
לְעוֹלָם בְּרִיתוֹ: כֹּחַ מַעֲשָׂיו הִגִּיד לְעַמּוֹ לָתֵת לָהֶם נַחֲלַת גּוֹיִם:
מַעֲשֵׂי יָדָיו אֱמֶת וּמִשְׁפָּט נֶאֱמָנִים כָּל־פִּקּוּדָיו: סְמוּכִים לָעַד לְעוֹלָם
עֲשׂוּיִם בֶּאֱמֶת וְיָשָׁר: פְּדוּת | שָׁלַח לְעַמּוֹ צִוָּה־לְעוֹלָם בְּרִיתוֹ קָדוֹשׁ
וְנוֹרָא שְׁמוֹ: רֵאשִׁית חָכְמָה | יִרְאַת יְהֹוָה שֵׂכֶל טוֹב לְכָל־עֹשֵׂיהֶם
תְּהִלָּתוֹ עֹמֶדֶת לָעַד:

Halleluyah Odeh Adonai Bechol-Levav; Besod Yesharim Ve'edah.
Gedolim Ma'asei Adonai Derushim. Lechol-Cheftzeihem. Hod-
Vehadar Po'olo; Vetzidkato. Omedet La'ad. Zecher Asah
Lenifle'otav; Chanun Verachum Adonai Teref Natan Lire'av; Yizkor
Le'olam Berito. Koach Ma'asav Higid Le'ammo; Latet Lahem.
Nachalat Goyim. Ma'asei Yadav Emet Umishpat; Ne'emanim. Chol-
Pikudav. Semuchim La'ad Le'olam; Asuyim. Be'emet Veyashar.
Pedut Shalach Le'ammo. Tzivah-Le'olam Berito; Kadosh Venora
Shemo. Reshit Chochmah Yir'at Adonai Sechel Tov
Lechol-'Oseihem; Tehilato. Omedet La'ad.

Halleluyah. א I will give thanks to Hashem with my whole heart, ב In the council of the upright, and in the congregation. ג The works of Hashem are great, ד Searched out by all of them that have delight in them. ה His work is glory and majesty; ו And His righteousness endures forever. ז He has made a memorial for His wonderful works; ח Hashem is gracious and full of compassion. ט He has given food to them that fear Him; י He will ever be mindful of His covenant. כ He has declared to His people the power of His works, ל In giving them the heritage of the nations. מ The works of His hands are truth and justice; נ All His precepts are sure. ס They are established forever and ever, ע They are done in truth and uprightness. פ He has sent redemption to His people; צ He has commanded His covenant forever; **ק** Holy and awesome is His name. **ר** The fear of Hashem is the beginning of wisdom; **ש** All those that practice it gain good understanding; **ת** His praise endures forever.

And on Chol HaMoed Pesach say:

Psalms 114

בְּצֵאת יִשְׂרָאֵל מִמִּצְרָיִם בֵּית יַעֲקֹב מֵעַם לֹעֵז: הָיְתָה יְהוּדָה לְקָדְשׁוֹ יִשְׂרָאֵל מַמְשְׁלוֹתָיו: הַיָּם רָאָה וַיָּנֹס הַיַּרְדֵּן יִסֹּב לְאָחוֹר: הֶהָרִים רָקְדוּ כְאֵילִים גְּבָעוֹת כִּבְנֵי־צֹאן: מַה־לְּךָ הַיָּם כִּי תָנוּס הַיַּרְדֵּן תִּסֹּב לְאָחוֹר: הֶהָרִים תִּרְקְדוּ כְאֵילִים גְּבָעוֹת כִּבְנֵי־צֹאן: מִלִּפְנֵי אָדוֹן חוּלִי אָרֶץ מִלִּפְנֵי אֱלוֹהַּ יַעֲקֹב: הַהֹפְכִי הַצּוּר אֲגַם־מָיִם חַלָּמִישׁ לְמַעְיְנוֹ־מָיִם:

Betzet Yisra'el Mimitzrayim Beit Ya'akov Me'am Lo'ez. Hayetah Yehudah Lekodsho Yisra'el Mamshelotav. Hayam Ra'ah Vayanos Hayarden Yissov Le'achor. Heharim Rakedu Che'eilim Geva'ot Kivnei Tzon. Mah Lecha Hayam Ki Tanus Hayarden Tissov Le'achor. Heharim Tirkedu Che'eilim Geva'ot Kivnei Tzon. Millifnei Adon Chuli Aretz Millifnei Eloah Ya'akov. Hahofechi Hatzur Agam Mayim Challamish Lema'yeno Mayim.

When Yisrael came forth out of Mitzrayim, The house of Yaakov from a people of strange language; Yehudah became His Sanctuary, Yisrael His dominion. The sea saw it, and fled; The Yarden turned backward. The mountains skipped like rams, The hills like young sheep. What ails you, Oh sea, that you flee? You Yarden, that you turn backward? You mountains, that you skip like rams; You hills, like young sheep? Tremble, earth, at the presence of Hashem, At the presence of the God of Yaakov; Who turned the rock into a pool of water, the flint into a fountain of waters.

And on Chol HaMoed Sukkot; Shavuot, and Shemini Atzeret / Simchat Torah say:

Psalms 122

שִׁיר הַמַּעֲלוֹת לְדָוִד שָׂמַחְתִּי בְּאֹמְרִים לִי בֵּית יְהֹוָה נֵלֵךְ: עֹמְדוֹת הָיוּ רַגְלֵינוּ בִּשְׁעָרַיִךְ יְרוּשָׁלָיִם: יְרוּשָׁלַם הַבְּנוּיָה כְּעִיר שֶׁחֻבְּרָה־לָּהּ יַחְדָּו: שֶׁשָּׁם עָלוּ שְׁבָטִים שִׁבְטֵי־יָהּ עֵדוּת לְיִשְׂרָאֵל לְהֹדוֹת לְשֵׁם יְהֹוָה: כִּי שָׁמָּה | יָשְׁבוּ כִסְאוֹת לְמִשְׁפָּט כִּסְאוֹת לְבֵית דָּוִד: שַׁאֲלוּ שְׁלוֹם יְרוּשָׁלָ͏ִם יִשְׁלָיוּ אֹהֲבָיִךְ: יְהִי־שָׁלוֹם בְּחֵילֵךְ שַׁלְוָה בְּאַרְמְנוֹתָיִךְ: לְמַעַן אַחַי וְרֵעָי אֲדַבְּרָה־נָּא שָׁלוֹם בָּךְ: לְמַעַן בֵּית־יְהֹוָה אֱלֹהֵינוּ אֲבַקְשָׁה טוֹב לָךְ:

Shir Hama'alot Ledavid Samachti Be'omerim Li Beit Adonai Nelech. Omedot Hayu Ragleinu Bish'arayich Yerushalayim. Yerushalayim Habenuyah Ke'ir Shechuberah

Lah Yachdav. Shesham Alu Shevatim Shivtei Yah Edut Leyisra'el Lehodot Leshem
Adonai. Ki Shamah Yashevu Chis'ot Lemishpat Kis'ot Leveit David. Sha'alu Shelom
Yerushalayim Yishlayu Ohavayich. Yehi Shalom Becheilech Shalvah
Be'armenotayich. Lema'an Achai Vere'ai Adaberah Na Shalom Bach. Lema'an Beit
Adonai Eloheinu Avakshah Tov Lach.

A Song of Ascents; of David. I rejoiced when they said to me: 'Let us go to the
House of Hashem.' Our feet are standing within your gates, Yerushalayim;
Yerushalayim, that is built as a city that is compact together; Where the tribes went
up, even the tribes of Hashem, as a testimony to Yisrael, to give thanks to the name
of Hashem. For there were set thrones for judgment, the thrones of the House of
David. Pray for the peace of Yerushalayim; May they that love You prosper. Peace
be within your walls, and prosperity within your palaces. For my brothers and
companions' sakes, I will now say: 'Peace be within you.' For the sake of the House
of Hashem our God I will seek your good.

And say Kaddish Yehei-Shelama:

Kaddish is only recited in a minyan (ten men). אמן denotes when the congregation responds "Amen"
together out loud. According to the Shulchan Arukh, the congregation says "Yehei Shemeh Rabba"
to "Yitbarach" out loud together without interruption, and also that one should respond "Amen"
after "Yitbarach." (SA, OC 55,56) This is not the common custom today. Though many are
accustomed to answering according to their own custom, it is advised to respond in the custom of
the one reciting to avoid not fragmenting into smaller groups. ("Lo Titgodedu" - BT, Yevamot 13b /
SA, OC 493, Rema / MT, Avodah Zara 12:15)

יִתְגַּדַּל וְיִתְקַדַּשׁ שְׁמֵהּ רַבָּא. אמן בְּעָלְמָא דִּי בְרָא. כִּרְעוּתֵהּ. וְיַמְלִיךְ
מַלְכוּתֵהּ. וְיַצְמַח פֻּרְקָנֵהּ. וִיקָרֵב מְשִׁיחֵהּ. אמן בְּחַיֵּיכוֹן וּבְיוֹמֵיכוֹן
וּבְחַיֵּי דְכָל בֵּית יִשְׂרָאֵל. בַּעֲגָלָא וּבִזְמַן קָרִיב. וְאִמְרוּ אָמֵן. אמן יְהֵא
שְׁמֵהּ רַבָּא מְבָרַךְ לְעָלַם וּלְעָלְמֵי עָלְמַיָּא יִתְבָּרַךְ. וְיִשְׁתַּבַּח.
וְיִתְפָּאַר. וְיִתְרוֹמַם. וְיִתְנַשֵּׂא. וְיִתְהַדָּר. וְיִתְעַלֶּה. וְיִתְהַלָּל שְׁמֵהּ
דְקֻדְשָׁא. בְּרִיךְ הוּא. אמן לְעֵלָּא מִן כָּל בִּרְכָתָא שִׁירָתָא. תֻּשְׁבְּחָתָא
וְנֶחֱמָתָא. דַּאֲמִירָן בְּעָלְמָא. וְאִמְרוּ אָמֵן. אמן

Yitgadal Veyitkadash Shemeh Rabba. **Amen** Be'alema Di Vera.
Kir'uteh. Veyamlich Malchuteh. Veyatzmach Purkaneh. Vikarev
Meshicheh. **Amen** Bechayeichon Uveyomeichon Uvechayei Dechal-
Beit Yisra'el. Ba'agala Uvizman Kariv. Ve'imru Amen. **Amen** Yehei
Shemeh Rabba Mevarach Le'alam Ule'alemei Alemaya Yitbarach.
Veyishtabach. Veyitpa'ar. Veyitromam. Veyitnasse. Veyit'hadar.
Veyit'aleh. Veyit'hallal Shemeh Dekudsha. Berich Hu. **Amen** Le'ella

Min Kol Birchata Shirata. Tushbechata Venechemata. Da'amiran Be'alema. Ve'imru Amen. Amen

Glorified and sanctified be God's great name Amen throughout the world which He has created according to His will. May He establish His kingdom, hastening His salvation and the coming of His Messiah, Amen, in your lifetime and during your days, and within the life of the entire House of Yisrael, speedily and soon; and say, Amen. Amen May His great name be blessed forever and to all eternity. Blessed and praised, glorified and exalted, extolled and honored, adored and lauded is the name of the Holy One, blessed is He, Amen Beyond all the blessings and hymns, praises and consolations that are ever spoken in the world; and say, Amen. Amen

יְהֵא שְׁלָמָא רַבָּא מִן שְׁמַיָּא. חַיִּים וְשָׂבָע וִישׁוּעָה וְנֶחָמָה. וְשֵׁיזָבָא וּרְפוּאָה וּגְאוּלָה וּסְלִיחָה וְכַפָּרָה וְרֶוַח וְהַצָּלָה לָנוּ וּלְכָל עַמּוֹ יִשְׂרָאֵל. וְאִמְרוּ אָמֵן. אמן

Yehei Shelama Rabba Min Shemaya. Chayim Vesava Vishu'ah Venechamah. Vesheizava Urefu'ah Uge'ulah Uselichah Vechapparah Verevach Vehatzalah Lanu Ulechol Ammo Yisra'el. Ve'imru Amen. Amen

May abundant peace descend from heaven, with life and plenty, salvation, solace, liberation, healing and redemption, and forgiveness and atonement, enlargement and freedom, for us and all of God's people Yisrael; and say, Amen. Amen

---

One bows and takes three steps backwards, while still bowing. After three steps, while still bowing and before erecting, while saying, "Oseh Shalom Bimromav", turn one's face to the left, "Hu [Berachamav] Ya'aseh Shalom Aleinu", turn one's face to the right; then bow forward like a servant leaving his master. (SA, OC 123:1)

עוֹשֶׂה שָׁלוֹם בִּמְרוֹמָיו. הוּא בְּרַחֲמָיו יַעֲשֶׂה שָׁלוֹם עָלֵינוּ. וְעַל כָּל־עַמּוֹ יִשְׂרָאֵל. וְאִמְרוּ אָמֵן:

Oseh Shalom Bimromav. Hu Berachamav Ya'aseh Shalom Aleinu. Ve'al Kol-'Ammo Yisra'el. Ve'imru Amen.

Creator of peace in His high places, may He in His mercy create peace for us and for all Yisrael, and say Amen.

Aleinu

[*] denotes pausing and then bowing when saying "Va'anachnu Mistachavim".

Aleinu Leshabei'ach La'adon	עָלֵינוּ לְשַׁבֵּחַ לַאֲדוֹן
Hakol. Latet Gedullah Leyotzer	הַכֹּל. לָתֵת גְּדֻלָּה לְיוֹצֵר
Bereshit. Shelo Asanu Kegoyei	בְּרֵאשִׁית. שֶׁלֹּא עָשָׂנוּ כְּגוֹיֵי
Ha'aratzot. Velo Samanu	הָאֲרָצוֹת. וְלֹא שָׂמָנוּ
Kemishpechot Ha'adamah.	כְּמִשְׁפְּחוֹת הָאֲדָמָה.
Shelo Sam Chelkenu Kahem	שֶׁלֹּא שָׂם חֶלְקֵנוּ כָּהֶם
Vegoraleinu Kechal-Hamonam.	וְגוֹרָלֵנוּ כְּכָל־הֲמוֹנָם.
Shehem Mishtachavim Lahevel	שֶׁהֵם מִשְׁתַּחֲוִים לְהֶבֶל
Varik. Umitpallelim El-'El Lo	וָרִיק. וּמִתְפַּלְלִים אֶל־אֵל לֹא
Yoshia. *Va'anachnu	יוֹשִׁיעַ. *וַאֲנַחְנוּ
Mishtachavim Lifnei Melech	מִשְׁתַּחֲוִים לִפְנֵי מֶלֶךְ
Malchei Hamelachim Hakadosh	מַלְכֵי הַמְּלָכִים הַקָּדוֹשׁ
Baruch Hu. Shehu Noteh	בָּרוּךְ הוּא. שֶׁהוּא נוֹטֶה
Shamayim Veyosed Aretz.	שָׁמַיִם וְיוֹסֵד אָרֶץ.
Umoshav Yekaro Bashamayim	וּמוֹשַׁב יְקָרוֹ בַּשָּׁמַיִם
Mima'al. Ushechinat Uzo	מִמַּעַל. וּשְׁכִינַת עֻזּוֹ
Begavehei Meromim. Hu	בְּגָבְהֵי מְרוֹמִים. הוּא
Eloheinu. Ve'ein Od Acher.	אֱלֹהֵינוּ. וְאֵין עוֹד אַחֵר.
Emet Malkeinu Ve'efes Zulato.	אֱמֶת מַלְכֵּנוּ וְאֶפֶס זוּלָתוֹ.
Kakatuv Batorah. Veyada'ta	כַּכָּתוּב בַּתּוֹרָה. וְיָדַעְתָּ
Hayom. Vahasheivota El-	הַיּוֹם וַהֲשֵׁבֹתָ אֶל־
Levavecha Ki Adonai Hu	לְבָבֶךָ כִּי יְהֹוָה הוּא
Ha'elohim. Bashamayim	הָאֱלֹהִים בַּשָּׁמַיִם
Mima'al. Ve'al-Ha'aretz	מִמַּעַל וְעַל־הָאָרֶץ
Mitachat; Ein Od.	מִתָּחַת אֵין עוֹד:

It is our obligation us to praise the Lord of all. To render greatness to the Former of creation. For He has not made us like the nations of the lands, nor set us to be like the families of the earth. Who has not given our portion like theirs and our lot like their masses that bow down to vanity and emptiness, "And pray to a god that does not save." *'But we bow before the supreme King of kings, the Holy One, blessed is He. Who stretches out the heavens and laid the foundations of the earth and His glorious seat is in the heavens above, and the presence of His might in the most exalted of heights. He is our God, there is no other. In truth our King, there is no one except Him. As it is written in the Torah: "This day know and lay it to your heart, that Hashem, He is God in the heavens above and on the earth beneath. There is no one else."

Al Ken Nekaveh Lach. Adonai	עַל כֵּן נְקַוֶּה לְּךָ. יְהֹוָה
Eloheinu. Lir'ot Meheirah	אֱלֹהֵינוּ. לִרְאוֹת מְהֵרָה
Betif'eret Uzach. Leha'avir	בְּתִפְאֶרֶת עֻזֶּךְ. לְהַעֲבִיר
Gilulim Min Ha'aretz.	גִּלּוּלִים מִן הָאָרֶץ.
Veha'elilim Karot Yikaretun.	וְהָאֱלִילִים כָּרוֹת יִכָּרֵתוּן.
Letakken Olam Bemalchut	לְתַקֵּן עוֹלָם בְּמַלְכוּת
Shaddai. Vechol-Benei Vasar	שַׁדַּי. וְכָל-בְּנֵי בָשָׂר
Yikre'u Vishmecha. Lehafnot	יִקְרְאוּ בִשְׁמֶךָ. לְהַפְנוֹת
Eleicha Kol-Rish'ei Aretz. Yakiru	אֵלֶיךָ כָּל-רִשְׁעֵי אָרֶץ. יַכִּירוּ
Veyede'u Kol-Yoshevei Tevel. Ki	וְיֵדְעוּ כָּל-יוֹשְׁבֵי תֵבֵל. כִּי
Lecha Tichra Kol-Berech. Tishava	לְךָ תִכְרַע כָּל-בֶּרֶךְ. תִּשָּׁבַע
Kol-Lashon. Lefaneicha. Adonai	כָּל-לָשׁוֹן. לְפָנֶיךָ. יְהֹוָה
Eloheinu Yichre'u Veyipolu.	אֱלֹהֵינוּ יִכְרְעוּ וְיִפֹּלוּ.
Velichvod Shimcha Yekar Yitenu.	וְלִכְבוֹד שִׁמְךָ יְקָר יִתֵּנוּ.
Vikabelu Chulam Et-'Ol	וִיקַבְּלוּ כֻלָּם אֶת-עֹל

Malchutecha. Vetimloch Aleihem	מַלְכוּתֶךָ. וְתִמְלוֹךְ עֲלֵיהֶם
Meheirah Le'olam Va'ed. Ki	מְהֵרָה לְעוֹלָם וָעֶד. כִּי
Hamalchut Shelecha Hi.	הַמַּלְכוּת שֶׁלְּךָ הִיא.
Ule'olemei Ad Timloch	וּלְעוֹלְמֵי עַד תִּמְלוֹךְ
Bechavod. Kakatuv Betoratach.	בְּכָבוֹד. כַּכָּתוּב בְּתוֹרָתֶךָ:
Adonai Yimloch Le'olam Va'ed.	יְהוָה ׀ יִמְלֹךְ לְעֹלָם וָעֶד:
Vene'emar. Vehayah Adonai	וְנֶאֱמַר. וְהָיָה יְהוָה
Lemelech Al-Kol-Ha'aretz;	לְמֶלֶךְ עַל־כָּל־הָאָרֶץ
Bayom Hahu. Yihyeh Adonai	בַּיּוֹם הַהוּא יִהְיֶה יְהוָה
Echad Ushemo Echad.	אֶחָד וּשְׁמוֹ אֶחָד:

Therefore we hope in You, Hashem our God, soon to see Your glorious might, to remove idols from the earth and the non-gods will be wholly cut down, to rectify the world with the kingdom of El Shaddai, and all children of flesh will call on Your name and all of the earth's wicked will turn to You. All that dwell on earth will understand and know that to You every knee must bend, and every tongue swear. Before You, Hashem our God, may all kneel and fall and give honor to Your glorious name. And they will all accept the yoke of Your kingdom. And may You speedily rule over them forever. For dominion is Yours, and forever You will reign in glory, as is written in Your Torah, "Hashem will reign forever and ever." For, it is said, "Hashem will be King over all the earth; and on that day Hashem will be One and His name One."

Uvetoratecha Adonai Eloheinu	וּבְתוֹרָתְךָ יְהוָה אֱלֹהֵינוּ
Katuv Lemor. Shema Yisra'el;	כָּתוּב לֵאמֹר. שְׁמַע יִשְׂרָאֵל
Adonai Eloheinu Adonai Echad.	יְהוָה אֱלֹהֵינוּ יְהוָה אֶחָד:

And in Your Torah, Hashem our God, it is written: Hear O Yisrael Hashem our God, Hashem is One.

Seudah Sh'lishit / Third Meal

סעודה שלישית

One should be very careful to fulfill the precept of eating the third meal on Shabbat, and it may be fulfilled by just partaking of food the size of an egg. The time to eat the third meal is when the time to hold the Shabbat Mincha Services has come (the sixth and a half hour onward). (SA 291) According to the Shulchan Arukh, women are obligated in the Third Meal.

Some have the custom (BTH', BT Shabbat 33b:8) of circling, to his right (when he is facing, conter-clockwise) the table with 2 myrtle branches, holding them together, making the appropriate blessing for sweet smelling trees (borei atzei vesamim), smelling them and saying:

זָכוֹר וְשָׁמוֹר בְּדִיבּוּר אֶחָד נֶאֶמְרוּ:

Remember and keep [the Shabbat] were said in one utterance.

And also say:

רֵיחַ נִיחוֹחַ אִשֶּׁה לַיהוה:

A soothing fragrance to Hashem.

Some say before:

אַתְקִינוּ סְעוּדָתָא דִמְהֵימְנוּתָא שְׁלֵימָתָא חֶדְוָתָא דְמַלְכָּא קַדִּישָׁא. אַתְקִינוּ סְעוּדָתָא דְמַלְכָּא. דָּא הִיא סְעוּדָתָא דְמַלְכָּא קַדִּישָׁא זְהִיר אַנְפִּין (וְעַתִּיקָא קַדִּישָׁא וַחֲקַל תַּפּוּחִין קַדִּישִׁין אַתְיָן לְסַעֲדָא בַּהֲדֵיהּ):

Atkinu Se'udata Dimheimnuta Sheleimata Chedvata Demalka Kaddisha: Atkinu Se'udata Demalka. Da Hi Se'udata Demalka Kaddisha Za'eir Anpin (Ve'atika Kaddisha Vachakal Tappuchin Kaddishin Atyan Lesa'ada Bahadeih):

Psalms 23

מִזְמוֹר לְדָוִד יְהֹוָה רֹעִי לֹא אֶחְסָר: בִּנְאוֹת דֶּשֶׁא יַרְבִּיצֵנִי עַל מֵי מְנֻחוֹת יְנַהֲלֵנִי: נַפְשִׁי יְשׁוֹבֵב יַנְחֵנִי בְמַעְגְּלֵי־צֶדֶק לְמַעַן שְׁמוֹ: גַּם כִּי־אֵלֵךְ בְּגֵיא צַלְמָוֶת לֹא־אִירָא רָע כִּי־אַתָּה עִמָּדִי שִׁבְטְךָ וּמִשְׁעַנְתֶּךָ הֵמָּה יְנַחֲמֻנִי: תַּעֲרֹךְ לְפָנַי | שֻׁלְחָן נֶגֶד צֹרְרָי דִּשַּׁנְתָּ בַשֶּׁמֶן רֹאשִׁי כּוֹסִי רְוָיָה אַךְ | טוֹב וָחֶסֶד יִרְדְּפוּנִי כָּל־יְמֵי חַיָּי וְשַׁבְתִּי בְּבֵית־יְהֹוָה לְאֹרֶךְ יָמִים:

Mizmor Ledavid; Adonai Ro'i. Lo Echsar. Bin'ot Deshei Yarbitzeni; Al Mei Menuchot Yenahaleini. Nafshi Yeshovev; Yancheini Vema'gelei-Tzedek. Lema'an Shemo. Gam Ki-'Elech Begei

Tzalmavet Lo-'Ira Ra'. Ki-'Attah Immadi; Shivtecha Umish'antecha. Hemah Yenachamuni. Ta'aroch Lefanai Shulchan. Neged Tzorerai; Dishanta Vashemen Roshi. Kosi Revayah Ach Tov Vachesed Yirdefuni Chol-Yemei Chayai; Veshavti Beveit-Adonai Le'orech Yamim.

A Psalm of David. Hashem is my Shepherd; I will not want. He makes me to lie down in green pastures; He leads me beside the still waters. He restores my soul; He guides me in straight paths for His name's sake. Even though I walk through the valley of the shadow of death, I will fear no evil, for You are with me; Your rod and Your staff, they comfort me. You prepare a table before me in the presence of my enemies; You have anointed my head with oil; my cup runs over. Surely goodness and mercy will follow me all the days of my life; And I will dwell in the House of Hashem forever.

Some say:

וַיֹּאמֶר מֹשֶׁה אִכְלֻהוּ הַיּוֹם כִּי־שַׁבָּת הַיּוֹם לַיהֹוָה הַיּוֹם לֹא תִמְצָאֻהוּ בַּשָּׂדֶה: רְאוּ כִּי־יְהֹוָה נָתַן לָכֶם הַשַּׁבָּת עַל־כֵּן הוּא נֹתֵן לָכֶם בַּיּוֹם הַשִּׁשִּׁי לֶחֶם יוֹמָיִם שְׁבוּ | אִישׁ תַּחְתָּיו אַל־יֵצֵא אִישׁ מִמְּקֹמוֹ בַּיּוֹם הַשְּׁבִיעִי: וַיִּשְׁבְּתוּ הָעָם בַּיּוֹם הַשְּׁבִיעִי: עַל־כֵּן בֵּרַךְ יְהֹוָה אֶת־יוֹם הַשַּׁבָּת וַיְקַדְּשֵׁהוּ:

Vayomer Mosheh Ichluhu Hayom Ki Shabbat Hayom L'Adonai Hayom Lo Timtza'uhu Bassadeh. Re'u Ki Adonai Natan Lachem Hashabbat Al Ken Hu Noten Lachem Bayom Hashishi Lechem Yomayim Shevu Ish Tachtav Al Yetze Ish Mimekomo Bayom Hashevi'i. Vayishbetu Ha'am Bayom Hashevi'i. Al Ken Berach Adonai Et Yom Hashabbat Vaykadeshehu.

And Moshe said: 'Eat that today; for today is a Shabbat to Hashem; today you will not find it in the field. See that Hashem has given you the Shabbat; so He gives you on the sixth day the bread of two days; let every man abide in his place, let no man go out of his place on the seventh day. So the people rested on the seventh day. Therefore Hashem blessed the Shabbat day, and sanctified it. (Ex. 16:25, 29-30, 20:11)

Savri Maranan!

סַבְרִי מָרָנָן:

And answer:

Le'chayim!

לְחַיִּים:

To life!

Gentlemen, with your attention!

Baruch Attah Adonai Eloheinu Melech

ברוּךְ אַתָּה יְהוָה אֱלֹהֵינוּ מֶלֶךְ

Ha'olam Borei Pri Hagefen.

הָעוֹלָם. בּוֹרֵא פְּרִי הַגָּפֶן:

Blessed are You, Hashem our God, King of the universe, Who creates the fruit of the vine.

Before Third Meal, some say:

לְשֵׁם יְחוּד קוּדְשָׁא בְּרִיךְ הוּא וּשְׁכִינְתֵּיהּ. בִּדְחִילוּ וּרְחִימוּ. וּרְחִימוּ וּדְחִילוּ. לְיַחֲדָא שֵׁם יוֹ"ד קֵ"י בְּוָא"ו קֵ"י בְּיִחוּדָא שְׁלִים (יהוה) בְּשֵׁם כָּל יִשְׂרָאֵל. הנה אנכי בא לקיים מצות סעודה שלישית של שבת והיא כנגד יעקב אב של שבעים נפש. ובזכותו נצול ממלחמת גוג ומגוג. ויקויים בנו מקרא שכתוב והאכלתיך נחלת יעקב אביך. נחלה בלי מצרים. ובכן בכח סגלת ג' סעודות אלו יתקן פגמנו בסעודות הרשות ומאכלות אסורות. וִיהִי נֹעַם אֲדֹנָי אֱלֹהֵינוּ עָלֵינוּ וּמַעֲשֵׂה יָדֵינוּ כּוֹנְנָה עָלֵינוּ וּמַעֲשֵׂה יָדֵינוּ כּוֹנְנֵהוּ:

Zohar, Parashat Yitro

תא חזי בכל שתא יומי דשבתא. כד מטא שעתא דצלותא דמנחה. דינא תקיפא שלטא. וכל דינין מתערין. אבל ביומא דשבתא. כד מטא עדן דצלותא דמנחה. רעוא דרעוין אשתכח. ועתיקא קדישא גליא רצון דילה. וכל דינין מתכפין. ומשתכח רעותא וחדו בכלא. ובהאי רצון. אסתלק משה. נביאה מהימנא קדישא מעלמא. בגין למנדע. דלא בדינא אסתלק. וההיא שעתא ברצון דעתיקא קדישא נפק נשמתה. ואתטמר ביה. בגין כך. ולא ידע איש את קברתו כתיב. מה עתיקא קדישא. טמיר מכל טמירין.

ולא ידעין עלאין ותתאין. אוף הכא. האי נשמתא דאתטמר בהאי רצון.
דאתגליא בשעתא דצלותא דמנחה דשבתא. כתיב ולא ידע איש את
קברתו והוא טמיר מכל טמירין דעלמא. ודינא לא שלטא ביה. זכאה
חולקיה דמשה. תאנא. בהאי יומא. דאוריתא מתעטרא ביה. מתעטרא
בכלא. בכל אנון פקודין בכל אנון גזרין ועונשין. בשבעין ענפין דנהורא.
דזהרין מכל סטרא וסטרא. מאן חמי. ענפין דנפקין מכל ענפא וענפא.
חמשא קימין בגו אילנא. כלהו אנפין בהו אחידן. מאן חמי. אנן תרעין
דמתפתחין בכל סטרא וסטרא. כלהו מזדהרין ונהרין. בההוא נהורא דנפיק
ולא פסיק. קל כרוזא נפיק. אתערו קדישי עליונין. אתערו עמא קדישא.
דאתבחרו לעלא ותתא. אתערו חדותא לקדמות מאריכון. אתערו בחדותא
שלימתא. אזדמנו בתלת חדוון. דתלת אבהן. אזדמנו לקדמות מהימנותא
דחדוה דכל חדותא. זכאה חולקכון. ישראל קדישין. בעלמא דין ובעלמא
דאתי. דא הוא ירותא לכון. מכל עמים עובדי עבודה זרה. ועל דא כתיב.
ביני ובין בני ישראל. אמר רבי יהודה. הכי הוא ודאי. ועל דא כתיב זכור
את יום השבת לקדשו וכתיב קדשים תהיו כי קדוש אני יהוה. וכתיב.
וקראת לשבת ענג לקדוש יהוה מכבד. תאנא. בהאי יומא. כל נשמתיהון
דצדיקיא. מתעדנין בתפנוקי עתיקא קדישא. סתימא דכל סתימין. ורוחא
חדא דא מענוגא דההוא עתיקא מתפשטא בכלהו עלמין. וסלקא ונחתא.
ומתפשטא לכלהו בני קדישין. לכלהו נטורי אוריתא. וניחין בניחא שלים.
ומתנשי מכלהו. כל רוגזין. כל דינין. וכל פולחנין קשין. הדא הוא דכתיב.
ביום הניח יהוה לך מעצבך ומרגזך ומן העבדה הקשה. בגיני כך. שקיל
שבתא לקבל אוריתא. וכל דנטיר שבתא. כאלו נטיר אוריתא כלה. וכתיב
אשרי אנוש יעשה זאת ובן אדם יחזיק בה שמר שבת מחללו ושמר ידו
מעשות כל רָע. אשתמע. דמאן דנטיר שבתא. כמאן דנטיר אוריתא כלה.
ברוך יהוה לעולם אמן ואמן:

It is a custom for some to read the Mishnah, Tractate Shabbat, Ch. 17-24

Some have a custom of reciting Psalms 95, 118:25-29, 119, 120-134, 16,144,67, 73, 72 and 104 (on Rosh Chodesh)

Pirkei Avot - Shabbat Mincha

פרקי אבות

Chapter 1

כָּל־יִשְׂרָאֵל יֵשׁ לָהֶם חֵלֶק לָעוֹלָם הַבָּא. שֶׁנֶּאֱמַר: וְעַמֵּךְ כֻּלָּם צַדִּיקִים לְעוֹלָם יִירְשׁוּ אָרֶץ נֵצֶר מַטָּעוֹ (מַטָּעַי) מַעֲשֵׂה יָדַי לְהִתְפָּאֵר:

All Yisrael have a portion in the world to come, as it is said, "And Your people will be all righteous; they will inherit the land forever, the branch of my planting, the work of my hands, that I may be glorified." (Isaiah 60:21)

א. מֹשֶׁה קִבֵּל תּוֹרָה מִסִּינַי. וּמְסָרָהּ לִיהוֹשֻׁעַ. וִיהוֹשֻׁעַ לִזְקֵנִים. וּזְקֵנִים לִנְבִיאִים. וּנְבִיאִים מְסָרוּהָ לְאַנְשֵׁי כְנֶסֶת הַגְּדוֹלָה. הֵם אָמְרוּ שְׁלשָׁה דְבָרִים: הֱווּ מְתוּנִים בַּדִּין. וְהַעֲמִידוּ תַלְמִידִים הַרְבֵּה. וַעֲשׂוּ סְיָג לַתּוֹרָה:

1. Moshe received the Torah on Sinai, and handed it down to Yehoshua; Yehoshua to the elders; the elders to the prophets; and the prophets handed it down to the Anshei Kenesset HaGedolah (Men of the Great Assembly). They said three things: Be deliberate in Judgment; raise up many disciples, and make a fence around the Torah.

ב. שִׁמְעוֹן הַצַּדִּיק הָיָה מִשְּׁיָרֵי כְנֶסֶת הַגְּדוֹלָה. הוּא הָיָה אוֹמֵר. עַל שְׁלשָׁה דְבָרִים הָעוֹלָם עוֹמֵד: עַל הַתּוֹרָה. וְעַל הָעֲבוֹדָה. וְעַל גְּמִילוּת חֲסָדִים:

2. Shimon HaTzaddik (the righteous) was one of the last survivors of the Kenesset HaGedolah (Great Assembly). He used to say, The world stands on three things: on the Torah, on the Temple service, and on the practice of gemilut chasadim (acts of loving-kindness).

ג. אַנְטִיגְנוֹס אִישׁ סוֹכוֹ. קִבֵּל מִשִּׁמְעוֹן הַצַּדִּיק. הוּא הָיָה אוֹמֵר.
אַל תִּהְיוּ כַעֲבָדִים הַמְשַׁמְּשִׁין אֶת־הָרַב עַל מְנָת לְקַבֵּל פְּרָס. אֶלָּא
הֱווּ כַעֲבָדִים הַמְשַׁמְּשִׁין אֶת־הָרַב שֶׁלֹּא עַל מְנָת לְקַבֵּל פְּרָס. וִיהִי
מוֹרָא שָׁמַיִם עֲלֵיכֶם:

3. Antignos of Socho received the tradition from Shimon
HaTzaddik. He used to say, Do not be like the servants who minister
to their master on the condition of receiving a reward; and let the
fear of Heaven be upon you.

ד. יוֹסֵי בֶּן־יוֹעֶזֶר אִישׁ צְרֵדָה. וְיוֹסֵי בֶּן־יוֹחָנָן אִישׁ יְרוּשָׁלַיִם. קִבְּלוּ
מֵהֶם. יוֹסֵי בֶּן־יוֹעֶזֶר אִישׁ צְרֵדָה אוֹמֵר. יְהִי בֵיתְךָ בֵּית־וַעַד
לַחֲכָמִים. וֶהֱוֵי מִתְאַבֵּק בַּעֲפַר רַגְלֵיהֶם. וֶהֱוֵי שׁוֹתֶה בַצָּמָא
אֶת־דִּבְרֵיהֶם:

4. Yosei ben Yo'ezer, of Tzeredah, and Yosei ben Yochanan, of
Yerushalayim received the tradition from them. Yosei ben Yo'ezer, of
Tzeredah, said, Let your house be a meeting house for the wise; sit
in the midst of the dust of their feet, and drink their words with
thirst.

ה. יוֹסֵי בֶּן־יוֹחָנָן אִישׁ יְרוּשָׁלַיִם אוֹמֵר. יְהִי בֵיתְךָ פָּתוּחַ לִרְוָחָה.
וְיִהְיוּ עֲנִיִּים בְּנֵי בֵיתֶךָ. וְאַל תַּרְבֶּה שִׂיחָה עִם הָאִשָּׁה. בְּאִשְׁתּוֹ
אָמְרוּ. קַל וָחֹמֶר בְּאֵשֶׁת חֲבֵרוֹ. מִכָּאן אָמְרוּ חֲכָמִים. כָּל־הַמַּרְבֶּה
שִׂיחָה עִם הָאִשָּׁה. גּוֹרֵם רָעָה לְעַצְמוֹ. וּבָטֵל מִדִּבְרֵי תוֹרָה. וְסוֹפוֹ
יוֹרֵשׁ גֵּהִנָּם:

5. Yosei ben Yochanan, of Yerushalayim, said, Let your house be
open wide; let the poor be the members of your household, and do
not engage in much gossip with women. This applies even to one's
own wife; how much more then to the wife of one's neighbor. Hence
the sages say, Whoever engages in much gossip with women brings

evil on himself, neglects the study of the Torah, and will in the end inherit Gehinnom.

ו. יְהוֹשֻׁעַ בֶּן־פְּרַחְיָה וְנִתַּאי הָאַרְבֵּלִי. קִבְּלוּ מֵהֶם. יְהוֹשֻׁעַ בֶּן־פְּרַחְיָה אוֹמֵר. עֲשֵׂה לְךָ רַב. וּקְנֵה לְךָ חָבֵר. וֶהֱוֵי דָן אֶת־כָּל־הָאָדָם לְכַף זְכוּת:

6. Yehoshua ben Perachyah, and Nittai, the Arbelite, received the tradition from the preceding. Yehoshua ben Perachyah, used to say, get for your studies both a teacher and a fellow student. Judge all men charitably.

ז. נִתַּאי הָאַרְבֵּלִי אוֹמֵר. הַרְחֵק מִשָּׁכֵן רָע. וְאַל תִּתְחַבֵּר לְרָשָׁע. וְאַל תִּתְיָאֵשׁ מִן הַפֻּרְעָנוּת:

7. Nittai of the Arbelite said, keep away from an evil neighbor. Have no association with an evil man. Do not doubt eventual retribution.

ח. יְהוּדָה בֶּן־טַבַּאי וְשִׁמְעוֹן בֶּן־שָׁטַח קִבְּלוּ מֵהֶם. יְהוּדָה בֶּן־טַבַּאי אוֹמֵר. אַל־תַּעַשׂ עַצְמְךָ כְּעוֹרְכֵי הַדַּיָּנִין. וּכְשֶׁיִּהְיוּ בַעֲלֵי־הַדִּינִין עוֹמְדִים לְפָנֶיךָ. יִהְיוּ בְעֵינֶיךָ כִּרְשָׁעִים. וּכְשֶׁנִּפְטָרִים מִלְּפָנֶיךָ. יִהְיוּ בְעֵינֶיךָ כְּזַכָּאִין. כְּשֶׁקִּבְּלוּ עֲלֵיהֶם אֶת־הַדִּין:

8. Yehudah ben Tabbai and Shimon ben Shatach received the tradition from Yehoshua and Nittai. Yehudah ben Tabbai used to say, when sitting as judge do not act the counsel's part. While the litigants stand before you, regard them both as guilty; but when the case is decided, regard them as innocent, cleared by the decision which they have accepted.

ט. שִׁמְעוֹן בֶּן־שָׁטַח אוֹמֵר. הֱוֵי מַרְבֶּה לַחֲקוֹר אֶת־הָעֵדִים. וֶהֱוֵי זָהִיר בִּדְבָרֶיךָ. שֶׁמָּא מִתּוֹכָם יִלְמְדוּ לְשַׁקֵּר:

9. Shimon ben Shatach would say, examine the witnesses thoroughly, and be very exact with your words, in case through them the witnesses find opportunity for giving false testimony.

י. שְׁמַעְיָה וְאַבְטַלְיוֹן קִבְּלוּ מֵהֶם. שְׁמַעְיָה אוֹמֵר. אֱהוֹב
אֶת־הַמְּלָאכָה. וּשְׂנָא אֶת־הָרַבָּנוּת. וְאַל תִּתְוַדַּע לָרָשׁוּת:

10. Shemayah and Avtalyon received the tradition from them (Yehudah and Shimon). Shemayah said, love work. Hate (a position of) lordship, and do not make yourself known to those in political authority.

יא. אַבְטַלְיוֹן אוֹמֵר. חֲכָמִים. הִזָּהֲרוּ בְדִבְרֵיכֶם. שֶׁמָּא תָחוּבוּ חוֹבַת
גָּלוּת. וְתִגְלוּ לִמְקוֹם מַיִם הָרָעִים. וְיִשְׁתּוּ הַתַּלְמִידִים הַבָּאִים
אַחֲרֵיכֶם וְיָמוּתוּ. וְנִמְצָא שֵׁם־שָׁמַיִם מִתְחַלֵּל:

11. Avtalyon used to say, sages, be careful in your words, in case you condemn yourselves to exile to some place where the waters of learning are impure; then the disciples who follow you will drink and die and the Heavenly Name will be profaned.

יב. הִלֵּל וְשַׁמַּאי קִבְּלוּ מֵהֶם. הִלֵּל אוֹמֵר. הֱוֵי מִתַּלְמִידָיו שֶׁל
אַהֲרֹן. אוֹהֵב שָׁלוֹם. וְרוֹדֵף שָׁלוֹם. אוֹהֵב אֶת־הַבְּרִיּוֹת. וּמְקָרְבָן
לַתּוֹרָה:

12. Hillel and Shammai received the tradition from them (Shemayah and Avtalyon). Hillel was known to say, be of the disciples of Aharon, loving peace and pursuing peace, loving your fellow men and drawing them near to the Torah.

יג הוּא הָיָה אוֹמֵר. נְגִיד שְׁמָא אֲבַד שְׁמֵהּ. וּדְלָא מוֹסִיף יָסֵף.
וּדְלָא יָלִיף קְטָלָא חַיָּב. וּדְאִשְׁתַּמַּשׁ בְּתָגָא חֲלָף:

13. He used to say, He who seeks fame destroys his name. Increase knowledge or be decreased. He who does not study is not worthy of life. He who undermines the crown of the Torah to worldly uses will pass away.

יד. הוּא הָיָה אוֹמֵר. אִם אֵין אֲנִי לִי מִי לִי. וּכְשֶׁאֲנִי לְעַצְמִי מָה אֲנִי. וְאִם לֹא עַכְשָׁיו. אֵימָתַי:

14. He used to say, If I am not for myself, who is for me? But if I am for myself alone, what am I? And if not now, when?

טו. שַׁמַּאי אוֹמֵר. עֲשֵׂה תוֹרָתְךָ קֶבַע. אֱמוֹר מְעַט וַעֲשֵׂה הַרְבֵּה. וֶהֱוֵי מְקַבֵּל אֶת־כָּל־ הָאָדָם בְּסֵבֶר פָּנִים יָפוֹת:

15. Shammai would say, make your study of the Torah a regular duty. Say little, but do much. Receive all men with friendly countenance.

טז. רַבָּן גַּמְלִיאֵל הָיָה אוֹמֵר. עֲשֵׂה לְךָ רַב. וְהִסְתַּלֵּק מִן הַסָּפֵק. וְאַל תַּרְבֶּה לְעַשֵּׂר אֲמָדוֹת:

16. Rabban Gamliel used to say, get a teacher so that you are free of doubt. And do not be accustomed to tithe by rough estimation.

יז. שִׁמְעוֹן בְּנוֹ אוֹמֵר. כָּל־יָמַי גָּדַלְתִּי בֵין הַחֲכָמִים. וְלֹא מָצָאתִי לַגּוּף טוֹב אֶלָּא שְׁתִיקָה. וְלֹא הַמִּדְרָשׁ הוּא הָעִקָּר אֶלָּא הַמַּעֲשֶׂה. וְכָל־הַמַּרְבֶּה דְבָרִים מֵבִיא חֵטְא:

17. Shimon son of Rabban Gamliel was known to say, All of my days I have grown up among the sages and I have found nothing better for a man than silence. Not learning, but doing is the essential. Indulging over many words brings sin.

יח. רַבָּן שִׁמְעוֹן בֶּן־גַּמְלִיאֵל אוֹמֵר. עַל־שְׁלֹשָׁה דְבָרִים הָעוֹלָם עוֹמֵד: עַל־הַדִּין וְעַל־הָאֱמֶת וְעַל־הַשָּׁלוֹם. שֶׁנֶּאֱמַר: אֱמֶת וּמִשְׁפַּט שָׁלוֹם שִׁפְטוּ בְּשַׁעֲרֵיכֶם:

18. Rabban Shimon ben Gamliel used to say, the world is supported on three pillars — truth, justice and peace, even as it says, "Every man speak the truth with his neighbor; execute the judgment of truth and peace in your gates;" (Zech. 8:16)

רַבִּי חֲנַנְיָא בֶּן־עֲקַשְׁיָא אוֹמֵר: רָצָה הַקָּדוֹשׁ בָּרוּךְ הוּא לְזַכּוֹת אֶת־יִשְׂרָאֵל. לְפִיכָךְ הִרְבָּה לָהֶם תּוֹרָה וּמִצְוֹת. שֶׁנֶּאֱמַר: יְהֹוָה חָפֵץ לְמַעַן צִדְקוֹ יַגְדִּיל תּוֹרָה וְיַאְדִּיר:

Rabbi Chananya ben Akashya used to say, the Holy One, blessed is He, wishing to make Yisrael more worthy, enlarged for them with Torah and its commandments. For so it is said, "Hashem was pleased, for His righteousness' sake, To make the Torah great and glorious." (Isaiah 42:21)

כָּל־יִשְׂרָאֵל יֵשׁ לָהֶם חֵלֶק לָעוֹלָם הַבָּא. שֶׁנֶּאֱמַר: וְעַמֵּךְ כֻּלָּם צַדִּיקִים לְעוֹלָם יִירְשׁוּ אָרֶץ נֵצֶר מַטָּעוֹ (מַטָּעַי) מַעֲשֵׂה יָדַי לְהִתְפָּאֵר:

All Yisrael have a portion in the world to come, as it is said, "And Your people will be all righteous; they will inherit the land forever, the branch of my planting, the work of my hands, that I may be glorified." (Isaiah 60:21)

Chapter 2

א. רַבִּי אוֹמֵר. אֵיזוֹהִי דֶרֶךְ יְשָׁרָה שֶׁיָּבוֹר לוֹ הָאָדָם. כָּל־שֶׁהִיא תִפְאֶרֶת לְעוֹשֶׂיהָ. וְתִפְאֶרֶת לוֹ מִן הָאָדָם. וֶהֱוֵי זָהִיר בְּמִצְוָה קַלָּה כְּבַחֲמוּרָה. שֶׁאֵין אַתָּה יוֹדֵעַ מַתַּן שְׂכָרָן שֶׁל מִצְוֹת. וֶהֱוֵי מְחַשֵּׁב הֶפְסֵד מִצְוָה כְּנֶגֶד שְׂכָרָהּ. וּשְׂכַר עֲבֵרָה כְּנֶגֶד הֶפְסֵדָהּ. וְהִסְתַּכֵּל

בִּשְׁלֹשָׁה דְבָרִים. וְאִי אַתָּה בָא לִידֵי עֲבֵרָה: דַע מַה־לְמַעְלָה מִמְּךָ. עַיִן רוֹאָה וְאֹזֶן שׁוֹמַעַת. וְכָל־מַעֲשֶׂיךָ בַּסֵּפֶר נִכְתָּבִין:

1. "Rabbi" used to say, Which is the right way that a man should choose? Whatever honors the One who made it and brings him honor from his fellow men. Be careful with a light commandment as with a weighty one, for you do not know the reward of each commandment. Account any loss involved in observing a commandment against its reward, and account any benefit which comes through a transgression against the moral loss. Think on three things, and you will not come into the power of sin: — Know what is above you — a seeing eye, a hearing ear and all of your actions set down on record.

ב. רַבָּן גַּמְלִיאֵל בְּנוֹ שֶׁל רַבִּי יְהוּדָה הַנָּשִׂיא אוֹמֵר. יָפֶה תַלְמוּד תּוֹרָה עִם־דֶּרֶךְ אֶרֶץ. שֶׁיְּגִיעַת שְׁנֵיהֶם מְשַׁכַּחַת עָוֹן. וְכָל־תּוֹרָה שֶׁאֵין עִמָּהּ מְלָאכָה. סוֹפָהּ בְּטֵלָה וְגוֹרֶרֶת עָוֹן. וְכָל־הָעֲמֵלִים עִם־הַצִּבּוּר. יִהְיוּ עֲמֵלִים עִמָּהֶם לְשֵׁם שָׁמַיִם. שֶׁזְּכוּת אֲבוֹתָם מְסַיְּעָתַן. וְצִדְקָתָם עוֹמֶדֶת לָעַד. וְאַתֶּם. מַעֲלֶה אֲנִי עֲלֵיכֶם שָׂכָר הַרְבֵּה. כְּאִלּוּ עֲשִׂיתֶם:

2. Rabban Gamliel, his son, was known to say, excellent is the study of Torah together with worldly occupation, for their combined actions do not allow one to think on sin. All study of Torah not combined with work induces sin and in the end will be useless. Let all who labor with the community to do so for Heaven's sake; for the merit of their forefathers upholds them and their righteousness endures forever. To you who do communal work, God says, "I attribute to you great reward as if the work were solely yours."

ג. הֱווּ זְהִירִין בָּרָשׁוּת. שֶׁאֵין מְקָרְבִין לוֹ לְאָדָם אֶלָּא לְצֹרֶךְ עַצְמָן. נִרְאִין כְּאוֹהֲבִין בִּשְׁעַת הֲנָאָתָן. וְאֵין עוֹמְדִין לוֹ לְאָדָם בִּשְׁעַת דָּחְקוֹ:

3. Be cautious with those in political authority, for they draw a man on only for their own ends. They appear as friends when it profits them, but they do not stand by a man in the hour of his need.

ד. הוּא הָיָה אוֹמֵר. עֲשֵׂה רְצוֹנוֹ כִּרְצוֹנֶךָ. כְּדֵי שֶׁיַּעֲשֶׂה רְצוֹנְךָ כִּרְצוֹנוֹ. בַּטֵּל רְצוֹנְךָ מִפְּנֵי רְצוֹנוֹ. כְּדֵי שֶׁיְּבַטֵּל רְצוֹן אֲחֵרִים מִפְּנֵי רְצוֹנֶךָ.

4. He was also known to say, do His will as your will, that He may do your will as His will. Set aside your will before His will, that He may set aside the will of others before your will.

ה. הִלֵּל אוֹמֵר. אַל תִּפְרוֹשׁ מִן הַצִּבּוּר. וְאַל תַּאֲמֵן בְּעַצְמְךָ עַד יוֹם מוֹתֶךָ. וְאַל תָּדִין אֶת־חֲבֵרְךָ עַד שֶׁתַּגִּיעַ לִמְקוֹמוֹ. וְאַל תֹּאמַר דָּבָר שֶׁאִי אֶפְשָׁר לִשְׁמוֹעַ. שֶׁסּוֹפוֹ לְהִשָּׁמַע. וְאַל תֹּאמַר לִכְשֶׁאֶפָּנֶה אֶשְׁנֶה. שֶׁמָּא לֹא תִפָּנֶה:

5. Hillel used to say, do not stay apart from the community. Do not trust yourself until the day of your death. Do not judge your fellow until you come to his situation. Do not say that it is unintelligible for it to be understood ultimately. Do not say, "When I have leisure I will study", in case you will have not have leisure.

ו. הוּא הָיָה אוֹמֵר. אֵין בּוּר יְרֵא חֵטְא. וְלֹא עַם הָאָרֶץ חָסִיד. וְלֹא הַבַּיְשָׁן לָמֵד. וְלֹא הַקַּפְּדָן מְלַמֵּד. וְלֹא כָּל־הַמַּרְבֶּה בִּסְחוֹרָה מַחְכִּים. וּבְמָקוֹם שֶׁאֵין אֲנָשִׁים. הִשְׁתַּדֵּל לִהְיוֹת אִישׁ:

6. He would say, an empty-headed man will not be fearful of sin, or an ignorant man pious, or the timid man learn, or the irate be a teacher, or the one engrossed in business a scholar. Where there are no men, strive to be a man.

ז. אַף הוּא רָאָה גֻּלְגֹּלֶת אַחַת שֶׁצָּפָה עַל־פְּנֵי הַמַּיִם. אָמַר לָהּ. עַל
דְּאַטֵּפְתְּ אַטְפוּךְ. וְסוֹף מְטַיְפַיִךְ יְטוּפוּן:

7. Seeing a skull floating on the water, he said to it, because you
drowned, you have been drowned, and in the end they who
drowned you will themselves be drowned.

ח. הוּא הָיָה אוֹמֵר. מַרְבֶּה בָשָׂר. מַרְבֶּה רִמָּה. מַרְבֶּה נְכָסִים.
מַרְבֶּה דְאָגָה. מַרְבֶּה נָשִׁים. מַרְבֶּה כְשָׁפִים. מַרְבֶּה שְׁפָחוֹת. מַרְבֶּה
זִמָּה. מַרְבֶּה עֲבָדִים. מַרְבֶּה גָזֵל. מַרְבֶּה תוֹרָה. מַרְבֶּה חַיִּים. מַרְבֶּה
יְשִׁיבָה. מַרְבֶּה חָכְמָה. מַרְבֶּה עֵצָה. מַרְבֶּה תְבוּנָה. מַרְבֶּה צְדָקָה.
מַרְבֶּה שָׁלוֹם. קָנָה שֵׁם טוֹב. קָנָה לְעַצְמוֹ. קָנָה לוֹ דִבְרֵי תוֹרָה.
קָנָה לוֹ חַיֵּי הָעוֹלָם הַבָּא.

8. He used to say, the more flesh, the more worms; the more
property, the more worry; the more women, the more witchcraft;
the more maid-servants, the more lewdness; the more men-servants,
the more robbery. But the more Torah, the more life; the more
study, the more wisdom; the more counsel, the more
understanding; the more righteousness, the more peace. Gain a
good name and, for yourself, you have gained it; but gain knowledge
of the Torah and you have gained life in the world to come.

ט. רַבָּן יוֹחָנָן בֶּן־זַכַּאי קִבֵּל מֵהִלֵּל וּמִשַּׁמַּאי. הוּא הָיָה אוֹמֵר. אִם
לָמַדְתָּ תוֹרָה הַרְבֵּה. אַל תַּחֲזִיק טוֹבָה לְעַצְמְךָ. כִּי לְכָךְ נוֹצָרְתָּ:

9. Rabban Yochanan ben Zakkai received the tradition from Hillel
and Shammai. He used to say, you have learned Torah abundantly,
do not prescribe any merit to yourself, because this is what you were
created for.

י. חֲמִשָּׁה תַלְמִידִים הָיוּ לוֹ לְרַבָּן יוֹחָנָן בֶּן־זַכַּאי. וְאֵלּוּ הֵן: רַבִּי אֱלִיעֶזֶר בֶּן־הוֹרְקָנוֹס. רַבִּי יְהוֹשֻׁעַ בֶּן־חֲנַנְיָא. רַבִּי יוֹסֵי הַכֹּהֵן. רַבִּי שִׁמְעוֹן בֶּן־נְתַנְאֵל וְרַבִּי אֶלְעָזָר בֶּן־עֲרָךְ.

10. Rabban Yochanan ben Zakkai had five disciples, Rabbi Eliezer ben Hyrcanus, Rabbi Yehoshua ben Chananya, Rabbi Yosei the priest, Rabbi Shimon ben Natanel and Rabbi Elazar ben Arach.

יא. הוּא הָיָה מוֹנֶה שְׁבָחָן: רַבִּי אֱלִיעֶזֶר בֶּן־הוֹרְקָנוֹס. בּוֹר סוּד שֶׁאֵינוֹ מְאַבֵּד טִפָּה. רַבִּי יְהוֹשֻׁעַ בֶּן־חֲנַנְיָא. אַשְׁרֵי יוֹלַדְתּוֹ. רַבִּי יוֹסֵי הַכֹּהֵן. חָסִיד. רַבִּי שִׁמְעוֹן בֶּן־נְתַנְאֵל. יְרֵא חֵטְא. רַבִּי אֶלְעָזָר בֶּן־עֲרָךְ. כְּמַעְיָן הַמִּתְגַּבֵּר.

11. He used to recall their quality: Eliezer ben Hyrcanus is a plastered cistern that does not lose a drop. Yehoshua ben Chananya — happy is she who gave birth to him. Rabbi Yosei the priest, is a pious man. Shimon ben Natanel is a fearer of sin. Elazar ben Arach is like a spring flowing with ever sustained vigor.

יב. הוּא הָיָה אוֹמֵר. אִם יִהְיוּ כָל־חַכְמֵי יִשְׂרָאֵל בְּכַף מֹאזְנַיִם. וֶאֱלִיעֶזֶר בֶּן־הוֹרְקָנוֹס בְּכַף שְׁנִיָּה. מַכְרִיעַ אֶת־כֻּלָּם. אַבָּא שָׁאוּל אוֹמֵר מִשְּׁמוֹ. אִם יִהְיוּ כָל־חַכְמֵי יִשְׂרָאֵל בְּכַף מֹאזְנַיִם. וֶאֱלִיעֶזֶר בֶּן־הוֹרְקָנוֹס אַף עִמָּהֶם. וְאֶלְעָזָר בֶּן־עֲרָךְ בְּכַף שְׁנִיָּה. מַכְרִיעַ אֶת־כֻּלָּם.

12. He said further, were all the sages of Yisrael in one scale of the balance and Eliezer ben Hyrcanus in the other, he would outweigh all the rest. But Abba Shaul reported him as saying that were all the sages of Yisrael together with Eliezer ben Hyrcanus in one scale of the balance and Elazar ben Arach in the other, he would outweigh all the rest.

יג. אָמַר לָהֶם. צְאוּ וּרְאוּ אֵיזוֹהִי דֶרֶךְ טוֹבָה שֶׁיִּדְבַּק בָּהּ הָאָדָם. רַבִּי אֱלִיעֶזֶר אוֹמֵר. עַיִן טוֹבָה. רַבִּי יְהוֹשֻׁעַ אוֹמֵר. חָבֵר טוֹב. רַבִּי יוֹסֵי אוֹמֵר. שָׁכֵן טוֹב. רַבִּי שִׁמְעוֹן אוֹמֵר. הָרוֹאֶה אֶת־הַנּוֹלָד. רַבִּי אֶלְעָזָר אוֹמֵר. לֵב טוֹב. אָמַר לָהֶם. רוֹאֶה אֲנִי אֶת־דִּבְרֵי אֶלְעָזָר בֶּן־עֲרָךְ מִדִּבְרֵיכֶם. שֶׁבִּכְלָל דְּבָרָיו דִּבְרֵיכֶם.

13. He said to them, go out and see which is the best way for a man to cleave to. Rabbi Eliezer said, a good eye. Rabbi Yehoshua said, a good friend. Rabbi Yosei said, a good neighbor. Rabbi Shimon said, one who forsees the consequence of an action. Rabbi Elazar said, a good heart. Upon this he said to them, I approve the words of Elazar ben Arach the most, because in them the sayings of the rest of you are comprehended.

יד. אָמַר לָהֶם. צְאוּ וּרְאוּ אֵיזוֹהִי דֶרֶךְ רָעָה שֶׁיִּתְרַחֵק מִמֶּנָּה הָאָדָם. רַבִּי אֱלִיעֶזֶר אוֹמֵר. עַיִן רָעָה. רַבִּי יְהוֹשֻׁעַ אוֹמֵר. חָבֵר רָע. רַבִּי יוֹסֵי אוֹמֵר. שָׁכֵן רָע. רַבִּי שִׁמְעוֹן אוֹמֵר. הַלֹּוֶה וְאֵינוֹ מְשַׁלֵּם. אֶחָד הַלֹּוֶה מִן הָאָדָם. כְּלֹוֶה מִן הַמָּקוֹם. שֶׁנֶּאֱמַר: לֹוֶה רָשָׁע וְלֹא יְשַׁלֵּם וְצַדִּיק חוֹנֵן וְנוֹתֵן: רַבִּי אֶלְעָזָר אוֹמֵר. לֵב רָע. אָמַר לָהֶם. רוֹאֶה אֲנִי אֶת־דִּבְרֵי אֶלְעָזָר בֶּן־עֲרָךְ מִדִּבְרֵיכֶם. שֶׁבִּכְלָל דְּבָרָיו דִּבְרֵיכֶם.

14. Again he said to them, go out and see which is the evil way that a man should shun. Rabbi Eliezer said, an evil eye. Rabbi Yehoshua said, an evil associate. Rabbi Yosei said, an evil neighbor. Rabbi Shimon said, to borrow and not repay, whether from man or from God, - it is the same whether one borrows from man or from the All-present God, as it says, "The wicked borrow and does not repay, but the righteous deal graciously and gives." Rabbi Eleazar said, an evil heart. Said Rabban Yochanan ben Zakkai, I approve the words of Elazar ben Arach the most because in them the sayings of the rest of you are comprehended.

טו. הֵם אָמְרוּ שְׁלֹשָׁה דְבָרִים. רַבִּי אֱלִיעֶזֶר אוֹמֵר. יְהִי כְבוֹד חֲבֵרְךָ חָבִיב עָלֶיךָ כְּשֶׁלָּךְ. וְאַל תְּהִי נֹחַ לִכְעוֹס. וְשׁוּב יוֹם אֶחָד לִפְנֵי מִיתָתְךָ. וֶהֱוֵי מִתְחַמֵּם כְּנֶגֶד אוּרָן שֶׁל חֲכָמִים. וֶהֱוֵי זָהִיר בְּגַחַלְתָּן שֶׁלֹּא תִכָּוֶה. שֶׁנְּשִׁיכָתָן נְשִׁיכַת שׁוּעָל. וַעֲקִיצָתָן עֲקִיצַת עַקְרָב. וּלְחִישָׁתָן לְחִישַׁת שָׂרָף. וְכָל־דִּבְרֵיהֶם כְּגַחֲלֵי אֵשׁ:

15. Each of them said three things. Rabbi Eliezer said, Let your friend's honor be as dear to you as your own, and do not be easily moved to anger. Repent one day before your death. Warm yourself at the fire of the sages. But beware of their glowing coals, in case you are burnt, for their bite is the bite of a fox, and their sting is the scorpion's sting, and their hiss is the serpent's hiss, and all their words are like coals of fire.

טז. רַבִּי יְהוֹשֻׁעַ אוֹמֵר. עַיִן הָרָע וְיֵצֶר הָרָע וְשִׂנְאַת הַבְּרִיּוֹת. מוֹצִיאִין אֶת־הָאָדָם מִן הָעוֹלָם:

16. Rabbi Yehoshua would say, an evil eye, the evil inclination and hatred of the creation remove one from the world.

יז. רַבִּי יוֹסֵי אוֹמֵר. יְהִי מָמוֹן חֲבֵרְךָ חָבִיב עָלֶיךָ כְּשֶׁלָּךְ. וְהַתְקֵן עַצְמְךָ לִלְמוֹד תּוֹרָה. שֶׁאֵינָה יְרֻשָּׁה לָךְ. וְכָל־מַעֲשֶׂיךָ יִהְיוּ לְשֵׁם שָׁמָיִם:

17. Rabbi Yosei used to say, Let your neighbor's money as precious to you as your own. Set yourself to learn Torah, for it does not come to you as an inheritance. Let all of your actions for the sake of Heaven.

יח. רַבִּי שִׁמְעוֹן אוֹמֵר. הֱוֵי זָהִיר בִּקְרִיאַת שְׁמַע וּבִתְפִלָּה. וּכְשֶׁאַתָּה מִתְפַּלֵּל. אַל תַּעַשׂ תְּפִלָּתְךָ קֶבַע. אֶלָּא רַחֲמִים וְתַחֲנוּנִים

לִפְנֵי הַמָּקוֹם. שֶׁנֶּאֱמַר: כִּי־חַנּוּן וְרַחוּם הוּא אֶרֶךְ אַפַּיִם וְרַב־חֶסֶד וְנִחָם עַל־הָרָעָה: וְאַל תְּהִי רָשָׁע בִּפְנֵי עַצְמֶךָ:

18. Rabbi Shimon was known to say, be careful in reading the Shema and in prayer. When you pray, do not make your prayer fixed, but as an appeal of mercy and grace before the All-Present One, as it says, "You are a gracious God, and compassionate, long-suffering, and abundant in mercy, and You repent of the evil." (Jonah 4:2) Do not be evil in your own sight. /

יט. רַבִּי אֶלְעָזָר אוֹמֵר. הֱוֵי שָׁקוּד לִלְמוֹד תּוֹרָה. וְדַע מַה־שֶּׁתָּשִׁיב לָאֶפִּיקוֹרוֹס. וְדַע. לִפְנֵי מִי אַתָּה עָמֵל. וְנֶאֱמָן הוּא בַּעַל מְלַאכְתְּךָ. שֶׁיְשַׁלֶּם לְךָ שְׂכַר פְּעֻלָּתֶךָ:

19. Rabbi Elazar said, be alert in the study of Torah. Know what to answer an unbeliever. Know before whom you are laboring and who is the Master of your work who will pay you the wages of your labor.

כ. רַבִּי טַרְפוֹן אוֹמֵר. הַיּוֹם קָצֵר. וְהַמְּלָאכָה מְרֻבָּה. וְהַפּוֹעֲלִים עֲצֵלִים. וְהַשָּׂכָר הַרְבֵּה. וּבַעַל הַבַּיִת דּוֹחֵק:

20. Rabbi Tarfon used to say, the day is short, the work is great, and the laborers are lazy, and the reward is abundant and the Master of the house is pressing.

כא. הוּא הָיָה אוֹמֵר. לֹא עָלֶיךָ הַמְּלָאכָה לִגְמוֹר. וְלֹא־אַתָּה בֶן־חוֹרִין לְהִבָּטֵל מִמֶּנָּה. אִם לָמַדְתָּ תּוֹרָה הַרְבֵּה. נוֹתְנִין לְךָ שָׂכָר הַרְבֵּה. וְנֶאֱמָן הוּא בַּעַל מְלַאכְתְּךָ. שֶׁיְשַׁלֶּם לְךָ שְׂכַר פְּעֻלָּתֶךָ. וְדַע. שֶׁמַּתַּן שְׂכָרָן שֶׁל צַדִּיקִים לֶעָתִיד לָבוֹא:

21. He used to say, it is not incumbent on you to complete the work, but you are not free to abandon it. If you have learned much Torah, you will be given abundant reward, for the Master of your work is trustworthy to pay you the reward of your labor. But know that the giving of the reward to the righteous is in the time to come.

רַבִּי חֲנַנְיָא בֶּן־עֲקַשְׁיָא אוֹמֵר: רָצָה הַקָּדוֹשׁ בָּרוּךְ הוּא לְזַכּוֹת אֶת־יִשְׂרָאֵל.
לְפִיכָךְ הִרְבָּה לָהֶם תּוֹרָה וּמִצְוֹת. שֶׁנֶּאֱמַר: יְהֹוָה חָפֵץ לְמַעַן צִדְקוֹ יַגְדִּיל
תּוֹרָה וְיַאְדִּיר:

Rabbi Chananya ben Akashya used to say, the Holy One, blessed is He, wishing to make Yisrael more worthy, enlarged for them with Torah and its commandments. For so it is said, "Hashem was pleased, for His righteousness' sake, To make the Torah great and glorious." (Isaiah 42:21)

כָּל־יִשְׂרָאֵל יֵשׁ לָהֶם חֵלֶק לָעוֹלָם הַבָּא. שֶׁנֶּאֱמַר: וְעַמֵּךְ כֻּלָּם צַדִּיקִים לְעוֹלָם
יִירְשׁוּ אָרֶץ נֵצֶר מַטָּעוֹ (מַטָּעַי) מַעֲשֵׂה יָדַי לְהִתְפָּאֵר:

All Yisrael have a portion in the world to come, as it is said, "And Your people will be all righteous; they will inherit the land forever, the branch of my planting, the work of my hands, that I may be glorified."(Isaiah 60:21)

Chapter 3

א. עֲקַבְיָא בֶּן־מַהֲלַלְאֵל אוֹמֵר. הִסְתַּכֵּל בִּשְׁלשָׁה דְבָרִים. וְאֵין
אַתָּה בָא לִידֵי עֲבֵרָה: דַע מֵאַיִן בָּאתָ. וּלְאָן אַתָּה הוֹלֵךְ. וְלִפְנֵי מִי
אַתָּה עָתִיד לִתֵּן דִּין וְחֶשְׁבּוֹן. מֵאַיִן בָּאתָ. מִטִּפָּה סְרוּחָה. וּלְאָן
אַתָּה הוֹלֵךְ. לִמְקוֹם עָפָר רִמָּה וְתוֹלֵעָה. וְלִפְנֵי מִי אַתָּה עָתִיד לִתֵּן
דִּין וְחֶשְׁבּוֹן. לִפְנֵי מֶלֶךְ מַלְכֵי הַמְּלָכִים. הַקָּדוֹשׁ בָּרוּךְ הוּא:

1. Akavya ben Mahalalel used to say, think on three things and you will not come into the power of sin: Know from where you come, where you are going, and before Whom you are destined to give an accounting. From where you come? From a putrefying drop. Where you are going? To the place of dust and worms. Before Whom you are destined to give an accounting? Before the supreme King of kings, the Holy One, blessed is He.

ב. רַבִּי חֲנִינָא סְגַן הַכֹּהֲנִים אוֹמֵר. הֱוֵי מִתְפַּלֵּל בִּשְׁלוֹמָהּ שֶׁל מַלְכוּת. שֶׁאִלְמָלֵא מוֹרָאָהּ. אִישׁ אֶת־רֵעֵהוּ חַיִּים בָּלָעוּ:

2. Rabbi Chanina, the deputy high-priest, would say, pray for the welfare of the government, for were it not for respect for it, men would swallow one another alive.

ג. רַבִּי חֲנִינָא בֶּן־תְּרַדְיוֹן אוֹמֵר. שְׁנַיִם שֶׁיּוֹשְׁבִין וְאֵין בֵּינֵיהֶם דִּבְרֵי תוֹרָה. הֲרֵי זֶה מוֹשַׁב לֵצִים. שֶׁנֶּאֱמַר: וּבְמוֹשַׁב לֵצִים לֹא יָשָׁב: אֲבָל שְׁנַיִם שֶׁיּוֹשְׁבִין וְיֵשׁ בֵּינֵיהֶם דִּבְרֵי תוֹרָה. שְׁכִינָה שְׁרוּיָה בֵינֵיהֶם. שֶׁנֶּאֱמַר: אָז נִדְבְּרוּ יִרְאֵי יְהֹוָה אִישׁ אֶל־רֵעֵהוּ וַיַּקְשֵׁב יְהֹוָה וַיִּשְׁמָע וַיִּכָּתֵב סֵפֶר זִכָּרוֹן לְפָנָיו לְיִרְאֵי יְהֹוָה וּלְחֹשְׁבֵי שְׁמוֹ: אֵין לִי אֶלָּא שְׁנַיִם. מִנַּיִן אֲפִלּוּ אֶחָד. שֶׁיּוֹשֵׁב וְעוֹסֵק בַּתּוֹרָה. שֶׁהַקָּדוֹשׁ בָּרוּךְ הוּא קוֹבֵעַ לוֹ שָׂכָר. שֶׁנֶּאֱמַר: יֵשֵׁב בָּדָד וְיִדֹּם כִּי נָטַל עָלָיו:

3. Rabbi Chananya ben Teradyon used to say, when two sit together and interchange no words of Torah, they are a meeting of scorners, concerning whom it is said, "The godly man does not sit in the seat of scorners." (Ps. 1:1) But when two sit together and words of Torah pass between them, the Divine Presence rests on them. As is said, "Then those who revere Hashem spoke with one another, and Hashem listened and heard, and it was written before Him in the book of remembrance for those who revere Hashem and think on His name." (Malachi 3:16) This applies to two. What verse can be used to show that the Holy One, blessed is He, determines, a reward for even one who sits and occupies himself with the Torah? As it says, "Let him sit alone and keep silent, because He has laid it upon him." (Lam. 3:28)

ד. רַבִּי שִׁמְעוֹן אוֹמֵר. שְׁלֹשָׁה שֶׁאָכְלוּ עַל שֻׁלְחָן אֶחָד וְלֹא אָמְרוּ
עָלָיו דִּבְרֵי תוֹרָה. כְּאִלּוּ אָכְלוּ מִזִּבְחֵי מֵתִים. שֶׁנֶּאֱמַר: כִּי
כָל־שֻׁלְחָנוֹת מָלְאוּ קִיא צֹאָה בְּלִי מָקוֹם: אֲבָל שְׁלֹשָׁה שֶׁאָכְלוּ עַל
שֻׁלְחָן אֶחָד וְאָמְרוּ עָלָיו דִּבְרֵי תוֹרָה. כְּאִלּוּ אָכְלוּ מִשֻּׁלְחָנוֹ שֶׁל
מָקוֹם. שֶׁנֶּאֱמַר: וַיְדַבֵּר אֵלַי זֶה הַשֻּׁלְחָן אֲשֶׁר לִפְנֵי יְהֹוָה:

4. Rabbi Shimon said, three who have eaten together at table and
have said over it no words of Torah are as though they had eaten of
sacrifices to the dead, as it says, "For all tables are full of filthy
vomit, and no place is clean." (Isaiah 28:8) But three who have eaten
together at table and have said over it words of Torah are as though
they had eaten of the table of God, as it says "And he said to me:
'This is the table that is before Hashem.' (Ezekiel 41:22)

ה. רַבִּי חֲנִינָא בֶּן־חֲכִינַאי אוֹמֵר. הַנֵּעוֹר בַּלַּיְלָה. וְהַמְהַלֵּךְ בַּדֶּרֶךְ
יְחִידִי. וּמְפַנֶּה לִבּוֹ לְבַטָּלָה. הֲרֵי זֶה מִתְחַיֵּב בְּנַפְשׁוֹ:

5. Rabbi Chanina ben Chachina used to say, he who awakens by
night and gives his heart to idle thoughts, or he who walks alone
and gives his heart to idle thoughts, endangers his life.

ו. רַבִּי נְחוּנְיָא בֶּן־הַקָּנָה אוֹמֵר. כָּל־הַמְקַבֵּל עָלָיו עֹל תּוֹרָה.
מַעֲבִירִין מִמֶּנּוּ עֹל מַלְכוּת וְעֹל דֶּרֶךְ אֶרֶץ. וְכָל־הַפּוֹרֵק מִמֶּנּוּ עֹל
תּוֹרָה. נוֹתְנִין עָלָיו עֹל מַלְכוּת וְעֹל דֶּרֶךְ אֶרֶץ:

6. Rabbi Nechunya ben Hakanah was known to say, whoever
accepts the yoke of Torah has removed from him the yoke of
government and the yoke of worldly affairs; but he who casts off the
yoke of Torah will find himself bearing the yokes of government and
of worldly affairs.

ז. רַבִּי חֲלַפְתָּא אִישׁ כְּפַר חֲנַנְיָא אוֹמֵר. עֲשָׂרָה שֶׁיּוֹשְׁבִין וְעוֹסְקִין בַּתּוֹרָה. שְׁכִינָה שְׁרוּיָה בֵינֵיהֶם. שֶׁנֶּאֱמַר: אֱלֹהִים נִצָּב בַּעֲדַת־אֵל. וּמִנַּיִן אֲפִלּוּ חֲמִשָּׁה. שֶׁנֶּאֱמַר: וַאֲגֻדָּתוֹ עַל־אֶרֶץ יְסָדָהּ. וּמִנַּיִן אֲפִלּוּ שְׁלֹשָׁה. שֶׁנֶּאֱמַר: בְּקֶרֶב אֱלֹהִים יִשְׁפֹּט: וּמִנַּיִן אֲפִלּוּ שְׁנַיִם. שֶׁנֶּאֱמַר: אָז נִדְבְּרוּ יִרְאֵי יְהֹוָה אִישׁ אֶל־רֵעֵהוּ וַיַּקְשֵׁב יְהֹוָה וַיִּשְׁמָע. וּמִנַּיִן אֲפִלּוּ אֶחָד. שֶׁנֶּאֱמַר: בְּכָל־הַמָּקוֹם אֲשֶׁר אַזְכִּיר אֶת־שְׁמִי אָבוֹא אֵלֶיךָ וּבֵרַכְתִּיךָ:

7. Rabbi Chalafta ben Dosa of Kfar Chananya used to say, ten who sit down and occupy themselves with the Torah, the Divine Presence rests among them, as it is said, "God stands in the congregation of God." (Ps. 82:1) Even if there are five? As it says, "And He has established His troop upon the earth." (Amos 9:6) Even also of three? As it says, "God judges in the midst of the judges." (Ps. 82:1) Even also of two? As it says, "Then those who revere Hashem spoke with one another and Hashem listened and heard." (Malachi 3:16) And what suggests it even of one? As it says, "In every place where I cause My name to be mentioned I will come to you and bless you." (Ex. 20:21)

ח. רַבִּי אֶלְעָזָר אִישׁ בַּרְתּוֹתָא אוֹמֵר. תֶּן לוֹ מִשֶּׁלּוֹ. שֶׁאַתָּה וְשֶׁלְּךָ שֶׁלּוֹ. וְכֵן בְּדָוִד הוּא אוֹמֵר. כִּי מִמְּךָ הַכֹּל וּמִיָּדְךָ נָתַנּוּ לָךְ:

8. Rabbi Elazar of Bartota would say, give to Him from what is His, for you and what is yours are His. As so by David when he says, "For all things come from You, and of Your own we have given You." (I Chron. 29:14)

ט. רַבִּי יַעֲקֹב אוֹמֵר. הַמְהַלֵּךְ בַּדֶּרֶךְ וְשׁוֹנֶה. וּמַפְסִיק מִמִּשְׁנָתוֹ וְאוֹמֵר: מַה־נָּאֶה אִילָן זֶה. וּמַה־נָּאֶה נִיר זֶה. מַעֲלֶה עָלָיו הַכָּתוּב. כְּאִלּוּ מִתְחַיֵּב בְּנַפְשׁוֹ:

9. Rabbi Yaakov used to say, one who is studying Torah as he walks by the way and who stops his study to say, "How beautiful is this tree, or this fertile ground," the scripture regards as if he has forfeited his life. (For the words of the Shema declare, "You will speak of them when You walk by the way").

י. רַבִּי דוֹסְתַּאי בְּרַבִּי יַנַּאי מִשׁוּם רַבִּי מֵאִיר אוֹמֵר. כָּל־הַשּׁוֹכֵחַ דָּבָר אֶחָד מִמִּשְׁנָתוֹ. מַעֲלֶה עָלָיו הַכָּתוּב כְּאִלּוּ מִתְחַיֵּב בְּנַפְשׁוֹ. שֶׁנֶּאֱמַר: רַק הִשָּׁמֶר לְךָ וּשְׁמֹר נַפְשְׁךָ מְאֹד פֶּן־תִּשְׁכַּח אֶת־הַדְּבָרִים אֲשֶׁר־רָאוּ עֵינֶיךָ. יָכוֹל אֲפִלּוּ תָּקְפָה עָלָיו מִשְׁנָתוֹ. תַּלְמוּד לוֹמַר: וּפֶן־יָסוּרוּ מִלְּבָבְךָ כָּל יְמֵי חַיֶּיךָ. הָא אֵינוֹ מִתְחַיֵּב בְּנַפְשׁוֹ. עַד שֶׁיֵּשֵׁב וִיסִירֵם מִלִּבּוֹ:

10. Rabbi Dostai bar Yannai would say in Rabbi Meir's name, one who forgets anything of his Torah-learning is as though he has forfeited his life. As it says, "Only take guard to yourself, and keep your soul diligently, in case you forget the things which your eyes saw," (Deut. 4:9) In case you would think that this applies even when the learning has been too hard, the verse continues, "and in case they depart from your heart all the days of your life;" So, a person's guilt is not established until he deliberately and purposely sits down and removes them from his heart.

יא. רַבִּי חֲנִינָא בֶּן־דּוֹסָא אוֹמֵר. כָּל־שֶׁיִּרְאַת חֶטְאוֹ קוֹדֶמֶת לְחָכְמָתוֹ. חָכְמָתוֹ מִתְקַיֶּמֶת. וְכָל־ שֶׁחָכְמָתוֹ קוֹדֶמֶת לְיִרְאַת חֶטְאוֹ. אֵין חָכְמָתוֹ מִתְקַיֶּמֶת:

11. Rabbi Chanina ben Dosa used to say, everyone for whom fear of sin takes precedence over learning, for him that learning will endure; but everyone whose learning takes precedence over his fear of sin, his learning will not endure.

יב. הוּא הָיָה אוֹמֵר. כָּל־שֶׁמַּעֲשָׂיו מְרֻבִּין מֵחָכְמָתוֹ. חָכְמָתוֹ מִתְקַיֶּמֶת. וְכָל־ שֶׁחָכְמָתוֹ מְרֻבָּה מִמַּעֲשָׂיו. אֵין חָכְמָתוֹ מִתְקַיֶּמֶת:

12. He used to say also, everyone whose works are greater than his learning, his learning will endure, but everyone whose learning is greater than his works, his learning will not endure.

יג. הוּא הָיָה אוֹמֵר. כָּל־שֶׁרוּחַ הַבְּרִיּוֹת נוֹחָה הֵימֶנּוּ. רוּחַ הַמָּקוֹם נוֹחָה הֵימֶנּוּ. וְכָל־שֶׁאֵין רוּחַ הַבְּרִיּוֹת נוֹחָה הֵימֶנּוּ. אֵין רוּחַ הַמָּקוֹם נוֹחָה הֵימֶנּוּ:

13. He also used to say, in everyone in whom the spirit of his fellow-men takes pleasure, the spirit of the All-Present also takes pleasure; but everyone in whom the spirit of his fellow-men does not take pleasure, the spirit of the All-Present does not take pleasure in him.

יד. רַבִּי דוֹסָא בֶּן־הַרְכִּינָס אוֹמֵר. שֵׁנָה שֶׁל שַׁחֲרִית. וְיַיִן שֶׁל צָהֳרַיִם. וְשִׂיחַת הַיְלָדִים. וִישִׁיבַת בָּתֵּי כְנֵסִיּוֹת שֶׁל עַמֵּי הָאָרֶץ. מוֹצִיאִין אֶת־הָאָדָם מִן הָעוֹלָם:

14. Rabbi Dosa ben Harkinas said, morning sleep, mid-day wine, children's talk and frequenting the houses of assembly of the ignorant take a man out of the world.

טו. רַבִּי אֶלְעָזָר הַמּוֹדָעִי אוֹמֵר. הַמְחַלֵּל אֶת־הַקֳּדָשִׁים. וְהַמְבַזֶּה אֶת־הַמּוֹעֲדוֹת. וְהַמַּלְבִּין פְּנֵי חֲבֵרוֹ בָּרַבִּים. וְהַמֵּפֵר בְּרִיתוֹ שֶׁל אַבְרָהָם אָבִינוּ. עָלָיו הַשָּׁלוֹם. וְהַמְגַלֶּה פָנִים בַּתּוֹרָה שֶׁלֹּא כַהֲלָכָה. אַף־עַל־פִּי שֶׁיֵּשׁ בְּיָדוֹ תּוֹרָה וּמַעֲשִׂים טוֹבִים. אֵין לוֹ חֵלֶק לְעוֹלָם הַבָּא:

15. Rabbi Elazar of Modi'in would say, he who profanes holy things, he who despises the festivals, he who publicly shames his fellow-

man, he who makes void the covenant of our father Avraham, and who casually interprets the Torah in conflict with the halachah. Such a person, even though he has knowledge of the Torah and good deeds, has no share in the world to come.

טז. רַבִּי יִשְׁמָעֵאל אוֹמֵר. הֱוֵי קַל לְרֹאשׁ וְנֹחַ לְתִשְׁחֹרֶת. וֶהֱוֵי מְקַבֵּל אֶת־כָּל־הָאָדָם בְּשִׂמְחָה:

16. Rabbi Yishmael used to say, be prompt to a superior and flexible under oppression. And receive every man with joy.

יז. רַבִּי עֲקִיבָא אוֹמֵר. שְׂחוֹק וְקַלּוּת רֹאשׁ. מַרְגִּילִין אֶת־הָאָדָם לְעֶרְוָה. מַסֹּרֶת. סְיָג לַתּוֹרָה. מַעַשְׂרוֹת. סְיָג לָעֹשֶׁר. נְדָרִים. סְיָג לַפְּרִישׁוּת. סְיָג לַחָכְמָה. שְׁתִיקָה:

17. Rabbi Akiva was known to say, laughing and joking lead a man on to indecency. Tradition is a safeguarding fence to the Torah; tithes are a fence to wealth, vows a fence to abstinence; silence is a fence to wisdom.

יח. הוּא הָיָה אוֹמֵר. חָבִיב אָדָם שֶׁנִּבְרָא בְּצֶלֶם. חִבָּה יְתֵרָה נוֹדַעַת לוֹ שֶׁנִּבְרָא בְּצֶלֶם. שֶׁנֶּאֱמַר: כִּי בְּצֶלֶם אֱלֹהִים עָשָׂה אֶת־הָאָדָם: חֲבִיבִין יִשְׂרָאֵל שֶׁנִּקְרְאוּ בָנִים לַמָּקוֹם. חִבָּה יְתֵרָה נוֹדַעַת לָהֶם שֶׁנִּקְרְאוּ בָנִים לַמָּקוֹם. שֶׁנֶּאֱמַר: בָּנִים אַתֶּם לַיהֹוָה אֱלֹהֵיכֶם. חֲבִיבִין יִשְׂרָאֵל שֶׁנִּתַּן לָהֶם כְּלִי חֶמְדָּה. חִבָּה יְתֵרָה נוֹדַעַת לָהֶם. שֶׁנִּתַּן לָהֶם כְּלִי חֶמְדָּה שֶׁבּוֹ נִבְרָא הָעוֹלָם. שֶׁנֶּאֱמַר: כִּי לֶקַח טוֹב נָתַתִּי לָכֶם תּוֹרָתִי אַל־תַּעֲזֹבוּ:

18. He used to say, beloved is man that he is created in the image of God; but greater yet is the love that this has been made known to him, as it says, "in the image of God He made man." (Gen. 9:6) Beloved are Yisrael that they are called children of God; but greater yet is the love that this has been made known to them, as it says, "You are children of Hashem your God." (Deut. 14:1) Beloved are Yisrael that there has been given to them the precious instrument of the world's creation; but greater is the love that this has been made known to them, as it says, "For I give you good teaching; Do not forsake my Torah." (Prov. 4:2)

יט. הַכֹּל צָפוּי. וְהָרְשׁוּת נְתוּנָה. וּבְטוֹב הָעוֹלָם נִדּוֹן. וְהַכֹּל לְפִי רֹב הַמַּעֲשֶׂה:

19. Everything is foreseen yet free choice is given to man. The world is judged with goodness, but everything is according to the amount of one's work.

כ. הוּא הָיָה אוֹמֵר. הַכֹּל נָתוּן בְּעֵרָבוֹן. וּמְצוּדָה פְרוּסָה עַל־כָּל־הַחַיִּים. הַחֲנוּת פְּתוּחָה. וְהַחֶנְוָנִי מַקִּיף. וְהַפִּנְקָס פָּתוּחַ. וְהַיָּד כּוֹתֶבֶת. וְכָל־הָרוֹצֶה לִלְווֹת יָבֹא וְיִלְוֶה. וְהַגַּבָּאִים מַחֲזִירִין תָּדִיר בְּכָל־יוֹם. וְנִפְרָעִין מִן־הָאָדָם מִדַּעְתּוֹ וְשֶׁלֹּא מִדַּעְתּוֹ. וְיֵשׁ לָהֶם עַל מַה שֶּׁיִּסְמוֹכוּ. וְהַדִּין דִּין אֱמֶת. וְהַכֹּל מְתֻקָּן לִסְעֻדָה:

20. He would also say, everything is given in pledge, and a net is spread for all of the living. The shop is open, the hand writes, and any who wish to borrow may come and borrow. But the collectors go around daily all the time and exact payment with or without consent, for they have the warrant on which they rely, since the judgment is a true judgment. And everything is prepared for a feast.

כא. רַבִּי אֶלְעָזָר בֶּן־עֲזַרְיָה אוֹמֵר. אִם אֵין תּוֹרָה. אֵין דֶּרֶךְ אֶרֶץ. אִם אֵין דֶּרֶךְ אֶרֶץ. אֵין תּוֹרָה. אִם אֵין חָכְמָה. אֵין יִרְאָה. אִם אֵין יִרְאָה. אֵין חָכְמָה. אִם אֵין בִּינָה. אֵין דַּעַת. אִם אֵין דַּעַת. אֵין בִּינָה. אִם אֵין קֶמַח. אֵין תּוֹרָה. אִם אֵין תּוֹרָה. אֵין קֶמַח:

21. Rabbi Eleazar ben Azaryah said, where there is no Torah there is no way of life, and where there is no way of life there is no Torah. Where there is no wisdom there is no reverence, and where there is no reverence there is no wisdom. Where there is no knowledge there is no understanding, and where there is no understanding there is no knowledge. Where there is no food there is no Torah, and where there is no Torah there is no food.

כב. הוּא הָיָה אוֹמֵר. כָּל־שֶׁחָכְמָתוֹ מְרֻבָּה מִמַּעֲשָׂיו. לְמָה הוּא
דוֹמֶה. לְאִילָן שֶׁעֲנָפָיו מְרֻבִּין וְשָׁרָשָׁיו מוּעָטִין. וְהָרוּחַ בָּאָה וְעוֹקַרְתּוֹ
וְהוֹפַכְתּוֹ עַל פָּנָיו. שֶׁנֶּאֱמַר: וְהָיָה כְּעַרְעָר בָּעֲרָבָה וְלֹא יִרְאֶה
כִּי־יָבוֹא טוֹב וְשָׁכַן חֲרֵרִים בַּמִּדְבָּר אֶרֶץ מְלֵחָה וְלֹא תֵשֵׁב: אֲבָל
כָּל־שֶׁמַּעֲשָׂיו מְרֻבִּין מֵחָכְמָתוֹ. לְמָה הוּא דוֹמֶה. לְאִילָן שֶׁעֲנָפָיו
מוּעָטִין וְשָׁרָשָׁיו מְרֻבִּין. שֶׁאֲפִלּוּ כָּל־הָרוּחוֹת שֶׁבָּעוֹלָם בָּאוֹת
וְנוֹשְׁבוֹת בּוֹ. אֵין מְזִיזִין אוֹתוֹ מִמְּקוֹמוֹ. שֶׁנֶּאֱמַר: וְהָיָה כְּעֵץ שָׁתוּל
עַל־פַּלְגֵי מָיִם. וְעַל יוּבַל יְשַׁלַּח שָׁרָשָׁיו. וְלֹא יִרְאֶה כִּי יָבֹא חֹם.
וְהָיָה עָלֵהוּ רַעֲנָן. וּבִשְׁנַת בַּצֹּרֶת לֹא יִדְאָג. וְלֹא יָמִישׁ מֵעֲשׂוֹת פֶּרִי:

22. He would also say, he whose wisdom exceeds his works, to what is he like? A tree with abundant branches and whose roots are few. The wind blows, uproots it and it lies on it face, as it says, "For he will be like a tamarisk in the desert, And will not see when good comes; But will inhabit the parched places in the wilderness, A salt land and not inhabited." (Jer. 17:6) But he whose works exceed his wisdom, what is he like? A tree with few branches and abundant roots. Though all the winds in the world come and blow against it, they can not budge it from its place, as it says, "For he will be like a tree planted by the waters, And that spreads out its roots by the river, And will not see when heat comes, But its foliage will be luxuriant; And will not be anxious in the year of drought, Neither will it stop from yielding fruit." (Jer. 17:8)

כג. רַבִּי אֶלְעָזָר בֶּן חִסְמָא אוֹמֵר. קִנִּין וּפִתְחֵי נִדָּה. הֵן הֵן גּוּפֵי הֲלָכוֹת. תְּקוּפוֹת וְגִימַטְרִיָּאוֹת. פַּרְפְּרָאוֹת לַחָכְמָה:

23. Rabbi Elazar Hisma used to say, the offerings of birds and purification of women from personal uncleanness—they are the body of halachot (main-course); but the calculation of the equinoxes and gematria—these are the desserts of wisdom.

רַבִּי חֲנַנְיָא בֶּן־עֲקַשְׁיָא אוֹמֵר: רָצָה הַקָּדוֹשׁ בָּרוּךְ הוּא לְזַכּוֹת אֶת־יִשְׂרָאֵל. לְפִיכָךְ הִרְבָּה לָהֶם תּוֹרָה וּמִצְוֹת. שֶׁנֶּאֱמַר: יְהֹוָה חָפֵץ לְמַעַן צִדְקוֹ יַגְדִּיל תּוֹרָה וְיַאְדִּיר:

Rabbi Chananya ben Akashya used to say, the Holy One, blessed is He, wishing to make Yisrael more worthy, enlarged for them with Torah and its commandments. For so it is said, "Hashem was pleased, for His righteousness' sake, To make the Torah great and glorious." (Isaiah 42:21)

כָּל־יִשְׂרָאֵל יֵשׁ לָהֶם חֵלֶק לָעוֹלָם הַבָּא. שֶׁנֶּאֱמַר: וְעַמֵּךְ כֻּלָּם צַדִּיקִים לְעוֹלָם יִירְשׁוּ אָרֶץ נֵצֶר מַטָּעוֹ (מַטָּעַי) מַעֲשֵׂה יָדַי לְהִתְפָּאֵר:

All Yisrael have a portion in the world to come, as it is said, "And Your people will be all righteous; they will inherit the land forever, the branch of my planting, the work of my hands, that I may be glorified." (Isaiah 60:21)

Chapter 4

א. בֶּן־זוֹמָא אוֹמֵר. אֵיזֶהוּ חָכָם. הַלּוֹמֵד מִכָּל־אָדָם. שֶׁנֶּאֱמַר: מִכָּל־מְלַמְּדַי הִשְׂכַּלְתִּי. כִּי עֵדְוֹתֶיךָ שִׂיחָה לִי. אֵיזֶהוּ גִבּוֹר. הַכּוֹבֵשׁ אֶת־יִצְרוֹ. שֶׁנֶּאֱמַר: טוֹב אֶרֶךְ אַפַּיִם מִגִּבּוֹר וּמֹשֵׁל בְּרוּחוֹ מִלֹּכֵד עִיר: אֵיזֶהוּ עָשִׁיר. הַשָּׂמֵחַ בְּחֶלְקוֹ. שֶׁנֶּאֱמַר: יְגִיעַ כַּפֶּיךָ כִּי תֹאכֵל אַשְׁרֶיךָ וְטוֹב לָךְ: אַשְׁרֶיךָ בָּעוֹלָם הַזֶּה. וְטוֹב לָךְ לָעוֹלָם הַבָּא. אֵיזֶהוּ מְכֻבָּד. הַמְכַבֵּד אֶת־הַבְּרִיּוֹת. שֶׁנֶּאֱמַר: כִּי־מְכַבְּדַי אֲכַבֵּד וּבֹזַי יֵקָלּוּ:

1. Ben Zoma used to say, who is wise? He who learns from all men, as it says, "I have gained understanding from all of my teachers;" (Ps. 119:99) Who is strong? He who controls his passions, as it says, "He that is slow to anger is better than the mighty; And he that rules his spirit (is better) than he that takes a city." (Prov. 16:32) Who is rich? One who rejoices in his lot, as it says, "When You eat the labor of your hands, you will be happy, and it will be well with you." (Ps. 128:2) "You will be happy" in this world, "and it will be well with you" for the world to come. Who is honored? He who honors his fellow-men, as it says, "For those that honor Me I will honor, and they that despise Me will be lightly esteemed."

ב. בֶּן־עַזַּאי אוֹמֵר. הֱוֵי רָץ לְמִצְוָה קַלָּה כְּבַחֲמוּרָה. וּבוֹרֵחַ מִן הָעֲבֵרָה. שֶׁמִּצְוָה גוֹרֶרֶת מִצְוָה. וַעֲבֵרָה גוֹרֶרֶת עֲבֵרָה. שֶׁשְּׂכַר מִצְוָה – מִצְוָה. וּשְׂכַר עֲבֵרָה – עֲבֵרָה:

2. Ben Azai would say, run to fulfill even a light commandment and flee from transgression; for one commandment leads to another, one transgression leads to another, the reward of a commandment is another commandment, while the reward of a transgression is a transgression.

ג. הוּא הָיָה אוֹמֵר. אַל תְּהִי בָז לְכָל־אָדָם. וְאַל תְּהִי מַפְלִיג לְכָל־דָּבָר. שֶׁאֵין לְךָ אָדָם שֶׁאֵין לוֹ שָׁעָה. וְאֵין לְךָ דָבָר שֶׁאֵין לוֹ מָקוֹם:

3. He also used to say, do not despise any man and do not hold anything impossible, for there is no man that does not have his hour, and there is no thing that does not have its place.

ד. רַבִּי לְוִיטַס אִישׁ יַבְנֶה אוֹמֵר. מְאֹד מְאֹד הֱוֵי שְׁפַל רוּחַ. שֶׁתִּקְוַת אֱנוֹשׁ רִמָּה:

4. Rabbi Levitas the man of Yavneh was known to say, "Be exceeding humble, for the hope of man is the worm."

ה. רַבִּי יוֹחָנָן בֶּן־בְּרוֹקָה אוֹמֵר. כָּל־הַמְחַלֵּל שֵׁם שָׁמַיִם בַּסֵּתֶר. נִפְרָעִין מִמֶּנּוּ בְּגָלוּי. אֶחָד שׁוֹגֵג וְאֶחָד מֵזִיד בְּחִלּוּל הַשֵּׁם:

5. Rabbi Yohanan ben Berokah used to say, whoever profanes the name of Heaven in secret will pay the penalty in public, whether committed involuntarily or willfully, it is the same in profaning the name.

ו. רַבִּי יִשְׁמָעֵאל בְּנוֹ אוֹמֵר. הַלּוֹמֵד עַל מְנָת לְלַמֵּד. מַסְפִּיקִין בְּיָדוֹ לִלְמוֹד וּלְלַמֵּד. וְהַלּוֹמֵד עַל מְנָת לַעֲשׂוֹת. מַסְפִּיקִין בְּיָדוֹ לִלְמוֹד וּלְלַמֵּד. לִשְׁמוֹר וְלַעֲשׂוֹת:

6. Rabbi Yishmael, his son, used to say, he who learns in order to teach will be enabled both to learn and teach, but he who learns in order to practice will be enabled to learn, to teach and to practice.

ז. רַבִּי צָדוֹק אוֹמֵר. אַל תִּפְרוֹשׁ מִן הַצִּבּוּר. וְאַל תַּעַשׂ עַצְמְךָ כְּעוֹרְכֵי הַדַּיָּנִין. וְאַל תַּעֲשֶׂהָ עֲטָרָה לְהִתְגַּדֵּל בָּהּ. וְלֹא קַרְדֹּם לַחְפּוֹר בָּהּ. וְכָךְ הָיָה הִלֵּל אוֹמֵר. וּדְאִשְׁתַּמֵּשׁ בְּתַגָּא חֲלָף. הָא לָמַדְתָּ. כָּל־הַנֶּהֱנֶה מִדִּבְרֵי תוֹרָה. נוֹטֵל חַיָּיו מִן הָעוֹלָם:

7. Rabbi Tzadok said, do not seperate yourself from the congregation, and do not make yourselves like lawyers, do not make the Torah a crown to praise yourself, or a spade to dig with. Likewise Hillel used to say, he who makes worldly use of the crown of the Torah will pass away. So also have you learned that anyone who exploits the teachings of the Torah removes himself from the world of life.

ח. רַבִּי יוֹסֵי אוֹמֵר. כָּל־הַמְכַבֵּד אֶת־הַתּוֹרָה. גּוּפוֹ מְכֻבָּד עַל הַבְּרִיּוֹת. וְכָל־הַמְחַלֵּל אֶת־הַתּוֹרָה. גּוּפוֹ מְחֻלָּל עַל הַבְּרִיּוֹת:

8. Rabbi Yosei used to say, everyone who honors the Torah will himself be honored by men, and everyone who dishonors the Torah will himself be dishonored by men.

ט. רַבִּי יִשְׁמָעֵאל בְּנוֹ אוֹמֵר. הַחוֹשֵׂךְ עַצְמוֹ מִן הַדִּין. פּוֹרֵק מִמֶּנּוּ אֵיבָה וְגֵזֶל וּשְׁבוּעַת שָׁוְא. וְהַגַּס לִבּוֹ בְּהוֹרָאָה. שׁוֹטֶה רָשָׁע וְגַס רוּחַ:

9. Rabbi Yishmael his son said, he who shuns the office of judge escapes enmity, theft and perjury, while he who presumptuously lays down decisions is arrogant, a fool, wicked and of an arrogant spirit.

י. הוּא הָיָה אוֹמֵר. אַל תְּהִי דָן יְחִידִי. שֶׁאֵין דָּן יְחִידִי אֶלָּא אֶחָד. וְאַל תֹּאמַר. קַבְּלוּ דַעְתִּי. שֶׁהֵן רַשָּׁאִין. וְלֹא אָתָּה:

10. He used to say, do not judge alone, for there is but One who may judge alone. Do not say, "accept my opinion," for they have the right to decide, not you.

יא. רַבִּי יוֹנָתָן אוֹמֵר. כָּל־הַמְקַיֵּם אֶת־הַתּוֹרָה מֵעוֹנִי. סוֹפוֹ לְקַיְּמָהּ מֵעֹשֶׁר. וְכָל־הַמְבַטֵּל אֶת־הַתּוֹרָה מֵעֹשֶׁר. סוֹפוֹ לְבַטְּלָהּ מֵעוֹנִי:

11. Rabbi Yonatan said, everyone who fulfills the Torah in poverty will in the end fulfill it in wealth, and everyone who disregards the Torah in wealth will in the end disregard it in poverty.

יב. רַבִּי מֵאִיר אוֹמֵר. הֱוֵי מְמַעֵט בָּעֵסֶק וַעֲסֹק בַּתּוֹרָה. וֶהֱוֵי שְׁפַל רוּחַ בִּפְנֵי כָל־אָדָם. וְאִם בָּטַלְתָּ מִן הַתּוֹרָה. יֶשׁ לְךָ בְּטֵלִים הַרְבֵּה כְּנֶגְדֶּךָ. וְאִם עָמַלְתָּ בַּתּוֹרָה. יֶשׁ לוֹ שָׂכָר הַרְבֵּה לִתֶּן לָךְ:

12. Rabbi Meir used to say, diminish your business and occupy yourself with the Torah. Be humble of spirit before all men. If you have neglected the Torah, there are many more causes for neglecting it before you; but if you have labored in the Torah, God has rich reward to give you.

יג. רַבִּי אֱלִיעֶזֶר בֶּן־יַעֲקֹב אוֹמֵר. הָעוֹשֶׂה מִצְוָה אַחַת. קוֹנֶה לוֹ פְּרַקְלִיט אֶחָד. וְהָעוֹבֵר עֲבֵרָה אַחַת. קוֹנֶה לוֹ קַטֵּגוֹר אֶחָד. תְּשׁוּבָה וּמַעֲשִׂים טוֹבִים. כִּתְרִיס בִּפְנֵי הַפֻּרְעָנוּת:

13. Rabbi Eliezer son of Yaakov was known to say: he who performs one commandment acquires for himself one advocate. while he who commits one transgression acquires one accuser. Teshuvah (repentance) and good deeds are as a shield against punishment.

יד. רַבִּי יוֹחָנָן הַסַּנְדְּלָר אוֹמֵר. כָּל־כְּנֵסִיָּה שֶׁהִיא לְשֵׁם שָׁמַיִם. סוֹפָהּ לְהִתְקַיֵּם. וְשֶׁאֵינָהּ לְשֵׁם שָׁמַיִם. אֵין סוֹפָהּ לְהִתְקַיֵּם:

14. Rabbi Yohanan the sandal maker said every assembly which is for the name of Heaven will, in the end, be established; but that which is not for the name of Heaven will, in the end, not be established.

טו. רַבִּי אֶלְעָזָר בֶּן־שַׁמּוּעַ אוֹמֵר. יְהִי כְבוֹד תַּלְמִידְךָ חָבִיב עָלֶיךָ כְּשֶׁלָּךְ. וּכְבוֹד חֲבֵרְךָ כְּמוֹרָא רַבָּךְ. וּמוֹרָא רַבָּךְ כְּמוֹרָא שָׁמָיִם:

15. Rabbi Elazar ben Shamua said, let the honor of your disciple be as precious to you as the honor of your colleague, the honor of your colleague as precious to you as the respect for your teacher, and the respect for your teacher as precious to you as your fear of Heaven.

טז. רַבִּי יְהוּדָה אוֹמֵר. הֱוֵי זָהִיר בְּתַלְמוּד. שֶׁשִּׁגְגַת תַּלְמוּד עוֹלָה זָדוֹן:

16. Rabbi Yehudah used to say, be careful in learning, for error in learning amounts to deliberate sin.

יז. רַבִּי שִׁמְעוֹן אוֹמֵר. שְׁלשָׁה כְתָרִים הֵם. כֶּתֶר תּוֹרָה וְכֶתֶר כְּהֻנָּה וְכֶתֶר מַלְכוּת. וְכֶתֶר שֵׁם טוֹב עוֹלֶה עַל גַּבֵּיהֶן:

17. Rabbi Shimon would say, there are three crowns, the crown of the Torah, the crown of the priesthood and the crown of kingdom; but the crown of the good name ascends above them.

יח. רַבִּי נְהוֹרַאי אוֹמֵר. הֱוֵי גוֹלֶה לִמְקוֹם תּוֹרָה. וְאַל תֹּאמַר שֶׁהִיא תָבוֹא אַחֲרֶיךָ. שֶׁחֲבֵרֶיךָ יְקַיְּמוּהָ בְּיָדֶךָ. וְאֶל־בִּינָתְךָ אַל תִּשָּׁעֵן:

18. Rabbi Nehorai used to say, wander out to a place of the Torah, and do not say that it will follow you, for it is your fellow students who establish it through you, so "And do not lean upon your own understanding." (Proverbs 3:5)

יט. רַבִּי יַנַּאי אוֹמֵר. אֵין בְּיָדֵינוּ לֹא מִשַּׁלְוַת הָרְשָׁעִים. וְאַף לֹא מִיִּסּוּרֵי הַצַּדִּיקִים:

19. Rabbi Yannai said, it is not in our hands to explain either the prosperous security of the wicked, or the sufferings of the righteous.

כ. רַבִּי מַתְיָא בֶּן־חָרָשׁ אוֹמֵר. הֱוֵי מַקְדִּים בִּשְׁלוֹם כָּל־אָדָם. וֶהֱוֵי זָנָב לָאֲרָיוֹת. וְאַל תְּהִי רֹאשׁ לַשּׁוּעָלִים:

20. Rabbi Mattyah ben Cheresh used to say, be the first to greet every man. Be a tail of lions, not a head of foxes.

כא. רַבִּי יַעֲקֹב אוֹמֵר. הָעוֹלָם הַזֶּה דּוֹמֶה לִפְרוֹזְדוֹר בִּפְנֵי הָעוֹלָם הַבָּא. הַתְקֵן עַצְמְךָ בִּפְרוֹזְדוֹר כְּדֵי שֶׁתִּכָּנֵס לַטְּרַקְלִין:

21. Rabbi Yaakov would say, this world is like an entrance hallway to the world to come; prepare yourself in the entrance hallway so that you can enter the banquet hall.

כב. הוּא הָיָה אוֹמֵר. יָפָה שָׁעָה אַחַת בִּתְשׁוּבָה וּמַעֲשִׂים טוֹבִים בָּעוֹלָם הַזֶּה. מִכָּל־חַיֵּי הָעוֹלָם הַבָּא. וְיָפָה שָׁעָה אַחַת שֶׁל קוֹרַת רוּחַ בָּעוֹלָם הַבָּא. מִכָּל־חַיֵּי הָעוֹלָם הַזֶּה:

22. He also would say, better is one hour in teshuvah and good deeds in this world than all the life of the world to come; but better is one hour of spiritual rest in the world to come than all the life of this world.

כג. רַבִּי שִׁמְעוֹן בֶּן־אֶלְעָזָר אוֹמֵר. אַל תְּרַצֶּה אֶת־חֲבֵרְךָ בִּשְׁעַת כַּעֲסוֹ. וְאַל תְּנַחֲמֵהוּ בְּשָׁעָה שֶׁמֵּתוֹ מֻטָּל לְפָנָיו. וְאַל תִּשְׁאַל לוֹ בִּשְׁעַת נִדְרוֹ. וְאַל תִּשְׁתַּדֵּל לִרְאוֹתוֹ בִּשְׁעַת קַלְקָלָתוֹ:

23. Rabbi Shimon son of Elazar was known to say, do not appease your fellow-man in the moment of his wrath, or comfort him in the hour that his dead lies before him, or question him at the hour of his vow, and do not strive to see him in the time of his humiliation.

כד. שְׁמוּאֵל הַקָּטָן אוֹמֵר: בִּנְפֹל אוֹיִבְךָ אַל תִּשְׂמָח. וּבִכָּשְׁלוֹ אַל־יָגֵל לִבֶּךָ. פֶּן־יִרְאֶה יהוה וְרַע בְּעֵינָיו. וְהֵשִׁיב מֵעָלָיו אַפּוֹ:

24. Shemuel the Little said, "Do not rejoice when your enemy falls, And do not let your heart be glad when he stumbles; In case Hashem sees it, and it displeases Him, And He turns away His wrath from him." (Prov. 24:18)

כה. אֱלִישָׁע בֶּן־אֲבוּיָה אוֹמֵר. הַלּוֹמֵד יֶלֶד לְמָה הוּא דוֹמֶה. לִדְיוֹ כְתוּבָה עַל נְיָר חָדָשׁ. וְהַלּוֹמֵד זָקֵן לְמָה הוּא דוֹמֶה. לִדְיוֹ כְתוּבָה עַל נְיָר מָחוּק:

25. Elisha ben Avuyah used to say, he who learns when a child, what is he like? He is like ink written on fresh paper. But one who learns when old, what is he like? He is like ink written on rubbed paper.

כו. רַבִּי יוֹסִי בַר־יְהוּדָה. אִישׁ כְּפַר הַבַּבְלִי אוֹמֵר. הַלּוֹמֵד מִן הַקְּטַנִּים. לְמָה הוּא דוֹמֶה. לְאוֹכֵל עֲנָבִים קֵהוֹת. וְשׁוֹתֶה יַיִן מִגִּתּוֹ. וְהַלּוֹמֵד מִן הַזְּקֵנִים. לְמָה הוּא דוֹמֶה. לְאוֹכֵל עֲנָבִים בְּשׁוּלוֹת. וְשׁוֹתֶה יַיִן יָשָׁן:

26. Rabbi Yosei bar Yehudah of Kefar HaBavli said, he who learns from the young, what is he like? He is like one who eats unripe grapes and drinks wine fresh from his vats. But he who learns from elders, what is he like? He is like one who eats ripe grapes and drinks old wine.

כז. רַבִּי מֵאִיר אוֹמֵר. אַל תִּסְתַּכֵּל בַּקַּנְקַן. אֶלָּא בְמַה־שֶׁיֵּשׁ בּוֹ. יֵשׁ קַנְקַן חָדָשׁ מָלֵא יָשָׁן. וְיָשָׁן שֶׁאֲפִלּוּ חָדָשׁ אֵין בּוֹ:

27. "Rabbi" would say, do not look on the flask but on what it contains; for there is a new flask containing old wine, and an old flask which does not contains even new wine.

כח. רַבִּי אֶלְעָזָר הַקַּפָּר אוֹמֵר. הַקִּנְאָה וְהַתַּאֲוָה וְהַכָּבוֹד. מוֹצִיאִין אֶת־הָאָדָם מִן הָעוֹלָם:

28. Rabbi Elazar HaKappar was known to say, jealousy, lust and ambition remove a man from the world.

כט. הוּא הָיָה אוֹמֵר. הַיִּלּוֹדִים לָמוּת. וְהַמֵּתִים לַחֲיוֹת. וְהַחַיִּים
לִדּוֹן. לֵידַע. וּלְהוֹדִיעַ. וּלְהִוָּדַע. שֶׁהוּא אֵל. הוּא הַיּוֹצֵר. הוּא
הַבּוֹרֵא. הוּא הַמֵּבִין. הוּא הַדַּיָּן. הוּא הָעֵד. הוּא בַּעַל־דִּין. הוּא
עָתִיד לָדוּן. בָּרוּךְ הוּא. שֶׁאֵין לְפָנָיו לֹא עַוְלָה. וְלֹא שִׁכְחָה. וְלֹא
מַשּׂוֹא פָנִים. וְלֹא מִקַּח שֹׁחַד. וְדַע. שֶׁהַכֹּל לְפִי הַחֶשְׁבּוֹן. וְאַל
יַבְטִיחֲךָ יִצְרְךָ. שֶׁהַשְּׁאוֹל בֵּית מָנוֹס לָךְ. שֶׁעַל כָּרְחֲךָ אַתָּה נוֹצָר.
וְעַל כָּרְחֲךָ אַתָּה נוֹלָד. וְעַל כָּרְחֲךָ אַתָּה חַי. וְעַל כָּרְחֲךָ אַתָּה מֵת.
וְעַל כָּרְחֲךָ אַתָּה עָתִיד לִתֵּן דִּין וְחֶשְׁבּוֹן. לִפְנֵי מֶלֶךְ מַלְכֵי הַמְּלָכִים.
הַקָּדוֹשׁ בָּרוּךְ הוּא:

29. He also used to say, they who are born are destined to die, but
the dead will be revived, and all living are to be judged, to become
aware, to know and to make known that He is God, blessed is He,
that He is the Maker, He is the Creator, He is He who understands
all. He is the Judge, He is the Witness, He is the Prosecutor. He will
hold judgment, and before Him there is no iniquity or forgetting, or
respect of persons or the taking of bribes, for all is His. Know that
for all there is an accounting. Do not let your desire assure you that
the grave will be an escape for you, for involuntarily you were
created, involuntarily you were born, involuntarily you are alive,
involuntarily you will die, involuntarily you are destined to give an
accounting before the supreme King of kings, the Holy One, blessed
is He.

רַבִּי חֲנַנְיָא בֶּן־עֲקַשְׁיָא אוֹמֵר: רָצָה הַקָּדוֹשׁ בָּרוּךְ הוּא לְזַכּוֹת אֶת־יִשְׂרָאֵל.
לְפִיכָךְ הִרְבָּה לָהֶם תּוֹרָה וּמִצְוֹת. שֶׁנֶּאֱמַר: יְהֹוָה חָפֵץ לְמַעַן צִדְקוֹ יַגְדִּיל
תּוֹרָה וְיַאְדִּיר:

Rabbi Chananya ben Akashya used to say, the Holy One, blessed is He, wishing to
make Yisrael more worthy, enlarged for them with Torah and its commandments.
For so it is said, "Hashem was pleased, for His righteousness' sake, To make the
Torah great and glorious." **(Isaiah 42:21)**

כָּל־יִשְׂרָאֵל יֵשׁ לָהֶם חֵלֶק לָעוֹלָם הַבָּא. שֶׁנֶּאֱמַר: וְעַמֵּךְ כֻּלָּם צַדִּיקִים לְעוֹלָם יִירְשׁוּ אָרֶץ נֵצֶר מטעו (מַטָּעַי) מַעֲשֵׂה יָדַי לְהִתְפָּאֵר:

All Yisrael have a portion in the world to come, as it is said, "And Your people will be all righteous; they will inherit the land forever, the branch of my planting, the work of my hands, that I may be glorified." (Isaiah 60:21)

Chapter 5

א. בַּעֲשָׂרָה מַאֲמָרוֹת נִבְרָא הָעוֹלָם. וּמַה תַּלְמוּד לוֹמַר. וַהֲלֹא בְּמַאֲמָר אֶחָד יָכוֹל לְהִבָּרְאוֹת. אֶלָּא לְהִפָּרַע מִן הָרְשָׁעִים שֶׁמְּאַבְּדִין אֶת־ הָעוֹלָם. שֶׁנִּבְרָא בַעֲשָׂרָה מַאֲמָרוֹת. וְלִתֵּן שָׂכָר טוֹב לַצַּדִּיקִים שֶׁמְּקַיְּמִין אֶת־הָעוֹלָם. שֶׁנִּבְרָא בַעֲשָׂרָה מַאֲמָרוֹת:

1. With ten divine utterances the world was created. What does this teach us? Could it not have been created with one utterance? It is to make known the punishment that will happen to the wicked who destroy the world that was created with ten utterances, as well as the good reward that will be bestowed on the just who preserve the world that was created with ten utterances.

ב. עֲשָׂרָה דוֹרוֹת מֵאָדָם וְעַד נֹחַ. לְהוֹדִיעַ כַּמָּה אֶרֶךְ אַפַּיִם לְפָנָיו. שֶׁכָּל־הַדּוֹרוֹת הָיוּ מַכְעִיסִין וּבָאִין. עַד שֶׁהֵבִיא עֲלֵיהֶם אֶת־מֵי הַמַּבּוּל.

2. There were Ten generations from Adam to Noach to make known God's patience; for every one of those generations continued provoking Him, until in the end He brought on them, the waters of the flood.

ג. עֲשָׂרָה דוֹרוֹת מִנֹּחַ וְעַד אַבְרָהָם. לְהוֹדִיעַ כַּמָּה אֶרֶךְ אַפַּיִם לְפָנָיו. שֶׁכָּל־הַדּוֹרוֹת הָיוּ מַכְעִיסִין וּבָאִין. עַד שֶׁבָּא אַבְרָהָם אָבִינוּ וְקִבֵּל שָׂכָר כֻּלָּם:

3. There were Ten generations from Adam to Noach to make known God's patience; for every one of those generations continued provoking Him, until in the end our father Avraham came and received the reward they all should have earned.

ד. עֲשָׂרָה נִסְיוֹנוֹת נִתְנַסָּה אַבְרָהָם אָבִינוּ וְעָמַד בְּכֻלָּם. לְהוֹדִיעַ כַּמָּה חִבָּתוֹ שֶׁל אַבְרָהָם אָבִינוּ:

4. Ten times was our father Avraham tested and he withstood all of the tests, to make known how great his love of God was.

ה. עֲשָׂרָה נִסִּים נַעֲשׂוּ לַאֲבוֹתֵינוּ בְמִצְרָיִם. וַעֲשָׂרָה עַל הַיָּם. עֶשֶׂר מַכּוֹת הֵבִיא הַקָּדוֹשׁ בָּרוּךְ הוּא עַל הַמִּצְרִיִּים בְּמִצְרַיִם. וְעֶשֶׂר עַל הַיָּם.

5. Ten miracles were done for our ancestors in Mitzrayim and ten by the Sea of Reeds. Ten plagues the Holy One, blessed is He, brought: on the Egyptians in Mitzrayim and ten more by the Sea of Reeds.

ו. עֲשָׂרָה נִסְיוֹנוֹת נִסּוּ אֲבוֹתֵינוּ אֶת־הַקָּדוֹשׁ בָּרוּךְ הוּא בַּמִּדְבָּר. שֶׁנֶּאֱמַר: וַיְנַסּוּ אֹתִי זֶה עֶשֶׂר פְּעָמִים וְלֹא שָׁמְעוּ בְּקוֹלִי:

6. Ten times our ancestors in the wilderness tried the Holy One, blessed is He, even as He said, "They have tried Me these ten times and have not listened to My voice."

ז. עֲשָׂרָה נִסִּים נַעֲשׂוּ לַאֲבוֹתֵינוּ בְּבֵית־הַמִּקְדָּשׁ. לֹא הִפִּילָה אִשָּׁה מֵרֵיחַ בְּשַׂר הַקֹּדֶשׁ. וְלֹא הִסְרִיחַ בְּשַׂר הַקֹּדֶשׁ מֵעוֹלָם. וְלֹא נִרְאָה זְבוּב בְּבֵית הַמִּטְבָּחַיִם. וְלֹא אֵרַע קֶרִי לְכֹהֵן גָּדוֹל בְּיוֹם הַכִּפּוּרִים. וְלֹא כִבּוּ הַגְּשָׁמִים אֵשׁ שֶׁל עֲצֵי הַמַּעֲרָכָה. וְלֹא נָצְחָה הָרוּחַ אֶת־עַמּוּד הֶעָשָׁן. וְלֹא נִמְצָא פְסוּל בָּעֹמֶר. וּבִשְׁתֵּי הַלֶּחֶם וּבְלֶחֶם

הַפָּנִים. עוֹמְדִים צְפוּפִים וּמִשְׁתַּחֲוִים רְוָחִים. וְלֹא הִזִּיק נָחָשׁ וְעַקְרָב
בִּירוּשָׁלַיִם מֵעוֹלָם. וְלֹא אָמַר אָדָם לַחֲבֵרוֹ. צַר לִי הַמָּקוֹם שֶׁאָלִין
בִּירוּשָׁלָיִם:

7. Ten miracles were done for our ancestors in connection with the Temple: no woman miscarried from the odor of the flesh of the offerings; the holy flesh never became putrid; no fly was ever seen in the place of slaughter; no unclean accident ever happened to the Kohan Hagadol (High Priest) on Yom Kippur; rain never quenched the fire of the wood arranged on the altar; wind never dispersed the column of smoke; no defilement was ever found in the offering of the Omer of barley, or in the two loaves of the first fruits (of the wheat harvest), or in the showbread; though the people stood pressed together they could freely prostrate themselves; neither snake or scorpion ever injured anyone in Yerushalayim, and no one ever said to his neighbor, "There is no room for me to lodge in Yerushalayim."

ח. עֲשָׂרָה דְבָרִים נִבְרְאוּ בְעֶרֶב שַׁבָּת בֵּין הַשְּׁמָשׁוֹת. וְאֵלּוּ הֵן: פִּי
הָאָרֶץ. וּפִי הַבְּאֵר. וּפִי הָאָתוֹן. וְהַקֶּשֶׁת. וְהַמָּן. וְהַמַּטֶּה. וְהַשָּׁמִיר.
וְהַכְּתָב. וְהַמִּכְתָּב. וְהַלּוּחוֹת. וְיֵשׁ אוֹמְרִים. אַף הַמַּזִּיקִין. וּקְבוּרָתוֹ
שֶׁל מֹשֶׁה. וְאֵילוֹ שֶׁל אַבְרָהָם אָבִינוּ. וְיֵשׁ אוֹמְרִים. אַף צְבָת בִּצְבָת
עֲשׂוּיָה:

8. Ten things were created at twilight on the eve of the first Shabbat —the mouth of the earth (to be opened for Korah and his followers); the mouth of the well (to be opened for Moshe); the mouth of the donkey (to be opened for Bilam); the rainbow (of Noach); the manna; Aharon's staff; the shamir (which split the stones for the Temple); the letter, the writing (the inscription on the tablets of stone), and the tablets themselves. Some include also the destroying spirits, the grave of Moshe, and the ram of Avraham, and others add tongs made with tongs.

ט. שִׁבְעָה דְבָרִים בְּגֹלֶם וְשִׁבְעָה בְּחָכָם. חָכָם. אֵינוֹ מְדַבֵּר לִפְנֵי מִי
שֶׁהוּא גָדוֹל מִמֶּנּוּ בְּחָכְמָה וּבְמִנְיָן. וְאֵינוֹ נִכְנָס לְתוֹךְ דִּבְרֵי חֲבֵרוֹ.
וְאֵינוֹ נִבְהָל לְהָשִׁיב. שׁוֹאֵל כָּעִנְיָן וּמֵשִׁיב כַּהֲלָכָה. וְאוֹמֵר עַל
רִאשׁוֹן רִאשׁוֹן וְעַל אַחֲרוֹן אַחֲרוֹן. וְעַל מַה שֶּׁלֹּא שָׁמַע אוֹמֵר לֹא
שָׁמַעְתִּי. וּמוֹדֶה עַל הָאֱמֶת. וְחִלּוּפֵיהֶן בְּגֹלֶם:

9. Seven are the characteristics of an uncultured-man and seven those of a wise-man. The wise-man does not speak before him who is greater than him in wisdom; he does not interrupt; he is not hasty to answer; he questions according to the subject matter and answers in keeping with the halacha; he speaks of the first things first and of the last things last; where he has not understood he says, "I do not understand it."; he acknowledges that which is true. The reverse of all of these attributes marks an uncultured-man.

י. שִׁבְעָה מִינֵי פֻּרְעָנִיּוֹת בָּאִין לָעוֹלָם. עַל שִׁבְעָה גוּפֵי עֲבֵרָה.
מִקְצָתָן מְעַשְּׂרִין וּמִקְצָתָן אֵינָן מְעַשְּׂרִין. רָעָב שֶׁל בַּצֹּרֶת בָּא.
מִקְצָתָן רְעֵבִים וּמִקְצָתָן שְׂבֵעִים. גָּמְרוּ שֶׁלֹּא לְעַשֵּׂר. רָעָב שֶׁל
מְהוּמָה וְשֶׁל בַּצֹּרֶת בָּא. וְשֶׁלֹּא לִטּוֹל אֶת־הַחַלָּה. רָעָב שֶׁל כְּלָיָה
בָּא.

10. Seven forms of punishment come into the world for seven main transgressions. If some give their tithes and others do not, a famine ensues from drought, and some suffer hunger while others are full. If they all determine to give no tithes, a famine ensues from tumult and drought. Famine comes with extermination when men have resolved not to give the offering of the first of the dough. (Num. 15:20)

יא. דֶּבֶר בָּא לָעוֹלָם עַל־מִיתוֹת הָאֲמוּרוֹת בַּתּוֹרָה שֶׁלֹּא נִמְסְרוּ
לְבֵית דִּין. וְעַל פֵּרוֹת שְׁבִיעִית. חֶרֶב בָּאָה לָעוֹלָם. עַל עִנּוּי הַדִּין.
וְעַל עִוּוּת הַדִּין. וְעַל הַמּוֹרִים בַּתּוֹרָה שֶׁלֹּא כַהֲלָכָה: חַיָּה רָעָה

בָּאָה לְעוֹלָם. עַל שְׁבוּעַת שָׁוְא. וְעַל חִלּוּל הַשֵּׁם. גָּלוּת בָּאָה לְעוֹלָם. עַל עוֹבְדֵי עֲבוֹדָה זָרָה. וְעַל גִּלּוּי עֲרָיוֹת. וְעַל שְׁפִיכוּת דָּמִים. וְעַל שְׁמִטַּת הָאָרֶץ.

11. Pestilence descends upon the world for those capital offenses detailed in the Torah, which are not given over to the court, and for the violation of the law regarding the fruits of the seventh year. (Lev. 25:1-7) The sword visits the earth because of delayed justice and perversion of justice, and because of those who decide questions of the Torah, not according to halacha. Evil beasts come into the world for false oaths and Chilul Hashem (desecration of God's name). Exile comes to the world because of idolatry, immorality, bloodshed, and neglect to give release to the soil in the sabbatical year.

יב. בְּאַרְבָּעָה פְרָקִים הַדֶּבֶר מִתְרַבֶּה. בָּרְבִיעִית. וּבַשְּׁבִיעִית. וּבְמוֹצָאֵי שְׁבִיעִית. וּבְמוֹצָאֵי הֶחָג שֶׁבְּכָל־שָׁנָה וְשָׁנָה. בָּרְבִיעִית. מִפְּנֵי מַעֲשַׂר עָנִי שֶׁבַּשְּׁלִישִׁית. בַּשְּׁבִיעִית. מִפְּנֵי מַעֲשַׂר עָנִי שֶׁבַּשִּׁשִּׁית. בְּמוֹצָאֵי שְׁבִיעִית. מִפְּנֵי פֵרוֹת שְׁבִיעִית. בְּמוֹצָאֵי הֶחָג שֶׁבְּכָל־שָׁנָה וְשָׁנָה. מִפְּנֵי גֶזֶל מַתְּנוֹת עֲנִיִּים:

12. There are four periods when pestilence increases: in the fourth year, the seventh year, after the close of the seventh year and at the close of Sukkot every year. In the fourth and seventh years because of failure in the third and sixth years, to give the tithe of the poor that is then due; (Deut. 14:28-29) After the close of the seventh year because of failure to leave the fruits of the seventh year for all; at the close of Sukkot every year because of robbing the poor of the harvest gifts that are due to them.

יג. אַרְבַּע מִדּוֹת בָּאָדָם: הָאוֹמֵר שֶׁלִּי שֶׁלִּי. וְשֶׁלְּךָ שֶׁלָּךְ. זוֹ מִדָּה בֵּינוֹנִית. וְיֵשׁ אוֹמְרִים. זוֹ מִדַּת סְדוֹם. שֶׁלִּי שֶׁלָּךְ. וְשֶׁלְּךָ שֶׁלִּי. עַם

הָאָרֶץ. שֶׁלִּי שֶׁלָּךְ. וְשֶׁלְּךָ שֶׁלָּךְ. חָסִיד. שֶׁלִּי שֶׁלִּי. וְשֶׁלְּךָ שֶׁלִּי. רָשָׁע:

13. There are four types of men: he who says what is mine is mine and what is yours is yours, this is the average man, though some say this is a type of Sedom. He who says what is mine is yours and what is yours is mine is an Am Ha'aretz (ignorant, uneducated). He who says what is mine is yours and what is yours is yours is pious. But he who says what is yours is mine and what is mine is mine is a wicked-man.

יד. אַרְבַּע מִדּוֹת בַּדֵּעוֹת: נֹחַ לִכְעוֹס וְנֹחַ לִרְצוֹת. יָצָא הֶפְסֵדוֹ בִשְׂכָרוֹ. קָשֶׁה לִכְעוֹס וְקָשֶׁה לִרְצוֹת. יָצָא שְׂכָרוֹ בְהֶפְסֵדוֹ. קָשֶׁה לִכְעוֹס וְנֹחַ לִרְצוֹת. חָסִיד. נֹחַ לִכְעוֹס וְקָשֶׁה לִרְצוֹת. רָשָׁע:

14. There are four temperaments of men: easily angered and easily appeased, his loss is cancelled by his gain. Angered with difficulty but appeased with difficulty, his gain is cancelled by his loss. Angered with difficulty and easily appeased, he is pious. Easily angered and appeased with difficulty, he is a wicked-man.

טו. אַרְבַּע מִדּוֹת בְּתַלְמִידִים: מָהִיר לִשְׁמוֹעַ וּמָהִיר לְאַבֵּד. יָצָא שְׂכָרוֹ בְהֶפְסֵדוֹ. קָשֶׁה לִשְׁמוֹעַ וְקָשֶׁה לְאַבֵּד. יָצָא הֶפְסֵדוֹ בִשְׂכָרוֹ. מָהִיר לִשְׁמוֹעַ וְקָשֶׁה לְאַבֵּד. זֶה חֵלֶק טוֹב. קָשֶׁה לִשְׁמוֹעַ וּמָהִיר לְאַבֵּד. זֶה חֵלֶק רָע:

15. There are four characteristics found among disciples: quick to learn and quick to forget, his gain is cancelled by his loss. Slow to learn and slow to forget, his loss is cancelled by his gain. Quick to learn and slow to forget, his is a good portion. Slow to learn and quick to forget, his is an evil portion.

טז. אַרְבַּע מִדּוֹת בְּנוֹתְנֵי צְדָקָה: הָרוֹצֶה שֶׁיִּתֵּן וְלֹא יִתְּנוּ אֲחֵרִים. עֵינוֹ רָעָה בְּשֶׁל אֲחֵרִים. יִתְּנוּ אֲחֵרִים וְהוּא לֹא יִתֵּן. עֵינוֹ רָעָה בְּשֶׁלּוֹ. יִתֵּן וְיִתְּנוּ אֲחֵרִים. חָסִיד. לֹא יִתֵּן וְלֹא יִתְּנוּ אֲחֵרִים. רָשָׁע:

16. There are four traits characterizing those who give tzedakah (charity): he who wishes to give but does not wish others to give, his eye is evil toward others. He who wishes that others should give and he not, his eye is evil against what is his own. He who wishes himself to give and others to give is pious. He who wishes neither to give or that others should give is a wicked-man.

יז. אַרְבַּע מִדּוֹת בְּהוֹלְכִים לְבֵית הַמִּדְרָשׁ: הוֹלֵךְ וְאֵינוֹ עוֹשֶׂה. שְׂכַר הֲלִיכָה בְּיָדוֹ. עוֹשֶׂה וְאֵינוֹ הוֹלֵךְ. שְׂכַר מַעֲשֶׂה בְּיָדוֹ. הוֹלֵךְ וְעוֹשֶׂה. חָסִיד. לֹא הוֹלֵךְ וְלֹא עוֹשֶׂה. רָשָׁע:

17. There are four characteristics among those who attend the house of study: he who attends but does not practice has the reward of his going. He who practices but does not attend has the reward of his practicing. He who both attends and practices is pious. But he who does not attend or practice is a wicked-man.

יח. אַרְבַּע מִדּוֹת בְּיוֹשְׁבִים לִפְנֵי חֲכָמִים: סְפוֹג וּמַשְׁפֵּךְ. מְשַׁמֶּרֶת וְנָפָה. סְפוֹג. שֶׁהוּא סוֹפֵג אֶת־הַכֹּל. מַשְׁפֵּךְ. שֶׁמַּכְנִיס בְּזוֹ וּמוֹצִיא בְזוֹ. מְשַׁמֶּרֶת. שֶׁמּוֹצִיאָה אֶת־הַיַּיִן וְקוֹלֶטֶת אֶת־הַשְּׁמָרִים. וְנָפָה. שֶׁמּוֹצִיאָה אֶת־הַקֶּמַח וְקוֹלֶטֶת אֶת־הַסֹּלֶת:

18. There are four characteristics among those who sit in the presence of the sages: the sponge, the funnel, the strainer, and the sieve. The sponge which absorbs everything, the funnel which receives in one ear and lets out at the other, the strainer which lets through the good wine and retains the dregs, and the sieve which eliminates the coarse meal and collects the fine flour.

יט. כָּל־אַהֲבָה שֶׁהִיא תְלוּיָה בְדָבָר. בָּטֵל דָּבָר בְּטֵלָה אַהֲבָה. וְשֶׁאֵינָהּ תְּלוּיָה בְדָבָר. אֵינָהּ בְּטֵלָה לְעוֹלָם. אֵיזוֹ הִיא אַהֲבָה שֶׁהִיא תְלוּיָה בְדָבָר. זוֹ אַהֲבַת אַמְנוֹן וְתָמָר. וְשֶׁאֵינָהּ תְּלוּיָה בְדָבָר. זוֹ אַהֲבַת דָּוִד וִיהוֹנָתָן:

19. When love is dependent on a consideration, if that cause disappears so does the love; but a love which is free from ulterior interest will never come to nothing. What is an example of such a dependent love? That of Amnon for Tamar, and an example of a love that is free of all ulterior consideration is that of David and Yehonatan.

כ. כָּל־מַחֲלֹקֶת שֶׁהִיא לְשֵׁם שָׁמַיִם. סוֹפָהּ לְהִתְקַיֵּם. וְשֶׁאֵינָהּ לְשֵׁם שָׁמַיִם. אֵין סוֹפָהּ לְהִתְקַיֵּם. אֵיזוֹ הִיא מַחֲלֹקֶת שֶׁהִיא לְשֵׁם שָׁמַיִם. זוֹ מַחֲלֹקֶת הִלֵּל וְשַׁמַּאי. וְשֶׁאֵינָהּ לְשֵׁם שָׁמַיִם. זוֹ מַחֲלֹקֶת קֹרַח וְכָל־עֲדָתוֹ:

20. Every difference of opinion which is in the name of Heaven will in the end be established, but that which is not in the name of Heaven will in the end not be established. What is an example of such a difference of opinion in the name of Heaven? The controversies between Hillel and Shammai, and an example of a difference that is not in the name of Heaven is the dispute of Korach and his followers with Moshe.

כא. כָּל־הַמְזַכֶּה אֶת־הָרַבִּים. אֵין חֵטְא בָּא עַל יָדוֹ. וְכָל־הַמַּחֲטִיא אֶת־הָרַבִּים. אֵין מַסְפִּיקִין בְּיָדוֹ לַעֲשׂוֹת תְּשׁוּבָה. מֹשֶׁה זָכָה וְזִכָּה אֶת־הָרַבִּים. זְכוּת הָרַבִּים תָּלוּי בּוֹ. שֶׁנֶּאֱמַר: צִדְקַת יְהֹוָה עָשָׂה וּמִשְׁפָּטָיו עִם־יִשְׂרָאֵל: יָרָבְעָם בֶּן־נְבָט חָטָא וְהֶחֱטִיא אֶת־הָרַבִּים. חֵטְא הָרַבִּים תָּלוּי בּוֹ. שֶׁנֶּאֱמַר: עַל־חַטֹּאות יָרָבְעָם אֲשֶׁר חָטָא וַאֲשֶׁר הֶחֱטִיא אֶת־יִשְׂרָאֵל:

21. Whoever leads the masses in the right path will not occasion any sin; but whosoever leads the masses astray will not be able to do teshuvah for all the wrong he occasions. So Moshe was virtuous and he led the masses in the right path, and their merit is ascribed to him, as it says, "He executed the righteousness of Hashem, And His ordinances with Yisrael." (Deut. 33:21) But Yaravam son of Nevat who sinned and led the masses astray, the sin of the masses is ascribed to him, as it says, "for the sins of Yaravam which he sinned, and where he made Yisrael to sin;" (I Kings 15:30)

כב. כָּל־מִי שֶׁיֵּשׁ בּוֹ שְׁלֹשָׁה דְבָרִים הַלָּלוּ. הוּא מִתַּלְמִידָיו שֶׁל אַבְרָהָם אָבִינוּ. וּשְׁלֹשָׁה דְבָרִים אֲחֵרִים. הוּא מִתַּלְמִידָיו שֶׁל בִּלְעָם הָרָשָׁע. עַיִן טוֹבָה. וְרוּחַ נְמוּכָה. וְנֶפֶשׁ שְׁפָלָה מִתַּלְמִידָיו שֶׁל אַבְרָהָם אָבִינוּ. עַיִן רָעָה. וְרוּחַ גְּבוֹהָה. וְנֶפֶשׁ רְחָבָה – מִתַּלְמִידָיו שֶׁל בִּלְעָם הָרָשָׁע. מַה־בֵּין תַּלְמִידָיו שֶׁל אַבְרָהָם אָבִינוּ לְתַלְמִידָיו שֶׁל בִּלְעָם הָרָשָׁע. תַּלְמִידָיו שֶׁל אַבְרָהָם אָבִינוּ. אוֹכְלִין בָּעוֹלָם הַזֶּה. וְנוֹחֲלִין בָּעוֹלָם הַבָּא. שֶׁנֶּאֱמַר: לְהַנְחִיל אֹהֲבַי|יֵשׁ וְאֹצְרֹתֵיהֶם אֲמַלֵּא: אֲבָל תַּלְמִידָיו שֶׁל בִּלְעָם הָרָשָׁע יוֹרְשִׁין גֵּהִנָּם. וְיוֹרְדִין לִבְאֵר שַׁחַת. שֶׁנֶּאֱמַר: וְאַתָּה אֱלֹהִים | תּוֹרִדֵם | לִבְאֵר שַׁחַת אַנְשֵׁי דָמִים וּמִרְמָה לֹא־יֶחֱצוּ יְמֵיהֶם וַאֲנִי אֶבְטַח־בָּךְ:

22. Whoever possesses these three qualities is of the disciples of our father Avraham, but whoever has the other three qualities is of Bilam the wicked. A generous (good) eye, a humble spirit and a meek (lowly) soul are of the disciples of Avraham, our father. An evil eye, arrogantly superior (high) spirit and desirous and lustful (wide) soul, is of the disciples of the wicked Bilam. What is the difference between the disciples of the Bilam the wicked and of the Avraham our father? The disciples of our father Avraham enjoy this world and inherit the world to come, as it says, "That I may cause those that love me to inherit substance, And that I may fill their treasuries." (Prov. 8:21) But the disciples of Balaam the wicked inherit Gehinnom and descend down into the pit of destruction, as it says, "But You, God, will bring them down into the pit of destruction; Men of blood and deceit will not live out half their days; But as for me, I will trust in You." (Ps. 55:24)

כג. יְהוּדָה בֶן־תֵּימָא אוֹמֵר. הֱוֵי עַז כַּנָּמֵר. וְקַל כַּנֶּשֶׁר. וְרָץ כַּצְּבִי. וְגִבּוֹר כָּאֲרִי. לַעֲשׂוֹת רְצוֹן אָבִיךָ שֶׁבַּשָּׁמָיִם: הוּא הָיָה אוֹמֵר. עַז פָּנִים לְגֵהִנָּם. וּבֹשֶׁת פָּנִים לְגַן עֵדֶן. יְהִי רָצוֹן מִלְּפָנֶיךָ. יהוה אֱלֹהֵינוּ וֵאלֹהֵי אֲבוֹתֵינוּ. שֶׁתִּבְנֶה בֵית־הַמִּקְדָּשׁ בִּמְהֵרָה בְיָמֵינוּ. וְתֵן חֶלְקֵנוּ בְּתוֹרָתֶךָ:

23. Yehudah ben Teimah used to say, be as strong as the leopard, as swift as the eagle, as nimble as the gazelle, and as mighty as the lion to do the will of Your Father in Heaven. He used also to say, the arrogant are (destined) for Gehinnom, but the shame-faced are (destined) for Gan Eden. May it be Your will, Hashem our God and God of our fathers, that the Temple be rebuilt speedily in our days, and grant us our portion in Your Torah.

כד. הוּא הָיָה אוֹמֵר. בֶּן־חָמֵשׁ שָׁנִים לַמִּקְרָא. בֶּן־עֶשֶׂר לַמִּשְׁנָה. בֶּן־שְׁלֹשׁ עֶשְׂרֵה לַמִּצְוֹת. בֶּן־חֲמֵשׁ עֶשְׂרֵה לַתַּלְמוּד. בֶּן־שְׁמוֹנֶה עֶשְׂרֵה לַחֻפָּה. בֶּן־עֶשְׂרִים לִרְדּוֹף. בֶּן שְׁלֹשִׁים לַכֹּחַ. בֶּן־אַרְבָּעִים לַבִּינָה. בֶּן־חֲמִשִּׁים לָעֵצָה. בֶּן־שִׁשִּׁים לַזִּקְנָה. בֶּן שִׁבְעִים לַשֵּׂיבָה. בֶּן־שְׁמוֹנִים לַגְּבוּרָה. בֶּן־תִּשְׁעִים לָשׁוּחַ. בֶּן־מֵאָה. כְּאִלּוּ מֵת וְעָבַר וּבָטֵל מִן־הָעוֹלָם:

24. He would also say, at five years for the Scriptures, at ten for the Mishnah, at thirteen for the commandments, at fifteen for the Talmud, at eighteen for marriage, at twenty for one's life's pursuit, at thirty for mature strength, at forty for understanding, at fifty for counsel, at sixty for old age, at seventy for grey hair, at eighty for exceeding strength, at ninety for being hunched (beneath the weight of years), and at a hundred as though one were already dead and passed away completely from the world.

כה. בֶּן־בַּג בַּג אוֹמֵר. הֲפֹךְ בָּהּ וַהֲפֹךְ בָּהּ. דְּכֹלָּא בָהּ. וּבָהּ תֶּחֱזֵי. וְסִיב וּבְלֵה בָּהּ. וּמִנָּהּ לָא תְזוּעַ. שֶׁאֵין לְךָ מִדָּה טוֹבָה הֵימֶנָּה:

25. Ben Bag Bag said (about the Torah), turn it and turn it over again, for everything is in it. Contemplate it, grow old and wear out in it, and do not budge from it, for you have no better rule than it.

כו. בֶּן־הֵא הֵא אוֹמֵר: לְפוּם צַעֲרָא. אַגְרָא:

26. Ben Heh Heh used to say, according to the suffering is the reward.

רַבִּי חֲנַנְיָא בֶּן־עֲקַשְׁיָא אוֹמֵר: רָצָה הַקָּדוֹשׁ בָּרוּךְ הוּא לְזַכּוֹת אֶת־יִשְׂרָאֵל. לְפִיכָךְ הִרְבָּה לָהֶם תּוֹרָה וּמִצְוֹת. שֶׁנֶּאֱמַר: יְהֹוָה חָפֵץ לְמַעַן צִדְקוֹ יַגְדִּיל תּוֹרָה וְיַאְדִּיר:

Rabbi Chananya ben Akashya used to say, the Holy One, blessed is He, wishing to make Yisrael more worthy, enlarged for them with Torah and its commandments. For so it is said, "Hashem was pleased, for His righteousness' sake, To make the Torah great and glorious." (Isaiah 42:21)

כָּל־יִשְׂרָאֵל יֵשׁ לָהֶם חֵלֶק לָעוֹלָם הַבָּא. שֶׁנֶּאֱמַר: וְעַמֵּךְ כֻּלָּם צַדִּיקִים לְעוֹלָם יִירְשׁוּ אָרֶץ נֵצֶר מַטָּעוֹ (מַטָּעַי) מַעֲשֵׂה יָדַי לְהִתְפָּאֵר:

All Yisrael have a portion in the world to come, as it is said, "And Your people will be all righteous; they will inherit the land forever, the branch of my planting, the work of my hands, that I may be glorified." (Isaiah 60:21)

Chapter 6

שָׁנוּ חֲכָמִים בִּלְשׁוֹן הַמִּשְׁנָה. בָּרוּךְ שֶׁבָּחַר בָּהֶם וּבְמִשְׁנָתָם:

The sages taught also the following in the style of the Mishnah. Blessed is He who chose them and their teaching.

א. רַבִּי מֵאִיר אוֹמֵר. כָּל־הָעוֹסֵק בַּתּוֹרָה לִשְׁמָהּ. זוֹכֶה לִדְבָרִים הַרְבֵּה. וְלֹא עוֹד. אֶלָּא שֶׁכָּל־הָעוֹלָם כֻּלּוֹ כְּדַאי הוּא לוֹ. נִקְרָא רֵעַ. אָהוּב. אוֹהֵב אֶת־הַמָּקוֹם. אוֹהֵב אֶת־הַבְּרִיּוֹת. מְשַׂמֵּחַ אֶת־הַמָּקוֹם. מְשַׂמֵּחַ אֶת־הַבְּרִיּוֹת. וּמַלְבַּשְׁתּוֹ עֲנָוָה וְיִרְאָה. וּמַכְשַׁרְתּוֹ לִהְיוֹת צַדִּיק. וְחָסִיד. וְיָשָׁר וְנֶאֱמָן. וּמְרַחַקְתּוֹ מִן הַחֵטְא. וּמְקָרַבְתּוֹ לִידֵי זְכוּת. וְנֶהֱנִין מִמֶּנּוּ עֵצָה וְתוּשִׁיָּה. בִּינָה וּגְבוּרָה. שֶׁנֶּאֱמַר: לִי־עֵצָה וְתוּשִׁיָּה אֲנִי בִינָה לִי גְבוּרָה: וְנוֹתֶנֶת לוֹ מַלְכוּת וּמֶמְשָׁלָה וְחִקּוּר דִּין. וּמְגַלִּין לוֹ רָזֵי תוֹרָה. וְנַעֲשָׂה כְמַעְיָן הַמִּתְגַּבֵּר וּכְנָהָר שֶׁאֵינוֹ פּוֹסֵק. וְהֹוֶה צָנוּעַ. וְאֶרֶךְ רוּחַ. וּמוֹחֵל עַל עֶלְבּוֹנוֹ. וּמְגַדַּלְתּוֹ וּמְרוֹמַמְתּוֹ עַל־כָּל־הַמַּעֲשִׂים:

1. Rabbi Meir used to say, whosoever occupies himself with the Torah for its own sake merits many things; not only so, but the whole world is indebted to him. He is called friend, beloved, lover of God and lover of mankind. He rejoices God and man. The Torah clothes him with modesty and reverence, and fits him to be righteous, pious, upright and faithful. It holds him far from sin and draws him near to virtue. Through him men enjoy advice and sound wisdom, understanding and might, as it says, "Counsel is mine, and sound wisdom; I am understanding, power is mine." (Prov. 8:14) It gives him sovereignty and dominion and discernment into judgement. To him the secrets of the Torah are revealed. He becomes as a never-failing spring or a river of constant flow. He is modest and patient, overlooking insults, for it magnifies and exalts him above all deeds.

ב. אָמַר רַבִּי יְהוֹשֻׁעַ בֶּן־לֵוִי. בְּכָל־יוֹם וָיוֹם בַּת קוֹל יוֹצֵאת מֵהַר
חוֹרֵב וּמַכְרֶזֶת וְאוֹמֶרֶת. אוֹי לָהֶם לַבְּרִיּוֹת מֵעֶלְבּוֹנָהּ שֶׁל תּוֹרָה.
שֶׁכָּל־מִי שֶׁאֵינוֹ עוֹסֵק בַּתּוֹרָה. נִקְרָא נָזוּף. שֶׁנֶּאֱמַר: נֶזֶם זָהָב בְּאַף
חֲזִיר אִשָּׁה יָפָה וְסָרַת טָעַם: וְאוֹמֵר: וְהַלֻּחֹת מַעֲשֵׂה אֱלֹהִים הֵמָּה
וְהַמִּכְתָּב מִכְתַּב אֱלֹהִים הוּא חָרוּת עַל־הַלֻּחֹת: אַל תִּקְרָא חָרוּת
אֶלָּא חֵרוּת. שֶׁאֵין לְךָ בֶּן־חוֹרִין. אֶלָּא מִי שֶׁעוֹסֵק בְּתַלְמוּד תּוֹרָה.
וְכָל־מִי שֶׁעוֹסֵק בְּתַלְמוּד תּוֹרָה. הֲרֵי זֶה מִתְעַלֶּה. שֶׁנֶּאֱמַר:
וּמִמַּתָּנָה נַחֲלִיאֵל וּמִנַּחֲלִיאֵל בָּמוֹת:

2. Rabbi Yehoshua ben Levi would say, every day a heavenly voice resounds from Mount Horev and proclaims, "Woe to mankind for the contempt of the Torah." For whoever does not occupy himself with the Torah is censured. As it says, 'As a ring of gold in a swine's snout, so is a fair woman that turns aside from discretion.' (Prov. 11:22) And it says, "And the tablets were the work of God, and the writing was the writing of God, engraven upon the tablets." Do not read *charuth* (engraven), but *cheruth* (freedom), for there is no free man except he who engages with the study of Torah. And whoever engages in the study of Torah, they transcends, as it says: "From Mattanah (the gift of the Torah) to Nahaliel (the inheritance of God) and from Nahaliel to Bamot (the heights)." (Numbers 21:19)

ג. הַלּוֹמֵד מֵחֲבֵרוֹ פֶּרֶק אֶחָד. אוֹ הֲלָכָה אַחַת. אוֹ פָּסוּק אֶחָד. אוֹ
דִבּוּר אֶחָד. אוֹ אֲפִלּוּ אוֹת אַחַת. צָרִיךְ לִנְהָג בּוֹ כָּבוֹד. שֶׁכֵּן מָצִינוּ
בְּדָוִד מֶלֶךְ יִשְׂרָאֵל. שֶׁלֹּא לָמַד מֵאֲחִיתֹפֶל אֶלָּא שְׁנֵי דְבָרִים בִּלְבַד.
קְרָאוֹ רַבּוֹ. אַלּוּפוֹ וּמְיֻדָּעוֹ. שֶׁנֶּאֱמַר: וְאַתָּה אֱנוֹשׁ כְּעֶרְכִּי אַלּוּפִי
וּמְיֻדָּעִי: וַהֲלֹא דְבָרִים קַל וָחֹמֶר. וּמַה־דָּוִד מֶלֶךְ יִשְׂרָאֵל. שֶׁלֹּא לָמַד
מֵאֲחִיתֹפֶל אֶלָּא שְׁנֵי דְבָרִים בִּלְבָד. קְרָאוֹ רַבּוֹ. אַלּוּפוֹ וּמְיֻדָּעוֹ.
הַלּוֹמֵד מֵחֲבֵרוֹ פֶּרֶק אֶחָד. אוֹ הֲלָכָה אַחַת. אוֹ פָּסוּק אֶחָד. אוֹ
דִבּוּר אֶחָד. אוֹ אֲפִלּוּ אוֹת אַחַת. עַל אַחַת כַּמָּה וְכַמָּה שֶׁצָּרִיךְ

לִנְהוֹג בּוֹ כָּבוֹד. וְאֵין כָּבוֹד אֶלָּא תוֹרָה. שֶׁנֶּאֱמַר: כָּבוֹד חֲכָמִים יִנְחָלוּ. וּתְמִימִים יִנְחֲלוּ טוֹב: וְאֵין טוֹב אֶלָּא תוֹרָה. שֶׁנֶּאֱמַר: כִּי לֶקַח טוֹב נָתַתִּי לָכֶם תּוֹרָתִי אַל־תַּעֲזֹבוּ:

3. He who learns from his fellow a single chapter, or one law or one verse or saying, or even a single letter, must show him honor. For so we find with David, King of Yisrael, who having learned from Ahitophel, and yet regarded him as his master, his companion and familiar friend, as it says, "But it was you, a man my equal, my companion, and my familiar friend;" (Ps. 55:14) It is an argument a fortiori, that if David, King of Yisrael who learned from Ahitophel only a couple of worldly matters yet called him his companion and familiar friend, how much the more honor must be shown by the one who learns from his associate, but a single chapter, law, or verse or saying, or even a single letter of Torah. For honor is nothing but Torah, as it says, "The wise will inherit honor" (Prov. 3:35) and "the whole-hearted will inherit good." (Prov. 28:10) And good is nothing but the Torah, as it says, "For I give you a good teaching; Do not forsake my Torah." (Prov. 4:2)

ד. כָּךְ הִיא דַרְכָּהּ שֶׁל תוֹרָה. פַּת בְּמֶלַח תֹּאכֵל. וּמַיִם בִּמְשׂוּרָה תִשְׁתֶּה. וְעַל הָאָרֶץ תִּישָׁן. וְחַיֵּי צַעַר תִּחְיֶה. וּבַתּוֹרָה אַתָּה עָמֵל. אִם אַתָּה עֹשֶׂה כֵּן. אַשְׁרֶיךָ וְטוֹב לָךְ. אַשְׁרֶיךָ בָּעוֹלָם הַזֶּה. וְטוֹב לָךְ לְעוֹלָם הַבָּא:

4. The way of the Torah is this: A morsel of bread and salt to eat, water by ration to drink, sleep on the ground, and live a life of hardship while you toil in the Torah. If you will so do, "You will be happy and it will be well with you." (Prov. 4:2) Happy are you in this world, and it will be well with you for the world to come.

ה. אַל תְּבַקֵּשׁ גְּדֻלָּה לְעַצְמְךָ. וְאַל תַּחְמוֹד כָּבוֹד. יוֹתֵר מִלִּמּוּדְךָ עֲשֵׂה. וְאַל תִּתְאַוֶּה לְשֻׁלְחָנָם שֶׁל מְלָכִים. שֶׁשֻּׁלְחָנְךָ גָּדוֹל מִשֻּׁלְחָנָם. וְכִתְרְךָ גָּדוֹל מִכִּתְרָם. וְנֶאֱמָן הוּא בַּעַל מְלַאכְתְּךָ. שֶׁיְּשַׁלֶּם לְךָ שְׂכַר פְּעֻלָּתֶךָ:

5. Do not seek greatness for yourself, and do not crave honor. Practice more than you learn. Do not yearn for the table of kings, for your table is greater than theirs, and your crown greater than theirs, while the Master of your work is faithful to pay you the reward of your activity.

ו. גְּדוֹלָה תוֹרָה יוֹתֵר מִן הַכְּהֻנָּה וּמִן הַמַּלְכוּת. שֶׁהַמַּלְכוּת נִקְנֵית בִּשְׁלֹשִׁים מַעֲלוֹת. וְהַכְּהֻנָּה נִקְנֵית בְּעֶשְׂרִים וְאַרְבָּעָה. וְהַתּוֹרָה נִקְנֵית בְּאַרְבָּעִים וּשְׁמוֹנָה דְבָרִים. וְאֵלּוּ הֵן: בְּתַלְמוּד. בִּשְׁמִיעַת הָאֹזֶן. בַּעֲרִיכַת שְׂפָתַיִם. בְּבִינַת הַלֵּב. בְּאֵימָה. בְּיִרְאָה. בַּעֲנָוָה. בְּשִׂמְחָה. בְּטָהֳרָה. בְּשִׁמּוּשׁ חֲכָמִים. בְּדִקְדּוּק חֲבֵרִים. בְּפִלְפּוּל הַתַּלְמִידִים. בְּיִשּׁוּב בְּמִקְרָא בְּמִשְׁנָה. בְּמִעוּט סְחוֹרָה. בְּמִעוּט דֶּרֶךְ אֶרֶץ. בְּמִעוּט תַּעֲנוּג. בְּמִעוּט שֵׁנָה. בְּמִעוּט שִׂיחָה. בְּמִעוּט שְׂחוֹק. בְּאֶרֶךְ אַפַּיִם. בְּלֵב טוֹב. בֶּאֱמוּנַת חֲכָמִים. וּבְקַבָּלַת הַיִּסּוּרִין. הַמַּכִּיר אֶת־מְקוֹמוֹ. וְהַשָּׂמֵחַ בְּחֶלְקוֹ. וְהָעוֹשֶׂה סְיָג לִדְבָרָיו. וְאֵינוֹ מַחֲזִיק טוֹבָה לְעַצְמוֹ. אָהוּב. אוֹהֵב אֶת־הַמָּקוֹם. אוֹהֵב אֶת־הַבְּרִיּוֹת. אוֹהֵב אֶת־הַצְּדָקוֹת. אוֹהֵב אֶת־הַמֵּישָׁרִים. אוֹהֵב אֶת־הַתּוֹכָחוֹת. וּמִתְרַחֵק מִן הַכָּבוֹד. וְלֹא מֵגִיס לִבּוֹ בְּתַלְמוּדוֹ. וְאֵינוֹ שָׂמֵחַ בְּהוֹרָאָה. נוֹשֵׂא בְעֹל עִם חֲבֵרוֹ. וּמַכְרִיעוֹ לְכַף זְכוּת. וּמַעֲמִידוֹ עַל הָאֱמֶת. וּמַעֲמִידוֹ עַל הַשָּׁלוֹם. וּמִתְיַשֵּׁב לִבּוֹ בְּתַלְמוּדוֹ. שׁוֹאֵל וּמֵשִׁיב. שׁוֹמֵעַ וּמוֹסִיף. הַלּוֹמֵד עַל מְנָת לְלַמֵּד. וְהַלּוֹמֵד עַל מְנָת לַעֲשׂוֹת. הַמַּחְכִּים אֶת־רַבּוֹ. וְהַמְכַוֵּן אֶת־שְׁמוּעָתוֹ. וְהָאוֹמֵר

דָּבָר בְּשֵׁם אוֹמְרוֹ. הָא לָמַדְתָּ. שֶׁכָּל־הָאוֹמֵר דָּבָר בְּשֵׁם אוֹמְרוֹ. מֵבִיא גְאֻלָּה לָעוֹלָם. שֶׁנֶּאֱמַר: וַתֹּאמֶר אֶסְתֵּר לַמֶּלֶךְ בְּשֵׁם מָרְדֳּכָי:

6. The Torah is greater than the priesthood or royalty, for royalty is attained through thirty qualifications, the priesthood through twenty-four, but Torah is attainable through forty-eight, and they are: study, listening of the ear, ordering of the lips, understanding and insight of the heart, awe, reverence, humility, joyousness, association with sages, attaching oneself with fellow students, discussion with disciples, steadiness in study of the Scripture and Mishnah; by moderation in business, minimizing worldly interests, minimizing indulgence, minimizing sleep, minimizing converse, minimizing joking; by patience, a good heart, faith in the sages, acceptance of chastisements, knowing one's place, rejoicing in one's lot, setting a limit to one's words, not claiming merit for oneself, being beloved, loving God, loving one's fellow-men, loving the right course, loving rectitude and reproof, keeping oneself far from honors, not boasting in one's learning, not delighting to lay down the law, bearing the yoke with one's fellow student, judging him favorably, establishing him in the truth and in peace, by being composed in one's study, questioning and answering, hearing and adding to what one hears, learning in order to teach, learning in order to practice, enlightening one's teacher, ordering well that which one hears, and repeating a saying in the name of him who said it. For you have learned, that whoever repeats a saying in the name of its author brings deliverance to the world. As it says, "and Esther told the king of it in Mordechai's name." (Esther 2:22)

ז. גְּדוֹלָה תוֹרָה. שֶׁהִיא נוֹתֶנֶת חַיִּים לְעֹשֶׂיהָ בָּעוֹלָם הַזֶּה וּבָעוֹלָם הַבָּא. שֶׁנֶּאֱמַר: כִּי־חַיִּים הֵם לְמֹצְאֵיהֶם וּלְכָל־בְּשָׂרוֹ מַרְפֵּא: וְאוֹמֵר: רִפְאוּת תְּהִי לְשָׁרֶּךָ וְשִׁקּוּי לְעַצְמוֹתֶיךָ: וְאוֹמֵר: עֵץ־חַיִּים הִיא לַמַּחֲזִיקִים בָּהּ וְתֹמְכֶיהָ מְאֻשָּׁר: וְאוֹמֵר: כִּי | לִוְיַת חֵן הֵם לְרֹאשֶׁךָ

וַעֲנָקִים לְגַרְגְּרֹתֶךָ: וְאוֹמֵר: תִּתֵּן לְרֹאשְׁךָ לִוְיַת־חֵן עֲטֶרֶת תִּפְאֶרֶת
תְּמַגְּנֶךָ: וְאוֹמֵר: כִּי־בִי יִרְבּוּ יָמֶיךָ וְיוֹסִיפוּ לְּךָ שְׁנוֹת חַיִּים: וְאוֹמֵר:
אֹרֶךְ יָמִים בִּימִינָהּ בִּשְׂמֹאולָהּ עֹשֶׁר וְכָבוֹד: וְאוֹמֵר: כִּי אֹרֶךְ יָמִים
וּשְׁנוֹת חַיִּים וְשָׁלוֹם יוֹסִיפוּ לָךְ: וְאוֹמֵר: דְּרָכֶיהָ דַרְכֵי־נֹעַם
וְכָל־נְתִיבוֹתֶיהָ שָׁלוֹם:

7. Great is Torah, for it gives life to the one who fulfills it both in this world and in the world to come, as it says, "life to those that find them, And health to all their flesh." (Prov. 4:11) "It will be health to your navel, And refreshing to your bones." (Prov. 3:8) And again, "She is a tree of life to them that lay hold of her, And happy is everyone that clings to her." (Prov. 3:18) And again, "For they will be an ornament of grace to your head, And chains around your neck." (Prov. 1:9) And again, "She will give your head an ornament of grace; A crown of glory she will bestow on you." (Prov. 4:9) And again, "For by me your days will be multiplied, and the years of your life will be increased." (Prov. 9:11) And again, "Length of days is in her right hand; In her left hand are riches and honor." (Prov. 3:16) And again, "For length of days, and years of life, And peace, they will add to you." (Prov. 3:2)

ח. רַבִּי שִׁמְעוֹן בֶּן־יְהוּדָה מִשּׁוּם רַבִּי שִׁמְעוֹן בֶּן־יוֹחַאי אוֹמֵר. הַנּוֹי.
וְהַכֹּחַ. וְהָעֹשֶׁר. וְהַכָּבוֹד. וְהַחָכְמָה. וְהַזִּקְנָה. וְהַשֵּׂיבָה. וְהַבָּנִים.
נָאֶה לַצַּדִּיקִים וְנָאֶה לָעוֹלָם. שֶׁנֶּאֱמַר: עֲטֶרֶת תִּפְאֶרֶת שֵׂיבָה בְּדֶרֶךְ
צְדָקָה תִּמָּצֵא: וְאוֹמֵר: עֲטֶרֶת חֲכָמִים עָשְׁרָם. וְאוֹמֵר: עֲטֶרֶת זְקֵנִים
בְּנֵי בָנִים וְתִפְאֶרֶת בָּנִים אֲבוֹתָם: וְאוֹמֵר: תִּפְאֶרֶת בַּחוּרִים כֹּחָם
וַהֲדַר זְקֵנִים שֵׂיבָה: וְאוֹמֵר: וְחָפְרָה הַלְּבָנָה וּבוֹשָׁה הַחַמָּה כִּי־מָלַךְ
יְהוָה צְבָאוֹת בְּהַר צִיּוֹן וּבִירוּשָׁלַם וְנֶגֶד זְקֵנָיו כָּבוֹד: רַבִּי שִׁמְעוֹן
בֶּן־מְנַסְיָא אוֹמֵר. אֵלּוּ שֶׁבַע מִדּוֹת שֶׁמָּנוּ חֲכָמִים לַצַּדִּיקִים. כֻּלָּם
נִתְקַיְּמוּ בְּרַבִּי וּבְבָנָיו:

8. Rabbi Shimon ben Yehudah said in the name of Rabbi Shimon ben Yochai, "Beauty, strength, wealth, honor, wisdom, old age, and a hoary head and children are suitable for the righteous and for the world, as it says, "The hoary head is a crown of glory, It is found in the way of righteousness." (Prov. 16:31) "The glory of young men is their strength; and the beauty of old men is the hoary head." (Prov. 20:29) "The crown of the wise is their riches." (Prov. 14:24) "Children's children are the crown of old men; And the glory of children are their fathers." (Prov. 17:6) And it is said, "Then the moon will be confounded, and the sun ashamed; For Hashem of hosts will reign in mount Tziyon, And in Yerushalayim, and before His elders will be glory." (Isaiah 24:23)

ט. רַבִּי שִׁמְעוֹן בֶּן־מְנַסְיָא אוֹמֵר. אֵלּוּ שֶׁבַע מִדּוֹת שֶׁמָּנוּ חֲכָמִים לַצַּדִּיקִים. כֻּלָּם נִתְקַיְּמוּ בְּרַבִּי וּבְבָנָיו:

9. Rabbi Shimon ben Menasya said, these seven qualities which the sages enumerated for the righteous were all realized in "Rabbi" and his sons.

י. אָמַר רַבִּי יוֹסֵי בֶּן־קִסְמָא. פַּעַם אַחַת הָיִיתִי מְהַלֵּךְ בַּדֶּרֶךְ. וּפָגַע בִּי אָדָם אֶחָד. וְנָתַן לִי שָׁלוֹם. וְהֶחֱזַרְתִּי לוֹ שָׁלוֹם. אָמַר לִי. רַבִּי. מֵאֵיזֶה מָקוֹם אַתָּה. אָמַרְתִּי לוֹ. מֵעִיר גְּדוֹלָה שֶׁל חֲכָמִים וְשֶׁל סוֹפְרִים אָנִי. אָמַר לִי. רַבִּי. רְצוֹנְךָ שֶׁתָּדוּר עִמָּנוּ בִּמְקוֹמֵנוּ. וַאֲנִי אֶתֵּן לְךָ אֶלֶף אֲלָפִים דִּינְרֵי זָהָב וַאֲבָנִים טוֹבוֹת וּמַרְגָּלִיּוֹת. אָמַרְתִּי לוֹ. בְּנִי. אִם אַתָּה נוֹתֵן לִי כָּל־כֶּסֶף וְזָהָב וַאֲבָנִים טוֹבוֹת וּמַרְגָּלִיּוֹת שֶׁבָּעוֹלָם. אֵינִי דָר אֶלָּא בִמְקוֹם תּוֹרָה. לְפִי שֶׁבִּשְׁעַת פְּטִירָתוֹ שֶׁל אָדָם. אֵין מְלַוִּין לוֹ לְאָדָם. לֹא כֶסֶף וְלֹא זָהָב וְלֹא אֲבָנִים טוֹבוֹת וּמַרְגָּלִיּוֹת. אֶלָּא תוֹרָה וּמַעֲשִׂים טוֹבִים בִּלְבָד. שֶׁנֶּאֱמַר: בְּהִתְהַלֶּכְךָ | תַּנְחֶה אֹתָךְ בְּשָׁכְבְּךָ תִּשְׁמֹר עָלֶיךָ וַהֲקִיצוֹתָ הִיא תְשִׂיחֶךָ: בְּהִתְהַלֶּכְךָ | תַּנְחֶה אֹתָךְ. בָּעוֹלָם הַזֶּה. בְּשָׁכְבְּךָ תִּשְׁמֹר עָלֶיךָ.

בַּקֶּבֶר. וַהֲקִיצוֹתָ הִיא תְשִׂיחֶךָ. לְעוֹלָם הַבָּא. וְכֵן כָּתוּב בְּסֵפֶר
תְּהִלִּים עַל יְדֵי דָוִד מֶלֶךְ יִשְׂרָאֵל. טוֹב־לִי תוֹרַת־פִּיךָ מֵאַלְפֵי זָהָב
וָכֶסֶף: וְאוֹמֵר: לִי הַכֶּסֶף וְלִי הַזָּהָב נְאֻם יְהוָה צְבָאוֹת:

10. Rabbi Yosei ben Kisma said, once when I was journeying on the way a man met me and hailed me with the greeting of "Shalom," and I replied, "Shalom" Said he to me, "Rabbi, from what place did you come from?" I said to him, "I come from a city great in sages and scribes." He said to me, "Rabbi, if you will dwell with us in our place, I will give you a thousand thousands of gold pieces, and pearls and precious stones." I said to him, "And if you gave me all the silver, gold, pearls and precious stones in the world, I would not dwell except in a place where there is Torah. And so it is written in the Book of Psalms by David, King of Yisrael, "The Torah of Your mouth is better to me than thousands of gold and silver." (Ps. 119:72) and not only so, at the time of man's leaving this world, neither silver or gold or pearls or precious stones accompany him, but only Torah and good deeds, as it says, "When you walk, it will lead you, When you lie down, it will watch over you; And when you awake, it will talk with you." (Prov. 6:22) "When you walk, it will lead you" in this world; "When you lie down, it will watch over you" in the grave, "And when you awake, it will talk with you" in the life to come. And it says, "The silver is Mine, and the gold is Mine, says Hashem of hosts." (Haggai 2:8)

יא. חֲמִשָּׁה קִנְיָנִים קָנָה הַקָּדוֹשׁ בָּרוּךְ הוּא בְּעוֹלָמוֹ. וְאֵלּוּ הֵן:
תּוֹרָה קִנְיָן אֶחָד. שָׁמַיִם וָאָרֶץ קִנְיָן אֶחָד. אַבְרָהָם קִנְיָן אֶחָד.
יִשְׂרָאֵל קִנְיָן אֶחָד. בֵּית־הַמִּקְדָּשׁ קִנְיָן אֶחָד. תּוֹרָה קִנְיָן אֶחָד מִנַּיִן.
דִּכְתִיב: יְהוָה קָנָנִי רֵאשִׁית דַּרְכּוֹ קֶדֶם מִפְעָלָיו מֵאָז: שָׁמַיִם וָאָרֶץ
קִנְיָן אֶחָד מִנַּיִן. דִּכְתִיב: כֹּה אָמַר יְהוָה הַשָּׁמַיִם כִּסְאִי וְהָאָרֶץ הֲדֹם
רַגְלָי אֵי־זֶה בַיִת אֲשֶׁר תִּבְנוּ־לִי וְאֵי־זֶה מָקוֹם מְנוּחָתִי: וְאוֹמֵר:
מָה־רַבּוּ מַעֲשֶׂיךָ | יְהוָה כֻּלָּם בְּחָכְמָה עָשִׂיתָ מָלְאָה הָאָרֶץ קִנְיָנֶךָ:

אַבְרָהָם קִנְיָן אֶחָד מִנַּיִן. דִּכְתִיב: וַיְבָרְכֵהוּ וַיֹּאמַר בָּרוּךְ אַבְרָם לְאֵל
עֶלְיוֹן קֹנֵה שָׁמַיִם וָאָרֶץ: יִשְׂרָאֵל קִנְיָן אֶחָד מִנַּיִן. דִּכְתִיב: עַד־יַעֲבֹר
עַמְּךָ יְהֹוָה עַד־יַעֲבֹר עַם־זוּ קָנִיתָ: וְאוֹמֵר: לִקְדוֹשִׁים אֲשֶׁר־בָּאָרֶץ
הֵמָּה וְאַדִּירֵי כָּל־חֶפְצִי־בָם: בֵּית־הַמִּקְדָּשׁ קִנְיָן אֶחָד מִנַּיִן. דִּכְתִיב:
מָכוֹן לְשִׁבְתְּךָ פָּעַלְתָּ יְהֹוָה מִקְדָּשׁ אֲדֹנָי כּוֹנְנוּ יָדֶיךָ: וְאוֹמֵר: וַיְבִיאֵם
אֶל־גְּבוּל קָדְשׁוֹ הַר־זֶה קָנְתָה יְמִינוֹ:

11. Five possessions did the Holy One, blessed is He, acquire in His world, and they are: the Torah, heaven and earth, Avraham, Yisrael, and the Temple. Where do we know this of the Torah? Because it is written, "Hashem made me as the beginning of His way, The first of His works of old." (Proverbs 8:22) Heaven and earth, because it is written, "So says Hashem: The heaven is My Throne, and the earth is My footstool; where is the house that you may build to Me? And where is the place that may be My resting-place?" (Isaiah 66:1) And it says, "How manifold are Your works, Hashem. In wisdom You have made them all; The earth is full of Your possessions." (Psalms 104:24) Avraham, because it is written, "And he blessed him, and said: 'Blessed is Avram of God Most High, Maker of heaven and earth;'" Yisrael, as it says, "Until Your people pass over, Hashem, Until the people pass over that You have acquired." (Ex. 15:16) As it says, "As for the holy that are in the earth, They are the mighty in whom is all my delight." (Psalms 16:3) There of the Temple? As it is said, "The place, Hashem, which You have made for You to dwell in, The Sanctuary, Hashem, which Your hands have established." (Ex. 15:17) And it says, "And He brought them to His holy border, To the mountain, which His right hand had acquired." (Psalms 78:54)

יב. כָּל־מַה־שֶּׁבָּרָא הַקָּדוֹשׁ בָּרוּךְ הוּא בְּעוֹלָמוֹ. לֹא בָרָא אֶלָּא
לִכְבוֹדוֹ. שֶׁנֶּאֱמַר: כֹּל הַנִּקְרָא בִשְׁמִי וְלִכְבוֹדִי בְּרָאתִיו יְצַרְתִּיו
אַף־עֲשִׂיתִיו: וְאוֹמֵר: יְהֹוָה יִמְלֹךְ לְעֹלָם וָעֶד:

12. All that the Holy One, blessed is He, created in His world, He created only for His glory, as it says, "Everyone that is called by My name, and whom I have created for My glory, I have formed him, I have made him." (Is. 43:7) And it says, "Hashem will reign forever and ever." (Ex. 15:18)

רַבִּי חֲנַנְיָא בֶּן־עֲקַשְׁיָא אוֹמֵר: רָצָה הַקָּדוֹשׁ בָּרוּךְ הוּא לְזַכּוֹת אֶת־יִשְׂרָאֵל. לְפִיכָךְ הִרְבָּה לָהֶם תּוֹרָה וּמִצְוֹת. שֶׁנֶּאֱמַר: יְהֹוָה חָפֵץ לְמַעַן צִדְקוֹ יַגְדִּיל תּוֹרָה וְיַאְדִּיר:

Rabbi Chananya ben Akashya used to say, the Holy One, blessed is He, wishing to make Yisrael more worthy, enlarged for them with Torah and its commandments. For so it is said, "Hashem was pleased, for His righteousness' sake, To make the Torah great and glorious." (Isaiah 42:21)

כָּל־יִשְׂרָאֵל יֵשׁ לָהֶם חֵלֶק לְעוֹלָם הַבָּא. שֶׁנֶּאֱמַר: וְעַמֵּךְ כֻּלָּם צַדִּיקִים לְעוֹלָם יִירְשׁוּ אָרֶץ נֵצֶר מטעו (מַטָּעַי) מַעֲשֵׂה יָדַי לְהִתְפָּאֵר:

All Yisrael have a portion in the world to come, as it is said, "And Your people will be all righteous; they will inherit the land forever, the branch of my planting, the work of my hands, that I may be glorified." (Isaiah 60:21)

MOTZA'EI SHABBAT / SHABBAT EVENING PRAYER

The ideal time to pray Arvit is after the emergence of three stars [in a line]. Although many have a custom of starting directly after sundown, one should make sure that the recital of the Shema is after the emergence of the stars. (SA, OC 235) It can be said until about 72 minutes before sunrise. Motza'ei Shabbat should be said at a later hour than the weekday, in order to add from the common to the holy.

On the evening of Rosh Chodesh, Barchi Nafshi is recited (Psalms 104, located in the Rosh Chodesh section.) On Chol HaMoed Sukkot, some recite Ps. 42 and 43. Motzaei Shabbat Chol HaMoed Pesach, some recite Ps. 107. On Hanukkah some recite Ps. 30 (below).

On Hanukkah some say:

Psalms 30

מִזְמוֹר שִׁיר־חֲנֻכַּת הַבַּיִת לְדָוִד: אֲרוֹמִמְךָ יְהֹוָה כִּי דִלִּיתָנִי וְלֹא־שִׂמַּחְתָּ אֹיְבַי
לִי: יְהֹוָה אֱלֹהָי שִׁוַּעְתִּי אֵלֶיךָ וַתִּרְפָּאֵנִי: יְהֹוָה הֶעֱלִיתָ מִן־שְׁאוֹל נַפְשִׁי חִיִּיתַנִי
מִיּוֹרְדִי (מִיָּרְדִי)־בוֹר: זַמְּרוּ לַיהֹוָה חֲסִידָיו וְהוֹדוּ לְזֵכֶר קָדְשׁוֹ: כִּי רֶגַע | בְּאַפּוֹ
חַיִּים בִּרְצוֹנוֹבָעֶרֶב יָלִין בֶּכִי וְלַבֹּקֶר רִנָּה: וַאֲנִי אָמַרְתִּי בְשַׁלְוִי בַּל־אֶמּוֹט
לְעוֹלָם: יְהֹוָה בִּרְצוֹנְךָ הֶעֱמַדְתָּה לְהַרְרִי עֹז הִסְתַּרְתָּ פָנֶיךָ הָיִיתִי נִבְהָל: אֵלֶיךָ
יְהֹוָה אֶקְרָא וְאֶל־אֲדֹנָי אֶתְחַנָּן: מַה־בֶּצַע בְּדָמִי בְּרִדְתִּי אֶל שָׁחַת הֲיוֹדְךָ עָפָר
הֲיַגִּיד אֲמִתֶּךָ: שְׁמַע־יְהֹוָה וְחָנֵּנִי יְהֹוָה הֱיֵה־עֹזֵר לִי: הָפַכְתָּ מִסְפְּדִי לְמָחוֹל לִי
פִּתַּחְתָּ שַׂקִּי וַתְּאַזְּרֵנִי שִׂמְחָה: לְמַעַן | יְזַמֶּרְךָ כָבוֹד וְלֹא יִדֹּם יְהֹוָה אֱלֹהַי
לְעוֹלָם אוֹדֶךָּ:

Mizmor Shir-Chanukkat Habayit Ledavid. Aromimcha Adonai Ki Dillitani; Velo-Simachta Oyevai Li. Adonai Elohai; Shiva'ti Eleicha. Vatirpa'eni. Adonai He'elita Min-She'ol Nafshi; Chiyitani. Miyordi-Vor. Zameru L'Adonai Chasidav; Vehodu. Lezecher Kodsho. Ki Rega' Be'appo Chayim Birtzonobba'erev Yalin Bechi. Velaboker Rinah. Va'ani Amarti Veshalvi; Bal-'Emot Le'olam. Adonai Birtzonecha He'emadtah Lehareri Oz Histarta Faneicha. Hayiti Nivhal. Eleicha Adonai Ekra; Ve'el-' Adonai. Etchanan. Mah-Betza Bedami Beridti El Shachat Hayodecha Afar; Hayagid Amitecha. Shema'-Adonai Vechoneni; Adonai Heyeh-'Ozeir Li. Hafachta Mispedi Lemachol Li Pittachta Sakki; Vate'azereini Simchah. Lema'an Yezamercha Chavod Velo Yidom; Adonai Elohai. Le'olam Odeka.

A Psalm; a Song at the Dedication of the House of David. I will extol You, Hashem, for You have raised me up, and have not suffered my enemies to rejoice over me. Hashem my God, I cried to You, and You healed me; Oh Hashem, You brought up my soul from Sheol; You did keep me alive, that I should not go down to the pit. Sing praise to Hashem, His godly ones, and give thanks to His holy name. For His anger is but for a moment, His favor is for a life-time; weeping may come for the night, but joy comes in the morning. Now I had said in my security: 'I will never be moved.' You had established, Hashem, in Your favor my mountain as a stronghold — You hid Your face; I was afraid. To You, Hashem, did I call, and to Hashem I made supplication: 'What profit is there in my blood, when I go down to the pit? Will the dust praise You? Will it declare Your truth? Hear, Hashem, and be gracious to me; Hashem, be my helper.' You turned my mourning into dancing; You loosed my sackcloth, and girded me with gladness; So that my glory may sing praise to You, and not be silent; Hashem my God, I will give thanks to You forever.

Some say before:

יְהֹוָה צְבָאוֹת עִמָּנוּ מִשְׂגָּב־לָנוּ אֱלֹהֵי יַעֲקֹב סֶלָה: יְהֹוָה צְבָאוֹת
אַשְׁרֵי אָדָם בֹּטֵחַ בָּךְ: יְהֹוָה הוֹשִׁיעָה הַמֶּלֶךְ יַעֲנֵנוּ בְיוֹם־קָרְאֵנוּ: מִי
יִתֵּן מִצִּיּוֹן יְשׁוּעַת יִשְׂרָאֵל בְּשׁוּב יְהֹוָה שְׁבוּת עַמּוֹ יָגֵל יַעֲקֹב יִשְׂמַח
יִשְׂרָאֵל: וּתְשׁוּעַת צַדִּיקִים מֵיְהֹוָה מָעוּזָּם בְּעֵת צָרָה: וַיַּעְזְרֵם יְהֹוָה
וַיְפַלְּטֵם יְפַלְּטֵם מֵרְשָׁעִים וְיוֹשִׁיעֵם כִּי־חָסוּ בוֹ: אַךְ צַדִּיקִים יוֹדוּ
לִשְׁמֶךָ יֵשְׁבוּ יְשָׁרִים אֶת־פָּנֶיךָ:

Adonai Tzeva'ot Imanu Misgav Lanu Elohei Ya'akov Selah. Adonai Tzeva'ot Ashrei Adam Boteach Bach. Adonai Hoshi'ah Hamelech Ya'aneinu Veyom Kor'enu: Mi Yiten Mitziyon Yeshu'at Yisra'el Beshuv Adonai Shevut Ammo Yagel Ya'akov Yismach Yisra'el. Uteshu'at Tzaddikim Meyehvah Ma'uzam Be'et Tzarah. Vaya'zerem Adonai Vayfalletem Yefalletem Meresha'im Veyoshi'em Ki Chasu Vo. Ach Tzaddikim Yodu Lishmecha Yeshevu Yesharim Et Paneicha.

Hashem of hosts is with us; the God of Yaakov is our Stronghold. Hashem of hosts, happy is the man who trusts in You. Hashem, save; may the King answer us in the day that we call. Oh that the salvation of Yisrael would come out of Zion. When Hashem turns the captivity of His people, let Yaakov rejoice, let Yisrael be glad. But the salvation of the righteous is from Hashem; He is their stronghold in the time of trouble. And Hashem helps them, and delivers them; He delivers them from the wicked, and saves them, because they have taken refuge in Him. Surely the righteous will give thanks to Your name; The upright will dwell in Your presence. (Ps. 46:12, 84:13, 20:10, 14:7, 37:39-40, 140:14)

Some say:

לְשֵׁם יְחוּד קוּדְשָׁא בְּרִיךְ הוּא וּשְׁכִינְתֵּיהּ. בִּדְחִילוּ וּרְחִימוּ. וּרְחִימוּ וּדְחִילוּ. לְיַחֲדָא שֵׁם יוֹ"ד קֵ"י בְּוָא"ו קֵ"י בְּיִחוּדָא שְׁלִים (יהוה) בְּשֵׁם כָּל יִשְׂרָאֵל. הִנֵּה אֲנַחְנוּ בָּאִים לְהִתְפַּלֵּל תְּפִלַּת עַרְבִית שֶׁתִּקֵּן יַעֲקֹב אָבִינוּ עָלָיו הַשָּׁלוֹם. עִם כָּל הַמִּצְוֹת הַכְּלוּלוֹת בָּהּ לְתַקֵּן אֶת שׁוֹרְשָׁהּ בִּמְקוֹם עֶלְיוֹן. לַעֲשׂוֹת נַחַת רוּחַ לְיוֹצְרֵנוּ וְלַעֲשׂוֹת רְצוֹן בּוֹרְאֵנוּ. וִיהִי נֹעַם אֲדֹנָי אֱלֹהֵינוּ עָלֵינוּ וּמַעֲשֵׂה יָדֵינוּ כּוֹנְנָה עָלֵינוּ וּמַעֲשֵׂה יָדֵינוּ כּוֹנְנֵהוּ:

Hatzi-Kaddish / Half Kaddish

Kaddish is only recited in a minyan (ten men). אמן denotes when the congregation responds "Amen" together out loud. According to the Shulchan Arukh, the congregation says "Yehei Shemeh Rabba" to "Yitbarach" out loud together without interruption, and also that one should respond "Amen" after "Yitbarach." (SA, OC 55,56) This is not the common custom today. Though many are accustomed to answering according to their own custom, it is advised to respond in the custom of the one reciting to avoid not fragmenting into smaller groups. ("Lo Titgodedu" - BT, Yevamot 13b / SA, OC 493, Rema / MT, Avodah Zara 12:15)

יִתְגַּדַּל וְיִתְקַדַּשׁ שְׁמֵהּ רַבָּא. אמן בְּעָלְמָא דִּי בְרָא. כִּרְעוּתֵהּ. וְיַמְלִיךְ מַלְכוּתֵהּ. וְיַצְמַח פֻּרְקָנֵהּ. וִיקָרֵב מְשִׁיחֵהּ. אמן בְּחַיֵּיכוֹן וּבְיוֹמֵיכוֹן וּבְחַיֵּי דְכָל בֵּית יִשְׂרָאֵל. בַּעֲגָלָא וּבִזְמַן קָרִיב. וְאִמְרוּ אָמֵן. אמן יְהֵא שְׁמֵיהּ רַבָּא מְבָרַךְ לְעָלַם וּלְעָלְמֵי עָלְמַיָּא יִתְבָּרַךְ. וְיִשְׁתַּבַּח. וְיִתְפָּאַר. וְיִתְרוֹמַם. וְיִתְנַשֵּׂא. וְיִתְהַדָּר. וְיִתְעַלֶּה. וְיִתְהַלָּל שְׁמֵהּ דְּקֻדְשָׁא. בְּרִיךְ הוּא. אמן לְעֵלָּא מִן כָּל בִּרְכָתָא שִׁירָתָא. תֻּשְׁבְּחָתָא וְנֶחֱמָתָא. דַּאֲמִירָן בְּעָלְמָא. וְאִמְרוּ אָמֵן. אמן

Yitgadal Veyitkadash Shemeh Rabba. Amen Be'alema Di Vera.
Kir'uteh. Veyamlich Malchuteh. Veyatzmach Purkaneh. Vikarev
Meshicheh. Amen Bechayeichon Uveyomeichon Uvechayei Dechal-
Beit Yisra'el. Ba'agala Uvizman Kariv. Ve'imru Amen. Amen Yehei
Shemeh Rabba Mevarach Le'alam Ule'alemei Alemaya Yitbarach.
Veyishtabach. Veyitpa'ar. Veyitromam. Veyitnasse. Veyit'hadar.
Veyit'aleh. Veyit'hallal Shemeh Dekudsha. Berich Hu. Amen Le'ella
Min Kol Birchata Shirata. Tushbechata Venechemata. Da'amiran
Be'alema. Ve'imru Amen. Amen

Glorified and sanctified be God's great name Amen throughout the world which He has created according to His will. May He establish His kingdom, hastening His salvation and the coming of His Messiah, ^{Amen}, in your lifetime and during your days, and within the life of the entire House of Yisrael, speedily and soon; and say, Amen. ^{Amen} May His great name be blessed forever and to all eternity. Blessed and praised, glorified and exalted, extolled and honored, adored and lauded is the name of the Holy One, blessed is He, ^{Amen} Beyond all the blessings and hymns, praises and consolations that are ever spoken in the world; and say, Amen. ^{Amen}

Congregation and Chazan:

וְהוּא רַחוּם יְכַפֵּר עָוֹן וְלֹא־יַשְׁחִית וְהִרְבָּה לְהָשִׁיב אַפּוֹ וְלֹא־יָעִיר כָּל־חֲמָתוֹ: יְהֹוָה הוֹשִׁיעָה הַמֶּלֶךְ יַעֲנֵנוּ בְיוֹם־קָרְאֵנוּ:

Vehu Rachum YeChapeir Avon Velo Yashchit Vehirbah Lehashiv Appo Velo Ya'ir Kol Chamato. Adonai Hoshi'ah HaMelech Ya'Aneinu Veyom Kor'enu:

But He, being full of compassion, forgives iniquity, and does not destroy; many times He turns His anger away, And does not stir up all His wrath. Hashem, save; may the King answer us in the day that we call. (Psalms 78:38, 20:10)

Barechu

Barechu / Call to Prayer is recited only with 10 men (minyan).

The Chazan says:

בָּרְכוּ אֶת יְהֹוָה הַמְבֹרָךְ:

Barechu Et Adonai Hamevorach.

Bless Hashem, the blessed One.

The kahal answers:

בָּרוּךְ יְהֹוָה הַמְבֹרָךְ לְעוֹלָם וָעֶד:

Baruch Adonai Hamevorach Le'olam Va'ed.

Blessed is Hashem Who is blessed for all eternity.

The Chazan says:

בָּרוּךְ יְהֹוָה הַמְבֹרָךְ לְעוֹלָם וָעֶד:

Baruch Adonai Hamevorach Le'olam Va'ed.

Blessed is Hashem Who is blessed for all eternity.

Ma'ariv Aravim

Baruch Attah Adonai Eloheinu	בָּרוּךְ אַתָּה יְהֹוָה אֱלֹהֵינוּ
Melech Ha'olam. Asher Bidvaro	מֶלֶךְ הָעוֹלָם. אֲשֶׁר בִּדְבָרוֹ
Ma'ariv Aravim Bechochmah.	מַעֲרִיב עֲרָבִים בְּחָכְמָה.
Potei'ach She'arim Bitvunah.	פּוֹתֵחַ שְׁעָרִים בִּתְבוּנָה.
Meshaneh Itim. Umachalif Et-	מְשַׁנֶּה עִתִּים. וּמַחֲלִיף אֶת־
Hazmanim. Umesader Et-	הַזְּמַנִּים. וּמְסַדֵּר אֶת־
Hakochavim	הַכּוֹכָבִים
Bemishmeroteihem Barakia'.	בְּמִשְׁמְרוֹתֵיהֶם בָּרָקִיעַ.
Kirtzono. Borei Yomam Valailah.	כִּרְצוֹנוֹ. בּוֹרֵא יוֹמָם וָלַיְלָה.
Golel Or Mipenei Choshech	גּוֹלֵל אוֹר מִפְּנֵי חֹשֶׁךְ
Vechoshech Mipenei Or.	וְחֹשֶׁךְ מִפְּנֵי אוֹר.
Hama'avir Yom Umevi Lailah.	הַמַּעֲבִיר יוֹם וּמֵבִיא לָיְלָה.
Umavdil Bein Yom Uvein	וּמַבְדִּיל בֵּין יוֹם וּבֵין
Lailah. Adonai Tzeva'ot Shemo.	לָיְלָה. יְהֹוָה צְבָאוֹת שְׁמוֹ:
Baruch Attah Adonai Hama'ariv	בָּרוּךְ אַתָּה יְהֹוָה הַמַּעֲרִיב
Aravim.	עֲרָבִים:

Blessed are You, Hashem our God, King of the universe, Who with His word brings on evenings; with wisdom opens the gates of the heavens, and with understanding changes the cycles of time and the seasons. And set the stars in their watches in the sky according to His will. He creates day and night, recedes light before darkness and darkness before light. He removes the day and brings on night and separates between day and night. Hashem of hosts is Your name. Blessed are You, Hashem Who brings on evening.

Ahavat Olam

Ahavat Olam Beit Yisra'el	אַהֲבַת עוֹלָם בֵּית יִשְׂרָאֵל
Ammecha Ahaveta. Torah	עַמְּךָ אָהָבְתָּ. תּוֹרָה
Umitzvot Chukkim Umishpatim	וּמִצְוֹת חֻקִּים וּמִשְׁפָּטִים
Otanu Limadta. Al-Ken Adonai	אוֹתָנוּ לִמַּדְתָּ. עַל־כֵּן יְהֹוָה
Eloheinu. Beshachevenu	אֱלֹהֵינוּ. בְּשָׁכְבֵנוּ
Uvekumenu Nasiach	וּבְקוּמֵנוּ נָשִׂיחַ
Bechukkeicha. Venismach	בְּחֻקֶּיךָ. וְנִשְׂמַח
Vena'aloz Bedivrei Talmud	וְנַעֲלֹז בְּדִבְרֵי תַלְמוּד
Toratecha Umitzvoteicha	תוֹרָתֶךָ וּמִצְוֹתֶיךָ
Vechukkoteicha Le'olam Va'ed.	וְחֻקּוֹתֶיךָ לְעוֹלָם וָעֶד.
Ki-Hem Chayeinu Ve'orech	כִּי־הֵם חַיֵּינוּ וְאֹרֶךְ
Yameinu. Uvahem Nehgeh	יָמֵינוּ. וּבָהֶם נֶהְגֶּה
Yomam Valailah. Ve'ahavatecha	יוֹמָם וָלָיְלָה. וְאַהֲבָתְךָ
Lo Tasur Mimenu Le'olamim.	לֹא תָסוּר מִמֶּנּוּ לְעוֹלָמִים:
Baruch Attah Adonai Ohev	בָּרוּךְ אַתָּה יְהֹוָה אוֹהֵב
Et-'Ammo Yisra'el.	אֶת־עַמּוֹ יִשְׂרָאֵל:

With love everlasting You have loved the House of Yisrael, Your people. You have taught us Your Torah, and commandments, statutes and judgments; and therefore, Hashem our God, when we lie down and when we rise up, we will speak of Your statutes, rejoicing and delighting in learning the words of Your Torah, and Your commandments and statutes for all time. For they are our life and our length of days, and on them we will meditate by day and by night. May Your love never depart from us forever. Blessed are You, Hashem Who loves His people Yisrael.

LAWS OF RECITING THE SHEMA

One who recites the Shema, but did not have intention during the first verse, 'Shema Yisrael', one did not fulfill their obligation. As for the rest, if they read during the specified time and did not have intention, they have fulfilled their obligation. One should recite the Shema with intention, awe, fear, shaking and trembling. The custom is to place one's hands over their face during the recitation of the first verse in order that one will not look at something else that will prevent him from directing his heart. (SA, OC 59-61)

The Shema
Deuteronomy 6:4-9

One covers their eyes and says:

שְׁמַ֖ע יִשְׂרָאֵ֑ל יְהֹוָ֥ה אֱלֹהֵ֖ינוּ יְהֹוָ֥ה | אֶחָֽד:

Shema Yisrael; Adonai Eloheinu Adonai Echad.
"Hear, O Yisrael, Hashem is our God, Hashem is One."

Whisper silently:

בָּרוּךְ שֵׁם כְּבוֹד מַלְכוּתוֹ לְעוֹלָם וָעֶד:
Baruch Shem Kevod Malchuto Le'olam Va'ed.
Blessed is His name and glorious kingdom forever and ever.

Ve'ahavta

וְאָהַבְתָּ֕ אֵ֖ת יְהֹוָ֣ה אֱלֹהֶ֑יךָ בְּכָל־לְבָבְךָ֥ וּבְכָל־נַפְשְׁךָ֖ וּבְכָל־מְאֹדֶֽךָ׃ וְהָי֞וּ הַדְּבָרִ֣ים הָאֵ֗לֶּה אֲשֶׁ֨ר אָנֹכִ֧י מְצַוְּךָ֛ הַיּ֖וֹם עַל־לְבָבֶֽךָ׃ וְשִׁנַּנְתָּ֣ם לְבָנֶ֔יךָ וְדִבַּרְתָּ֖ בָּ֑ם בְּשִׁבְתְּךָ֤ בְּבֵיתֶ֨ךָ֙ וּבְלֶכְתְּךָ֣ בַדֶּ֔רֶךְ וּֽבְשָׁכְבְּךָ֖ וּבְקוּמֶֽךָ׃ וּקְשַׁרְתָּ֥ם לְא֖וֹת עַל־יָדֶ֑ךָ וְהָי֥וּ לְטֹטָפֹ֖ת בֵּ֥ין עֵינֶֽיךָ׃ וּכְתַבְתָּ֛ם עַל־מְזֻז֥וֹת בֵּיתֶ֖ךָ וּבִשְׁעָרֶֽיךָ׃

Ve'ahavta Et Adonai Eloheicha; Bechol-Levavecha Uvechol-
Nafshecha Uvechol-Me'odecha. Vehayu Hadevarim Ha'eleh. Asher
Anochi Metzavecha Hayom Al-Levavecha. Veshinantam Levaneicha.
Vedibarta Bam; Beshivtecha Beveitecha Uvelechtecha Vaderech.
Uveshochbecha Uvekumecha. Ukeshartam Le'ot Al-Yadecha;
Vehayu Letotafot Bein Eineicha. Uchetavtam Al-Mezuzot Beitecha
Uvish'areicha.

And you will love Hashem your God with all your heart, and with all your soul, and with all your might. And these words, which I command you this day, will be upon your heart; and you will teach them diligently to your children, and will talk of them when you sit in your house, and when you walk by the way, and when you lie down, and when you rise up. And you will bind them for a sign on your hand, and they will be for frontlets between your eyes. And you will write them on the doorposts of your house, and on your gates.

Vehayah Im-shamoa

וְהָיָ֗ה אִם־שָׁמֹ֤עַ תִּשְׁמְעוּ֙ אֶל־מִצְוֺתַ֔י אֲשֶׁ֧ר אָנֹכִ֛י מְצַוֶּ֥ה אֶתְכֶ֖ם הַיּ֑וֹם לְאַהֲבָ֞ה אֶת־יְהֹוָ֤ה אֱלֹֽהֵיכֶם֙ וּלְעָבְד֔וֹ בְּכָל־לְבַבְכֶ֖ם וּבְכָל־נַפְשְׁכֶֽם׃ וְנָתַתִּ֧י מְטַֽר־אַרְצְכֶ֛ם בְּעִתּ֖וֹ יוֹרֶ֣ה וּמַלְק֑וֹשׁ וְאָסַפְתָּ֣ דְגָנֶ֔ךָ וְתִירֹֽשְׁךָ֖ וְיִצְהָרֶֽךָ׃ וְנָתַתִּ֛י עֵ֥שֶׂב בְּשָׂדְךָ֖ לִבְהֶמְתֶּ֑ךָ וְאָכַלְתָּ֖ וְשָׂבָֽעְתָּ׃ הִשָּׁ֣מְר֣וּ לָכֶ֔ם פֶּ֥ן יִפְתֶּ֖ה לְבַבְכֶ֑ם וְסַרְתֶּ֗ם וַעֲבַדְתֶּם֙ אֱלֹהִ֣ים אֲחֵרִ֔ים וְהִשְׁתַּחֲוִיתֶ֖ם לָהֶֽם׃ וְחָרָ֨ה אַף־יְהֹוָ֜ה בָּכֶ֗ם וְעָצַ֤ר אֶת־הַשָּׁמַ֨יִם֙

וְלֹא־יִהְיֶה מָטָר וְהָאֲדָמָה לֹא תִתֵּן אֶת־יְבוּלָהּ וַאֲבַדְתֶּם מְהֵרָה מֵעַל
הָאָרֶץ הַטֹּבָה אֲשֶׁר יְהוָה נֹתֵן לָכֶם: וְשַׂמְתֶּם אֶת־דְּבָרַי אֵלֶּה
עַל־לְבַבְכֶם וְעַל־נַפְשְׁכֶם וּקְשַׁרְתֶּם אֹתָם לְאוֹת עַל־יֶדְכֶם וְהָיוּ
לְטוֹטָפֹת בֵּין עֵינֵיכֶם. וְלִמַּדְתֶּם אֹתָם אֶת־בְּנֵיכֶם לְדַבֵּר בָּם בְּשִׁבְתְּךָ
בְּבֵיתֶךָ וּבְלֶכְתְּךָ בַדֶּרֶךְ וּבְשָׁכְבְּךָ וּבְקוּמֶךָ: וּכְתַבְתָּם עַל־מְזוּזוֹת בֵּיתֶךָ
וּבִשְׁעָרֶיךָ: לְמַעַן יִרְבּוּ יְמֵיכֶם וִימֵי בְנֵיכֶם עַל הָאֲדָמָה אֲשֶׁר נִשְׁבַּע
יְהוָה לַאֲבֹתֵיכֶם לָתֵת לָהֶם כִּימֵי הַשָּׁמַיִם עַל־הָאָרֶץ:

Vehayah Im-Shamoa Tishme'u El-Mitzvotai. Asher Anochi Metzaveh
Etchem Hayom; Le'ahavah Et-Adonai Eloheichem Ule'avdo. Bechol-
Levavchem Uvechol-Nafshechem. Venatati Metar-'Artzechem Be'ito
Yoreh Umalkosh; Ve'asafta Deganecha. Vetiroshecha Veyitzharecha.
Venatati Esev Besadecha Livhemtecha; Ve'achalta Vesava'eta.
Hishameru Lachem. Pen Yifteh Levavchem; Vesartem. Va'avadtem
Elohim Acherim. Vehishtachavitem Lahem. Vecharah Af-Adonai
Bachem. Ve'atzar Et-Hashamayim Velo-Yihyeh Matar. Veha'adamah.
Lo Titen Et-Yevulah; Va'avadtem Meheirah. Me'al Ha'aretz Hatovah.
Asher Adonai Noten Lachem. Vesamtem Et-Devarai Eleh. Al-
Levavchem Ve'al-Nafshechem; Ukeshartem Otam Le'ot Al-Yedchem.
Vehayu Letotafot Bein Eineichem. Velimadtem Otam Et-Beneichem
Ledaber Bam; Beshivtecha Beveitecha Uvelechtecha Vaderech.
Uveshochbecha Uvekumecha. Uchetavtam Al-Mezuzot Beitecha
Uvish'areicha. Lema'an Yirbu Yemeichem Vimei Veneichem. Al
Ha'adamah. Asher Nishba Adonai La'avoteichem Latet Lahem;
Kimei Hashamayim Al-Ha'aretz.

And it will come to pass, if you will observe My commandments
which I command you this day, to love Hashem your God, and to
serve Him with all your heart and with all your soul, that I will give
the rain of your land in its season, the former rain and the latter
rain, that you may gather in your corn, and your wine, and your oil.
And I will give grass in your fields for your cattle, and you will eat
and be satisfied. Be cautious, in case your heart is deceived, and you
turn aside, and serve other gods, and worship them; and the anger
of Hashem is kindled against you, and He shut up the heaven, so
that there will be no rain, and the ground will not yield her fruit; and
you perish quickly from off the good land which Hashem gives you.

Therefore you will lay up these words in your heart and in your soul; and you will bind them for a sign upon your hand, and they will be for frontlets between your eyes. And you will teach them to your children, talking of them, when you sit in your house, and when you walk by the way, and when you lie down, and when you rise up. And you will write them on the doorposts of your house, and on your gates; that your days may be multiplied, and the days of your children, upon the land which Hashem swore to your fathers to give them, as the days of the heavens above the earth. (Deuteronomy 11:13-21)

Numbers 15:37-41

וַיֹּאמֶר יְהֹוָה אֶל־מֹשֶׁה לֵּאמֹר: דַּבֵּר אֶל־בְּנֵי יִשְׂרָאֵל וְאָמַרְתָּ אֲלֵהֶם וְעָשׂוּ לָהֶם צִיצִת עַל־כַּנְפֵי בִגְדֵיהֶם לְדֹרֹתָם וְנָתְנוּ עַל־צִיצִת הַכָּנָף פְּתִיל תְּכֵלֶת: וְהָיָה לָכֶם לְצִיצִת וּרְאִיתֶם אֹתוֹ וּזְכַרְתֶּם אֶת־כָּל־מִצְוֹת יְהֹוָה וַעֲשִׂיתֶם אֹתָם וְלֹא־תָתוּרוּ אַחֲרֵי לְבַבְכֶם וְאַחֲרֵי עֵינֵיכֶם אֲשֶׁר־אַתֶּם זֹנִים אַחֲרֵיהֶם: לְמַעַן תִּזְכְּרוּ וַעֲשִׂיתֶם אֶת־כָּל־מִצְוֹתָי וִהְיִיתֶם קְדֹשִׁים לֵאלֹהֵיכֶם: אֲנִי יְהֹוָה אֱלֹהֵיכֶם אֲשֶׁר הוֹצֵאתִי אֶתְכֶם מֵאֶרֶץ מִצְרַיִם לִהְיוֹת לָכֶם לֵאלֹהִים אֲנִי יְהֹוָה אֱלֹהֵיכֶם: אֱמֶת.

Vayomer Adonai El-Mosheh Lemor. Daber El-Benei Yisra'el Ve'amarta Aleihem. Ve'asu Lahem Tzitzit Al-Kanfei Vigdeihem Ledorotam; Venatenu Al-Tzitzit Hakanaf Petil Techelet. Vehayah Lachem Letzitzit Ure'item Oto Uzechartem Et-Chol-Mitzvot Adonai Va'asitem Otam; Velo-Taturu Acharei Levavchem Ve'acharei Eineichem. Asher-'Attem Zonim Achareihem. Lema'an Tizkeru. Va'asitem Et-Chol-Mitzvotai; Vihyitem Kedoshim Leloheichem. Ani Adonai Eloheichem. Asher Hotzeti Etchem Me'eretz Mitzrayim. Lihyot Lachem Lelohim; Ani Adonai Eloheichem. Emet.

And Hashem spoke to Moshe, saying: Speak to the children of Yisrael, and command them to make tzitzit on the corners of their garments throughout their generations, and that they put a thread

of tekhelet with the tzitzit of each corner. And they will be to you for
tzitzit, that you may look upon them, and remember all the
commandments of Hashem, and do them; and that you do not go
about after your own heart and your own eyes, after which you go
whoring; that you may remember and do all My commandments,
and be holy to your God. I am Hashem your God, Who brought you
out of the land of Mitzrayim, to be your God: I am Hashem your
God. It is true.

יְהוָה אֱלֹהֵיכֶם אֱמֶת:

Adonai Eloheichem Emet.

Hashem, your God, is true.

Emet Ve'Emunah

וֶאֱמוּנָה כָּל־זֹאת וְקַיָּם עָלֵינוּ. כִּי הוּא יְהוָה אֱלֹהֵינוּ וְאֵין זוּלָתוֹ.
וַאֲנַחְנוּ יִשְׂרָאֵל עַמּוֹ. הַפּוֹדֵנוּ מִיַּד מְלָכִים. הַגֹּאֲלֵנוּ מַלְכֵּנוּ מִכַּף
כָּל־עָרִיצִים. הָאֵל הַנִּפְרָע לָנוּ מִצָּרֵינוּ. הַמְשַׁלֵּם גְּמוּל לְכָל־אֹיְבֵי
נַפְשֵׁנוּ. הַשָּׂם נַפְשֵׁנוּ בַּחַיִּים. וְלֹא נָתַן לַמּוֹט רַגְלֵנוּ. הַמַּדְרִיכֵנוּ עַל
בָּמוֹת אוֹיְבֵינוּ. וַיָּרֶם קַרְנֵנוּ עַל־כָּל־שֹׂונְאֵינוּ. הָאֵל הָעֹשֶׂה לָנוּ נְקָמָה
בְּפַרְעֹה. בְּאוֹתוֹת וּבְמוֹפְתִים בְּאַדְמַת בְּנֵי חָם. הַמַּכֶּה בְעֶבְרָתוֹ
כָּל־בְּכוֹרֵי מִצְרָיִם. וַיּוֹצֵא אֶת־עַמּוֹ יִשְׂרָאֵל מִתּוֹכָם לְחֵרוּת עוֹלָם.
הַמַּעֲבִיר בָּנָיו בֵּין גִּזְרֵי יַם־סוּף. וְאֶת־רוֹדְפֵיהֶם וְאֶת־שֹׂונְאֵיהֶם
בִּתְהוֹמוֹת טִבַּע. רָאוּ בָנִים אֶת־גְּבוּרָתוֹ. שִׁבְּחוּ וְהוֹדוּ לִשְׁמוֹ.
וּמַלְכוּתוֹ בְרָצוֹן קִבְּלוּ עֲלֵיהֶם. מֹשֶׁה וּבְנֵי יִשְׂרָאֵל לְךָ עָנוּ שִׁירָה
בְּשִׂמְחָה רַבָּה. וְאָמְרוּ כֻלָּם. מִי־כָמֹכָה בָּאֵלִם יְהוָה מִי כָּמֹכָה
נֶאְדָּר בַּקֹּדֶשׁ נוֹרָא תְהִלֹּת עֹשֵׂה פֶלֶא: מַלְכוּתְךָ יְהוָה אֱלֹהֵינוּ רָאוּ
בָנֶיךָ עַל הַיָּם. יַחַד כֻּלָּם הוֹדוּ וְהִמְלִיכוּ וְאָמְרוּ. יְהוָה | יִמְלֹךְ לְעֹלָם

וָעֶד: וְנֶאֱמַר. כִּי־פָדָה יְהוָה אֶת־יַעֲקֹב וּגְאָלוֹ מִיַּד חָזָק מִמֶּנּוּ: בָּרוּךְ
אַתָּה יְהוָה גָּאַל יִשְׂרָאֵל:

Ve'emunah Kol-Zot Vekayam Aleinu. Ki Hu Adonai Eloheinu Ve'ein
Zulato. Va'anachnu Yisra'el Ammo. Hapodenu Miyad Melachim.
Hago'alenu Malkeinu Mikaf Kol-'Aritzim. Ha'el Hanifra Lanu
Mitzareinu. Hamshalem Gemul Lechol-'Oyevei Nafshenu. Hassam
Nafshenu Bachayim. Velo Natan Lamot Raglenu. Hamadricheinu Al
Bamot Oyeveinu. Vayarem Karnenu Al-Kol-Sone'einu. Ha'el
Ha'oseh Lanu Nekamah Befar'oh. Be'otot Uvemofetim Be'admat
Benei Cham. Hamakeh Ve'evrato Kol-Bechorei Mitzrayim. Vayotzi
Et-'Ammo Yisra'el Mitocham Lecherut Olam. Hama'avir Banav Bein
Gizrei Yam-Suf. Ve'et-Rodefeihem Ve'et-Sone'eihem Bit'homot Tiba.
Ra'u Vanim Et-Gevurato. Shibechu Vehodu Lishmo. Umalchuto
Veratzon Kibelu Aleihem. Mosheh Uvenei Yisra'el Lecha Anu Shirah
Besimchah Rabah. Ve'ameru Chulam. Mi-Chamochah Ba'elim
Hashem Mi Kamochah Ne'dar Bakodesh; Nora Tehillot Oseh Fele.
Malchutecha Adonai Eloheinu Ra'u Vaneicha Al Hayam. Yachad
Kulam Hodu Vehimlichu Ve'ameru. Adonai Yimloch Le'olam Va'ed.
Vene'emar. Ki-Fadah Adonai Et-Ya'akov; Uge'alo Miyad Chazak
Mimenu. Baruch Attah Adonai Ga'al Yisra'el.

Trustworthy is all of this, and binding upon us, that He is Hashem
our God with none besides Him, and we Yisrael are His people. He
redeems us from the hand of kings, our King Who redeems us from
the hand of all oppressors. The God Who ransoms us from
adversaries, Who brings retribution on all enemies of our souls. "He
set our soul in life, And has not allowed our feet to slip." He has
guided us upon high places of our enemies, And has raised our
strength above all who hated us. The God Who performed
vengeance on Pharaoh or us by signs and wonders in the land of the
sons of Cham. In His wrath He struck all the first-born of Mitzrayim,
And brought out His people Yisrael to everlasting freedom. He led
His children between the divided Sea of Reeds, and sank their
pursuers and enemies in the depths. His children praised His power;
they sang gave thanks to His name and with willingly accepted His
kingship. Then, to You, Moshe and all the children of Yisrael sang,
proclaiming with great joy, "Who is like You, Hashem, among the

gods, Who is like You, glorified in holiness, You are awesome in praise, working wonders." By the sea, Hashem our God, Your children beheld Your kingdom; all together they gave thanks to You, proclaiming Your kingship, and it is said, "Hashem will reign forever and ever." And also declared Yirmiyahu, Your prophet, "Hashem will surely redeem Yaakov, And rescue him from the hand of one stronger than him." (Jeremiah 31:10) Blessed are You, Hashem Who redeemed Yisrael.

Hashkiveinu

הַשְׁכִּיבֵנוּ אָבִינוּ לְשָׁלוֹם. וְהַעֲמִידֵנוּ מַלְכֵּנוּ לְחַיִּים טוֹבִים וּלְשָׁלוֹם. וּפְרוֹשׂ עָלֵינוּ סֻכַּת שְׁלוֹמֶךָ. וְתַקְּנֵנוּ מַלְכֵּנוּ בְּעֵצָה טוֹבָה מִלְּפָנֶיךָ. וְהוֹשִׁיעֵנוּ מְהֵרָה לְמַעַן שְׁמֶךָ. וְהָגֵן בַּעֲדֵנוּ. וְהָסֵר מֵעָלֵינוּ מַכַּת אוֹיֵב. דֶּבֶר. חֶרֶב. חוֹלִי. צָרָה. רָעָה. רָעָב. וְיָגוֹן. וּמַשְׁחִית. וּמַגֵּפָה. שְׁבוֹר וְהָסֵר הַשָּׂטָן מִלְּפָנֵינוּ וּמֵאַחֲרֵינוּ. וּבְצֵל כְּנָפֶיךָ תַּסְתִּירֵנוּ. וּשְׁמוֹר צֵאתֵנוּ וּבוֹאֵנוּ לְחַיִּים טוֹבִים וּלְשָׁלוֹם מֵעַתָּה וְעַד עוֹלָם: כִּי אֵל שׁוֹמְרֵנוּ וּמַצִּילֵנוּ אָתָּה מִכָּל דָּבָר רָע וּמִפַּחַד לָיְלָה. בָּרוּךְ אַתָּה יהוה שׁוֹמֵר אֶת עַמּוֹ יִשְׂרָאֵל לָעַד אָמֵן.

Hashkiveinu Avinu Leshalom. Veha'amidenu Malkeinu Lechayim Tovim Uleshalom. Uferos Aleinu Sukkat Shelomecha. Vetakenenu Malkeinu Be'etzah Tovah Milfaneicha. Vehoshi'enu Meheirah Lema'an Shemecha. Vehagen Ba'adenu. Vehaseir Me'aleinu Makat Oyev. Dever. Cherev. Choli. Tzarah. Ra'ah. Ra'av. Veyagon. Umashchit. Umagefah. Shevor Vehaseir Hasatan Millefaneinu Ume'achareinu. Uvetzel Kenafeicha Tastirenu. Ushemor Tzetenu Uvo'enu Lechayim Tovim Uleshalom Me'attah Ve'ad Olam. Ki El Shomerenu Umatzilenu Attah Mikol Davar Ra Umipachad Lailah. Baruch Attah Adonai Shomer Et 'Ammo Yisra'el La'ad. Amen.

Our Father, lay us down in peace and raise us up, our King, to a good life and peace. And spread over us Your shelter of peace and direct us with good council before You, our King. And save us speedily for Your name's sake. And remove from us the strike of an enemy, pestilence, sword, illness, distress, evil, famine, sorrow and destruction and plague. Break and remove the Satan from before us and from behind us. And shelter us in the shadow of Your wings and guard our going out and our coming in, for a good life and peace now and forever. For You are God, our Guardian and our Deliverer from every evil thing and from dread of the night. Blessed are You, Hashem Who guards His people Yisrael forever. Amen.

And recite Hatzi-Kaddish:

Kaddish is only recited in a minyan (ten men). אמן denotes when the congregation responds "Amen" together out loud. According to the Shulchan Arukh, the congregation says "Yehei Shemeh Rabba" to "Yitbarach" out loud together without interruption, and also that one should respond "Amen" after "Yitbarach." (SA, OC 55,56) This is not the common custom today. Though many are accustomed to answering according to their own custom, it is advised to respond in the custom of the one reciting to avoid not fragmenting into smaller groups. ("Lo Titgodedu" - BT, Yevamot 13b / SA, OC 493, Rema / MT, Avodah Zara 12:15)

יִתְגַּדַּל וְיִתְקַדַּשׁ שְׁמֵהּ רַבָּא. אמן בְּעָלְמָא דִּי בְרָא. כִּרְעוּתֵהּ. וְיַמְלִיךְ מַלְכוּתֵהּ. וְיַצְמַח פֻּרְקָנֵהּ. וִיקָרֵב מְשִׁיחֵהּ. אמן בְּחַיֵּיכוֹן וּבְיוֹמֵיכוֹן וּבְחַיֵּי דְכָל בֵּית יִשְׂרָאֵל. בַּעֲגָלָא וּבִזְמַן קָרִיב. וְאִמְרוּ אָמֵן. אמן יְהֵא שְׁמֵיהּ רַבָּא מְבָרַךְ לְעָלַם וּלְעָלְמֵי עָלְמַיָּא יִתְבָּרַךְ. וְיִשְׁתַּבַּח. וְיִתְפָּאַר. וְיִתְרוֹמַם. וְיִתְנַשֵּׂא. וְיִתְהַדָּר. וְיִתְעַלֶּה. וְיִתְהַלָּל שְׁמֵהּ דְּקֻדְשָׁא. בְּרִיךְ הוּא. אמן לְעֵלָּא מִן כָּל בִּרְכָתָא שִׁירָתָא. תֻּשְׁבְּחָתָא וְנֶחֱמָתָא. דַּאֲמִירָן בְּעָלְמָא. וְאִמְרוּ אָמֵן. אמן

Yitgadal Veyitkadash Shemeh Rabba. **Amen** Be'alema Di Vera. Kir'uteh. Veyamlich Malchuteh. Veyatzmach Purkaneh. Vikarev Meshicheh. **Amen** Bechayeichon Uveyomeichon Uvechayei Dechal-Beit Yisra'el. Ba'agala Uvizman Kariv. Ve'imru Amen. **Amen** Yehei Shemeh Rabba Mevarach Le'alam Ule'alemei Alemaya Yitbarach. Veyishtabach. Veyitpa'ar. Veyitromam. Veyitnasse. Veyit'hadar. Veyit'aleh. Veyit'hallal Shemeh Dekudsha. Berich Hu. **Amen** Le'ella Min Kol Birchata Shirata. Tushbechata Venechemata. Da'amiran Be'alema. Ve'imru Amen. **Amen**

Glorified and sanctified be God's great name ᴬᵐᵉⁿ throughout the world which He has created according to His will. May He establish His kingdom, hastening His salvation and the coming of His Messiah, ᴬᵐᵉⁿ, in your lifetime and during your days, and within the life of the entire House of Yisrael, speedily and soon; and say, Amen. ᴬᵐᵉⁿ May His great name be blessed forever and to all eternity. Blessed and praised, glorified and exalted, extolled and honored, adored and lauded is the name of the Holy One, blessed is He, ᴬᵐᵉⁿ Beyond all the blessings and hymns, praises and consolations that are ever spoken in the world; and say, Amen. ᴬᵐᵉⁿ

LAWS OF AMIDAH

When one gets up to pray if he was standing outside the Land of Yisrael, he should turn his face toward the Land of Yisrael and focus also on Yerushalayim and the Temple and the Holy of Holies. One who is not able to determine the directions, [should] direct one's heart to their Father in Heaven. One should consider oneself as if one is standing in the Beit Hamikdash, and in one's heart, one should be directed upward towards Heaven. One who prays needs to intend in their heart the meaning of the words which are coming out of their mouth. They should think as if the Divine Presence is before them, and remove all distracting thoughts from themselves, until their thoughts and intention are pure in their prayer. (SA, OC 94, 95, 98) These are the blessings at which we bow: in Avot, at the beginning and at the end; in Modim, at the beginning and at the end. And if you come to bow at the end of every blessing or at the beginning, we teach him to not bow but in the middle, one can bow. One needs to bend until all the vertebrae in his spine are bent. His head should stay straight and submissive. One should not bow too much until his mouth is opposite his belt. If he is sick or old and cannot bow, he should humble his head, that is enough. Bow at "Baruch" and stand up at Hashem's name. (SA, OC 113,114) One shoul
d position one's feet next to each other as though they are one, in order to imitate angels, as it written regarding them: "their feet were a straight foot" (Ez. 1:7), which is to say their feet appeared as one foot. One should take three steps forward in the way of coming close and approaching a matter that must be done. (SA, OC 95, Rema)

Amidah / Shemoneh Esrei - Motza'ei Shabbat

Take three steps forward and say:

Adonai Sefatai Tiftach; Ufi. Yagid
Tehilatecha.

אֲדֹנָי שְׂפָתַי תִּפְתָּח וּפִי יַגִּיד
תְּהִלָּתֶךָ:

Hashem, open my lips, that my mouth may declare Your praise.

Avot / Fathers

Bow at "Baruch Attah" / "Blessed are You". Raise up at Adonai / Hashem.

Baruch Attah Adonai Eloheinu

בָּרוּךְ אַתָּה יְהֹוָה אֱלֹהֵינוּ

Velohei Avoteinu. Elohei

וֵאלֹהֵי אֲבוֹתֵינוּ. אֱלֹהֵי

Avraham. Elohei Yitzchak.

אַבְרָהָם. אֱלֹהֵי יִצְחָק.

Velohei Ya'akov. Ha'el Hagadol

וֵאלֹהֵי יַעֲקֹב. הָאֵל הַגָּדוֹל

Hagibor Vehanorah. El Elyon.

הַגִּבּוֹר וְהַנּוֹרָא. אֵל עֶלְיוֹן.

Gomel Chasadim Tovim. Koneh

גּוֹמֵל חֲסָדִים טוֹבִים. קוֹנֵה

Hakol. Vezocher Chasdei Avot.

הַכֹּל. וְזוֹכֵר חַסְדֵּי אָבוֹת.

Umevi Go'el Livnei Veneihem

וּמֵבִיא גוֹאֵל לִבְנֵי בְנֵיהֶם

Lema'an Shemo Be'ahavah.

לְמַעַן שְׁמוֹ בְּאַהֲבָה:

Blessed are You, Hashem our God and God of our fathers, God of
Avraham, God of Yitzchak and God of Yaakov; the great, mighty
and revered God, most high God, Who bestows lovingkindness.
Master of all things; Who remembers the kindnesses of our fathers,
and Who will bring a redeemer to their children's children for the
sake of His name in love.

During the 10 days of repentance (Rosh Hashanah to Yom Kippur) add:

Zochrenu Lechayim. Melech Chafetz

זָכְרֵנוּ לְחַיִּים. מֶלֶךְ חָפֵץ

Bachayim. Katevenu Besefer Chayim.

בַּחַיִּים. כָּתְבֵנוּ בְּסֵפֶר חַיִּים.

Lema'anach Elohim Chayim.

לְמַעַנְךָ אֱלֹהִים חַיִּים.

Remember us to life, King Who delights in life; inscribe us in the book of life for
Your sake, Oh living God.

Bow at "Baruch Attah" / Blessed are You. Raise up at Adonai / Hashem.

Melech Ozeir Umoshia	מֶלֶךְ עוֹזֵר וּמוֹשִׁיעַ
Umagen. Baruch Attah Adonai	וּמָגֵן: בָּרוּךְ אַתָּה יְהֹוָה
Magen Avraham.	מָגֵן אַבְרָהָם:

King, Supporter, and Savior and Shield. Blessed are You, Hashem, Shield of Avraham.

Gevurot / Powers

We [in Yisrael] begin to say "Mashiv Haruach" in the second blessing of the Amidah from the Musaf [Additional] Service of the last day of Sukkot, and conclude at the Musaf [Additional] Service of the first day of Pesach. On the first day of Pesach the congregation still says it in the Musaf Service, but the Reader stops saying it then. In lands outside of Yisrael, [in the Birkhat HaShanim / Blessing for the Years,] we begin to pray for rain in the Arvit (Evening) Service of the sixtieth day after the New Moon of Tishrei, and in Yisrael we begin to say it in the evening of the seventh day of Cheshvan, and it is said until the Afternoon Service on the day preceding the first day of Passover. If one prayed for rain in the summer, or if one omitted to pray for it in the winter, he must repeat the Amidah again. If one said "Morid Hageshem" in the summer time, he must repeat again from the beginning of the blessing. If he already concluded the blessing, he must read the entire Amidah again. Likewise in the winter, if he omitted it, he must begin all over again. (SA, OC 117)

Attah Gibor Le'olam Adonai.	אַתָּה גִבּוֹר לְעוֹלָם אֲדֹנָי.
Mechayeh Meitim Attah. Rav	מְחַיֶּה מֵתִים אַתָּה. רַב
Lehoshia.	לְהוֹשִׁיעַ.

You, Hashem, are mighty forever; You revive the dead; You are powerful to save.

B'ketz: Morid Hatal.	בקיץ: מוֹרִיד הַטָּל.
B'choref: Mashiv Haruach Umorid	בחורף: מַשִּׁיב הָרוּחַ וּמוֹרִיד
Hageshem.	הַגָּשֶׁם.

In summer: You cause the dew to fall.

In winter: You cause the wind to blow and the rain to fall.

Mechalkel Chayim Bechesed.	מְכַלְכֵּל חַיִּים בְּחֶסֶד.
Mechayeh Meitim Berachamim	מְחַיֶּה מֵתִים בְּרַחֲמִים

Rabim. Somech Nofelim. Verofei	רַבִּים. סוֹמֵךְ נוֹפְלִים. וְרוֹפֵא
Cholim. Umatir Asurim.	חוֹלִים. וּמַתִּיר אֲסוּרִים.
Umekayem Emunato Lishenei	וּמְקַיֵּם אֱמוּנָתוֹ לִישֵׁנֵי
Afar. Mi Chamocha Ba'al	עָפָר. מִי כָמוֹךְ בַּעַל
Gevurot. Umi Domeh Lach.	גְּבוּרוֹת. וּמִי דוֹמֶה לָּךְ.
Melech Memit Umechayeh	מֶלֶךְ מֵמִית וּמְחַיֶּה
Umatzmiach Yeshu'ah.	וּמַצְמִיחַ יְשׁוּעָה.

You sustain the living with kindness, and revive the dead with great mercy; You support all who fall, and heal the sick; You set the captives free, and keep faith with those who sleep in the dust. Who is like You, Master of power? Who resembles You, Oh King? You bring death and restore life, and cause salvation to flourish.

During the 10 days of repentance (Rosh Hashanah to Yom Kippur) add:

Mi Chamocha Av Harachaman. Zocher	מִי כָמוֹךְ אָב הָרַחֲמָן. זוֹכֵר
Yetzurav Berachamim Lechayim.	יְצוּרָיו בְּרַחֲמִים לְחַיִּים.

Who is like You, merciful Father? In mercy You remember Your creatures to life.

Vene'eman Attah Lehachayot	וְנֶאֱמָן אַתָּה לְהַחֲיוֹת
Meitim. Baruch Attah Adonai	מֵתִים: בָּרוּךְ אַתָּה יְהֹוָה
Mechayeh Hameitim.	מְחַיֵּה הַמֵּתִים:

And You are faithful to revive the dead. Blessed are You, Hashem, Who revives the dead.

Kedushat HaShem / Holiness of the Name

Attah Kadosh Veshimcha	אַתָּה קָדוֹשׁ וְשִׁמְךָ
Kadosh. Ukedoshim Bechol-	קָדוֹשׁ. וּקְדוֹשִׁים בְּכָל-
Yom Yehalelucha Selah. Baruch	יוֹם יְהַלְלוּךָ סֶלָה: בָּרוּךְ
Attah Adonai Ha' El Hakadosh.	אַתָּה יְהֹוָה הָאֵל הַקָּדוֹשׁ:

You are holy and Your name is holy, and the holy-ones will praise
You every day, selah. Blessed are You, Hashem, The Holy God.

During the 10 days of repentance (Rosh Hashanah to Yom Kippur) say:

Hamelech Hakadosh.   הַמֶּלֶךְ הַקָּדוֹשׁ:

The Holy King.

If one is unsure or forgot if they said, repeat the Amidah. If it was immediately said after, it is fulfilled.

Binah / Understanding

Attah Chonen Le'adam Da'at   אַתָּה חוֹנֵן לְאָדָם דַּעַת

Umlamed Le'enosh Binah.   וּמְלַמֵּד לֶאֱנוֹשׁ בִּינָה.

You favor man with knowledge, and teach mortals understanding.

On Motza'ei Shabbat the following is added:

אַתָּה חוֹנַנְתָּנוּ יְהֹוָה אֱלֹהֵינוּ מַדָּע וְהַשְׂכֵּל. אַתָּה אָמַרְתָּ לְהַבְדִּיל בֵּין קֹדֶשׁ
לְחֹל וּבֵין אוֹר לְחֹשֶׁךְ וּבֵין יִשְׂרָאֵל לָעַמִּים. וּבֵין יוֹם הַשְּׁבִיעִי לְשֵׁשֶׁת יְמֵי
הַמַּעֲשֶׂה. כְּשֵׁם שֶׁהִבְדַּלְתָּנוּ יְהֹוָה אֱלֹהֵינוּ מֵעַמֵּי הָאֲרָצוֹת וּמִמִּשְׁפְּחוֹת
הָאֲדָמָה. כָּךְ פְּדֵנוּ וְהַצִּילֵנוּ מִשָּׂטָן רָע וּמִפֶּגַע רָע. וּמִכָּל גְּזֵרוֹת קָשׁוֹת וְרָעוֹת
הַמִּתְרַגְּשׁוֹת לָבֹא בָּעוֹלָם.

Attah Chonantanu Adonai Eloheinu Madda Vehaskel. Attah Amarta Lehavdil Bein
Kodesh Lechol Uvein Or Lechoshech Uvein Yisra'el La'ammim. Uvein Yom
Hashevi'i Lesheshet Yemei Hama'aseh. Keshem Shehivdaltanu Adonai Eloheinu
Me'ammei Ha'aratzot Umimishpechot Ha'adamah. Kach Pedenu Vehatzileinu
Misatan Ra Umipega Ra. Umikol Gezerot Kashot Vera'ot Hamitraggeshot Lavo
Va'olam.

You have endowed us, Hashem, our God, with knowledge and understanding; You
said to separate between the holy and the common; between light and darkness;
between Yisrael and other nations; and between the seventh day and the six days
of labor. And as You have separated us, Hashem our God, from the peoples of the
lands, and from the families of the earth; so redeem us and deliver us from the evil
adversary, evil occurrences, and from all severe and hurtful decrees, and evil things
which may come to the world.

Vechanenu Me'ltecha	וְחָנֵּנוּ מֵאִתְּךָ
Chochmah Binah Vada'at.	חָכְמָה בִּינָה וָדָעַת
Baruch Attah Adonai Chonen	בָּרוּךְ אַתָּה יְהַוֹה חוֹנֵן
Hada'at.	הַדָּעַת:

Graciously grant us wisdom, understanding and knowledge from
You. Blessed are You, Hashem, gracious Giver of knowledge.

Teshuvah / Repentance

Hashiveinu Avinu Letoratecha.	הֲשִׁיבֵנוּ אָבִינוּ לְתוֹרָתֶךָ.
Vekarevenu Malkeinu	וְקָרְבֵנוּ מַלְכֵּנוּ
La'avodatecha. Vehachazirenu	לַעֲבוֹדָתֶךָ. וְהַחֲזִירֵנוּ
Bitshuvah Shelemah Lefaneicha.	בִּתְשׁוּבָה שְׁלֵמָה לְפָנֶיךָ:
Baruch Attah Adonai Harotzeh	בָּרוּךְ אַתָּה יְהֶוֶה הָרוֹצֶה
Bitshuvah.	בִּתְשׁוּבָה:

Restore us, our Father, to Your Torah; draw us near, our King, to
Your service; cause us to return in perfect repentance before You.
Blessed are You, Hashem, Who desires repentance.

Selichah / Forgiveness

Selach Lanu Avinu Ki Chatanu.	סְלַח לָנוּ אָבִינוּ כִּי חָטָאנוּ.
Mechol Lanu Malkeinu Ki	מְחֹל לָנוּ מַלְכֵּנוּ כִּי
Fasha'enu. Ki El Tov Vesalach	פָשָׁעְנוּ. כִּי אֵל טוֹב וְסַלָּח
Attah. Baruch Attah Adonai	אָתָּה: בָּרוּךְ אַתָּה יְהֶוֶה
Chanun Hamarbeh Lisloach.	חַנּוּן הַמַּרְבֶּה לִסְלֹחַ:

Forgive us, our Father, for we have sinned; pardon us, our King, for we have transgressed; for You are a good and forgiving God. Blessed are You, Hashem, Who is gracious and ever forgiving.

Ge'ulah / Redemption

Re'eh Na Ve'aneyenu. Verivah	רְאֵה נָא בְעָנְיֵנוּ. וְרִיבָה
Rivenu. Umaher Lego'aleinu	רִיבֵנוּ. וּמַהֵר לְגָאֲלֵנוּ
Ge'ulah Shelemah Lema'an	גְאוּלָה שְׁלֵמָה לְמַעַן
Shemecha. Ki El Go'el Chazak	שְׁמֶךָ. כִּי אֵל גּוֹאֵל חָזָק
Attah. Baruch Attah Adonai	אָתָּה: בָּרוּךְ אַתָּה יְהֹוָה
Go'el Yisra'el.	גּוֹאֵל יִשְׂרָאֵל:

Look upon our affliction and fight our cause; and hasten to redeem us completely for Your name's sake, for You are a strong and redeeming God. Blessed are You, Hashem, Redeemer of Yisrael.

Refuah / Healing

Refa'enu Adonai Venerafe.	רְפָאֵנוּ יְהֹוָה וְנֵרָפֵא.
Hoshi'enu Venivashe'ah. Ki	הוֹשִׁיעֵנוּ וְנִוָּשֵׁעָה. כִּי
Tehillateinu Attah. Veha'aleh	תְהִלָּתֵנוּ אָתָּה. וְהַעֲלֵה
Aruchah Umarpei Lechol-	אֲרוּכָה וּמַרְפֵּא לְכָל־
Tachalu'einu Ulechol-	תַּחֲלוּאֵינוּ וּלְכָל־
Mach'oveinu Ulechol-	מַכְאוֹבֵינוּ וּלְכָל־
Makoteinu. Ki El Rofei Rachman	מַכּוֹתֵינוּ. כִּי אֵל רוֹפֵא רַחְמָן
Vene'eman Attah. Baruch Attah	וְנֶאֱמָן אָתָּה: בָּרוּךְ אַתָּה

Adonai Rofei Cholei Ammo
Yisra'el.

יְהֹוָה רוֹפֵא חוֹלֵי עַמּוֹ
יִשְׂרָאֵל:

Heal us, Hashem, and we will be healed; save us and we will be saved; for You are our praise. And bring healing and a cure to all of our ailments and wounds; for You are the faithful and merciful God Who heals. Blessed are You, Hashem, Who heals the sick of Your people Yisrael.

Birkat HaShanim / Blessing for the Years

In Summer:

בַּקַּיִץ:

Barecheinu Adonai Eloheinu

בָּרְכֵנוּ יְהֹוָה אֱלֹהֵינוּ

Bechol-Ma'asei Yadeinu.

בְּכָל־מַעֲשֵׂי יָדֵינוּ.

Uvarech Shenateinu Betalelei

וּבָרֵךְ שְׁנָתֵנוּ בְּטַלְלֵי

Ratzon Berachah Unedavah.

רָצוֹן בְּרָכָה וּנְדָבָה.

Utehi Acharitah Chayim Vesava

וּתְהִי אַחֲרִיתָהּ חַיִּים וְשָׂבָע

Veshalom Kashanim Hatovot

וְשָׁלוֹם כַּשָּׁנִים הַטּוֹבוֹת

Livrachah. Ki El Tov Umeitiv

לִבְרָכָה. כִּי אֵל טוֹב וּמֵטִיב

Attah Umevarech Hashanim.

אַתָּה וּמְבָרֵךְ הַשָּׁנִים:

Baruch Attah Adonai Mevarech
Hashanim.

בָּרוּךְ אַתָּה יְהֹוָה מְבָרֵךְ
הַשָּׁנִים:

Bless us, our Father, in all the work of our hands, and bless our year with favoring dews of blessing and abundance. May it's result be life, plenty and satisfaction and peace like the good years which You have blessed. For You, God, are good and You do good, blessing the years. Blessed are You, Hashem Who blesses the years.

In Winter: בְּחוֹרֶף:

Barech Aleinu Adonai Eloheinu	בָּרֵךְ עָלֵינוּ יְהֹוָה אֱלֹהֵינוּ
Et-Hashanah Hazot Ve'et-Kol-	אֶת־הַשָּׁנָה הַזֹּאת וְאֶת־כָּל־
Minei Tevu'atah Letovah. Veten	מִינֵי תְבוּאָתָהּ לְטוֹבָה. וְתֵן
Tal Umatar Livrachah Al Kol-	טַל וּמָטָר לִבְרָכָה עַל כָּל־
Penei Ha'adamah. Veraveh	פְּנֵי הָאֲדָמָה. וְרַוֵּה
Penei Tevel Vesabba Et-Ha'olam	פְּנֵי תֵבֵל וְשַׂבַּע אֶת־הָעוֹלָם
Kulo Mituvach. Umalei Yadeinu	כֻּלּוֹ מִטּוּבָךְ. וּמַלֵּא יָדֵינוּ
Mibirchoteicha Ume'osher	מִבִּרְכוֹתֶיךָ וּמֵעֹשֶׁר
Mattenot Yadeicha. Shamerah	מַתְּנוֹת יָדֶיךָ. שָׁמְרָה
Vehatzilah Shanah Zo Mikol-	וְהַצִּילָה שָׁנָה זוֹ מִכָּל־
Davar Ra'. Umikal-Minei	דָּבָר רָע. וּמִכָּל־מִינֵי
Mashchit Umikal-Minei	מַשְׁחִית וּמִכָּל־מִינֵי
Fur'anut. Va'aseh Lah Tikvah	פֻּרְעָנוּת. וַעֲשֵׂה לָהּ תִּקְוָה
Tovah Ve'acharit Shalom. Chus	טוֹבָה וְאַחֲרִית שָׁלוֹם. חוּס
Verachem Aleiha Ve'al Kol-	וְרַחֵם עָלֶיהָ וְעַל כָּל־
Tevu'atah Ufeiroteiha.	תְּבוּאָתָהּ וּפֵירוֹתֶיהָ.
Uvarechah Begishmei Ratzon	וּבָרְכָהּ בְּגִשְׁמֵי רָצוֹן
Berachah Unedavah. Utehi	בְּרָכָה וּנְדָבָה. וּתְהִי
Acharitah Chayim Vesava	אַחֲרִיתָהּ חַיִּים וְשָׂבָע
Veshalom. Kashanim Hatovot	וְשָׁלוֹם. כַּשָּׁנִים הַטּוֹבוֹת
Livrachah. Ki El Tov Umeitiv	לִבְרָכָה. כִּי אֵל טוֹב וּמֵטִיב
Attah Umevarech Hashanim.	אַתָּה וּמְבָרֵךְ הַשָּׁנִים.
Baruch Attah Adonai Mevarech	בָּרוּךְ אַתָּה יְהֹוָה מְבָרֵךְ
Hashanim.	הַשָּׁנִים:

Hashem our God, bless for us this year with all its varied produce,
for good. Send dew and rain to bless the face of the entire earth,

and water the surface of the earth, and satisfy the whole world with
Your goodness. Fill our hands with Your blessings and the rich gifts
of Your hands. Guard and deliver this year from all evil, and from all
disaster and from all chaos, and make it a year of good hope and a
peaceful ending. Have pity and compassion on this year and all its
increase and fruits. Bless the year with rains of favor, blessing and
generosity, and may its end be life, satisfaction and peace, like the
good years which You have blessed. For You God, are good and You
do good, blessing the years. Blessed are You, Hashem Who blesses
the years.

Galuyot / Ingathering of Exiles

Teka Beshofar Gadol	תְּקַע בְּשׁוֹפָר גָּדוֹל
Lecheruteinu. Vesa Nes	לְחֵרוּתֵנוּ. וְשָׂא נֵס
Lekabetz Galyoteinu.	לְקַבֵּץ גָּלֻיּוֹתֵינוּ.
Vekabetzeinu Yachad Me'arba	וְקַבְּצֵנוּ יַחַד מֵאַרְבַּע
Kanfot Ha'aretz Le'artzenu.	כַּנְפוֹת הָאָרֶץ לְאַרְצֵנוּ:
Baruch Attah Adonai Mekabetz	בָּרוּךְ אַתָּה יְהֹוָה מְקַבֵּץ
Nidchei Ammo Yisra'el.	נִדְחֵי עַמּוֹ יִשְׂרָאֵל:

Sound the great shofar for our freedom; lift up the banner to bring
our exiles; And gather us together from the four corners of the earth
into our land. Blessed are You, Hashem, Who gathers the dispersed
of His people Yisrael.

Birkat HaDin / Restoration of Justice

Hashivah Shofeteinu	הָשִׁיבָה שׁוֹפְטֵינוּ

Kevarishonah. Veyo'atzeinu	כְּבָרִאשׁוֹנָה. וְיוֹעֲצֵינוּ
Kevatechillah. Vehaseir Mimenu	כְּבַתְּחִלָּה. וְהָסֵר מִמֶּנּוּ
Yagon Va'anachah. Umeloch	יָגוֹן וַאֲנָחָה. וּמְלוֹךְ
Aleinu Meheirah Attah Adonai	עָלֵינוּ מְהֵרָה אַתָּה יְהֹוָה
Levadecha. Bechesed	לְבַדְּךָ. בְּחֶסֶד
Uverachamim. Betzedek	וּבְרַחֲמִים. בְּצֶדֶק
Uvemishpat. Baruch Attah	וּבְמִשְׁפָּט: בָּרוּךְ אַתָּה
Adonai Melech Ohev Tzedakah	יֹהוָוֹהוּ מֶלֶךְ אוֹהֵב צְדָקָה
Umishpat.	וּמִשְׁפָּט:

Restore our judges as at first, and our counselors as at the beginning; remove from us sorrow and sighing; reign over us speedily, Hashem, You alone in kindness and mercy; and with righteousness and with justice. Blessed are You, Hashem, King Who loves righteousness and justice.

During the 10 days of repentance (Rosh Hashanah to Yom Kippur) say:

Hamelech Hamishpat.	הַמֶּלֶךְ הַמִּשְׁפָּט:

The King, The Judge.

Birkat HaMinim / Blessing Against the Heretics

Laminim Velamalshinim Al-Tehi	לַמִּינִים וְלַמַּלְשִׁינִים אַל־תְּהִי
Tikvah. Vechol-Hazeidim Kerega	תִּקְוָה. וְכָל־הַזֵּדִים כְּרֶגַע
Yovedu. Vechol-'Oyeveicha	יֹאבֵדוּ. וְכָל־אֹיְבֶיךָ
Vechol-Sone'eicha Meheirah	וְכָל־שׂוֹנְאֶיךָ מְהֵרָה
Yikaretu. Umalchut Harish'ah	יִכָּרֵתוּ. וּמַלְכוּת הָרִשְׁעָה
Meheirah Te'akeir Uteshaber	מְהֵרָה תְעַקֵּר וּתְשַׁבֵּר
Utechalem Vetachni'em	וּתְכַלֵּם וְתַכְנִיעֵם

Bimheirah Veyameinu. Baruch

Attah Adonai Shoveir Oyevim

Umachnia Zeidim. (Minim)

בִּמְהֵרָה בְיָמֵינוּ: בָּרוּךְ

אַתָּה יְהֹוָה שׁוֹבֵר אוֹיְבִים

וּמַכְנִיעַ זֵדִים: (מִינִים)

For the heretics and the slanderers let there be no hope, and all of the arrogant disappear in an instant. May all of Your enemies and all of those who hate You quickly be cut off, and the evil government uprooted, and broken, and humbled and subdued quickly in our days. Blessed are You, Hashem, Who breaks enemies and subdues the arrogant. (heretics)

Tzaddikim / The Righteous

Al Hatzaddikim Ve'al

Hachasidim. Ve'al She'erit

Ammecha Beit Yisra'el. Ve'al

Peleitat Beit Sofereihem. Ve'al

Gerei Hatzedek Ve'aleinu.

Yehemu Na Rachameicha.

Adonai Eloheinu. Veten Sachar

Tov Lechol-Habotechim

Beshimcha Be'emet. Vesim

Chelkenu Imahem. Ule'olam Lo

Nevosh Ki Vecha Vatachenu.

Ve'al Chasdecha Hagadol

Be'emet Nish'aneinu. Baruch

Attah Adonai Mish'an Umivtach

Latzaddikim.

עַל הַצַּדִּיקִים וְעַל

הַחֲסִידִים. וְעַל שְׁאֵרִית

עַמְּךָ בֵּית יִשְׂרָאֵל. וְעַל

פְּלֵיטַת בֵּית סוֹפְרֵיהֶם. וְעַל

גֵּרֵי הַצֶּדֶק וְעָלֵינוּ.

יֶהֱמוּ נָא רַחֲמֶיךָ.

יְהֹוָה אֱלֹהֵינוּ. וְתֵן שָׂכָר

טוֹב לְכָל־הַבּוֹטְחִים

בְּשִׁמְךָ בֶּאֱמֶת. וְשִׂים

חֶלְקֵנוּ עִמָּהֶם. וּלְעוֹלָם לֹא

נֵבוֹשׁ כִּי בְךָ בָטָחְנוּ.

וְעַל חַסְדְּךָ הַגָּדוֹל

בֶּאֱמֶת נִשְׁעָנְנוּ: בָּרוּךְ

אַתָּה יהוווהו מִשְׁעָן וּמִבְטָח

לַצַּדִּיקִים:

On the righteous and on the pious and on the remainders of Your people, the House of Yisrael, and over the remnant of their scribes; over the righteous converts and over us may Your mercy be aroused. Hashem our God, grant a good reward to all who truly trust in Your name, and place our portion among them; may we never come to shame, for in You we trust and on Your great kindness we faithfully rely. Blessed are You, Hashem, the support and trust of the righteous.

Boneh Yerushalayim / Builder of Yerushalayim

Tishkon Betoch Yerushalayim	תִּשְׁכּוֹן בְּתוֹךְ יְרוּשָׁלַיִם
Irecha Ka'asher Dibarta.	עִירְךָ כַּאֲשֶׁר דִּבַּרְתָּ.
Vechisei David Avdecha	וְכִסֵּא דָוִד עַבְדְּךָ
Meheirah Betochah Tachin.	מְהֵרָה בְּתוֹכָהּ תָּכִין.
Uveneh Otah Binyan Olam	וּבְנֵה אוֹתָהּ בִּנְיַן עוֹלָם
Bimheirah Veyameinu. Baruch	בִּמְהֵרָה בְיָמֵינוּ: בָּרוּךְ
Attah Adonai Boneh	אַתָּה יְהֹוָה בּוֹנֵה
Yerushalayim.	יְרוּשָׁלָיִם:

May Your presence dwell in Yerushalayim, Your city, as You have promised; establish soon the throne of David, Your servant, within it, And rebuild it soon, in our days, as an everlasting structure. Blessed are You, Hashem, Builder of Yerushalayim.

Birkhat David / Prayer for Davidic Reign

Et Tzemach David Avdecha	אֶת צֶמַח דָּוִד עַבְדְּךָ
Meheirah Tatzmiach. Vekarno	מְהֵרָה תַצְמִיחַ. וְקַרְנוֹ

Tarum Bishu'atecha. Ki	תָּרוּם בִּישׁוּעָתֶךָ. כִּי
Lishu'atecha Kivinu Kol-Hayom.	לִישׁוּעָתְךָ קִוִּינוּ כָּל־הַיּוֹם:
Baruch Attah Adonai Matzmiach	בָּרוּךְ אַתָּה יְהֹוָה מַצְמִיחַ
Keren Yeshu'ah.	קֶרֶן יְשׁוּעָה:

Speedily cause the offspring of Your servant David to flourish, and let his horn be exalted in Your salvation, for we hope in Your salvation every day. Blessed are You, Hashem, Who flourishes the horn of salvation.

Tefillah / Acceptance of Prayer

Shema Koleinu. Adonai	שְׁמַע קוֹלֵנוּ. יְהֹוָה
Eloheinu. Av Harachaman.	אֱלֹהֵינוּ. אָב הָרַחֲמָן.
Rachem Aleinu. Vekabel	רַחֵם עָלֵינוּ. וְקַבֵּל
Berachamim Uveratzon Et-	בְּרַחֲמִים וּבְרָצוֹן אֶת־
Tefillateinu. Ki El Shome'ah	תְּפִלָּתֵנוּ. כִּי אֵל שׁוֹמֵעַ
Tefillot Vetachanunim Attah.	תְּפִלּוֹת וְתַחֲנוּנִים אָתָּה.
Umilfaneicha Malkeinu. Reikam	וּמִלְּפָנֶיךָ מַלְכֵּנוּ. רֵיקָם
Al-Teshivenu. Chonenu	אַל־תְּשִׁיבֵנוּ. חָנֵּנוּ
Va'aneinu Ushema Tefillateinu.	וַעֲנֵנוּ וּשְׁמַע תְּפִלָּתֵנוּ. כִּי אַתָּה
Ki Attah Shome'ah Tefillat Kol-	שׁוֹמֵעַ תְּפִלַּת כָּל־
Peh. Baruch Attah Adonai	פֶּה: בָּרוּךְ אַתָּה יְהֹוָה
Shome'ah Tefillah.	שׁוֹמֵעַ תְּפִלָּה:

Hear our voice, Hashem our God. Merciful Father, have compassion upon us. And accept our prayers with mercy and favor, for You are God Who hears to prayers and supplications. And from before You, our King, do not leave us empty-handed, but be gracious to us and hear our prayers. For You hear the prayer of every mouth. Blessed are You, Hashem Who hears prayer.

Avodah / Temple Service

Retzeh Adonai Eloheinu	רְצֵה יְהֹוָה אֱלֹהֵינוּ
Be'ammecha Yisra'el Velitfilatam	בְּעַמְּךָ יִשְׂרָאֵל וְלִתְפִלָּתָם
She'eh. Vehasheiv Ha'avodah	שְׁעֵה. וְהָשֵׁב הָעֲבוֹדָה
Lidvir Beitecha. Ve'ishei Yisra'el	לִדְבִיר בֵּיתֶךָ. וְאִשֵּׁי יִשְׂרָאֵל
Utefilatam. Meheirah Be'ahavah	וּתְפִלָּתָם. מְהֵרָה בְּאַהֲבָה
Tekabel Beratzon. Utehi	תְקַבֵּל בְּרָצוֹן. וּתְהִי
Leratzon Tamid Avodat Yisra'el	לְרָצוֹן תָּמִיד עֲבוֹדַת יִשְׂרָאֵל
Ammecha.	עַמֶּךָ:

Be favorable, Hashem our God, on Your people Yisrael and regard their prayers. And the service to the Sanctuary of Your House, and the fire offerings of Yisrael, and their prayers accept soon with love. And may the service of Your people, Yisrael, always be favorable.

On Rosh Chodesh and Chol HaMoed Passover and Sukkot say:

Ya'aleh Veyavo

אֱלֹהֵינוּ וֵאלֹהֵי אֲבוֹתֵינוּ. יַעֲלֶה וְיָבֹא. וְיַגִּיעַ וְיֵרָאֶה. וְיֵרָצֶה וְיִשָּׁמַע. וְיִפָּקֵד וְיִזָּכֵר. זִכְרוֹנֵנוּ וְזִכְרוֹן אֲבוֹתֵינוּ. זִכְרוֹן יְרוּשָׁלַיִם עִירָךְ. וְזִכְרוֹן מָשִׁיחַ בֶּן־דָּוִד עַבְדָּךְ. וְזִכְרוֹן כָּל־עַמְּךָ בֵּית יִשְׂרָאֵל לְפָנֶיךָ. לִפְלֵיטָה. לְטוֹבָה. לְחֵן. לְחֶסֶד וּלְרַחֲמִים. לְחַיִּים טוֹבִים וּלְשָׁלוֹם. בְּיוֹם:

Eloheinu Velohei Avoteinu. Ya'aleh Veyavo. Veyagia Veyera'eh. Veyeratzeh Veyishama'. Veyipaked Veyizacher. Zichronenu Vezichron Avoteinu. Zichron Yerushalayim Irach. Vezichron Mashiach Ben-David Avdach. Vezichron Kol-'Ammecha Beit Yisra'el Lefaneicha. Lifleitah. Letovah. Lechein. Lechesed Ulerachamim. Lechayim Tovim Uleshalom. Beyom:

Our God, and God of our fathers, may it rise, and come, arrive, appear, find favor, and be heard, and be considered, and be remembered our remembrance and the remembrance of our fathers, Yerushalayim Your city, the remembrance of Messiah ben David Your servant, and the remembrance of all Your people of the House of Yisrael before You for deliverance, for good favor, for kindness and mercy, for good life and for peace. On this day of:

On Rosh Chodesh:

רֹאשׁ חֹדֶשׁ הַזֶּה.

Rosh Chodesh Hazeh.

Rosh Chodesh (New Moon).

On Pesach:

חַג הַמַּצּוֹת הַזֶּה. בְּיוֹם מִקְרָא קֹדֶשׁ הַזֶּה.

Chag Hamatzot Hazeh. Beyom Mikra Kodesh Hazeh.

The Festival of Matzot. on this day of holy convocation.

On Sukkot:

חַג הַסֻּכּוֹת הַזֶּה. בְּיוֹם מִקְרָא קֹדֶשׁ הַזֶּה.

Chag Hasukkot Hazeh. Beyom Mikra Kodesh Hazeh.

The Festival of Sukkot. on this day of holy convocation.

לְרַחֵם בּוֹ עָלֵינוּ וּלְהוֹשִׁיעֵנוּ. זָכְרֵנוּ יְהוָה אֱלֹהֵינוּ בּוֹ לְטוֹבָה. וּפָקְדֵנוּ בּוֹ
לִבְרָכָה. וְהוֹשִׁיעֵנוּ בוֹ לְחַיִּים טוֹבִים. בִּדְבַר יְשׁוּעָה וְרַחֲמִים. חוּס וְחָנֵּנוּ.
וַחֲמוֹל וְרַחֵם עָלֵינוּ. וְהוֹשִׁיעֵנוּ כִּי אֵלֶיךָ עֵינֵינוּ. כִּי אֵל מֶלֶךְ חַנּוּן וְרַחוּם אָתָּה:

Lerachem Bo Aleinu Ulehoshi'enu. Zochrenu Adonai Eloheinu Bo Letovah.
Ufokdenu Vo Livrachah. Vehoshi'enu Vo Lechayim Tovim. Bidvar Yeshu'ah
Verachamim. Chus Vechanenu. Vachamol Verachem Aleinu. Vehoshi'enu Ki Eleicha
Eineinu. Ki El Melech Chanun Verachum Attah.

to have mercy upon us and save us. Remember us, Hashem our God, on it for good.
Be mindful of us on it for blessing and save us on it for a life of good. With the
promise of salvation and mercy, show us pity, and be gracious to us and have
compassion and mercy on us and save us. For our eyes are lifted towards You, for
You, God, are a gracious and merciful King.

Attah Berachameicha Harabim.	וְאַתָּה בְּרַחֲמֶיךָ הָרַבִּים.
Tachpotz Banu Vetirtzenu.	תַּחְפֹּץ בָּנוּ וְתִרְצֵנוּ.
Vetechezeinah Eineinu	וְתֶחֱזֶינָה עֵינֵינוּ
Beshuvecha Letziyon	בְּשׁוּבְךָ לְצִיּוֹן
Berachamim. Baruch Attah	בְּרַחֲמִים: בָּרוּךְ אַתָּה
Adonai Hamachazir Shechinato	יְהוָה הַמַּחֲזִיר שְׁכִינָתוֹ
Letziyon.	לְצִיּוֹן.

And You, in Your abundant mercy, delight in us, and be favorable to
us, so that our eyes may witness Your return to Tziyon with mercy.

Blessed are You, Hashem Who returns His Presence to Tziyon.

Hoda'ah (Modim) / Thanksgiving

On Saying "Modim" / "We are Thankful" One Bows and begins to rise after "Adonai" / "Hashem".

Modim Anachnu Lach.	מוֹדִים אֲנַחְנוּ לָךְ.
She'attah Hu Adonai Eloheinu	שָׁאַתָּה הוּא יְהֹוָה אֱלֹהֵינוּ
Velohei Avoteinu Le'olam Va'ed.	וֵאלֹהֵי אֲבוֹתֵינוּ לְעוֹלָם וָעֶד.
Tzurenu Tzur Chayeinu	צוּרֵנוּ צוּר חַיֵּינוּ
Umagen Yish'enu Attah Hu.	וּמָגֵן יִשְׁעֵנוּ אַתָּה הוּא.
Ledor Vador Nodeh Lecha	לְדוֹר וָדוֹר נוֹדֶה לְּךְ
Unsapeir Tehilatecha. Al	וּנְסַפֵּר תְּהִלָּתֶךָ. עַל
Chayeinu Hamesurim	חַיֵּינוּ הַמְסוּרִים
Beyadecha. Ve'al Nishmoteinu	בְּיָדֶךָ. וְעַל נִשְׁמוֹתֵינוּ
Hapekudot Lach. Ve'al Niseicha	הַפְּקוּדוֹת לָךְ. וְעַל נִסֶּיךְ
Shebechol-Yom Imanu. Ve'al	שֶׁבְּכָל־יוֹם עִמָּנוּ. וְעַל
Nifle'oteicha Vetovoteicha	נִפְלְאוֹתֶיךָ וְטוֹבוֹתֶיךָ
Shebechol-'Et. Erev Vavoker	שֶׁבְּכָל־עֵת. עֶרֶב וָבֹקֶר
Vetzaharayim. Hatov. Ki Lo	וְצָהֳרָיִם. הַטּוֹב. כִּי לֹא
Chalu Rachameicha.	כָלוּ רַחֲמֶיךָ.
Hamerachem. Ki Lo Tamu	הַמְרַחֵם. כִּי לֹא תַמּוּ
Chasadeicha. Ki Me'olam	חֲסָדֶיךָ. כִּי מֵעוֹלָם
Kivinu Lach.	קִוִּינוּ לָךְ:

We are thankful to You, Hashem our God and the God of our fathers, forever. You are our strength and Rock of our life and the Shield of our salvation. In every generation we will thank You and recount Your praise for our lives which are given into Your hand, for our souls which are placed in Your care, and for Your miracles which are daily with us, and for Your wonders and goodness—evening, morning and noon. The Beneficent One, for Your mercies never end, Merciful One, for Your kindness has never ceased, for we have always placed our hope in You.

Modim Derabbanan

During the repetition, this is to be recited softly while the Chazan reads the Modim. Still bow at Modim as before.

מוֹדִים אֲנַחְנוּ לָךְ. שָׁאַתָּה הוּא יְהֹוָה אֱלֹהֵינוּ וֵאלֹהֵי אֲבוֹתֵינוּ. אֱלֹהֵי כָל בָּשָׂר. יוֹצְרֵנוּ יוֹצֵר בְּרֵאשִׁית. בְּרָכוֹת וְהוֹדָאוֹת לְשִׁמְךָ הַגָּדוֹל וְהַקָּדוֹשׁ. עַל שֶׁהֶחֱיִיתָנוּ וְקִיַּמְתָּנוּ. כֵּן תְּחַיֵּנוּ וּתְחָנֵּנוּ וְתֶאֱסוֹף גָּלְיוֹתֵינוּ לְחַצְרוֹת קָדְשֶׁךָ. לִשְׁמֹר חֻקֶּיךָ וְלַעֲשׂוֹת רְצוֹנֶךָ וּלְעָבְדְּךָ בְּלֵבָב שָׁלֵם. עַל שֶׁאֲנַחְנוּ מוֹדִים לָךְ. בָּרוּךְ אֵל הַהוֹדָאוֹת.

Modim Anachnu Lach. She'attah Hu Adonai Eloheinu Velohei Avoteinu. Elohei Chol Basar. Yotzreinu Yotzer Bereshit. Berachot Vehoda'ot Leshimcha Hagadol Vehakadosh. Al Shehecheyitanu Vekiyamtanu. Ken Techayeinu Utechanenu Vete'esof Galyoteinu Lechatzrot Kodshecha. Lishmor Chukkeicha Vela'asot Retzonecha Ule'avedecha Velevav Shalem. Al She'anachnu Modim Lach. Baruch El Hahoda'ot.

We are thankful to You, Hashem our God and the God of our fathers. God of all flesh, our Creator and Former of Creation, blessings and thanks to Your great and holy name, for You have kept us alive and sustained us; may You always grant us life and be gracious to us. And gather our exiles to Your holy courtyards to observe Your statutes, and to do Your will, and to serve You with a perfect heart. For this we thank You. Blessed is God of thanksgivings.

Al HaNissim

On Purim and Hanukkah an extra prayer is added here:

עַל הַנִּסִּים וְעַל הַפֻּרְקָן וְעַל הַגְּבוּרוֹת וְעַל הַתְּשׁוּעוֹת וְעַל הַנִּפְלָאוֹת וְעַל הַנֶּחָמוֹת שֶׁעָשִׂיתָ לַאֲבוֹתֵינוּ בַּיָּמִים הָהֵם בַּזְּמַן הַזֶּה:

Al Hanissim Ve'al Hapurkan Ve'al Hagevurot Ve'al Hateshu'ot Ve'al Hanifla'ot Ve'al Hanechamot She'asita La'avoteinu Bayamim Hahem Bazman Hazeh.

For the miracles, and for the triumphant liberation, and the mighty works, and for the deliverances, and for the wonders, and for the consolations which You have done for our fathers in those days at this season:

On Hanukkah:

בִּימֵי מַתִּתְיָה בֶן־יוֹחָנָן כֹּהֵן גָּדוֹל. חַשְׁמוֹנָאִי וּבָנָיו כְּשֶׁעָמְדָה מַלְכוּת יָוָן הָרְשָׁעָה עַל עַמְּךָ יִשְׂרָאֵל. לְשַׁכְּחָם תּוֹרָתֶךָ וּלְהַעֲבִירָם מֵחֻקֵּי רְצוֹנֶךָ. וְאַתָּה בְּרַחֲמֶיךָ הָרַבִּים עָמַדְתָּ לָהֶם בְּעֵת צָרָתָם. רַבְתָּ אֶת רִיבָם. דַּנְתָּ אֶת דִּינָם. נָקַמְתָּ אֶת נִקְמָתָם. מָסַרְתָּ גִבּוֹרִים בְּיַד חַלָּשִׁים. וְרַבִּים בְּיַד מְעַטִּים. וּרְשָׁעִים בְּיַד צַדִּיקִים. וּטְמֵאִים בְּיַד טְהוֹרִים. וְזֵדִים בְּיַד עוֹסְקֵי תוֹרָתֶךָ. לְךָ עָשִׂיתָ שֵׁם גָּדוֹל וְקָדוֹשׁ בְּעוֹלָמֶךָ. וּלְעַמְּךָ יִשְׂרָאֵל עָשִׂיתָ תְּשׁוּעָה גְדוֹלָה וּפֻרְקָן כְּהַיּוֹם הַזֶּה. וְאַחַר כָּךְ בָּאוּ בָנֶיךָ לִדְבִיר בֵּיתֶךָ. וּפִנּוּ אֶת־הֵיכָלֶךָ. וְטִהֲרוּ אֶת־מִקְדָּשֶׁךָ. וְהִדְלִיקוּ נֵרוֹת בְּחַצְרוֹת קָדְשֶׁךָ. וְקָבְעוּ שְׁמוֹנַת יְמֵי חֲנֻכָּה אֵלּוּ בְּהַלֵּל וּבְהוֹדָאָה. וְעָשִׂיתָ עִמָּהֶם נִסִּים וְנִפְלָאוֹת וְנוֹדֶה לְשִׁמְךָ הַגָּדוֹל סֶלָה:

Bimei Mattityah Ven-Yochanan Kohen Gadol. Chashmona'i Uvanav Keshe'amedah Malchut Yavan Haresha'ah Al Ammecha Yisra'el. Leshakecham Toratach Uleha'aviram Mechukkei Retzonach. Ve'attah Berachameicha Harabim Amadta Lahem Be'et Tzaratam. Ravta Et Rivam. Danta Et Dinam. Nakamta Et Nikmatam. Masarta Giborim Beyad Chalashim. Verabim Beyad Me'atim. Uresha'im Beyad Tzaddikim. Uteme'im Beyad Tehorim. Vezeidim Beyad Osekei Toratecha. Lecha Asita Shem Gadol Vekadosh Be'olamach. Ule'ammecha Yisra'el Asita Teshu'ah Gedolah Ufurkan Kehayom Hazeh. Ve'achar Kach Ba'u Vaneicha Lidvir Beitecha. Ufinu Et-Heichalecha. Vetiharu Et-Mikdashecha. Vehidliku Nerot Bechatzrot Kodshecha. Vekave'u Shemonat Yemei Chanukkah Elu Behallel Uvehoda'ah. Ve'asita Imahem Nissim Venifla'ot Venodeh Leshimcha Hagadol Selah.

Then in the days of Mattityahu ben-Yochanan, High Priest, the Hasmonean and his sons, when the cruel Greek power rose up against Your people, Yisrael, to make them forget Your Torah and transgress the statutes of Your will. And You, in Your great compassion, stood up for them in time of their trial to plead their cause and defend their judgment. Giving out retribution, delivered the strong into the hand of the weak, and the many into the hand of the few, and the wicked into the hand of the upright, and the impure into the hand of the pure, and tyrants into the hand of the devotees of Your Torah. You made for Yourself a great and holy name in Your world. And for Your people, Yisrael, You performed a great salvation and liberation as this very day. Then Your children came to the Sanctuary of Your House, cleared Your Temple, cleansed Your Sanctuary and kindled lights in Your courtyards, and they instituted these eight days of Hanukkah for praise and thanksgiving. And You did miracles and wonders for them, and we give thanks to Your great name, selah.

On Purim:

בִּימֵי מָרְדְּכַי וְאֶסְתֵּר בְּשׁוּשַׁן הַבִּירָה. כְּשֶׁעָמַד עֲלֵיהֶם הָמָן הָרָשָׁע. בִּקֵּשׁ לְהַשְׁמִיד לַהֲרֹג וּלְאַבֵּד אֶת־כָּל־הַיְּהוּדִים מִנַּעַר וְעַד זָקֵן טַף וְנָשִׁים בְּיוֹם אֶחָד.

בִּשְׁלשָׁה עָשָׂר לְחֹדֶשׁ שְׁנֵים עָשָׂר. הוּא חֹדֶשׁ אֲדָר. וּשְׁלָלָם לָבוֹז. וְאַתָּה בְּרַחֲמֶיךָ הָרַבִּים הֵפַרְתָּ אֶת־עֲצָתוֹ וְקִלְקַלְתָּ אֶת־מַחֲשַׁבְתּוֹ. וַהֲשֵׁבוֹתָ לּוֹ גְּמוּלוֹ בְּרֹאשׁוֹ. וְתָלוּ אוֹתוֹ וְאֶת־בָּנָיו עַל הָעֵץ. וְעָשִׂיתָ עִמָּהֶם נֵס וָפֶלֶא וְנוֹדֶה לְשִׁמְךָ הַגָּדוֹל סֶלָה:

Bimei Mordechai Ve'ester Beshushan Habirah. Keshe'amad Aleihem Haman Harasha. Bikesh Lehashmid Laharog Ule'abed Et-Kol-Hayehudim Mina'ar Ve'ad Zaken Taf Venashim Beyom Echad. Bishloshah Asar Lechodesh Sheneim Asar. Hu Chodesh Adar. Ushelalam Lavoz. Ve'attah Berachameicha Harabim Hefarta Et-'Atzato Vekilkalta Et-Machashavto. Vahasheivota Lo Gemulo Verosho. Vetalu Oto Ve'et-Banav Al Ha'etz. Ve'asita Imahem Nes Vafelei Venodeh Leshimcha Hagadol Selah.

In the days of Mordechai and Ester in Shushan, the capital, the wicked Haman rose up and sought to destroy, slay and utterly annihilate all of the Yehudim, both young and old, women and children, on one day, on the thirteenth day of the twelfth month, which is the month of Adar, and to plunder their possessions. But You in Your great mercy You broke his plan and spoiled his designs, causing them to recoil on his own head, and they hanged him and his sons on the gallows. And You did miracles and wonders for them, and we give thanks to Your great name, selah.

Ve'al Kulam Yitbarach.	וְעַל כֻּלָּם יִתְבָּרַךְ.
Veyitromam. Veyitnasse. Tamid.	וְיִתְרוֹמָם. וְיִתְנַשֵּׂא. תָּמִיד.
Shimcha Malkeinu. Le'olam	שִׁמְךָ מַלְכֵּנוּ. לְעוֹלָם
Va'ed. Vechol-Hachayim	וָעֶד. וְכָל־הַחַיִּים
Yoducha Selah.	יוֹדוּךָ סֶלָה:

For all these acts, may Your name, our King, be blessed, extolled and exalted forever. And all of the living will thank You, selah.

During the 10 days of repentance (Rosh Hashanah to Yom Kippur) say:

Uchetov Lechayim Tovim Kol Benei Veritecha.

וּכְתֹב לְחַיִּים טוֹבִים כָּל בְּנֵי בְרִיתֶךָ.

Inscribe all of Your people of the covenant for a happy life.

Bow at "Baruch Attah" / "Blessed are You". Raise up at Adonai / Hashem.

Vihalelu Vivarechu Et-Shimcha	וִיהַלְלוּ וִיבָרְכוּ אֶת־שִׁמְךָ
Hagadol Be'emet Le'olam Ki Tov.	הַגָּדוֹל בֶּאֱמֶת לְעוֹלָם כִּי טוֹב.
Ha'el Yeshu'ateinu Ve'ezrateinu	הָאֵל יְשׁוּעָתֵנוּ וְעֶזְרָתֵנוּ

Selah. Ha'el Hatov. Baruch Attah
Adonai Hatov Shimcha Ulecha
Na'eh Lehodot.

סֶלָה. הָאֵל הַטּוֹב: בָּרוּךְ אַתָּה
יְהֹוָה הַטּוֹב שִׁמְךָ וּלְךָ
נָאֶה לְהוֹדוֹת:

And they will praise and bless Your great and good name sincerely, forever. For You are good, the God of our salvation and our help forever, the Good God. Blessed are You, Hashem, Your name is good and to You it is good to give thanks.

Sim Shalom / Grant Peace

Sim Shalom Tovah Uverachah.

שִׂים שָׁלוֹם טוֹבָה וּבְרָכָה.

Chayim Chein Vachesed

חַיִּים חֵן וָחֶסֶד

Verachamim. Aleinu Ve'al Kol-

וְרַחֲמִים. עָלֵינוּ וְעַל כָּל־

Yisra'el Ammecha. Uvarecheinu

יִשְׂרָאֵל עַמֶּךָ. וּבָרְכֵנוּ

Avinu Kulanu Ke'echad Be'or

אָבִינוּ כֻּלָּנוּ כְּאֶחָד בְּאוֹר

Paneicha. Ki Ve'or Paneicha

פָּנֶיךָ. כִּי בְאוֹר פָּנֶיךָ

Natata Lanu Adonai Eloheinu

נָתַתָּ לָנוּ יְהֹוָה אֱלֹהֵינוּ

Torah Vechayim. Ahavah

תּוֹרָה וְחַיִּים. אַהֲבָה

Vachesed. Tzedakah

וָחֶסֶד. צְדָקָה

Verachamim. Berachah

וְרַחֲמִים. בְּרָכָה

Veshalom. Vetov Be'eineicha

וְשָׁלוֹם. וְטוֹב בְּעֵינֶיךָ

Levarecheinu Ulevarech Et-

לְבָרְכֵנוּ וּלְבָרֵךְ אֶת־

Kol-'Ammecha Yisra'el. Berov

כָּל־עַמְּךָ יִשְׂרָאֵל. בְּרֹב

Oz Veshalom.

עֹז וְשָׁלוֹם:

Grant peace, goodness and blessing, a life of grace, and kindness and mercy, to us and to all Yisrael, Your people. And bless us, our Father, all as one with the light of Your countenance; for with the light of Your countenance You have given us, Hashem our God, a Torah and life, love and kindness, righteousness and mercy, blessing and peace. May it be good in Your eyes to bless us and bless all of Your people, Yisrael, with abundant strength and peace.

During the 10 days of repentance (Rosh Hashanah to Yom Kippur) say:

Uvesefer Chayim. Berachah Veshalom.	וּבְסֵפֶר חַיִּים. בְּרָכָה וְשָׁלוֹם.
Ufarnasah Tovah Vishu'ah	וּפַרְנָסָה טוֹבָה וִישׁוּעָה
Venechamah. Ugezerot Tovot. Nizacher	וְנֶחָמָה. וּגְזֵרוֹת טוֹבוֹת. נִזָּכֵר
Venikkatev Lefaneicha. Anachnu	וְנִכָּתֵב לְפָנֶיךָ. אֲנַחְנוּ
Vechol Ammecha Beit Yisra'el.	וְכָל עַמְּךָ בֵּית יִשְׂרָאֵל.
Lechayim Tovim Uleshalom.	לְחַיִּים טוֹבִים וּלְשָׁלוֹם.

May we and all Yisrael Your people be remembered and inscribed before You in the book of life and blessing, peace and prosperity, for a happy life and for peace.

Baruch Attah Adonai	בָּרוּךְ אַתָּה יהוווהו
Hamevarech Et Ammo Yisra'el	הַמְבָרֵךְ אֶת עַמּוֹ יִשְׂרָאֵל
Bashalom. Amen.	בַּשָּׁלוֹם. אָמֵן:

Blessed are You, Hashem, Who blesses His people Yisrael with peace. Amen.

Yihyu Leratzon Imrei-Fi Vehegyon Libi	יִהְיוּ לְרָצוֹן אִמְרֵי־פִי וְהֶגְיוֹן לִבִּי
Lefaneicha; Adonai Tzuri Vego'ali.	לְפָנֶיךָ יְהֹוָה צוּרִי וְגֹאֲלִי:

May the words of my mouth and the meditation of my heart find favor before You, Hashem my Rock and my Redeemer.

Elohai. Netzor Leshoni Meira	אֱלֹהַי. נְצֹר לְשׁוֹנִי מֵרָע
Vesiftotai Midaber Mirmah.	וּשְׂפָתַי מִדַּבֵּר מִרְמָה.
Velimkalelai Nafshi Tidom.	וְלִמְקַלְלַי נַפְשִׁי תִדֹּם.
Venafshi Ke'afar Lakol Tihyeh.	וְנַפְשִׁי כֶּעָפָר לַכֹּל תִּהְיֶה.
Petach Libi Betoratecha.	פְּתַח לִבִּי בְּתוֹרָתֶךָ.
Ve'acharei Mitzvoteicha Tirdof	וְאַחֲרֵי מִצְוֹתֶיךָ תִּרְדֹּף
Nafshi. Vechol-Hakamim Alai	נַפְשִׁי. וְכָל־הַקָּמִים עָלַי
Lera'ah. Meheirah Hafer	לְרָעָה. מְהֵרָה הָפֵר
Atzatam Vekalkel	עֲצָתָם וְקַלְקֵל
Machshevotam. Aseh Lema'an	מַחְשְׁבוֹתָם. עֲשֵׂה לְמַעַן
Shemach. Aseh Lema'an	שְׁמֶךָ. עֲשֵׂה לְמַעַן
Yeminach. Aseh Lema'an	יְמִינָךְ. עֲשֵׂה לְמַעַן
Toratach. Aseh Lema'an	תּוֹרָתָךְ. עֲשֵׂה לְמַעַן
Kedushatach. Lema'an	קְדֻשָּׁתָךְ. לְמַעַן
Yechaletzun Yedideicha;	יֵחָלְצוּן יְדִידֶיךָ
Hoshi'ah Yeminecha Va'Aneni.	הוֹשִׁיעָה יְמִינְךָ וַעֲנֵנִי:

My God, guard my tongue from evil, and my lips from speaking deceit. And to those who curse me may my soul be silent; and may my soul be like the dust to all. Open my heart to Your Torah, that my soul may follow after Your commandments. And all that rise to do evil against me, speedily nullify their plan, and spoil their thoughts. Do it for the sake of Your name; do it for the sake of Your right hand; do it for the sake of Your Torah, do it for the sake of Your holiness. That Your beloved may be rescued, save with Your right hand and answer me. (Ps. 60:7)

Yihyu Leratzon Imrei-Fi Vehegyon Libi
Lefaneicha; Adonai Tzuri Vego'ali.

יִהְיוּ לְרָצוֹן | אִמְרֵי־פִי וְהֶגְיוֹן לִבִּי
לְפָנֶיךָ יְהֹוָה צוּרִי וְגֹאֲלִי:

May the words of my mouth and the meditation of my heart find favor before You,
Hashem my Rock and my Redeemer.

Oseh Shalom

One bows and takes three steps backwards, while still bowing. After three steps, while still bowing
and before erecting, while saying, "Oseh Shalom Bimromav", turn one's face to the left, "Hu
[Berachamav] Ya'aseh Shalom Aleinu", turn one's face to the right; [face forward and] then bow
forward like a servant leaving his master. (SA, OC 123:1)

Oseh Shalom On the 10 Days of

Repentance: (Hashalom) Bimromav,

Hu Berachamav Ya'aseh Shalom

Aleinu, Ve'al Kol-'Ammo

Yisra'el, Ve'imru Amen.

עוֹשֶׂה שָׁלוֹם
בעשי"ת (הַשָּׁלוֹם) בִּמְרוֹמָיו.
הוּא בְּרַחֲמָיו יַעֲשֶׂה שָׁלוֹם
עָלֵינוּ. וְעַל כָּל־עַמּוֹ
יִשְׂרָאֵל. וְאִמְרוּ אָמֵן:

Creator of On the 10 Days of Repentance: (the) peace in His high places, may
He in His mercy create peace for us and for all Yisrael, and say
Amen.

Yehi Ratzon Milfaneicha Adonai
Eloheinu Velohei Avoteinu. Shetivneh
Beit Hamikdash Bimheirah Veyameinu.
Veten Chelkenu Vetoratach La'asot
Chukkei. Retzonach Ule'avedach
Belevav Shalem.

יְהִי רָצוֹן מִלְּפָנֶיךָ יְהֹוָה
אֱלֹהֵינוּ וֵאלֹהֵי אֲבוֹתֵינוּ. שֶׁתִּבְנֶה
בֵּית הַמִּקְדָּשׁ בִּמְהֵרָה בְיָמֵינוּ.
וְתֵן חֶלְקֵנוּ בְּתוֹרָתֶךָ לַעֲשׂוֹת
חֻקֵּי רְצוֹנָךְ וּלְעָבְדָךְ
בְּלֵבָב שָׁלֵם:

May it be Your will, Hashem our God and God of our fathers, that the Beit
HaMikdash be speedily rebuilt in our days, and grant us a share in Your Torah so
we may fulfill the statutes of Your will and serve You with a whole heart.

Yehi Shem

יְהִי שֵׁם יְהֹוָה מְבֹרָךְ מֵעַתָּה וְעַד־עוֹלָם: מִמִּזְרַח־שֶׁמֶשׁ עַד־מְבוֹאוֹ מְהֻלָּל שֵׁם
יְהֹוָה: רָם עַל־כָּל־גּוֹיִם | יְהֹוָה עַל הַשָּׁמַיִם כְּבוֹדוֹ: יְהֹוָה אֲדֹנֵינוּ מָה־אַדִּיר
שִׁמְךָ בְּכָל־הָאָרֶץ:

Yehi Shem Adonai Mevorach; Me'attah. Ve'ad-'Olam. Mimizrach-Shemesh Ad-
Mevo'o; Mehulal. Shem Adonai Ram Al-Chol-Goyim Adonai Al Hashamayim
Kevodo. Adonai Adoneinu; Mah-'Adir Shimcha. Bechol-Ha'aretz.

Blessed is the name of Hashem from this time forward and forever. From the rising
of the sun to it's going down, Hashem's name is to be praised. Hashem, our Lord,
How glorious is Your name in all of the earth. (Psalms 113:2-4, 8:2)

And say Hatzi-Kaddish:

> Kaddish is only recited in a minyan (ten men). אמן denotes when the congregation responds "Amen"
> together out loud. According to the Shulchan Arukh, the congregation says "Yehei Shemeh Rabba"
> to "Yitbarach" out loud together without interruption, and also that one should respond "Amen"
> after "Yitbarach." (SA, OC 55,56) This is not the common custom today. Though many are
> accustomed to answering according to their own custom, it is advised to respond in the custom of
> the one reciting to avoid not fragmenting into smaller groups. ("Lo Titgodedu" - BT, Yevamot 13b /
> SA, OC 493, Rema / MT, Avodah Zara 12:15)

יִתְגַּדַּל וְיִתְקַדַּשׁ שְׁמֵהּ רַבָּא. אמן בְּעָלְמָא דִּי בְרָא. כִרְעוּתֵהּ. וְיַמְלִיךְ
מַלְכוּתֵהּ. וְיַצְמַח פֻּרְקָנֵהּ. וִיקָרֵב מְשִׁיחֵהּ. אמן בְּחַיֵּיכוֹן וּבְיוֹמֵיכוֹן
וּבְחַיֵּי דְכָל בֵּית יִשְׂרָאֵל. בַּעֲגָלָא וּבִזְמַן קָרִיב. וְאִמְרוּ אָמֵן. אמן יְהֵא
שְׁמֵיהּ רַבָּא מְבָרַךְ לְעָלַם וּלְעָלְמֵי עָלְמַיָּא יִתְבָּרַךְ. וְיִשְׁתַּבַּח.
וְיִתְפָּאַר. וְיִתְרוֹמַם. וְיִתְנַשֵּׂא. וְיִתְהַדָּר. וְיִתְעַלֶּה. וְיִתְהַלָּל שְׁמֵהּ
דְּקֻדְשָׁא. בְּרִיךְ הוּא. אמן לְעֵלָּא מִן כָּל בִּרְכָתָא שִׁירָתָא. תֻּשְׁבְּחָתָא
וְנֶחֱמָתָא. דַּאֲמִירָן בְּעָלְמָא. וְאִמְרוּ אָמֵן. אמן

Yitgadal Veyitkadash Shemeh Rabba. Amen Be'alema Di Vera.
Kir'uteh. Veyamlich Malchuteh. Veyatzmach Purkaneh. Vikarev
Meshicheh. Amen Bechayeichon Uveyomeichon Uvechayei Dechal-
Beit Yisra'el. Ba'agala Uvizman Kariv. Ve'imru Amen. Amen Yehei
Shemeh Rabba Mevarach Le'alam Ule'alemei Alemaya Yitbarach.
Veyishtabach. Veyitpa'ar. Veyitromam. Veyitnasse. Veyit'hadar.
Veyit'aleh. Veyit'hallal Shemeh Dekudsha. Berich Hu. Amen Le'ella
Min Kol Birchata Shirata. Tushbechata Venechemata. Da'amiran
Be'alema. Ve'imru Amen. Amen

Glorified and sanctified be God's great name ^{Amen} throughout the world which He has created according to His will. May He establish His kingdom, hastening His salvation and the coming of His Messiah, ^{Amen}, in your lifetime and during your days, and within the life of the entire House of Yisrael, speedily and soon; and say, Amen. ^{Amen} May His great name be blessed forever and to all eternity. Blessed and praised, glorified and exalted, extolled and honored, adored and lauded is the name of the Holy One, blessed is He, ^{Amen} Beyond all the blessings and hymns, praises and consolations that are ever spoken in the world; and say, Amen. ^{Amen}

Some say:

הריני מכין עצמי לקבל אור תוספת קדושת שבת לימי החול, ואתקדש בעזרת השם יתברך בימי החול מקדשת השבת כמו שצוונו יהוה אלהינו בתורתו הקדושה והתקדשתם והייתם קדושים. ויהי רצון מלפניך יהוה אלהי ואלהי אבותי שיעלה לפניך כאלו כונתי בכל הכונות הראויות לכוין בזה:

שׁוּבָה יְהֹוָה עַד־מָתָי וְהִנָּחֵם עַל־עֲבָדֶיךָ: שַׂבְּעֵנוּ בַבֹּקֶר חַסְדֶּךָ וּנְרַנְּנָה וְנִשְׂמְחָה בְּכָל־יָמֵינוּ: שַׂמְּחֵנוּ כִּימוֹת עִנִּיתָנוּ שְׁנוֹת רָאִינוּ רָעָה: יֵרָאֶה אֶל־עֲבָדֶיךָ פָעֳלֶךָ וַהֲדָרְךָ עַל־בְּנֵיהֶם: וִיהִי נֹעַם אֲדֹנָי אֱלֹהֵינוּ עָלֵינוּ וּמַעֲשֵׂה יָדֵינוּ כּוֹנְנָה עָלֵינוּ וּמַעֲשֵׂה יָדֵינוּ כּוֹנְנֵהוּ:

Shuvah Adonai Ad-Matai; Vehinachem. Al-'Avadeicha. Sabe'einu
Vaboker Chasdecha; Uneranenah Venismechah. Bechol-Yameinu.
Samecheinu Kimot Initanu; Shenot. Ra'inu Ra'ah. Yera'eh
El-'Avadeicha Fo'olecha; Vahadarecha. Al-Beneihem. Vihi No'am
Adonai Eloheinu. Aleinu Uma'aseh Yadeinu Konenah Aleinu;
Uma'aseh Yadeinu. Konenehu.

Return, Hashem; how long? Have compassion on Your servants. Satisfy us in the morning with Your mercy; That we may rejoice and

be glad all our days. Make us glad according to the days that You
have afflicted us, According to the years that we have seen evil. Let
Your work appear to Your servants, And Your glory upon their
children. And may the graciousness of Hashem our God be on us;
Establish also upon us the work of our hands; and the work of our
hands, establish it. (Psalms 90:13-17)

Psalms 91

יֹשֵׁב בְּסֵתֶר עֶלְיוֹן בְּצֵל שַׁדַּי יִתְלוֹנָן: אֹמַר לַיהוָה מַחְסִי וּמְצוּדָתִי
אֱלֹהַי אֶבְטַח־בּוֹ: כִּי הוּא יַצִּילְךָ מִפַּח יָקוּשׁ מִדֶּבֶר הַוּוֹת: בְּאֶבְרָתוֹ
יָסֶךְ לָךְ וְתַחַת־כְּנָפָיו תֶּחְסֶה צִנָּה וְסֹחֵרָה אֲמִתּוֹ: לֹא־תִירָא מִפַּחַד
לַיְלָה מֵחֵץ יָעוּף יוֹמָם: מִדֶּבֶר בָּאֹפֶל יַהֲלֹךְ מִקֶּטֶב יָשׁוּד צָהֳרָיִם:
יִפֹּל מִצִּדְּךָ אֶלֶף וּרְבָבָה מִימִינֶךָ אֵלֶיךָ לֹא יִגָּשׁ: רַק בְּעֵינֶיךָ תַבִּיט
וְשִׁלֻּמַת רְשָׁעִים תִּרְאֶה: כִּי־אַתָּה יְהוָה מַחְסִי עֶלְיוֹן שַׂמְתָּ מְעוֹנֶךָ:
לֹא־תְאֻנֶּה אֵלֶיךָ רָעָה וְנֶגַע לֹא־יִקְרַב בְּאָהֳלֶךָ: כִּי מַלְאָכָיו יְצַוֶּה־לָּךְ
לִשְׁמָרְךָ בְּכָל־דְּרָכֶיךָ: עַל־כַּפַּיִם יִשָּׂאוּנְךָ פֶּן־תִּגֹּף בָּאֶבֶן רַגְלֶךָ:
עַל־שַׁחַל וָפֶתֶן תִּדְרֹךְ תִּרְמֹס כְּפִיר וְתַנִּין: כִּי בִי חָשַׁק וַאֲפַלְּטֵהוּ
אֲשַׂגְּבֵהוּ כִּי־יָדַע שְׁמִי: יִקְרָאֵנִי וְאֶעֱנֵהוּ עִמּוֹ־אָנֹכִי בְצָרָה אֲחַלְּצֵהוּ
וַאֲכַבְּדֵהוּ: אֹרֶךְ יָמִים אַשְׂבִּיעֵהוּ וְאַרְאֵהוּ בִּישׁוּעָתִי:

Yoshev Beseter Elyon; Betzel Shaddai. Yitlonan. Omar. L'Adonai
Machsi Umetzudati; Elohai. Evtach-Bo. Ki Hu Yatzilecha Mippach
Yakush. Midever Havot. Be'evrato Yasech Lach Vetachat-Kenafav
Techseh; Tzinah Vesocherah Amito. Lo-Tira Mipachad Lailah;
Mechetz. Ya'uf Yomam. Midever Ba'ofel Yahaloch; Miketev. Yashud
Tzohorayim. Yippol Mitzidecha Elef. Urevavah Miminecha; Eleicha.
Lo Yigash. Rak Be'eineicha Tabbit; Veshilumat Resha'im Tir'eh.
Ki-'Attah Adonai Machsi; Elyon. Samta Me'onecha. Lo-Te'uneh
Eleicha Ra'ah; Venega'. Lo-Yikrav Be'oholecha. Ki Mal'achav
Yetzaveh-Lach; Lishmorcha. Bechol-Deracheicha. Al-Kapayim
Yissa'unecha; Pen-Tiggof Ba'even Raglecha. Al-Shachal Vafeten
Tidroch; Tirmos Kefir Vetanin. Ki Vi Chashak Va'afalletehu;

Asagevehu. Ki-Yada Shemi. Yikra'eni Ve'e'enehu. Immo-'Anochi
Vetzarah; Achalletzehu. Va'achabedehu. Orech Yamim Asbi'ehu;
Ve'ar'ehu. Bishu'ati.

You that dwells in the shadow of the Most High, And abides in the
shadow of the Almighty; I will say of Hashem, Who is my refuge and
my fortress, My God, in Whom I trust, That He will deliver you from
the snare of the fowler, And from the harmful pestilence. He will
cover you with His wings, And under His wings you will take refuge;
His truth is a shield and a buckler. You will not be afraid of the terror
by night, or of the arrow that flies by day; Of the pestilence that
walks in darkness, or of the destruction that wastes at noon. A
thousand may fall at Your side, And ten thousand at Your right
hand; It will not come near you. Only with your eyes you will behold,
And see the recompense of the wicked. For you have made Hashem
your Habitation, Even the Most High, Who is my refuge. No evil will
happen to you, Neither will any plague come near to your tent. For
He will give His angels charge over you, To keep you in all your ways.
They will bear you upon their hands, Lest you dash your foot
against a stone. You will tread upon the lion and asp; The young
lion and the serpent you will trample under feet. Because he has set
his love upon Me, therefore I will deliver him; I will set him on high,
because he has known My name. He will call on Me, and I will
answer him; I will be with him in trouble; I will rescue him, and bring
him to honor. With long life I will satisfy him, And make Him behold
My salvation.

Some repeat the last line two times.

Next, **Ve'attah Kadosh** is recited. This is Uva Letziyon with the first two verses omitted. One should
be very careful to say the kedushah of Uva Letziyon with kavanah (intention). (SA, OC 132:1) It is
ideal to say this kedusha seated and with a minyan (10 men). If one says this by himself, it should be
recited like one would read from the Torah with cantillation.

Ve'attah Kadosh

Ve'attah Kadosh; Yoshev. Tehillot	וְאַתָּה קָדוֹשׁ יֹושֵׁב תְּהִלּוֹת
Yisra'el. Vekara Zeh El-Zeh	יִשְׂרָאֵל: וְקָרָא זֶה אֶל־זֶה
Ve'amar. **Kadosh Kadosh**	וְאָמַר קָדוֹשׁ	קָדוֹשׁ
Kadosh Adonai Tzeva'ot; Melo	קָדוֹשׁ יְהֹוָה צְבָאוֹת מְלֹא
Chol-Ha'aretz Kevodo.	כָל־הָאָרֶץ כְּבוֹדוֹ:
Umekabelin Dein Min Dein	וּמְקַבְּלִין דֵּין מִן דֵּין
Ve'amerin. Kaddish Bishmei	וְאָמְרִין: קַדִּישׁ בִּשְׁמֵי
Meroma Illa'ah Beit Shechineteh.	מְרוֹמָא עִלָּאָה בֵּית שְׁכִינְתֵּהּ.
Kaddish Al Ar'a Ovad	קַדִּישׁ עַל אַרְעָא עוֹבַד
Gevureteh. Kaddish Le'alam	גְּבוּרְתֵּהּ. קַדִּישׁ לְעָלַם
Ule'alemei Alemaya. Adonai	וּלְעָלְמֵי עָלְמַיָּא. יְהֹוָה
Tzeva'ot Malya Chol-'Ar'a Ziv	צְבָאוֹת מַלְיָא כָל-אַרְעָא זִיו
Yekareh. Vatissa'eni Ruach.	יְקָרֵהּ: וַתִּשָּׂאֵנִי רוּחַ
Va'eshma Acharai. Kol Ra'ash	וָאֶשְׁמַע אַחֲרַי קוֹל רַעַשׁ
Gadol; **Baruch Kevod-Adonai**	גָּדוֹל בָּרוּךְ כְּבוֹד־יְהֹוָה
Mimekomo. Unetalatni Rucha.	מִמְּקוֹמוֹ: וּנְטָלַתְנִי רוּחָא.
Ushema'it Batrai Kal Zia Sagi	וּשְׁמָעִית בַּתְרַי קָל זִיעַ שַׂגִּיא
Dimshabechin Ve'amerin. Berich	דִּמְשַׁבְּחִין וְאָמְרִין: בְּרִיךְ
Yekara Da'Adonai Me'atar Beit	יְקָרָא דַיהֹוָה מֵאֲתַר בֵּית
Shechineteh. **Adonai Yimloch**	שְׁכִינְתֵּהּ: יְהֹוָה	יִמְלֹךְ
Le'olam Va'ed. Adonai	לְעָלָם וָעֶד: יְהֹוָה
Malchuteih Ka'im Le'alam	מַלְכוּתֵיהּ קָאִים לְעָלַם
Ule'alemei Alemaya. Adonai	וּלְעָלְמֵי עָלְמַיָּא: יְהֹוָה
Elohei Avraham Yitzchak	אֱלֹהֵי אַבְרָהָם יִצְחָק
Veyisra'el Avoteinu. Shomrah-	וְיִשְׂרָאֵל אֲבֹתֵינוּ שָׁמְרָה־

Zot Le'olam. Leyetzer	זֹאת לְעוֹלָם לְיֵצֶר
Machshevot Levav Ammecha;	מַחְשְׁבוֹת לְבַב עַמֶּךָ
Vehachein Levavam Eleicha.	וְהָכֵן לְבָבָם אֵלֶיךָ:
Vehu Rachum Yechapeir Avon	וְהוּא רַחוּם ׀ יְכַפֵּר עָוֹן
Velo-Yashchit Vehirbah Lehashiv	וְלֹא־יַשְׁחִית וְהִרְבָּה לְהָשִׁיב
Appo; Velo-Ya'ir. Chol-Chamato.	אַפּוֹ וְלֹא־יָעִיר כָּל־חֲמָתוֹ:
Ki-'Attah Adonai Tov Vesalach;	כִּי־אַתָּה אֲדֹנָי טוֹב וְסַלָּח
Verav-Chesed Lechol-Kore'eicha.	וְרַב־חֶסֶד לְכָל־קֹרְאֶיךָ:
Tzidkatecha Tzedek Le'olam;	צִדְקָתְךָ צֶדֶק לְעוֹלָם
Vetoratecha Emet. Titen Emet	וְתוֹרָתְךָ אֱמֶת: תִּתֵּן אֱמֶת
Leya'akov. Chesed Le'avraham;	לְיַעֲקֹב חֶסֶד לְאַבְרָהָם
Asher-Nishba'ta La'avoteinu	אֲשֶׁר־נִשְׁבַּעְתָּ לַאֲבֹתֵינוּ
Mimei Kedem. Baruch Adonai	מִימֵי קֶדֶם: בָּרוּךְ אֲדֹנָי
Yom Yom Ya'amas-Lanu. Ha'el	יוֹם ׀ יוֹם יַעֲמָס־לָנוּ הָאֵל
Yeshu'atenu Selah. Adonai	יְשׁוּעָתֵנוּ סֶלָה: יְהֹוָה
Tzeva'ot Imanu; Misgav-Lanu	צְבָאוֹת עִמָּנוּ מִשְׂגָּב־לָנוּ
Elohei Ya'akov Selah. Adonai	אֱלֹהֵי יַעֲקֹב סֶלָה: יְהֹוָה
Tzeva'ot; Ashrei Adam. Boteach	צְבָאוֹת אַשְׁרֵי אָדָם בֹּטֵחַ
Bach. Adonai Hoshi'ah;	בָּךְ: יְהֹוָה הוֹשִׁיעָה
Hamelech. Ya'aneinu Veyom-	הַמֶּלֶךְ יַעֲנֵנוּ בְיוֹם־
Kor'enu.	קָרְאֵנוּ:

"For You are holy and are enthroned amidst the praises of Yisrael."
"The angels called one to another, and said, **Holy, Holy, Holy is
Hashem of hosts, The fullness of all the earth is His glory."** And
they receive word from each other and say, Holy in the highest
heavens, the abode of His Divine Presence. Holy upon earth the
work of His mighty power. Holy forever and to all eternity, is

Hashem of hosts. The whole earth is full of His glorious splendor. "Then a spirit lifted me and behind me I heard a mighty sound, **'Blessed is Hashem's glory from His Abode.'"** Then the spirit raised me and I heard behind me a mighty moving sound of those who uttered His praise, proclaiming, 'Blessed is the glory of Hashem from the abiding place of His Divine Presence.' **"Hashem will reign forever and ever."** The rule of Hashem is established forever and ever. "Oh Hashem God of Avraham, Yitzchak and Yisrael, our fathers, forever preserve this as the inward thoughts of the heart of Your people and direct their hearts toward You. For He being merciful, will forgive iniquity and not destroy, yes, many times He averts His anger and does not awaken all of His wrath. For You, Hashem, are good and forgiving, and abounding in mercy to all who call upon You. Your righteousness is everlasting righteousness, and Your Torah is truth. You give truth to Yaakov, kindness to Avraham, As You have sworn to our fathers from ancient days. Blessed is Hashem, day to day He bears our burdens, The God of our salvation forever. Hashem of hosts is with us, The God of Yaakov is our high refuge forever. Hashem of hosts, Happy is the man who trusts in You. Hashem, save us, May the King answer us on the day when we call."

Baruch Eloheinu Shebera'anu	בָּרוּךְ אֱלֹהֵינוּ שֶׁבְּרָאָנוּ
Lichvodo. Vehivdilanu Min	לִכְבוֹדוֹ. וְהִבְדִּילָנוּ מִן
Hato'im. Venatan Lanu Torat	הַתּוֹעִים. וְנָתַן לָנוּ תּוֹרַת
Emet. Vechayei Olam Nata	אֱמֶת. וְחַיֵּי עוֹלָם נָטַע
Betocheinu. Hu Yiftach Libenu	בְּתוֹכֵנוּ. הוּא יִפְתַּח לִבֵּנוּ
Betorato. Veyasim Belibeinu	בְּתוֹרָתוֹ. וְיָשִׂים בְּלִבֵּנוּ
Ahavato Veyir'ato La'asot	אַהֲבָתוֹ וְיִרְאָתוֹ לַעֲשׂוֹת
Retzono Ule'avedo Belevav	רְצוֹנוֹ וּלְעָבְדוֹ בְּלֵבָב

Shalem. Lo Niga Larik. Velo	שָׁלֵם. לֹא נִיגַע לָרִיק. וְלֹא
Neled Labehalah. Yehi Ratzon	נֵלֵד לַבֶּהָלָה. יְהִי רָצוֹן
Milfaneicha Adonai Eloheinu	מִלְּפָנֶיךָ יְהוָה אֱלֹהֵינוּ
Velohei Avoteinu Shenishmor	וֵאלֹהֵי אֲבוֹתֵינוּ שֶׁנִּשְׁמֹר
Chukkeicha Umitzvoteicha	חֻקֶּיךָ וּמִצְוֹתֶיךָ
Ba'olam Hazeh. Venizkeh	בָּעוֹלָם הַזֶּה. וְנִזְכֶּה
Venichyeh Venirash Tovah	וְנִחְיֶה וְנִירַשׁ טוֹבָה
Uverachah Lechayei Ha'olam	וּבְרָכָה לְחַיֵּי הָעוֹלָם
Haba. Lema'an Yezamercha	הַבָּא: לְמַעַן	יְזַמֶּרְךָ
Chavod Velo Yidom; Adonai	כָבוֹד וְלֹא יִדֹּם יְהוָה
Elohai. Le'olam Odeka. Adonai	אֱלֹהַי לְעוֹלָם אוֹדֶךָּ: יְהוָה
Chafetz Lema'an Tzidko; Yagdil	חָפֵץ לְמַעַן צִדְקוֹ יַגְדִּיל
Torah Veya'dir. Veyivtechu Vecha	תּוֹרָה וְיַאְדִּיר: וְיִבְטְחוּ בְךָ
Yodei Shemecha; Ki Lo-'Azavta	יוֹדְעֵי שְׁמֶךָ כִּי לֹא־עָזַבְתָּ
Doresheicha Adonai. Adonai	דֹרְשֶׁיךָ יְהוָה: יְהוָה
Adoneinu; Mah-'Adir Shimcha.	אֲדֹנֵינוּ מָה־אַדִּיר שִׁמְךָ
Bechol-Ha'aretz. Chizku	בְּכָל־הָאָרֶץ: חִזְקוּ
Veya'ametz Levavchem; Chol-	וְיַאֲמֵץ לְבַבְכֶם כָּל־
Hamyachalim. L'Adonai.	הַמְיַחֲלִים לַיהוָה:

Blessed is our God, Who has created us for His glory, and has separated us from those that go astray, and has given to us the Torah of truth and planted everlasting life in our midst. May He open our hearts to His Torah, and place love and fear of Him within our hearts, to do His will and serve Him with a perfect heart, that we may not labor in vain, or bring forth confusion. May it be Your will, Hashem our God and God of our fathers, that we may keep Your statutes and commandments in this world and may we merit and live and inherit happiness and blessing for the life of the world to come. To the end that my glory may sing to You, and not be silent. Hashem my God, I will give thanks to You forever. It pleased Hashem, for His righteousness' sake, to magnify the Torah and to make it glorious. And those that know Your name will put their trust in You; for You have not forsaken those that seek You, Hashem. Oh Hashem, our Lord, How glorious is Your name in all of the earth. Be strong, and let your heart take courage, all of you that wait for Hashem.

Kaddish Titkabbal

Kaddish is only recited in a minyan (ten men). אמן denotes when the congregation responds "Amen" together out loud. According to the Shulchan Arukh, the congregation says "Yehei Shemeh Rabba" to "Yitbarach" out loud together without interruption, and also that one should respond "Amen" after "Yitbarach." (SA, OC 55,56) This is not the common custom today. Though many are accustomed to answering according to their own custom, it is advised to respond in the custom of the one reciting to avoid not fragmenting into smaller groups. ("Lo Titgodedu" - BT, Yevamot 13b / SA, OC 493, Rema / MT, Avodah Zara 12:15)

יִתְגַּדַּל וְיִתְקַדַּשׁ שְׁמֵהּ רַבָּא. אמן בְּעָלְמָא דִּי בְרָא. כִרְעוּתֵהּ. וְיַמְלִיךְ
מַלְכוּתֵהּ. וְיַצְמַח פֻּרְקָנֵהּ. וִיקָרֵב מְשִׁיחֵהּ. אמן בְּחַיֵּיכוֹן וּבְיוֹמֵיכוֹן
וּבְחַיֵּי דְכָל בֵּית יִשְׂרָאֵל. בַּעֲגָלָא וּבִזְמַן קָרִיב. וְאִמְרוּ אָמֵן. אמן יְהֵא
שְׁמֵיהּ רַבָּא מְבָרַךְ לְעָלַם וּלְעָלְמֵי עָלְמַיָּא יִתְבָּרַךְ. וְיִשְׁתַּבַּח.
וְיִתְפָּאַר. וְיִתְרוֹמַם. וְיִתְנַשֵּׂא. וְיִתְהַדָּר. וְיִתְעַלֶּה. וְיִתְהַלָּל שְׁמֵהּ
דְּקֻדְשָׁא. בְּרִיךְ הוּא. אמן לְעֵלָּא מִן כָּל בִּרְכָתָא שִׁירָתָא. תֻּשְׁבְּחָתָא
וְנֶחֱמָתָא. דַּאֲמִירָן בְּעָלְמָא. וְאִמְרוּ אָמֵן. אמן

Yitgadal Veyitkadash Shemeh Rabba. **Amen** Be'alema Di Vera.
Kir'uteh. Veyamlich Malchuteh. Veyatzmach Purkaneh. Vikarev
Meshicheh. **Amen** Bechayeichon Uveyomeichon Uvechayei Dechal-
Beit Yisra'el. Ba'agala Uvizman Kariv. Ve'imru Amen. **Amen** Yehei
Shemeh Rabba Mevarach Le'alam Ule'alemei Alemaya Yitbarach.
Veyishtabach. Veyitpa'ar. Veyitromam. Veyitnasse. Veyit'hadar.
Veyit'aleh. Veyit'hallal Shemeh Dekudsha. Berich Hu. **Amen** Le'ella
Min Kol Birchata Shirata. Tushbechata Venechemata. Da'amiran
Be'alema. Ve'imru Amen. **Amen**

Glorified and sanctified be God's great name Amen throughout the world which He has created according to His will. May He establish His kingdom, hastening His salvation and the coming of His Messiah, Amen, in your lifetime and during your days, and within the life of the entire House of Yisrael, speedily and soon; and say, Amen. Amen May His great name be blessed forever and to all eternity. Blessed and praised, glorified and exalted, extolled and honored, adored and lauded is the name of the Holy One, blessed is He, Amen Beyond all the blessings and hymns, praises and consolations that are ever spoken in the world; and say, Amen. Amen

תִּתְקַבַּל צְלוֹתָנָא וּבָעוּתָנָא. עִם צְלוֹתְהוֹן וּבָעוּתְהוֹן דְּכָל בֵּית
יִשְׂרָאֵל. קֳדָם אֲבוּנָא דְבִשְׁמַיָּא וְאַרְעָא. וְאִמְרוּ אָמֵן. אָמֵן

Titkabbal Tzelotana Uva'utana. Im Tzelotehon Uva'utehon Dechol Beit Yisra'el. Kodam Avuna Devishmaya Ve'ar'a. Ve'imru Amen. Amen

May the prayer and supplication of the whole House of Yisrael be accepted before their Father in heaven, and say, Amen. Amen

יְהֵא שְׁלָמָא רַבָּא מִן שְׁמַיָּא. חַיִּים וְשָׂבָע וִישׁוּעָה וְנֶחָמָה. וְשֵׁיזָבָא
וּרְפוּאָה וּגְאוּלָה וּסְלִיחָה וְכַפָּרָה וְרֶוַח וְהַצָּלָה לָנוּ וּלְכָל עַמּוֹ
יִשְׂרָאֵל. וְאִמְרוּ אָמֵן. אָמֵן

Yehei Shelama Rabba Min Shemaya. Chayim Vesava Vishu'ah Venechamah. Vesheizava Urefu'ah Uge'ulah Uselichah Vechapparah Verevach Vehatzalah Lanu Ulechol Ammo Yisra'el. Ve'imru Amen. Amen

May abundant peace descend from heaven, with life and plenty, salvation, solace, liberation, healing and redemption, and forgiveness and atonement, enlargement and freedom, for us and all of God's people Yisrael; and say, Amen. Amen

---

One bows and takes three steps backwards, while still bowing. After three steps, while still bowing and before erecting, while saying, "Oseh Shalom Bimromav", turn one's face to the left, "Hu [Berachamav] Ya'aseh Shalom Aleinu", turn one's face to the right; then bow forward like a servant leaving his master. (SA, OC 123:1)

עוֹשֶׂה שָׁלוֹם בִּמְרוֹמָיו. הוּא בְּרַחֲמָיו יַעֲשֶׂה שָׁלוֹם עָלֵינוּ. וְעַל
כָּל־עַמּוֹ יִשְׂרָאֵל. וְאִמְרוּ אָמֵן:

Oseh Shalom Bimromav. Hu Berachamav Ya'aseh Shalom Aleinu.
Ve'al Kol-'Ammo Yisra'el. Ve'imru Amen.

Creator of peace in His high places, may He in His mercy create
peace for us and for all Yisrael, and say Amen.

Some count the Omer at this point. Some wait till after the Aleinu.

Psalms 121

שִׁיר לַמַּעֲלוֹת אֶשָּׂא עֵינַי אֶל־הֶהָרִים מֵאַיִן יָבֹא עֶזְרִי: עֶזְרִי מֵעִם
יְהֹוָה עֹשֵׂה שָׁמַיִם וָאָרֶץ: אַל־יִתֵּן לַמּוֹט רַגְלֶךָ אַל־יָנוּם שֹׁמְרֶךָ: הִנֵּה
לֹא־יָנוּם וְלֹא יִישָׁן שׁוֹמֵר יִשְׂרָאֵל: יְהֹוָה שֹׁמְרֶךָ יְהֹוָה צִלְּךָ עַל־יַד
יְמִינֶךָ: יוֹמָם הַשֶּׁמֶשׁ לֹא־יַכֶּכָּה וְיָרֵחַ בַּלָּיְלָה: יְהֹוָה יִשְׁמָרְךָ מִכָּל־רָע
יִשְׁמֹר אֶת־נַפְשֶׁךָ: יְהֹוָה יִשְׁמָר־צֵאתְךָ וּבוֹאֶךָ מֵעַתָּה וְעַד־עוֹלָם:

Shir Lamma'alot Essa Einai El-Heharim; Me'ayin. Yavo Ezri. Ezri
Me'im Adonai Oseh. Shamayim Va'aretz. Al-Yiten Lamot Raglecha;
Al-Yanum. Shomerecha. Hineh Lo-Yanum Velo Yishan; Shomer.
Yisra'el. Adonai Shomerecha; Hashem Tzillecha. Al-Yad Yeminecha.
Yomam. Hashemesh Lo-Yakekah. Veyareach Balailah. Adonai
Yishmorcha Mikol-Ra'; Yishmor. Et-Nafshecha. Adonai Yishmor-
Tzetecha Uvo'echa; Me'attah. Ve'ad-'Olam.

A Song of Ascents. I will lift up my eyes to the mountains: From
where will my help come? My help comes from Hashem, Who made
heaven and earth. He will not suffer Your foot to be moved; He that
keeps You will not slumber. Behold, He that keeps Yisrael neither
slumbers or sleeps. Hashem is your Guardian; Hashem is Your
shade on Your right hand. The sun will not harm you by day, or the
moon by night. Hashem will keep you from all evil; He will keep your
soul. Hashem will guard your going out and your coming in, From
this time and forever.

And on Chol HaMoed Pesach say:

Psalms 114

בְּצֵאת יִשְׂרָאֵל מִמִּצְרָיִם בֵּית יַעֲקֹב מֵעַם לֹעֵז: הָיְתָה יְהוּדָה לְקָדְשׁוֹ יִשְׂרָאֵל מַמְשְׁלוֹתָיו: הַיָּם רָאָה וַיָּנֹס הַיַּרְדֵּן יִסֹּב לְאָחוֹר: הֶהָרִים רָקְדוּ כְאֵילִים גְּבָעוֹת כִּבְנֵי־צֹאן: מַה־לְּךָ הַיָּם כִּי תָנוּס הַיַּרְדֵּן תִּסֹּב לְאָחוֹר: הֶהָרִים תִּרְקְדוּ כְאֵילִים גְּבָעוֹת כִּבְנֵי־צֹאן: מִלִּפְנֵי אָדוֹן חוּלִי אָרֶץ מִלִּפְנֵי אֱלוֹהַּ יַעֲקֹב: הַהֹפְכִי הַצּוּר אֲגַם־מָיִם חַלָּמִישׁ לְמַעְיְנוֹ־מָיִם:

Betzet Yisra'el Mimitzrayim Beit Ya'akov Me'am Lo'ez. Hayetah Yehudah Lekodsho Yisra'el Mamshelotav. Hayam Ra'ah Vayanos Hayarden Yissov Le'achor. Heharim Rakedu Che'eilim Geva'ot Kivnei Tzon. Mah Lecha Hayam Ki Tanus Hayarden Tissov Le'achor. Heharim Tirkedu Che'eilim Geva'ot Kivnei Tzon. Millifnei Adon Chuli Aretz Millifnei Eloah Ya'akov. Hahofechi Hatzur Agam Mayim Challamish Lema'yeno Mayim.

When Yisrael came forth out of Mitzrayim, The house of Yaakov from a people of strange language; Yehudah became His Sanctuary, Yisrael His dominion. The sea saw it, and fled; The Yarden turned backward. The mountains skipped like rams, The hills like young sheep. What ails you, Oh sea, that you flee? You Yarden, that you turn backward? You mountains, that you skip like rams; You hills, like young sheep? Tremble, earth, at the presence of Hashem, At the presence of the God of Yaakov; Who turned the rock into a pool of water, the flint into a fountain of waters.

And on Chol HaMoed Sukkot; Shavuot, and Shemini Atzeret / Simchat Torah say:

Psalms 122

שִׁיר הַמַּעֲלוֹת לְדָוִד שָׂמַחְתִּי בְּאֹמְרִים לִי בֵּית יְהוָה נֵלֵךְ: עֹמְדוֹת הָיוּ רַגְלֵינוּ בִּשְׁעָרַיִךְ יְרוּשָׁלָ͏ִם: יְרוּשָׁלַ͏ִם הַבְּנוּיָה כְּעִיר שֶׁחֻבְּרָה־לָּהּ יַחְדָּו: שֶׁשָּׁם עָלוּ שְׁבָטִים שִׁבְטֵי־יָהּ עֵדוּת לְיִשְׂרָאֵל לְהֹדוֹת לְשֵׁם יְהוָה: כִּי שָׁמָּה | יָשְׁבוּ כִסְאוֹת לְמִשְׁפָּט כִּסְאוֹת לְבֵית דָּוִד: שַׁאֲלוּ שְׁלוֹם יְרוּשָׁלָ͏ִם יִשְׁלָיוּ אֹהֲבָיִךְ: יְהִי־שָׁלוֹם בְּחֵילֵךְ שַׁלְוָה בְּאַרְמְנוֹתָיִךְ: לְמַעַן אַחַי וְרֵעָי אֲדַבְּרָה־נָּא שָׁלוֹם בָּךְ: לְמַעַן בֵּית־יְהוָה אֱלֹהֵינוּ אֲבַקְשָׁה טוֹב לָךְ:

Shir Hama'alot Ledavid Samachti Be'omerim Li Beit Adonai Nelech. Omedot Hayu Ragleinu Bish'arayich Yerushalayim. Yerushalayim Habenuyah Ke'ir Shechuberah Lah Yachdav. Shesham Alu Shevatim Shivtei Yah Edut Leyisra'el Lehodot Leshem Adonai. Ki Shamah Yashevu Chis'ot Lemishpat Kis'ot Leveit David. Sha'alu Shelom Yerushalayim Yishlayu Ohavayich. Yehi Shalom Becheilech Shalvah Be'armenotayich. Lema'an Achai Vere'ai Adaberah Na Shalom Bach. Lema'an Beit Adonai Eloheinu Avakshah Tov Lach.

A Song of Ascents; of David. I rejoiced when they said to me: 'Let us go to the House of Hashem.' Our feet are standing within your gates, Yerushalayim; Yerushalayim, that is built as a city that is compact together; Where the tribes went up, even the tribes of Hashem, as a testimony to Yisrael, to give thanks to the name of Hashem. For there were set thrones for judgment, the thrones of the House of David. Pray for the peace of Yerushalayim; May they that love You prosper. Peace be within your walls, and prosperity within your palaces. For my brothers and companions' sakes, I will now say: 'Peace be within you.' For the sake of the House of Hashem our God I will seek your good.

Kaddish Yehei-Shelama

Kaddish is only recited in a minyan (ten men). אמן denotes when the congregation responds "Amen" together out loud. According to the Shulchan Arukh, the congregation says "Yehei Shemeh Rabba" to "Yitbarach" out loud together without interruption, and also that one should respond "Amen" after "Yitbarach." (SA, OC 55,56) This is not the common custom today. Though many are accustomed to answering according to their own custom, it is advised to respond in the custom of the one reciting to avoid not fragmenting into smaller groups. ("Lo Titgodedu" - BT, Yevamot 13b / SA, OC 493, Rema / MT, Avodah Zara 12:15)

יִתְגַּדַּל וְיִתְקַדַּשׁ שְׁמֵהּ רַבָּא. אמן בְּעָלְמָא דִּי בְרָא. כִרְעוּתֵהּ. וְיַמְלִיךְ מַלְכוּתֵהּ. וְיַצְמַח פֻּרְקָנֵהּ. וִיקָרֵב מְשִׁיחֵהּ. אמן בְּחַיֵּיכוֹן וּבְיוֹמֵיכוֹן וּבְחַיֵּי דְכָל בֵּית יִשְׂרָאֵל. בַּעֲגָלָא וּבִזְמַן קָרִיב. וְאִמְרוּ אָמֵן. אמן יְהֵא שְׁמֵהּ רַבָּא מְבָרַךְ לְעָלַם וּלְעָלְמֵי עָלְמַיָּא יִתְבָּרַךְ. וְיִשְׁתַּבַּח. וְיִתְפָּאַר. וְיִתְרוֹמַם. וְיִתְנַשֵּׂא. וְיִתְהַדָּר. וְיִתְעַלֶּה. וְיִתְהַלָּל שְׁמֵהּ דְּקֻדְשָׁא. בְּרִיךְ הוּא. אמן לְעֵלָּא מִן כָּל בִּרְכָתָא שִׁירָתָא. תֻּשְׁבְּחָתָא וְנֶחֱמָתָא. דַּאֲמִירָן בְּעָלְמָא. וְאִמְרוּ אָמֵן. אמן

Yitgadal Veyitkadash Shemeh Rabba. Amen Be'alema Di Vera. Kir'uteh. Veyamlich Malchuteh. Veyatzmach Purkaneh. Vikarev Meshicheh. Amen Bechayeichon Uveyomeichon Uvechayei Dechal-Beit Yisra'el. Ba'agala Uvizman Kariv. Ve'imru Amen. Amen Yehei Shemeh Rabba Mevarach Le'alam Ule'alemei Alemaya Yitbarach. Veyishtabach. Veyitpa'ar. Veyitromam. Veyitnasse. Veyit'hadar. Veyit'aleh. Veyit'hallal Shemeh Dekudsha. Berich Hu. Amen Le'ella Min Kol Birchata Shirata. Tushbechata Venechemata. Da'amiran Be'alema. Ve'imru Amen. Amen

Glorified and sanctified be God's great name ^{Amen} throughout the world which He has created according to His will. May He establish His kingdom, hastening His salvation and the coming of His Messiah, ^{Amen}, in your lifetime and during your days, and within the life of the entire House of Yisrael, speedily and soon; and say, Amen. ^{Amen} May His great name be blessed forever and to all eternity. Blessed and praised, glorified and exalted, extolled and honored, adored and lauded is the name of the Holy One, blessed is He, ^{Amen} Beyond all the blessings and hymns, praises and consolations that are ever spoken in the world; and say, Amen. ^{Amen}

יְהֵא שְׁלָמָא רַבָּא מִן שְׁמַיָּא. חַיִּים וְשָׂבָע וִישׁוּעָה וְנֶחָמָה. וְשֵׁיזָבָא וּרְפוּאָה וּגְאוּלָה וּסְלִיחָה וְכַפָּרָה וְרֶוַח וְהַצָּלָה לָנוּ וּלְכָל עַמּוֹ יִשְׂרָאֵל. וְאִמְרוּ אָמֵן. אָמֵן

Yehei Shelama Rabba Min Shemaya. Chayim Vesava Vishu'ah
Venechamah. Vesheizava Urefu'ah Uge'ulah Uselichah
Vechapparah Verevach Vehatzalah Lanu Ulechol Ammo Yisra'el.
Ve'imru Amen. ^{Amen}

May abundant peace descend from heaven, with life and plenty, salvation, solace, liberation, healing and redemption, and forgiveness and atonement, enlargement and freedom, for us and all of God's people Yisrael; and say, Amen. ^{Amen}

One bows and takes three steps backwards, while still bowing. After three steps, while still bowing and before erecting, while saying, "Oseh Shalom Bimromav", turn one's face to the left, "Hu [Berachamav] Ya'aseh Shalom Aleinu", turn one's face to the right; then bow forward like a servant leaving his master. (SA, OC 123:1)

עוֹשֶׂה שָׁלוֹם בִּמְרוֹמָיו. הוּא בְּרַחֲמָיו יַעֲשֶׂה שָׁלוֹם עָלֵינוּ. וְעַל כָּל־עַמּוֹ יִשְׂרָאֵל. וְאִמְרוּ אָמֵן:

Oseh Shalom Bimromav. Hu Berachamav Ya'aseh Shalom Aleinu.
Ve'al Kol-'Ammo Yisra'el. Ve'imru Amen.

Creator of peace in His high places, may He in His mercy create peace for us and for all Yisrael, and say Amen.

The Barechu / Call to Prayer

Barechu is only said with 10 men (a minyan).

The Oleh / Reader:

בָּרְכוּ אֶת יְהֹוָה הַמְבֹרָךְ:

Barechu Et Adonai Hamevorach.

Bless Hashem, Who is forever blessed.

The kahal / congregation:

בָּרוּךְ יְהֹוָה הַמְבֹרָךְ לְעוֹלָם וָעֶד:

Baruch Adonai Hamevorach Le'olam Va'ed.

Blessed is Hashem Who is blessed for all eternity.

The Oleh and Chazan:

בָּרוּךְ יְהֹוָה הַמְבֹרָךְ לְעוֹלָם וָעֶד:

Baruch Adonai Hamevorach Le'olam Va'ed.

Blessed is Hashem Who is blessed for all eternity.

Aleinu

[*] denotes pausing and then bowing when saying "Va'anachnu Mistachavim".

Aleinu Leshabei'ach La'adon	עָלֵינוּ לְשַׁבֵּחַ לַאֲדוֹן
Hakol. Latet Gedullah Leyotzer	הַכֹּל. לָתֵת גְּדֻלָּה לְיוֹצֵר
Bereshit. Shelo Asanu Kegoyei	בְּרֵאשִׁית. שֶׁלֹּא עָשָׂנוּ כְּגוֹיֵי
Ha'aratzot. Velo Samanu	הָאֲרָצוֹת. וְלֹא שָׂמָנוּ
Kemishpechot Ha'adamah. Shelo	כְּמִשְׁפְּחוֹת הָאֲדָמָה. שֶׁלֹּא
Sam Chelkenu Kahem	שָׂם חֶלְקֵנוּ כָּהֶם
Vegoraleinu Kechal-Hamonam.	וְגוֹרָלֵנוּ כְּכָל־הֲמוֹנָם.
Shehem Mishtachavim Lahevel	שֶׁהֵם מִשְׁתַּחֲוִים לְהֶבֶל

Varik. Umitpallelim El-'El Lo	וָרִיק. וּמִתְפַּלְּלִים אֶל־אֵל לֹא
Yoshia. *Va'anachnu	יוֹשִׁיעַ. *וַאֲנַחְנוּ
Mishtachavim Lifnei Melech	מִשְׁתַּחֲוִים לִפְנֵי מֶלֶךְ
Malchei Hamelachim Hakadosh	מַלְכֵי הַמְּלָכִים הַקָּדוֹשׁ
Baruch Hu. Shehu Noteh	בָּרוּךְ הוּא. שֶׁהוּא נוֹטֶה
Shamayim Veyosed Aretz.	שָׁמַיִם וְיוֹסֵד אָרֶץ.
Umoshav Yekaro Bashamayim	וּמוֹשַׁב יְקָרוֹ בַּשָּׁמַיִם
Mima'al. Ushechinat Uzo	מִמַּעַל. וּשְׁכִינַת עֻזּוֹ
Begavehei Meromim. Hu	בְּגָבְהֵי מְרוֹמִים. הוּא
Eloheinu. Ve'ein Od Acher. Emet	אֱלֹהֵינוּ. וְאֵין עוֹד אַחֵר.
Malkeinu Ve'efes Zulato.	אֱמֶת מַלְכֵּנוּ וְאֶפֶס זוּלָתוֹ.
Kakatuv Batorah. Veyada'ta	כַּכָּתוּב בַּתּוֹרָה. וְיָדַעְתָּ
Hayom. Vahasheivota El-	הַיּוֹם וַהֲשֵׁבֹתָ אֶל־
Levavecha Ki Adonai Hu	לְבָבֶךָ כִּי יְהֹוָה הוּא
Ha'elohim. Bashamayim	הָאֱלֹהִים בַּשָּׁמַיִם
Mima'al. Ve'al-Ha'aretz	מִמַּעַל וְעַל־הָאָרֶץ
Mitachat; Ein Od.	מִתָּחַת אֵין עוֹד:

It is our obligation us to praise the Lord of all. To render greatness to the Former of creation. For He has not made us like the nations of the lands, nor set us to be like the families of the earth. Who has not given our portion like theirs and our lot like their masses that bow down to vanity and emptiness, "And pray to a god that does not save." *But we bow before the supreme King of kings, the Holy One, blessed is He. Who stretches out the heavens and laid the foundations of the earth and His glorious seat is in the heavens above, and the presence of His might in the most exalted of heights. He is our God, there is no other. In truth our King, there is no one except Him. As it is written in the Torah: "This day know and lay it to your heart, that Hashem, He is God in the heavens above and on the earth beneath. There is no one else."

Al Ken Nekaveh Lach. Adonai	עַל כֵּן נְקַוֶּה לְךָ. יְהֹוָה
Eloheinu. Lir'ot Meheirah	אֱלֹהֵינוּ. לִרְאוֹת מְהֵרָה
Betif'eret Uzach. Leha'avir	בְּתִפְאֶרֶת עֻזָּךְ. לְהַעֲבִיר
Gilulim Min Ha'aretz.	גִּלּוּלִים מִן הָאָרֶץ.
Veha'elilim Karot Yikaretun.	וְהָאֱלִילִים כָּרוֹת יִכָּרֵתוּן.
Letakken Olam Bemalchut	לְתַקֵּן עוֹלָם בְּמַלְכוּת
Shaddai. Vechol-Benei Vasar	שַׁדַּי. וְכָל־בְּנֵי בָשָׂר
Yikre'u Vishmecha. Lehafnot	יִקְרְאוּ בִשְׁמֶךָ. לְהַפְנוֹת
Eleicha Kol-Rish'ei Aretz. Yakiru	אֵלֶיךָ כָּל־רִשְׁעֵי אָרֶץ. יַכִּירוּ
Veyede'u Kol-Yoshevei Tevel. Ki	וְיֵדְעוּ כָּל־יוֹשְׁבֵי תֵבֵל. כִּי
Lecha Tichra Kol-Berech.	לְךָ תִּכְרַע כָּל־בֶּרֶךְ. תִּשָּׁבַע
Tishava Kol-Lashon. Lefaneicha.	כָּל־לָשׁוֹן. לְפָנֶיךָ. יְהֹוָה
Adonai Eloheinu Yichre'u	אֱלֹהֵינוּ יִכְרְעוּ וְיִפֹּלוּ.
Veyipolu. Velichvod Shimcha	וְלִכְבוֹד שִׁמְךָ יְקָר יִתֵּנוּ.
Yekar Yitenu. Vikabelu Chulam	וִיקַבְּלוּ כֻלָּם אֶת־עֹל
Et-'Ol Malchutecha. Vetimloch	מַלְכוּתֶךָ. וְתִמְלוֹךְ עֲלֵיהֶם
Aleihem Meheirah Le'olam	מְהֵרָה לְעוֹלָם וָעֶד. כִּי
Va'ed. Ki Hamalchut Shelecha	הַמַּלְכוּת שֶׁלְּךָ הִיא.
Hi. Ule'olemei Ad Timloch	וּלְעוֹלְמֵי עַד תִּמְלוֹךְ
Bechavod. Kakatuv Betoratach.	בְּכָבוֹד. כַּכָּתוּב בְּתוֹרָתֶךָ:
Adonai Yimloch Le'olam Va'ed.	יְהֹוָה ׀ יִמְלֹךְ לְעֹלָם וָעֶד:
Vene'emar. Vehayah Adonai	וְנֶאֱמַר. וְהָיָה יְהֹוָה
Lemelech Al-Kol-Ha'aretz;	לְמֶלֶךְ עַל־כָּל־הָאָרֶץ
Bayom Hahu. Yihyeh Adonai	בַּיּוֹם הַהוּא יִהְיֶה יְהֹוָה
Echad Ushemo Echad.	אֶחָד וּשְׁמוֹ אֶחָד:

Therefore we hope in You, Hashem our God, soon to see Your glorious might, to remove idols from the earth and the non-gods will be wholly cut down, to rectify the world with the kingdom of El Shaddai, and all children of flesh will call on Your name and all of the earth's wicked will turn to You. All that dwell on earth will understand and know that to You every knee must bend, and every tongue swear. Before You, Hashem our God, may all kneel and fall and give honor to Your glorious name. And they will all accept the yoke of Your kingdom. And may You speedily rule over them forever. For dominion is Yours, and forever You will reign in glory, as is written in Your Torah, "Hashem will reign forever and ever." For, it is said, "Hashem will be King over all the earth; and on that day Hashem will be One and His name One."

Uvetoratecha Adonai Eloheinu	בְּתוֹרָתְךָ יְהֹוָה אֱלֹהֵינוּ
Katuv Lemor. Shema Yisra'el;	כָּתוּב לֵאמֹר. שְׁמַע יִשְׂרָאֵל
Adonai Eloheinu Adonai Echad.	יְהֹוָה אֱלֹהֵינוּ יְהֹוָה אֶחָד:

And in Your Torah, Hashem our God, it is written: Hear O Yisrael Hashem our God, Hashem is One.

At this point some Count the Omer (referring to section in the back) in the seven weeks after Pesach. Many also recite Birkhat HaLevanah (The Blessing of the Moon) within the first half of new month, depending on the custom. (Refer to section in the back for instructions).

Before Havdalah - Motsa'ei Shabbat

Eliyahu HaNavi

Before Havdalah some:

אֵלִיָּהוּ הַנָּבִיא. אֵלִיָּהוּ הַתִּשְׁבִּי. אֵלִיָּהוּ הַגִּלְעָדִי. בִּמְהֵרָה יָבֹא אֵלֵינוּ
עִם מָשִׁיחַ בֶּן דָּוִד:

Eliyahu Hanavi. Eliyahu Hatishbi. Eliyahu Hagil'adi. Bimheirah Yavo
Eleinu Im Mashiach Ben David:

Eliyahu, the prophet, Eliyahu, the Tishbite. He will come to us
speedily with Messiah ben David.

אִישׁ אֲשֶׁר קִנֵּא לְשֵׁם הָאֵל אֵלִיָּהוּ הַנָּבִיא. אִישׁ בִּשַּׂר שָׁלוֹם עַל יַד
יְקוּאֵל אֵלִיָּהוּ הַנָּבִיא. אִישׁ גָּשׁ וַיְכַפֵּר עַל בְּנֵי יִשְׂרָאֵל. אֵלִיָּהוּ
הַנָּבִיא זָכוּר לְטוֹב:

Ish Asher Kine Leshem Ha'el Eliyahu Hanavi. Ish Bussar Shalom Al
Yad Yekui'el Eliyahu Hanavi. Ish Gash Vaychapeir Al Benei Yisra'el.
Eliyahu Hanavi Zachur Letov:

He was the man who was zealous for the name of God; to whom
tidings of peace were delivered by the hand of Yekuthiel; he was the
man who drew near and made expiation for the children of Yisrael.
Eliyahu, the prophet may his name be of good memory.

אִישׁ דּוֹרוֹת שְׁנֵים עָשָׂר רָאוּ עֵינָיו אֵלִיָּהוּ הַנָּבִיא. אִישׁ הַנִּקְרָא בַּעַל
שֵׂעָר בְּסִימָנָיו אֵלִיָּהוּ הַנָּבִיא. אִישׁ וְאֵזוֹר עוֹר אָזוּר בְּמָתְנָיו. אֵלִיָּהוּ
הַנָּבִיא זָכוּר לְטוֹב:

Ish Dorot Sheneim Asar Ra'u Einav Eliyahu Hanavi. Ish Hanikra
Ba'al Se'ar Besimanav Eliyahu Hanavi. Ish Ve'ezor Or Azur
Bematenav. Eliyahu Hanavi Zachur Letov:

He was the man whose eyes beheld twelve generations; who was
known, and called a hairy man, girt with a girdle of leather about his
loins. Eliyahu, the prophet may his name be of good memory.

אִישׁ זָעַף עַל עוֹבְדֵי חַמָּנִים אֵלִיָּהוּ הַנָּבִיא. אִישׁ חָשׁ וְנִשְׁבַּע מִהְיוֹת
גִּשְׁמֵי מְעוֹנִים אֵלִיָּהוּ הַנָּבִיא. אִישׁ טַל וּמָטָר עָצַר שָׁלשׁ שָׁנִים.
אֵלִיָּהוּ הַנָּבִיא זָכוּר לְטוֹב:

Ish Za'af Al Ovedei Chamanim Eliyahu Hanavi. Ish Chash Venishba
Mihyot Gishmei Me'onim Eliyahu Hanavi. Ish Tal Umatar Atzar
Shalosh Shanim. Eliyahu Hanavi Zachur Letov:

He was the man who was angry with the worshippers of the images
of the sun; the man who in haste swore, that no rain should descend
from the heavens. He was the man who withheld dew and rain for
three years. Eliyahu, the prophet may his name be of good memory.

אִישׁ יָצָא לִמְצֹא לְנַפְשׁוֹ נַחַת אֵלִיָּהוּ הַנָּבִיא. אִישׁ כִּלְכְּלוּהוּ
הָעוֹרְבִים וְלֹא מֵת לַשַּׁחַת אֵלִיָּהוּ הַנָּבִיא. אִישׁ לְמַעֲנוֹ נִתְבָּרְכוּ כַּד
וְצַפַּחַת. אֵלִיָּהוּ הַנָּבִיא זָכוּר לְטוֹב:

Ish Yatza Limtzo Lenafsho Nachat Eliyahu Hanavi. Ish Kilkeluhu
Ha'orevim Velo Met Lashachat Eliyahu Hanavi. Ish Lema'ano
Nitbarechu Kad Vetzappachat. Eliyahu Hanavi Zachur Letov:

He was the man who went out to seek rest for his soul; the man who
was fed by the ravens, and preserved from death; the man for whom
the barrel and cruse were blessed. Eliyahu, the prophet may his
name be of good memory.

אִישׁ מוּסָרָיו הִקְשִׁיבוּ כְּמֵהִים אֵלִיָּהוּ הַנָּבִיא. אִישׁ נֶעֱנָה בָאֵשׁ
מִשְּׁמֵי גְבוֹהִים אֵלִיָּהוּ הַנָּבִיא. אִישׁ שָׂחוּ אַחֲרָיו יְהֹוָה הוּא
הָאֱלֹהִים. אֵלִיָּהוּ הַנָּבִיא זָכוּר לְטוֹב:

Ish Musarav Hikshivu Chemehim Eliyahu Hanavi. Ish Ne'enah
Va'esh Mishemei Gevohim Eliyahu Hanavi. Ish Sachu Acharav
Adonai Hu Ha'elohim. Eliyahu Hanavi Zachur Letov:

He was the man whose rebuke was attended to by those who were
humbled; the man who was answered by fire from the highest
heavens; tho man after whom they proclaimed "Hashem, He is
God." Eliyahu, the prophet may his name be of good memory.

אִישׁ עָתִיד לְהִשְׁתַּלֵּחַ מִשְּׁמֵי עֲרָבוֹת אֵלִיָּהוּ הַנָּבִיא. אִישׁ פָּקִיד עַל
כָּל בְּשׂוֹרוֹת טוֹבוֹת אֵלִיָּהוּ הַנָּבִיא. אִישׁ צִיר נֶאֱמָן לְהָשִׁיב לֵב
בָּנִים עַל אָבוֹת. אֵלִיָּהוּ הַנָּבִיא זָכוּר לְטוֹב:

Ish Atid Lehishtalleach Mishemei Aravot Eliyahu Hanavi. Ish Pakid
Al Kol Besorot Tovot Eliyahu Hanavi. Ish Tzir Ne'eman Lehashiv Lev
Banim Al Avot. Eliyahu Hanavi Zachur Letov:

He is the man destined to be sent from the highest heavens; the man
specially appointed to bring good tidings; the man who will be a
faithful messenger to turn the heart of the children to the fathers.
Eliyahu, the prophet may his name be of good memory.

אִישׁ קָרָא קַנֹּא קִנֵּאתִי לַיהֹוָה בִּתְפְאָרָה אֵלִיָּהוּ הַנָּבִיא. אִישׁ רָכַב
עַל סוּסֵי אֵשׁ וְעָלָה בַּסְעָרָה אֵלִיָּהוּ הַנָּבִיא. אִישׁ שֶׁלֹּא טָעַם טַעַם
מִיתָה וּקְבוּרָה. אֵלִיָּהוּ הַנָּבִיא זָכוּר לְטוֹב:

Ish Kara Kano Kineti L'Adonai Betif'arah Eliyahu Hanavi. Ish Rachav
Al Susei Esh Ve'alah Vasse'arah Eliyahu Hanavi. Ish Shelo Ta'am
Ta'am Mitah Ukevurah. Eliyahu Hanavi Zachur Letov:

He was the man who proclaimed, "I have been very zealous for the
God of glory"; the man who rode on horses of fire in a whirlwind;
the man who tasted neither death or burial. Eliyahu, the prophet
may his name be of good memory.

תִּשְׁבִּי תַּצִּילֵנוּ מִפִּי אֲרָיוֹת אֵלִיָּהוּ הַנָּבִיא. תְּבַשְּׂרֵנוּ בְּשׂוֹרוֹת טוֹבוֹת
בְּמוֹצָאֵי שַׁבָּתוֹת אֵלִיָּהוּ הַנָּבִיא. תְּשַׂמְּחֵנוּ בָנִים עַל אָבוֹת. אֵלִיָּהוּ
הַנָּבִיא זָכוּר לְטוֹב:

Tishbi Tatzilenu Mipi Arayot Eliyahu Hanavi. Tevaserenu Besorot
Tovot Bemotza'ei Shabbatot Eliyahu Hanavi. Tesamecheinu Banim
Al Avot. Eliyahu Hanavi Zachur Letov:

Deliver us from the devouring mouth of lions; bring good tidings to
us at the close of the Shabbat. Cause us to rejoice all together, both
fathers and children. Eliyahu, the prophet may his name be of good
memory.

אִישׁ תִּשְׁבִּי עַל שְׁמוֹ נִקְרָא אֵלִיָּהוּ הַנָּבִיא. תַּצְלִיחֵנוּ עַל יָדוֹ בַּתּוֹרָה
אֵלִיָּהוּ הַנָּבִיא. תַּשְׁמִיעֵנוּ מִפִּיו בְּשׂוֹרָה טוֹבָה בִּמְהֵרָה אֵלִיָּהוּ
הַנָּבִיא. תּוֹצִיאֵנוּ מֵאֲפֵלָה לְאוֹרָה. אֵלִיָּהוּ הַנָּבִיא זָכוּר לְטוֹב:

Ish Tishbi Al Shemo Nikra Eliyahu Hanavi. Tatzlicheinu Al Yado
Batorah Eliyahu Hanavi. Tashmi'enu Mipiv Besorah Tovah Bimheirah
Eliyahu Hanavi. Totzi'enu Me'afelah Le'orah. Eliyahu Hanavi Zachur
Letov:

He was the man called by the additional name of Tishbite. Cause us
to prosper through him in Your Torah; let us speedily hear the good
tidings from his mouth. Bring us out from darkness to light. Eliyahu,
the prophet may his name be of good memory.

אַשְׁרֵי מִי שֶׁרָאָה פָנָיו בַּחֲלוֹם אַשְׁרֵי הוּא. אַשְׁרֵי מִי שֶׁנָּתַן לוֹ
שָׁלוֹם וְהֶחֱזִיר לוֹ שָׁלוֹם אַשְׁרֵי הוּא. יְהֹוָה יְבָרֵךְ אֶת עַמּוֹ בַשָּׁלוֹם.
אֵלִיָּהוּ הַנָּבִיא זָכוּר לְטוֹב:

Ashrei Mi Shera'ah Fanav Bachalom Ashrei Hu. Ashrei Mi Shenatan
Lo Shalom Vehechezir Lo Shalom Ashrei Hu. Adonai Yevarech Et
Ammo Vashalom. Eliyahu Hanavi Zachur Letov:

Happy is he who has seen him in a dream; happy is he who greeted
him with peace, to whom he returned the greeting of peace. May
Hashem bless His people with peace. Eliyahu the prophet is
remembered well. Eliyahu, the prophet may his name be of good
memory.

כַּכָּתוּב הִנֵּה אָנֹכִי שֹׁלֵחַ לָכֶם אֵת אֵלִיָּה הַנָּבִיא לִפְנֵי בּוֹא יוֹם יְהֹוָה
הַגָּדוֹל וְהַנּוֹרָא: וְהֵשִׁיב לֵב־אָבוֹת עַל־בָּנִים וְלֵב בָּנִים עַל־אֲבוֹתָם:

Kakatuv Hineh Anochi Sholeach Lachem Et Eliyah Hanavi Lifnei Bo
Yom Adonai Hagadol Vehanora. Veheshiv Lev Avot Al Banim Velev
Banim Al Avotam:

As it is written', "Behold, I will send you Eliyahu, the prophet, before
the coming of the great and tremendous day of Hashem. And he
will turn the heart of the fathers to the children, and the heart of the
children to their fathers."

Continue with petitions for the coming week.

Eloheinu Velohei Avoteinu.	אֱלֹהֵינוּ וֵאלֹהֵי אֲבוֹתֵינוּ.
Besiman Tov Uvemazal Tov	בְּסִימָן טוֹב וּבְמַזָּל טוֹב
Hachel Aleinu Et Sheshet Yemei	הָחֵל עָלֵינוּ אֶת שֵׁשֶׁת יְמֵי
Hama'aseh Habai'm Likratenu	הַמַּעֲשֶׂה הַבָּאִים לִקְרָאתֵנוּ
Leshalom. Chasuchim Mikol	לְשָׁלוֹם. חֲשׂוּכִים מִכָּל־
Chet Vafesha. Umenukkim Mikol	חֵטְא וָפֶשַׁע. וּמְנֻקִּים
Avon Ve'ashmah Varesha.	מִכָּל־עָוֹן וְאַשְׁמָה וָרֶשַׁע.
Umedubbakim Betalmud Torah	וּמְדֻבָּקִים בְּתַלְמוּד תּוֹרָה
Uma'asim Tovim. Vachanunim	וּמַעֲשִׂים טוֹבִים. וַחֲנוּנִים
Chochmah Binah Vada'at	חָכְמָה בִּינָה וָדַעַת
Me'itecha. Vetashmi'enu Vahem	מֵאִתְּךָ. וְתַשְׁמִיעֵנוּ בָהֶם
Sason Vesimchah. Velo Ta'aleh	שָׂשׂוֹן וְשִׂמְחָה. וְלֹא תַעֲלֶה
Kin'atenu Al Lev Adam. Velo	קִנְאָתֵנוּ עַל לֵב אָדָם. וְלֹא
Kin'at Adam Ta'aleh Al Libenu.	קִנְאַת אָדָם תַּעֲלֶה עַל לִבֵּנוּ.
Malkeinu Veloheinu. Sim	מַלְכֵּנוּ וֵאלֹהֵינוּ. שִׂים
Berachah Revachah	בְּרָכָה רְוָחָה
Vehatzlachah Bechol Ma'aseh	וְהַצְלָחָה בְּכָל־מַעֲשֵׂה
Yadeinu. Vechol Hayo'etz Aleinu	יָדֵינוּ. וְכָל־הַיּוֹעֵץ עָלֵינוּ
Ve'al Ammecha Beit Yisra'el	וְעַל עַמְּךָ בֵּית יִשְׂרָאֵל
Etzah Tovah. Umachashavah	עֵצָה טוֹבָה. וּמַחֲשָׁבָה
Tovah. Ammetzo. Barecho.	טוֹבָה. אַמְּצוֹ. בָּרְכוֹ.
Gadelo. Kayemo. Kayem Atzato.	גַּדְּלוֹ. קַיְּמוֹ. קַיֵּם עֲצָתוֹ.
Kadavar Shene'emar Yiten Lecha	כַּדָּבָר שֶׁנֶּאֱמַר יִתֶּן־לְךָ
Chilvavecha Vechol Atzatecha	כִלְבָבֶךָ וְכָל־עֲצָתְךָ
Yemalle. Vene'emar Vetigzar	יְמַלֵּא: וְנֶאֱמַר וְתִגְזַר־
Omer Veyakam Lach Ve'al	אֹמֶר וְיָקָם לָךְ וְעַל־

Deracheicha Nagah Or: Vechol	דְּרָכֶיךָ נָגַהּ אוֹר: וְכָל־
Hayo'etz Aleinu Ve'al Ammecha	הַיּוֹעֵץ עָלֵינוּ וְעַל עַמְּךָ
Beit Yisra'el Etzah She'einah	בֵּית יִשְׂרָאֵל עֵצָה שֶׁאֵינָהּ
Tovah Umachashavah She'einah	טוֹבָה וּמַחֲשָׁבָה שֶׁאֵינָהּ
Tovah. (Abedo. Battelo. Gade'o.	טוֹבָה. (אַבְּדוֹ. בַּטְּלוֹ. גַּדְּעוֹ.
Hafero.) Hafer Atzato. Kadavar	הֲפֵרוֹ.) הָפֵר עֲצָתוֹ. כַּדָּבָר
Shene'emar Adonai Hefir Atzat	שֶׁנֶּאֱמַר יְהֹוָה הֵפִיר עֲצַת־
Goyim Heni Machshevot	גּוֹיִם הֵנִיא מַחְשְׁבוֹת
Ammim: Vene'emar Utzu Etzah	עַמִּים: וְנֶאֱמַר עֻצוּ עֵצָה
Vetufar Daberu Davar Velo	וְתֻפָר דַּבְּרוּ דָבָר וְלֹא
Yakum Ki Imanu El: Ufetach	יָקוּם כִּי עִמָּנוּ אֵל: וּפְתַח
Lanu Adonai Eloheinu Bazeh	לָנוּ יְהֹוָה אֱלֹהֵינוּ בָּזֶה
Hashavua' Uvechol Shavua'	הַשָּׁבוּעַ וּבְכָל־שָׁבוּעַ
Veshavua':	וְשָׁבוּעַ:

Our God, and the God of our fathers, with good sign and fortune, let us begin the six days of labor which now approach us, freed from all sin and transgression; and purified from all iniquity, trespass, and wickedness; in which we may adhere to the study of the Torah, and perform good and worthy deeds. Grant us knowledge, understanding, and prudence; and cause us on them to hear joy and gladness, but do not allow others to envy us, neither we envy others. Our King and our God, Send blessing, abundance, and prosperity to all the work of our hands; and whoever gives good counsel, or entertains favorable thoughts for us, or for Your people Yisrael; Strengthen, bless, exalt and establish him, and confirm his counsel, according as it is written, "He will grant you according to your own heart, And fulfill all of your counsel." (Psalms 20:5) And it is said, "You will also decree a thing, and it will be established to you, And light will shine upon your ways." (Job 22:28) But whoever counsels anything that is not good, or conceives any thought that is not good concerning us, or Your people, the House of Yisrael, (destroy him, cancel him, cut him down, annul him) frustrate his counsel; according as it is said, "Hashem brings the counsel of the nations to nothing; He makes the thoughts of the peoples to be of no effect." (Psalms 33:10) It is also said, "Take counsel together, and it will be brought to nothing; Speak the word, and it will not stand; For God is with us." (Isaiah 8:10) Hashem our God, may it be Your will to open for us, on this, and every week:

Sha'arei Orah. Sha'arei	שַׁעֲרֵי אוֹרָה. שַׁעֲרֵי
Verachah. Sha'arei Gilah.	בְרָכָה. שַׁעֲרֵי גִילָה.
Sha'arei Ditzah. Sha'arei De'ah.	שַׁעֲרֵי דִיצָה. שַׁעֲרֵי דֵעָה.
Sha'arei Hod Vehadar. Sha'arei	שַׁעֲרֵי הוֹד וְהָדָר. שַׁעֲרֵי
Va'ad Tov. Sha'arei Zimrah.	וַעַד טוֹב. שַׁעֲרֵי זִמְרָה.
Sha'arei Chedvah. Sha'arei	שַׁעֲרֵי חֶדְוָה. שַׁעֲרֵי
Chemlah. Sha'arei Chein	חֶמְלָה. שַׁעֲרֵי חֵן
Vachesed. Sha'arei Chayim	וָחֶסֶד. שַׁעֲרֵי חַיִּים
Tovim. Sha'arei Tovah. Sha'arei	טוֹבִים. שַׁעֲרֵי טוֹבָה. שַׁעֲרֵי
Yeshu'ah. Sha'arei Chapparah.	יְשׁוּעָה. שַׁעֲרֵי כַפָּרָה.
Sha'arei Chalkalah. Sha'arei	שַׁעֲרֵי כַלְכָּלָה. שַׁעֲרֵי
Limmud Torah Lishmah. Sha'arei	לִמּוּד תוֹרָה לִשְׁמָה. שַׁעֲרֵי
Mazon. Sha'arei Mechilah.	מָזוֹן. שַׁעֲרֵי מְחִילָה.
Sha'arei Nechamah. Sha'arei	שַׁעֲרֵי נֶחָמָה. שַׁעֲרֵי
Selichah. Sha'arei Ezrah. Sha'arei	סְלִיחָה. שַׁעֲרֵי עֶזְרָה. שַׁעֲרֵי
Fedut. Sha'arei Farnasah Tovah.	פְדוּת. שַׁעֲרֵי פַרְנָסָה טוֹבָה.
Sha'arei Tzedakah. Sha'arei	שַׁעֲרֵי צְדָקָה. שַׁעֲרֵי
Tzoholah. Sha'arei Komemiyut.	צָהֳלָה. שַׁעֲרֵי קוֹמְמִיּוּת.

Sha'arei Refu'ah Sheleimah.	שַׁעֲרֵי רְפוּאָה שְׁלֵימָה.
Sha'arei Shalom. Sha'arei	שַׁעֲרֵי שָׁלוֹם. שַׁעֲרֵי
Shalvah. Sha'arei Torah. Sha'arei	שַׁלְוָה. שַׁעֲרֵי תוֹרָה. שַׁעֲרֵי
Tefillah. Sha'arei Teshuvah.	תְפִלָּה. שַׁעֲרֵי תְשׁוּבָה.
Sha'arei Teshu'ah:	שַׁעֲרֵי תְשׁוּעָה:

the gates of light, the gates of blessing, the gates of rejoicing, the gates of happiness, the gates of knowledge, the gates of splendor and glory, the gates of good counsel, the gates of song, the gates of gladness, the gates of grace and kindness, the gates of good life; the gates of goodness, the gates of salvation, the gates of atonement, the gates of support, the gates of study of Torah for its own sake, the gates of sustenance, the gates of forgiveness, the gates of consolation, the gates of pardon, the gates of help, the gates of rescue, the gates of good livelihood, the gates of justice, the gates of exultation, the gates of uprightness, the gates of complete healing, the gates of peace, the gates of security; the gates of Torah, the gates of prayer, the gates of repentance, and deliverance;

Kedichtiv Uteshu'at Tzaddikim	כְּדִכְתִיב וּתְשׁוּעַת צַדִּיקִים
Mey'Adonai Ma'uzam Be'et	מֵיהֹוָה מָעוּזָּם בְּעֵת
Tzarah. Vaya'zerem Adonai	צָרָה: וַיַּעְזְרֵם יְהֹוָה
Vayfalletem Yefalletem	וַיְפַלְּטֵם יְפַלְּטֵם
Meresha'im Veyoshi'em Ki	מֵרְשָׁעִים וְיוֹשִׁיעֵם כִּי־
Chasu Vo. Vene'emar Chasaf	חָסוּ בוֹ: וְנֶאֱמַר חָשַׂף
Adonai Et Zeroa' Kodsho	יְהֹוָה אֶת־זְרוֹעַ קָדְשׁוֹ
Le'einei Kol Hagoyim Vera'u Kol	לְעֵינֵי כָּל־הַגּוֹיִם וְרָאוּ כָּל־
Afsei Aretz Et Yeshu'at Eloheinu.	אַפְסֵי־אָרֶץ אֵת יְשׁוּעַת אֱלֹהֵינוּ:
Vene'emar Kol Tzofayich Nase'u	וְנֶאֱמַר קוֹל צֹפַיִךְ נָשְׂאוּ
Kol Yachdav Yeranenu Ki Ayin	קוֹל יַחְדָּו יְרַנֵּנוּ כִּי עַיִן

Be'ayin Yir'u Beshuv Adonai	בְּעַיִן יִרְאוּ בְּשׁוּב יְהֹוָה
Tziyon. Vekayem Lanu Adonai	צִיּוֹן: וְקַיֶּם לָנוּ יְהֹוָה
Eloheinu Mikra Shekatuv. Mah	אֱלֹהֵינוּ מִקְרָא שֶׁכָּתוּב. מַה־
Navu Al Heharim Raglei	נָּאווּ עַל־הֶהָרִים רַגְלֵי
Mevaser Mashmia Shalom	מְבַשֵּׂר מַשְׁמִיעַ שָׁלוֹם
Mevaser Tov Mashmia' Yeshu'ah	מְבַשֵּׂר טוֹב מַשְׁמִיעַ יְשׁוּעָה
Omer Letziyon Malach	אֹמֵר לְצִיּוֹן מָלַךְ
Elohayich.	אֱלֹהָיִךְ:

as it is written, "But the salvation of the righteous is from Hashem: He is their strength in the time of trouble. Hashem will also help and deliver them; He will deliver them from the wicked, and save them, because they trust in Him." It is also said, "Hashem has made bare His holy arm in the sight of all the nations, and all the ends of the earth will see the salvation of our God." And it is said, "Your watchmen lift up their voice, with one voice they will sing together: for face to face they will see when Hashem returns to Tziyon." And confirm to us, Hashem, our God, the sentence which is written, "How beautiful upon the mountains are the feet of the messenger of good news, That announces peace, the harbinger of good news, That announces salvation; That says to Tziyon: 'Your God reigns.' (Isaiah 52:7)

Havdalah / Seperation

One should say Havdalah while sitting. [Though many stand.] One holds the wine in the right hand and the spices (it is customary to use myrtle whenever one can) in the left and makes the blessing over the wine. Then he places the spice in the right hand and the wine in the left and says the blessing over the spice and returns the wine to his right hand. (SA, OC 296)

רִאשׁוֹן לְצִיּוֹן הִנֵּה הִנָּם וְלִירוּשָׁלַ͏ִם מְבַשֵּׂר אֶתֵּן: אַל־תִּשְׂמְחִי אֹיַ֫בְתִּי לִי כִּי נָפַלְתִּי קָמְתִּי כִּי־אֵשֵׁב בַּחֹשֶׁךְ יְהֹוָה אוֹר לִי: לַיְּהוּדִים הָיְתָה אוֹרָה וְשִׂמְחָה וְשָׂשֹׂן וִיקָר: וַיְהִי דָוִד לְכָל־דְּרָכָו מַשְׂכִּיל וַיהֹוָה עִמּוֹ: וְנֹחַ מָצָא חֵן בְּעֵינֵי יְהֹוָה: כֵּן נִמְצָא חֵן וְתִמְצָאוּ חֵן וְשֵׂכֶל טוֹב בְּעֵינֵי אֱלֹהִים וְאָדָם:

Rishon Letziyon Hineh Hinam Velirushalayim Mevaser Etten:
Layehudim Hayetah Orah Vesimchah Vesason Vikar. Uchetiv Vayhi
David Lechol Derachav Maskil Va'Adonai Immo. Ken Yihyeh Imanu:
Venoach Matza Chein Be'einei Adonai: Kn Nimtza Chein Vesechel
B'einei Elohim Ve'adam:

The first will say to Tziyon, Behold they are here; and to Yerushalayim, I will give a messenger of good news: (Is. 41:27) "The Jews had light and gladness, and joy and honor." (Esther 8:16) And as it is written, "And David had great success in all his ways; and Hashem was with him." (I Samuel 18:14) But Noach found grace in the eyes of Hashem. (Genesis 6:8) Yes, you will find grace and you will find grace and good favor In the sight of God and man. (Proverbs 3:4)

קוּמִי אוֹרִי כִּי בָא אוֹרֵךְ וּכְבוֹד יְהֹוָה עָלַיִךְ זָרָח: כִּי־הִנֵּה הַחֹשֶׁךְ יְכַסֶּה־אֶרֶץ וַעֲרָפֶל לְאֻמִּים וְעָלַיִךְ יִזְרַח יְהֹוָה וּכְבוֹדוֹ עָלַיִךְ יֵרָאֶה:

Kumi Ori Ki Va Orech Uchevod Adonai Alayich Zarach. Ki-Hinneh
Hachoshech Yechasseh-Eretz Va'arafel Le'ummim Ve'alayich Yizrach
Adonai Uchevodo Alayich Yera'eh.

Arise, shine, for your light has come, And the glory of Hashem has risen upon you. For, behold, darkness will cover the earth, And gross darkness the peoples; But upon you Hashem will arise, And His glory will be seen upon you. (Isaiah 60:1-2)

Kindle a light, bring some aromatic spice and fill a cup with wine; take it in the right hand and say:

כּוֹס־יְשׁוּעוֹת אֶשָּׂא וּבְשֵׁם יְהֹוָה אֶקְרָא:

Kos Yeshu'ot Essa Uveshem Adonai Ekra.

I will lift up the cup of salvation, And call upon the name of Hashem.

(Psalms 116:13)

אָנָּא יְהֹוָה הוֹשִׁיעָה נָּא. אָנָּא יְהֹוָה הוֹשִׁיעָה נָּא:

Ana Adonai Hoshi'ah Na. Ana Adonai Hoshi'ah Na:

Please Hashem, Save Now. Please Hashem, Save Now.

אָנָּא יְהֹוָה הַצְלִיחָה נָּא. אָנָּא יְהֹוָה הַצְלִיחָה נָּא:

Ana Adonai Hatzlichah Na. Ana Adonai Hatzlichah Na.

Please Hashem, Give Success Now. Please Hashem, Give Success Now.

Some say "Hatzlicheinu" and others say "Baruch Haba".

הַצְלִיחֵנוּ הַצְלִיחַ דְּרָכֵינוּ הַצְלִיחַ לִמּוּדֵינוּ וּשְׁלַח בְּרָכָה רְוָחָה וְהַצְלָחָה בְּכָל־מַעֲשֵׂה יָדֵינוּ. כְּדִכְתִיב יִשָּׂא בְרָכָה מֵאֵת יְהֹוָה וּצְדָקָה מֵאֱלֹהֵי יִשְׁעוֹ: לַיְּהוּדִים הָיְתָה אוֹרָה וְשִׂמְחָה וְשָׂשֹׂן וִיקָר: וּכְתִיב וַיְהִי דָוִד לְכָל־דְּרָכָו מַשְׂכִּיל וַיהֹוָה עִמּוֹ: כֵּן יִהְיֶה עִמָּנוּ: וְנֹחַ מָצָא חֵן בְּעֵינֵי יְהֹוָה: כֵּן נִמְצָא חֵן וְשֵׂכֶל בְּעֵינֵי אֱלֹהִים וְאָדָם:

Hatzlicheinu Hatzliach Deracheinu Hatzliach Limmudeinu Ushelach Berachah Revachah Vehatzlachah Bechol Ma'aseh Yadeinu. Kedichtiv Yissa Verachah Me'et Adonai Utzedakah Me'elohei Yish'o: Layehudim Hayetah Orah Vesimchah Vesason Vikar. Uchetiv Vayhi David Lechol Derachav Maskil Va'Adonai Immo. Ken Yihyeh Imanu: Venoach Matza Chein Be'einei Adonai: Kn Nimtza Chein Vesechel B'einei Elohim Ve'adam:

Give us success and prosper our matters and our Torah learning and send blessing, abundance and success to all our undertakings. As it is written, "He will receive a blessing from Hashem, and righteousness from the God of his salvation." **(Psalms 24:5)** "The Jews had light and gladness, and joy and honor." **(Esther 8:16)** And as it is written, "And David had great success in all his ways; and Hashem was with him." (I Samuel 18:14) But Noach found grace in the eyes of Hashem. (Genesis 6:8) Yes, you will find grace and you will find grace and good favor in the sight of God and man. (Proverbs 3:4)

בָּרוּךְ הַבָּא בְּשֵׁם יְהוָֹה בֵּרַכְנוּכֶם מִבֵּית יְהוָֹה: אֵל | יְהוָֹה וַיָּאֶר־לָנוּ
אִסְרוּ־חַג בַּעֲבֹתִים עַד־קַרְנוֹת הַמִּזְבֵּחַ: אֵלִי אַתָּה וְאוֹדֶךָ אֱלֹהַי
אֲרוֹמְמֶךָ: הוֹדוּ לַיהוָֹה כִּי־טוֹב כִּי לְעוֹלָם חַסְדּוֹ:

Baruch Haba Beshem Adonai Berachnuchem Mibeit Adonai. El Adonai Vayaer-Lanu Isru-Chag Ba'avotim Ad-Karnot Hamizbe'ach. Eli Attah Ve'odeka Elohai Aromemeka. Hodu L'Adonai Ki-Tov Ki Le'olam Chasdo.

Blessed is he that comes in the name of Hashem; We bless you out of the House of Hashem. Hashem is God, and has given us light; Order the festival procession with boughs, even to the horns of the altar. You are my God, and I will give thanks to You; You are my God, I will exalt You. Give thanks to Hashem, for He is good, For His mercy endures forever. (Ps. 118:26-29)

The one making the blessing says:

Savri Maranan!   סַבְרִי מָרָנָן:

Gentlemen, with your attention!

And answer:

Le'chayim!   לְחַיִּים:

To life!

Baruch Attah Adonai Eloheinu   בָּרוּךְ אַתָּה יְהוָֹה. אֱלֹהֵינוּ

Melech Ha'olam Borei Pri   מֶלֶךְ הָעוֹלָם. בּוֹרֵא פְּרִי

Hagefen.   הַגָּפֶן:

Blessed are You, Hashem our God, King of the universe, Who creates the fruit of the vine.

On the evening of Yom Tov, which is not Saturday, there are no blessings on the spices or on the candle.

Baruch Attah Adonai Eloheinu

Melech Ha'olam Borei Minei

Vesamim:

בָּרוּךְ אַתָּה יְהֹוָה אֱלֹהֵינוּ

מֶלֶךְ הָעוֹלָם. בּוֹרֵא מִינֵי

בְשָׂמִים:

Blessed are You, Hashem our God, King of the universe, Who creates various spices.

It is a custom to hold one's hand towards the lighted candle and look at the palm of one's hands and one's nails (SA, OC 298), and then say:

Baruch Attah Adonai Eloheinu

Melech Ha'olam Borei Me'orei

Ha'esh:

בָּרוּךְ אַתָּה יְהֹוָה אֱלֹהֵינוּ

מֶלֶךְ הָעוֹלָם. בּוֹרֵא מְאוֹרֵי

הָאֵשׁ:

Blessed are You, Hashem our God, King of the universe, Who creates the lights of the fire.

Baruch Attah Adonai Eloheinu

Melech Ha'olam Hamavdil Bein

Kodesh Lechol. Uvein Or

Lechoshech. Uvein Yisra'el

La'ammim. Uvein Yom

Hashevi'i Lesheshet Yemei

Hama'aseh. Baruch Attah

Adonai Hamavdil Bein Kodesh

Lechol:

בָּרוּךְ אַתָּה יְהֹוָה אֱלֹהֵינוּ

מֶלֶךְ הָעוֹלָם. הַמַּבְדִּיל בֵּין

קֹדֶשׁ לְחוֹל. וּבֵין אוֹר

לְחֹשֶׁךְ. וּבֵין יִשְׂרָאֵל

לָעַמִּים. וּבֵין יוֹם

הַשְּׁבִיעִי לְשֵׁשֶׁת יְמֵי

הַמַּעֲשֶׂה. בָּרוּךְ אַתָּה

יְהֹוָה הַמַּבְדִּיל בֵּין קֹדֶשׁ

לְחוֹל:

Blessed are You, Hashem our God, King of the universe, Who makes a distinction between holy and common; between light and darkness; between Yisrael and other nations; and between the seventh day and the six days of labor. Blessed are You, Hashem, Who makes a distinction between holy and common.

Some say (SA, OC 299:7, Rema):

After Blessing for Wine

בָּרוּךְ אַתָּה יְהֹוָה אֱלֹהֵינוּ מֶלֶךְ הָעוֹלָם. עַל הַגֶּפֶן וְעַל פְּרִי הַגֶּפֶן וְעַל תְּנוּבַת הַשָּׂדֶה. וְעַל אֶרֶץ חֶמְדָּה טוֹבָה וּרְחָבָה. שֶׁרָצִיתָ וְהִנְחַלְתָּ לַאֲבוֹתֵינוּ. לֶאֱכֹל מִפִּרְיָהּ וְלִשְׂבֹּעַ מִטּוּבָהּ. רַחֵם יְהֹוָה אֱלֹהֵינוּ עָלֵינוּ. וְעַל יִשְׂרָאֵל עַמֶּךָ. וְעַל יְרוּשָׁלַיִם עִירָךְ. וְעַל הַר צִיּוֹן מִשְׁכַּן כְּבוֹדָךְ. וְעַל מִזְבָּחָךְ וְעַל הֵיכָלָךְ. וּבְנֵה יְרוּשָׁלַיִם עִיר הַקֹּדֶשׁ. בִּמְהֵרָה בְיָמֵינוּ. וְהַעֲלֵנוּ לְתוֹכָהּ. וְשַׂמְּחֵנוּ בְּבִנְיָנָהּ. וּנְבָרֶכְךָ עָלֶיהָ בִּקְדֻשָּׁה וּבְטָהֳרָה.

Baruch Attah Adonai Eloheinu Melech Ha'olam Al Hagefen Ve'al Peri Hagefen Ve'al Tenuvat Hassadeh. Ve'al Eretz Chemdah Tovah Urechavah. Sheratzita Vehinchalta La'avoteinu. Le'echol Mipiryah Velisboa' Mituvah. Rachem Adonai Eloheinu Aleinu. Ve'al Yisra'el Amach. Ve'al Yerushalayim Irach. Ve'al Har Tziyon Mishkan Kevodach. Ve'al Mizbachach Ve'al Heichalach. Uveneh Yerushalayim Ir Hakodesh. Bimheirah Veyameinu. Veha'alenu Letochah. Vesamecheinu Bevinyanah. Unevarechach Aleiha Bikdushah Uvetaharah.

Blessed are You, Hashem our God, King of the universe, for the fruit of the vine and produce of the field, for the lovely and spacious land which You granted to our fathers as a heritage to eat of its fruit and enjoy its good gifts. Have mercy, Hashem our God, on Yisrael Your people, on Yerushalayim Your city, on Tziyon the abode of Your majesty, on Your Altar and Your Temple. Rebuild the holy city of Yerushalayim speedily in our days. Bring us there and gladden us with the restoration of our land; may we eat of its fruit and enjoy its good gifts; may we bless You for it in holiness and purity.

On Rosh Chodesh:

וְזָכְרֵנוּ לְטוֹבָה בְּיוֹם רֹאשׁ חֹדֶשׁ הַזֶּה.

Vezacherenu Letovah Beyom Rosh Chodesh Hazeh.

And be mindful of us on this New Moon day.

On Rosh Hashanah:

וְזָכְרֵנוּ לְטוֹבָה בְּיוֹם הַזִּכָּרוֹן הַזֶּה.

Vezochrenu Letovah Beyom Hazikaron Hazeh.

And be mindful of us on this Day of Remembrance.

On Pesach:

וְשַׂמְּחֵנוּ בְּיוֹם חַג הַמַּצּוֹת הַזֶּה. בְּיוֹם טוֹב מִקְרָא קֹדֶשׁ הַזֶּה.

Vesamecheinu Beyom Chag Hamatzot Hazeh. Beyom Tov Mikra Kodesh Hazeh.

Grant us joy on this Festival of Unleavened Bread, this Festival Day of holy convocation.

On Shavuot:

וְשַׂמְּחֵנוּ בְּיוֹם חַג הַשָּׁבוּעוֹת הַזֶּה בְּיוֹם טוֹב מִקְרָא קֹדֶשׁ הַזֶּה.

Vesamecheinu Beyom Chag Hashavu'ot Hazeh Beyom Tov Mikra Kodesh Hazeh.

Grant us joy on this Festival of Weeks, this Festival Day of holy convocation.

On Sukkot:

וְשַׂמְּחֵנוּ בְּיוֹם הַסֻּכּוֹת הַזֶּה. בְּיוֹם טוֹב מִקְרָא קֹדֶשׁ הַזֶּה.

Vesamecheinu Beyom Hasukkot Hazeh. Beyom Tov Mikra Kodesh Hazeh.

Grant us joy on this Festival of Tabernacles, this Festival Day of holy convocation.

On Shemini Atzeret:

וְשַׂמְּחֵנוּ בְּיוֹם שְׁמִינִי חַג עֲצֶרֶת הַזֶּה בְּיוֹם טוֹב מִקְרָא קֹדֶשׁ הַזֶּה.

Vesamecheinu Beyom Shemini Chag Atzeret Hazeh Beyom Tov Mikra Kodesh Hazeh.

Grant us joy on this Festival of Eighth Day Feast, this Festival Day of holy convocation.

כִּי אַתָּה טוֹב וּמֵטִיב לַכֹּל. וְנוֹדֶה לְּךָ עַל הָאָרֶץ וְעַל פְּרִי הַגֶּפֶן (גַּפְנָהּ) בָּרוּךְ אַתָּה יְהֹוָה עַל הָאָרֶץ וְעַל פְּרִי הַגֶּפֶן: (גַּפְנָהּ:)

Ki Attah Tov Umeitiv Lakol. Venodeh Lecha Al Ha'aretz Ve'al Peri Hagefen **Of Yisrael:** (Hagafnah). Baruch Attah Adonai Al Ha'aretz Ve'al Peri Hagefen **Of Yisrael:** (Hagafnah).

For You are good and beneficent to all; and we will give You thanks for the land, and for the fruit of the vine. **Of Yisrael:** (And for the fruit of its vine.) Blessed are You, Hashem, for the land, and for the fruit of the vine. **Of Yisrael:** (And for the fruit of its vine.)

If Rosh Chodesh or within the first 15 days of the month, some say Birkhat HaLevanah / The Blessing of the Moon, at the back of the Siddur (page 705).

Veyiten Lecha

וְיִתֶּן־לְךָ֙ הָאֱלֹהִ֔ים מִטַּל֙ הַשָּׁמַ֔יִם וּמִשְׁמַנֵּ֖י הָאָ֑רֶץ וְרֹ֥ב דָּגָ֖ן וְתִירֹֽשׁ: יַֽעַבְד֣וּךָ עַמִּ֗ים וישתחו (וְיִֽשְׁתַּחֲו֣וּ) לְךָ֙ לְאֻמִּ֔ים הֱוֵ֤ה גְבִיר֙ לְאַחֶ֔יךָ וְיִשְׁתַּחֲו֥וּ לְךָ֖ בְּנֵ֣י אִמֶּ֑ךָ אֹרְרֶ֣יךָ אָר֔וּר וּֽמְבָרֲכֶ֖יךָ בָּרֽוּךְ:

Veyiten Lecha Ha'elohim Mittal Hashamayim Umishmanei Ha'aretz
Verov Dagan Vetirosh. Ya'avducha Ammim Veyishtachavu Lecha
Le'ummim Heveh Gevir Le'acheicha Veyishtachavu Lecha Benei
Imecha Orereicha Arur Umevarecheicha Baruch.

May God give you of the dew of heaven, And of the fat places of the
earth, and plenty of corn and wine. May peoples serve you, And
nations bow down to you. Be lord over your brothers, And may your
mother's sons bow down to you. Cursed is everyone that curses
you, And blessed is everyone that blesses you. (Genesis 27:28-29)

וְאֵ֤ל שַׁדַּי֙ יְבָרֵ֣ךְ אֹֽתְךָ֔ וְיַפְרְךָ֖ וְיַרְבֶּ֑ךָ וְהָיִ֖יתָ לִקְהַ֥ל עַמִּֽים: וְיִתֶּן־לְךָ֙ אֶת־בִּרְכַּ֣ת אַבְרָהָ֗ם לְךָ֖ וּלְזַרְעֲךָ֣ אִתָּ֑ךְ לְרִשְׁתְּךָ֙ אֶת־אֶ֣רֶץ מְגֻרֶ֔יךָ אֲשֶׁר־נָתַ֥ן אֱלֹהִ֖ים לְאַבְרָהָֽם:

Ve'el Shaddai Yevarech Otecha Veyafrecha Veyarbecha Vehayita
Likhal Ammim. Veyiten Lecha Et Birkhat Avraham Lecha
Ulezar'acha Ittach Lerishtecha Et Eretz Megureicha Asher Natan
Elohim Le'avraham.

And God Almighty bless you, and make you fruitful, and multiply
you, that you may be a congregation of peoples; and give you the
blessing of Avraham, to you, and to your seed with you; that you
may inherit the land of your sojourning, which God gave to
Avraham.' (Genesis 28:4)

מֵאֵ֨ל אָבִ֜יךָ וְיַעְזְרֶ֗ךָ וְאֵ֤ת שַׁדַּי֙ וִיבָרְכֶ֔ךָ בִּרְכֹ֤ת שָׁמַ֙יִם֙ מֵעָ֔ל בִּרְכֹ֥ת תְּה֖וֹם רֹבֶ֣צֶת תָּ֑חַת בִּרְכֹ֥ת שָׁדַ֖יִם וָרָֽחַם: בִּרְכֹ֣ת אָבִ֗יךָ גָּֽבְרוּ֙ עַל־בִּרְכֹ֣ת הוֹרַ֔י עַֽד־תַּאֲוַ֖ת גִּבְעֹ֣ת עוֹלָ֑ם תִּֽהְיֶ֙יןָ֙ לְרֹ֣אשׁ יוֹסֵ֔ף וּלְקָדְקֹ֖ד נְזִ֥יר אֶחָֽיו:

Me'el Avicha Veya'zerekka Ve'et Shaddai Vivarechekka Birchot
Shamayim Me'al Birchot Tehom Rovetzet Tachat Birchot Shadayim
Varacham. Birchot Avicha Gaveru Al Birchot Horai Ad Ta'avat Giv'ot
Olam Tihyeina Lerosh Yosef Ulekodkod Nezir Echav.

Even by the God of your father, who will help you, And by the
Almighty, who will bless you, With blessings of heaven above,
Blessings of the deep that couches beneath, Blessings of the
breasts, and of the womb. The blessings of your father are mighty
beyond the blessings of my progenitors to the utmost bound of the
everlasting hills; They will be on the head of Yosef, And on the
crown of the head of the prince among his brothers. (Genesis 49:25-26)

וַאֲהֵבְךָ֙ וּבֵרַכְךָ֣ וְהִרְבֶּ֔ךָ וּבֵרַ֣ךְ פְּרִי־בִטְנְךָ֣ וּפְרִי־אַדְמָתֶ֗ךָ דְּגָֽנְךָ֤ וְתִירֹֽשְׁךָ֙
וְיִצְהָרֶ֔ךָ שְׁגַר־אֲלָפֶ֖יךָ וְעַשְׁתְּרֹ֣ת צֹאנֶ֑ךָ עַ֚ל הָֽאֲדָמָ֔ה אֲשֶׁר־נִשְׁבַּ֥ע
לַֽאֲבֹתֶ֖יךָ לָ֥תֶת לָֽךְ: בָּר֥וּךְ תִּֽהְיֶ֖ה מִכָּל־הָֽעַמִּ֑ים לֹא־יִהְיֶ֥ה בְךָ֛ עָקָ֥ר
וַֽעֲקָרָ֖ה וּבִבְהֶמְתֶּֽךָ: וְהֵסִ֧יר יְהֹוָ֛ה מִמְּךָ֖ כָּל־חֹ֑לִי וְכָל־מַדְוֵי֩ מִצְרַ֨יִם
הָֽרָעִ֜ים אֲשֶׁ֣ר יָדַ֗עְתָּ לֹ֤א יְשִׂימָם֙ בָּ֔ךְ וּנְתָנָ֖ם בְּכָל־שֹׂנְאֶֽיךָ:

Va'ahevecha Uverachcha Vehirbecha Uverach Peri Vitnecha Uferi
Admatecha Deganecha Vetiroshecha Veyitzharecha Shegar
Alafeicha Ve'ashterot Tzonecha Al Ha'adamah Asher Nishba
La'avoteicha Latet Lach. Baruch Tihyeh Mikol Ha'ammim Lo Yihyeh
Vecha Akar Va'akarah Uvivhemtecha. Vehesir Adonai Mimecha Kol
Choli Vechol Madvei Mitzrayim Hara'im Asher Yada'ta Lo Yesimam
Bach Unetanam Bechol Sone'eicha.

And He will love you, and bless you, and multiply you; He will also
bless the fruit of your body and the fruit of your land, your corn and
your wine and your oil, the increase of your herd and the young of
your flock, in the land which He swore to your fathers to give you.
You will be blessed above all peoples; there will be no male or
female barren among you, or among your cattle. And Hashem will
take away from you all sickness; and He will put none of the evil
diseases of Mitzrayim, which you know, upon you, but will lay them
upon all of them that hate you. (Deut. 7:13-15)

בָּרוּךְ אַתָּה בָּעִיר וּבָרוּךְ אַתָּה בַּשָּׂדֶה: בָּרוּךְ פְּרִי־בִטְנְךָ וּפְרִי
אַדְמָתְךָ וּפְרִי בְהֶמְתֶּךָ שְׁגַר אֲלָפֶיךָ וְעַשְׁתְּרוֹת צֹאנֶךָ: בָּרוּךְ טַנְאֲךָ
וּמִשְׁאַרְתֶּךָ: בָּרוּךְ אַתָּה בְּבֹאֶךָ וּבָרוּךְ אַתָּה בְּצֵאתֶךָ: יִתֵּן יְהֹוָה
אֶת־אֹיְבֶיךָ הַקָּמִים עָלֶיךָ נִגָּפִים לְפָנֶיךָ בְּדֶרֶךְ אֶחָד יֵצְאוּ אֵלֶיךָ
וּבְשִׁבְעָה דְרָכִים יָנוּסוּ לְפָנֶיךָ: יְצַו יְהֹוָה אִתְּךָ אֶת־הַבְּרָכָה בַּאֲסָמֶיךָ
וּבְכֹל מִשְׁלַח יָדֶךָ וּבֵרַכְךָ בָּאָרֶץ אֲשֶׁר־יְהֹוָה אֱלֹהֶיךָ נֹתֵן לָךְ:

Baruch Attah Ba'ir Uvaruch Attah Bassadeh. Baruch Peri Vitnecha
Uferi Admatecha Uferi Vehemtecha Shegar Alafeicha Ve'ashterot
Tzonecha. Baruch Tan'acha Umish'artecha. Baruch Attah Bevo'echa
Uvaruch Attah Betzetecha. Yiten Adonai Et Oyeveicha Hakamim
Aleicha Niggafim Lefaneicha Bederech Echad Yetze'u Eleicha
Uveshiv'ah Derachim Yanusu Lefaneicha. Yetzav Adonai Itecha Et
Haberachah Ba'asameicha Uvechol Mishlach Yadecha Uverachcha
Ba'aretz Asher Adonai Eloheicha Noten Lach.

Blessed will you be in the city, and blessed will you be in the field.
Blessed will be the fruit of your body, and the fruit of your land, and
the fruit of your cattle, the increase of your herd, and the young of
your flock. Blessed will be your basket and your kneading-trough.
Blessed will you be when you come in, and blessed will you be when
you go out. Hashem will cause your enemies that rise up against you
to be smitten before you; they will come out against you one way,
and will flee before you seven ways. Hashem will command the
blessing with you in your barns, and in all that you put your hand to;
and He will bless you in the land which Hashem your God gives you.
(Deuteronomy 28:3-8)

יִפְתַּח יְהֹוָה | לְךָ אֶת־אוֹצָרוֹ הַטּוֹב אֶת־הַשָּׁמַיִם לָתֵת מְטַר־אַרְצְךָ
בְּעִתּוֹ וּלְבָרֵךְ אֵת כָּל־מַעֲשֵׂה יָדֶךָ וְהִלְוִיתָ גּוֹיִם רַבִּים וְאַתָּה לֹא
תִלְוֶה: אַשְׁרֶיךָ יִשְׂרָאֵל מִי כָמוֹךָ עַם נוֹשַׁע בַּיהֹוָה מָגֵן עֶזְרֶךָ
וַאֲשֶׁר־חֶרֶב גַּאֲוָתֶךָ וְיִכָּחֲשׁוּ אֹיְבֶיךָ לָךְ וְאַתָּה עַל־בָּמוֹתֵימוֹ תִדְרֹךְ:

Yiftach Adonai Lecha Et Otzaro Hatov Et Hashamayim Latet Metar
Artzecha Be'ito Ulevarech Et Kol Ma'aseh Yadecha Vehilvita Goyim
Rabim Ve'attah Lo Tilveh. Ashreicha Yisra'el Mi Chamocha Am

Nosha Badonai Magen Ezrecha Va'asher Cherev Ga'avatecha
Veyikachashu Oyeveicha Lach Ve'attah Al Bamoteimo Tidroch.

Hashem will open to you His good treasure the heavens to give the
rain of your land in its season, and to bless all the work of your
hand; and you will lend to many nations, but you will not borrow.
Happy are you, Yisrael, who is like you? A people saved by Hashem,
The Shield of your help, And that is the sword of your excellency.
And your enemies will dwindle away before you; And you will tread
on their high places. (Deut. 28:12, 33:29)

יִשְׂרָאֵל נוֹשַׁע בַּיהוָה תְּשׁוּעַת עוֹלָמִים לֹא־תֵבֹשׁוּ וְלֹא־תִכָּלְמוּ
עַד־עוֹלְמֵי עַד:

Yisra'el Nosha B'Adonai Teshu'at Olamim Lo Tevoshu Velo Tikalemu
Ad Olemei Ad.

Yisrael, that is saved by Hashem with an everlasting salvation; You
will not be ashamed or confounded forever.

וַאֲכַלְתֶּם אָכוֹל וְשָׂבוֹעַ וְהִלַּלְתֶּם אֶת־שֵׁם יְהוָה אֱלֹהֵיכֶם אֲשֶׁר־עָשָׂה
עִמָּכֶם לְהַפְלִיא וְלֹא־יֵבֹשׁוּ עַמִּי לְעוֹלָם: וִידַעְתֶּם כִּי בְקֶרֶב יִשְׂרָאֵל
אָנִי וַאֲנִי יְהוָה אֱלֹהֵיכֶם וְאֵין עוֹד וְלֹא־יֵבֹשׁוּ עַמִּי לְעוֹלָם:

Va'achaltem Achol Vesavoa' Vehillaltem Et Shem Adonai
Eloheichem Asher Asah Imachem Lehafli Velo Yevoshu Ammi
Le'olam. Vida'tem Ki Vekerev Yisra'el Ani Va'ani Adonai Eloheichem
Ve'ein Od Velo Yevoshu Ammi Le'olam.

And you will eat your fill And praise the name of Hashem your God
Who dealt so wondrously with you— My people will be ashamed no
more. And you will know That I am in the midst of Yisrael: That I,
Hashem, am your God and there is no other. And My people will be
ashamed no more." (Joel 2, 26-27)

וּפְדוּיֵי יְהוָה יְשֻׁבוּן וּבָאוּ צִיּוֹן בְּרִנָּה וְשִׂמְחַת עוֹלָם עַל־רֹאשָׁם שָׂשׂוֹן
וְשִׂמְחָה יַשִּׂיגוּ וְנָסוּ יָגוֹן וַאֲנָחָה:

Ufeduyei Adonai Yeshuvun Uva'u Tziyon Berinah Vesimchat Olam
Al Rosham Sason Vesimchah Yassigu Venasu Yagon Va'anachah.

And the ransomed of Hashem will return, And come with shouting to Tziyon, crowned with everlasting joy. They will attain joy and gladness, while sorrow and sighing flee. (Isaiah 35:10)

כִּי־בְשִׂמְחָה תֵצֵאוּ וּבְשָׁלוֹם תּוּבָלוּן הֶהָרִים וְהַגְּבָעוֹת יִפְצְחוּ לִפְנֵיכֶם רִנָּה וְכָל־עֲצֵי הַשָּׂדֶה יִמְחֲאוּ־כָף:

Ki Vesimchah Tetze'u Uveshalom Tuvalun Heharim Vehageva'ot Yiftzechu Lifneichem Rinah Vechol Atzei Hassadeh Yimcha'u Chaf.

For you will go out with joy, And be led forth with peace; The mountains and the hills will break out before you into singing, And all the trees of the field will clap their hands. (Isaiah 55:12)

הִנֵּה אֵל יְשׁוּעָתִי אֶבְטַח וְלֹא אֶפְחָד כִּי־עָזִּי וְזִמְרָת יָהּ יְהֹוָה וַיְהִי־לִי לִישׁוּעָה: וּשְׁאַבְתֶּם־מַיִם בְּשָׂשׂוֹן מִמַּעַיְנֵי הַיְשׁוּעָה: וַאֲמַרְתֶּם בַּיּוֹם הַהוּא הוֹדוּ לַיהֹוָה קִרְאוּ בִשְׁמוֹ הוֹדִיעוּ בָעַמִּים עֲלִילֹתָיו הַזְכִּירוּ כִּי נִשְׂגָּב שְׁמוֹ: זַמְּרוּ יְהֹוָה כִּי גֵאוּת עָשָׂה מִידַעַת (מוּדַעַת) זֹאת בְּכָל־הָאָרֶץ: צַהֲלִי וָרֹנִּי יוֹשֶׁבֶת צִיּוֹן כִּי־גָדוֹל בְּקִרְבֵּךְ קְדוֹשׁ יִשְׂרָאֵל:

Hineh El Yeshu'ati Evtach Velo Efchad Ki Ozi Vezimrat Yah Adonai Vayhi Li Lishu'ah. Ushe'avtem Mayim Besason Mima'aynei Hayeshu'ah. Va'amartem Bayom Hahu Hodu L'Adonai Kir'u Vishmo Hodi'u Va'ammim Alilotav Hazkiru Ki Nisgav Shemo. Zameru Adonai Ki Ge'ut Asah Muda'at Zot Bechol Ha'aretz. Tzahali Varoni Yoshevet Tziyon Ki Gadol Bekirbech Kedosh Yisra'el.

Behold, God is my salvation; I will trust, and will not be afraid; For God, Hashem is my strength and song; And He has become my salvation. Therefore, with joy, you will draw water out of the wells of salvation. And in that day you will say: 'Give thanks to Hashem, proclaim His name, declare His works among the peoples, Make mention that His name is exalted. Sing to Hashem; for He has done gloriously; This is made known in all the earth. Cry aloud and shout, you inhabitant of Tziyon, For great is the Holy One of Yisrael in the midst of you. (Isaiah 12:2-6)

וְאָמַר בַּיּוֹם הַהוּא הִנֵּה אֱלֹהֵינוּ זֶה קִוִּינוּ לוֹ וְיוֹשִׁיעֵנוּ זֶה יְהֹוָה קִוִּינוּ
לוֹ נָגִילָה וְנִשְׂמְחָה בִּישׁוּעָתוֹ:

Ve'amar Bayom Hahu Hineh Eloheinu Zeh Kivinu Lo Veyoshi'enu
Zeh Adonai Kivinu Lo Nagilah Venismechah Bishu'ato.

And it will be said in that day: 'Behold, this is our God, For Whom
we waited, that He might save us; This is Hashem, for Whom we
waited, We will be glad and rejoice in His salvation.' (Isaiah 25:9)

בּוֹרֵא נוב (נִיב) שְׂפָתָיִם שָׁלוֹם | שָׁלוֹם לָרָחוֹק וְלַקָּרוֹב אָמַר יְהֹוָה
וּרְפָאתִיו:

Borel Niv Sefatayim Shalom Shalom Larachok Velakarov Amar
Adonai Urefativ.

Peace, peace, to him that is far off and to him that is near, Says
Hashem that creates the fruit of the lips; And I will heal him. (Isaiah
57:19)

וְרוּחַ לָבְשָׁה אֶת־עֲמָשַׂי רֹאשׁ השלושים (הַשָּׁלִישִׁים) לְךָ דָוִיד
וְעִמְּךָ בֶן־יִשַׁי שָׁלוֹם | שָׁלוֹם לְךָ וְשָׁלוֹם לְעֹזְרֶךָ כִּי עֲזָרְךָ אֱלֹהֶיךָ
וַיְקַבְּלֵם דָּוִיד וַיִּתְּנֵם בְּרָאשֵׁי הַגְּדוּד:

Veruach Laveshah Et Amasai Rosh Hashalishim Lecha David
Ve'imecha Ben Yishai Shalom Shalom Lecha Veshalom Le'ozerecha
Ki Azarecha Eloheicha Vaykabelem David Vayitenem Berashei
Hagedud.

Then the spirit seized Amasai, chief of the captains: "We are yours,
David, On your side, son of Yishai; At peace, at peace with you, And
at peace with him who supports you, for your God supports you."
So David accepted them, and placed them at the head of his band.
(1 Chronicles 12:19)

Some recite the following verses:

וַאֲמַרְתֶּם כֹּה לֶחָי וְאַתָּה שָׁלוֹם וּבֵיתְךָ שָׁלוֹם וְכֹל אֲשֶׁר־לְךָ שָׁלוֹם:

Va'amartem Koh Lechai Ve'attah Shalom Uveitcha Shalom Vechol
Asher Lecha Shalom.

And so you will say: To life! peace be both to you, and peace be to your house, and peace be to all that you have. (1 Samuel 25:6)

בָּרוּךְ הַגֶּבֶר אֲשֶׁר יִבְטַח בַּיהֹוָה וְהָיָה יְהֹוָה מִבְטַחוֹ. יְהֹוָה עֹז לְעַמּוֹ
יִתֵּן יְהֹוָה | יְבָרֵךְ אֶת־עַמּוֹ בַשָּׁלוֹם:

Baruch Hagever Asher Yivtach Badonai Vehayah Adonai Mivtacho.
Adonai Oz Le'ammo Yiten Adonai Yevarech Et Ammo Vashalom.

Blessed is the man that trusts in Hashem, And whose trust Hashem is. Hashem will give strength to His people; Hashem will bless His people with peace. (Jeremiah 17:7, Psalms 29:11)

אֵלִיָּהוּ הַנָּבִיא זָכוּר לְטוֹב:

Eliyahu Hanavi Zachur Letov:
Eliyahu the Prophet, may he be remembered for good.

Pizmonim for Motzei Shabbat

פזמונים למוצאי שבת

Hamavdil Bein Kodesh L'Chol
R. Isaac ibn Ghayat

הַמַּבְדִּיל בֵּין קֹדֶשׁ לְחוֹל. חַטֹּאתֵינוּ יִמְחוֹל. זַרְעֵנוּ וְכַסְפֵּנוּ יַרְבֶּה
כַחוֹל. וְכַכּוֹכָבִים בַּלָּיְלָה:

Hamavdil Bein Kodesh Lechol. Chatoteinu Yimchol. Zar'enu
Vechaspenu Yarbeh Chachol. Vechakochavim Balailah:

Oh God, Who did with love divide, our days of toil from days of
peace. Forgive our sins this eventide. And grant our seed in strength
increase, Even as the sand, even as the light. Radiant from the stars
of night.

יוֹם פָּנָה כְּצֵל תֹּמֶר. אֶקְרָא לָאֵל עָלַי גּוֹמֵר. יוֹם אֲשֶׁר אָמַר שׁוֹמֵר.
אָתָא בֹקֶר וְגַם לָיְלָה:

Yom Panah Ketzel Tomer. Ekra La'el Alai Gomer. Yom Asher Amar
Shomer. Ata Voker Vegam Lailah:

The day declines, and swifter flies, than flies the palm tree's shade; I
call on You, Whose hand each need supplies: What though the
shadows around me fall, The watchman cries, 'Behold the light.
Triumphant over the hosts of night.'

צִדְקָתְךָ כְּהַר תָּבוֹר. עֲלֵי פְּשָׁעַי עָבוֹר תַּעֲבוֹר. כְּיוֹם אֶתְמוֹל כִּי
יַעֲבֹר. וְאַשְׁמוּרָה בַלָּיְלָה:

Tzidkatecha Kehar Tavor. Alei Fesha'ai Avor Ta'avor. Keyom Etmol Ki
Ya'avor. Ve'ashmurah Valailah:

Oh God, Your righteousness is as strong as Tavor's peak, unmoved
forever; Forgive our sin, forget our wrong, Pass over by our guilt, as
yesterday. Forever passes from our sight, Or as a watch of the night.

חָלְפָה עוֹנַת מִנְחָתִי. מִי יִתֵּן מְנוּחָתִי. יָגַעְתִּי בְאַנְחָתִי. אַשְׂחֶה
בְכָל־לַיְלָה:

Chalefah Onat Minchati. Mi Yiten Menuchati. Yaga'ti Ve'anchati.
Ascheh Vechol Layelah:

No longer can offering purge, My sin-seared soul in Tziyon's shrine;
No sacrifice my plea can urge, Ah, would that rest were truly mine;
Worn out with sighs, distraught with fright, My tears drench my
couch at night.

קוֹלִי שִׁמְעָה בַּל יֻנְטָל. פְּתַח לִי שַׁעַר הַמְּנֻטָּל. שֶׁראֹשִׁי נִמְלָא טָל.
קְוֻצּוֹתַי רְסִיסֵי לָיְלָה:

Koli Shim'ah Bal Yuntal. Petach Li Sha'ar Hamenuttal. Sheroshi
Nimla Tal. Kevutzotai Resisei Lailah:

Oh hear my voice, receive my cry, Let my prayer not be cast away;
Open to me the gate on high, listen to the sacred Bridegroom's lay,
Behold my head with raindrops bright, My glistening locks with dew
of night.'

הֵעָתֵר נוֹרָא וְאָיוֹם. אֲשַׁוֵּעַ תְּנָה פִדְיוֹם. בְּנֶשֶׁף בְּעֶרֶב יוֹם. בְּאִישׁוֹן
לָיְלָה:

Hei'ateir Nora Ve'ayom. Ashavea' Tenah Fidyom. Beneshef Be'erev
Yom. Be'ishon Lailah:

Most revered God, most awesome Lord, be entreated of us this
hour; Our hearts with fervent prayers outpoured. Implore Your wise
redeeming power. Now in the dusk fight our fight, even, in the
blackness of the night.

קְרָאתִיךָ יָהּ הוֹשִׁיעֵנִי. אוֹרַח חַיִּים תּוֹדִיעֵנִי. מִדַּלּוּת תְּבַצְּעֵנִי. מִיּוֹם
וְעַד לָיְלָה:

Keraticha Yah Hoshi'eni. Orach Chayim Todi'eni. Middalut
Tevatze'eni. Miyom Ve'ad Lailah:

Save us, Lord, we call on You, save. Make known to us the path of
life, From wasting sickness, from the grave. Deliver us, from war and

strife, From daily cares, from evil plight, In lonesome silence of the night.

טַהֵר טִנּוּף מַעֲשַׂי. פֶּן יֹאמְרוּ מַכְעִיסַי. אַיֵּה אֱלֹוֹהַּ עוֹשַׂי. נוֹתֵן זְמִירוֹת בַּלָּיְלָה:

Taher Tinuf Ma'asai. Pen Yomru Mach'isai. Ayeh Eloah Osai. Noten Zemirot Balailah:

Purge my soul from blot and stain, From thoughts unclean, Lord, set me free, lest mockers cry with glad refrain: Where is the God of purity, Who made me with His strength and might, The God Who gives songs at night?

נַחְנוּ בְיָדְךָ כַּחֹמֶר. סְלַח נָא עַל קַל וָחֹמֶר. יוֹם לְיוֹם יַבִּיעַ אֹמֶר. וְלַיְלָה לְלַיְלָה:

Nachnu Veyadecha Kachomer. Selach Na Al Kal Vachomer. Yom Leyom Yabbia' Omer. Velayelah Lelailah:

Within Your hand as clay we live, mould us to Your sovereign will, Our sins both light and grave forgive. We are Your chosen people still; Age will to age Your Word recite, Day to Day, Night to Night.

Some add:

אֵל פּוֹדֶה מִכָּל־צָר. קְרָאנוּךָ מִן הַמֵּצָר. יָדְךָ לֹא תִקְצָר. לֹא יוֹם וְלֹא לָיְלָה:

El Podeh Mikol Tzar. Keranucha Min Hametzar. Yadecha Lo Tiktzar. Lo Yom Velo Lailah:

Rescue us from all distress. We call out to You from a place confined. Your hand will never rest. Not during the day and not during the night:

מִיכָאֵל שַׂר יִשְׂרָאֵל. אֵלִיָּהוּ וְגַבְרִיאֵל. בֹּאוּ נָא עִם הַגּוֹאֵל. קוּמוּ בַּחֲצִי הַלָּיְלָה:

Micha'el Sar Yisra'el. Eliyahu Vegavri'el. Bo'u Na Im Hago'el. Kumu Vachatzi Halailah:

Micha'el, the Minister of Yisrael. Eliyahu and Gavriel. With the Redeemer, please come. Arise in the middle of the night, before the sun:

מִימִינֵנוּ מִיכָאֵל. וּמִשְּׂמאלֵנוּ גַּבְרִיאֵל. וְעַל רֹאשֵׁנוּ שְׁכִינַת אֵל. בְּכָל־יוֹם וּבְכָל־לָיְלָה:

Miminenu Micha'el. Umissemolenu Gavri'el. Ve'al Roshenu Shechinat El. Bechol Yom Uvechol Lailah:

Mikhael is to our right. And to our left is Gavriel. And over our heads the presence of God. Every day and every night:

תְּנָה לָנוּ שָׁבוּעַ טוֹב. רַעֲנָן כְּגַן רָטוֹב. וּמֵיְהֹוָה יָבוֹא הַטּוֹב. כָּל־הַיּוֹם וְכָל־הַלָּיְלָה:

Tenah Lanu Shavua' Tov. Ra'anan Kegan Ratov. Umey'Adonai Yavo Hatov. Kol Hayom Vechol Halailah:

Give us a good week. Fresh as a watered garden might. And from Him will come the good. Every day and every night:

יְבוֹרַךְ הַבַּיִת הַזֶּה. מִפִּי נָבִיא וְגַם חוֹזֶה. כִּי כֵן יְצַוֶּה אֱלֹהֵינוּ זֶה. לְשָׁמְרוֹ יוֹמָם וָלָיְלָה:

Yevorach Habayit Hazeh. Mipi Navi Vegam Chozeh. Ki Chein Yetzaveh Eloheinu Zeh. Leshomro Yomam Valailah:

Bless this house. From the mouth of a prophet and also a seer. For so our God has commanded this. He will guard it day and night:

הַמַּבְדִּיל בֵּין מַיִם לְמַיִם. יְחַיֵּנוּ מִיּוֹמָיִם. יַרְאֵנוּ בְּטוּב יְרוּשָׁלָיִם. וְלִמְשׁוֹל בַּיּוֹם וּבַלָּיְלָה:

Hamavdil Bein Mayim Lemayim. Yechayenu Miyomayim. Yar'enu Betuv Yerushalayim. Velimshol Bayom Uvalailah:

Seperate, water between water. Be more gracious than other days. Show us the prospering of Yerushalayim. And rule the day and the night.

B'Motzaei Yom Menuchah
R. Jacob Menuy

בְּמוֹצָאֵי יוֹם מְנוּחָה. הַמְצֵא לְעַמְּךָ רְוָחָה. שְׁלַח תִּשְׁבִּי לְנֶאֱנָחָה. וְנָסוּ יָגוֹן וַאֲנָחָה:

Bemotza'ei Yom Menuchah. Hamtze Le'ammecha Revachah. Shelach Tishbi Lene'enachah. Venasu Yagon Va'anachah:

At the close of the day of rest, Oh grant relief to Your people; Send Eliyahu to the distressed, That grief and sighs may flee away;

יָאֲתָה לְךָ צוּרִי. לְקַבֵּץ עַם מְפֻזָּרִי. מִיַּד גּוֹי אַכְזָרִי. אֲשֶׁר כָּרָה לִי שׁוּחָה: (בְּמוֹצָאֵי)

Ya'atah Lecha Tzuri. Lekabetz Am Mefuzari. Miyad Goy Achzari. Asher Karah Li Shuchah: (Bemotza'ei)

It is suitable You, my Creator, To gather my scattered people From amidst a cruel nation that is digging pitfalls for me.

עֵת דּוֹדִים תְּעוֹרֵר אֵל. לְמַלֵּט עַם אֲשֶׁר שׁוֹאֵל. רְאוֹת טוּבְךָ בְּבוֹא גּוֹאֵל. לְשֶׂה פְּזוּרָה נִדָּחָה: (בְּמוֹצָאֵי)

Et Dodim Te'orer El. Lemallet Am Asher Sho'el. Re'ot Tuvcha Bevo Go'el. Leseh Pezurah Niddachah: (Bemotza'ei)

Oh God, do You arouse Your love, To save a people that asks to see Your grace, when a redeemer comes to Your dispersed, unhappy flock.

קְרָא יֶשַׁע לְעַם נְדָבָה. אֵל דָּגוּל מֵרְבָבָה. יְהִי הַשָּׁבוּעַ הַבָּא. לִישׁוּעָה וְלִרְוָחָה: (בְּמוֹצָאֵי)

Kera Yesha Le'am Nedavah. El Dagul Merevavah. Yehi Hashavua' Haba. Lishu'ah Velirvachah: (Bemotza'ei)

Proclaim freedom to a noble people, You Who are worshipped by myriads; May this coming week be given to deliverance and relief.

בַּת צִיּוֹן הַשְּׁכוּלָה. אֲשֶׁר הִיא הַיּוֹם גְּעוּלָה. מְהֵרָה תִּהְיֶה בְּעוּלָה. אֵם הַבָּנִים שְׂמֵחָה: (בְּמוֹצָאֵי)

Bat Tziyon Hashechulah. Asher Hi Hayom Ge'ulah. Meheirah
Tihyeh Be'ulah. Em Habanim Shomechah: (Bemotza'ei)
The bereaved city of Tziyon, Held today in utter contempt, May she
soon be populated— A happy mother of children.

מַעְיָנוֹת אֲזַי יְזוּבוּן. וּפְדוּיִים עוֹד יְשׁוּבוּן. וּמִי יֶשַׁע יִשְׁאֲבוּן. וְהַצָּרָה
נִשְׁכָּחָה: (בְּמוֹצָאֵי)
Ma'yanot Azai Yezuvun. Ufeduyim Od Yeshuvun. Umi Yesha
Yish'avun. Vehatzarah Nishkachah: (Bemotza'ei)
The fountains will then be flowing; Those freed by the Lord will
return; They will draw water that saves, And trouble will soon be
forgotten.

נְחֵה עַמְּךָ כְּאָב רַחֲמָן. יְצַפְצְפוּ עַם לֹא אַלְמָן. דְּבַר יְהֹוָה אֲשֶׁר
נֶאֱמָן. בַּהֲקִימְךָ הַבְטָחָה: (בְּמוֹצָאֵי)
Necheh Ammecha Ke'av Rachaman. Yetzaftzfu Am Lo Alman. Devar
Adonai Asher Ne'eman. Bahakimcha Havtachah: (Bemotza'ei)
Merciful Father, guide Your people; Let a people, unbereft, say That
the word of God is faithful, When You will have kept Your promise.

וִידִידִים פְּלִיטֵי חֶרֶץ. נְגִינָתָם יִפְצְחוּ בְמֶרֶץ. בְּלִי צְוָחָה וּבְלִי פֶרֶץ.
אֵין יוֹצֵאת וְאֵין צְוָחָה: (בְּמוֹצָאֵי)
Vididim Pelitei Cheretz. Neginatam Yiftzchu Bemeretz. Beli
Tzvachah Uveli Feretz. Ein Yotzet Ve'ein Tzevachah: (Bemotza'ei)
Your loved ones, escaping ruin, Will break into vigorous song —
Without alarm, without havoc, No surrender and no panic.

יְהִי הַחֹדֶשׁ הַזֶּה. כִּנְבוּאַת אָבִי חוֹזֶה. וְיִשָּׁמַע בְּבַיִת זֶה. קוֹל שָׂשׂוֹן
וְקוֹל שִׂמְחָה: (בְּמוֹצָאֵי)
Yehi Hachodesh Hazeh. Kinvu'at Avi Chozeh. Veyishama Bevayit
Zeh. Kol Sasson Vekol Simchah: (Bemotza'ei)
May the vision of the great seer, Yirmiyahu, come to pass this
month; May in this household be heard the sound of joy and
gladness.

חֲזָק יְמַלֵּא מִשְׁאֲלוֹתֵינוּ. אַמִּיץ יַעֲשֶׂה בַּקָּשָׁתֵנוּ. וְהוּא יִשְׁלַח בְּכָל מַעֲשֵׂה יָדֵינוּ. בְּרָכָה רְוָחָה וְהַצְלָחָה: (בְּמוֹצָאֵי)

Chazak Yemallei Mish'aloteinu. Ammitz Ya'aseh Bakashatenu. Vehu Yishlach Bechol Ma'aseh Yadeinu. Berachah Revachah Vehatzlachah: **(Bemotza'ei)**

May God fulfill our petitions, The Almighty do what we ask; May He prosper all our efforts, And send us blessings and success.

בְּמוֹצָאֵי יוֹם גִּילָה. שִׁמְךָ נוֹרָא עֲלִילָה. שְׁלַח תִּשְׁבִּי לְעַם סְגֻלָּה. רֶוַח שָׂשׂוֹן וַהֲנָחָה: (בְּמוֹצָאֵי)

Bemotza'ei Yom Gilah. Shimcha Nora Alilah. Shelach Tishbi Le'am Segullah. Revach Sason Vahanachah: **(Bemotza'ei)**

At the close of the joyous day, Send Eliyahu to Your chosen people. You whose deeds are awe-inspiring;

קוֹל צָהֳלָה וְרִנָּה. שְׂפָתֵינוּ אָז תְּרַנֶּנָּה. אָנָּא יְהֹוָה הוֹשִׁיעָה נָּא אָנָּא יְהֹוָה הַצְלִיחָה נָּא: (בְּמוֹצָאֵי)

Kol Tzoholah Verinah. Shofateinu Az Teranenah. Ana Adonai Hoshi'ah Na Ana Adonai Hatzlichah Na: **(Bemotza'ei)**

Send relief, joy and a release. Then will our lips joyfully chant: Hashem, save us; Hashem, prosper us.

Amar Adonai L'Yaakov

אָמַר יְהֹוָה לְיַעֲקֹב. אַל תִּירָא עַבְדִּי יַעֲקֹב:

Amar Adonai Leya'akov. Al Tira Avdi Ya'akov:

Hashem said to Yaakov. Fear not, my servant Yaakov.

בָּחַר יְהֹוָה בְּיַעֲקֹב. גָּאַל יְהֹוָה אֶת יַעֲקֹב. דָּרַךְ כּוֹכָב מִיַּעֲקֹב.

Bachar Adonai Beya'akov. Ga'al Adonai Et Ya'akov. Darach Kochav Miya'akov.

Hashem has chosen Yaakov. Hashem has redeemed Yaakov. A star has risen from Yaakov.

הַבָּאִים יַשְׁרֵשׁ יַעֲקֹב. וְיֵרְדְּ מִיַּעֲקֹב. זְכֹר אֵלֶּה יַעֲקֹב.

Habai'm Yashresh Ya'akov. Veyered Miya'akov. Zechor Eleh Ya'akov.

Then will Yaakov take root. Out of Yaakov will one rule. Remember this, Oh Yaakov.

חֶדְוַת יְשׁוּעוֹת יַעֲקֹב. טֹבוּ אֹהָלֶיךָ יַעֲקֹב. יוֹרוּ מִשְׁפָּטֶיךָ לְיַעֲקֹב.

Chedvat Yeshu'ot Ya'akov. Tovu Ohaleicha Ya'akov. Yoru Mishpateicha Leya'akov.

Joyous triumph will Yaakov have. Goodly are your tents, Oh Yaakov. Your laws are taught to Yaakov.

כִּי לֹא נַחַשׁ בְּיַעֲקֹב. לֹא הִבִּיט אָוֶן בְּיַעֲקֹב. מִי מָנָה עֲפַר יַעֲקֹב.

Ki Lo Nachash Beya'akov. Lo Hibit Aven Beya'akov. Mi Manah Afar Ya'akov.

There is no sorcery with Yaakov. None has seen iniquity in Yaakov. Who has counted Yaakov's masses?

נִשְׁבַּע יְהֹוָה לְיַעֲקֹב. סְלַח נָא לַעֲוֹן יַעֲקֹב. עַתָּה הָשֵׁב שְׁבוּת יַעֲקֹב.

Nishba Adonai Leya'akov. Selach Na La'avon Ya'akov. Attah Hasheiv Shevut Ya'akov.

Hashem has made promise to Yaakov. Pardon the sins of Yaakov. Bring back now the captivity of Yaakov.

פָּדָה יְהֹוָה אֶת יַעֲקֹב. צַוֵּה יְשׁוּעוֹת יַעֲקֹב. קוֹל קוֹל יַעֲקֹב.

Padah Adonai Et Ya'akov. Tzaveh Yeshu'ot Ya'akov. Kol Kol Ya'akov.

Hashem redeems Yaakov. Command the salvation of Yaakov. The voice is the voice of Yaakov.

רָנּוּ שִׂמְחָה לְיַעֲקֹב. שָׁב יְהֹוָה אֶת שְׁבוּת יַעֲקֹב. תִּתֵּן אֱמֶת לְיַעֲקֹב.

Ranu Simcha Leya'akov. Shav Adonai Et Shevut Ya'akov. Titen Emet Leya'akov.

Sing with gladness for Yaakov. Hashem restores the pride of Yaakov. You will grant kindness to Yaakov.

Some sing:

<u>Psalms 121</u>

Shir. Lamma'alot Essa Einai El-	שִׁיר לַמַּעֲלוֹת אֶשָּׂא עֵינַי אֶל־
Heharim; Me'ayin. Yavo Ezri.	הֶהָרִים מֵאַיִן יָבֹא עֶזְרִי:
Ezri Me'im Adonai Oseh.	עֶזְרִי מֵעִם יְהֹוָה עֹשֵׂה
Shamayim Va'aretz. Al-Yiten	שָׁמַיִם וָאָרֶץ: אַל־יִתֵּן
Lamot Raglecha; Al-Yanum.	לַמּוֹט רַגְלֶךָ אַל־יָנוּם
Shomerecha. Hineh Lo-Yanum	שֹׁמְרֶךָ: הִנֵּה לֹא־יָנוּם
Velo Yishan; Shomer. Yisra'el.	וְלֹא יִישָׁן שׁוֹמֵר יִשְׂרָאֵל:
Adonai Shomerecha; Hashem	יְהֹוָה שֹׁמְרֶךָ יְהֹוָה
Tzillecha. Al-Yad Yeminecha.	צִלְּךָ עַל־יַד יְמִינֶךָ:
Yomam. Hashemesh Lo-	יוֹמָם הַשֶּׁמֶשׁ לֹא־
Yakekah. Veyareach Balailah.	יַכֶּכָּה וְיָרֵחַ בַּלָּיְלָה:
Adonai Yishmorcha Mikol-Ra';	יְהֹוָה יִשְׁמָרְךָ מִכָּל־רָע
Yishmor. Et-Nafshecha. Adonai	יִשְׁמֹר אֶת־נַפְשֶׁךָ: יְהֹוָה
Yishmor-Tzetecha Uvo'echa;	יִשְׁמָר־צֵאתְךָ וּבוֹאֶךָ
Me'attah. Ve'ad-'Olam.	מֵעַתָּה וְעַד־עוֹלָם:

A Song of Ascents. I will lift up my eyes to the mountains: From where will my help come? My help comes from Hashem, Who made heaven and earth. He will not suffer Your foot to be moved; He that keeps You will not slumber. Behold, He that keeps Yisrael neither slumbers or sleeps. Hashem is your Guardian; Hashem is Your shade on Your right hand. The sun will not harm you by day, or the moon by night. Hashem will keep you from all evil; He will keep your soul. Hashem will guard your going out and your coming in, From this time and forever.

Seudah Revi'it / Fourth Meal

סעודה רביעית

> One should arrange their table in order to show respect and escort out the Shabbat. The blessing of wine in havdalah exempts a blessing for the meal. (BT Shabbat 119b, SA, OC 300:1)

Before the fourth meal, some say:

אַתְקִינוּ סְעֻדָּתָא דִּמְהֵימְנוּתָא דָּא הִיא סְעֻדָּתָא רְבִיעָאָה דְּדָוִד מַלְכָּא מְשִׁיחָא:

Atkinu Se'udata Dimheimnuta Da Hi Se'udata Revi'a'ah Dedavid Malka Meshicha:

לְשֵׁם יִחוּד קוּדְשָׁא בְּרִיךְ הוּא וּשְׁכִינְתֵּיהּ. בִּדְחִילוּ וּרְחִימוּ. וּרְחִימוּ וּדְחִילוּ. לְיַחֲדָא שֵׁם יוֹ"ד קֵ"י בְּוָא"וֹ קֵ"י בְּיִחוּדָא שְׁלִים (יהוה) בְּשֵׁם כָּל יִשְׂרָאֵל. הנה אנכי בא לסעוד סעודה רביעית של שבת ללוות את המלכא וללוות הנפש יתירה בחינת חיה שבה המסתלקת עתה. ולהשאיר ברכה בכל סעודותינו בששת ימי החול ולהשאיר בהם מקדושת השבת. ובכן בכח סגולתה שמרנו כאישון בת עין ובצל כנפיך תסתירנו והושיענו מצער חבוט הקבר ותשכין את נפשנו רוחנו ונשמתנו במשכנות מבטחים. וִיהִי נֹעַם אֲדֹנָי אֱלֹהֵינוּ עָלֵינוּ וּמַעֲשֵׂה יָדֵינוּ כּוֹנְנָה עָלֵינוּ וּמַעֲשֵׂה יָדֵינוּ כּוֹנְנֵהוּ:

ROSH CHODESH

ראש חודש

Barchi Nafshi - Rosh Chodesh

Some communities say Barchi Nafshi (Psalms 104) on Rosh Chodesh at the end of Mincha after the Song of the Day, Beginning of Arvit and before Shabbat.

Psalms 104

בָּרְכִי נַפְשִׁי אֶת־יְהֹוָה יְהֹוָה אֱלֹהַי גָּדַלְתָּ מְּאֹד הוֹד וְהָדָר לָבָשְׁתָּ:
עֹטֶה־אוֹר כַּשַּׂלְמָה נוֹטֶה שָׁמַיִם כַּיְרִיעָה: הַמְקָרֶה בַמַּיִם עֲלִיּוֹתָיו
הַשָּׂם־עָבִים רְכוּבוֹ הַמְהַלֵּךְ עַל־כַּנְפֵי־רוּחַ: עֹשֶׂה מַלְאָכָיו רוּחוֹת
מְשָׁרְתָיו אֵשׁ לֹהֵט: יָסַד־אֶרֶץ עַל־מְכוֹנֶיהָ בַּל־תִּמּוֹט עוֹלָם וָעֶד:
תְּהוֹם כַּלְּבוּשׁ כִּסִּיתוֹ עַל־הָרִים יַעַמְדוּ־מָיִם: מִן־גַּעֲרָתְךָ יְנוּסוּן
מִן־קוֹל רַעַמְךָ יֵחָפֵזוּן: יַעֲלוּ הָרִים יֵרְדוּ בְקָעוֹת אֶל־מְקוֹם זֶה | יָסַדְתָּ
לָהֶם: גְּבוּל־שַׂמְתָּ בַּל־יַעֲבֹרוּן בַּל־יְשֻׁבוּן לְכַסּוֹת הָאָרֶץ: הַמְשַׁלֵּחַ
מַעְיָנִים בַּנְּחָלִים בֵּין הָרִים יְהַלֵּכוּן: יַשְׁקוּ כָּל־חַיְתוֹ שָׂדָי יִשְׁבְּרוּ
פְרָאִים צְמָאָם: עֲלֵיהֶם עוֹף־הַשָּׁמַיִם יִשְׁכּוֹן מִבֵּין עֳפָאיִם יִתְּנוּ־קוֹל:
מַשְׁקֶה הָרִים מֵעֲלִיּוֹתָיו מִפְּרִי מַעֲשֶׂיךָ תִּשְׂבַּע הָאָרֶץ: מַצְמִיחַ
חָצִיר | לַבְּהֵמָה וְעֵשֶׂב לַעֲבֹדַת הָאָדָם לְהוֹצִיא לֶחֶם מִן־הָאָרֶץ: וְיַיִן |
יְשַׂמַּח לְבַב־אֱנוֹשׁ לְהַצְהִיל פָּנִים מִשָּׁמֶן וְלֶחֶם לְבַב־אֱנוֹשׁ יִסְעָד:
יִשְׂבְּעוּ עֲצֵי יְהֹוָה אַרְזֵי לְבָנוֹן אֲשֶׁר נָטָע: אֲשֶׁר־שָׁם צִפֳּרִים יְקַנֵּנוּ
חֲסִידָה בְּרוֹשִׁים בֵּיתָהּ: הָרִים הַגְּבֹהִים לַיְּעֵלִים סְלָעִים מַחְסֶה
לַשְׁפַנִּים: עָשָׂה יָרֵחַ לְמוֹעֲדִים שֶׁמֶשׁ יָדַע מְבוֹאוֹ: תָּשֶׁת־חֹשֶׁךְ וִיהִי
לָיְלָה בּוֹ־תִרְמֹשׂ כָּל־חַיְתוֹ־יָעַר: הַכְּפִירִים שֹׁאֲגִים לַטָּרֶף וּלְבַקֵּשׁ
מֵאֵל אָכְלָם: תִּזְרַח הַשֶּׁמֶשׁ יֵאָסֵפוּן וְאֶל־מְעוֹנֹתָם יִרְבָּצוּן: יֵצֵא אָדָם
לְפָעֳלוֹ וְלַעֲבֹדָתוֹ עֲדֵי־עָרֶב: מָה־רַבּוּ מַעֲשֶׂיךָ | יְהֹוָה כֻּלָּם בְּחָכְמָה
עָשִׂיתָ מָלְאָה הָאָרֶץ קִנְיָנֶךָ: זֶה | הַיָּם גָּדוֹל וּרְחַב יָדָיִם שָׁם־רֶמֶשׂ
וְאֵין מִסְפָּר חַיּוֹת קְטַנּוֹת עִם־גְּדֹלוֹת: שָׁם אֳנִיּוֹת יְהַלֵּכוּן לִוְיָתָן

זֶה־יָצַרְתָּ לְשַׂחֶק־בּוֹ: כֻּלָּם אֵלֶיךָ יְשַׂבֵּרוּן לָתֵת אָכְלָם בְּעִתּוֹ: תִּתֵּן
לָהֶם יִלְקֹטוּן תִּפְתַּח יָדְךָ יִשְׂבְּעוּן טוֹב: תַּסְתִּיר פָּנֶיךָ יִבָּהֵלוּן תֹּסֵף
רוּחָם יִגְוָעוּן וְאֶל־עֲפָרָם יְשׁוּבוּן: תְּשַׁלַּח רוּחֲךָ יִבָּרֵאוּן וּתְחַדֵּשׁ פְּנֵי
אֲדָמָה: יְהִי כְבוֹד יְהֹוָה לְעוֹלָם יִשְׂמַח יְהֹוָה בְּמַעֲשָׂיו: הַמַּבִּיט
לָאָרֶץ וַתִּרְעָד יִגַּע בֶּהָרִים וְיֶעֱשָׁנוּ: אָשִׁירָה לַיהֹוָה בְּחַיָּי אֲזַמְּרָה
לֵאלֹהַי בְּעוֹדִי: יֶעֱרַב עָלָיו שִׂיחִי אָנֹכִי אֶשְׂמַח בַּיהֹוָה: יִתַּמּוּ
חַטָּאִים ׀ מִן־הָאָרֶץ וּרְשָׁעִים ׀ עוֹד אֵינָם בָּרְכִי נַפְשִׁי אֶת־יְהֹוָה
הַלְלוּיָהּ:

Barchi Nafshi Et Adonai Adonai Elohai Gadalta Me'odhod Vehadar
Lavasheta. Oteh Or Kassalmah Noteh Shamayim Kayeri'ah.
Hamkareh Vammayim Aliyotav Hassam Avim Rechuvo
Hamehallech Al Kanfei Ruach. Oseh Mal'achav Ruchot Mesharetav
Esh Lohet. Yasad Eretz Al Mechoneiha Bal Timot Olam Va'ed. Tehom
Kallevush Kissito Al Harim Ya'amdu Mayim. Min Ga'aratecha
Yenusun Min Kol Ra'amcha Yechafezun. Ya'alu Harim Yeredu
Veka'ot El Mekom Zeh Yasadta Lahem. Gevul Samta Bal Ya'avorun
Bal Yeshuvun Lechasot Ha'aretz. Hameshalleach Ma'yanim
Banechalim Bein Harim Yehallechun. Yashku Kol Chayto Sadai
Yishberu Fera'im Tzema'am. Aleihem Of Hashamayim Yishkon
Mibein Ofayim Yitenu Kol. Mashkeh Harim Me'aliyotav Miperi
Ma'aseicha Tisba Ha'aretz. Matzmiach Chatzir Labehemah Ve'esev
La'avodat Ha'adam Lehotzi Lechem Min Ha'aretz. Veyayin
Yesamach Levav Enosh Lehatzhil Panim Mishamen Velechem Levav
Enosh Yis'ad. Yisbe'u Atzei Adonai Arzei Levanon Asher Nata. Asher
Sham Tziporim Yekanenu Chasidah Beroshim Beitah. Harim
Hagevohim Laye'elim Sela'im Machseh Lashfanim. Asah Yareach
Lemo'adim Shemesh Yada Mevo'o. Tashet Choshech Vihi Lailah Bo
Tirmos Kol Chayto Ya'ar. Hakkefirim Sho'agim Lattaref Ulevakesh
Me'el Ochlam. Tizrach Hashemesh Ye'asefun Ve'el Me'onotam
Yirbatzun. Yetze Adam Lefo'olo Vela'avodato Adei Arev. Mah Rabbu
Ma'aseicha Adonai Kulam Bechochmah Asita Male'ah Ha'aretz
Kinyanecha. Zeh Hayam Gadol Urechav Yadayim Sham Remes
Ve'ein Mispar Chayot Ketanot Im Gedolot. Sham Oniyot
Yehallechun Livyatan Zeh Yatzarta Lesachek Bo. Kulam Eleicha
Yesaberun Latet Ochlam Be'ito. Titen Lahem Yilkotun Tiftach
Yadecha Yisbe'un Tov. Tastir Paneicha Yibahelun Tosef Rucham
Yigva'un Ve'el Afaram Yeshuvun. Teshallach Ruchacha Yibare'un

Utechadesh Penei Adamah. Yehi Chevod Adonai Le'olam Yismach
Adonai Bema'asav. Hamabbit La'aretz Vatir'ad Yigga Beharim
Veye'eshanu. Ashirah L'Adonai Bechayai Azamerah Lelohai Be'odi.
Ye'erav Alav Sichi Anochi Esmach Badonai. Yitamu Chata'im Min
Ha'aretz Uresha'im Od Einam Barchi Nafshi Et Adonai Halleluyah.

Bless Hashem, Oh my soul. Hashem my God, You are very great;
You are clothed with glory and majesty. Who covers Yourself with
light as with a garment, Who stretches out the heavens like a
curtain; Who lays the beams of Your upper chambers in the waters,
Who makes the clouds Your chariot, Who walks upon the wings of
the wind; Who makes winds Your messengers, the flaming fire Your
ministers. Who established the earth upon its foundations, that it
should not be moved forever and ever; You covered it with the deep
as with a garment; the waters stood above the mountains. At Your
rebuke they fled, at the voice of Your thunder they hasted away—
The mountains rose, the valleys sank down—To the place which You
established for them; You set a bound which they should not pass
over, That they might not return to cover the earth. Who sends out
springs into the valleys; They run between the mountains; They give
drink to every beast of the field, The wild donkeys quench their
thirst. Beside them dwell the birds of the sky, From among the
branches they sing. Who waters the mountains from Your upper
chambers; The earth is full of the fruit of Your works. Who causes
the grass to spring up for the cattle, And herb for the service of
man; To bring forth bread from out of the earth, And wine that
makes the heart of man glad, Making the face brighter than oil, And
bread that sustains man's heart. The trees of Hashem have their fill,
The cedars of Levanon, which He has planted; in it, the birds make
their nests; As for the stork, the fir-trees are her house. The high
mountains are for the wild goats; The rocks are a refuge for the
badgers. Who appointed the moon for moadim (appointed times);
The sun knows his going down. You make darkness, and it is night,
Where all the beasts of the forest creep out. The young lions roar
after their prey, And seek their food from God. The sun arises, they

slink away, and couch in their dens. Man goes out to his work and to his labor until the evening. How manifold are Your works, Hashem. In wisdom You have made them all; The earth is full of Your creatures. So is this sea, great and wide, in it are creeping things innumerable, Living creatures, both small and great. There the ships go; There is Livyatan, whom You have formed to play in it. All of them wait for You, that You may give them their food in due season. You give it to them, they gather it; You open Your hand, they are satisfied with good. You hide Your face, they vanish; You withdraw their breath, they perish, and return to their dust. You send out Your spirit, they are created; and You renew the face of the earth. May the glory of Hashem endure forever; let Hashem rejoice in His works. Who looks on the earth, and it trembles; He touches the mountains, and they smoke. I will sing to Hashem as long as I live; I will sing praise to my God while I have any being. Let my meditation be sweet to Him; as for me, I will rejoice in Hashem. Let sinners cease out of the earth, and let the wicked be no more. Bless Hashem, Oh my soul. Halleluyah.

Order of Prayers - Rosh Chodesh

Service is as usual for Arvit, Shacharit and Mincha with Ya'aleh Ve'yavo inserted into the Amidah. If Ya'aleh Ve'yavo was omitted in the Evening Service, he does not need to say the Amidah again, but if it was omitted in Shacharit or Mincha then it must be said again. (SA. OC 422) After the repetition of Amidah is recited, then Hallel is said without a blessing and the noted sections omitted below.

HALLEL FOR ROSH CHODESH AND MOADIM

הלל לראש חודש ולמועדים

On Rosh Hodesh Hallel is said without a blessing with certain sections omitted. The full Hallel is recited on Pesach - the first two nights and days of Pesach (only the first night and day in Yisrael), on Shavuot, Sukkot - all seven days, on Shemini Atzeret and Simchat Torah, and on Hanukkah - all eight days. Hallel is recited while standing. (SA, OC 422)

Birshut Morai Verabotai:

בִּרְשׁוּת מוֹרַי וְרַבּוֹתַי:

With the permission of my teachers and masters:

Answer: Shamayim!

עונים: שָׁמַיִם.

Answer: (By) Heaven!

And the Chazan and the people bless. On days when the Hallel is not completed, skip this:

Baruch Attah Adonai Eloheinu

בָּרוּךְ אַתָּה יְהֹוָה אֱלֹהֵינוּ

Melech Ha'olam Asher

מֶלֶךְ הָעוֹלָם. אֲשֶׁר

Kideshanu Bemitzvotav.

קִדְּשָׁנוּ בְּמִצְוֹתָיו

Vetzivanu Ligmor Et Hahallel:

וְצִוָּנוּ לִגְמוֹר אֶת הַהַלֵּל:

Blessed are You, Hashem our God, King of the universe, Who has sanctified us with His commandments and commanded us to recite the Hallel.

Psalms 113

הַלְלוּיָהּ | הַלְלוּ עַבְדֵי יְהֹוָה הַלְלוּ אֶת־שֵׁם יְהֹוָה: יְהִי שֵׁם יְהֹוָה מְבֹרָךְ מֵעַתָּה וְעַד־עוֹלָם: מִמִּזְרַח־שֶׁמֶשׁ עַד־מְבוֹאוֹ מְהֻלָּל שֵׁם יְהֹוָה: רָם עַל־כָּל־גּוֹיִם | יְהֹוָה עַל הַשָּׁמַיִם כְּבוֹדוֹ: מִי כַּיהֹוָה

אֱלֹהֵינוּ הַמַּגְבִּיהִי לָשָׁבֶת: הַמַּשְׁפִּילִי לִרְאוֹת בַּשָּׁמַיִם וּבָאָרֶץ: מְקִימִי
מֵעָפָר דָּל מֵאַשְׁפֹּת יָרִים אֶבְיוֹן: לְהוֹשִׁיבִי עִם־נְדִיבִים עִם נְדִיבֵי
עַמּוֹ: מוֹשִׁיבִי | עֲקֶרֶת הַבַּיִת אֵם־הַבָּנִים שְׂמֵחָה הַלְלוּיָהּ:

Halleluyah Hallelu Avdei Adonai Hallelu Et Shem Adonai. Yehi
Shem Adonai Mevorach Me'attah Ve'ad Olam. Mimizrach Shemesh
Ad Mevo'o Mehulal Shem Adonai. Ram Al Kol Goyim Adonai Al
Hashamayim Kevodo. Mi Ka'Adonai Eloheinu Hamagbihi Lashavet.
Hamashpili Lir'ot Bashamayim Uva'aretz. Mekimi Me'afar Dal
Me'ashpot Yarim Evyon. Lehoshivi Im Nedivim Im Nedivei Ammo.
Moshivi Akeret Habayit Em Habanim Semechah Halleluyah.

Halleluyah. Praise, you servants of Hashem, Praise the name of
Hashem. Blessed is the name of Hashem From this time and forever.
From the rising of the sun to the going down of it Hashem's name is
to be praised. Hashem is high above all nations, His glory is above
the heavens. Who is like Hashem our God, That is enthroned on
high, That looks down low upon heaven and upon the earth? Who
raises up the poor out of the dust, And lifts up the needy out of the
dunghill; That He may set him with princes, Even with the princes of
His people. Who makes the barren woman to dwell in her house as a
joyful mother of children. Halleluyah.

Psalms 114

בְּצֵאת יִשְׂרָאֵל מִמִּצְרָיִם בֵּית יַעֲקֹב מֵעַם לֹעֵז: הָיְתָה יְהוּדָה לְקָדְשׁוֹ
יִשְׂרָאֵל מַמְשְׁלוֹתָיו: הַיָּם רָאָה וַיָּנֹס הַיַּרְדֵּן יִסֹּב לְאָחוֹר: הֶהָרִים
רָקְדוּ כְאֵילִים גְּבָעוֹת כִּבְנֵי־צֹאן: מַה־לְּךָ הַיָּם כִּי תָנוּס הַיַּרְדֵּן תִּסֹּב
לְאָחוֹר: הֶהָרִים תִּרְקְדוּ כְאֵילִים גְּבָעוֹת כִּבְנֵי־צֹאן: מִלִּפְנֵי אָדוֹן
חוּלִי אָרֶץ מִלִּפְנֵי אֱלוֹהַּ יַעֲקֹב: הַהֹפְכִי הַצּוּר אֲגַם־מָיִם חַלָּמִישׁ
לְמַעְיְנוֹ־מָיִם:

Betzet Yisra'el Mimitzrayim Beit Ya'akov Me'am Lo'ez. Hayetah
Yehudah Lekodsho Yisra'el Mamshelotav. Hayam Ra'ah Vayanos
Hayarden Yissov Le'achor. Heharim Rakedu Che'eilim Geva'ot

Kivnei Tzon. Mah Lecha Hayam Ki Tanus Hayarden Tissov Le'achor. Heharim Tirkedu Che'eilim Geva'ot Kivnei Tzon. Millifnei Adon Chuli Aretz Millifnei Eloah Ya'akov. Hahofechi Hatzur Agam Mayim Challamish Lema'yeno Mayim.

When Yisrael came forth out of Mitzrayim, The house of Yaakov from a people of strange language; Yehudah became His Sanctuary, Yisrael His dominion. The sea saw it, and fled; The Yarden turned backward. The mountains skipped like rams, The hills like young sheep. What ails you, Oh sea, that you flee? You Yarden, that you turn backward? You mountains, that you skip like rams; You hills, like young sheep? Tremble, earth, at the presence of Hashem, At the presence of the God of Yaakov; Who turned the rock into a pool of water, the flint into a fountain of waters.

Psalms 115

On days when the Hallel is not completed, skip this (first part of Psalm):

לֹא לָנוּ יְהֹוָה לֹא לָנוּ כִּי־לְשִׁמְךָ תֵּן כָּבוֹד עַל־חַסְדְּךָ עַל־אֲמִתֶּךָ: לָמָּה יֹאמְרוּ הַגּוֹיִם אַיֵּה־נָא אֱלֹהֵיהֶם: וֵאלֹהֵינוּ בַשָּׁמָיִם כֹּל אֲשֶׁר־חָפֵץ עָשָׂה: עֲצַבֵּיהֶם כֶּסֶף וְזָהָב מַעֲשֵׂה יְדֵי אָדָם: פֶּה־לָהֶם וְלֹא יְדַבֵּרוּ עֵינַיִם לָהֶם וְלֹא יִרְאוּ: אָזְנַיִם לָהֶם וְלֹא יִשְׁמָעוּ אַף לָהֶם וְלֹא יְרִיחוּן: יְדֵיהֶם | וְלֹא יְמִישׁוּן רַגְלֵיהֶם וְלֹא יְהַלֵּכוּ לֹא־יֶהְגּוּ בִּגְרוֹנָם: כְּמוֹהֶם יִהְיוּ עֹשֵׂיהֶם כֹּל אֲשֶׁר־בֹּטֵחַ בָּהֶם: יִשְׂרָאֵל בְּטַח בַּיהֹוָה עֶזְרָם וּמָגִנָּם הוּא: בֵּית אַהֲרֹן בִּטְחוּ בַיהֹוָה עֶזְרָם וּמָגִנָּם הוּא: יִרְאֵי יְהֹוָה בִּטְחוּ בַיהֹוָה עֶזְרָם וּמָגִנָּם הוּא:

Lo Lanu Adonai Lo Lanu Ki Leshimcha Ten Kavod Al Chasdecha Al Amitecha. Lamah Yomru Hagoyim Ayeh Na Eloheihem. Veloheinu Vashamayim Kol Asher Chafetz Asah. Atzabeihem Kesef Vezahav Ma'aseh Yedei Adam. Peh Lahem Velo Yedaberu Einayim Lahem Velo Yir'u. Oznayim Lahem Velo Yishma'u Af Lahem Velo Yerichun. Yedeihem Velo Yemishun Ragleihem Velo Yehallechu Lo Yehgu Bigronam. Kemohem Yihyu Oseihem Kol Asher Boteach Bahem. Yisra'el Betach B'Adonai Ezram Umaginam Hu. Beit Aharon Bitchu

B'Adonai Ezram Umaginam Hu. Yir'ei Adonai Bitchu B'Adonai
Ezram Umaginam Hu.

Not to us, Hashem, not to us, But to Your name give glory, For Your
mercy, and for Your truth's sake. Why should the nations say:
'Where is their God now?' But our God is in the heavens; Whatever
pleased Him He has done. Their idols are silver and gold, The work
of men's hands. They have mouths, but they do not speak; Eyes
have they, but they do not see; They have ears, but they do not hear;
They have noses, but they do not smell; They have hands, but they
cannot handle; They have feet, but they cannot walk; Neither can
they speak with their throat. They that make them will be like them;
Even, everyone that trusts in them. Yisrael, trust in Hashem. He is
their Help and their Shield. House of Aharon, trust in Hashem. He is
their Help and their Shield. You that fear Hashem, trust in Hashem.
He is their Help and their Shield.

On days when the Hallel is not completed, continue here:

יְהֹוָה זְכָרָנוּ יְבָרֵךְ יְבָרֵךְ אֶת־בֵּית יִשְׂרָאֵל יְבָרֵךְ אֶת־בֵּית אַהֲרֹן: יְבָרֵךְ
יִרְאֵי יְהֹוָה הַקְּטַנִּים עִם־הַגְּדֹלִים: יֹסֵף יְהֹוָה עֲלֵיכֶם עֲלֵיכֶם
וְעַל־בְּנֵיכֶם: בְּרוּכִים אַתֶּם לַיהֹוָה עֹשֵׂה שָׁמַיִם וָאָרֶץ: הַשָּׁמַיִם
שָׁמַיִם לַיהֹוָה וְהָאָרֶץ נָתַן לִבְנֵי־אָדָם: לֹא הַמֵּתִים יְהַלְלוּ־יָהּ וְלֹא
כָּל־יֹרְדֵי דוּמָה: וַאֲנַחְנוּ | נְבָרֵךְ יָהּ מֵעַתָּה וְעַד־עוֹלָם הַלְלוּ יָהּ:

Adonai Zecharanu Yevarech Yevarech Et Beit Yisra'el Yevarech Et Beit
Aharon. Yevarech Yir'ei Adonai Haketanim Im Hagedolim. Yosef
Adonai Aleichem Aleichem Ve'al Beneichem. Beruchim Attem
L'Adonai Oseh Shamayim Va'aretz. Hashamayim Shamayim
L'Adonai Veha'aretz Natan Livnei Adam. Lo Hameitim Yehallelu-Yah
Velo Kol Yoredei Dumah. Va'anachnu Nevarech Yah Me'attah Ve'ad
Olam Hallelu Yah.

Hashem has been mindful of us, He will bless— He will bless the
House of Yisrael; He will bless the house of Aharon. He will bless
them that fear Hashem, Both small and great. May Hashem increase
you more and more, You and your children. May you be blessed by
Hashem, Who made heaven and earth. The heavens are the heavens

of Hashem; But the earth He has given to the children of men. The dead do not praise Hashem, Neither any that go down into silence; But we will bless Hashem from this time and forever. Halleluyah.

Psalms 116

On days when the Hallel is not finished, skip this (first part of Psalm):

אֲהַבְתִּי כִּי־יִשְׁמַע | יְהֹוָה אֶת־קוֹלִי תַּחֲנוּנָי: כִּי־הִטָּה אָזְנוֹ לִי וּבְיָמַי אֶקְרָא: אֲפָפוּנִי | חֶבְלֵי־מָוֶת וּמְצָרֵי שְׁאוֹל מְצָאוּנִי צָרָה וְיָגוֹן אֶמְצָא: וּבְשֵׁם־יְהֹוָה אֶקְרָא אָנָּה יְהֹוָה מַלְּטָה נַפְשִׁי: חַנּוּן יְהֹוָה וְצַדִּיק וֵאלֹהֵינוּ מְרַחֵם: שֹׁמֵר פְּתָאיִם יְהֹוָה דַּלֹּתִי וְלִי יְהוֹשִׁיעַ: שׁוּבִי נַפְשִׁי לִמְנוּחָיְכִי כִּי־יְהֹוָה גָּמַל עָלָיְכִי: כִּי חִלַּצְתָּ נַפְשִׁי מִמָּוֶת אֶת־עֵינִי מִן־דִּמְעָה אֶת־רַגְלִי מִדֶּחִי: אֶתְהַלֵּךְ לִפְנֵי יְהֹוָה בְּאַרְצוֹת הַחַיִּים: הֶאֱמַנְתִּי כִּי אֲדַבֵּר אֲנִי עָנִיתִי מְאֹד: אֲנִי אָמַרְתִּי בְחָפְזִי כָּל־הָאָדָם כֹּזֵב:

Ahavti Ki Yishma Adonai Et Koli Tachanunai. Ki Hittah Ozno Li Uveyamai Ekra. Afafuni Chevlei Mavet Umetzarei She'ol Metza'uni Tzarah Veyagon Emtza. Uveshem Adonai Ekra Anah Adonai Malletah Nafshi. Chanun Adonai Vetzaddik Veloheinu Merachem. Shomer Petayim Adonai Daloti Veli Yehoshia'. Shuvi Nafshi Limnuchayechi Ki Adonai Gamal Alayechi. Ki Chilatzta Nafshi Mimavet Et Eini Min Dim'ah Et Ragli Middechi. Ethallech Lifnei Adonai Be'artzot Hachayim. He'emanti Ki Adaber Ani Aniti Me'od. Ani Amarti Vechofzi Kol Ha'adam Kozev.

I love that Hashem hears my voice and my supplications. Because He has inclined His ear to me, Therefore I will call on Him all of my days. The cords of death encompassed me, and the straits of Sheol took hold on me; I found trouble and sorrow. But I called on the name of Hashem: 'I implore You, Hashem, deliver my soul.' Gracious is Hashem, and righteous; Yes, our God is compassionate. Hashem preserves the simple; I was brought low, and He saved me. Return, my soul, to Your rest; For Hashem has dealt bountifully with you.

For you have delivered my soul from death, My eyes from tears, And my feet from stumbling. I will walk before Hashem In the lands of the living. I trusted even when I spoke: 'I am greatly afflicted.' I said in my haste: 'All men are liars.'

On days when the Hallel is not completed, continue here:

מָה־אָשִׁיב לַיהוָה כָּל־תַּגְמוּלוֹהִי עָלָי: כּוֹס־יְשׁוּעוֹת אֶשָּׂא וּבְשֵׁם יְהוָה אֶקְרָא: נְדָרַי לַיהוָה אֲשַׁלֵּם נֶגְדָה־נָּא לְכָל־עַמּוֹ: יָקָר בְּעֵינֵי יְהוָה הַמָּוְתָה לַחֲסִידָיו: אָנָּה יְהוָה כִּי־אֲנִי עַבְדֶּךָ אֲנִי־עַבְדְּךָ בֶּן־אֲמָתֶךָ פִּתַּחְתָּ לְמוֹסֵרָי: לְךָ־אֶזְבַּח זֶבַח תּוֹדָה וּבְשֵׁם יְהוָה אֶקְרָא: נְדָרַי לַיהוָה אֲשַׁלֵּם נֶגְדָה־נָּא לְכָל־עַמּוֹ: בְּחַצְרוֹת | בֵּית יְהוָה בְּתוֹכֵכִי יְרוּשָׁלַםִ הַלְלוּיָהּ:

Mah Ashiv L'Adonai Kol Tagmulohi Alai. Kos Yeshu'ot Essa Uveshem Adonai Ekra. Nedarai L'Adonai Ashalem Negdah Na Lechol Ammo. Yakar Be'einei Adonai Hamavetah Lachasidav. Anah Adonai Ki Ani Avdecha Ani Avdecha Ben Amatecha Pittachta Lemoserai. Lecha Ezbach Zevach Todah Uveshem Adonai Ekra. Nedarai L'Adonai Ashalem Negdah Na Lechol Ammo. Bechatzrot Beit Adonai Betochechi Yerushalayim Halleluyah.

How can I repay to Hashem all of His bountiful dealings toward me? I will lift up the cup of salvation, And call upon the name of Hashem. I will pay my vows to Hashem, even, in the presence of all His people. Precious in the sight of Hashem is the death of His holy-ones. I implore You, Hashem, for I am Your servant; I am Your servant, the son of Your handmaid; You have released my bands. I will offer to You the sacrifice of thanksgiving, And will call on the name of Hashem. I will pay my vows to Hashem, even, in the presence of all His people; in the courts of Hashem's house, in the midst of you, Yerushalayim. Halleluyah.

Psalms 117

הַלְלוּ אֶת־יְהֹוָה כָּל־גּוֹיִם שַׁבְּחוּהוּ כָּל־הָאֻמִּים: כִּי גָבַר עָלֵינוּ |
חַסְדּוֹ וֶאֱמֶת־יְהֹוָה לְעוֹלָם הַלְלוּיָהּ:

Hallelu Et Adonai Kol Goyim Shabechuhu Kol Ha'ummim. Ki Gavar
Aleinu Chasdo Ve'emet Adonai Le'olam Halleluyah.

Praise Hashem, all nations; Acclaim Him, all peoples. For His mercy
is great toward us; And the truth of Hashem endures forever.
Halleluyah.

Psalms 118

הוֹדוּ לַיהֹוָה כִּי־טוֹב כִּי לְעוֹלָם חַסְדּוֹ:

Hodu L'Adonai Ki Tov Ki Le'olam Chasdo.

Give thanks to Hashem, for He is good, For His mercy endures
forever.

יֹאמַר־נָא יִשְׂרָאֵל כִּי לְעוֹלָם חַסְדּוֹ:

Yomar Na Yisra'el Ki Le'olam Chasdo.

So let Yisrael now say, For His mercy endures forever:

יֹאמְרוּ־נָא בֵית־אַהֲרֹן כִּי לְעוֹלָם חַסְדּוֹ:

Yomeru Na Veit Aharon Ki Le'olam Chasdo.

So let the house of Aharon now say, For His mercy endures forever.

יֹאמְרוּ־נָא יִרְאֵי יְהֹוָה כִּי לְעוֹלָם חַסְדּוֹ:

Yomeru Na Yir'ei Adonai Ki Le'olam Chasdo.

So let them now that fear Hashem say, For His mercy endures
forever.

מִן־הַמֵּצַר קָרָאתִי יָּהּ עָנָנִי בַמֶּרְחָב יָהּ: יְהֹוָה לִי לֹא אִירָא
מַה־יַּעֲשֶׂה לִי אָדָם: יְהֹוָה לִי בְּעֹזְרָי וַאֲנִי אֶרְאֶה בְשֹׂנְאָי: טוֹב
לַחֲסוֹת בַּיהֹוָה מִבְּטֹחַ בָּאָדָם: טוֹב לַחֲסוֹת בַּיהֹוָה מִבְּטֹחַ בִּנְדִיבִים:

כָּל־גּוֹיִם סְבָבוּנִי בְּשֵׁם יְהֹוָה כִּי אֲמִילַם: סַבּוּנִי גַם־סְבָבוּנִי בְּשֵׁם
יְהֹוָה כִּי אֲמִילַם: סַבּוּנִי כִדְבוֹרִים דֹעֲכוּ כְּאֵשׁ קוֹצִים בְּשֵׁם יְהֹוָה כִּי
אֲמִילַם: דָּחֹה דְחִיתַנִי לִנְפֹּל וַיהֹוָה עֲזָרָנִי: עָזִּי וְזִמְרָת יָהּ וַיְהִי־לִי
לִישׁוּעָה: קוֹל | רִנָּה וִישׁוּעָה בְּאָהֳלֵי צַדִּיקִים יְמִין יְהֹוָה עֹשָׂה חָיִל:
יְמִין יְהֹוָה רוֹמֵמָה יְמִין יְהֹוָה עֹשָׂה חָיִל: לֹא־אָמוּת כִּי־אֶחְיֶה
וַאֲסַפֵּר מַעֲשֵׂי יָהּ: יַסֹּר יִסְּרַנִּי יָּהּ וְלַמָּוֶת לֹא נְתָנָנִי: פִּתְחוּ־לִי
שַׁעֲרֵי־צֶדֶק אָבֹא־בָם אוֹדֶה יָּהּ: זֶה־הַשַּׁעַר לַיהֹוָה צַדִּיקִים יָבֹאוּ בוֹ:

Min Hametzar Karati Yah Anani Vammerchav Yah. Adonai Li Lo Ira
Mah Ya'aseh Li Adam. Adonai Li Be'ozerai Va'ani Er'eh Vesone'ai.
Tov Lachasot Badonai Mibetoach Ba'adam. Tov Lachasot Badonai
Mibetoach Bindivim. Kol Goyim Sevavuni Beshem Adonai Ki
Amilam. Sabbuni Gam Sevavuni Beshem Adonai Ki Amilam.
Sabbuni Chidvorim Do'achu Ke'esh Kotzim Beshem Adonai Ki
Amilam. Dachoh Dechitani Linpol Va'Adonai Azarani. Ozi Vezimrat
Yah Vayhi Li Lishu'ah. Kol Rinah Vishu'ah Be'oholei Tzaddikim
Yemin Adonai Osah Chayil. Yemin Adonai Romemah Yemin Adonai
Osah Chayil. Lo Amut Ki Echyeh Va'asaper Ma'asei Yah. Yassor
Yisserani Yah Velamavet Lo Netanani. Pitchu Li Sha'arei Tzedek Avo
Vam Odeh Yah. Zeh Hasha'ar L'Adonai Tzaddikim Yavo'u Vo.

Out of my restriction I called on Hashem; He answered me with
great enlargement. Hashem is for me; I will not fear; What can man
do to me? Hashem is for me as my Helper; And I will gaze on them
that hate me. It is better to take refuge in Hashem than to trust in
man. It is better to take refuge in Hashem than to trust in princes.
All nations encircled me; In the name of Hashem I will cut them off.
They encircle me, yes, they surround me; In the name of Hashem I
will cut them off. They surround me like bees; They will be
quenched as the fire of thorns; In the name of Hashem I will cut
them off. You thrusted at me that I might fall; But Hashem helped
me. Hashem is my strength and song; And He is become my
salvation. The voice of rejoicing and salvation is in the tents of the
righteous; The right hand of Hashem does valiantly. The right hand
of Hashem is exalted; The right hand of Hashem does valiantly. I
will not die, but live, and declare the works of Hashem. Hashem has

disciplined me greatly; But He has not given me over to death. Open to me the gates of righteousness; I will enter into them, I will give thanks to Hashem. This is the gate of Hashem; The righteous will enter into it.

אוֹדְךָ כִּי עֲנִיתָנִי וַתְּהִי־לִי לִישׁוּעָה: אוֹדְךָ כִּי עֲנִיתָנִי וַתְּהִי־לִי לִישׁוּעָה: אֶבֶן מָאֲסוּ הַבּוֹנִים הָיְתָה לְרֹאשׁ פִּנָּה: אֶבֶן מָאֲסוּ הַבּוֹנִים הָיְתָה לְרֹאשׁ פִּנָּה: מֵאֵת יְהֹוָה הָיְתָה זֹּאת הִיא נִפְלָאת בְּעֵינֵינוּ: מֵאֵת יְהֹוָה הָיְתָה זֹּאת הִיא נִפְלָאת בְּעֵינֵינוּ: זֶה־הַיּוֹם עָשָׂה יְהֹוָה נָגִילָה וְנִשְׂמְחָה בוֹ: זֶה־הַיּוֹם עָשָׂה יְהֹוָה נָגִילָה וְנִשְׂמְחָה בוֹ:

Odecha Ki Anitani Vatehi Li Lishu'ah. Odecha Ki Anitani Vatehi Li Lishu'ah. Even Ma'asu Habonim Hayetah Lerosh Pinah. Even Ma'asu Habonim Hayetah Lerosh Pinah. Me'et Adonai Hayetah Zot Hi Niflat Be'eineinu. Me'et Adonai Hayetah Zot Hi Niflat Be'eineinu. Zeh Hayom Asah Adonai Nagilah Venismechah Vo. Zeh Hayom Asah Adonai Nagilah Venismechah Vo.

I will give thanks to You, for You have answered me, and have become my salvation. The stone which the builders rejected has become the chief corner-stone. This is Hashem's doing; It is marvelous in our eyes. This is the day which Hashem has made; We will rejoice and be glad in it.

אָנָּא יְהֹוָה הוֹשִׁיעָה נָּא. אָנָּא יְהֹוָה הוֹשִׁיעָה נָּא:

Ana Adonai Hoshi'ah Na. Ana Adonai Hoshi'ah Na:
Hashem, save now. Hashem, save now.

אָנָּא יְהֹוָה הַצְלִיחָה נָּא. אָנָּא יְהֹוָה הַצְלִיחָה נָּא:

Ana Adonai Hatzlichah Na. Ana Adonai Hatzlichah Na.
Hashem, prosper us now. Hashem, prosper us now.

בָּרוּךְ הַבָּא בְּשֵׁם יְהֹוָה בֵּרַכְנוּכֶם מִבֵּית יְהֹוָה: בָּרוּךְ הַבָּא בְּשֵׁם יְהֹוָה בֵּרַכְנוּכֶם מִבֵּית יְהֹוָה: אֵל | יְהֹוָה וַיָּאֶר לָנוּ אִסְרוּ־חַג

בַּעֲבֹתִים עַד־קַרְנוֹת הַמִּזְבֵּחַ: אֵל | יְהֹוָה וַיָּאֶר לָנוּ אִסְרוּ־חַג
בַּעֲבֹתִים עַד־קַרְנוֹת הַמִּזְבֵּחַ: אֵלִי אַתָּה וְאוֹדֶךָּ אֱלֹהַי אֲרוֹמְמֶךָּ: אֵלִי
אַתָּה וְאוֹדֶךָּ אֱלֹהַי אֲרוֹמְמֶךָּ: הוֹדוּ לַיהֹוָה כִּי־טוֹב כִּי לְעוֹלָם חַסְדּוֹ:
הוֹדוּ לַיהֹוָה כִּי־טוֹב כִּי לְעוֹלָם חַסְדּוֹ:

Baruch Haba Beshem Adonai Berachnuchem Mibeit Adonai. Baruch
Haba Beshem Adonai Berachnuchem Mibeit Adonai. El Adonai
Vayaer Lanu Isru Chag Ba'avotim Ad Karnot Hamizbe'ach. El
Adonai Vayaer Lanu Isru Chag Ba'avotim Ad Karnot Hamizbe'ach.
Eli Attah Ve'odekka Elohai Aromemekka. Eli Attah Ve'odekka Elohai
Aromemekka. Hodu L'Adonai Ki Tov Ki Le'olam Chasdo. Hodu
L'Adonai Ki Tov Ki Le'olam Chasdo.

Blessed is he that comes in the name of Hashem; We bless you out
of the House of Hashem. Hashem is God, and has given us light;
Order the festival procession with boughs, even to the horns of the
altar. You are my God, and I will give thanks to You; You are my God,
I will exalt You. Give thanks to Hashem, for He is good, for His
mercy endures forever. Give thanks to Hashem, for He is good, for
His mercy endures forever.

On days when the Hallel is not completed, this closing blessing is omitted as well:

Yehallelucha Adonai Eloheinu	יְהַלְלוּךָ יְהֹוָה אֱלֹהֵינוּ
Kol Ma'aseicha. Vachasideicha	כָּל מַעֲשֶׂיךָ. וַחֲסִידֶיךָ
Vetzaddikim Osei Retzonecha	וְצַדִּיקִים עוֹשֵׂי רְצוֹנֶךָ
Ve'ammecha Beit Yisra'el. Kulam	וְעַמְּךָ בֵּית יִשְׂרָאֵל. כֻּלָּם
Berinah Yodu Vivarechu	בְּרִנָּה יוֹדוּ וִיבָרְכוּ
Vishabechu Vifa'aru Et Shem	וִישַׁבְּחוּ וִיפָאֲרוּ אֶת שֵׁם
Kevodecha. Ki Lecha Tov	כְּבוֹדֶךָ. כִּי לְךָ טוֹב
Lehodot. Uleshimcha Na'im	לְהוֹדוֹת. וּלְשִׁמְךָ נָעִים.
Lezamer. Ume'olam Ve'ad Olam	לְזַמֵּר. וּמֵעוֹלָם וְעַד עוֹלָם.

Attah El. Baruch Attah Adonai

אַתָּה אֵל. בָּרוּךְ אַתָּה יְהֹוָה

Melech Mehulal Batishbachot.

מֶלֶךְ מְהֻלָּל בַּתִּשְׁבָּחוֹת.

Amen:

אָמֵן:

All of Your works, Hashem our God, will praise You; Your pious servants, the righteous who perform Your will, and Your people, the House of Yisrael, will altogether, with joyful song, give thanks, bless, praise, and laud Your glorious name: for it is good to give thanks to You, and pleasant to sing praise to Your name, for You are God from everlasting to everlasting. Blessed are You, Hashem,   King adored with praises. Amen.

Some say:

Yehi Shem

יְהִי שֵׁם יְהֹוָה מְבֹרָךְ מֵעַתָּה וְעַד־עוֹלָם: מִמִּזְרַח־שֶׁמֶשׁ עַד־מְבוֹאוֹ מְהֻלָּל שֵׁם יְהֹוָה: רָם עַל־כָּל־גּוֹיִם | יְהֹוָה עַל הַשָּׁמַיִם כְּבוֹדוֹ: יְהֹוָה אֲדֹנֵינוּ מָה־אַדִּיר שִׁמְךָ בְּכָל־הָאָרֶץ:

Yehi Shem Adonai Mevorach; Me'attah. Ve'ad-'Olam. Mimizrach-Shemesh Ad-Mevo'o; Mehulal. Shem Adonai Ram Al-Chol-Goyim Adonai Al Hashamayim Kevodo. Adonai Adoneinu; Mah-'Adir Shimcha. Bechol-Ha'aretz.

Blessed is the name of Hashem from this time forward and forever. From the rising of the sun to it's going down, Hashem's name is to be praised. Hashem, our Lord, How glorious is Your name in all of the earth. (Psalms 113:2-4, 8:2)

And the Cantor says Kaddish Titkabbal, and on Hanukkah say Hatzi-Kaddish:

Kaddish Titkabbal

Kaddish is only recited in a minyan (ten men). אמן denotes when the congregation responds "Amen" together out loud. According to the Shulchan Arukh, the congregation says "Yehei Shemeh Rabba" to "Yitbarach" out loud together without interruption, and also that one should respond "Amen" after "Yitbarach." (SA, OC 55,56) This is not the common custom today. Though many are accustomed to answering according to their own custom, it is advised to respond in the custom of the one reciting to avoid not fragmenting into smaller groups. ("Lo Titgodedu" - BT, Yevamot 13b / SA, OC 493, Rema / MT, Avodah Zara 12:15)

יִתְגַּדַּל וְיִתְקַדַּשׁ שְׁמֵהּ רַבָּא. אמן בְּעָלְמָא דִּי בְרָא. כִּרְעוּתֵהּ. וְיַמְלִיךְ מַלְכוּתֵהּ.
וְיַצְמַח פֻּרְקָנֵהּ. וִיקָרֵב מְשִׁיחֵהּ. אמן בְּחַיֵּיכוֹן וּבְיוֹמֵיכוֹן וּבְחַיֵּי דְכָל בֵּית
יִשְׂרָאֵל. בַּעֲגָלָא וּבִזְמַן קָרִיב. וְאִמְרוּ אָמֵן. אמן יְהֵא שְׁמֵהּ רַבָּא מְבָרַךְ לְעָלַם
וּלְעָלְמֵי עָלְמַיָּא יִתְבָּרַךְ. וְיִשְׁתַּבַּח. וְיִתְפָּאַר. וְיִתְרוֹמַם. וְיִתְנַשֵּׂא. וְיִתְהַדָּר.
וְיִתְעַלֶּה. וְיִתְהַלָּל שְׁמֵהּ דְּקֻדְשָׁא. בְּרִיךְ הוּא. אמן לְעֵלָּא מִן כָּל בִּרְכָתָא
שִׁירָתָא. תֻּשְׁבְּחָתָא וְנֶחֱמָתָא. דַּאֲמִירָן בְּעָלְמָא. וְאִמְרוּ אָמֵן. אמן

Yitgadal Veyitkadash Shemeh Rabba. Amen Be'alema Di Vera. Kir'uteh. Veyamlich
Malchuteh. Veyatzmach Purkaneh. Vikarev Meshicheh. Amen Bechayeichon
Uveyomeichon Uvechayei Dechal-Beit Yisra'el. Ba'agala Uvizman Kariv. Ve'imru
Amen. Amen Yehei Shemeh Rabba Mevarach Le'alam Ule'alemei Alemaya
Yitbarach. Veyishtabach. Veyitpa'ar. Veyitromam. Veyitnasse. Veyit'hadar. Veyit'aleh.
Veyit'hallal Shemeh Dekudsha. Berich Hu. Amen Le'ella Min Kol Birchata Shirata.
Tushbechata Venechemata. Da'amiran Be'alema. Ve'imru Amen. Amen

Glorified and sanctified be God's great name Amen throughout the world which He
has created according to His will. May He establish His kingdom, hastening His
salvation and the coming of His Messiah, Amen, in your lifetime and during your
days, and within the life of the entire House of Yisrael, speedily and soon; and say,
Amen. Amen May His great name be blessed forever and to all eternity. Blessed and
praised, glorified and exalted, extolled and honored, adored and lauded is the
name of the Holy One, blessed is He, Amen Beyond all the blessings and hymns,
praises and consolations that are ever spoken in the world; and say, Amen. Amen

תִּתְקַבַּל צְלוֹתָנָא וּבָעוּתָנָא. עִם צְלוֹתְהוֹן וּבָעוּתְהוֹן דְּכָל בֵּית יִשְׂרָאֵל. קֳדָם
אֲבוּנָא דְּבִשְׁמַיָּא וְאַרְעָא. וְאִמְרוּ אָמֵן. אמן

Titkabbal Tzelotana Uva'utana. Im Tzelotehon Uva'utehon Dechol Beit Yisra'el.
Kodam Avuna Devishmaya Ve'ar'a. Ve'imru Amen. Amen

May the prayer and supplication of the whole House of Yisrael be accepted before
their Father in heaven, and say, Amen. Amen

יְהֵא שְׁלָמָא רַבָּא מִן שְׁמַיָּא. חַיִּים וְשָׂבָע וִישׁוּעָה וְנֶחָמָה. וְשֵׁיזָבָא וּרְפוּאָה
וּגְאוּלָה וּסְלִיחָה וְכַפָּרָה וְרֶוַח וְהַצָּלָה לָנוּ וּלְכָל עַמּוֹ יִשְׂרָאֵל. וְאִמְרוּ אָמֵן. אמן

Yehei Shelama Rabba Min Shemaya. Chayim Vesava Vishu'ah Venechamah.
Vesheizava Urefu'ah Uge'ulah Uselichah Vechapparah Verevach Vehatzalah Lanu
Ulechol Ammo Yisra'el. Ve'imru Amen. Amen

May abundant peace descend from heaven, with life and plenty, salvation, solace,
liberation, healing and redemption, and forgiveness and atonement, enlargement
and freedom, for us and all of God's people Yisrael; and say, Amen. Amen

One bows and takes three steps backwards, while still bowing. After three steps, while still bowing
and before erecting, while saying, "Oseh Shalom Bimromav", turn one's face to the left, "Hu
[Berachamav] Ya'aseh Shalom Aleinu", turn one's face to the right; then bow forward like a servant
leaving his master. (SA, OC 123:1)

עוֹשֶׂה שָׁלוֹם בעשי״ת (הַשָּׁלוֹם) בִּמְרוֹמָיו. הוּא בְּרַחֲמָיו יַעֲשֶׂה שָׁלוֹם עָלֵינוּ. וְעַל
כָּל־עַמּוֹ יִשְׂרָאֵל. וְאִמְרוּ אָמֵן:

Oseh Shalom **On the 10 days of repentance:** (Hashalom) Bimromav, Hu Berachamav
Ya'aseh Shalom Aleinu, Ve'al Kol-'Ammo Yisra'el, Ve'imru Amen.

Creator of **On the 10 days of repentance:** (the) peace in His high places, may He in His
mercy create peace for us and for all Yisrael, and say Amen.

Some say these verses three times after Hallel:

וְאַבְרָהָם זָקֵן בָּא בַּיָּמִים וַיהוָה בֵּרַךְ אֶת־אַבְרָהָם בַּכֹּל:

Ve'avraham Zaken Ba Bayamim Va'Adonai Berach Et Avraham Bakol.

And Avraham was old, well stricken in age; and Hashem had blessed Avraham in all
things. (Gen. 24:1)

And then say:

יְהוָה יִשְׁמְרֵנִי וִיחַיֵּנִי. כֵּן יְהִי רָצוֹן מִלְּפָנֶיךָ אֱלֹהִים חַיִּים וּמֶלֶךְ עוֹלָם אֲשֶׁר
בְּיָדוֹ נֶפֶשׁ כָּל חַי אָמֵן כֵּן יְהִי רָצוֹן:

Adonai Yishmereni Vichayeni. Ken Yehi Ratzon Milfaneicha Elohim Chayim
Umelech Olam Asher Beyado Nefesh Kol Chai Amen Ken Yehi Ratzon:

Watch over me and give me life. So may it be Your will, living God and eternal King,
in His hand is the soul of all living things; (Job 12:10) Amen, may it be so.

Kriyat HaTorah / The Torah Reading - Rosh Chodesh Shabbat

The Torah Reading Service now follows the respective day (Shabbat Shacharit, Torah Reading, start with "Yehi Adonai Eloheinu Imanu"). Torah Reading for the portion is as normal, Maftir is listed and shown below, except for Rosh Chodesh Elul: Isaiah 54:11-55:55. If Rosh Chodesh falls on a Sunday, the haftorah read on Shabbat is I Sam. 20:18-42. (SA, OC 425)

Torah Reading: Normal weekly portion

Maftir: Numbers 28:9-15

Haftorah: Isaiah 66:1-24

וּבְיוֹם֙ הַשַּׁבָּ֔ת שְׁנֵֽי־כְבָשִׂ֥ים בְּנֵֽי־שָׁנָ֖ה תְּמִימִ֑ם וּשְׁנֵ֣י עֶשְׂרֹנִ֗ים סֹ֧לֶת מִנְחָ֛ה בְּלוּלָ֥ה בַשֶּׁ֖מֶן וְנִסְכּֽוֹ: עֹלַ֤ת שַׁבַּת֙ בְּשַׁבַּתּ֔וֹ עַל־עֹלַ֥ת הַתָּמִ֖יד וְנִסְכָּֽהּ:

Uveyom Hashabbat Shenei Chevasim Benei Shanah Temimim Ushenei Esronim Solet Minchah Belulah Vashemen Venisko. Olat Shabbat Beshabbato Al Olat Hatamid Veniskah.

And on the Shabbat day two male lambs of the first year without blemish, and two tenth parts of an ephah of fine flour for a meal-offering, mingled with oil, and the drink-offering of it. This is the burnt-offering of every Shabbat, beside the continual burnt-offering, and the drink-offering of it.

וּבְרָאשֵׁי֙ חָדְשֵׁיכֶ֔ם תַּקְרִ֥יבוּ עֹלָ֖ה לַֽיהֹוָ֑ה פָּרִ֨ים בְּנֵֽי־בָקָ֤ר שְׁנַ֙יִם֙ וְאַ֣יִל אֶחָ֔ד כְּבָשִׂ֧ים בְּנֵֽי־שָׁנָ֛ה שִׁבְעָ֖ה תְּמִימִֽם: וּשְׁלֹשָׁ֣ה עֶשְׂרֹנִ֗ים סֹ֤לֶת מִנְחָה֙ בְּלוּלָ֣ה בַשֶּׁ֔מֶן לַפָּ֖ר הָֽאֶחָ֑ד וּשְׁנֵ֣י עֶשְׂרֹנִ֗ים סֹ֤לֶת מִנְחָה֙ בְּלוּלָ֣ה בַשֶּׁ֔מֶן לָאַ֖יִל הָֽאֶחָֽד: וְעִשָּׂרֹ֣ן עִשָּׂר֗וֹן סֹ֤לֶת מִנְחָה֙ בְּלוּלָ֣ה בַשֶּׁ֔מֶן לַכֶּ֖בֶשׂ הָֽאֶחָ֑ד עֹלָה֙ רֵ֣יחַ נִיחֹ֔חַ אִשֶּׁ֖ה לַֽיהֹוָֽה: וְנִסְכֵּיהֶ֗ם חֲצִ֣י הַהִ֞ין יִֽהְיֶ֣ה לַפָּ֗ר וּשְׁלִישִׁ֤ת הַהִין֙ לָאַ֔יִל וּרְבִיעִ֥ת הַהִ֛ין לַכֶּ֖בֶשׂ יָ֑יִן זֹ֣את עֹלַ֥ת חֹ֙דֶשׁ֙ בְּחָדְשׁ֔וֹ לְחָדְשֵׁ֖י הַשָּׁנָֽה: וּשְׂעִ֨יר עִזִּ֥ים אֶחָ֛ד לְחַטָּ֖את לַֽיהֹוָ֑ה עַל־עֹלַ֧ת הַתָּמִ֛יד יֵֽעָשֶׂ֖ה וְנִסְכּֽוֹ:

Uveroshei Chodsheichem Takrivu Olah L'Adonai Parim Benei Vakar
Shenayim Ve'ayil Echad Kevasim Benei Shanah Shiv'ah Temimim.
Usheloshah Esronim Solet Minchah Belulah Vashemen Lappar
Ha'echad Ushenei Esronim Solet Minchah Belulah Vashemen
La'ayil Ha'echad. Ve'issaron Issaron Solet Minchah Belulah
Vashemen Lakeves Ha'echad Olah Reiach Nichoach Isheh
L'Adonai. Veniskeihem Chatzi Hahin Yihyeh Lappar Ushelishit
Hahin La'ayil Urevi'it Hahin Lakeves Yayin Zot Olat Chodesh
Bechodsho Lechodshei Hashanah. Use'ir Izim Echad Lechatat
L'Adonai Al Olat Hatamid Ye'aseh Venisko.

And on your new moons you will present a burnt-offering to
Hashem: two young bulls, and one ram, seven male lambs of the
first year without blemish; and three-tenth parts of an ephah of fine
flour for a meal-offering, mingled with oil, for each bull; and two
tenth parts of fine flour for a meal-offering, mingled with oil, for the
one ram; and a several tenth part of fine flour mingled with oil for a
meal-offering to every lamb; for a burnt-offering of a sweet savor, an
offering made by fire to Hashem. And their drink-offerings will be
half a hin of wine for a bull, and the third part of a hin for the ram,
and the fourth part of a hin for a lamb. This is the burnt-offering of
every new moon throughout the months of the year. And one male
goat for a sin-offering to Hashem; it will be offered beside the
continual burnt-offering, and the drink-offering of it.

After the Haftorah reading, continue with the normal Shabbat Shacharit Service, concluding the
Torah Service until Musaf. Then continue with Musaf here.

Musaf / Additional Service - Rosh Chodesh

The chazan recites Hatzi-Kaddish:

Kaddish is only recited in a minyan (ten men). אמן denotes when the congregation responds "Amen" together out loud. According to the Shulchan Arukh, the congregation says "Yehei Shemeh Rabba" to "Yitbarach" out loud together without interruption, and also that one should respond "Amen" after "Yitbarach." (SA, OC 55,56) This is not the common custom today. Though many are accustomed to answering according to their own custom, it is advised to respond in the custom of the one reciting to avoid not fragmenting into smaller groups. ("Lo Titgodedu" - BT, Yevamot 13b / SA, OC 493, Rema / MT, Avodah Zara 12:15)

יִתְגַּדַּל וְיִתְקַדַּשׁ שְׁמֵהּ רַבָּא. אמן בְּעָלְמָא דִּי בְרָא. כִרְעוּתֵהּ. וְיַמְלִיךְ מַלְכוּתֵהּ. וְיַצְמַח פֻּרְקָנֵהּ. וִיקָרֵב מְשִׁיחֵהּ. אמן בְּחַיֵּיכוֹן וּבְיוֹמֵיכוֹן וּבְחַיֵּי דְכָל בֵּית יִשְׂרָאֵל. בַּעֲגָלָא וּבִזְמַן קָרִיב. וְאִמְרוּ אָמֵן. אמן יְהֵא שְׁמֵהּ רַבָּא מְבָרַךְ לְעָלַם וּלְעָלְמֵי עָלְמַיָּא יִתְבָּרַךְ. וְיִשְׁתַּבַּח. וְיִתְפָּאַר. וְיִתְרוֹמַם. וְיִתְנַשֵּׂא. וְיִתְהַדָּר. וְיִתְעַלֶּה. וְיִתְהַלָּל שְׁמֵהּ דְּקֻדְשָׁא. בְּרִיךְ הוּא. אמן לְעֵלָּא מִן כָּל בִּרְכָתָא שִׁירָתָא. תֻּשְׁבְּחָתָא וְנֶחֱמָתָא. דַּאֲמִירָן בְּעָלְמָא. וְאִמְרוּ אָמֵן. אמן

Yitgadal Veyitkadash Shemeh Rabba. Amen Be'alema Di Vera. Kir'uteh. Veyamlich Malchuteh. Veyatzmach Purkaneh. Vikarev Meshicheh. Amen Bechayeichon Uveyomeichon Uvechayei Dechal-Beit Yisra'el. Ba'agala Uvizman Kariv. Ve'imru Amen. Amen Yehei Shemeh Rabba Mevarach Le'alam Ule'alemei Alemaya Yitbarach. Veyishtabach. Veyitpa'ar. Veyitromam. Veyitnasse. Veyit'hadar. Veyit'aleh. Veyit'hallal Shemeh Dekudsha. Berich Hu. Amen Le'ella Min Kol Birchata Shirata. Tushbechata Venechemata. Da'amiran Be'alema. Ve'imru Amen. Amen

Glorified and sanctified be God's great name Amen throughout the world which He has created according to His will. May He establish His kingdom, hastening His salvation and the coming of His Messiah, Amen, in your lifetime and during your days, and within the life of the entire House of Yisrael, speedily and soon; and say, Amen. Amen May His great name be blessed forever and to all eternity. Blessed and praised, glorified and exalted, extolled and honored, adored and lauded is the name of the Holy One, blessed is He, Amen Beyond all the blessings and hymns, praises and consolations that are ever spoken in the world; and say, Amen. Amen

Amidah - Musaf / Additional Service - Rosh Chodesh Shabbat

Take three steps forward and say:

Adonai Sefatai Tiftach; Ufi. Yagid
Tehilatecha.

אֲדֹנָי שְׂפָתַי תִּפְתָּח וּפִי יַגִּיד
תְּהִלָּתֶךָ:

Hashem, open my lips, that my mouth may declare Your praise.

Avot / Fathers

Bow at "Baruch Attah" / "Blessed are You". Raise up at Adonai / Hashem.

Baruch Attah Adonai Eloheinu

בָּרוּךְ אַתָּה יְהוָה אֱלֹהֵינוּ

Velohei Avoteinu. Elohei

וֵאלֹהֵי אֲבוֹתֵינוּ. אֱלֹהֵי

Avraham. Elohei Yitzchak.

אַבְרָהָם. אֱלֹהֵי יִצְחָק.

Velohei Ya'akov. Ha'el Hagadol

וֵאלֹהֵי יַעֲקֹב. הָאֵל הַגָּדוֹל

Hagibor Vehanorah. El Elyon.

הַגִּבּוֹר וְהַנּוֹרָא. אֵל עֶלְיוֹן.

Gomel Chasadim Tovim. Koneh

גּוֹמֵל חֲסָדִים טוֹבִים. קוֹנֵה

Hakol. Vezocher Chasdei Avot.

הַכֹּל. וְזוֹכֵר חַסְדֵי אָבוֹת.

Umevi Go'el Livnei Veneihem

וּמֵבִיא גוֹאֵל לִבְנֵי בְנֵיהֶם

Lema'an Shemo Be'ahavah.

לְמַעַן שְׁמוֹ בְּאַהֲבָה:

Blessed are You, Hashem our God and God of our fathers, God of Avraham, God of Yitzchak and God of Yaakov; the great, mighty and revered God, most high God, Who bestows lovingkindness. Master of all things; Who remembers the kindnesses of our fathers, and Who will bring a redeemer to their children's children for the sake of His name in love.

Bow at "Baruch Attah" / Blessed are You. Raise up at Adonai / Hashem.

Melech Ozeir Umoshia

מֶלֶךְ עוֹזֵר וּמוֹשִׁיעַ

Umagen. Baruch Attah Adonai

וּמָגֵן: בָּרוּךְ אַתָּה יְהוָה

Magen Avraham.

מָגֵן אַבְרָהָם:

King, Supporter, and Savior and Shield. Blessed are You, Hashem, Shield of Avraham.

Gevurot / Powers

We [in Yisrael] begin to say "Mashiv Haruach" in the second blessing of the Amidah from the Musaf [Additional] Service of the last day of Sukkot, and conclude at the Musaf [Additional] Service of the first day of Pesach. On the first day of Pesach the congregation still says it in the Musaf Service, but the Reader stops saying it then. In lands outside of Yisrael, [in the Birkhat HaShanim / Blessing for the Years,] we begin to pray for rain in the Arvit (Evening) Service of the sixtieth day after the New Moon of Tishrei, and in Yisrael we begin to say it in the evening of the seventh day of Cheshvan, and it is said until the Afternoon Service on the day preceding the first day of Passover. If one prayed for rain in the summer, or if one omitted to pray for it in the winter, he must repeat the Amidah again. If one said "Morid Hageshem" in the summer time, he must repeat again from the beginning of the blessing. If he already concluded the blessing, he must read the entire Amidah again. Likewise in the winter, if he omitted it, he must begin all over again. (SA, OC 117)

Attah Gibor Le'olam Adonai.	אַתָּה גִבּוֹר לְעוֹלָם אֲדֹנָי.
Mechayeh Meitim Attah. Rav	מְחַיֶּה מֵתִים אַתָּה. רַב
Lehoshia.	לְהוֹשִׁיעַ.

You, Hashem, are mighty forever; You revive the dead; You are powerful to save.

B'ketz: Morid Hatal.	בקיץ: מוֹרִיד הַטָּל.
B'choref: Mashiv Haruach Umorid	בחורף: מַשִּׁיב הָרוּחַ וּמוֹרִיד
Hageshem.	הַגָּשֶׁם.

In summer: You cause the dew to fall.

In winter: You cause the wind to blow and the rain to fall.

Mechalkel Chayim Bechesed.	מְכַלְכֵּל חַיִּים בְּחֶסֶד.
Mechayeh Meitim Berachamim	מְחַיֶּה מֵתִים בְּרַחֲמִים
Rabim. Somech Nofelim. Verofei	רַבִּים. סוֹמֵךְ נוֹפְלִים. וְרוֹפֵא
Cholim. Umatir Asurim.	חוֹלִים. וּמַתִּיר אֲסוּרִים.
Umekayem Emunato Lishenei	וּמְקַיֵּם אֱמוּנָתוֹ לִישֵׁנֵי

Afar. Mi Chamocha Ba'al	עָפָר. מִי כָמוֹךָ בַּעַל
Gevurot. Umi Domeh Lach.	גְּבוּרוֹת. וּמִי דוֹמֶה לָךְ.
Melech Memit Umechayeh	מֶלֶךְ מֵמִית וּמְחַיֶּה
Umatzmiach Yeshu'ah.	וּמַצְמִיחַ יְשׁוּעָה.

You sustain the living with kindness, and revive the dead with great mercy; You support all who fall, and heal the sick; You set the captives free, and keep faith with those who sleep in the dust. Who is like You, Master of power? Who resembles You, Oh King? You bring death and restore life, and cause salvation to flourish.

Vene'eman Attah Lehachayot	וְנֶאֱמָן אַתָּה לְהַחֲיוֹת
Meitim. Baruch Attah Adonai	מֵתִים: בָּרוּךְ אַתָּה יְהֹוָה
Mechayeh Hameitim.	מְחַיֵּה הַמֵּתִים:

And You are faithful to revive the dead. Blessed are You, Hashem, Who revives the dead.

Kedusha

Kedusha is said only in a minyan (10 men). If one is not available, skip to "Holiness". It is proper to position one's feet together at the time one is reciting Kedushah with the prayer-leader. On Weekday Chol HaMoed (Intermediate days between Festivals) brackets are omitted, [*] lines only are read for Chol HaMoed.

Keter Yitenu Lecha. Adonai	כֶּתֶר יִתְּנוּ לְךָ. יְהֹוָה
Eloheinu. Mal'achim Hamonei	אֱלֹהֵינוּ. מַלְאָכִים הֲמוֹנֵי
Ma'lah. Im Ammecha Yisra'el	מַעְלָה. עִם עַמְּךָ יִשְׂרָאֵל
Kevutzei Mattah. Yachad Kulam	קְבוּצֵי מַטָּה. יַחַד כֻּלָּם
Kedushah Lecha Yeshalleshu.	קְדֻשָּׁה לְךָ יְשַׁלֵּשׁוּ.
Kadavar Ha'amur Al Yad	כַּדָּבָר הָאָמוּר עַל יַד
Nevi'ach Vekara Zeh El Zeh	נְבִיאָךְ וְקָרָא זֶה אֶל־זֶה

Ve'amar **Kadosh Kadosh Kadosh**	וְאָמַר קָדוֹשׁ | קָדוֹשׁ קָדוֹשׁ
Adonai Tzeva'ot Melo Chol	יְהֹוָה צְבָאוֹת מְלֹא כָל־
Ha'aretz Kevodo. Kevodo Male	הָאָרֶץ כְּבוֹדוֹ: כְּבוֹדוֹ מָלֵא
Olam. Umesharetav Sho'alim	עוֹלָם. וּמְשָׁרְתָיו שׁוֹאֲלִים
Ayeh Mekom Kevodo	אַיֵּה מְקוֹם כְּבוֹדוֹ
Leha'aritzo: Le'ummatam	לְהַעֲרִיצוֹ: לְעֻמָּתָם
Meshabechim Ve'omerim **Baruch**	מְשַׁבְּחִים וְאוֹמְרִים בָּרוּךְ
Kevod Adonai Mimekomo.	כְּבוֹד־יְהֹוָה מִמְּקוֹמוֹ:
Mimekomo Hu Yifen	מִמְּקוֹמוֹ הוּא יִפֶן
Berachamav Le'ammo	בְּרַחֲמָיו לְעַמּוֹ
Hameyachadim Shemo Erev	הַמְיַחֲדִים שְׁמוֹ עֶרֶב
Vavoker. Bechol Yom Tamid	וָבֹקֶר. בְּכָל יוֹם תָּמִיד
Omerim Pa'amayim Be'ahavah	אוֹמְרִים פַּעֲמַיִם בְּאַהֲבָה
Shema Yisra'el Adonai Eloheinu	שְׁמַע יִשְׂרָאֵל יְהֹוָה אֱלֹהֵינוּ
Adonai Echad. Hu Eloheinu. Hu	יְהֹוָה | אֶחָד: הוּא אֱלֹהֵינוּ. הוּא
Avinu. Hu Malkeinu. Hu	אָבִינוּ. הוּא מַלְכֵּנוּ. הוּא
Moshi'enu. Hu Yoshi'enu	מוֹשִׁיעֵנוּ. הוּא יוֹשִׁיעֵנוּ
Veyig'alenu Shenit.	וְיִגְאָלֵנוּ שֵׁנִית.
Veyashmi'enu Berachamav	וְיַשְׁמִיעֵנוּ בְּרַחֲמָיו
Le'einei Kol Chai Lemor. Hen	לְעֵינֵי כָּל חַי לֵאמֹר. הֵן
Ga'alti Etchem Acharit Kereshit	גָּאַלְתִּי אֶתְכֶם אַחֲרִית כְּרֵאשִׁית
Lihyot Lachem Lelohim. **Ani**	לִהְיוֹת לָכֶם לֵאלֹהִים. אֲנִי
Adonai Eloheichem: Uvedivrei	יְהֹוָה אֱלֹהֵיכֶם: וּבְדִבְרֵי
Kodshecha Katuv Lemor **Yimloch**	קָדְשְׁךָ כָּתוּב לֵאמֹר יִמְלֹךְ
Adonai Le'olam Elohayich	יְהֹוָה | לְעוֹלָם אֱלֹהַיִךְ
Tziyon Ledor Vador Halleluyah:	צִיּוֹן לְדֹר וָדֹר הַלְלוּיָהּ:

To You, Hashem our God, will the heavenly host of angels above, with Your people Yisrael assembled beneath, give a crown; all with one accord will thrice proclaim the holy praise to You, according to the word spoken by Your prophet, "And one cried to another, and said, **"Holy, holy, holy is Hashem of hosts, the whole earth is full of His glory."** His glory fills the world, and His ministering angels enquire. Where is the place of His glory that they may worship Him with awe? While those angels turning towards each other continue praising and saying: **"Blessed is the glory of Hashem from His place."** From His place may He turn to His people with mercy, who evening and morning daily proclaim the unity of His name, by repeating twice every day with love, **"Hear, O Yisrael. Hashem is our God, Hashem is One."** He is our God, He is our Father, He is our King, He is our Savior; He will save and redeem us a second time, and through His infinite mercy will let us hear when He will proclaim in the presence of all living, Behold, I have now redeemed you in the latter times, as at the beginning, to be your God. **"I am Hashem your God."** And in Your holy Word it is written, saying, **"Hashem will reign forever, your God, Tziyon, from generation to generation. Halleluyah."**

Kedushat HaShem / Holiness of the Name

Attah Kadosh Veshimcha אַתָּה קָדוֹשׁ וְשִׁמְךָ
Kadosh. Ukedoshim Bechol- קָדוֹשׁ. וּקְדוֹשִׁים בְּכָל־
Yom Yehalelucha Selah. Baruch יוֹם יְהַלְלוּךָ סֶּלָה: בָּרוּךְ
Attah Adonai Ha' El Hakadosh. אַתָּה יְהֹוָה הָאֵל הַקָּדוֹשׁ:

You are holy and Your name is holy, and the holy-ones will praise You every day, selah. Blessed are You, Hashem, The Holy God.

Kedushat HaYom / Holiness of the Day

Attah Yatzarta Olamecha	אַתָּה יָצַרְתָּ עוֹלָמְךָ
Mikedem. Killita Melachtecha	מִקֶּדֶם. כִּלִּיתָ מְלַאכְתְּךָ
Bayom Hashevi'i. Bacharta	בַּיּוֹם הַשְּׁבִיעִי. בָּחַרְתָּ
Banu Mikol Ha'ummot Veratzita	בָּנוּ מִכָּל הָאֻמּוֹת וְרָצִיתָ
Banu Mikol Halleshonot.	בָּנוּ מִכָּל הַלְּשׁוֹנוֹת.
Vekidashtanu Bemitzvoteicha.	וְקִדַּשְׁתָּנוּ בְּמִצְוֹתֶיךָ.
Vekeravtanu Malkeinu	וְקֵרַבְתָּנוּ מַלְכֵּנוּ
La'avodatecha. Veshimcha	לַעֲבוֹדָתֶךָ. וְשִׁמְךָ
Hagadol Vehakadosh Aleinu	הַגָּדוֹל וְהַקָּדוֹשׁ עָלֵינוּ
Karata. Vatiten Lanu Adonai	קָרָאתָ. וַתִּתֶּן לָנוּ יְהֹוָה
Eloheinu Be'ahavah Shabbatot	אֱלֹהֵינוּ בְּאַהֲבָה שַׁבָּתוֹת
Limnuchah Veroshei Chodashim	לִמְנוּחָה וְרָאשֵׁי חֳדָשִׁים
Lechapparah. Ulefi Shechatanu	לְכַפָּרָה. וּלְפִי שֶׁחָטָאנוּ
Lefaneicha Adonai Eloheinu	לְפָנֶיךָ יְהֹוָה אֱלֹהֵינוּ
Velohei Avoteinu. Charevah	וֵאלֹהֵי אֲבוֹתֵינוּ. חָרְבָה
Irenu Veshamem Mikdashenu.	עִירֵנוּ וְשָׁמֵם מִקְדָּשֵׁנוּ.
Vegalah Yekarenu. Venuttal	וְגָלָה יְקָרֵנוּ. וְנִטַּל
Kavod Mibeit Chayeinu. Ve'ein	כָּבוֹד מִבֵּית חַיֵּינוּ. וְאֵין
Anachnu Yecholim Lehakriv	אֲנַחְנוּ יְכוֹלִים לְהַקְרִיב
Lefaneicha Korban. Velo	לְפָנֶיךָ קָרְבָּן. וְלֹא
Chohen Sheyechapeir	כֹהֵן שֶׁיְּכַפֵּר
Ba'adenu:	בַּעֲדֵנוּ:

You have formed Your world from old. You completed Your work on the seventh-day. You have chosen us from all the nations, and favored us from all the tongues: and sanctified us with Your commandments, and brought us near, our King, to Your service and have proclaimed upon us Your great and holy name. And You gave us, Hashem our God, with love, Shabbatot for rest and the Rosh Chodesh (New Moon) Days for atonement. But because we sinned before You, Hashem our God and the God of our fathers, our city has been made desolate, and our Holy Mikdash wasted; our honor carried into exile, and the glory removed from the House of our life. And we are unable to offer before You a sacrifice, nor can a Kohen atone for us.

Yehi Ratzon Milfaneicha Adonai	יְהִי רָצוֹן מִלְּפָנֶיךָ יְהֹוָה
Eloheinu Velohei Avoteinu.	אֱלֹהֵינוּ וֵאלֹהֵי אֲבוֹתֵינוּ.
Sheta'alenu Vesimchah	שֶׁתַּעֲלֵנוּ בְשִׂמְחָה
Le'artzenu Vetita'enu Bigvulenu.	לְאַרְצֵנוּ וְתִטָּעֵנוּ בִּגְבוּלֵנוּ.
Vesham Na'aseh Lefanecha Et	וְשָׁם נַעֲשֶׂה לְפָנֶיךָ אֶת
Karebenot Chovoteinu. Temidim	קָרְבְּנוֹת חוֹבוֹתֵינוּ. תְּמִידִים
Kesidram Umusafim	כְּסִדְרָם וּמוּסָפִים
Kehilchatam. Et Musefei Yom	כְּהִלְכָתָם. אֶת מוּסְפֵי יוֹם
Hashabbat Hazeh. Veyom Rosh	הַשַּׁבָּת הַזֶּה. וְיוֹם רֹאשׁ
Hachodesh Hazeh. Na'aseh	הַחֹדֶשׁ הַזֶּה. נַעֲשֶׂה
Venakriv Lefaneicha Be'ahavah	וְנַקְרִיב לְפָנֶיךָ בְּאַהֲבָה
Kemitzvat Retzonach. Kemo	כְּמִצְוַת רְצוֹנָךְ. כְּמוֹ
Shekatavta Aleinu Betoratach Al	שֶׁכָּתַבְתָּ עָלֵינוּ בְּתוֹרָתָךְ עַל
Yedei Mosheh Avdach Ka'amur:	יְדֵי מֹשֶׁה עַבְדָּךְ כָּאָמוּר:

May it be Your will, Hashem our God and God of our fathers, to bring us up with joy to our land, and to plant us in our own territory; and there we will offer in Your presence, bring the offerings of our duty; the continual offerings according to their order and the Musaf (additional) offerings according to their laws. The Musaf offering of this day of rest and of this day of Rosh Chodesh we will offer before You with love according to the commands of Your will, as You have written concerning us in Your Torah, by the hand of Moshe, Your servant; as it is said:

וּבְיוֹם הַשַּׁבָּת שְׁנֵי־כְבָשִׂים בְּנֵי־שָׁנָה תְּמִימִם וּשְׁנֵי עֶשְׂרֹנִים סֹלֶת מִנְחָה בְּלוּלָה בַשֶּׁמֶן וְנִסְכּוֹ: עֹלַת שַׁבַּת בְּשַׁבַּתּוֹ עַל־עֹלַת הַתָּמִיד וְנִסְכָּהּ:

Uveyom Hashabbat Shenei Chevasim Benei Shanah Temimim Ushenei Esronim Solet Minchah Belulah Vashemen Venisko. Olat Shabbat Beshabbato Al Olat Hatamid Veniskah.

And on the Shabbat day two male-lambs of the first year without blemish, and two tenth parts of an ephah of fine flour for a meal-offering, mingled with oil, and the drink-offering accordingly. This is the burnt-offering of every Shabbat, beside the continual burnt-offering, and the drink-offering of it. (Num. 28:9-10)

וּבְרָאשֵׁי חָדְשֵׁיכֶם תַּקְרִיבוּ עֹלָה לַיהֹוָה פָּרִים בְּנֵי־בָקָר שְׁנַיִם וְאַיִל אֶחָד כְּבָשִׂים בְּנֵי־שָׁנָה שִׁבְעָה תְּמִימִם: וּמִנְחָתָם וְנִסְכֵּיהֶם כַּמְדֻבָּר: שְׁלֹשָׁה עֶשְׂרֹנִים לַפָּר וּשְׁנֵי עֶשְׂרֹנִים לָאַיִל וְעִשָּׂרוֹן לַכֶּבֶשׂ. וְיַיִן כְּנִסְכּוֹ. וְשָׂעִיר לְכַפֵּר. וּשְׁנֵי תְמִידִים כְּהִלְכָתָם:

Uveroshei Chodsheichem Takrivu Olah L'Adonai Parim Benei Vakar Shenayim Ve'ayil Echad Kevasim Benei Shanah Shiv'ah Temimim. Uminchatam Veniskeihem Kammedubbar: Sheloshah Esronim Lappar Ushenei Esronim La'ayil Ve'issaron Lakeves. Veyayin Kenisko. Vesa'ir Lechapeir. Ushenei Temidim Kehilchatam.

And on your new moons you will present a burnt-offering to Hashem: two young bulls, and one ram, seven male lambs of the first year without blemish; and their meal-offering and drink-offerings according to it. Three tenths of a hin for each bull, two tenths of a hin for the ram, and a tenths of a hin for every lamb, and wine according to the drink-offering of it; a goat for an atonement, and the two daily offerings, according to their institution. (Num.28:11-14)

Eloheinu Velohei Avoteinu.	אֱלֹהֵינוּ וֵאלֹהֵי אֲבוֹתֵינוּ.
Chadesh Aleinu Et Hachodesh	חַדֵּשׁ עָלֵינוּ אֶת הַחֹדֶשׁ
Hazeh Letovah Velivrachah.	הַזֶּה לְטוֹבָה וְלִבְרָכָה.
Lesason Ulesimchah. Lishu'ah	לְשָׂשׂוֹן וּלְשִׂמְחָה. לִישׁוּעָה
Ulenechamah. Lefarnasah	וּלְנֶחָמָה. לְפַרְנָסָה
Ulechalkalah. Lechayim Tovim	וּלְכַלְכָּלָה. לְחַיִּים טוֹבִים
Uleshalom. Limchilat Chet.	וּלְשָׁלוֹם. לִמְחִילַת חֵטְא.
Velislichat Avon. **In A Leap Year:**	וְלִסְלִיחַת עָוֹן. בשנה מעוברת אומרים:
(Ulechapparat Pesha.) Veyihyeh	(וּלְכַפָּרַת פֶּשַׁע.) וְיִהְיֶה
Rosh Chodesh Hazeh Sof Vaketz	רֹאשׁ חֹדֶשׁ הַזֶּה סוֹף וָקֵץ
Lechol Tzaroteinu. Techillah	לְכָל צָרוֹתֵינוּ. תְּחִלָּה וְרֹאשׁ
Varosh Lefidyon Nafshenu. Ki	לְפִדְיוֹן נַפְשֵׁנוּ. כִּי
Ve'ammecha Yisra'el Mikol	בְעַמְּךָ יִשְׂרָאֵל מִכָּל
Ha'ummot Bacharta. Vechukkei	הָאֻמּוֹת בָּחַרְתָּ. וְחֻקֵּי
Roshei Chodashim Lahem	רָאשֵׁי חֳדָשִׁים לָהֶם
Kava'eta:	קָבָעְתָּ:

Our God, and the God of our fathers, renew this month for good and for blessing; for gladness and for joy; for salvation and for consolation; for maintenance and for sustenance; for good life and for peace, for forgiveness of sin and for pardon of iniquity. **In a leap year:** (and for atonement of transgression.) And may this new month be the end and termination of all our troubles, the opening and beginning of the redemption of our souls; for Your people, Yisrael, You chose from all nations and have appointed for them the statutes of Rosh Chodesh.

Yismechu Vemalchutach	יִשְׂמְחוּ בְמַלְכוּתָךְ
Shomerei Shabbat Vekore'ei	שׁוֹמְרֵי שַׁבָּת וְקוֹרְאֵי
Oneg. Am Mekadeshei Shevi'i.	עֹנֶג. עַם מְקַדְּשֵׁי שְׁבִיעִי.
Kulam Yisbe'u Veyit'anegu	כֻּלָּם יִשְׂבְּעוּ וְיִתְעַנְּגוּ
Mituvach. Vehashevi'i Ratzita	מִטּוּבָךְ. וְהַשְּׁבִיעִי רָצִיתָ
Bo Vekidashto. Chemdat Yamim	בּוֹ וְקִדַּשְׁתּוֹ. חֶמְדַּת יָמִים
Oto Karata. Zecher Lema'aseh	אוֹתוֹ קָרָאתָ. זֵכֶר לְמַעֲשֵׂה
Vereshit:	בְרֵאשִׁית:

They will rejoice in Your rule, those who keep Shabbat and call it a delight. A people who sanctify the seventh day, they will all be satisfied and delight in Your goodness. And the seventh, You desired it, and sanctified it, declaring it "the desired of days", a memorial to the work of Creation.

Eloheinu Velohei Avoteinu.	אֱלֹהֵינוּ וֵאלֹהֵי אֲבוֹתֵינוּ.
Retzeh Na Bimnuchatenu.	רְצֵה נָא בִמְנוּחָתֵנוּ.
Kadeshenu Bemitzvoteicha. Sim	קַדְּשֵׁנוּ בְּמִצְוֹתֶיךָ. שִׂים
Chelkenu Betoratach. Sabe'einu	חֶלְקֵנוּ בְּתוֹרָתֶךָ. שַׂבְּעֵנוּ
Mituvach. Same'ach Nafshenu	מִטּוּבָךְ. שַׂמֵּחַ נַפְשֵׁנוּ
Bishu'atach. Vetaher Libenu	בִּישׁוּעָתֶךָ. וְטַהֵר לִבֵּנוּ
Le'avdecha Ve'emet.	לְעָבְדְּךָ בֶּאֱמֶת.
Vehanchilenu Adonai Eloheinu	וְהַנְחִילֵנוּ יְהֹוָה אֱלֹהֵינוּ
Be'ahavah Uveratzon Shabbat	בְּאַהֲבָה וּבְרָצוֹן שַׁבָּת
Kodshecha. Veyanuchu Vo Kol-	קָדְשֶׁךָ. וְיָנוּחוּ בוֹ כָּל
Yisra'el Mekadeshei Shemecha.	יִשְׂרָאֵל מְקַדְּשֵׁי שְׁמֶךָ.
Baruch Attah Adonai Mekadesh	בָּרוּךְ אַתָּה יְהֹוָה מְקַדֵּשׁ

Hashabbat Veyisrael Veroshei	הַשַּׁבָּת וְיִשְׂרָאֵל וְרָאשֵׁי
Chadashim.	חֳדָשִׁים:

Our God, God of our fathers, be pleased with our rest. Sanctify us through Your commandments and grant our portion in Your Torah. Content us with Your goodness. Rejoice our soul with Your salvation. And make our heart pure to serve You in truth. Cause us to inherit, Hashem our God, Your holy Shabbat with love and favor; and grant rest on it to all Yisrael who sanctify Your name. Blessed are You, Hashem Who sanctifies the Shabbat and Yisrael and the days of Rosh Chodesh.

Avodah / Temple Service

Retzeh Adonai Eloheinu	רְצֵה יְהוָה אֱלֹהֵינוּ
Be'ammecha Yisra'el Velitfilatam	בְּעַמְּךָ יִשְׂרָאֵל וְלִתְפִלָּתָם
She'eh. Vehasheiv Ha'avodah	שְׁעֵה. וְהָשֵׁב הָעֲבוֹדָה
Lidvir Beitecha. Ve'ishei Yisra'el	לִדְבִיר בֵּיתֶךָ. וְאִשֵּׁי יִשְׂרָאֵל
Utefilatam. Meheirah Be'ahavah	וּתְפִלָּתָם. מְהֵרָה בְּאַהֲבָה
Tekabel Beratzon. Utehi	תְקַבֵּל בְּרָצוֹן. וּתְהִי
Leratzon Tamid Avodat Yisra'el	לְרָצוֹן תָּמִיד עֲבוֹדַת יִשְׂרָאֵל
Ammecha. Ve'attah	עַמֶּךָ. וְאַתָּה
Berachameicha Harabim.	בְּרַחֲמֶיךָ הָרַבִּים.
Tachpotz Banu Vetirtzenu.	תַּחְפֹּץ בָּנוּ וְתִרְצֵנוּ.
Vetechezeinah Eineinu	וְתֶחֱזֶינָה עֵינֵינוּ
Beshuvecha Letziyon	בְּשׁוּבְךָ לְצִיּוֹן
Berachamim. Baruch Attah	בְּרַחֲמִים. בָּרוּךְ אַתָּה
Adonai Hamachazir Shechinato	יְהוָה הַמַּחֲזִיר שְׁכִינָתוֹ
Letziyon:	לְצִיּוֹן:

Be favorable, Hashem our God, on Your people Yisrael and regard their prayers. And the service to the Sanctuary of Your House, and the fire offerings of Yisrael, and their prayers accept soon with love. And may the service of Your people, Yisrael, always be favorable. And You, in Your abundant mercy, delight in us, and be favorable to us, so that our eyes may witness Your return to Tziyon with mercy. Blessed are You, Hashem Who returns His Presence to Tziyon.

Hoda'ah (Modim) / Thanksgiving

On Saying "Modim" / "We are Thankful" One Bows and begins to rise after "Adonai" / "Hashem".

Modim Anachnu Lach. She'attah	מוֹדִים אֲנַחְנוּ לָךְ. שָׁאַתָּה
Hu Adonai Eloheinu Velohei	הוּא יְהֹוָה אֱלֹהֵינוּ וֵאלֹהֵי
Avoteinu Le'olam Va'ed. Tzurenu	אֲבוֹתֵינוּ לְעוֹלָם וָעֶד. צוּרֵנוּ
Tzur Chayeinu Umagen Yish'enu	צוּר חַיֵּינוּ וּמָגֵן יִשְׁעֵנוּ
Attah Hu. Ledor Vador Nodeh	אַתָּה הוּא. לְדוֹר וָדוֹר נוֹדֶה
Lecha Unsapeir Tehilatecha. Al	לְךָ וּנְסַפֵּר תְּהִלָּתֶךָ. עַל
Chayeinu Hamesurim	חַיֵּינוּ הַמְּסוּרִים
Beyadecha. Ve'al Nishmoteinu	בְּיָדֶךָ. וְעַל נִשְׁמוֹתֵינוּ
Hapekudot Lach. Ve'al Niseicha	הַפְּקוּדוֹת לָךְ. וְעַל נִסֶּיךָ
Shebechol-Yom Imanu. Ve'al	שֶׁבְּכָל־יוֹם עִמָּנוּ. וְעַל
Nifle'oteicha Vetovoteicha	נִפְלְאוֹתֶיךָ וְטוֹבוֹתֶיךָ
Shebechol-'Et. Erev Vavoker	שֶׁבְּכָל־עֵת. עֶרֶב וָבֹקֶר
Vetzaharayim. Hatov. Ki Lo	וְצָהֳרָיִם. הַטּוֹב. כִּי לֹא
Chalu Rachameicha.	כָלוּ רַחֲמֶיךָ.
Hamerachem. Ki Lo Tamu	הַמְרַחֵם. כִּי לֹא תַמּוּ
Chasadeicha. Ki Me'olam Kivinu	חֲסָדֶיךָ. כִּי מֵעוֹלָם קִוִּינוּ
Lach.	לָךְ:

We are thankful to You, Hashem our God and the God of our
fathers, forever. You are our strength and Rock of our life and the
Shield of our salvation. In every generation we will thank You and
recount Your praise for our lives which are given into Your hand, for
our souls which are placed in Your care, and for Your miracles which
are daily with us, and for Your wonders and goodness—evening,
morning and noon. The Beneficent One, for Your mercies never
end, Merciful One, for Your kindness has never ceased, for we have
always placed our hope in You.

Modim Derabbanan

During the repetition, this is to be recited softly while the Chazan reads the Modim. Still bow at Modim as before.

מוֹדִים אֲנַחְנוּ לָךְ. שָׁאַתָּה הוּא יְהֹוָה אֱלֹהֵינוּ וֵאלֹהֵי אֲבוֹתֵינוּ. אֱלֹהֵי כָל בָּשָׂר.
יוֹצְרֵנוּ יוֹצֵר בְּרֵאשִׁית. בְּרָכוֹת וְהוֹדָאוֹת לְשִׁמְךָ הַגָּדוֹל וְהַקָּדוֹשׁ. עַל שֶׁהֶחֱיִיתָנוּ
וְקִיַּמְתָּנוּ. כֵּן תְּחַיֵּנוּ וּתְחָנֵּנוּ וְתֶאֱסוֹף גָּלְיוֹתֵינוּ לְחַצְרוֹת קָדְשֶׁךָ. לִשְׁמֹר חֻקֶּיךָ
וְלַעֲשׂוֹת רְצוֹנֶךָ וּלְעָבְדְּךָ בְּלֵבָב שָׁלֵם. עַל שֶׁאֲנַחְנוּ מוֹדִים לָךְ. בָּרוּךְ אֵל
הַהוֹדָאוֹת.

Modim Anachnu Lach. She'attah Hu Adonai Eloheinu Velohei Avoteinu. Elohei
Chol Basar. Yotzreinu Yotzer Bereshit. Berachot Vehoda'ot Leshimcha Hagadol
Vehakadosh. Al Shehecheyitanu Vekiyamtanu. Ken Techayeinu Utechanenu
Vete'esof Galyoteinu Lechatzrot Kodshecha. Lishmor Chukkeicha Vela'asot
Retzonecha Ule'avedecha Velevav Shalem. Al She'anachnu Modim Lach. Baruch El
Hahoda'ot.

We are thankful to You, Hashem our God and the God of our fathers. God of all
flesh, our Creator and Former of Creation, blessings and thanks to Your great and
holy name, for You have kept us alive and sustained us; may You always grant us life
and be gracious to us. And gather our exiles to Your holy courtyards to observe
Your statutes, and to do Your will, and to serve You with a perfect heart. For this we
thank You. Blessed is God of thanksgivings.

Al HaNissim

On Purim and Hanukkah an extra prayer is added here:

עַל הַנִּסִּים וְעַל הַפֻּרְקָן וְעַל הַגְּבוּרוֹת וְעַל הַתְּשׁוּעוֹת וְעַל הַנִּפְלָאוֹת וְעַל
הַנֶּחָמוֹת שֶׁעָשִׂיתָ לַאֲבוֹתֵינוּ בַּיָּמִים הָהֵם בַּזְּמַן הַזֶּה:

Al Hanissim Ve'al Hapurkan Ve'al Hagevurot Ve'al Hateshu'ot Ve'al Hanifla'ot Ve'al
Hanechamot She'asita La'avoteinu Bayamim Hahem Bazman Hazeh.

For the miracles, and for the triumphant liberation, and the mighty works, and for the deliverances, and for the wonders, and for the consolations which You have done for our fathers in those days at this season:

On Hanukkah:

בִּימֵי מַתִּתְיָהוּ בֶּן־יוֹחָנָן כֹּהֵן גָּדוֹל. חַשְׁמוֹנָאִי וּבָנָיו כְּשֶׁעָמְדָה מַלְכוּת יָוָן הָרְשָׁעָה עַל עַמְּךָ יִשְׂרָאֵל. לְשַׁכְּחָם תּוֹרָתֶךָ וּלְהַעֲבִירָם מֵחֻקֵּי רְצוֹנֶךָ. וְאַתָּה בְּרַחֲמֶיךָ הָרַבִּים עָמַדְתָּ לָהֶם בְּעֵת צָרָתָם. רַבְתָּ אֶת רִיבָם. דַּנְתָּ אֶת דִּינָם. נָקַמְתָּ אֶת נִקְמָתָם. מָסַרְתָּ גִבּוֹרִים בְּיַד חַלָּשִׁים. וְרַבִּים בְּיַד מְעַטִּים. וּרְשָׁעִים בְּיַד צַדִּיקִים. וּטְמֵאִים בְּיַד טְהוֹרִים. וְזֵדִים בְּיַד עוֹסְקֵי תוֹרָתֶךָ. לְךָ עָשִׂיתָ שֵׁם גָּדוֹל וְקָדוֹשׁ בְּעוֹלָמֶךָ. וּלְעַמְּךָ יִשְׂרָאֵל עָשִׂיתָ תְּשׁוּעָה גְדוֹלָה וּפֻרְקָן כְּהַיּוֹם הַזֶּה. וְאַחַר כָּךְ בָּאוּ בָנֶיךָ לִדְבִיר בֵּיתֶךָ. וּפִנּוּ אֶת־הֵיכָלֶךָ. וְטִהֲרוּ אֶת־מִקְדָּשֶׁךָ. וְהִדְלִיקוּ נֵרוֹת בְּחַצְרוֹת קָדְשֶׁךָ. וְקָבְעוּ שְׁמוֹנַת יְמֵי חֲנֻכָּה אֵלּוּ בְּהַלֵּל וּבְהוֹדָאָה. וְעָשִׂיתָ עִמָּהֶם נִסִּים וְנִפְלָאוֹת וְנוֹדֶה לְשִׁמְךָ הַגָּדוֹל סֶלָה:

Bimei Mattityah Ven-Yochanan Kohen Gadol. Chashmona'i Uvanav Keshe'amedah Malchut Yavan Haresha'ah Al Ammecha Yisra'el. Leshakecham Toratach Uleha'aviram Mechukkei Retzonach. Ve'attah Berachameicha Harabim Amadta Lahem Be'et Tzaratam. Ravta Et Rivam. Danta Et Dinam. Nakamta Et Nikmatam. Masarta Giborim Beyad Chalashim. Verabim Beyad Me'atim. Uresha'im Beyad Tzaddikim. Uteme'im Beyad Tehorim. Vezeidim Beyad Osekei Toratecha. Lecha Asita Shem Gadol Vekadosh Be'olamach. Ule'ammecha Yisra'el Asita Teshu'ah Gedolah Ufurkan Kehayom Hazeh. Ve'achar Kach Ba'u Vaneicha Lidvir Beitecha. Ufinu Et-Heichalecha. Vetiharu Et-Mikdashecha. Vehidliku Nerot Bechatzrot Kodshecha. Vekave'u Shemonat Yemei Chanukkah Elu Behallel Uvehoda'ah. Ve'asita Imahem Nissim Venifla'ot Venodeh Leshimcha Hagadol Selah.

Then in the days of Mattityahu ben-Yochanan, High Priest, the Hasmonean and his sons, when the cruel Greek power rose up against Your people, Yisrael, to make them forget Your Torah and transgress the statutes of Your will. And You, in Your great compassion, stood up for them in time of their trial to plead their cause and defend their judgment. Giving out retribution, delivered the strong into the hand of the weak, and the many into the hand of the few, and the wicked into the hand of the upright, and the impure into the hand of the pure, and tyrants into the hand of the devotees of Your Torah. You made for Yourself a great and holy name in Your world. And for Your people, Yisrael, You performed a great salvation and liberation as this very day. Then Your children came to the Sanctuary of Your House, cleared Your Temple, cleansed Your Sanctuary and kindled lights in Your courtyards, and they instituted these eight days of Hanukkah for praise and thanksgiving. And You did miracles and wonders for them, and we give thanks to Your great name, selah.

On Purim:

בִּימֵי מָרְדְּכַי וְאֶסְתֵּר בְּשׁוּשַׁן הַבִּירָה. כְּשֶׁעָמַד עֲלֵיהֶם הָמָן הָרָשָׁע. בִּקֵּשׁ לְהַשְׁמִיד לַהֲרֹג וּלְאַבֵּד אֶת־כָּל־הַיְּהוּדִים מִנַּעַר וְעַד זָקֵן טַף וְנָשִׁים בְּיוֹם אֶחָד. בִּשְׁלֹשָׁה עָשָׂר לְחֹדֶשׁ שְׁנֵים עָשָׂר. הוּא חֹדֶשׁ אֲדָר. וּשְׁלָלָם לָבוֹז. וְאַתָּה בְּרַחֲמֶיךָ הָרַבִּים הֵפַרְתָּ אֶת־עֲצָתוֹ וְקִלְקַלְתָּ אֶת־מַחֲשַׁבְתּוֹ. וַהֲשֵׁבוֹתָ לּוֹ גְּמוּלוֹ בְּרֹאשׁוֹ. וְתָלוּ אוֹתוֹ וְאֶת־בָּנָיו עַל הָעֵץ. וְעָשִׂיתָ עִמָּהֶם נֵס וָפֶלֶא וְנוֹדֶה לְשִׁמְךָ הַגָּדוֹל סֶלָה:

Bimei Mordechai Ve'ester Beshushan Habirah. Keshe'amad Aleihem Haman Harasha. Bikesh Lehashmid Laharog Ule'abed Et-Kol-Hayehudim Mina'ar Ve'ad Zaken Taf Venashim Beyom Echad. Bishloshah Asar Lechodesh Sheneim Asar. Hu Chodesh Adar. Ushelalam Lavoz. Ve'attah Berachameicha Harabim Hefarta Et-'Atzato Vekilkalta Et-Machashavto. Vahasheivota Lo Gemulo Verosho. Vetalu Oto Ve'et-Banav Al Ha'etz. Ve'asita Imahem Nes Vafelei Venodeh Leshimcha Hagadol Selah.

In the days of Mordechai and Ester in Shushan, the capital, the wicked Haman rose up and sought to destroy, slay and utterly annihilate all of the Yehudim, both young and old, women and children, on one day, on the thirteenth day of the twelfth month, which is the month of Adar, and to plunder their possessions. But You in Your great mercy You broke his plan and spoiled his designs, causing them to recoil on his own head, and they hanged him and his sons on the gallows. And You did miracles and wonders for them, and we give thanks to Your great name, selah.

Ve'al Kulam Yitbarach.	וְעַל כֻּלָּם יִתְבָּרַךְ.
Veyitromam. Veyitnasse. Tamid.	וְיִתְרוֹמַם. וְיִתְנַשֵּׂא. תָּמִיד.
Shimcha Malkeinu. Le'olam	שִׁמְךָ מַלְכֵּנוּ. לְעוֹלָם
Va'ed. Vechol-Hachayim	וָעֶד. וְכָל־הַחַיִּים
Yoducha Selah.	יוֹדוּךָ סֶלָה:

For all these acts, may Your name, our King, be blessed, extolled and exalted forever. And all of the living will thank You, selah.

Bow at "Baruch Attah" / "Blessed are You". Raise up at Adonai / Hashem.

Vihalelu Vivarechu Et-Shimcha	וִיהַלְלוּ וִיבָרְכוּ אֶת־שִׁמְךָ
Hagadol Be'emet Le'olam Ki Tov.	הַגָּדוֹל בֶּאֱמֶת לְעוֹלָם כִּי טוֹב.

Ha'el Yeshu'atenu Ve'ezratenu
Selah. Ha'el Hatov. Baruch Attah
Adonai Hatov Shimcha Ulecha
Na'eh Lehodot.

הָאֵל יְשׁוּעָתֵנוּ וְעֶזְרָתֵנוּ
סֶלָה. הָאֵל הַטּוֹב: בָּרוּךְ אַתָּה
יְהֹוָה הַטּוֹב שִׁמְךָ וּלְךָ
נָאֶה לְהוֹדוֹת:

And they will praise and bless Your great and good name sincerely,
forever. For You are good, the God of our salvation and our help
forever, the Good God. Blessed are You, Hashem, Your name is
good and to You it is good to give thanks.

Birkhat Kohanim / The Priestly Blessing

*If there is more than one Kohen present, start here. If there is not, start with Eloheinu Velohei
Avoteinu:*

Some say:

לְשֵׁם יִחוּד קוּדְשָׁא בְּרִיךְ הוּא וּשְׁכִינְתֵּיהּ. בִּדְחִילוּ וּרְחִימוּ. וּרְחִימוּ וּדְחִילוּ.
לְיַחֲדָא שֵׁם יוֹ"ד קֵ"י בְּוָא"ו קֵ"י בְּיִחוּדָא שְׁלִים (יהוה) בְּשֵׁם כָּל יִשְׂרָאֵל.
הִנֵּה אָנֹכִי מוּכָן וּמְזוּמָּן לְקַיֵּים מִצְוַת עֲשֵׂה לְבָרֵךְ אֶת יִשְׂרָאֵל בִּרְכַּת כֹּהֲנִים
בִּנְשִׂיאוּת כַּפִּים לַעֲשׂוֹת נַחַת רוּחַ לְיוֹצְרֵנוּ וּלְהַמְשִׁיךְ שֶׁפַע וּבְרָכָה לְכָל
הָעוֹלָמוֹת הַקְּדוֹשִׁים. וִיהִי נֹעַם אֲדֹנָי אֱלֹהֵינוּ עָלֵינוּ וּמַעֲשֵׂה יָדֵינוּ כּוֹנְנָה עָלֵינוּ
וּמַעֲשֵׂה יָדֵינוּ כּוֹנְנֵהוּ:

The Kohanim stand on the pulpit after Modim Derabbanan and say:

יְהִי רָצוֹן מִלְפָנֶיךָ יְהֹוָה אֱלֹהֵינוּ וַאלֹהֵי אֲבוֹתֵינוּ שֶׁתִּהְיֶה בְּרָכָה זוֹ שֶׁצִּוִּיתָנוּ
לְבָרֵךְ אֶת־עַמְּךָ יִשְׂרָאֵל בְּרָכָה שְׁלֵמָה וְלֹא יִהְיֶה בָהּ מִכְשׁוֹל וְעָוֹן מֵעַתָּה וְעַד
עוֹלָם:

Yehi Ratzon Milfaneicha Adonai Eloheinu Velohei Avoteinu Shetihyeh Berachah Zo
Shetzivitanu Levarech Et-'Ammecha Yisra'el Berachah Shelemah Velo Yihyeh Vah
Michshol Ve'avon Me'attah Ve'ad Olam.

May it be Your Will, Hashem our God, that this blessing which You have
commanded us to bless Your people Yisrael with will be a perfect blessing. May
there not be in it any stumbling or perverseness from now and forever.

Then they say the blessing. If there is more than one Kohen, the leader calls them, "Kohanim!".

בָּרוּךְ אַתָּה יְהֹוָה אֱלֹהֵינוּ מֶלֶךְ הָעוֹלָם. אֲשֶׁר קִדְּשָׁנוּ בִּקְדֻשָּׁתוֹ שֶׁל־אַהֲרֹן.
וְצִוָּנוּ לְבָרֵךְ אֶת־עַמּוֹ יִשְׂרָאֵל בְּאַהֲבָה:

Baruch Attah Adonai Eloheinu Melech Ha'olam Asher Kideshanu Bikdushato Shel-
Aharon. Vetzivanu Levarech Et-'Ammo Yisra'el Be'ahavah. Amen.

Blessed are You Hashem our God, King of the universe, Who has sanctified us with
the sanctification of Aharon and commanded us to bless His people, Yisrael, with
love.

The congregation answers:

אָמֵן:

Amen.

And the Chazan and the Kohanim say after him exactly:

Yevarechecha Adonai Veyishmerecha.
יְבָרֶכְךָ יְהֹוָה וְיִשְׁמְרֶךָ:

And answer: Amen
וְעוֹנִים: אָמֵן:

Hashem bless you and keep you. **And answer:** Amen

Ya'er Adonai Panav Eleicha Vichuneka.
יָאֵר יְהֹוָה | פָּנָיו אֵלֶיךָ וִיחֻנֶּךָּ:

And Answer: Amen
וְעוֹנִים: אָמֵן:

Hashem make His countenance shine upon you, and be gracious to you. **And answer:**
Amen

Yissa Adonai Panav Eleicha. Veyasem
יִשָּׂא יְהֹוָה | פָּנָיו אֵלֶיךָ וְיָשֵׂם

Lecha Shalom. **And answer:** Amen
לְךָ שָׁלוֹם: וְעוֹנִים: אָמֵן:

Hashem lift up His countenance towards you and give you peace. **And answer:** Amen

When the Chazan begins the Sim Shalom below, the Kohanim face toward the Ark and say:

רִבּוֹן הָעוֹלָמִים עָשִׂינוּ מַה שֶּׁגָּזַרְתָּ עָלֵינוּ. עֲשֵׂה אַתָּה מַה שֶׁהִבְטַחְתָּנוּ.
הַשְׁקִיפָה מִמְּעוֹן קָדְשְׁךָ מִן־הַשָּׁמַיִם וּבָרֵךְ אֶת־עַמְּךָ אֶת־יִשְׂרָאֵל:

Ribon Ha'olamim Asinu Mah Shegazarta Aleinu. Aseh Attah Mah-Shehivtachetanu.
Hashkifah Mime'on Kodshecha Min-Hashamayim. Uvarech Et-'Ammecha Et-
Yisra'el.

Sovereign of the universe, We have done what You have decreed for us, You have
done as You promised. "Look down from Your holy Habitation, from heaven, and
bless Your people Yisrael." (Deut. 26:15)

Eloheinu Velohei Avoteinu

If there are no Kohanim, the Chazan recites a substitute blessing:

Eloheinu Velohei Avoteinu.	אֱלֹהֵינוּ וֵאלֹהֵי אֲבוֹתֵינוּ.
Barecheinu Baberachah	בָּרְכֵנוּ בַּבְּרָכָה
Hamshuleshet Batorah	הַמְשֻׁלֶּשֶׁת בַּתּוֹרָה
Haketuvah Al Yedei Mosheh	הַכְּתוּבָה עַל יְדֵי מֹשֶׁה
Avdach. Ha'amurah Mipi	עַבְדָּךְ. הָאֲמוּרָה מִפִּי
Aharon Uvanav Hakohanim Im	אַהֲרֹן וּבָנָיו הַכֹּהֲנִים עַם
Kedosheicha Ka'amur.	קְדוֹשֶׁיךָ כָּאָמוּר:

Our God, God of our fathers, bless us with the threefold blessing
written in the Torah by Your servant Moshe, and spoken by the
mouth of Aharon and his descendants Your consecrated Kohanim:

Yevarechecha Adonai	יְבָרֶכְךָ יְהֹוָה
Veyishmerecha. **And answer:** Ken	וְיִשְׁמְרֶךָ: ועונים: כֵּן
Yehi Ratzon.	יְהִי רָצוֹן:

Hashem bless you and keep you. **And answer:** May this be His will.

Ya'er Adonai Panav Eleicha	יָאֵר יְהֹוָה	פָּנָיו אֵלֶיךָ
Vichuneka. **And answer:** Ken Yehi	וִיחֻנֶּךָּ: ועונים: כֵּן יְהִי
Ratzon.	רָצוֹן:

Hashem make His countenance shine upon you, and be gracious to
you. **And answer:** May this be His will.

Yissa Adonai Panav Eleicha.	יִשָּׂא יְהֹוָה	פָּנָיו אֵלֶיךָ
Veyasem Lecha Shalom.	וְיָשֵׂם לְךָ שָׁלוֹם:
And answer: Ken Yehi Ratzon.	ועונים: כֵּן יְהִי רָצוֹן:

Hashem lift up His countenance towards you and give you peace.
And answer: May this be His will.

Vesamu Et-Shemi Al-Benei
Yisra'el; Va'ani Avarechem.

וְשָׂמוּ אֶת־שְׁמִי עַל־בְּנֵי
יִשְׂרָאֵל וַאֲנִי אֲבָרְכֵם:

And they will set My name upon the Children of Yisrael, and I will
bless them.

Sim Shalom / Grant Peace

Sim Shalom Tovah Uverachah.

שִׂים שָׁלוֹם טוֹבָה וּבְרָכָה.

Chayim Chein Vachesed

חַיִּים חֵן וָחֶסֶד

Verachamim. Aleinu Ve'al Kol-

וְרַחֲמִים. עָלֵינוּ וְעַל כָּל־

Yisra'el Ammecha. Uvarecheinu

יִשְׂרָאֵל עַמֶּךָ. וּבָרְכֵנוּ

Avinu Kulanu Ke'echad Be'or

אָבִינוּ כֻּלָּנוּ כְּאֶחָד בְּאוֹר

Paneicha. Ki Ve'or Paneicha

פָּנֶיךָ. כִּי בְאוֹר פָּנֶיךָ

Natata Lanu Adonai Eloheinu

נָתַתָּ לָּנוּ יְהֹוָה אֱלֹהֵינוּ

Torah Vechayim. Ahavah

תּוֹרָה וְחַיִּים. אַהֲבָה

Vachesed. Tzedakah

וְחֶסֶד. צְדָקָה

Verachamim. Berachah

וְרַחֲמִים. בְּרָכָה

Veshalom. Vetov Be'eineicha

וְשָׁלוֹם. וְטוֹב בְּעֵינֶיךָ

Levarecheinu Ulevarech Et-

לְבָרְכֵנוּ וּלְבָרֵךְ אֶת־

Kol-'Ammecha Yisra'el. Berov

כָּל־עַמְּךָ יִשְׂרָאֵל. בְּרֹב

Oz Veshalom. Baruch Attah

עֹז וְשָׁלוֹם: בָּרוּךְ אַתָּה יהוווהו

Adonai Hamevarech Et Ammo

הַמְבָרֵךְ אֶת עַמּוֹ

Yisra'el Bashalom. Amen.

יִשְׂרָאֵל בַּשָּׁלוֹם. אָמֵן:

Grant peace, goodness and blessing, a life of grace, and kindness
and mercy, to us and to all Yisrael, Your people. And bless us, our
Father, all as one with the light of Your countenance; for with the
light of Your countenance You have given us, Hashem our God, a
Torah and life, love and kindness, righteousness and mercy,

blessing and peace. May it be good in Your eyes to bless us and bless all of Your people, Yisrael, with abundant strength and peace. Blessed are You, Hashem, Who blesses His people Yisrael with peace. Amen.

Yihyu Leratzon Imrei-Fi Vehegyon Libi Lefaneicha; Adonai Tzuri Vego'ali.

יִהְיוּ לְרָצוֹן | אִמְרֵי־פִי וְהֶגְיוֹן לִבִּי לְפָנֶיךָ יְהֹוָה צוּרִי וְגֹאֲלִי:

May the words of my mouth and the meditation of my heart find favor before You, Hashem my Rock and my Redeemer.

The chazan's repetition ends here; personal / individual continue:

Elohai. Netzor Leshoni Meira

אֱלֹהַי. נְצֹר לְשׁוֹנִי מֵרָע

Vesiftotai Midaber Mirmah.

וּשְׂפָתַי מִדַּבֵּר מִרְמָה.

Velimkalelai Nafshi Tidom.

וְלִמְקַלְלַי נַפְשִׁי תִדֹּם.

Venafshi Ke'afar Lakol Tihyeh.

וְנַפְשִׁי כֶּעָפָר לַכֹּל תִּהְיֶה.

Petach Libi Betoratecha.

פְּתַח לִבִּי בְּתוֹרָתֶךָ.

Ve'acharei Mitzvoteicha Tirdof

וְאַחֲרֵי מִצְוֹתֶיךָ תִרְדֹּף

Nafshi. Vechol-Hakamim Alai

נַפְשִׁי. וְכָל־הַקָּמִים עָלַי

Lera'ah. Meheirah Hafer Atzatam

לְרָעָה. מְהֵרָה הָפֵר עֲצָתָם

Vekalkel Machshevotam. Aseh

וְקַלְקֵל מַחְשְׁבוֹתָם. עֲשֵׂה

Lema'an Shemach. Aseh

לְמַעַן שְׁמֶךָ. עֲשֵׂה

Lema'an Yeminach. Aseh

לְמַעַן יְמִינֶךָ. עֲשֵׂה

Lema'an Toratach. Aseh Lema'an

לְמַעַן תּוֹרָתֶךָ. עֲשֵׂה לְמַעַן

Kedushatach. Lema'an

קְדֻשָּׁתֶךָ. לְמַעַן

Yechaletzun Yedideicha;

יֵחָלְצוּן יְדִידֶיךָ

Hoshi'ah Yeminecha Va'aneni.

הוֹשִׁיעָה יְמִינְךָ וַעֲנֵנִי:

My God, guard my tongue from evil, and my lips from speaking deceit. And to those who curse me may my soul be silent; and may my soul be like the dust to all. Open my heart to Your Torah, that my soul may follow after Your commandments. And all that rise to do evil against me, speedily nullify their plan, and spoil their thoughts. Do it for the sake of Your name; do it for the sake of Your right hand; do it for the sake of Your Torah, do it for the sake of Your holiness. That Your beloved may be rescued, save with Your right hand and answer me. (Ps. 60:7)

Yihyu Leratzon Imrei-Fi Vehegyon Libi

Lefaneicha; Adonai Tzuri Vego'ali.

יִהְיוּ לְרָצוֹן | אִמְרֵי־פִי וְהֶגְיוֹן לִבִּי לְפָנֶיךָ יְהֹוָה צוּרִי וְגֹאֲלִי:

May the words of my mouth and the meditation of my heart find favor before You, Hashem my Rock and my Redeemer.

Oseh Shalom

One bows and takes three steps backwards, while still bowing. After three steps, while still bowing and before erecting, while saying, "Oseh Shalom Bimromav", turn one's face to the left, "Hu [Berachamav] Ya'aseh Shalom Aleinu", turn one's face to the right; [face forward and] then bow forward like a servant leaving his master. (SA, OC 123:1)

Oseh Shalom Bimromav, Hu

Berachamav Ya'aseh Shalom

Aleinu, Ve'al Kol-'Ammo

Yisra'el, Ve'imru Amen.

עוֹשֶׂה שָׁלוֹם בִּמְרוֹמָיו. הוּא בְּרַחֲמָיו יַעֲשֶׂה שָׁלוֹם עָלֵינוּ. וְעַל כָּל־עַמּוֹ יִשְׂרָאֵל. וְאִמְרוּ אָמֵן:

Creator of peace in His high places, may He in His mercy create peace for us and for all Yisrael, and say Amen.

Yehi Ratzon Milfaneicha Adonai	יְהִי רָצוֹן מִלְּפָנֶיךָ יְהוָה
Eloheinu Velohei Avoteinu. Shetivneh	אֱלֹהֵינוּ וֵאלֹהֵי אֲבוֹתֵינוּ. שֶׁתִּבְנֶה
Beit Hamikdash Bimheirah Veyameinu.	בֵּית הַמִּקְדָּשׁ בִּמְהֵרָה בְיָמֵינוּ.
Veten Chelkenu Vetoratach La'asot	וְתֵן חֶלְקֵנוּ בְּתוֹרָתָךְ לַעֲשׂוֹת
Chukkei. Retzonach Ule'avedach	חֻקֵּי רְצוֹנָךְ וּלְעָבְדָךְ
Belevav Shalem.	בְּלֵבָב שָׁלֵם:

May it be Your will, Hashem our God and God of our fathers, that the Beit HaMikdash be speedily rebuilt in our days, and grant us a share in Your Torah so we may fulfill the statutes of Your will and serve You with a whole heart.

Yehi Shem

יְהִי שֵׁם יְהוָה מְבֹרָךְ מֵעַתָּה וְעַד־עוֹלָם: מִמִּזְרַח־שֶׁמֶשׁ עַד־מְבוֹאוֹ מְהֻלָּל שֵׁם יְהוָה: רָם עַל־כָּל־גּוֹיִם | יְהוָה עַל הַשָּׁמַיִם כְּבוֹדוֹ: יְהוָה אֲדֹנֵינוּ מָה־אַדִּיר שִׁמְךָ בְּכָל־הָאָרֶץ:

Yehi Shem Adonai Mevorach; Me'attah. Ve'ad-'Olam. Mimizrach-Shemesh Ad-Mevo'o; Mehulal. Shem Adonai Ram Al-Chol-Goyim Adonai Al Hashamayim Kevodo. Adonai Adoneinu; Mah-'Adir Shimcha. Bechol-Ha'aretz.

Blessed is the name of Hashem from this time forward and forever. From the rising of the sun to it's going down, Hashem's name is to be praised. Hashem, our Lord, How glorious is Your name in all of the earth. (Psalms 113:2-4, 8:2)

And say Kaddish Titkabbal:

Kaddish is only recited in a minyan (ten men). אמן denotes when the congregation responds "Amen" together out loud. According to the Shulchan Arukh, the congregation says "Yehei Shemeh Rabba" to "Yitbarach" out loud together without interruption, and also that one should respond "Amen" after "Yitbarach." (SA, OC 55,56) This is not the common custom today. Though many are accustomed to answering according to their own custom, it is advised to respond in the custom of the one reciting to avoid not fragmenting into smaller groups. ("Lo Titgodedu" - BT, Yevamot 13b / SA, OC 493, Rema / MT, Avodah Zara 12:15)

יִתְגַּדַּל וְיִתְקַדַּשׁ שְׁמֵהּ רַבָּא. אמן בְּעָלְמָא דִּי בְרָא. כִרְעוּתֵהּ. וְיַמְלִיךְ מַלְכוּתֵהּ. וְיַצְמַח פֻּרְקָנֵהּ. וִיקָרֵב מְשִׁיחֵהּ. אמן בְּחַיֵּיכוֹן וּבְיוֹמֵיכוֹן וּבְחַיֵּי דְכָל בֵּית יִשְׂרָאֵל. בַּעֲגָלָא וּבִזְמַן קָרִיב. וְאִמְרוּ אָמֵן. אמן יְהֵא שְׁמֵיהּ רַבָּא מְבָרַךְ לְעָלַם וּלְעָלְמֵי עָלְמַיָּא יִתְבָּרַךְ. וְיִשְׁתַּבַּח. וְיִתְפָּאַר. וְיִתְרוֹמַם. וְיִתְנַשֵּׂא. וְיִתְהַדָּר.

וְיִתְעַלֶּה. וְיִתְהַלָּל שְׁמֵהּ דְּקֻדְשָׁא. בְּרִיךְ הוּא. אמן לְעֵלָּא מִן כָּל בִּרְכָתָא

שִׁירָתָא. תֻּשְׁבְּחָתָא וְנֶחֱמָתָא. דַּאֲמִירָן בְּעָלְמָא. וְאִמְרוּ אָמֵן. אמן

Yitgadal Veyitkadash Shemeh Rabba. **Amen** Be'alema Di Vera. Kir'uteh. Veyamlich
Malchuteh. Veyatzmach Purkaneh. Vikarev Meshicheh. **Amen** Bechayeichon
Uveyomeichon Uvechayei Dechal-Beit Yisra'el. Ba'agala Uvizman Kariv. Ve'imru
Amen. **Amen** Yehei Shemeh Rabba Mevarach Le'alam Ule'alemei Alemaya
Yitbarach. Veyishtabach. Veyitpa'ar. Veyitromam. Veyitnasse. Veyit'hadar. Veyit'aleh.
Veyit'hallal Shemeh Dekudsha. Berich Hu. **Amen** Le'ella Min Kol Birchata Shirata.
Tushbechata Venechemata. Da'amiran Be'alema. Ve'imru Amen. **Amen**

Glorified and sanctified be God's great name **Amen** throughout the world which He
has created according to His will. May He establish His kingdom, hastening His
salvation and the coming of His Messiah, **Amen**, in your lifetime and during your
days, and within the life of the entire House of Yisrael, speedily and soon; and say,
Amen. **Amen** May His great name be blessed forever and to all eternity. Blessed and
praised, glorified and exalted, extolled and honored, adored and lauded is the
name of the Holy One, blessed is He, **Amen** Beyond all the blessings and hymns,
praises and consolations that are ever spoken in the world; and say, Amen. **Amen**

תִּתְקַבַּל צְלוֹתַנָא וּבָעוּתַנָא. עִם צְלוֹתְהוֹן וּבָעוּתְהוֹן דְּכָל בֵּית יִשְׂרָאֵל. קֳדָם

אֲבוּנָא דְּבִשְׁמַיָּא וְאַרְעָא. וְאִמְרוּ אָמֵן. אמן

Titkabbal Tzelotana Uva'utana. Im Tzelotehon Uva'utehon Dechol Beit Yisra'el.
Kodam Avuna Devishmaya Ve'ar'a. Ve'imru Amen. **Amen**

May the prayer and supplication of the whole House of Yisrael be accepted before
their Father in heaven, and say, Amen. **Amen**

יְהֵא שְׁלָמָא רַבָּא מִן שְׁמַיָּא. חַיִּים וְשָׂבָע וִישׁוּעָה וְנֶחָמָה. וְשֵׁיזָבָא וּרְפוּאָה

וּגְאוּלָה וּסְלִיחָה וְכַפָּרָה וְרֶוַח וְהַצָּלָה לָנוּ וּלְכָל עַמּוֹ יִשְׂרָאֵל. וְאִמְרוּ אָמֵן. אמן

Yehei Shelama Rabba Min Shemaya. Chayim Vesava Vishu'ah Venechamah.
Vesheizava Urefu'ah Uge'ulah Uselichah Vechapparah Verevach Vehatzalah Lanu
Ulechol Ammo Yisra'el. Ve'imru Amen. **Amen**

May abundant peace descend from heaven, with life and plenty, salvation, solace,
liberation, healing and redemption, and forgiveness and atonement, enlargement
and freedom, for us and all of God's people Yisrael; and say, Amen. **Amen**

> One bows and takes three steps backwards, while still bowing. After three steps, while still bowing
> and before erecting, while saying, "Oseh Shalom Bimromav", turn one's face to the left, "Hu
> [Berachamav] Ya'aseh Shalom Aleinu", turn one's face to the right; then bow forward like a servant
> leaving his master. (SA, OC 123:1)

עוֹשֶׂה שָׁלוֹם בעשי״ת (הַשָּׁלוֹם) בִּמְרוֹמָיו. הוּא בְּרַחֲמָיו יַעֲשֶׂה שָׁלוֹם עָלֵינוּ. וְעַל

כָּל־עַמּוֹ יִשְׂרָאֵל. וְאִמְרוּ אָמֵן:

Oseh Shalom **On the 10 days of repentance:** (Hashalom) Bimromav, Hu Berachamav
Ya'aseh Shalom Aleinu, Ve'al Kol-'Ammo Yisra'el, Ve'imru Amen.

Creator of **On the 10 days of repentance:** (the) peace in His high places, may He in His mercy create peace for us and for all Yisrael, and say Amen.

The rest of the service now follows the normal Shabbat Musaf service from after the above Yehi Shem after the Amidah. Start from Kaddish Titkabbal, Kol Yisrael, etc. after the Amidah and continue until the end.

Sheva Berakhot / The Seven Blessings

סדר שבע ברכות

This is the order of the service for under the wedding canopy. During the seven days of rejoicing for a bride and group it is customary when a zimmun (3 men) is present, that the seven blessings are recited afterwards. The first blessing over the wine is then recited last.

Savri Maranan!

סַבְרִי מָרָנָן:

Gentlemen, with your attention!

And those present answer:

Le'chayim!

לְחַיִּים:

To life!

Baruch Attah Adonai Eloheinu

בָּרוּךְ אַתָּה יְהֹוָה אֱלֹהֵינוּ

Melech Ha'olam Borei Pri

מֶלֶךְ הָעוֹלָם. בּוֹרֵא פְּרִי

Hagefen:

הַגָּפֶן:

Blessed are You, Hashem our God, King of the universe, Who creates the fruit of the vine.

Baruch Attah Adonai Eloheinu

בָּרוּךְ אַתָּה יְהֹוָה אֱלֹהֵינוּ

Melech Ha'olam Shehakol Bara

מֶלֶךְ הָעוֹלָם. שֶׁהַכֹּל בָּרָא

Lichvodo:

לִכְבוֹדוֹ:

Blessed are You, Hashem our God, King of the universe, Who has created everything for His glory.

Baruch Attah Adonai Eloheinu

בָּרוּךְ אַתָּה יְהֹוָה אֱלֹהֵינוּ

Melech Ha'olam Yotzer

מֶלֶךְ הָעוֹלָם. יוֹצֵר

Ha'Adam:

הָאָדָם:

Blessed are You, Hashem our God, King of the universe; the Creator of man.

Baruch Attah Adonai Eloheinu	בָּרוּךְ אַתָּה יְהֹוָה אֱלֹהֵינוּ
Melech Ha'olam Asher Yatzar Et	מֶלֶךְ הָעוֹלָם. אֲשֶׁר יָצַר אֶת־
Ha'adam Betzalmo. Betzelem	הָאָדָם בְּצַלְמוֹ. בְּצֶלֶם
Demut Tavnito. Vehitkin Lo	דְּמוּת תַּבְנִיתוֹ. וְהִתְקִין לוֹ
Mimenu Binyan Adei Ad.	מִמֶּנּוּ בִּנְיַן עֲדֵי־עַד.
Baruch Attah Adonai Yotzer	בָּרוּךְ אַתָּה יְהֹוָה יוֹצֵר
Ha'Adam:	הָאָדָם:

Blessed are You, Hashem our God, King of the universe; Who has formed man in Your image; in the image of the likeness of Your form, and has prepared out of him an everlasting establishment.

Sos Tasis Vetagel Akarah	שׂוֹשׂ תָּשִׂישׂ וְתָגֵל עֲקָרָה
Bekibutz Baneiha Letochah	בְּקִבּוּץ בָּנֶיהָ לְתוֹכָה
Bimheirah Besimchah. Baruch	בִּמְהֵרָה בְּשִׂמְחָה. בָּרוּךְ
Attah Adonai Mesame'ach	אַתָּה יְהֹוָה מְשַׂמֵּחַ
Tziyon Bevaneiha:	צִיּוֹן בְּבָנֶיהָ:

She who was barren will surely rejoice and be glad, at the gathering of her children to her speedily. Blessed are You, Hashem, Who causes Tziyon to rejoice through her children.

Same'ach Tesamach Re'im	שַׂמֵּחַ תְּשַׂמַּח רֵעִים
Ahuvim Kesamechacha Yetzircha	אֲהוּבִים כְּשַׂמֵּחֲךָ יְצִירְךָ
Began Eden Mikedem.	בְּגַן עֵדֶן מִקֶּדֶם.

Baruch Attah Adonai

בָּרוּךְ אַתָּה יְהֹוָה

Mesame'ach Chatan Vechallah:

מְשַׂמֵּחַ חָתָן וְכַלָּה:

May this loving couple delight in the joy You caused Your creation
of ancient times in the Garden of Eden. Blessed are You, Hashem,
Who causes the bridegroom and bride to rejoice.

Baruch Attah Adonai Eloheinu

בָּרוּךְ אַתָּה יְהֹוָה אֱלֹהֵינוּ

Melech Ha'olam Asher Bara

מֶלֶךְ הָעוֹלָם. אֲשֶׁר בָּרָא

Sason Vesimchah. Chatan

שָׂשׂוֹן וְשִׂמְחָה. חָתָן

Vechallah. Gilah Rinah Ditzah

וְכַלָּה. גִּילָה רִנָּה דִּיצָה

Vechedvah. Ahavah Ve'achvah.

וְחֶדְוָה. אַהֲבָה וְאַחֲוָה.

Shalom Vere'ut. Meheirah

שָׁלוֹם וְרֵעוּת. מְהֵרָה

Adonai Eloheinu Yishama

יְהֹוָה אֱלֹהֵינוּ יִשָּׁמַע

Be'arei Yehudah Uvechutzot

בְּעָרֵי יְהוּדָה וּבְחוּצוֹת

Yerushalayim. Kol Sason Vekol

יְרוּשָׁלָיִם. קוֹל שָׂשׂוֹן וְקוֹל

Simchah. Kol Chatan Vekol

שִׂמְחָה. קוֹל חָתָן וְקוֹל

Kallah. Kol Mitzhalot Chatanim

כַּלָּה. קוֹל מִצְהֲלוֹת חֲתָנִים

Mechuppatam. Une'arim

מֵחֻפָּתָם. וּנְעָרִים

Mimishteh Neginatam. Baruch

מִמִּשְׁתֵּה נְגִינָתָם. בָּרוּךְ

Attah Adonai Mesame'ach

אַתָּה יְהֹוָה מְשַׂמֵּחַ

Hechatan Im Hakallah

הֶחָתָן עִם הַכַּלָּה

Umatzliach:

וּמַצְלִיחַ:

Blessed are You, Hashem our God, King of the universe; Who has
created joy and gladness, bridegroom and bride, love and fraternity,
delight and pleasure, peace and fellowship; grant speedily, Hashem
our God, that there be heard in the cities of Yehudah, and in the
streets of Yerushalayim, the voice of joy and of gladness; the voice

of the bridegroom and bride; the voice of jubilant bridegrooms at their wedding, and of youths at musical banquets. Blessed are You, Hashem, Who brings happiness to the bridegroom and bride; and Who brings them success.

The leader of Birkhat HaMazon raises his cup and says (Kaf HaChayim 190:3):

כּוֹס־יְשׁוּעוֹת אֶשָּׂא וּבְשֵׁם יְהֹוָה אֶקְרָא:

Kos-Yeshuot Esah Uveshem Adonai Ekrah:

I will lift up the cup of salvations, And call on the name of Hashem. **(Ps. 116:13)**

Savri Maranan!   סַבְרִי מָרָנָן:

Gentlemen, with your attention!

And those present answer:

Le'chayim!   לְחַיִּים:

To life!

Baruch Attah Adonai Eloheinu   בָּרוּךְ אַתָּה יְהֹוָה אֱלֹהֵינוּ

Melech Ha'olam Borei Pri   מֶלֶךְ הָעוֹלָם. בּוֹרֵא פְּרִי

Hagefen: הַגָּפֶן:

Blessed are You, Hashem our God, King of the universe, Who creates the fruit of the vine.

Then, the wine in the two cups is mixed together. Then each assigned cup owner drinks from his cup. The cup for the seven blessings is given to the groom and bride to drink, and the cup for Birkhat HaMazon is given to those in attendance to drink.

SEDER BRIT MILAH / ORDER OF CIRCUMCISION

סדר ברית מילה

Some pray before:

לְשֵׁם יְחוּד קוּדְשָׁא בְּרִיךְ הוּא וּשְׁכִינְתֵּיה. בִּדְחִילוּ וּרְחִימוּ. וּרְחִימוּ וּדְחִילוּ. לְיַחֲדָא שֵׁם יוֹ"ד קֵ"י בְּוָא"ו קֵ"י בְּיְחוּדָא שְׁלִים (יהוה) בְּשֵׁם כָּל יִשְׂרָאֵל. הנה אנכי בא למול תינוק זה (ואבי יאמר: למול את בני) לקים מצות עשה כמו שנאמר. זאת בריתי אשר תשמרו ביני וביניכם ובין זרעך אחריך המול לכם כל־זכר: להכניסו בבריתו של אברהם אבינו ולהכניסו בחולקא טבא דקדשא בריך הוא. ויהא רעוא דקדשא בריך הוא בהאי קרבנא ויתרעי ביה. ויזכה לעשר חפות רומין שעתיד קדשא בריך הוא למעבד לצדיקיא לעלמא דאתי כדכתיב: אשרי תבחר ותקרב ישכן חצריך נשבעה בטוב ביתך קדוש היכלך: ועתה בעונותינו חרבה עירנו ושמם בית מקדשנו ואין לנו קרבנות שיכפרו בעדנו. יְהִי רָצוֹן שֶׁיְהֵא נֶחְשָׁב דַּם הַבְּרִית הַזֶּה כְּאִלּוּ בָּנִיתִי מִזְבֵּחַ וְהֶעֱלֵיתִי עָלָיו עוֹלוֹת וּזְבָחִים. יִהְיוּ לְרָצוֹן אִמְרֵי־פִי וְהֶגְיוֹן לִבִּי לְפָנֶיךָ יְהֹוָה צוּרִי וְגֹאֲלִי: וִיהִי נֹעַם אֲדֹנָי אֱלֹהֵינוּ עָלֵינוּ וּמַעֲשֵׂה יָדֵינוּ כּוֹנְנָה עָלֵינוּ וּמַעֲשֵׂה יָדֵינוּ כּוֹנְנֵהוּ:

In some congregations the sandak then prays:

לְשֵׁם יְחוּד קוּדְשָׁא בְּרִיךְ הוּא וּשְׁכִינְתֵּיה. בִּדְחִילוּ וּרְחִימוּ. וּרְחִימוּ וּדְחִילוּ. לְיַחֲדָא שֵׁם יוֹ"ד קֵ"י בְּוָא"ו קֵ"י בְּיְחוּדָא שְׁלִים (יהוה) בְּשֵׁם כָּל יִשְׂרָאֵל. הנה אנכי בא להיות סנדק ואהיה כסא ומזבח לעשות על ירכי המילה. ויהי רצון מלפניך יהוה אלהינו ואלהי אבותינו שיהיה מזבח כפרה ותכפר על כל חטאתי עונותי ופשעי ובפרט מה שפגמתי בירכי ובאות ברית קדש. ותעלה עלינו כאלו כוונונו כל הכוונות הראויות לכוין ולתקן את שרשה במקום עליון לעשות נחת רוח ליוצרנו ולעשות רצון בוראנו. וִיהִי נֹעַם אֲדֹנָי אֱלֹהֵינוּ עָלֵינוּ וּמַעֲשֵׂה יָדֵינוּ כּוֹנְנָה עָלֵינוּ וּמַעֲשֵׂה יָדֵינוּ כּוֹנְנֵהוּ:

When the baby is brought to the synagogue, the assembly stands and says:

בָּרוּךְ הַבָּא בְּשֵׁם יְהֹוָה:

Baruch Haba Beshem Adonai:

Blessed is he that comes in the name of Hashem: (Psalms 118:26)

And when the father of the son takes the baby in his arms says:

שָׂשׂ אָנֹכִי עַל־אִמְרָתֶךָ כְּמוֹצֵא שָׁלָל רָב: זִבְחֵי אֱלֹהִים רוּחַ נִשְׁבָּרָה לֵב־נִשְׁבָּר וְנִדְכֶּה אֱלֹהִים לֹא תִבְזֶה: הֵיטִיבָה בִרְצוֹנְךָ אֶת־צִיּוֹן תִּבְנֶה חוֹמוֹת יְרוּשָׁלָ͏ִם: אָז תַּחְפֹּץ זִבְחֵי־צֶדֶק עוֹלָה וְכָלִיל אָז יַעֲלוּ עַל־מִזְבַּחֲךָ פָרִים:

Sas Anochi Al Imratecha Kemotze Shalal Rav. Zivchei Elohim Ruach Nishbarah Lev Nishbar Venidkeh Elohim Lo Tivzeh. Heitivah Virtzonecha Et Tziyon Tivneh Chomot Yerushalayim. Az Tachpotz Zivchei Tzedek Olah Vechalil Az Ya'alu Al Mizbachaca Farim.

I rejoice at Your word, As one that finds great spoil. The sacrifices of God are a broken spirit; a broken and a contrite heart, God, You will not despise. Do good in Your favor to Tziyon; build the walls of Yerushalayim. Then You will delight in the sacrifices of righteousness, in burnt-offering and whole offering; Then will they offer bulls upon Your Altar. (Psalms 119:162, 51:19-21)

And after the father of the son says:

אַשְׁרֵי | תִּבְחַר וּתְקָרֵב יִשְׁכֹּן חֲצֵרֶיךָ.

Ashrei Tivchar Utekarev Yishkon Chatzereicha.

Happy is the man Whom You choose, and bring near, that he may dwell in Your courts. (Psalms 65:5)

And those standing then answer:

נִשְׂבְּעָה בְּטוּב בֵּיתֶךָ קְדֹשׁ הֵיכָלֶךָ:

Nisbe'ah Betuv Beitecha Kedosh Heichalecha.

May we be satisfied with the goodness of Your House, the holy place of Your Temple. (Psalms 65:5)

In Eretz-Israel it is customary to add these verses:

אִם־אֶשְׁכָּחֵךְ יְרוּשָׁלָ͏ִם תִּשְׁכַּח יְמִינִי: תִּדְבַּק־לְשׁוֹנִי | לְחִכִּי° אִם־לֹא אֶזְכְּרֵכִי
אִם־לֹא אַעֲלֶה אֶת־יְרוּשָׁלַ͏ִם עַל רֹאשׁ שִׂמְחָתִי:

Im Eshkachech Yerushalayim Tishkach Yemini. Tidbak Leshoni Lechikki Im Lo Ezkerechi Im Lo A'aleh Et Yerushalayim Al Rosh Simchati.

If I forget you, Oh Yerushalayim, let my right hand forget her cunning. Let my tongue cleave to the roof of my mouth, if I don't remember you; if I don't set Yerushalayim above my most chief joy. (Psalms 137:5-6)

The following is recited by the father and then those in attendance:

שְׁמַע יִשְׂרָאֵל יְהֹוָה אֱלֹהֵינוּ יְהֹוָה | אֶחָד:

Shema Yisra'el Adonai Eloheinu Adonai Echad.

Hear, O Yisrael. Hashem is our God, Hashem is One.

יְהֹוָה מֶלֶךְ, יְהֹוָה מָלָךְ יְהֹוָה | יִמְלֹךְ לְעֹלָם וָעֶד: ב׳ פעמים

Adonai Melech, Adonai Malach Adonai Yimloch Le'olam Va'ed:

Hashem is King, Hashem was King, Hashem will reign forever and ever. 2x

אָנָּא יְהֹוָה הוֹשִׁיעָה נָּא: ב׳ פעמים

Ana Adonai Hoshi'ah Na:

Hashem, save now. 2x

אָנָּא יְהֹוָה הַצְלִיחָה נָּא: ב׳ פעמים

Ana Adonai Hatzlichah Na:

Hashem, prosper us now. 2x

The father of the son says now to appoint the mohel as his agent:

הֲרֵינִי מְמַנֶּה אוֹתְךָ שָׁלִיחַ לָמוּל אֶת־בְּנִי:

Hareini Memaneh Otecha Shaliach Lamul Et-Beni:

I hereby appoint you as my agent to circumcise my son.

The father of the son says:

בִּרְשׁוּת מוֹרַי וְרַבּוֹתַי:

Birshut Morai Verabotai:

With the permission of my teachers and masters:

He then says while standing:

Baruch Attah Adonai Eloheinu	בָּרוּךְ אַתָּה יְהֹוָה אֱלֹהֵינוּ
Melech Ha'olam Asher	מֶלֶךְ הָעוֹלָם. אֲשֶׁר
Kideshanu Bemitzvotav	קִדְּשָׁנוּ בְּמִצְוֹתָיו
Vetzivanu Lehachniso Bivrito	וְצִוָּנוּ לְהַכְנִיסוֹ בִּבְרִיתוֹ
Shel Avraham Avinu:	שֶׁל אַבְרָהָם אָבִינוּ:

Blessed are You, Hashem our God, King of the universe, Who has sanctified us with His commandments, and commanded us to introduce my son into the covenant of Avraham our father.

And the congregation and the Mohel says:

Keshem Shehichnasto Laberit.	כְּשֵׁם שֶׁהִכְנַסְתּוֹ לַבְּרִית.
Kach Tizkeh Lehachniso Latorah	כָּךְ תִּזְכֶּה לְהַכְנִיסוֹ לַתּוֹרָה
Velamitzvot Velachuppah	וְלַמִּצְוֹת וְלַחֻפָּה
Ulema'asim Tovim:	וּלְמַעֲשִׂים טוֹבִים:

Even as he has been introduced into the covenant, so may he be introduced to the Torah, and to the chuppah, and to a life of good deeds.

The sandak says sits on the chair and placed the baby on his lap, and says:

זֶה הַכִּסֵּא שֶׁל אֵלִיָּהוּ הַנָּבִיא מַלְאַךְ הַבְּרִית זָכוּר לַטּוֹב:

Zeh Hakisse Shel Eliyahu Hanavi Mal'ach Haberit Zachur Latov:

This is the throne of Eliyahu the prophet, the messenger of the covenant, of blessed memory:

And the mohel will receive the baby and place it on the godfather's knees and before circumcision he will bless:

Baruch Attah Adonai Eloheinu   בָּרוּךְ אַתָּה יְהֹוָה אֱלֹהֵינוּ

Melech Ha'olam Asher   מֶלֶךְ הָעוֹלָם. אֲשֶׁר

Kideshanu Bemitzvotav   קִדְּשָׁנוּ בְּמִצְוֹתָיו

Vetzivanu Al Hamilah: וְצִוָּנוּ עַל הַמִּילָה:

Blessed are You, Hashem our God, King of the universe, Who has sanctified us with His commandments, and commanded us concerning circumcision.

And after circumcision the father of the son will bless:

Baruch Attah Adonai Eloheinu   בָּרוּךְ אַתָּה יְהֹוָה אֱלֹהֵינוּ

Melech Ha'olam Shehecheyanu   מֶלֶךְ הָעוֹלָם. שֶׁהֶחֱיָינוּ

Vekiyemanu Vehigi'anu Lazman   וְקִיְּמָנוּ וְהִגִּיעָנוּ לַזְּמַן

Hazeh: הַזֶּה:

Blessed are You, Hashem our God, King of the universe, Who has kept us in life and preserved us and enabled us to reach this time.

And the mohel or another person takes a glass of wine and greets:

Savri Maranan!

סַבְרִי מָרָנָן:

Gentlemen, with your attention!

And those present answer:

Le'chayim!

לְחַיִּים:

To life!

Baruch Attah Adonai Eloheinu

בָּרוּךְ אַתָּה יְהֹוָה אֱלֹהֵינוּ

Melech Ha'olam Borei Pri

מֶלֶךְ הָעוֹלָם. בּוֹרֵא פְּרִי

Hagefen:

הַגָּפֶן:

Blessed are You, Hashem our God, King of the universe, Who creates the fruit of the vine.

And then he takes myrtle and blesses:

Baruch Attah Adonai Eloheinu

בָּרוּךְ אַתָּה יְהֹוָה אֱלֹהֵינוּ

Melech Ha'olam Borei Atzei

מֶלֶךְ הָעוֹלָם. בּוֹרֵא עֲצֵי

Vesamim.

בְשָׂמִים:

Blessed are You, Hashem our God, King of the universe, Who creates sweet smelling woods.

Baruch Attah Adonai Eloheinu

בָּרוּךְ אַתָּה יְהֹוָה אֱלֹהֵינוּ

Melech Ha'olam Asher Kidesh

מֶלֶךְ הָעוֹלָם. אֲשֶׁר קִדֵּשׁ

Yedid Mibeten Vechok Bish'ero

יְדִיד מִבֶּטֶן וְחֹק בִּשְׁאֵרוֹ

Sam. Vetze'etza'av Chatam Be'ot

שָׂם. וְצֶאֱצָאָיו חָתַם בְּאוֹת

Berit Kodesh. Al Ken Bischar Zo.

בְּרִית קֹדֶשׁ. עַל כֵּן בִּשְׂכַר זוֹ.

El Chai Chelkenu Tzurenu.	אֵל חַי חֶלְקֵנוּ צוּרֵנוּ.
Tzaveh Lehatzil Yedidut Zera	צַוֵּה לְהַצִּיל יְדִידוּת זֶרַע
Kodesh She'erenu Mishachat.	קֹדֶשׁ שְׁאֵרֵנוּ מִשַּׁחַת.
Lema'an Berito Asher Sam	לְמַעַן בְּרִיתוֹ אֲשֶׁר שָׂם
Bivsarenu. Baruch Attah Adonai	בִּבְשָׂרֵנוּ. בָּרוּךְ אַתָּה יְהֹוָה
Koret Haberit:	כּוֹרֵת הַבְּרִית:

Blessed are You, Hashem our God, King of the universe; Who sanctified the beloved from the womb, and ordained a statute for His lineage, and sealed His offspring with the sign of the holy covenant. Therefore as a reward for it, the living God, our Portion and Rock, has commanded the deliverance of the beloved holy seed of our lineage from destruction, for the sake of the covenant, which He has put in our flesh. Blessed are You, Hashem, Maker of the covenant.

He drinks from the glass and says. And when the Father blesses, he says the brackets:

[**] At this point the Mohel gives a few drops of wine to the child

אֱלֹהֵינוּ וֵאלֹהֵי אֲבוֹתֵינוּ קַיֵּם אֶת הַיֶּלֶד (בְּנִי) הַזֶּה לְאָבִיו (לִי)
וּלְאִמּוֹ וְיִקָּרֵא שְׁמוֹ בְּיִשְׂרָאֵל (פְּלוֹנִי). יִשְׂמַח הָאִישׁ (יְהִי רָצוֹן
שֶׁאֶשְׂמַח בְּיוֹצֵא חֲלָצַי) בְּיוֹצֵא חֲלָצָיו. וְתָגֵל הָאִשָּׁה בִּפְרִי בִטְנָהּ
כָּאָמוּר: יִשְׂמַח־אָבִיךָ וְאִמֶּךָ וְתָגֵל יוֹלַדְתֶּךָ: וְנֶאֱמַר: וָאֶעֱבֹר עָלַיִךְ
וָאֶרְאֵךְ מִתְבּוֹסֶסֶת בְּדָמָיִךְ וָאֹמַר לָךְ בְּדָמַיִךְ חֲיִי ** וָאֹמַר לָךְ
בְּדָמַיִךְ חֲיִי: וְנֶאֱמַר: זָכַר לְעוֹלָם בְּרִיתוֹ דָּבָר צִוָּה לְאֶלֶף דּוֹר: אֲשֶׁר
כָּרַת אֶת־אַבְרָהָם וּשְׁבוּעָתוֹ לְיִשְׂחָק: וַיַּעֲמִידֶהָ לְיַעֲקֹב לְחֹק
לְיִשְׂרָאֵל בְּרִית עוֹלָם: הוֹדוּ לַיהֹוָה כִּי־טוֹב כִּי לְעוֹלָם חַסְדּוֹ:
(פְּלוֹנִי) זֶה הַקָּטָן. אֱלֹהִים יְגַדְּלֵהוּ. כְּשֵׁם שֶׁנִּכְנַס לַבְּרִית כָּךְ יִכָּנֵס
לַתּוֹרָה וְלַמִּצְוֹת וְלַחֻפָּה וּלְמַעֲשִׂים טוֹבִים. וְכֵן יְהִי רָצוֹן וְנֹאמַר
אָמֵן:

Eloheinu Velohei Avoteinu Kayem Et Hayeled (Beni) Hazeh Le'aviv
(Li) Ule'immo Veyikare Shemo Beyisra'el (Peloni). Yismach Ha'Ish If
The Father Performs The Circumcision Personally: (Yehi Ratzon She'esmach Beyotze
Chalatzai) Beyotze Chalatzav. Vetagel Ha'ishah Bifri Vitnah Ka'amur:
Yismach Avicha Ve'imecha Vetagel Yoladtecha. Vene'emar: Va'e'evor
Alayich Va'er'ech Mitboseset Bedamayich Va'omar Lach
Bedamayich Chayi ** Va'omar Lach Bedamayich Chayi. Vene'emar:
Zachar Le'olam Berito Davar Tzivah Le'elef Dor. Asher Karat Et
Avraham Ushevu'ato Leyischak. Vaya'amideha Leya'akov Lechok
Leyisra'el Berit Olam. Hodu L'Adonai Ki Tov Ki Le'olam Chasdo.
(Peloni) Zeh Hakkatan. Elohim Yegadelehu. Keshem Shenichnas
Laberit Kach Yikanes Latorah Velamitzvot Velachuppah Ulema'asim
Tovim. Vechein Yehi Ratzon Venomar Amen:

Our God, and God of our fathers, preserve this child (my son) to his
father (to me) and mother; and his name will be called in Yisrael
(name of child). May the father rejoice in him who proceeds from his
loins If the father performs the circumcision personally: May it be His will that I rejoice
in my offspring), and the mother be glad with the fruit of her womb;
as it is said "Your father and mother will rejoice, and they who gave
birth to you will be glad." It is also said, "And I passed by you, and
saw you wallowing in your own blood; and I said to you, In your own
blood you will live; ** and I said to you, In your own blood you will
live." (Ezekiel 16:6) And it is said, "He has remembered His covenant
forever, the word which he commanded to a thousand generations;
which He covenanted with Avraham, and likewise His oath to
Yitzchak, which he confirmed to Yaakov as a statute; to Yisrael as an
everlasting covenant, give thanks to Hashem, for He is good, for His
mercy endures forever." (Psalms 105:8) May God cause this young (name
of child) to grow up prosperously; and even as he has been
introduced into Your covenant, so may he be initiated into the
practice of the Torah and of the precepts, into the chuppah, and to
good deeds. May it be the Divine Will, and let us say, Amen.

Psalms 128

שִׁיר הַמַּעֲלוֹת אַשְׁרֵי כָּל־יְרֵא יְהוָה הַהֹלֵךְ בִּדְרָכָיו: יְגִיעַ כַּפֶּיךָ כִּי
תֹאכֵל אַשְׁרֶיךָ וְטוֹב לָךְ: אֶשְׁתְּךָ | כְּגֶפֶן פֹּרִיָּה בְּיַרְכְּתֵי בֵיתֶךָ בָּנֶיךָ
כִּשְׁתִלֵי זֵיתִים סָבִיב לְשֻׁלְחָנֶךָ: הִנֵּה כִי־כֵן יְבֹרַךְ גָּבֶר יְרֵא יְהוָה:
יְבָרֶכְךָ יְהוָה מִצִּיּוֹן וּרְאֵה בְּטוּב יְרוּשָׁלָ‍ִם כֹּל יְמֵי חַיֶּיךָ: וּרְאֵה־בָנִים
לְבָנֶיךָ שָׁלוֹם עַל־יִשְׂרָאֵל:

Shir Hama'alot Ashrei Kol Yere Adonai Haholech Bidrachav. Yegia'
Kappeicha Ki Tochel Ashreicha Vetov Lach. Eshtecha Kegefen
Poriyah Beyarkete Veitecha Baneicha Kishtilei Zeitim Saviv
Leshulchanecha. Hineh Chi Chein Yevorach Gaver Yere Adonai.
Yevarechecha Adonai Mitziyon Ure'eh Betuv Yerushalayim Kol
Yemei Chayeicha. Ure'eh Vanim Levaneicha Shalom Al Yisra'el.

A Song of Ascents. Happy is everyone that fears Hashem, That
walks in His ways. When you eat the labor of your hands, Happy you
will be, and it will be well with you. Your wife will be as a fruitful vine,
in the innermost parts of your house; Your children like olive plants,
around your table. Behold, surely will the man be blessed that fears
Hashem. May Hashem bless you out of Tziyon; And may you see the
good of Yerushalayim all the days of your life; And see your
children's children. Peace be upon Yisrael.

And say Kaddish Yehei-Shelama.

Kaddish is only recited in a minyan (ten men). אמן denotes when the congregation responds "Amen"
together out loud. According to the Shulchan Arukh, the congregation says "Yehei Shemeh Rabba"
to "Yitbarach" out loud together without interruption, and also that one should respond "Amen"
after "Yitbarach." (SA, OC 55,56) This is not the common custom today. Though many are
accustomed to answering according to their own custom, it is advised to respond in the custom of
the one reciting to avoid not fragmenting into smaller groups. ("Lo Titgodedu" - BT, Yevamot 13b /
SA, OC 493, Rema / MT, Avodah Zara 12:15)

יִתְגַּדַּל וְיִתְקַדַּשׁ שְׁמֵהּ רַבָּא. אמן בְּעָלְמָא דִּי בְרָא. כִּרְעוּתֵהּ. וְיַמְלִיךְ
מַלְכוּתֵהּ. וְיַצְמַח פֻּרְקָנֵהּ. וִיקָרֵב מְשִׁיחֵהּ. אמן בְּחַיֵּיכוֹן וּבְיוֹמֵיכוֹן
וּבְחַיֵּי דְכָל בֵּית יִשְׂרָאֵל. בַּעֲגָלָא וּבִזְמַן קָרִיב. וְאִמְרוּ אָמֵן. אמן יְהֵא

שְׁמֵהּ רַבָּא מְבָרַךְ לְעָלַם וּלְעָלְמֵי עָלְמַיָּא יִתְבָּרַךְ. וְיִשְׁתַּבַּח.
וְיִתְפָּאַר. וְיִתְרוֹמַם. וְיִתְנַשֵּׂא. וְיִתְהַדָּר. וְיִתְעַלֶּה. וְיִתְהַלָּל שְׁמֵהּ
דְּקֻדְשָׁא. בְּרִיךְ הוּא. אָמֵן לְעֵלָּא מִן כָּל בִּרְכָתָא שִׁירָתָא. תֻּשְׁבְּחָתָא
וְנֶחֱמָתָא. דַּאֲמִירָן בְּעָלְמָא. וְאִמְרוּ אָמֵן. אָמֵן

Yitgadal Veyitkadash Shemeh Rabba. Amen Be'alema Di Vera.
Kir'uteh. Veyamlich Malchuteh. Veyatzmach Purkaneh. Vikarev
Meshicheh. Amen Bechayeichon Uveyomeichon Uvechayei Dechal-
Beit Yisra'el. Ba'agala Uvizman Kariv. Ve'imru Amen. Amen Yehei
Shemeh Rabba Mevarach Le'alam Ule'alemei Alemaya Yitbarach.
Veyishtabach. Veyitpa'ar. Veyitromam. Veyitnasse. Veyit'hadar.
Veyit'aleh. Veyit'hallal Shemeh Dekudsha. Berich Hu. Amen Le'ella
Min Kol Birchata Shirata. Tushbechata Venechemata. Da'amiran
Be'alema. Ve'imru Amen. Amen

Glorified and sanctified be God's great name Amen throughout the world which He has created according to His will. May He establish His kingdom, hastening His salvation and the coming of His Messiah, Amen, in your lifetime and during your days, and within the life of the entire House of Yisrael, speedily and soon; and say, Amen. Amen May His great name be blessed forever and to all eternity. Blessed and praised, glorified and exalted, extolled and honored, adored and lauded is the name of the Holy One, blessed is He, Amen Beyond all the blessings and hymns, praises and consolations that are ever spoken in the world; and say, Amen. Amen

יְהֵא שְׁלָמָא רַבָּא מִן שְׁמַיָּא. חַיִּים וְשָׂבָע וִישׁוּעָה וְנֶחָמָה. וְשֵׁיזָבָא
וּרְפוּאָה וּגְאוּלָה וּסְלִיחָה וְכַפָּרָה וְרֶוַח וְהַצָּלָה לָנוּ וּלְכָל עַמּוֹ
יִשְׂרָאֵל. וְאִמְרוּ אָמֵן. אָמֵן

Yehei Shelama Rabba Min Shemaya. Chayim Vesava Vishu'ah
Venechamah. Vesheizava Urefu'ah Uge'ulah Uselichah
Vechapparah Verevach Vehatzalah Lanu Ulechol Ammo Yisra'el.
Ve'imru Amen. Amen

May abundant peace descend from heaven, with life and plenty, salvation, solace, liberation, healing and redemption, and forgiveness and atonement, enlargement and freedom, for us and all of God's people Yisrael; and say, Amen. Amen

> One bows and takes three steps backwards, while still bowing. After three steps, while still bowing and before erecting, while saying, "Oseh Shalom Bimromav", turn one's face to the left, "Hu [Berachamav] Ya'aseh Shalom Aleinu", turn one's face to the right; then bow forward like a servant leaving his master. (SA, OC 123:1)

עוֹשֶׂה שָׁלוֹם בִּמְרוֹמָיו. הוּא בְּרַחֲמָיו יַעֲשֶׂה שָׁלוֹם עָלֵינוּ. וְעַל
כָּל־עַמּוֹ יִשְׂרָאֵל. וְאִמְרוּ אָמֵן:

Oseh Shalom Bimromav. Hu Berachamav Ya'aseh Shalom Aleinu.
Ve'al Kol-'Ammo Yisra'el. Ve'imru Amen.

Creator of peace in His high places, may He in His mercy create peace for us and for all Yisrael, and say Amen.

Zeved HaBat (Naming Ceremony of a Daughter) - Shabbat Shacharit

The word Zeved translates to precious gift. When the mother comes, or brings the child, to the synagogue, follow the service of Birkhat Hagomel and close it by this form of blessing the child. Without the final psalm, this is the form used if the child is named when the father is called to the Sefer Torah.

יוֹנָתִי בְּחַגְוֵי הַסֶּלַע בְּסֵתֶר הַמַּדְרֵגָה הַרְאִינִי אֶת־מַרְאַיִךְ הַשְׁמִיעִנִי אֶת־קוֹלֵךְ כִּי־קוֹלֵךְ עָרֵב וּמַרְאֵיךְ נָאוֶה:

Yonati Bechagvei Hassela Beseter Hamadregah Har'ini Et Mar'ayich Hashmi'ini Et Kolech Ki Kolech Arev Umar'eich Naveh.

"Oh my dove, in the cleft of the rocks, Hidden by the cliff, Let me see your face, Let me hear your voice; For your voice is sweet and your face is beautiful." (Song of Songs 2:14)

מִי שֶׁבֵּרַךְ אִמּוֹתֵינוּ. שָׂרָה. רִבְקָה. רָחֵל וְלֵאָה וּמִרְיָם הַנְּבִיאָה וַאֲבִיגַיִל. וְאֶסְתֵּר הַמַּלְכָּה בַּת אֲבִיחַיִל. הוּא יְבָרֵךְ אֶת הַיַּלְדָּה הַנְּעִימָה הַזֹּאת. וְיִקָּרֵא שְׁמָהּ (פְּלוֹנִית בַּת פְּלוֹנִי) בְּמַזָּל טוֹב וּבְשָׁעַת בְּרָכָה. וִיגַדְלָהּ בִּבְרִיאוּת שָׁלוֹם וּמְנוּחָה. וִיזַכֶּה אֶת־אָבִיהָ וְאֶת־אִמָּהּ לִרְאוֹת בְּשִׂמְחָתָהּ וּבְחֻפָּתָהּ. בְּבָנִים זְכָרִים. עֹשֶׁר וְכָבוֹד. דְּשֵׁנִים וְרַעֲנַנִּים יְנוּבוּן בְּשֵׂיבָה. וְכֵן יְהִי רָצוֹן וְנֹאמַר אָמֵן:

Mi Sheberach Imoteinu. Sarah. Rivkah. Rachel Vele'ah Umiryam Hanevi'ah Va'avigayil. Ve'ester Hamalkah Bat Avichayil. Hu Yevarech Et Hayaldah Hane'imah Hazot. Veyikare Shemah (Pelonit Bat Peloni) Bemazal Tov Uvish'at Berachah. Vigadelah Vivri'ut Shalom Umenuchah. Vizakeh Le'aviha Ule'imah Lir'ot Besimchatah Uvechuppatah. Bevanim Zecharim. Osher Vechavod. Deshenim Vera'ananim Yenuvun Beseivah. Vechen Yehi Ratzon Venomar Amen:

May He Who blessed our mothers Sarah, Rivkah, Rachel and Leah, Miryam the prophetess, Avigail, and Esther the queen, bless also this darling child. And may her name be called ___ daughter of ___. May He bless her to grow up in health, peace and happiness. May He give to her mother and father the joy of seeing her happily married, a radiant mother of children, rich in honor and joy to a ripe old age. May this be the will of God, and let us say, Amen.

SEFIRAT HAOMER / COUNTING OF THE OMER

ספירת העומר

From the 2nd Day of Passover to until the night before Shavuot, the Omer is counted after Arvit Prayer in the evening when it is dark.

Many say the following prayer:

לְשֵׁם יִחוּד קוּדְשָׁא בְּרִיךְ הוּא וּשְׁכִינְתֵּיהּ. בִּדְחִילוּ וּרְחִימוּ. וּרְחִימוּ וּדְחִילוּ.
לְיַחֲדָא שֵׁם יוֹ"ד קֵ"י בְּוָא"ו קֵ"י בְּיִחוּדָא שְׁלִים (יהוה) בְּשֵׁם כָּל יִשְׂרָאֵל.
הִנֵּה אֲנַחְנוּ בָּאִים לְקַיֵּם מִצְוַת עֲשֵׂה שֶׁל סְפִירַת הָעֹמֶר כְּדִכְתִיב (בליל מ"ט ידלג
פסוקים אלה. עד שבעה שבועות. ויאמר לתקן שורש מצוה זו וכו') וּסְפַרְתֶּם לָכֶם מִמָּחֳרַת הַשַּׁבָּת מִיּוֹם
הֲבִיאֲכֶם אֶת־עֹמֶר הַתְּנוּפָה שֶׁבַע שַׁבָּתוֹת תְּמִימֹת תִּהְיֶינָה: עַד מִמָּחֳרַת
הַשַּׁבָּת הַשְּׁבִיעִת תִּסְפְּרוּ חֲמִשִּׁים יוֹם וְהִקְרַבְתֶּם מִנְחָה חֲדָשָׁה לַיהוָה:
וְנֶאֱמַר. שִׁבְעָה שָׁבֻעֹת תִּסְפָּר לָךְ מֵהָחֵל חֶרְמֵשׁ בַּקָּמָה תָּחֵל לִסְפֹּר שִׁבְעָה
שָׁבֻעוֹת: לְתַקֵּן שֹׁרֶשׁ מִצְוָה זוֹ בְּמָקוֹם עֶלְיוֹן עִם כָּל הַמִּצְוֹת הַכְּלוּלוֹת בָּהּ.
לַעֲשׂוֹת נַחַת רוּחַ לְיוֹצְרֵנוּ וְלַעֲשׂוֹת רָצוֹן בּוֹרְאֵנוּ. יַעֲלֶה לְפָנָיו כְּאִלּוּ כִּוַּנְנוּ כָּל
הַכַּוָּנוֹת הָרְאוּיוֹת לְכַוֵּן בָּזֶה: וִיהִי נֹעַם אֲדֹנָי אֱלֹהֵינוּ עָלֵינוּ וּמַעֲשֵׂה יָדֵינוּ כּוֹנְנָה
עָלֵינוּ וּמַעֲשֵׂה יָדֵינוּ כּוֹנְנֵהוּ:

Leshem Yichud Kudsha Berich Hu Ushechinteih. Bidchilu Urechimu. Urechimu Udechilu. Leyachada Shem Yod Key BeVav Key Beyichuda Shelim Beshem Kol Yisra'el. Hineh Anachnu Ba'im Lekayem Mitzvat Aseh Shel Sefirat Ha'omer Kedichtiv **(On the night of Matan Torah (Shavuot) skip these verses, up to "Shiv'ah Shavu'ot", and say "Letakken Shoresh Mitzvah", etc.)** Usefartem Lachem Mimochorat Hashabbat Miyom Havi'achem Et Omer Hatenufah Sheva Shabbatot Temimot Tihyeinah. Ad Mimochorat Hashabbat Hashevi'it Tisperu Chamishim Yom Vehikravtem Minchah Chadashah Ladonai. Vene'emar. Shiv'ah Shavu'ot Tispar Lach Mehachel Chermesh Bakamah Tachel Lispor Shiv'ah Shavu'ot. Letaken Shoresh Mitzvah Zo Bemakom Elyon Im Kol Hamitzvot Hakelulot Bah. La'asot Nachat Ruach Leyotzreinu Vela'asot Retzon Bore'enu. Ya'aleh Lefanav Che'ilu Kivanu Chol Hakavanot Hare'uyot Lechaven Bazeh: Vihi No'am Adonai Eloheinu Aleinu Uma'aseh Yadeinu Konenah Aleinu Uma'aseh Yadeinu Konenehu. **(Lev. 23:15-16, Deut.16:19)**

Some say:

יְהוָה יִגְמֹר בַּעֲדִי יְהוָה חַסְדְּךָ לְעוֹלָם מַעֲשֵׂי יָדֶיךָ אַל־תֶּרֶף: אֶקְרָא לֵאלֹהִים
עֶלְיוֹן לָאֵל גֹּמֵר עָלָי: וְאֶעֱבֹר עָלַיִךְ וָאֶרְאֵךְ מִתְבּוֹסֶסֶת בְּדָמָיִךְ וָאֹמַר לָךְ
בְּדָמַיִךְ חֲיִי וָאֹמַר לָךְ בְּדָמַיִךְ חֲיִי: בָּרְכִי נַפְשִׁי אֶת־יְהוָה יְהוָה אֱלֹהַי גָּדַלְתָּ
מְּאֹד הוֹד וְהָדָר לָבָשְׁתָּ: עֹטֶה־אוֹר כַּשַּׂלְמָה נוֹטֶה שָׁמַיִם כַּיְרִיעָה:

Adonai Yigmor Ba'adi Adonai Chasdecha Le'olam Ma'asei Yadeicha Al Teref. Ekra
Lelohim Elyon La'el Gomer Alai. Va'e'evor Alayich Va'er'ech Mitboseset
Bedamayich Va'omar Lach Bedamayich Chayi Va'omar Lach Bedamayich Chayi.
Barchi Nafshi Et Adonai Adonai Elohai Gadalta Me'od Hod Vehadar Lavasheta.
Oteh Or Kassalmah Noteh Shamayim Kayeri'ah.

Hashem will accomplish that which concerns me; Your mercy, Hashem, endures
forever; Do not forsake the work of Your own hands. I will cry to God Most high; to
God that accomplishes it for me. And when I passed by you, and saw you
wallowing in your blood, I said to you: In your blood, live; yes, I said to you: In your
blood, live; Bless Hashem, Oh my soul. Hashem, my God, You are very great; You
are clothed with glory and majesty. Who covers Yourself with light as with a
garment, Who stretches out the heavens like a curtain. (Ps. 138:8, 57:3, Ez. 16:6, Ps.
104:1-2)

Birshut Morai Verabotai: בִּרְשׁוּת מוֹרַי וְרַבּוֹתַי:

With the permission of my teachers and masters:

Answer: Shamayim!   עונים: שָׁמַיִם.

Answer: (By) Heaven!

And the Chazan and the people bless:

Baruch Attah Adonai Eloheinu   בָּרוּךְ אַתָּה יְהֹוָה אֱלֹהֵינוּ

Melech Ha'olam Asher   מֶלֶךְ הָעוֹלָם. אֲשֶׁר

Kideshanu Bemitzvotav   קִדְּשָׁנוּ בְּמִצְוֹתָיו

Vetzivanu Al Sefirat Ha'Omer: וְצִוָּנוּ עַל סְפִירַת הָעֹמֶר:

And say: Hayom and say the count: ואומרים הַיּוֹם וכו' ואחר הספירה אומר:

Blessed are You, Hashem our God, King of the universe, Who has
sanctified us with His commandments, and has given us command
concerning the counting of the O'mer. (Continue down and say "HaYom..." and
the day to count. Continue afterwards with Psalm 67, etc.)

16th of Nissan

Hayom Yom Echad La'omer: הַיּוֹם יוֹם אֶחָד לָעֹמֶר:

Today is the first day of the Omer.

17th of Nissan

Hayom Shenei Yamim La'omer:

הַיּוֹם שְׁנֵי יָמִים לָעֹמֶר:

Today is the second day of the Omer.

18th of Nissan

Hayom Sheloshah Yamim La'omer:

הַיּוֹם שְׁלֹשָׁה יָמִים לָעֹמֶר:

Today is the third day of the Omer.

19th of Nissan

Hayom Arba'ah Yamim La'omer:

הַיּוֹם אַרְבָּעָה יָמִים לָעֹמֶר:

Today is the fourth day of the Omer.

20th of Nissan

Hayom Chamishah Yamim La'omer:

הַיּוֹם חֲמִשָּׁה יָמִים לָעֹמֶר:

Today is the fifth day of the Omer.

21st of Nissan

Hayom Shishah Yamim La'omer:

הַיּוֹם שִׁשָּׁה יָמִים לָעֹמֶר:

Today is the sixth day of the Omer.

22nd of Nissan

Hayom Shiv'ah Yamim La'omer
Shehem Shavua' Echad:

הַיּוֹם שִׁבְעָה יָמִים לָעֹמֶר
שֶׁהֵם שָׁבוּעַ אֶחָד:

Today is the seventh day of the Omer, which is one week.

23rd of Nissan

Hayom Shemonah Yamim La'omer
Shehem Shavua' Echad Veyom Echad:

הַיּוֹם שְׁמוֹנָה יָמִים לָעֹמֶר
שֶׁהֵם שָׁבוּעַ אֶחָד וְיוֹם אֶחָד:

Today is the seventh day of the Omer, which is one week and one day.

24th of Nissan

Hayom Tish'ah Yamim La'omer Shehem
Shavua' Echad Ushenei Yamim:

הַיּוֹם תִּשְׁעָה יָמִים לָעֹמֶר שֶׁהֵם
שָׁבוּעַ אֶחָד וּשְׁנֵי יָמִים:

Today is the ninth day of the Omer, which is one week and two days.

25th of Nissan

Hayom Asarah Yamim La'omer Shehem

Shavua' Echad Usheloshah Yamim:

הַיּוֹם עֲשָׂרָה יָמִים לָעֹמֶר שֶׁהֵם שָׁבוּעַ אֶחָד וּשְׁלֹשָׁה יָמִים:

Today is the tenth day of the Omer, which is one week and three days.

26th of Nissan

Hayom Achad Asar Yom La'omer

Shehem Shavua' Echad Ve'arba'ah

Yamim:

הַיּוֹם אַחַד עָשָׂר יוֹם לָעֹמֶר שֶׁהֵם שָׁבוּעַ אֶחָד וְאַרְבָּעָה יָמִים:

Today is the eleventh day of the Omer, which is one week and four days.

27th of Nissan

Hayom Sheneim Asar Yom La'omer

Shehem Shavua' Echad Vachamishah

Yamim:

הַיּוֹם שְׁנֵים עָשָׂר יוֹם לָעֹמֶר שֶׁהֵם שָׁבוּעַ אֶחָד וַחֲמִשָּׁה יָמִים:

Today is the twelfth day of the Omer, which is one week and five days.

28th of Nissan

Hayom Sheloshah Asar Yom La'omer

Shehem Shavua' Echad Veshishah

Yamim:

הַיּוֹם שְׁלֹשָׁה עָשָׂר יוֹם לָעֹמֶר שֶׁהֵם שָׁבוּעַ אֶחָד וְשִׁשָּׁה יָמִים:

Today is the thirteenth day of the Omer, which is one week and six days.

29th of Nissan

Hayom Arba'ah Asar Yom La'omer

Shehem Shenei Shavu'ot:

הַיּוֹם אַרְבָּעָה עָשָׂר יוֹם לָעֹמֶר שֶׁהֵם שְׁנֵי שָׁבוּעוֹת:

Today is the fourteenth day of the Omer, which is two weeks.

30th of Nissan

Hayom Chamishah Asar Yom La'omer

Shehem Shenei Shavu'ot Veyom Echad:

הַיּוֹם חֲמִשָּׁה עָשָׂר יוֹם לָעֹמֶר שֶׁהֵם שְׁנֵי שָׁבוּעוֹת וְיוֹם אֶחָד:

Today is the fifteenth day of the Omer, which is two weeks and one day.

1st of Iyar

Hayom Shishah Asar Yom La'omer

Shehem Shenei Shavu'ot Ushenei

Yamim:

הַיּוֹם שִׁשָּׁה עָשָׂר יוֹם לָעֹמֶר
שֶׁהֵם שְׁנֵי שָׁבוּעוֹת וּשְׁנֵי
יָמִים:

Today is the sixteenth day of the Omer, which is two weeks and two days.

2nd of Iyar

Hayom Shiv'ah Asar Yom La'omer

Shehem Shenei Shavu'ot Usheloshah

Yamim:

הַיּוֹם שִׁבְעָה עָשָׂר יוֹם לָעֹמֶר
שֶׁהֵם שְׁנֵי שָׁבוּעוֹת וּשְׁלֹשָׁה
יָמִים:

Today is the seventeenth day of the Omer, which is two weeks and three days.

3rd of Iyar

Hayom Shemonah Asar Yom La'omer

Shehem Shenei Shavu'ot Ve'arba'ah

Yamim:

הַיּוֹם שְׁמוֹנָה עָשָׂר יוֹם לָעֹמֶר
שֶׁהֵם שְׁנֵי שָׁבוּעוֹת וְאַרְבָּעָה
יָמִים:

Today is the eighteenth day of the Omer, which is two weeks and four days.

4th of Iyar

Hayom Tish'ah Asar Yom La'omer

Shehem Shenei Shavu'ot Vachamishah

Yamim:

הַיּוֹם תִּשְׁעָה עָשָׂר יוֹם לָעֹמֶר
שֶׁהֵם שְׁנֵי שָׁבוּעוֹת וַחֲמִשָּׁה
יָמִים:

Today is the nineteenth day of the Omer, which is two weeks and five days.

5th of Iyar

Hayom Esrim Yom La'omer Shehem

Shenei Shavu'ot Veshishah Yamim:

הַיּוֹם עֶשְׂרִים יוֹם לָעֹמֶר שֶׁהֵם
שְׁנֵי שָׁבוּעוֹת וְשִׁשָּׁה יָמִים:

Today is the twentieth day of the Omer, which is two weeks and six days.

6th of Iyar

Hayom Echad Ve'esrim Yom La'omer

Shehem Sheloshah Shavu'ot:

הַיּוֹם אֶחָד וְעֶשְׂרִים יוֹם לָעֹמֶר
שֶׁהֵם שְׁלֹשָׁה שָׁבוּעוֹת:

Today is the twenty-first day of the Omer, which is three weeks.

Hayom Shenayim Ve'esrim Yom

La'omer Shehem Sheloshah Shavu'ot

Veyom Echad:

הַיּוֹם שְׁנַיִם וְעֶשְׂרִים יוֹם

לָעֹמֶר שֶׁהֵם שְׁלשָׁה שָׁבוּעוֹת

וְיוֹם אֶחָד:

Today is the twenty-second day of the Omer, which is three weeks and one day.

Hayom Sheloshah Ve'esrim Yom

La'omer Shehem Sheloshah Shavu'ot

Ushenei Yamim:

הַיּוֹם שְׁלשָׁה וְעֶשְׂרִים יוֹם

לָעֹמֶר שֶׁהֵם שְׁלשָׁה שָׁבוּעוֹת

וּשְׁנֵי יָמִים:

Today is the twenty-third day of the Omer, which is three weeks and two days.

Hayom Arba'ah Ve'esrim Yom La'omer

Shehem Sheloshah Shavu'ot

Usheloshah Yamim:

הַיּוֹם אַרְבָּעָה וְעֶשְׂרִים יוֹם לָעֹמֶר

שֶׁהֵם שְׁלשָׁה שָׁבוּעוֹת

וּשְׁלשָׁה יָמִים:

Today is the twenty-fourth day of the Omer, which is three weeks and three days.

Hayom Chamishah Ve'esrim Yom

La'omer Shehem Sheloshah Shavu'ot

Ve'arba'ah Yamim:

הַיּוֹם חֲמִשָּׁה וְעֶשְׂרִים יוֹם

לָעֹמֶר שֶׁהֵם שְׁלשָׁה שָׁבוּעוֹת

וְאַרְבָּעָה יָמִים:

Today is the twenty-fifth day of the Omer, which is three weeks and four days.

Hayom Shishah Ve'esrim Yom La'omer

Shehem Sheloshah Shavu'ot

Vachamishah Yamim:

הַיּוֹם שִׁשָּׁה וְעֶשְׂרִים יוֹם לָעֹמֶר

שֶׁהֵם שְׁלשָׁה שָׁבוּעוֹת

וַחֲמִשָּׁה יָמִים:

Today is the twenty-sixth day of the Omer, which is three weeks and five days.

Hayom Shiv'ah Ve'esrim Yom La'omer

Shehem Sheloshah Shavu'ot Veshishah

Yamim:

הַיּוֹם שִׁבְעָה וְעֶשְׂרִים יוֹם לָעֹמֶר

שֶׁהֵם שְׁלשָׁה שָׁבוּעוֹת וְשִׁשָּׁה

יָמִים:

Today is the twenty-seventh day of the Omer, which is three weeks and six days.

13th of Iyar

Hayom Shemonah Ve'esrim Yom

La'omer Shehem Arba'ah Shavu'ot:

הַיּוֹם שְׁמוֹנָה וְעֶשְׂרִים יוֹם
לָעֹמֶר שֶׁהֵם אַרְבָּעָה שָׁבוּעוֹת:

Today is the twenty-eighth day of the Omer, which is four weeks.

14th of Iyar

Hayom Tish'ah Ve'esrim Yom La'omer

Shehem Arba'ah Shavu'ot Veyom

Echad:

הַיּוֹם תִּשְׁעָה וְעֶשְׂרִים יוֹם לָעֹמֶר
שֶׁהֵם אַרְבָּעָה שָׁבוּעוֹת וְיוֹם
אֶחָד:

Today is the twenty-ninth day of the Omer, which is four weeks and one day.

15th of Iyar

Hayom Sheloshim Yom La'omer

Shehem Arba'ah Shavu'ot Ushenei

Yamim:

הַיּוֹם שְׁלשִׁים יוֹם לָעֹמֶר
שֶׁהֵם אַרְבָּעָה שָׁבוּעוֹת וּשְׁנֵי
יָמִים:

Today is the thirtieth day of the Omer, which is four weeks and two days.

16th of Iyar

Hayom Echad Usheloshim Yom

La'omer Shehem Arba'ah Shavu'ot

Usheloshah Yamim:

הַיּוֹם אֶחָד וּשְׁלשִׁים יוֹם
לָעֹמֶר שֶׁהֵם אַרְבָּעָה שָׁבוּעוֹת
וּשְׁלשָׁה יָמִים:

Today is the thirty-first day of the Omer, which is four weeks and three days.

17th of Iyar

Hayom Shenayim Usheloshim Yom

La'omer Shehem Arba'ah Shavu'ot

Ve'arba'ah Yamim:

הַיּוֹם שְׁנַיִם וּשְׁלשִׁים יוֹם
לָעֹמֶר שֶׁהֵם אַרְבָּעָה שָׁבוּעוֹת
וְאַרְבָּעָה יָמִים:

Today is the thirty-second day of the Omer, which is four weeks and four days.

18th of Iyar

Hayom Sheloshah Usheloshim Yom

Lal'omer Shehem Arba'ah Shavu'ot

Vachamishah Yamim:

הַיּוֹם שְׁלֹשָׁה וּשְׁלֹשִׁים יוֹם
לָעֹמֶר שֶׁהֵם אַרְבָּעָה שָׁבוּעוֹת
וַחֲמִשָּׁה יָמִים:

Today is the thirty-third day of the Omer, which is four weeks and five days.

19th of Iyar

Hayom Arba'ah Usheloshim Yom

La'omer Shehem Arba'ah Shavu'ot

Veshishah Yamim:

הַיּוֹם אַרְבָּעָה וּשְׁלֹשִׁים יוֹם
לָעֹמֶר שֶׁהֵם אַרְבָּעָה שָׁבוּעוֹת
וְשִׁשָּׁה יָמִים:

Today is the thirty-fourth day of the Omer, which is four weeks and six days.

20th of Iyar

Hayom Chamishah Usheloshim Yom

La'omer Shehem Chamishah Shavu'ot:

הַיּוֹם חֲמִשָּׁה וּשְׁלֹשִׁים יוֹם
לָעֹמֶר שֶׁהֵם חֲמִשָּׁה שָׁבוּעוֹת:

Today is the thirty-fifth day of the Omer, which is five weeks.

21st of Iyar

Hayom Shishah Usheloshim Yom

La'omer Shehem Chamishah Shavu'ot

Veyom Echad:

הַיּוֹם שִׁשָּׁה וּשְׁלֹשִׁים יוֹם
לָעֹמֶר שֶׁהֵם חֲמִשָּׁה שָׁבוּעוֹת
וְיוֹם אֶחָד:

Today is the thirty-sixth day of the Omer, which is five weeks and one day.

23rd of Iyar

Hayom Shiv'ah Usheloshim Yom

La'omer Shehem Chamishah Shavu'ot

Ushenei Yamim:

הַיּוֹם שִׁבְעָה וּשְׁלֹשִׁים יוֹם
לָעֹמֶר שֶׁהֵם חֲמִשָּׁה שָׁבוּעוֹת
וּשְׁנֵי יָמִים:

Today is the thirty-seventh day of the Omer, which is five weeks and two days.

24th of Iyar

Hayom Shemonah Usheloshim Yom

La'omer Shehem Chamishah Shavu'ot

Usheloshah Yamim:

הַיּוֹם שְׁמוֹנָה וּשְׁלֹשִׁים יוֹם
לָעֹמֶר שֶׁהֵם חֲמִשָּׁה שָׁבוּעוֹת
וּשְׁלֹשָׁה יָמִים:

Today is the thirty-eighth day of the Omer, which is five weeks and three days.

25th of Iyar

Hayom Tish'ah Usheloshim Yom

La'omer Shehem Chamishah Shavu'ot

Ve'arba'ah Yamim:

הַיּוֹם תִּשְׁעָה וּשְׁלֹשִׁים יוֹם

לָעֹמֶר שֶׁהֵם חֲמִשָּׁה שָׁבוּעוֹת

וְאַרְבָּעָה יָמִים:

Today is the thirty-ninth day of the Omer, which is five weeks and four days.

26th of Iyar

Hayom Arba'im Yom La'omer Shehem

Chamishah Shavu'ot Vachamishah

Yamim:

הַיּוֹם אַרְבָּעִים יוֹם לָעֹמֶר שֶׁהֵם

חֲמִשָּׁה שָׁבוּעוֹת וַחֲמִשָּׁה

יָמִים:

Today is the fortieth day of the Omer, which is five weeks and five days.

27th of Iyar

Hayom Echad Ve'arba'im Yom La'omer

Shehem Chamishah Shavu'ot Veshishah

Yamim:

הַיּוֹם אֶחָד וְאַרְבָּעִים יוֹם לָעֹמֶר

שֶׁהֵם חֲמִשָּׁה שָׁבוּעוֹת וְשִׁשָּׁה

יָמִים:

Today is the forty-first day of the Omer, which is five weeks and six days.

28th of Iyar

Hayom Shenayim Ve'arba'im Yom

La'omer Shehem Shishah Shavu'ot:

הַיּוֹם שְׁנַיִם וְאַרְבָּעִים יוֹם

לָעֹמֶר שֶׁהֵם שִׁשָּׁה שָׁבוּעוֹת:

Today is the forty-second day of the Omer, which is six weeks.

29th of Iyar

Hayom Sheloshah Ve'arba'im Yom

La'omer Shehem Shishah Shavu'ot

Veyom Echad:

הַיּוֹם שְׁלֹשָׁה וְאַרְבָּעִים יוֹם

לָעֹמֶר שֶׁהֵם שִׁשָּׁה שָׁבוּעוֹת

וְיוֹם אֶחָד:

Today is the forty-third day of the Omer, which is six weeks and one day.

30th of Iyar

Hayom Arba'ah Ve'arba'im Yom

La'omer Shehem Shishah Shavu'ot

Ushenei Yamim:

הַיּוֹם אַרְבָּעָה וְאַרְבָּעִים יוֹם

לָעֹמֶר שֶׁהֵם שִׁשָּׁה שָׁבוּעוֹת

וּשְׁנֵי יָמִים:

Today is the forty-fourth day of the Omer, which is six weeks and two days.

1st of Sivan

Hayom Chamishah Ve'arba'im Yom
La'omer Shehem Shishah Shavu'ot
Usheloshah Yamim:

הַיוֹם חֲמִשָּׁה וְאַרְבָּעִים יוֹם
לָעְמֶר שֶׁהֵם שִׁשָּׁה שָׁבוּעוֹת
וּשְׁלֹשָׁה יָמִים:

Today is the forty-fifth day of the Omer, which is six weeks and three days.

2nd of Sivan

Hayom Shishah Ve'arba'im Yom
La'omer Shehem Shishah Shavu'ot
Ve'arba'ah Yamim:

הַיוֹם שִׁשָּׁה וְאַרְבָּעִים יוֹם
לָעְמֶר שֶׁהֵם שִׁשָּׁה שָׁבוּעוֹת
וְאַרְבָּעָה יָמִים:

Today is the forty-sixth day of the Omer, which is six weeks and four days.

3rd of Sivan

Hayom Shiv'ah Ve'Arba'im Yom
La'omer Shehem Shishah Shavu'ot
Vachamishah Yamim:

הַיוֹם שִׁבְעָה וְאַרְבָּעִים יוֹם
לָעְמֶר שֶׁהֵם שִׁשָּׁה שָׁבוּעוֹת
וַחֲמִשָּׁה יָמִים:

Today is the forty-seventh day of the Omer, which is six weeks and five days.

4th of Sivan

Hayom Shemonah Ve'arba'im Yom
La'omer Shehem Shishah Shavu'ot
Veshishah Yamim:

הַיוֹם שְׁמוֹנָה וְאַרְבָּעִים יוֹם
לָעְמֶר שֶׁהֵם שִׁשָּׁה שָׁבוּעוֹת
וְשִׁשָּׁה יָמִים:

Today is the forty-eighth day of the Omer, which is six weeks and six days.

5th of Sivan

Hayom Tish'ah Ve'arba'im Yom La'omer
Shehem Shiv'ah Shavu'ot:

הַיוֹם תִּשְׁעָה וְאַרְבָּעִים יוֹם לָעְמֶר
שֶׁהֵם שִׁבְעָה שָׁבוּעוֹת:

Today is the forty-ninth day of the Omer, which is seven weeks.

Continue with Harachaman, Psalms 67 and Ana Bechoach. If one counted after Kaddish Titkabbal in Shacharit, continue with Psalms 121. If one counted after Aleinu, the service is now concluded.

After counting the omer say:

Harachaman Yachazir Beit

Hamikdash Limkomah

Bimheirah Beyameinu:

הָרַחֲמָן יַחֲזִיר בֵּית
הַמִּקְדָּשׁ לִמְקוֹמָה
בִּמְהֵרָה בְיָמֵינוּ:

May the Most Merciful restore the service of the Beit HaMikdash to its place, speedily in our days.

Psalms 67 / Lamnatzeach Binginot

לַמְנַצֵּחַ בִּנְגִינֹת מִזְמוֹר שִׁיר: אֱלֹהִים יְחָנֵּנוּ וִיבָרְכֵנוּ יָאֵר פָּנָיו אִתָּנוּ סֶלָה: לָדַעַת בָּאָרֶץ דַּרְכֶּךָ בְּכָל־גּוֹיִם יְשׁוּעָתֶךָ: יוֹדוּךָ עַמִּים | אֱלֹהִים יוֹדוּךָ עַמִּים כֻּלָּם: יִשְׂמְחוּ וִירַנְּנוּ לְאֻמִּים כִּי־תִשְׁפֹּט עַמִּים מִישֹׁר וּלְאֻמִּים | בָּאָרֶץ תַּנְחֵם סֶלָה: יוֹדוּךָ עַמִּים | אֱלֹהִים יוֹדוּךָ עַמִּים כֻּלָּם: אֶרֶץ נָתְנָה יְבוּלָהּ יְבָרְכֵנוּ אֱלֹהִים אֱלֹהֵינוּ: יְבָרְכֵנוּ אֱלֹהִים וְיִירְאוּ אֹתוֹ כָּל־אַפְסֵי־אָרֶץ:

Lamnatzeach Binginot. Mizmor Shir. Elohim. Yechonenu Vivarecheinu; Ya'er Panav Itanu Selah. Lada'at Ba'aretz Darkecha; Bechol-Goyim. Yeshu'atecha. Yoducha Ammim Elohim; Yoducha. Ammim Kulam. Yismechu Viranenu. Le'ummim Ki-Tishpot Ammim Mishor; Ule'ummim Ba'aretz Tanchem Selah. Yoducha Ammim Elohim; Yoducha. Ammim Kulam. Eretz Natenah Yevulah; Yevarecheinu. Elohim Eloheinu. Yevarecheinu Elohim; Veyire'u Oto. Chol-'Afsei-'Aretz.

For the Leader; with string-music. A Psalm, a Song. May God be gracious to us, and bless us; May He cause His face to shine toward us; Selah. That Your way may be known upon earth, Your salvation among all nations. Let the people give thanks to You, Oh God; Let the peoples give thanks to You, all of them. Let the nations be glad and sing for joy; For You will judge the people with equity, And lead the nations on earth. Selah. Let the people give thanks to You, Oh God; Let the peoples give thanks to You, all of them. The earth has yielded her increase; May God, our own God, bless us. May God bless us; And let all the ends of the earth fear Him.

Ana Bechoach

אָנָּא בְּכֹחַ. גְּדוּלַת יְמִינֶךָ. תַּתִּיר צְרוּרָה:

Ana Bechoach. Gedulat Yeminecha. Tatir Tzerurah.

By the great power of Your right hand, Oh set the captive free.

קַבֵּל רִנַּת. עַמְּךָ שַׂגְּבֵנוּ. טַהֲרֵנוּ נוֹרָא:

Kabel Rinat. Ammecha Sagveinu. Tahareinu Nora.

God of awe, accept Your people's prayer; strengthen us, cleanse us.

נָא גִבּוֹר. דּוֹרְשֵׁי יִחוּדֶךָ. כְּבָבַת שָׁמְרֵם:

Na Gibor. Doreshei Yichudecha. Kevavat Shamerem.

Almighty God, guard as the apple of the eye those who seek You.

בָּרְכֵם טַהֲרֵם. רַחֲמֵי צִדְקָתֶךָ. תָּמִיד גָּמְלֵם:

Barechem Taharem. Rachamei Tzidkatecha. Tamid Gamelem.

Bless them, cleanse them, pity them; forever grant them Your truth.

חֲסִין קָדוֹשׁ. בְּרֹב טוּבְךָ. נַהֵל עֲדָתֶךָ:

Chasin Kadosh. Berov Tuvecha. Nahel Adatecha.

Almighty and holy, in Your abundant goodness, guide Your people.

יָחִיד גֵּאֶה. לְעַמְּךָ פְּנֵה. זוֹכְרֵי קְדֻשָּׁתֶךָ:

Yachid Ge'eh. Le'ammecha Feneh. Zocherei Kedushatecha.

Supreme God, turn to Your people who are mindful of Your holiness.

שַׁוְעָתֵנוּ קַבֵּל. וּשְׁמַע צַעֲקָתֵנוּ. יוֹדֵעַ תַּעֲלוּמוֹת:

Shav'ateinu Kabel. Ushema Tza'akateinu. Yodea Ta'alumot.

Accept our prayer, hear our cry, You Who knows secret thoughts.

And Say Silently:

בָּרוּךְ, שֵׁם כְּבוֹד מַלְכוּתוֹ, לְעוֹלָם וָעֶד:

Baruch, Shem Kevod Malchuto, Le'olam Va'ed

Blessed is the Name of His glorious kingdom forever and ever.

SEDER BIRKHAT HALEVANAH / ORDER OF THE BLESSING OF THE MOON

Upon beholding the New Moon, one must say the blessing "asher bema'amaro", etc. (One should not consecrate the moon unless the moon is shining). The blessing should be said preferably on Shabbat night. (This is only true when Saturday night occur before the tenth of the month, then we have to wait till Shabbat night, but if it fall after the tenth of the month, we do not need to wait). The blessing should not be recited before seven days after its conjunction has passed. (The moon should not be consecrated before the Ninth of Av, only at the conclusion of it; and not before Yom Kippur, only at the conclusion of it). How long may we wait say the blessing over it? Up to the sixteenth day of its conjunction, the sixteenth day not included. (And it should not be consecrated before the half of twenty-nine (twelve hours, twenty-two and 11.18 minutes from the conjunction). (SA, OC 426)

Psalms 19

לַמְנַצֵּחַ מִזְמוֹר לְדָוִד: הַשָּׁמַיִם מְסַפְּרִים כְּבוֹד־אֵל וּמַעֲשֵׂה יָדָיו
מַגִּיד הָרָקִיעַ: יוֹם לְיוֹם יַבִּיעַ אֹמֶר וְלַיְלָה לְּלַיְלָה יְחַוֶּה־דָּעַת:
אֵין־אֹמֶר וְאֵין דְּבָרִים בְּלִי נִשְׁמָע קוֹלָם: בְּכָל־הָאָרֶץ | יָצָא קַוָּם
וּבִקְצֵה תֵבֵל מִלֵּיהֶם לַשֶּׁמֶשׁ שָׂם־אֹהֶל בָּהֶם: וְהוּא כְּחָתָן יֹצֵא
מֵחֻפָּתוֹ יָשִׂישׂ כְּגִבּוֹר לָרוּץ אֹרַח: מִקְצֵה הַשָּׁמַיִם | מוֹצָאוֹ וּתְקוּפָתוֹ
עַל־קְצוֹתָם וְאֵין נִסְתָּר מֵחַמָּתוֹ: תּוֹרַת יְהוָה תְּמִימָה מְשִׁיבַת נָפֶשׁ
עֵדוּת יְהוָה נֶאֱמָנָה מַחְכִּימַת פֶּתִי: פִּקּוּדֵי יְהוָה יְשָׁרִים מְשַׂמְּחֵי־לֵב
מִצְוַת יְהוָה בָּרָה מְאִירַת עֵינָיִם: יִרְאַת יְהוָה | טְהוֹרָה עוֹמֶדֶת לָעַד
מִשְׁפְּטֵי־יְהוָה אֱמֶת צָדְקוּ יַחְדָּו: הַנֶּחֱמָדִים מִזָּהָב וּמִפַּז רָב
וּמְתוּקִים מִדְּבַשׁ וְנֹפֶת צוּפִים: גַּם־עַבְדְּךָ נִזְהָר בָּהֶם בְּשָׁמְרָם עֵקֶב
רָב: שְׁגִיאוֹת מִי־יָבִין מִנִּסְתָּרוֹת נַקֵּנִי: גַּם מִזֵּדִים | חֲשֹׂךְ עַבְדֶּךָ
אַל־יִמְשְׁלוּ־בִי אָז אֵיתָם וְנִקֵּיתִי מִפֶּשַׁע רָב: יִהְיוּ לְרָצוֹן | אִמְרֵי־פִי
וְהֶגְיוֹן לִבִּי לְפָנֶיךָ יְהוָה צוּרִי וְגֹאֲלִי:

Lamnatzeach, Mizmor Ledavid. Hashamayim, Mesaperim Kevod-El; Uma'aseh Yadav, Maggid Harakia. Yom Leyom Yabbia Omer; Velaylah Lelaylah, Yechaveh-Da'at. Ein-'Omer Ve'ein Devarim; Beli, Nishma Kolam. Bechol-Ha'aretz Yatza Kavam, Uviktzeh Tevel Mileihem; Lashemesh, Sam-'Ohel Bahem. Vehu, Kechaton Yotzei Mechuppato; Yasis Kegibor, Larutz Orach. Miktzeh Hashamayim

Motza'o, Utekufato Al-Ketzotam; Ve'ein Nistar, Mechamato. Torat Adonai Temimah Meshivat Nafesh; Edut Adonai Ne'emanah, Machkimat Peti. Pikudei Adonai Yesharim Mesamechei-Lev; Mitzvat Adonai Barah, Me'irat Einayim. Yir'at Adonai Tehorah Omedet La'ad Mishpetei-Adonai Emet; Tzadeku Yachdav. Hanechemadim, Mizahov Umipaz Rav; Umetukim Midevash, Venofet Tzufim. Gam-Avdecha Nizhar Bahem; Beshomram, Ekev Rav. Shegi'ot Mi-Yavin; Ministarot Nakkeni. Gam Mizeidim Chasoch Avodecha, Al-Yimshelu-Vi Az Eitam; Venikkeiti, Mippesha Rav. Yihyu Leratzon Imrei-Fi Vehegyon Libi Lefaneicha; Adonai Tzuri Vego'ali.

For the Leader. A Psalm of David. The heavens declare the glory of God, and the firmament shows the work of His hands; Day to day utters speech, and night to night reveals knowledge; There is no speech, there are no words, neither is their voice heard. Their line is gone out through all the earth, and their words to the end of the world. In them He has set a tent for the sun, Which is as a bridegroom coming out of his chamber, and rejoices as a strong man to run his course. His going out is from the end of the heaven, and his circuit to the ends of it; and there is nothing hidden from the heat of it. The Torah of Hashem is perfect, restoring the soul; the testimony of Hashem is sure, making wise the simple. The precepts of Hashem are right, rejoicing the heart; the commandment of Hashem is pure, enlightening the eyes. The fear of Hashem is clean, enduring forever; the ordinances of Hashem are true, they are righteous altogether; More to be desired are they than gold, even than much fine gold; sweeter also than honey and the honeycomb. Also by them is Your servant warned; in keeping of them there is great reward. Who can discern his errors? Cleanse me from hidden faults. Keep back Your servant from presumptuous sins, that they may not have dominion over me; then I will be faultless, and I will be clear from great transgression. Let the words of my mouth and the meditation of my heart be acceptable before You, Hashem, my Rock, and my Redeemer.

צוּרִי בָּעוֹלָם הַזֶּה וְגוֹאֲלִי לְעוֹלָם הַבָּא. וְכָל־קַרְנֵי רְשָׁעִים אֲגַדֵּעַ
תְּרוֹמַמְנָה קַרְנוֹת צַדִּיק:

Tzuri Ba'olam Hazeh Vego'ali La'olam Haba. Vechol Karnei
Resha'im Agadea' Teromamnah Karnot Tzaddik.

My rock in this world and my redeemer in the world to come. All the
horns of the wicked I will also cut off; But the horns of the righteous
will be lifted up. (Psalms 75:11)

Psalms 148:1-6

הַלְלוּיָהּ | הַלְלוּ אֶת־יְהֹוָה מִן־הַשָּׁמַיִם הַלְלוּהוּ בַּמְּרוֹמִים: הַלְלוּהוּ
כָל־מַלְאָכָיו הַלְלוּהוּ כָּל־צְבָאָו: הַלְלוּהוּ שֶׁמֶשׁ וְיָרֵחַ הַלְלוּהוּ
כָּל־כּוֹכְבֵי אוֹר: הַלְלוּהוּ שְׁמֵי הַשָּׁמָיִם וְהַמַּיִם אֲשֶׁר | מֵעַל הַשָּׁמָיִם:
יְהַלְלוּ אֶת־שֵׁם יְהֹוָה כִּי הוּא צִוָּה וְנִבְרָאוּ: וַיַּעֲמִידֵם לָעַד לְעוֹלָם
חָק־נָתַן וְלֹא יַעֲבוֹר:

Halleluyah Halelu Et-Adonai Min-Hashamayim; Halleluhu.
Bameromim. Halleluhu Chol-Mal'achav; Halleluhu. Chol-Tzeva'av.
Halleluhu Shemesh Veyareach; Halleluhu. Chol-Kochevei Or.
Halleluhu Shemei Hashamayim; Vehamayim. Asher Me'al
Hashamayim. Yehalelu Et-Shem Adonai Ki Hu Tzivah Venivra'u.
Vaya'amidem La'ad Le'olam; Chok-Natan. Velo Ya'avor.

Halleluyah. Praise Hashem from the heavens; Praise Him in the
heights. Praise Him, all His angels; Praise Him, all His hosts. Praise
Him, sun and moon; Praise Him, all stars of light. Praise Him,
heavens of heavens, And waters that are above the heavens. Let
them praise the name of Hashem; For He commanded, and they
were created. He also established them forever and ever; He made a
decree which will not be transgressed. (Psalms 148:1-6)

Look upon the moon and recite the verses. When reciting the blessing after, do not look upon the
moon.

כִּי־אֶרְאֶה שָׁמֶיךָ מַעֲשֵׂה אֶצְבְּעֹתֶיךָ יָרֵחַ וְכוֹכָבִים אֲשֶׁר כּוֹנָנְתָּה׃
יְהֹוָה אֲדֹנֵינוּ מָה־אַדִּיר שִׁמְךָ בְּכָל־הָאָרֶץ׃

Ki-Er'eh Shameicha Ma'aseh Etzbe'oteicha; Yareach Vechochavim.
Asher Konanetah. Adonai Adoneinu; Mah-'Adir Shimcha. Bechol-
Ha'aretz.

When I behold Your heavens, the work of Your fingers, The moon
and the stars, which You have established; Hashem, our Lord, How
glorious is Your name in all of the earth. (Psalms 8:4, 8:5)

Some say before the blessing:

לְשֵׁם יְחוּד קוּדְשָׁא בְּרִיךְ הוּא וּשְׁכִינְתֵּיהּ. בִּדְחִילוּ וּרְחִימוּ. וּרְחִימוּ וּדְחִילוּ.
לְיַחֲדָא שֵׁם יוֹ"ד קֵ"י בְּוָא"ו קֵ"י בְּיִחוּדָא שְׁלִים (יהוה) בְּשֵׁם כָּל יִשְׂרָאֵל.
הנה אנחנו באים לברך ברכת הלבנה כמו שתקנו לנו רבותינו זכרונם
לברכה. עם כל־המצות הכלולות בה. לתקן את שורשה במקום עליון.
לעשות נחת רוח ליוצרנו ולעשות רצון בוראנו. וִיהִי נֹעַם אֲדֹנָי אֱלֹהֵינוּ עָלֵינוּ
וּמַעֲשֵׂה יָדֵינוּ כּוֹנְנָה עָלֵינוּ וּמַעֲשֵׂה יָדֵינוּ כּוֹנְנֵהוּ׃

From this point on one should not look at the moon.

Baruch Attah Adonai Eloheinu	בָּרוּךְ אַתָּה יְהֹוָה אֱלֹהֵינוּ
Melech Ha'olam Asher	מֶלֶךְ הָעוֹלָם. אֲשֶׁר
Bema'amaro Bara Shechakim	בְּמַאֲמָרוֹ בָּרָא שְׁחָקִים
Uveruach Piv Kol Tzeva'am.	וּבְרוּחַ פִּיו כָּל צְבָאָם.
Chok Uzeman Natan Lahem	חֹק וּזְמַן נָתַן לָהֶם
Shelo Yeshanu Et Tafkidam.	שֶׁלֹּא יְשַׁנּוּ אֶת תַּפְקִידָם.
Sasim Usemechim La'asot	שָׂשִׂים וּשְׂמֵחִים לַעֲשׂוֹת
Retzon Koneihem. Po'el Emet	רְצוֹן קוֹנֵיהֶם. פּוֹעֵל
Sheppe'ulato Emet. Velalevanah	אֱמֶת שֶׁפְּעֻלָּתוֹ אֱמֶת. וְלַלְּבָנָה
Amar Shetitchadesh. Ateret	אָמַר שֶׁתִּתְחַדֵּשׁ. עֲטֶרֶת

Tif'eret La'amusei Vaten.	תִּפְאֶרֶת לַעֲמוּסֵי בָטֶן.
Sheggam Hem Atidim	שֶׁגַּם הֵם עֲתִידִים
Lehitchadesh Kemotah Ulefa'er	לְהִתְחַדֵּשׁ כְּמוֹתָהּ וּלְפָאֵר
Leyotzeram Al Shem Kevod	לְיוֹצְרָם עַל שֵׁם כְּבוֹד
Malchuto. Baruch Attah Adonai	מַלְכוּתוֹ. בָּרוּךְ אַתָּה יְהֹוָה
Mechadesh Chadashim.	מְחַדֵּשׁ חֳדָשִׁים:

Blessed are You, Hashem our God, King of the universe, Who with His word You created the heavens, and with a breath from His mouth, all of their hosts. A law and appointed times He gave them, so that they should not deviate from their position. They rejoice and are glad to perform the will of their Creator. The Worker is true, and His work is true. To the moon He said it should renew her crown of splendor monthly to those brought up from the womb, for they are destined to be renewed like her, to praise their Creator, for the glorious name of His kingdom. Blessed are You, Hashem Who renews the months.

Recite three times:

בְּסִימָן טוֹב תְּהִי לָנוּ וּלְכָל יִשְׂרָאֵל:

Besiman Tov Tehi Lanu Ulechol Yisra'el.

May the new moon herald an auspicious month for us and all Yisrael.

Baruch Yotzerich. Baruch Osich.	בָּרוּךְ יוֹצְרִיךְ. בָּרוּךְ עוֹשִׂיךְ.
Baruch Konich. Baruch Bore'ich.	בָּרוּךְ קוֹנִיךְ. בָּרוּךְ בּוֹרְאִיךְ.
Keshem She'anachnu	כְּשֵׁם שֶׁאֲנַחְנוּ
Merakkedim Kenegdich. Ve'ein	מְרַקְּדִים כְּנֶגְדִּיךְ. וְאֵין
Anachnu Yecholim Liga Bich.	אֲנַחְנוּ יְכוֹלִים לִגַּע בִּיךְ.

Kach Im Yerakedu Acherim	כָּךְ אִם יְרַקְּדוּ אֲחֵרִים
Kenegdenu Lehazikenu. Lo	כְּנֶגְדֵּנוּ לְהַזִּיקֵנוּ. לֹא
Yuchelu Liga Banu. Velo Yishletu	יוּכְלוּ לִגַּע בָּנוּ. וְלֹא יִשְׁלְטוּ
Vanu. Velo Ya'asu Vanu Shum	בָּנוּ. וְלֹא יַעֲשׂוּ בָנוּ שׁוּם
Roshem. Tipol Aleihem Eimatah	רֹשֶׁם. תִּפֹּל עֲלֵיהֶם אֵימָֽתָה
Vafachad. Bigdol Zero'acha	וָפַֽחַד. בִּגְדֹל זְרוֹעֲךָ
Yidemu Ka'aven;. Ka'aven	יִדְּמוּ כָּאָֽבֶן: כָּאָֽבֶן
Yidemu. Zero'acha Bigdol.	יִדְּמוּ. זְרוֹעֲךָ בִּגְדָל.
Vafachad Eimatah Aleihem Tipol.	וָפַֽחַד אֵימָֽתָה עֲלֵיהֶם תִּפֹּל:

Blessed is He Who formed you, blessed is He Who produced you, blessed is He Who owns you, blessed is He Who created you. Were we with our utmost effort to spring towards the moon, we could not touch it. So, if men have evil intentions towards us, may they not come near to us. "Terror and dread falls upon them; By the greatness of Your arm they are as still as a stone". Even, still as a stone may they be before Your saving power, And may dread and terror fall upon them. (Exodus 15:16)

דָּוִד מֶֽלֶךְ יִשְׂרָאֵל חַי וְקַיָּם. שלש פעמים

David Melech Yisra'el Chai Vekayam.

King David of Yisrael lives forever. (3x)

אָמֵן שלש פעמים נֶֽצַח שלש פעמים סֶֽלָה שלש פעמים וָעֶד שלש פעמים

Amen (3x) Netzach (3x) Selah (3x) Va'ed (3x)

לֵב טָהוֹר בְּרָא־לִי אֱלֹהִים וְרֽוּחַ נָכוֹן חַדֵּשׁ בְּקִרְבִּי: שבע פעמים

Lev Tahor Bera-Li Elohim; Veruach Nachon. Chadesh Bekirbi.

Create me a clean heart, God; and renew a steadfast spirit within me. (7X)

Psalms 121

שִׁיר לַמַּעֲלוֹת אֶשָּׂא עֵינַי אֶל־הֶהָרִים מֵאַיִן יָבֹא עֶזְרִי: עֶזְרִי מֵעִם
יְהֹוָה עֹשֵׂה שָׁמַיִם וָאָרֶץ: אַל־יִתֵּן לַמּוֹט רַגְלֶךָ אַל־יָנוּם שֹׁמְרֶךָ: הִנֵּה
לֹא־יָנוּם וְלֹא יִישָׁן שׁוֹמֵר יִשְׂרָאֵל: יְהֹוָה שֹׁמְרֶךָ יְהֹוָה צִלְּךָ עַל־יַד
יְמִינֶךָ: יוֹמָם הַשֶּׁמֶשׁ לֹא־יַכֶּכָּה וְיָרֵחַ בַּלָּיְלָה: יְהֹוָה יִשְׁמָרְךָ מִכָּל־רָע
יִשְׁמֹר אֶת־נַפְשֶׁךָ: יְהֹוָה יִשְׁמָר־צֵאתְךָ וּבוֹאֶךָ מֵעַתָּה וְעַד־עוֹלָם:

Shir. Lamma'alot Essa Einai El-Heharim; Me'ayin. Yavo Ezri. Ezri
Me'im Adonai Oseh. Shamayim Va'aretz. Al-Yiten Lamot Raglecha;
Al-Yanum. Shomerecha. Hineh Lo-Yanum Velo Yishan; Shomer.
Yisra'el. Adonai Shomerecha; Adonai Tzillecha. Al-Yad Yeminecha.
Yomam. Hashemesh Lo-Yakekah. Veyareach Balailah. Adonai
Yishmorcha Mikol-Ra'; Yishmor. Et-Nafshecha. Adonai Yishmor-
Tzetecha Uvo'echa; Me'attah. Ve'ad-'Olam.

A Song of Ascents. I will lift up my eyes to the mountains: From
where will my help come? My help comes from Hashem, Who made
heaven and earth. He will not suffer Your foot to be moved; He that
keeps You will not slumber. Behold, He that keeps Yisrael neither
slumbers or sleeps. Hashem is your Guardian; Hashem is Your
shade on Your right hand. The sun will not harm you by day, or the
moon by night. Hashem will keep you from all evil; He will keep your
soul. Hashem will guard your going out and your coming in, From
this time and forever.

Psalms 150

הַלְלוּיָהּ | הַלְלוּ־אֵל בְּקָדְשׁוֹ הַלְלוּהוּ בִּרְקִיעַ עֻזּוֹ: הַלְלוּהוּ
בִגְבוּרֹתָיו הַלְלוּהוּ כְּרֹב גֻּדְלוֹ: הַלְלוּהוּ בְּתֵקַע שׁוֹפָר הַלְלוּהוּ בְּנֵבֶל
וְכִנּוֹר: הַלְלוּהוּ בְּתֹף וּמָחוֹל הַלְלוּהוּ בְּמִנִּים וְעֻגָב: הַלְלוּהוּ
בְצִלְצְלֵי־שָׁמַע הַלְלוּהוּ בְּצִלְצְלֵי תְרוּעָה: כֹּל הַנְּשָׁמָה תְּהַלֵּל יָהּ
הַלְלוּיָהּ:

Halleluyah Halelu-'El Bekod'sho; Halleluhu. Birkia Uzo. Halleluhu
Vigvurotav; Halleluhu. Kerov Gudlo. Halleluhu Beteka Shofar;
Halleluhu. Benevel Vechinor. Halleluhu Betof Umachol; Halleluhu.
Beminim Ve'ugav. Halleluhu Vetziltzelei-Shama'; Halleluhu.
Betziltzelei Teru'ah. Kol Haneshamah Tehallel Yah. Halleluyah. Kol
Haneshamah Tehallel Yah. Halleluyah.

Halleluyah. Praise God in His Sanctuary; Praise Him in the
firmament of His power. Praise Him for His mighty acts; Praise Him
according to His abundant greatness. Praise Him with the blast of
the shofar; Praise Him with the psaltery and harp. Praise Him with
the timbrel and dance; Praise Him with stringed instruments and
the pipe. Praise Him with the loud-sounding cymbals; Praise Him
with the clanging cymbals. Let everything that has breath praise
Hashem. Halleluyah.

Sanhedrin 42

תָּנָא דְּבֵי רְבִי יִשְׁמָעֵאל אִלְמָלֵי לֹא זָכוּ בְנֵי יִשְׂרָאֵל אֶלָּא לְהַקְבִּיל פְּנֵי אֲבִיהֶם
שֶׁבַּשָּׁמַיִם פַּעַם אַחַת בַּחֹדֶשׁ דַּיָּם. אָמַר אַבַּיֵי. הֶלְכָּךְ נִימְרִינְהוּ מֵעֹמֶד:

Tana Devei Ribi Yishma'el Ilmalei Lo Zachu Venei Yisra'el Ela Lehakbil Penei
Avihem Shebashamayim Pa'am Achat Bachodesh Dayam. Amar Abayei Helechach
Nimrinhu Me'omed:

In the school of Rabbi Yishmael it was taught: If Yisrael should only have the
meritorious act of receiving the glory of their heavenly Father once a month, it
would be sufficient. Abayei said: Therefore we must pronounce the above blessing
standing.

Some say:

Makkot 23b

רַבִּי חֲנַנְיָא בֶּן־עֲקַשְׁיָא אוֹמֵר: רָצָה הַקָּדוֹשׁ בָּרוּךְ הוּא לְזַכּוֹת אֶת־יִשְׂרָאֵל.
לְפִיכָךְ הִרְבָּה לָהֶם תּוֹרָה וּמִצְוֹת. שֶׁנֶּאֱמַר: יְהֹוָה חָפֵץ לְמַעַן צִדְקוֹ יַגְדִּיל
תּוֹרָה וְיַאְדִּיר:

Ribi Chananya Ben Akashya Omer: Ratzah Hakadosh Baruch Hu Lezakkot Et
Yisra'el. Lefichach Hirbah Lahem Torah Umitzvot. Shene'emar: Adonai Chafetz
Lema'an Tzidko Yagdil Torah Veya'dir.

Rabbi Chananya ben Akashya used to say, the Holy One, blessed is He, wishing to make Yisrael more worthy, enlarged for them with Torah and its commandments. For so it is said, "Hashem was pleased, for His righteousness' sake, To make the Torah great and glorious." (Isaiah 42:21)

And now say Kaddish Al Yisrael:

Kaddish is only recited in a minyan (ten men). אמ denotes when the congregation responds "Amen" together out loud. According to the Shulchan Arukh, the congregation says "Yehei Shemeh Rabba" to "Yitbarach" out loud together without interruption, and also that one should respond "Amen" after "Yitbarach." (SA, OC 55,56) This is not the common custom today. Though many are accustomed to answering according to their own custom, it is advised to respond in the custom of the one reciting to avoid not fragmenting into smaller groups. ("Lo Titgodedu" - BT, Yevamot 13b / SA, OC 493, Rema / MT, Avodah Zara 12:15)

יִתְגַּדַּל וְיִתְקַדַּשׁ שְׁמֵהּ רַבָּא. אמ בְּעָלְמָא דִּי בְרָא. כִּרְעוּתֵהּ. וְיַמְלִיךְ מַלְכוּתֵהּ. וְיַצְמַח פֻּרְקָנֵהּ. וִיקָרֵב מְשִׁיחֵהּ. אמ בְּחַיֵּיכוֹן וּבְיוֹמֵיכוֹן וּבְחַיֵּי דְכָל בֵּית יִשְׂרָאֵל. בַּעֲגָלָא וּבִזְמַן קָרִיב. וְאִמְרוּ אָמֵן. אמ יְהֵא שְׁמֵיהּ רַבָּא מְבָרַךְ לְעָלַם וּלְעָלְמֵי עָלְמַיָּא יִתְבָּרַךְ. וְיִשְׁתַּבַּח. וְיִתְפָּאַר. וְיִתְרוֹמַם. וְיִתְנַשֵּׂא. וְיִתְהַדָּר. וְיִתְעַלֶּה. וְיִתְהַלָּל שְׁמֵהּ דְּקֻדְשָׁא. בְּרִיךְ הוּא. אמ לְעֵלָּא מִן כָּל בִּרְכָתָא שִׁירָתָא. תֻּשְׁבְּחָתָא וְנֶחֱמָתָא. דַּאֲמִירָן בְּעָלְמָא. וְאִמְרוּ אָמֵן. אמ

Yitgadal Veyitkadash Shemeh Rabba. **Amen** Be'alema Di Vera. Kir'uteh. Veyamlich Malchuteh. Veyatzmach Purkaneh. Vikarev Meshicheh. **Amen** Bechayeichon Uveyomeichon Uvechayei Dechal-Beit Yisra'el. Ba'agala Uvizman Kariv. Ve'imru Amen. **Amen** Yehei Shemeh Rabba Mevarach Le'alam Ule'alemei Alemaya Yitbarach. Veyishtabach. Veyitpa'ar. Veyitromam. Veyitnasse. Veyit'hadar. Veyit'aleh. Veyit'hallal Shemeh Dekudsha. Berich Hu. **Amen** Le'ella Min Kol Birchata Shirata. Tushbechata Venechemata. Da'amiran Be'alema. Ve'imru Amen. **Amen**

Glorified and sanctified be God's great name **Amen** throughout the world which He has created according to His will. May He establish His kingdom, hastening His salvation and the coming of His Messiah, **Amen**, in your lifetime and during your days, and within the life of the entire House of Yisrael, speedily and soon; and say, Amen. **Amen** May His great name be blessed forever and to all eternity.

Blessed and praised, glorified and exalted, extolled and honored, adored and lauded is the name of the Holy One, blessed is He, Amen Beyond all the blessings and hymns, praises and consolations that are ever spoken in the world; and say, Amen. Amen

עַל יִשְׂרָאֵל וְעַל רַבָּנָן. וְעַל תַּלְמִידֵיהוֹן וְעַל כָּל תַּלְמִידֵי תַלְמִידֵיהוֹן. דְּעָסְקִין בְּאוֹרַיְתָא קַדִּשְׁתָּא. דִּי בְאַתְרָא הָדֵין וְדִי בְכָל אֲתַר וַאֲתַר. יְהֵא לָנָא וּלְהוֹן וּלְכוֹן חִנָּא וְחִסְדָּא וְרַחֲמֵי. מִן קֳדָם מָארֵי שְׁמַיָּא וְאַרְעָא וְאִמְרוּ אָמֵן. אמן

Al Yisra'el Ve'al Rabbanan. Ve'al Talmideihon Ve'al Kol Talmidei Talmideihon. De'asekin Be'orayta Kaddishta. Di Ve'atra Hadein Vedi Vechal Atar Va'atar. Yehei Lana Ulehon Ulechon China Vechisda Verachamei. Min Kodam Marei Shemaya Ve'ar'a Ve'imru Amen. Amen

May we of Yisrael together with our rabbis, their disciples and pupils, and all who engage in the study of holy Torah here and everywhere, find gracious favor and mercy from their Father Who is in heaven; and say, Amen. Amen

יְהֵא שְׁלָמָא רַבָּא מִן שְׁמַיָּא. חַיִּים וְשָׂבָע וִישׁוּעָה וְנֶחָמָה. וְשֵׁיזָבָא וּרְפוּאָה וּגְאוּלָה וּסְלִיחָה וְכַפָּרָה וְרֶוַח וְהַצָּלָה לָנוּ וּלְכָל עַמּוֹ יִשְׂרָאֵל. וְאִמְרוּ אָמֵן. אמן

Yehei Shelama Rabba Min Shemaya. Chayim Vesava Vishu'ah Venechamah. Vesheizava Urefu'ah Uge'ulah Uselichah Vechapparah Verevach Vehatzalah Lanu Ulechol Ammo Yisra'el. Ve'imru Amen. Amen

May abundant peace descend from heaven, with life and plenty, salvation, solace, liberation, healing and redemption, and forgiveness and atonement, enlargement and freedom, for us and all of God's people Yisrael; and say, Amen. Amen

---

One bows and takes three steps backwards, while still bowing. After three steps, while still bowing and before erecting, while saying, "Oseh Shalom Bimromav", turn one's face to the left, "Hu [Berachamav] Ya'aseh Shalom Aleinu", turn one's face to the right; then bow forward like a servant leaving his master. (SA, OC 123:1)

עוֹשֶׂה שָׁלוֹם בִּמְרוֹמָיו. הוּא בְּרַחֲמָיו יַעֲשֶׂה שָׁלוֹם עָלֵינוּ. וְעַל
כָּל־עַמּוֹ יִשְׂרָאֵל. וְאִמְרוּ אָמֵן:

Oseh Shalom Bimromav. Hu Berachamav Ya'aseh Shalom Aleinu.
Ve'al Kol-'Ammo Yisra'el. Ve'imru Amen.

Creator of peace in His high places, may He in His mercy create
peace for us and for all Yisrael, and say Amen.

After Kaddish some say:

וְהָיָה אוֹר־הַלְּבָנָה כְּאוֹר הַחַמָּה וְאוֹר הַחַמָּה יִהְיֶה שִׁבְעָתַיִם כְּאוֹר
שִׁבְעַת הַיָּמִים בְּיוֹם חֲבֹשׁ יְהֹוָה אֶת־שֶׁבֶר עַמּוֹ וּמַחַץ מַכָּתוֹ יִרְפָּא:
וָתַעְדִּי זָהָב וָכֶסֶף וּמַלְבּוּשֵׁךְ שׁשִׁי (שֵׁשׁ) וָמֶשִׁי וְרִקְמָה סֹלֶת וּדְבַשׁ
וָשֶׁמֶן אכלתי (אָכָלְתְּ) וַתִּיפִי בִּמְאֹד מְאֹד וַתִּצְלְחִי לִמְלוּכָה:

Vehayah Or-Halevanah Ke'or Hachamah. Ve'or Hachamah Yihyeh
Shiv'atayim. Ke'or Shiv'at Hayamim; Beyom. Chavosh Adonai Et-
Shever Ammo. Umachatz Makato Yirpa. Vata'di Zahav Vachesef.
Umalbushech Shesh Vameshi Verikmah. Solet Udevash Vashemen
Chlt Vatifi Bim'od Me'od. Vatitzlechi Limluchah.

Moreover the light of the moon will be as the light of the sun, And
the light of the sun will be sevenfold, as the light of the seven days,
In the day that Hashem binds up the bruise of His people, And heals
the stroke of their wound. So were you decked with gold and silver;
and your raiment was of fine linen, and silk, and richly woven work;
you ate fine flour, and honey, and oil; and you did turn exceeding
beautiful, and you attained royal estate. (Isaiah 30:26, Ezekiel 16:13)

ואומרים שלש פעמים: שָׁלוֹם עֲלֵיכֶם.

Shalom Aleichem. (say three times)
Peace be with you. (say three times

TORAH READINGS FOR SPECIAL DAYS

Rosh Chodesh
Numbers 28:1–15

Fast Days
Exodus 32:11–14, 34:1–10

Tisha B'Av / 9th of Av
Shacharit: Deuteronomy 4:25–40
Minchah: Exodus 32:11-14

Hanukkah – Day 1
Sephardim: Numbers 6:22–7:17
Ashkenazim: Numbers 7:1–17

Hanukkah – Days 2–7
Read the offering for the respective day, Numbers 7:18-53.

On Rosh Chodesh, read the Rosh Chodesh reading from the 1st Torah scroll, and the Hanukkah reading from the 2nd Torah scroll.

Hanukkah – Day 8
Numbers 7:54-8:4

Purim
Exodus 17:8-16

TORAH READINGS FOR SPECIAL SHABBATOT

Shabbat Rosh Chodesh
Numbers 28:9-15

Shabbat Hanukkah
Read the the passage for Shabbat Rosh Chodesh from the 2nd Torah scroll and for Hanukkah from the third.

Parashat Shekalim
Exodus 30:11-16
If Rosh Chodesh falls on Parashat Shekalim, the passage for Rosh Chodesh is read from the 2nd Torah scroll and Parashat Shekalim from the third.

Parashat Zakhor
Deuteronomy 25:17-19

Parashat Parah
Numbers 19:1-22

Parashat HaChodesh
Exodus 12:1-20
If Parashat HaChodesh falls on Rosh Chodesh, the passage for Rosh Chodesh is read from the 2nd Torah scroll and Parashat HaChodesh from the third.

Purim on Shabbat
(in Walled Cities)
Exodus 17:8-16
Haftarah: Same as Shabbat Zakhor.
(Deuteronomy 25:17-19)

TORAH READINGS FOR YOM TOV / FESTIVALS

Pesach - Day 1
Exodus 12:21-51
On Shabbat, Sephardim read Exodus
12:14-51
Maftir: Numbers 28:16-25

Day 2
Leviticus 22:26-23:44
In Israel: Revi'i (2nd Torah scroll):
Numbers 28:19-25
In the Diaspora: Maftir: Same as Day 1.

Day 3
Exodus 13:1-16
Revi'i (2nd Torah scroll): Numbers
28:19-25

Day 4
Exodus 22:24-23:19
(If it falls on a Sunday, Sephardim read the
passage for Day 3.)
Revi'i (2nd Torah scroll): Numbers
28:19-25

Day 5
Exodus 34:1-26
(If it falls on a Monday, Sephardim read the
passage for Day 4.)
Revi'i (2nd Torah scroll): Numbers
28:19-25

Day 6
Numbers 9:1-14
Revii (2nd Torah scroll): Numbers
28:19-25

Shabbat Chol HaMoed
Pesach
Exodus 33:12-34:26
Maftir: Numbers 28:19-25

Day 7
Exodus 13:17-15:26
Maftir: Numbers 28:19-25

Day 8 (Diaspora)
Deuteronomy 15:19-16:17
On Shabbat: Deuteronomy 14:22-16:17
Maftir: Numbers 28:19-25

Shavuot - Day
Exodus 19:1-20:23
Maftir: Numbers 28:26-31

Day 2 - (Diaspora)
Deuteronomy 15:19-16:17
On Shabbat: Deuteronomy 14:22-16:17
Maftir: Same as Day 1.

Rosh Hashanah Day 1
Genesis 21:1-34
Maftir: Numbers 29:1-6

Day 2
Genesis 22:1-24
Maftir: Same as Day 1.

Yom Kippur
Shacharit: Leviticus 16:1-34
Maftir: Numbers 29:7-11
Mincha: Leviticus 18:1-30

Sukkot - Day 1
Leviticus 22:26-23:44
Maftir: Numbers 29:12-16

Day 2
Israel: Numbers 29:17-19
Diaspora: Same as day 1.

Day 3
Israel: Numbers 29:20-22

Diaspora: Numbers 29:17-25

Day 4
Israel: Numbers 29:23-25
Diaspora: Numbers 29:20-28

Day 5
Israel: Numbers 29:26-28
Diaspora: Numbers 29:23-31

Day 6
Israel: Numbers 29:29-31
Diaspora: Numbers 29:26-34

Day 7 - Hoshana Rabbah
Israel: Numbers 29:32-34
Diaspora: Numbers 29:26-34
Shabbat Chol HaMoed: Exodus
33:12-34:26

Sukkot
Maftir: Read the offering for the
respective day (in the Diaspora adding
the offering for the previous day)

Shemini Atzeret - (Diaspora)
Deuteronomy 15:19-16:17
On Shabbat: Deuteronomy 14:22-16:17
Maftir: Numbers 29:35-30:1

Simchat Torah
1st Torah scroll: Deuteronomy
33:1-34:12
(Israel and Diaspora) 2nd Torah scroll:
Genesis 1:1-2:3
Third Torah scroll (Maftir): Numbers
29:35-30:1

HAFTAROT READINGS

Bereshit
Sephardim: Isaiah 42:5-21
Ashkenazim: Isaiah 42:5-43:10

Noach
Sephardim: Isaiah 54:1-54:10
Ashkenazim: Isaiah 54:1-55:5

Lekh-Lekha
Isaiah 40:27-41:16

Vayera
Sephardim: II Kings 4:1-23
Ashkenazim: II Kings 4:1-37

Chayei Sara
I Kings 1:1-31

Toldot
Malachi 1:1-2:7

Vayetze
Sephardim: Hosea 11:7-12:12
Ashkenazim: Hosea 12:13-14:10

Vayishlach
Obadiah 1:1-21

Vayeshev
Amos 2:6-3:8

Miketz
I Kings 3:15-4:1

Vayigash
Ezekiel 37:15-28

Vayechi
I Kings 2:1-12

Shemot
Sephardim: Jeremiah 1:1-2:3
Ashkenazim: Isaiah 27:6-28:13 and
29:22-23

Va'era
Ezekiel 28:25-29:21

Bo
Jeremiah 46:13-28

Beshalach
Sephardim: Judges 5:1-31
Ashkenazim: Judges 4:4-5:31

Yitro
Sephardim: Isaiah 6:1-13
Ashkenazim: Isaiah 6:1-7:6, and 9:5-6

Mishpatim
Jeremiah 34:8-22 and 33:25-26

Teruma
1 Kings 5:26-6:13

Tetzaveh
Ezekiel 43:10-27

Ki Tisa
Sephardim: I Kings 18:20-39
Ashkenazim: I Kings 18:1-39

Vayak'hel
Sephardim: I Kings 7:13-26
Ashkenazim: I Kings 7:40-50

Pekudei (or Vayak'hel-Pikudei)
Sephardim: I Kings 7:40-50
Ashkenazim: I Kings 7:51-8:21

Vayikra
Isaiah 43:21-44:23

Tzav
Jeremiah 7:21-8:3 and 9:22-23

Shemini
Sephardim: I Samuel 6:1-19
Ashkenazim: I Samuel 6:1-7:17

Tazria
II Kings 4:42-5:19

Metzora (or Tazria-Metzora)
II Kings 7:3-20

Acharei Mot
Sephardim: Ezekiel 22:1-16
Ashkenazim: Ezekiel 22:1-19

Kedoshim (or Acharei Mot-Kedoshim)
Sephardim: Ezekiel 20:2-20
Ashkenazim: Amos 9:7-9:15

Emor
Ezekiel 44:15-31

Behar
Jeremiah 32:6-27

Behukotai (or Behar-Behukotai)
Jeremiah 16:19-17:14

Bemidbar
Hosea 2:1-22

Naso
Judges 13:2-25

Beha'alotekha
Zechariah 2:14-4:7

Shelach
Joshua 2:1-24

Korach
I Samuel 11:14-12:22

Chukat
Judges 11:1-33

Balak (or Chukat-Balak)
Micah 5:6-6:8

Pinhas (before 17 Tamuz)
I Kings 18:46-19:21

Shabbat following 17 Tammuz - (Pinhas or Matot)
Jeremiah 1:1-2:3

Masei (or Mattot-Masei)
Jeremiah 2:4-28 and...
(for Sephardim) 4:1-2
(for Ashkenazim) 3:4

Devarim
Isaiah 1:1-27

Va'etchanan
Isaiah 40:1-26

Ekev
Isaiah 49:14-51:3

Re'eh
Isaiah 54:11-55:5

Shoftim
Isaiah 51:12-52:12

Ki Tetzeh
Isaiah 54:1-10

Ki Tavo
Isaiah 60:1-22

Nitzavim (or Nitzavim-Vayelekh)
Isaiah 61:10-63:9

Vayelekh
Isaiah 55:6 - 56:8

Shabbat Shuvah (Vayelekh or Haazinu)
Sephardim: Hosea 14:2-10 and Micah 7:18-20
Ashkenazim: Hosea 14:2-10 and Joel 2:15-27
Some also read Micah 7:18-20 or Joel 2:15-27

Ha'azinu (after Yom Kippur)
II Samuel 22:1-51

Vezot Haberachah
Sephardim: Joshua 1:1-9
Ashkenazim: Joshua 1:1-18

HAFTAROT FOR SPECIAL SHABBATOT AND HOLIDAYS

Shabbat Rosh Chodesh
Isaiah 66:1-24

Shabbat Erev Rosh Chodesh
I Samuel 20:18-42

Shabbat Hanukkah
1st: Zechariah 2:14-4:7
2nd: I Kings 7:40-50

Fast Day Minha
Isaiah 55:6-56:8

Parashat Shekalim
Sephardim: II Kings 11:17-12:17
Ashkenazim: II Kings 12:1-17

Parashat Zakhor
Sephardim: I Samuel 15:1-34
Ashkenazim: I Samuel 15:2-34

Parashat Parah
Sephardim: Ezekiel 36:16-36
Ashkenazim: Ezekiel 36:16-38

Parashat HaChodesh
Sephardim: Ezekiel 45:18-46:15
Ashkenazim: Ezekiel 45:16-46:18

Shabbat HaGadol
Malachi 3:4-24

Pesach - Day 1
(Some start with Joshua 3:5-7)
Joshua 5:2-6:1 and 6:27

Pesach - Day 2 - (Diaspora)
II Kings 23:1-9 and 23:21-25

Shabbat Chol HaMoed Pesach
Ezekiel 37:1-17

Pesach - Day 7
II Samuel 22:1-51

Pesach - Day 8 - (Diaspora)
Isaiah 10:32-12:6

Shavuot Day 1
Ezekiel 1:1-28 and 3:12

Shavuot Day 2 - (Diaspora)
Habakkuk 2:20-3:19

Tisha B'Av / 9th of Av - Shaharit
Jeremiah 8:13-9:23

Tisha B'Av / 9th of Av - Mincha
Sephardim: Hosea 14:2-10
Some add Joel 2:15-27 and Micah 7:18-20
Ashkenazim: Isaiah 55:6-56:8

Rosh HaShanah - Day 1
I Samuel 1:1-2:10

Rosh HaShanah - Day 2
Jeremiah 31:1-19

Yom Kippur - Shacharit
Isaiah 57:14-58:14

Yom Kippur - Minchah
The Book of Jonah and Micah 7:18-20

Sukkot - Day 1
Zechariah 14:1-21

Sukkot - Day 2 - (Diaspora)
I Kings 8:2-21

Shabbat Chol HaMoed
Sukkot
Ezekiel 38:18-39:16

Shemini Atzeret
Sephardim: I Kings 8:54-66
Ashkenazim: I Kings 8:54-9:1

Simchat Torah
Sephardim: Joshua 1:1-9
Ashkenazim: Joshua 1:1-18

SIDDUR

סדור נר תמיד

NER TAMID

TRANSLITERATED SEPHARDIC SIDDUR

SHABBAT

עץ אחד
EITZ ECHAD

Siddur Ner Tamid
© 2021 Eitz Echad LLC
All rights reserved.

No part of this publication may be reproduced, stored in a retrieval system, stored in a database and / or published in any form or by any means, electronic, mechanical, photocopying, recording or otherwise, without the prior written permission of the publisher. For licensing inquiry please message: eitzechad@outlook.com

Officially copyrighted with the U.S. Copyright office on 2021-08-10: TXu002274596

Editing, format design and layout, artwork were all made in-house by Eitz Echad in the United States of America.

WWW.EITZECHAD.COM